I0605468

Writing from a faithfully evangelical Christian approach, Michael Wilkins provides a thorough, wide-ranging, comprehensive, and up-to-date work on Matthean theology that will profit all interpreters of Matthew's Gospel.

—*Craig S. Keener,* Professor of Biblical Studies,
Asbury Theological Seminary

Mike Wilkins has marinated in the Gospel of Matthew for nearly fifty years. Thus, as readers we are the beneficiaries of his mature exegetical and theological reflection on the Gospel. Wilkins's study is comprehensive, exploring the history, structure, content, theology, and relevance of the Gospel of Matthew. Wilkins's work is also written in a clear and accessible way, making it one of the most valuable studies of Matthew's Gospel today.

—*Thomas Schreiner,* James Buchanan Harrison Professor of New Testament,
The Southern Baptist Theological Seminary

Michael Wilkins's contribution to this series rewards readers with an all-encompassing and insightful presentation of Matthew's theological vision. His fair and balanced interpretation derives from his esteemed lifetime of research on this gospel is both clear, vibrant and inspirational. It is destined to be a valued resource for pastors, teachers, and students alike.

—*David E. Garland,* Professor Emeritus, George W. Truett Theological Seminary,
Baylor University

Michael Wilkins has devoted his entire scholarly career to mining the riches of the Gospel of Matthew for its witness to the person, proclamation, and passion of Jesus Messiah. In this deeply learned volume, Wilkins caps off a lifetime of study by providing a comprehensive analysis of the central message and major themes of this much-celebrated, Testament-bridging Gospel. In Matthew, as Wilkins demonstrates, we receive a portrait of Jesus who is shown to be both the son of David (Israel's long-awaited king who comes to bless the nation, and indeed all nations, through his beneficent and self-giving reign), and the God-Man (the preexisting, incarnate Son of God who fulfills and sacrificially embodies Israel's law). It is this Jesus who has authoritatively yet mercifully entered human history and called to himself disciples, that they might imitate him through love and allegiance. Thus, Jesus Messiah is no ordinary rabbi; he is our gracious Lord by whose presence God indeed remains "with us." Because Matthew's Gospel, as Wilkins persuasively shows, is nothing short of a manual on discipleship, the careful reader will find in this study a robust tutorial on how to follow faithfully after our beloved Master and Messiah. Highly recommended for students, pastors, and scholars!

—*John K. Goodrich,* Academic Dean and Professor of Biblical Studies,
Compass Bible Institute

It makes sense that a dedicated New Testament and, in particular, Matthean scholar would provide this volume to comprehensively articulate Matthew's theology. Wilkins's life work and exegetical skills have been devoted to knowing the mind and thought of this apostle of Christ and his Gospel. With his proven and distinguished scholarship, Wilkins engages the reader, be they an academician, university student, ministry colleague, or the curiously interested.

—*Joanne Jung,* Professor of Biblical and Theological Studies,
Biola University

In this comprehensive study of Matthean theology, Mike Wilkins draws deeply from his career-long passion for the First Gospel. With the mind of a scholar and the heart of a pastor, Wilkins finds in Matthew a reliable testimony to the historical Jesus, theological instruction for Matthew's first-century community, and God's authoritative word for the church today.

—*Mark L. Strauss,* University Professor of New Testament,
Bethel Seminary

This is a clearly-written, superbly-researched volume that will be a treasure to the study of Matthew. Wilkins adeptly guides the reader through the apostle's portrait of the Messiah in its historical, theological, and modern discipleship contexts. Filled with big-picture insights and exegetical nuggets, *A Theology of Matthew's Gospel* is a valuable resource for both ministry and classroom use.

—*Daniel K. Eng,* Associate Professor of New Testament,
Western Seminary

*A Theology of Matthew's Gospel* is as solidly evangelical as it is richly pastoral; complete in its scholarship but not complex. Michael J. Wilkins sees the Gospel of Matthew as a manual for following Jesus as a disciple who is always and forever subordinate to the Master. Those wishing to do likewise have found a reliable guide in this new book.

—*Daniel M. Gurtner,* Professor of New Testament,
Gateway Seminary

Not every study of biblical theology can be fortified with extraordinarily deep and wide reading, based on decades of classroom experience, informed by sagacious judgment, and produced as a labor of love and devotion to its subject. But what a scholarly blessing it is that Wilkins's *A Theology of Matthew's Gospel* is just such a book.

—*Fred Sanders,* Professor of Theology,
Torrey Honors College, Biola University

Understanding Matthew's Gospel is like navigating a beautiful mountain range: The breathtaking views are only won through an arduous climb. A guide like Michael Wilkins makes the hike worthwhile. Built upon decades of study, this theology of Matthew enables the reader to understand Matthew's thought in its breadth and depth. Wilkins exegetes the text, reviews the history of interpretation, and surveys central themes, all the while shepherding the reader in their walk with Jesus Messiah. After reading the text of Matthew itself, read this book, and you will appreciate the beautiful view like never before.

—*Michael H. Burer,* Dean of Faculty, Professor of New Testament Studies,
Dallas Theological Seminary

As the crowning achievement of his distinguished career, Michael Wilkins has produced an impressive and uniquely detailed survey of Matthew's theology that has no equal. The author of several commentaries on Matthew, Wilkins makes excellent use of his exegetical skills in this enterprise. And his special interest over many years in Matthew's teaching on discipleship is highlighted. Evident throughout is the desire to hear and to obey. Readers will not only be informed, but edified, blessed, and challenged by this remarkable volume.

—*Donald A. Hagner,* George Eldon Ladd Professor Emeritus of New Testament,
Fuller Theological Seminary

This volume is a gift to the church. In it Michael Wilkins pours in a lifetime of study and the result is a deeper appreciation and understanding for a Gospel that has often been a cornerstone for the understanding of all Jesus is.

—*Darrell L. Bock,* Executive Director for Cultural Engagement Hendricks Center
Senior Research Professor of New Testament Studies,
Dallas Theological Seminary

We have in Michael Wilkins's learned study of the Gospel of Matthew a lifetime of scholarly engagement with the text in its original language and with the best of scholarship, ancient and modern. Professor Wilkins moves from topic to topic with expertise and insight. The result is a rich and satisfying treatment of a writing that profoundly impacted the early Church.

—*Craig A. Evans,* Distinguished Research Professor,
The Bible Seminary

The work of a lifetime by one of the world's leading exegetes on the Gospel of Matthew, this book is a rare combination of accumulated wisdom, stellar scholarship and passionate spirituality that will help the reader discover the glorious richness of one of the most treasured writings of the Christian faith.

—*Andrew T. Loke,* Associate Professor,
Hong Kong Baptist University

Wilkins's work on Matthew is one of the most thorough, evenhanded, and faithful readings of Matthew that I have read. He focuses on history, theology, and literature and thus presents a multilayered reading that will serve readers of the Gospel for years to come.

—*Patrick Schreiner,* Associate Professor of New Testament and Biblical Theology,
Midwestern Baptist Theological Seminary

In an extensive examination of the theology of Matthew's Gospel, Mike Wilkins argues that Matthew can be simultaneously a work of accurate history, meaningful theology, and relevant literature. Wilkins's literary investigation of Matthew's theology uncovers the Gospel to be a manual on discipleship to Jesus Messiah even now for the church in the twenty-first century. Highly recommended.

—*Douglas S. Huffman,* Dean of the School of Theology and Professor of New Testament,
University of Northwestern-St. Paul

Michael Wilkins has written a definitive presentation of the theology of the First Gospel. His exegetical analysis is rooted in deep research, his theological discussions are both comprehensive and focused, his evaluations of variegated theories on a host of hermeneutical questions are both fair and balanced as well as decisive, and his style is eminently readable. Students, pastors, and scholars will be richly rewarded when they study the Gospel of Matthew with the help of this magnificent volume.

—*Eckhard J. Schnabel,* Mary F. Rockefeller Distinguished Professor of New Testament Emeritus,
Gordon-Conwell Theological Seminar

*Jesus Immanuel; Messiah of the Kingdom of Heaven, Israel, and the Church*

# A THEOLOGY OF MATTHEW'S GOSPEL

BIBLICAL THEOLOGY OF THE NEW TESTAMENT

MICHAEL J. WILKINS

Andreas J. Köstenberger,
General Editor

ZONDERVAN ACADEMIC

*A Theology of Matthew's Gospel*


Published by Zondervan, 3950 Sparks Drive SE, Suite 101, Grand Rapids, Michigan, 49546, USA. Zondervan is a registered trademark of The Zondervan Corporation, L.L.C., a wholly owned subsidiary of HarperCollins Christian Publishing, Inc.

Requests for information should be addressed to customercare@harpercollins.com.

Zondervan titles may be purchased in bulk for educational, business, fundraising, or sales promotional use. For information, please email SpecialMarkets@Zondervan.com.

---

Library of Congress Cataloging-in-Publication Data

Names: Wilkins, Michael J., author. | Köstenberger, Andreas J., 1957- general editor.
Title: A theology of Matthew's gospel : Jesus Immanuel ; Messiah of the kingdom of heaven, Israel, and the church / Michael J. Wilkins ; Andreas . Köstenberger, general editor.
Description: Grand Rapids, Michigan : Zondervan Academic, [2025] | Series: Biblical theology of the New Testament | Includes bibliographical references and index.
Identifiers: LCCN 2024051511 (print) | LCCN 2024051512 (ebook) | ISBN 9780310270874 (hardcover) | ISBN 9780310172734 (ebook)
Subjects: LCSH: Bible. Matthew--Theology. | Jesus Christ--Messiahship--Biblical teaching.
Classification: LCC BS2575.52 .C66 2022 (print) | LCC BS2575.52 (ebook) | DDC 226.2--dc23/eng/20250215
LC record available at https://lccn.loc.gov/2024051511
LC ebook record available at https://lccn.loc.gov/2024051512

---



HarperCollins Publishers, Macken House, 39/40 Mayor Street Upper, Dublin 1, D01 C9W8, Ireland (https://www.harpercollins.com)

*Cover design: Rob Monacelli*
*Cover photo: Public Domain*
*Interior design: Kait Lamphere*
*Interior typesetting: Sara Colley*

*Printed in the United States of America*

---

25 26 27 28 29 30 31 32 33 34 35 36 37 38 39 /TRM/ 19 18 17 16 15 14 13 12 11 10 9 8 7 6 5 4 3 2 1

*To*

*Lynne Alison Melia Wilkins*

*who for more than fifty-four years it has been my privilege*

*to have known you as the love of my life, wife*

*and partner in loving our daughters and granddaughters,*

*best friend, and lifelong companion on this journey with Jesus*

*and to*

*the faculty, staff, and students of*

*Talbot School of Theology, Biola University*

*whom I have been privileged to know for more than fifty years as*

*valued colleagues, trusted coworkers, and fellow learners*

# CONTENTS

## PART 4: ***Final Matters***

# CONTENTS (DETAILED)

## PART 3: *Major Themes in Matthew's Theology*

# SERIES PREFACE

THE BIBLICAL THEOLOGY of the New Testament series consists of eight distinct volumes covering the entire New Testament. Each volume is devoted to an in-depth exploration of a given New Testament writing, or group of writings, within the context of the theology of the New Testament, and ultimately of the entire Bible. While each corpus requires an approach that is suitable for the writing(s) studied, all volumes include:

(1) a survey of recent scholarship and of the state of research
(2) a treatment of the relevant introductory issues
(3) a thematic commentary following the narrative flow of the document(s)
(4) a treatment of important individual themes
(5) discussions of the relationship between a particular writing and the rest of the New Testament and the Bible

While Biblical Theology is a relatively new academic discipline and one that has often been hindered by questionable presuppositions, doubtful methodology, and/or flawed execution, the field is one of the most promising avenues of biblical and theological research today. In essence, Biblical Theology engages in the study of the biblical texts while giving careful consideration to the historical setting in which a given piece of writing originated. It seeks to locate and relate the contributions of the respective biblical documents along the lines of the continuum of God's salvation historical program centered in the coming and salvific work of Christ. It also endeavors to ground the theological exploration of a given document in a close reading of the respective text(s), whether narrative, discourse, or some other type of literature.

By providing in-depth studies of the diverse, yet complementary perspectives of the New Testament writings, the Biblical Theology of the New Testament series aims to make a significant contribution to the study of the major interrelated themes of Scripture in a holistic, context-sensitive, and spiritually nurturing manner. Each volume is written by a scholar who has written a major commentary or monograph on the corpus covered. The generous page allotment allows for an in-depth investigation. While coming from diverse academic backgrounds and institutional affiliations, the contributors share a commitment to an evangelical faith and a respect for the authority of Scripture. They also have in common a conviction that the canon of Scripture is ultimately unified, not contradictory.

In addition to contributing to the study of individual New Testament writings and to the study of the New Testament and ultimately of Scripture as a whole, the series also seeks to make a methodological contribution, showing how Biblical Theology ought to be conducted. In each case, the way in which the volume is conceived reflects careful consideration of the nature of a given piece or body of writings. The complex interrelationships between the three so-called "Synoptic Gospels"; the two-volume nature of Luke-Acts; the relationship between John's Gospel, letters, and the book of Revelation; the thirteen letters making up the Pauline corpus; and the theologies of Peter, James, and Jude, as well as Hebrews, each presents unique challenges and opportunities.

In the end, it is hoped that the volumes will pay tribute to the multifaceted nature of divine revelation contained in Scripture. As G. B. Caird puts it:

> The question we must ask is not whether these books all say the same thing, but whether they all bear witness to the same Jesus and through him to the many splendoured wisdom of the one God. . . . We shall neither attempt to press all our witnesses into a single mould nor captiously complain that one seems at some points deficient in comparison with another. What we shall do is rejoice that God has seen fit to establish His gospel at the mouth of so many independent witnesses. The music of the New Testament choir is not written to be sung in unison.[1]

In this spirit, the contributors offer their work as a humble aid to a greater appreciation of the magnificent scriptural symphony of God.

Andreas J. Köstenberger, series editor
Wake Forest, NC

1. G. B. Caird, *New Testament Theology*, compl. and ed. L. D. Hurst (Oxford: Clarendon, 1995), 24.

# AUTHOR'S PREFACE

**WRITING THIS VOLUME** on Matthew's Gospel has been a privilege and an obligation. It has been a privilege to focus much of my academic study and teaching on the Gospels, with Matthew as a special focus. To cap my academic work by writing a biblical theology of Matthew's Gospel is a privilege for which I am eternally grateful. Biblical theology as I have developed it here is undertaken on three horizons: the horizon of the historical Jesus, the horizon of Matthew and his community, and the horizon of the contemporary reader. These horizons are debated methodologically by scholars, but the perspectives of these horizons have guided my scholarly work and also my academic and pastoral work. As I have walked with Jesus in his first-century historical setting through Matthew's meticulous written reflections, as I have been instructed through Matthew's theological intentions for his community, and as I have opened myself to allow Matthew's insights to Jesus's identity and mission to penetrate to my heart, soul, mind, and strength, I have been changed. I live with that privilege as a driving force.

And the privilege then impels my writing as an obligation. I do not write as a pastime or a hobby or a means of advancing my academic or professional reputation or standing. I write as an obligation to Jesus Christ, to bear witness to his sacrificial life. I write as an obligation to clearly hear Matthew's message for the church. And I write as an obligation to the present-day church, to attempt to show how the historical Jesus lives as "God with us" as much today as he always has in communities that have been blessed to study Matthew's Gospel. And then, in turn, the obligation becomes a privilege.

Much of my teaching, writing, thinking, and pastoral guidance has come from the study of Matthew's Gospel. I have preached and taught through Matthew's Gospel in many contexts around the world. I have written commentaries, academic monographs, and articles on Matthew's Gospel and related topics. These writings naturally overlap at places with the various introductory issues and theological topics in this volume. I have sometimes used the wording of these earlier projects in this volume. I have always revised the earlier projects, which I indicate in the footnotes to this volume. For example, in Chapter 4 I develop a Literary and Theological Reading of the entirety of Matthew's Gospel that has been informed by my past work on Matthew's Gospel. The theological themes surfaced in the context of that narrative reading are developed in full elsewhere in the Chapter(s) that are devoted to that particular theological theme (e.g., Christology [Chapters 7-8]; Kingdom of heaven [Chapter 9]; etc.). Some overlap and even duplication will be inevitable, but I venture to keep such to a minimum.

I especially have been privileged to have taught Matthew's Gospel to undergraduate, graduate, and doctoral students in many different institutions, but primarily at Talbot School of Theology, Biola University. I first came to Biola as a new believer, a "Jesus freak" (!), and remained there for the next 50+ years as a student, then professor, chair of the New Testament department, dean of the faculty, and retiring as distinguished professor. I can't name all of those over the years who influenced me, but I thank a few, who are friends and more. Dennis Dirks, my fellow dean for over twenty years. Clint Arnold, one of my closest colleagues and collaborators. Bob Saucy (†), one of my most trusted mentors. J. P. Moreland and Scott Rae, my philosopher buddies and visionaries. Clyde Cook (†) and Barry Corey, presidents and dear friends. And then I thank the many faculty and staff colleagues I had the privilege of helping come to campus to join in making Talbot/Biola the dream institution it has become. What a privilege to serve our Lord Jesus together! To the faculty, staff, and students of this wonderful institution, I dedicate this book.

And I have been privileged also to teach on the Gospel of Matthew to the church. My first experience was as pastor of a church plant, Carlsbad Community Evangelical Free Church (now North Coast). Then as pastor of Cayucos Community Evangelical Free Church. And then for over twenty years on the (adjunct) pastoral staff at San Clemente Presbyterian Church. I have also had the privilege to teach on Matthew's Gospel to adult ministries, such as Hume Lake Christian Camps, Forest Home Christian Camps, and Mount Hermon Christian Camps. Almost everything I have ever written on Matthew's Gospel has been exposed to these various pastoral and teaching settings.

This volume has been many years in the making. I give special thanks to Zondervan Academic, through which much of my publishing work has come to life, for their patience and guidance. I have been privileged to experience the professional and personal care at Zondervan of a wonderful core of editors, including Stan Gundry, Ed van der Maas, Verlyn Verbrugge, Jack Kuhatschek, Jack Kragt, and Lee Fields especially on this project, among many others. The leadership has recently gone to Katya Covrett, with whom my wife and I have enjoyed long friendships and professional care. Thank you, Katya, for your encouragement and professional leadership.

Preeminently I thank the Lord Jesus for finding me and saving me—a very disturbed, angry, and misguided young soul, just back from fighting in the war in Viet Nam. The grace of God is the gift of life and is the enablement to live a new life (Titus 3:1–8). I can only thank him for saving me and giving me the life that enabled me to understand more clearly the gospel of Jesus Christ and to write this book on the theology of the Gospel of Matthew.

And no less preeminently, I thank my wife, Lynne, for allowing God to guide me to you. Thank you for allowing me to enter your life as a very disturbed young man and allowing God to give us life together for now over fifty-four years. I could never have done what I have done, including writing this book, without your constant presence, encouragement, exasperation at my plodding , and support for my work. Our joy together has been to raise two wonderful daughters, Michelle and Wendy, and to be blessed by their husbands, Dan and Jason, and now to revel in our granddaughters, Melia and Ava. Thank you, Lynne, for the journey. To you again I dedicate this book.

Michael J. Wilkins
San Clemente, California

# Abbreviations

Abbreviations for books of the Bible, Second Temple Jewish literature, rabbinic works, papyri, early church writings, classical works, and similar materials are readily available in sources such as *The SBL Handbook of Style* and are included here where considered necessary. The *SBL Handbook of Style* is the standard for abbreviations in this book.

| | |
|---|---|
| AABSSS | Anglican Association of Biblical Scholars Study Series |
| AB | Anchor Bible |
| Abbott-Smith | Abbott-Smith, G. *A Manual Greek Lexicon of the New Testament.* New York: Charles Scribner's Sons, 1922. |
| *ABD* | *Anchor Bible Dictionary.* David Noel Freedman, Editor in Chief. New York: Doubleday, 1992 |
| ABRL | Anchor Bible Reference Library |
| AcBib | Academia Biblica |
| ACCSNT | Ancient Christian Commentary on Scripture: New Testament |
| ACNT | Augsburg Commentary on the New Testament |
| *Ag. Ap.* | *Against Apion* (Josephus) |
| AJEC | Ancient Judaism and Early Christianity |
| *ALGNT* | *Analytical Lexicon of the Greek New Testament.* Timothy Friberg, Barbara Friberg, Neva F. Miller. Grand Rapids, Baker, 2000 |
| AnBib | Analecta Biblica |
| ANCTRTBS | Ashgate New Critical Thinking in Religion, Theology and Biblical Studies |
| *ANF* | *Ante-Nicene Fathers*, ed. Alexander Roberts and James Donaldson |
| *ANRW* | *Aufstieg und Niedergang der römischen Welt: Geschichte und Kultur Rom im Spiegel der neueren Forschung.* Hildegard Temporini and Wolfgang Hause, eds. Part 2, Principat. Berlin: de Gruyter, 1972– |
| *Ant.* | *Jewish Antiquities* (Josephus) |
| ANTC | Abingdon New Testament Commentaries |
| ASBT | Acadia Studies in Bible and Theology |
| *AThRSup* | *Anglican Theological Review Supplement Series* |
| AYBRL | Anchor Yale Bible Reference Library |
| b. | Babylonian Talmud |

| | |
|---|---|
| *BBR* | *Bulletin for Biblical Research* |
| *BBRSup* | *Bulletin for Biblical Research Supplements* |
| BDAG | Bauer, W., F. W. Danker, W. F. Arndt, and F. W. Gingrich. *A Greek-English Lexicon of the New Testament and Other Early Christian Literature.* 3rd ed. Chicago: University of Chicago Press, 2000 |
| BDB | Brown, Francis, S. R. Driver, and Charles A. Briggs. *A Hebrew and English Lexicon of the Old Testament* |
| BDF | Blass, Friedrich, Albert Debrunner, and Robert W. Funk. *A Greek Grammar of the New Testament and Other Early Christian Literature.* Chicago: University of Chicago Press, 1961 |
| *BEB* | *Baker Encyclopedia of the Bible.* 2 vols. Walter A. Elwell, ed. Grand Rapids: Baker Book House, 1988 |
| BECNT | Baker Exegetical Commentary on the New Testament |
| BETL | Bibliotheca Ephemeridum Theologicarum Lovaniensium |
| *Bib* | *Biblica* |
| BibInt | Biblical Interpretation Series |
| BibleRec | The Bible and Its Reception |
| BibSem | The Biblical Seminar |
| *BiPa* | *Biblia Patristica: Index des citations et allusions bibliques dans la littérature patristique.* Paris: Centre national de la recherche scientifique, 1975 |
| BMSSEC | Baylor-Mohr Siebeck Studies in Early Christianity |
| BRLA | Brill Reference Library of Judaism |
| *BSac* | *Bibliotheca Sacra* |
| BST | The Bible Speaks Today |
| *BTB* | *Biblical Theology Bulletin* |
| BTCB | Brazos Theological Commentary on the Bible |
| BTL | Biblical Theology for Life |
| BZNW | Beihefte zur Zeitschrift für die neutestamentliche Wissenschaft und die Kunde der älteren Kirche |
| CBET | Contributions to Biblical Exegesis and Theology |
| *CBQ* | *Catholic Biblical Quarterly* |
| CCL | Corpus Christianorum Series Latina |
| CCR | Cambridge Companions to Religion |
| CNT | Commentaire du Nouveau Testament |
| ConBNT | Coniectanea Neotestamentica or Coniectanea Biblica: New Testament Series |
| CRINT | Compendia rerum iudaicarum ad Novum Testamentum |
| *CTR* | *Criswell Theological Review* |
| *CurBR* | *Currents in Biblical Research* |
| *CurBS* | *Currents in Research: Biblical Studies* |

Danby — Herbert Danby, trans. and ed. *The Mishnah*. Oxford: Oxford University Press, 1933
*DBI* — *Dictionary of Biblical Imagery*. Edited by Leland Ryken, James C. Wilhoit, and Tremper Longman III. Downers Grove: InterVarsity, 1998
*Dial.* — *Dialogus cum Tryphone* (Justin Martyr)
Did. — Didache
*DJBP* — *Dictionary of Judaism in the Biblical Period: 450 B.C.E. to 600 C.E.* Edited by Jacob Neusner and William Scott Green. Peabody, MA: Hendrickson, 1999
*DJG*[1] — *Dictionary of Jesus and the Gospels*. Edited by Joel B. Green, Scot McKnight, and I. Howard Marshall. Downers Grove: InterVarsity, 1992
*DJG*[2] — *Dictionary of Jesus and the Gospels*. Edited by Joel B. Green, Jeannine K. Brown, and Nicholas Perrin. 2nd ed. Downers Grove: InterVarsity, 2013
*DLNTD* — *Dictionary of the Later New Testament and Its Developments*. Edited by Ralph P. Martin and Peter H. Davids. Downers Grove: InterVarsity, 1997
*DNTB* — *Dictionary of New Testament Background*. Edited by Craig A. Evans and Stanley E. Porter. Downers Grove: InterVarsity, 2000
*DPL* — *Dictionary of Paul and His Letters*. Edited by Gerald F. Hawthorne, Ralph P. Martin, and Daniel G. Reid. Downers Grove: InterVarsity, 1993
*DSD* — *Dead Sea Discoveries*
EBC — Expositor's Bible Commentary. Edited by Frank E. Gaebelein. 12 vols. Grand Rapids: Zondervan, 1979 (cf. REBC)
*EBR* — *Encyclopedia of the Bible and Its Reception*. Edited by Hans-Josef Klauck et al. Berlin: de Gruyter, 2009–
EBS — Essentials of Biblical Studies
EBT — Explorations in Biblical Theology
EBTC — Evangelical Biblical Theology Commentary
ECC — Eerdmans Critical Commentary
ECL — Early Christianity and Its Literature
*EDB* — *Eerdmans Dictionary of the Bible*. Edited by David Noel Freedman, Allen C. Myers, and Astrid B. Beck. Grand Rapids: Eerdmans, 2000
*EDBT* — *Evangelical Dictionary of Biblical Theology*. Edited by Walter A. Elwell. Grand Rapids: Baker, 1996
*EDEJ* — *Eerdmans Dictionary of Early Judaism*. Edited by John J. Collins and Daniel C. Harlow. Grand Rapids: Eerdmans, 2010
*EDSS* — *Encyclopedia of the Dead Sea Scrolls*. Edited by Lawrence H. Schiffman and James C. VanderKam. 2 vols. Oxford: Oxford University Press, 2000
EEC — Evangelical Exegetical Commentary
*EJR* — *Encyclopedia of the Jewish Religion*. Edited by R. J. Zwi Werblowsky and Geoffrey Wigoder. New York: Adama, 1986

| | |
|---|---|
| EKKNT | Evangelisch-katholischer Kommentar zum Neuen Testament |
| ESBT | Essential Studies in Biblical Theology |
| ESEC | Emory Studies in Early Christianity |
| esp. | especially |
| *ETL* | *Ephemerides Theologicae Lovanienses* |
| ETSMS | Evangelical Theological Society Monograph Series |
| *EuroJTh* | *European Journal of Theology* |
| *EvQ* | *Evangelical Quarterly* |
| exp. | expanded |
| *ExpTim* | *Expository Times* |
| FET | Foundations of Evangelical Theology |
| *Fr. Matt.* | *Fragmenta ex commentarii in evangelium Matthaei* (Origen) |
| *FzB* | *Forschung zur Bibel* |
| GNC | Good News Commentary |
| GNS | Good News Studies |
| HACB | Holman Apologetics Commentary on the Bible |
| *Haer.* | *Adversus haereses* (Irenaeus) |
| HBT | Horizons in Biblical Theology |
| Hermeneia | Hermeneia—A Critical and Historical Commentary on the Bible |
| *HeyJ* | *Heythrop Journal* |
| *Hist. eccl.* | *Ecclesiastical History* (Eusebius) |
| *HSHJ* | *Handbook for the Study of the Historical Jesus* |
| HTANT | Historisch-Theologische Auslegung Neues Testament |
| *HTR* | *Harvard Theological Review* |
| HUT | Hermeneutische Untersuchungen zur Theologie |
| *HvTSt* | *Hervormde Teologiese Studies* |
| HvTStSup | Hervormde Teologiese Studies Supplementum |
| ICC | International Critical Commentary |
| *IEJ* | *Israel Exploration Journal* |
| Ign. *Eph.* | Ignatius, *To the Ephesians* |
| Ign. *Magn.* | Ignatius, *To the Magnesians* |
| Ign. *Phld.* | Ignatius, *To the Philadelphians* |
| Ign. *Pol.* | Ignatius, *To Polycarp* |
| Ign. *Smyrn.* | Ignatius, *To the Smyrnaeans* |
| *Int* | *Interpretation* |
| IVBS | International Voices in Biblical Studies |
| *DTBYML* | *A Dictionary of the Targumim, the Babli and Yerushalmi, and the Midrashic Literature.* Marcus Jastrow. 2 vols. London: Luzac & Co.; New York: G. P. Putnam's Sons, 1903 |

| | |
|---|---|
| *JBL* | *Journal of Biblical Literature* |
| *JBRec* | *Journal of the Bible and Its Reception* |
| JCT | Jewish and Christian Texts |
| *JECH* | *Journal of Early Christian History* |
| *JETS* | *Journal of the Evangelical Theological Society* |
| *JJMJS* | *Journal of the Jesus Movement in Its Jewish Setting: From the First to the Seventh Century* |
| *JSHJ* | *Journal for the Study of the Historical Jesus* |
| *JSJ* | *Journal for the Study of Judaism in the Persian, Hellenistic, and Roman Periods* |
| JSJSup | Journal for the Study of Judaism in the Persian, Hellenistic, and Roman Periods Supplement Series |
| *JSNT* | *Journal for the Study of the New Testament* |
| JSNTSup | Journal for the Study of the New Testament Supplement Series |
| *JSP* | *Journal for the Study of the Pseudepigrapha* |
| JSPSup | Journal for the Study of the Pseudepigrapha Supplement Series |
| *JTS* | *Journal of Theological Studies* |
| *J.W.* | *Jewish War* (Josephus) |
| LATCS | Los Angeles Theology Conference Series |
| *LBD* | *Lexham Bible Dictionary*, Logos edition |
| LBRS | Lexham Bible Reference Series |
| LBS | Linguistic Biblical Studies |
| LCL | Loeb Classical Library |
| LEC | Library of Early Christianity |
| *LGCG* | *Lexham Geographic Commentary on the Gospels*. Edited by Barry J. Beitzel, with Kristopher A. Lyle. Bellingham, WA: Lexham, 2016 |
| LHJS | Library of Historical Jesus Studies |
| *Life* | *The Life* (Josephus) |
| LNTS | Library of New Testament Studies |
| LSJ | Liddell, Henry George, Robert Scott, and Henry Stuart Jones. *A Greek-English Lexicon*. 9th ed. with revised supplement. Oxford: Clarendon, 1996 |
| LSTS | Library of Second Temple Studies |
| *LTW* | *Lexham Theological Wordbook*. Edited by Douglas Mangum, Derek R. Brown, Rachel Klippenstein, and Rebekkah Hurst. Bellingham, WA: Lexham, 2014 |
| m. | Mishnah. Normally citing *The Mishnah*. Translated by Herbert Danby. Oxford: Oxford University Press, 1933 |
| MBI | Methods in Biblical Interpretation |
| MNTS | McMaster New Testament Studies |
| NAC | New American Commentary |
| NACSBT | NAC Studies in Bible and Theology |

| | |
|---|---|
| *NBD*[3] | *New Bible Dictionary*. Edited by D. R. W. Wood, I. Howard Marshal, J. D. Douglas, and N. Hillyer. 3rd ed. Downers Grove, IL: InterVarsity, 1996 |
| NCB | New Century Bible |
| n.d. | no date |
| *NDBT* | *New Dictionary of Biblical Theology: Exploring the Unity and Diversity of Scripture*. Edited by T. Desmond Alexander, Brian S. Rosner, D. A. Carson, and Graeme Goldsworthy. Downers Grove, IL: InterVarsity, 2000 |
| *Neot* | *Neotestamentica* |
| *NIB* | *New Interpreter's Bible*. Edited by Leander E. Keck. 12 vols. Nashville: Abingdon, 1994–2004 |
| NIBCNT | New International Biblical Commentary, New Testament |
| NICNT | New International Commentary on the New Testament |
| NICOT | New International Commentary on the Old Testament |
| *NIDNTT* | *New International Dictionary of New Testament Theology*. Edited by Colin Brown. 5 vols. Grand Rapids: Zondervan, 1975–1978 |
| *NIDNTTE* | *New International Dictionary of New Testament Theology and Exegesis*. 2nd ed. Edited by Moíses Silva. 5 vols. Grand Rapids: Zondervan, 2014 |
| *NIDOTTE* | *New International Dictionary of Old Testament Theology and Exegesis*. Edited by Willem A. VanGemeren. 5 vols. Grand Rapids: Zondervan, 1997 |
| NIGTC | New International Greek Testament Commentary |
| NIVAC | New International Version Application Commentary |
| *NovT* | *Novum Testamentum* |
| NovTSup | Supplements to Novum Testamentum |
| *NPNF*[2] | *Nicene and Post-Nicene Fathers*, Series 2. Edited by Philip Schaff. 1886–1889. 14 vols. Repr. Peabody, MA: Hendricksen, 1994 |
| NS | New Series |
| NSBT | New Studies in Biblical Theology |
| NSD | New Studies in Dogmatics |
| NT | New Testament |
| NTAbh | Neutestamentliche Abhandlungen |
| NTC | New Testament Commentary |
| NTGJC | New Testament Gospels in Their Judaic Contexts |
| NTL | New Testament Library |
| NTM | New Testament Message |
| NTMon | New Testament Monographs |
| NTP | Novum Testamentum Patristicum |
| NTS | New Testament Studies |
| NTTS | New Testament Tools and Studies |
| OBT | Overtures to Biblical Theology |

| | |
|---|---|
| *OHC* | *Oxford Handbook of Christology*. Edited by Francesca Aran Murphy and Troy A. Stefano. Oxford: Oxford University Press, 2015 |
| OT | Old Testament |
| *OTP* | *Old Testament Pseudepigrapha*. James E. Charlesworth. 2 vols. New York; London: Yale University Press, 1983 |
| Paideia | Paideia Commentaries on the New Testament |
| passim | located at various places and throughout a work |
| PBM | Paternoster Biblical Monographs |
| PNTC | Pillar New Testament Commentary |
| PTMS | Princeton Theological Monograph Series |
| QD | Quaestiones Disputatae |
| R5AS | Refo500 Academic Studies |
| *R&T* | *Religion and Theology* |
| RAD | Reformed Academic Dissertations |
| RAS | Reformed Academic Studies |
| RCIT | Reclaiming the Christian Intellectual Tradition |
| REBC | Revised Expositor's Bible Commentary. Edited by Tremper Longman III and David E. Garland. 13 vols. Grand Rapids: Zondervan, 2010 (cf. EBC) |
| *RevExp* | *Review and Expositor* |
| SANACS | Society of Asian North American Christian Studies |
| SBEC | Studies in the Bible and Early Christianity |
| *SBET* | *Scottish Bulletin of Evangelical Theology* |
| SBIR | Studies of the Bible and Its Reception |
| *SBJT* | *Southern Baptist Journal of Theology* |
| SBL | Studies in Biblical Literature |
| SBLDS | Society of Biblical Literature Dissertation Series |
| SBLMS | Society of Biblical Literature Monograph Series |
| SBLSP | Society of Biblical Literature Seminar Papers |
| SBLSymS | Society of Biblical Literature Symposium Series |
| SBT | Studies in Biblical Theology |
| *SCJR* | *Studies in Christian-Jewish Relations*, e-journal of the Council of Centers on Jewish-Christian Relations, Boston College |
| SGBC | Story of God Bible Commentary |
| SHBC | Smyth & Helwys Bible Commentary |
| SHBCSS | Smyth & Helwys Bible Commentary Supplemental Series |
| SJSJ | Supplements to the Journal for the Study of Judaism |
| *SJT* | *Scottish Journal of Theology* |
| SM | Sermon on the Mount |
| SNTI | Studies in New Testament Interpretation |

| | |
|---|---|
| SNTSMS | Society for New Testament Studies Monograph Series |
| SNTW | Studies of the New Testament and Its World |
| SP | Sacra Pagina |
| SPNT | Studies on Personalities of the New Testament |
| SSBT | Studies in Scripture and Biblical Theology |
| STDJ | Studies on the Texts of the Desert of Judah |
| SubBi | Subsidia Biblica |
| SWBA | Social World of Biblical Antiquity |
| *TBD* | *Tyndale Bible Dictionary.* Walter A. Elwell and Philip Wesley Comfort. Wheaton, IL: Tyndale House Publishers, 2001 |
| *TCGNT*[2] | *Textual Commentary on the Greek New Testament: A Companion Volume to the UBS' Greek New Testament (Fourth Revised Edition).* 2nd ed. Edited by Bruce M. Metzger. Stuttgart: German Bible Society, 1994 |
| *TDNT* | *Theological Dictionary of the New Testament.* Edited by Gerhard Kittel and Gerhard Friedrich. Tranlated by Geoffrey W. Bromiley. 10 vols. Grand Rapids: Eerdmans, 1964–1976 |
| *TDOT* | *Theological Dictionary of the Old Testament.* Edited by G. Johannes Botterweck and Helmer Ringgren. Translated by John T. Willis et al. 17 vols. Grand Rapids: Eerdmans, 1974–2006 |
| TEBC | The Earth Bible Commentary Series |
| TENTS | Texts and Editions for New Testament Study |
| TGST | Tesi Gregoriana, Serie Teologia |
| *Them* | *Themelios* |
| THNTC | Two Horizons New Testament Commentary |
| TNTC | Tyndale New Testament Commentary |
| TPINTC | Trinity Press International New Testament Commentaries |
| *TynBul* | *Tyndale Bulletin* |
| UBS[4] | *The Greek New Testament,* United Bible Society, 4th ed. Edited by Barbar Aland et al. Stuttgart: Deutsche Bibelgesellschaft and United Bible Societies, 1994 |
| UBS[5] | *The Greek New Testament,* United Bible Society, 5th ed. Edited by Barbar Aland et al. Stuttgart: Deutsche Bibelgesellschaft and United Bible Societies, 2014 |
| *VT* | *Vetus Testamentum* |
| VTSup | Vetus Testamentum Supplements |
| WBBC | Wiley Blackwell Bible Commentaries |
| WBC | Word Biblical Commentaries |
| *WTJ* | *Westminster Theological Journal* |
| WTT | Westar Tools and Translations |
| WUNT | Wissenschaftliche Untersuchungen zum Neuen Testament |
| *WW* | *Word and World* |

| | |
|---|---|
| *ZDBT* | *Zondervan Dictionary of Bible Themes.* Martin H. Manser, Alister E. McGrath, J. I. Packer, Donald J. Wiseman, eds. Grand Rapids: Zondervan, 2009 |
| ZECNT | Zondervan Exegetical Commentary on the New Testament |
| *ZIBBC* | *Zondervan Illustrated Bible Backgrounds Commentary* |
| *ZKT* | *Zeitschrift für katholische Theologie* |
| *ZNT* | *Zeitschrift für Neues Testament* |
| *ZNW* | *Zeitschrift für die neutestamentliche Wissenschaft und die Kunde der älteren Kirche* |
| *ZPEB* | *Zondervan Pictorial Encyclopedia of the Bible.* Edited by Merrill C. Tenney. 5 vols. Grand Rapids: Zondervan, 1975 |
| *ZTK* | *Zeitschrift für Theologie und Kirche* |

*Part 1*

# Introductory Matters as a Foundation for Matthew's Theology

*Chapter 1*

# INTRODUCING MATTHEW'S GOSPEL

## *History, Theology and Literature*

### BIBLIOGRAPHY

**Aune, David E.**, ed. *The Gospel of Matthew in Current Study: Studies in Memory of William G. Thompson, S.J.* Grand Rapids: Eerdmans, 2001. **Bauckham, Richard J.**, ed. *The Gospels for All Christians: Rethinking the Gospel Audiences.* Grand Rapids: Eerdmans, 1998. ———. "The Gospels as Testimony to Jesus Christ: A Contemporary View of Their Historical Value." Pages 55–70 in *OHC*. ———. *Jesus and the Eyewitnesses: The Gospels as Eyewitness Testimony.* 2nd ed. 2006; Grand Rapids: Eerdmans, 2017. **Bird, Michael F.** "New Testament Theology Re-Loaded: Integrating Biblical Theology and Christian Origins." *TynBul* 60.2 (2009): 265–91. **Blomberg, Craig L.** *A New Testament Theology.* Waco, TX: Baylor University Press, 2018. **Bock, Darrell L., and J. Ed Komoszewski**, eds. *Jesus, Skepticism, and the Problem of History: Criteria and Context in the Study of Christian Origins.* Grand Rapids: Zondervan, 2019. **Bockmuehl, Markus.** "The Gospels on the Presence of Jesus." Pages 87–102 in *OHC*. **Boxall, Ian.** *Discovering Matthew: Content, Interpretation, Reception.* Discovering Biblical Texts. Grand Rapids: Eerdmans, 2015. ———. *Matthew Through the Centuries.* WBBC. Hoboken, NJ: Wiley, 2019. **Burridge, Richard A.** *What Are the Gospels? A Comparison with Graeco-Roman Biography.* 25th anniversary (3rd) ed. 1992; 2004; Waco, TX: Baylor University Press, 2018. **Carson, D. A.**, ed. *The Enduring Authority of the Christian Scriptures.* Grand Rapids: Eerdmans, 2016. **Deines, Roland.** "The Recognition of God's Acts in History in the Gospel of Matthew: An Exercise in Salvation History." Pages 311–50 in Roland Deines, Acts *of God in History: Studies Towards Recovering a Theological Historiography.* Edited by Christoph Ochs and Peter Watts. WUNT 317. Tübingen: Mohr Siebeck, 2013. **Evans, Craig A.** "'The Book of the Genesis of Jesus Christ': The Purpose of Matthew in Light of the Incipit." Pages 61–72 in *Biblical Interpretation in Early Christian Gospels.* Vol. 2 of *The Gospel of Matthew.* Edited by Thomas R. Hatina. LNTS 310. London: T&T Clark, 2008. **Feinberg, John S.** *Light in a Dark Place: The Doctrine of Scripture.* FET. Wheaton, IL: Crossway, 2018.

**France, R. T.** *Matthew: Evangelist and Teacher.* Grand Rapids: Zondervan, 1989. **Frankemölle, Hubert.** *Jahwe-Bund und Kirche Christi: Studien zur Form- und Traditionsgeschichte des 'Evangelius' nach Matthäus.* NTAbh. Münster, DE: Aschendorff, 1974. **Grudem, Wayne.** *Systematic Theology: An Introduction to Biblical Doctrine.* 2nd ed. Grand Rapids: Zondervan, 2020. **Gurtner, Daniel M.** "The Gospel of Matthew from Stanton to Present: A Survey of Some Recent Developments." Pages 23–38 in *Jesus, Matthew's Gospel and Early Christianity: Studies in Memory of Graham N. Stanton.* Edited by Daniel M. Gurtner, Joel Willitts, and Richard A. Burridge. LNTS 435. London: T&T Clark, 2011. **Hagner, Donald A.** "Matthew: Christian Judaism or Jewish Christianity?" Pages 263–82 in *The Face of New Testament Studies: A Survey of Recent Research.* Edited by Scot McKnight and Grant R. Osborne. Grand Rapids: Baker Academic, 2004. **Hengel, Martin.** *The Four Gospels and the One Gospel of Jesus Christ: An Investigation of the Collection and Origin of the Canonical Gospels.* Translated by John Bowden. Harrisburg, PA: Trinity Press International, 2000. **Kealy, Sean P.** *Matthew's Gospel and the History of Biblical Interpretation.* 2 vols. Mellen Biblical Press Series 55a and 55b. New York: Mellen, 1997. **Keener, Craig S.** *Christobiography: Memory, History, and the Reliability of the Gospels.* Grand Rapids: Eerdmans, 2019. **Kirk, J. R. Daniel.** "Conceptualising Fulfilment in Matthew." *TynBul* 59.1 (2008): 77–98. **Klink, Edward W., III, and Darian R. Lockett.** *Understanding Biblical Theology: A Comparison of Theory and Practice.* Grand Rapids: Zondervan, 2012. **Ladd, George Eldon.** *A Theology of the New Testament.* Rev. ed. Edited by Donald A. Hagner. 1974; Grand Rapids: Eerdmans, 1993. **Lemcio, Eugene E.** *The Past of Jesus in the Gospels.* SNTSMS 68. Cambridge: Cambridge University Press, 1991. **Luz, Ulrich.** *The Theology of the Gospel of Matthew.* Translated by J. Bradford Robinson. New Testament Theology. Cambridge: Cambridge University Press, 1995. **Marshall, I. Howard.** "Matthew's Theological Story." Pages 95–111 in *New Testament Theology: Many Witnesses, One Gospel.* Downers Grove, IL: InterVarsity, 2004. **Martin, Ralph P.** *New Testament Foundations: A Guide for Christian Students. Volume 1: The Four Gospels.* Grand Rapids: Eerdmans, 1975. **Massaux, Édouard.** *The Influence of the Gospel of Saint Matthew on Christian Literature before Saint Irenaeus, Book 1: The First Ecclesiastical Writers.* Translated by Norman J. Belval and Suzanne Hecht. Edited by Arthur J. Bellinzoni. New Gospel Studies 5/1. 1950; Macon, GA: Mercer, 1990. **Morgan, Robert, and John Barton.** *Biblical Interpretation.* The Oxford Bible Series. Oxford: Oxford University Press, 1988. **Pennington, Jonathan T.** *Reading the Gospels Wisely: A Narrative and Theological Introduction.* Grand Rapids: Baker Academic, 2012. **Powell, Mark Allan,** ed. *Methods for Matthew.* MBI. Cambridge: Cambridge University Press, 2009. **Quarles, Charles L.** *A Theology of Matthew: Jesus Revealed as Deliverer, King, and Incarnate Creator.* Explorations in Biblical Theology. Phillipsburg, NJ: P&R, 2013. **Rosner, Brian S.** "Biblical Theology." *DNBT* 3–11. **Schröter, Jens.** *Jesus of Nazareth: Jew from Galilee, Savior of the World.* Translated by Wayne Coppins and S. Brian Pounds. BMSSEC. Waco, TX: Baylor University

Press, 2014. ———. "The Quest for the Historical Jesus: Current Debates and Prospects." *Early Christianity* 11 (2020): 283–96. **Senior, Donald.** *What Are They Saying About Matthew?* Rev. and exp. ed. New York: Paulist, 1996. ———. "Directions in Matthean Studies." Pages 5–21 in *The Gospel of Matthew in Current Study: Studies in Memory of William G. Thompson, S.J.* Edited by David E. Aune. Grand Rapids: Eerdmans, 2001. ———. "Matthew at the Crossroads of Early Christianity: An Introductory Assessment." Pages 3–24 in *The Gospel of Matthew at the Crossroads of Early Christianity*. Edited by Donald Senior. BETL CCXLIII. Leuven: Peeters, 2011. **Sim, David C.** "Matthew: The Current State of Research." Pages 33–51 in *Mark and Matthew I. Comparative Readings: Understanding the Earliest Gospels in Their First Century Settings*. Edited by Eve-Marie Becker and Anders Runesson. WUNT 271. Tübingen: Mohr Siebeck, 2011. **Spadaro, Martin C.** *Reading Matthew as the Climactic Fulfillment of the Hebrew Story*. Eugene, OR: Wipf & Stock, 2015. **Stanton, Graham N.** "The Origin and Purpose of Matthew's Gospel: Matthean Scholarship from 1945–1980." Pages 9–75 in *Studies in Matthew and Early Christianity*. Reprint. Edited by Markus Bockmuehl and David Lincicum. WUNT 309. Tübingen: Mohr Siebeck, 2013. ———, ed. *The Interpretation of Matthew*. 2nd ed. Studies in New Testament Interpretation. Edinburgh: T&T Clark, 1995. ———. "The Early Reception of Matthew's Gospel: New Evidence from Papyri?" Pages 42–61 in *The Gospel of Matthew in Current Study: Studies in Memory of William G. Thompson, S.J.* Edited by David E. Aune. Grand Rapids: Eerdmans, 2001. **Thielman, Frank.** *Theology of the New Testament: A Canonical and Synthetic Approach*. Grand Rapids: Zondervan, 2005. **Thiselton, Anthony C.** *New Horizons in Hermeneutics: The Theory and Practice of Transforming Biblical Reading*. Grand Rapids: Zondervan, 1992. ———. *The Two Horizons: New Testament Hermeneutics and Philosophical Description*. Grand Rapids: Eerdmans, 1980. **Treier, Daniel J.** "Biblical Theology and/or Theological Interpretation of Scripture? Defining the Relationship." *SJT* 61.1 (2008): 16–31. **Vos, Geerhardus.** *Biblical Theology: Old and New Testaments*. Grand Rapids: Eerdmans, 1948. **Watson, Francis.** *The Fourfold Gospel: A Theological Reading of the New Testament Portraits of Jesus*. Grand Rapids: Baker Academic, 2016. **Wilkins, Michael J., and Erik Thoennes.** *Biblical and Theological Studies: A Student's Guide*. RCIT. Wheaton, IL: Crossway, 2018. **Wright, N. T., and Michael F. Bird.** *The New Testament in Its World: An Introduction to the History, Literature, and Theology of the First Christians*. Grand Rapids: Zondervan, 2019. **Yarbrough, Robert W.** *The Salvation Historical Fallacy? Reassessing the History of New Testament Theology*. History of Biblical Interpretation Series 2. Leiderdorp, NL: Deo, 2004. ———. "Salvation History." Pages 45–58 in *God's Glory Revealed in Christ: Essays on Biblical Theology in Honor of Thomas R. Schreiner*. Edited by Denny Burk, James M. Hamilton Jr., and Brian Vickers. Nashville: B&H, 2019. **Yieh, John Yueh-Han.** *One Teacher: Jesus' Teaching Role in Matthew's Gospel Report*. BZNW 124. Berlin: de Gruyter, 2004. ———. *Conversations with Scripture: The Gospel of Matthew*. AABSSS. New York: Morehouse, 2012.

# 1.1 INTRODUCTION TO MATTHEW'S GOSPEL: HISTORY, THEOLOGY, AND LITERATURE

## 1.1.1 The Influence of Matthew's Gospel in Church History

We are embarking on a historical and theological journey through one of the most treasured writings of the Christian faith: the Gospel according to the apostle Matthew.

The Gospel of Matthew, according to citations found in early Christian writers, was the most widely read and frequently used of any of the four Gospels in the formative years of the church. D. H. Williams, a leading authority on patristic use of Matthew's Gospel, states, "In the early Church, the Gospel according to St. Matthew received more commentary and sermons than any of the other three gospels."[1] Early church history scholar Édouard Massaux asserts that the Gospel of Matthew could easily be called "the Gospel par excellence" as the most important of the four Gospels for the first centuries of the church.[2] In the introduction to his comprehensive survey of Matthean studies throughout church history, Sean Kealy states, "Although much is disputed in detail, there is no doubt that Matthew's Gospel quickly became the most popular Gospel in the post-apostolic church."[3] He notes that an examination of biblical references in the early church fathers from the first two centuries shows that they make seventy references to Matthew, twenty-seven to Mark, sixty to Luke, and thirty-seven to John.[4]

Manlio Simonetti, a renowned expert in patristic literature, states of Matthew's Gospel, "It is no exaggeration to state that the faithful who lived between the end of the first and the end of the second centuries came to know the words and deeds of Christ on the basis of this text."[5]

And Matthean scholar Graham Stanton declares, "Matthew's Gospel was more widely used and more influential in the early Church than any of the other Gospels."[6] He points to the seven earliest surviving papyri of Matthew's Gospel, all dated no later

1. D. H. Williams, trans. and ed., *Matthew: Interpreted by Early Christian Commentators*, Church's Bible (Grand Rapids: Eerdmans, 2018), xxiii. See also D. Jeffrey Bingham, *Irenaeus' Use of Matthew's Gospel in Adversus Haereses*, Traditio Exegetica Graeca 7 (Leuven: Peeters, 1997); and especially on the Valentinian reception of the Gospel of Matthew, see David W. Jorgensen, *Treasure Hidden in a Field: Early Christian Reception of the Gospel of Matthew*, SBIR 6 (Berlin: de Gruyter, 2016).

2. Édouard Massaux, *The Influence of the Gospel of Saint Matthew on Christian Literature before Saint Irenaeus, Book 1: The First Ecclesiastical Writers*, ed. Arthur J. Bellinzoni, trans. Norman J. Belval and Suzanne Hecht, New Gospel Studies 5/1 (1950; Macon, GA: Mercer University Press, 1990), xxi. So also Orthodox Church NT scholar Metropolitan Hilarion (Alfeyev) of Volokolamsk, "The Gospel of Matthew in Church Tradition and Modern Scholarship," in *The Gospel of Matthew in its Historical and Theological Context: Papers from the International Conference in Moscow, September 24 to 28, 2018*, ed. Mikhail Seleznev, William R. G. Loader, and Karl-Wilhelm Niebuhr, WUNT 459 (Tübingen: Mohr Siebeck, 2021), 3–16.

3. Sean P. Kealy, *Matthew's Gospel and the History of Biblical Interpretation*, 2 vols., Mellen Biblical Press Series 55a and 55b (Lewiston, NY: Mellen, 1997), 1:5.

4. Kealy, *Matthew's Gospel*, 5, citing *Biblia Patristica: Index des citations et allusions bibliques dans la littérature patristique* (Paris: Centre national de la recherche scientifique, 1975).

5. Manlio Simonetti, ed., *Matthew 1–13*, ACCSNT Ia (Downers Grove: InterVarsity, 2001), xxxvii.

6. Graham N. Stanton, ed., *The Interpretation of Matthew*, 2nd ed., SNTI (Edinburgh: T&T Clark, 1995), 1.

than the middle of the third century AD, as evidence of the widespread use of the first Gospel in private and in public settings in the early church.[7]

Origen was perhaps the greatest intellectual in the third century church and the most influential of the Greek church fathers. Origen's last preserved exegetical work is his *Commentary on Matthew*, covering the entire Gospel in twenty-five books, giving access to Origen's most mature theological thinking as he interacts with Matthew's Gospel.[8]

Many Matthean scholars, including Ulrich Luz, and church historians, including Wolf-Dietrich Köhler, likewise contend that Matthew's Gospel was the most important Gospel for much of church history.[9] Ian Boxall demonstrates through a study of *Wirkungsgeschichte*—the history of influence or reception history—how Matthew's Gospel has inspired such divergent political, spiritual, and cultural figures as Francis of Assisi, John Ruskin, Leo Tolstoy, Dietrich Bonhoeffer, Mahatma Gandhi, Dorothy L. Sayers, and Pier Paolo Pasolini.[10] Matthew's Gospel has retained its appeal throughout the centuries and has exerted a powerful influence on the church.[11]

### 1.1.2 Fulfillment: The Bridge Between the Testaments

There is no existing listing of the four Gospels or extant canonical collection that does not position Matthew first at the head of the New Testament canonical order. One of the reasons for its positioning immediately succeeding the Old Testament canonical material, and thus at the head of the New Testament canon, may well have been Matthew's use of the Old Testament—especially his editorial comments concerning the "fulfillment" of particular Old Testament texts.[12] As such, Williams refers to Matthew as "the Gospel of fulfillment."[13] The recurring Matthean refrain, "This was to fulfill what was spoken by the prophet," heralds Matthew as a prominent bridge between the Testaments, demonstrating that where the record of the old covenant ends is where Matthew's Gospel becomes the bridge to the record of where the new covenant is established. In that light, one primary reason why this Gospel is so important is

7. Graham N. Stanton, "The Early Reception of Matthew's Gospel: New Evidence from Papyri?," in *The Gospel of Matthew in Current Study: Studies in Memory of William G. Thompson, S.J.*, ed. David E. Aune (Grand Rapids: Eerdmans, 2001), 42–61. These are among the Oxyrhynchus papyri published in 1997 and 1998: 𝔓1, 𝔓45, 𝔓53, 𝔓64 + 𝔓67, 𝔓77, 𝔓103, 𝔓104.

8. Ian Boxall, "Origen's Commentary on Matthew and the Reception of Matthew's Gospel," in *The Composition, Theology, and Early Reception of Matthew's Gospel*, ed. Joseph Verheyden, Jens Schröter, and David C. Sim, WUNT 477 (Tübingen: Mohr Siebeck, 2022), 321–40.

9. Ulrich Luz, *Matthew 1–7: A Commentary*, trans. Wilhelm C. Linss (Minneapolis: Augsburg Fortress, 1989), 81; Wolf-Dietrich Köhler, *Die Rezeption des Matthäusevangeliums in der Zeit vor Irenäus*, WUNT 2/24 (Tübingen: Mohr Siebeck, 1987). See also D. Jeffrey Bingham, *Irenaeus' Use of Matthew's Gospel in Adversus Haereses*, Traditio Exegetica Graeca 7 (Leuven: Peeters, 1997).

10. Ian Boxall, *Matthew Through the Centuries*, WBBC (Hoboken, NJ: Wiley, 2019), esp. 1–37; and Ian Boxall, *Discovering Matthew: Content, Interpretation, Reception*, Discovering Biblical Texts (Grand Rapids: Eerdmans, 2015), 1–45.

11. For brief historical surveys, see Williams, *Matthew*, xxiii–xxviii; Simonetti, *Matthew 1–13*, xxxvii–xli; Boxall, *Matthew Through the Centuries*, 1–37.

12. David Allen, *According to the Scriptures: The Death of Christ in the Old Testament and the New* (London: SCM, 2018), 53.

13. Williams, *Matthew*, xxiii.

because of its verification from the fulfillment of Old Testament Scripture that Jesus was the long-awaited Messiah of Israel who had brought salvation to the Jews but also to all of humanity in the new covenant. The early church quite likely placed Matthew first in the New Testament canon precisely because of its value as a bridge between the Testaments.

### 1.1.3 Jesus's Arrival in Human History

But Jesus Messiah had arrived in Israel with little fanfare. He was associated with the fiery, popular prophet, John the Baptist, but that became a dangerous association, since John was beheaded by the Roman puppet ruler of Galilee, Herod Antipas. Like John the Baptist, Jesus Messiah soon became quite popular with the people, attracting thousands to hear his message, to experience his healing miracles, and to be challenged by his preaching about the arrival of the kingdom of heaven. But also, like John the Baptist, Jesus Messiah soon became the target of opposition from the religious and political powers in Israel. That opposition escalated dramatically, until sadly, in the third year of his ministry during the Passover season, Jesus Messiah was arrested, tried by both the Jewish religious establishment and the Roman occupying government, and executed by crucifixion.

At first this seemed to put an end to the messianic movement surrounding Jesus. But very soon rumors began circulating that Jesus Messiah had been resurrected, that he had appeared to his followers, and that what he had preached about the arrival of the kingdom of heaven was true. He really was the Messiah of Israel and the Savior of humanity. His message was soon spread throughout the Mediterranean world by his followers. Pockets of Jews became followers of Jesus Messiah in Palestine, in the increasingly important gathering of Judaism in Syria Antioch, and even in Rome, the hated center of Roman imperialism. Wherever diaspora Judaism had settled, it soon was impacted by the persistent, and even pervasive, incursions of Jewish Christians, sparking division with those who rejected the message regarding Jesus Messiah.

But as happened in his own earthly ministry, Jesus Messiah's message soon created divisions among those who heard. Emperor Claudius had been troubled by the fast-spreading Christian movement, which Suetonius (*Claudius* 25.4) apparently records as behind the dispute over one "Chrestus" in Rome in the AD 40s. This well could have been a dispute between Jews and Christians over the preaching about Jesus Messiah.[14] Christians claimed that Jesus was raised from the dead and pointed to an empty tomb. Jews countered with the story of a stolen body. Frustrated with both

14. Cf. Craig S. Keener, *Acts: An Exegetical Commentary, Volume 3: 15:1–23:35* (Grand Rapids: Baker, 2014), 2681–711, esp. 2708–11; also, F. F. Bruce, *The Acts of the Apostles: Greek Text with Introduction and Commentary*, 3rd ed. (Grand Rapids: Eerdmans, 1990), 391.

sides, Claudius expelled all the Jews from Rome, which included Jewish Christians (Acts 18:2).[15]

Claudius then had a local governor set up the famous "Nazareth Inscription." It is a stone slab with a decree from Caesar (Claudius?) warning of capital punishment for those violating tombs, and points to the seriousness with which disturbing graves and moving dead bodies was held in the ancient world. It may also give some insight to the events in Matthew's narrative, if it was erected (as some propose) in AD 50 in Nazareth in response to the controversy between Jews and Christians about Jesus's empty tomb.[16] This would be consistent with Matthew's statement that the Jews continued to circulate a story about Jesus's body being stolen by his disciples (see Matt 28:11–15). The early Christian apologist Justin Martyr indicates that such stories were still being circulated nearly a century later (ca. AD 150; *Dialogue with Trypho* 108.2).[17]

### 1.1.4 Matthew's First Audience

It is amid these kinds of controversies that the first Gospel was written. Craig Evans points to the very first verse and suggests that it functions as an incipit or a sort of title that directs the reader to the author's purpose for writing.[18] We will examine this more directly later, but we can indeed see that the first verse indicates that Matthew intends his Gospel to establish Jesus's identity as the Messiah, the heir to the promises of Israel's throne through King David, and heir to the promises of blessing to all the nations through the patriarch Abraham.

So, this first Gospel offers evangelistic hope in Jesus's message of the gospel to Jews, contending that they should turn to Jesus as their long-awaited Messiah (Matt 11:2–6). But strikingly, Matthew's Gospel also offers evangelistic hope to gentiles, emphasizing that salvation through Jesus Messiah is available to all the nations (28:19).

Matthew's Gospel further serves as an apologetic tool to both Jewish and gentile Christians. It encourages Jewish Christians to stand firm in the face of opposition from their Jewish countrypersons and from gentile pagans, knowing that Jesus Messiah has fulfilled the promised arrival of the kingdom of heaven. And it encourages gentile Christians to humbly accept their inclusion at the banquet table with Abraham, Isaac,

15. For discussion of these circumstances, see Ben Witherington III, *The Acts of the Apostles: A Socio-Rhetorical Commentary* (Grand Rapids: Eerdmans, 1998), 538–45.

16. The slab is said to have been found in Nazareth in 1878 but dated to the first century BC through its Greek script-type. It is in the possession of the Bibliotheque Nationale in Paris. See photo in E. M. Blaiklock, "Nazareth Decree," *ZPEB* 4:391–92. For careful discussion, see Bruce M. Metzger, "The Nazareth Inscription Again," in *New Testament Studies: Philological, Versional, and Patristic*, NTTS 10 (Leiden: Brill, 1980), 75–92; E. M. Blaiklock, *The Archaeology of the New Testament*, rev. and updated ed. (Nashville: Thomas Nelson, 1984), 70–71.

17. David L. Turner, *Matthew*, BECNT (Grand Rapids: Baker Academic, 2008), 685–86.

18. Craig A. Evans, "'The Book of the Genesis of Jesus Christ': The Purpose of Matthew in Light of the Incipit," in *Biblical Interpretation in Early Christian Gospels, Volume 2: The Gospel of Matthew*, ed. Thomas R. Hatina, LNTS 310 (London: T&T Clark, 2008), 61–72.

and Jacob in the kingdom of heaven (8:11), now knowing that the children of God are all those who do the will of Jesus's Father in heaven (12:48–50).

Against the backdrop of a world that is increasingly hostile to Christianity, the author of the Gospel of Matthew solidifies his church's identity as the true people of God who transcend ethnic, economic, and religious barriers to find oneness in their adherence to Jesus Messiah. His Gospel becomes a manual, or *enchiridion*, on discipleship, as Jew and gentile are made disciples of Jesus Messiah and learn to obey all that he commanded his original disciples.[19]

## 1.2 FOUNDATIONAL ASSUMPTIONS

We now turn to clarify two foundational assumptions that guide our study of Matthew's Gospel.[20] These are discussed more fully elsewhere in this volume, but here it is helpful simply to get them out into the open.

### 1.2.1 Matthew's Gospel Is a Divine-Human Book

In the first place, even as our Lord Jesus Christ, the living Word of God (cf. John 1:1, 14; Rev 19:13), is one person in two natures, divine and human, so the Bible, the written Word of God (cf. Exod 32:16; 2 Tim 3:16), is one book in two natures, divine and human: it is a divine-human book.[21] It is divine because it was God-breathed, and it is human because God used human authors to write down his words. This is not "dictation" but rather the Spirit of God guiding and superintending the writers of Scripture so that the very words, and all the words, contain without error the truth that God intended to communicate to humans. The humanness of Matthew is retained by the Spirit in the uniqueness of Matthew's style, vocabulary, purposes, rhetoric, experiences, and background, but the accuracy of the text reflects the Spirit's guidance and superintendence of Matthew's writing.[22]

19. We will explore this more thoroughly later. See John Yueh-Han Yieh, *Conversations with Scripture: The Gospel of Matthew*, AABSSS (New York: Morehouse, 2012), 6–12; *One Teacher: Jesus' Teaching Role in Matthew's Gospel Report*, BZNW 124 (Berlin: de Gruyter, 2004).

20. For my similar, yet briefer, discussion, see Michael J. Wilkins and Erik Thoennes, *Biblical and Theological Studies: A Student's Guide*, RCIT (Wheaton, IL: Crossway, 2018), 75–79.

21. For a very careful and thorough theological discussion of the Bible as a divine-human book as inspired by the Holy Spirit, see John S. Feinberg, *Light in a Dark Place: The Doctrine of Scripture*, FET (Wheaton, IL: Crossway, 2018), 183–228. I agree with Feinberg, who suggests that the analogy of Scripture as a divine-human book to Jesus as the divine-human person should be used only in a loose way so as to avoid pressing the analogy too far (see Feinberg, *Light*, 219–228). For a pastoral exploration of this analogy, see John R. W. Stott, *Culture and the Bible* (Downers Grove: InterVarsity, 1979); and *Authentic Christianity: From the Writings of John Stott*, ed. Timothy Dudley-Smith (Downers Grove: InterVarsity, 1995).

22. For discussion, see Wayne Grudem, *Systematic Theology: An Introduction to Biblical Doctrine*, 2nd ed. (Grand Rapids: Zondervan, 2020), 31–38. For a recent—and potent—exploration by a significant array of scholars of the many facets of the inspiration and authority of Scripture, see D. A. Carson, ed., *The Enduring Authority of the Christian Scriptures* (Grand Rapids: Eerdmans, 2016).

Matthew alludes to this phenomenon in at least two of his famous "fulfillment quotations." In 1:22 and 2:15 Matthew uses the prepositional phrases "by the Lord" (*hypo kyriou*) and "through the prophet" (*dia tou prophētou*) to underline the divine agency implicit in the participial phrase "what was said" (*to rhēthen*).

> "All this took place to fulfill what the Lord had said through the prophet." (1:22)

> "And so was fulfilled what the Lord had said through the prophet." (2:15)

This should be understood as a "divine" or "theological" passive to indicate the dual authorship of Scripture[23] where the human prophet is the channel through whom the divine agency speaks and writes (cf. 15:4–7; 22:43–44).[24] Matthew's Gospel is inspired—God-breathed—even as the Old Testament prophetic writings were inspired.

Therefore, as we read Matthew's Gospel, we are hearing God speak to us through a human author, and our methods for reading it and gaining insight to its meaning will need to emphasize both aspects. Consequently, on the one hand, this is a truly spiritual endeavor as we listen to God speak through the human author Matthew. And on the other hand, this is an equally human endeavor as we listen through human language and interact with the written text of the Bible much like we interact with other written texts. As we enter into the world of a theology of Matthew's Gospel, it is awe-inspiring to know that we are hearing God speak to us through a human who has been impacted by God himself and we can be impacted directly as well.

Jerome's love of Scripture drove him to provide us with the Vulgate translation. It is a powerful version that has formed varieties of Christians throughout the ages. Jerome states forcefully, "For if, as Paul says, *Christ is the power of God and the wisdom of God, and if the man who does not know Scripture does not know the power and wisdom of God, then ignorance of Scripture is ignorance of Christ.*"[25] His statement is a powerful impetus to diligently study the written Word to know even more fully the living Word, Jesus Messiah.

In like manner, one of the most important New Testament scholars of the modern era, Peter Stuhlmacher, professor emeritus of New Testament at the University of Tübingen, contends for the full inspiration of Scripture on the basis that it is a divine-human book. This is quite remarkable because Stuhlmacher was trained by Ernst Käsemann, who in turn had been trained by Rudolf Bultmann, one of the most influential New Testament scholars of the twentieth century. Bultmann relied on

23. Daniel B. Wallace, *Greek Grammar Beyond the Basics: An Exegetical Syntax of the New Testament* (Grand Rapids: Zondervan, 1996), 437–38.

24. Cf. Turner, *Matthew*, 21.

25. Excerpt from Jerome's *Commentary on Isaiah* 1.2 (Scheck, CCL 73, 1–3). My emphasis.

demythologizing, an approach he developed interpreting existentially what he deemed the mythological elements in the New Testament. However, in a stunning reversal, Stuhlmacher emphatically accentuated the divine-human nature of Scripture. He emphasizes that, according to the tradition held in common by the major Orthodox, Catholic, and Protestant churches, "the biblical doctrine of inspiration instructs people to read the Holy Scripture as a thoroughly human but also a thoroughly divine book, and so to be ready to experience how the word of God in this book can be heard not only by past but also by present generations."[26] Stuhlmacher's emphasis of the human and the divine in Scripture is astounding, given his training, and stands as an important guideline as we study the divine-human Word that is the Gospel of Matthew.

### 1.2.2 Matthew's Gospel Is History, Theology, and Literature

A second important foundational assumption that guides my approach to this study is that Matthew's Gospel is at once history, theology, and literature.

As *history*, Matthew intends his Gospel to be a trustworthy record of what happened in the arrival of Jesus Messiah in antiquity. We are undertaking this project with the assumption that God has acted in history, and Matthew, and indeed all four of the canonical gospel writers, set as his/their purpose, at least in part, to record an accurate account of God's saving activities, which Richard Bauckham contends is based upon eyewitness testimony to Jesus Christ.[27] Palmer Robertson recreates how Matthew may have been led by God to write his eyewitness account of Jesus Messiah's life: "a Gospel carefully structured to enhance the reader's ability to grasp the consummative significance of every aspect of Jesus' life and ministry as the son of David, the Christ, the Son of the living God."[28]

As *theology*, Matthew gives a unique theological interpretation of what happened in history.[29] In his theological investigation of Matthew, Charles Quarles states,

26. Peter Stuhlmacher, *Biblical Theology of the New Testament*, trans. and ed. Daniel P. Bailey, with collaboration of Jostein Ådna (Grand Rapids: Eerdmans, 2018), 800.

27. Richard J. Bauckham, "The Gospels as Testimony to Jesus Christ: A Contemporary View of Their Historical Value," in *OHC*, 55–70. More fully, Richard J. Bauckham, *Jesus and the Eyewitnesses: The Gospels as Eyewitness Testimony*, 2nd ed. (2006; Grand Rapids: Eerdmans, 2017). For recent emphases upon the historical reliability of the Gospels, including Matthew, see Darrell L. Bock and J. Ed Komoszewski, eds., *Jesus, Skepticism, and the Problem of History: Criteria and Context in the Study of Christian Origins* (Grand Rapids: Zondervan, 2019). Similarly, Michal Dinkler treats the gospels as "rhetorically shaped narratives that claim to be reliable records of recent events"; see Michal Beth Dinkler, "What Is a Genre?," in *Modern and Ancient Literary Criticism of the Gospels: Continuing the Debate on Gospel Genre(s)*, ed. Robert Matthew Calhoun, David P. Moessner, and Tobias Nicklas, WUNT 451 (Tübingen: Mohr Siebeck, 2020), 77–96; here, 92.

28. O. Palmer Robertson, *Christ of the Consummation: A New Testament Biblical Theology*, vol. 1 of *The Testimony of the Four Gospels*, 3 vols. (Phillipsburg, NJ: P&R, 2022), 314.

29. A helpful wrestle with this issue is found in Michael F. Bird, "New Testament Theology Re-Loaded: Integrating Biblical Theology and Christian Origins," *TynBul* 60.2 (2009): 265–91, who examines the problem of balancing the historical and theological components of New Testament theology and argues for a "Theology of the New Covenant," where theology emerges out of the interface of canon and community.

"Rediscovery of biblical theology best begins with a rediscovery of who Jesus is and why he came. . . . Matthew clearly articulates Jesus's identity as our God, our Savior, and our King in memorable, even gripping, ways."[30]

And as *literature*, Matthew composes a document in which he communicates to readers/hearers the story of Jesus by employing literary elements in his text such as plot, setting, intertextuality, and characterization, by which he intends to propel his audience to belief and action.[31] In articulating the value of literary approaches to Scripture, Douglas Estes suggests that the literary approach encourages the biblical interpreter to take the reader seriously, as well as to better understand the contextual impacts on reading Scripture in general. "The Bible comes alive with its impact on audiences and situations, not just its original historical context, and this liveliness is now/once again a legitimate means of exploration within critical, biblical scholarship."[32]

The last one hundred years of New Testament scholarship have seen periods where each of these three elements—history, theology, and literature—has reigned supreme in the interpretative task. However, when one is emphasized to the exclusion of the others, it tends to produce a myopic or blinkered perspective of the text. But by valuing the insights derived from each lens—history, theology, and literature—and by balancing the insights from each and allowing them to inform and enhance each other, the insights produced are more expansive than even the sum of the three parts. It is now increasingly emphasized that when these three approaches are employed simultaneously, a more realistic understanding of the text is produced.[33]

Therefore, an important foundational assumption that informs my approach is that Matthew is diligent to accurately record what happened in history and interpret those historical events theologically for his readers in an artful literary manner that communicates the story of Jesus for audiences of all generations and all worldviews because this is the story of God's redemptive activity for all people.

30. Charles L. Quarles, *A Theology of Matthew: Jesus Revealed as Deliverer, King, and Incarnate Creator*, EBT (Phillipsburg, NJ: P&R, 2013), 2.

31. For helpful recent studies, see e.g., Douglas Mangum and Douglas Estes, eds., *Literary Approaches to the Bible*, Lexham Methods Series (Bellingham, WA: Lexham, 2018); and Jeannine K. Brown, *The Gospels as Stories: A Narrative Approach to Matthew, Mark, Luke, and John* (Grand Rapids: Baker Academic, 2020).

32. Douglas Estes, "Introduction: The Literary Approach to the Bible," in *Literary Approaches to the Bible*, ed. Douglas Mangum and Douglas Estes (Bellingham, WA: Lexham, 2018), loc. 798, Kindle edition.

33. This threefold approach is the focus of Robert Morgan and John Barton, "History, Literature, and Theology," in their classic volume *Biblical Interpretation*, Oxford Bible Series (Oxford: Oxford University Press, 1988), ch. 6; and Andreas J. Köstenberger with Richard D. Patterson, *Invitation to Biblical Interpretation: Exploring the Hermeneutical Triad of History, Literature, and Theology*, ITS, 2nd ed. (Grand Rapids: Kregel, 2021). This threefold emphasis is also found in recent studies of OT texts, as in Ehud Ben Zvi, *History, Literature and Theology in the Book of Chronicles*, BibleWorld (Equinox: Sheffield, 2006; Abingdon, UK: Routledge, 2014), 2–19; in a recent NT survey by N. T. Wright and Michael F. Bird, *The New Testament in Its World: An Introduction to the History, Literature, and Theology of the First Christians* (Grand Rapids: Zondervan, 2019), 47–83; in a NT introduction by Mark Allan Powell, *Introducing the New Testament: A Historical, Literary, and Theological Survey* (Grand Rapids: Baker Academic, 2009); and is also the focus of an exploration of Johannine theology by Andreas J. Köstenberger, "A Hermeneutical Triad: History, Language or Literature, and Theology," in *A Theology of John's Gospel and Letters*, BTNT (Grand Rapids: Zondervan, 2009), 42–47.

Consequently, Matthew's Gospel is simultaneously a historical, theological, and literary document. This is an important foundational assumption that guides my understanding of the way in which Matthew has composed his Gospel and will in turn guide this entire study. In large part these three correspond to the three horizons of Matthew's Gospel that we now discuss.

## 1.3 The Three Horizons of Matthew's Gospel

These two assumptions—Matthew is a divine-human Gospel and Matthew is a historical, theological, and literary document—lead us to read this Gospel on three interdependent "horizons." Scholars have various technical definitions in hermeneutical theory for the concept of "horizon," but Anthony Thiselton notes in his classic volume, *The Two Horizons*, that "in common parlance 'horizon' is used metaphorically to denote the limits of thought dictated by a given viewpoint or perspective."[34] This means viewing the text from particular vantage points.[35]

The two horizons that most biblical scholars emphasize are the horizon of the ancient biblical text and the horizon of the modern reader or hearer. Thiselton emphasizes, "The goal of biblical hermeneutics is to bring about an active and meaningful engagement between the interpreter and text, in such a way that the interpreter's own horizon is re-shaped and enlarged."[36] In the Two Horizons New Testament Commentary series, which draws upon the discipline of theological interpretation of Scripture, the focus is on the horizons of theological exegesis and theological reflection. The commentary on Matthew's Gospel by Jeannine Brown and Kyle Roberts thus emphasizes the priority of the text and its biblical authority but also the interpreter's own interpretive locations and privilege.[37]

In a slightly different direction, when discussing preaching from the Gospels, Sidney Greidanus also emphasizes two horizons, but he focuses on the horizon of the historical activities of Jesus and the horizon of the Gospel writer and his audience.[38]

Here I will conflate these emphases to emphasize the three horizons that correspond with history, theology, and literature—i.e., the horizon of the historical Jesus, the horizon of Matthew the evangelist and his intended audience(s), and the horizon of the contemporary reader(s).[39] Recent approaches to biblical theology have wrestled with

34. Anthony C. Thiselton, *The Two Horizons: New Testament Hermeneutics and Philosophical Description* (Grand Rapids: Eerdmans, 1980), xix, 15.

35. Anthony C. Thiselton, *New Horizons in Hermeneutics: The Theory and Practice of Transforming Biblical Reading* (Grand Rapids: Zondervan, 1992), 46.

36. Thiselton, *Two Horizons*, 15.

37. Jeannine K. Brown and Kyle Roberts, *Matthew*, THNTC (Grand Rapids: Eerdmans, 2018), 3–5. See also the series description of the general editor, Joel B. Green, in the forematter, *Matthew*, i.

38. Sidney Greidanus, *The Modern Preacher and the Ancient Text: Interpreting and Preaching Biblical Literature* (Grand Rapids: Eerdmans, 1988) 300–6; "Preaching from the Gospels," *DJG*[1] 625–30. Greidanus emphasizes two horizons but also includes the reader's own horizon, which I refer to as the third horizon.

39. See also Thiselton, *New Horizons*, 604–19.

the balance of the first two horizons, history and theology, and how those relate to the third horizon, its application in the life of the modern reader.[40] We will approach these horizons in our study of Matthew's Gospel in the following manner:

> **The Three Horizons of Matthew's Gospel**
>
> - **First Horizon: "The Mission of Jesus Messiah to Israel and the World"**—*The horizon of Jesus's historical ministry.* Matthew provides for us a record of God's activities in history in the arrival of Jesus Messiah and the kingdom of heaven.
> - **Second Horizon: "Matthew's Theological Presentation of Jesus Messiah"**—*The horizon of Matthew's theological perspective for his audience(s).* Here we attempt to understand and isolate Matthew's unique theological perspective of God's activities in history in Jesus Messiah.
> - **Third Horizon: "A Manual on Discipleship to Jesus Messiah for the Twenty-First Century"**—*The horizon of today's reader(s).* Here we attempt to capture the significance of the perspective of today's reader's understanding of Jesus Messiah's activities in history and Matthew's theological perspective for the contemporary church.

## 1.3.1 First Horizon: The Mission of Jesus Messiah to Israel and the World

The *first horizon* is Jesus's historical ministry, or what I refer to as "The Mission of Jesus Messiah to Israel and the World." Here we focus on the question, "What did God do in history in the activities of Jesus Messiah?"

### *1.3.1.1 What Did God Do in History in Jesus Messiah?*

The chief focal point for Matthew's Gospel is to concentrate on God's activities in history in the arrival of Jesus Messiah and the kingdom of heaven. Here we view the unfolding mission of Jesus Messiah to his people Israel, with the universal implications that will result for all the nations.[41] We try to place ourselves in the first-century historical setting to see and hear Jesus as would those who followed him around the

40. For a careful and helpful overview of five "types" of biblical theology as either "more historical" or "more theological" in concern and practice, see Edward W. Klink III and Darian R. Lockett, *Understanding Biblical Theology: A Comparison of Theory and Practice* (Grand Rapids: Zondervan, 2012). See also a brief but helpful discussion of the relationship of History and Theology, an exegetical methodology study of Matthew's Gospel in D. A. Carson, "Matthew," in *Matthew–Mark*, REBC 9 (Grand Rapids: Zondervan, 2010), 29–34.

41. An important issue here that is beyond the scope of this study is the Quest for the Historical Jesus, which especially was pursued in the twentieth century and the early twenty-first century. For an important overview, see Pierpaolo Bertalotto, Gabriele Boccaccini, and James H. Charlesworth, eds., "The

countryside. History is of vital importance in understanding the Gospels because they record what actually took place in space and time. The Gospel writers were either witnesses or recorders of the heart of the Christian message that God had acted in history. The evangelists were not reading post-Easter theology back into the pre-Easter portions of their narratives.[42] The Gospel writers were, as Ralph Martin states graphically, "reporting solid history, and the chief actor in their drama was a flesh-and-blood character, living a human life under Palestinian skies."[43] This historical record was the basis of the evangelists' faith, who wished to impart historical truth (e.g., Luke 1:1–4).

That is the first horizon of Matthew's Gospel that we will view as we walk through his narrative of Jesus's ministry. In the first horizon we look at the Jesus of history and attempt to see Matthew's perspective of Jesus. We note that Jesus is understood by Matthew to be the Messiah of Israel's expectations and that Jesus has a mission of establishing the kingdom of heaven in Israel, and in the world.[44]

**On the horizon of Jesus's historical ministry we are asking questions such as:**

- What were the religious, social, military, political, etc. circumstances in Israel at the time Jesus began his ministry? In the Near Eastern region? In the broader Mediterranean world?
- What were Jesus's salvation historical purposes for his ministry?
- What were Jesus's purposes in his teaching ministry?
- What were the circumstances of Jesus's audiences? What impact did Jesus intend to make upon the audiences (disciples, crowds, religious leaders)?
- What response did Jesus intend to elicit from the audiences? What if the audience was made up of his disciples, of the crowds generally, or of the religious leaders?

Historical Jesus: Contemporary Interpreters and New Perspectives," *Henoch* 32.2 (2010): 250–330. For evangelical treatments, see Darrell L. Bock and Robert L. Webb, eds., *Key Events in the Life of the Historical Jesus: A Collaborative Exploration of Context and Coherence*, WUNT 247 (Tübingen: Mohr Siebeck, 2009), and Michael J. Wilkins and J. P. Moreland, eds., *Jesus Under Fire: Modern Scholarship Reinvents the Historical Jesus* (Grand Rapids: Zondervan, 1995).

42. For elaboration on the pre- and post-Easter use of terminology by the evangelists in their narratives to distinguish Jesus's time from their own, see Eugene E. Lemcio, *The Past of Jesus in the Gospels*, SNTSMS 68 (Cambridge: Cambridge University Press, 1991). One contender that the evangelists deliberately shaped myths about Jesus into historical discourse to maximize their believability for their ancient audiences is M. David Litwa, *How the Gospels Became History: Jesus and Mediterranean Myths*, Synkrisis (New Haven, CT: Yale University Press, 2019), a view I reject for reasons we explore below.

43. Ralph P. Martin, *New Testament Foundations: A Guide for Christian Students. Volume 1: The Four Gospels* (Grand Rapids: Eerdmans, 1975), 43.

44. For a recent, balanced overview, see Jens Schröter, "The Quest for the Historical Jesus: Current Debates and Prospects," *Early Christianity* 11 (2020): 283–96; and the blog by Michael F. Bird, "Jens Schröter on the Jesus of History and the Christ of Faith," *Euangelion* (May 10, 2021), https://www.patheos.com/blogs/euangelion/2021/05/16990/.

### *1.3.1.2 Salvation/Redemption History*

This historical perspective has been a distinguishing aspect of evangelical approaches to doing biblical theology. In the mid-twentieth century Geerhardus Vos described biblical theology as "that branch of Exegetical Theology which deals with the process of the self-revelation of God deposited in the Bible."[45] Later, my first doctoral supervisor, George Eldon Ladd, expanded upon that description by saying that

> Biblical Theology is that discipline which sets forth the message of the books of the Bible in their historical setting. . . . Biblical Theology has the task of expounding the theology found in the Bible in its own historical setting, and its own terms, categories and thought forms. . . . It is basically the description and interpretation of the divine activity within the scene of human history that seeks humanity's redemption.[46]

Ladd's approach influenced a generation of evangelical scholars. This has led to what is described as a "salvation-historical" or "redemptive-historical" approach to Biblical Theology. We seek to discover inductively from the canonical literature of the Old and New Testaments God's progressive self-revelation of how he has acted in history to seek the salvation and redemption of humanity.

Robert Yarbrough emphasizes that a salvation-history approach is an important method to develop a whole-Bible approach to biblical theology. He emphasizes that "salvation history" refers to the historical process, attested throughout Scripture, "through which God brought, is bringing, and will bring about the redemption of his people and the world, transforming the current state of things into the eternal order foretold by Old Testament prophets and Christ the Messiah himself."[47] Frank Thielman likewise contends, "Taken together, the four gospels give special emphasis to Jesus' death as an atonement, an exaltation, and a necessary step in the inevitable progress of salvation history."[48]

Roland Deines uses Matthew's Gospel for understanding salvation history as a theological understanding of history through which the people of God are able to participate in God's history. He points to Jesus's expectation in Matthew 16:1–4 that the Pharisees should recognize the signs of the times, which indicates that the acts of

---

45. Geerhardus Vos, *Biblical Theology: Old and New Testaments* (Grand Rapids: Eerdmans, 1948), 5.

46. George Eldon Ladd, *A Theology of the New Testament*, rev. ed. (Grand Rapids: Eerdmans, 1993), 20–21.

47. Robert W. Yarbrough, "Salvation History," in *God's Glory Revealed in Christ: Essays on Biblical Theology in Honor of Thomas R. Schreiner*, ed. Denny Burk, James M. Hamilton Jr., and Brian Vickers (Nashville: B&H, 2019), 45. For his extensive treatment of this theme that builds upon his doctoral dissertation and decades of reflection, see Robert W. Yarbrough, *The Salvation Historical Fallacy? Reassessing the History of New Testament Theology*, History of Biblical Interpretation Series 2 (Leiderdorp, NL: Deo, 2004).

48. Frank Thielman, *The Theology of the New Testament: A Canonical and Synthetic Approach* (Grand Rapids: Zondervan, 2005), 206.

God are recognizable since God has been revealed in history. Deines contends that God manifests himself in the historical process, and it is our obligation to attempt to describe the past as meaningful history within the setting of a theistic worldview. He argues that it is plausible, reasonable, and worthwhile to write history "based on the assumption that God acted, is acting and will act in the lives of individuals, as well as in larger social bodies like families, the Church, the people of Israel, in particular, and perhaps within other peoples *qua* peoples as well."[49]

On this first horizon we explore Matthew's record of the activities of Jesus in his overall earthly ministry and in his death, burial, and resurrection as he fulfills the promises to Israel and to the world by accomplishing salvation for his people. It is also on this horizon that we see God's future activities as he consummates his plan of salvation in the return of Jesus to gather his people into their heavenly and earthly rewards and bring judgment to those who have rejected him.

#### *1.3.1.3 The Historical Intent of Matthew and the Four Gospels*

We could say that this is the intent of the four Gospels as a whole and individually, as they attempt to communicate to their audiences the essence and particulars of Jesus's historical ministry. Luke's Gospel makes this explicit as is stated in his opening explanation of his purpose in writing: "so that you may know *the exact truth* about the things you have been taught" (Luke 1:1–4 [NASB]; my emphasis). I have undertaken this project with the assumption that God has acted in history, and Matthew, and all four of the canonical Gospel writers, have as their purpose to record an accurate account of God's saving activities.[50]

The Bible is our primary textbook for this horizon, but in developing a theology of Matthew's Gospel we employ other evidence of history, such as archaeology, secular writings, religious traditions, sociological and anthropological studies, and general revelation. These other sources put God's activities into their historical context. We will see in the next horizon that there is diversity in the various biblical authors' perspectives, but here we emphasize that this first horizon gives a unified record of God's activities in history. It is on this horizon we place ourselves in the sweep of history to see and hear God as he brought salvation for his people, established his covenants, reconciled men and women to himself, and fulfilled his promises to us as he inaugurated his kingdom on earth.

49. Roland Deines, "The Recognition of God's Acts in History in the Gospel of Matthew: An Exercise in Salvation History," in Roland Deines, *Acts of God in History: Studies Towards Recovering a Theological Historiography*, ed. Christoph Ochs and Peter Watts, WUNT 317 (Tübingen: Mohr Siebeck, 2013), 21. With regard to accessing the historical Jesus, see Roland Deines, "Can the 'Real' Jesus Be Identified with the Historical Jesus? A Review of the Pope's Challenge to Biblical Scholarship and the Various Reactions It Provoked," *Didaskalia: Revista da Faculdade de Teologia/Lisboa* 39 (2009): 11–46.

50. See Bauckham, "The Gospels as Testimony to Jesus Christ," 55–70; Bauckham, *Jesus and the Eyewitnesses.*

In this volume, I explore the unfolding life and mission of Jesus Messiah, giving attention to the relationship of the Old Testament, commenting briefly on the common features that Matthew shares with the other evangelists but focusing on Matthew's record of Jesus. Here especially Matthew causes us to see how Jesus ministered to his people Israel, but with the universal implications that will result for all the nations. We will try to place ourselves in the first-century historical setting to attempt to see and hear Jesus as would those who followed him around the Palestinian countryside.

### 1.3.2 Second Horizon: Matthew's Theological Presentation of Jesus Messiah

The *second horizon* is Matthew's theological perspective on historical data, or what I refer to as "Matthew's Theological Presentation of Jesus Messiah." Here we focus on the question, "What is the *meaning* of Matthew's record of God's activities in history?"

The second horizon builds on the first horizon and gives special attention to Matthew's unique perspective of Jesus's historical life and ministry. The apostle Matthew had followed Jesus as one of the Twelve, and out of all that he experienced and saw and heard, he had specific purposes in selecting events and sayings of Jesus that he wished to pass on to his audience, in which he instructs his community with regard to their own particular issues.

#### *1.3.2.1 History and Theology*

In the light of this discussion of the first two horizons of Matthew's Gospel, we see that the Gospel records are both historical *and* theological documents. What the evangelists wrote was historical, but as Howard Marshall contends, "Their interest was not that of a historian concerned with the past merely for its own sake, but that of the Christian for whom the past is significant because of its character as salvation history."[51] They wanted to acquaint their readers with what had actually happened in history so that they might know the certainty of the things about which they had been instructed (Luke 1:4) and so come to faith in Jesus as the Christ and Son of God (John 20:30–31). Marshall goes on to say, "The writing of history and the proclamation of a message are not two incompatible activities; on the contrary, the content of the message is a historical narrative about the action of God in a historical person."[52]

Matthew likewise narrates his record in such a way as to interpret the events of history. We see this explicitly in the very first chapters of this Gospel as Matthew looks back on certain events in Jesus's early life and provides a theological interpretation for

51. I. Howard Marshall, "Jesus in the Gospels," in *Introductory Articles*, EBC 1 (Grand Rapids: Zondervan, 1979), 518–19.

52. Marshall, "Jesus in the Gospels," 519.

his readers. For example, after Matthew records the angel's explanation of the historical conception of Jesus he provides his theological explanation: "All this took place to fulfill what the Lord had said through the prophet: 'The virgin will conceive and give birth to a son, and they will call him Immanuel' (which means 'God with us')" (Matt 1:22–23).

#### *1.3.2.2 The Meaning of the Facts of History*

A recovery of the bare facts of history was not enough for the evangelists, including Matthew. They wished to so present the facts that their readers would understand the meaning of Jesus's life and ministry, namely, that he was indeed the Christ, who is their Savior. The authors, led by the Holy Spirit, presented materials that focused on their purpose of declaring Jesus to be the Messiah, the Savior. The apostle John tells his audience that out of the vast historical materials about Jesus's life and ministry that were available, he selected facts and wrote his Gospel with a theological purpose: "These are written so that you may believe that Jesus is the Christ, the Son of God, and that by believing you may have life in his name" (John 20:31). Thus, John tells us that he writes purposefully and theologically.

This is the essence of the second horizon for Matthew's Gospel as well. We see in Matthew's unique record of Jesus's conception and birth a statement from the angel about his mother Mary, "She will give birth to a son, and you are to give him the name Jesus, because he will save his people from their sins" (Matt 1:21). Matthew has selected from his knowledge of Jesus's early life an incident that gives theological clarity about Jesus's historical mission: to save his people from their sins. This establishes a theological agenda that Matthew will unfold for his audience in his narrative of Jesus's life and ministry. This is an example of how Matthew interprets theologically for his audience the historical mission of Jesus.

In the second horizon we look at what Matthew wants his readers to understand about Jesus and how that is to impact their lives. The second horizon is where we ascertain Matthew's unique perspective as he instructs his community with regard to their own particular issues. For this we draw upon Matthew's own background and emphases and those of his community. This is the heart of Matthew's theological perspective. Matthew did not create historical data to substantiate Jesus's messianic identity or satisfy his audience's desires, but he did view Jesus's life from his own unique perspective. Each of the evangelists wished to present the facts of history in such a way that they would convince their readers that Jesus was indeed the Messiah and Savior. As the Messiah, Jesus has claim to all authority in heaven and on earth, and therefore has full authority to call all men and women to a relationship with him as his disciples. As they respond and become his disciples, they are to be baptized and then taught to obey everything he commanded (28:18–20).

### *1.3.2.3 Approaches to Biblical Theology*[53]

Palmer Robertson observes that New Testament biblical theology deals with the whole of the revelational truth found in the documents of the New Testament and this material has been approached in three basic ways.[54]

In the **topical or thematic approach** a set of topics, generally but not always derived from the discipline of systematic theology, becomes the basis for the examination and organization of the materials of the New Testament. Typically, subjects treated include, among others, God, man, sin, salvation, the Christian life, the church, and eschatology.[55]

In the **biblical-book approach** the various authors or books of the New Testament are treated in sequence, generally following a chronological order or as the books are arranged in the New Testament.[56]

Following the **redemptive-historical approach** the effort is made to reconstruct the progress of redemptive history and revelation through the various periods of the New Testament era.[57]

Though various New Testament theologies will generally fall under one of these three categories, something of a mixture or blending of approaches is inevitable. Each of these three approaches has its own strengths and weaknesses.

Our approach in this second horizon will be explored in two distinct biblical theological fashions because we focus on one particular biblical book, the Gospel of Matthew.

First, we will walk through Matthew's Gospel as he unfolds his theological perspective of Jesus and his ministry in a linear, literary fashion. We will trace the development of Matthew's theology through a thematic commentary that proceeds unit by unit from the beginning of Matthew's Gospel to its conclusion, which will allow us to trace the unfolding of various theological themes and their interconnectedness throughout the book. That is the task of Part 2, Chapter 4, and is the approach of Ulrich Luz in his *Theology of the Gospel of Matthew*.[58]

53. What looks to be a helpful volume was published too late for use here, but I list it for the readers' attention: Andreas J. Köstenberger and Gregory Goswell, *Biblical Theology: A Canonical, Thematic, and Ethical Approach* (Wheaton, IL: Crossway, 2023).

54. Robertson, *Christ of the Consummation*, 48–49.

55. Robertson suggests that Donald Guthrie and Thomas Schreiner are representatives of this approach. See Donald Guthrie, *New Testament Theology* (Leicester, UK: Inter-Varsity Press, 1981). Guthrie combines a topical approach with a historically progressive perspective by tracing the topics through the various stages of NT unfolding. Cf. also Thomas R. Schreiner, *New Testament Theology: Magnifying God in Christ* (Grand Rapids: Baker Academic, 2008).

56. Robertson suggests that George Ladd, Howard Marshall, and Leon Morris are representative of this approach. See Ladd, *A Theology of the New Testament*; I. Howard Marshall, *New Testament Theology: Many Witnesses, One Gospel* (Downers Grove, IL: IVP Academic, 2004); Leon Morris, *New Testament Theology* (Grand Rapids: Zondervan, 1986).

57. Robertson suggests that radically different results following this method may be seen by comparing two classic works: Vos, *Biblical Theology: Old and New Testaments*, and Rudolf Bultmann, *Theology of the New Testament*, 2 vols. (New York: Scribner's Sons, 1955).

58. Ulrich Luz, *The Theology of the Gospel of Matthew*, trans. J. Bradford Robinson, New Testament Theology (Cambridge: Cambridge University Press, 1993).

Then in Part 3, Chapters 5–17, we will trace Matthew's theology topically, providing a presentation of the major theological themes of Matthew's Gospel, such as Christology, the kingdom of heaven, Israel and the church, discipleship, etc. This is similar to the approach of R. T. France in his *Matthew: Evangelist and Teacher*.[59]

I. Howard Marshall in his section on "Matthew's Theological Story" combines both of these approaches in a literary narrative segment and in a thematic topical segment.[60] This dual approach to Matthew's second horizon is the methodology of this present volume, as is the case in all the volumes in this series. In both of these approaches we understand that the evangelists were intending either to awaken or to strengthen the faith of their readers.

#### *1.3.2.4 Theological Biography*

We will discuss more fully the literary genre of Matthew's Gospel in the next chapter, but here we suggest that all four Gospels reflect aspects of common Greco-Roman biographical literature or "lives" (*bioi*) of famous ancient figures.[61] But in the Gospels of the New Testament we have a literary form that goes beyond other ancient literature in important ways that get at the core of the message that is truly the "good news" of God to his people. Jonathan Pennington advances this line of reasoning by offering a fuller definition of "Gospel": "Our canonical Gospels are the *theological, historical, and aretological (virtue-forming) biographical narratives that retell the story and proclaim the significance of Jesus Christ, who through the power of the Spirit is the Restorer of God's reign*."[62] This helps to situate the direction that our study will take in exploring how the second horizon gives us Matthew's unique perspectives of the meaning of God's activities in history.

**On this second horizon of the author Matthew and his audience we ask additional questions:**

- What were the circumstances of the author?
- Why did the author record his material in the way that he recorded it?
- What were the circumstances of the readers?
- Why did the author write what he wrote to them in the particular manner he wrote?
- What response did the author expect from his readers?

59. R. T. France, *Matthew: Evangelist and Teacher* (Grand Rapids: Zondervan, 1989).

60. I. Howard Marshall, "Matthew's Theological Story," in *New Testament Theology*, 95–111.

61. The leading voice in the exploration of the gospels as "biographies" or "lives" (*bioi*) for the last 25 years is Richard A. Burridge, especially in his *What Are the Gospels? A Comparison with Graeco-Roman Biography*, 25th anniversary (3rd) ed. (Waco, TX: Baylor University Press, 2018).

62. Jonathan T. Pennington, *Reading the Gospels Wisely: A Narrative and Theological Introduction* (Grand Rapids: Baker Academic, 2012), 35; emphasis his.

The audience of this second horizon includes all those whom Matthew expected to read and hear his gospel record. But it goes beyond that original audience to include others in the first century and those in the succeeding two millennia, including readers today. Here is where we read expectantly, attempting to glean theology from Matthew that will shape our understanding of Jesus Messiah as Matthew unfolds his message. On this horizon we understand Matthew's Gospel as a portrait of Jesus Messiah, the son of David, the son of Abraham (1:1), and Immanuel, God with us always (1:23; 28:20), as we experience life in the kingdom of heaven. We will see that Matthew's Gospel is formulated to be a manual on discipleship to Jesus, the one who holds all authority (28:18–20), and it places expectations upon our lives today as his disciples just as it did upon the first-century audience.

We begin to see a clue to the unique point of view of each author on both of these levels simply by reading the first verse(s) of each Gospel. Notice how strikingly different each Gospel begins.

| **Matthew 1:1** | **Mark 1:1** | **Luke 1:1–4** | **John 1:1** |
|---|---|---|---|
| This is the genealogy of Jesus the Messiah the son of David, the son of Abraham: | The beginning of the good news about Jesus the Messiah, the Son of God, | Many have undertaken to draw up an account of the things that have been fulfilled among us, just as they were handed down to us by those who from the first were eyewitnesses and servants of the word. With this in mind, since I myself have carefully investigated everything from the beginning, I too decided to write an orderly account for you, most excellent Theophilus, so that you may know the certainty of the things you have been taught. | In the beginning was the Word, and the Word was with God, and the Word was God. |

### *1.3.2.5 The Fourfold Gospel*

As discussed above, each of the Gospels gives an accurate recounting of the historical details of Jesus's life and ministry, yet each offers a unique perspective on the life and ministry of Jesus for the particular needs of the audience to which it is addressed.[63]

63. Although each Gospel most likely had an original audience to which it was addressed, the Gospels were not intended exclusively for any one particular community but were written with an eye to the broader audience that would be reached as each of the Gospels was circulated. This is the helpful thesis of recent scholarship, as in Richard Bauckham, ed., *The Gospels for All Christians: Rethinking the Gospel Audiences* (Grand Rapids: Eerdmans, 1998), and Hengel, *The Four Gospels and the One*

Francis Watson contends for the significance of the fourfold Gospel's plural form by showing that in its plurality it bears definitive witness to what God has done in Jesus Christ. Watson focuses on reading the Gospels as a group rather than in isolation and explains that the fourfold Gospel is greater than, and other than, the sum of its individual parts.[64]

But he would also contend that each has a powerful message of its own, as we can see clearly from these opening verses. The early church drew on the symbolism found in Ezekiel and Revelation of four living creatures around the divine throne to represent the emphases of the four gospels—the human, the lion, the calf, and the eagle—which is instructive for us as well.[65] Watson states, "These plural yet complementary perspectives are integral to the fourfold gospel, and we may follow the lead of its earlier readers in tracing them back to the divergent gospel openings."[66]

### *1.3.2.6 Fulfillment*

We observed earlier that Matthew's Gospel was always placed first in canonical collections because its emphasis on "fulfillment," causing it to be seen by many as a natural bridge between the Testaments as "the Gospel of fulfillment."[67] Matthew demonstrates that the hopes of Israel and the writings of the Old Testament Scriptures are fulfilled in the arrival of Jesus Messiah. David Nienhuis concurs: "To begin the NT canon with Matthew is to begin a *New* Testament that can be understood only as the fulfillment of what has come before."[68] Blomberg also isolates "fulfillment" as the central theme in Matthew's theological agenda. He states, "Matthew's emphasis on fulfillment of the Scriptures in general, the Law in particular, and righteousness throughout pervades his Gospel and dominates his volume more so than any other NT book."[69]

Among others who find that "fulfillment" is at the center of Matthew's theology is R. T. France. He says of Matthew's theological perspective as centered in the arrival of Jesus Messiah, that with his coming to be "God with us" a new age has dawned, and nothing can ever be the same again. "Henceforward it is in Jesus that all God's purposes, including his purpose for his people Israel, are centered. . . . In all these areas,

*Gospel of Jesus Christ* : An Investigation of the Collection and Origin of the Canonical Gospels (Harrisburg, PA: Trinity Press International, 2000), 34–115.

64. Francis Watson, *The Fourfold Gospel: A Theological Reading of the New Testament Portraits of Jesus* (Grand Rapids: Baker Academic, 2016), 1–22.

65. Watson, *Fourfold Gospel*, 21. Watson devotes a full chapter to each of these symbolic referents. I draw on his summary but add my own reflections here on each of the gospel portraits.

66. Watson, *Fourfold Gospel*, 20.

67. Williams, *Matthew*, xxiii.

68. David R. Nienhuis, *A Concise Guide to Reading the New Testament: A Canonical Introduction* (Grand Rapids: Baker Academic, 2018), 22; his emphasis.

69. Craig L. Blomberg, *A New Testament Theology* (Waco, TX: Baylor University Press, 2018), 381. See also Martin C. Spadaro, *Reading Matthew as the Climactic Fulfillment of the Hebrew Story* (Eugene, OR: Wipf & Stock, 2015), passim; J. R. Daniel Kirk, "Conceptualising Fulfilment in Matthew," *TynBul* 59.1 (2008): 77–98; Grant R. Osborne, *Matthew*, ZECNT (Grand Rapids: Zondervan, 2010), 38–39.

as in the presentation of Jesus himself, Matthew proclaims *fulfillment in Jesus.*"[70] When he considers the many attempts to find Matthew's central theme, France avers, "The theme I propose is that of 'fulfillment.'"[71]

We will explore the theme of "fulfillment" at length in Chapter 5—"The Old Testament and Jesus Messiah in Matthew's Gospel: Fulfillment"—but here I suggest that on Matthew's second horizon, "fulfillment" is a central theme that gets to the heart of Matthew's theological core.

### 1.3.3 Third Horizon: A Manual on Discipleship to Jesus Messiah for the Twenty-First Century

The third horizon is the contemporary reader's perspective of Matthew's Gospel, or what I refer to as "A Manual on Discipleship to Jesus Messiah for the Twenty-First Century." Here we attend to the questions, "What is the contemporary significance of Matthew's Gospel for today's readers?" "How has Matthew artfully developed and structured his literary creation to communicate historical and theological truth in such a way as to have relevance for readers of all the ages?"

The third horizon is the present-day reader's perspective of Matthew's Gospel, and the reader's interaction with the first two horizons. Here we attempt to capture the significance of Matthew's understanding of Jesus Messiah's activities in history for the contemporary church.[72]

#### *1.3.3.1 A Matthean Biblical Theology of "Jesus Immanuel, God with Us"*

From that broad understanding of biblical theology, we move to a Matthean biblical theology for the church and today's readers.

Matthew begins his Gospel by referring to Jesus as Immanuel, "God with us" (1:23), and concludes his Gospel with Jesus's declaration, "I am with you always, to the very end of the age" (28:20). There is no more radical claim than understanding that Jesus is God incarnate, who came to be with his people, and now in his risen and ascended position with the Father remains with his people. That was the essence of discipleship to Jesus in the first century in both the first and second horizons and remains the privilege of Christians today as we walk with Jesus in the world of the twenty-first century.

70. R. T. France, "Matthew, Mark, and Luke," in Ladd, *Theology of the New Testament*, 228; emphasis his.

71. France, *Matthew: Evangelist and Teacher*, 166.

72. Brian S. Rosner, "Biblical Theology," *NDBT* 10; emphasis his. Sigurd Grindheim sees the unifying theme of the canonical OT and NT to be "the good news of Jesus Christ"; see Sigurd Grindheim, *Introducing Biblical Theology* (London: Bloomsbury, 2013), 1; Andrew Naselli gives his longer definition of biblical theology: "Biblical theology is a way of analyzing and synthesizing the Bible that makes organic, salvation-historical connections with the whole canon on its own terms, especially regarding how the Old and New Testaments progress, integrate, and climax in Christ"; Andrew David Naselli, "Question One: 'What Do We Mean by "Biblical Theology"?,'" in *40 Questions About Biblical Theology*, Jason S. DeRouchie, Oren R. Martin, and Andrew David Naselli (Grand Rapids: Kregel Academic, 2020), loc. 266, Kindle edition. Similarly, see James M. Hamilton Jr., *What Is Biblical Theology? A Guide to the Bible's Story, Symbolism, and Patterns* (Wheaton, IL: Crossway, 2014), 16.

Markus Bockmuehl emphasizes that Matthew is the most resolute of the evangelists in affirming the presence of the living Jesus in and with the church in its life and mission after Easter. Matthew is aware of the tension of absence, but he affirms Jesus as always present. Matthew never articulates precisely how this is, and does not resort to materializing or localizing that presence with a narrowly sacramental focus.[73] Bockmuehl states that between the two endpoints of his great *inclusio* of "God with us" (1:23; 28:20), "the cumulative effect of Matthew's narrative delivers an affirmation of presence far stronger and richer than the religious commonplace of anonymous divine providence or assistance."[74] He asserts that "the same Jesus who was Emmanuel as Mary's child promises his abiding presence in the Church's internal discernment and outreach to the world, and especially in their welcome and service of the least of his brothers and sisters."[75]

This third horizon explores the contemporary *significance* of God's activities in history as Jesus is "God with us" (1:23), as he is now "with [us] always" (28:20) in our discipleship to him, and as he is "with [us]" (18:20) as the church gathers in his name. Such is the radical significance of living in the presence of Jesus.[76]

**On this third horizon of today's readers, we address the following kinds of questions:**

- What significance does the "genealogy of Jesus the Messiah the son of David, the son of Abraham" (1:1) have for people of the twenty-first century who often have no clue as to their own genealogy, let alone one for a person 2,000 years ago?
- What is the relevance of the historical material for us today? For example, what is the contemporary significance of Jesus's historical death on the cross? Matthew will present the historical data, but not always offer explanation.
- Are there biblical principles in Matthew's narrative that have relevance for readers today? What should we make of Jesus's interactions with the religious leaders of the first century? What is Matthew intending for leaders in his own community, and

73. Markus Bockmuehl, "The Gospels on the Presence of Jesus," in *OHC*, 94–95.

74. Bockmuehl, "The Gospels on the Presence of Jesus," *OHC*, 95.

75. Bockmuehl, "The Gospels on the Presence of Jesus," *OHC*, 95.

76. The christological, discipleship, and ecclesiastical significance of the expressions "God with us" (1:23), "I am with you always" (28:20), and "there am I among them" (18:20) is the focus of at least the following Matthean scholars: Hubert Frankemölle, *Jahwe-Bund und Kirche Christi: Studien zur Form- und Traditionsgeschichte des 'Evangelius' nach Matthäus*, NTAbh (Münster: Aschendorff, 1974), Andries G. van Aarde, *God-With-Us: The Dominant Perspective in Matthew's Story, And Other Essays*, HvTStSup 5 (Pretoria, South Africa: University of Pretoria, 1994), and David D. Kupp, *Matthew's Emmanuel: Divine Presence and God's People in the First Gospel*, SNTSMS 90 (Cambridge: Cambridge University Press, 1996). We will explore this theme more fully in Chapter 7, Christology in Matthew's Gospel: Jesus Immanuel Is More Than a Man.

ours, to derive from Jesus's scathing denunciations of the religious leaders, and his careful training of the Twelve?

- Do teachings of Jesus have relevance to our situation today? Matthew records two passages in which Jesus gives instruction on divorce. What is the relevance for our marriages in the twenty-first century?
- How does Matthew's perspective inform our understanding of Jesus and enrich our worldview today?
- How does Matthew's perspective on Jesus's life fulfilling the Old Testament prophecies inform our understanding of the relationship of the Old and New Testaments, and the relationship between Israel and the church today?
- What is the significance of Matthew's record of Jesus calling the four brothers to follow him and the implications for what we give up or not in our discipleship to him?
- How should we understand the inclusion of women accompanying Jesus and the Twelve to Jerusalem for the final days, and how does that guide our understanding of the Great Commission?

In a sense, on this third horizon we view the Bible as an open window through which we can place one foot in the biblical world and walk with the biblical characters, while keeping the other foot firmly planted in our contemporary world and applying principles and truths and warnings from their lives to our own.

## 1.3.4 Learning from the Three Horizons

There are particular issues that stand out from which we can learn from these three horizons.

### *1.3.4.1 Learning from the First Horizon: The Mission of Jesus Messiah to Israel and the World*

There are contemporary issues and circumstances that make reading the first horizon of the Bible, both Old Testament and New Testament, immediately relevant to us. For example, when reading the Old Testament, we see that David was the king of Israel and one of the most important historical figures of the Old Testament. We may not relate to his royal roles, but many of his personal experiences in his relationship with God and other humans can speak directly into our own lives. For example, when David was confronted by Nathan the prophet regarding his sinful act of adultery with Bathsheba, he wrote a psalm of repentance, which serves an example of repentance for all of us when he says, "For you will not delight in sacrifice, or I would give it; you will not be pleased with a burnt offering. The sacrifices of God are a broken spirit; a broken and contrite heart, O God, you will not despise" (Ps 51:16–17). David exemplifies for us that God desires from each of us not simply more religious activity, but a pure heart.

Likewise, when we come to the New Testament one of the first figures to appear in Matthew's historical narrative is the thundering prophet, John the Baptist. John declared the arrival of the kingdom of heaven and castigated the religious leaders for their shameless hypocrisy in coming for baptism. Yet when John was imprisoned, he saw that Jesus was apparently not initiating the kingdom in the way that he anticipated, and he sent his followers to question Jesus. Jesus's reaction to John's questioning was, "Blessed is anyone who does not stumble on account of me" (Matt 11:6). Each of us can have expectations of the way that we think that Jesus should operate in the world and in our own lives, and we can learn from John's experience. We similarly should not allow our unmet expectations of how God should act to cause us to inappropriately question Jesus. Here we attempt to draw the significance of the first horizon and how our own actions today can be informed from what Matthew records had occurred in history in the experience of John the Baptist.

#### *1.3.4.2 Learning from the Second Horizon: Matthew's Theological Presentation of Jesus Messiah*

We likewise learn from the second horizon. Matthew has peered into the historical ministry of Jesus and uniquely records this perspective on Jesus—that he is God, and that he will always be with those who have declared their commitment to him as his disciples—and this informs us as disciples of Jesus Immanuel on the third horizon. Matthew has developed his literary creation in such a way as to show his unique theological perspective of Jesus for readers of all the ages.

As we work our way through Matthew's Gospel, we will profit from his perspective of the historical unfolding of Jesus's life and mission from conception to commission. This will be the focus in Chapter 4: "A Literary and Theological Reading of Matthew's Gospel."

Then, in Chapters 5 through 17 we will focus on the various loci of theological topics most relevant to Matthew's Gospel.

#### *1.3.4.3 Learning from the Third Horizon: A Manual on Discipleship to Jesus Messiah for the Twenty-First Century*

I illustrate the interconnectedness of the three horizons to my classes by asking for three volunteers to come to the front of the class. The three students stand facing the classroom but spread out to the left, center, and right. Then I ask each to hold up their hands as if they each were holding a window through which they were looking at the classroom. The class must stay looking straight ahead and may not move their heads.

I stand by the volunteer who is angled to the left of the class. I then say that if that were the only window through which the volunteer could view the class, she might think that this was a very odd group of students: it appears that this is a class that had only right ears.

Then I move to the volunteer on the right side of the classroom facing the students who are seated. Without the students moving their heads, the volunteer to the right looks at the class through the imaginary window. It is the same number of students, still dressed the same, still seated in the same seats, but now the volunteer has a quite different perspective. If this was the only window through which he could look at the class, he might assume that this was a class that had only left ears.

Then I move to the center volunteer, who is also holding an imaginary window. From this vantage point she can see that this is a classroom with students that actually have both left and right ears.

Then I move to the back of the room and enlist another volunteer. Without the class moving their heads, the volunteer holds up an imaginary window through which he views the class. He observes that this is a class with the same number of students, dressed similarly, sitting in the same seats. But if this was the only window to view the students, he might conclude that this is a class that has members with two ears, but with no faces!

This little exercise helps illustrate that the three volunteers in the front represent Matthew, Mark, and Luke—the Synoptic Gospels. They are called Synoptic Gospels (Gr. *synoptikos: syn* ["together"] + *optikos* ["view"]) because they view Jesus's life and ministry from a similar perspective, but they also record unique features from their unique perspectives. The volunteer standing at the back of the class represents the Gospel of John, written many years after the Synoptic Gospels, most likely having had access to the Synoptics, and writing intentionally to complement and supplement their accounts with his very unique perspective of Jesus's historical life and ministry.

The third horizon is that of contemporary readers who look through the windows of the Gospels from their unique perspectives. It is an enriching experience to view the first horizon through the individual perspectives of the second horizons of Matthew, Mark, Luke, and John. Our privilege in this current study is to peer intently through Matthew's window and view the historical ministry of Jesus from Matthew's perspective and understand from his manual how to make disciples of Jesus Messiah for the twenty-first century. We are really not that different as humans from those of the first two horizons—i.e., those involved in the historical ministry of Jesus, and Matthew's perspective of what happened in history. But there are contemporary issues and circumstances that we must address that make the reading of Matthew immediately relevant.

These are the issues that we will attempt to address as we explore the three horizons of Matthew's Gospel.

## 1.4 CLOSING OBSERVATIONS: MATTHEW'S GOSPEL AS A MANUAL ON DISCIPLESHIP

### 1.4.1 Humility and Conviction in Reading Matthew's Gospel

As discussed above, I approach Matthew's Gospel as a divine-human product that contains the truth of God's salvation-historical program. Therefore, I understand there to be real meaning in Matthew's Gospel that I can access through what Kevin Vanhoozer calls a "hermeneutics of humility and conviction."[77] He asks the question, "Just how confident can we be as interpreters that we have discovered the meaning of the text rather than ourselves and our own projections? The short response is to say both that *our knowledge must be tempered by humility, and that our skepticism must be countered by conviction*."[78]

Humility combats the prideful arrogance of my particular interpretative location. Conviction is commitment to my interpretation because I believe it to be faithful to the meaning of the biblical text. Go too far in either direction and I commit what Vanhoozer calls the two deadly interpretative sins: pride and sloth. He says of his book *Is There a Meaning in This Text?*, "this book will have succeeded if it has established the possibility of a reading [of the biblical text] that yields knowledge while resisting both temptations [pride and sloth], a reading that would be both humble yet confident."[79]

This careful interpretative balance will guide our journey through Matthew's Gospel as we attempt to understand his theological perspective.

As will be seen, my interaction with these theological perspectives will at times overlap. For example, in Chapter 4 I will develop a Literary and Theological Reading of the entirety of Matthew's Gospel. The theological themes surfaced in the context of that narrative reading will be developed in full elsewhere in the chapter(s) that are devoted to that particular theological theme. Some overlap and even duplication will be inevitable, but I endeavor to keep such to a minimum.

### 1.4.2 Matthew as a Manual on Discipleship to Jesus in the Kingdom of Heaven

As will be seen, my interaction with these theological themes means that they reappear in other chapters. Some overlap and even duplication will be inevitable, but I endeavor to keep such to a minimum.

We noted above that Matthew begins his Gospel by referring to Jesus as Immanuel,

77. Kevin J. Vanhoozer, *Is There a Meaning in This Text? The Bible, The Reader, and the Morality of Literary Knowledge* (Grand Rapids: Zondervan, 1998), 462.

78. Vanhoozer, *Is There a Meaning in This Text?*, 462 (emphasis original). For an overview of recent critical approaches to the biblical text, see Eryl W. Davies, *Biblical Criticism: A Guide for the Perplexed*, Guides for the Perplexed (London: Bloomsbury T&T Clark, 2013).

79. Vanhoozer, *Is There a Meaning in This Text?*, 462.

"God with us" (1:23), and concludes his Gospel with Jesus's declaration, "I am with you always, to the very end of the age" (28:20). In my view, a significant part of Matthew's overall intention in writing is to show how Jesus came to initiate a discipleship relationship to him in the kingdom of heaven. Discipleship to Jesus was not a phenomenon that was restricted to the first century. Discipleship to Jesus is the central transformational relationship for the church, and Matthew's Gospel directs us in our experience of growing in that relationship in the twenty-first century.

Matthew's Gospel is intended, at least in part, as a resource tool to help Jesus's disciples in their task of making and developing future disciples. I refer to it as "a manual on discipleship." Matthew points to Jesus to be the supreme Lord and Teacher of the disciples and emphasizes that Jesus's life and teaching produced in them obedience to and understanding of the truth of God's revelation. That same obedience and understanding will continue to be the hallmark of disciples in the ongoing age. Matthew's Gospel is readily usable for this purpose, especially as he has clarified the nature of the kingdom of heaven in Jesus's ministry. Like Jesus did in his ministry, we are to call people to repent and believe in the gospel of the kingdom of heaven. That is how they become disciples. And then we are to enfold them into the family of faith as they are baptized, publicly declaring their allegiance to Jesus and identifying with the community of disciples. It is in carrying out the directive of the final participle of the Great Commission that we have our ongoing directive for our discipleship to Jesus: "teaching them to obey everything I have commanded you" (28:20).

For much of church history, the Gospel of Matthew was used as one of the primary catechetical tools for teaching disciples how to obey all that Jesus commanded.[80] With its alternating sections of narrative and discourse, this Gospel gives perhaps the most complete picture in writing of Jesus's actions and the most complete collection of his sayings. I will discuss this more fully in Chapter 10—"Discipleship in Matthew's Gospel: Salvation, Righteousness, and Transformation"—but here we note that the alternating sections of six major narratives and five major discourses that comprise the structure of Matthew's Gospel fully display the life of Jesus and the declarations of Jesus that are directed toward the development of his disciples, and are intended as instruction in, and clarification of, what it meant to be Jesus's unique kind of disciple. It is therefore at least in part a manual on discipleship. That is a significant purpose behind the writing of Matthew's Gospel, and it is the purpose of the resurrected Jesus in calling us to carry out fully his Great Commission.

The six narratives reveal Jesus's true identity in his actions and deeds. In the five discourses Jesus gives in word his instructions, commands, parables, directives, and

80. Donald Guthrie, *New Testament Introduction*, 3rd ed. (Downers Grove, IL: InterVarsity, 1970), 21; Williams, *Matthew*, xxiii.

prophecies that will guide his followers in our discipleship to Jesus until the end of the age.

Therefore, the largest compilation available to us of all that Jesus commanded, which includes all that he did and said, is collected by Matthew in this Gospel so that it can be passed on to succeeding generations of the church. Since discipleship is basically equivalent to teaching on spiritual formation and sanctification that we find elsewhere in Scripture, Matthew has provided us an invaluable tool for our growth in discipleship, the Christian life. This compilation has provided a wholistic presentation of the kind of discipleship that was to be taught to all disciples as the basis for full-orbed obedience to Christ.

But the final saying of Jesus in this Gospel is what gives us the greatest assurance that we can carry out his purpose in our lives, because he promises unconditionally, "And surely I am with you always, to the very end of the age" (28:20). Our discipleship to the risen Jesus continues to be our greatest source of comfort, power, and security. As Matthew demonstrates over and over in this Gospel, the arrival of Jesus began the greatest revolution that history has ever known. It is a revolution that begins in the heart, where Jesus enters in and begins the transformation. But then it extends to every area of our lives, so that our physical, emotional, mental, and relational life is impacted by the power of the kingdom of heaven. To demonstrate the reality of this revolution was Matthew's purpose, and I pray that as we initiate the study of this magnificent Gospel, our lives will be revolutionized as well.

*Chapter 2*

# The Context of Matthew's Gospel

## *Author, Place of Writing, Community Participants, Reception, Genre, Composition*

### Bibliography

**Bailey, Kenneth E.** "Informal Controlled Oral Tradition and the Synoptic Gospels." *Asia Journal of Theology* 5.1 (1991): 34–54. **Bauckham, Richard J.**, ed. "The Gospels as Testimony to Jesus Christ: A Contemporary View of Their Historical Value." Pages 55–70 in *OHC*. ———. *The Gospels for All Christians: Rethinking the Gospel Audiences*. Grand Rapids: Eerdmans, 1998. ———. *Jesus and the Eyewitnesses: The Gospels as Eyewitness Testimony*. 2nd ed. 2006; Grand Rapids: Eerdmans, 2017. **Bauer, David R.** *The Gospel of the Son of God: An Introduction to Matthew*. Downers Grove, IL: InterVarsity, 2019. **Baum, Armin D.** "The Anonymity of the New Testament History Books: A Stylistic Device in the Context of Greco-Roman and Ancient Near Eastern Literature." *NovT* 50.2 (2008): 120–42. **Bennema, Cornelis.** "The Ethnic Conflict in Early Christianity: An Appraisal of Bauckham's Proposal on the Antioch Crisis and the Jerusalem Council." *JETS* 56.4 (2013): 753–63. ———. "Early Christian Identity Formation Amidst Conflict." *JECH* 5:1 (2015): 26–48. **Bernier, Jonathan.** *Rethinking the Dates of the New Testament: The Evidence for Early Composition*. Grand Rapids: Baker Academic, 2022. **Bird, Michael F.** "Jesus and the 'Partings of the Ways.'" Pages 1183–215 in vol. 2 of *HSHJ*. Edited by Tom Holmén and Stanley E. Porter. 4 vols. Leiden: Brill. 2011. **Bockmuehl, Markus.** "New Testament *Wirkungsgeschichte* and the Early Christian Appeal to Living Memory." Pages 341–68 in *Memory in the Bible and Antiquity*. The Fifth Durham-Tübingen Research Symposium (Durham, September 2004). WUNT 212. Edited by Loren T. Stuckenbruck, Stephen C. Barton, and Benjamin G. Wold. Tübingen: Mohr Siebeck, 2007. **Bridge, Edward.** "Christians and Jews in Antioch." Pages 208–36 in *Into All the World: Emergent Christianity in Its Jewish and Greco-Roman Context*. Edited by Mark Harding and Alanna Nobbs. Grand Rapids: Eerdmans, 2017. **Burnet, Régis.** *Exegesis and History of Reception: Reading the New Testament Today with the Readers of the Past*. WUNT 455. Tübingen: Mohr Siebeck, 2021. **Burridge, Richard A.** *What Are the Gospels? A Comparison with Graeco-Roman Biography*. 25th anniversary (3rd) ed. Waco, TX: Baylor University Press, 2018. **Carson, D. A., and Douglas J. Moo.** *An Introduction to the New Testament.* 2nd ed. Grand Rapids: Zondervan, 2005. **Cohen, Akiva.** *Matthew and the Mishnah: Redefining Identity and Ethos in the Shadow of the Second Temple's Destruction.* WUNT 2/418. Tübingen: Mohr Siebeck, 2016. **Dennert, Brian C.** *John the Baptist and the Jewish Setting of Matthew.* WUNT 2/403. Tübingen: Mohr Siebeck, 2015. **Donaldson, Terence L.** *Gentile Christian Identity from Cornelius to Constantine: The Nations, the Parting of the Ways, and Roman Imperial Ideology.* Grand Rapids: Eerdmans, 2020. **Drimbe, Amiel.** *The Church of Antioch and the Eucharistic Traditions (ca. 35–130 CE).* WUNT 2/529. Tübingen: Mohr Siebeck, 2020. **Dungan, David Laird.** *A History of the Synoptic Problem: The Canon, the Text, the Composition, and the Interpretation of the Gospels.* ABRL. New York: Doubleday, 1999. **Dunn, James D. G.** *Jesus Remembered.* Vol. 1 of *Christianity in the Making.* Grand Rapids: Eerdmans, 2003. **Eve, Eric.** *Behind the Gospels: Understanding the Oral Tradition.* Minneapolis: Fortress, 2014. **Gathercole, Simon J.** "The Alleged Anonymity of the Canonical Gospels." *JTS* 69.2 (2018): 447–76. ———. "The Earliest Manuscript Title of Matthew's Gospel (BnF Suppl. gr. 1120 ii 3 / 𝔓[4])." *NovT* 54.3 (2012): 209–35. ———. *The Gospel and the Gospels: Christian Proclamation and Early Jesus Books.* Grand Rapids: Eerdmans, 2022. ———. "The Titles of the Gospels in the Earliest New Testament Manuscripts." *ZNW* 104.1 (2013): 33–76. **Gurtner, Daniel M.** "The Gospel of Matthew from Stanton to Present: A Survey of Some Recent Developments." Pages 23–38 in *Jesus, Matthew's Gospel and Early Christianity: Studies in Memory of Graham N. Stanton.* Edited by Daniel M. Gurtner, Joel Willitts, and Richard A. Burridge. LNTS 435. London: T&T Clark, 2011. **Guthrie, Donald.** *New Testament Introduction.* 4th rev. ed. Downers Grove, IL: InterVarsity, 1990. **Hagner, Donald A.** "Determining the Date of Matthew." Pages 76–92 in *Jesus, Matthew's Gospel and Early Christianity: Studies in Memory of Graham N. Stanton.* Edited by Daniel M. Gurtner, Joel Willitts, and Richard A. Burridge. LNTS 435. London: T&T Clark, 2011. ———. *The New Testament: A Historical and Theological Introduction.* Grand Rapids: Baker Academic, 2012. **Hengel, Martin.** *The Four Gospels and the One Gospel of Jesus Christ: An Investigation of the Collection and Origin of the Canonical Gospels.* Translated by John Bowden. Harrisburg, PA: Trinity Press International, 2000. **Howard, George.** *Hebrew Gospel of Matthew.* Macon, GA: Mercer University Press, 1995. **Keener, Craig S.** *Christobiography: Memory, History, and the Reliability of the Gospels.* Grand Rapids: Eerdmans, 2019. **Kirk, Alan.** *Q in Matthew: Ancient Media, Memory, and Early Scribal Transmission of the Jesus Tradition.* LNTS 564. London: Bloomsbury T&T Clark, 2016. **Klink, Edward W., III,** ed. *The Audience of the Gospels: The Origin and Function of the Gospels in Early Christianity.* LNTS 353. London: T&T Clark, 2010. **Konradt, Matthias.** *Israel, Church and the Gentiles in the Gospel of Matthew.* Translated by Kathleen Ess. Baylor–Mohr Siebeck Studies in Early Christianity. Waco, TX: Baylor University Press, 2014. **Kümmel, Werner Georg.** *Introduction to The New Testament.* Translated by Howard Clark Kee. Rev. ed. Nashville: Abingdon, 1973. **Lau, Theresa Yu Chui Siang.** "Reading the Gospel of Matthew as a Gospel of the Jerusalem Council." PhD diss., University of Melbourne, Centre for Jewish History and

Culture, 2006. **Litfin, Bryan M.** *After Acts: Exploring the Lives and Legends of the Apostles.* Chicago: Moody, 2015. **McIver, Robert K.** *Mainstream or Marginal? The Matthean Community in Early Christianity.* Friedensauer Schriftenreihe 12. Berlin: Peter Lang, 2012. **McKnight, Scot.** "Matthew as 'Gospel.'" Pages 59–75 in *Jesus, Matthew's Gospel and Early Christianity: Studies in Memory of Graham N. Stanton.* Edited by Daniel M. Gurtner, Joel Willitts, and Richard A. Burridge. LNTS 435. London: T&T Clark, 2011. **Nicklas, Tobias.** "From Gospel Book to Virtual Reality: A Neglected Aspect of the Gospel of Matthew's Ancient Reception History." Pages 17–28 in *The Gospel of Matthew in its Historical and Theological Context: Papers from the International Conference in Moscow, September 24 to 28, 2018.* WUNT 459. Edited by Mikhail Seleznev, William R. G. Loader, and Karl-Wilhelm Niebuhr. Tübingen: Mohr Siebeck, 2021. **Overman, Andrew J.** *Matthew's Gospel and Formative Judaism: The Social World of the Matthean Community.* Minneapolis: Fortress, 1990. **———.** "Matthew, Gospel of." Pages 922b–924b in *The Eerdmans Dictionary of Early Judaism.* Grand Rapids: Eerdmans, 2010. **Park, Wongi.** *The Politics of Race and Ethnicity in Matthew's Passion Narrative.* Cham, Switzerland: Palgrave Macmillan, 2019. **Pierce, Madison N., Andrew J. Byers, and Simon Gathercole,** eds. *Gospel Reading and Reception in Early Christian Literature.* Cambridge: Cambridge University Press, 2022. **Porter, Stanley E. and Bryan R. Dyer,** eds. *The Synoptic Problem: Four Views.* Grand Rapids: Baker Academic, 2016. **Powell, Mark Allan.** *Introducing the New Testament: A Historical, Literary, and Theological Survey.* Grand Rapids: Baker Academic, 2009. **Quarles, Charles L.** "The Oath Formulas of Matthew 23:16–22 as Evidence for a Pre-70 Date of Composition for Matthew's Gospel." *TynBul* 72 (2021): 1–24. **Robinson, J. A. T.** *Redating the New Testament.* Philadelphia: Westminster, 1976. **Rodríguez, Rafael.** *Structuring Early Christian Memory: Jesus in Tradition, Performance and Text.* LNTS 407. London: Bloomsbury T&T Clark, 2010. **Runesson, Anders.** "Rethinking Early Jewish-Christian Relations: Matthean Community History as Pharisaic Intragroup Conflict." *JBL* 127.1 (2008): 95–132. **Saldarini, Anthony J.** "The Gospel of Matthew and Jewish-Christian Conflict in the Galilee." Pages 23–38 in *The Galilee in Late Antiquity.* Edited by Lee I. Levine. New York: Jewish Theological Seminary of America, 1992. **———.** *Matthew's Christian-Jewish Community.* Chicago: University of Chicago, 1994. **Shanks, Monte Allen.** *Papias and the New Testament.* Eugene, OR: Pickwick, 2013. **Shelton, W. Brian.** *Quest for the Historical Apostles: Tracing Their Lives and Legacies.* Grand Rapids: Baker Academic, 2018. **Sim, David C.** *The Gospel of Matthew and Christian Judaism: The History and Social Setting of the Matthean Community.* Edinburgh: T&T Clark, 1998. **———.** "The Gospel of Matthew and Galilee: An Evaluation of an Emerging Hypothesis." *ZNW* 107.2 (2016): 141–69. **Slee, Michelle.** *The Church in Antioch in the First Century CE: Communion and Conflict.* JSNTS 244. London: Sheffield, 2003. **Stanton, Graham N.** "The Origin and Purpose of Matthew's Gospel: Matthean Scholarship from 1945–1980." Pages 9–75 in *Studies in Matthew and Early Christianity.* Edited by Markus Bockmuehl and David Lincicum. WUNT 309. Tübingen: Mohr Siebeck, 2013. **Stark, Rodney.** "Antioch as the Social Location for Matthew's Gospel." Pages 189–210 in *Social History of the Matthean*

*Community: Cross-Disciplinary Approaches*. Edited by David L. Balch. Minneapolis: Fortress, 1991. **Tamfu, Dieudonné.** "Jesus' Kingly Blessings for the Nations: A Missiological Understanding of Matthew 1:1." *Journal of Global Christianity* 1.1 (2015): 79–91. **Tuckett, Christopher M.** "Matthew: The Social and Historical Context—Jewish Christian and/or Gentile?" Pages 99–129 in *The Gospel of Matthew at the Crossroads of Early Christianity*. Edited by Donald Senior. BETL CCXLIII. Leuven: Peeters, 2011. **Vine, Cedric E. W.** *The Audience of Matthew: An Appraisal of the Local Audience Thesis*. LNTS 496. London: Bloomsbury T&T Clark, 2014. **Wenham, John.** *Redating Matthew, Mark and Luke: A Fresh Assault on the Synoptic Problem*. Downers Grove, IL: InterVarsity, 1992. **Wilkins, Michael J., and Erik Thoennes.** *Biblical and Theological Studies: A Student's Guide*. RCIT. Wheaton, IL: Crossway, 2018.

## 2.1 Introduction to the Context of Matthew's Gospel

While the overall purpose of this book is to examine the theology of the Gospel of Matthew, other factors influence this project, including introductory matters such as authorship, the date and place of writing, the identity and location of the community participants who first heard/read this Gospel, its reception by the early church, and attempting to understand how the Gospel of Matthew came to be written.

For example, our conclusion regarding the date of writing of this Gospel impacts our conclusion regarding authorship, which in turn affects our understanding of various theological matters in Matthew. Many Matthean scholars today conclude—for reasons that we will address below—that this Gospel was written after AD 70 toward the end of the first century. This dating makes it unlikely that Matthew the apostle actually wrote this Gospel himself. This conclusion then impacts our understanding of the trustworthiness of Matthean accounts of Jesus's life and ministry and teaching. This also throws into confusion the virtually unanimous testimony of the early church leaders that Matthew the apostle was the author. Therefore, in this chapter we will briefly establish some of the important parameters that will serve as a frame of reference for our study of the theology of Matthew's Gospel.

## 2.2 The Author and Date of Writing

In the wider world of Matthean scholarship, a growing consensus is that the apostle Matthew did not write the first Gospel.[1] Ulrich Luz states flatly, "We do not know

1. For a chart listing "Opinions on the Authorship of Matthew," primarily in the twentieth century up to 1985, see W. D. Davies and Dale C. Allison Jr., *A Critical and Exegetical Commentary on the Gospel According to Saint Matthew*, 3 vols., ICC (Edinburgh: T&T Clark, 1988, 1991, 1997), 1:10–11. The three primary opinions of authorship that they list are (1) the apostle Matthew, (2) a Jewish Christian, or (3) a gentile Christian.

the author."[2] Eugene Boring expands, "Practically all critical scholars consider the evidence against apostolic authorship to be overwhelming."[3] Werner Kümmel states that apostolic authorship is "completely impossible."[4] And even the evangelical scholar John Nolland can state, "The composition of the canonical Gospel by the apostle Matthew, though never questioned in the early centuries, is most unlikely."[5]

Several points of evidence against apostolic authorship are often used to discount Matthew as author. (1) Since the author does not self-identify, the first Gospel is itself anonymous. (2) The title affixed to the document, "The Gospel According to Matthew," is not original to the text but is a later addition attempting to establish its apostolic authority. (3) If the dominant "two-source" theory is held as the explanation for the Synoptic problem and the origin of the first Gospel, it is inconceivable that an apostle and eyewitness, Matthew, would rely on a non-apostle and non-eyewitness, Mark. Matthew's use of Mark and Q as sources undercuts its claim to eyewitness testimony. (4) The Greek language in which the Gospel of Matthew was composed appears to be the native language of the author and is of higher quality than would have been used by a first-century Palestinian Jew. (5) Many scholars today conclude that Matthew was written after AD 70 and the destruction of the Jerusalem temple, which then makes it unlikely that the apostle Matthew would still be alive.[6]

The traditional position, that Matthew the apostle wrote the first Gospel, responds to these objections in the following ways.

### 2.2.1 The Gospels Were Never Anonymous

A first argument against Matthean authorship is that since the author does not self-identify, the first Gospel is itself anonymous.

***Response***: To a modern reader the lack of an original title identifying the author and the lack of any self-identifying reference to the author within the body of the document may seem to indicate it is anonymous. However, to the original hearers/readers the Gospels were not anonymous. To allude to the Gospels as anonymous is imprecise.[7]

In the first place, the evangelists were not writing letters to far-off church communities to which were attached the names of the addressees and senders. That is

2. Luz, *Matthew 1–7*, 59.

3. M. Eugene Boring, "Matthew: Introduction, Commentary, and Reflections," in *NIB* 8 (Nashville: Abingdon, 1995), 106.

4. Werner Georg Kümmel, *Introduction to the New Testament*, rev. ed., trans. Howard Clark Kee (Nashville: Abingdon, 1973), 121.

5. John Nolland, *The Gospel of Matthew*, NIGTC (Grand Rapids: Eerdmans, 2005), 4.

6. For recent voices that are skeptical of Matthew as author, see Boring, "Matthew," 106–7; Luz, *Matthew 1–7*, 59–60; Matthias Konradt, *The Gospel According to Matthew*, trans. M. Eugene Boring (Waco, TX: Baylor University Press, 2020), 17–20; Donald Senior, *Matthew*, ANTC (Nashville: Abingdon, 1998), 21–22; R. Alan Culpepper, *Matthew: A Commentary*, NTL (Louisville: Westminster John Knox, 2021), 59–88; Charles H. Talbert, *Matthew*, Paideia (Grand Rapids: Baker Academic, 2010), 3–4; Walter T. Wilson, *The Gospel of Matthew: Matthew 1–13*, ECC (Grand Rapids: Eerdmans, 2012), loc. 605–18, Kindle.

7. For a recent discussion of anonymity and attribution of authorship of all the Gospels, see Simon J. Gathercole, "The Alleged Anonymity of the Canonical Gospels," *JTS* 69.2 (2018): 447–76, especially the chart on 473.

what we find in the letters that Paul or Peter or John wrote to churches in which they identified themselves to the recipients of their letters. Quite differently than writing letters, the evangelists were compiling gospel stories for churches of which they were active participants and leaders. They quite likely stood among the assembly and first read their Gospel accounts themselves.[8]

Second, as a written document, Matthew's Gospel first resided in the community of which Matthew was a member, with no need for the name to be attached. To attach his name as author would have been unnecessary because his audience knew his identity.

Third, it may have even been seen as inappropriate to attach his name to his account, since the gospel story is not about him. The primary intention was not to assert his own leadership authority but to record for his audience the matchless story of the life and ministry and teaching of Jesus.[9]

Fourth, as Matthew's Gospel began to circulate, the person transporting the document would have certainly passed it on to churches with an accompanying statement such as, "Here is Matthew's record of the life and ministry of Jesus." The earliest circulation of the document outside his own community would have been accompanied with full knowledge of the author Matthew's identity. There is never any sense that the first Gospel was anonymous or written by anyone else.

On this basis, the most likely conclusion to be drawn is that the attribution of authorship to Matthew is original. Gathercole argues regarding the names of the authors attached to our four Gospels, "that as far back as we can go, and probably from the beginning, these were the names attached to the Gospels."[10] The names associated with the four Gospels, including Matthew, are original, and "in the light of these arguments, other hypotheses will have to be ventured besides anonymous publication."[11] While they do not commit themselves to Matthean authorship, Davies and Allison state, "There was, as far as we know, no challenge in early Christian times to the Matthean authorship of the First Gospel."[12]

## 2.2.2 Apostolic, Divine Authority Ascribed to Matthew's Gospel

A second argument against Matthean authorship is that the title affixed to the document, "The Gospel According to Matthew," is not original to the text but is a later addition attempting to establish its apostolic authority.

8. For further discussion of the significance of this perspective, see below in this chapter, Place of Writing and the Community Participants.

9. Armin D. Baum, "The Anonymity of the New Testament History Books: A Stylistic Device in the Context of Greco-Roman and Ancient Near Eastern Literature," *NovT* 50.2 (2008): 120–42, argues similarly for the evangelists' deep conviction concerning the ultimate priority of their subject matter, the narrative of the life of Jesus Christ, but he does so arguing for their anonymity.

10. Gathercole, "Alleged Anonymity," 474.

11. Gathercole, "Alleged Anonymity," 476.

12. Davies and Allison, *Matthew*, 1:14. The most to which Davies and Allison will commit themselves is that "the author of the First Gospel was a member of the Jewish people" (1:58).

***Response***: While the title "Gospel According to Matthew" (i.e., ευαγγελιον κατα μαθθαιος) as we know it in our current Greek texts may come at a later date,[13] early church literature from the late first century and early second century is virtually unanimous in ascribing apostolic, divine authority to Matthew's Gospel.[14]

*Didache and Barnabas.* Toward the end of the first century, the Didache (ca. AD 100) demonstrates direct knowledge of the first Gospel, quoting it more than any of the other three Gospels: e.g., citing the two great commandments (Didache 1.2; Matt 22:37–39); citing passages from the Sermon on the Mount (Didache 1.3b–2.1[15]); and quoting the Lord's Prayer (cf. Didache 8:2; Matt 6:9–11). A few years later the letter of Pseudo-Barnabas (ca. AD 130) cites a saying from the first Gospel with the phrase "as it is written," a well-known introductory reference to divinely inspired Scripture.[16] The author states, "We too should pay attention, lest, as it is written, 'many of us were found called, but few chosen'" (Barnabas 4.14=Matt 22:14).

*Papias.* The earliest explicit, and perceived by some as the most important, of the early church traditions that point to Matthew as the author of this Gospel comes from Papias early in the second century. Papias was bishop of Hierapolis in Asia Minor and lived approximately AD 60–130. Tradition holds that Papias was a hearer of the apostle John, the son of Zebedee, and later was a companion of Polycarp (Irenaeus, *Haer.* 5.33.3–4). He was quoted and endorsed by the church historian Eusebius (ca. AD 325): "And this is what he [Papias] says about Matthew: 'And so Matthew composed (*synetaxato*) the sayings (*ta logia*) in the Hebrew [Aramaic] tongue (*Hebraidi dialektō*) and each one interpreted [or translated] (*hērmēneusen*) them to the best of his ability" (Eusebius, *Hist. Eccl.* 3.39.16).[17] There is considerable debate over the meaning and significance of Papias's statement. Among the interpretations of his statement are the following:[18]

13. Martin Hengel has argued well that the Gospels, including Matthew, always had their headings: see Martin Hengel, *The Four Gospels and the One Gospel of Jesus Christ* (Harrisburg, PA: Trinity Press International, 2000), 48–53, 76–78. But his reasoning encounters difficulty in the fact that there is no textual evidence for the headings occurring in our earliest manuscripts. Most Matthean scholars have concluded that the headings were affixed sometime in the second or third century. Gathercole evaluated a fragment containing Matthew's title and suggests that it comes from the "late second/early third century," which he argues makes it the earliest extant manuscript title of Matthew's Gospel and may even be our earliest manuscript title for any Gospel. See Simon J. Gathercole, "The Earliest Manuscript Title of Matthew's Gospel (BnF Suppl. gr. 1120 ii 3 / 𝔓[4])," *NovT* 54.3 (2012): 209–35, here 234–35.

14. Cf. Talbert, *Matthew*, 3: "Ancient tradition was unanimous. Modern historical scholarship is dubious."

15. Didache 1.2=Matt 7:12; Didache 1.3=Matt 5:44, 46–47; Didache 1.4b=Matt 5:39; Didache 1.4c=Matt 5:48; Didache 1.4d=Matt 5:40–41; Didache 1.5=Matt 5:26.

16. E.g., 1 Kgs 2:3; Acts 7:42; Mark 1:2; Rom 2:24.

17. Ματθαῖος μὲν οὖν Ἑβραΐδι διαλέκτῳ τὰ λόγια συνετάξατο, ἡρμήνευσεν δ' αὐτὰ ὡς ἦν δυνατὸς ἕκαστος.

18. For helpful, brief discussions, see D. A. Carson and Douglas J. Moo, *An Introduction to the New Testament*, 2nd ed. (Grand Rapids: Zondervan, 2005), 142–50; Scot McKnight, "Matthew, Gospel of," *DJG*[1] 526–28; Jeannine K. Brown, "Matthew, Gospel of," *DJG*[2] 570–84; Donald Guthrie, *New Testament Introduction*, 4th rev. ed. (Downers Grove, IL: InterVarsity, 1990), 43–53; Monte Allen Shanks, *Papias and the New Testament* (Eugene, OR: Pickwick, 2013), 193–99.

1. In the early church this was understood to mean that Matthew wrote a Gospel in Hebrew/Aramaic, and that others translated it into their own languages. We will see below that Irenaeus and Origin confirmed this line of thought.
2. More recently this has been interpreted to mean that the apostle Matthew authored an original Hebrew/Aramaic Gospel that was later translated into Greek by an unknown Christian, or else Matthew himself translated the earlier work. The Greek Gospel is substantially the same as the Hebrew/Aramaic Gospel.[19]
3. Matthew himself composed an original Aramaic collection of the sayings of Jesus (some suggest identified with Q, others suggest that it refers to the collection of Matthew's discourses; others that it signifies the Old Testament quotations in Matthew, perhaps a *testimonia* source), and this was later translated and augmented with Markan traditions.[20]
4. In contrast to Mark's unordered, Greek *chreia*-style[21] Gospel, Papias contends that Matthew composed a more Jewish, orderly-styled Gospel. The original language, then, is of no concern to Papias. Matthew was composed originally in Greek and in a Jewish style.[22]

Papias's statement is, as is seen above, notoriously difficult to interpret. But a couple of points may help give us direction. First, *logia*, in "Matthew collected the oracles (*logia*)," refers to the entire Gospel, not only to a supposed Q or to the Matthean discourses. This is suggested because Eusebius's previous reference to Mark as an "arrangement of the Lord's oracles (*logia*)" (*Hist. Eccl.* 3.39.15 [Lake, LCL]) used *logia* to refer to the entire Gospel of Mark. Hence, it should be interpreted to mean the entire Gospel of Matthew here, including Jesus's words and deeds.[23]

Second, even though the early tradition of Papias may suggest that Matthew wrote some kind of Hebrew/Aramaic account of the Gospel, the Gospel we now have does *not* show evidence of being a translation; e.g., why would Matthew have given the Semitic originals and Greek translations of a *few* terms, such as "Immanuel" (1:23) and "Golgotha" (27:33), if the whole Gospel were a translation from Hebrew or Aramaic? It is possible that Matthew first composed some kind of Hebrew account and later published a Greek edition which we now have, quickly superseding the older.[24]

---

19. See Guthrie, *New Testament Introduction*, 47–53.

20. See Hagner, *Matthew 1–13*, xxvii.

21. A *chreia* (pl. *chreiai*) is a saying or act that is well-aimed or apt, expressed concisely, attributed to a person, and regarded as useful for living. An example of a *chreia* is: "Diogenes the philosopher, on being asked by someone how he could become famous, responded: 'By worrying as little as possible about fame'" (see D. F. Watson, "Chreia/Aphorism," *DJG*[1] 104).

22. See Gundry, *Matthew*, 619–20; McKnight, "Matthew," 527–28.

23. Carson and Moo, *Introduction*, 147; Shanks, *Papias and the New Testament*, 193–99.

24. For a thorough study of a proposed "Hebrew Gospel" and its relationship to Matthew's Gospel, see James R. Edwards, *The Hebrew Gospel and the Development of the Synoptic Tradition* (Grand Rapids: Eerdmans, 2009), esp. ch. 8.

While Papias's statement is difficult and has been interpreted differently, for our purposes it is a significant early voice confirming Matthew as author of a Gospel. Osborne observes, "The major point is that Papias is the earliest source for Matthew writing a Gospel (or Ur-Gospel)."[25] We will continue this discussion below.

*Irenaeus*. Somewhat later in the second century, Irenaeus, bishop of Lyons in Gaul, cited Matthew (e.g., Irenaeus, *Haer.* 1.26.1–2; 3.9.1–3). Irenaeus was born in Asia Minor in approximately AD 135, studied under Polycarp, bishop of Smyrna, and according to tradition died as a martyr around AD 200. Irenaeus refers several times to Matthew, Mark, Luke, and John. In one of his five monumental books against the Gnostic heresies (ca. AD 175), Irenaeus states,

> Matthew also issued a written Gospel among the Hebrews in their own dialect, while Peter and Paul were preaching at Rome, and laying the foundations of the Church. After their departure, Mark, the disciple and interpreter of Peter, did also hand down to us in writing what had been preached by Peter. Luke also, the companion of Paul, recorded in a book the Gospel preached by him. Afterwards, John, the disciple of the Lord, who also had leaned upon his breast, did himself publish a Gospel during his residence at Ephesus in Asia. (Irenaeus, *Haer.*, 3.1.1 [*ANF* 1:414])

In Irenaeus we have clear connections between these authors and the Gospels that we know under these names because he refers to the beginning of each Gospel in connection with each name (*Haer.* 3.11.8; cf. *Demonstration of the Apostolic Preaching* 34; 94).[26]

These church leaders either knew the apostolic community directly, or were taught by those associated with the apostles, and so were directly aware of the origins of the Gospels. This is striking when we compare Matthew and the other Gospels with the epistle to the Hebrews. By approximately the beginning of the third century no fewer than four different suggestions for the authorship of Hebrews had been made—Paul, Barnabas, Clement of Rome, and Luke.[27] Gathercole states, "This sort of diversity is exactly what we do not find in references to the authorship of the Gospels."[28]

25. Osborne, *Matthew*, 34. Exploring the possibility of a Hebrew Ur-Gospel written by Matthew and interacting with Papias and Irenaeus, see Armin D. Baum, *Einleitung in das Neue Testament*, Evangelien und Apostelgeschichte (Gießen, Germany: Brunnen, 2017), 219–62, 902–14. On the possibility of a Hebrew version of Matthew, see George Howard, *Hebrew Gospel of Matthew* (Macon, GA: Mercer University Press, 1995); but this Hebrew rendering of Matthew's Gospel appears to be a secondary work, based on earlier medieval traditions, and is therefore not considered primitive.

26. Gathercole, "Alleged Anonymity," 466. See also Joseph Verheyden, "Irenaeus and the Gospel of Matthew," in *The Composition, Theology, and Early Reception of Matthew's Gospel*, ed. Joseph Verheyden, Jens Schröter, and David C. Sim, WUNT 477 (Tübingen: Mohr Siebeck, 2022), 289–320.

27. See Paul Ellingworth, *The Epistle to the Hebrews: A Commentary on the Greek Text*, NIGTC (Grand Rapids: Eerdmans, 1993), 3–15; Harold W. Attridge, *Hebrews: A Commentary on the Epistle to the Hebrews*, Hermeneia (Philadelphia: Fortress, 1989), 1–6.

28. Gathercole, "Alleged Anonymity," 475.

No competing tradition assigning the first Gospel to any other author has survived, if any ever existed. Subsequent authors (e.g., Hippolytus, Tertullian, Cyprian, Novatian) cite the Gospel of Matthew regularly as inspired Scripture on the same level as the Old Testament.[29]

*Gospel of Thomas.* Another allusion to Matthew is found in the Gnostic Gospel of Thomas (ca. AD 140–180): "Jesus said to his disciples: 'Make a comparison and tell me: who am I like?' Simon Peter said to him: 'You are like a righteous angel.' Matthew said to him: 'You are like a wise philosopher.' Thomas said to him: 'Teacher, my mouth cannot let me say at all what you are like'" (Gospel of Thomas 13).[30] Matthew appears to be an authoritative spokesman, alongside Peter. The reference to Matthew here occurs in a logion that is heavily influenced by Matthew's Gospel (cf. Gospel of Thomas 8 with Matt 13:47–51; Gospel of Thomas 9 with Matt 13:3–9).[31] Some have also conjectured that the reference on Matthew's part to Jesus as a "wise philosopher" might reflect a perspective on the Christology of Matthew. Gathercole states, "Since Matthew is known for little else in early Christianity besides being an evangelist, there is a high degree of probability that this dialogue in *Thomas* presupposes not just a Gospel attributed to Matthew, but one which has attained a certain level of authority."[32]

Taken altogether, the first two centuries AD have a good deal more references to Gospel authors than is commonly realized. The most common attestation is to John and Matthew in the top two, with Mark and Luke in the lower tier, facts that roughly fit together with the evidence from the papyri as well as with the relative frequency of biblical references from the period.[33] The apostolic authority and identity of Matthew as the author of the Gospel that bears his name are fully attested well before the dates of our earliest extant textual titles.

### 2.2.3 Congruency of Matthew with Gospel Sources

A third argument against Matthean authorship of the first Gospel by some modern scholars is based on their assumptions of the priority of Mark and the "two-source theory," and they consider it inconceivable that an apostle and eyewitness (Matthew) would rely on a non-apostle (Mark), and a source Q.[34] Matthew's use of Mark and Q as sources would undercut its claim to eyewitness testimony.

***Response***: However, this appears to read our modern mindset into the first-century church situation. In the first place, granting that the "two-source theory" is

29. Simonetti, *Matthew 1–13*, xxxvii.

30. See Bart D. Ehrman and Zlatko Pleše, *The Apocryphal Gospels: Texts and Translations* (Oxford: Oxford University Press, 2011), 313.

31. Simon J. Gathercole, *The Composition of the Gospel of Thomas* (Cambridge: Cambridge University Press, 2012), 169–77.

32. Gathercole, "Alleged Anonymity," 469–70.

33. Gathercole, "Alleged Anonymity," 472. Gathercole points also to Larry W. Hurtado, *The Earliest Christian Artifacts: Manuscripts and Christian Origins* (Grand Rapids: Eerdmans, 2006), 20.

34. E.g., Luz, *Matthew*, 1:59; Senior, *Matthew*, 21–22; Boxall, *Discovering Matthew*, 4–5; Boring, "Matthew," 106–7; Konradt, *Matthew*, 17; Culpepper, *Matthew*, 69; W. Wilson, *Matthew 1–13*, loc. 605–18, Kindle.

the dominant resolution of the Synoptic problem, it should not be construed to be a mechanical understanding of Matthew's use of his sources. It is certainly understandable that if Matthew had access to Mark's Gospel, he would have been eager to consult it, because as Papias and Irenaeus noted, the apostle Peter was a significant source for Mark's Gospel. Eusebius cites Papias: "And this is what the elder used to say, 'When Mark was the interpreter [or: *translator*] of Peter, he wrote down accurately everything that he recalled of the Lord's words and deeds'" (Eusebius, *Hist. eccl.* 3.39.15 [Ehrman, LCL]). And Irenaeus states,

> Matthew also issued a written Gospel among the Hebrews in their own dialect, while Peter and Paul were preaching at Rome, and laying the foundations of the Church. After their departure, Mark, the disciple and interpreter of Peter, did also hand down to us in writing what had been preached by Peter. (Irenaeus, *Haer.*, 3.1.1 [*ANF* 1:414])

Therefore, according to extremely early tradition, the Gospel of Mark is essentially apostolic. Gundry then puts forward the logical question: "Is it too hard to think that one apostle took material that came from a fellow apostle? Of course not—especially since the apostle borrowed from was none else than the foremost among the twelve."[35] If Matthew did have access to Mark's Gospel, Mark represented Peter's authoritative account and would certainly only give an added apostolic weight to Matthew's account.

Second, as we will argue below, the developing oral tradition regarding Jesus Messiah's life and ministry was a significant body of material that Peter and Matthew had watched develop and had monitored in the nearly thirty years that they had preached and taught in Jerusalem and Antioch and Rome since the foundation of the early church. And all that we really know about Q is that it is the material found in Matthew and Luke that is not found in Mark. It is easily accounted for on the basis of the developing oral tradition that Matthew and Luke accessed. This is the basis of the Gospels' narratives and recollections of Jesus's life and ministry.

### 2.2.4 Matthew's Gospel Reflects the Jewishness of Jesus's Life and Ministry

A fourth argument often lodged against Matthean authorship is that the Greek language in which the Gospel of Matthew was composed appears to be the native language of the author and is of higher quality than would have been used by a first-century Palestinian Jew.[36]

---

35. Gundry, *Matthew*, 621.

36. E.g., Boring, "Matthew," 106–7; Luz, *Matthew*:59–60; Senior, *Matthew*, 22; W. Wilson, *Matthew 1–13*, loc. 605–18, Kindle.

***Response***: This argument does not cohere with a number of things known of Jewish life in the Galilee region during Jesus's life and ministry. In the first place, (1) Matthew's position as a tax collector (9:9) would have required him to be fluent in both Aramaic/Hebrew and Greek. His "tax collector's booth" (*to telōnion*) was probably located on one of the main trade highways near Capernaum, collecting tolls for Herod Antipas from the commercial traffic traveling through this area. This would have required Matthew to be able to converse and write fluidly in Aramaic with the Jewish populace and in Greek with travelers and merchants.

(2) Likewise, as the Gospel first crossed racial and linguistic barriers, Matthew's background in Aramaic/Hebrew and Greek for both preaching and writing "squares with the notion of a gospel written in Greek that nevertheless could draw on Semitic sources."[37]

(3) Further, many scholars see in 13:52 a subtle self-reference by the author: "Therefore every scribe who has been trained for the kingdom of heaven is like a master of a house, who brings out of his treasure what is new and what is old" (ESV). This is not a scribe in the rabbinical sense, but a scribe in the secular sense—a well-educated writer.[38] As a tax collector, Matthew would have been trained in secular scribal techniques, and as a Galilean Jewish Christian he would have been able to interpret the life of Jesus from the perspective of the Old Testament expectations.[39] The name Levi may be an indication that he was from the tribe of Levi and therefore familiar with Levitical practices.[40]

The evidence accumulates to indicate that Matthew the apostle was well equipped to compile notes from his calling and time with Jesus and assemble a Gospel in Greek after some thirty years of preaching and teaching the gospel.[41]

### 2.2.5 Dating of Matthew's Gospel

A fifth argument against Matthean scholarship focuses on the date of writing. If Matthew can cite a saying of Jesus about the destruction of the temple, then Jesus's sayings and the writing of Matthew must be after the fact since prophecy of an event is not probable or even possible. This is often not expressed strongly or openly, but it is a significant issue for many critical scholars.[42]

Therefore, if the Gospel is being written after AD 70, as is assumed, a widely accepted hypothesis among critical scholars is that the author of the first Gospel lived

37. Carson and Moo, *Introduction*, 148.

38. For discussion, see Carson and Moo, *Introduction*, 148.

39. Cf. France, *Matthew: Evangelist and Teacher*, 70–74.

40. W. F. Albright and C. S. Mann, *Matthew*, AB 26 (Garden City, New York: Doubleday, 1971), CLXXVII–CLXXVIII, CLXXXIII–CLXXXIV.

41. See also Carson and Moo, *Introduction*, 140–50; Osborne, *Matthew*, 33–35.

42. W. Wilson, *Matthew 1–13*, loc. 605–18, Kindle.

at the end of the first century. Davies and Allison state unequivocally, "Matthew was almost certainly written between A.D. 70 and A.D. 100, in all probability between A.D. 80 and 95."[43] This makes it unlikely that the apostle Matthew would still be alive.[44] Many critical scholars therefore conclude that it is unlikely that Matthew the apostle is the author of the document that bears his name.

***Response***: On the other hand, the traditional early dating of Matthew's Gospel is upheld today by many evangelical scholars.[45] Early church tradition, found in the church father Irenaeus (ca. AD 175) indicates that Matthew wrote his Gospel while Paul and Peter were still alive ministering together in Rome. Irenaeus writes: "Matthew also issued a written Gospel among the Hebrews in their own dialect, while Peter and Paul were preaching at Rome, and laying the foundations of the Church" (Irenaeus, *Haer.* 3.1.1 [*ANF* 1:414]). This points to Matthew writing before the destruction of Jerusalem in AD 70. That testimony was accepted for much of church history.

Let us now consider each argument for and against a late dating.

### *2.2.5.1 Allusions to the Destruction of Jerusalem and the Temple*

It is said by many critical scholars that possible allusions to the destruction of Jerusalem in Jesus's rebuke of the religious leaders reflect the situation following the Jewish war of AD 66–73. For example, in Jesus's debates with the Pharisees in the temple area he states: "The king was enraged. He sent his army and destroyed those murderers and burned their city" (22:7). In his final diatribe against the scribes and Pharisees, Jesus states: "Jerusalem, Jerusalem, you who kill the prophets and stone those sent to you, how often I have longed to gather your children together, as a hen gathers her chicks under her wings, and you were not willing. Look, your house is left to you desolate" (23:37–38).

Further, Jesus gives a prophecy of the abomination of desolation standing in the inner sanctums of the temple and the ensuing devastation: "So when you see standing in the holy place 'the abomination that causes desolation,' spoken of through the

43. Davies and Allison, *Matthew*, 1:138.

44. Senior, *Matthew*, 22; Talbert, *Matthew*, 4; John Kampen, *Matthew Within Sectarian Judaism*, AYBRL (New Haven, CT: Yale University Press, 2019), esp. 38–67; Élian Cuvillier, *L'évangile de Matthieu*, in *Le Nouveau Testament Commenté*, ed. Camille Focant and Daniel Marguerat (Paris/Geneva: Bayard/Labor et Fides, 2012), 4.

45. E.g., Blomberg, *Matthew*, 41–42; Carson, "Matthew," 43–45; Evans, *Matthew*, 4–5; R. T. France, *The Gospel of Matthew*, NICNT (Grand Rapids: Eerdmans, 2007), 18–19; Gundry, *Matthew*, 599–609; Leon Morris, *The Gospel According to Matthew*, PNTC (Grand Rapids: Eerdmans, 1992), 8–11; Nolland, *Matthew*, 14–17; Osborne, *Matthew*, 35; Charles L. Quarles, "The Oath Formulas of Matthew 23:16–22 as Evidence for a Pre-70 Date of Composition for Matthew's Gospel," *TynBul* 72 (2021): 1–24. For an excellent overview of dating options, and with a slight lean toward early dating, see Donald A. Hagner, "Determining the Date of Matthew," in *Jesus, Matthew's Gospel and Early Christianity: Studies in Memory of Graham N. Stanton*, ed. Daniel M. Gurtner, Joel Willitts, and Richard A. Burridge, LNTS 435 (London: T&T Clark, 2011), 76–92; Gerhard Maier, *Das Evangelium des Matthäus, Kapitel 1–14*, HTANT 5 (Witten/Giessen: SCM R. Brockhaus/Brunnen, 2015), 17–20; Amiel Drimbe, *The Church of Antioch and the Eucharistic Traditions (ca. 35–130 CE)*, WUNT 2/529 (Tübingen: Mohr Siebeck, 2020), esp. 96–97.

prophet Daniel—let the reader understand—then let those who are in Judea flee to the mountains" (24:15–16). This prophecy is used to indicate that Matthew is writing after the events of the destruction of the temple in AD 70 anywhere up to the end of the first century or the beginning of the second century.[46] Thus these events constitute a *vaticinium ex eventu* ("prophecy after the event") in the minds of some interpreters.

Luz is representative of this interpretative approach. In his exegesis of the final discourse, Matthew 24–25, Luz distinguishes between history and eschatology. "Is our text to be interpreted historically or eschatologically: Does it speak of the destruction of Jerusalem in 70 CE and of other experiences from the time of its composition? Or does it speak of the final tribulations, of the Antichrist and of the return of Christ?"[47] While not usually stated, the underlying assumption appears to be that Jesus does not speak prophetically of the future and Matthew does not record prophesied forecasts of future events—i.e., if an event in Matthew's Gospel speaks of the future, it must be past history. The assumption is that when one finds a narrative of the destruction of the temple in Matthew's Gospel, it must be recorded history, not predicted eschatology. And therefore, Matthew must have written his Gospel after AD 70 with the destruction of the temple and the burning of the city.

***Response***: The arguments for a late dating of Matthew's Gospel largely dismiss Jesus Messiah's ability to give predictive prophesy and Matthew's ability to recall such a prophesy. If predictive prophesy is a possibility for Jesus Messiah, and if Matthew can record such a prophesy, then there is no necessity to simply dismiss out of hand Matthean authorship before AD 70 and during the lifetime of the apostle Matthew. Supernatural capabilities characterized Jesus's life and ministry, and to call into question his predictive prophecies is unnecessarily skeptical.

And Jesus was not the first to make predictions of the doom of Jerusalem and/or the temple. Several predictions are found in intertestamental literature. Evans cites, for example, the Testament of Levi: "your holy places will be made desolate" (T. Levi 16:4; cf. 15:1); the Testament of Judah: "destruction . . . slaughter . . . plunder . . . consumption of God's sanctuary by fire" (T. Judah 23:3); and the Sibylline Oracles:

> But again the kings of the peoples will launch an attack together against this land, bringing doom upon themselves, for they will want to destroy the Temple of the Great God and most excellent men when they enter the land. The abominable

46. E.g., Luz, *Matthew*, 3:183–4; Eduard Schweizer, *The Good News According to Matthew*, trans. David E. Green (Richmond, VA: John Knox, 1975), 15–17; Culpepper, *Matthew*, 609–11; Boring, "Matthew,"105–6, 439; Senior, *Matthew*, 266–67; Konradt, *Matthew*, 23, 356–57; Anna Case-Winters, *Matthew*, Belief (Louisville: Westminster John Knox, 2015), 2–3; Akiva Cohen, *Matthew and the Mishnah: Redefining Identity and Ethos in the Shadow of the Second Temple's Destruction*, WUNT 2/418 (Tübingen: Mohr Siebeck, 2016), passim; esp. 40–59, placing Matthew at the beginning of the second century.

47. Luz, *Matthew*, 3:184.

kings, each one with his throne and faithless people, will set them up around the city. (Sibylline Oracles 3:665 [Collins, *OTP* 1:377])

Evans cites others (e.g., *Lives of Prophets* 10:10; 12:1) and then states, "Although there are some who have expressed skepticism, many, if not most, scholars accept these traditions as authentic predictions of the temple's doom."[48] He adds that Josephus himself claims that he foresaw the temple's destruction (Josephus, *J.W.* 3.351–52; 6.109; 6.311) and that rabbinic literature also contains traditions of predictions of the temple's destruction, especially in the story of Johanan ben Zakkai (y. Sotah 6.3; cf. b. Yoma 39b; Avot of Rabbi Natan 4.5).

Carson and Moo similarly conclude that the language of Matthew 22:7, especially the reference to the burning of the city, is the standard language of both the Old Testament and the Roman world describing punitive military assaults against rebellious cities. Given that Jesus foresaw the destruction of Jerusalem (as did many prophets before him), the language he used does not depend on specific detailed knowledge as to how things actually turned out in AD 70. Carson and Moo point to the argument of scholars that the synoptic prophecies about the fall of Jerusalem, including Matthew 22:7, are so restrained that they *must* have been written before 70. Otherwise, we should expect to see some indication that the prophecies had actually been fulfilled.[49]

As a prophet, Jesus was warning Israel that the religious center of worship, the temple, would soon be destroyed if they did not repent. The firm belief in Jesus as Messiah in both the first century and today comes at least in part from the fact that his prophecies bear witness to his messianic identity. Therefore, the conclusion that Matthew's Gospel was written before the destruction of Jerusalem and the temple in AD 70 is the evidence we see as the most convincing testimony to Jesus's messianic identity.

### *2.2.5.2 Mark and Matthew*

Similar to the discussion regarding Matthew's Gospel, the Gospel of Mark is often dated post-AD 70 because of Jesus's predictive prophesy of the destruction of Jerusalem and the temple in AD 70 (Mark 13:1–14). It is argued that Mark is reflecting back on historical events that have already transpired. Joel Marcus is uncertain whether Mark knows that the temple has been demolished or whether he is merely positive that it *will* be destroyed very soon and thus dates the composition as early as AD 69 or as late as AD 74–75.[50] Francis Moloney takes it further and views Mark 13 as like a

48. Evans, *Matthew*, 400.

49. Carson and Moo, *Introduction*, 153; emphasis original. Citing J. A. T. Robinson, *Redating the New Testament* (Philadelphia: Westminster, 1976), ch. 2. See also Jonathan Bernier, *Rethinking the Dates of the New Testament: The Evidence for Early Composition* (Grand Rapids: Baker Academic, 2022), ch. 1.

50. Joel Marcus, *Mark 1–8: A New Translation with Introduction and Commentary*, AB 27A (New York: Doubleday, 1999), 38–39.

window into Markan circumstances. Consequently, in his view one of the hard facts is that Mark's Gospel was written shortly after the fall of Jerusalem in the year 70.[51] As a result of this reasoning, it is argued that if Mark is one of Matthew's sources, and if Mark is dated post-AD 70, then Matthew must be dated post-AD 70 and quite likely post-AD 80. Davies and Allison reason similarly that since they believe that the first evangelist knew and used the Gospel of Mark, Matthew's Gospel "was almost certainly composed after A.D. 70."[52]

***Response***: The arguments for early dating of Matthew would also apply to the arguments regarding the early dating of Mark. Despite the majority of critical scholars dating the eschatological discourse of Mark 13 after AD 70, Adele Collins finds clues that Mark considers the discourse to record prophecy of future events and concludes: "Since the 'desolating sacrilege' and the destruction of the temple seem to belong to the future from the point of view of the evangelist, the Gospel was probably written before 70 CE."[53] Jesus's prophecies of the destruction of Jerusalem and the temple were faithfully rendered by Mark prior to AD 70. Therefore, even if Matthew, writing pre-AD 70, used Mark as one of his sources, also writing pre-AD 70, the prophecy is upheld.[54]

### *2.2.5.3 The "Church" (*Ekklēsia*) in Matthew*

It is only in Matthew's Gospel that the "church" (*ekklēsia*) is mentioned. In 16:18 Matthew records a saying of Jesus in which he declares to Peter, "And I tell you that you are Peter, and on this rock I will build my church, and the gates of Hades will not overcome it." And in 18:17 Jesus speaks of the discipline to be exerted on sinning disciples: "If they still refuse to listen, tell it to the church; and if they refuse to listen even to the church, treat them as you would a pagan or a tax collector." This consciousness of building the church and allusions to church hierarchy and discipline are signs of a later date when the church was fully functioning.[55]

***Response***: These texts regarding the "church" in Matthew's Gospel say nothing about church order that we see later when overseers and deacons are in evidence. In his letters, Ignatius appears to be the first to discuss the "monarchical bishop/episcopate" in the local congregation. He describes a three-tiered ministry of bishops (*episkopoi*), elders (*presbyteroi*), and deacons (*diakonoi*) in each church. The central role of the bishop organizationally has a theological rationale, in that the bishop is nothing less than

51. Francis J. Moloney, *The Gospel of Mark: A Commentary* (Peabody, MA: Hendrickson, 2002), 13–14.

52. Davies and Allison, *Matthew*, 1:131.

53. Adela Yarbro Collins, *Mark: A Commentary*, Hermeneia (Minneapolis: Fortress, 2007), 14.

54. See Hagner, "Determining the Date of Matthew," 82–83.

55. Luz, *Matthew* 2:449–57; L. Michael White, "Crisis Management and Boundary Maintenance: The Social Location of the Matthean Community," in *Social History of the Matthean Community*, ed. David L. Balch (Minneapolis: Fortress, 1991), 211–247; here 221–28.

God's representative to the congregation.[56] Note Ignatius's advice to the congregation: "Be eager to do everything in godly harmony, the bishop presiding in the place of God and the presbyters in the place of the council of the apostles and the deacons, who are especially dear to me, since they have been entrusted with the ministry of Jesus Christ" (Ign. *Magn.* 6.1 [Holmes]). This is far different than what we see in the Matthean texts. The church as it is foreseen in Matthew is merely the messianic community, and the discipline pictured in Matthew 18 envisions basic principles that Jesus Messiah gives that are applicable in even the earliest stages of the messianic community.[57] These sayings of Jesus regarding the "church" represent Matthew's record of Jesus Messiah's predictive instructions for later developments of the messianic community.

#### *2.2.5.4 Matthew's Community and Judaism*

The multiple times that the expression "their synagogue(s)" (*synagōgē autōn*; 4:23; 9:35; 10:17; 12:9; 13:54) or "your synagogue(s)" (*synagōgais hymōn*; 23:34) occurs is taken by many recent critical scholars to indicate that Matthew is alluding to a current distinction between Matthew's community and the Judaism of his time. Some see this as a debate *within* Judaism (*intra muros*, "within the walls"), so that Matthew's community is still a subset within Judaism. Others see this as an indication of a separation *from* Judaism (*extra muros*, "outside the walls"), indicating that there is a consummate break between the community the evangelist addressed and the Judaism of his time.[58] Either way, many scholars use this discussion to indicate a date of writing late in the first century after the destruction of Jerusalem.[59]

***Response***: I will discuss this at greater length in Chapter 12. But here I observe that the tensions between Jews and Christians go back to the historical Jesus and his earthly mission of bringing salvation to Israel, and the resultant rejection of Jesus by Israel. The reasons the leaders of Israel give for demanding Jesus's death are that he was a false prophet, he committed blasphemy, and that he was the Messiah whom they rejected. His debates with the leaders of Israel touched upon the pillars of Judaism—God, torah, election, and the temple. We will see below that these illustrate the primary points of contention between Jews and Christians.

The questions remain as to why Matthew would mention several Jewish rituals such as the washing of hands, the temple tax, and offerings in the temple, and so often center on the Sadducees, who disappeared after AD 70, unless he was writing before

56. Michael W. Holmes, *The Apostolic Fathers: Greek Texts and English Translations*, 3rd ed. (Grand Rapids: Baker Academic, 2007), 168.

57. Carson and Moo, *Introduction*, 154.

58. E.g., Cuvillier, *L'évangile de Matthieu*, 4.

59. For the view of a later dating of Matthew that draws upon the later conflict between the Jewish and Jewish-Christian communities, see Anthony J. Saldarini, *Matthew's Christian-Jewish Community* (Chicago: University of Chicago Press, 1994). See also Robert T. Fortna, *The Gospel of Matthew*, Scholar's Bible 3 (Santa Rosa, CA: Polebridge, 2005), 12–19; Powell, *Introducing the New Testament*, 107–9.

the destruction of the temple.[60] Although Jesus himself remained within the orbit of a "common Judaism," his attitudes and actions pushed those boundaries to the point that he incurred violent opposition from other Jews.[61] And these continued in the earliest days of the church, as the book of Acts illustrates, long before the events of AD 70. Matthew records actual tensions that he observed as an apostle traveling with Jesus Messiah.

### 2.2.6 Conclusion

The testimony of the early church fathers to the apostolic authorship of the Synoptic Gospels, Matthew, Mark, and Luke, cannot be overlooked lightly.[62] All of the evidence uniformly supports the belief that Matthew (the tax collector turned disciple), Mark (the companion of Peter and Paul), and Luke (Paul's "beloved physician") were the authors of the Gospels attributed to them. It is difficult to conceive why Christians as early as the latter part of the first century and the beginning decades of the second century would ascribe these Gospels to three such unlikely candidates if they did not in fact write them. Mark and Luke were not among Jesus's twelve apostles. Mark is best known for abandoning Paul (Acts 13:13; cf. 15:37–40), and Luke is particularly obscure, being mentioned by name only once in the New Testament (Col 4:14). Matthew, while an apostle, is also best known for a negative characteristic—his unconscionable past as a tax collector (Matt 9:9–13). Tax collectors were considered traitorous to their nation.

Since the early church father Irenaeus (ca. AD 175) indicates that Matthew wrote his Gospel while Paul and Peter were still alive ministering together in Rome (Irenaeus, *Haer.* 3.1.1), the traditional dating has usually settled on the late 50s or early 60s. Matthew tells us that as of the time he writes the "field of blood" in Jerusalem continued to be called by that name (27:8). He also records that the chief priests and elders devised a plan to have the soldiers say that Jesus's disciples came during the night and stole his body away while they were asleep, a "story has been spread among the Jews to this day" (28:15 ESV). These show Matthew's continual connection with conditions in Palestine and hint that this is prior to the devastation in Jerusalem at AD 70.

A broad range of evangelical scholars posit a pre-AD 70 Matthean authorship of the First Gospel. Some understand the Gospel to have been written in response to the Neronian persecution, AD 65–67.[63] Others posit a dating more generally in the latter half of the 60s, especially after the outbreak of the Jewish revolt in AD 66 yet before the destruction of the temple in AD 70.[64] Still others see a dating of Matthew's Gospel

60. Osborne, *Matthew*, 35.

61. See the discussion of Michael F. Bird, "Jesus and the 'Partings of the Ways,'" in vol. 2 of *HSHJ*, ed. Tom Holmén and Stanley E. Porter, 4 vols. (Leiden: Brill, 2011), 1183–215.

62. This testimony of the apostolic fathers applies to John and his Gospel as well, but we treat here only the Synoptic Gospels, which have similar issues behind them.

63. See Gundry, *Matthew*, 599–609; Osborne, *Matthew*, 35.

64. See Carson, "Matthew," 43–45; France, *Matthew*, NICNT, 18–19; Nolland, *Matthew*, 14–17; Turner, *Matthew*, 13–14; Evans, *Matthew*, 4–5; Drimbe, *Church of Antioch*, esp. 96–97.

in the late AD 50s to early 60s.[65] A creative postulate puts the dating in the context of the Jerusalem Council, around AD 48.[66] And one innovative proposal puts the dating very early, to around AD 40.[67] As I will discuss below under 2.7, The Development of the Written Gospel of Matthew, I believe the most persuasive dating of Matthew's Gospel is prior to AD 70, and more specifically the late AD 50s or early 60s.[68]

## 2.3 MATTHEW, THE DISCIPLE AND THE APOSTLE

The list of the twelve disciples in Matthew's Gospel refers to him as "Matthew the tax collector," which harks back to the incident when Jesus called Matthew while he was sitting in the tax office (cf. 9:9; 10:3). When recounting the call, the First Gospel refers to him as "Matthew" (9:9), while Mark's Gospel refers to him as "Levi, son of Alphaeus" (Mark 2:14), and Luke's Gospel refers to him as "Levi" (Luke 5:27). Speculation surrounds the reason for the variation, but most scholars suggest that this tax collector had two names, Matthew Levi, either from birth or from the time of his conversion.[69] Dual naming was common in Roman Palestine, and since Matthew was a common name, it is plausible that an individual could be called both Levi and Matthew. Some have attempted to show that *Levi* was not one of the Twelve and therefore different from *Matthew*, but this is unwarranted speculation since the circumstances of the calling are the same in Matthew and Mark-Luke.[70]

The name Levi may be an indication that he was from the tribe of Levi and therefore familiar with Levitical practices.[71] Mark's record of the calling refers to him as the "son of Alphaeus" (Mark 2:14), which some have understood to mean that he was the brother of the apostle James son of Alphaeus (cf. Mark 3:18). But since the other pairs of brothers are specified to be brothers and linked as such, it is unlikely that Matthew Levi and James were brothers.

65. See Blomberg, *Matthew*, 41–42; Blomberg, *New Testament Theology*, 341–42; Robinson, *Redating the New Testament*, 86–117; Maier, *Matthäus*, 1:17–20.

66. E.g., Theresa Yu Chui Siang Lau, "Reading the Gospel of Matthew as a Gospel of the Jerusalem Council" (PhD diss., University of Melbourne, Centre for Jewish History and Culture, 2006).

67. E.g., John Wenham, *Redating Matthew, Mark and Luke: A Fresh Assault on the Synoptic Problem* (Downers Grove, IL: InterVarsity, 1992), 223–24. See also the redating of papyrus fragments in Magdalen College, Oxford ($\mathfrak{P}^{64}$) to ca. AD 60 by papyrologist Carsten Peter Thiede, "Papyrus Magdalen Greek 17 (Gregory-Aland $\mathfrak{P}^{64}$)," *TynBul* 64 (1995): 29–42, which led to his conclusion that Matthew was written in the 50s or earlier. See also the highly unfavorable review by Peter M. Head, "The Date of the Magdalen Papyrus of Matthew (*P. MAGD. GR.* 17=$P^{64}$): A Response to C. P. Thiede," *TynBul* 46 (1995): 251–85.

68. A recent, fascinating study places the dating of Matthew's Gospel between AD 45–59; see Bernier, *Rethinking the Dates of the New Testament*, 84; for discussion, see chs. 1–2.

69. For example, D. A. Carson leans toward "Matthew Levi" being a double name given to him from birth since he does not see any evidence for "Matthew" being a Christian name (Carson, "Matthew," 262–63), while Donald Hagner suggests that the name "Matthew" was given to Levi after his conversion (Hagner, *Matthew 1–13*, 237–38).

70. For a treatment of the evidence equating Matthew and Levi as one person see France, *Matthew: Evangelist and Teacher*, 66–70; W. Brian Shelton, *Quest for the Historical Apostles: Tracing Their Lives and Legacies* (Grand Rapids: Baker Academic, 2018), 189–90.

71. Albright and Mann, *Matthew*, CLXXVII–CLXXVIII, CLXXXIII–CLXXXIV.

Matthew Levi was called to follow Jesus while he was sitting in the tax collector's booth. This booth was probably located on one of the main trade highways near Capernaum, collecting tolls for Herod Antipas from the commercial traffic journeying through this area, whether it was on the roadways or through the waterways of the Jordan River and the Sea of Galilee. Matthew's collaboration with Herod Antipas in support of Roman interests would not have gone unnoticed by his fellow Jews in Capernaum and the Galilean region. Especially with Jewish leaders and the political zealotry, and almost certainly with the general Jewish populace, Matthew would have conflicted ideologically. And tax collectors generally were fairly wealthy and were despised by the local populace (cf. Zacchaeus; Luke 19:1–10).[72]

Particularly among the rebellion-oriented Jews, Matthew would have been considered a traitor. Was he a conniving materialist out for his own wealth, a cunning conspirator with the puppet for the Romans, Herod Antipas, or a blatant turncoat to his Jewish heritage and loyalties? He could be all of these, or there could be some other motivation behind his collaboration with the Romans. The text does not tell us.

But when Jesus, the Jewish Messiah, calls Matthew Levi, the Jewish tax collector for the Romans, the scene is one of intrigue and outrage: intrigue by Jesus's other disciples as to why Jesus would call such a person, and outrage by the extremist Jews as to why Jesus would call such a traitor. But immediately Matthew followed Jesus. And stunningly he arranged a banquet for Jesus at his home, to which were invited a large crowd of other tax collectors and sinners. Luke tells us that it was Matthew who arranged the banquet at Matthew's own home (Luke 5:29–30), whereas Matthew does not give us that information (Matt 9:10–11). By omitting his own name, this could be deemed a criterion of humility that supports Matthew's own authorship of the Gospel bearing his name. And it also may give us a glimpse into the personal humility of the disciple himself.[73]

Matthew's calling and response were completely out of the ordinary and required nothing short of a miraculous turnaround in this tax collector's life. Bryan Litfin compares Matthew's transformation to that of John Newton, the faithless seaman and slave trader who became an Anglican minister and hymn writer, best known for his hymn "Amazing Grace."[74] Litfin states of Matthew: "The pen that once kept false and abusing ledger books was used instead to record the greatest story ever told."[75] Amazing grace does indeed characterize the origin of Matthew Levi's transformation.

Little else is known of Matthew Levi, except for the widely attested tradition that he is the author of the Gospel that now bears his name (see discussion above). As a tax

72. Shelton, *Quest for the Historical Apostles*, 188.

73. Shelton, *Quest for the Historical Apostles*, 191.

74. Bryan M. Litfin, *After Acts: Exploring the Lives and Legends of the Apostles* (Chicago: Moody, 2015), 39.

75. Litfin, *After Acts*, 39.

collector he would have been trained in secular scribal techniques, and as a Galilean Jewish Christian he would have been able to interpret the life of Jesus from the perspective of the Old Testament expectations. This is especially true if the name Levi indicates coming from the tribe of that name.[76]

Matthew's career in the apostolic age is based on traditions of the church fathers as well as apocryphal and legendary accounts. Eusebius says that Matthew first preached to "Hebrews" and then to "others." His first ministry concentrated in Palestine and Syria, with much of his ministry centered in Antioch. Other points of ministry included places such as Persia and Parthia, which is where he may have gone after his ministry in Antioch, Syria (Eusebius, *Hist. eccl.* 3.24.6).

Eusebius reports that Pantanaeus, a missionary to India, found a copy of Matthew's Gospel in Hebrew there about AD 180. Eusebius writes of the missionaries in India:

> Pantanaeus was one of these, and is said to have gone to India. It is reported that among persons there who knew of Christ, he found the Gospel according to Matthew, which had anticipated his own arrival. For Bartholomew, one of the apostles, had preached to them, and left with them the writing of Matthew in the Hebrew language, which they had preserved till that time.[77]

The traditions are mixed regarding Matthew's death, with some saying that he died a martyr's death and others saying that he died a natural death.

Clement of Alexandria quotes Heracleon, a Valentinian expositor of the mid-second century, and one of the earliest commentators on the New Testament, as saying that Matthew died naturally, not being tried before a magistrate, which is the image that is conjured up by the idea of Christian martyrdom (*Stromata* 4.9). Hippolytus of Rome, active in the late second and early third century, writes the following: "And Matthew wrote the Gospel in the Hebrew tongue, and published it at Jerusalem, and fell asleep at Hierees, *a town* of Parthia" (Hippolytus, *On the Twelve Apostles* 7 [*ANF* 5:255]).

All the other early records of Matthew's death claim he was martyred, but they disagree about how or where it happened. The early church fathers claim variously he was burned, stoned, stabbed, or beheaded for his faith.

An account of Matthew's death in the Martyrdom of St. Matthew the Apostle is considered legendary and probably originated in the third or fourth century.[78] The account states that at Jesus's command, Matthew goes to "Myrna," called "the city of the man-eaters," where he is to visit the church founded by the apostle Andrew. The king of the city is outraged that his wife, his son, and his son's wife have been exorcized

76. Cf. France, *Matthew: Evangelist and Teacher*, 70–74.

77. Eusebius, *Hist. eccl*, 5.10.3 (*NPNF*[2] 1:225).

78. "The Acts and Martydom of St. Matthew the Apostle," *ANF* 8:528–34. On dating see *ANF* 8: v–vi.

of demons by Matthew and they have become Matthew's followers. The king resolves to have Matthew burned to death and gives these instructions:

> Having laid him, therefore, on the ground on his back, and stretched him out, pierce his hands and feet with iron nails, and cover him over with paper, having smeared it with dolphins' oil, and cover him up with brimstone and asphalt and pitch, and *put* tow and brushwood above. Thus apply the fire to him; and if any of the same tribe with him rise up against you, he shall get the same punishment. (*ANF* 8:531, italics original)

But the fire that was intended to consume Matthew is miraculously turned into the form of a great and dreadful dragon and goes against his persecutors and their gods before he himself dies. Later the author writes,

> We all saw Matthew rising up, as it were, from the bed, and going into heaven, led by the hand by a beautiful boy [the Lord Jesus Christ]; and twelve men in shining garments came to meet him, having never-fading and golden crowns on their head; and we saw how that child crowned Matthew, so as to be like them, and in a flash of lightning they went away to heaven. (*ANF* 8:532)

According to another legend, the apostle was killed on the orders of the king of Ethiopia, Hirticus, while celebrating Mass at the altar. Hirticus wished to marry his own niece Iphigenia, the abbess of a convent and therefore the bride of Christ. When the apostle Matthew forbade the marriage, Hirticus had him murdered by a soldier sent by the wicked king.[79]

These legends are quite different than the portraits of the apostles, including Matthew, found in the canonical Gospels. These legends point to a faithful and powerful apostle Matthew, but they give us little historical information and certainty.

## 2.4 Place of Writing and the Community Participants

We have concluded that the apostle Matthew wrote the Gospel that bears his name and that it was composed prior to the destruction of Jerusalem and the temple in AD 70,

79. This legend is behind *The Martyrdom of Saint Matthew* (AD 1599–1600), a painting by the Italian master painter Michelangelo Merisi da Caravaggio, located in the Contarelli Chapel of the church San Luigi dei Francesi in Rome, where it hangs opposite *The Calling of Saint Matthew* and beside the altarpiece *The Inspiration of Saint Matthew*. For background see *Encyclopedia Britannica*, "Caravaggio: Italian Painter," by Andrew Graham-Dixon, last updated March 7, 2025, https://www.britannica.com/biography/Caravaggio and also see the Caravaggio website https://www.caravaggio.org.

perhaps in the late 50s or early 60s. We now turn our attention to the place of writing and the composition of the community for whom Matthew wrote his gospel account of Jesus Messiah.

I have suggested above that the evangelists were compiling gospel stories for churches of which they were active participants and leaders. Matthew quite likely stood among the assembly and first read his Gospel account to his community, perhaps over a period of time as he diligently composed his Gospel story. This is quite different than what we find in the epistles of the New Testament, where Paul or James or Peter or John wrote to far-off church communities and needed to identify themselves to the recipients of their letters. Matthew was likely a member of the community for which he was writing a lasting document that recorded the life and ministry of his Savior and Lord. In this section we will focus our attention on attempting to identify the place of writing and the makeup of the community participants. These topics are intertwined with the conclusions above regarding authorship and date of writing.

### 2.4.1 Place of Writing of Matthew's Gospel

Matthew Levi, the former Jewish tax collector, displays significant Jewish emphases in his Gospel. Matthew has particular concern for the distinctiveness of Israel and for the fulfillment of the Old Testament and promises to Israel. At the same time, Matthew's Gospel displays openness to gentiles and that the gospel is now universally accessible to Jews and gentiles.[80] Those concerns will help guide us in our search for the identification of where Matthew and his community are located, and therefore where the Gospel of Matthew was written.

This is a difficult task, however, because there is no explicit mention of the location or identity of the recipients in the Gospel itself. Matthean scholars have been especially inventive and far-reaching in proposing locations for this Gospel. Among those put forward are Alexandria (Egypt),[81] Phoenicia (Mediterranean coast of Syria),[82] Edessa (Syrian desert),[83] Damascus (lower Syria),[84] Caesarea Maritima (Palestinian coastline),[85] Caesarea Philippi (upper Galilee),[86] Capernaum (central Galilee),[87] Jerusalem or in nearby Palestine (Judea),[88] and the general regions of

80. Konradt, *Matthew*, 18; Graham N. Stanton, *A Gospel for a New People: Studies in Matthew* (Edinburgh: T&T Clark, 1992), 278–83.

81. S. G. F. Brandon, *The Fall of Jerusalem and the Christian Church* (London: SPCK, 1951), 217–43; Sjef van Tilborg, *The Jewish Leaders in Matthew* (Leiden: Brill, 1972), 172.

82. George D. Kilpatrick, *The Origins of the Gospel According to St. Matthew* (Oxford: Clarendon, 1946), 130–34.

83. Benjamin W. Bacon, *Studies in Matthew* (London: Holt, 1930), 15–23; Robert E. Osborne, "The Provenance of Matthew's Gospel," *Studies in Religion / Sciences Religieuses* 3.3 (1973): 220–35.

84. Konradt, *Matthew*, 23.

85. Benedict T. Viviano, "Where Was the Gospel According to St. Matthew Written?," *CBQ* 41 (1979) 533–46.

86. Viviano, "Where Was the Gospel According to St. Matthew Written?," 533–46.

87. Witherington, *Matthew*, 27–28.

88. Willoughby C. Allen, *A Critical and Exegetical Commentary on the Gospel According to S. Matthew*, ICC, 3rd ed. (Edinburgh: T&T Clark, 1912), 34–35; France, *Matthew: Evangelist and Teacher*, 93–94: "general locality, Palestine"; Maier, *Matthäus*, 1:24–25.

Transjordan (lands east of the Jordan River).[89] None of these creative proposals has won wide endorsement.[90]

Currently there are two primary locations that are preferred as the place of origin of the Matthean community. The first is the region of Galilee, and some of those who favor this general provenance have suggested Sepphoris, Tiberias, or Capernaum as possible locations. The second is the general area of Syria, with many scholars opting for Antioch, the provincial capital and one of the largest metropolitan areas in the Roman Empire. The latter proposal, Antioch in Syria, has been the traditional proposal in the twentieth century, but the former, Galilee, has received significant recent attention.

#### *2.4.1.1 Galilee*

A growing number of scholars regard it as likely that Matthew was written in Galilee. Andrew Overman is often noted as one of the first to offer Palestine as the likely provenance of the Gospel of Matthew.[91] Within Palestine he narrows the provenance to the general region of Galilee. He then indicates that the language and some of the imagery within Matthew suggest a city in Galilee, with Tiberias or Sepphoris as the most likely specific location. He ultimately tends toward Sepphoris because of the important role it played in nascent rabbinic Judaism.[92]

Overman gives only brief attention to the provenance of Matthew's Gospel but suggests that the major arguments in favor of Galilee are as follows.

1. The struggle with formative Judaism is especially evident in Galilee, and Galilee played a central role in early rabbinic Judaism. Overman points to several places in Matthew where he suggests that conflict with formative Judaism is a current issue (e.g., 5:17) and that the Matthean community is turning away from formative Judaism toward other nations or people (e.g., 21:43; 28:19).[93]
2. Matthew seems to know Galilee well, and essentially limits the activity of the Jesus movement to Galilee. For Overman this seems to be one more reflection of Matthew's setting and world, which has made its way into his gospel story.[94]

89. H. D. Slingerland, "The Transjordanian Origin of Matthew's Gospel," *JSNT* 3 (1979): 18–28; Graham N. Stanton, "The Origin and Purpose of Matthew's Gospel: Matthean Scholarship from 1945 to 1980," *ANRW* 25.3:1941–42.

90. For extended discussion and critique of each see Davies and Allison, *Matthew*, 1:138–47; David C. Sim, *The Gospel of Matthew and Christian Judaism: The History and Social Setting of the Matthean Community* (Edinburgh: T&T Clark, 1998), 31–62; and most recently Drimbe, *Church of Antioch*, 84–102; Drimbe offers a helpful chart of proposals (85–86). One who is skeptical of community reconstructions is Cedric E. W. Vine, *The Audience of Matthew: An Appraisal of the Local Audience Thesis*, LNTS 496 (London: Bloomsbury T&T Clark, 2014), 207.

91. Andrew J. Overman, *Matthew's Gospel and Formative Judaism: The Social World of the Matthean Community* (Minneapolis: Fortress, 1990), 158–61.

92. Overman, *Matthew's Gospel and Formative Judaism*, 159n20.

93. Overman, *Matthew's Gospel and Formative Judaism*, 158.

94. Overman, *Matthew's Gospel and Formative Judaism*, 159.

3. The Pharisees, who are imported by Matthew into his Gospel story, are the Galilean Pharisees who represent the actual competitors of Matthew's community.[95]

Several scholars have followed Overman's lead and build on these three arguments.[96] For example, some observe that Matthew uses the term *polis* ("city") more extensively than Mark (twenty-six vs. eight times), suggesting an urban setting. And Matthew writes in good Koine Greek, which is seen by some as natural for a setting in Galilee where Greek was the second language of choice.[97] Others observe that a Galilean, or perhaps generally Palestinian setting for Matthew and his Gospel appears to be the traditional view of the early church, as numerous patristic authors followed Papias,[98] assuming that Matthew was originally in Aramaic.[99] Gale concludes that Matthew's audience was a conservative Christian community located in Galilee that still believed the laws of Torah were valid and required strict adherence. He concludes that the Matthean church was located near Sepphoris and was a wealthy, urban, and learned community comprised of many scribes.[100]

However, not all have been convinced of a Galilean setting for Matthew's Gospel. Davies and Allison state that "the community in which [Matthew] lived as he wrote his Gospel was not, in all probability, in Palestine."[101] David Sim has launched the most extensive critical evaluation of the proposed Galilean setting of Matthew's Gospel. He holds to a post-70 date of composition, so his arguments are influenced by that view. His arguments against Galilee as the provenance of writing are: (1) There is meager evidence for any types of Jesus-believers in Galilee in the late first century.[102] (2) The Gospel of Matthew was written in Greek and was based upon Greek sources, so it is unlikely that a Christian author in Galilee would have written a Greek Gospel to an Aramaic-speaking Christian community.[103] (3) The massive destruction and depopulation that characterized Galilee during the war initially must have had a substantial social and economic impact on cities like Sepphoris, making it unlikely that the significant community of Matthew's audience would have survived that war.[104] (4) The only

95. Overman, *Matthew's Gospel and Formative Judaism*, 159.

96. Daniel J. Harrington, *The Gospel of Matthew*, SP 1 (Collegeville, MN: Michael Glazier, 1991), 73–74; Anthony J. Saldarini, "The Gospel of Matthew and Jewish-Christian Conflict in the Galilee," in *The Galilee in Late Antiquity*, ed. Lee I. Levine (New York: Jewish Theological Seminary of America, 1992), 23–38, here 26–27; Paul Hertig, *Matthew's Narrative Use of Galilee in the Multicultural and Missiological Journeys of Jesus*, Mellen Biblical Press Series 46 (Lewiston, NY: Mellen, 1998), 60–65; Aaron M. Gale, *Redefining Ancient Borders: The Jewish Scribal Framework of Matthew's Gospel* (London: T&T Clark, 2005), 40–63; Witherington, *Matthew*, 21–28.

97. Witherington, *Matthew*, 25–28; Gale, *Redefining Ancient Borders*, 111–61.

98. Eusebius, *Hist. eccl.* 3.39.16.

99. E.g., Irenaeus, *Haer.* 3.1.1; Eusebius, *Hist. eccl.* 3.24.6; 3.25.5; 5.8.2; 5.10.3; 6.25.3–4; Jerome, *Vir. ill.* 3, 36.

100. Gale, *Redefining Ancient Borders*, 162–67.

101. Davies and Allison, *Matthew*, 1:140–41.

102. David C. Sim, "The Gospel of Matthew and Galilee: An Evaluation of an Emerging Hypothesis," *ZNW* 107.2 (2016): 141–69, here 155–59.

103. Sim, "Matthew and Galilee," 159–63.

104. Sim, "Matthew and Galilee," 163–65.

unique Matthean episode about Jesus in Galilee is the tradition concerning the temple tax and its accompanying miracle story in 17:24–27; hence there is no decisive evidence for Matthew's access to unique, local Galilean material.[105]

Sim has offered a sound critique of the theory of a Galilean provenance for Matthew's Gospel. My perspective, since I contend for a pre-70 dating of Matthew, would differ in that I would point out that all the arguments for a Galilean provenance are based on conditions following the war. I believe that is an unnecessary perspective. Rather, as I have stated as an assumption earlier, Matthew is writing good history and reflecting on the conditions at the time of Jesus's historical ministry. Therefore, since the evidence in favor of the Galilean hypothesis is rather meager and strong arguments can be raised against it, and since, while growing in popularity, it has not yet challenged the dominant view, I conclude that Matthew was written somewhere in Syria and most probably in Antioch. To that argument we now turn.

#### *2.4.1.2 Antioch*

The hypothesis of Antioch in ancient Syria as the provenance of the Gospel of Matthew was first proposed among modern scholars by B. H. Streeter in his classic study of the origins of the four Gospels.[106] It quickly attracted support and established itself firmly as the majority view and still enjoys this prominent position in current Matthean scholarship, although the degree of commitment to its probability varies.[107] For example, Davies and Allison state, "So while, in our judgement, the First Gospel was probably put together for the church of Antioch, this conclusion remains no more than the best educated guess."[108] Carson and Moo conclude, "In short, we cannot be certain of the geographic provenance of this gospel. Syria is perhaps the most likely suggestion, but nothing of importance hangs on the decision."[109] But as we will see below, more confidence in the Antiochene provenance is garnered by other scholars.[110]

Following the general arguments first proposed by Streeter, Michelle Slee helpfully

105. Sim, "Matthew and Galilee," 165–67.

106. B. H. Streeter, *The Four Gospels: A Study of Origins*, 4th rev. ed. (London: Macmillan: 1930), 500–523.

107. Schweizer, *The Good News According to Matthew*, 15–17; Davies and Allison, *Matthew*, 1:143–147; Sim, *Matthew and Christian Judaism*, 53–62; Rodney Stark, "Antioch as the Social Location for Matthew's Gospel," in *Social History of the Matthean Community: Cross-Disciplinary Approaches*, ed. David L. Balch (Minneapolis: Fortress, 1991), 189–210; Gundry, *Matthew*, 609; Hagner, *Matthew 1–13*, lxxv; Keener, *Matthew* (2009), 41–42; Michelle Slee, *The Church in Antioch in the First Century CE: Communion and Conflict*, JSNTS 244 (London: Sheffield, 2003), 118–22; Luz, *Matthew* 3:56–58; Carson and Moo, *Introduction*,151–52; Dennis C. Duling, *A Marginal Scribe: Studies in the Gospel of Matthew in Social-Scientific Perspective*, Matrix 7 (Eugene, OR: Cascade, 2012), 38–40; and Seán Freyne, *The Jesus Movement and Its Expansion: Meaning and Mission* (Grand Rapids: Eerdmans, 2014), 296–97; Drimbe, *Church of Antioch*, 109–10; W. Wilson, *Matthew 1–13*, loc. 618–33, Kindle.

108. Davies and Allison, *Matthew*, 1:146–47.

109. Carson and Moo, *Introduction*, 152.

110. For a careful evaluation of the current state of research, see Edward Bridge, "Christians and Jews in Antioch," in *Into All the World: Emergent Christianity in Its Jewish and Greco-Roman Context*, ed. Mark Harding and Alanna Nobbs (Grand Rapids: Eerdmans, 2017), 208–36.

identifies and summarizes the six arguments accepted by most scholars who favor Antioch.[111]

(1) The testimonies of Papias and Irenaeus indicate from an early date that the Gospel of Matthew was believed to have originated in the East rather than in Rome or in Asia Minor.

(2) The Gospel did not originally have a name of the author attached, so its early spread and acceptance could be explained by the influential and mission-oriented church that stood behind its text, since this would have facilitated the rapid spread of the Gospel to other areas. Moreover, acceptance of the Gospel in these other areas would be almost assured if it was known to have originated in a particularly prestigious church, especially one that was deemed to have apostolic authority. This church was not Jerusalem, since the Gospel was composed in Greek, after the AD 70s (in her view).

(3) The Gospel contains both positive and negative statements in regard to the mission to the gentiles, which indicates conflicts and disputes over this issue inside the Matthean community. Antioch was the scene of bitter conflicts and disputes on this very issue, and it was in the Antioch church that one could find many different groups adopting various positions on the issue of gentile entry to the church. The tension in the Gospel of Matthew in regard to this mission is suggestive of an Antiochene provenance.

(4) The Jewish character of the text also points to Antioch, a city that was predominantly gentile yet had a very large Jewish population. A background in Antioch would explain *both* the Jewishness of the Gospel and the references to gentiles.

(5) Peter is given an important role in the Gospel, which accords well with the apostle's status and influence in Antioch. Peter's actions appear to have influenced the decision of the majority of Jewish Christians in Antioch to separate themselves from gentile Christians (Gal 2:11–14). Eusebius records a tradition in the fourth century that the first bishop of Antioch was Peter (Eusebius, *Hist. eccl.* 3.36.2; cf. Jerome, *Vir. ill.* 1, 16), who was succeeded by Evodius and then by the well-known martyr Ignatius of Antioch, who died in the reign of Trajan (ca. 108; Eusebius, *Hist. eccl.* 3.22).

(6) It is likely that the Gospel which Ignatius, bishop of Antioch, was familiar with was the Gospel of Matthew.[112] Since there is no indication that Ignatius was familiar with any of the other Gospels known to us, the written Gospel known to Ignatius is the Gospel of Matthew, to which at times he may be referring when he uses the word

111. Slee, *Church in Antioch*, 118–22.

112. For a cautious assessment, see Paul Foster, "Ignatius of Antioch's Reception of the Gospel of Matthew," in *The Composition, Theology, and Early Reception of Matthew's Gospel*, ed. Joseph Verheyden, Jens Schröter, and David C. Sim, WUNT 477 (Tübingen: Mohr Siebeck, 2022), 249–87. For the view that "texts in Ignatius of Antioch which bear a definite literary contact" with the written Gospel of Matthew, see Massaux, *Influence of the Gospel of Saint Matthew*, 85–96; here 85. For a discussion of four texts from the Ignatian letters that "supply clear proof of the dependence of Ignatius on the Gospel of Matthew" (cf. Ign. *Smyrn.* 1.1; *Phld.* 3.1; *Pol.* 2.2; *Eph.* 19.2–3), see John P. Meier, "Matthew and Ignatius: A Response to William R. Schoedel," in *Social History of the Matthean Community: Cross-Disciplinary Approaches*, ed. by David L. Balch (Minneapolis: Fortress, 1991), 178–86; here 180.

"gospel."[113] Ignatius of Antioch only knew one "Gospel," and that was the Gospel of Matthew.[114] This again might point to the Gospel having been composed in Antioch.

Amiel Drimbe contends that the six arguments originally proposed by Streeter and summarized by Slee are also accepted by Meier,[115] Davies and Allison,[116] Sim,[117] and many others, which constitutes a scholarly consensus today. Nine decades after Streeter first proposed them, these six arguments have stood the test of time.[118]

(7) In addition to these six arguments, Drimbe argues that the Didache should become the seventh argument for Antioch as the provenance of Matthew's Gospel. The Didache and the Gospel of Matthew are closely related.[119] After over a hundred and thirty years of research, the Antiochene provenance of the Didache is widely accepted.[120] Drimbe then observes that there is also the growing consensus that the Didache and Matthew's Gospel "evolved" together, since the Didache inserts material from both pre-Matthean sources and the written Gospel in its final form. "Therefore, the complex literary connections between the two writings has led an international group of fifty-five scholars of related fields (New Testament, early Christianity, Second Temple Judaism, Patristic studies, liturgical studies) to conclude that Matthew and the Didache originated 'from the same Jewish-Christian milieu,' which most probably was Antioch."[121]

### *2.4.1.3 Conclusion*

While we have still not arrived at absolute certainty, these seven arguments in my view favor a provenance of Matthew's Gospel in Antioch. A final quote from John Meier puts the Matthean connection to Antioch in perspective when the overall history of development is considered, including Ignatius. He argues that the simplest and most obvious solution is that Ignatius knew and used Matthew, which he may actually refer to at times as *euangelion*. Meier offers that, once accepted, this position

113. Schoedel suggests that oral material from Matthew was a source for Ignatius: William R. Schoedel, *Ignatius of Antioch: A Commentary on the Letters of Ignatius of Antioch*, ed. Helmut Koester, Hermeneia (Philadelphia: Fortress, 1985), 9–10.

114. The significant points of comparison are the following: Ign. *Smyrn.* 1.1 (cf. Matt 3:15); Ign. *Eph.* 6.1 (cf. Matt 10:25; 13:27, 52; 20:1); Ign. *Eph.* 19.1–2 (cf. Matt 2:2); Ign. *Pol.* 2.2 (cf. Matt 10:16b).

115. John P. Meier, "Antioch," in *Antioch and Rome: New Testament Cradles of Catholic Christianity*, ed. Raymond E. Brown and John P. Meier (New York: Paulist, 2004), 12–86.

116. Davies and Allison, *Matthew*, 143–147.

117. Sim, "Matthew and Galilee," 167–68.

118. Drimbe, *Church of Antioch*, 109–10.

119. See Jonathan A. Draper, "Conclusion: Missing Pieces in the Puzzle or Wild Goose Chase? A Retrospect and Prospect," in *The Didache: A Missing Piece of the Puzzle in Early Christianity*, ed. Jonathan A. Draper and Clayton N. Jefford, ECL 14 (Atlanta: Society of Biblical Literature, 2015), 534–36.

120. Cf. Clayton N. Jefford, "Introduction: Dynamics, Methodologies, and Progress in Didache Studies," in *The Didache: A Missing Piece of the Puzzle in Early Christianity*, ed. Jonathan A. Draper and Clayton N. Jefford, ECL 14 (Atlanta: Society of Biblical Literature, 2015), 4–8.

121. Drimbe, *Church of Antioch*, 110–11. Drimbe cites Huub van de Sandt, ed., *Matthew and the Didache: Two Documents from the Same Jewish-Christian Milieu?* (Minneapolis: Fortress, 2005); Huub van de Sandt and Jürgen K. Zangenberg, ed., *Matthew, James, and Didache: Three Related Documents in Their Jewish and Christian Settings*, SBLSymS 45 (Atlanta: Society of Biblical Literature, 2008).

has tremendous implications for drawing up a history of the church in Antioch that reaches from Barnabas and Paul, through Matthew, to Ignatius. "Such a genealogy gives the Matthean church a 'before' and 'after,' forebears and progeny, and thus supplies a framework for writing the social history of the Matthean community in Syria."[122]

## 2.4.2 Matthew's Message for His Community

While we still do not have absolute certainty of the provenance of Matthew's Gospel, the highly influential church at Antioch in ancient Syria (modern Turkey), with its large Jewish-Christian and gentile-Christian contingents (cf. Acts 11:19–26; 13:1–3), as we have seen above, has often been recognized as the original audience of those who first heard/read Matthew's Gospel.[123] This is confirmed in part because of the first Gospel's influence upon Ignatius, the bishop of Antioch, and upon the Didache. But Matthew's message was equally relevant for the fledgling church throughout the ancient world and appears to have been disseminated fairly quickly.

Antioch had a large, wealthy Jewish population in the first century (Josephus, *J.W.* 7.43).[124] These Jews endowed beautifully decorated synagogues, and "constantly attracting to their religious ceremonies multitudes of Greeks" (*J.W.* 7.45 [Thackery, LCL]). The first mention of Antioch in the New Testament is in reference to Nicolaus, a proselyte to the Jewish faith from Antioch (Acts 6:5). He accepted Christ and was subsequently appointed as one of seven men to oversee the needs of Hellenist widows in Jerusalem in the early days of the church.

The church in Antioch saw a large influx of gentile believers in the mid-AD 30s (probably former God-fearers—gentiles who were attracted to Jewish monotheism, e.g., Acts 10:22), due to the evangelism by some Greek-speaking Jewish believers (Acts 8:1, 4; 11:19–26). Disciples of Jesus who fled the persecutions in Jerusalem soon spread the gospel and after arriving in Antioch "spoke to Greeks also" (Acts 11:20).[125] So the church in Antioch, established in the mid-30s by the scattered "Hellenists" (i.e., Greek-speaking Jews; cf. Acts 6:1) from Jerusalem, consisted of a mix of Jewish and gentile Christians (Acts 8:1, 4; 11:19–21).

This missionary activity resulted in "a great number" (Acts 11:21) of gentile conversions and prompted the church in Jerusalem to send Barnabas to Antioch to monitor the progress. Barnabas, impressed by the large number of converts and probably aware of Paul's commission to preach to gentiles (Acts 26:17), brought Paul from Tarsus

122. Meier, "Matthew and Ignatius," 186.

123. Cf. also Keener, *Matthew* (2009), 41–42.

124. For background, see Frederick W. Norris, "Antioch of Syria," *ABD* 1:265–69; John McRay, "Antioch," *Eerdmans Dictionary of the Bible*, ed. David Noel Freedman, Allen C. Myers, and Astrid B. Beck (Grand Rapids: Eerdmans, 2000), 67–68.

125. Cornelis Bennema, "The Ethnic Conflict in Early Christianity: An Appraisal of Bauckham's Proposal on the Antioch Crisis and the Jerusalem Council," *JETS* 56.4 (2013): 753–63.

to work in Antioch. They worked together in this gentile center (Acts 11:26), which subsequently became the sponsoring church for Paul's missionary journeys to the gentile world (13:3; 15:40; 18:22–23). The term "Christian" (follower of the Christ/Messiah)[126] was first applied to the disciples of Jesus in this city (Acts 11:26).[127]

One of the most remarkable events in the early church relating to ethnic distinctions occurred in Antioch. Peter joined Paul in Antioch, where he used to eat with the gentiles in the church. But when a contingent from James arrived in Antioch, Peter began to draw back and separate himself from the gentiles because he was afraid of those who belonged to the circumcision group (Gal 2:12). Paul accused Peter of acting hypocritically (2:13). In this highly dramatic situation, Paul "opposed him to his face, because he stood condemned" (2:11), rebuking Peter "in front of them all" (2:14). This then led to the Jerusalem Council's arbitration of circumcision for gentile converts.[128]

It is this background that contributes to many scholars conjecturing that Matthew the apostle wrote his Gospel to the Jewish-gentile Christian community in Antioch. But without further evidence, this remains conjecture. But what can we make of the participants for whom Matthew wrote his Gospel?

#### *2.4.2.1 Jewish Participants*

There is evidence in the first Gospel of a message for a Jewish readership.[129] On the positive side, a long-standing perspective of Matthew's Gospel is that the person responsible for penning this document has Jewish concerns in view, which are evident from the opening verses.[130] The incipit, which focuses on the "beginnings of Jesus Messiah, the son of David, the son of Abraham" (1:1, author's translation), would have great relevance to a Jewish audience.

The immediately following genealogy traces Jesus Messiah's lineage from Abraham, Isaac, and Jacob, through David the king of Israel and the ensuing generations of Israel's kings (1:2–17), up to the arrival of the magi from the east asking, "Where is the one who has been born king of the Jews?" (2:2). The arrival of Jesus Messiah is the fulfillment of the hopes and dreams of the people of Israel. And then Matthew displays the unique "fulfillment" quotations and allusions from the Old Testament (e.g., 1:21–23; 2:14–15,

126. Michael J. Wilkins, "Belief/Believer" and "Christian," *ABD* 1:656–57, 925–26.

127. James D. G. Dunn, *Beginning from Jerusalem*, vol. 2 of *Christianity in the Making* (Grand Rapids: Eerdmans, 2009), 301–8, 383–85.

128. See Richard Bauckham, "James, Peter, and the Gentiles," in *The Missions of James, Peter, and Paul: Tensions in Early Christianity*, ed. Bruce Chilton and Craig Evans, NovTSup 115 (Leiden: Brill, 2005), 91–142; Eckhard J. Schnabel, *Early Christian Mission*, 2 vols. (Downers Grove, IL: InterVarsity, 2004), 2:1069–72; Dunn, *Beginning from Jerusalem*, 301–2; Bennema, "Ethnic Conflict in Early Christianity," 753–63.

129. Konradt, *Matthew*, 17–20.

130. For a thorough discussion of the "Jewishness" of Matthew's Gospel, see Christopher M. Tuckett, "Matthew: The Social and Historical Context—Jewish Christian and/or Gentile?," in *The Gospel of Matthew at the Crossroads of Early Christianity*, ed. Donald Senior, BETL 243 (Leuven: Peeters, 2011), 99–129.

17–18, 23), where the focus is upon Jesus Messiah as the fulfillment of Israel's hopes and Scriptures.[131]

On the negative side, Matthew does not include asides in Mark's Gospel where Mark explains Jewish practices. For example, when Mark narrates an incident where Jesus's disciples were eating food "with hands that were defiled, that is, unwashed" (Mark 7:2), he expands upon the narrative with an explanation (Mark 7:3–4). This appears to indicate that Mark's readers were unfamiliar with these Jewish practices and needed explanation. However, when Matthew narrates the same incident, he does not include this explanation, which may indicate that Matthew's readers were familiar with these Jewish practices.[132] This is especially forceful if Matthew had access to Mark's Gospel and eliminated this explanation.

Early church fathers indicate that Matthew was in direct contact with the Jewish community. Eusebius includes a statement from Irenaeus (ca. AD 130–202) that indicates close knowledge of the Jewish community (Eusebius, *Hist. eccl.* 5.8.2 = Irenaeus, *Haer.* 3.1.1). This may indicate that Matthew communicated the gospel both orally and in written form to the Jewish and/or Jewish-Christian community. Eusebius also notes Origen's (ca. AD 184–253) understanding that Matthew wrote "for those who from Judaism came to believe, composed as it was in the Hebrew language" (Eusebius, *Hist. eccl.* 6.25.4 [Lake, LCL]). Eusebius himself (ca. AD 323) also indicated his view that "Matthew had first preached to Hebrews, and when he was on the point of going to others he transmitted in writing in his native language the Gospel according to himself" (Eusebius, *Hist. eccl.* 3.24.5–6 [Lake, LCL]).

### *2.4.2.2 Gentile Participants*

There is also evidence in the first Gospel of a message for a gentile audience.[133] Matthew calls Jesus the "son of David" in his opening verse, but he also calls him the "son of Abraham." Matthew mentions David sixteen times throughout his Gospel,[134] but he also mentions Abraham seven times (1:1, 2, 17; 3:9 [2x]; 8:11; 22:32). In tracing the ancestry not only to David but also to Abraham, Matthew holds a light of hope to the entire world. The covenant God made with Abraham established Israel as his

131. Nicholas G. Piotrowski, *Matthew's New David at the End of Exile: A Socio-Rhetorical Study of Scriptural Quotations*, NovTSup 170 (Leiden: Brill, 2016).

132. Robert McIver pushes this a bit too far, in my opinion, by suggesting that Matthew's community had a high regard for law and practiced Sabbath observance, as well as observing the distinction between clean and unclean foods, and the community was therefore likely mainstream early Christianity. See Robert K. McIver, *Mainstream or Marginal? The Matthean Community in Early Christianity*, Friedensauer Schriftenreihe Series 12 (Berlin: Peter Lang, 2012).

133. As somewhat of a reaction to the emphasis on the Jewish dimensions of Matthew's Gospel, see the emphasis on the Hellenistic/gentile dimensions in Robert S. Kinney, *Hellenistic Dimensions of the Gospel of Matthew: Background and Rhetoric*, WUNT 2/414 (Tübingen: Mohr Siebeck, 2016).

134. Matthew 1:1, 6 [2x], 17, 20; 9:27; 12:3, 23; 15:22; 20:30, 31; 21:9, 15; 22:42, 43, 45.

chosen people, but it also was a promise that his line would be a blessing to all the nations (Gen 12:1–3; 22:18).[135]

At a very early stage of Jesus's ministry and Matthew's narrative we find a staggering reversal of ethnic and religious expectations: a gentile is healed, a promise of gentile inclusion to the kingdom of heaven is revealed, and the nation of Israel is warned of exclusion from God's program of redemption if they do not repent (Matt 8:10–12). The gentile centurion understands that Jesus is the hoped-for deliverer, whom Israel as a nation should have recognized. Jesus's statement both singles out the centurion for exemplary faith, but also censures Israel for its lack of faith. This is not only extraordinary praise for a gentile but contains an indictment of Israel for lack of faith, so the praise and indictment turn to language of promise to gentiles and judgment against Israel (8:11). This certainly must have shocked Jesus's audience and is a stark reminder to Matthew's readers of the nature of discipleship to Jesus.

### *2.4.2.3 A Jewish-Gentile Christian Community*

The first (1:1) and final verses (28:18–20) of Matthew's Gospel can operate as a frame that emphasizes the Jewish-gentile orientation of the author's purposes in writing.[136] The very first verse gives the direction—it is a book that establishes Jesus's identity as the Messiah, the heir to the promises of Israel's throne through king David, and heir to the promises of blessing to all the nations through the patriarch Abraham. The final verses climactically declare Jesus's Great Commission to make disciples of all the nations, including both Jews and gentiles (28:18–20).

So, this first Gospel serves as an evangelistic tool to Jews, contending that they should turn to Jesus as their long-awaited Messiah, but also to gentiles, emphasizing that salvation through Jesus Messiah is available to all the nations. This first Gospel also serves as an apologetic tool to Jewish-Christians, encouraging them to stand firm in the face of opposition from their Jewish countrypersons and from gentile pagans, knowing that Jesus Messiah has fulfilled the promised arrival of the kingdom of heaven.

Against the backdrop of a world that is increasingly hostile to Christianity, the author solidifies his church's identity as the true people of God, who transcend ethnic, economic, and religious barriers to find oneness in their adherence to Jesus Messiah. His Gospel becomes a manual on discipleship, as Jew and gentile are made disciples of Jesus Messiah and learn to obey all that he commanded his original disciples.

135. See, e.g., M. Daniel Carroll R., "Blessing the Nations: Toward a Biblical Theology of Mission from Genesis," *BBR* 10.1 (2000): 17–34; Richard J. Erickson, "Joseph and the Birth of Isaac in Matthew 1," *BBR* 10.1 (2000): 35–51.

136. Hagner, *Matthew 1–13*, 9–10; Morris, *Matthew*, 20–21; Dieudonné Tamfu, "Jesus' Kingly Blessings for the Nations: A Missiological Understanding of Matthew 1:1," *Journal of Global Christianity* 1.1 (2015): 79–91.

### 2.4.2.3.1 Salvation-Historical "Particularism" and "Universalism"

The terms "particularism" and "universalism" indicate that Matthew's Gospel lays striking emphasis upon both the fulfillment of the promises of salvation to a particular people, Israel, and the fulfillment of the universal promise of salvation to all the peoples of the earth. The church, made up of every nationality, has cherished this Gospel because Matthew aims to record the continuation of the history of salvation to all the nations. His introductory statement, that Jesus Christ is both the "son of David" and the "son of Abraham" (1:1), is the preliminary indication that salvation promises made both through David to God's chosen people, Israel (e.g., 2 Sam 7:8–17), and through Abraham to all peoples (Gen 12:1–3; 22:18), have been fulfilled through the life and ministry of Jesus Christ, the promised Savior of all nations.

Matthew's Gospel alone points explicitly to Jesus's intention to go first to the lost sheep of the house of Israel (10:5–6; 15:24), showing historically how God's promise of salvation to Israel was indeed fulfilled. And yet the promises made to Abraham that he would be a blessing to all the nations are also fulfilled as Jesus extends salvation to the gentiles (cf. 21:43; 28:19). The church throughout the ages has found assurance in Matthew's Gospel that God truly keeps his promises to his people.

### 2.4.2.3.2 The New Community of Faith

Facing the threat of gathering Roman persecution within a pagan world, Matthew addresses a church that is representative of the emerging community of faith. The community apparently has a large membership of Jewish-Christians who are familiar with temple activities and the Jewish religious system. But it also has a large contingent of gentile Christians who are discovering their heritage of faith in God's universal promise of salvation.[137] The church has consistently found in Matthew's Gospel a call to a new community that transcends ethnic and religious barriers to find oneness in its adherence to Jesus Messiah. The church has continually been challenged by Matthew's message that former barriers to discipleship have now been abolished.

The offer of discipleship found in the Great Commission broke down the same barriers that Jesus broke down all through his earthly ministry. Restrictions on the basis of gender, ethnicity, social status, and religious practice were abolished, so that now women and men, Jew and gentile, rich and poor, clean and unclean all have been called to be disciples of Jesus. With Matthew's clear understanding of the Old Testament and Jewish practices, his Gospel has held a radical position in sustaining Jesus's call to "all who are weary and burdened" (11:28). Keener clarifies, "But most of

137. For a thorough study of the Matthean community and its relationship to Pharisaic Judaism, but with different conclusions than here, see Anders Runesson, "Rethinking Early Jewish-Christian Relations: Matthean Community History as Pharisaic Intragroup Conflict," *JBL* 127.1 (2008): 95–132.

all, Matthew probably functions as a discipling manual, a 'handbook' of Jesus' basic life and teaching, relevant to a Jewish-Christian community engaged in the gentile mission and deadlocked in a scriptural polemic with their local synagogue communities."[138]

Matthew alone among the evangelists uses the term *ekklēsia*, which later became the common term to designate the church. He emphasizes explicitly that God's program of salvation history will find its continuation in the present age as Jesus builds his universal church (16:18) and maintains his presence within its local assembly (18:15–20; cf. 28:20). Whoever responds to his invitation (22:10) is brought within the church to enjoy his fellowship and demonstrate the true community of faith. A new kind of identity is forged in Matthew's presentation of his Gospel. Cornelis Bennema emphasizes that the Christian identity is a unifying identity that incorporates diverse identities—ethnic, national, and cultural—and converges them toward Christ in terms of beliefs, practices, behavior, and ethos.[139]

This is the Christian identity that Matthew advocates for his community—a community that was the early example of breaking down the walls that separated Jew and gentile before the advent of the gospel of Jesus Christ.

## 2.5 GENRE

"Genre" (French: "kind" or "sort") refers to a particular type or category of literature, art, music, film, etc. Literary genre is a distinctive type or category of literary composition, such as epic, tragedy, biography, poetry, comedy, novel, and short story.[140] When we come to the literature of the New Testament there are a number of common literary genres, including poetry, historical narrative, parable, letter, etc. Each genre is characterized by certain grammatical, structural, and lexical features that help convey the meaning and purpose of the discourse.

When examining the Gospels of the New Testament, many have tried fitting them into the genre of other ancient literature. Among those proposed are Greek aretalogy (stories of the miraculous deeds of a godlike hero, such as *The Life of Apollonius of Tyana*), saga (extended narrative re-creation of historical events, such as the *Iliad* and *Odyssey* of Homer), legend (a traditional tale thought to have a historical basis, such as the story of the Oracle at Delphi), or Jewish midrash (viewing the personages and circumstances of the Bible in the light of the contemporary history of the time, such as the Genesis Rabbah).

But the most popular, and deemed most defensible, is that the Gospels are related to the Greek biography.[141] Many New Testament scholars now suggest that all four

138. Keener, *Matthew* (2009), 51.

139. Cornelis Bennema, "Early Christian Identity Formation Amidst Conflict," *JECH* 5:1 (2015): 26–48; here 43.

140. *Encyclopedia Britannica*, "Genre," last updated March 7, 2025, https://www.britannica.com/art/genre-literature.

141. Carson and Moo, *Introduction*, 114.

Gospels reflect aspects of common Greco-Roman biographical literature or "lives" (*bioi*) of famous ancient figures. The leading voice in the exploration of the Gospels as "biographies" or "lives" (*bioi*) is Richard Burridge.[142] He argues that the genre of biography was a very broad one in antiquity, and broad enough to encompass the Gospels of the New Testament,[143] including the Gospel of Matthew.[144] After his survey of Matthean scholarship in the last twenty-five years, Burridge declares, "the biographical hypothesis has not only become accepted but increasingly assumed and used for further research."[145] I think that most Matthean scholars would concur, and would explore various other expressions of biographical hypotheses. For example, Armin Baum suggests that the four New Testament Gospels are biographies of Jesus in Old Testament biographical and historiographical style and rabbinic style with comparatively slight Greco-Roman influences.[146] Burridge and Keener would emphasize the Greco-Roman *bioi* tradition and its relevance for gospel studies but would also include Jewish literary influence.[147]

I would include that in the Gospels of the New Testament we have a literary form that goes beyond other ancient literature in important ways that get at the core of the message that is truly the "good news" of God to his people. Martin Hengel makes an important distinction regarding the Gospels of the New Testament, which will guide our study of the theology of Matthew's Gospel.

> By the standards of antiquity they are βίοι [*bioi*], but as "saving event" they have a unique, one might almost say incomparable, character. Ordinary biographies do not contain a message of faith which is decisive for eternal life and the last judgment. That is what is completely new about the "genre" Gospel.[148]

Simon Gathercole argues that there are substantial differences of theological content between the New Testament Gospels and noncanonical Gospels. He shows how the Gospels of Matthew, Mark, Luke, and John each include four key points that formed

142. Burridge, *What Are the Gospels?* A recent voice taking this further is Craig S. Keener, *Christobiography: Memory, History, and the Reliability of the Gospels* (Grand Rapids: Eerdmans, 2019). A relatively appreciative critique of Keener's approach is found in Sarah E. Rollens, "Major Review: *Christobiography: Memory, History, and the Reliability of the Gospels* by Craig S. Keener," *Interpretation* 75.2 (2021): 164–66. For surveys of the literature on the "genre of the gospels" see Burridge, *What Are the Gospels?*, 1–112; Judith A. Diehl, "What is a 'Gospel'? Recent Studies in the Gospel Genre," *CurBR* 9.2 (2011): 171–99.

143. Burridge, *What Are the Gospels?*, 53–77.

144. For a survey of recent Matthean scholarship and how Burridge declares that "the biographical hypothesis has not only become accepted but increasingly assumed and used for further research," see Richard A. Burridge, "Matthew and Gospel Genre: A Critical Review of the Last 25 Years, 1993–2018," in Seleznev, Loader, and Niebuhr, *The Gospel of Matthew in Its Historical and Theological Context*, WUNT 459 (Tübingen: Mohr Siebeck, 2021), 47–74; here 58.

145. Burridge, *What Are the Gospels?*, I.16.

146. Armin D. Baum, "Biographics of Jesus in Old Testament and Rabbinic Style: The Genre of the New Testament Gospels," in *The Earliest Perceptions of Jesus in Context: Essays in Honour of John Nolland on His 70th Birthday*, ed. Aaron W. White, Craig A. Evans, and David Wenham, LNTS 566 (London: Bloomsbury T&T Clark, 2018), 33–58; here 58.

147. Burridge, *What Are the Gospels?*, 37–77; Keener, *Christobiography*, e.g., 155–57.

148. Hengel, *Four Gospels*, 266n368.

the core of early Christian preaching and teaching: Jesus's identity as messiah, the saving death of Jesus, the resurrection of Jesus, and Scripture's foretelling of the Christ event.[149] These set the canonical Gospels apart from other ancient biographies.[150] This helps to situate the direction that our study will take us to gain Matthew's unique perspectives of the meaning of God's activities in history.

Scot McKnight, in his creative way, concludes an essay he wrote on "Matthew as 'Gospel'" with the following words: "The first Gospel 'gospels.'"[151] He places Matthew in the genre of *bioi* (biography), but he takes his overriding cue from the term "gospel" itself. He writes, "Matthew 'gospels' because he tells a saving Story of Jesus that fulfills Israel's Story. The Gospel involves declaring the salvation of Israel from its oppressing burdens through Jesus as its Messiah."[152] In this way, we understand the relationship of the spelling of "gospel" and "Gospel." The "gospel" (4:23; 9:35) is the unique saving message about Jesus Messiah, and the "Gospel" (24:14; 26:13)[153] is the written declaration of that unique saving message about Jesus Messiah from the unique perspectives of the individual authors, Matthew, Mark, Luke, and John.

Coupled with our discussion above of the identity of Matthew's community, we do well to heed the caution of David Bauer and not place more emphasis upon the community than upon the focus of Matthew's Gospel, which is Jesus. Bauer points to the "obsession" in recent Matthean scholarship to reconstruct the community of Matthew and to interpret the Gospel of Matthew in light of that community reconstruction. Such a venture runs the risk of mistakenly insinuating that the Gospel of Matthew is primarily about Matthew's church rather than about Jesus himself.[154]

Matthew was engaged in a creative and dynamic act of theological reception as he reflected upon the life and ministry of Jesus in the light of the Old Testament Scriptures.[155] The audience of Matthew's Gospel comprises all those that Matthew expected to hear and to read his Gospel record, including, as we discussed above, the mix of Jewish-Christian and gentile-Christian disciples.[156] Richard Bauckham has

149. Simon J. Gathercole, *The Gospel and the Gospels: Christian Proclamation and Early Jesus Books* (Grand Rapids: Eerdmans, 2022). See also Pennington, *Reading the Gospels Wisely*, 35.

150. Recently Francis Watson has tried to loosen the distinctiveness of the term *gospel* and make a more inclusive relationship to the non-canonical gospels, which I see as problematic. See Francis Watson, *What Is a Gospel?* (Grand Rapids: Eerdmans, 2022).

151. Scot McKnight, "Matthew as 'Gospel,'" in Gurtner, Willitts, and Burridge, eds., *Jesus, Matthew's Gospel*, 59–75; here 75.

152. McKnight, "Matthew as 'Gospel,'" 74.

153. McKnight agrees with Graham Stanton that at 24:14 and 26:13 Matthew may well be calling his writing "the Gospel." Cf. McKnight, "Matthew as 'Gospel,'" 74, and Graham N. Stanton, *Gospel Truth? New Light on Jesus and the Gospels* (Valley Forge, PA: Trinity Press International, 1995), 98.

154. David R. Bauer, *The Gospel of the Son of God: An Introduction to Matthew* (Downers Grove, IL: InterVarsity, 2019), "Form and Genre," loc. 606–29, Kindle.

155. See Madison N. Pierce, Andrew J. Byers, Simon Gathercole, eds., *Gospel Reading and Reception in Early Christian Literature* (Cambridge: Cambridge University Press, 2022), esp. 1–10.

156. A helpful, brief overview of recent scholarship on the relationship of Matthew's community to the Jewish community is found in Brian C. Dennert, *John the Baptist and the Jewish Setting of Matthew*, WUNT 2/403 (Tübingen: Mohr Siebeck, 2015), esp. 2–7. For more extensive recent scholarship, see Robert K. McIver, *Mainstream or Marginal? The Matthean Community in*

convinced most Gospels scholars that the evangelists' intent was to provide a message that goes beyond that original audience to focus on others in the first century.[157] But importantly, Blomberg emphasizes a both/and approach: Matthew's purpose included writing his Gospel for his localized community but he did so with a broader audience in mind.[158] This incorporates also those in the succeeding two millennia, including readers today. Here is where we read expectantly, attempting to glean theology from Matthew that will shape our understanding of Jesus Messiah as Matthew unfolds his message. Here we understand Matthew's Gospel as a portrait of Jesus Messiah, the son of David, the son of Abraham (1:1), and Immanuel, God with us always (1:23; 28:20) as we experience life in the kingdom of heaven. We will see that Matthew's Gospel is formulated to be a manual on discipleship to Jesus, the one who holds all authority (28:18–20), and it places expectations upon our lives today as his disciples as it did upon the first-century audience.[159]

## 2.6 RECEPTION-HISTORY OF MATTHEW'S GOSPEL

In Chapter 1 we explored looking through the windows of the Gospels. Additionally, today we also have our own lenses. I read (and write about) Matthew's Gospel as a white, male, evangelical, Western scholar/pastor. These, at least in part, are the lenses that make up my interpretative and social location. They do not *determine* how I read the biblical text, but they should be acknowledged as elements that *influence* my reading. These social locations can provide helpful nuances in the way that I interpret and apply Matthew's Gospel to my own life. On the other hand, they can unduly cloud my understanding of the biblical text. We truly are in an era of global Christianity, and we

*Early Christianity*, Friedensauer Schriftenreihe 12 (Berlin: Peter Lang, 2012), and Terence L. Donaldson, *Gentile Christian Identity from Cornelius to Constantine: The Nations, the Parting of the Ways, and Roman Imperial Ideology* (Grand Rapids: Eerdmans, 2020), esp. ch. 4.

157. Richard Bauckham, "For Whom Were the Gospels Written?," in *The Gospels for All Christians: Rethinking the Gospel Audiences*, ed. Richard Bauckham (Grand Rapids: Eerdmans, 1998), 9–48. For a specific challenge to what she sees as a simple dichotomy between "specific" and "indefinite" readers, see Margaret M. Mitchell, "Patristic Counter-Evidence to the Claim that 'The Gospels Were Written for All Christians,'" *NTS* 51.1 (2005): 36–79. For a defense of Bauckham's thesis, see Michael F. Bird, "Bauckham's *The Gospel For All Christians* Revisited," *EuroJTh* 15.1 (2006): 5–13; and Edward W. Klink III, ed., *The Audience of the Gospels: The Origin and Function of the Gospels in Early Christianity*, LNTS 353 (London: T&T Clark, 2010); in this volume edited by Klink, Bauckham himself offers a response to Mitchell; see Richard Bauckham, "Is There Patristic Counter-Evidence? A Response to Margaret Mitchell," 68–110. Cedric Vine follows Bauckham and is skeptical of community reconstructions: "In summary, local community reconstructions currently represent inadequate readings of the Gospel in that they result from a hermeneutical process that is highly ambiguous, are selective, if not abusive, in their treatment of plot and characterisation, and operate with an overly simplistic conception of the nature of audience experience that fails to incorporate the dynamics of aurality and an audience awareness of other early Christian traditions." See Vine, *Audience of Matthew*, 207.

158. Craig L. Blomberg, "The Gospels for Specific Communities *and* All Christians," in Klink, *Audience of the Gospels*, 111–33. For another helpful emphasis on this wider audience, see Justin Marc Smith, *Why Bíος? On the Relationship Between Gospel Genre and Implied Audience*, LNTS 518 (London: Bloomsbury T&T Clark, 2015).

159. See also Keener, *Matthew* (2009), 51.

have the opportunity to learn from others and read the Bible through the eyes of many different interpreters and see how the Bible impacts their social and cultural contexts.[160]

An example is Matthew's understanding of discipleship to Jesus. Discipleship in the ancient Greco-Roman and Jewish world was primarily a professional male apprenticeship to a teacher or rabbi with the ultimate goal of the disciple becoming a teacher or rabbi. However, Jesus established a very different form of discipleship, which we will explore in full in Chapter 10.

As a white, Western scholar, do I fully appreciate the significance of Jesus establishing his form of discipleship that was not a scholarly apprenticeship but a permanent transformational relationship available to all people—male, female, Jew, gentile, rich, poor? What was it like for women to follow Jesus, when in that first-century Jewish culture no women were allowed to enter into discipleship to a rabbi? How well do I appreciate the radical nature of Jesus's new kind of discipleship to include gentiles alongside of Jews? And do I really understand the mind-boggling phenomenon that Jesus was not just another human leader, but truly the fully divine and human Messiah, "God with us" as our Savior and Lord? As we attempt to find biblical principles for our discipleship to Jesus for today, we will need to have as objective an understanding as possible of the first two horizons in order to find relevance on the third horizon.

The past fifty years have witnessed a virtual explosion of scholarship on Matthew's Gospel on all three horizons. This scholarly explosion has built upon the preceding two millennia of church history, and has included all the spectra of Christian experience, including liberal to fundamentalist theology, male and female perspectives, colonial and post-colonial analyses, ecological and economical engagement, international perspectives, etc. This scholarship also includes the many hermeneutical and methodological approaches to the text of Matthew's Gospel. Surveys of this scholarship have been numerous and help us to see the influence of Matthew's Gospel throughout the last two millennia.[161]

160. For a recent, provocative article that sketches what the author describes as the deficiencies and challenges of the movement from monoracial to multiracial biblical studies, see Wongi Park, "Multiracial Biblical Studies," *JBL* 140.3 (2021): 435–59. See also Wongi Park, *The Politics of Race and Ethnicity in Matthew's Passion Narrative* (Cham, Switzerland: Palgrave Macmillan, 2019), esp. ch. 5, "Proposing an Alternative Narrative: An Ethnoracial Reading of Matthew 26–27," 107–48. In my view he forces his interpretive scheme too far as he critiques leading Matthean scholars (e.g., R. T. France and Donald Hagner) for their "traditional religious-theological interpretations" of Matthew's Gospel (e.g., Park, *Politics of Race and Ethnicity*, 15–46).

161. For select surveys in chronological order: Graham N. Stanton, "The Origin and Purpose of Matthew's Gospel: Matthean Scholarship from 1945–1980," in *Studies in Matthew and Early Christianity*, ed. Markus Bockmuehl and David Lincicum, WUNT 309 (Tübingen: Mohr Siebeck, 2013), 9–75; Donald Senior, *What Are They Saying About Matthew?*, rev. and exp. ed. (New York: Paulist, 1996); David R. Bauer, "The Interpretation of Matthew's Gospel in the Twentieth Century," *Summary of the Proceedings of the American Theological Library Association* [St. Meinrad, IN] 42 (1988): 119–45; R. T. France, "Matthew's Gospel in Recent Study," *Them* 14.2 (1989): 41–46; John Riches, *Matthew*, T&T Clark Study Guides (London: T&T Clark, 1996); Kealy, *Matthew's Gospel*; Aune, ed. *Gospel of Matthew*; Gurtner, "Gospel of Matthew from Stanton to Present," 23–38; David C. Sim, "Matthew: The Current State of Research," in *Mark and Matthew I. Comparative Readings: Understanding*

Tobias Nicklas, a specialist in the area of reception history,[162] states that "probably no other early Christian writing was more influential than the Gospel of Matthew."[163] He is an editor of the international project *Novum Testamentum Patristicum* Commentary Series (NTP),[164] which tries to offer a complete documentation of New Testament receptions in ancient Christianity. In following chapters, we look briefly at scholars from a variety of interpretative and social locations to see how they interpret elements of Matthew's Gospel. This will help illustrate for us how others interpret the horizon of the historical Jesus and the horizon of Matthew's perspective. These lenses come from a variety of different interpretative and social locations, representing early interpreters in reception history, different theological backgrounds, different gender perspectives, those from different ecclesial traditions, and those from different international locations, including majority world readings of Matthew.

One of the originators of the reception-history approach to texts was philosopher Hans-Georg Gadamer (1900–2002), whose significant contributions are many, but especially philosophical hermeneutics in his classic work, *Truth and Method*. He introduced the term *Wirkungsgeschichte*, often translated "reception history," for the critical history of the impact or effect of a text.[165] Especially for texts like Scripture, New Testament scholar Richard Burridge suggests that their subsequent history and impact upon generations of believers may be more important than the original audience.[166] Markus Bockmuehl suggests that *Wirkungsgeschichte* points to a two-way interaction between the biblical text and its readers, and may more appropriately be translated "the history of a text's effects." He states, "Rightly understood as the history of the text's effects (and not merely its 'reception'), *Wirkungsgeschichte* speaks of how Scripture has interpreted us, the readers."[167]

---

*the Earliest Gospels in Their First Century Settings*, ed. Eve-Marie Becker and Anders Runesson, WUNT 271 (Tübingen: Mohr Siebeck, 2011), 33–51; Elaine M. Wainwright, with Robert J. Myles and Carlos Olivares, *Matthew: An Introduction and Study Guide, The* Basileia *of the Heavens Is Near at Hand*, T&T Clark Study Guides to the New Testament 1 (London: Bloomsbury T&T Clark, 2017); see also Elaine M. Wainwright, "Matthew, The Gospel of," in *The Cambridge Dictionary of Christianity*, ed. Daniel Patte (Cambridge: Cambridge University Press, 2010), 778–79; J. Brown and Roberts, *Matthew*, 267–522, nearly half of their volume is devoted to two theological sections: "Thinking Theologically with Matthew" and "Constructive Theological Engagement with Matthew," which are theological engagements with recent Matthean scholarship.

162. See e.g., Tobias Nicklas, "Zwischen Redaktion und 'Neuinszenierung'": Vom Umgang erzählender Evangelien des 2. Jahrhunderts mit ihren Vorlagen," in *Gospels and Gospel Traditions in the Second Century: Experiments in Reception*, ed. Jens Schröter, Tobias Nicklas, and Joseph Verheyden, in collaboration with Katharina Simunovic, BZNW 235 (Berlin: de Gruyter, 2019), 311–30.

163. Tobias Nicklas, "From Gospel Book to Virtual Reality: A Neglected Aspect of the Gospel of Matthew's Ancient Reception History," in Seleznev, Loader, and Niebuhr, *The Gospel of Matthew in Its Historical and Theological Context*, WUNT 459 (Tübingen: Mohr Siebeck, 2021), 17–28; here 17.

164. See https://www.uni-regensburg.de/theology/novum-testamentum-patristicum/home/index.html.

165. Hans-Georg Gadamer, *Truth and Method*, 2nd rev. ed., trans. and rev. Joel Weinsheimer and Donald G. Marshall (1960; New York: Continuum, 2004), esp. 299–306.

166. Richard A. Burridge, "Who Writes, Why, and For Whom?," in *The Written Gospel*, ed. Markus Bockmuehl and Donald A. Hagner (Cambridge: Cambridge University Press, 2005), 110.

167. Markus Bockmuehl, "New Testament *Wirkungsgeschichte*

Régis Burnet provides a recent discussion of exegesis and the discipline of history of reception (*Wirkungsgeschichte*). He proposes "renewing the dialogue with tradition, i.e., with the readings of the past—from the Fathers of the Church to the 21st-century exegetes—with a definition of the term 'reading' broad enough to include literary and poetic works, plastic works, music, and even popular culture."[168] He provides examples from specific New Testament passages and figures such as Judas Iscariot and Mary Magdalene. While we may not agree with some of his underlying methods or methodologies, his is a worthy objective.

## 2.7 THE DEVELOPMENT OF THE WRITTEN GOSPEL OF MATTHEW

Building on the preceding discussions of authorship, dating, community, genre, and reception history, we now inquire into the development of the written document that we know as the Gospel of Matthew, and the relationship of the Gospel of Matthew to the other written Gospels. Today we have four written documents that God has preserved for us. They give similar yet different perspectives of the life and ministry of Jesus Messiah. The author of each Gospel account was concerned to record the life and ministry of Jesus Messiah for his own particular audience. Ancient church tradition tells us much about the authorship and destination of each Gospel, but it tells us very little about the period of time between the first preaching of the gospel on Pentecost and the time of the appearance of the first written document, approximately thirty years later. How did the gospel circulate, and how was it preserved?

### 2.7.1 Synopsis

Of special interest in this regard in our study is the relationship of the first three Gospels—Matthew, Mark, and Luke—called the "Synoptic Gospels." The English adjective *synoptic* comes from the Greek term *synopsis*, which means viewing or seeing together the life and ministry of Jesus from a common point of view.[169] A synopsis presents parallel texts from each of the Gospels in vertical columns side by side in

and the Early Christian Appeal to Living Memory," in *Memory in the Bible and Antiquity*, Fifth Durham-Tübingen Research Symposium (Durham, September 2004), ed. Loren T. Stuckenbruck, Stephen C. Barton, and Benjamin G. Wold, WUNT 212 (Tübingen: Mohr Siebeck, 2007), 341–68, here 343. See also a full volume that explores reception history in Eve-Marie Becker and Anders Runesson, eds., *Mark and Matthew II. Comparative Readings: Reception History, Cultural Hermeneutics, and Theology*, WUNT 304 (Tübingen: Mohr Siebeck, 2013).

168. Régis Burnet, *Exegesis and History of Reception: Reading the New Testament Today with the Readers of the Past*, WUNT 455 (Tübingen: Mohr Siebeck, 2021), 6.

169. For discussion see Robert H. Stein, *Studying the Synoptic Gospels: Origin and Interpretation*, 2nd ed. (Grand Rapids: Baker Academic, 2001), esp. 17–25.

order to compare and contrast the accounts of the life and ministry of Jesus and the individual evangelists' narrative.[170] The chart below is what a synopsis looks like for the four Gospels' accounts of Jesus's arrest. Notice the similarity of all four, but also the distinct difference of John's account.

| Matt 26:51–52 | Mark 14:47 | Luke 22:49–51 | John 18:10–11 |
|---|---|---|---|
| | | When Jesus' followers saw what was going to happen, they said, "Lord, should we strike with our swords?" | |
| With that, one of Jesus' companions reached for his sword, drew it out and struck the servant of the high priest, cutting off his ear. | Then one of those standing near drew his sword and struck the servant of the high priest, cutting off his ear. | And one of them struck the servant of the high priest, cutting off his right ear. | Then Simon Peter, who had a sword, drew it and struck the high priest's servant, cutting off his right ear. (The servant's name was Malchus.) |
| "Put your sword back in its place," Jesus said to him, "for all who draw the sword will die by the sword." | | But Jesus answered, "No more of this!" And he touched the man's ear and healed him. | Jesus commanded Peter, "Put your sword away! Shall I not drink the cup the Father has given me?" |

### 2.7.2 Synoptic Gospels

Matthew, Mark, and Luke are called Synoptic Gospels because they view the life and ministry of Jesus from a common perspective different from that of John, the writer of the fourth Gospel. The Synoptic Gospels are three works that have distinct similarities in their picture of Jesus Christ. In general, they follow the same outline and record similar material.

#### *2.7.2.1 Distinct Similarities Between the Synoptic Gospels*

Mark Strauss has charted the differences between the Synoptic Gospels and the Gospel of John as follows:[171]

170. Donald A. Hagner, *The New Testament: A Historical and Theological Introduction* (Grand Rapids: Baker Academic, 2012), 131–32. The synopsis that has Greek text and English translation (RSV) on opposite pages is helpful for most students: Kurt Aland, ed., *Synopsis of the Four Gospels: Greek-English Edition of the Synopsis Quattuor Evangeliorum*, 12th ed. (Freiburg: German Bible Society, 2001).

171. Mark L. Strauss, *Four Portraits, One Jesus: A Survey of Jesus and the Gospels* (Grand Rapids: Zondervan, 2007), 25.

| Synoptics | John |
|---|---|
| (1) Emphasize the Galilean setting of the initial part of Jesus's ministry. | (1) Considerable movement between Galilee and Judea. |
| (2) Little information given to determine the length of Jesus's ministry. Much of the material could fit in a single year. | (2) Mentions at least three Passover feasts (2:13; 6:4; 13:1; possibly 5:1), suggesting a ministry of at least 2½ to 3 years. |
| (3) Emphasize Jesus's teaching in parables, short sayings, and epigrams. | (3) Relates long speeches by Jesus, dialogues with his opponents, and interviews with individuals. |
| (4) Jesus's teaching centers on the theme of the kingdom of God. Healings and exorcisms demonstrate the power of the kingdom and the dawn of eschatological salvation. | (4) Jesus's teaching focuses on himself and the Son's revelation of the Father. Signs or miracles reveal Jesus's identity and glorify the Father. Frequently mentions eternal life. |

The Synoptic Gospels present Jesus of Nazareth as a unique person with a unique ministry to accomplish. They then proceed to proclaim the good news about him by recounting events and teachings organized around the four periods of Jesus's public ministry.

- **Period of preparation:** the ministry of John the Baptist, the baptism of Jesus, and the temptation of Jesus (Matt 3:1–4:1; Mark 1:2–13; Luke 3:1–4:13)
- **Ministry in Galilee** (Matt 4:12–18:35; Mark 1:14–9:50; Luke 4:14–9:50)
- **Journey to Judea and ministry in and around Judea** (Matt 19:1–20:34; Mark 10:1–52; Luke 9:51–19:27)
- **Final week in Jerusalem, death, and resurrection** (Matt 21:1–28:20; Mark 11:1–16:8 [20]; Luke 19:28–24:53)

Notice also that the Synoptic Gospels have some striking agreements in the structure of certain events. In the story of the paralytic let down through the roof, all three break their narratives by inserting a parenthesis at the same place, while John does not record the event.

| Matt 9:6 | Mark 2:10–11 | Luke 5:24 |
|---|---|---|
| But I want you to know that the Son of Man has authority on earth to forgive sins." *So he said to the paralyzed man,* "Get up, take your mat and go home." | But I want you to know that the Son of Man has authority on earth to forgive sins." *So he said to the man,* "I tell you, get up, take your mat and go home." | But I want you to know that the Son of Man has authority on earth to forgive sins." *So he said to the paralyzed man,* "I tell you, get up, take your mat and go home." |

### *2.7.2.2 Differences Within the Synoptic Gospels*

One's reaction to seeing these similarities might be to say they should be expected if all three are accurately recording the truth of what occurred. But what of the differences?

#### 2.7.2.2.1 Material Peculiar to Individual Gospels

Each Gospel contains material that is peculiar or unique to it.[172] This is especially true of Matthew and Luke. The birth stories in Matthew and Luke are entirely different (Matt 1:18–2:23 and Luke 1:5–2:52). Both Gospels give genealogies (Matt 1:1–17; Luke 3:23–38), but their lists are different, and they appear in different contexts. Only Matthew records the incident of Peter walking on the water (14:28–31) and the coin in the fish's mouth (17:24–27), while the material in Luke 9:51–18:14 is unique to the Third Gospel.

Using a percentage basis, over a century ago B. F. Westcott[173] tabulated the peculiarities and coincidences of the four Gospels. "Peculiarities" refers to material that is unique to each Gospel, and "Coincidences" refers to material that is shared with the other Gospels. Most of Mark's Gospel is shared with the other Gospels, while the majority of John's Gospel is unique to his account.

| Gospel | Peculiarities | Concordances |
|---|---|---|
| | *Material Unique to Each Gospel* | *Material Shared with Other Gospels* |
| Mark | 7 | 93 |
| Matthew | 42 | 58 |
| Luke | 59 | 41 |
| John | 92 | 8 |

#### 2.7.2.2.2 Differences in Parallel Accounts

**Three temptations of Jesus.** Matthew's order of Jesus's temptations in the wilderness (Matt 4:1–13) differs from the order given in Luke's account (Luke 4:1–13), while Mark says nothing about the different temptations (Mark 1:12–13). Both Matthew and Luke give the temptation of bread first, but then reverse the next two. This is an important example of each evangelist narrating incidents for his particular purpose. Matthew seems to be intent upon narrating chronological sequence, while Luke seems to have a more theological purpose in placing the temple temptation last.[174] This does not, however, mean that either evangelist alters the historical record of the temptations, as is implied by some scholars.[175]

**Healing of a centurion's servant at Capernaum.** Matthew pictures the centurion as personally bringing his request to Jesus (Matt 8:5–13), while Luke relates that the

172. Guthrie, *New Testament Introduction*, 122.

173. B. F. Westcott, *An Introduction to the Study of the Gospels*, 8th ed. (London: Macmillan, 1898), 195, citing William Stroud, *Harmony of the Gospels*, 117.

174. Cf. I. Howard Marshall, *Commentary on Luke*, NIGTC (Grand Rapids: Eerdmans, 1978), 166–67; John Nolland, *Luke 1–9:20*, WBC (Dallas: Word, 1989), 180–81.

175. N. H. Taylor, "The Temptation of Jesus on the Mountain: A Palestinian Christian Polemic against Agrippa I," *JSNT* 83 (2001): 27–49.

centurion made his request through Jewish elders sent to intercede on his behalf (Luke 7:1–10). Luke's greater detail relates that the centurion sent word to Jesus through two groups of his representatives, first some Jewish elders (7:3), and then some friends (7:6). Luke tells us further that these groups of Jewish advocates came on behalf of the gentile centurion out of gratitude to him, because he had been responsible for building a synagogue for the Jewish people. The reason for sending others on his behalf lies in the centurion's recognition of his own unworthiness (7:7) as a gentile to approach Jesus.

**Jesus's sermon.** Matthew's record of the Sermon on the Mount (Matt 5–7) is considerably longer than the Sermon on the Plain recorded in Luke (Luke 6:20–49), with some of the material in Luke not found in Matthew's account, and some of Matthew's account of the Sermon found scattered elsewhere in Luke. Reconciling the similarities and differences has led to different conclusions by interpreters. (1) The similarities lead some to assert that Matthew and Luke present two distinct summaries of the same message given by Jesus.[176] (2) The differences lead others to suggest that Matthew and Luke record two different sermons, which were given by Jesus on separate occasions when he repeated some of the same or similar content.[177]

The first view is strengthened by observing the same general context, the general order, and the similar geographical setting (mountainous area) of both sermons. The second view is strengthened by recalling that Jesus went about teaching and preaching all through the countryside of Galilee for nearly two years, and he almost certainly repeated much of the same content on numerous occasions. Since nothing of great importance relies on the solution to this question, it may be best to say that until further insight is gained either the first or second view is acceptable.

### 2.7.3 Synoptic Problem

A comparison of the contents of the Synoptic Gospels therefore reveals both close resemblance and striking divergence. How is the remarkable, complex comingling of agreements and disagreements among Matthew, Mark, and Luke to be explained? Why are the first three Gospels so much alike? How are the differences to be explained, and if one is different, why? These are the questions that give rise to the discussion of the origin of the Gospels, especially focusing on the discussion of the Synoptic Problem.

The so-called Synoptic Problem deals with the investigation of the relationship

176. E.g., Carson, "Matthew," 152–58; Darrell L. Bock, *Luke 1:1–9:50*, BECNT (Grand Rapids: Baker Books, 1994), 553; Robert L. Thomas and Stanley N. Gundry, *The NIV Harmony of the Gospels* (New York: HarperCollins, 1988), 70–71, note c.

177. E.g., Morris, *Matthew*, 93; Blomberg, *Matthew*, 96.

between the Synoptic Gospels, especially attempting to explain the similarities and differences between these documents. The similarities and differences between the Synoptic Gospels suggest literary dependence to many scholars. This may have involved writers using the same written sources or drawing upon one or both of the other Synoptic Gospels.

A supplementary element advanced by many is that in addition to the three Synoptic Gospels is a source called Q ("Q" comes from the German word for "source," *Quelle*), a hypothetical oral, or some say written, narrative of certain accounts of Jesus's life and ministry. The phenomenon called Q represents the places where Matthew and Luke have material that is not found in Mark. That coincidence is the only *fact*.

The inquiry into the relationship among the Synoptic Gospels, usually on the literary level, attempts to explain the similarities and differences found in the Synoptic Gospels by articulating a theory of their relationships to one another.[178] Stanley Porter and Bryan Dyer assembled four renowned scholars to debate the principal ways of attempting to solve the Synoptic Problem.[179] This will provide us a brief overview of the primary hypotheses.

### *2.7.3.1 Two-Source Hypothesis*

Craig Evans articulates and defends the **two-source hypothesis**, which has been the dominant theory for much of the last one hundred years. This hypothesis contends that the Gospel of Mark was written first and became the principal narrative source of the Gospels of Matthew and Luke. The two-source hypothesis also holds that Matthew and Luke made use of a second major non-Markan source, which is chiefly comprised of the teaching of Jesus. This source is usually referred to as Q.[180] This latter source, Q, most scholars suggest, has been lost to us.

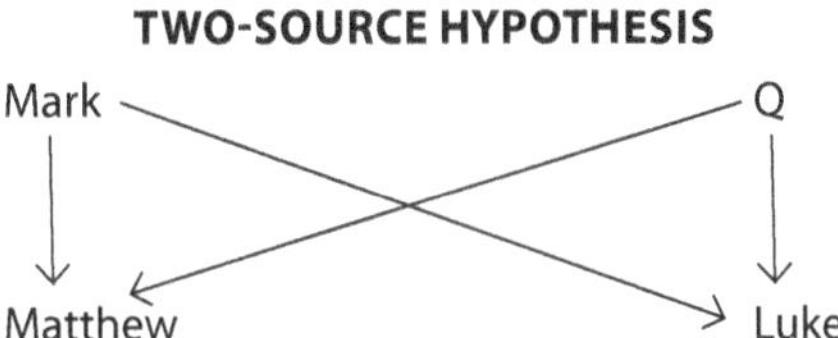


*The two-source hypothesis also recognizes that Matthew and Luke incorporate within their Gospels material that is unique to their documents ("M" and "L"). This is often diagramed as the "four-document hypothesis."*

178. David Laird Dungan, *A History of the Synoptic Problem: The Canon, the Text, the Composition, and the Interpretation of the Gospels*, ABRL (New York: Doubleday, 1999), 2–3.

179. Stanley E. Porter and Bryan R. Dyer, eds., *The Synoptic Problem: Four Views* (Grand Rapids: Baker Academic, 2016), 13.

180. Craig A. Evans, "The Two Source Hypothesis," in Porter

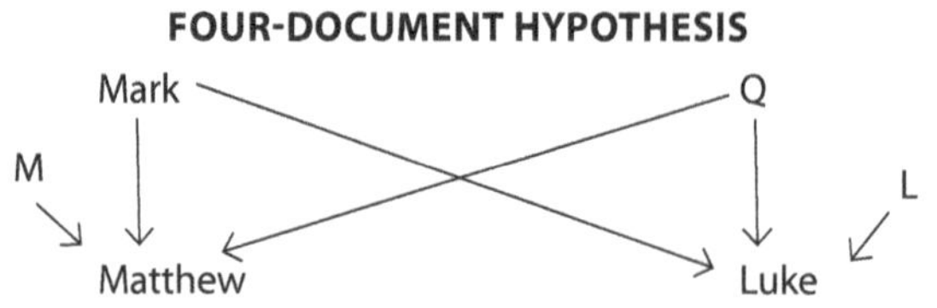

**FOUR-DOCUMENT HYPOTHESIS**

Mark → Matthew; Mark → Luke; Q → Matthew; Q → Luke; M → Matthew; L → Luke

*The four-source hypothesis is basically the same as the two-source hypothesis plus the additional features of unique Matthean material and unique Lukan material. Most advocates of the two-source hypothesis would concur.[181] Evans poses and answers the following question:*

> Why is the two-source hypothesis the dominant view among New Testament scholars? It is the dominant view because most scholars believe that it offers the best explanation of the data. This is not to say that everything is neatly explained; no theory of the relationships of the Synoptic Gospels is free from difficulty. It is only to say that most scholars find that the Two Source Hypothesis encounters the fewest difficulties and, more importantly, offers greater explanatory power.[182]

### *2.7.3.2 Farrer Hypothesis*

Mark Goodacre advocates the **Farrer hypothesis**, which is a challenge to the existence of Q as a source, but strongly advocates the priority of Mark as a source for both Matthew and Luke. This latter point is similar to the two-source hypothesis. However, the Farrar hypothesis starkly differs, suggesting that Matthew draws upon Mark and then Luke draws upon both Mark and Matthew. This is where the Farrar hypothesis differs: it eliminates Q, because Luke draws upon Matthew, dispensing with the need to account for the places where Matthew has material that is not found in Mark.[183]

and Dyer, *Synoptic Problem*, 27. See also Stein, *Studying the Synoptic Gospels*, 143–52. For the most recent detailed study of the existence of Q material in Matthew in the defense of the two-source hypothesis, see Alan Kirk, *Q in Matthew: Ancient Media, Memory, and Early Scribal Transmission of the Jesus Tradition*, LNTS 564 (London: Bloomsbury T&T Clark, 2016). See also James M. Robinson, Paul Hoffmann, and John S. Kloppenborg, eds., *The Critical Edition of Q: Synopsis Including the Gospels of Matthew and Luke, Mark and Thomas, with English, German and French Translations of Q and Thomas*, Hermeneia (Minneapolis: Fortress, 2000).

181. Porter and Dyer, *Synoptic Problem*, 16.

182. Evans, "Two Source Hypothesis," 27–28.

183. Mark Goodacre, "The Farrer Hypothesis," in Porter and Dyer, *Synoptic Problem*, 47–48. See also Mark Goodacre, *The Synoptic Problem: A Way Through the Maze*, BibSem 80 (London: Sheffield Academic, 2001).

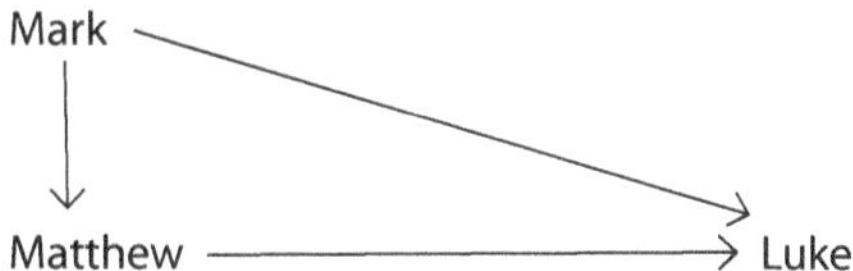


One of the cases made against Q being an actual source is that it is primarily a rendering of Jesus's sayings, that he is only a sage, not a miracle worker.[184] In the reconstructed source is one healing of a centurion servant (Q 7:10), one allusion to Jesus's overall healing ministry (Q 7:22), and one exorcism (Q 11:14). Q does not include the Gospel narratives of Jesus's miraculous birth, nor of Jesus's passion and resurrection. Therefore, Q partisans contend that the authors of Q knew nothing about the way Jesus died or about the stories of an empty tomb. Or if they knew, they did not care to reproduce them as historical events. Consequently, there is no historical basis for an atonement doctrine in Q theology.[185] All of this leads to many scholars rejecting Q as a document that represents a Christian community's understanding of who Jesus was. An interesting perspective is given by New Testament scholar John Meier:

> I cannot help thinking that biblical scholarship would be greatly advanced if every morning all exegetes would repeat as a mantra: "Q is a hypothetical document whose exact extension, wording, originating community, strata, and stages of redaction cannot be known." This daily devotion might save us flights of fancy that are destined, in my view, to end in skepticism.[186]

### *2.7.3.3 Two-Gospel Hypothesis*

David Peabody undertakes advocacy of the **two-Gospel hypothesis**. This hypothesis proposes that Matthew's Gospel was written first, Luke later utilized Matthew's Gospel and a considerable amount of non-Matthean source material, while Mark, writing third, utilized both Matthew's and Luke's Gospels as primary sources and blended or "conflated" them, with the addition of very little other source material.[187]

184. For recent critiques of Q, see Mark Goodacre, *The Case Against Q: Studies in Markan Priority and the Synoptic Problem* (Harrisburg, PA: Trinity Press International, 2002); Mark Goodacre and Nicholas Perrin, eds., *Questioning Q: A Multidimensional Critique* (Downers Grove, IL: InterVarsity, 2004).

185. For advocates of Q as the earliest Gospel, see John S. Kloppenborg, *Q Parallels: Synopsis, Critical Notes and Concordance* (Sonoma: Polebridge, 1988); John S. Kloppenborg, *Q, The Earliest Gospel: An Introduction to the Original Stories and Sayings of Jesus* (Louisville: Westminster John Knox, 2008), esp. ch. 3: "What a Difference Difference Makes." See also Burton L. Mack, *The Lost Gospel: The Book of Q and Christian Origins* (San Francisco: HarperSanFrancisco, 1993).

186. John P. Meier, *Mentor, Message, and Miracles*, vol. 2 of *A Marginal Jew: Rethinking the Historical Jesus*, ABRL (New Haven, CN: Yale University Press, 1994), 178.

187. David Barrett Peabody, "The Two Gospel Hypothesis," in Porter and Dyer. *Synoptic Problem*, 67–68.

An earlier version of this hypothesis is known as the Griesbach hypothesis, and in the 1960s–1970s a version appeared that was championed by William Farmer and his followers.[188]

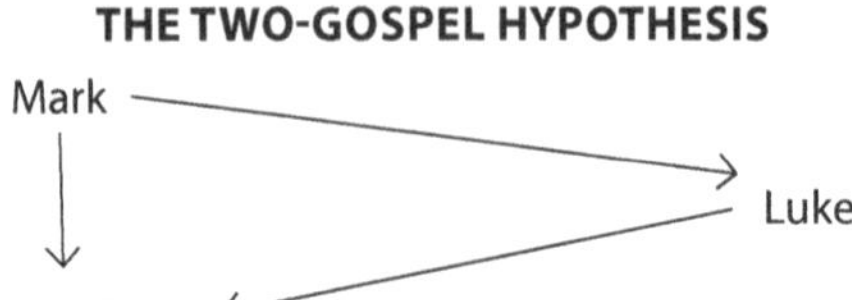


This hypothesis has the advantage of building on much of church history's belief that Matthew was the first Gospel written and making unnecessary the postulating of an actual source Q.

### *2.7.3.4 Orality-and-Memory Hypothesis*

Rainer Riesner explores the very complex **orality-and-memory hypothesis.**[189] The three prior hypotheses heavily emphasize the literary relationships between the Gospels. The orality-and-memory hypothesis emphasizes that an "oral" gospel lay behind the Synoptic Gospels. This oral gospel commenced with the original twelve apostles/disciples, especially emphasizing the role of the apostle Peter. The apostolic preaching in Jerusalem is the basis for this originally Aramaic oral gospel, and as the witness spread it was memorized and re-preached. This oral gospel spread throughout Palestine before extending outward.

This original oral gospel was used to assist the earliest preachers and evangelists, especially including the apostle Paul, in the spread of the gospel message. It was orally translated into Greek to preach to the gentile community with some changes in presentation and emphasis to effectively communicate to the gentile audience.

This basic Aramaic gospel, with its Greek translations, formed the main source for the Synoptic Gospels, each evangelist using the material according to his own audience and purpose. Matthew produced a genuine Palestinian gospel, Mark under the influence of Peter recorded a modified Palestinian Gospel, and Luke reflected a Pauline gospel. The literary differences between them were conditioned by the respective author's training and ability.[190]

188. William R. Farmer, *The Synoptic Problem: A Critical Analysis* (New York: Macmillan, 1964).

189. Rainer Riesner, "Orality and Memory Hypothesis," in Porter and Dyer, *Synoptic Problem*, 89–111.

190. Riesner, "Orality and Memory Hypothesis," 89–111.

**THE ORALITY-AND-MEMORY HYPOTHESIS THE FOLLOWING CHART IS ADAPTED FROM RIESNER, "ORALITY AND MEMORY HYPOTHESIS," 107.**

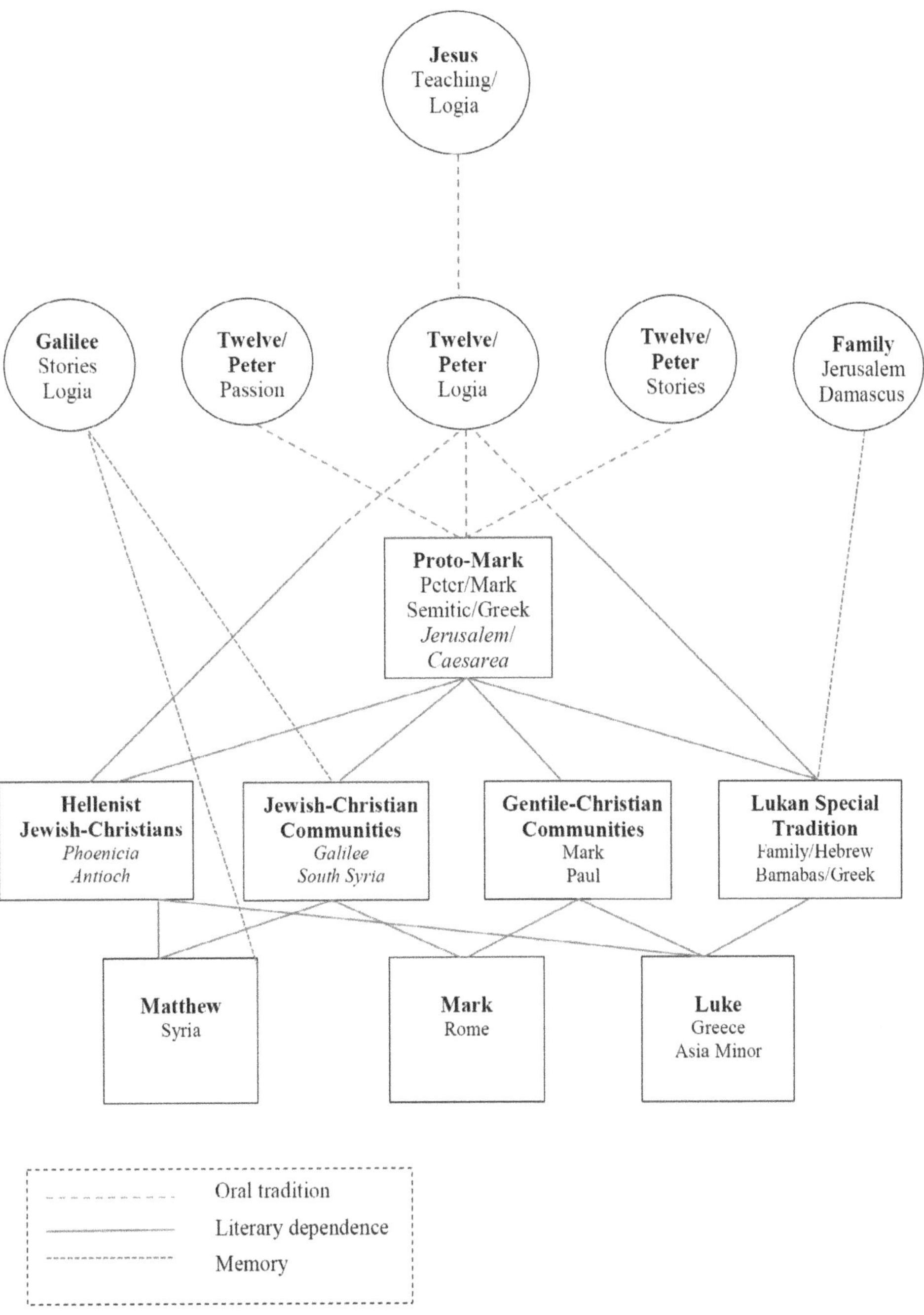

### 2.7.4 Conservative Assumptions

My purpose here is not to focus on the Synoptic Problem, but to explore how the various hypotheses contribute to understand how Matthew came to be written.[191] The literature on this is massive and I have followed and partaken of its fruit for the last nearly fifty years. The following is my take on the way the accounts about Jesus (oral and written) developed. I especially emphasize the developing oral tradition in an oral culture that lies behind the written Gospels. Before we look at a theory of how Matthew and the Gospels came to be written, we will start with assumptions that may help with some of the difficulties.

#### *2.7.4.1 The Holy Spirit*

While each writer took great pains to compose a document that taxed his abilities as a human author, the Holy Spirit was at work guiding his thoughts, bringing to mind certain details and arranging the form to coincide with truth. John recorded these words of Jesus spoken during his last night with the disciples: "But the Advocate, the Holy Spirit, whom the Father will send in my name, will teach you all things and will remind you of everything I have said to you" (John 14:26). And in the same discourse, Jesus declared: "But when he, the Spirit of truth, comes, he will guide you into all the truth. He will not speak on his own; he will speak only what he hears, and he will tell you what is yet to come" (16:13; cf. vv. 12–15).

What guides me here theologically is known as the "concursive" theory of the inspiration of Scripture. This theory emphasizes the dual authorship of Scripture—the Holy Spirit and the human author. God superintended the process of composing the Scriptures so that the end result establishes his divine intention, without overriding the human authors and their intentions. Paul Feinberg emphasizes that the Holy Spirit's role was to reveal the truths to be written and guide and superintend the authors so that their words coincided with truth.[192]

#### *2.7.4.2 Historical Account*

We should expect many similarities of detail throughout the Gospels' accounts if the authors are recording truth. If there was no similarity of detail, we would wonder if any of them were acquainted with things the way they actually occurred. Luke guides us to understand that the evangelists were intent upon passing on an accurate record of what happened in history. Luke writes, "It seemed fitting for me as well, having investigated everything carefully from the beginning, to write it out for you in an orderly sequence,

191. James D. G. Dunn, "How Did Matthew Go About Composing His Gospel?," in Gurtner, Willitt, and Burridge, *Jesus, Matthew's Gospel*, 39–58.

192. Feinberg, *Light in a Dark Place*, 202.

most excellent Theophilus; so that you may know the exact truth about the things you have been taught" (Luke 1:3–4 NASB).

#### *2.7.4.3 Individual Perspectives*

Many divergences are bound to occur in the various Gospel accounts because of the unique individuality of the three authors. Each would give a similar account for the two reasons just discussed, but differences would naturally occur as they expressed their individual personalities and perspectives of the truth.

We need to be careful in the largely speculative attempt to understand the origin of the Gospels, and these three assumptions will be profitable to add perspective.

### 2.7.5 A Tentative Theory of the Origins of Matthew and the Other Gospels

In this section I will lay out part of my understanding of the way in which Matthew's Gospel developed as a written document. I will include here the relationship of Matthew as a written Gospel to the other Gospels.

#### *2.7.5.1 Jesus's Life and Ministry*

We start with ***Jesus's life and ministry***. The apostles were eyewitnesses of Jesus's life and ministry. This was crucial for the distinctive of them being called apostles (cf. Acts 1:21–26). They had a striking memory of Jesus's story. The apostolic preachers (e.g., Peter in Acts 2) gave most prominence to the passion material, with a certain emphasis connected to the events and teaching of Jesus. This stage of the development of the Gospels, including Matthew, was oral. N. T. Wright emphasizes that since the culture of Jesus's time was primarily oral and securely retentive, it safeguarded the memory of what Jesus said and did.[193] In this Jewish oral culture, where memorization was a standard of daily and religious life, the earliest disciples would have been focused on remembering their Messiah and Lord and passing on that memory to others.

#### *2.7.5.2 The Preaching of the Passion*

The earliest message about Jesus given by the apostolic band was the ***passion***, as we can see from the earliest preaching accounts in Acts. This is the ***kerygma***. If we

193. N. T. Wright, *Jesus and the Victory of God*, vol. 2 of *Christian Origins and the Question of God* (Minneapolis: Fortress, 1996), 133–37. For a treatment of the oral tradition as background to the development of Matthew's Gospel, see Riesner's position above. See also Kenneth E. Bailey, "Informal Controlled Oral Tradition and the Synoptic Gospels," *Asia Journal of Theology* 5.1 (1991): 34–54; James D. G. Dunn, *Jesus Remembered*, vol. 1 of *Christianity in the Making* (Grand Rapids: Eerdmans, 2003), esp. 139–335; Dunn, *The Oral Gospel Tradition* (Grand Rapids: Eerdmans, 2013); Rafael Rodríguez, *Structuring Early Christian Memory: Jesus in Tradition, Performance and Text*, LNTS 407 (London: Bloomsbury T&T Clark, 2010); Eric Eve, *Behind the Gospels: Understanding the Oral Tradition* (Minneapolis: Fortress, 2014); Bauckham, *Jesus and the Eyewitnesses*.

look at percentages of the Gospels given over to the Passion Week, it comprises 25 to 48 percent of their materials. This became a standardized message to unbelievers, but also to believers.

**PERCENTAGE OF MATERIAL IN EACH GOSPEL NARRATING THE PASSION**

- Matthew: chs. 21–28 (28.5%)
- Mark: chs. 11–16 (37.5%)
- Luke: chs. 19–24 (25%)
- John: chs. 12–21 (47.6%)

The apostles are the first to preach the gospel, focusing on the passion, as eyewitnesses and those passing on the tradition.

### *2.7.5.3 Teaching Disciples to Obey All Jesus Commanded*

What was needed for new believers, according to the Great Commission, after they were baptized, was ***teaching (didachē)***. Disciples, new and old, needed to be *taught* to *obey* all that Jesus had originally commanded (cf. Matt 28:18–20). The apostles were the ones commissioned with this; so, all that Jesus had spent time "commanding them," in word and deed, they now taught new believers so that they could obey Jesus's truth about life (cf. John 8:31–32). This "teaching what Jesus commanded" continues through the faithfully rendered oral tradition.

### *2.7.5.4 The Narrative of Jesus's Life Story*

The rest of the ***narrative*** of Jesus's life story could now be supplied. We understand that the earliest disciples were gathered away in Jerusalem for some period of time. Among them were Mary, Jesus's mother, and Jesus's brothers (Acts 1:14), who would have been able to fill in all the blanks of Jesus's life to give a full portrait of Jesus. This apostolic band was gathered there in Jerusalem for upward of nearly twenty years (the Apostolic Council was in approximately AD 49), plenty of time for them to memorize massive amounts of Jesus's passion, teaching, and narrative life story and pass it on through oral rendering. This would also include the telling of a story that would include commonly told editorial comments.

### *2.7.5.5 Interpretation of Jesus's Life*

Next would come ***interpretation*** of Jesus's life, especially in the light of the Old Testament, similar to the way that Jesus spent forty days prior to his ascension interpreting his life for them in the light of the Old Testament (Luke 24:44–49; Acts 1:1–5). This is what we see Matthew doing for his Jewish audience (see esp. Matt 1–2). This is the powerful part of giving a story to the people of God to understand God's dealings with humanity from the very beginning. This oral interpretation of Jesus's life would have occurred during the time the church was primarily in Jerusalem.

### *2.7.5.6 The Standardized, Fixed Oral Tradition*

What now results is what I call the ***standardized, fixed oral tradition*** of the early church about Jesus.

- It is *standardized* because it was told over and over again by the passionate new church.
- It became *fixed* because any errant variation would quickly become corrected by the eyewitness apostles.
- And it was oral, indicating that this was the period of time before the documents that we know as the Gospels were written. This does not exclude notes that may have been taken during Jesus's lifetime by the apostles, or during this basic time period.

But on the other hand, there would be freedom to vary the basic storyline for the needs of a given audience any time the story was told.

- For example, if giving the story to Hellenistic Jews, the story would vary, helping them to reaffirm their roots in the Old Testament.
- It would vary if told to orthodox Jews who would connect with the way that Jesus Messiah affirmed the Law and the Prophets but without elevating oral tradition.
- It would vary if told to God-fearing gentiles, affirming their belief in the expected Coming One who is Jesus Messiah.
- And it would vary if being told to children or to old people.

This was an oral culture, where telling stories was the stock of daily life. As this developed over ten to twenty years, each person telling the story, especially the apostles, would have been able to retell the entire account of Jesus's life verbatim with ease. As time passed, the oral tradition became a stable recounting of the good news of Jesus Messiah, his message, mission, and impact.

Kenneth Bailey, followed by N. T. Wright, similarly refers to this as "the world of *informal but controlled oral tradition*."[194] The tradition is *informal* in that anyone can join in, provided they have been a part of the community to qualify as true members. The oral tradition is *controlled* in that "the whole community knows the traditions well enough to check whether serious innovation is being smuggled in, and to object if it is."[195] The community ordered its life and thought by telling and retelling important events

194. Bailey, "Informal Controlled Oral Tradition," 34–54 (emphasis original). See also N. T. Wright, *Jesus and the Victory of God*, 134.

195. N. T. Wright, *Jesus and the Victory of God*, 134.

that he made them who they were.[196] And the good news of Jesus's life and ministry were the most important events in their lifetime and throughout Christian history.

### *2.7.5.7 Circulating Tradition of Jesus*

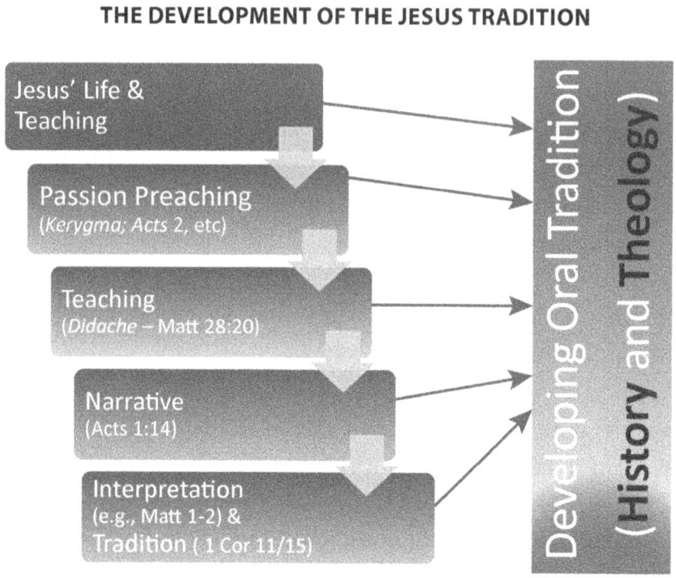

**THE DEVELOPMENT OF THE JESUS TRADITION**

Jesus' Life & Teaching

Passion Preaching (*Kerygma; Acts 2, etc*)

Teaching (*Didache* – Matt 28:20)

Narrative (Acts 1:14)

Interpretation (e.g., Matt 1-2) & Tradition ( 1 Cor 11/15)

Developing Oral Tradition (History and Theology)

The ***apostle Paul*** is an important witness to the way in which this ***tradition*** was circulating in the church. He repeats for the Corinthians two pieces of oral material to remind his audience of what they have already heard, i.e., he presupposes that they will recognize this material. Because we can isolate it out of his letters, the way he describes, we then are able to reconstruct what that early body of material would have looked like at a time before it was ever written down.

One of these early pieces of oral material is 1 Corinthians 11, where Paul describes Jesus instituting the Last Supper.

> For I received from the Lord what I also passed on to you: The Lord Jesus, on the night he was betrayed, took bread, and when he had given thanks, he broke it and said, "This is my body, which is for you; do this in remembrance of me." In the same way, after supper he took the cup, saying, "This cup is the new covenant in my blood; do

196. N. T. Wright, *Jesus and the Victory of God*, 133–37.

> this, whenever you drink it, in remembrance of me." For whenever you eat this bread and drink this cup, you proclaim the Lord's death until he comes. (1 Cor 11:23–26)

The other is 1 Corinthians 15, where Paul describes the story of the death, burial, resurrection, and resurrection appearances of Jesus, which is the earliest account that we have in any written form.

> For what I received I passed on to you as of first importance: that Christ died for our sins according to the Scriptures, that he was buried, that he was raised on the third day according to the Scriptures, and that he appeared to Cephas, and then to the Twelve. After that, he appeared to more than five hundred of the brothers and sisters at the same time, most of whom are still living, though some have fallen asleep. Then he appeared to James, then to all the apostles, and last of all he appeared to me also, as to one abnormally born. (1 Cor 15:3–8)

This is what Paul himself had heard and passed on over a period of several years. It is one of those little blocks of material in Paul's letters that pushes us that much further back toward the historical time of Jesus. Paul writes this letter probably from Ephesus, early in AD 55. Keeping in mind that Paul's conversion and time in Damascus (Acts 9:1–25) occurred around AD 33–34, he would have had access to and been influenced by the earliest standardized oral tradition of Jesus's life that was circulating in the church for the next ten to thirty years while he wrote his epistles. This is some twenty-five years after the gospel was first preached by the apostles in Jerusalem and had traveled as far as Corinth in Greece. His epistles would have been subject to censure by the apostolic church if they were not in line with the Jesus tradition. Paul was a recipient of direct revelation and the oral tradition of Jesus Messiah's message, mission, and activities. He presupposes that the Corinthians had also been recipients of this oral tradition.

#### *2.7.5.8 The Gospel in Writing*

As the apostles were growing older, no longer sure that Jesus would return in their lifetime, they were gripped by the necessity to put in ***writing*** this most important message for the next generations. It would have been a relatively simple task to put into writing the story that they wanted to tell because of the extended time they had been retelling the account.

#### *2.7.5.9 Mark's Gospel?*

If ***Mark*** wrote first, ca. AD 55–60, he wrote with twenty-five-plus years of experience in both hearing and passing on the story of Jesus. In an oral culture he could easily have had the entire story memorized, with the ability to make variations to suit the needs of his audiences. He also writes as Peter's amanuensis, according to early church tradition. Writing would be a relatively easy task in the first-century setting.

#### *2.7.5.10 Matthew's Gospel*

As ***Matthew*** writes, either first or second, in ca. AD 55–60, he writes from his own eyewitness perspective, as well as with twenty-five-plus years of experience as part of the apostolic band that standardized and fixed the developing oral tradition. He writes especially to interpret the story of Jesus in the light of the Old Testament for his Jewish-Christian and gentile-Christian audience. On the one hand, we might suggest that Matthew wrote first because of the nearly unanimous early church tradition to that effect. On the other hand, we might suggest that Matthew wrote with Mark as a reference, in addition to his own resources (as eyewitness and apostolic guardian of the tradition). It seems easier to account for Matthew expanding upon Mark, than Mark condensing Matthew (especially with the variation of arrangement).

#### *2.7.5.11 Luke's Gospel*

***Luke*** then writes to give an accurate account that would suit the needs of his audience, Theophilus. Theophilus appears to be a Greek official,[197] who may well have some influence in protecting or advancing the Christian community. Luke writes to Theophilus "so that [he] may know the exact truth about the things [he has] been taught" (Luke 1:4, NASB).[198] Luke researched everything available to put together an account of Jesus that would be convincing to this apparently Christian gentile official, who was either in danger of recanting or else needed written documentation to use as support for the Christian community.

The most plausible explanation for the abrupt ending of Acts (despite a variety of other recent suggestions) is still that Luke was writing at the very time of the events he describes in Acts 28—during Paul's two-year house arrest in Rome. No other explanation convincingly accounts for why Acts 19–28 devotes ten whole chapters to the events leading up to and including Paul's arrest and trials, only to leave us completely in the dark about the outcome of his appeal to Caesar. But if Luke did not know that outcome because Caesar had not yet tried Paul's case, then his omission is understandable. If Luke wrote Acts while Paul was still awaiting the result of his appeal to Rome, we must date that book to no later than AD 62.[199] Then Luke's Gospel, as the first of his two-part work, must be dated to the same year or even earlier.

197. The name *Theophilos*, Θεόφιλος, is Greek, not Latin or Hebrew. The expression "most excellent" (*kratistos*, κράτιστος) leans toward addressing a Greek official.

198. *Asphaleia*, ἀσφάλεια, means "certainty, truth" and it is used in other literature as a legal term for "proof, security" ("ἀσφάλεια," Abbott-Smith, 66; cf. "ἀσφάλεια," BDAG 147).

199. Cf. esp. Colin J. Hemer, *The Book of Acts in the Setting of Hellenistic History*, ed. Conrad H. Gempf (Tübingen: Mohr, 1989), 365–410.

### *2.7.5.12 All Three Synoptic Gospels Were Composed Within About Thirty Years of Christ's Death*

The evidence suggests that ***all three Gospels were composed within about thirty years of Christ's death*** (probably AD 30) and well within the period of time when people could check up on the accuracy of the facts they contain. This is supported by the testimony of Christians as early as Irenaeus near the end of the second century, who attributes the writing of Matthew and Mark to the first generation of church history, i.e., before the fall of Jerusalem to Rome in AD 70. Irenaeus states, "Matthew also issued a written Gospel among the Hebrews in their own dialect, while Peter and Paul were preaching at Rome, and laying the foundations of the Church" (Irenaeus, *Haer.* 3.1.1 [*ANF* 1:414]). Since these two apostles were martyred under Nero sometime between AD 64 and 68, the writing of Matthew would have been sometime prior to their deaths. Irenaeus continues by discussing Mark, "After their departure, Mark, the disciple and interpreter of Peter, did also hand down to us in writing what had been preached by Peter" (*Haer.* 3.1.1 [*ANF* 1:414]). Some take this to mean that Mark wrote after Peter's death, but "departure" may refer to his leaving Rome to travel somewhere else, prior to his death. But even if it does not, the perfect participle "what he had written" suggests that only the *transmission* and not the writing of Mark's Gospel took place after Peter's "departure."[200]

### *2.7.5.13 The Phenomenon Called Q*

**The phenomenon called Q** represents the places where Matthew and Luke share material not found in Mark. That coincidence is the only *fact.* It easily can be accounted for by Matthew and Luke tapping into the developing oral tradition at the same point. I do not lean toward seeing it as a separate circulating written document, especially when we see how difficult it is to postulate Matthew using the same Q document as Luke, but then simply scattering the sayings all throughout his document, differently than Luke, who has large bodies of Q material in sequence. All that we can say with certainty is that Q is the material that Matthew and Luke happen to share but that does not occur in Mark. Another possibility is that Q could have been the original Aramaic notes of Matthew on Jesus's teachings that he had jotted down to supplement the oral tradition of the passion story, and Luke had access to those notes. And as we saw in the discussion above of the Farrer hypothesis, Luke may have used Matthew's Gospel as one of his sources, which would account for supposed Q material in Matthew and Luke.

### *2.7.5.14 Variations and Similarities*

Each author would have easily been able to make ***variations*** needed for their particular audiences. If they had access to each other's documents, then they almost certainly

200. Robert H. Gundry, *Mark: A Commentary on His Apology for the Cross* (Grand Rapids: Eerdmans, 1993), 1042–43.

would have referenced each other to make the enterprise easier and give more assurance of accuracy. But having written sources before them was not an absolute necessity. In an oral culture, as we have seen above, the memorization of the basic story line would give ***similarity*** and uniformity. Similarity of detail between the Synoptics, even down to "editorial asides," could be accounted for by the memorization of the standardized, fixed, oral tradition. Stories certainly would have contained such editorial asides for effect in the telling of the story.

### *2.7.5.15 John's Gospel*

As the apostle ***John*** approached the end of his life, he undertook to write a very different kind of account of Jesus's life and ministry. He appears to be intentionally supplementing and complementing the Synoptic Gospels by filling in where they do not comment on Jesus's life. Ninety-two percent of John's Gospel material is unique to his account. He supplies an account of the first year of Jesus's ministry, including the Cana wedding, the first cleansing of the temple, the preaching and baptizing ministry of Jesus and his disciples, and the interaction with the Samaritan woman. John also supplies for us extended accounts of Jesus's teaching not found in the Synoptic Gospels, including the Upper Room Discourse (John 14–17). The most reliable early tradition suggests a date for John around the AD 90s (Irenaeus, *Haer.* 2.22.5; Eusebius, *Hist. Eccl.* 3.23.1–4).[201]

**THE DEVELOPMENT OF THE JESUS TRADITION**

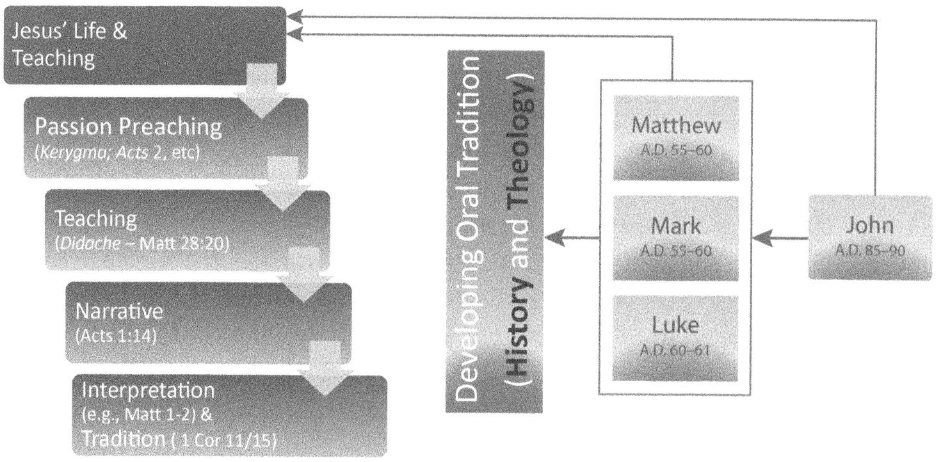

Jesus' Life & Teaching
Passion Preaching (*Kerygma*; Acts 2, etc)
Teaching (*Didache* – Matt 28:20)
Narrative (Acts 1:14)
Interpretation (e.g., Matt 1-2) & Tradition (1 Cor 11/15)
Developing Oral Tradition (History and Theology)
Matthew A.D. 55–60
Mark A.D. 55–60
Luke A.D. 60–61
John A.D. 85–90

201. While there is some uncertainty among the later Christian writers whether this is John the apostle or a different John who is called "the elder" (or "presbyter") who was a disciple of John the apostle, I believe the evidence points toward this being John the apostle. For discussion see D. A. Carson, *The Gospel According to John* (Grand Rapids: Eerdmans, 1991), 68–81. See also Martin Hengel, *The Johannine Question* (Philadelphia: Trinity, 1990).

### *2.7.5.16 Far Closer to the Original Events than Many Ancient Biographies*

One can now see that with the traditional dating of the writing of the Synoptic Gospels, and even with John, ***we are far closer to the original events than with many ancient biographies***. For example, the two earliest biographers of Alexander the Great, Arrian (born ca. AD 89–died ca. 160) and Plutarch (ca. AD 46–119), wrote more than four hundred years after Alexander's death in 323 BC, yet historians generally consider them to be reasonably trustworthy. Fabulous legends about the life of Alexander did develop over time, but for the most part only in the several centuries *after* these two writers.[202]

The evidence suggests that the Gospels were written by people in a position to report accurate historical information.[203] Richard Bauckham states,

> I have argued that the New Testament evidence points to a formally controlled tradition, such as can be found in many oral societies, but also that, in the period up to the writing of the Gospels, we must also reckon with the eyewitnesses. While the events of Jesus's story were within living memory, the eyewitnesses, many of whom were well known in the Christian movement, are likely to have been regarded as the accessible sources and authoritative guardians of the traditions that they themselves had formulated at the beginning.[204]

## 2.8 CONCLUSION

We have attempted to develop the context of Matthew's Gospel. Here is what I have concluded:

- the author is Matthew Levi
- the person is the apostle Matthew, former tax collector, eyewitness to the majority of Jesus Messiah's earthly ministry, crucifixion, resurrection, and risen ministry, and himself an apostolic witness
- the date of writing, perhaps the late AD 50s or early 60s
- the place of writing, perhaps northern Syria, and perhaps the city of Antioch in Syria

202. Cf. further Robin L. Fox, *The Search for Alexander* (Boston: Little, 1980).

203. Major evangelical New Testament introductions have repeatedly provided appropriate support for the early dating of the Gospels. See, e.g., Guthrie, *New Testament Introduction*, 28–135; Carson and Moo, *Introduction*, 134–224; Andreas J. Köstenberger, L. Scott Kellum, and Charles L. Quarles, *The Cradle, the Cross, and the Crown: An Introduction to the New Testament* (Nashville: B&H, 2009), 101–328.

204. Richard J. Bauckham, "The Gospels as Testimony to Jesus Christ: A Contemporary View of Their Historical Value," in *OHC*, 59. See also Birger Gerhardsson, *The Reliability of the Gospel Tradition* (Peabody, MA: Hendrickson, 2001).

- the genre of Matthew's Gospel is similar to that of a biography, but focused on the *euangelion*, the gospel of Jesus Messiah, which brings the kingdom of heaven to earth and transformation for his disciples and the hope of transformation to the world
- the written Gospel of Matthew is from the apostolic eyewitness, former traitor-tax collector turned radical disciple of Jesus Messiah, the apostle Matthew, who shares in the developing oral and written tradition regarding Jesus Messiah

We now turn to a discussion of the structure and a literary/theological reading of Matthew's Gospel. In Chapter 3 we will first attempt to discern the structure of Matthew's Gospel. Then in Chapter 4 we will proceed unit by unit and trace the unfolding of various major theological themes and their interconnectedness throughout the book.

*Part 2*

# LITERARY/ THEOLOGICAL FOUNDATIONS FOR UNDERSTANDING MATTHEW'S THEOLOGY

*Chapter 3*

# THE STRUCTURE OF MATTHEW'S GOSPEL

## *A Manual on Discipleship*

### BIBLIOGRAPHY

**Allison, Dale C., Jr.** "Matthew's First Two Words (Matt. 1:1)." Pages 157–62 in *Studies in Matthew: Interpretation Past and Present*. Baker Academic, 2005. ———. "Structure, Biographical Impulse, and the *Imitatio Christi*." Pages 135–55 in *Studies in Matthew: Interpretation Past and Present*. Baker Academic, 2005. **Baasland, Ernst.** *Parables and Rhetoric in the Sermon on the Mount. New Approaches to a Classical Text*. WUNT 351. Tübingen: Mohr Siebeck, 2015. **Bacon, Benjamin W.** *Studies in Matthew*. New York: Henry Holt, 1930. **Bauer, David R.** *The Structure of Matthew's Gospel: A Study in Literary Design*. JSNTSS 31. Sheffield: Sheffield Academic, 1988. **Brown, Jeannine K.** "Direct Engagement of the Reader in Matthew's Discourses: Rhetorical Techniques and Scholarly Consensus." *NTS* 51.1 (2005): 19–35. **Carter, Warren.** "Kernels and Narrative Blocks: The Structure of Matthew's Gospel." *CBQ* 54.3 (1992): 463–82. **Derickson, Gary W.** "Matthew's Chiastic Structure and Its Dispensational Implications." *BSac* 163 (2006): 423–37. **Kingsbury, Jack Dean.** *Matthew: Structure, Christology, Kingdom*. 2nd ed. Minneapolis: Fortress, 1989. **Marguerat, Daniel.** "'Livre de la genèse de Jésus Christ' (Mt 1,1): Commencer l'évangile selon Matthieu." Pages 177–91 in *Fins et commencements—Renvois et interactions: Mélanges offerts à Michel Gourgues*. Edited by Maxime Allard, Emmanuel Durand, and Marie de Lovinfosse. BTS 35. Leuven: Peeters, 2018. **Olmstead, Wesley G.** *Matthew's Trilogy of Parables: The Nation, the Nations and the Reader in Matthew 21:28–22:14*. SNTSMS 127. Cambridge: Cambridge University Press, 2003. **Pizzuto, Vincent A.** "The Structural Elegance of Matthew 1–2: A Chiastic Proposal." *CBQ* 74.4 (2012): 712–37. **Powell, Mark Allan.** "The Plot and Subplots of Matthew's Gospel." *NTS* 38.2 (1992): 187–204. ———. "Toward a Narrative-Critical Understanding of Matthew's Gospel." *Int* 46.4 (1992): 341–46. **Smith, Christopher R.** "Literary Evidences of a Fivefold Structure in the Gospel of Matthew." *NTS* 43.4 (1997): 540–51. **Weren, Wim J. C.** *Studies in Matthew's Gospel: Literary Design, Intertextuality, and Social Setting*. BibInt 130. Leiden: Brill, 2014. **Wilson, Walter T.** *Healing in the Gospel of Matthew: Reflections on Method and Ministry*. Minneapolis: Fortress, 2014.

## 3.1 A Structural and Literary/Theological Reading of the Structure of Matthew's Gospel

*The Greatest Story Ever Told* is a 1965 American epic film that is a retelling of the biblical account about Jesus Messiah from his nativity at Bethlehem through to his ascension. Academy Award-winning producer and director George Stevens made it his goal to have the film fulfill its headline. The writers of the New Testament Gospels made it their goal that their accounts of the greatest story ever told were correct, "so that you might know the exact truth about the things you have been taught" (Luke 1:4 NASB). New Testament scholar Ben Witherington declares, "Their interpretations were all in agreement that 'his story' is true 'history'—indeed, the most important history of all, a history that changed and is changing the world."[1] Therefore, in my view, the descriptor "greatest" is not just a cliché. It is God's greatest story of God entering human history in the person of his Son, Jesus Messiah, to redeem humanity.[2]

Matthew's Gospel is one of the four sources for this Greatest Story. And Matthew wrote his story to identify, defend, and promote Jesus of Nazareth as the Davidic Messiah who fulfilled the Old Testament expectations of human redemption. Edward Meadors notes the elements of God's greatest story when he describes Matthew's purpose in writing his Gospel: "Matthew's Gospel told the story of Jesus's genealogy, birth, baptism, temptations, Galilean ministry, journey to Jerusalem, arrest, trial, crucifixion, resurrection, and ascension, so that early Christians could know the story of their Lord, follow him more obediently, and make Christlike disciples as he had called them to do."[3]

In this chapter and the following chapter, I undertake an investigation into the structure of this Gospel and a literary and theological reading of Matthew's Gospel.[4] Here we view Matthew's perspective of God's activities in Jesus's unfolding earthly ministry. We will trace these themes through a linear perspective of Matthew's narrative and see how various theological themes surfaced as Jesus's ministry unfolded. That is the theological level of Matthew's perspective of what God was doing in history through Jesus's activities.

After writing his exegetical commentary on Matthew's Gospel, Ulrich Luz developed

---

1. Ben Witherington III, *Invitation to the New Testament: First Things* (Oxford: Oxford University Press, 2013), 18.

2. Witherington, *Invitation to the New Testament*, 18.

3. Edward P. Meadors, "What Did Matthew Really Care About?," in *What the New Testament Authors Really Cared About: A Survey of Their Writings*, ed. Kenneth Berding and Matt Williams (Grand Rapids: Kregel, 2008), 24.

4. This section, as well as the other sections and chapters, draws upon my prior writings on Matthew, especially my "Matthew," in *Matthew, Mark, Luke*, vol. 1 of *ZIBBC*, 4 vols. (Grand Rapids: Zondervan, 2002), 2–203, and my *Matthew*, NIVAC (Grand Rapids: Zondervan, 2004). I have not brought over all the documentation footnotes, but especially attempted to update my work by documenting in the footnotes newer research. At all points I encourage the reader to consult both commentaries for fuller exegesis and exposition.

his theology of the Gospel of Matthew with just this approach.[5] He chose to follow the Matthean narrative account and write Matthew's theological story of Jesus in the manner of Richard A. Edwards[6] and Jack Dean Kingsbury.[7] Luz explains that he chose this latter approach because he is "convinced that the Gospel of Matthew is a *story* of Jesus that can only be understood when one retraces it and tries to grasp what it wished to convey to its intended readers."[8]

In our overall study of Matthew's theology in this book, we will employ both approaches, as did for example I. Howard Marshall.[9] In much of the remainder of our study in this book, I will take a theologically topical approach to understanding Matthew's theology, similar to the approaches of Josef Ernst[10] and R. T. France,[11] and more recently by Udo Schnelle,[12] Charles Quarles,[13] and Craig Blomberg.[14]

But in this and the following chapter, I will trace the unfolding of Matthew's theological themes as they develop in his telling of the story of Jesus, an approach taken by Edwards and Kingsbury noted above, and more recently in the theological commentaries of Stanley Hauerwas, Richard Swanson, Jeannine Brown and Kyle Roberts, and Mark Alan Powell.[15]

## 3.2 A Structural Outline of Matthew's Gospel

An important issue when undertaking a literary and theological reading of Matthew's Gospel is to try to determine how the book is structured. Most students of Matthew's Gospel recognize the alternating sections of "narrative" and "discourse." The six narratives (chs. 1–4; 8–9; 11–12; 14–17; 19–23; 26–28) recount the fullness of Jesus Messiah's earthly life and ministry from his conception and early life and ministry to his death, burial, and resurrection. Each discourse is introduced with a Matthean introductions that identifies the audience that Jesus addresses. Each of the five discourses addresses Jesus's disciples (5:1–2; 10:5; 13:10, 18:1; 24:1–3), while the first and third include the crowds (5:1–2; 13:2–3). Matthew signals the conclusion of each discourse and the transition to narrative of Jesus's life with the same phrase—"And when Jesus

5. Ulrich Luz, *Theology of the Gospel of Matthew*, trans. J. Bradford Robinson, NTT (Cambridge: Cambridge University Press, 1993), xi.

6. Richard A. Edwards, *Matthew's Story of Jesus* (Philadelphia: Fortress, 1985).

7. Jack Dean Kingsbury, *Matthew as Story*, 2nd ed. (Philadelphia: Fortress, 1988).

8. Luz, *Theology of the Gospel of Matthew*, xi.

9. Marshall, *New Testament Theology*, 95–128.

10. Josef Ernst, *Matthäus: Ein theologisches Portrait* (Düsseldorf: Patmos, 1989).

11. France, *Matthew: Evangelist and Teacher*.

12. Udo Schnelle, *Theology of the New Testament*, trans. M. Eugene Boring (Grand Rapids: Baker Academic, 2007), 429–63.

13. Quarles, *Theology of Matthew*.

14. Blomberg, *New Testament Theology*, 341–82.

15. Stanley Hauerwas, *Matthew*, BTCB (Grand Rapids: Brazos, 2006); Swanson, *Provoking the Gospel of Matthew*; Jeannine K. Brown and Kyle Roberts, *Matthew*, THNTC (Grand Rapids: Eerdmans, 2018); Mark Allan Powell, *Matthew*, Interpretation Bible Commentary (Louisville: Westminster John Knox Press, 2023).

finished these"—and then inserts a description of the discourse as "sayings" (*logous*; 7:28), "instructions" (*diatassōn*; 11:1), "parables" (*parabolas*; 13:53), "sayings" (*logous*; 19:1), or "sayings" (*logous*; 26:1). While most scholars acknowledge the narratives and discourses, the intended structure and its meaning of Matthew's Gospel has been debated for decades.[16] Representative of this debate are the following approaches.

### 3.2.1 Five Books

Noting the five discourses with the preceding narratives, Benjamin Bacon proposed that Matthew divided his Gospel into five blocks that are so independent of each other that they can be considered as five books, analogous to the five books of Moses, the Pentateuch.[17] Each discourse (D) is preceded by an introductory narrative section (N) that always forms a whole with the relevant discourse. In total, this pattern occurs five times, so that Matthew consists of five books, of which the first begins in 3:1 and the last ends in 25:46. The five books are framed by a preamble (chs. 1–2) and an epilogue (chs. 26–28).

| | |
|---|---|
| Preamble | 1:1–2:23 |
| Book 1 | 3:1–4:25 (N) and 5:1–7:27 (D); formula: 7:28–29 |
| Book 2 | 8:1–9:35 (N) and 9:36–10:42 (D); formula: 11:1 |
| Book 3 | 11:2–12:50 (N) and 13:1–52 (D); formula: 13:53 |
| Book 4 | 13:54–17:20 (N) and 17:22–18:35 (D); formula: 19:1a |
| Book 5 | 19:1b–22:46 (N) and 23:1–25:46 (D); formula: 26:1 |
| Epilogue | 26:3–28:20 |

Bacon's observations regarding the overall structure of narrative-discourse have been followed by a number of scholars.[18] And Moses typology in Matthew has been observed by many scholars, and there are obvious allusions to Moses (e.g., 17:1–9).[19] But in my view the stronger is Israel typology fulfilled in Jesus,[20] and links between the five discourses and the five books of Moses are minimal.[21]

16. For a wide-ranging overview, see David R. Bauer, *The Structure of Matthew's Gospel: A Study in Literary Design*, JSNTSup 31 (Sheffield: Sheffield Academic, 1988), 11–55. For brief updating and overviews see Donald A. Hagner, *New Testament*, 197–200; and Wim J. C. Weren, *Studies in Matthew's Gospel: Literary Design, Intertextuality, and Social Setting*, BibInt 130 (Leiden: Brill, 2014), 13–23.

17. Benjamin W. Bacon, *Studies in Matthew* (New York: Henry Holt, 1930), 80–81.

18. E.g., Christopher R. Smith, "Literary Evidence of a Fivefold Structure in the Gospel of Matthew," *NTS* 43 (1997): 540–51; Raymond E. Brown, *An Introduction to the New Testament*, ABRL (New York: Doubleday, 1997), 172.

19. E.g., Dale C. Allison, *The New Moses: A Matthean Typology* (Minneapolis: Fortress, 1993); R. T. France, *The Gospel of Matthew*, NICNT (Grand Rapids: Eerdmans, 2007), e.g., 63–64; Turner, *Matthew*, 149.

20. For Israel typology fulfilled in Jesus, see Kirk, "Conceptualising Fulfilment in Matthew," 77–98; Nolland, *Matthew*, e.g., 123; Osborne, *Matthew*, e.g., 99. Patrick Schreiner (*Matthew, Disciple and Scribe: The First Gospel and Its Portrait of Jesus* [Grand Rapids: Baker Academic, 2019]) has a multilayered portrait of Jesus in that he emphasizes the Moses typology (pp. 131–68), but also emphasizes the Israel typology and presents Jesus's life as the fulfillment of the OT story of Israel and how Jesus brings new life in the NT (pp. 207–39). "[Jesus] is Israel, but the better Israel" (p. 239).

21. Suggested by Carson, "Matthew," 76; Ben Witherington

### 3.2.2 A Story in Three Movements

A number of scholars, prominent among them Jack Dean Kingsbury and David Bauer,[22] were at the forefront of narrative approaches to Matthew's structure. They point to the parallelism between 4:17 and 16:21, where both verses open with the phrase "from that time he began" (*apo tote ērxato*) followed by an infinitive and a brief summary of the content of Jesus's words. They suggest that these verses serve as the captions of two long sections about Jesus's proclamation of the kingdom and about his journey to Jerusalem for his passion, death, and resurrection. From this perspective, the story of Jesus Messiah in Matthew's Gospel consists of three movements:

I. 1:1–4:16 The Person of Jesus Messiah
II. 4:17–16:20 The Proclamation of Jesus Messiah
III. 16:21–28:20 The Passion, Death, and Resurrection of Jesus Messiah

The majority of Matthean scholarship recognize the repeated refrain[23] but remain skeptical as to whether such a subtle expression marks an intended overall indicator of Matthew's structure.[24] While its appearance obviously marks a crucial transition in the narrative, it is doubtful that it would have held much significance for an aural audience, separated as far apart as are the two occurrences.

### 3.2.3 Macrostructure

A more comprehensive narrative approach to Matthew's Gospel followed the lead of Seymour Chatman in his general theory of narrative in both verbal and visual media.[25] Early followers, after the work of Kingsbury and Bauer, included Frank Matera, Brendan Byrne, and Warren Carter, who focused on understanding the plot of the Gospel.[26]

III, *Matthew*, SHBC (Macon, GA: Smyth & Helwys, 2006), 15–17. Witherington submits that at times Matthew may even delete Mosaic motifs found in the Markan source material (*Mattthew*, 291).

22. Jack Dean Kingsbury, *Matthew: Structure, Christology, Kingdom*, 2nd ed. (Minneapolis: Fortress, 1989), 40–93; David R. Bauer, *The Structure of Matthew's Gospel: A Study in Literary Design*, JSNTSS 31 (Sheffield: Sheffield Academic, 1988), 73–108. A more recent adherent is Jeffrey A. Gibbs, *Matthew 1:1–11:1*, Concordia Commentary (St Louis, MO: Concordia, 2006), 38–47.

23. Weren acknowledges the role of these phrases within Matthew's structure but goes on to develop a much more complex macrosyntactic structure (*Studies in Matthew's Gospel*, 22–41).

24. For critiques see Dale C. Allison Jr., "Structure, Biographical Impulse, and the *Imitatio Christi*," *Studies in Matthew: Interpretation Past and Present* (Grand Rapids: Baker Academic, 2005), 136; Weren, *Studies in Matthew's Gospel*, 18–22.

25. Seymour Chatman, *Story and Discourse: Narrative Structure in Fiction and Film* (Ithaca, NY: Cornell University Press, 1978).

26. Frank J. Matera, "The Plot of Matthew's Gospel," *CBQ* 49 (1987), 233–53; following Matera is Brendan Byrne, *Lifting the Burden: Reading Matthew's Gospel in the Church Today* (Collegeville, MN: Liturgical, 2004), 9–16; Warren Carter, "Kernels and Narrative Blocks: The Structure of Matthew's Gospel," *CBQ* 54.3 (1992): 463–81. Carter develops the larger narrative structure by isolating "kernels" and "satellites" that advance the plot. He explains: "Kernels are significant and major 'branching points,' events that advance the plot. They are the absolutely crucial parts of the narrative structure, which if deleted, would destroy the narrative logic. Satellites are minor events that derive from kernels and which work out and elaborate kernels" (467).

More recently, Wim Weren acknowledges the role of the phrase "from that time he began" (*apo tote ērxato*; 4:17; 16:21) within Matthew's structure but goes on to develop a much more complex macro-syntactic structure that includes temporal and topographical information and specific literary features such as "plot," "kernels," and "hinges." He suggests that what is new about his hypothesis is that it provides a layered image of the structure of Matthew's Gospel. At the first level, the structure is still coarse; at the second and third levels, the structure of the *corpus* (4:18–25:46) is presented gradually in more detail. Also new in his approach is the insight that five passages function as hinges (4:12–17; 11:2–30; 16:13–28; 21:1–17; 26:1–16). "Such a hinge text is linked with both the sequence that precedes it and the one that follows it. The size of these sequences is relatively large at the first level. At the second level, they are smaller and, at the third level, even smaller still."[27] Weren renders the macrostructure of Matthew in the following scheme, the various parts of which he provides with headings.

<table>
<tr><th colspan="7">Overview of the Macrostructure of Matthew's Gospel (Weren Wim)[28]</th></tr>
<tr><td>1:1–4:11<br>Overture: Jesus's origin, identity, and mission</td><td>4:12–17<br>Hinge: Jesus's mission begins in Capernaum</td><td colspan="3">4:18–25:46<br>Corpus: Ministry; five lengthy discourses</td><td>26:1–16<br>Hinge: Jesus is anointed and will be handed over</td><td>26:17–28:20<br>Finale: suffering, death, and resurrection; start of the disciples' mission to all nations</td></tr>
<tr><td colspan="3">4:18–16:12<br>Move away from Jerusalem and Judea</td><td>16:13–28<br>Hinge: the Son of God is a suffering Messiah</td><td colspan="3">17:1–25:46<br>Journey to Jerusalem and work there</td></tr>
<tr><td>4:18–11:1<br>Calling of the four fishermen; Messiah in word and deed; sending out of the twelve</td><td>11:2–30<br>Hinge: review of the work of John and Jesus</td><td>12:1–16:12<br>The kingdom: hidden and revealed</td><td></td><td>17:1–20:34<br>Journey to Jerusalem to suffer and die there</td><td>21:1–17<br>Hinge: Arrival in Jerusalem and first confrontations in the temple</td><td>21:18–25:46<br>Jesus is active in Jerusalem</td></tr>
</table>

Weren's complex development of the structure helps to blend narrative and geographical features of Matthew's Gospel. But the blurring of the discourses as the *corpus* of Jesus's ministry does not help to isolate the distinctives of the spoken ministry of Jesus.

27. Weren, *Studies in Matthew's Gospel*, 40.

28. Weren, *Studies in Matthew's Gospel*, 41.

### 3.2.4 Chiastic Structure

Some scholars detect a symmetrical chiastic structure in Matthew, whether in micro-sections as in Vincent Pizzuto,[29] or in macro-overviews that build on the alternation of narrative and discourse sections as in the following by Gary Derickson:[30]

A Demonstration of Jesus's Qualifications as King (chs. 1–4)
  B Sermon on the Mount: Who Can Enter His Kingdom (chs. 5–7)
    C Miracles and Instruction (chs. 8–9)
      D Instruction to the Twelve: Authority and Message for Israel (ch. 10)
        E Opposition: The Nation's Rejection of the King (chs. 11–12)
          F Parables of the Kingdom: The Kingdom Postponed (ch. 13)
        E′ Opposition: The Nation's Rejection of the King (chs. 14–17)
      D′ Instruction to the Twelve: Authority and Message for the Church (ch. 18)
    C′ Miracles and Instruction (chs. 19–23)
  B′ Olivet Discourse: When the Kingdom Will Come (chs. 24–25)
A′ Demonstration of Jesus's Qualifications as King (chs. 26–28)

Scholars are often dubious about how the motifs of the narratives, such as the infancy narrative (chs. 1–4) and the crucifixion and resurrection narrative correspond chiastically, and no consensus has emerged regarding Matthew's overall chiastic structure.[31]

### 3.2.5 The Structure of Narrative and Discourse Contributes to a Manual on Discipleship to Jesus Messiah

Building in part on the above observations of Matthew's structure, I suggest that the most obvious elements of Matthew's Gospel, the alternating sections of discourse and narrative, lead us to Matthew's purpose in writing: to provide for his readers *Jesus's words to obey* and *Jesus's example to follow*. Early on historically, Clement of Alexandria noted that Jesus Messiah is our true Teacher, and therefore Matthew's Gospel with its alternating segments of words and narratives of Jesus's life offers "that

29. Vincent A. Pizzuto, "The Structural Elegance of Hagner, Matthew 1–2: A Chiastic Proposal," *CBQ* 74.4 (2012): 712–37.

30. Gary W. Derickson, "Matthew's Chiastic Structure and Its Dispensational Implications," *BSac* 163 (2006): 423–37.

31. Cf. Hagner, *New Testament*, 198–99. See H. J. Bernard Combrink, "Structure of the Gospel of Matthew as Narrative," *TynBul* 34 (1983): 61–91, who combines a chiastic structure with a broader perspective in which the narrative plot of Matthew consists of the following three elements: (1) Setting (1:1–4:17); (2) Complication (4:18–25:46); (3) Resolution (26:1–28:20) (Combrink, "Structure," 75).

which assumes the form of counselling to obedience, and that which is presented in the form of example." [32]

A wide spectrum of Matthean scholars from a variety of interpretative perspectives contend that any attempt to understand the structure of the gospel must acknowledge the striking appearance of the five discourses (chs. 5–7; 10; 13; 18; 24–25).[33] Such diverse perspectives contend that the five discourses signal some form of intended structure in Matthew's Gospel.[34] Matthew signals the conclusion of each discourse with the recurring identical formula: "When Jesus had finished" (*egeneto hote etelesen ho Iēsous*) (7:28; 11:1; 13:53; 19:1; 26:1). This formula-ending transitions to the following narrative of Jesus's life and mission. A wide number of scholars then conclude that the structure of alternating sections of discourse and narrative is the most secure base for ascertaining Matthew's organizational agenda.[35]

Additionally, by noting that all five of Jesus's major discourses are addressed at least in part to Jesus's disciples (5:2; 10:1–5; 13:10; 18:1; 24:1–4),[36] and that in the concluding Great Commission Jesus states that disciples are to be taught "to obey everything I have commanded you" (28:20), the narrative-discourse structure leads us to understand Matthew's Gospel to be at least in part a manual on discipleship to Jesus Messiah in the kingdom of heaven.[37] The goal of teaching disciples is obedience to what Jesus commanded, so that their lives increasingly become like him (cf. 10:24–25; 2 Cor 3:18; Rom 8:29). Jesus is here addressing the first disciples, including at least the

32. Clement of Alexandria, *Paedagogus* 1.2.2 (*ANF*, 2:209). See also Dale C. Allison Jr., *Studies in Matthew* (Grand Rapids: Baker Academic, 2005), 154. Clement expands upon this theme elsewhere more generally: "For what else do we say is incumbent on the rational creature—I mean man—than the contemplation of the Divine? I say, too, that it is requisite to contemplate human nature, and to live as the truth directs, and to admire the Instructor and His injunctions, as suitable and harmonious to each other. According to which image also we ought, conforming ourselves to the Instructor, and making the word and our deeds agree, to live a real life" (Clement of Alexandria, *Paedagogus* 1.12 [*ANF*, 2:235]).

33. See esp. Jeannine K. Brown, "Direct Engagement of the Reader in Matthew's Discourses: Rhetorical Techniques and Scholarly Consensus," *NTS* 51.1 (2005): 19–35; esp. 20.

34. Matthew 23 has been problematic for some scholars. Witherington is a minority proponent of six discourses, contending that ch. 23 is "a stand-alone discourse offered to a different audience and in a different setting than the apocalyptic discourse in Matthew 24–25" (Witherington, *Matthew*, 15). On the other hand, Jason Hood ("Matthew 23–25: The Extent of Jesus' Fifth Discourse," *JBL* 128.3 [Fall 2009]: 527–43) argues for the unity of Matt 23–25 and suggests that there are five discourses, with chs. 23–25 as one discourse. Space does not allow for full discussion here, but arguments against Witherington's suggestion would be that ch. 23 does not have the stereotyped conclusion found in the other discourses, and ch. 23 concludes the debates with the religious leaders in chs. 21–22 and is a final warning against and condemnation of their failed leadership. An argument against Hood's proposal is that the subject matter of ch. 23 is markedly different from the eschatological material of chs. 24–25, and the introductory verses in 24:1–3 set it off from ch. 23.

35. E.g., Carson, "Matthew," 75–84; Davies and Allison, *Matthew*, 1:58–72; Osborne, *Matthew*, 41–47; Turner, *Matthew*, 9–10; James D. G. Dunn, *Jesus According to the New Testament* (Grand Rapids: Eerdmans, 2019), 35; W. Wilson, *Matthew 1–13*, loc. 633–68, Kindle.

36. C. Smith ("Fivefold Structure," 543–45) emphasizes that the phrase "his disciples came to him" (varied slightly in each use) is discourse-introductory in four of the discourses: 5:1; 13:10; 18:1 and 24:1. In the mission discourse, Jesus calls the disciples to himself (10:1). See also David Barr, "The Drama of Matthew's Gospel," *Theology Digest* 24 (1976): 349–59, esp. 351, 358n14.

37. This discipleship thematic structure is briefly noted also by Nienhuis, *A Concise Guide to Reading the New Testament*, 22–24; see also Allison, "Structure, Biographical Impulse," 135–55.

Eleven (Matt 28:16), so he indicates that everything that he had previously commanded them, they are to teach other disciples.

And we should observe that Jesus does not reduplicate "teaching." He does not say that they are to *teach* (*didaskō*) disciples to obey everything he *taught* them. Rather, they are to *teach* disciples to obey everything he *commanded* them (*entellō*). The verb "commanded" (*entellō*) in this context has an all-inclusive sense.[38] All of Jesus's life that he communicated by word of mouth and by his life and actions is included in what he commanded them. The verb *entellō* unifies Jesus's words and deeds and therefore recalls the entirety that Matthew has recorded of Jesus's life. Everything involved in the revelation brought in and through Jesus's life ministry is included in his command to teach disciples to obey.[39]

This surfaces the transformative message of the New Testament that unites the Gospels and the Epistles. Transformed to be like Jesus the Master is the message of Jesus (cf. 10:24–25; Luke 6:40), Paul (Rom 8:29; 2 Cor 3:18), John (John 3:3, 16; 1 John 3:2), and Peter (2 Pet 1:3). As we see the life and ministry of Jesus and hear the words of Jesus and receive their truth, the Spirit of God causes us to be born anew and to experience continual transformation from the inside out to become like Jesus.

Matthew organizes his story of Jesus in alternating sections of narratives and discourses to reveal Jesus as the Messiah at Work and Messiah in Word. In the six *narratives*, Matthew reveals Jesus's true identity in his deeds and introduces themes that will lead to instructions to Jesus's disciples in the discourses.[40] The narratives provide the example that Jesus's disciples are commanded to obey. In the five *discourses*, Matthew records Jesus's instructions, commands, parables, directives, and prophecies that will guide his followers in their discipleship to Jesus until the end of the age. Combined, the narratives of Jesus's life provide Jesus's example to follow, and the discourses give Jesus's instructions to obey, and are the basis of our ongoing transformation to become like Jesus. Dale Allison states it well: "The crucial moral imperatives are imaginatively and convincingly incarnated, which is exactly what the First Gospel supplies. . . . Ephraem put it this way: 'What he taught us, Christ first did, and by this went before us, so that we might follow him.'"[41]

We will discuss this more fully in the thematic unfolding of Matthew's Gospel, and in the chapters below on Discipleship in Matthew's Gospel (Ch. 10) and on Mission and Commission in Matthew's Gospel (Ch. 15), but here I offer a glimpse at what I believe to be Matthew's intended overall structure.

38. Gottlob Schrenk, "ἐντέλλομαι, ἐντολή," *TDNT* 2:545.

39. Davies and Allison, *Matthew*, 3:686.

40. Cf. C. Smith, "Fivefold Structure," 545.

41. Allison, "Structure, Biographical Impulse," 154–55 and n71. Allison cites Saint Ephraem the Syrian, *An Exposition of the Gospel* 62 (*Corpus Scriptorum Christianorum Orientalium* 291, Scriptores Armeniaci 5, ed. G.A. Egan [Leuven: Peeters, 1968], 48).

| **"Teaching Them to Obey All I Commanded You"—Matthew's** Narrative-*Discourse* **Structure of** The Life and Ministry of Jesus Messiah as the Transformational Model of Discipleship **and** *Jesus's Oral Guidance for Discipleship to Jesus Messiah in the Kingdom of heaven* | |
|---|---|
| Narrative 1 (chs. 1–4) | Jesus Immanuel: The Messiah of Israel and the Hope of gentiles |
| *Discourse 1* (chs. 5–7) | *Kingdom Discipleship to Jesus Messiah: Sermon on the Mount for* Kingdom-life Disciples |
| Narrative 2 (chs. 8–9) | Jesus Messiah Demonstrates the Power of the Kingdom of Heaven in His Miraculous Ministry |
| *Discourse 2* (ch. 10) | *Mission-Driven Discipleship in the Kingdom of Heaven: Mission Mandate for* Mission-Driven Disciples |
| Narrative 3 (chs. 11–12) | Jesus Messiah Experiences Opposition from the Religious Leadership of Israel |
| *Discourse 3* (ch. 13) | *Clandestine Kingdom Discipleship in the Kingdom: Parables of the Mysteries of the Messianic Kingdom for* Clandestine-Kingdom Disciples |
| Narrative 4 (chs. 14–17) | Jesus Messiah's Divine Identity Is Demonstrated—He Is the Son of God Who Will Be the Crucified Messiah |
| *Discourse 4* (ch. 18): | *Community Discipleship within the CHURCH and the* CHURCH*: Community Prescription for* Church-Oriented *Disciples* |
| Narrative 5 (chs. 19–23) | Jesus Messiah Asserts Divine Authority over Israel and Its Leadership |
| *Discourse 5* (chs. 24–25) | *The* Eschatological Forecast *Develops What It Means to Be* Expectant-Sojourner *Disciples (chs. 24–25).* |
| Narrative 6 (chs. 26–28) | Jesus Messiah Is Crucified and Risen with a Divine Commission |

*Chapter 4*

# A Literary and Theological Reading of Matthew's Gospel

## Bibliography

**Allison, Dale C., Jr.** "Matthew's First Two Words (Matt. 1:1)." Pages 157–62 in *Studies in Matthew: Interpretation Past and Present*. Baker Academic, 2005. **Bauer, David R.** *The Gospel of the Son of God: An Introduction to Matthew*. Downers Grove, IL: InterVarsity, 2019. **Beilby, James, and Paul R. Eddy,** eds. *The Nature of the Atonement: Four Views*. Downers Grove, IL: InterVarsity, 2006. **Bock, Darrell L.** *Blasphemy and Exaltation in Judaism: The Charge Against Jesus in Mark 14:53–65*. Grand Rapids: Baker Academic, 2000. **Bray, Gerald.** *God Is Love: A Biblical and Systematic Theology*. Wheaton, IL: Crossway, 2012. **Brown, Raymond E.** *The Birth of the Messiah: A Commentary on the Infancy Narratives in the Gospels of Matthew and Luke*. New updated. ABRL. New York: Doubleday, 1993. ———. *The Death of the Messiah: From Gethsemane to the Grave. A Commentary on the Passion Narratives in the Four Gospels*. ABRL. New York: Doubleday, 1994. **Chapman, David W.** *Ancient Jewish and Christian Perceptions of Crucifixion*. WUNT 2/244. Tübingen: Mohr Siebeck, 2008. **Chapman, David W., and Eckhard J. Schnabel.** *The Trial and Crucifixion of Jesus: Texts and Commentary*. WUNT 344. Tübingen: Mohr Siebeck, 2015. **Cooper, Ben.** *Incorporated Servanthood: Commitment and Discipleship in the Gospel of Matthew*. LNTS 490. London: T&T Clark, 2013. **Craig, William Lane.** *The Atonement*. Elements in the Philosophy of Religion. Cambridge: Cambridge University Press, 2018. **Dunn, James D. G.** *Jesus According to the New Testament*. Grand Rapids: Eerdmans, 2019. **Evans, Craig A.** "'The Book of the Genesis of Jesus Christ': The Purpose of Matthew in Light of the Incipit." Pages 61–72 in *Biblical Interpretation in Early Christian Gospels, Volume 2: The Gospel of Matthew*. Edited by Thomas R. Hatina. LNTS 310. London: T&T Clark, 2008. **Gupta, Nijay K.** *The Lord's Prayer*. SHBCSS. Macon, GA: Smyth and Helwys, 2017. **Hengel, Martin.** *Crucifixion: In the Ancient World and the Folly of the Message of the Cross*. ET. Philadelphia: Fortress, 1977. **Keith, Chris, and Larry W. Hurtado,** eds. *Jesus Among Friends and Enemies: A Historical and Literary Introduction to Jesus in the Gospels*. Grand Rapids: Baker Academic, 2011. **Köstenberger, Andreas J., and Justin Taylor, with Alexander Stewart.** *The Final Days of Jesus: The Most Important Week of the Most Important Person Who Ever Lived*. Wheaton, IL: Crossway, 2014. **Marshall, I. Howard.** "Matthew's Theological

Story." Pages 95–111 in *New Testament Theology: Many Witnesses, One Gospel*. Downers Grove: InterVarsity, 2004. **McKnight, Scot.** *Jesus and His Death: Historiography, the Historical Jesus, and Atonement Theory*. Waco, TX: Baylor University Press, 2005. **Pennington, Jonathan T.** *The Sermon on the Mount and Human Flourishing: A Theological Commentary*. Grand Rapids: Baker Academic, 2017. **Perrin, Nicholas.** *Jesus the Priest*. Grand Rapids: Baker Academic, 2018. ———. *Jesus the Temple*. Grand Rapids: Baker Academic, 2010. **Schnabel, Eckhard J.** *Early Christian Mission*. Vol. 1 of *Jesus and the Twelve*. Downers Grove, IL: InterVarsity, 2004. ———. *Jesus in Jerusalem: The Last Days*. Grand Rapids: Eerdmans, 2018. **Snodgrass, Klyne R.** *Stories with Intent: A Comprehensive Guide to the Parables of Jesus*. Grand Rapids: Eerdmans, 2008. **Turner, David L.** *Israel's Last Prophet: Jesus and the Jewish Leaders in Matthew 23*. Minneapolis: Fortress, 2015. **Verseput, Donald J.** *The Rejection of the Humble Messianic King: A Study of the Composition of Matthew 11–12*. European University Studies 291. Frankfurt am Main: Peter Lang, 1986. **Wenham, John.** *Easter Enigma: Are the Resurrection Accounts in Conflict?* 2nd ed. Grand Rapids: Baker, 1992. **Wilkins, Michael J.** "Peter's Declaration of Jesus' Identity in Caesarea Philippi." Pages 293–381 in *Key Events in the Life of the Historical Jesus: A Collaborative Exploration of Context and Coherence*. Edited by Darrell L. Bock and Robert L. Webb. WUNT 247. Tübingen: Mohr Siebeck, 2009. **Wilkins, Michael J., and J. P. Moreland,** eds. *Jesus Under Fire: Modern Scholarship Reinvents the Historical Jesus*. Grand Rapids: Zondervan, 1995. **Wilson, Alistair I.** *When Will These Things Happen? A Study of Jesus as Judge in Matthew 21–25*. PBM. Carlisle, UK: Paternoster, 2004. **Witherington, Ben, III.** *Invitation to the New Testament: First Things*. Oxford: Oxford University Press, 2013. **Wright, N. T.** *The Resurrection of the Son of God*. Vol. 3 of *Christian Origins and the Question of God*. Minneapolis: Fortress, 2003.

## 4.1 THE ARRIVAL IN HISTORY OF JESUS MESSIAH (1:1–2:23)

On the surface of the Mediterranean world lay the famed *pax Romana* (Latin "Roman peace"), a condition of comparative calm throughout the Mediterranean world that originated with the reign of Caesar Augustus (27 BC–AD 14) and lasted at least to the reign of Marcus Aurelius (AD 161–180).

But as the Roman historian Tacitus observes, the peace that Augustus inaugurated did not bring with it freedom for all of his subjects. Many throughout the land hoped for change.[1] Tides of revolution continually swirled just below the surface, and periodically rose to disturb the so-called peace of the Roman Empire.

In one of the remote regions of the empire, where a variety of disturbances repeatedly surfaced, the hoped-for freedom finally arrived in a most unexpected way. A rival to

1. Cornelius Tacitus, *The Annals of Imperial Rome* 1.4.

Augustus was born in Israel. But this rival did not appear with fanfare, nor would he challenge directly the military and political might of Rome. Even many of his own people would become disappointed with the revolution that he would bring, because it was a revolution of the heart, not a revolution of swords or chariots.

This was the revolution brought by Jesus, the long-awaited Messiah of Israel. Matthew's Gospel, the first in the canonical order that tells Jesus's story, harks back upon a long history of anticipation within Israel. His recounting elucidates how Jesus's life and ministry fulfilled the promises of the Old Testament prophets but clarifies how Jesus also disappointed many of the misplaced expectations of the people. This ultimately brought him to be crucified. But in the end, he was raised from the dead and brought the hope and peace for which humanity longed.

### 4.1.1 Jesus Messiah Brings a New Beginning for Humanity (1:1)

Matthew introduces his Gospel by recalling the beginning of the grand story of the Bible: "The book of the genealogy of Jesus Christ, the son of David, the son of Abraham" (1:1 ESV). The word "genealogy" (NIV and most translations) is from the Greek noun *genesis*, or "beginnings," which in this context indicates "an account of someone's life." Ulrich Luz refers to the opening verse as a "curious title," because the reader cannot tell what it refers to. Does it refer to the genealogy, the entire prologue, the first chapter, or the entire Gospel?[2] Luz concludes that "the book of the *genesis*" introduces the genealogy but also the entire book to follow. Daniel Marguerat understands the first verse to have a "metanarrative function": Matthew's Gospel can only be understood in the light of the Scripture of Israel, but at the same time it presents another origin, another beginning, from which everything will have to be looked at—a story that has its source in Jesus Christ.[3] With Luz and Marguerat, I understand Matthew's expression "the book of the *genesis*" to serve as a heading for the genealogy (1:2–17) as well as an introduction to the entire story to follow: this is a new beginning with the arrival of Jesus the Messiah and the kingdom of heaven.[4]

#### *4.1.1.1 A Record of the Beginnings of Jesus, the Messiah (1:1)*

When the Gospels of the New Testament are compared with other writings of antiquity, one well-known characteristic comes to the light: the authors of the Gospels wrote on two levels. One level was the historical presentation of Jesus, and the other

2. Luz, *Theology of the Gospel of Matthew*, 23.

3. Daniel Marguerat, "'Livre de la genèse de Jésus Christ' (Mt 1,1): Commencer l'évangile selon Matthieu," in *Fins et commencements—Renvois et interactions: Mélanges offerts à Michel Gourgues*, ed. Maxime Allard, Emmanuel Durand, and Marie de Lovinfosse, BTS 35 (Leuven: Peeters, 2018), 177–191, here 178.

4. See the chart in Ch. 1. Cf. Dale C. Allison Jr., "Matthew's First Two Words (*Matt.* 1:1)," in *Studies in Matthew*, 157–162; Frank Crüsemann, "Kontinuität im Neuanfang Oder: Der Anfang des Neuen Testamentes in der Perspektive des Alten," in *Der Anfang des Neuen Testaments: Matthäus 1–4 neu entdeckt. Ein Kommentar mit Beiträgen zum Gespräch*, ed. Frank Crüsemann, Claudia Janssen, and Rainer Kessler (Stuttgart: Kohlhammer, 2019), 27.

level involved the author's perspective on Jesus that addressed the needs and concerns of the evangelist's own audience. On both of these levels, the evangelists were intending either to awaken or to strengthen the faith of their readers.[5] We begin to see a clue to the unique point of view of each author on both of these levels by simply reading the first verse(s) of each Gospel.[6]

As discussed in Chapter 1, each of the Gospels gives an accurate recounting of the historical details of Jesus's life and ministry, yet each offers a unique perspective on the life and ministry of Jesus for the particular needs of the audience to which it is addressed.

#### *4.1.1.2 Jesus Messiah Is the Son of David and the Son of Abraham (1:1)*

Likewise, Matthew's opening verse gives an important clue to the overall purpose and perspective that he will take in the writing of his Gospel. Matthew's opening words had special significance to those in his audience with a Jewish background, who traced their ancestry through the covenants God made with Israel. The name "Jesus" (Gr. *Iēsous*) was a common Jewish name that meant "Yahweh saves." From the outset, Matthew calls Jesus "Messiah" (Gr. *Christos*), which meant "anointed one." The designation harks back to David as the anointed king of Israel's past and is associated with the covenant promise of an "anointed one" who would be the hope for Israel's future (2 Sam 7:11–16). Matthew also calls Jesus the "son of David," the descendant from David's royal lineage who would reestablish the throne in Jerusalem and the kingdom of Israel.

But Matthew's opening words also had special significance to those in his audience with a gentile background. The final designation of Jesus is that he is the "son of Abraham," recalling the covenant promise God made with the father of Israel to bless the nation as his chosen people, and also to bless all the nations of the earth through Abraham's line.

Consequently, the designations of Jesus serve at the very beginning as an indication of an important key to interpreting this Gospel.[7] Matthew emphasizes the way in which Jesus's ministry brought fulfillment of God's covenant to the particular people of Israel (e.g., 10:6; 15:24). Yet he will weave into his story a message to those from all nations, detailing how the arrival of Jesus brought fulfillment to the universal hope of salvation for all people (cf. 21:43; 28:19), because he is the heir to the universal covenantal blessing established through the patriarch Abraham. This theme of promise to all the

5. See, e.g., David E. Aune, *The New Testament in Its Literary Environment*, LEC (Philadelphia: Westminster, 1987), 59–63.

6. Evans, "'Book of the Genesis,'" 61–72; see also Davies and Allison, *Matthew*, 1:149–60.

7. Evans, "'Book of the Genesis,'" 61–72.

nations will become increasingly pronounced in Matthew's Gospel and will come to a climax in the concluding commission (28:18–20).[8]

### 4.1.2 Jesus Messiah's Genealogy (1:2–17)

As the heading flows directly into the genealogy, Matthew unfolds the lineage of Jesus, the one whom he has identified as the Messiah. Genealogies were important in the ancient world and played an especially significant role for the people of Israel. The Old Testament reveals that the Jews kept extensive genealogies, which served generally as a record of a family's descendants but were used for practical and legal purposes to establish a person's heritage, inheritance, legitimacy, and rights.[9]

There are several basic differences between the genealogical record found in Matthew's Gospel (1:2–17) and that found in Luke's Gospel (Luke 3:23–38).[10] Scholars have suggested various explanations for the differences, but two basic options surface. (1) The first view emphasizes generally that Matthew gives Jesus's line through his father Joseph, while Luke gives Jesus's line through his mother Mary. (2) The second basic view emphasizes that the focus is on Joseph in both genealogies, but for different purposes.

One plausible explanation may be a combination of these two primary views. While the differences between the two genealogies remain somewhat unsolvable with the information that we now possess, it does seem clear that Matthew intends to demonstrate Jesus's legal claim to the throne of David. David's greater Son, the anticipated Davidic messianic king, has arrived with the birth of Jesus.[11]

#### *4.1.2.1 Heroes and Villains*

The genuineness—and unlikeliness—of this genealogy must have stunned Matthew's readers.[12] Jesus's ancestors were humans with all the foibles, yet potentials, of everyday people. And God worked through them to bring about his plan of salvation. There is no pattern of righteousness in the lineage of Jesus. We find adulterers, harlots, heroes, and gentiles. Wicked Rehoboam was the father of wicked Abijah, who was the

8. Paul Foster, *Community, Law and Mission in Matthew's Gospel*, WUNT 2/177 (Tübingen: Mohr Siebeck, 2004), 220.

9. Cf. Richard L. Rohrbaugh, "The Social Function of Genealogies in the New Testament and Its World," in *To Set at Liberty: Essays on Early Christianity and Its Social World in Honor of John H. Elliott*, ed. Stephen K. Black, SWBA 11 (Sheffield: Sheffield Phoenix Press, 2014); Marshall D. Johnson, *The Purpose of Biblical Genealogies with Special Reference to the Setting of the Genealogies of Jesus*, 2nd. ed., SNTSMS 8 (Cambridge: Cambridge University Press, 1988).

10. For discussion, see Raymond E. Brown, *The Birth of the Messiah: A Commentary on the Infancy Narratives in the Gospels of Matthew and Luke*, new updated ed., ABRL (New York: Doubleday, 1993), 84–95; David R. Bauer, "The Literary and Theological Function of the Genealogy in Matthew's Gospel," in *Treasures New and Old: Recent Contributions to Matthean Studies*, ed. David R. Bauer and Mark Allan Powell, SBLSS 1 (Atlanta: Scholars, 1996), 129–59.

11. Cf. 22:41–46; 2 Sam. 7:12–16; Pss 89:19–29, 35–37; 110:1–7; 132:11–12.

12. Marguerat refers to it as a "strange genealogy": "une étrange généalogie." Marguerat, "'Livre de la genèse de Jésus Christ' (Mt 1,1)," 178.

father of good King Asa. Asa was the father of the good King Jehoshaphat (1:8), who was the father of wicked King Joram.

And so, at the very start of his Gospel, Matthew points his readers beyond the personal qualifications of individuals who belong to the line of the Messiah. Instead, he focuses on the faithfulness of God to bring about his plan of salvation. And as will be made clear throughout Matthew's story of Jesus's life and ministry, it was God's overwhelming love for his people that energized his faithfulness. This will become the explicit message of Matthew's story about Jesus Messiah.

#### *4.1.2.2 Women and Men*

The inclusion of the five women in Jesus's genealogy is often recognized as another clue to Matthew's emphasis. Women were not always included in Old Testament genealogies, because the emphasis was usually upon tracing descent through men as the head of the family. When women were included, there was usually some particular reason.[13] The speculation about Matthew's purpose has a long history,[14] but he seems to have a variety of reasons for including five women in Jesus's genealogy. Something positive can be said for each of the following, although it may be difficult to narrow Matthew's purpose to any one alone.

(1) Women had experienced increasing marginalization and even abuse within Jewish society. Jesus's line included Tamar, a woman who wrongfully had been denied motherhood by the deceitfulness of men. The women in the genealogy represent the gender equality that had been denied them within much of Jewish culture.[15] From the beginning Jesus came to restore the personal equality and dignity of women with men.

(2) Tamar, Rahab, and Bathsheba had reputations for morally indiscreet behavior and character. They are examples of women sinners Jesus came to save, a powerful statement about the offer of salvation to those of any gender.[16]

(3) The first four women may have been gentiles, although the ethnicity of Tamar and Bathsheba is unclear.[17] It is clear however that Ruth was a Moabitess, and to the tenth generation a Moabite was not to be admitted to the congregation (Deut 23:3). Matthew may be indicating that salvation is a possibility for every ethnic group, which is a strong motif in this Gospel (8:5–13; 28:18–20). Jesus Messiah, who could not

13. E.g., Richard Bauckham, "The Gentile Foremothers of the Messiah," in *Gospel Women: Studies of the Named Women in the Gospels* (Grand Rapids: Eerdmans, 2002), 17–46.

14. For summaries with evaluations of the various views, see Johnson, *Purpose of Biblical Genealogies*, 152–79; Brown, *Birth of the Messiah*, 71–74; Davies and Allison, *Matthew*, 1:170–72; John C. Hutchison, "Women, Gentiles, and the Messianic Mission in Matthew's Genealogy," *BSac* 158 (2001): 152–64.

15. Beverly Roberts Gaventa, *Mary: Glimpses of the Mother of Jesus* (Columbia: University of South Carolina Press, 1995), 33–39; Wim J. Weren, "The Five Women in Matthew's Genealogy," *CBQ* 59.2 (1997): 288–305.

16. Morris, *Matthew*, 23.

17. The ethnicity of Bathsheba is clouded because she is mentioned only by her former husband's name; cf. John Nolland, "The Four (Five) Women and Other Annotations in Matthew's Genealogy," *NTS* 43 (1997): 527–39.

have male gentiles in his ancestry, nonetheless had gentile ancestors in these women, suggesting his suitability as the Messiah for gentiles as well as for Jews.[18]

(4) The women had unusual marriages, sexual scandal in their past, or suspicions of having had illegitimate children. Matthew may be disarming prejudice against Mary's circumstances by those Jews who might forget their own history, even as he refutes charges of illegitimacy against Mary (1:18–25).[19]

(5) These women each represent a crucial period in Israel's history when a gentile displayed extraordinary faith in contrast to Jews who lacked courage and faith: Tamar versus Judah's disloyalty, Rahab versus the wilderness generation's faithlessness as exemplified by Achan, Ruth versus the unfaithful Israelites at the time of the judges as exemplified in the "friend" (Ruth 4:1), and Uriah versus David's sinfulness against Bathsheba. The messianic line was preserved—even through gentiles—when Israel was unfaithful.[20]

#### *4.1.2.3 The Culmination of Matthew's Genealogy in Jesus Messiah (1:16–17)*

The overriding importance of Matthew's opening verses is to understand that God is faithful to his covenant promises to Israel and to all the nations. With the birth of Jesus Messiah, the dawning of salvation has arrived for all people, of whatever ethnicity, gender, or status. Indeed, by including these unexpected names in the messianic genealogy, Matthew shows that God can use anyone—however marginalized or despised—to bring about his purposes. Against the backdrop of a world that was increasingly hostile to Christianity, Matthew solidifies his church's identity as the true people of God, who transcend ethnic, economic, and religious barriers to find oneness in their adherence to Jesus Messiah.

### 4.1.3 The Angelic Announcement of the Conception of Jesus Messiah (1:18–21)

At the start of this crucial narrative section, Matthew signals with a mild adversative (*de*; 1:18) that he has come to the central focus and purpose for listing the preceding genealogy—the conception and birth of the Messiah. Carson states, "All the preceding generations have been listed, 'but' the birth of Jesus comes into a class of its own."[21]

18. Luz, *Matthew*, 1:83–85; Richard Bauckham, "Tamar's Ancestry and Rahab's Marriage: Two Problems in the Matthean Genealogy," *NovT* 37.4 (1995): 313; Keener, *Matthew* (2009), 78–81.

19. Brown, *Birth of the Messiah*, 71–74; Edwin D. Freed, "The Women in Matthew's Genealogy," *JSNT* 29 (1987): 3–19; Craig L. Blomberg, "The Liberation of Illegitimacy: Women and Rulers in Matthew 1–2," *BTB* 21.4 (1991): 145–50; Hagner, *Matthew 1–13*, 10; Davies and Allison, *Matthew*, 1:170–72.

20. Hutchison, "Women, Gentiles, and the Messianic Mission in Matthew's Genealogy," 152–64.

21. Carson, "Matthew," 106n18.

Jesus is both son of David and son of Abraham (1:1) but also is now revealed to be the Son of God.[22]

The marriage customs of general Jewish culture at that time usually included two basic phases of the relationship—the betrothal and the wedding.[23] As was the custom, Joseph and Mary were pledged to each other in a period of "betrothal" or "engagement," a weightier undertaking than is found in many current cultures. Within the betrothal there were two stages. The first stage of betrothal involved the choosing of a spouse. According to Jewish custom, parents of a young man chose a young woman to be engaged to their son. The second stage of betrothal involved official arrangements and a prenuptial agreement before witnesses, a legally binding contract that could only be broken by a formal process of divorce. The expressions "husband" and "wife" were used during this stage to refer to betrothed partners. Sexual unfaithfulness with another person during betrothal was considered adultery, and the penalty for adultery was death by stoning—a public and shameful penalty. In a formal ceremony about a year after the betrothal, the marriage proper was initiated.[24]

Mary is legally betrothed to Joseph, but he discovers that she is about four months pregnant, having spent about three months with her "relative" Elizabeth (Luke 1:36, 56).[25] Mary seems to Joseph to be an adulteress, so he decides to "divorce her quietly." His decision is a compassionate one. He intends to maintain his personal righteousness yet wants to save her from disgrace.

God sends an angel in a dream to reassure Joseph of Mary's innocence and reveal that the baby's conception was from the Holy Spirit.[26] He instructs Joseph to give the baby the name Jesus, which means "Yahweh saves," drawing on Jesus's mission to save his people from their sins (1:21).[27]

#### *4.1.3.1 The Prophesied Immanuel (1:22–23)*

The phrase "All this took place to fulfill" (Matt 1:22) is a pattern Matthew repeats throughout his Gospel to point to an event or teaching of Jesus that fulfills an Old

22. The emphasis in this important pericope continues to be upon Jesus's genealogical links, but Matthew introduces also the Son of God motif, which will become explicit later in the narrative (e.g., 3:17). Kingsbury, *Matthew as Story*, 49–58; Birger Gerhardsson, "The Christology of Matthew," in *Who Do You Say That I Am? Essays on Christology; In Honor of Jack Dean Kingsbury*, ed. Mark Allan Powell and David R. Bauer (Westminster John Knox, 1999), 21–23.

23. See Joachim Jeremias, *Jerusalem in the Time of Jesus: An Investigation into Economic and Social Conditions During the New Testament Period*, ET (Philadelphia: Fortress, 1969), 363–68; Victor P. Hamilton, "Marriage (OT and ANE)," *ABD* 4:559–69.

24. See m. Ketubbot 5:2; m. Nedarim 10:5.

25. For discussion of the place of Mary the mother of Jesus in the biblical narratives, see Chris Maunder, "Mary and the Gospel Narratives," in *The Oxford Handbook of Mary*, ed. Chris Maunder, Oxford Handbooks (Oxford: Oxford University Press, 2019), 21–39.

26. William J. Subash, *The Dreams of Matthew 1:18–2:23: Tradition, Form, and Theological Investigation*, Studies in Biblical Literature 149 (New York: Peter Lang, 2012), esp. 165–68. For analysis of the passage and traditions of the "angel of the Lord," see Kristian A. Bendoraitis, *"Behold, the Angels Came and Served Him": A Compositional Analysis of Angels in Matthew*, LNTS 523 (London: Bloomsbury, 2015), 22–43.

27. Jeffrey Siker, *Sin in the New Testament*, EBS (Oxford: Oxford University Press, 2019), 53.

Testament passage. Here, Jesus's miraculous conception and birth fulfills the prophecy of Isaiah 7:14. The prophecy was immediately fulfilled when a young virgin married and gave birth to a son named Immanuel, but the same sign also held promise of a future virgin who would bear a messianic figure named Immanuel, "God with us." The prophecy is now fulfilled in Jesus Immanuel, indicating what he will do (Jesus, "God saves"), and who he is (Immanuel, "God with us"). Matthew will conclude his Gospel with the same theme as Jesus promises to be "with" his disciples until the end of the age (28:20).

#### *4.1.3.2 The Human/Divine Jesus Messiah*

Matthew's presentation of the birth narrative supports with firmness the fact of the virgin birth as announced to Joseph by the angel of the Lord. Matthew also attests to both human and divine natures in the remarkable conception of Jesus. The child has a human lineage through King David and the patriarch Abraham (1:1–17), a human name, "Jesus," by which he identifies with "his people" (1:21), and a human birth (1:25). But the child also has a divine relationship through the Holy Spirit (1:23), a divine description, "Immanuel, God with us" (1:22), and a divine origin through the Holy Spirit in his conception by his virgin mother (1:18, 20).[28]

Without giving details, the angelic announcement makes clear that the mode of conception will not be by any ordinary human means, but by a totally unparalleled action of the Holy Spirit. Matthew does not theorize how such a conception could take place, but merely presents it as historically authentic. Matthew understood that there was something both natural and supernatural about Jesus in his conception, birth, and development. He presents the virgin conception and birth of Jesus as an accepted fact, thus accounting for the astounding truth that God has taken on human nature and is now with his people. It is only this God-Man who, as Matthew's story unfolds, could save his people from their sins, which should cause them to reflect in unending gratitude, and to worship him as Jesus, "God saves," and Immanuel, "God with us."

### 4.1.4 The Identity of Jesus Messiah (1:22–2:23)

Matthew introduces a theme in chapter 1 that becomes one of the leading characteristics of the narrative of chapter 2. The theme is exposed in his regularly recurring fulfillment formula—"And so was fulfilled what the Lord had said through the prophet" (e.g., 2:14). Matthew's two horizons are revealed in this formula. As he looks back and records the historical details of the earthly life of Jesus (first horizon), he looks beyond to the Old Testament Scriptures and declares to his readers that Jesus's life fulfills

28. For discussion, see Andreas J. Köstenberger and Alexander E. Stewart, *The First Days of Jesus: The Story of the Incarnation* (Wheaton, IL: Crossway, 2015), 45–59; and Stephen J. Wellum, *God the Son Incarnate: The Doctrine of Christ*, FET (Wheaton, IL: Crossway, 2016), 209–45.

ancient prophetic pronouncements (second horizon). This theme is a significant clue to understanding Matthew's purpose for writing his Gospel. He varies the theme from direct predictive prophecy to analogical (or typological) correspondence to demonstrate the way that Jesus fulfills Old Testament prophecies. Both ways give a more complete picture of Jesus as the anticipated Messiah of Israel.

#### *4.1.4.1 Immanuel: God with Us (1:23)*

The first occurrence of the fulfillment formula points to Jesus's conception and birth, which fulfills the predictive prophecy of the messianic deliverer who would be born of a virgin. The child will be known as Immanuel, which prepares Matthew's readers for the incarnational truth guaranteed in the birth of the child Jesus, that "God [is] with us" (1:22–23; cf. Isa 7:14).

The significance of Matthew's interpretation of Jesus's name, Immanuel, "God with us," therefore, cannot be overstated. God has come to be with his people to fulfill the deepest meaning of the covenant. In Jesus, God is now with his people personally as their Savior. This theme will form the heart of a personal relationship of Jesus with his followers that will characterize his unique form of discipleship (see on 4:18–22).[29]

#### *4.1.4.2 Born in Bethlehem, the Ruler Who Will Shepherd My People Israel (2:6)*

The second occurrence of the fulfillment formula indicates that Jesus's birth in Bethlehem of Judea fulfills the predictive prophecy of the coming Messiah who will be born in David's own ancient birthplace and who will rule and shepherd the people of Israel (2:6; cf. Mic 5:2; 2 Sam 5:2). Jesus is *Christos* (Matt 1:1), a designation that harks back to David as the anointed king of Israel's past and is associated with the covenant promise of an "anointed one" who would be the hope for Israel's future (2 Sam 7:11–16).

#### *4.1.4.3 Out of Egypt I Called My Son (2:15)*

The third fulfillment formula declares that Jesus fulfills analogically/typologically the correspondence between Israel as God's son being rescued and delivered from Egypt by God, and Jesus as God's Son being protected from harm as he goes down and comes back from Egypt under divine protection (2:15; Hos 11:1). The covenant with Israel that was initiated with the Passover and exodus is now fulfilled in the arrival of Jesus to initiate the new covenant.[30]

29. For this OT theme in relationship to the appearance of Jesus, see Michael J. Wilkins, *Following the Master: A Biblical Theology of Discipleship* (Grand Rapids: Zondervan, 1992), 51–69, esp. 57 and 66. Also drawing upon this relationship in Matt 1 with the birth of the "God-with-Us" Messiah, but more critically, is Kupp, *Matthew's Emmanuel*, 157–75.

30. See Richard B. Hays, "Figural Exegesis and the Retrospective Re-cognition of Israel's Story," *BBR* 29.1 (2019): 32–48; esp. 38–39.

#### *4.1.4.4 Bethlehem's Grieving Mothers (2:17–18)*

The fourth fulfillment formula affirms that Jesus's life events fulfill analogically/typologically the correspondence between Israel's mothers sorrowing over their exiled children at the time of the Babylonian captivity and Bethlehem's grieving mothers at the slaughter of the innocent boys. Herod's attempts to eliminate the newborn king of the Jews correspond analogically to an earlier attempt by a foreign power to wipe out God's chosen people, but Jesus's advent also marks the arrival of the comfort to Israel that had been promised to the Jews who had been sent into exile in Babylon (Matt 2:17–18; Jer 31:15).[31]

#### *4.1.4.5 He Shall Be Called a "Nazarene" (2:23)*

The fifth occurrence of the fulfillment formula reveals that Jesus's hometown roots in Nazareth point toward his identity as the One who fulfills both the direct prophecy of the messianic Branch, a king from David's line who will judge with righteousness and strike the earth with the rod (Matt 2:23; cf. Isa 11:1–5; also Jer 23:5; etc.), and also the direct prophecy of a messianic suffering servant who would be despised (Matt 2:23; cf. Isa 52–53).

Matthew paints a bold picture of Jesus by drawing together strands of prophecy from the Old Testament that challenge sectarian expectations within Israel. Jesus is as much as any of them could have hoped for, but he is far more. He is the incarnate God who has come to be their King.

## 4.2 John the Baptist and Jesus Messiah Prepare for the Appearance of the Messianic Kingdom of Heaven (3:1–17)

### 4.2.1 John the Baptist Arrives (3:1–12)

John the Baptist was an important historical figure linking God's saving activity in the Old Testament and his saving activity in the ministry of Jesus. John's preaching calls people to repent, because the kingdom of heaven is at hand. In the Old Testament, repentance called for a change in a person's attitude toward God, which impacted one's actions and overall direction in life. External signs of repentance regularly included confession, abandonment of sin, and prayers of remorse.

#### *4.2.1.1 Kingdom of Heaven (3:1–6)*

The phrase "kingdom of heaven" is interchangeable with the expression "kingdom of God" in the other Gospels (cf. 19:23–24; Mark 10:24–25; Luke 18:24–25), but in

31. Hays, "Figural Exegesis," 38–39.

Matthew it also uniquely emphasizes that those who will choose to follow the Coming One must align themselves with the coming radical heavenly kingdom.[32] John the Baptist's message is unique because the kingdom of heaven has come near to people in the person of the soon-arriving Messiah. John is calling people to clear obstacles out of their lives that might hinder their reception of the Messiah and his kingdom. It was no easy matter to go out into the wilderness, especially for the city-dwellers of Jerusalem. But gripped by John's startling declaration of the nearness of God's kingdom, they demonstrate their repentance by confessing their sins.

#### *4.2.1.2 The Impact of the Kingdom of Heaven (3:7–12)*

John's popularity also drew some religious leaders, Pharisees and Sadducees mentioned here for the first time in Matthew's Gospel, to investigate this prophetic figure. John denounces both groups as a "brood of vipers." Vipers were proverbial for their subtle approach and attack, and John sees through these groups' ulterior motives in joining the crowd. Superficial religious activity and pedigree can blind a person to inner spiritual deficiencies before God. Just as the decisive identifier of a good tree is the health of its fruit, the decisive identifier of sincere faith is the fruit of repentance. Those lacking genuine repentance, like these Pharisees and Sadducees, will face God's wrath, the judgment that the Messiah will bring.[33]

John's role is to act as the herald who points to the main event, the appearance of Jesus, the messianic deliverer who will inaugurate God's kingdom on earth. John baptizes the repentant with water to prepare them for Jesus's arrival. Despite his significant ministry, John knows he is but a mere servant to the One to come. John's baptism will be superseded when the Messiah baptizes the repentant with the blessing of the Holy Spirit. Those who are unreceptive to the Messiah will be baptized with the judgment of eternal fire. Though many have come to receive John's baptism, the coming Jesus Messiah will separate the sincere from the superficial.

### 4.2.2 The Appearance of Jesus Messiah for Baptism by John the Baptist (3:13–17)

When Jesus goes to the desert to receive John's baptism, John initially tries to deter him because he recognizes Jesus as the "more powerful" One who brings the messianic

32. A majority of commentators conclude that the expressions are interchangeable; e.g., Blomberg, *New Testament Theology*, 366–68. Some have suggested that Matthew intends an additional aspect in his use of the phrase kingdom of heaven; e.g., Jonathan T. Pennington, *Heaven and Earth in the Gospel of Matthew*, NovTSup 126 (Leiden: Brill, 2007). See discussion below in my Chapter 9, The Kingdom of Heaven Comes to Earth in Matthew's Gospel.

33. For analysis of the messianic implications, see Richard Bauckham, "The Messianic Interpretation of Isa. 10:34 in the Dead Sea Scrolls, 2 Baruch and the Preaching of John the Baptist," *DSD* 2.2 (1995): 202–16.

baptism. John consents after Jesus asserts his water baptism will "fulfill all righteousness." The term "fulfill" (*plēroō*) continues the theme of "fulfillment" that has been so prominent in the beginning narrative of Matthew's Gospel.[34]

Righteousness (*dikaiosynē*) is an important concept in Matthew's Gospel.[35] With these words, "fulfill all righteousness," Jesus reveals that God's saving activity, which was prophesied throughout the Old Testament, is now being fulfilled with the inauguration of Jesus's ministry, a ministry that will culminate in his death on the cross. Jesus's baptism is an endorsement of John's ministry and message, and links Jesus's cause to John's. The focus on "righteousness" forms an *inclusio* between 3:15 and 21:32. This *inclusio* links eschatologically the ministries of Jesus and John, although in Jesus there is an innovation of a unique form of righteousness.[36] Although Jesus needs no repentance or cleansing, through water baptism he identifies with the sinful humanity he came to save as our substitute (cf. 2 Cor 5:21).[37]

Upon Jesus's baptism, God opens the heavens and anoints Jesus with a visible manifestation of his Spirit. God's voice from heaven audibly confirms the existing relationship between Jesus the unique Son and God the heavenly Father: Jesus is the Father's beloved Son. The clearest expression of the oneness between the Father and the Son is the love between them. And now the Father is pleased to send his Son to carry out his divine mission to bring salvation to the nations. The anointing and pronouncement formally confirms Jesus's messianic identity as Israel's true king, and commissions him as God's righteous servant for the public ministry he will now carry out in the power and presence of the Spirit, and which will be sustained by the Father's love for him.

### *4.2.2.1 The Mind-Boggling Truth of Jesus as Son of God (3:17)*

Modern Christian readers are probably a bit too familiar with Jesus to recognize how difficult it was for people in the first century, including even his own disciples, to comprehend fully who he was. But as one scholar observes, Jesus's coming into the world is the most stupendous event in human history.[38] It is not just the religious significance of Jesus's ministry to which he refers. He refers especially to the stupendous truth that God actually became a human and lived among us. Matthew writes to recount the good news of the incarnation's reality. We should note two points here.

34. See Chapter 5 below: The Old Testament and Jesus Messiah in Matthew's Gospel: Fulfillment.

35. Cf. 3:15; 5:6, 10, 20; 6:1, 33; 21:32.

36. See François Batuafe Ngole, *L'accomplissement de toute Justice: Approche pragmatique du procès dialogique entre Jésus et Jean-Baptiste dans l'Évangile de Matthieu*, Publications Universitaires Europeénnes 23.956 (Frankfurt am Main: Peter Lang, 2017), esp. 328–30.

37. See Nicholas Perrin, *Jesus the Priest* (Grand Rapids: Baker Academic, 2018), 54–90.

38. Malcolm Muggeridge, *Jesus: The Man Who Lives* (New York: Harper and Row, 1975), 1.

#### 4.2.2.1.1 A Veiled Trinitarianism (3:16–17)

In this one baptismal passage, we have the appearance of the Spirit, the presence of the Son, and the voice of the Father. As Leon Morris states, "Matthew certainly has trinitarian interest."[39] Matthew will conclude his Gospel with another Trinitarian allusion in Jesus's instruction that new disciples are to be baptized in the singular name of the Father, Son, and Holy Spirit (28:19).[40] For Matthew, the reality of the incarnation now makes clear God's revelation through the prophets: Jesus is the divine Son of God.[41]

#### 4.2.2.1.2 The Role of the Spirit (3:11, 16)

John the Baptist said that Jesus would baptize with the Holy Spirit and fire, and now in his baptism Jesus is anointed by the Spirit. This inaugurates the age of the Spirit foretold by the prophet Joel (Joel 2:28–29). The consistent christological picture in the New Testament reveals Jesus as a person who was fully divine in his essence and attributes during his time on earth, yet he did not operate in glorious display of his deity. Rather, he lived a fully human life in the power of the Spirit, giving his followers the ultimate example of a Spirit-led and empowered life, the example of how true human life is to be lived.[42]

## 4.3 Jesus Messiah Begins to Advance the Messianic Kingdom (4:1–25)

After his baptism, Jesus enters his ministry as the Spirit-anointed and Father-confirmed messianic deliverer. But before Jesus begins his public ministry, the Spirit leads him to the wilderness to undergo temptations. Increasingly, Matthew allows us to see that the Spirit is no impersonal force. The Spirit is the personal agent who will be intimately involved in empowering Jesus every step of the way in his earthly life. The Spirit will be Jesus's source of strength to overcome the temptations and to inaugurate his ministry.

### 4.3.1 Temptations of the Messiah (4:1–11)

Entering for the first time on the scene of Matthew's story is *ho diabolos*, "the devil," Jesus's real adversary, or, as he will be called later, Satan (4:10; 12:26; 16:23). The temptations are his diabolical attempt to foil God's plan for humanity's redemption. The word "tempted" is the verb *peirazō*, which can mean either "tempt" or "test."[43] Scripture

39. Morris, *Matthew*, 68.

40. Frederick Dale Bruner, *Matthew: The Christbook, Matthew 1–12*, vol. 1 of *Matthew: A Commentary*, 2 vols., rev. and exp. ed. (Grand Rapids: Eerdmans, 2004), 108.

41. See Brandon D. Crowe, "The Trinity and the Gospel of Matthew," in *The Essential Trinity: New Testament Foundations and Practical Relevance*, ed. Brandon D. Crowe and Carl R. Truman (Phillipsburg, NJ: P&R, 2017), 25–43.

42. See Daniel M. Doriani, *Matthew*, Reformed Expository Commentary (Phillipsburg, NJ: P&R, 2008), 1:61.

43. "πειράζω," BDAG 646. This is true as well for the noun, *peirasmos*, which can mean either "temptation" or "test."

is clear that God never *tempts* anyone to do evil, but he does allow circumstances to *test* a person's character (cf. Jas 1:13). The difference is the intended outcome of the act: a temptation intends a failure, whereas a test intends a strengthening. Although Satan aims to disqualify Jesus as sinless Savior and obedient Son, God uses Satan's evil intention for good: to strengthen Jesus for his messianic role.

Jesus's forty days of fasting in the wilderness corresponds to Israel's forty years of testing in the wilderness (Deut 8:2–3). Israel should have trusted God at his word that he would care for them. Where Israel failed, Jesus will now prove to be victorious.

#### *4.3.1.1 First Temptation: Personal—Turning Stones into Bread (4:3–4)*

The devil's first temptation attacks Jesus's personal trust in the Father's will. It is the Father's will for Jesus to be in the wilderness to fast, so this is the devil's attempt to get Jesus to misuse his power as the Son of God and act against the Father's will for the Son. It is not the Father's will for Jesus to acquire food miraculously in the wilderness. Jesus has come to live a truly human life, one that goes through the normal means of acquiring food. For Jesus to have turned the stones into bread would lead Jesus outside of the Father's will for the Son's experience.

#### *4.3.1.2 Second Temptation: National—Jumping Off the Temple Pinnacle (4:5–7)*

The devil's second temptation attacks Jesus's trust in the Father's love for him. The devil tries to manipulate Jesus into proving the Father's love by intentionally throwing himself in harm's way. As a tactic, the devil blatantly misuses Scripture. But true faith makes no such demands, and Jesus needs no proof of the love the Father has already declared (3:17).

If the first temptation attacks the personal life of the Son in relationship to the Father's will, the second temptation is an attack on the Son's national responsibility. By taking Jesus to the temple, the devil is likely tempting Jesus to test the Father's will for his messianic reception. If Jesus were to cast himself off the high place of the temple and the angels rescued him, think of the reaction of the people! This is a very devilish temptation for Jesus to gain the following of the nation Israel by a spectacular display at the central place of Israel's religion, the temple. But Jesus is not to gain a following in that way. His following will come by obediently proclaiming the gospel of the kingdom of God and suffering whatever consequences may come.

#### *4.3.1.3 Third Temptation: Universal—Worshiping Satan (4:8–10)*

The devil's third temptation attacks the very reason Jesus laid aside his own glory to come to earth. Jesus's mission is to gather the nations into the kingdom of God. But before Jesus sits on the throne of God's kingdom, he must suffer and hang upon the cross. So, the devil offers him a shortcut that bypasses the suffering: give up the will of the Father in heaven and worship the devil on earth. Satan's real objective is to acquire worship for himself. This is the essence of sin because it supplants God, the only one worthy of worship. Worshiping God tangibly demonstrates that a person has given over the rule of his or her own life to God's will.

### 4.3.2 Jesus Messiah Begins His Galilean Ministry (4:12–25)

#### *4.3.2.1 Jesus Messiah's Message (4:17)*

Jesus begins his ministry by preaching the same message of repentance as John the Baptist: "Repent, for the kingdom of heaven has come near" (4:17). We noted above that the phrase "kingdom of heaven" is interchangeable with the expression "kingdom of God" in the other Gospels (cf. 19:23–24; Mark 10:24–25; Luke 18:24–25), but in Matthew it also uniquely emphasizes that those who will obey Jesus's summons must align themselves with the coming radical heavenly kingdom.

Within Israel many expected imminent judgment and restoration to be dispensed with the arrival of the Coming One, looking for God's wrath to be poured out on the unrighteous, and for his blessing to be poured out on the righteous. When people heard Jesus announce that the kingdom of heaven was near, they expected Jesus to inaugurate the kind of kingdom consistent with their hopes.

But God's ways are not always what humans expect. Jesus will indeed fulfill the prophetic hope. But he will bring this hope to complete fulfillment only when he returns as the Son of Man in glory (cf. 24:29–31). This dual phenomenon is what scholars today generally refer to as the "already-not yet" nature of the presence of the kingdom. Jesus has *already* inaugurated the kingdom, but it has *not yet* reached its final form.

#### *4.3.2.2 Jesus Messiah Calls Fishers of Men (4:18–22)*

The kingdom of heaven advances in a unique way as Jesus calls fishermen to join him. In the ancient world, rabbis did not typically call for people to follow them, so we begin to see here that Jesus initiates a unique form of discipleship.[44] The normal pattern in Israel was for a prospective disciple to approach a rabbi and ask to study with him (e.g., 8:19). In the early stage of the Jesus movement various people came to Jesus in similar fashion (e.g., John 1:38, 49; 3:2).

But at the inauguration of his kingdom mission Jesus establishes a new pattern, because he is the one who takes the initiative to seek out and issue a call to these brothers

44. Cf. James D. G. Dunn, *Jesus' Call to Discipleship* (Cambridge: Cambridge University Press, 1992); Michael J. Wilkins, *The Concept of Disciple in Matthew's Gospel: As Reflected in the Use of the Term* Μαθητής, NovTSup 59 (Leiden: Brill, 1988), esp. chs. 1–3.

to enter a permanent relationship with him.[45] The brothers Simon Peter and Andrew obey Jesus's call to change their primary occupation from fishing for fish to fishing for human souls. Similarly, the brothers James and John relinquish their commitment to the family business, their assets, and their livelihood to join Jesus's messianic mission. Peter, Andrew, James, and John will become the inner circle among the twelve disciples around Jesus as he goes throughout Israel proclaiming the arrival of the kingdom of heaven. Jesus is enlisting workers to join him in his kingdom mission.

#### *4.3.2.3 Jesus Messiah Displays the Gospel of the Kingdom (4:23–25)*

Jesus goes through Galilee teaching his disciples and proclaiming the message of the "gospel of the kingdom" (4:23). Matthew uses the noun "gospel" (*euangelion*) only four times, and three of those four occur in the phrase "gospel of the kingdom," found only in Matthew. The real "good news" is that the age of the kingdom of God has finally dawned in the ministry of Jesus.

And this good news is not only taught and preached, but it is also demonstrated as Jesus was "healing" every disease and sickness among the people. Healing signals once again that Jesus has authority over the powers of this world and confirms the reality of the arrival of the kingdom of God (see on 11:4–6).

### 4.3.3 Jesus's Call

On the historical level, the call of the brothers serves foremost to highlight Jesus's authority as the inaugurator of the kingdom who is enlisting workers for the kingdom mission. The brothers' response illustrates how obedience is the only appropriate response to Jesus's authoritative call.

But not every disciple of Jesus was called to leave behind his or her occupation. One of the more striking examples we see later is Joseph of Arimathea. He was a disciple of Jesus, but he retained his position in society and the political establishment of Jerusalem. He also had great wealth, which allowed him to offer an indispensable service to Jesus at the moment of greatest need. Joseph was uniquely able to provide a burial tomb for the crucified Savior (cf. 27:57–60).

Nor did the brothers' immediate obedience deny either common sense or appropriate accountability to their personal, family, and professional responsibilities. Although they "left everything," Peter continued to live in his own home with his wife and mother-in-law and quite likely his brother Andrew and his family (8:14–15). There is a sense in which Peter and the rest of the Twelve will give up everything to play their foundational role in the church (cf. 19:27), yet we never hear of them abandoning their

45. Martin Hengel, *The Charismatic Leader and His Followers*, trans. J. C. G Greig (New York: Crossroad, 1981), 42–57.

responsibilities to provide for their families. The apostle Paul will rebuke later believers who were ministerial busybodies and who were not caring for the needs of their family (2 Thess. 3:6–13; 1 Tim. 5:8).

## 4.4 The Authoritative Message of Messiah: Kingdom Life for His Disciples (5:1–7:29)

### *First Discourse: "Kingdom-Life Proclamation"—Sermon on the Mount*

Matthew will continue to narrate the activities of Jesus's ministry, but he now turns to record an extensive message that develops in detail the kind of life that is available to those who respond to the announcement of the arrival of the kingdom of God.

This first of Jesus's discourses, traditionally called the Sermon on the Mount, is undoubtedly the most widely known of his messages. Jesus began his public ministry by announcing the good news of the arrival of the kingdom of heaven and calling his first followers. Now he gives his first monumental message.

### 4.4.1 The Setting of the Sermon on the Mount (5:1–2)

When Jesus saw the crowds, he went up onto the mountain. Then his disciples came to him and he taught them. This is a clear clue as to the intent of the Sermon. It is instruction for his disciples on discipleship to Jesus in the kingdom of heaven.

Matthew specifies three primary groups of people around Jesus in his earthly ministry: his disciples, the religious leaders, and the crowd.[46] The *disciples* are those who have come to Jesus for salvation and made a commitment to Jesus as the Messiah. The *religious leaders* are Jesus's opponents for much of his ministry, represented especially by the scribes and Pharisees (12:22–32).[47] The *crowd* is the basically neutral, though curious, group of people who are astounded by his teaching and ministry (7:28–29), but who have not yet made a commitment to him.

The disciples are *with* Jesus, the religious leaders are *against* him, and the crowd stands in the middle as not yet having made a decision either for or against him.

In this sermon, Jesus has an eye on all three groups. The message for his disciples is instruction on discipleship to Jesus. The message for the religious leaders is warning

46. Wilkins, *Concept of Disciple*, esp. 163–72; Wilkins, *Following the Master*, 179–83. For a similar perspective, see J. R. C. Cousland, *The Crowds in the Gospel of Matthew*, NovTSup 102 (Leiden: Brill, 2002).

47. For a brief discussion of historical portraits of the Jewish leaders both outside of the Gospels and within the narrative world of the Gospels, see Anthony Le Donne, "The Jewish Leaders," in *Jesus Among Friends and Enemies: A Historical and Literary Introduction to Jesus in the Gospels*, ed. Chris Keith and Larry W. Hurtado (Grand Rapids: Baker Academic, 2011), 199–217.

or rebuke for their opposition to him. And the message for the crowd includes an invitation to become disciples and experience life in the kingdom of heaven.

Now, in his first sermonic message, Jesus gives a powerful statement of the reality and availability of kingdom life for his disciples, which includes practical instruction on how to carry out kingdom life. Jesus expounds upon the radical reality of everyday discipleship lived in the presence and power of the kingdom of heaven.

#### *4.4.2.1 The Sermon on the Mount Delineates the Foundation of Our Discipleship to Jesus*

The kind of kingdom life elucidated in the Sermon on the Mount is the foundation for each Christian's personal discipleship to Jesus. The mandate of the Great Commission that concludes Matthew's Gospel is to "make disciples" of all the nations (28:19). As a person is converted, he or she becomes a disciple of Jesus, which is synonymous with being a Christian. The final participle of the Great Commission directs new disciples to be taught to obey everything that Jesus commanded (28:20). And the Sermon on the Mount is the first major teaching of Jesus found in the Gospel, delineating the core of what it means to live as Jesus's disciple.

I emphasize this especially to counteract some who understand discipleship to be reserved for an advanced stage of commitment. From the biblical point of view, all Christians are disciples, so the teaching in the Sermon on the Mount is not for a few more-committed believers. This is the heart of Jesus's teaching for all Christians.

### 4.4.2 The Essence of Kingdom Life for Disciples of Jesus in All Eras

Throughout church history expositors have subjected the Sermon on the Mount to a variety of interpretations.[48] But a majority of interpreters, with some variation, understand the it to be the declaration of the essence of life in the kingdom of heaven for all true believers. In line with our understanding of the audiences around Jesus, the Sermon is primarily addressed to Jesus's disciples and is instruction on discipleship

48. For brief, helpful overviews of the history of interpretation, see Robert A. Guelich, *The Sermon on the Mount: A Foundation for Understanding* (Waco, TX: Word, 1982), 14–22; Daniel M. Doriani, *The Sermon on the Mount: The Character of a Disciple* (Phillipsburg, NJ: P&R, 2006), 1–12; Charles L. Quarles, *Sermon on the Mount: Restoring Christ's Message to the Modern Church*, NACSBT (Nashville: B&H, 2011), 4–11; Scot McKnight, *Sermon on the Mount*, SGBC (Grand Rapids: Zondervan, 2013), 1–14; and Jonathan T. Pennington, *The Sermon on the Mount and Human Flourishing: A Theological Commentary* (Grand Rapids: Baker Academic, 2017), 1–16. More extensive surveys are found in Hans Dieter Betz, *The Sermon on the Mount: A Commentary on the Sermon on the Mount, Including the Sermon on the Plain (Matthew 5:3—7:27 and Luke 6:20–49)*, Hermeneia (Minneapolis: Fortress, 1995), 1–44; Jeffrey P. Greenman, Timothy Larsen, and Stephen R. Spencer, eds., *The Sermon on the Mount Through the Centuries: From the Early Church to John Paul II* (Grand Rapids: Brazos, 2007); Clarence Bauman, *The Sermon on the Mount: The Modern Quest for Its Meaning* (Macon, GA: Mercer, 1985); and Warren S. Kissinger, *The Sermon on the Mount: A History of Interpretation and Bibliography* (Metuchen, NJ: Scarecrow, 1975). For an attempt to root the Sermon on the Mount parabolically and in Greek rhetoric, see Ernst Baasland, *Parables and Rhetoric in the Sermon on the Mount: New Approaches to a Classical Text*, WUNT 351 (Tübingen: Mohr Siebeck, 2015).

and life in the kingdom. It can be designated as training in Christian discipleship for believers of all eras.

It is primarily *instruction* for disciples about how life is to be lived on this earth in the light of the radical truth that the kingdom of heaven has arrived. The Sermon is the first basic instruction in Matthew's Gospel for those who have made a commitment to Jesus and his proclamation of the gospel of the kingdom, offering them instruction about life in the kingdom.

We also see that the Sermon is a *warning* to the religious leaders, primarily the scribes and the Pharisees, of their fate if they continue their hypocritical leadership. At virtually every point in the Sermon we must determine how Jesus confronts an erroneous interpretation or a hypocritical application of the Old Testament that was being advanced by the scribes and the Pharisees.

But the Sermon also holds out an enticing *example* of kingdom life that is available to those who have not yet made a decision for or against Jesus. In the Sermon Jesus extends an invitation to the crowds to become Jesus's disciples and enter the kingdom and experience kingdom life (e.g., 5:20). His teaching was a tantalizing attraction to the crowds who were within hearing range, but who had not yet made a commitment to him. But it is also a warning to the crowd not to follow the hypocritical leadership of the scribes and Pharisees.

#### *4.4.2.2 The Sermon on the Mount Is the Realistic, Though Ideal, Model of the Christian Life*

The Sermon on the Mount gives the ideal of discipleship (e.g., 5:48), yet that goal is set within a realistic understanding of everyday human life as it will be transformed through participation in new covenant life (26:26–29). The new covenant that Jesus inaugurates includes both forgiveness of sins and transformation of lives because it is the basis of Spirit-produced regeneration and spiritual growth (cf. Ezek 36:26–32; Titus 3:4–7).

The ideal life that Jesus lives and teaches becomes the goal that all his disciples are to strive toward in this life. The emphasis in the Sermon will be on inside-out transformation. Jesus will continually go to inner motivation, not external performance. The inner life will naturally transform the outer life. The heart that treasures the kingdom of heaven above all else will be the starting point for transformation of the entire life.

### 4.4.3 The Beatitudes of the Kingdom of Heaven (5:3–12)

The Beatitudes open the Sermon on the Mount with a sober yet dazzling vision of the operation of the kingdom of heaven among God's people. More than simply a formal literary introduction, the Beatitudes give a summarizing declaration of the essence of the Sermon's message, giving in a nutshell the way in which the kingdom of God makes its impact upon the lives of those who respond to it. The character of this kingdom life contravenes the values that most people hold dear, because God's blessing rests upon the unlikely ones—the poor in spirit, the mourners, the meek, the persecuted.[49] Jesus's disciples embody God's alternative reality through these character qualities of the Beatitudes of the kingdom of heaven.[50]

### 4.4.3.1 "Blessed"

The word "beatitude" is derived from the Latin *beatitudo*, translating Matthew's Greek word *makarios*, which traditionally has been rendered into English as "blessed." This does not mean a conferral of blessing, nor an exhortation to live a life worthy of blessing, but rather is an acknowledgment that the ones indicated are blessed from God's perspective. To be "blessed" is more than to be happy. Blessedness belongs to those who respond to Jesus's ministry and come into a vital relationship with God.

### 4.4.3.2 The Structure of the Beatitudes

The overall structure of the Beatitudes gives an important clue to their theme. The first and the eighth beatitudes (5:3, 10) form bookends, an example of the common Hebrew literary devise called an *inclusio*, because the causal clause of the first beatitude is repeated in the last beatitude—"for theirs *is* the kingdom of heaven" (cf. 5:3, 10). The repetition of the present-tense clause ("for theirs *is*") signals the main theme of the Beatitudes: the blessedness of the kingdom of heaven is a present possession and operation among those who respond to Jesus's ministry.

However, the second through seventh beatitudes (5:4–9) have a future tense in the causal clause of each beatitude (e.g., 5:4: "for they *will be* comforted"), indicating that the kingdom is a future expectation and hope as well as a present possession.

### 4.4.3.3 The Message of the Beatitudes

As Jesus's disciples face the daily challenges lived in the everyday realities of a fallen world, they must choose to reject the evil path and allow the Spirit of God to produce these Christlike characteristics in them.[51] A brief summary of each of the seven Beatitudes reveals their powerful message.[52]

49. Richard B. Hays, *The Moral Vision of the New Testament—Community, Cross, New Community: A Contemporary Introduction to New Testament Ethics* (San Francisco: HarperSanFrancisco, 1996), 321.

50. For a complex, yet helpful discussion of discipleship to Jesus as "theocentric commitment" articulated in the Beatitudes, see Ben Cooper, *Incorporated Servanthood: Commitment and Discipleship in the Gospel of Matthew*, LNTS 490 (London: T&T Clark, 2013), summarized 252–56.

51. John Stott, *The Beatitudes: Developing Spiritual Character* (Downers Grove: InterVarsity, 1998).

52. See the excellent overview by Peter W. Gosnell, *The Ethical Vision of the Bible: Learning Good from Knowing God* (Downers Grove, IL: InterVarsity, 2014), 228.

1. The poor in spirit (5:3) are those who recognize their need for God's help, embracing abject humility. Those who confess their spiritual bankruptcy, rather than claiming spiritual self-sufficiency, live in the power of the kingdom.
2. Sin—personal and corporate—produces spiritual, emotional, or financial bankruptcy. Such bankruptcy produces mourning: grief over one's own wretched condition. The arrival of the kingdom of heaven will bring the blessing of God's comfort to those who mourn their bankruptcy and receive God's gift of forgiveness (5:4).
3. The meek are the "gentle," those who do not assert themselves over others in order to advance their own causes, but who will nonetheless inherit the earth (5:5). The meek willingly suppress the right to exert personal power.
4. Those who hunger and thirst for righteousness will recognize that God is the ultimate source of real righteousness. They will be satisfied by responding to his invitation to be in relationship with him and will long for morally right actions in a crooked world (5:6).
5. The merciful show kindness to those in need and demonstrate forgiveness toward the guilty. The mercy that they show others will be shown toward them (5:7).
6. The pure in heart are those whose pursuit of purity affects every area of life. They have set their hearts on God instead of external religious righteousness (5:8).
7. Those who promote God's messianic peace will receive the ultimate reward of being called sons of God because they reflect the character of their heavenly Father (5:9).
8. Those who are persecuted because of righteousness are those who are wrongly treated for their stand for the gospel message. Since Jesus himself will experience opposition and persecution, his disciples should expect the same. Their reward may not come on earth but will surely come in heaven (5:10–12).

As Jesus's disciples face the daily challenges lived in the everyday realities of a fallen world, they must choose to reject the evil path and allow the Spirit of God to produce these Christlike characteristics in them.

The Beatitudes that Jesus issues to start the Sermon on the Mount are *pronouncements of blessing* on those waiting for God's messianic activity, but also are *pronouncements of condemnation* on the religious establishment who have attempted to secure God's blessing through their own efforts. At the same time, the Beatitudes are *instructions* for Jesus's disciples about the life that is truly "blessed" from God's perspective. As such, the Beatitudes contrast Jesus's values with the values of the world, and the values of the religious establishment that takes pride in its accomplishments apart from the life of the kingdom of heaven.

The Beatitudes are neither means of entering the kingdom nor means of advancing in the kingdom. They are expressions of Spirit-produced kingdom life, revealing to the entire world that God is advancing as he has begun a transformation in Jesus's disciples. They are guidelines of God's values, which give the parameters of God's transformational standards that guide disciples' lives. This transformation by God is why Jesus calls the disciples "blessed."

### 4.4.4 Salt and Light (5:13–16)

The metaphors of salt and light (5:13–16) are the first explicit indication that the presence of the kingdom produces changed lives. As Jesus's disciples go out into the world as salt, the proof of the reality of their profession is in the nature of their lives.[53] True disciples cannot lose what has made them disciples, because they have become changed persons, made new by the life of the kingdom of heaven.

Jesus's disciples, called to be the light of the world, have the kingdom life within them as a living testimony to those in the world who do not yet have the light. Disciples' good works are produced by the light-life from God, not of their own making, because those who see them in action will glorify their Father in heaven.

### 4.4.5 Jesus and the Messianic Kingdom in Relation to the Law (5:17–20)

The next section has four verses that provide a crucial key to the interpretation of the Sermon but also in many ways a crucial key to understanding Jesus's inauguration of the kingdom and, by extension, an understanding of Matthew's purpose for writing his Gospel.

#### *4.4.5.1 Jesus Fulfills the Law (5:17–19)*

Jesus's announcement of the arrival of the kingdom of heaven (4:17) might be interpreted by some as though he was starting a new work that would bring him into conflict with the Old Testament Scriptures. But Jesus categorically declares, "Do not think that I have come to abolish the Law and the Prophets" (5:17). The expression "the Law and the Prophets" is a way of referring to the entire Hebrew Scriptures (7:12; 11:13; 22:40; cf. Rom 3:21), and the expression "Do not think" indicates that Jesus is countering a suspicion that he is attempting to set aside God's former revelation with his announcement of the arrival of the kingdom of God. Such an attempt would be the ultimate mark of a heretic.[54]

The term "fulfill" has already become in Matthew's narrative an important indicator of Jesus's significance in God's historical program, because Jesus's life and ministry fulfill Old Testament prophecies and expectations (e.g., Matt 1:22–23; 2:15, 17–18,

53. Emphasizing the universalistic mission to gentiles is Boris Paschke, *Particularism and Universalism in the Sermon on the Mount: A Narrative-Critical Analysis of Matthew 5–7 in the Light of Matthew's View on Mission*, NTAbh NS 56 (Münster: Aschendorff, 2012), e.g., 59–117.

54. Keener, *Matthew* (2009), 176n46.

23; 4:14–16). Here Jesus declares that he has come to fulfill *all* the Old Testament Scripture. The idea of "fulfillment" is more than his obedience (i.e., keeping the Law), although that is included. Jesus himself is the fulfillment of predictions of the coming Messiah and certain anticipated roles, including his forthcoming sacrificial death for the sins of the world. Jesus has come to actualize the Scripture, and his interpretation and application of the Old Testament Scripture completes and clarifies God's intent and meaning through it. All that the Old Testament intended to communicate about God's will and hopes and future for humanity finds its full meaning and accomplishment in Jesus's ministry and teaching.

Jesus's statement in verse 18 confirms the full authority of the Old Testament as Scripture as a valid expression of God's will for all ages (2 Tim 3:15–16), even down to the smallest components of the written text.

#### *4.4.5.2 "Inside-Out" Righteousness (5:20)*

Jesus's declaration in verse 20 was stunning, because the Pharisees and teachers of the Law were the epitome of ethical righteousness. They were committed to fulfilling the demands of the Old Testament through their elaborate oral tradition. Their scrupulous adherence to the written and oral law was legendary in Israel, and yet Jesus says that it did not gain them entrance to the kingdom of heaven.

Jesus's disciples are called to a different *kind* and *quality* of righteousness, not an increased quantity. Kingdom righteousness operates from the inside out, not the outside in, a principle that is fully in line with Old Testament understandings of righteousness and purification (e.g., Ps 51:2, 7, 10). Righteousness belongs to the realm of grace. Jesus's proclamation of good news is that the kingdom of heaven is now available to those who respond to him. God's saving activity has arrived on the earthly scene to deliver his people, and this will produce a radical change in their lives.

### 4.4.6 Jesus's Declarative Fulfillment of the Law (5:21–48)

The next section of the Sermon on the Mount is commonly referred to as "the antitheses," because six times we hear similar recurring statements, "You have heard it said . . . *but I say to you.*" Jesus's declaration is the antithesis of what has gone before. This has been mistakenly interpreted by some to mean that Jesus makes his teaching the antithesis of the Old Testament itself.

But as we look closely at each, we see that Jesus is contrasting *his interpretation* of the Old Testament with *faulty interpretations* and/or *applications* of the Old Testament, especially by the scribes and Pharisees. In each of the antitheses, Jesus demonstrates how the Old Testament is to be properly interpreted and applied, and thus, how the Law and the Prophets are fulfilled (cf. 5:17).

This elevates Jesus above all interpreters, making his pronouncements equivalent with Scripture itself. These next sections of the Sermon on the Mount demonstrate that Jesus's interpretation of the Old Testament is the antithesis of the religious leaders' faulty interpretations.[55] By living in accordance with the true intent and motive of the Law, disciples of Jesus will continually live a righteousness that surpasses that of the scribes and Pharisees.

#### *4.4.6.1 Murder . . . Nurturing Relationships (5:21–26)*

Jesus addresses first the current understanding of the sixth commandment of the Decalogue, "You shall not murder" (Exod 20:13; Deut 5:17). It carries the idea of killing with premeditation and deliberateness. A faulty interpretation of the commandment would say that avoiding homicide fulfills the obligation of the Law. However, Jesus's declarative statement, "But I tell you," introduces three ways that a person's life is removed from him or her besides the physical act of murder: inappropriate anger, public ridicule, and public contempt. In each case, punishment is due, ranging from eternal fiery judgment (5:22) to prison (5:25).[56]

Jesus uses these scenarios to emphasize the seriousness of the problem of anger. Unreconciled anger is the inner equivalency of murder, which is a sin debt impossible to repay. To leave problems unreconciled is to allow the sin that has been created to continue to destroy relationships between people.

The true disciple not only avoids murder but is transformed so that one does not strip away the personhood and identity of others through anger or defamation (5:21–23), and one continually produces reconciliation in offended relationships (5:23–26).[57]

#### *4.4.6.2 Adultery . . . Marital Oneness (5:27–30)*

Adultery was considered one of the most serious offenses because it broke the marriage relationship, a union that reflects the covenant relationship between God and his people. Oneness with a wife means that her husband gives himself to her and her alone. When a man even looks with desire at another woman, he has rejected his wife and given himself to another. The disciple of Jesus not only shuns physical acts of adultery, but he is so completely committed to God's purpose for marriage that he has eyes and hands for only for his spouse, and he disciplines his every thought and action to be singly focused on her alone.

55. One who tends unduly to minimize Jesus's criticism of the scribes and Pharisees is Reinhard Neudecker, *Moses Interpreted by the Pharisees and Jesus: Matthew's Antitheses in the Light of Early Rabbinic Literature*, SubBi 44 (Rome: Gregorian and Biblical Press, 2012), e.g., 129–30.

56. Alan W. Gomes, *40 Questions About Heaven and Hell*, 40 Questions (Grand Rapids: Kregel, 2018), 318–19.

57. For the complicated relationship of the sayings in 5:21–22 to 5:23–26 see Pennington, *Sermon on the Mount*, 182–85.

### *4.4.6.3 Divorce . . . Marriage Sanctity Inviolate (5:31–32)*

Marital unfaithfulness consists of any sinful activity that intentionally breaks the marriage relationship.[58] Disciples of Jesus not only respect the purity of the marital relationship but have God's values for the original design for marriage and are unreservedly committed to its permanence and sanctity.[59]

### *4.4.6.4 Oaths . . . Transparent Honesty (5:33–37)*

When making an oath, people would invoke God's name, or substitutes for it, to guarantee the truth of what one said. But Jesus's disciples are not to swear any oath at all. Instead, they should be people of such integrity that their word is sufficiently trustworthy. Jesus's disciples do not need to give an oath as an additional confirmation of their trustworthiness, because their faithful lives continually confirm the reliability of their word.[60]

### *4.4.6.5 Eye for an Eye . . . Servanthood (5:38–42)*

The "law of retaliation" was God's means of providing justice and purging evil from among his people (cf. Deut 19:20–21). It was intended to prevent inappropriate punishment and was imposed by civil authorities rather than individuals.[61] Jesus uses four illustrations from the everyday affairs of his disciples under oppression to emphasize that his disciples are to serve those who offend them.[62] The disciple of Jesus is so secure in her/his transformed kingdom identity that when she/he is wronged she/he does not merely adhere to legal retribution, but uses every opportunity to serve others, both good and evil people, so that the reality of God's grace in her/his life woos them to the kingdom of heaven.

### *4.4.6.6 Love and Hatred . . . Unconditional Commitment (5:43–47)*

God's hatred of evil was a central theme in the Old Testament. Because God hates evil, those who embody evil are understood to be God's enemies, and it was natural to hate God's enemies (cf. Ps 139:21–22). However, although God hates evil, he also loves every one of his creatures and intends to bring reconciliation. All who respond to God's will in the ministry of Jesus are children of the heavenly Father. With the sun and rain, God shows grace and care for all his creatures, so his disciples are to love both neighbor and enemy.[63]

---

58. For discussion of the cultural context, see William R. G. Loader, "Did Adultery Mandate Divorce? A Reassessment of Jesus' Divorce Logia," *NTS* 61.1 (2015): 67–78.

59. For a brief biblical theology of marriage and Jesus's perspective of God's original intent, with practical implications, see Raymond C. Ortlund Jr., *Marriage and the Mystery of the Gospel*, Short Studies in Biblical Theology (Wheaton, IL: Crossway, 2016), esp. 79–85.

60. John P. Meier, "Did the Historical Jesus Prohibit All Oaths? Part 1," *JSHJ* 5.2 (2007): 175–204.

61. For discussion of the cultural context, see James F. Davis, *Lex Talionis in Early Judaism and the Exhortation of Jesus in Matthew 5.38–42*, JSNT 281 (London: T&T Clark, 2005).

62. E.g., Guelich, *Sermon on the Mount*, 220.

63. See Ernst Baasland, "Mission and Love of Enemy: Matthew 5:43–44 and Luke 6:27–28, 35 (2 Clem. 13.3; Diogn. 5) in

#### *4.4.6.7 Conclusion: The Pursuit of Perfection (5:48)*

Matthew concludes the declarations of the antitheses with a stunning statement: "you shall be perfect." The statement holds out an emphatic *goal* that is to shape the disciples' entire life—they are to set nothing less than the perfection of God as the ultimate objective of their behavior, thoughts, and will. Further, the statement also implies a *promise*, because the Father is not only the divine goal but also the divine enabler. Jesus's disciples are to pursue the perfection that is God himself.[64] Jesus's statement implies a realistically ideal goal that Jesus's disciples are to pursue with restful dissatisfaction in this life until their final perfection in eternity. Matthew records climactically that Jesus's disciples have experienced the powerfully life-changing presence of the kingdom of heaven in such a way that their progressive transformation into the image of Jesus the Son of God secures their progressive growth into the very perfection of God the Father.

### 4.4.7 Public Kingdom Spirituality in Religious Life (6:1–18)

Matthew now records three examples of Jewish pious acts (giving to the needy, prayer, fasting) to make one primary point: obedience in public does not guarantee a reward from God, because one's *motive* is more important than outward activity.

These three are representative ways that discipleship to Jesus surpasses the external, legalistic, pious life of the leading religious figures of Jesus's day. Obedience is central to Jesus's form of discipleship, as it was to other forms of discipleship within Judaism, but Jesus calls his followers to adhere to the *motive* behind obedience to the Old Testament, not simply to carry out external compliance. In common parlance today, "hypocrites" are those who *say one thing and do another*, but here Jesus censures the religious leaders, especially the Pharisees, for a particular form of hypocrisy: *doing right things* for the *wrong reasons*. Our motives reveal who we truly are.

#### *4.4.7.1 Giving to the Needy (6:2–4)*

Giving to the needy was one of the pillars of religious life. But the religious leaders have a hidden motivation and give to the needy to gain public adulation and to enhance their reputation within the religious establishment. The tragic irony is that by choosing to receive their reward of public and professional acclaim, they will receive no reward from God.

#### *4.4.7.2 Praying (6:5–15)*

A second primary practice of Jewish piety was prayer. At set times of prayer pious Jews would stop what they were doing and pray, some discreetly, but others with

Its Graeco-Roman Context," in *The Church and Its Mission in the New Testament and Early Christianity: Essays in Memory of Hans Kvalbein*, ed. David E. Aune and Reidar Hvalvik, WUNT 404 (Tübingen: Mohr Siebeck, 2018), 63–83.

64. Cf. France, *Gospel of Matthew*, 228–29.

pretentious display. This kind of hypocritical prayer receives the same reward as hypocritical almsgiving: since they want acclaim from people, that is all the reward those who pray this way receive (cf. 6:2). Jesus clarifies that God cannot be manipulated by the performance of ritual prayers.

#### *4.4.7.3 The Model Prayer for Disciples: "The Lord's Prayer" (6:9–13)*

In distinction from the hypocritical prayers of the Jewish religious leaders and the babbling prayers of pagans, Jesus gives an example of how his disciples should pray.[65] The prayer is offered not so much as a command to pray but as an invitation to share in the prayer life of Jesus himself.[66] While it is commonly referred to as "The Lord's Prayer," it is actually "the disciple's prayer" because it is an example for disciples to follow in their regular prayer life.[67] It as a model of what a disciple's prayer life will emulate. However, Jesus does not necessitate verbatim repetition of these words, because frequent repetitive use may lead to the sin of formalism that he here condemns.[68]

The prayer Jesus sets forth has a beginning invocation and six petitions that give proper priorities for prayer.[69] The prayer begins by invoking God as Father. Jesus's disciples are invited into the intimacy of the Son with his Father in the new community of faith.[70]

1. The first petition is directed toward God's name. His name signifies his person. The purpose of hallowing God's name is that God would be "sanctified" or set apart as holy among all people and in all actions, that God would be treated with the highest honor.
2. In the second petition, the disciples pray "your kingdom come," aligning themselves with God's kingdom movement and seeking God's power in furthering its ultimate fulfillment.
3. The third petition speaks of God's will—wherever the kingdom of heaven exerts its presence, God's will is experienced.[71]

65. C. Clifton Black, *The Lord's Prayer*, Interpretation (Louisville: Westminster John Knox, 2018). Black gives a helpful overview of prayer in the ancient world: "The Religious World of the Lord's Prayer" (3–28).

66. N. T. Wright, "The Lord's Prayer as a Paradigm of Christian Prayer," in *Into God's Presence: Prayer in the New Testament*, ed. Richard N. Longenecker, MNTS (Grand Rapids: Eerdmans, 2001), 132.

67. M. M. B. Turner, "Prayer in the Gospels and Acts," in *Teach Us to Pray: Prayer in the Bible and the World*, ed. D. A. Carson (Grand Rapids: Baker, 1990), 64. Hence the title in Jeffrey B. Gibson, *The Disciples' Prayer: The Prayer Jesus Taught in Its Historical Setting* (Minneapolis: Fortress, 2015).

68. See Michael J. Wilkins, "Prayer," *DLNTD* 947.

69. Three helpful recent studies are Nijay K. Gupta, *The Lord's Prayer*, SHBCSS (Macon, GA: Smyth and Helwys, 2017); Black, *Lord's Prayer*, 2018; and Charles Nathan Ridlehoover, *The Lord's Prayer and the Sermon on the Mount in Matthew's Gospel*, LNTS 616 (London: T&T Clark, 2020).

70. See David E. Garland, "The Lord's Prayer in the Gospel of Matthew," *RevExp* 89 (1992): 215–28, esp. 217–19; Perrin, *Jesus the Priest*, esp. 39.

71. A link with Jesus's Gethsemane prayer for God's will is important to note.

4. The fourth petition addresses the disciples' daily bread, which refers to all of a believer's needs, both physical and spiritual. Disciples are to be concerned with one day at a time, relying on God for their daily provision.
5. The fifth petition addresses the disciples' debts of sin. Sin creates a "debt" to God that cannot be repaid. Jesus's disciples have responded to his charge to repent and have received forgiveness for their debts. Those who receive forgiveness are so grateful to God that they in turn eagerly forgive those who sin against them.
6. The final petition addresses the disciples' battle with evil forces. The word "temptation" can be used for either temptation or testing. Disciples should pray either for relief from testing or that their testing would not become an occasion for temptation (cf. Exod 16:4; Deut 8:16; 1 Pet 1:7). Satan's influence is behind every attempt to turn a testing into a temptation to evil.

Jesus concludes his instruction on prayer by reiterating the emphasis of the fifth petition on forgiving others (cf. 6:14–15 with 6:12). Salvation does not rest on human merits, but only on the grace and mercy of God. Once disciples have received forgiveness and salvation, they are to forgive with the same forgiveness with which they have been forgiven. This is the evidence that they are indeed forgiven (see also on 18:21–35).[72]

#### *4.4.7.4 Fasting (6:16–18)*

A third practice of Jewish piety was fasting. Jesus assumes that his disciples will fast. But religious discipline is not for others to see. Rather than making a public display of fasting, which would negate its spiritual value, Jesus's disciples are to celebrate life while fasting.

### 4.4.8 Personal Kingdom Spirituality in the Everyday World (6:19–34)

The key saying of this section is Jesus's famous imperative, "But seek first his kingdom and his righteousness" (6:33). It continues the overall priority and teaching of the Sermon on the Mount. The present section continues the teaching on the pursuit of kingdom righteousness, but here the spotlight is on the kind of personal interior life that Jesus's disciples will experience in their everyday world (6:19–34).

#### *4.4.8.1 Choose Your Master: God or Wealth (6:19–24)*

Material wealth was often seen in Israel as a sign of God's blessing and one's reward for obedience. But with wealth comes the danger of having a false sense of security or an inaccurate assessment of one's spiritual standing before God. The heart represents

72. See Isaac Kahwa Mbabazi, *The Significance of Interpersonal Forgiveness in the Gospel of Matthew* (Eugene, OR: Pickwick, 2013), Kindle edition, ch. 5, "The Rhetoric of Interpersonal Forgiveness in Matt 6:9–15."

the core of a person's being, the real inner person. What a person values is driven by the nature of a person's heart (see 5:8, 28). The material possessions that some people value are all subject to the destructive effects of this world. But those who are truly righteous value the greatest treasure in heaven, God himself. One who sets his heart on God sets a healthy trajectory for discipleship.

The eye is the conduit to the heart. When the eye focuses on something of value, it becomes the conduit that fills the heart with what has been focused on.[73] If the eye is fixed on what is good, the heart is filled with the light of God's treasure. But if the eye covets earthly treasure, then the heart will be filled with darkness.[74] Wealth is a rival god, and Satan uses greed and covetousness to ensnare people in idolatry. So, Jesus calls his disciples to make a choice: to love, serve and devote themselves completely to God, or be mastered by Satan.

#### *4.4.8.2 Choose Your Provider: God or Worry (6:25–34)*

If God is going to be the Master whom the disciples truly love and serve (6:24), then some implications immediately follow. In particular, this Master will take care of Jesus's disciples' basic needs so that they can give attention to more important issues of life, especially summed up in the expression, "Seek first his kingdom and his righteousness" (6:33).

Worrying is a sign of "little faith," which is not the *absence* of faith but a *deficiency* of faith. Instead of worrying, disciples are to make the kingdom of God the center of their continual, daily priorities. As they pursue this, they will have all of their needs met by their ever-caring, ever-watching heavenly Father.

### 4.4.9 Interpersonal Kingdom Spirituality in Community Relationships (7:1–12)

Jesus now shifts from warning his disciples about their own personal temptations concerning wealth and worry to the temptations that can surface in their relationships with each other. This carries forward his theme about the nature of real kingdom life for his disciples.

#### *4.4.9.1 Judging Others Inappropriately (7:1–5)*

In this context, "judging" refers to setting oneself over others and pronouncing their guilt. Jesus warns his disciples against making their own opinions and their way of doing things the absolute standard. Such judging usurps the place of God, who alone is the judge.

73. See Davies and Allison (*Matthew*, 1:639–41) for discussion of the background. See John H. Elliott, *Introduction, Mesopotamia, and Egypt*, vol. 1 of *Beware the Evil Eye: The Evil Eye in the Bible and the Ancient World*, 4 vols. (Eugene, OR: Cascade, 2015).

74. Hagner, *Matthew 1–13*, 159.

The metaphor of the speck illustrates the hypocrisy of a disciple who thinks he clearly sees the sins of his brother, yet has not seen his own blatantly self-righteous, condemning attitude. Disciples bear the responsibility of helping one another remove sin from each other's lives (cf. 18:15–20). But first they need to examine themselves and receive God's spiritual healing.

### *4.4.9.2 Evaluating Others Appropriately (7:6)*

The opposite problem of hypocritical judgment is naïve acceptance. Jesus warns his disciples not to waste the precious message of the kingdom on those who do not appreciate its value (cf. 13:45–46). "Pearls" symbolize the value of the message of the kingdom of heaven (see on 13:45–46). Something so valuable should not be given to those who have no appreciation for such precious truths; their nature is demonstrated by their rejection of the message of the gospel. Disciples' mistaken zeal for proclaiming the gospel to them may result in ridicule, or worse.

### *4.4.9.3 God's Guidance in Our Relationship to Others (7:7–12)*

Through the divine enablement that is supplied by God as Jesus's disciples pray, they will be able to avoid the extremes of judging and of being gullible. With God's divine enablement, Jesus's disciples are to be merciful and slow to judge, yet wisely discerning and observant. They will be able to see the true character of people and deal with them accordingly (7:1–6). And divine enablement will be supplied as disciples pray (7:7–8).

In the imperatives "ask, seek, knock," Jesus indicates a rising scale of intensity in one's prayers, and points to the persistent manner of life lived before the Father. Jesus's disciples are to ask the Father continually as a manner of life, to be constantly responsible in pursuing God's will, and to maintain an unremitting determination in expecting the Father to answer.

### *4.4.9.4 The Golden Rule (7:12)*

The primary teaching of the Sermon on the Mount is drawing to a close, so Jesus takes the whole way of life in the kingdom to its zenith in one precept: "So in everything, do to others what you would have them do to you, for this sums up the Law and the Prophets" (7:12; Luke 6:31). The maxim is commonly called the "Golden Rule." The Golden Rule summarizes the essence of God's will for his people in the Old Testament, and now provides a summary of God's will for Jesus's disciples. Jesus thus indicates that the discipleship that he inaugurates fulfills the deepest inclination of humans who are created in the image of God.

But whereas other expressions of this saying in the ancient world indicate *ethical aspiration*, Jesus declares that the Golden Rule is the *normative manifestation* of his disciples' kingdom life. The inauguration of kingdom life enables his disciples to live life the way God intended it to be lived. As such the Golden Rule truly "sums up the Law and the Prophets" (7:12; cf. 5:17–20) because it localizes the motivating force for discipleship in the changed heart of the disciples.

### 4.4.10 Warning! With Jesus or Against Him (7:13–27)

The disciples have been the primary object of Jesus's teaching in the Sermon on the Mount (cf. 5:1–2), but throughout he has had an eye on the crowds and religious leaders. He continues to extend an invitation to the crowds to enter the kingdom of heaven, and he continues to caution both his disciples and the crowds about the erroneous leadership of the religious establishment, especially the scribes and the Pharisees (cf. 5:20).

He concludes the Sermon with warnings that are directed to all three groups—there are eternal consequences of the arrival of the kingdom of heaven. He warns his disciples to examine themselves to be sure that they are truly members of the kingdom of heaven, and not simply ones who profess allegiance, because the decision is eternal. He warns the crowds to carefully consider the alternative of following him or following the popular religious leadership, because an eternal destiny is at stake. And he warns the religious establishment, especially the scribes and Pharisees, about their culpability for leading the people in the wrong direction, because there will be eternal repercussions.

In each of the four basic warnings there is a choice to be made—are you with Jesus or against him? There is no middle ground, no other choice, and a decision must be made, because there are eternal consequences.

#### *4.4.10.1 Narrow and Broad Gates and Roads (7:13–14)*

Entrance into the life of the kingdom of heaven is through the narrow gate, that is, through Jesus alone. The "narrow road" indicates the life of discipleship that ensues. Those who follow the example of the religious leaders in seeking outward righteousness and the approval of humans are on the road to destruction—eternal separation from God. Jesus continues to hold open the narrow gate to life in the kingdom of heaven and invites those still outside to embark on a life of following him. But he warns those who choose the wide gate that the popular broad road will lead to destruction.

#### *4.4.10.2 True and False Prophets (7:15–20)*

Disciples should beware of leaders who claim to be sent from God and to speak for him but who give their own message that leads the people astray. The prophet's fruit is his work and life, which will indicate whether his message is consistent with the kingdom life of righteousness. Those who choose Jesus will find the inner source of transformation that will produce the good fruit of life. But those who choose to follow the prophetic voices of this world that hype a promise of life will only take themselves into the fires of hell.

#### *4.4.10.3 True and False Disciples (7:21–23)*

Not only will false prophets enter the community, but some within the community itself will be false disciples. Jesus warns that a verbal confession of Jesus as Lord can mask an unrepentant heart. False disciples may gain power in Jesus's name, but their activities are meaningless because they deceive themselves and other believers with spectacular displays. Jesus says he will condemn false disciples to hell, a judgment only God can make. Jesus calls all to obey the will of his Father and come to Jesus as their only Lord, but also warns all not to chase after spectacular manifestations of spirituality that will result in eternal banishment.

#### *4.4.10.4 Wise and Foolish Builders (7:24–27)*

Jesus closes his sermon with a parable that calls for a decision between him and the religious establishment. He draws a dividing line between him and any other foundation of life. Disciples build their lives on the bedrock of Jesus and his kingdom message, regardless of cultural or religious weather. Like the foolish man, the religious establishment advocated a form of surface righteousness that masked a flimsy foundation of religious hypocrisy. Jesus challenges all to build their lives on him as their solid rock. Otherwise, the pleasant ease of their life will fool them into not preparing for the storms that will come in this life, and which will ultimately wash them away into the desolation of the afterlife.

#### *4.4.10.5 The Reaction of the Crowds (7:28–29)*

The crowd's astonishment indicates a variety of emotional responses to Jesus's words, though not a commitment to his messianic ministry. To obey his command is to come out of the crowd and become his disciple. The amazement of the crowds at his teaching underscores the authority with which Jesus has spoken throughout the Sermon on the Mount, and so the final spotlight is on Jesus himself. Matthew wants his readers to see that Jesus's words have authority because of who he is. But simple amazement is not the same as allegiance to Jesus.

## 4.5 THE AUTHORITATIVE POWER OF MESSIAH: KINGDOM POWER DEMONSTRATED (8:1–9:38)

The Sermon on the Mount and the two subsequent chapters are sandwiched between two almost identical summaries of Jesus's ministry of preaching, teaching, and healing (cf. 4:23–25 and 9:35–36). Those summaries are called a literary *inclusio* because, like two bookends, they set off the material between them. This leads many to the conclusion that the Sermon on the Mount and the chapters of Jesus's miracles form a literary diptych, or double panel, of the ministry of Jesus. So, Matthew brings together several miracle stories to show that Jesus not only has a great messianic message, but also has a great messianic mission.[75] Jesus is not only Messiah in Word (chs. 5–7) but is also Messiah at Work in his miraculous deeds (chs. 8–9). These miracles demonstrate that the kingdom of God has arrived in the messianic ministry of Jesus.[76]

The miracles as they are found in chapters 8–9 are not in the chronological order followed by standard harmonies of Jesus's life.[77] This is an indication that Matthew had theological purposes in mind as he gathered these miracle stories together in one place. As is typical of Matthew's emphasis, this arrangement highlights both authoritative Christology and discipleship. Each miracle highlights particular aspects of Jesus's person and mission as the central figure of the narrative, and then the sayings clarify how discipleship to Jesus demands an allegiance to him and his calling that is strikingly different from other extant forms of discipleship in the ancient world.[78]

### 4.5.1 Healing the Marginalized (8:1–17)

In three brief scenes, Matthew demonstrates how Jesus's messianic ministry brings restoration to people who were often marginalized within Jewish culture: lepers (8:1–4), gentiles (8:5–13), and women (8:14–15). In this way Jesus breaks down purity, ethnic, and gender barriers so that all may respond to his invitation to the kingdom of heaven.

#### *4.5.1.1 Purity Boundaries (8:1–4)*

The first miracle is cleansing the leper, transcending purity boundaries. Instead of causing Jesus to become unclean himself, Jesus's touch brings healing and ritual cleansing. Jesus instructs the man to fulfill the law required for lepers to reenter society (Lev 14:57).

#### *4.5.1.2 Ethnic Boundaries (8:5–13)*

The second miracle is the healing of the gentile centurion's servant, transcending ethnic boundaries. The centurion displays exemplary faith in Jesus, recognizing Jesus to be the messianic deliverer who can heal on the authority of his word alone. This faith results in his servant's healing. This faith is what Israel lacked. Gentile peoples across the world who believe in Jesus will join Israel's patriarchs in ultimate celebration

75. Evert-Jan Vledder, *Conflict in the Miracle Stories: A Socio-Exegetical Study of Matthew 8 and 9*, JSNTSup 152 (Sheffield: Sheffield Academic, 1997.

76. For an overview of Matthew's perspective of Jesus's miracles, with special reference to Matthew 8–9, see Graham H. Twelftree, *Jesus the Miracle Worker: A Historical and Theological Study* (Downers Grove. IL: InterVarsity, 1999), 102–24; Walter T. Wilson, *Healing in the Gospel of Matthew: Reflections on Method and Ministry* (Minneapolis: Fortress, 2014). And more broadly, Craig S. Keener, *Miracles: The Credibility of the New Testament Accounts*, 2 vols. (Grand Rapids: Baker Academic, 2011).

77. E.g., Thomas and Gundry, *NIV Harmony*, 22–26.

78. For a similar understanding see Blomberg, *Matthew*, 136–37.

in the kingdom of heaven (cf. Isa 25:6–9; 56:3–8). But the original "subjects of the kingdom"—descendants of the patriarchs—will lose their place and face judgment unless they follow the path of faith that the centurion has exemplified.[79]

#### *4.5.1.3 Gender Boundaries (8:14–17)*

The third miracle involves Peter's mother-in-law. She was in the throes of a severe, feverish illness, and Jesus heals her with a simple touch. Jesus's personal presence commands authority over this diseased-ravaged world. By Jesus healing her and receiving her service, gender boundaries of discipleship are transcended.[80]

### 4.5.2 Expected Discipleship Disappointed (8:18–22)

The following incident is a special scene in Matthew's Gospel, reflecting an early stage of the Jesus movement where two individuals come forward, already apparently Jesus's disciples but deficient in their understanding of what exactly discipleship to Jesus entails.[81]

The first is a teacher of the law who wants to attach himself to Jesus to further his professional ambition. Jesus's response clarifies that his ministry as the Son of Man will not result in the comforts of an institutional establishment.

The second is an early follower of Jesus with mixed priorities. Jesus elevates his call to "follow me" above all other allegiances. Those who would follow must set aside anything that gets in the way of total commitment to him and the new family of faith he is creating. This demands wise thinking. Jesus's disciples must continue to be guided by God's mandate to honor their parents, but the supremacy of Jesus as their Master must always be heeded.[82] This was a typical struggle in that culture, trying to balance responsibility to family with commitment to God, because on several occasions Jesus challenges the crowd and even his own disciples not to have any family commitment take priority over commitment to him (10:37–39; Luke 14:25–26).[83]

### 4.5.3 Overpowering Satan's Strongholds (8:23–9:8)

Jesus continues to invade and overpower three of Satan's primary strongholds.[84]

---

79. See J. Paul Tanner, "The 'Outer Darkness' in Matthew's Gospel: Shedding Light on an Ominous Warning," *BSac* 174 (2017): 445–59.

80. Warren Carter, "The Disciples," in Keith and Hurtado, *Jesus Among Friends and Enemies*, 81–102, esp. 84–86.

81. Jack Dean Kingsbury, "On Following Jesus: The 'Eager' Scribe and the 'Reluctant' Disciple (Matthew 8.18–22)," *NTS* 34 (1988): 47–52, esp. 49.

82. See Hagner, *Matthew 1–13*, 218.

83. For discussion of the social setting, see Joseph H. Hellerman, *The Ancient Church as Family* (Minneapolis: Fortress, 2001), 72–73.

84. Douglas Sean O'Donnell, *Matthew: All Authority in Heaven and on Earth*, Preaching the Word (Wheaton, IL: Crossway, 2013), 221–29. O'Donnell focuses on the first two; I include the third as Jesus overpowers three of Satan's primary strongholds.

#### *4.5.3.1 Authority over Nature (8:23–27)*

The disciples fear for their lives in the storm but turn to Jesus as "Lord" to save them. Their "little faith" is a deficiency in understanding and trusting completely who Jesus is. Jesus calls them to better understand who he is and to act upon it. He commands the winds and the waves with a "rebuke," in the same way that God "rebukes" the sea in the Old Testament and demonstrates his sovereign control over all of nature (2 Sam 22:16; Ps 18:15). The disciples are increasing in their understanding of who Jesus is, but still do not fully grasp his true nature.

#### *4.5.3.2 Authority over the Spirit World (8:28–34)*

Jesus and his disciples enter gentile territory and are met with two violently demon-possessed men. The demons immediately recognize Jesus's true identity as the Son of God. They know that their stronghold is being invaded, even though it is not yet time for God's final judgment over Satan's forces. The request of the demons to enter the pigs has an added sinister purpose. Demons are known to cause injury and pain to God's creatures (e.g., 17:14–20), and they do whatever they can to stimulate opposition to Jesus and his invasion of Satan's stronghold. Jesus allows the demons to escape destruction when he frees the two men, but it costs the gentile town the loss of a large herd of pigs being raised for market. The townspeople push Jesus away, valuing their pigs more than their own people.

#### *4.5.3.3 Authority over Sin (9:1–8)*

Having heard of his supernatural ability to heal, some people bring to him a paralyzed man. Jesus forgives the paralyzed man's sins, and the scribes immediately accuse Jesus of blasphemy—dishonoring God by taking upon himself the prerogative of God, because forgiving sins is something only God can do. Jesus argues that it is easier to pronounce forgiveness of sins than to heal because there is no visible way to confirm it. Jesus's claim to have authority on earth to forgive sins is tantamount to claiming his deity, and Jesus backs this claim with the hard evidence of healing.

### 4.5.4 Unexpected Discipleship Revealed (9:9–17)

Jesus's messianic mission has not unfolded as many may have expected.

#### *4.5.4.1 Calling Matthew and Other Sinners (9:9–13)*

Jesus has a meal with Matthew and other tax collectors. Also included at the dinner are "sinners." Sinners were people who lived a lifestyle disobedient to the will of God, especially in the eyes of law-abiding Jews like the Pharisees.[85] The Pharisees consider

85. For background to the various uses of "sinner" in the Gospels, see Michael J. Wilkins, "Sinner," *DJG*[1] 757–60; Keener, *Matthew* (2009), 294–96.

themselves to be "healthy" before God because of their self-righteousness, but they are blind to their real sinfulness before God. Jesus's merciful offer of salvation and fellowship to the sinfully sick like tax collectors and sinners threatens the Pharisees' way of life, yet this is the core of Jesus's mission.[86]

#### *4.5.4.2 Discipleship and Religious Traditions (9:14–17)*

Jesus alludes to himself as Israel's divine bridegroom of the Old Testament, Yahweh (cf. Isa 62:5; Hos 2:19–20).[87] The arrival of the kingdom of heaven in Jesus fulfills the Old Testament promises to Israel, which is cause for rejoicing. It is therefore not an appropriate time to fast. Jesus has not come to patch up traditional practices of righteousness within religious Judaism; rather, he has come to offer real growth in kingdom righteousness. Just as new forms are needed for the new wine of the kingdom, new practices are needed for the new life of discipleship to Jesus.

### 4.5.5 Unexpected Miracles Demonstrate Extraordinary Compassion (9:18–34)

Although it astounds the crowds and provokes opposition from the religious establishment, the unexpected nature of Jesus's messianic mission will model for his disciples how compassion for the harassed and helpless should compel them to minister to the crowds with the gospel and power of the kingdom of heaven (9:35–38).

#### *4.5.5.1 The Dead Have Life (9:18–26)*

A synagogue leader humbles himself before Jesus with an incredible request: to raise his dead daughter to life. Not only does he recognize Jesus's authority, but he also demonstrates profound faith in Jesus, since Jesus has not yet raised anyone from the dead in his ministry (9:18–19).

As Jesus follows the synagogue leader to his home, a woman approaches him with a disease in which the menstrual flow is abnormally prolonged and causes anemia. Through healing her, Jesus removes the public stigma of her disease, facilitating her reentry into the life of the community (9:20–22).[88]

At the home of the synagogue leader, Jesus sends away the funeral mourners and brings the girl to life with a touch. Touching a corpse rendered a person ritually unclean for seven days (Num 19:11–21). Jesus's touch, however, makes the unclean clean (Matt 9:23–26).

86. Benjamin J. Ribbens, "Whose 'Mercy'? What 'Sacrifice'? A Proposed Reading of Matthew's Hosea 6:6 Quotations," *BBR* 28.3 (2018): 381–404.

87. Phillip J. Long, *Jesus the Bridegroom: The Origin of the Eschatological Feast as a Wedding Banquet in the Synoptic Gospels* (Eugene, OR: Wipf & Stock, 2013).

88. Keener, *Matthew* (2009), 301–5.

### *4.5.5.2 The Blind Have Sight (9:27–31)*

Two blind men follow Jesus, calling him the "Son of David," a reference to the promise of the messianic deliverer from David's line whose kingdom would have no end and whose coming would bring healing to the blind (cf. Isa 29:18; 35:5). Blindness was one of the grimmest maladies in the ancient world and considered to be only a little less serious than being dead, primarily because there was no known cure and because of the severe hardship that it placed upon the blind person and family.[89] But these blind men see Jesus's true identity and are the first to call Jesus by the title "Son of David."[90] By contrast, the Pharisees are spiritually blind and cannot see that God is doing something unique in Israel through Jesus. Lacking eyes of faith, they attribute Jesus's power to the devil (9:32–34).

### *4.5.5.3 The Mute Have Voice (9:32–34)*

The third and final miracle in these collections of miracle stories involved both healing and exorcism. The exorcism of the demon and the concurrent healing of muteness is one of the most powerful demonstrations that the kingdom of heaven has finally arrived. It is the sign that the crowd understands to be unique in the history of Israel (9:33).

But without eyes of faith, the religious leaders cannot see beyond their parochial experience to recognize that God is doing something unique in Israel in the word and work of Jesus's inauguration of the kingdom of heaven. So, they gather their opposition to Jesus, both protecting their religious domain and thinking that they are protecting the people from Jesus. The teachers of the law have accused Jesus of blasphemy (9:3), and now the Pharisees make the accusation that Jesus casts out demons by the "prince of demons." They will reiterate that charge later where they will identify him as Beelzebul (see 12:24–48).

## 4.5.6 The Messiah at Work Enlists Workers (9:35–38)

As he continues his teaching and healing ministry through Galilee, Jesus is moved with compassion on the crowds because the Jewish religious leaders have failed to give proper spiritual care for the people's tremendous needs. Suffering under Roman oppression and the difficulties of daily life, they are like harassed sheep. But they are also like a bountiful harvest in need of harvesters.

89. Twelftree, *Jesus the Miracle Worker*, 83–84.

90. Cf. Wayne S. Baxter, "Healing and the 'Son of David': Matthew's Warrant," *NovT* 48.1 (2006): 36–50; Jiří Dvořáček, *The Son of David in Matthew's Gospel in the Light of the Solomon as Exorcist Tradition*, WUNT 2/415 (Tübingen: Mohr Siebeck, 2016); H. Daniel Zacharias, *Matthew's Presentation of the Son of David: Davidic Tradition and Typology in the Gospel of Matthew*, T&T Clark Biblical Studies (London: Bloomsbury T&T Clark, 2017), 81–82.

# 4.6 The Authoritative Mission of Messiah's Messengers (10:1–42)

## *Second Discourse: "The Mission Mandate"*

After Jesus tells his disciples to pray to the "Lord of the harvest" for workers (9:38), he himself answers their prayer by calling the Twelve to embark on their mission. As the *twelve disciples* (10:1), they will embark on a mission to Israel during Jesus's earthly ministry. Yet as the *twelve apostles* (10:2), they will extend the mission to include gentiles.[91]

### 4.6.1 The Mandate to the Twelve Disciples/Apostles (10:1–4)

The term *apostle* has a significantly different meaning than the word *disciple. Disciple* is the term used to designate all those who have believed in Jesus, while the title *apostle* designates those who have been commissioned to be his representatives. This is a clue to the role of the Twelve. As disciples, the Twelve are the examples of what Jesus accomplishes in all believers; as apostles, the Twelve are set aside as the leaders within the new movement. Therefore, this mission discourse is directed to all disciples/ believers, with special instructions for leaders.

In this second of Jesus's discourses, the Mission Mandate, Matthew provides us with a crucial collection of Jesus's instructions for "mission-driven disciples." The discourse describes how Jesus's disciples (then and now) are to go out to share and live the message of the gospel of the kingdom of heaven in an alien and often hostile world.

### 4.6.2 Instructions for the Short-Term Mission to Israel (10:5–15)

In the instructions to the disciples/apostles, Jesus focuses first on their short-term mission to Israel during Jesus's earthly ministry. Jesus prohibits the Twelve from going to gentiles or Samaritans on this short-term mission. They are to restrict their outreach to the lost sheep of the house of Israel. This demonstrates that Jesus's coming as the Messiah fulfills the promises given to Israel and accomplishes God's initial program of salvation.[92]

As the Twelve go out, their mission will replicate Jesus's own mission. The power of the missionary disciples to perform miraculous works is an extension of Jesus's own

91. Eckhard J. Schnabel, *Early Christian Mission* (Downers Grove, IL: InterVarsity, 2004), 1:263–315; Jostein Ådna, "The Mission to Israel and the Nations: The Understanding of Mission in the Gospel of Matthew Reconsidered," in Aune and Hvalvik, *Church and Its Mission*, 45–60; and Matthias Konradt, *Israel, Church and the Gentiles in the Gospel of Matthew*, trans. Kathleen Ess, BMSSEC (Waco, TX: Baylor University Press, 2014), 74–87.

92. J. Julius Scott, "Gentiles and the Ministry of Jesus: Further Observations on Matt. 10:5–6; 15:21–28," *JETS* 33.2 (1990): 161–69; Ådna, "Mission to Israel and the Nations," 45–60. For background on the relations between Jews and Samaritans, see Gary N. Knoppers, *Jews and Samaritans: The Origins and History of Their Early Relations* (Oxford: Oxford University Press, 2013); in the NT era, esp. 220–39.

power. The disciples received the gift of the kingdom of heaven freely from Jesus, so they must likewise share the good news of the kingdom freely with the lost sheep of Israel.

Support for their mission is the responsibility of those who receive their ministry.[93] A worthy person (10:11–13) is someone who responds positively to the message proclaimed by the disciples. Those individuals, homes, or cities that receive the greeting of peace recognize the Twelve as emissaries of God.[94]

When Jesus instructs the Twelve (10:14–15) to "shake off dust from [their] feet" when they leave a house or town that refuses to listen to their message, this is a sign that they have completely removed from themselves the uncleanness of unrepentant people. The act symbolizes judgment on those rejecting the kingdom message.[95]

### 4.6.3 Instructions for the Long-Term Mission to the World (10:16–23)

With verse 16, Jesus's commissioning begins to change—now the disciples are the sheep among wolves; he switches from present to future tense; and he warns them of the persecution that missionary disciples will endure as they witness to gentiles. These changes indicate that Jesus was not only giving instructions for the short-term mission to Israel during Jesus's earthly ministry (10:5–15), but he is also giving them instructions for the long-term mission to Jews and gentiles throughout this age.[96]

And it also indicates that persecution will come throughout this age while they proclaim the gospel of the kingdom. But Jesus promises that the Spirit, the empowering force in Jesus's own life, will speak through his disciples in the moment of their most difficult opposition, and they will experience the fullness of the kingdom's salvation.

As Jesus comforts the missionary disciples, he obliquely comforts Israel as well: "Truly I tell you, you will not finish going through the towns of Israel before the Son of Man comes" (10:23). "Matthew views the mission to Israel as still incomplete."[97] Jesus's statement indicates that there will be a continuing mission to Israel alongside the mission to the gentiles until Jesus returns at the end of this age (see on 28:18–20).[98]

93. See Eugene Eung-Chun Park, "Cynic Itinerant Philosophers and Galilean Wandering Missionaries in Matthew," in *Reading a Tendentious Bible: Essays in Honor of Robert B. Coote*, ed. Marvin L. Chaney, Uriah Y. Kim, and Annette Schellenberg, Hebrew Bible Monographs 66 (Sheffield: Sheffield Pheonix, 2014), 125–39.

94. Osborne, *Matthew*, 379–81.

95. Turner, *Matthew*, 271–72.

96. Cf. Osborne, *Matthew*, 386–87.

97. Evans, *Matthew*, 224.

98. Hans Kvalbein, "Has Matthew Abandoned the Jews? A Contribution to a Disputed Issue in Recent Scholarship," in *The Mission of the Early Church to Jews and Gentiles*, ed. Jostein Ådna and Hans Kvalbein, WUNT 127 (Tübingen: Mohr Siebeck, 2000), 45–62. See also Konradt, *Israel, Church and the Gentiles*, 74–87; Blomberg, *Matthew*, 176; Davies and Allison, *Matthew*, 2:189–90; Keener, *Matthew* (2009), 324–25; Nolland, *Matthew*, 428–29; David L. Turner, *Israel's Last Prophet: Jesus and the Jewish Leaders in Matthew 23* (Minneapolis: Fortress, 2015), 193–95.

### 4.6.4 Characteristics of Missionary Disciples (10:24–42)

As Jesus concludes prophesying about the worldwide mission, he gives instructions about the characteristics of true missionary disciples in 10:24–42, which has relevance for disciples at all times in history. First, we should expect to be treated in the same way that Jesus was treated. If he was wrongly accused, we can expect to be also (10:24–25). Second, do not fear. If the heavenly Father gives constant supervision to insignificant creatures such as sparrows, surely he will also care for every need of missionary disciples (10:26–31). Third, do not deny your allegiance to Jesus. The easiest way to avoid persecution would be to deny Jesus. Jesus calls us to courageously declare our allegiance to him (10:32–33). Fourth, we must expect division in our own families from those who deny Jesus (10:34–37). Fifth, continually take up the cross. The cross was the Father's will for the Son's life, and speaking metaphorically, Jesus declares that to take up our cross means to take up God's will for our lives and continually experience the new life that discipleship to Jesus promises (10:38–39). Finally, to receive Jesus's disciples is to receive Jesus himself, because we go out with Jesus's message and authority (10:40–42).

## 4.7 OPPOSITION TO THE MESSIAH EMERGES (11:1–12:50)

### 4.7.1 John the Baptist and Jesus (11:1–15)

As the months go by, all does not seem to be unfolding as John the Baptist may have expected.[99]

#### *4.7.1.1 John the Baptist Questions Jesus (11:2–6)*

John the Baptist does not oppose Jesus, but he apparently has begun to question whether Jesus is "the one who is to come" (11:3). John had expected the Coming One to bring blessing on those who repented and judgment on those who did not. Instead, John lies in prison awaiting execution for publicly challenging the morality of Herod Antipas (cf. Matt 14). Having been imprisoned at Antipas's fortress of Machaerus for a year or more, John sends his disciples to try to find out whether Jesus really is the Messiah. John needed to have his understanding of the messianic program reconfirmed.[100]

Jesus replies that his ministry should be clear proof of his identity. His works fulfill Isaiah's prophecies that the promised Messiah's miraculous ministry would cause the blind to see, the lame to walk, leprosy to be cured, the deaf to hear, and the dead to be raised (11:4–5).[101] And the good news is preached to the poor. Jesus's ministry should

99. See Donald J. Verseput, *The Rejection of the Humble Messianic King: A Study of the Composition of Matthew 11–12*, European University Studies 291 (Frankfurt am Main: Peter Lang, 1986).

100. Witherington, *Christology of Jesus*, 43.

101. Craig S. Keener, "'The Dead are Raised' (Matthew 11:5 // Luke 7:22): Resuscitation Accounts in the Gospels and Eyewitness Testimony," *BBR* 25.1 (2015): 55–79.

be proof that he is the Messiah, which is a mild rebuke of John (11:20–24; cf. John 3:31–36; 5:25–35). John and his disciples must use eyes of faith to recognize Jesus's messianic identity.

#### *4.7.1.2 Jesus's Tribute to John the Baptist (11:7–19)*

In these next verses, we see the complexity of God's plan of redemption. John was greater than any Old Testament prophet because he had the privilege of preparing the way for the Messiah and the kingdom of heaven. Yet, John is a transitional figure. He prepared the way for the Coming One, but the implication is that he will not live to see and experience the full arrival of the kingdom's establishment.[102]

Jesus's institution of the new covenant in his blood, which is poured out for the forgiveness of sin, is a dividing line. Jesus's crucifixion, resurrection, ascension and sending of the Spirit at Pentecost brings the arrival of the kingdom's redemptive life. But John will be executed before the arrival of those events. John is the greatest of those born during the Old Testament era because of his crucial role in preparing the way for the Messiah and his kingdom. John's mission was great because of the greatness of the One he introduced. But those in the kingdom of heaven are greater because of their privilege to have actually entered the kingdom of heaven. Even the least in the kingdom of heaven can point to Jesus as the messianic deliverer more clearly than John. And the least in the kingdom of heaven have experienced firsthand the forgiveness of their sins and the transformation of regeneration by the Spirit that characterizes this age.[103]

### 4.7.2 The Privileged Unrepentant Cities (11:20–24)

Then Jesus turns to condemn the Galilean cities of Chorazin, Bethsaida, and Capernaum because they have rejected Jesus's mission. The people in these towns have witnessed most of Jesus's miracles, but they have not repented. Then surprisingly, Jesus indicates that the pagan, gentile cities of Tyre and Sidon, and even the proverbial city of sin, Sodom, would have repented had they witnessed what these Jewish towns have seen. Had they received the privilege of witnessing Jesus's miracles firsthand, they would have been gripped by the gospel and repented. So, the privileged Jewish cities stand condemned.

102. The majority of interpreters follow this reasoning, including Blomberg, *Matthew*, 187; Carson, "Matthew," 306–7; R. T. France, *Matthew: An Introduction and Commentary*, TNTC 1 (Downers Grove, IL: InterVarsity Press, 1985), 194–95; Hagner, *Matthew 1–13*, 305–6; Morris, *Matthew*, 280–81.

103. For recent discussion that encodes both phrases as indicting Herod Antipas, see Matthew W. Bates, "Cryptic Codes and a Violent King: A New Proposal for Matthew 11:12 and Luke 16:16–18," *CBQ* 75.1 (2013): 74–93. See also Blomberg, *Matthew*, 187–88; Davies and Allison, *Matthew*, 2:256; France, *Matthew*, NICNT, 195–96; Hagner, *Matthew 1–13*, 306–7, Morris, *Matthew*, 281–82; Witherington, *Matthew*, 233–34.

## 4.7.3 An Invitation to a Relationship with the Father and the Son (11:25–30)

We now come to one of the most theologically powerful passages in Matthew's Gospel. Jesus indicates that in both his incarnate and eternal state, Jesus and the Father *know* each other in an exclusive way, which in biblical language means that they experience an exclusive relationship. For Jesus, the Father is "my Father." They enjoy a direct, intuitive, and immediate knowledge that is grounded in their relationship as Father and Son. And this implies powerfully that this is *divine knowledge*. What the Father and the Son share stands apart from all human relationships and all human knowledge.

Jesus then goes on to state that although the Son knows the Father in an exclusive way, all those who come to Jesus can know the Father as well. This entails taking on Jesus's yoke of discipleship, which promises rest from the burden of religious regulation and human oppression. Discipleship to Jesus brings relief from the burden of Pharisaic regulations, but it is not lawlessness. He says, "For my yoke is easy and my burden is light" (11:30). The two clauses are in synonymous parallelism to emphasize Jesus's way of discipleship. Discipleship to Jesus is an easy or serviceable yoke because his teaching equips us most effectively to live out God's will in the way that life was designed by God to be lived. And further, discipleship to Jesus is not the oppressive burden of Pharisaic legalism (23:4), but instead turns the load of life into one that is manageable (cf. Gal 6:5). Discipleship to Jesus is not essentially a religious obligation.[104] Our discipleship to Jesus is an intimate relationship with the One who calls (11:28–29).

## 4.7.4 Confrontations with the Pharisees Regarding the Sabbath (12:1–14)

The scribes and the Pharisees are convinced that Jesus's ministry is not from God. So out of their self-deceived sense of duty to protect the people, they set out to trap Jesus into being condemned of outright, flagrant violations of the Law.

They first focus on violations of the Sabbath.[105] Along with circumcision and dietary laws, practicing the Sabbath was one of the most distinctive characteristics of the Jewish

104. Huub van de Sandt, "Matthew 11,28–30: Compassionate Law Interpretation in Wisdom Language," in Senior, *The Gospel of Matthew at the Crossroads*, 313–37. Contra Matthew W. Mitchell, "The Yoke Is Easy, but What of Its Meaning? A Methodological Reflection Masquerading as a Philological Discussion of Matthew 11:30," *JBL* 135.2 (2016): 321–40, who suggests, "That the yoke, a biblical and ancient Near Eastern symbol of servitude and subservience, is a symbol of religious obligation and commitment in Matthew seems uncontestable" (339).

105. For a helpful study that verifies the historicity and clarifies the meaning of Jesus's actions on the Sabbath, see Michael H. Burer, *Divine Sabbath Work*, BBRSup 5 (Winona Lake, IN: Eisenbrauns, 2012). For the relevance of the Sabbath for contemporary Christians, see Christopher John Donato, ed., *Perspectives on the Sabbath: Four Views* (Nashville: B&H, 2011).

people. God had instituted the Sabbath as a day of rest and holiness, so he gave the Israelites the commandment that no work was to be performed on the Sabbath. The Pharisees' interpretation of this commandment gave rise to an extensive set of oral laws to keep people from violating the Sabbath.

When the Pharisees see Jesus's disciples picking some grain to eat, they accuse them of breaking the law. One later rabbinic ruling stated that there were thirty-nine main classes of work that were prohibited on the Sabbath, among them, "sowing, ploughing, reaping, binding sheaves, threshing, winnowing, cleansing crops, grinding, sifting" (m. Shabbat 7:2). The disciples could have been guilty of several of these in the eyes of the Pharisees as they plucked grain heads, separated the chaff from the grain, and ground the grain in their hands to prepare it to eat.[106]

Jesus uses the Old Testament to clear his disciples from the Pharisees' charge. Twelve loaves of bread were prepared for the tabernacle on each Sabbath as an offering. This consecrated bread was to be eaten only by the priests (Lev 24:5–9). However, Scripture did not condemn David for eating the bread during his escape from Saul.

God intended the law to serve his people, not for people to serve the law. Jesus's response to the Pharisees takes the argument one step further by quoting a second time from Hosea 6:6 (cf. Matt 9:13): "If you had known what these words mean, 'I desire mercy, not sacrifice,' you would not have condemned the innocent" (12:7). Out of his great mercy, God instituted the Sabbath to give his creatures rest from daily burdens. If the Pharisees had truly understood God's law, they ought to have extended mercy, not demanded more sacrifice.[107] Jesus does not challenge the Sabbath law itself but the Pharisees' interpretation of it. Jesus reminds the Pharisees and Jesus's disciples that it is his interpretation of the Law that goes to the intent and motive of God's giving the Law.[108]

### 4.7.5 God's Spirit-Anointed Servant (12:15–21)

In another fulfillment quotation from Isaiah, Matthew shows that Jesus's actions prove his messianic identity: Jesus is the gentle, Spirit-endowed, suffering servant, the one chosen by God to advance God's mission of justice to the nations (Isa 42:1–4). Jesus "proclaims justice" through his message of the arrival of the kingdom of heaven, which is a humble invitation to the harassed and helpless people, as well as a sentence of judgment on the rulers of this world.

106. Keener, *Matthew* (2009), 351–54.

107. For theological significance see Yong-Eui Yang, *Jesus and the Sabbath in Matthew's Gospel*, JSNTSup 139 (Sheffield: Sheffield Academic, 1997), 305–6. Somewhat differently, see Ribbens, "Whose 'Mercy'? What 'Sacrifice'?," 381–404.

108. Nicholas Perrin, *Jesus the Temple* (Grand Rapids: Baker Academic, 2010), 60–61. For a helpful discussion that does not give a solid conclusion, see Eyal Regev, *The Temple in Early Christianity: Experiencing the Sacred*, AYBRL (New Haven, CT: Yale University Press, 2019), esp. 176–99.

### 4.7.6 Confrontations with the Pharisees over the Source of Jesus's Miraculous Power (12:22–29)

When Jesus exorcises a man blind and mute from demon-possession, the exorcism causes the man to be healed. The people watching are amazed, wondering if the messianic Son of David they assumed would be a mighty warrior could be this gentle healer.[109]

The power of the Spirit of God in battling Satan's demons tangibly confirms the arrival of the kingdom of God through Jesus. Jesus has bound Satan, the "strong man," by inaugurating the kingdom and is now "plundering his house" by setting the demon-possessed free. The eschatological victory of the kingdom of God is now manifested in Jesus's exorcisms.[110] And drawing further on Matthew's reference to Isaiah's servant (Matt 12:18), Jesus is "empowered by the Spirit for a ministry of mercy and justice to bring about Israel's restoration and consequently (and subsequently) the inclusion of the nations."[111]

### 4.7.7 Jesus on Offense (12:30–45)

There is no middle ground with Jesus: either he is the Messiah, or he is not. To attribute to Satan what is accomplished by the power of the Spirit of God through Jesus Messiah is to commit the sin of blasphemy. Blasphemy involves flagrant, willful, persistent rejection of the work of the Spirit of God. The Pharisees attempt to hide their own blasphemy by calling Jesus a blasphemer. But Jesus reveals their true colors: they blaspheme the Spirit because their hearts are evil.[112]

The unpardonable sin is not one flippant transgression. Rather it is a heart sin of unchangeable rejection whereby the Jewish leaders rejected the ministry of the Holy Spirit in their lives. This sin can be committed only by non-believers who consciously and willfully reject the ministry of the Holy Spirit bearing witness to the reality of Jesus as the Savior and leading them to salvation. By yielding to the Spirit's convicting work a person can be led to repentance. But to reject continually the Spirit's work will result in a person never being able to reach that point. Ultimately, once a person has either hardened his or her heart to an irretrievable point in this life or has died without repenting, the chance for forgiveness has passed.

---

109. See Baxter, "Healing and the 'Son of David,'" 36–50; Zacharias, *Matthew's Presentation of the Son of David*, 83–84.

110. Jesse P. Nickel, "Jesus, the Isaianic Servant Exorcist: Exploring the Significance of Matthew 12:18–21 in the Beelzebul Pericope," *ZNW* 107.2 (2016): 170–85. For one who argues that Jesus's main role is to "bring justice" in the Matthean Isaiah reference, see Elizabeth R. Hayes, "The One Who Brings Justice: Conceptualizing the Role of 'The Servant' in Isaiah 42:1–4 and Matthew 12:15–21," in *Let Us Go Up to Zion: Essays in Honour of H. G. M. Williamson on the Occasion of His Sixty-Fifth Birthday*, ed. Iain Provan and Mark Boda, VTSup 153 (Leiden: Brill, 2012), 143–52.

111. Jeannine K. Brown, "Matthew's Christology and Isaiah's Servant: A Fresh Look at a Perennial Issue," in *Treasures New & Old: Essays in Honor of Donald A. Hagner*, ed. Carl S. Sweatman and Clifford B. Kvidahl, GlossaHouse Festschrift Series 1 (Wilmore, KY: GlossaHouse, 2018), 93–106; here 101.

112. For background, see Michael P. Knowles, "Serpents, Scribes, and Pharisees," *JBL* 133.1 (2014): 165–78.

### 4.7.8 Jesus's Disciples Are His True Family (12:46–50)

Jesus will not be deterred from his messianic mission, even if it means disrupting biological loyalties. Jesus is not abolishing biological family ties but is demonstrating the priority of a person's commitment to him and the kingdom of heaven. He is establishing a new spiritual family of disciples in relationship to him and to the Father.

Jesus specifies the central feature that creates and characterizes his spiritual family: "For whoever does the will of my Father in heaven is my brother and sister and mother" (12:49–50). The theme of "doing the will of the heavenly Father" is a motif that runs throughout Matthew's Gospel and reflects deep Jewish roots (cf. 6:10; 7:21; 18:14; 21:31; 26:42).[113] Jesus declares that whoever has obeyed his call to enter the kingdom of heaven and has become his disciple is part of the new family of God. The will of the Father means obedience to the call to the kingdom of heaven that will result in true righteousness. A person's genealogical relationship to Israel did not guarantee a place in the kingdom of heaven, and neither does a person's family relationship. Each individual must respond to the will of the Father and obey Jesus's call to the kingdom and become his disciple.

The implication of this individual responsibility is that Jesus intentionally broadens the gender references to include women as his disciples by not only referring to mother and brother, but by bringing in "sister" as well.[114] For the first explicit time, Jesus indicates that his message and ministry initiates a unique form of discipleship. Within Judaism at that time, especially among the rabbis, only men could become a disciple of a rabbi and study Torah.

But with Jesus, any person—woman or man, young or old, gentile or Jew—who responds to the gospel of the kingdom and believes on Jesus for eternal life is his disciple. Therefore, discipleship to Jesus is not to be defined by rabbinic models, but in relationship to Jesus, which means obedience to the will of the Father.[115] This is the hallmark of Jesus's disciples, whatever the family, whatever the gender.

## 4.8 MYSTERIES OF THE MESSIANIC KINGDOM REVEALED IN PARABLES (13:1–58)

### *THIRD DISCOURSE: "PARABOLIC DISCLOSURES"*

Jesus is now more than halfway through his earthly ministry. He has developed a significant following of disciples. And Matthew has shown that an increasing number of

113. Senior, *Matthew*, 145.
114. Hagner, *Matthew 1–13*, 360.
115. See Michael J. Wilkins, "Women in the Teaching and Example of Jesus," in *Women and Men in Ministry: A Complementary Perspective*, ed. Robert L. Saucy and Judith K. TenElshof (Chicago: Moody, 2001), 91–112.

religious leaders are gathering in their opposition to Jesus. But here we will see that there is still a large group, the crowds, who have not yet made a decision either for or against him. So, Jesus employs an important spiritual communicative tool—the parable—that will test the hearts of hearers to display whether they are with Jesus, or against him.

This is not the first time that Jesus has spoken in parables (see e.g., 7:1–27; 9:15–17), but now it becomes a significant tool to teach and to test.[116] Underlying the term "parable" is the Hebrew *mašal*, which refers to a wide spectrum of ideas that are based on comparison or analogy.[117] As used by Jesus, the parable is a way of communicating truth through a narrative analogy in the service of moral or spiritual argument.

This is the third discourse of Jesus that Matthew has collected in his Gospel—the Parabolic Disclosures (ch. 13). The Parabolic Disclosures develop what it means to be "clandestine-kingdom disciples." The kingdom of heaven is not here in an overtly powerful way, so Matthew wants to emphasize for his readers then and now that Jesus's disciples will not externally look that much different from the world around them, but internally they have been radically impacted by the arrival of the kingdom of heaven.

Through these parables Jesus reveals to his disciples the secrets of the kingdom of heaven, making known that during this age the kingdom will exist in a hidden form. It will be an undercover kingdom, not the overpowering political, militaristic, and dominant cultural manifestation of God's rule that many expected (13:31–33). So, the parables reveal what it means for Jesus's disciples to live as kingdom subjects in a world that has not yet experienced the fully consummated kingdom of heaven.

### 4.8.1 The Parable of the Sower and the Soils (13:3b–9)

Jesus begins with a story about agriculture. But it is actually a parable about the operation of the kingdom of heaven in this world. The emphasis in this parable is on the seed, which is the message of the kingdom, and the response to the seed as it is sown in different types of soil.[118] The soils indicate different ways that different kinds

116. For excellent overviews of Jesus and parables, see Klyne R. Snodgrass, *Stories with Intent: A Comprehensive Guide to the Parables of Jesus* (Grand Rapids: Eerdmans, 2008), and Craig L. Blomberg, *Interpreting the Parables* (Downers Grove, IL: InterVarsity, 1990). On a more popular level, and very helpful, see Michelle Lee-Barnewall, *Surprised by the Parables: Growing in Grace through the Stories of Jesus* (Bellingham, WA: Lexham, 2020). From varied interpretative perspectives, see also Ruben Zimmermann, "Parables in Matthew: Tradition, Interpretation, and Function in the Gospel," in *An Early Reader of Mark and Q*, ed. Joseph Verheyden and Gilbert van Belle, BTS 21 (Leuven: Peeters, 2016), 159–86; John P. Meier, *Probing the Authenticity of the Parables*, vol. 5 of *A Marginal Jew: Rethinking the Historical Jesus*, 5 vols., AYBRL (New Haven, CT: Yale University Press, 2016); Richard Lischer, *Reading the Parables*, Interpretation (Louisville: Westminster John Knox, 2018); Stephen I. Wright, *Jesus the Storyteller* (London: SPCK, 2014; repr., Louisville: Westminster John Knox, 2015); Peter Yaw Oppong-Kumi, *Matthean Sets of Parables*, WUNT 2/340 (Tübingen: Mohr Siebeck, 2013).

117. For an overview of the relationship to Jewish usage, see Geza Vermes, *The Religion of Jesus the Jew* (Minneapolis: Fortress, 1993), 90–97. For an extensive discussion of parables within Jewish rabbinic literature, see David Stern, *Parables in Midrash: Narrative and Exegesis in Rabbinic Literature* (Cambridge, MA: Harvard University Press, 1991).

118. Donald A. Hagner, "Matthew's Parables of the Kingdom (*Matthew 13:1–52*)," in *The Challenge of Jesus' Parables*, ed. Richard N. Longenecker (Grand Rapids: Eerdmans, 2000), 106.

of people receive the message of the kingdom, but it is only those who produce fruit who are truly sons and daughters of the kingdom.

### 4.8.2 Jesus's Purpose for Speaking in Parables (13:10–17)

After giving the parable, Jesus's disciples come to him and ask, "Why do you speak to them [the crowds] in parables?" (13:10). They recognize that Jesus's primary intended audience is the crowds. Jesus indicates the different purposes for the different kinds of people around him.

- For those in the crowd who are receptive to Jesus's message, the parables stimulate their spiritual heart and that prompts them to pursue the truth from Jesus.
- For those in the crowd who are unreceptive, the parables actually harden their spiritual heart against the truth of the parables, which will ultimately cause them to turn away from Jesus.
- For the disciples, as they hear the parable it produces spiritual receptivity, and they come and ask Jesus for understanding.

The parables have imbedded within them spiritual truths about the "mysteries of the kingdom of heaven." The mysteries or "secrets" are not that God would establish his kingdom, which was a well-known prophetic hope within Israel, but that it has arrived in a form different than what had been anticipated.

Many in Israel hoped for the kingdom of God to arrive with power and military might to overthrow the rulers of this world. Instead, the arrival of the kingdom will be shown in the following parables as hidden from those without eyes of faith. This is a secret now being revealed in veiled speech to God's chosen, who are Jesus's disciples.

So, Jesus's parables *test* the hearts of listeners. To those who are responsive, the parables offer *instruction* about the kingdom of God and the life of discipleship. To those who are unresponsive, the parables harden their hearts so that ultimately they turn away from the kingdom of God.

### 4.8.3 Summary of Jesus's Teaching on the Parables of the Mysteries of the Kingdom of Heaven

Jesus gives seven parables in the discourse that reveal the mysteries of the kingdom of heaven. The power that Jesus brought with his announcement of the arrival of the kingdom of heaven did not have the perception of power that many people expected.[119]

119. Lischer, *Reading the Parables*, 1–27.

So Jesus clarifies with his parables that the kingdom of heaven has secret truths associated with it.

#### *4.8.3.1 The Parable of the Sower and the Soils (13:1–9, 18–23)*

The parable of the sower and the soils indicates that the kingdom of heaven is hidden but powerful in its spiritual transformational working. We will know the power of the kingdom as we see fruit in the transformed lives of Jesus's disciples throughout this age.[120] Jesus does not explicitly identify the fruit, but in this context, it likely refers to the transformation of a person who has encountered the kingdom of heaven. The character of the person who "understands" the message—receives it into his/her heart—will experience the transformation of kingdom life, the very life that Jesus described in the Sermon on the Mount (e.g., 5:3–16, 20–48). The fruit produced is the outward evidence of the reality of the inward life of the kingdom of God.

#### *4.8.3.2 The Parables of the Mustard Seed and the Yeast (13:31–33)*

The parables of the mustard seed and the yeast combine to indicate the surprising appearance of the kingdom of heaven during this age. It is small and inconspicuous in its beginning, but it will bring the reality of salvation from sin to all those who dare to come to it with eyes of faith and an open heart.[121]

#### *4.8.3.3 The Parables of the Hidden Treasure and the Costly Pearl (13:44–46)*

The parables of the hidden treasure and the costly pearl declare the immeasurable value of the kingdom of heaven. The supreme worth of the treasure of the kingdom is unseen by others and it is worth far more than any sacrifice one might make to acquire it. And life in the kingdom is worth far more than all our former accumulated wealth.[122]

#### *4.8.3.4 The Parables of the Wheat and Weeds and of the Dragnet (13:24–30, 36–43, 47–50)*

Finally, the parables of the wheat and weeds and of the dragnet combine to show that God's judgment of the evil one and his followers is certain, and will come with power, but it may not always appear that way during this age until Jesus returns.[123] The final arrival of the kingdom of heaven will then extend its net throughout the world.

---

120. For the already-not yet conception of the kingdom in Jewish thought, see Alexander E. Stewart, "The Temporary Messianic Kingdom in Second Temple Judaism and the Delay of the Parousia: Psalm 110:1 and the Development of Early Christian Inaugurated Eschatology," *JETS* 59.2 (2016): 255–70.

121. Snodgrass, *Stories with Intent*, 235.

122. For an emphasis on the dubious merchant/outsider who becomes an insider who epitomizes the values of the kingdom, see Ernest van Eck, *Parables of Jesus the Galilean: Stories of a Social Prophet*, Matrix (Eugene, OR: Wipf & Stock, 2016), esp. 208–26.

123. Hagner, "Matthew's Parables of the Kingdom," 110; Vermes, *Religion of Jesus the Jew*, 100.

Jesus's return in glorious power to liberate this sin-sick world is a concrete promise that energizes us and gives us purpose for our own lives.[124]

In this remarkable series of parables, Jesus reveals that the kingdom of heaven has arrived with power, but it is a hidden, spiritual, transformational power. This is what discipleship to Jesus will be like in this age of the clandestinely inaugurated, but not fully consummated, kingdom of heaven.[125]

## 4.9 The Full Identity of the Messiah Revealed (13:54–16:20)

Jesus gives increasing clarification to his disciples of his identity as Messiah.

### 4.9.1 Jesus Rejected at Nazareth (13:54–58)

Jesus returns to his hometown of Nazareth, likely to demonstrate to his family that although he is establishing a new spiritual family with his disciples, this does not negate his biological family. His burgeoning reputation as a teacher allows him to teach in his hometown synagogue, but the townspeople are not receptive to his teaching. They are familiar with Jesus's human roots and family, which tends to diminish the honor they should give him. The people's hard-heartedness is an obstacle to their faith, which prevents them from receiving Jesus's healing ministry.

### 4.9.2 John the Baptist Beheaded by Herod Antipas (14:1–12)

Matthew now gives a historical flashback to the time of John the Baptist's execution at the order of Herod Antipas. Antipas had fallen in love with his half-brother Philip's wife, Herodias, who was also his half-niece. Herodias divorced Philip, Antipas divorced his wife, and Antipas and Herodias married. John the Baptist publicly condemned Antipas for these actions. Such a marriage would have been considered an incestuous affront to the Law (Lev 18:16; 20:21). John was imprisoned in Antipas's fortress at Machaerus. Herodias used this opportunity to eliminate a threat to her husband's reign, the accusing voice of John the Baptist. Although John was a prophet revered by the people, the quisling Antipas capitulated and had him executed.

### 4.9.3 Compassionate Healer and Supplier (14:13–21)

Jesus's popularity has not diminished, and a large crowd follows him on foot along the shore, bringing their sick for him to heal. This isolated place where the crowd gathered for Jesus to heal their sick becomes the scene of the climactic feeding of the

124. Blomberg, *Interpreting the Parables*, 202.

125. See also Stephen I. Wright, "Hearing the Stories through Matthew," in *Jesus the Storyteller*, 69–76.

five thousand.[126] The disciples' pooled resources consist of small loaves of bread and a couple fish, sufficient only for one person's afternoon meal. Miraculously, the resources are multiplied until all the people are satisfied. Jesus shows that in the face of huge need, disciples must look not to their small human resources but to the greatness of God's resources.[127]

### 4.9.4 The Son of God Is Worshiped (14:22–36)

About three miles out onto the lake, the disciples have been battling a storm all night when Jesus comes to them, walking on the water. Seeing him, the disciples are afraid, thinking that some evil spirit is attempting to deceive them. Jesus gives them immediate assurance that it is no deceptive evil spirit but truly their Master (14:27).

Jesus's reassuring words, "It is I" (lit., "I am" [*egō eimi*]) may allude to the voice of Yahweh from the bush (Exod 3:14) and the voice of assurance to Israel of the Lord's identity and presence as their Savior (Isa 43:10–13). These words hint of Jesus's divine identity.[128] At Jesus's call, Peter gets out of the boat and begins walking toward Jesus. But noticing the wind, his fear overtakes him, and he begins to sink. Peter cries out for Jesus's help, recognizing that the Lord who could walk on water is also the one who can save him from sinking.

Jesus immediately catches him by the hand to rescue him, and then says to Peter, "You of little faith, why did you doubt?" (14:31). "Little faith" (*oligopistos*) is not the same as "no faith" (*apistos*; cf. 17:17). A person who had no faith would not recognize Jesus and call out to him. Peter has faith; it is just not functioning properly. It is ineffective faith (cf. 17:20). Peter's faith was effective enough to motivate him, but not effective enough to sustain him. Faith is not like a commodity of which Peter needs more. Rather, faith is consistent trust in Jesus to accomplish that to which Peter is called. Effective faith would have caused him to keep his eyes firmly focused on Jesus instead of on the dangers of the wind-swept sea.

When Jesus and Peter enter the boat, the storm immediately ceases. In the context of such works of divine significance, the disciples are gripped with the reality that Jesus is much more than they had understood—he is the Son of God, and so they worship him, an action reserved only for deity. This is the first time the disciples address Jesus as the Son of God, and their immediate worship shows their growing comprehension of Jesus's relationship as the true Son of the Father, God.[129]

---

126. See Mark 6:32–44; Luke 9:10–17; John 6:1–15.

127. For a discussion of the background and comparisons with Mark and John, see Roger David Aus, *Feeding the Five Thousand: Studies in the Judaic Background of Mark 6:30–44 par. and John 6:1–15*, Studies in Judaism (Lanham, MD: University Press of America, 2010).

128. Brian D. McPhee, "Walk, Don't Run: Jesus's Water Walking Is Unparalleled in Greco-Roman Mythology," *JBL* 135.4 (2016): 763–77.

129. David Peterson, *Engaging with God: A Biblical Theology of Worship* (Downers Grove: InterVarsity, 1992), 85–86. For a very careful analysis of "worship" language in relationship to Jesus in 14:22–33, see Joshua E. Leim, *Matthew's Theological Grammar: The Father and the Son*, WUNT 2/402 (Tübingen: Mohr Siebeck,

### 4.9.5 Peter as Example and Leader

At this juncture in Matthew's Gospel narrative Peter will begin to play an increasingly important role. In the next five chapters, Matthew will narrate five incidents in which Peter figures prominently that are found nowhere else in the Gospels (14:28–31; 15:15; 16:17–19; 17:24–27; 18:21). And the focus is twofold.

In the first place, Matthew will focus upon Peter's personal life and characteristics as an example of the way in which Jesus transforms his disciples. Peter becomes an example for all disciples of the developmental process of discipleship to Jesus. But second, Matthew will focus on Peter's leadership role and the way that Jesus develops him into the kind of leader who will be instrumental in the coming church. Peter becomes an example for leaders of the developmental process of leadership under Jesus. In these two ways, Matthew emphasizes Peter's increasingly important responsibility.[130] But Matthew also shows how Peter is both an imperfect disciple and a leader who is in process of development.[131]

### 4.9.6 The Traditions of the Jewish Elders (15:1–9)

Jesus is creating a stir among the people of Galilee with his teaching and interpretation of the Old Testament. The ministry of Jesus has disturbed the local Pharisees (12:2), so they apparently sent word to the highest level of Pharisaic leadership in Jerusalem, who arrive in Galilee to confront Jesus about the practices of his disciples violating the "tradition of the elders" (15:2)—the interpretations of Scripture made by past esteemed rabbis that were passed on to later generations.[132]

### 4.9.7 Purity and Impurity from the Heart (15:10–20)

Jesus calls out the Pharisees for their hypocrisy. They perform external religious rituals without an inner heart of worship. Jesus declares that the heart is the real source of spiritual purity or impurity. Food or ceremonial purification rites do not affect a person's spiritual purity. The spiritual heart is tainted with sin and must be cleansed, which will then produce lives that exemplify purity in words, thoughts, motivations, deeds, and relationships.

2015), esp. ch. 5. For a comparison of this statement and the statement of the Roman centurion at the crucifixion scene, see Andrew R. Angel, "*Crucifixus Vincens*: The 'Son of God' as Divine Warrior in Matthew," *CBQ* 73.2 (2011): 299–317.

130. See Wilkins, "Matthew's Theological Understanding of Simon Peter," in *Concept of Disciple*, 173–216; Pheme Perkins, *Peter: Apostle for the Whole Church*, Studies on Personalities of the New Testament (Columbia, SC: University of South Carolina Press, 1994), 18–21.

131. Hans F. Bayer, *Apostolic Bedrock: Christology, Identity, and Character Formation According to Peter's Canonical Testimony*, PBM (Milton Keynes, UK: Paternoster, 2016), esp. ch. 9, 229–67. See also Joseph Verheyden, "Rock and Stumbling Block: The Fate of Matthew's Peter," in Senior, *Matthew at the Crossroads*, 263–311; Timothy Wiarda, *Peter in the Gospels: Pattern, Personality, and Relationship*, WUNT 2/127 (Tübingen: Mohr Siebeck, 2000).

132. Samuel Sandmel, *Judaism and Christian Beginnings* (New York: Oxford, 1978), 103.

## 4.9.8 Healer and Provider for Gentiles (15:21–39)

Jesus has completed this phase of his Jewish Galilean ministry, so he withdraws to gentile regions. In a highly dramatic scene, a Canaanite woman approaches Jesus, pleading for his miraculous ministry of exorcism for her daughter. Canaanites were pagan gentiles, but Jesus's reputation has preceded him. The woman comes to Jesus for her daughter's healing instead of going to her local temple dedicated to Eshmun, a pagan god of healing.[133] Intriguingly, she demonstrates familiarity with Jewish messianic tradition by calling Jesus "Son of David" and calling for his merciful, miraculous ministry of exorcism for her daughter.[134]

Jesus does not immediately reply, which the disciples apparently take as his refusal. Jesus is not demonstrating ethnic bigotry against gentiles but maintaining his commitment to fulfill the mission for which he was sent. He must first go to the nation of Israel, so that gentiles will glorify God for the fulfillment of his promises made to his people.

But the woman is very persistent in her request. Jesus uses a common metaphor of a dog to indicate the contrast between God's care for those of his family and those who are not.[135] He is not condoning the use of a derogatory title, as the response of the woman indicates. The woman continues the metaphor but uses it to emphasize that dogs too had a caring relationship with their masters.

This is a very perceptive woman. She has already confessed Jesus as the messianic son of David. Now she draws upon the Abrahamic covenant to seek the aid of Jesus Messiah. She recognizes that although Israel receives the primary blessings of the covenant, gentiles also were to be the recipient of blessing through them.

Jesus's reply at first seems somewhat harsh, given the desperate condition of her daughter, but in a sense he was testing her. Would she see through the salvation-historical distinction between Israel and the gentiles and recognize that God ultimately desires to bring healing to all people? She passes the test because she acknowledges that as the Messiah of Israel Jesus is the master of all, and he will care for the needs of all, whether Jew or gentile. Her response is called by Jesus an exercise of "great faith," which was rewarded by her daughter being healed that very hour. Even though God has a program, he responds to true faith.[136]

133. Cf. John J. Rousseau and Rami Arav, "Tyre and Sidon," in *Jesus and His World: An Archaeological and Cultural Dictionary* (Minneapolis: Fortress, 1995), 327–28.

134. Cf. Donald J. Verseput, "The Davidic Messiah and Matthew's Jewish Christianity," *SBLSP* 34 (1995): 102–16; Baxter, "Healing and the 'Son of David,'" 36–50; Dvořáček, *Son of David in Matthew's Gospel*, esp. part 2; Zacharias, *Matthew's Presentation of the Son of David*, 84–85, 102–3.

135. See Jacob Neusner and William Scott Green, "Dog," *DJBP* 172; Ryken et al., "Animals," "Dogs," *DBI* 29, 213–14.

136. Gail R. O'Day, "Surprised by Faith: Jesus and the Canaanite Woman," in *A Feminist Companion to Matthew*, ed. Amy-Jill Levine, with Marianne Blickenstaff (Cleveland: Pilgrim, 2004), 114–25; cf. Glenna S. Jackson, *Have Mercy on Me: The Story of the Canaanite Woman in Matthew 15.21–28*, JSNTSup 228 (London: Sheffield, 2002).

### 4.9.9 Feeding the Four Thousand (15:29–39)

Jesus remains in a gentile region, now along the Sea of Galilee in the Decapolis (cf. Mark 7:31). Crowds gather around him again to seek miraculous healing. As Jesus heals the needy, these gentiles glorify the God of Israel. As in the feeding of the five thousand, Jesus uses the disciples' small resources to provide plentifully for the people's needs. The number seven of loaves and baskets of leftovers here may symbolize the completion or fullness of God meeting the needs of all peoples, now including gentiles.[137] As Israel rejects Jesus's invitation to the kingdom, growing numbers of gentiles receive his message and healing. This is a preview of the worldwide mission to all the nations.

### 4.9.10 Evil Spiritual Leaven of the Religious Leaders (16:1–12)

Jesus has performed many miracles openly, some of which the religious leaders witnessed firsthand (cf. 12:9–14, 22). To those with eyes of faith, his miracles are signs that validate his identity as the Messiah. If the religious leaders were open to God's message, they had enough of a sign that Jesus truly is the Messiah. Instead, their hard hearts rejected the miracles' authenticating power and they used those same miracles as the basis of the charge that he is a satanic instrument (12:24). Recognizing their evil motive, Jesus refuses to fall into their trap of giving them further ammunition to use against him, except for the sign of Jonah: just as Jonah's appearance was God's sign to the people of Nineveh, Jesus's resurrection from the dead will be the sign of judgment on all those who refuse to repent at Jesus's proclamation of the arrival of God's kingdom.[138]

### 4.9.11 Peter Declares Jesus to Be the Christ, the Son of the Living God (16:13–20)

Leaving Jewish Galilee, Jesus travels with his disciples to the gentile Greco-Roman area of Caesarea Philippi. Jesus asks his disciples not only what the people have gleaned about his identity as the Son of Man, but also what they themselves have come to understand. The people's perceptions are in line with one of Israel's popular messianic expectations about a great prophet that would arise.

When Jesus asks the disciples for their own conclusion, Peter acts as spokesman for the Twelve and boldly declares Jesus to be the Messiah, the Son of the living God.[139] In an area teeming with ancient cults and emperor worship, Peter's proclamation is significant. He declares that Jesus is not only the Messiah, but he is the living Son of the God, unlike these pagan gods.[140]

---

137. Cf. Hagner, *Matthew 14–28*, 451–52; cf. Carson, "Matthew," 409.

138. Hans F. Bayer, *Jesus' Predictions of Vindication and Resurrection: The Provenance, Meaning, and Correlation of the Synoptic Predictions*, WUNT 2/20 (Tübingen: Mohr Siebeck, 1986), 141–45, 182.

139. For my full discussion of this passage, see Michael J. Wilkins, "Peter's Declaration of Jesus' Identity in Caesarea Philippi," in Bock and Webb, *Key Events*, 293–381; and Wilkins, "Matthew's Theological Understanding of Simon Peter," 173–216.

140. For a good overview, see Elaine A. Phillips, "Peter's Declaration at Caesarea Philippi," in *Lexham Geographic Commentary*

Peter spoke for the group, but Jesus addresses Peter directly. He declares that Peter's confession came about by direct revelation from Jesus's divine Father.[141] Then Jesus creates a wordplay to show Peter's role in the foundation of the church: "You are Peter (*Petros* = Eng. "rock"), and on this rock (*petra* = Eng. "bedrock") I will build my church." This saying has been interpreted in three primary ways: (1) the wordplay refers to Peter individually, who will play a foundational role in the establishment of Jesus's church;[142] (2) the wordplay refers to an *aspect* of Peter[143]—the truth of the confession[144] and/or the leadership of Peter[145]—that is the rock upon which the church will be built; (3) Jesus refers to *himself* as the rock upon which the church will be built, similar to the way that other New Testament passages refer to Christ as the "rock"[146] and the "foundation"[147] of the church.[148]

Each view has its strengths, but I agree with most scholars that Jesus intended Peter as the antecedent to "this rock" upon which he will build Jesus's church.[149] Peter will play a foundational role in the establishment of his church. The second-person singular verb form and personal pronouns, plus the specification of his human name, indicate that the stress is on Peter personally: "And I tell *you* [*soi*] that *you are Peter* [*sy ei Petros*]. . . . I will give *to you* [*soi*] . . . whatever *you bind* [*dēsēs*] . . . whatever *you loose* [*lysēs*]" (16:18–19). This is a notion consistent with the way in which from the beginning Peter was spokesman and leader of the Twelve. Here Jesus points ahead to the time when Peter the rock is given the authority to admit entrance to the kingdom of heaven through preaching the gospel to Jews on Pentecost, to Samaritans, and to gentiles (Acts 2; 8; 10).

Jews, Samaritans, and gentiles now comprise Jesus's church, which Jesus builds, but it will come about through the foundational activity of the apostles and prophets (Eph 2:20). Peter will be a rock-leader among the apostles, but once his foundational role is finished, he passes off the scene of the record of the early church in Acts. Peter has authority to declare the terms under which God grants entrance to, and exclusion

---

*on the Gospels*, ed. Barry J. Beitzel, with Kristopher A. Lyle (Bellingham, WA: Lexham, 2016), 286–97.

141. For primary emphasis on Peter as one who is an "apocalyptic seer" for God, see Markley, *Peter—Apocalyptic Seer: The Influence of the Apocalypse Genre on Matthew's Portrayal of Peter*, WUNT 2/348 (Tübingen: Mohr Siebeck, 2013), 191–215.

142. This was the interpretation of most of the early church fathers, although very early many fought against its use for establishing any kind of papacy (e.g., Ignatius, Justin, Origen, Tertullian, Cyprian, Firmilian).

143. This view was held early in church history by John Chrysostom and attested to by Origen, Eusebius, Ambrose, and Theodore of Mopsuestia (cf. Cullmann, *Peter*, 162; Brown, Donfried, and Reumann, *Peter*, 93 and n216).

144. Chrys C. Caragounis, *Peter and the Rock*, BZNW 58 (Berlin: de Gruyter, 1990), esp. 88–119.

145. R. V. G. Tasker, *The Gospel According to St. Matthew: An Introduction and Commentary*, TNTC (Grand Rapids: Eerdmans, 1961), 162; Evans, *Matthew*, 313–14.

146. E.g., 21:42, but here the term used is *lithos*; 1 Cor 10:4, where the term used is *petra*.

147. E.g., 1 Cor 3:11; 1 Pet 2:4–8.

148. This view was held as early as Origen and Augustine, and was also the major view of Luther, Calvin, and many of the Reformers (Cullmann, *Peter*, 162–63). Recent adherents include Gundry, *Mattthew*, 334.

149. This is the dominant view held of those of a broad confessional background, such as Albright and Mann, *Matthew*, 647; Carson, "Matthew," 418–19; Davies and Alison, *Matthew*, 2:628–32; France, *Matthew*, TNTC, 254–55; Morris, *Matthew*, 422–24; Nolland, *Matthew*, 667–83; Osborne, *Matthew*, 627–28; Stendahl, "Matthew," 787; Turner, *Matthew*, 404–5.

from, the kingdom, the same authority given to the church in preaching the gospel (cf. Matt 18:18; John 20:23). Jesus promises that not even demonic powers or death will overpower the church.

### 4.9.12 Tell No One That He Is the Christ (16:20)

When he finishes his declaration to Peter, Jesus instructs his disciples to keep his identity as the Messiah private. A regular feature of Jesus's ministry has been to demand secrecy about his identity and mission (see on 8:4; cf. 9:30; 12:16; 16:20; 17:9). He carefully avoided stirring up in the crowds a misunderstanding of his messianic identity. The title "Christ/Messiah" carried for the populace connotations of political-military liberation, and they could easily misunderstand his message to mean that he had come to begin the revolution. Peter's confession has released Jesus's identity as the Messiah/Christ, but it is still subject to misunderstanding by the crowds, and even by his own disciples, as even Peter will soon display. So, Jesus warns his disciples not to disclose to the crowds that he is the Messiah. His message must be understood to focus on entrance into the kingdom of heaven, which will come about as the people are loosed from their sins, and not at this time the establishment of an earthly kingdom.

## 4.10 THE SUFFERING OF THE MESSIAH REVEALED (16:21–17:27)

The revelation of Jesus's true identity by his heavenly Father to Peter is now matched by Jesus's revelation of his true mission to the group of disciples.

### 4.10.1 Jesus Messiah Predicts His Suffering and Resurrection (16:21–23)

For the first time, Jesus predicts his arrest and crucifixion—the first of four times that he will make this prediction (16:21; 17:22–23; 20:17–19; 26:2). But as much as he tries to get his disciples to understand the necessity of his mission, they continually misapprehend its significance.[150] Now he reveals that his earthly mission must involve suffering, and more. Rather than being the *conquering* Messiah, in his present earthly mission he will be the *crucified and risen* Messiah.

Shocked at the idea of his master's suffering, Peter audaciously steps forward, likely once again as spokesman for the rest of the shocked disciples, to try to save his Master from the announced fate of suffering. Jesus turns and rebukes Peter as "Satan." Satan had tried to tempt Jesus away from carrying out the Father's will at the start of his

150. Bayer, *Jesus' Predictions of Vindication and Resurrection*, 182–88.

earthly ministry (see on 4:1–11), and now he uses a different strategy. He tries to hinder Jesus's mission through Peter, one of Jesus's very own disciples, the one who had just prior to this been privy to a revelation from God the Father (16:17). Through Peter, Satan tries to hinder Jesus's mission by tempting Peter to focus on human concerns and create a stumbling block for Jesus on his mission to the cross. Without consistency in relying upon the Father's revelation, Peter the rock becomes Peter the stumbling stone.[151]

### 4.10.2 The Cost of Discipleship (16:24–26)

Jesus now teaches his disciples one of the central principles of discipleship to him: a disciple must take up his own cross and follow Jesus (cf. 10:38). The horror of the cross will be Jesus's tragic fate.[152] But in what must have been to the disciples a shocking shift of emphasis, he uses the cross and crucifixion as an image of discipleship. Although the image is often understood by modern Christians as bearing up under some personal hardship or life's cruel fate, as used here by Jesus the cross has a much more profound significance: one must die to his or her own will and take up God's will (cf. 16:25–26). The person who tries to hold on to his or her own will for his or her life, rejecting what God desires for him or her, will ultimately lose all that he or she is attempting to protect.

### 4.10.3 The Son of Man Coming in His Kingdom (16:27–28)

Jesus's second coming at the end of the age will mean judgment for those who have not taken up the cross and reward for those who have. Some present with Jesus will see the Son of Man "coming in his kingdom," which likely points to Peter, James, and John witnessing Jesus's transfiguration just a few days later.

### 4.10.4 The Beloved, Transfigured Son (17:1–13)

A week after Jesus predicts his death, he takes his inner circle of disciples with him up a high mountain, likely Mount Hermon, near Caesarea Philippi.[153] The disciples watch as Jesus is "transfigured." Jesus experiences a physical transformation that is visible to the disciples. It was a reminder of Jesus's preincarnate glory (John 1:14; 17:5; Phil 2:6–7) and a preview of his coming exaltation (2 Pet 1:16–18; Rev 1:16). Jesus is transfigured to reveal his divine nature and to radiate the glory that is his as God. This is a true Christophany, or revelation of Jesus's divine nature.

The transfiguration of Jesus that reveals his divine glory is seconded by the

151. Tracing the history of the reception of Matthew's Peter, see Verheyden, "Rock and Stumbling Block," 263–311.

152. David W. Chapman, "Perceptions of Crucifixion Among Jews and Christians in the Ancient World" *TynBul* 51.2 (2000): 313–16; Chapman, *Ancient Jewish and Christian Perceptions of Crucifixion*, WUNT 2/244 (Tübingen: Mohr Siebeck, 2008).

153. See Benjamin A. Foreman, "The Geographical Significance of the Transfiguration," *LGCG*, 298–307. See also A. D. A. Moses, *Matthew's Transfiguration Story and Jewish-Christian Controversy*, JSNTSup 122 (Sheffield: Sheffield Academic, 1996).

appearance of two of the greatest Old Testament figures, Moses and Elijah. Their arrival represents the Law and the Prophets witnessing to Jesus as the Messiah who fulfills the Old Testament (cf. Matt 5:17) and who has the eschatological role of initiating the kingdom of God (4:17). Their appearance on the mountain with Jesus indicates the greatness of Jesus, who transcends them both as the One who will be declared the Son of God.[154] But God the Father now pronounces the same public endorsement of Jesus his beloved Son that was given at his baptism. Jesus is the embodied Son of God, so the disciples must listen to him to understand his messianic mission.[155]

### 4.10.5 Sons of the Kingdom and "Faith" (17:14–23)

As Jesus and his inner circle rejoin the other disciples down the mountain, they find that a crowd has been drawn to an argument about the disciples' failed attempt to heal an epileptic boy. The boy's father respects Jesus as an esteemed master and anticipates that Jesus can extend mercy to heal his son. He had assumed Jesus's disciples had the ability to heal as well, but his confidence is dashed.

Jesus rebukes the whole current generation of people because they have not as a whole placed their faith in Jesus as the anticipated Messiah. He describes the generation of that day as being "without faith" (17:17) whereas his disciples have "little faith" (17:20). Having authority over the demonic source of this illness, Jesus rebukes the demon causing the epilepsy. The demon is exorcised, and the boy is immediately healed.

The disciples were unable to drive out the demon because their faith in Jesus and his mission is still defective. That Jesus is not talking about the *amount* of the disciples' faith is indicated by the analogy to the smallest of all seeds, the mustard seed. Instead of amount, Jesus points to the *effectiveness* of faith. The smallest faith can accomplish the greatest deeds, like moving a mountain, if it is properly focused upon God's will for it to happen.

### 4.10.6 Paying the Temple Tax (17:24–27)

The temple is the Father's own house, so as the Son of God his Father, Jesus is exempt from the temple tax. And Jesus's disciples, who are now part of the Father's family (12:48–50), are likewise exempt. This is a profound christological statement, indicating not only Jesus's relationship by analogy to his Father, the ultimate King, but also indicating the way in which he is the fulfillment of the Law. There will be in the future no sacrifice in the temple because his sacrificial service will fulfill the need for the final sacrifice (cf. Heb 7:26–28). Hence, there will be no temple tax for Jesus's disciples.[156]

154. Randall E. Otto, "The Fear Motivation in Peter's Offer to Build τρεῖς σκηνάς," *WTJ* 59.1 (1997): 101–12.

155. Cf. Markus Öhler, "The Expectation of Elijah and the Presence of the Kingdom of God," *JBL* 118.3 (1999): 461–76.

156. Some take this too far to advocate for Matthew's community a political subversiveness to Roman authority; cf. Warren Carter, "Paying the Tax to Rome as Subversive Praxis: Matthew 17.24–27," *JSNT* 76 (1999): 3–31.

But to avoid offending the conscience of those who have not experienced this exemption, they will pay the tax regardless. To make a striking impression on his disciples that they would long remember, Jesus instructs Peter to throw out a fishing line and there he will find the coin for paying the tax, provided miraculously in a fish. The miracle is both foreknowledge (cf. 21:2) and divine provision, and is a sign for the disciples, an indication of Jesus's superiority to the temple (cf. 12:6). The age of God's kingdom has dawned.[157]

## 4.11 THE COMMUNITY OF THE MESSIAH REVEALED (18:1–20:34)

### *FOURTH DISCOURSE: "COMMUNITY PRESCRIPTION"*

### 4.11.1 Characteristics of Life in the Kingdom Community (18:1–35)

This fourth discourse, the Community Prescription, delineates the church as the community of disciples that witness to the reality of the presence of the kingdom of God throughout this age. Much of this prescription for the community of disciples is unique to Matthew, especially noted by the occurrence of the term *ekklēsia* ("church"), which appears in the Gospels only in Matthew, here for the second and final time (18:17; cf. 16:18). The disciples' witness as the community of the church comes both through their declaration of the gospel message and through their example of living out the gospel message as a family of faith that is characterized by humility, purity, accountability, discipline, reconciliation, restoration, and forgiveness.

#### *4.11.1.1 The Greatness of Humility (18:1–4)*

Matthew tells us that the event that precipitates the community discourse is a surprising question from Jesus's disciples about who is greatest in the kingdom of heaven (18:1). The ambition to achieve greatness is a pursuit central to human accomplishment, and on the strictly natural level it is not an inappropriate pursuit. But when Jesus had spoken of "greatness," he had meant the honor of serving God by preparing for the Messiah and of experiencing the arrival of the blessings of the new covenant through his blood. The disciples had misunderstood him to mean the greatness that comes from human endeavor and heroic accomplishments. One of the primary topics throughout this community discourse will be the revision of the disciples' understanding to

157. For defense of the historicity of this event, see Gertraud Harb, "Matthew 17.24–27 and Its Value for Historical Jesus Research," *JSHJ* 8.3 (2010): 254–74.

think the way that God thinks about greatness rather than the way that humans typically think.[158]

Jesus places a little child in the middle of the disciples and indicates that both entrance to the kingdom and greatness in the kingdom is like the humility of a child. Childlike humility consists of vulnerability and complete dependence on the parents.[159] Those who wish to enter the kingdom must turn away from their own power and self-seeking attitude, and in childlike humility call upon God's mercy.[160]

#### *4.11.1.2 Shelter for Childlike Disciples and Angelic Protection of Little Ones (18:5–10)*

Jesus indicates that in the same way one must humbly receive God's mercy in order to enter the kingdom of heaven and become his disciple (18:1–4), once one becomes Jesus's disciple that same kind of humility must continue to characterize one's life of discipleship (18:5).[161] Jesus not only encourages care for humble disciples, but also warns any who would take advantage of them that his disciples will have the strength, protection, and invincibility of the kingdom of God to shelter them as they serve their Master in this world (18:6–7). He uses hyperbole to emphasize that sin must be dealt with radically so that it is removed from the disciple's life before it leads to final judgment (18:8–9).

He also warns anyone who might try to take advantage of his little ones that the heavenly Father uses angels to care for childlike disciples (18:10). The value of "the little ones" is amplified through Mathew's portrayal of angels as mediators of God's care toward earthly beings.[162]

#### *4.11.1.3 Divine Search for Lost Sheep (18:12–14)*

Not only does the Father employ angels to protect his little ones, but he himself will expend every effort to bring about a wandering disciple's safe return to obedient discipleship. In Jesus's parable, the wandering sheep is a believer, and finding a lost sheep produces incredible joy. This joy does not mean the lost sheep is more valuable than the other sheep, but it indicates the love and care the Father has toward all those in his family, even those who go astray.

---

158. See Jeannine K. Brown, *The Disciples in Narrative Perspective: The Portrayal and Function of the Matthean Disciples*, AcBib 9 (Atlanta: SBL Press, 2002), esp. 147–52.

159. John Aranda Cabrido, "A Typology for Discipleship: The Narrative Function of παιδίον in Matthew's Story of Jesus," *ABR* 57 (2009): 47–60.

160. Warren Carter, *Households and Discipleship: A Study of Matthew 19–20*, JSNTSup 103 (Sheffield: JSOT, 1994), 96–97; Don Garlington, "Who Is the Greatest?" *JETS* 53.2 (2010): 287–316.

161. See Frederick Dale Bruner, *Matthew: The Churchbook, Matthew 1–12*, vol. 2 of *Matthew: A Commentary*, 2 vols., rev. and exp. ed. (Grand Rapids: Eerdmans, 2007), 207–12.

162. Bendoraitis, "*Behold, the Angels Came*," esp. ch. 6. See also Graham A. Cole, *Against the Darkness: The Doctrine of Angels, Satan, and Demons*, FET (Wheaton, IL: Crossway, 2019), 71–73.

### *4.11.1.4 Disciplining Wayward Disciples (18:15–20)*

This next passage, which is unique to Matthew's Gospel, follows logically from the preceding warnings about sin committed by disciples. In this passage, Jesus gives four steps of discipline that the community must apply to sinful situations. The ultimate aim is not punishment but restoration to the path of discipleship.

(1) The first step for disciplining a sinning disciple is a personal confrontation with the person who has sinned to lay out his or her fault. Jesus emphasizes that the entire encounter is sensitive. It must be undertaken with privacy so that if it is resolved, there would not be undue attention given to the tragedy of committed sin by a member of the community.

(2) If the brother or sister does not repent, the second step is to bring one or two other disciples to witness the confrontation and confirm whether or not there is repentance (not eyewitnesses to the sin committed; cf. Deut 19:15).

(3) If the sinning brother or sister refuses to repent in front of the witnesses, the third step is to bring the unrepentant disciple before the church to listen to the church's admonishment.

(4) If the brother or sister still refuses to repent of his or her sin, the fourth step is for the community to treat the sinning member as a "pagan" or "tax collector," common titles for those who consciously rebel against God and his people.

Some suggest that the sinning person is not to be allowed to participate in any activities of the church. However, since unbelievers, such as "pagans and tax collectors," are encouraged to come to the assembly to hear the gospel message, it must mean something other than strict removal. Rather, the directive "let him be to you as a Gentile and a tax collector" (18:17 ESV) is best carried out when the church considers the sinning individual not to be a believer. Confessing disciples who live with unconfessed sin indicate by their lives that they are not truly members of Jesus's spiritual discipleship family and are not to be allowed to enjoy the fellowship of the family. They should be treated like non-believers, with the same compassion and urgency of having them exercise repentance, yet not extended the same openness to the inner fellowship of the community that is reserved for fellow disciples. The intent is to involve the body of believers in trying to get the sinning brother or sister to acknowledge personal sin, repent, and be restored to full participation in the community.

The authority to declare the terms under which God forgives the sin of wayward disciples is extended to the entire community of disciples (cf. 16:19). Jesus promises his divine presence among his disciples when they seek agreement in decisions of church discipline.[163]

---

163. For discussion of the "I am with you" theme here, see Kupp, *Matthew's Emmanuel*, 176–200.

#### *4.11.1.5 Forgiveness in the Community Toward Sinning Disciples (18:21–35)*

Realizing that there may be some within the community who put on a show of repentance yet continue to sin, Peter asks whether there is a limit to forgiveness. Within Judaism, forgiving someone three times was enough to show a forgiving spirit (Amos 1:3; 2:6; Job 33:29–30). Peter's suggestion of seven times shows significant generosity.

Jesus's response is not about a specific number, but an instruction to forgive without keeping count. He illustrates this with a parable in which a servant owes his king an incalculable debt. When the servant begs for mercy, the king takes pity on him and cancels the debt. The debt's cancellation is a powerful display of the forgiveness that God extends toward those whose sin has offended him. After the servant is pardoned, he finds a fellow servant who owes him a much smaller debt. But the first servant refuses to forgive the debt and punishes the man. The first servant's true nature is revealed in his actions. The king rebukes the first servant for his wickedness and imprisons him, which alludes to an eternal destiny of judgment for those who fail to demonstrate mercy. A transformed heart produces a changed life that renders to others the same mercy and forgiveness one receives from God.[164]

### 4.11.2 The Sanctity of Marriage in the Community (19:1–12)

There was significant debate within Pharisaical schools over the lawful basis for divorce, so they test Jesus by asking, "Is it lawful for a man to divorce his wife for any and every reason?" (19:3).[165] The expression "for any and every reason" (*kata pasan aitian*) is unique to Matthew, reflecting his remembrance of this controversy among the Pharisees at the time.

Jesus avoids the Pharisees' debates, going back to creation to demonstrate God's original intention for the institution of marriage. Marriage was to be a permanent bond of a man and a woman into one new union consecrated by becoming one flesh.[166] Although marriage as God intended it was permanent, Moses allowed for divorce as an exception to protect the non-offending partner and to protect the institution of marriage from becoming an indecent sham. Jesus states that adultery is when a person has committed *porneia*, which the NIV appropriately renders "marital unfaithfulness." The semantic range of *porneia* includes whatever intentionally divides the marital relationship, possibly including related sexual sins such as incest, prostitution, or molestation, but conceivably including actions such as violent domestic physical abuse.[167]

---

164. See Mbabazi, *Significance of Interpersonal Forgiveness*, Kindle edition, ch. 6.

165. For a full-length treatment that concludes with pastoral implications, see David Instone-Brewer, *Divorce and Remarriage in the Bible: The Social and Literary Context* (Grand Rapids: Eerdmans, 2002).

166. See Ortlund, *Marriage and the Mystery*, 79–85.

167. Nolland, *Matthew*, 244–45.

## 4.11.3 Valuing the Kingdom Community (19:13–20:34)

### *4.11.3.1 The Kingdom Community Belongs to Children (19:13–15)*

Jesus once again turns prevailing societal values on their head to show that the low position of children in society illustrates the humility necessary for entrance into the kingdom of God (19:14; see 18:1–5). Childlikeness is not only a prerequisite for entrance to the kingdom (18:3) but is a necessary lifetime characteristic for Jesus's disciples. As weak, defenseless, vulnerable children they will continue to maintain dependence upon their heavenly Father for the purpose, power, and significance of their life of discipleship to Jesus.[168]

### *4.11.3.2 The Tragedy of the Rich Young Man (19:16–22)*

A religious leader, possibly a Pharisee, approaches Jesus addressing him as "teacher" (19:16), a respectful title that acknowledges Jesus's mastery of Scripture. He asks Jesus what righteous deed he must perform in order to have assurance of eternal life. Only by understanding that God alone is good can one see that good deeds do not obtain eternal life. Obedience does not earn eternal life, but those who would have eternal life will humbly obey the Law out of childlike faith in God's goodness.

Jesus lists several commandments, which represent the entire Law. Understanding Jesus's meaning, the man knows his obedience to the Law is complete, yet he senses there is something he still lacks. Jesus knows the man's wealth has become his means to personal identity, to his power, to his sense of purpose and meaning in life. It has, in a very real sense, become his god. Jesus calls him to exchange the god of wealth for following Jesus as the one true God who has "fulfilled" the Law.[169] The man departs with sadness because Jesus has pinpointed the issue. He knows that rejecting Jesus's invitation is a decision that has eternal consequences.[170]

Wealth is a heady intoxicant, because it provides counterfeits that deceive a person into thinking that he or she does not need God. But even in such a case God can break through a seemingly impenetrable hard heart. With an extreme illustration of a camel going through the eye of a needle, Jesus says that even what seems absurdly impossible is possible with God.

### *4.11.3.3 The Gracious Reward for Those Who Follow Jesus (19:23–30)*

Jesus acknowledges to Peter and the other disciples that they will receive rewards for their sacrifice in following Jesus. Jesus indicates a future time of renewal when the Twelve will participate in the final establishment of the kingdom of God on the earth, when Israel will be restored to the land and the Twelve will rule with Jesus Messiah over the renewal of

168. Carter, *Households and Discipleship*, 113–14.

169. Wesley G. Olmstead, "Jesus, the Eschatological Perfection of Torah, and the *imitatio Dei* in Matthew," in *Torah Ethics and Early Christian Identity*, ed. Susan J. Wendel and David M. Miller (Grand Rapids: Eerdmans, 2016), 43–58.

170. Joseph H. Hellerman, "Wealth and Sacrifice in Early Christianity: Revisiting Mark's Presentation of Jesus' Encounter with the Rich Young Ruler," *TrinJ* 21NS (2000): 143–64.

all things (19:28).[171] Although "judging" can indicate condemnation of Israel for rejecting Jesus as national Messiah,[172] the idea of Jesus as the Son of Man and the Twelve ruling or governing is paramount (cf. Rev 3:21; 20:6). Condemning Israel would bring no great pleasure to the disciples, but reward would, which was the point of Peter's request (Matt 19:27).[173] The twelve disciples will judge the twelve tribes in the sense of shepherding them (cf. Pss. Sol. 17:26), not punishing them.[174] This apparently speaks to the political reconstitution of a twelve-tribe nation state in the restored Davidic kingdom.[175]

All those who give up the god of their lives to follow Jesus will receive the full realization of their inheritance of eternal life. But inheritance is a gift, not an earned reward. Those who serve for the purpose of gaining rewards will be last; but those who serve purely out of obedience and gratitude to Jesus will be first (cf. 20:16).

#### *4.11.3.4 The Parable of the Vineyard Workers: Gratitude for Eternal Life and Service in the Kingdom Community (20:1–16)*

The landowner calls out the workers' self-centered envy. Rather than begrudging the landowner's generosity, the workers should have simply been grateful for being hired at all. Disciples must not measure their worth by what they have done and what they have sacrificed.[176] Focusing on rewards and comparing oneself with others will cause disciples to question the wisdom and generosity of God. Instead of being motivated by "fairness" or "reward," the most noble of motivations is "gratitude."[177] And the profound significance of gratitude is that it impacts not just the one toward whom we should be grateful but all other relationships as well.

#### *4.11.3.5 The Example of Jesus for Community Sacrifice, Suffering, and Service (20:20–28)*

As Jesus gives his third prediction of his impending crisis in Jerusalem (20:17–19), the mother of Zebedee's sons comes up to Jesus with her sons and, "kneeling down, asked a favor of him . . . 'Grant that one of these two sons of mine may sit at your right and the other at your left in your kingdom'" (20:20–21). This woman has been a faithful follower of Jesus. Later identified as Salome, she is among the women who attends Jesus at the cross and witnesses the empty tomb (cf. 27:56; Mark 15:40; 16:1).

171. Cf. Robert L. Saucy, *The Case for Progressive Dispensationalism: The Interface Between Dispensational and Non-Dispensational Theology* (Grand Rapids: Zondervan, 1993), 267–69.

172. See Carson, "Matthew," 480–81; cf. George R. Beasley-Murray, *Jesus and the Kingdom of God* (Grand Rapids: Eerdmans, 1986), 275–76.

173. See Konradt, *Israel, Church, and the Gentiles*, 259–63. Evans, *Matthew*, 348.

174. Evans, *Matthew*, 348.

175. See Keener, *Matthew* (2009), 479–80; Joel Willitts, "Zionism in the Gospel of Matthew," in *The New Christian Zionism: Fresh Perspectives on Israel and the Land*, ed. Gerald R. McDermott (Downers Grove: InterVarsity, 2016), 138.

176. So also B. Rod Doyle, "The Place of the Parable of the Labourers in the Vineyard in Matthew 20:1–16," *Australian Biblical Review* 42 (1994): 39–58.

177. For a somewhat different approach but with similar conclusions, see Nathan Eubank, "What Does Matthew Say About Divine Recompense? On the Misuse of the Parable of the Workers in the Vineyard (20:1–16)," *JSNT* 35.3 (2013): 242–62.

The best clarification of the listings of the women identifies Salome as the sister of Mary, Jesus's mother (cf. John 19:25). So, she is Jesus's aunt, and her sons, James and John, are his cousins on his mother's side.[178]

Jesus asks James and John if they will share in suffering for the kingdom. The "cup" refers figuratively to one's divinely appointed destiny, whether blessing or disaster. Here it refers to Jesus's forthcoming suffering. Misunderstanding him, they respond with bravado. Jesus confirms that they will indeed share in both suffering and blessing if they submit to the Father's will for their future. The other disciples are indignant because James and John have attempted to use an unfair kinship advantage to get what they themselves had also wanted.

Jesus gathers the disciples together to overturn their sense of ambition. From a human perspective, it is better to rule than to serve, so servants and slaves were two of the lowest positions in society. Jesus reverses their status in the community of disciples. Disciples who aim to be great in the kingdom must arrange their lives with the ambition to serve others.

The ultimate model for the disciples' ambition is Jesus's own life of service. But in a dramatic extension, Jesus states that as the Son of Man he will "give his life as a ransom for many" (20:28). He will exchange his life as a substitute for all those who will accept his payment for their sins. "Jesus's righteous deed is here described not just as an example—though it is that too—but as a vicarious payment on behalf of others."[179]

#### *4.11.3.6 Jesus Messiah, the Son of David, Mercifully Heals Two Blind Men in Jericho en Route to Jerusalem (20:29–34)*

The blind men understand Jesus to be the "Son of David," a reference to the promise of the messianic deliverer from the line of David whose kingdom would have no end (2 Sam 7:12–16; cf. Pss. Sol. 17:23).[180] The messianic age promised to bring healing to the blind (Isa 29:18; 35:5; 42:7), which Jesus told John the Baptist was one of the signs that he indeed was the expected one (Matt 11:2–6). So, these blind men ask for the gift of messianic mercy that would heal their blindness.[181]

## 4.12 THE MESSIAH ASSERTS HIS AUTHORITY OVER JERUSALEM (21:1–23:39)

### 4.12.1 Climactic Entry into Jerusalem: Jesus's Authority as Messiah (21:1–11)

As Jesus arrives in Jerusalem, his messianic ministry enters its climactic final week.[182]

178. Cf. George R. Beasley-Murray, *John*, 2nd ed., WBC 36 (Nashville, TN: Nelson,1999), 348–49; D. A. Carson, *Gospel According to John* (Grand Rapids: Eerdmans, 1991), 616.

179. Nathan Eubank, *Wages of Cross-Bearing and Debt of Sin: The Economy of Heaven in Matthew's Gospel*, BZNW 196 (Berlin: de Gruyter, 2013), 161. Just what that "ransom" entails we will discuss more fully in Chapter 14 below, "The Death and Resurrection of Jesus Messiah: Forgiveness and New Life."

180. Dvořáček, *The Son of David in Matthew's Gospel*, esp. part 2.

181. Zacharias, *Matthew's Presentation of the Son of David*, 85–86, 102–3.

182. For a comprehensive study of the final week of Jesus's life,

His entrance into Jerusalem on a donkey fulfills the prophecy of Zech 9:9, "Your king comes to you, gentle and riding on a donkey" (Matt 21:5). The time has come for Jesus to declare openly that he is the righteous Davidic Messiah, fulfilling the messianic prophecy of Zechariah.[183] The quotation of the Zechariah prophecy indicates the nature of Jesus's arrival—he comes as the righteous one who offers salvation, not as a conquering military leader. He comes with reconciliation, as did rulers who sometimes rode a donkey in times of peace (Judg 5:10; 1 Kgs 1:33). Jesus delineates from the moment of his entrance that he has not come to bring military conquest.[184]

But as Jesus enters the city, the crowd cries out "Hosanna" (21:9), "O save." They receive Jesus as their anticipated Davidic king, whom they believe will miraculously save them from Roman oppression. They spread their cloaks on the ground before Jesus, symbolizing their submission to Jesus as king. They wave palm branches that symbolize Jewish nationalism and victory.

The "whole city" is in an uproar (21:10), but it includes a mixed group. Some recognize Jesus's entrance as a fulfillment of messianic prophecy. Some are merely curious, caught up in the excitement over the prophet from Galilee who's been causing such a stir. But Jerusalem's religious establishment are watching for a way to get rid of Jesus, because they see him as one who has come to usurp their power and threaten national security.

### 4.12.2 Temple Actions: Jesus's Pronouncement on the Temple Establishment (21:12–17)

Matthew records that Jesus went to the temple after his entrance to Jerusalem. There is much to commend the view that in historical ministry Jesus twice went to the temple with a message to Israel and its leadership.[185] He had cleared the temple at the beginning of his ministry as a warning to Israel's leaders (John 2:13–17). When he arrives at the temple again at the end of his ministry, it's clear that the religious establishment has failed to lead Israel to repentance.[186] The temple leadership have abused the temple, conducting commercial activity that often exploited the disadvantaged. In this second clearing of the temple, Jesus rebukes the corruption, which is a pronouncement of

---

see Eckhard J. Schnabel, *Jesus in Jerusalem: The Last Days* (Grand Rapids: Eerdmans, 2018). For a semi-popular focus on the events of the cross and resurrection culminating Jesus's final week, see Craig A. Evans and N. T. Wright, *Jesus, the Final Days: What Really Happened*, ed. Troy A. Miller (Louisville: Westminster John Knox, 2009). For a popular study, see Andreas J. Köstenberger and Justin Taylor, with Alexander Stewart, *The Final Days of Jesus: The Most Important Week of the Most Important Person Who Ever Lived* (Wheaton, IL: Crossway, 2014). For a skeptical survey, see Marcus J. Borg and John Dominic Crossan, *The Last Week: A Day-by-Day Account of Jesus's Final Week in Jerusalem* (New York: HarperCollins, 2006).

183. Osborne, *Matthew*, 754–55.

184. Clay Alan Ham, *The Coming King and the Rejected Shepherd: Matthew's Reading of Zechariah's Messianic Hope*, NTMon 4 (Sheffield: Sheffield Phoenix, 2006), 112–14.

185. For a cogent rationale for two cleansings based on sociological data, see Edward W. Klink III, *John*, ZECNT (Grand Rapids: Zondervan, 2016), 176–79. For an emphasis upon historical reasoning, see Andreas Köstenberger, *John*, BECNT (Grand Rapids: Baker Academic, 2004), 111; Leon Morris, *The Gospel According to John*, rev. ed., NICNT (Grand Rapids: Eerdmans, 1995), 166–69; Carson, *Gospel According to John*, 176–78.

186. Evaluating the Johannine temple action in the light of the synoptic versions and seeing Jesus's body as temple, see Jacob Chanikuzhy, *Jesus, the Eschatological Temple: An Exegetical Study of Jn 2,13–22 in the Light of the Pre 70 C.E. Eschatological Temple*

judgment upon Israel's leadership and a rejection of their authority.[187] The blind and lame had been prevented from full access to the temple, because they were considered "unclean" by the religious establishment. By healing them, Jesus shows his authority to purify all who desire to approach God in worship.[188]

### 4.12.3 Cursing the Fig Tree: Jesus's Judgment of the Nation (21:18–22)

The tree that should have been producing the sweetest figs was unproductive, with no figs at all. This becomes an appropriate object for Jesus to use to indicate Israel's spiritual condition, providing a striking lesson for the disciples. Now that Israel, especially represented by its religious leadership, had perverted the temple practices and had not repented at the appearance of Jesus Messiah proclaiming the arrival of the kingdom of heaven, Israel was being judged by God. The cursing of the unproductive fig tree is a fitting object lesson to highlight Israel's unrepentance.

### 4.12.4 Controversies in the Temple Court over Jesus's Authority (21:23–22:46)

#### *4.12.4.1 Three Parables of Condemnation Directed Toward the Religious Leadership of Israel (21:23–22:14)*

After the religious leaders question his authority, Jesus gives three extended parables that reveal God's judgment upon them for not fulfilling their responsibility among the people to respond to his invitation to the kingdom of God (21:28–22:14).[189] Jesus counters their question with one of his own, laying a logical trap: if the religious leaders refute the divine origin of John the Baptist's highly popular prophetic ministry, they risk alienating the people (21:24). But because John had pointed to Jesus as the Messiah, any admission that John's authority came from God would validate Jesus's authority to say and do whatever he wishes, even in the temple. The Jewish leaders' unwillingness to admit the truth reveals their duplicity (21:25–27).

##### 4.12.4.1.1 The Parable of the Two Sons: The Religious Leadership Did Not Repent and Enter the Kingdom of God (21:28–32)

Jesus then gives a parable of two sons. The son that first refused to work in the vineyard but later obeyed is like those in Israel who were once outwardly disobedient

---

*Hopes and the Synoptic Temple Actions*, CBET (Leuven: Peeters, 2012), esp. ch. 3, 233–330.

187. France, *Matthew*, TNTC, 300–3; Osborne, *Matthew*, 761–64; Morris, *Matthew*, 525–26; Davies and Allison, *Matthew*, 3:133–37; E. P. Sanders, *Jesus and Judaism* (Philadelphia: Fortress, 1985), 61–69; Steven M. Bryan, *Jesus and Israel's Traditions of Judgement and Restoration*, SNTSMS 117 (Cambridge: Cambridge University Press. 2002).

188. For a discussion of the historicity of the synoptic actions, see Perrin, *Jesus the Temple*, 82–92.

189. For a close reading, see Wesley G. Olmstead, *Matthew's Trilogy of Parables: The Nation, the Nations and the Reader in Matthew 21:28–22:14*, SNTSMS 127 (Cambridge: Cambridge University Press, 2003).

(e.g., tax collectors and prostitutes), but eventually obeyed God's call of repentance through John. The son that initially consented to work in the vineyard, but failed to act, is like Israel's leaders who were outwardly obedient to the law but failed to demonstrate real obedience to God's message through Jesus.

#### 4.12.4.1.2 The Parable of the Wicked Tenants: God Takes Away the Kingdom from Israel for Not Producing the Fruit of the Kingdom (21:33–46)[190]

Jesus intensifies his rebuke with another parable that reveals the Jewish leaders' hostility toward God's message.[191] Like tenants of a vineyard, Israel's leaders were installed to guide God's people so that the nation would produce spiritual fruit. Through this parable, Jesus publicly asserts his divine sonship to the religious leadership and foretells what they will do to him. They will condemn him as a messianic pretender and have him killed by the gentiles.

Because the religious leaders have been irresponsible in their obligations and have rejected God's messengers, including his Son, their privileged role in caring for God's kingdom will be taken away and given to a people producing its fruits (21:43). This will not abolish the promises made to Israel nationally, but it does point to the transition of leadership and prominence that will be given to the disciples of Jesus in the outworking of God's kingdom program in the present age. The kingdom of God will produce its fruit in the new nation of Jesus's disciples, composed of both Jews and gentiles.[192] Jesus's disciples represent the fulfillment in part of the promises to Israel, and they now functionally perform the role that Israel had performed, but they do not replace Israel nor become Israel.

#### 4.12.4.1.3 The Parable of the Wedding Banquet: God Judges Appropriately All Responses to the Invitation to the Kingdom of Heaven (22:1–14)

Jesus continues his debates with the religious leaders with a third parable that makes plain the consequences they face for rejecting his invitation to repent and enter the kingdom of heaven. The first part of the parable points to those religious leaders who reject the invitation to the wedding with trivial excuses. Others abuse and even kill the king's servants. Their actions are not merely insulting but treasonous, and the king's rage and form of punishment are appropriate for such open rebellion (22:1–7). Even though he does not mention the destruction of the temple here, Jesus may be prophesying the

190. Klyne R. Snodgrass, "Recent Research on the Parable of the Wicked Tenants: An Assessment," *IBR* 8 (1998): 187–215; Snodgrass, "The Wicked Tenants," in *Stories with Intent*, 276–99.

191. Erin K. Vearncombe, "Redistribution and Reciprocity: A Socio-Economic Interpretation of the Parable of the Labourers in the Vineyard (Matthew 20.1–15)," *JSHJ* 8.3 (2010): 199–236.

192. For a fuller overview of these issues, see Chapters 12–13 below, and Michael J. Wilkins, "The Consideration of a Future for Israel in the Light of the Apparently Bleak Consequences for Negative Responses to Jesus's Ministry in the Gospel of Matthew," in *The Future Restoration of Israel: A Response to Supersessionism*, ed. Stanley E. Porter and Alan E. Kurschner, McMaster Biblical Studies Series 10 (Eugene, OR: Wipf & Stock; Hamilton, Ontario: McMaster Divinity College Press Press, 2023), 313–40.

destruction of Jerusalem and the judgment of the religious establishment in AD 70, a theme to which he will return in the eschatological discourse (cf. 24:1–3).

The second part of the parable (22:8–10) takes an unimaginable turn. It is not the externally righteous but the sinners who are received into the kingdom of heaven. The wedding guests gathered from the streets correspond to the sinners, tax collectors, and gentiles who respond to Jesus's gracious invitation into the kingdom.

The third part of the parable (22:11–14) focuses on one of the guests who has gained entrance to the wedding but arrives inappropriately dressed. The man's speechlessness implies that he had access to the appropriate attire but had declined to wear it. His actions reveal that he has refused Jesus's invitation to the kingdom, resulting in eternal judgment.

A pithy statement gives a concluding pronouncement to the parable of the wedding feast, but also to the three preceding parables generally: "For many are invited, but few are chosen" (22:14). The term "chosen" is an alternative expression for Jesus's true disciples. While Jesus gave an open invitation to the kingdom, from the divine perspective it is only God's sovereign choice that effects salvation. From a human perspective it is only those who respond to the call appropriately that are part of the banquet. Israel and her religious leadership lose their privileged position because they are held responsible for rejecting Jesus's invitation. Any who insult God's gracious offer of the kingdom of heaven by presuming upon it without honoring the Son will receive due judgment.

### *4.12.4.2 Four Debates with the Religious Leaders Concerning Jesus's Authority and Identity (22:15–46)*

#### 4.12.4.2.1 Tribute in the Kingdom: Paying Taxes to Caesar—Scribes of the Pharisees and Herodians (22:15–22)

These disciples of the Pharisees apparently are the Pharisees' pawns.[193] They advance with fawning deference, attempting to disarm Jesus so that they might trap him. The disciples of the Pharisees are joined by the Herodians in this sinister maneuvering.[194] Taxes were a volatile issue in Israel. If Jesus answered that it was appropriate to pay taxes to Caesar, he would be cast into disfavor among the tax-burdened people. If Jesus answered that it was not appropriate, his words could be used to accuse him of insurrection against the Roman Empire.

Jesus saw through their hypocritical ploy because he knew[195] the evil behind their motivation (22:18). Jesus uses the denarius coin for paying taxes to make a profound

193. See Wilkins, *Concept of Disciple*, 106–7, 114.

194. See Meier, *Companions and Competitors*, 560–65; Nikos Kokkinos, *The Herodian Dynasty: Origins, Role Society and Eclipse*, JSPSup 30 (Sheffield: Sheffield Academic, 1998).

195. Cf. 12:15; 18:8; 26:10 for Jesus's form of special knowledge.

counterpoint. God as Creator has sovereign claim over all creation and everything in it. Giving to God what is God's requires good stewardship of all he has created. It includes respecting governing authorities in a way that honors primary allegiance to God.

#### 4.12.4.2.2 Marriage at the Resurrection—Sadducees (22:23–33)

Jesus rebukes the Sadducees for their faulty understanding of the concept of resurrection and for denying the reality of the resurrection. To deny the resurrection is to deny the power of God to raise the dead to life. Their ignorance of the whole Hebrew Scriptures dramatically impairs their understanding of the way life is to be lived here and in the hereafter.

#### 4.12.4.2.3 The Greatest Commandments—A Legal Expert of the Pharisees (22:34–40)

These are the greatest commandments because they go to the essence of the way God has created humans to live: giving oneself to God and others to fulfill God's purposes for us as the crown of his creation in displaying in our lives the glory of God's kingdom on earth. The kingdom life that Jesus inaugurates fulfills the deepest inclination of humans who are created in the image of God. Kingdom life enables his disciples to live life the way God intended it to be lived, which means living responsibly in relationship to God and others.[196]

#### 4.12.4.2.4 The Son of David—Pharisees (22:41–46)

Jesus goes on the offensive by challenging the Pharisees' ability to interpret one of the most important messianic texts in the Old Testament—Psalm 110:1: "The Lord said to my Lord: 'Sit at my right hand until I put your enemies under your feet'" (Matt 22:44). If they cannot rightly interpret this text, they cannot possibly understand his true identity. So, Jesus presses them further. David himself, inspired by the Holy Spirit, says that the coming Messiah is not merely his special human descendant, but also his "Lord." David's descendant bears a unique relationship to God, seated at the highest position of privilege and authority at God's right hand.[197]

The Jews did not generally believe that the Messiah would be divine, but here Jesus confounds them by showing that as David called Messiah "son" and "LORD" (Ps 2:7; 110:1), Messiah is indeed his human descendant. But he sustains a divine relationship to Yahweh. Throughout Jesus's ministry his unique relationship to God as the Son of God has been increasingly revealed, an incredible truth that true disciples increasingly

196. Eugene Eung-Chun Park, "An Unintended Reader's Response to Matthew 22:34–40," *Sacra Scripta* 9.1 (2011): 7–25.

197. For discussion of the historicity of this saying of Jesus, see Benjamin Sargent, *David Being a Prophet: The Contingency of Scripture upon History in the New Testament*, BZNW 207 (Berlin: de Gruyter, 2014), esp. 92–128.

come to realize (14:33; 16:16; 17:6–6).[198] Jesus prods the Pharisees to go beyond the pat answer of their tradition and understand that David's descendant is more than his human progeny; he is the Lord, the Son of Man of Daniel's prophecy (22:43–45).

### 4.12.5 Warnings and Woes of Judgment Against the Scribes and Pharisees (23:1–39)

Now Jesus gives a final scathing denunciation of their defective leadership. First, Jesus gives a series of warnings to the disciples and crowds not to follow the defective leadership of the scribes and Pharisees. Then he will turn directly to the scribes and Pharisees and pronounce a series of woes upon them for their destructive leadership. Matthew highlights these warnings and woes as a culmination of the judgment upon Israel's leadership that has been building since Jesus's climactic entrance into Jerusalem and the events in the temple.[199]

#### *4.12.5.1 Warning Disciples and Crowds About the Scribes and Pharisees (23:1–12)*

Jesus first addresses the crowds and his disciples to warn them of the false leadership that the teachers of the law and the Pharisees have given, and to warn them not to follow their false example (23:1–12).

##### 4.12.5.1.1 First Warning: Demanding Legalistic Performance (23:1–4)

All Scripture is to be obeyed, and Jesus recognizes the Pharisees' official capacity to teach Scripture in a proper manner. But Jesus condemns their oral tradition when it incorrectly interprets the intent of the Old Testament and inappropriately supplants it by creating obligations that were more burdensome than Scripture itself.

##### 4.12.5.1.2 Second Warning: Pretentious Public Displays of Piety (23:5–7)

The Pharisees' concern for religious garments and positioning for public prominence is a show designed to enhance their own reputation among the people, rather than point the peoples' attention to God.

##### 4.12.5.1.3 Third Warning: Exploiting Titles (23:8–10)

The ultimate goal of a disciple of a rabbi was to become a rabbi himself at the end of his course of study and initiation—it was essentially the pursuit of a profession. But

198. For a careful analysis of this passage and the resulting theological implications, see Leim, *Matthew's Theological Grammar*, esp. chapter 6: "The Father and the Son," 176–233.

199. For discussion of Matthew's heightened polemic with the Jewish leaders, see Layang Seng Ja, *The Pharisees in Matthew 23 Reconsidered*, Langham Monographs (Carlisle, UK: Langham, 2018); Turner, *Israel's Last Prophet*; Kenneth G. C. Newport, *The Sources and Sitz im Leben of Matthew 23*, JSNT 117 (Sheffield: Sheffield Academic, 1995); David E. Garland, *The Intention of Matthew 23*, NovTSup 52 (Leiden: Brill, 1979).

with Jesus a new form of discipleship emerges. A disciple of Jesus would always be a disciple of Jesus, because Jesus alone is Teacher and Master. And discipleship to Jesus is essentially the growth in a relationship to Jesus. Jesus's disciples are not to seek out honorific titles or personal authority as teacher or master over other disciples, because as the Messiah, Jesus alone is their ultimate authority.

#### *4.12.5.2 Woes on the Teachers of the Law and the Pharisees (23:13–39)*

The interjection "woe" (*ouai*) is a mixed cry of regret, compassion, sorrow, and denunciation. When Jesus seven times cries out, "Woe unto you," he is deploring the miserable condition in which the Pharisees now find themselves, which lies especially in their hypocrisy and spiritual blindness. But he is also pronouncing the fate that they have brought upon themselves.[200] They, of all, are least aware of the judgment that awaits them, living in a fool's paradise while thinking that they are the epitome of religious blessedness, when all along they continue down the path of destruction with the people of Israel following close behind. They have abused their responsibility for leadership in the nation by refusing Jesus's invitation to the kingdom of God and for leading Israel to doom. (1) As false leaders, the scribes and Pharisees are not leading the people to God but are leading them away from the kingdom of heaven. (2) Zealous to win people to their own brand of Judaism, these Pharisaic leaders place their followers under their particularly burdensome code of conduct in the oral law. (3) The Pharisees had developed a complicated series of rulings regarding vows and oaths. Jesus's criticism was that they had the most important matters reversed with the less important and that they were giving more attention to the smallest details of the law than the principle of the law. (4) Their narrow focus on ceremonial detail consumes so much of their attention that they neglect the daily exercise of more important matters, such as bringing justice to those who are wronged. (5) The heart is the source of all thoughts, motives, and actions. The Pharisees' emphasis on external piety only brings external purity. In order to be truly pure, they need to first purify their hearts. And the only genuine purification is through the power of the kingdom of heaven. (6) Jesus's charge is that the teachers of the law and Pharisees have given themselves the appearance of having avoided unrighteousness by their attention to their many legal requirements. But they are instead inwardly unrighteous, because they have not attended to the transformation of the heart that could have come by responding to Jesus. (7) Their hypocrisy lies in the inconsistency between honoring the dead prophets and secretly plotting to execute contemporary ones, like Jesus.

200. Norman Hillyer, "Woe (Οὐαί)," *NIDNTT* 3:1051–54.

#### *4.12.5.3 Final Invective: Murderers of the Righteous (23:33–36)*

Like the wicked people in Israel's history who spilled innocent blood, the religious leaders of this generation will continue spilling innocent blood, specifically that of Jesus and his messengers.

#### *4.12.5.4 Lament over Jerusalem (23:37–39)*

The term "Jerusalem" now includes a reference to the whole nation of Israel for whom Jesus was deeply burdened. Jerusalem stands condemned for eliminating God's messengers, yet Jesus has compassion for the nation. He longs to protect them from the coming judgment, but they have determined their own fate. Jesus's final address to the people is a prophecy that identifies himself as the Messiah, Israel's Savior, the one who will come to his people again after a time of judgment. At that time, they will have no other choice but to acknowledge him as Lord, either in great joy or in great sorrow.

## 4.13 THE DELAY, RETURN, AND JUDGMENT OF MESSIAH (24:1–25:46)

### *FIFTH [OLIVET] DISCOURSE: "ESCHATOLOGICAL FORECAST"*

On the Mount of Olives Jesus gives his fifth discourse recorded in Matthew's Gospel. This fifth discourse is the Eschatological Forecast (chs. 24–25). Jesus reveals to the disciples the consequences for the temple and the people of Israel for not repenting at the arrival of the kingdom: the temple will be destroyed, and Israel will be punished.[201] The discourse also points to his return in glory to prepare them for the interval before the return of the Son of Man. This discourse describes how Jesus's disciples are to live each day in this age of the already-not-yet consummation of the kingdom of God in expectant preparation for his return with power.

This fifth discourse has a specific intention to give to his disciples a basic prophetic overview of the events to transpire in the near and distant future. But Jesus's intent is not primarily to give a timetable—he focuses especially on the attitudes and character qualities that guide their discipleship to him for the days and years ahead when he would no longer be with them physically.

201. For a helpful study of Jesus as judge in Matthew, see Alistair I. Wilson, *When Will These Things Happen? A Study of Jesus as Judge in Matthew 21–25*, PBM (Carlisle, UK: Paternoster, 2004).

### 4.13.1 Interpreting the Eschatological Discourse

Jesus's eschatological forecast has produced an almost dizzying array of interpretations. The primary issue is to understand, from our vantage point, what has already been fulfilled in history, and what is yet to be fulfilled in the future.

(1) On the one extreme is the preterist (past perspective) view, which suggests that virtually all the events that Jesus prophesies in this discourse were fulfilled in the first century, primarily with the fall of Jerusalem and the destruction of the temple in AD 70.[202]

(2) On the other extreme is the futurist view, which suggests that virtually all of the events of the discourse are fulfilled in the future when Israel is once again reestablished in God's purposes.[203]

(3) The position taken in this volume is a mediating one: Jesus intentionally intertwines historical and eschatological fulfillment in the discourse. There is comprehensive theological cohesion in the discourse between Jesus's treatment of the fall of Jerusalem and the parousia, but there is no clear dividing point between historical and eschatological fulfillment.[204] The resolution is that the two are purposely intertwined under what some call a "double reference" prophecy or "prophetic foreshortening," where the near event serves as a partial fulfillment and symbol for the fulfillment of far events.[205] In this view the events of 24:4–14 are a general description of the life of the church during this age, perhaps with some increase of activity in 24:9–14. But at 24:15 begins a double reference to events that will be partially fulfilled at AD 70 with the destruction of the temple and Jerusalem and culminate in the future fulfillment of the complex of events surrounding the return of Jesus—the abomination that causes desolation, the end of the age, and the parousia.

This general mediating position has been adopted by a wide range of interpreters, perhaps "a majority of conservative sources."[206] Majority certainly does not always signify accuracy, but here it indicates that caution against going too far in either direction seems to be the wisest course of interpreting Jesus's prophecy. In the discourse, Jesus warns of first-century historical judgment on Israel for rejecting the invitation to the kingdom. But Jesus also upholds guidance for his disciples and the fulfillment of the covenantal promises to Israel to be restored to the land, which ushers in the reign of the messianic kingdom. In my view, the fifth discourse is an eschatological forecast of events fulfilled partially in the first century but brought to their final fulfillment with the events surrounding the return of Jesus Messiah in glory.

202. E.g., France, *Matthew*, TNTC, 333–46; France, *Matthew*, NICNT, 889–94.

203. See Louis Barbieri Jr., "Matthew," in vol. 2 of *The Bible Knowledge Commentary*, 2 vols., ed. John F. Walvoord and Roy B. Zuck (Wheaton, IL: Victor, 1983), 76–78.

204. Morris, *Matthew*, 593–94n4. See also Jeffrey A. Gibbs, *Jerusalem and Parousia: Jesus' Eschatological Discourse in Matthew's Gospel* (St. Louis: Concordia Academic, 2000).

205. Ladd, *Theology*, 198.

206. David L. Turner, "The Structure and Sequence of Matthew 24:1–41: Interaction with Evangelical Treatments," *Grace Theological Journal* 10.1 (1989): 9.

### 4.13.2 The Setting of the Discourse (24:1–3)

We may see three basic parts to Jesus's discourse. (1) Part one describes events, generally chronological, that indicate conditions prior to Jesus's return (24:4–14), and conditions that will accompany the coming of Jesus (24:15–31). (2) Part two gives lessons on watching, waiting, and being prepared for the coming of Jesus (24:32–25:30). (3) Part three concludes the discourse with a warning of judgment and a promise of reward at the time of Jesus's second coming (25:31–46).

### 4.13.3 Sufferings Throughout This Age (24:4–8)

As Jesus looks ahead to the future of his disciples, he warns them that many events might deceive them into thinking that the end of the age has arrived. But all of these events are general characteristics of this age of birth pains. Jesus explicitly emphasizes that neither false messiahs, nor wars, nor global conflicts, nor famines nor earthquakes are to be seen as indicators of the end of the age. These are conditions that will affect the entire world throughout this age.

### 4.13.4 Sufferings of Jesus's Disciples (24:9–13)

Jesus's disciples will have the privilege of carrying his name during this age, but they will also suffer for it because the hatred that is directed at Jesus will naturally fall on his followers. Through persecution the faith of Jesus's disciples will be tested. Jesus here indicates that disciples who remain firmly committed to him will not be consumed by persecution, even if they should experience physical death. He promises that they will experience the kingdom salvation of full blessing and peace when he returns.

### 4.13.5 Preaching the Gospel to All Nations (24:14)

One explicit condition must be met before Jesus returns: the gospel of the kingdom must be proclaimed in the entire world to all the nations. During Jesus's earthly ministry the disciples' mission was restricted to Israel (cf. 10:5–7) in fulfillment of the Davidic covenant. The future mission shifts to all the nations, which will fulfill the Abrahamic covenant, but it will include a continued outreach to Israel (see on 10:23; 28:19).[207] This future mission is inaugurated with the risen Jesus's "Great Commission" (28:16–20), but it is prophesied both here in the Olivet discourse and earlier in the missionary discourse (10:16–23).[208] This worldwide proclamation was fulfilled in part during the first century with the preaching of Paul throughout the then-known world (e.g., Rom 15:19), which contributes to the imminence of Jesus's return.[209]

207. Cf. Wayne A. Brindle, "'To the Jew First': Rhetoric, Strategy, History, or Theology?," *BSac* 159 (2002): 221–33.

208. For comparison of these mission directives, see Vicky Balabanski, "Mission in Matthew Against the Horizon of Matthew 24," *NTS* 54.2 (2008): 161–75.

209. E.g., Blomberg, *Matthew*, 356–57.

The urgency of worldwide missionary activity is demanded by recognizing that the final fulfillment of Jesus's statement in 24:14 awaits the eschatological arrival of the events of great tribulation, to which Jesus now turns. Jesus's disciples are to give themselves urgently to the task of preaching the gospel of the kingdom throughout this present age, because we cannot fully discern when it has finally reached into all of the world to all of the nations.[210] Each new generation of nations does bring with it a new mission field. But once this proclamation has been fulfilled in God's timing, the beginning of the time of tribulation on the earth will begin.

### 4.13.6 Description of "Great Tribulation" (24:15–28)

Moving from general characteristics of this age, Jesus points to an event prophesied in Dan 9:27, "the abomination that causes desolation." Rather than having been completely realized in the activities of Antiochus IV Epiphanes or any other time, Jesus quotes Daniel directly to clarify that the fulfillment of the "abomination that causes desolation" is yet future.[211] This event prophesies of the destruction of the temple in AD 70, but also foreshadows a future time of eschatological defilement and destruction. Jesus gives a mixture of prophetic elements that speak both to his present generation and to the future.

The appearance of the abomination of desolation launches a period of "great tribulation" (24:21). The destruction of Jerusalem in AD 70 was horrific, but this vision of human depravity will be completed in the future with horrors that are unequaled. But God is in control even in these days of horror. The "great tribulation" will not last indefinitely, because God will bring this period to an end for the sake of the elect.

During the time of great tribulation there will be an unprecedented rise of miracle-working false messiahs and prophets. Disciples must not be deceived. These messianic pretenders are pawns of the enemy of God. Jesus warns his disciples not to believe those "in the wilderness" or "in the inner rooms" who say that they are the Messiah. Rather, the Son of Man will appear spectacularly, like lightning that is visible to all. Just as people from far and wide can spot high circling vultures converging on a carcass, so will the return of the Son of Man be visible to all when he comes to bring judgment on the deadness of this corrupt world.

### 4.13.7 Description of the Coming of the Son of Man (24:29–31)

Using typical apocalyptic imagery, Jesus describes the arrival of the end of the age in terms of great disturbances in the heavens (cf. Isa 13:10). This language may point to both physical phenomena as well as political and spiritual disruptions. Jesus's language

210. E.g., Davies and Allison, *Matthew*, 3:344; Morris, *Matthew*, 602.

211. For discussion of related issues, see Gleason L. Archer Jr., "Daniel," in *Daniel–Malachi*, EBC 7 (Grand Rapids: Zondervan, 1985), 111–21.

echoes Daniel's prophecy and points to his return at the end of the age (Dan 7:13–14).[212] Jesus is the Son of Man, the one to whom the Ancient of Days gives glory and power and designates to receive worship as the divine King. His return is the sign of the consummation of the age.[213] At this time he will gather the elect, all Jewish and gentile believers. These events most likely refer to his coming at the end of the tribulation, which would correspond with the time of judgment of the nations (25:31–46).

### 4.13.8 The Lesson of the Fig Tree (24:32–35)

A switch of emphasis now occurs. Up to this point there has been a combination of historical and eschatological features in answer to the questions about the destruction of the temple and his return and the end of the age. Jesus has given a descriptive overview of the entire age. But now he deals with attitudes that should characterize those who live during this age and await his coming. He teaches us to be alert for the signs he has given, which will forewarn us that the end is near. His words serve as a *warning* of the need for repentance before coming judgment, and as a *promise* of the summer to come, the age of blessedness and fruitfulness that his return will bring.[214]

### 4.13.9 The "Time" of Jesus's Coming (24:36–41)

In answer to the disciples' earlier question concerning the time of his coming, Jesus says, "No one knows about that day or hour" (24:36). The knowledge of his return was not given to angelic heavenly beings, whose knowledge, though apparently superhuman, is not unlimited. Their knowledge accords with what is God's will for them to know.[215]

And neither was it given to the Son to know the time of his return. This is an important christological statement—it is an example of Jesus voluntarily limiting his divine attributes. He willingly remains uninformed as to his return. The theological doctrine of the kenosis (cf. Phil 2:7, with the verb κενόω) generally contends that in Jesus's incarnation he voluntarily limited the use of his divine attributes so that he could experience full human life without in any sense giving up his deity or any of his divine attributes. It was only at the will of his Father that he could use his divine attributes. It was not the Father's will for him to know the date of his return during his time on earth. In his human consciousness Jesus restricted himself to normal human knowledge, while he always retained the attribute of omniscience in his divine nature.[216]

212. For background, see Brant James Pitre, *Jesus, the Tribulation, and the End of the Exile: Restoration Eschatology and the Origin of the Atonement*, WUNT 2/204 (Tübingen: Mohr Siebeck, 2005).

213. Stewart, "Temporary Messianic Kingdom," 255–70.

214. Kenneth E. Guenter, "'This Generation' in the Trilogy of Matthew 24:34–35," *BSac* 175 (2018): 174–94.

215. For an overview, see Millard J. Erickson, *Christian Theology*, 3rd ed. (Grand Rapids: Baker Academic, 2013), 410–11.

216. An overview of the theological issues can be found in any standard systematic theology, such as Erickson, *Christian Theology*, 637, 644–53; or Grudem, *Systematic Theology*, esp. 684–90.

On other occasions he demonstrates supernatural knowledge of the present and the future.[217]

The unexpectedness of the coming of the Son of Man means that people will be like those of Noah's generation (24:37–39). They were more concerned with everyday activities than with spiritual realities, so they were caught off-guard by God's judgment in the flood. Jesus gives two images that illustrate the unexpectedness of his return: two men in a field and two women grinding. The images depict the same truth: the Son of Man will gather his disciples to enjoy the fullness of the kingdom; those left behind will experience his judgment.[218]

### 4.13.10 The Parable of the Homeowner and the Thief (24:42–44)

In the parable of the homeowner and the thief, Jesus draws a comparison between his coming and the unexpectedness of a thief's activity to teach *preparedness*. Since the timing of the Son of Man's coming is unknown, like a responsible homeowner thwarting a thief his disciples should keep vigilant watch throughout this age.

### 4.13.11 The Parable of Two Kinds of Servants (24:45–51)

The parable of the two kinds of servants emphasizes *faithfulness*. Jesus stresses the deep division between those who are ready for his return and those who are not; between those who receive blessing and those who receive judgment when the Son of Man comes. The true nature of the servants is revealed by their actions, which indicates their faithfulness or unfaithfulness during their master's absence. The parable serves to contrast true and false believers and addresses the consequences of those who show by their lives that they are deserving of blessing or judgment.[219]

### 4.13.12 The Parable of the Ten Virgins (25:1–13)

The parable of the ten virgins teaches *readiness* in the light of the unknown time of the coming of the Son of Man. Jesus, as the messianic Son of Man, is pictured as a bridegroom proceeding to his wedding banquet. The wise virgins were prepared for what could be a long wait, so when the bridegroom arrived, they were ready to go with him to the banquet. On the other hand, the foolish virgins were shut out, rejected by the bridegroom, because they were unprepared.[220] As in the preceding parable, this is a distinction between two types of people—those who are truly disciples of Jesus, and

217. E.g., John 2:4; 4:17–18; 6:70; 11:4, 11; 13:10–11, 38.

218. For an interpretation that reverses the image, see Benjamin L. Merkle, "Who Will Be Left Behind? Rethinking the Meaning of Matthew 24:40–41 and Luke 17:34–35," *WTJ* 72.1 (2010): 169–79.

219. Timothy A. Friedrichsen, "A Note on διχοτομήσει αὐτὸν (Luke 12:46 and the Parallel in Matthew 24:51)," *CBQ* 63.2 (2001): 258–64; esp. 262.

220. Ruben Zimmermann, *Puzzling the Parables of Jesus: Methods and Interpretation* (Minneapolis: Fortress, 2015), 261–92.

those who are not. Disciples of Jesus will be ready for the arrival of the Son of Man. The destiny of those who are not ready is outside the shut door.

### 4.13.13 The Parable of the Talents (25:14–30)

In the parable of the talents, Jesus adds *industriousness* to the list of profitable character qualities seen in those who await his return. When the master returns, he gives equal praise to the first and second servant. The praise does not depend on the total amount earned, but on each individual's responsible stewardship in living up to his or her potential. Both servants receive an identical share of the master's joy as a result of their faithfulness. The third servant's actions (25:24–27) primarily stem from his own attitude toward his master. The way he perceived his master as a "hard man" produced alienation, mistrust, fear, and laziness. Had he truly loved his master, he would have been more industrious. The third servant represents a false disciple whose laziness reveals the lack of a real love for Jesus and who will ultimately be deserving of hell.

### 4.13.14 Judgment at the End (25:31–46)

The third and final section of the Olivet Discourse emphasizes the promise of reward for those admitted into the kingdom and the warning of judgment for those who are excluded. Jesus, the Son of Man, will come again in glory as both judge and king over all the peoples of every nation throughout history.

The sheep on the king's right (25:34–39) are individuals who have truly believed the gospel. They are blessed of the Father and called righteous. Their blessing consists of their inheritance, which is the kingdom that they now receive. Their surprise indicates that these were not meritorious acts to gain favor but genuine acts of mercy. Jesus here calls his disciples "brothers" (25:40), meaning the term refers to all Christians. But "the least" points explicitly to needy Christians. In caring for their brothers, especially the needy among them, they have served Jesus himself and confirmed that they are truly Jesus's sheep.

The goats on the king's left (25:41–45) are individuals who never believed the gospel. They are called "you who are cursed" and are condemned to eternal punishment because they failed to demonstrate mercy to Jesus through care for Jesus's brothers in need.

Many, whatever their understanding of a literal earthly thousand year reign of Christ and his kingdom, understand this judgment scene to be the same as that occurring at the end of this earthly age, just prior to the eternal state (Rev 20:11–13).[221] Many others understand this judgment to take place prior to the inauguration of the earthly

221. Erickson, *Christian Theology*, 1102–3; Hagner, *Matthew 14–28*, 742–43; Blomberg, *Matthew*, 376; Morris, *Matthew*, 634–35.

millennial kingdom by Jesus, who now will rule over those who are blessed to enter that reign with him.[222] The evidence is scanty either way, but the important point throughout this scene is clear—judgment will come.[223] It is a final warning of eternal punishment for those who reject Jesus. But it is also a promise of eternal life for those who accept his invitation to the kingdom.

## 4.14 THE CRUCIFIED MESSIAH (26:1–27:66)

### 4.14.1 Matthew's Portrait of the Crucified Messiah

Matthew's intricate portrait of Jesus develops its sharpest relief and richest colors in these final chapters of his Gospel. As the spotlight of history focuses on the final events of Jesus's life, Matthew draws our attention to Jesus once again as Messiah, but in a tragically ironic way.[224] Jesus is the Messiah, but in a way that baffled his own followers, disappointed the crowds, and enraged the religious leaders. He is the crucified Messiah.

### 4.14.2 Jesus's Prediction and the Plot of the Religious Leaders (26:1–5)

For the fourth time Jesus predicts his arrest and crucifixion (26:2; cf. 16:21; 17:22–23; 20:17–19). Here he connects his death with the celebration of Passover. The Jewish Passover was celebrated annually to commemorate Israel's miraculous deliverance from bondage in Egypt. Paul later recognizes the spiritual significance by referring to Jesus as "our Passover lamb" (1 Cor 5:7).

### 4.14.3 Jesus Anointed at Bethany (26:6–13)

In reminiscing a scene from earlier that week, Matthew describes the extravagant homage given to Jesus by Mary, one of his female disciples (cf. John 12:3). The woman's act of homage stands out conspicuously against the plotting of the high priest Caiaphas and his cronies, and the duplicity of Jesus's own disciple, Judas.

During a meal at the home of Simon, the leper who had been healed by Jesus, Mary anoints Jesus with pure nard, an expensive perfume oil reserved for a solemn and special act of devotion.[225] The disciples view her actions as a waste, arguing that the value of the perfume could have been used to address a concrete problem: care for the poor. Jesus comes to Mary's defense. Jesus tells his disciples that she has performed an act of homage far more significant than even she knew. She unknowingly has begun the

222. E.g., Eugene W. Pond, "The Background and Timing of the Judgment of the Sheep and Goats," *BSac* 159 (2002): 201–20; R. Saucy, *The Case for Progressive Dispensationalism*, 130.

223. See Gomes, *40 Questions About Heaven and Hell*, 292–93; David C. Sim, *Apocalyptic Eschatology in the Gospel of Matthew*, SNTSMS 88 (Cambridge: Cambridge University Press, 1996), 130–39.

224. Inhee C. Berg, *Irony in the Matthean Passion Narrative*; Karl McDaniel, *Experiencing Irony in the First Gospel: Suspense, Surprise and Curiosity*, LNTS 488 (London: Bloomsbury, 2013).

225. Rousseau and Arav, "Ointments, Perfumes," in *Jesus and His World*, 216–20.

preparations for his burial, which will come sooner than any of them would consider possible. The beauty of Mary's worship paints a striking contrast to the male disciples of Jesus and their indignant reaction to the actions of this female follower of Jesus (26:8), and an even more stunning contrast to the religious leaders' conspiracy (26:2–5) and Judas's betrayal (26:14–16).[226]

### 4.14.4 Judas Arranges the Betrayal (26:14–16)

Judas's betrayal reveals his spiritual nature: he is not a true disciple. As Luke tells us, Satan had entered him, which prompted him to go to the temple authorities to arrange for Jesus's arrest (Luke 22:3–4). He was privileged to be included in Jesus's inner circle, yet he abuses his privilege for inconceivable treachery.

### 4.14.5 The Passover and the Lord's Supper (26:17–30)

Jesus's statement, "My appointed time is near," recognizes that he is on a divinely ordained timetable. He watches the clock of history tick toward his appointment with the cross and he readies himself to be fully prepared for that coming "hour" (cf. 26:45).[227]

Jesus had anticipated Judas's betrayal and even warned the disciples on their journey to Jerusalem (20:18; cf. John 6:71; 12:4). Nevertheless, Jesus's prediction comes as a distressing surprise. They would not expect that betrayal could come out of their tight-knit group that has experienced so much together for the last three years. Then Judas, the one who would betray him, said, "Surely you don't mean me, Rabbi?" Jesus answered, "You have said so" (26:25). Judas's insincere question indicts him when Jesus's reply confirms the truth he is trying to cover up.

Jesus now fulfills the symbolic significance of this meal by instituting what will traditionally be called "the Lord's Supper." With the bread and the cup, Jesus identifies himself as the fulfillment of the Passover sacrifice. The Passover lamb's blood opened the way for the redemption of God's people from Egypt.[228] Jesus's shed blood will open the way for the redemption of all humanity to enter into a new covenant relationship with God, fulfilling God's promise to Israel.[229] Jesus indicates that he must go away, but he also assures his disciples that he will return. When he returns, he will complete the establishment of God's kingdom, ushering in the peace and fellowship for which his disciples await, and the consolation promised to the people of Israel. The Lord's

226. Keener, *Matthew* (2009), 617–21.

227. Osborne, *Matthew*, 963–64.

228. For an overview of Second Temple Jewish practices, see Jacob Neusner and William Scott Green, eds., "Haggadah of Passover," *DJBP* 266–67; Robin Routledge, "Passover and Last Supper," *TynBul* 53.2 (2002): 203–21; Joachim Jeremias, *The Eucharistic Words of Jesus*, trans. Norman Perrin (London: SCM, 1966), 84–88. For an overview of contemporary Passover rituals, see "Haggadah, Passover," *EJR* 166–67.

229. Eugene H. Merrill, "Remembering: A Central Theme in Biblical Worship," *JETS* 43.1 (2000): 27–36.

Supper is a perpetual reminder of the work of redemption Jesus began on the cross and of his eventual return to bring that work to completion.

### 4.14.6 Gethsemane: Jesus's Agonizing Prayers (26:36–46)

After the meal, Jesus gives an ominous prediction to his disciples—that very night, their loyalty to him will falter. When their courage is put to the test they will run. But the promise to the disciples is that after they falter, they will be restored in fellowship with him. Peter, the leader and spokesperson among the Twelve, brashly insists that he will never desert Jesus. Jesus warns Peter that he will fail even more than the others. Before dawn arrives, he will have denied his discipleship to Jesus three times. But Peter does not listen to Jesus's warning or heed its caution, and his false bravado leads the rest of the disciples to join in on his insistent vow of loyalty.

On the Mount of Olives, Jesus and his disciples stop at a garden area called Gethsemane that they often frequented. Jesus asks his inner circle of disciples, Peter, James, and John, to stay awake with him while he prays so that they may support him in this time of overwhelming sorrow as he contemplates the cross. Jesus faces the most intense suffering imaginable as he will endure not simply physical death but the punishment for the sins of humanity. His heart is grieved at the prospect of impending forsakenness from his Father (27:46).

He did not ask the disciples to pray, but to watch with him. This reveals the depth of Jesus's human relationships that were necessary to sustain him in his time of greatest need with their fellowship, support, and encouragement as he went to his Father in prayer. It may be difficult to grasp that the Son of God had such needs, but to do so gives us a more adequate understanding of his incarnation.

In a posture of abject humility, Jesus lays his life before his Father. Jesus is facing the most severe temptation of his life: to bypass the cross, the "cup" of his life's mission on earth. Jesus had prophesied that he must endure this cup of crucifixion to accomplish the redemption of humanity. He wants only to obey his Father's will.[230] This is the landmark example of honesty and trustfulness in prayer.

After wrestling in prayer, Jesus returns to find the trio of disciples sleeping. They had been tasked to keep watch to support Jesus in his hour of need, but they succumbed to sleep and dropped their responsibility. Jesus chides them, calling them to continue in his charge to them and to pray that they may not fall into the temptation to fail again (26:40–41). Jesus goes away to pray a second and third time (26:42–44). Now he

230. For an attempt to see an intratextual link with the Lord's Prayer in Matthew, see James N. Neumann, "Thy Will Be Done: Jesus's Passion in the Lord's Prayer," *JBL* 138.1 (2019): 161–82. I agree that the link is important, yet not due to Matthean creation but Jesus's intention.

acknowledges that it is not possible to bypass the cup. He must drink its wrathful onslaught. As he prays, Jesus consciously submits to the Father's will.

## 4.14.7 Jesus Is Arrested (26:47–56)

The garden of Gethsemane had been a favorite meeting place for Jesus and the disciples, so Judas knew where to find Jesus. Judas leads a contingent of Roman soldiers and temple police. Matthew highlights his treachery by referring to Judas as "one of the Twelve." This is insider betrayal, an unbelievable exploitation of a trusted relationship.

As Jesus is arrested, Peter tries to defend him with his sword. But Jesus states, "all who draw the sword will die by the sword" (26:52). Jesus is not defenseless, nor is he resigned to fate. He has come to carry out God's plan of redemption that has been prophesied in "the Scriptures" (26:54). In obeying the Father's will, he will not resist the cross, even though he has authority to command angels to rescue him.

Jesus's pronouncement of the divine inevitability of these events should have caused the disciples to stand firm in their trust of God's control, but instead they all run away. Once again at Jesus's greatest time of personal need for human support, his closest followers deserts him. He faces the cross alone.

## 4.14.8 Jesus Before Caiaphas and the Sanhedrin (26:57–68)

Jesus is arrested and taken to the home of Caiaphas the high priest, where the Sanhedrin, the supreme ecclesiastical court of Israel, has already partially gathered. They saw Jesus as a threat to national security because of the popular excitement evoked by his radical ministry. The Romans exercised control over all judicial proceedings but allowed a certain amount of freedom to subjected peoples to try their own legal matters.[231] Peter follows at a distance to watch the proceedings.

### *4.14.8.1 False Witnesses (26:59–60)*

The Sanhedrin finds two witnesses who testify that Jesus had said "I am able to destroy the temple of God and rebuild it in three days." They are probably referring to a statement Jesus made when he cleared the temple (John 2:19). This statement was difficult enough for Jesus's own followers to understand, but easy to distort by those who were not sympathetic to his intention. The high priest viewed Jesus as exalting himself over the temple of God.

231. David W. Chapman and Eckhard J. Schnabel, *The Trial and Crucifixion of Jesus: Texts and Commentary*, WUNT 344 (Tübingen: Mohr Siebeck, 2015), part 1.

#### *4.14.8.2 Jesus Is Silent (26:63a)*

Such blatantly distorted charges could not be answered, because whatever he said to defend himself would have been further distorted. So, Jesus remains silent. But it is "a sovereign silence."[232] Throughout this long night Jesus has spoken of the divine inevitability of these events. The Scriptures have prophesied them, and the Father's will superintends them. The theme of silence is noted by the evangelists at various times during the trials, which fulfills the prophecy of Isa 53:7: "He was oppressed and afflicted, yet he did not open his mouth." This places the responsibility for his death back on his accusers.

#### *4.14.8.3 Jesus Is the Divine Son of Man (26:63b–64)*

Caiaphas tries to have Jesus publicly lay claim to the messianic title, for which he can then take Jesus to Pilate with charges of insurrection against Roman rule (27:2). Jesus replies, "You have said so" (26:64), which is an indirect way of making an affirmation that places the responsibility back upon Caiaphas.

Jesus's response affirms that he is the Messiah, but it allows him to go beyond Caiaphas's inadequate conception to give a further clarification of the kind of Messiah that he is, and in what way he is the Son of God. Jesus had avoided those kinds of titles in his ministry because of the way that they could be misunderstood. Now is the time for clarification. Jesus declares that he is not just a human messianic deliverer but the divine Son of Man foretold in Daniel's prophecy (Dan 7:13–14) and the object of the psalmist's reference to the divine figure who sits at the right hand of God (Ps 110:1–2).[233] Jesus confounds them by showing that he sustains a divine relationship to Yahweh.[234]

Jesus's astounding claim evokes a vehement response from Caiaphas: "He has spoken blasphemy" (26:65). Blasphemy here means that Jesus is asserting that he has a unique association with God and divine status as the Son of Man. It is a truthful claim by Jesus, but Caiaphas cannot believe it. From his hard-hearted perspective it is a crime deserving of death according to Jewish law.

### 4.14.9 Peter's Denials of Jesus (26:69–75)

Although Peter courageously stayed through the early morning hours in that hostile environment, when his own personal safety is threatened, his courage deserts him. With each accusation of his relationship to Jesus, his denial becomes more emphatic.

232. Hagner, *Matthew 14–28*, 799.

233. Raymond E. Brown, *The Death of the Messiah: From Gethsemane to the Grave. A Commentary on the Passion Narratives in the Four Gospels*, ABRL (New York: Doubleday, 1994), 1:523.

234. For discussion of the imagery, see Darrell L. Bock, *Blasphemy and Exaltation in Judaism: The Charge Against Jesus in Mark 14:53–65* (Grand Rapids: Baker Academic, 2000).

He first denies the servant girl's words, then denies Jesus with an oath. When Peter's Galilean accent gives him away, he even invokes curses of God's wrath upon himself to convince them he is not lying.

Just as Jesus had predicted, the rooster crows after Peter denies Jesus three times. At the sound, Peter recalls the promise he made to stand up for Jesus. The self-denial that caused Peter to reject all about himself that distinguished him as a follower of Jesus now is thrust upon him most deeply. He knows how reprehensibly cowardly and phony he is, and he goes outside and weeps bitterly.

### 4.14.10 Jesus Condemned by the Sanhedrin and Delivered to Pilate (27:1–2)

When morning came the chief priests and elders assembled so that they could give a more formal ratification of the pronouncement of blasphemy made against Jesus. One means of having final control over subjected people was that the Romans kept the death penalty under their own jurisdiction and reserved the right to step in on any case at any point and take over the proceedings. So, the Jewish leaders take Jesus to Pilate, the Roman prefect and governor of Judea.[235]

Handing over a Jewish citizen to a foreign power was considered a traitorous deed in Jewish practice. The obsession of the Sanhedrin to have Jesus executed was greater than the nationalistic aversion to betraying a fellow countryman to hostile foreign powers. This is a tragic testimony to the duplicitous relations that Caiaphas maintained with Pilate, knowing that the Romans would now carry out the Sanhedrin's desire to have Jesus eliminated.[236]

### 4.14.11 Judas's Remorse and Suicide (27:3–10)

Seeing Jesus condemned, Judas is seized with feelings of remorse. He attempts to reject the blood money he received for betraying him. However, Judas's feelings of remorse are not repentance. Judas was an unbeliever who chose suicide in order to escape the daily guilt of facing his actions for which he would not repent. The act of suicide itself is not the focus of condemnation, but rather the act of turning away from Jesus and betraying him. He was an unbeliever who had chosen suicide as the way of escaping the daily horror of facing his actions for which he would not repent.[237] He chose to meet his eternal condemnation.[238]

235. Chapman and Schnabel, *Trial and Crucifixion of Jesus*, part 2.

236. David Flusser, in collaboration with R. Steven Notley, *Jesus*, 3rd ed. (Jerusalem: Hebrew University Magnes Press, 2001), 205–6.

237. For one who sees repentance in Judas's actions, see Catherine Sider Hamilton, "The Death of Judas in Matthew: Matthew 27:9 Reconsidered," *JBL* 137.2 (2018): 419–37.

238. Senior, *Matthew*, 319; contra Kim Paffenroth, *Judas: Images of the Lost Disciple* (Louisville: Westminster John Knox, 2001), 111–18.

### 4.14.12 The Roman Trial of Jesus (27:11–26)

The religious crime of blasphemy is not sufficient for the Romans to impose the death penalty, so the Jewish leaders change the charges when they hand Jesus over to Pilate. They now charge him with making a claim to be "king of the Jews," which focuses on treason and insurrection. Pilate asks Jesus to confirm the charge, but while Jesus's answer affirms the question, it places the responsibility back upon Pilate to discern properly what the question implies. Jesus recognizes that the trial is a sham, so he does not reply.

#### *4.14.12.1 The Crowd, Barabbas, and Jesus (27:15–18)*

In an attempt to gain favor with the people, Pilate had initiated a custom in which he released a prisoner at Passover whom the crowds favored. Now he offers the crowd two options for release: Jesus, or Barabbas. As an "insurrectionist" (*lēstēs*), Barabbas may have belonged to a group of rural brigands stirring political and social unrest among the people. Social unrest was quite common, instigated in part by these insurrectionists.[239] It is important to note that the two criminals between whom Jesus was crucified were also called by this same term, "insurrectionist" (*lēstēs*) (27:38), a quite different sort of criminal than a common "thief" (*kleptēs*; 6:19; 24:43).[240] These insurrectionists were popular with the common people because they preyed upon the wealthy establishment of Israel and created havoc for the Roman government.

#### *4.14.12.2 The Dream of Pilate's Wife (27:19)*

Matthew inserts here another testimony of innocence. Because of a dream that Pilate's wife interprets as an omen, she contends that Jesus is a righteous man. Pilate's wife warns him not to sentence Jesus.

#### *4.14.12.3 The Religious Leaders, the Crowd, and Jesus's Blood (27:20–25)*

But Pilate does not heed her warning. Instead, Pilate listens to the crowd. Fearing a riot, Pilate washes his hands as an admission that he has not found anything in Jesus deserving of the death penalty. Pilate tried to escape the responsibility, but he cannot wash his hands of the matter. By not finding any guilt and still ordering Jesus to be executed, Pilate was guilty of the death of an innocent man.

The religious leaders of Israel persuade the crowds to demand that Barabbas be released, and that Jesus be crucified (cf. 27:20–25). Matthew then records the tragic declaration that as one "people" (*laos*) they answer, "His blood is on us and on our children!" (27:25). The people of that day, as in any day, are responsible for their own actions.[241]

---

239. Richard A. Horsley and John S. Hanson, *Bandits, Prophets, and Messiahs: Popular Movements at the Time of Jesus* (Minneapolis: Winton, 1985), 48–87. For a more recent discussion by Horsley of Jesus's role, see Richard A. Horsley, *The Prophet Jesus and the Renewal of Israel: Moving Beyond a Diversionary Debate* (Grand Rapids: Eerdmans, 2012).

240. See Michael J. Wilkins, "Barabbas," *ABD* 1:607.

241. Osborne, *Matthew*, 1021.

The apostle Peter in his first public sermon at Pentecost indicts the religious leaders, the Jewish crowds, and the Romans for Jesus's death (Acts 2:22–23; cf. 2:36; 3:17–19). Guilt is attributed to that generation and judgment exacted with the destruction of the temple and the city of Jerusalem in AD 70. But to those who acknowledge their guilt Peter's sermon also extends an offer of forgiveness of sins and salvation (2:37–41; 3:19–4:4). Thousands of Jewish people, including many priests, received that offer in the first days after Pentecost (2:41; 4:4; 6:7). Everyone is responsible for his or her own actions, but God's forgiveness awaits any who repent. It is not all Jews everywhere and forever who experienced judgment, but only those in Jerusalem or the land of Israel, and only that generation, who experienced judgment in AD 70.

### 4.14.13 Jesus Messiah Is Crucified (27:26–44)

The crucifixion narrative culminates a critical theme of this Gospel, a theme that marks a central purpose of Jesus's entire earthly mission—Jesus brings salvation from sin (cf. 1:21).

#### *4.14.13.1 The Soldiers Flog and Mock Jesus (27:26–31)*

With the Sabbath approaching, the Romans flog Jesus nearly to death so that he will not be left on the cross after sundown and the arrival of Sabbath. Jesus had suffered similar cruel taunting in the house of Caiaphas after he was condemned. There the high priest's guards played a brutal game with Jesus in order to ridicule his claim to prophecy (26:68); here the Roman soldiers play an even more brutal game to ridicule his claim to be the messianic King of Israel (27:29).[242]

#### *4.14.13.2 The Journey to Golgotha (27:32–34)*

Leaving the military quarters at Pilate's palace to crucify Jesus outside the city wall, the soldiers recognize that Jesus is so weakened from the flogging that he will not be able to carry the cross. The Roman soldiers conscript Simon, a pilgrim from Cyrene, to carry Jesus's crosspiece to Golgotha, the site of Jesus's execution.

#### *4.14.13.3 Jesus Is Crucified (27:35–38)*

At about nine o'clock in the morning, Jesus is crucified, nailed to a cross to undergo a painful, slow, humiliating execution by crucifixion.[243] Crucifixion was used both as a

242. Flusser, *Jesus*, 169.

243. The most important earlier historical study of crucifixion is Martin Hengel, *Crucifixion: In the Ancient World and the Folly of the Message of the Cross* (ET; Philadelphia: Fortress, 1977). But recent studies are immensely important, among them is David W. Chapman, *Ancient and Christian Perceptions of Crucifixion*, WUNT 2/244 (Tübingen: Mohr Siebeck, 2008); Gunnar Samuelsson, *Crucifixion in Antiquity: An Inquiry into the Background and Significance of the New Testament Terminology of Crucifixion*, 2nd ed., WUNT 2/310 (Tübingen: Mohr Siebeck, 2013); John Granger Cook, *Crucifixion in the Mediterranean World*, WUNT 2/327 (Tübingen: Mohr Siebeck, 2014); Chapman and Schnabel, *Trial and Crucifixion of Jesus.*

means of execution and for exposing an executed body to shame and humiliation. The soldiers divide Jesus's clothes among themselves and settle in to guard the execution, ensuring that none of Jesus's many followers attempt to rescue him.

The soldiers place a written charge above Jesus's head mocking his messianic claim: THIS IS JESUS, THE KING OF THE JEWS (27:37).[244] This acts as a deterrent to any Jews considering an uprising against Rome. Along with Jesus, they also crucify two *insurrectionists* or political rebels (*lēstai*). Pilate was apparently rounding up, arresting, and convicting people who were stirring up the crowds to insurrection.

### *4.14.13.4 The Mocking of Messiah (27:39–44)*

Convinced by the charges against Jesus, people begin to mock Jesus's claim of divine supernatural power.[245] The highest tiers of Israel's leadership have also followed Jesus out to Golgotha to hurl their final insults at him. Even the rebels crucified with Jesus deride him for what they determine is his false messianic claim. But darkness looms.

### *4.14.13.5 The Death of Jesus Messiah (27:45–50)*

At noon darkness falls that lasts for three hours. This is not a solar eclipse, for the Passover occurred at full moon. This is an act of God. The darkness that came over the land at the crucifixion scene displays God's displeasure on humanity for crucifying his Son, and most importantly God's judgment on evil.[246] At about the ninth hour, or three o'clock in the afternoon, Jesus cries out "My God, my God, why have you forsaken me?" (Ps 22:1). The crucifixion scene recalls the lament of King David. The Son of God must be separated from the Father in order to bear the sin of his people.

In his psalm, David goes on to recount his vindication (Ps 21:21–22), but Jesus's cry does not go that far. Matthew focuses on Jesus's abandonment, a theme that pervades the narrative.[247] Although Jesus will in truth be vindicated in his resurrection, Matthew calls us to ponder deeply his abandonment.[248] Jesus is being subjected to the separation from the Father that must accompany bearing the sin of his people (Matt 1:21; 20:28; 26:28). He now bears the divine retribution and punishment for sin, as the Father's cup of wrath is poured out on him in divine judgment of sin.[249]

244. A brief discussion of the historicity of the titulus is found in Wilkins, "Peter's Declaration," 345–47. For recent attempts to see Matthew's theological creativity in the titulus, see Tucker S. Ferda, "Matthew's *Titulus* and Psalm 2's King on Mount Zion," *JBL* 133.3 (2014): 561–81; Ferda, "The Soldiers' Inscription and the Angel's Word: The Significance of 'Jesus' in Matthew's Titulus," *NovT* 55.3 (2013): 221–31.

245. See David M. Moffitt, "Righteous Bloodshed, Matthew's Passion Narrative, and the Temple's Destruction: Lamentations as a Matthean Intertext," *JBL* 125.2 (2006): 299–320; esp. 319–20.

246. Michael J. Wilkins, "Darkness," *EDBT* 142–43; Hans Conzelmann, "σκότος, κ.τ.λ.," *TDNT* 7:423–45; H.-C Hahn, "Darkness," *NIDNTT* 1:420–25. For a discussion of the possible (new) covenant ratification aspect of the darkness of the death scene, see Greg Forbes, "Darkness Over All the Land: Theological Imagery in the Crucifixion Scene," *RTR* 66.2 (2007): 83–96.

247. E.g., M. Eugene Boring, "The Gospel of Matthew: Introduction, Commentary, and Reflections," in *NIB* 8 (Nashville: Abingdon, 1995), 492.

248. Cf. Davies and Allison, *Matthew*, 3:624–25.

249. See the helpful study of Jesus's lament from the cross

Jesus's divinely sustained humanity experienced consciously the full penalty of death for the sins of humanity. Earlier he had indicated to the disciples that the purpose of his life's mission was to be a "ransom for many" (20:28). Here we see that fateful prediction being carried out. This lays the foundation for the theological doctrine of "atonement," in which Jesus's sacrifice on the cross is one of "penal substitution" or "vicarious atonement"—Jesus suffers our punishment for our sin.[250] The penalty for sin is death (Rom 6:23), and in Jesus's separation from God the Father he experiences deathly punishment for the sins of humanity.

But even in the depth of Jesus's abandonment to his atoning sacrifice, he still knew that this experience was not one of despair—he still calls his Father "my God, my God."[251] The relational separation while bearing the sins of humanity could not separate him entirely from his Father because his consummate trust in his Father's will expects that he will not be abandoned forever and because the oneness of their ontology is indissoluble.

Jesus now yields his spirit to death out of his own volition (27:50). To the very end, Jesus is in full control over his destiny, even as he submits himself to the Father's will. This is the final voluntary demonstration of his divine dignity, in which he gives the irrevocable expenditure of his life for the sins of his people.

## 4.14.14 Testimonies to Jesus's Death (27:51–54)

Matthew immediately records several events that follow upon the death of Jesus, all of which give significant historical and theological testimony to explain the impact of Jesus's death.

### *4.14.14.1 The Temple (27:51)*

The first testimony comes from the temple. At the moment of Jesus's death, the curtain of the temple is torn in two. The sixty-foot-high curtain was split from top to bottom, which is a sign that God himself abolished the separation from the Holy of Holies, signifying that the new and living way was now open for all people to enter into the presence of God through the sacrifice of Jesus on the cross (cf. Eph 2:11–22;

---

by Rebekah Eklund, *Jesus Wept: The Significance of Jesus' Laments in the New Testament*, LNTS 515 (London: Bloomsbury T&T Clark, 2015), esp. 42–45.

250. For a "panel" discussion of four views of atonement maintained by four evangelical scholars, see James Beilby and Paul R. Eddy, eds., *The Nature of the Atonement: Four Views* (Downers Grove, IL: InterVarsity, 2006). I suggest that Thomas R. Schreiner's articulation of the "penal substitution" view is most satisfactory from a biblical, theological, and historical perspective. For recent full discussions of the doctrine of the atonement, see William Lane Craig, *The Atonement*, Elements in the Philosophy of Religion (Cambridge: Cambridge University Press, 2018); Eleonore Stump, *Atonement*, Oxford Studies in Analytic Theology (Oxford: Oxford University Press, 2019); David L. Allen, *The Atonement: A Biblical, Theological, and Historical Study of the Cross of Christ* (Nashville: B&H, 2019); Barry D. Smith, *The Meaning of Jesus' Death: Reviewing the New Testament's Interpretations* (London: Bloomsbury T&T Clark, 2017). For standard systematic treatments see Erickson, *Christian Theology*, 713–68; Grudem, *Systematic Theology*, 705–26.

251. Gerald L. Bray, *God Is Love: A Biblical and Systematic Theology* (Wheaton, IL: Crossway, 2012), 586.

Heb 10:20). The tear signifies the removal of separation between God and his people. Jesus's sacrifice on the cross fulfills the hopes expressed in Israel's temple sacrifice.

#### *4.14.14.2 The Dead (27:51b–53)*

The second testimony is a complex of earthquakes, splitting rocks, and raised bodies. At Jesus's death an earthquake occurs that breaks open the tombs. After Jesus's resurrection three days later, several pious Old Testament figures are also raised to life. As with the preceding miraculous testimonies, the supernatural raising of the bodies of these holy ones and their appearances in Jerusalem is striking testimony to Jesus's accomplished work on the cross, and thereafter his resurrection. Their miraculous resurrection testifies to the people in Jerusalem of Jesus's triumph over death through his own death and resurrection.[252]

#### *4.14.14.3 Gentiles (27:54)*

The third testimony following the death of Jesus is that of the centurion and the guards at the crucifixion scene. The centurion and his guards were accustomed to seeing crucifixions, but witnessing these cataclysmic events gives them insight into Jesus's identity as they exclaim: "Surely he was the Son of God!" Scholarly opinions vary as to the meaning of the exclamation, with some suggesting it is simply a pagan reaction and others suggesting that it is a response of fear.[253]

A more satisfactory understanding of the centurion's and his men's statement is that as little as they may have really understood, this was a true step of faith. The centurion was gaining an insight to Jesus's true identity. The charge of blasphemy from the Sanhedrin was in part lodged against Jesus's claim to be the Son of God, to which Jesus had responded with an affirmative (26:63–64). The centurion was certain to have known the various charges against Jesus because the military chain of command necessitates that he know about potential uprisings to rescue the convicted Jesus. As he watches the events unfold, the centurion and his men are overwhelmed by the realization that the identification was truthful. In this Jewish context, the centurion was struck by the confirmation that Jesus has a filial relationship to Israel's God.[254]

Matthew has given increasing emphasis to Jesus as Son of God since the Jewish trial that evinced cries of blasphemy (26:63–65). The centurion's evocation is in dramatic

252. For a recent, thorough study of these events that views them as historical with literary and theological significance, see Raymond M. Johnson, *I See Dead People: The Function of the Resurrection of the Saints in Matthew 27:51–54*, Reformed Academic Dissertations (Phillipsburg, NJ: P&R, 2019).

253. See Whitney T. Shiner, "The Ambiguous Pronouncement of the Centurion and the Shrouding of Meaning in Mark," *JSNT* 78 (2000): 3–22.

254. For a comparison of this declaration by the Roman centurion at the crucifixion scene with the declaration of the disciples when Jesus calmed the storm, see Angel, "*Crucifixus Vincens*," 299–317.

distinction from the religious leaders and the bystanders at the cross who had mocked Jesus for his claim to be the Son of God (27:40–43). It is a striking picture for Matthew's readers.

However much the centurion and his men understood by these words, Matthew's point is clear. The evaluative point of view of these Roman guards agrees with that of God the Father (3:17; 17:5), the disciples when Jesus calmed the storm (14:33), and Peter's declaration (16:16) that Jesus is the Son of God, a confession that is now given publicly.[255]

## 4.14.15 The Women Followers of Jesus (27:54–56)

All of the evangelists mention a group of women who followed and served Jesus in the Galilee region and who also followed him to Jerusalem, and witnessed the events of the final week, including bravely staying with Jesus to witness the crucifixion.[256] These women will also be the first witnesses to Jesus's resurrection.[257]

The expressions used to describe these women followers of Jesus concur with the evidence elsewhere that they were Jesus's disciples.[258] One of the revolutionary features of the form of discipleship that Jesus instituted concerned women who become some of Jesus's closest disciples. Women and men were originally created by God as humans who were equal and complementary coworkers in ruling God's creation for him (Gen 1:26–28). But in some circles within Judaism, because of misinterpretation of Scripture and cultural bias, women had lost their dignity, value, and worth. For women to be disciples of a great master was an unusual circumstance in Palestine of the first century.

Yet here we find another instance of the unique form of discipleship Jesus instituted. Jesus restores and reaffirms to women their dignity and worth as persons who are fully equal to men as humans created in the image of God. Distinctions among Jesus's disciples relate to function, not spiritual standing or commitment or essential personal worth. As Jesus has demonstrated, all those who are marginalized by the religious or social establishments now are invited to the level ground of discipleship to Jesus.

## 4.14.16 The Burial of Jesus Messiah (27:57–61)

### *4.14.16.1 Joseph of Arimathea (27:57–60)*

Joseph of Arimathea had also become a disciple of Jesus. Although he is called a disciple, he was not a part of the Twelve, but like the women, he is among the wider

255. Kingsbury, *Matthew as Story*, 90.

256. Matthew 27:55–56, 61; cf. Mark 15:40–41; Luke 23:49, 55–56; John 19:25–27.

257. Matthew 28:1; cf. Mark 16:1; Luke 24:1, 10–11; John 20:1–18.

258. Among those who argue that these characteristics imply that women are disciples of Jesus are In-Cheol Shin, "Matthew's Designation of the Role of Women as Indirectly Adherent Disciples," *Neotestamentica* 41.2 (2007): 399–415; Brown and Roberts, *Matthew*, 256–57; Keener, *Matthew* (2009), 688–91;

circle of Jesus's adherents.[259] He was a member of the Sanhedrin who did not consent to their actions against Jesus. His high standing allows him access to Pilate to ask for Jesus's body. Pilate evidently knew of Joseph's stature, because he releases Jesus's body to him immediately.

Jewish custom dictated that crucified bodies should be taken down before the Sabbath, which began at sundown that evening. Joseph begins burial procedures for Jesus in a new tomb of his own. The wealth of Joseph of Arimathea is attested in his having prepared a new family tomb, but little did he know that his new tomb had been sovereignly prepared for the sacred burial of his Master. Joseph begins preparing Jesus's body for burial by placing it in a clean linen cloth, or "shroud" (RSV; 27:59). After Jesus's body was laid in the tomb, Joseph rolled a large stone in front of the entrance to keep out ravaging animals (27:60).

#### *4.14.16.2 The Women's Sad Vigil (27:61)*

Matthew tells us that at least two of the women who had witnessed Jesus's crucifixion—Mary Magdalene and the "other Mary," whom Mark tells us was the mother of Joses (Mark 15:47)—sat opposite the tomb and witnessed the sad and lonely ceremony of preparation for burial. Prior to burial, out of respect and honor, the corpse was watched over (*shemirah*) and washed (*taharah*). The best conjecture is that the women who had followed Jesus from Galilee must have been close to Jesus's family, including Jesus's mother Mary and aunt Salome, both before and after the cross and into the early church (cf. Acts 1:14), and would have worked together with Joseph and Nicodemus to prepare the body for burial.[260]

### 4.14.17 The Guard at the Tomb (27:62–66)

The next day the chief priests and the Pharisees go to Pilate to make certain that Jesus does not rouse support even after his death. They have not forgotten Jesus's earlier claim that he would rise again after three days. They assume that Jesus's followers will try to continue his movement by perpetrating Jesus's deception, so they enlist the help of the Roman military to secure Jesus's tomb.

Matthew alone among the evangelists recounts this incident of securing Jesus's tomb. The fact that only Matthew records this incident leads some to doubt the historicity

---

Osborne, *Matthew*, 1047–48; Witherington, *Women in the Ministry of Jesus*, 122–23. Among those who argue that these characteristics do not imply that women are disciples is Janice Capel Andersen, "Matthew: Gender and Reading," *Semeia* 28 (1983): 18–24.

259. Cf. Ulrich Luz, "The Disciples in the Gospel According to Matthew," in *The Interpretation of Matthew*, ed. Graham N. Stanton, 2nd ed., SNTI (Edinburgh: T&T Clark, 1995), 115–48. The expression "adherents to Jesus" expresses the central meaning of the relationship in typical first century usage; cf. Wilkins, *Concept of Disciple*, 41–42, 124–25.

260. Cf. John Wenham, *Easter Enigma: Are the Resurrection Accounts in Conflict?* 2nd ed. (Grand Rapids: Baker, 1992), 60–67.

of this event.[261] But Matthew is writing for a Jewish-Christian audience that would have heard about the charges that were circulating among the Jews that Jesus's body had been stolen by his disciples (28:11–15), while the audiences of the other evangelists would not have been aware of such charges. Therefore, Matthew addresses a situation that is of unique, pressing concern to his readers.[262]

## 4.15 RESURRECTION AND COMMISSION OF THE MESSIAH (28:1–20)

Jesus's resurrection figures prominently in all four Gospels. While we do not have enough of the details to resolve all of the differences between the various accounts of the resurrection found in the Gospels and in Paul (esp. 1 Cor 15:1–8), their variations strengthen the truth that the evangelists are independent witnesses and that they are not attempting to reproduce a concocted deception.[263] The resurrection is the declaration that Jesus is who he said that he was, that what he came to accomplish at the cross was efficacious, and that he now lives to be the faithful Companion, Master, and Lord to all those who respond to his great commission.[264]

### 4.15.1 Women Disciples of Jesus Discover an Empty Tomb (28:1–4)

Matthew begins his narrative of the resurrection scenes by recounting how the women came to the tomb "after the Sabbath" at dawn on the first sunrise of the new week. This is the root of the later practice of Christians gathering on Sunday morning to worship the risen Jesus (e.g., 1 Cor 16:2).[265] Consistent with Jewish burial practices, the women would have assisted the family in preparing the body for burial. Jewish custom permitted both men and women to prepare corpses, with women allowed to attend to corpses of either gender, but men not allowed to attend to women's corpses.[266]

Another earthquake (cf. 27:51) now rocks the Jerusalem area, apparently before sunrise on the first day of the week when the women made their visit. Matthew alone relates that with the earthquake the angel of the Lord rolled away the stone, and he

261. E.g., Brown, *Death of the Messiah*, 1310–13; Davies and Allison, *Matthew*, 3:652–53.

262. Cf. Keener, *Matthew* (2009), 696–97; Carson, "Matthew," 654.

263. Cf. Morris, *Matthew*, 733; Hagner, *Matthew 14–28*, 868.

264. The literature on the resurrection is massive, but the following will give the reader a head start. For thorough studies of the historical and exegetical issues, see N. T. Wright, *Resurrection of the Son of God*; Michael R. Licona, *The Resurrection of Jesus: A New Historiographical Approach* (Downers Grove, IL: InterVarsity, 2010); Richard N. Longenecker, ed., *Life in the Face of Death: The Resurrection Message of the New Testament* (Grand Rapids: Eerdmans, 1998); and Matthew Levering, *Did Jesus Rise from the Dead? Historical and Theological Reflections* (Oxford: Oxford University Press, 2019).

265. Cf. Carson, "Matthew," 656–57; Davies and Allison, *Matthew*, 3:663; Hagner, *Matthew 14–28*, 868–69; Keener, *Matthew* (2009), 700; Morris, *Matthew*, 734n3.

266. Keener, *Matthew* (2009), 700.

sat upon it (28:2). The stone was rolled away not to let the risen Jesus out but to let the women in to witness the fact of the empty tomb. The stone that was sealed by the guards to assure that the body of Jesus would remain in the tomb now becomes the seat of triumph for the angel. The miraculous conception, birth, and infancy of Jesus were superintended by the angel of the Lord (1:20–21; 2:13, 19), so it is not surprising that the angel of the Lord (*angelos kyriou*; 28:2) now superintends the resurrection events, thereby framing Matthew's story of the divine message God gives to his people in the person of his Son, Jesus Christ. As in the infancy narrative, this angel is one of God's privileged messengers, perhaps Gabriel, who seems to have a special role in announcements.[267] In Luke's Gospel, Gabriel announces both the conception of John the Baptist to Zechariah and the conception of Jesus to Mary (Luke 1:11–20, 26–38).

The appearance of a fiery angel often terrified people (Judg 13:19–20; 4 Ezra 10:25–27), which is the case here also with the guards (28:4). This may indicate that they fainted from the shock of the angelic visitation.[268]

### 4.15.2 The Angel Announces the Resurrection of Jesus (28:5–7)

The angel calms the women and announces to them that Jesus is no longer in the tomb: he has been raised from the dead, just as Jesus had foretold. Jesus was not just raised spiritually; he was resurrected physically, because his body was no longer in the tomb. These events are so disorienting that the women will be filled with fear yet with unanticipated joy (cf. 28:8). The angel instructs them to go immediately and tell Jesus's disciples about this remarkable news and tell them that they will see him in Galilee. Here the expression "his disciples" probably refers to the Eleven.

One of the most important perspectives on the women here is that God used them as witnesses not only to the central redemptive act of history, Jesus's death on the cross, but also to the attestation of that act in his resurrection from the dead. Many scholars consider God's choice of these women as the first witnesses of Jesus's resurrection to be one of the bedrock authentications of the resurrection narratives and the historicity of the resurrection itself.[269] Since the women were present for Jesus's death on the cross and his burial by Joseph of Arimathea (cf. 27:55–56, 61), they could verify that he was truly dead, not just unconscious. Several of the women witnessed the sealing of the tomb,[270] and they are among the first witnesses of the empty tomb and the resurrected Jesus.[271] They are designated by both the angel and Jesus to be the ones

267. See Larry W. Hurtado, *One God, One Lord: Early Christian Devotion and Ancient Jewish Monotheism* (Philadelphia: Fortress, 1988), 71–92; Carol A. Newsom, "Gabriel," *ABD* 2:863; Carol A. Newsom and Duane F. Watson, "Angel," *ABD* 1:248–55.

268. Hagner, *Matthew 14–28*, 869.

269. E.g., Grant R. Osborne, "Women in Jesus' Ministry," *WTJ* 51 (1989): 270. For discussion of the broader issues, see William L. Craig, "Did Jesus Rise From the Dead?," in Wilkins and Moreland, *Jesus Under Fire*, 151–55.

270. Cf. Matt 27:60–61; Mark 15:46–47; Luke 23:55.

271. Matt 28:1–6; Mark 16:1–6; Luke 24:1–8; John 20:1–16.

who would carry their witness to the other disciples as the first to testify of the reality of the resurrection.[272]

### 4.15.3 The Risen Jesus Is Worshiped by the Women Disciples (28:8–10)

The women hurry off, and the physically resurrected Jesus meets them. Then the women's fear transforms into worship. By allowing this act of worship here and in Galilee (28:17), something which neither angels (Rev 22:8–9) nor apostles will allow (Acts 10:25–26; 14:11–15), Jesus accepts this acknowledgment of his deity. Only God is to be worshiped (cf. Acts 4:9–10; 14:33; Rev 22:9), and these women now prostrate themselves before the Risen One who is rightly to be accorded that divine honor. Jesus calms them and commissions them again to tell "my brothers" (Matt 28:10) to meet him in Galilee. The switch from "disciples" to "brothers" may be an indication of the larger group of disciples, who also will witness the risen Jesus (e.g., 1 Cor 15:6). The latter may explain the reaction of "some" who doubted (Matt 28:17).[273]

### 4.15.4 The Conspiracy to Deny the Truth of Jesus's Resurrection (28:11–15)

The religious leaders conspire together once again, fearing the potential threat to their powerbase if the truth of Jesus's resurrection becomes public. They pay the guards to circulate a false story among the Jews that casts Jesus's disciples negatively as conspirators deceiving the people with the news of Jesus's resurrection.

Matthew writes upward of thirty years after these events, and yet he states, "And this story has been widely circulated among the Jews to this very day" (28:15). This Matthean aside indicates that there was an active attempt by the Jewish leaders to counteract the increasingly widespread declaration that Jesus had been raised from the dead in vindication of his claim to be Messiah. Nearly a century later the rumor was still being spread among the Jews, as is evident in the writings of Justin Martyr (*Dial.* 108.2). The truth is often harder for a person to believe than a lie, and many fall for this conspiracy to avoid the radical truth of Jesus's resurrection.

### 4.15.5 The Risen Jesus Appears to His Disciples in Galilee (28:16–17)

This concluding paragraph (vv. 16–20) is unique to Matthew's Gospel and bears his unique emphases.[274] After hearing the women's news, the eleven disciples (now minus Judas) arrive in Galilee to meet with Jesus as instructed. Upon seeing Jesus, they have a mixed reaction of worship and hesitation.

272. Matt 28:10; Mark 16:7; John 20:17.

273. See Carson, "Matthew," 659. Hagner (*Matthew 14–28*, 874) questions the wider association.

274. Cf. Blomberg, *Matthew*, 429; Hagner, *Matthew 14–28*, 881–83; Keener, *Matthew* (2009), 715–21.

### 4.15.6 The Risen Jesus Gives His Great Commission to His Disciples (28:18–20)

The risen Jesus comes close to the Eleven and addresses their fears with his declaration of absolute authority throughout all heaven and earth. His authority assures the disciples' personal security but also forms the foundation for the exhortation to follow. As the one given all authority, Jesus gives his disciples the Great Commission, the mandate to make disciples of all the nations. Disciples of Jesus are to call other individuals into the same commitment to Jesus as their sole Master and Lord. Jesus's ministry in Israel was the beginning of what would be a universal invitation into the kingdom for all the peoples of the earth, including both Jews and gentiles.[275]

Individuals who become disciples are to be baptized in the name (singular) of the three persons of the Trinitarian Godhead. Baptism is a new disciple's public identification with God's new covenant family of faith. Teaching and obeying is the process by which disciples of Jesus are continually transformed, and the process of discipleship applies to everyone who responds to the gospel message. Everything that Jesus communicated in his words and conduct is to be taught and obeyed.

Jesus concludes the commission, and Matthew this Gospel, with the crucial element of discipleship: the abiding presence of the Master. Jesus's promise of his eternal presence with his disciples is fulfilled because he is Immanuel, "God with us" (e.g., 1:23; cf. 28:20). As Matthew has demonstrated over and over in this Gospel, the arrival of Jesus began the greatest revolution that history has ever known. It is a revolution that begins in the heart, where Jesus enters in and begins the transformation. But then it extends to every area of his disciples' lives, so that our physical, emotional, thought, and relational life is impacted by the power of the kingdom of heaven.

---

275. See Craig S. Keener, "Matthew's Missiology: Making Disciples of the Nations (Matthew 28:19–20)," *Asian Journal of Pentecostal Studies* 12.1 (2009): 3–20.

*Part 3*

# Major Themes in Matthew's Theology

*Chapter 5*

# The Old Testament and Jesus Messiah in Matthew's Gospel

## *Fulfillment*

### Bibliography

**Allen, David and Steve Smith,** eds. *Methodology in the Use of the Old Testament in the New: Context and Criteria*. LNTS 579. London: T&T Clark, 2020. **August, Jared M.** "'He Shall be Called a Nazarene': The Non-Citation of Matthew 2:23." *TynBul* 69.1 (2018): 63–74. **Beale, G. K.** "Finding Christ in the Old Testament." *JETS* 63.1 (2020): 25–50. ———. *Handbook on the New Testament Use of the Old Testament: Exegesis and Interpretation*. Grand Rapids: Baker Academic, 2012. **Beale, G. K., and D. A. Carson**, eds. *Commentary on the New Testament Use of the Old Testament*. Grand Rapids: Baker Academic, 2007. **Beaton, Richard.** *Isaiah's Christ in Matthew's Gospel*. SNTSMS 123. Cambridge: Cambridge University Press, 2002. **Berding, Kenneth, and Jonathan Lunde**, eds. *Three Views on the New Testament Use of the Old Testament*. Grand Rapids: Zondervan, 2008. **Blomberg, Craig L.** "Matthew." Pages 1–109 in *Commentary on the New Testament Use of the Old Testament*. Edited by G. K. Beale and D. A. Carson. Grand Rapids: Baker Academic, 2007. **Bock, Darrell L.** "Single Meaning, Multiple Contexts and Referents: The New Testament's Legitimate, Accurate, and Multifaceted Use of the Old." Pages 105–166 in *Three Views on the New Testament Use of the Old Testament*. Edited by Kenneth Berding and Jonathan Lunde. Grand Rapids: Zondervan, 2008. **Brown, Raymond.** *The* Sensus Plenior *of Sacred Scripture*. 1955; repr., 1960; repr., Eugene, OR: Wipf & Stock, 2008. **Chung, Woojin.** *Translation Theory and the Old Testament in Matthew: The Possibilities of Skopos Theory*. LBS 15. Leiden: Brill, 2017. **Deines, Roland.** "Did Matthew Know He Was Writing Scripture? Part 1 and 2." *EuroJTh* 22 (2013): 101–9 and 23 (2014): 3–12. ———. "Jesus and Scripture: Scripture and the Self-Understanding of Jesus." Pages 39–70 in *All That the Prophets Have Declared: The Appropriation of Scripture in the Emergence of Christianity*. Edited by Matthew R. Malcolm. Milton Keynes, UK: Paternoster, 2015. **Ellis, E. Earle.** "Jesus' Use of the Old Testament and the Genesis of New Testament Theology." *BBR* 3 (1993): 59–75. ———. *The Old Testament in Early Christianity: Canon and Interpretation in the Light of Modern Research*. WUNT 54. Tübingen: J. C. B. Mohr (Paul Siebeck), 1991. **Emadi,**

**Samuel.** "Intertextuality in New Testament Scholarship: Significance, Criteria, and the Art of Intertextual Reading. *CurBR* 14.1 (2015): 8–23. **Evans, Craig A.** *From Prophecy to Testament: The Function of the Old Testament in the New.* Peabody, MA: Hendrickson, 2004. ———. "New Testament Use of the Old Testament." Pages 96–104 in *A Handbook on the Jewish Roots of the Christian Faith.* Edited by Craig A. Evans and David Mishkin. Peabody, MA: Hendrickson, 2019. **France, R. T.** *Jesus and the Old Testament: His Application of Old Testament Passages to Himself and His Mission.* London: Tyndale, 1971. **Goldingay, John.** *Reading Jesus's Bible: How the New Testament Helps Us Understand the Old Testament.* Grand Rapids: Eerdmans, 2017. **Guelich, Robert A.** *The Sermon on the Mount: A Foundation for Understanding.* Waco, TX: Word, 1982. **Gundry, Robert H.** *The Use of the Old Testament in St Matthew's Gospel: With Special Reference to the Messianic Hope.* NovTSup 8. Leiden: Brill, 1975. **Hagner, Donald A.** "Matthew: Apostate, Reformer, Revolutionary?" *NTS* 49 (2003): 193–209. **Hays, Richard B.** *Echoes of Scripture in the Gospels.* Waco, TX: Baylor University Press, 2016. **Kaiser, Walter C., Jr.** "Single Meaning, Unified Referents: Accurate and Authoritative Citations of the Old Testament by the New Testament." Pages 45–104 in *Three Views on the New Testament Use of the Old Testament.* Edited by Kenneth Berding and Jonathan Lunde. Grand Rapids: Zondervan, 2008. **Kirk, J. R. Daniel.** "Conceptualising Fulfilment in Matthew." *TynBul* 59.1 (2008): 77–98. **Knowles, Michael P.** "Scripture, History, Messiah: Scriptural Fulfillment and the Fullness of Time in Matthew's Gospel." Pages 59–82 in *Hearing the Old Testament in the New Testament.* Edited by Stanley E. Porter. Grand Rapids: Eerdmans, 2006. **Lau, Theresa Yu Chui Siang.** "The Gospels and the Old Testament." Pages 155–80 in *The Content and Setting of the Gospel Tradition.* Edited by Mark Harding and Alanna Nobbs. Grand Rapids: Eerdmans, 2010. **Menken, Maarten J. J.** *Matthew's Bible: The Old Testament Text of the Evangelist.* BETL 173. Leuven: Peeters, 2004. **Miller, Robert J.** "How Matthew Helped Jesus Fulfill Prophecy." Pages 127–42 in *The Message of Jesus: John Dominic Crossan and Ben Witherington III in Dialogue.* Edited by Robert B. Stewart. Minneapolis: Fortress, 2013. ———. *Helping Jesus Fulfill Prophecy.* Eugene, OR: Cascade, 2015. **Moyise, Steve.** *Jesus and Scripture: Studying the New Testament Use of the Old Testament.* Grand Rapids: Baker Academic, 2010. ———. "Matthew's Bible in the Infancy Narrative." Pages 9–24 in *The Scriptures of Israel in Jewish and Christian Tradition.* Essays in Honour of Maarten J. J. Menken. Edited by Bart Koet, Steve Moyise and Joseph Verheyden. NovTSup 148. Leiden: Brill, 2013. **Porter, Stanley E.** *Sacred Tradition in the New Testament: Tracing Old Testament Themes in the Gospels and Epistles.* Grand Rapids: Baker Academic, 2016. **Quarles, Charles L.** *Midrash Criticism: Introduction and Appraisal.* Lanham, MD: University Press of America, 1997. **Sargent, Benjamin.** *David Being a Prophet: The Contingency of Scripture upon History in the New Testament.* BZNW 207. Berlin: de Gruyter, 2014. **Schreiner, Thomas R.** *New Testament Theology: Magnifying God in Christ.* Grand Rapids: Baker Academic, 2008. **Senior, Donald.** "The Lure of the Formula Quotations: Re-assessing Matthew's Use of the Old Testament with the Passion Narrative as a Test Case." Pages 89–115 in *Scriptures in the Gospels.* Edited by Christopher M. Tuckett. BETL

131. Leuven: Peeters, 1997. **Skarsaune, Oskar.** *The Proof from Prophecy: A Study in Justin Martyr's Proof-Text Tradition: Text-Type, Provenance, Theological Profile.* NovTSup 56. Leiden: Brill, 1987. **Soares-Prabhu, George M.** *The Formula Quotations in the Infancy Narratives of Matthew.* AnBib 63. Rome: Pontifical Biblical Press, 1976. **Stendahl, Krister.** *The School of St. Matthew and Its Use of the Old Testament.* 2nd ed. Lund: Gleerup, 1954. **Strecker, Georg.** *Der Weg der Gerechtigkeit: Untersuchung zur Theologie des Matthäus.* Göttingen: Vandenhoeck & Ruprecht, 1962. **Vanhoozer, Kevin J.** *Is There a Meaning in This Text? The Bible, the Reader, and the Morality of Literary Knowledge.* Grand Rapids: Zondervan, 1998. **Watts, Rikk E.** "Immanuel: Virgin Birth Proof Test or Programmatic Warning of Things to Come (Isa 7:14 in Matt 1:23)?" Pages 92–113 in *From Prophecy to Testament: The Function of the Old Testament in the New.* Edited by Craig A. Evans. Peabody, MA: Hendrickson, 2004. **Wegner, Paul D.** "How Many Virgin Births Are in the Bible? (Isaiah 7:14): A Prophetic Pattern Approach." *JETS* 54.3 (2011): 467–84. **Wellum, Stephen.** "From Alpha to Omega: A Biblical-Theological Approach to God the Son Incarnate." *JETS* 63.1 (2020): 71–94. **Witherington, Ben, III.** *Isaiah Old and New: Exegesis, Intertextuality, and Hermeneutics.* Minneapolis: Fortress, 2017. **Wright, N. T.** "Son of Man—Lord of the Temple? Gospel Echoes of Psalm 8 and the Ongoing Christological Challenge." Pages 77–96 in *The Earliest Perceptions of Jesus in Context: Essays in Honour of John Nolland on His 70th Birthday.* Edited by Aaron W. White, Craig A. Evans, and David Wenham. LNTS 566. London: Bloomsbury T&T Clark, 2018.

## 5.1 Introduction: Reading the Old Testament in Matthew's Gospel

With the entrance of Jesus to history, we have someone and something new on the human stage. Jesus is the Messiah of Israel, and he brings the kingdom of heaven to earth. At the same time, Jesus is the continuation and the fulfillment of what God has been establishing throughout history since the beginning of creation. Therefore, it is vital for us in our examination of the theology of Matthew's Gospel to understand Jesus's relationship with the Old Testament messages. How does Matthew present Jesus in relationship to the Old Testament? And how does Matthew understand Jesus in the light of contemporary Judaism and its relationship to the Old Testament? Stephen Westerholm remarks, "Scholars of the New Testament must seek to do justice both to what was new and distinctive about the message of Jesus and his followers, and to the wide areas of continuity it shared with the convictions and practices of other pious Jews."[1] This chapter attempts to do just that by seeing Matthew in relationship

1. Stephen Westerholm, *Law and Ethics in Early Judaism and the New Testament*, WUNT 383 (Tübingen: Mohr Siebeck, 2017), 2.

to the Old Testament, and to contemporary Judaism and its understanding of the Old Testament.

We noted in earlier chapters that Matthew is often perceived as having a distinctly Jewish orientation. One of the reasons that many interpreters set forth this proposal is because of Matthew's extensive use of the Hebrew Scriptures—the Old Testament—which is often seen as a key to his theological perspective. The Old Testament for Matthew was not "old" at all but centrally relevant to his understanding of how God has been at work in the mission of Jesus Messiah and in the community he established. If Matthew's Jesus can state unequivocally that he came not to abolish but to fulfill the Law and the Prophets (Matt 5:17), then it is doubtful that Matthew conceived of the Jewish Scriptures as "old," at least in the connotative sense of "antique, outmoded, quaint." David Turner contends, "Instead, Matthew viewed both the historical patterns and the prophetic oracles of the Hebrew Bible as filled with ultimate significance through the ministry and teaching of Jesus."[2]

In this chapter we examine Matthew's understanding of the Old Testament in the light of the ministry of Jesus Messiah. We will look at occurrences of the Old Testament in Matthew's Gospel, and then observe how Jesus and Matthew use those occurrences of the Old Testament, especially focusing on "fulfillment." In the next chapter, we will look at Matthew's understanding of the relevance of the Old Testament law for disciples of Jesus Messiah in current life in the kingdom of heaven.

This raises an important point regarding our use of terminology when referring to the Old Testament. The expression "Old Testament" does not occur in the New Testament. In Jesus's day and the early church, the Torah, Prophets, and Writings were simply "the Scriptures." Jews today often refer to their Scriptures as *Tanakh*, an acronym of the initial Hebrew letter of each of the Masoretic Text's three traditional subdivisions: *Torah* ("Teaching," or "the Five Books of Moses"), *Neviim* ("Prophets") and *Ketuvim* ("Writings")—which gives us *TaNaKh*.[3] The scholarly world today often refers to "the Hebrew Bible."

With the coming of Jesus and the initiation of the new covenant, the church developed a collection of written materials that they understood to be authoritative Scriptures (e.g., 2 Pet 3:16). These were placed alongside of the existing Hebrew Scriptures, and the new covenant Scriptures came to be called the New Testament and the Hebrew Scriptures the Old Testament. Some scholars prefer to use the expression "First Testament" and "Second Testament."[4] For some in Western cultures the phrase "Old Testament" can be viewed as something of a slight, perhaps implying that this

2. Turner, *Matthew*, 17.

3. R. J. Zwi Werblowsky and Geoffrey Wigoder, eds., "Tanakh," *EJR* 376.

4. E.g., and Second," *BTB* 17.2 (1987): 47–49. See also John Goldingay, *The First Testament: A New Translation* (Downers Grove: InterVarsity, 2018), who uses First Testament, but New Testament, not Second Testament.

this collection of writings is antique and outdated by the "New Testament."[5] All of the expressions used to refer to the Law, the Prophets, and the Writings have relevance, especially when in scholarly interaction with Jews today. However, I will use "Old Testament" and "New Testament" here because of their traditional, wide usage and general understanding, and so as not to undermine the significance of the connection of the new covenant with the New Testament.

The Old Testament is still one crucial part of God's revelation to his people, as much today as it was in the days of ancient Israel, and in the days of Matthew and the early church. For Matthew, what came to be called the Old Testament was God's word of revelation about his relationship with his people and how life should be lived. With the coming of Jesus Messiah and the kingdom of heaven, life will be lived in a new way, so Matthew carefully records Jesus Messiah's relationship to the Old Testament revelation, and how his disciples are now to live in relationship to it.

### 5.1.1 Matthew As a Bridge Between Old and New Testaments

From the opening lines of his story, Matthew provides a natural bridge between the Old Testament and New Testament. Matthew demonstrates repeatedly that Old Testament hopes, prophecies, and promises have now been fulfilled in the person and ministry of Jesus. The early church quite likely placed Matthew's Gospel first in the New Testament canon precisely because of its value as a bridge between the Testaments, demonstrating how the old covenant finds its fulfillment in the new covenant. Among the Gospels, Matthew has the clearest and most frequent links back to the Old Testament. Blomberg states, "Of the four, Matthew helped form the transition between the old and the new most smoothly."[6] Matthew's Gospel serves as a natural bridge from the Old Testament to the New Testament.

Roland Deines takes it one step further to suggest that as Matthew wrote his Gospel he knew that he was writing Scripture.[7] Deines suggests provocatively that New Testament authors, including Matthew, wrote to witness to what they had experienced as God's revelation in their own time. "They took this revelation as a continuation of what had happened in earlier times and this is why they used scriptural quotations so frequently to demonstrate the fundamental rooting of the new 'word' of God in that which already existed."[8] This suggestion is in line with evidence that other New Testament authors recognized that what was being written among them was indeed

5. John Goldingay, *Reading Jesus' Bible: How the New Testament Helps Us Understand the Old Testament* (Grand Rapids: Eerdmans, 2017), 1–3.

6. Craig L. Blomberg, "Matthew," in *Commentary on the New Testament Use of the Old Testament*, ed. G. K. Beale and D. A. Carson (Grand Rapids: Baker Academic, 2007), 2.

7. Roland Deines, "Did Matthew Know He Was Writing Scripture? Part 1," *EuroJTh* 22.2 (2013): 101–9; and "Part 2," *EuroJTh* 23.1 (2014): 3–12.

8. Deines, "Did Matthew Know He Was Writing Scripture? Part 2," 10.

Scripture—e.g., the author of 2 Peter referring to the writings of Paul (2 Pet 3:16). This is another indication of the significant place of Matthew as a bridge from Old Testament Scripture to New Testament Scripture.

This link to the Old Testament not only occurs in Matthew's commentary on and use of Israel's Scriptures but also in the way that, early in the history of the church, Matthew's Gospel was used as Scripture interpreting Old Testament Scripture. In the early church writing known as 2 Clement, we find what may be the earliest instance of a New Testament passage being quoted as Scripture.[9] In this homily, the author of 2 Clement gives a detailed interpretation of the text from Isa 54:12 (2 Clem. 2:1, 3) and then the author writes, "And another Scripture (*hētera graphē*) says, 'I have not come to call the righteous, but sinners.'" Christopher Tuckett notes that the author of 2 Clement here cites a saying from the Gospel of Matthew (2 Clem. 2:4=Matt 9:13) and places it on a par with Israel's Scriptures: it is "another Scripture."[10] We can see here that the process has already started whereby a Christian text—Matthew—is taking its place alongside an Old Testament text—Isaiah—and being considered as part of a developing Christian canon of Scripture. Thus, as early as 2 Clement in church history (ca. AD 95–140?), Matthew's Gospel is recognized to be Scripture in the same way as Isaiah's prophecy was regarded as Scripture. This demonstrates the immediate link of Matthew's Gospel with the Old Testament, providing a bridge to the New Testament.

Among the four Gospels, we find in Matthew's Gospel at least the following elements that provide a bridge from the Old Testament to the New:[11] (1) Matthew's Gospel references the Old Testament the most among the four Gospels; (2) it locates the person and mission of Jesus Messiah most explicitly in his Hebrew lineage (1:2–17); (3) it demonstrates most explicitly how activities in Jesus's life and mission—extending to the cross and beyond—fulfill Old Testament expectations (e.g., 2:4–6) and types (e.g., 2:15); (4) it is the only Gospel to reference the *ekklēsia* (16:18; 18:17) as Jesus's new discipleship community that he will now build; (5) and it is the only Gospel to address explicitly the leadership of Israel and state that there will be a transfer of guardianship of the kingdom of God to another *ethnos* producing its fruit (21:43). These are but a few of the ways that Matthew serves as a bridge between the Testaments.

These points have value as an indicator of the ways that we can explore the occurrence and use of the Old Testament in Matthew's Gospel.

9. Michael W. Holmes, ed., "Second Clement," in *The Apostolic Fathers: Greek Texts and Translations*, 3rd ed. (Grand Rapids: Baker Academic, 2007), 141n2.4.

10. Christopher Tuckett, *2 Clement: Introduction, Text, and Commentary*, Oxford Apostolic Fathers (Oxford: Oxford University Press, 2012), 42.

11. For a helpful perspective, see Goldingay, *Reading Jesus' Bible*, 1–3. Goldingay prefers "First Testament," but for convenience I will consistently use "Old Testament." For a useful overview of approaches to seeing Christ in the OT, including Goldingay's method in the light of other interpretative methodologies, see Brian J. Tabb and Andrew M. King, eds., *Five Views of Christ in the Old Testament: Genre, Authorial Intent, and the Nature of Scripture*, Counterpoints (Grand Rapids: Zondervan, 2022).

## 5.2 The Occurrence of the Old Testament in Matthew's Gospel

Matthew's Gospel arose within the frame of a culture derived chiefly from Israel's sacred texts and traditions. It is well known to contain the highest number of explicit quotations of Hebrew Scripture among the four Gospels. Besides incorporating all of Mark's quotations, Matthew has included in his narrative many more different forms of references to the Old Testament. Some of the evocations of the Hebrew Scriptures by Matthew are direct citations, others are indirect, referring to biblical texts, events, or characters without an explicit quotation formula or extended verbatim citation. This is the realm of "intertextuality," or as G. K. Beale prefers, "inner-biblical exegesis"[12] of Old and New Testaments.[13] Richard Hays suggests that we can roughly categorize the scriptural inner-biblical references in the Gospels by employing the terms "quotation," "allusion," and "echo," which are "approximate markers on the spectrum of intertextual linkage, moving from the most to the least explicit forms of reference."[14]

### 5.2.1 Definitions and Examples

There is much debate among scholars over these markers, especially concerning the meaning of "allusion" and "echo."[15] We will explore each briefly, then move on to examine the actual use of the Old Testament in Matthew's Gospel.

#### *5.2.1.1 Quotation*

Beale states that "a quotation is a direct citation of an OT passage that is easily recognizable by its clear and unique verbal parallelism."[16] Porter makes a distinction between a *formulaic quotation* and a *direct quotation*.[17] In a *formulaic quotation* the author introduces an Old Testament reference with some kind of formula, such as we find regularly in Matthew's unique "fulfillment" quotations. For example, when recounting the virginal conception of Mary, Matthew introduces the Old Testament quotation with the formulaic words, "All this took place to fulfill what the Lord had

12. G. K. Beale, *Handbook on the New Testament Use of the Old Testament: Exegesis and Interpretation* (Grand Rapids: Baker Academic, 2012), 40.

13. For a helpful survey of recent approaches to "intertextual reading" see Samuel Emadi, "Intertextuality in New Testament Scholarship: Significance, Criteria, and the Art of Intertextual Reading," *CurBR* 14.1 (2015): 8–23. For a collection of intertextual approaches, see B. J. Oropeza and Steve Moyise, eds., *Exploring Intertextuality: Diverse Strategies for New Testament Interpretation of Texts* (Eugene, OR: Cascade, 2016).

14. Richard B. Hays, *Echoes of Scripture in the Gospels* (Waco, TX: Baylor University Press, 2016), 10.

15. For overviews of the issues, see Beale, *Handbook*, 31–35; see also the extensive charts in Davies and Allison, *Matthew*, 1:34–57; Stanley E. Porter, *Sacred Tradition in the New Testament: Tracing Old Testament Themes in the Gospels and Epistles* (Grand Rapids: Baker Academic, 2016), 33–47. Porter also includes a fourth category, paraphrase: "An intentional and specific invoking of a definable passage, even if it is made in other words and in another form" (*Sacred Tradition*, 36). For our purposes we will concentrate on the above three: quotation, allusion, and echo.

16. Beale, *Handbook*, 29.

17. Porter, *Sacred Tradition*, 34–35.

said through the prophet" (1:22). Then Matthew quotes Isa 7:14: "The virgin will conceive and give birth to a son, and they will call him Immanuel" (Matt 1:23).

In a *direct quotation* the author cites an Old Testament passage without an introductory formula. For example, as Matthew recounts Jesus's horrific crucifixion, the only words that he records of Jesus from the cross are uttered in the loud cry, "*Eli, Eli, lema sabachthani?*" (27:46). This is a direct quotation of Ps 22:1 without any introductory formula. Then Matthew translates the expression into Greek for his readers, saying "which means 'My God, my God, why have you forsaken me?'" (27:46).

Matthew is well known to have the most citations of the Old Testament among the four Gospels.[18] The fifth revised edition of the United Bible Societies' *The Greek New Testament* includes An Index of Quotations: New Testament Order, listing the fifty-three citations that the editors have considered to be quotations (both formulaic and direct) of the Old Testament found in Matthew's Gospel.[19] In the chart below I give these fifty-three quotations, as well as ten allusions that some scholars consider to be quotations.[20] Thirty-seven citations are in a saying from Jesus, while sixteen occur in the narrative, coming either as Matthew's citation or citing a character in the narrative. I have also given a brief statement of the subject matter of the quotation and whether the citation comes in a saying of Jesus (thirty-seven instances) or is a citation in Matthew's narrative (sixteen instances).[21]

The editors of *The Greek New Testament* also list the quotations found in the other three Gospels: Mark (twenty-seven), Luke (twenty-five), and John (fourteen). Matthew has taken into his text virtually all of Mark's Old Testament quotations (with the possible exception of elements of Mark 12:32), but about twenty of Matthew's quotations are unique to his Gospel. Matthew's total of approximately fifty-three quotations compares to the sixty-six total in the other three Gospels combined. Richard Beaton states, "Matthew's use of the Old Testament is more thoroughgoing than that of the

18. For an examination of the text form of the OT quotations in Matthew, see Jan Joosten, "The Text of Old Testament Quotations in Matthew," in Seleznev, Loader, and Niebuhr, *The Gospel of Matthew in Its Historical and Theological Context*, WUNT 459 (Tübingen: Mohr Siebeck, 2021), 201–16.

19. "Index of Quotations: New Testament Order," in UBS[5], 860–61. Steve Moyise, *Jesus and Scripture: Studying the New Testament Use of the Old Testament* (Grand Rapids: Baker Academic, 2010), lists at least fifty-one OT quotations in Matthew.

20. The number of citations varies, depending on how a scholar renders what is a quotation. E.g., Richard Beaton asserts, "The frequent explicit citations, forty in all, implicit quotations, of which there are twenty-one, and numerous allusory references to the Old Testament are central to his narrative development"; Richard Beaton, *Isaiah's Christ in Matthew's Gospel*, SNTSMS 123 (Cambridge: Cambridge University Press, 2002), 17. Donald Senior counts sixty-one OT quotations: see "The Lure of the Formula Quotations: Re-assessing Matthew's Use of the Old Testament with the Passion Narrative as a Test Case," in *Scriptures in the Gospels*, ed. Christopher M. Tuckett, BETL 131 (Leuven: Peeters, 1997), 89–115. Hagner, *Matthew 1–13*, liv, states that "Matthew contains well over sixty explicit quotations from the OT."

21. For similar charts see Turner, *Matthew*, 18–19, who follows UBS[4], and Roland Deines, "Jesus and Scripture: Scripture and the Self-Understanding of Jesus," in *All That the Prophets Have Declared: The Appropriation of Scripture in the Emergence of Christianity*, ed. Matthew R. Malcolm (Milton Keynes, UK: Paternoster, 2015), 43–48. Deines ("Jesus and Scripture," 42–48) lists eighty-six citations of the OT (by my count), which includes quotations and various allusions to OT narrative incidents and figures (e.g., mentioning David fleeing from Saul and eating the shewbread from the temple in Nod).

other Synoptic Gospels."[22] This illustrates Matthew's focus on reinforcing his emphases with Old Testament support. Blomberg states, "Virtually every major theological emphasis of Matthew is reinforced with Old Testament support, often by the addition of segments of texts to the sources Matthew employed, most notably Mark."[23]

### *5.2.1.2 Table of Quotations of (with Some Allusions to) the Old Testament in Matthew's Gospel*

| | Matthew's Text | Person(s) Citing OT | Old Testament Text | Subject |
|---|---|---|---|---|
| 1 | 1:1–17 | Matthew | E.g., 1 Chr 1:1—3:24 | Genealogy of Jesus |
| 2 | 1:23a | Matthew | Isa 7:14 LXX | Virgin conception and birth |
| 3 | 1:23b | Matthew | Isa 8:8, 10 LXX | Immanuel, God with us |
| 4 | 2:6 | Chief priests and scribes | Mic 5:2 | Ruler born in Bethlehem |
| 5 | 2:15 | Matthew | Hos 11:1 | God's Son called out of Egypt |
| 6 | 2:18 | Matthew | Jer 31:15 | Rachel weeping in Ramah for murdered children |
| 7 | 2:23 | Matthew | OT prophets; Isa 53:2 | Jesus shall be called a Nazarene |
| 8 | 3:3 | Matthew | Isa 40:3 LXX | John the Baptist, a voice in the wilderness |
| 9 | 4:4 | Jesus | Deut 8:3 | Live not by bread alone |
| 10 | 4:6 | Satan | Ps 91:11–12 | Protecting angels |
| 11 | 4:7 | Jesus | Deut 6:16 | Do not tempt God |
| 12 | 4:10 | Jesus | Deut 6:13 | Worship and serve God only |
| 13 | 4:15–16 | Matthew | Isa 9:1–2 | Galilee of the gentiles |
| 14 | 5:21 | Jesus | Exod 20:13; Deut 5:17 | Sixth commandment: do not murder |
| 15 | 5:27 | Jesus | Exod 20:14; Deut 5:18 | Seventh commandment: do not commit adultery |
| 16 | 5:31 | Jesus | Deut 24:1 | Certificate of divorce |
| 17 | 5:33 | Jesus | Lev 19:12; Num 30:2 | Do not break oath, but fulfill vows |
| 18 | 5:38 | Jesus | Exod 21:24; Lev 24:20; Deut 19:21 | Eye for eye, tooth for tooth |
| 19 | 5:43 | Jesus | Lev 19:18 | Love your neighbor |
| 20 | 8:17 | Matthew | Isa 53:4 | Took our infirmities, bore our diseases |
| 21 | 9:13 | Jesus | Hos 6:6 | Mercy, not sacrifice |
| 22 | 10:35–36 | Jesus | Mic 7:6 | Family against one another |

*continued*

22. Beaton, *Isaiah's Christ in Matthew's Gospel*, 18.

23. Blomberg, "Matthew," 1.

| | Matthew's Text | Person(s) Citing OT | Old Testament Text | Subject |
|---|---|---|---|---|
| 23 | 11:10 | Jesus | Mal 3:1 (Ex 23:20) | Messenger preparing the way |
| 24 | 12:7 | Jesus | Hos 6:6 | Mercy, not sacrifice |
| 25 | 12:18–21 | Matthew | Isa 42:1–3 | Spirit-anointed servant of the Lord |
| 26 | 12:21 | Jesus | Isa 42:4 LXX | In his name the nations will put their hope |
| 27 | 12:40 | Jesus | Jonah 1:17 | Jonah three days and nights in belly of huge fish |
| 28 | 13:14–15 | Jesus | Isa 6:9–10 LXX | Seeing/hearing but not understanding or perceiving |
| 29 | 13:35 | Matthew | Ps 78:2 | Speaking in parables |
| 30 | 15:4a | Jesus | Exod 20:12; Deut 5:16 | Fifth commandment: honor father/mother |
| 31 | 15:4b | Jesus | Exod 21:17; Lev 20:9 | Speaking evil of parents |
| 32 | 15:8–9 | Jesus | Isa 29:13 LXX | Empty worship |
| 33 | 16:27 | Jesus | Prov 24:12 (allusion) | Son of Man judges |
| 34 | 17:10–11 | Jesus | Mal 4:5–6 (allusion) | Elijah comes before Messiah |
| 35 | 18:16 | Jesus | Deut 19:15 | Two or three witnesses |
| 36 | 19:4 | Jesus | Gen 1:27; 5:2 | Creation of man and woman |
| 37 | 19:5 | Jesus | Gen 2:24 | Inauguration of marriage |
| 38 | 19:7 | Pharisees | Deut 24:1 | Moses and certificate of divorce |
| 39 | 19:18–19 | Jesus | Exod 20:12–16; Deut 5:16–20 | Do not murder/Honor father/mother |
| 40 | 19:19 | Jesus | Lev 19:18 | Love your neighbor as yourself |
| 41 | 21:5 | Matthew | Isa 62:11; Zech 9:9 | Climactic entry of the king to Jerusalem |
| 42 | 21:9 | Crowds | Ps 118:25–26 | Blessed is he who comes in the name of the Lord |
| 43 | 21:13 | Jesus | Isa 56:7 | God's house of prayer |
| 44 | 21:13 | Jesus | Jer 7:11 (allusion) | Den of robbers |
| 45 | 21:16 | Jesus | Ps 8:3 LXX | Children giving praise |
| 46 | 21:42 | Jesus | Ps 118:22–23 | The rejected stone becomes the cornerstone |
| 47 | 22:24 | Sadducees | Deut 25:5 | Marrying a brother's widow |
| 48 | 22:32 | Jesus | Exod 3:6, 15 | The living God of Abraham, Isaac and Jacob |
| 49 | 22:37 | Jesus | Deut 6:5 | Love God with all your heart, soul, and mind |
| 50 | 22:39 | Jesus | Lev 19:18 | Love your neighbor as yourself |
| 51 | 22:44 | Jesus | Ps 110:1 | The Lord said to my Lord |

| | Matthew's Text | Person(s) Citing OT | Old Testament Text | Subject |
|---|---|---|---|---|
| 52 | 23:39 | Jesus | Ps 118:26 | He who comes in the name of the Lord |
| 53 | 24:15 | Jesus | Dan 9:27; 11:31 (allusions) | The abomination that causes desolation |
| 54 | 24:29 | Jesus | Isa 13:10; 34:4 (allusions) | The end of the age |
| 55 | 24:30 | Jesus | Dan 7:13 | Son of Man coming |
| 56 | 26:31 | Jesus | Zech 13:7 | Strike the shepherd |
| 57 | 26:56 | Jesus | writings of prophets (allusion) | Betrayed |
| 58 | 26:64a | Jesus | Ps 110:1 | LORD says to my lord: "Sit at my right hand" |
| 59 | 26:64b | Jesus | Dan 7:13 | Son of Man coming |
| 60 | 27:9–10 | Matthew | Zech 11:12–13 | Thirty pieces of silver |
| 61 | 27:35 | Matthew | Ps 22:18 (allusion) | Dividing garments by lot |
| 62 | 27:39 | Matthew | Ps 22:6–7 (allusion) | Despised by the people |
| 63 | 27: 42–43 | Chief priests, with the scribes and elders | Ps 22:8 (allusion) | Let God deliver him |
| 64 | 27:46 | Jesus | Ps 22:1 | My God, my God, why have you forsaken me |

### *5.2.1.3 Allusion*

The term *allusion* indicates passages with clear reference to the Old Testament, but they are woven into the new text rather than directly quoted. An allusion often imbeds words from the source text, or at least signals the reader to make a connection to the source text.[24] Porter defines allusion "as involving the indirect invoking of a person, place, literary work or the like, designed to bring the external person, place, literary work, or similar entity into the contemporary material."[25] This approach depends less on the respective Old Testament and New Testament texts' verbal similarity, although words can be used to make an allusion to Old Testament concepts. For example, Jesus's answer to John the Baptist's question in Matt 11:4–6 (cf. Luke 7:22) has a listing that reiterates to John's disciples that the way Jesus's ministry has unfolded (Matt 1–9) is in line with the prophetic promises: "Go back and report to John what you hear and see" (11:4). In Jesus's ministry are fulfilled Isaiah's prophecies that described the coming messianic ministry in these very terms and evoke images of the fulfillment of messianic hopes in the ministry of Jesus: the blind receive sight (Isa 29:18; 35:5; cf. Matt 9:27–32),

24. Hays, *Echoes of Scripture in the Gospels*, 10. See also Robert H. Gundry, *The Use of the Old Testament in St Matthew's Gospel: With Special Reference to the Messianic Hope*, NovTSup 8 (Leiden: Brill, 1975), 9.

25. Porter, *Sacred Tradition in the New Testament*, 39.

the lame walk (Isa 35:6; cf. Matt 15:30–31), those who have leprosy are cured (cf. Isa 53:4; cf. Matt 8:1–4), the deaf hear (Isa 29:18–19; 35:5; cf. Mark 7:32–37), the dead are raised (Isa 26:18–19; cf. Matt 10:8; Luke 7:11–17; John 11:1–44), and the good news is preached to the poor (Isa 61:1; Matt 5:3; Luke 14:13, 21). All of these descriptors combine to allude to the fulfillment of a multifaceted description of Old Testament concepts of the Coming One.

In addition to at least fifty-three *quotations*, Matthew has many more *allusions* to Old Testament texts. The United Bible Societies' *Greek New Testament* also has an appendix that gives an "Index of Allusions and Verbal Parallels."[26] The index does not make a distinction between allusion and echo. They also do not give a listing of the New Testament order as they do for quotations, but I have gone through and marked each allusion/verbal parallel of the Old Testament in Matthew's Gospel. According to my tabulation, there are at least 264 allusions/verbal parallels to the Old Testament in Matthew. I created a table below that gives the number of allusions/verbal parallels of each Old Testament book found in Matthew, along with one example of each allusion.

### *5.2.1.4 Table of the Number of Allusions/Verbal Parallels of Each Old Testament Book Found in Matthew, Along with One Example of Each Allusion*

| | **Old Testament Book** | **Number of Allusions/ Verbal Parallels** | **Example of an OT Citation** | **Matthean allusion** |
|---|---|---|---|---|
| 1 | Genesis | 17 | Gen 6:9–12 "This is the account of Noah and his family" | 24:37 "As it was in the days of Noah" |
| 2 | Exodus | 17 | Exod 3:16 "God of Abraham, Isaac, Jacob" | 22:32 "God of Abraham, Isaac, Jacob" |
| 3 | Leviticus | 15 | Lev 14:2 "law of the leprous person" | 8:4 "show yourself to the priest and offer the gift Moses commanded" |
| 4 | Numbers | 6 | Num 14:6 Joshua . . . Caleb . . . tore their clothes | 26:65 "high priest tore his clothes" |
| 5 | Deuteronomy | 16 | Deut 5:14 "the seventh day is a sabbath to the LORD your God" | 12:2 "Your disciples are doing what is unlawful on the Sabbath" |
| 6 | Joshua | 1 | Josh 22:5 "But be very careful to keep the commandment . . . to love the LORD your God" | 22:37–38 "Love the Lord your God with all your heart and with all your soul and with all your mind." |

26. "Index of Allusions and Verbal Parallels," UBS[5], 864–83.

| | Old Testament Book | Number of Allusions/ Verbal Parallels | Example of an OT Citation | Matthean allusion |
|---|---|---|---|---|
| 7 | Judges | 1 | Judg 13:5–7 "the boy is to be a Nazirite" | 2:23 "he would be called a Nazarene"[27] |
| 8 | Ruth | 5 | Ruth 4:12 "Perez, whom Tamar bore to Judah" | 1:3 "Judah the father of Perez, whose mother was Tamar |
| 9 | 1 Samuel | 2 | 1 Sam 14:45 "not a hair of his head will fall to the ground, for he did this today with God's help." | 10:30 "And even the very hairs of your head are all numbered." |
| 10 | 2 Samuel | 4 | 2 Sam 5:2 "And the LORD said to [David], 'You will shepherd my people Israel, and you will become their ruler.'" | 2:6 "Bethlehem . . . out of you will come a ruler who will shepherd my people Israel" |
| 11 | 1 Kings | 8 | 1 Kgs 8:13 "I have indeed built a magnificent temple for you, a place for you to dwell forever" | 23:21 "Anyone who swears by the temple swears by it and by the one who dwells in it" |
| 12 | 2 Kings | 5 | 2 Kgs 1:8 "He had a garment of hair and had a leather belt around his waist . . . That was Elijah the Tishbite." | 3:4 "John's clothes were made of camel's hair, and he had a leather belt around his waist." |
| 13 | 1 Chronicles | 9 | 1 Chr 1:34 "Abraham was the father of Isaac. The sons of Isaac: Esau and Israel" | 1:2 "Abraham was the father of Isaac, Isaac the father of Jacob," |
| 14 | 2 Chronicles | 7 | 2 Chr 9:1–12 "When the queen of Sheba heard of Solomon's fame, she came to Jerusalem to test him with hard questions." | 12:42 "The Queen of the South came from the ends of the earth to listen to Solomon's wisdom, and now something greater than Solomon is here." |
| 15 | Ezra | 2 | Ezra 3:2 "Joshua son of Jozadak and his fellow priests and Zerubbabel son of Shealtiel | 1:12 After the exile to Babylon: Jeconiah was the father of Shealtiel, Shealtiel the father of Zerubbabel, |
| 16 | Nehemiah | 1 | Neh 11:1 ". . . one out of every ten of them to live in Jerusalem, the holy city" | 4:5 "Then the devil took him to the holy city" |

*continued*

27. This is listed as a citation by the UBS[5] (Judges 13:5 by Matthew in 2:23), but more likely this alludes to the theme of the messianic Branch of the line of David, coupled with the theme of an unassuming Messiah with humble origins in the city of Nazareth. See discussion below.

| | Old Testament Book | Number of Allusions/ Verbal Parallels | Example of an OT Citation | Matthean allusion |
|---|---|---|---|---|
| 17 | Esther | 1 | Esth 4:1 "Mordecai . . . tore his clothes, put on sackcloth and ashes . . ." | 11:21 ". . . they would have repented long ago in sackcloth and ashes." |
| 18 | Job | 5 | Job 1:20 "Job got up and tore his robe and shaved his head." | 26:65 "The high priest tore his clothes . . ." |
| 19 | Psalms | 28 | Psa 2:7 "I will proclaim the LORD's decree: He said to me, 'You are my son; today I have become your father.'" | 3:17 "And a voice from heaven said, 'This is my Son, whom I love; with him I am well pleased.'" |
| 20 | Proverbs | 5 | Prov 2:4 ". . . and if you look for it as for silver and search for it as for hidden treasure" | 13:44 "The kingdom of heaven is like treasure hidden in a field." |
| 21 | Isaiah | 33 | Isa 5:1–2 "My loved one had a vineyard on a fertile hillside. [2] He dug it up and cleared it of stones and planted it with the choicest vines. He built a watchtower in it and cut out a winepress as well." | 21:33 "Listen to another parable: There was a landowner who planted a vineyard. He put a wall around it, dug a winepress in it and built a watchtower." |
| 22 | Jeremiah | 12 | Jer 6:16 ". . . ask where the good way is, and walk in it, and you will find rest for your souls." | 11:29 "Take my yoke upon you and learn from me, for I am gentle and humble in heart, and you will find rest for your souls." |
| 23 | Lamentations | 1 | Lam 2:15 "they scoff and shake their heads at Daughter Jerusalem" | 27:39 "Those who passed by hurled insults at him, shaking their heads" |
| 24 | Ezekiel | 12 | Ezek 13:10–12 "Rain will come in torrents, and I will send hailstones hurtling down, and violent winds will burst forth." | 7:27 "The rain came down, the streams rose, and the winds blew and beat against that house, and it fell with a great crash." |
| 25 | Daniel | 20 | Dan 2:44–45 "It will crush all those kingdoms and bring them to an end, but it will itself endure forever." | 21:44 "Anyone who falls on this stone will be broken to pieces; anyone on whom it falls will be crushed." |
| 26 | Joel | 5 | Joel 2:2 "Like dawn spreading across the mountains a large and mighty army comes, such as never was in ancient times nor ever will be in ages to come." | 24:21 "For then there will be great distress, unequaled from the beginning of the world until now—and never to be equaled again." |

| | Old Testament Book | Number of Allusions/ Verbal Parallels | Example of an OT Citation | Matthean allusion |
|---|---|---|---|---|
| 27 | Amos | 2 | Amos 1:9–10 "I will send fire on the walls of Tyre that will consume her fortresses." | 11:21–22 "But I tell you, it will be more bearable for Tyre and Sidon on the day of judgment than for you." |
| 28 | Jonah | 4 | Jonah 3:5 "The Ninevites believed God. A fast was proclaimed, and all of them, from the greatest to the least, put on sackcloth." | 12:41 "The men of Nineveh will stand up at the judgment with this generation and condemn it; for they repented at the preaching of Jonah, and now something greater than Jonah is here." |
| 29 | Micah | 2 | Mic 6:8 "And what does the LORD require of you? To act justly and to love mercy and to walk humbly with your God." | 23:23 "But you have neglected the more important matters of the law—justice, mercy and faithfulness." |
| 30 | Zephaniah | 1 | Zeph 1:3 "I will sweep away both man and beast; I will sweep away the birds in the sky and the fish in the sea—and the idols that cause the wicked to stumble." | 13:41 "The Son of Man will send out his angels, and they will weed out of his kingdom everything that causes sin and all who do evil." |
| 31 | Haggai | 2 | Hag 1:13 "'I am with you,' declares the LORD." | 28:20 "And surely I am with you always, to the very end of the age." |
| 32 | Zechariah | 11 | Zech 1:1 "the word of the LORD came to the prophet Zechariah son of Berekiah, the son of Iddo" | 23:35 ". . . to the blood of Zechariah son of Berekiah, whom you murdered between the temple and the altar." |
| 33 | Malachi | 4 | Mal 2:7–8 "But you have turned from the way and by your teaching have caused many to stumble; you have violated the covenant with Levi" | 23:3 "So you must be careful to do everything they tell you. But do not do what they do, for they do not practice what they preach." |
| | **Total** | 264 | | |

It is immediately evident that Matthew's Gospel is immersed in the Old Testament. Only five Old Testament books are not quoted or alluded to in Matthew: Ecclesiastes, Song of Solomon, Obadiah, Nahum, and Habakkuk. The *quotations* obviously reflect an author steeped in the Old Testament and equipped to interpret Jesus's life and ministry in the light of the Old Testament. But the *allusions* are no less indicative of the author's milieu. Robert Gundry states it well: "*An allusive quotation rather reflects the language and phrase-forms with which the writer is most familiar and in which he habitually thinks*—all the more so in the case of Jewish authors, whose education from childhood was steeped in OT lore."[28] The allusions are powerful demonstrations of Matthew's ability to interpret Jesus's life and ministry in the light of Old Testament expectations and hopes.

### *5.2.1.5 Echo*

An echo is a more subtle invocation of the Old Testament. This is perhaps the most debated of the criteria for seeing the New Testament use of the Old Testament,[29] since here we are moving from what Hays describes as "certain" (*quotation*) to "probable" (*allusion*), to "possible" (*echo*).[30] An echo is an abstract form of invocation. Porter contends, "I hold that the echo may be consciously intentional or unintentional, involving not paraphrase of a specific passage nor allusion to a person, place, literary work, etc., but by means of thematically related language invoking some more general notion or concept."[31] Theresa Lau proposes that "the evangelists are so immersed in Scripture that they naturally used many of its idioms and expressions as their own. Hence, many of the echoes can be quite unconscious and emerge from minds soaked in the scriptural heritage of Israel."[32]

Deines describes this as a "scripturally based world-view,"[33] in which the thought world and metaphorical and spiritual language of Jesus and the apostles were thoroughly and uniquely biblical—they lived in, with, and by Israel's master narrative, the Scriptures. They were part of a "scripturally created and inspired culture," so that they communicated from a "scripturally based world-view."[34] Being immersed in Scripture and allowing oneself to be guided and influenced by Scripture goes beyond simply quoting a specific text. Echoes of Scripture are found throughout all that they said and did. Jesus spoke and Matthew wrote out of a scripturally infused worldview in which the echoes of Scripture are found throughout all that they communicated.

For example, Jesus's saying that concludes the six antitheses in the Sermon on the Mount—"Be perfect [*teleios*], therefore, as your heavenly Father is perfect" (5:48)—appears to echo the concepts behind Lev 19:2, "Be holy because I, the LORD

28. Gundry, *Use of the Old Testament*, 3 (emphasis original).

29. See Beale, *Handbook*, 32; Hays, *Echoes of Scripture in the Gospels*, 10–12.

30. Richard B. Hays, *Echoes of Scripture in the Letters of Paul* (New Haven, CT: Yale University Press), 20–29. Hays lists seven criteria for detecting intertextual echoes (29–32), an approach Beale suggests is one of the best ways to discern and discuss the nature of echoes/allusions (*Handbook*, 33–34). Hays is not without his critics (see Porter, *Sacred Tradition*, 43–46).

31. Porter, *Sacred Tradition*, 45–46.

32. Theresa Yu Chui Siang Lau, "The Gospels and the Old Testament," in *The Content and Setting of the Gospel Tradition*, ed. Mark Harding and Alanna Nobbs (Grand Rapids: Eerdmans, 2010), 157–60.

33. Deines, "Jesus and Scripture," 42.

34. Deines, "Jesus and Scripture," 42.

your God, am holy," and the LXX of Deut 18:13, "You must be blameless ["perfect," *teleios*] before the Lord your God."[35] Jesus is not quoting nor necessarily alluding to these specific Old Testament texts, but the concepts inform his own specific directive that echoes the concepts found in the Old Testament. Deines draws two specific assumptions from this: "Hence, I take for granted that Jesus was part of this scripturally created and inspired culture, but I contend—and this is my second assumption—that he is also to be distinguished from this culture in a very special way as the *Lord of Scripture*."[36] We will see below that this is found especially in the ways in which Jesus declares that he *fulfills* the Old Testament Scriptures and the ways that he *pronounces* the abiding relevance of the Old Testament Scriptures.

We have indicated that an echo, in differentiation from a quotation or an allusion, is a more subtle and abstract invocation of a general notion or concept of an Old Testament text: "It may involve the inclusion of only a word or phrase that evokes, for the alert reader, a reminiscence of an earlier text."[37] N. T. Wright sees this occurring in the Son of Man language in Ps 8:3–6, which is echoed throughout Matthew's Gospel (e.g., Matt 9:5; 26:1, 64). Wright proposes that Matthew is presenting to his readers a "Son of Man" who is betrayed and will be crucified, but who will be vindicated, exalted, "so that, as in 28.18, matching 9.6, he is given 'all authority in heaven and on earth.' This narrative has exactly the same trajectory as the small story of 'the Son of Man' in Psalm 8 and indeed Daniel 7."[38] Wright refers to this as a "metaleptic echo," drawing on the work of Richard Hays, who has developed the theme of metalepsis, where a single word or line cited from a biblical passage may constitute an invitation to the reader to supply at least some of the larger context.[39]

Another example of "echo" may be found in the way that Matthew interacts with Isa 61. The UBS[5] appendix of allusions and verbal parallels lists Matt 5:4 in the Beatitudes of the Sermon on the Mount as an *allusion* to Isa 61:2–3. Michael Knowles goes one step further to suggest that there are further *echoes* of the language and vision of Isa 61 (LXX) in the Beatitudes. He draws attention to the following:[40]

35. E.g., Moyise, *Jesus and Scripture*, 38.

36. Deines, "Jesus and Scripture," 42.

37. Hays, *Echoes of Scripture in the Gospels*, 10.

38. N. T. Wright, "Son of Man—Lord of the Temple? Gospel Echoes of Psalm 8 and the Ongoing Christological Challenge," in White, Evans, and Wenham, *Earliest Perceptions of Jesus in Context*, 81–82.

39. N. T. Wright, "Son of Man—Lord of the Temple?," 78. See Hays, *Echoes of Scripture in the Gospels*, 11–12; Hays, *Echoes of Scripture in the Letters of Paul*, 20. This concept of metalepsis is similar to what Patrick Schreiner refers to as "shadow stories," which means a broadening from merely looking at lexical parallels but also considering the way that "the narrative as a whole is shaped in a way that imitates, duplicates, and replicates a previous story, not only individual pieces of it"; P. Schreiner, *Matthew, Disciple and Scribe*, 54–55.

40. Michael P. Knowles, "Scripture, History, Messiah: Scriptural Fulfillment and the Fullness of Time in Matthew's Gospel," in *Hearing the Old Testament in the New Testament*, ed. Stanley E. Porter, MNTS (Grand Rapids: Eerdmans, 2006), 67. See also Davies and Allison, *Matthew*, 1:436–39.

### *5.2.1.6 Table of the Beatitudes' Echoes of Isaiah 61 (LXX)*

| Matthew 5 | Isaiah 61 (LXX) |
|---|---|
| [3]"Blessed are the poor [*ptōchoi*] in spirit, for theirs is the kingdom of heaven." | [1]"The Spirit of the Sovereign LORD is on me, because the LORD has anointed me to proclaim good news to the poor [*ptōchois*]" |
| [4]"Blessed are those who mourn [*penthountes*], for they will be comforted [*paraklēthēsontai*]." | [2]"to comfort all who mourn [*parakalesai pantas tous penthountas*]" |
| [5]"Blessed are the meek, for they will inherit the earth [*klēronomēsousin tēn gēn*]." | [7]"they shall inherit the earth" [*klēronomēsousin tēn gēn*] |
| [6]"Blessed are those who hunger and thirst for righteousness [*dikaiosunēn*], for they will be filled." | [3]"They will be called oaks of righteousness [*dikaiosunēs*]" |
| [7]"Blessed are the merciful, for they will be shown mercy [*elethēsontai*]." | See below Isa 30:18 |
| [8]"Blessed are the pure in heart [*kardia*], for they will see God." | [1]"to bind up the brokenhearted [*kardia*]" |
| [12]"Rejoice and be glad [*agalliasthe*], because great is your reward in heaven" | [10]"my soul shall exult (*agalliasthō*] in my God." (ESV) |

The parallels of Matthew's text with Luke's version of the Beatitudes (Luke 7:22–23) have unique emphases in each Gospel that likely signify that Jesus's sayings were given on separate historical occasions. The significantly different settings of the Beatitudes in Matthew and Luke suggests that the echoes of Isaiah that are common to them do not derive from the evangelists, but rather derive from Jesus himself, who indicates by his echoes of scriptural language that his ministry is anticipated under prophetic expectation.[41]

Knowles broadens the scriptural scope to include "blessedness" language not only in Isa 61:1–2 but elsewhere, such as Ps 146:5, 7–9. These themes are frequent in the Psalms and also appear elsewhere in the septuagintal text of Isaiah, such as Isa 30:18: "Therefore the Lord (Heb. LORD) waits to be gracious to you, and therefore he exalts himself to show mercy [*eleēsai*] to you. For the LORD is a God of justice; blessed [*makarioi*] are all those who wait for him" (ESV).

Knowles adduces other parallels, which makes it increasingly difficult to trace many of Jesus's words to a single text from the Old Testament. Rather, Knowles concludes that Jesus intentionally echoes language that is generally characteristic of God's oft-repeated

41. Knowles, "Scripture, History, Messiah," 68. Others suggest that the provenance of Jesus's citations of the OT reside at the level of the evangelist or the early church. For discussion of other alternatives, with the conclusion that "the provenance of the quotation resides at the compositional stage, without negating the assumption that Jesus would have known and used the Scriptures in the practice of his religion," see Thomas R. Hatina, "The Provenance of Jesus' Quotations of Scripture from a Social Memory Perspective," in White, Evans, and Wenham, *Earliest Perceptions of Jesus*, 59–76, esp. 76. I see no compelling reason to deemphasize the origin of these echoes with Jesus himself.

promises of blessing, favor, and salvation for the weak and lowly. Isaiah 61:1–2 remains a prominent source for this theme, but we see elsewhere that the echoes are broadly thematic as much as text-specific.[42] As we will see below, Jesus sees himself and his ministry to have been anticipated under prophetic expectation of the Old Testament.

### 5.2.2 Summary

The occurrences in Matthew's Gospel of Old Testament quotations, allusions, and echoes give an indication of how Jesus understood his own ministry and how Matthew intentionally presented him to his audience for their growth in discipleship to Jesus. We cannot underestimate the influence of the Old Testament on Jesus's own ministry and on Matthew's thought and understanding of salvation history. Hays notes, "Matthew's language and imagery are from start to finish soaked in Scripture; he constantly presupposes the social and symbolic world rendered by the stories, songs, prophecies, laws, and wisdom teaching of Israel's sacred texts."[43] This scriptural backdrop in Matthew's Gospel helps us to understand Jesus's identity and life circumstances, and God's salvation-historical process involving Israel and the anticipated Messiah. It also helps us to understand Jesus's relationship to the people and leaders of Israel and to clarify the purposes and later consequences of his ministry.

We now extend our focus on the ways in which Matthew uses the Old Testament as the basis for his presentation of Jesus Messiah and his ministry. In particular, we look more closely at Matthew's use of "fulfillment," and the "relevance" of the Old Testament for life in the kingdom of heaven.

## 5.3 FULFILLMENT OF THE OLD TESTAMENT IN MATTHEW'S GOSPEL

Observant readers of Matthew's Gospel have long noted an intriguing characteristic in his emphasis upon "fulfillment." This emphasis occurs at the very beginning of his narrative. After recounting the genealogy of Jesus Messiah that shows his royal lineage (1:2–17), Matthew reveals that the conception of the infant Jesus is from the Holy Spirit. Then he states, "All this took place to fulfill what the Lord had said through the prophet: 'The virgin will conceive and give birth to a son, and they will call him Immanuel' (which means 'God with us')" (1:22–23). The term for "fulfill" is *plēroō*, which Matthew uses at least sixteen times.[44]

42. Knowles, "Scripture, History, Messiah," 69.

43. Hays, *Echoes of Scripture in the Gospels*, 109.

44. This should be compared to the occurrence of *plēroō* in the other Gospels: Mark = two times; Luke = nine times; John = fifteen times.

Ten times *plēroō* occurs in Matthew's well-known "fulfillment quotations" or "fulfillment formulas" or "reflection citations" to indicate Matthew's reflection upon the ways that Jesus's life and ministry fulfill the Old Testament: for example, "this took place to fulfill what the Lord had said through the prophet" (1:22; see the table in 5.3.3.1 below). Matthew uses this stereotyped formula to stress that specific events or aspects of Jesus's life "fulfill" an Old Testament text. Davies and Allison contend that the fulfillment of the Jewish Scriptures testifies to the authenticity of Matthew's story "and simultaneously shows that Matthew's religion is not a repudiation of the past but instead the goal of a long history: there is a unity between the old and new, a unity grounded in the divine purpose."[45]

The other six uses of *plēroō*, plus the use of the essentially synonymous verb *anaplēroō*, occur as sayings of Jesus, and are among the most important for understanding Jesus's relationship to the Old Testament (see the table at 5.3.2.1 below). Other quotations employing the term *gegraptai*, "it is written," in the introductory formula can also stress fulfillment.[46] The formula with *gegraptai* occurs at least nine times, eight of which appear as a saying of Jesus as he interprets his own life in the light of the Old Testament, as in his betrayal and impending death; e.g., "The Son of Man will go *just as it is written [gegraptai] about him.* But woe to that man who betrays the Son of Man! It would be better for him if he had not been born" (26:24; emphasis added).[47]

Most Matthean scholars emphasize that this theme of "fulfillment" is crucial for understanding Matthew's use of the Old Testament. Beaton contends, "There is a sound basis for the argument that the theme of fulfillment undergirds the Gospel from beginning to end."[48] France recognizes the potential danger of imposing an artificial theme on Matthew's Gospel in looking for a unifying thesis for his theological perspective. But France declares, "I remain convinced, however, that in the case of Matthew the theme I propose is one he himself would have accepted as summarizing his message, and one which has a clear content which is decisive for the whole orientation of Matthew's work. The theme I propose is that of 'fulfilment.'"[49] Blomberg similarly notes that "Matthew is the NT book that is most controlled by this topic" (i.e., fulfillment).[50] I indeed agree that for Matthew fulfillment is a central concern, especially highlighted in the following discussion of Jesus's own usage and of Matthew's interpretations.[51]

45. Davies and Allison, *Matthew*, 3:577. See their excursus on the formula quotations (3:573–77).

46. So Hagner, *Matthew 1–13*, lv.

47. This should be compared to the occurrence of *gegraptai* in the other gospels: Mark = nine times; Luke = nine times; John = two times.

48. Beaton, *Isaiah's Christ in Matthew's Gospel*, 18.

49. France, *Matthew: Evangelist and Teacher*, 166.

50. Blomberg, *New Testament Theology*, 345. Blomberg proposes that "fulfillment" is not only a central theme of Matthew's Gospel, but also can be seen as the center of New Testament theology overall; Blomberg, *New Testament Theology*, 1–16, 341–42, 353–65.

51. A full-length treatment of "fulfillment" in Matthew is given by Spadaro, *Reading Matthew as the Climactic Fulfillment of the Hebrew Story*.

### 5.3.1 Matthew's Understanding of "Fulfill"

Of the times that Matthew speaks of Old Testament Scripture as "fulfilled" (using the verb *plēroō*), it is always in reference to the Prophets.[52] Matthew uses the expression "fulfill what the Lord said through the prophet" in several different ways, which we will discuss below. It can indicate a direct prediction-fulfillment, in which the events of Jesus's earthly life and ministry bring to actualization predictive prophecy (e.g., 1:22–23). Or "fulfill" can indicate the way in which Jesus's earthly life and ministry is a divinely orchestrated analogical or typological correspondence or recapitulation of the nation of Israel's history (e.g., 2:15, 17–18). Or "fulfill" can indicate the way in which Jesus's life and teaching brings to its intended full meaning the entire Old Testament Scripture (e.g., 5:17–20).

Of note is the text form of the fulfillment quotations. When Matthew gives direct quotations from the Old Testament that are shared with Mark and Luke, they usually follow the LXX, which became the standard Greek version of the Old Testament used by the early church. But in the fulfillment quotations that are unique to Matthew, he appears not to follow the LXX. Gundry suggests that Matthew goes his particular way in offering his own free rendering of the Hebrew text, of which the formula quotations are the most prominent examples.[53] In another direction, Maarten Menken advances the hypothesis that very few of the differences between the LXX and his quotations were due to Matthew himself but were present in his scriptural text. He suggests that the text form of the fulfilment quotations is best explained as derived from a Septuagint text that was revised to make it better agree with the Hebrew and to improve the quality of its Greek. Menken suggests that the evangelist took these quotations from a continuous text that had developed in Jewish tradition.[54]

Alongside these varied perspectives as to the text-form, many suggestions have been offered as to the source of Matthew's formula quotations, but the primary options are as follows.[55]

(1) Krister Stendahl conjectured that the quotations came from a Matthean "school" that interpreted Old Testament texts in a manner similar to the pesher exegesis (i.e., "this current event is the fulfillment of that OT event") practiced at Qumran (e.g., the

52. See Craig A. Evans, "Fulfilling the Law and Seeking Righteousness in Matthew and in the Dead Sea Scrolls," in Gurtner, Willitts, and Burridge, *Jesus, Matthew's Gospel and Early Christianity*, 102–14.

53. Gundry, *Use of the Old Testament*, xi–xiii, 1–5, 155–59.

54. Maarten J. J. Menken, *Matthew's Bible: The Old Testament Text of the Evangelist*, BETL 173 (Leuven: Peeters, 2004), part 1 (e.g., 128, 146–48, 156–58). Menken suggests that later versions of Aquila, Symmachus, and Theodotion, as well as texts found at Qumran and Naḥal Ḥever, demonstrate a strong impulse in Judaism to bring the (known) Greek text into closer conformity to the (known) Hebrew text. For interaction with Menken's proposal, see Steve Moyise, "Matthew's Bible in the Infancy Narrative," in *The Scriptures of Israel in Jewish and Christian Tradition: Essays in Honour of Maarten J. J. Menken*, ed. Bart Koet, Steve Moyise, and Joseph Verheyden, NovTSup 148 (Leiden: Brill, 2013), passim.

55. Gundry lists several possibilities, some of which are rather obscure. He offers brief evaluation of each (*Use of the Old Testament*, 1–5) and then gives extended discussion of each (151–234). See also France, *Matthew: Evangelist and Teacher*, 172–81.

pesher "commentary" of 1QpHab).[56] Aside from the largely speculative existence of a "school" that generated a corporate production, the Qumran examples set forth are quite different in that they come from a continuous text (e.g., Habakkuk), rather than isolated quotations.[57] Also, the Qumran interpretations tended to make the original Old Testament context meaningless by focusing on current fulfillments. As Carson notes, "Even the most difficult passages in Matthew, such as 2:15, do not hint that the original OT meaning is void—in this case that the people of Israel were not called by God out of Egypt at the exodus."[58]

(2) Georg Strecker conjectured that the fulfillment-formula quotations came from a collection of *testimonia* (collections of Old Testament texts used for preaching and teaching) that Matthew had access to or that he compiled. Strecker based much of this theory on the *testimonia* found at Qumran.[59] Later church fathers also had a form of *testimonia*, used especially for debate.[60] However, the distinctive structure of Matthew's fulfillment quotations and the way that they fit so tightly into his narrative argue against such a loose collection of *testimonia*.[61]

(3) A more broadly accepted proposal, as illustrated in Gundry, suggests that the fulfillment formula quotations came from Matthew's own careful reflection upon the life of Jesus in the light of his understanding of the Old Testament.[62] This certainly does not exclude input from other sources, including the developing oral tradition of the early church, and from Jesus himself. Luke tells us that Jesus, both during his lifetime (e.g., Luke 4:16–21) and during his post-resurrection appearances (Luke 24:44–47; Acts 1:3), clarified to the disciples, including Matthew, how his ministry was the fulfillment of Old Testament Scriptures. In the concluding scenes from Luke's Gospel, he tells us that Jesus addressed the assembled disciples. "Everything must be fulfilled that is written about me in the Law of Moses, the Prophets and the Psalms" (Luke 24:44–47). Luke follows this with a statement from the opening verses of Acts: "After his suffering, [Jesus] presented himself to them and gave many convincing proofs that he was alive. He appeared to them over a period of forty days and spoke about the kingdom of God" (Acts 1:3).

---

56. Krister Stendahl, *The School of St. Matthew and Its Use of the Old Testament*, 2nd ed. (Lund: Gleerup, 1954), 50–85, 196–98. See also Richard N. Longenecker, *Biblical Exegesis in the Apostolic Period* (Grand Rapids: Eerdmans, 1975), 24–30, 180–84.

57. France, *Jesus and the Old Testament*, 206–7.

58. Carson, "Matthew," 52. See also Gundry, *Use of the Old Testament*, 155–59.

59. E.g., 4QTest and 4QFlor. See Georg Strecker, *Der Weg der Gerechtigkeit: Untersuchung zur Theologie des Matthäus* (Göttingen: Vandenhoeck & Ruprecht,1962), 49–85.

60. E.g., Justin [ca. 100–165], *1 Apol.* 33.1, 4–5 and Cyprian [ca. AD 200–258], *To Quirinius: Testimonies Against the Jews*. For a discussion of Justin's *testimonia* and his use of Matthew's Gospel, see Oskar Skarsaune, *The Proof from Prophecy: A Study in Justin Martyr's Proof-Text Tradition: Text-Type, Provenance, Theological Profile*, NovTSup 56 (Leiden: Brill, 1987), 7, 130, 163.

61. See George M. Soares-Prabhu, *The Formula Quotations in the Infancy Narratives of Matthew*, AnBib 63 (Rome: Pontifical Biblical Press, 1976), 67–73, 104; Osborne, *Matthew*, 39.

62. Cf. Gundry, *Use of the Old Testament*, 205–34. See also Roland Deines, "Jesus and the Torah according to the Gospel of Matthew," in Seleznev, Loader, and Niebuhr, *Gospel of Matthew*, 295–328, here 325–26.

By the time that Matthew was ready to compile his written record of Jesus Messiah's life and ministry, he had a unique background from which to draw. His immersion in the Old Testament as a Jewish youth and his stunning encounter with Jesus in his personal discipleship were coupled with upward of thirty years and more since the death and resurrection of Jesus Messiah to reflect upon the Old Testament and understand how Jesus was the fulfillment of its hopes and expectations. Matthew was a prime candidate to provide for his readers theological interpretation of the Old Testament in the light of Jesus's life and ministry.[63] And he does so in a variety of ways, as we will now discuss.

### *5.3.1.1 Jesus's Historical Life Fulfills Messianic Predictive Prophecy*

Sometimes the Old Testament texts cited in Matthew are clearly or at least plausibly messianic. In these cases, "fulfill" indicates the way in which the events of Jesus's earthly life and ministry bring to actualization predictive prophecy.[64] For example, Matthew cites the religious leaders' understanding of Old Testament prophecy to confirm that Jesus's birth in Bethlehem fulfills Micah's prophecy of the birthplace of a messianic deliverer from the line of David (cf. 2:1, 6 with Mic 5:1–5). Also, Matthew indicates that Jesus's climactic entry to Jerusalem riding on a donkey with a colt fulfills Zechariah's predictive messianic prophecy (cf. Matt 21:4–5, 9 with Zech 9:9–10).[65]

Predictive prophecy may be one particular expectation, as in Matt 1:22–23, where Jesus fulfills the prediction of a virgin-born messianic deliverer.[66] Or without citing a particular text, the fulfillment may be of a collective predictive subject as in Matt 2:23, where Old Testament prophetic strands point to significant, recognizable Old Testament themes. In this case we may find a double entendre that Matthew develops for his readers: the theme of the messianic Branch of the line of David who would bring deliverance to Israel, coupled with the theme of an unassuming Messiah with humble origins in the city of Nazareth.[67] Or Matthew may indicate, without citing an Old Testament text, that an activity in Jesus's life, such as coming for baptism by John the Baptist to "fulfill all righteousness" (3:15), indicates that this brings to

63. Cf. Gundry, *Use of the Old Testament*, 205–34.

64. For extended discussion of the use of OT prediction, see France, *Jesus and the Old Testament*, 83–163.

65. For a discussion of these texts, see Walter C. Kaiser Jr., *The Messiah in the Old Testament* (Grand Rapids: Zondervan, 1995), 151–54, 215–17; Michael F. Bird, *Jesus Is the Christ: The Messianic Testimony of the Gospels* (Downers Grove, IL: InterVarsity, 2012), 57–78; Clay Alan Ham, *Coming King and the Rejected Shepherd*, 39–47.

66. For discussion, see Carson, "Matthew," 95–106; Gundry, *Use of the Old Testament*, 89–92, 127–28; Ben Witherington III, *Isaiah Old and New: Exegesis, Intertextuality, and Hermeneutics* (Minneapolis: Fortress, 2017), 70–80.

67. For discussion, see Michael J. Wilkins, "Isaiah 53 in the Four Gospels," in *The Gospel According to Isaiah 53: Encountering the Suffering Servant in Jewish and Christian Theology*, ed. Darrell L. Bock and Mitch Glaser (Grand Rapids: Kregel, 2012), 109–32, esp. 115–19. See also Jared M. August, "'He Shall Be Called a Nazarene': The Non-Citation of Matthew 2:23," *TynBul* 69.1 (2018): 63–74.

actualization the collective Old Testament prophecy of future salvation-historical righteousness.[68]

### *5.3.1.2 Jesus's Life and Ministry Fulfill Typologically or Analogically Old Testament Salvation-Historical Patterns*

Matthew, however, does not usually operate on a direct *prediction-fulfillment* scheme. He regularly employs a form of *typology* to demonstrate through an analogy and/or forward-looking element or foreshadowing that the recurring patterns of God's activity in salvation history find their "fulfillment" especially in the person and activities and ministry of Jesus Messiah. In these cases, Matthew's use of "fulfill" indicates the way in which Jesus's earthly life and ministry corresponded analogically or typologically (some say recapitulated or repeated) to certain aspects of the national history of Israel. Typology then can be understood as earlier events establishing patterns that anticipate God's actions in future events. James Hamilton suggests that typological fulfillment in the life of Jesus "refers to the *fullest expression of a significant pattern of events*."[69]

Beale understands typology to include both analogy and a prophetic element.[70] France understands typology as a pattern of the dealings of God with humans in which his acts in the Old Testament present a pattern that can be seen to be repeated in New Testament events. This correspondence of Old Testament and New Testament is both historical (i.e., a correspondence of situation and meaning) and theological (i.e., an embodiment of the same principle of God's working).[71] It does not introduce into the Old Testament text a principle that was not already intelligible to the Old Testament readers, which prevents typology from degenerating into abstract allegory.[72]

This form of typology is apparently what Matthew has in view when he points to the flight of Jesus and his parents to Egypt and their later return and declares, "And so was fulfilled what the Lord had said through the prophet: 'Out of Egypt I called my son'" (2:15). This obviously is not direct prediction-fulfillment, as Hosea 11:1 does not even contain future-tense verbs, but simply declares a past event. It is difficult to see how

68. Cf. Keener, *Matthew* (2009), 132; Donald A. Hagner, "Righteousness in Matthew's Gospel," in *Worship, Theology, and Ministry in the Early Church: Essays in Honor of Ralph P. Martin*, ed. Michael J. Wilkins and Terence Paige, JSNTSup 87 (Sheffield: JSOT, 1992), 101–20.

69. James M. Hamilton Jr., "'The Virgin Will Conceive': Typological Fulfillment in Matthew 1:18–23," in *Built upon the Rock: Studies in the Gospel of Matthew*, ed. Daniel M. Gurtner and John Nolland (Grand Rapids: Eerdmans, 2008), 228–47, here 233 (emphasis original). See also his fuller work: James M. Hamilton Jr., *Typology—Understanding the Bible's Promise-Shaped Patterns: How Old Testament Expectations are Fulfilled in Christ* (Grand Rapids: Zondervan, 2022).

70. Beale, *Handbook on the New Testament Use of the Old Testament*, 14, which leads him to define typology as: "*the study of analogical correspondences among revealed truths about persons, events, institutions, and other things within the historical framework of God's special revelation, which, from a retrospective view, are of a prophetic nature and are escalated in their meaning*" (emphasis original).

71. France, *Jesus and the Old Testament*, 39.

72. See the careful discussion by Ardel Caneday, "Biblical Types: Revelation Concealed in Plain Sight to Be Disclosed—'These Things Occurred Typologically to Them and Were Written Down for Our Admonition,'" in *God's Glory Revealed in Christ: Essays on Biblical Theology in Honor of Thomas R. Schreiner*, ed. Denny Burk, James M. Hamilton Jr., and Brian J. Vickers (Nashville: B&H, 2019), esp. 154.

Hosea's reference back to the Exodus can imply for Matthew how Jesus's life fulfills what the prophet had said, unless we see that Matthew has a multifaceted perspective on the way that events in Jesus's life "fulfill" the Old Testament Scriptures.

Matthew is following here a standard, fairly conservative form of Jewish typology in interpreting the Scriptures. Blomberg describes this form of typology in the following way: "Key patterns of activity ascribed to God recur in striking, discernible patterns such that the believer can only affirm the same hand of God at work in both events. The apologetic is more subtle than with directly predictive prophecy but no less persuasive."[73]

Matthew draws an "analogical correspondence" between the events of the nation described by Hosea (Hos 11:1–2) and the events of Messiah's life (Matt 2:13–15), so that Jesus's calling from Egypt recapitulates Israel's exodus from Egypt.[74] As Matthew drew these correspondences he saw Jesus as the One who *actualizes* and *completes* all that God intended for the nation.[75] In the context of his prophecy, Hosea recounts how God had faithfully brought Israel out of Egypt in the exodus.[76] Matthew's point of comparison is the corporate solidarity between the nation Israel as God's son being rescued and delivered by God, and Jesus as the one who will be revealed to be God's "Son" *par excellence*, being rescued and delivered by God.[77] Jesus Messiah is not only the "son of David, son of Abraham" (1:1) but is God's Son, which points ahead to the unique manner in which the voice from heaven will specify Jesus as the beloved Son (3:17), the way in which the temptations are directed to the Son of God (4:3–10), the way in which Jesus's transfiguration prompts the voice from the cloud to again declare Jesus as his beloved Son (17:5), and the way in which Jesus will address God as his Father (26:39–42).

Further, Israel's wandering in the wilderness becomes a type of Jesus's wilderness testing when we see that the lessons Israel learned in the wilderness become the basis for Jesus's victory over Satan's temptations (4:1–11).[78] Old Testament authors consistently reminded the nation of Israel to look back to their redemption by God when he brought them out of Egypt.[79] The yearly Passover was a reminder, but also a promise, that God had provided a sacrificial lamb for his people Israel. As Matthew harks back to Hosea's recounting of God faithfully bringing Israel out of Egypt under divine protection (Hos

73. Blomberg, "Matthew," 2.

74. See Tracy L. Howard, "The Use of Hosea 11:1 in Matthew 2:15: An Alternative Solution," *BSac* 143 (1986): 314–28.

75. Howard, "Use of Hosea 11:1 in Matthew 2:15," 322.

76. Matthew gives both the ultimate origin and agency of the prophecy expressed with *hypo* "by" ("by the Lord" *hypo kyriou*) and the immediate agent of prophecy expressed with *dia* "through" ("through Jeremiah the prophet" *dia Ieremiou tou prophetou*), as in 1:22.

77. Kaiser, *Messiah in the Old Testament*, 35.

78. Blomberg, *Matthew*, 30; Carson, "Matthew," 140–43. For a discussion of "types" in the NT, see Caneday, "Biblical Types," 134–55.

79. E.g., Ps 78; 81; 105–6; Jer 2:6; 7:22–25; Ezek 20:1–20; Mic 6:1–4.

11:1), he points out how Jesus's infancy corresponds analogically to Israel's history. The life of Jesus is the historical completion of the process of redemption. No threat from any public official can thwart the process. Jesus coming out of Egypt is the recapitulation of the promise to Israel that redemption is at hand. Matthew saw striking parallels in the patterns of God's activities in history in ways he cannot attribute to coincidence. "Just as God brought the nation of Israel out of Egypt to inaugurate his original covenant with them, so again God is bringing the Messiah, who fulfills the hopes of Israel, out of Egypt as he is about to inaugurate his new covenant."[80] A substantial similarity exists between these two moments of redemptive history, and therefore the two are regarded as interconnected, forming one larger continuity. "The earlier is thus seen to foreshadow or anticipate the latter, which then becomes a kind of realization or fulfillment of the former."[81]

### *5.3.1.3* Sensus Plenior?

Matthew's understanding of Jesus Messiah brings us to a more complete and holistic understanding of God's activities in all of history, drawing a correspondence between the Old Testament and the New Testament. The original historical context of Israel's story provides a point of contact between God's recurring involvement in Israel's salvation and what he is doing now in Jesus's life and ministry. In a very real way, then, Matthew sees that generally the entire Old Testament, in Carson's words, "was preparing the way for Christ, anticipating him, pointing to him, leading up to him. When we ask how much of this forward-looking or 'prophetic' aspect in what they wrote the OT writers themselves recognized, the answer must vary with the particular text."[82]

This introduces another complicated issue, whether or not *sensus plenior* ("fuller sense" or "fuller meaning") is a valid hermeneutical principle to apply to Old Testament texts cited in the New Testament. Raymond Brown is one New Testament scholar who affirms the use of this principle as defined:

> The *sensus plenior* is that additional, deeper meaning, intended by God but not clearly intended by the human author, which is seen to exist in the words of a biblical text (or group of texts, or even a whole book) when they are studied in the light of further revelation or development in the understanding of revelation.[83]

80. Blomberg, *Matthew*, 67. Kaiser (*Messiah in the Old Testament*, 35) contends that the comparison is made only with respect to "my son" and not to being called "out of Egypt," but this seems to miss the larger comparison drawn between the two redemptive moments. See also John H. Sailhamer, "Hosea 11:1 and Matthew 2:15," *WTJ* 63 (2001): 83–92.

81. Hagner, *Matthew 1–13*, 36.

82. Carson, "Matthew," 53.

83. Raymond Brown, *The* Sensus Plenior *of Sacred Scripture* (Baltimore: St Mary's University Press, 1955; repr., Eugene, OR: Wipf & Stock, 2008), 92 (emphasis Brown's).

Kevin Vanhoozer suggests that

> to say that the Bible has a "fuller meaning" is to focus on the (divine) author's intended meaning at the level of the *canonical* act. Better said, *the canon as a whole becomes the unified act for which the divine intention serves as the unifying principle.* The divine intention *supervenes* on the intention of the human authors. . . . *The divine intention does not contravene the intention of the human author but rather supervenes upon it.*[84]

As such, Vanhoozer affirms a judicious use of the principle, apparently as the divine author works within the human author's intention to bring about a sovereign intention.[85]

Walter Kaiser is one Old Testament scholar who denies the principle of *sensus plenior*, contending that of any Old Testament text there is one plain, definite meaning that was intended by the author that can be discovered through the use of traditional exegetical methods. He poses the question:

> Should that meaning be limited to what the human writer of Scripture obtained as a result of standing in the revelatory counsel of God, or were there additional, or even alternative, meanings to be found that God somehow quietly incorporated into the text in some mysterious way, thus hiding them from the author, or perhaps even new meanings that the audience brought to the text on their own?[86]

I am sympathetic with Kaiser's concerns, especially the last. In an effort to harmonize the Old Testament text with its use in the New Testament, it is possible to impose a meaning on Old Testament passages that the author may never have intended. But, as we discussed in the opening chapter, when dealing with New Testament authors and their use of the Old Testament, we are in deep waters, because we are confronted with a unique phenomenon—the dual authorship of Scripture. Darrell Bock interacts with Kaiser's concerns and offers a response:

> The mention of the progress of revelation introduces an idea that is also a special feature of the concept of dual authorship, namely, that God progressively discloses his plan through history. This means that the force of earlier passages in God's plan becomes clearer and more developed as more of the plan is revealed in later events

84. Vanhoozer, *Is There a Meaning in This Text?*, 265 (emphasis original).

85. For further discussion, see Hagner, *New Testament*, 21–25.

86. Walter C. Kaiser Jr. "Single Meaning, Unified Referents: Accurate and Authoritative Citations of the Old Testament by the New Testament," in *Three Views on the New Testament Use of the Old Testament*, ed. Kenneth Berding and Jonathan Lunde (Grand Rapids: Zondervan, 2008), 45.

> and texts. This increase in clarity often involves the identification of new referents, to which the initial referents typologically point forward.[87]

God as author works within the human author to point forward to final fulfillment.[88]

When we turn to Matthew's use of the Old Testament, we see that Carson rejects an appeal to some hidden divine knowledge, but does suggest that a "fuller meaning" may be legitimate if we understand it to lie not in what any one text provides, but rather "the pattern of revelation up to that time—a pattern not yet adequately discerned."[89] For example, he suggests Hosea may have grasped the messianic nuance of the "son" language applied to Israel and David's promised heir (Hos 11:1), yet his purpose was not to apply this to a future messianic deliverer who would be called out of Egypt. Matthew picked up on one piece that Hosea understood (God's love for Israel as his son) and drew lessons from that piece of revelation when connected with others to provide a fuller picture of God's saving activity in Jesus.[90]

### *5.3.1.4 Moses or Israel?*

Another complicated issue when considering Matthew's use of typology concerns whether he intends the parallel to Jesus to be Moses or Israel. Some suggest that the analogy Matthew draws from Hosea, "Out of Egypt I called my son" (2:15), is intended to point to Jesus as a new and greater Moses: Matthew draws a significant, perhaps even central, theological parallel between Jesus and Moses.[91] Davies and Allison state, "The key to understanding Mt 1.18–2.23 is to be found in the haggadic traditions about Moses."[92] Raymond Brown goes further to point to the first five chapters of Matthew, where the infant Jesus faces the threat of murder at the hands of a tyrant, causing him to flee to Egypt, where he then undergoes his own exodus, wanders in the wilderness for forty days (cf. Moses's forty years) before his temptations, and then ascends a mountain and delivers the divine Law to the people.[93] In a full monograph, Dale Allison suggests that Matthew draws a strong theological typology between Jesus and Moses not only in the first few chapters, but throughout his Gospel. He states:

---

87. Darrell L. Bock, "Single Meaning, Multiple Contexts and Referents: The New Testament's Legitimate, Accurate, and Multifaceted Use of the Old," in Berding and Lunde, *Three Views on the New Testament Use of the Old Testament*, 114. For a very helpful overview of these issues, see William W. Klein, Craig L. Blomberg, and Robert L. Hubbard Jr., *Introduction to Biblical Interpretation*, 3rd ed. (Grand Rapids: Zondervan, 2017), 183–97.

88. For a thorough, and nuanced, discussion of a single, determinate meaning of Scripture, see Sargent, *David Being a Prophet*; Sargent, *Written for Our Learning*.

89. Carson, "Matthew," 120.

90. Carson, "Matthew," 119–20.

91. E.g., Davies and Allison, *Matthew*, 1:192–95; Mark D. Smith, "Of Jesus and Quirinius," *CBQ* 62.2 (2000): 278–93, see 291–93; Gundry, *Matthew*, 7, 33–35, 78–100, 593; E. P. Sanders, *The Historical Figure of Jesus* (New York: Penguin, 1993), 87–91.

92. Davies and Allison, *Matthew*, 1:192–95.

93. Brown, *Birth of the Messiah*, 228–32.

> Both Moses and Jesus were many things, and they occupied several common offices. Moses was the paradigmatic prophet-king, the Messiah's model, a worker of miracles, the giver of Torah, the mediator for Israel, and a suffering servant. And Jesus was similarly a suffering servant, the mediator for Israel, the giver of Torah, a worker of miracles, the Mosaic Messiah, and the eschatological prophet-king.[94]

This strong typological link is thus understood by many to be Matthew's christological emphasis upon Jesus as the "new Moses."[95]

However, while Moses was the primary leader in the exodus events, and he is highly regarded by Matthew (e.g., 17:3–4), others suggest that the more immediate and specifically identified analogy is between Jesus and *Israel* as God's people.[96] Nolland indicates that the Hosea quotation establishes an Israel typology: a little later in adult life Jesus will be called upon to relive the wilderness temptations of Israel (4:1–11), and now as an infant he retraces in his own life the foundational experience of Israel in being called by God out of Egypt.[97] So the emphasis is upon Israel as God's son, which Matthew sees typologically in Jesus as God's Son. The exodus demonstrated Israel's unique status as God's firstborn son. In the Old Testament, Israel the nation is the son of God (Exod 4:22–12; Jer 31:9, 20; Hos 1:10), and the Davidic kings are sons of God (2 Sam 7:14–15; Pss 2:6–7, 12; 72:1; 89:26–37), and God's special love and covenant loyalty are promised and demonstrated to both the nation and the kings. Turner stresses, "For Matthew, these themes are consummated in Jesus, whose individual life is an antitypical microcosm of macrocosmic typological Israel."[98]

Frank Thielman traces this typological theme of Israel and Jesus throughout Matthew's Gospel, where the evangelist implies in several passages that Jesus embodies the nation of Israel, recapitulating the nation's history and making the case that Jesus succeeded in obeying God where Israel failed.[99] Thielman traces this theme beginning in 2:14–23, following those scholars who understand that the "son" to whom Hosea referred was the nation of Israel itself, then typologically fulfilled in Jesus as God's Son. Jesus is the beloved Son in the baptism (3:15–17) and the transfiguration (17:5). He is obedient and victorious in the testings/temptations where the nation had failed (4:1–11). Matthew emphasizes that Jesus fulfills the role of the servant in Isaiah's four

94. Dale C. Allison Jr., *The New Moses: A Matthean Typology* (Minneapolis: Fortress, 1993), 275.

95. In addition to those cited above, see also E. P. Blair, *Jesus in the Gospel of Matthew* (Nashville: Abingdon, 1960), 124–37; Boring, "Matthew," 146–47; Roger David Aus, *Matthew 1–2 and the Virginal Conception: In Light of Palestinian and Hellenistic Judaic Traditions on the Birth of Israel's First Redeemer, Moses*, Studies in Judaism (Lanham, MD: University Press of America, 2004), passim; Talbert, *Matthew*, 37–39; Quarles, *Theology of Matthew*, 33–69.

96. E.g., Osborne, *Matthew*, 97–102; Carson, "Matthew," 117–20; Nolland, *Matthew*, 123; Turner, *Matthew*, 90–91; Evans, *Matthew*, 57–61; Blomberg, "Matthew," 8–10.

97. Nolland, *Matthew*, 123.

98. Turner, *Matthew*, 91.

99. Thielman, *Theology of the New Testament*, 95–97.

Servant Songs, where the servant is both an individual and the nation of Israel.[100] Jesus's healing ministry fulfills the servant's role in Isa 53:4, 11 (Matt 8:17). Jesus's death is "a ransom for many" (20:28) and corresponds to the vicarious, atoning nature of the servant's suffering. Thielman concludes, "Like the Servant, Jesus was everything that Israel should have been but was nevertheless numbered among the transgressors. His suffering, therefore, was not for his own sin but for the sins of others."[101]

I concur with France that Jesus as the new Moses is a typology of which Matthew is well aware. But Matthew uses it with considerable restraint. This typology is absorbed into a much richer conception of Jesus. "Jesus is not just 'another Moses,' but something far higher."[102] Jesus does not *give* a new law to his disciples on the Mount, but *fulfills* the Law (5:17–20), and gives instruction to his disciples on the way that they can obey the Law from the heart for inside-out transformation. This is something that Israel did not do, so Jesus gives the way that his disciples can fulfill what Israel did not.

### *5.3.1.5 God with His People*

We go one step further to suggest that the Old Testament theme of God with his people Israel finds explicit fulfillment in Jesus with his people, made up of all those from Israel and the nations who have followed Jesus in discipleship.[103] The ideal form of discipleship for Israel was for the nation to be in covenantal relationship with God. That ideal is richly expressed in the prophets as they look ahead to the time when Israel would have the ultimate realization of that relationship. Isaiah expresses the personalness of this as he tells the nation, "Although the Lord has given you bread of privation and water of oppression, *He*, your Teacher, will no longer hide Himself, but your eyes will behold your Teacher. And your ears will hear a word behind you, 'This is the way, walk in it,' whenever you turn to the right or to the left" (Isa 30:20–21 NASB, italics original). When giving the Law to Israel in the wilderness God stressed his covenantal intent: "I will walk among you and be your God, and you will be my people" (Lev 26:12). The nation was called to a relationship in which God was with his people.

The promise of a coming Davidic Messiah is intertwined with the promise that God himself would be with his people (e.g., Ezek 37:24–28). The significance of Matthew's interpretation of the meaning of Jesus's name—"Immanuel," "God with us" (1:23)—therefore, cannot be overstated. In Jesus, God has come to fulfill the deepest meaning of the covenant—God with his people as Master, Lord, and Savior. The centrality of God in the life of his people is also found in the epistles of the New Testament. The apostle Paul rightly understood the central place that God alone should

100. Thielman, *Theology of the New Testament*, 96–97. See also J. Brown, "Matthew's Christology and Isaiah's Servant," 93–106.

101. Thielman, *Theology of the New Testament*, 97.

102. France, *Matthew: Evangelist and Teacher*, 187.

103. See Wilkins, *Following the Master*, 56–57, 66–67.

have and explains the basis of differentiation between righteousness and wickedness, between believers and unbelievers: "As God has said: 'I will live with them and walk among them, and I will be their God, and they will be my people'" (2 Cor 6:16). The intimacy of the relationship cannot be overlooked. It is an intimacy that is fulfilled only when God, Jesus Messiah, is with his people.

### *5.3.1.6 History Prophesied or Prophecy Historicized?*

Another complicated issue when considering Matthew's use of "fulfillment" involves whether this is history prophesied or prophecy historicized. Some critics today charge Matthew with composing an account of Jesus's life that is a fanciful manipulation of facts to try and fit what prophets have said. The issue for us is whether we have in Matthew's Gospel a history that was prophesied, or prophecy that was made to look like it was actually fulfilled in history. That is, did Matthew write a historical record of Jesus's life and ministry that was prophesied in the Old Testament, or did Matthew write an account of Jesus's life and ministry that was made to look like it was prophesied? For example, John Dominic Crossan contends that when Matthew and the other evangelists wrote their passion narratives—the stories about Jesus's death—they reached back into Old Testament prophecies and manipulated the details to make it look like Jesus's death had been predicted: prophecy became *historicized*.[104]

The claim is that Matthew either fabricated details or else manipulated the facts to try to make it appear that Jesus's life and ministry fulfilled Old Testament prophecies about the coming of the Messiah. Elsewhere Crossan suggests that Matthew intentionally made up a life story about Jesus that fulfilled prophecies such as being born of a virgin in Bethlehem, or going to Egypt, or being raised in Nazareth.[105] He states, "I understand the virginal conception of Jesus to be a confessional statement about Jesus's status and not a biological statement about Mary's body. It is later faith in Jesus as an adult retrojected mythologically onto Jesus as an infant."[106]

Robert Miller likewise contends that Matthew created stories about Jesus to make it appear that he fulfilled Old Testament prophecies. In his study of Old Testament prophecy and its fulfillment in Matthew's Gospel, he states of his objectives, "First, we will examine how Matthew handled prophecy—or, more precisely, how he manipulated it—as he integrated the words of the prophets into his narrative. . . . Those prophecies can be fulfilled only because Matthew adds details from them into his narrative."[107]

My claim, along with many others, is the opposite: Jesus pointed to his own life and

104. John Dominic Crossan, *Who Killed Jesus? Exposing the Roots of Anti-Semitism in the Gospel Story of the Death of Jesus* (San Francisco: HarperSanFrancisco, 1996), ix–x.

105. E.g., John Dominic Crossan, *Jesus: A Revolutionary Biography* (San Francisco: HarperSanFrancisco, 1994), 15–21.

106. Crossan, *Jesus*, 23.

107. Robert J. Miller, "How Matthew Helped Jesus Fulfill Prophecy," in *The Message of Jesus: John Dominic Crossan and Ben Witherington III in Dialogue*, ed. Robert B. Stewart (Minneapolis: Fortress, 2013), 127, 131. See also Robert J. Miller, *Helping Jesus Fulfill Prophecy* (Eugene, OR: Cascade, 2015), 117.

ministry as a fulfillment of Old Testament prophecies.[108] And Matthew recorded accurately what Jesus said and what happened in the historical life and ministry of Jesus, and those events were the miraculous fulfillment of ancient prophecies regarding the coming Messiah. Evangelical scholars have satisfactorily answered charges of critics along four basic lines that I have distilled from my ongoing engagement with this discussion.[109]

In the first place, the creation of falsified historical accounts to substantiate a claim to prophetic fulfillment is not a staple of Jewish interpretive history. As a Jewish author, Matthew would not have had precedent for such a blatant disregard for Jewish interpretation of Old Testament prophecies. And he would have been subject to intense criticism from the Jewish interpretive community for falsifying predictive prophecy.

Second, the apostles, including Matthew, were so gripped by the reality of Jesus as the Messiah that they suffered persecution at the hands of the Jews, and most of them later experienced martyrdom. They were not going to suffer like this for a lie about a person who really was not the Messiah.

Third, when the Gospels were written and circulated, there were many people still living who had been alive when the events of Jesus life had occurred. They would have confronted Matthew with his fabrication. But no such record of this kind of accusation against Matthew surfaces from the ancient records.

Fourth, the Jewish people themselves would have used these kinds of fabrications as a way of discrediting the claims that Jesus was the Messiah. If Jesus had not been born in Bethlehem, or if his claim to being Messiah were not in line with Old Testament prophecies, they would have been readily denied by Jews who were familiar with the

108. Moyise (*Jesus and Scripture*, 5–11) discusses scholarly approaches to the subject of Jesus's use of Scripture by categorizing views as minimalist (Geza Vermes, John Dominic Crossan, Marcus Borg [pp. 9–11, ch. 5]), moderate (N. T. Wright, Dale Allison, James D. G. Dunn [pp. 8–9, ch. 6]), and maximalist (Charles Kimball, R. T. France [p. 7, ch. 7]). These labels refer to how Moyise understands the way that scholars view the reliability of the Gospels, including Matthew, in terms of preserving authentic appeals to Scripture by the historical Jesus (see Moyise, "Jesus and Scripture According to Matthew's Gospel," in *Jesus and Scripture*, 33–51). In this study I align myself with those who would be labeled "maximalists." I embrace this position because I understand the Gospels to convey historically reliable information both generally and specifically regarding the sayings of Jesus, including his citation of the OT. For discussion and defense of the authenticity of the Gospel records of Jesus's sayings, see Darrell L. Bock, "The Words of Jesus in the Gospels: Live, Jive, or Memorex?," in *Jesus Under Fire: Modern Scholarship Reinvents the Historical Jesus*, ed. Michael J. Wilkins and J. P. Moreland (Grand Rapids: Zondervan, 1995), 73–99. More generally, see Craig L. Blomberg, *The Historical Reliability of the Gospels*, 2nd ed. (Downers Grove, IL: InterVarsity, 2007).

109. For general overviews, see Darrell L. Bock and J. Ed Komoszewski, eds., *Jesus, Skepticism, and the Problem of History: Criteria and Context in the Study of Christian Origins* (Grand Rapids: Zondervan, 2019); Michael F. Bird, *How the Early Church Wrote the Story of Jesus* (Grand Rapids: Eerdmans, 2014). For popular discussion, see Peter J. Williams, *Can We Trust the Gospels?* (Wheaton, IL: Crossway, 2018). For a rebuttal of the scholarly charge that Matthew was a creative midrashic interpreter, see R. T. France, "Scripture, Tradition and History in the Infancy Narratives of Matthew," in *Studies of History and Tradition in the Four Gospels*, ed. R.T. France and David Wenham, vol. 2 of *Gospel Perspectives* (Sheffield: JSOT, 1981), 239–66; Blomberg, *Historical Reliability of the Gospels*, 75–87; Charles L. Quarles, *Midrash Criticism: Introduction and Appraisal* (Lanham, MD: University Press of America, 1997); "Midrash as Creative Historiography: Portrait of a Misnomer," *JETS* 39.3 (1996): 457–64; "The *Protoevangelium of James* as an Alleged Parallel to Creative Historiography in the Synoptic Birth Narratives," *BBR* 8 (1998): 139–49. For an overview of OT prophecies and their fulfillment in Jesus, see Kaiser, *Messiah in the Old Testament*, 13–35, 231–35, passim.

details. However, we do not hear of any such accusations, not even from the Talmud, which at points speaks derogatorily about Jesus and his followers, but never accuses them of falsification of Jesus's life to fit messianic prophecies.

I conclude that Matthew recorded accurately what happened in the historical life and ministry of Jesus, and those events were the miraculous fulfillment of ancient prophecies regarding the coming Messiah.

## 5.3.2 Jesus's Statements of the Fulfillment of the Old Testament

The four Gospels record Jesus quoting about fifty different Old Testament passages of Scripture, along with at least twice that number of allusions and echoes.[110] Of those quotations, thirty-seven are found in Matthew's Gospel,[111] providing the longest list of all four canonical Gospels.

In this section we look at the fulfillment citations by Jesus. In his historical ministry Jesus validated his person and mission by citing the ways that he fulfilled the Old Testament. Likewise, Matthew records that same apologetic thrust for his audience by drawing upon Jesus citing the ways in which he "fulfills" the Old Testament. This should not be surprising if we consider that Matthew's Gospel was written to address the questions and concerns in the minds of those followers of Jesus who came to faith in him from Judaism, as we discussed in Chapters 1 and 2.[112] Thus, Matthew's use of the Old Testament is based on Jesus Messiah's own use of the Old Testament, which validates the person and ministry of Jesus Messiah.

These are illustrated in the chart below, after which I will briefly comment on some of the most significant of these fulfillment sayings of Jesus.

### *5.3.2.1 Table of Fulfillment Formulas and References to the Old Testament by Jesus*

| | Jesus's citation in Matthew's Gospel | Term for "fulfill" (*plēroō*) | Old Testament text cited |
|---|---|---|---|
| 1) | 3:15 | *plērōsai* | Isa 53:11?—"Fulfill all righteousness" |
| 2) | 5:17 | *plērōsai* | "I have not come to abolish them but to fulfill them" (the Law and the Prophets) |
| 3) | 13:48 | *eplērōthē* | "When the net was full"—not significant |
| 4) | 23:32 | *plērōsate* | To the Pharisees: "Fill up, then, the measure of your fathers" (ESV) |

*continued*

110. Moyise, *Jesus and Scripture*, 122–23.

111. See 5.2.1.2 Table of Quotations of (with some Allusions to) the OT in Matthew's Gospel.

112. See also Deines, "Jesus and Scripture," 42; Craig A. Evans, "The Place of Jewish Scripture in Jesus' Teaching," in Stewart, *Message of Jesus*, 79–94. For additional discussion of the Jewish background of author and recipients, see Hagner, *New Testament*, 208–16.

| | Jesus's citation in Matthew's Gospel | Term for "fulfill" (*plēroō*) | Old Testament text cited |
|---|---|---|---|
| 5) | 26:54 | *plērōthōsin* | Jesus's statement about his betrayal and arrest: |
| 6) | 26:56 | *plērōthōsin* | Jesus's statement about his betrayal and arrest (cf. Isa 53; Zech 12–13) |
| | **Jesus's Citation in Matthew's Gospel** | ***anaplēroō*** | **Old Testament text cited** |
| 7) | 13:14–15 | *anaplēroutai* | Jesus's statement about the hard-heartedness of Israel (Isa 6:9–10) |
| | **Jesus's Citation in Matthew's Gospel** | ***gegraptai*** | **Old Testament text cited** |
| 8) | 4:4 | *gegraptai* | Deut 8:3: Jesus rebuffing temptation from Satan: |
| 9) | 4:6 | *gegraptai* | Psa 91:11, 12: Satan tempts Jesus, uses Scripture: |
| 10) | 4:7 | *gegraptai* | Deut 6:16: Jesus rebuffs Satan using Scripture: |
| 11) | 4:10 | *gegraptai* | Deut 6:13: Jesus rebuffs temptation from Satan: |
| 12) | 11:10 | *gegraptai* | Mal 3:1; cf. Mark 1:2: Jesus's declaration about John the Baptist |
| 13) | 21:13 | *gegraptai* | Isa 56:7 and Jer 7:11—Jesus clears the temple |
| 14) | 26:24 | *gegraptai* | Isa 42–53: Jesus in the Upper Room declaring his fate, and designating Judas as betrayer |
| 15) | 26:31 | *gegraptai* | Zech 13:7: Jesus declaring his fate and the denials of the disciples |

#### *5.3.2.2 Jesus's Baptism Fulfills All Righteousness (3:13–17)*

Why did Jesus come to be baptized by John the Baptist? Without a careful reading of the text one might conclude that Jesus thought that he also needed conversion and purification as did the crowd (3:2, 6).[113] But John quickly dispels that possibility, because he knew Jesus's identity as the One bringing the messianic baptism: "I need to be baptized by you, and do you come to me?" (3:14). Jesus is the more powerful One who inaugurates the kingdom that John has been proclaiming. Only at Jesus's insistence ("Let it be so now") does John consent to baptize Jesus, because, Jesus declares, "it is proper for us to do this to fulfill all righteousness" (3:15). Jesus's baptism has far more significance than we might think.

The expression "to fulfill" (*plērōsai*) continues the theme of "fulfillment" that has been so prominent in the beginning narrative of Matthew's Gospel. Jesus's conception, birth, and infancy fulfilled both specific and general prophecies (Matt 1–2), the appearance of John fulfills Old Testament expectations of the forerunner (3:3), and now Jesus's baptism "fulfills all righteousness."

113. Such is the speculative conclusion of the skeptical account of Jesus's life by Donald Spoto, *The Hidden Jesus: A New Life* (New York: St. Martin's, 1998), 45–46.

Righteousness (*dikaiosynē*) is an important concept in Matthew's Gospel.[114] Most likely Jesus means this in a salvation-historical sense. God's saving activity prophesied throughout the Old Testament is now being fulfilled with the inauguration of Jesus's ministry, culminating in his death on the cross (cf. Isa 53:11).[115] Jesus is expressing his obedience to God's plan of salvation that has been revealed in the Old Testament Scriptures and is being enacted through John the Baptist and Jesus in the inauguration of the kingdom of heaven.[116]

### *5.3.2.3 Jesus Rebuffs Temptations with Scripture (4:4–10)*

In Jesus's temptation scene, three times he uses Old Testament Scripture to rebuff Satan: "it is written" (*gegraptai*). And one time Satan likewise quotes the Old Testament to try to manipulate Jesus. Jesus succeeds in overcoming similar temptations where Adam and Eve failed, and the way that he succeeds becomes the example for the way that believers can succeed under similar types of temptations. We might summarize Jesus's example in the following way: *resist the devil in the power of the Spirit through the guidance of the Word to accomplish the will of God.*

**First temptation: 4:4 (Deut 8:3).** Jesus responds to Satan's challenge by quoting a passage from Deuteronomy, as he does in the following two temptations as well: "It is written: 'Man shall not live on bread alone, but on every word that comes from the mouth of God'" (4:4; cf. Deut 8:3). This demonstrates the link between Jesus's temptations and Israel's experience in the wilderness.

**Second temptation: 4:6–7 (Ps 91:11–12; Deut 6:16).** Satan approaches Jesus and states, "If you are the Son of God, throw yourself down. For it is written: 'He will command his angels concerning you, and they will lift you up in their hands, so that you will not strike your foot against a stone'" (4:6). The devil's quotation is a blatant misuse of Scripture to try to manipulate Jesus. The original Old Testament context does not imply that God will send protecting care for any and every harmful situation. Jesus sees through the devil's Scripture-twisting to the sinister motivation behind it, replying again with a quotation from the book of Deuteronomy: "It is also written: 'Do not put the Lord your God to the test'" (4:7).[117]

**Third temptation: 4:10 (Deut 6:13).** The Father's will for Jesus's life was the cross (see 16:21–27; 26:36–46), but Satan tries to sidetrack him from that mission by getting

114. Cf. 3:15; 5:6, 10, 20; 6:1, 33; 21:32. See below in Chapter 10, Discipleship in Matthew's Gospel.

115. Hagner, "Righteousness in Matthew's Gospel," 116–17.

116. Keener, *Matthew* (2009), 132; Francis Moloney, "Matthew 5:17–18 and the Matthean use of ΔΙΚΑΙΟΣΥΝΗ," in *Unity and Diversity in the Gospels and Paul: Essays in Honor of Frank J. Matera*, ed. Christopher W. Skinner and Kelly R. Iverson, ECL 7 (Atlanta: SBL Press, 2012), 33–54.

117. Christoph Kähler, "Satanischer Schriftgebrauch: Zur Hermeneutik von Mt 4,1–11/Lk 4, 1–13," *Theologische Literaturzeitung* 119.10 (1994): 857–68. This incident of the temptation of Jesus is unique in that it uses citations of Scripture and illustrates misuse of Scripture.

him to take a shortcut to gain the kingdom that would someday be his the hard way. Jesus emphatically declares, "Away from me, Satan! For it is written: 'Worship the Lord your God, and serve him only'" (4:10). In this response Jesus exerts his rightful authority over Satan by issuing his first command (cf. 16:23), and quotes for the third time the book of Deuteronomy (Deut 6:13). As powerful as Satan may be, and as frail as Jesus must be because of the extended fasting and the intensity of the temptations, Jesus vanquishes him with a word.

#### *5.3.2.4 Jesus Affirms the Old Testament and Is Himself Its Fulfillment by Bringing God's Old Testament Revelation to Its Intended Salvation-Historical Culmination and by Demonstrating Its Meaning and Intentions (5:17)*

For Matthew, the expression "fulfill" also indicates the way in which Jesus brings to its intended salvation-historical culmination the entire Old Testament Scripture, as he declares in the dramatic statement in the Sermon on the Mount, "Do not think that I have come to abolish the Law or the Prophets; I have not come to abolish them but to fulfill them" (5:17). Here Jesus declares that he has come to fulfill *all* of the Old Testament Scripture.

The exact meaning of the way in which Jesus has come "to fulfill" (*plērōsai*) the Law and the Prophets has been debated throughout the centuries, and a great deal has been written on the topic. Several major interpretations have been advocated in recent scholarship.[118]

(1) *Obedience.* Some suggest that Jesus fulfilled the Law by obeying its commands: he actualized it by doing it. Luz emphasizes that Jesus's obedient deeds fulfill the demands of the Law and the Prophets.[119] Bruner concurs by stating that "Jesus comes not just to preach the Law with brilliance but to fulfill it with obedience."[120]

118. For overviews of recent interpretations, see Guelich, *Sermon on the Mount*, 134–74; John P. Meier, *Law and Love*, vol. 4 of *A Marginal Jew: Rethinking the Historical Jesus*, ABRL (New Haven: Yale University Press, 2009), 40–47; Davies and Allison, *Matthew*, 1:484–87; Hagner, *Matthew 1–13*, 105–6; Luz, *Matthew*, 1:213–19; Osborne, *Matthew*, 182. For a helpful recent survey of the literature and study of *plēroō* in 5:17, see Bradley M. Trout, "The Nature of the Law's Fulfilment in Matthew 5:17–20: An Exegetical and Theological Study" (MA diss., North-West University, South Africa, 2015).

119. Luz, *Matthew*, 1:217–19. See also Adolf Schlatter, *Der Evangelist Matthäus* (Stuttgart: Calwer, 1929), 153; Keener, *Matthew* (2009), 177; Bruner, *Christbook*, 198–200. For a view that Matthew presents Jesus as Torah-observant as a guide for his Torah-observant community that is in involved in an *intra-muros* debate within Jewish communities, see Sim, *Matthew and Christian Judaism*, 118–27. Sim's focus is on Matthew's community, not the historical Jesus. Sim then takes this one step further to indicate that followers of Jesus must likewise be obedient to Torah: "The Matthean Jesus spells out unambiguously in 5:17–19 that the Torah, given by God to Moses at Mount Sinai, must be obeyed in full by his followers" (David C. Sim, "The Rise and Fall of the Gospel of Matthew," *Expository Times* 120.10 [2009]: 484). See also, among others, Anders Runesson, *Divine Wrath and Salvation in Matthew: The Narrative World of the First Gospel* (Minneapolis: Fortress, 2016), 68–101. For an overview of the debate, with a positive assessment given to Torah observance, see Sim, "Matthew: The Current State of Research," 33–51. For a negative assessment, see Roland Deines, "Not the Law but the Messiah: Law and Righteousness in the Gospel of Matthew—An Ongoing Debate," in *Built upon the Rock: Studies in the Gospel of Matthew*, ed. Daniel M. Gurtner and John Nolland (Grand Rapids: Eerdmans, 2008), 53–84. I follow the lead of Deines here.

120. Bruner, *Christbook*, 199.

(2) *Validation.* Others suggest that Jesus "established" or "validated" the Law by realizing it completely in his teaching and deeds.[121] William Loader contends that the intent of Jesus, in the light of the immediate context (5:18–20) as well as the larger context of the antitheses, "is confirming and upholding the validity of the Law and the Prophets."[122] Against the charge of being a lawbreaker, Jesus affirms the unending validity of the Law.

(3) *Intended meaning.* Still others contend that Jesus completed or filled up the Law's intended meaning in his own teaching and interpretation of Torah, thereby enabling kingdom people to live the Law more completely.[123] Jesus will demonstrate in the antitheses to follow (5:21–48) how the Law was intended to be lived from the heart, with external obedience alone a misinterpretation found among the teachers of the Law and Pharisees. With the arrival of the kingdom of heaven Jesus demonstrates in his teaching the intending meaning of the Law. Nolland notes that the fulfillment language represents a claim that Jesus's programmatic commitment is to enable God's people to live out the Law more effectively, not to undercut the role of the Law and the Prophets. "Matthew holds that Jesus offered . . . a new depth of insight into what the Law requires."[124] Jesus fulfills the Law and the Prophets as he leads his disciples to understand and obey the true intent of the Old Testament through his definitive interpretation of its true meaning.

(4) *Salvation-historical culmination.* And others argue that Jesus fulfills the Law by completing its "covenant promise" in bringing about a new redemptive-historical relationship with God. This points to an eschatological, salvation-historical culmination in Jesus and his announcement of the arrival of the kingdom of heaven. That to which the Law and the Prophets pointed is realized in Jesus.[125]

121. E.g., David Hill, *The Gospel of Matthew*, NCB (London: Oliphants, 1972), 117; David Wenham, "Jesus and the Law: An Exegesis on Matt. 5:17–20," *Them* 4 (1979), 92–96; J. Daryl Charles, "Garnishing with the 'Greater Righteousness': The Disciple's Relationship to the Law (Matthew 5:17–20)," *BBR* 12.1 (2002): 1–15.

122. William Loader, *Jesus' Attitude Towards the Law: A Study of the Gospels* (Grand Rapids: Eerdmans, 2002), 166.

123. E.g., Georg Strecker, *The Sermon on the Mount: An Exegetical Commentary*, trans. O. C. Dean Jr. (Nashville: Abingdon, 1988), 54–55; Hagner, *Matthew 1–13*, 105–6; Davies and Allison, *Matthew*, 1:485–86; Nolland, *Matthew*, 218–19; Betz, *Sermon on the Mount*, 178. Betz notes regarding the term *plēroō* and its Hebrew counterpart (קום), "The terms refer first to the recognition and implementation—or the refusal of recognition and implementation—of Holy Scripture as *legal authority*" (178; emphasis original). Betz cites a passage from the Mishnah as indicating the same sense: "'R. Jonathan said: He that fulfills the Law in poverty shall in the end fulfil it in wealth; and he that neglects the Law in wealth shall in the end neglect it in poverty" (m. Avot 4:9; Danby, *Mishnah*, 454 [Betz indicates Avot 4:11]). Betz adds regarding Avot 4, "The whole section deals with proper and improper ways of teaching the Torah" (Betz, *Sermon on the Mount*, 178n79).

124. Nolland, *Matthew*, 219.

125. E.g., C. F. D. Moule, "Fulfillment-Words in the New Testament: Use and Abuse," *NTS* 14 (1967–68): 294; Robert Banks, *Jesus and the Law in the Synoptic Tradition*, SNTSMS 28 (Cambridge: Cambridge University Press, 1975), 210; Douglas J. Moo, "Jesus and the Authority of the Mosaic Law," *JSNT* 20 (1984): 3–49; Guelich, *Sermon on the Mount*, 140; Turner, *Matthew*, 162–63; France, *Matthew*, NICNT, 181–84; France, *Matthew: Evangelist and Teacher*, 191–97; Witherington, *Matthew*, 126; Deines, "Not the Law," 74–77; Deines, "Jesus and Scripture," 52–53; Quarles, *Sermon on the Mount*, 91; Brandon D. Crowe, *The Last Adam: A Theology of the Obedient Life of Jesus in the Gospels* (Grand Rapids: Baker Academic, 2017), 91–93.

The first option is not satisfactory, because the verb *plēroō*, "fulfill," is not used in Matthew to describe obedience to the Law. Further, this view misses the nuance of "fill to the full" that is associated with the word in Matthew. And the context (5:21–48) refers to Jesus's authoritative pronouncements about the nature of the Law.[126]

Osborne suggests that the best understanding of Jesus's statement is through combining the last three.[127] The multiple ways that Jesus and Matthew use "fulfill" in this Gospel leads to this conclusion (e.g., direct prediction-fulfillment=1:22–23; typology=2:15; salvation-historical culmination=3:15). I mostly agree with Osborne but would emphasize them in reverse order.

This starts by stating that the primary emphasis should be placed on Jesus Messiah himself. He is the salvation-historical culmination of all that to which the Old Testament looked forward. As Wesley Olmstead indicates, "In Jesus, God has answered his promises and Israel's history has reached its climax. The time of fulfilment has come and the long-awaited, eschatological kingdom has dawned."[128] Jesus was the eschatological goal of the Law and the Prophets. Daniel Kirk conceptualizes "fulfilment" by perceiving Jesus reenacting the story of Israel as marked in the Law and Prophets (5:17). Jesus gives new substance to a narrative whose shape is given by the Scriptures of Israel. Jesus fulfills Israel's story by embodying and reenacting it.[129] The focus is now on Jesus, the one to whom the original story of the Law and the Prophets pointed. Matthew reiterates Jesus's conception of fulfillment that has a salvation-historical aspect—Israel's history anticipated the eschatological hopes that are made concrete in Jesus's ministry.

Following on the primary emphasis on Jesus Messiah's eschatological significance, the emphasis then flows to his authoritative pronouncement about the intended meaning of the Law and the Prophets. This in turn provides his validation of the Old Testament as the continuing revelation from God. Members of the kingdom of heaven will actualize the revelation of God in their own lives as they live in discipleship relationship with Jesus, who is the culmination of the Law and the Prophets. This brings the Law to its intended meaning in connection with its messianic fulfillment. Hagner contends that at the end of the Gospel Jesus calls his disciples to teach new disciples "to observe all that I have commanded you" (28:20). "They are finally called to obey not Torah, but Jesus. There is thus an important shift in Matthew that explains the newness of its perspective on the Law. To be sure, the Law remains significant for these Jewish Christians, but *only as it is taken up in the teaching of Jesus*."[130]

The teaching of Jesus by definition amounts to the new meaning of the Torah and

126. Moo, "Jesus and the Authority," 25–26; Hagner, *Matthew 1–13*, 105–6.

127. Osborne, *Matthew*, 182.

128. Olmstead, "Jesus, the Eschatological Perfection of Torah," 45.

129. Kirk, "Conceptualising Fulfilment in Matthew," 77–98, esp. 96.

130. Donald A. Hagner, "Matthew: Apostate, Reformer, Revolutionary?," *NTS* 49 (2003): 193–209, esp. 203 (emphasis original).

is hence paradoxically an affirmation of Jesus's loyalty to the Old Testament. This fits the context well, it maintains the commitment to the Law reflected in 5:18, and it affirms a new definition of the Law that comes with fulfillment.[131]

So, the idea of "fulfillment" in this saying of Jesus is more than Jesus's obedience (i.e., keeping the Law), or of completion, although those are included. The context, especially as worked out in the "antitheses" to follow (5:21–48), indicates that Jesus Messiah fulfills certain anticipated roles as the inaugurator of the kingdom of heaven, and his pronouncements regarding the Old Testament Scriptures complete and clarify God's intent and meaning through it.[132] All that the Old Testament intended to communicate about God's will and hopes and future[133] for humanity find their full meaning in Jesus. Jesus has come to actualize the Scripture and take his disciples to a deeper understanding of its intended meaning, and this in distinction from many of the leaders of Judaism. Deines asserts that Jesus's fulfillment of the Law and the Prophets takes place for Matthew neither only by his deeds nor by his teaching "but through his entire mission that includes his teaching, his deeds and especially his messianic works up to his death and resurrection (cf. the last two references for πληροῦν in 26:54, 56)."[134]

### *5.3.2.5 John the Baptist Fulfills the Role of Preparing for Jesus Messiah (11:9–10)*

Jesus here admonishes the crowds to recall that they went to the desert to see the first prophet for centuries sent from God to Israel. Jesus declares, "Yes, I tell you, and more than a prophet. This is the one about whom it is written (*gegraptai*): 'I will send my messenger ahead of you, who will prepare your way before you'" (11:9–10). John was like the prophets of the Old Testament because he was God's spokesperson who called the nation to repentance and declared God's program of salvation. But he was more than any prophet of the Old Testament because he was the one about whom a prophecy was given that it would be his privilege to be the prophet who would announce the arrival of the Messiah and the in-breaking of the kingdom of heaven. Because the prophecy of Mal 3:1 (cf. Mark 1:2) refers to preparing God's way, Jesus dramatically implies his own divine status, although it is doubtful that the crowds or even Jesus's disciples would have understood that distinction at this point in his ministry.[135]

Then Jesus makes an intriguing statement: "For all the Prophets and the Law

131. Hagner, *Matthew 1–13*, 106.

132. Helpful overviews are in Guelich, *Sermon on the Mount*, 138–42, and J. Daryl Charles, "The Greatest or the Least in the Kingdom? The Disciple's Relationship to the Law (Matt 5:17–20)," *Trinity Journal*, NS, 13 (1992): 139–62.

133. See Matt 11:13 where the Law and Prophets prophesy until the new age arrives with John.

134. Deines, "Not the Law," 75.

135. Gundry, *Matthew*, 214; Keener, *Matthew* (1999), 338. The form of the quotation may reflect influence from Exod 23:20 (Gundry, *Matthew*, 214), but the primary citation comes from Mal 3:1. By adding "your" to the second clause, "who will prepare *your* way before you," Jesus makes his own coming the coming of Yahweh and the eschatological day of Yahweh. It may have been a well-known *testimonium* in early Christianity (France, *Matthew*, NICNT, 194; France, *Jesus and the Old Testament*, 91–92, 155.

prophesied until John" (11:13). John is the culmination of a long history of prophecy throughout the Old Testament period that looked forward to the arrival of the messianic kingdom. The Law and the Prophets both have a prophetic role in pointing to Jesus Messiah. That prophetic hope has been realized in John's preparation for Jesus's inauguration of the kingdom of heaven.

### *5.3.2.6 Jesus Tests the Hearts of Israel with Parables (13:14–15)*

Jesus quotes Isa 6:9–10 to indicate that even as Israel had a long background of unbelief and rejection of God's prior prophets, so the crowd is now hardened against him (Matt 13:14–15). The crowd mirrors the people of Israel to whom the prophet Isaiah ministered. They rejected the message because they were spiritually deadened. The subordinating conjunction "lest" or "otherwise" (13:15; *mēpote*) denotes the purpose of the divine hardening.[136] The parables stimulate a hardening in those who have rejected Jesus which prohibits them from turning for God to heal them. The unbelievers among the crowd are like the Pharisees who have committed the unpardonable sin (12:31–32) and have sinned away their day of opportunity. The parables are given after the increasing rejection and opposition by Israel. God does not force anyone to accept the message of the kingdom, so the crowd's response to the parables is dictated by the nature of their heart. If a person in the crowd has no spiritual ears, his or her heart will be increasingly hardened and will turn away from Jesus and the healing that comes with the kingdom of heaven (4:23).

### *5.3.2.7 Clearing the Temple Condemns the Religious Leaders (21:13; 23:29–32)*

Jesus extends his authoritative pronouncement of judgment against the temple establishment, because they have misused the temple for commercial activity, instead of its intended spiritual activity. He declares, "It is written (*gegraptai*), 'My house will be called a house of prayer,' but you are making it a 'den of robbers'" (21:13). The religious leaders were treating the temple as robbers do their dens—a place of refuge for both the accumulation of illicitly gained wealth and for the plotting of future illegal activities. The term "robber" (*lestēs*) was not used for a common thief but for one who was an insurrectionist, such as Barabbas and the two robbers between whom Jesus was crucified, who fought against the Roman occupation.[137] This may be a subtle use of the term to indicate that the temple authorities were making it a nationalistic stronghold,[138] or more subtly, a place where they were insurrectionists against God's intended plan for the temple. The temple's primary purpose, as a house for communing with God,

136. "μήποτε," BDAG, 648.

137. Cf. Wilkins, "Barabbas," *ABD* 1:607.

138. Carson, "Matthew," 498–99; Hagner, *Matthew 14–28*, 601.

was lost in the frenzy of religious activity. The temple leadership stands condemned by Jesus in his use of Old Testament Scripture.

### *5.3.2.8 Jesus's Fate, Deniers, and Betrayer Anticipated (26:24, 31, 54)*

In four related passages, Jesus reveals how his fate, the denials of the disciples, and his betrayal are the fulfillment of Old Testament Scripture.

(1) The betrayal by Judas does not thwart God's plans but rather fits within them, because Jesus declares: "The Son of Man will go just as it is written [*gegraptai*] about him" (26:24). The divine certitude of his death is affirmed by Jesus's allusion to what "is written" about him, a reference to the various suffering servant Old Testament prophecies (Isa 42–53).[139] The Old Testament prophecies of a coming suffering servant were not widely held up as a primary expectation, not even among Jesus's own followers who were baffled at the possibility of Jesus being executed. But Jesus drives home the truth that the Scriptures had prophesied the coming of a slain Messiah. This points again to the profound interplay of God's sovereign control over all human activity with each human's personal responsibility and culpability for their own decisions.

(2) Along the way Jesus startles the disciples with another ominous prediction. "This very night you will all fall away on account of me" (26:31). This has been an evening of startling announcements, including the prediction that one of the Twelve would betray Jesus. But now he implicates all of them. Their failure has also been prophesied, as Jesus demonstrates by quoting the prophet Zechariah: "For it is written [*gegraptai*]: 'I will strike the shepherd, and the sheep of the flock will be scattered'" (26:31). The shepherd who is struck by the sword is the one described by the prophet as pierced (Zech 12:10; cf. Matt 24:30) and rejected (Zech 11). But the scene shifts in Zech 13:7, as this time Yahweh strikes the shepherd. This shepherd is identified as Yahweh's companion, who is side by side with Yahweh as his equal. As this messianic Shepherd is smitten, the sheep are scattered, which in the Zechariah context speaks to the dispersion of the Jews.[140] But Jesus sees that the prophecies of hardship will also fall on his disciples. He quotes Zech 13:7, with slight changes that follow the LXX,[141] to emphasize that even when God's actions are carried out by others, they are a result of his sovereign activity.

---

139. E.g., see on Matt 8:17; 12:17–21. See Markus Bockmuehl, "A 'Slain Messiah' in 4Q Serekh Milhamah (4Q285)?," *TynBul* 43.1 (1992): 155–69. Bockmuehl finds little expectation of a slain messiah within first-century Jewish interpretation of Old Testament prophecies, and probably none in the DSS, but posits it as a likelihood within wider Jewish circles (Bockmuehl, "A 'Slain Messiah'?," 167–69).

140. Kaiser, *Messiah in the Old Testament*, 226–27.

141. The quotation from Zech 13:7 follows the slight changes of the LXX, especially from second-person plural imperatives "strike the shepherd" and "scatter the sheep" to the first-person singular "I will scatter the sheep." This emphasizes that even when God's actions are carried out by others, they are a result of his sovereign activity. For comparison of the MT, LXX and Matthew, see Gleason L. Archer and G. C. Chirichigno, *Old Testament Quotations in the New Testament: A Complete Survey* (Chicago: Moody, 1983), 162–64.

(3) Jesus is not defenseless, nor is he resigned to fate: "But how then would the Scriptures be fulfilled [*plērōthōsin*] that say it must happen in this way?" (26:54). He has come to carry out God's plan of redemption that has been prophesied in "the Scriptures" (26:54). Jesus does not point to a particular prophetic passage, but to the Scriptures (plural) as a whole that indicate the purpose of his earthly ministry, which "must" (*dei*) lead him to the cross. This is "divine necessity."[142] There is no deviation nor exception to God's will. As was the point in the prayers at Gethsemane, obedience to the Father's will for his life is Jesus's ultimate desire, not pursuing his own.

(4) Jesus mocks the contingent that came out so heavily armed to arrest him because he has been within their reach right there in the temple precincts teaching throughout the week. Jesus declares to these representatives of the religious authorities that what they do deceptively God had ordained long ago: "But this has all taken place that the writings of the prophets might be fulfilled" (*plērōthōsin*; 26:56). In "the writings of the prophets," an expression found only here in the New Testament, God's spokespersons predicted the wickedness of Israel's religious leaders (see esp. Isa 53; Zech 12–13). His plan of redemption through the events of Jesus's crucifixion is divinely foretold, but those who carry out the evil deeds bear their own responsibility. The evil deeds of the religious establishment will accomplish God's plan, but it will be to their ultimate personal and national demise.

### 5.3.3 Matthew's Interpretation of Fulfillment of the Old Testament

We now come to a unique element that is well known by students of Matthew's Gospel—Matthew's ten fulfillment-formula quotations. In an earlier table (5.2.1.2 Table of Quotations of [with some Allusions to] the Old Testament in Matthew's Gospel), I listed fifty-three quotations in Matthew's Gospel. Thirty-seven quotations are in a saying from Jesus, while sixteen occur in the narrative, coming either as Matthew's quotation or citing a character in the narrative who quotes Old Testament Scripture.

But there are ten quotations that are mostly uniform in their construction, which has led to referring to them as "fulfillment-formula quotations" or "reflection citations" to indicate Matthew's reflection upon the ways that Jesus's life and ministry fulfill the Old Testament.[143] Each occurs with the verb *plēroō* ("fulfill"), the substantive participle *to rhēthen* ("what was spoken") is the subject, and the preposition *dia* ("through") expresses the means of the speech: "fulfills what was spoken *through* . . . " Five of the formulas are introduced by the conjunction *hina* ("so that," "in order that"; 1:22; 2:15; 4:14; 12:17; 21:4), three are introduced by *hopōs* ("so that"; 2:23; 8:17; 13:35) functioning similarly as a conjunction, and two by the adverb *tote* ("then"; 2:17; 27:9),

142. Hagner, *Matthew 14–28*, 790.

143. For a brief overview, see Donald Senior, *What Are They Saying About Matthew?*, rev. and exp. ed. (New York: Paulist, 1996), 51–61

functioning similarly to *hina* and *hopōs*. When Matthew uses *tote* it is followed by the aorist passive *indicative* form *eplērōthē* (2:17; 27:9), but when he uses *hina* and *hopōs* in the other eight formulas he uses the aorist passive *subjunctive* form *plērōthē*. The terms *hina* and *hopōs* are here used to express divine intention and are essentially synonymous, and *tote* appears to function in much the same way. Notice the striking regularity of Matthew's fulfillment-formula quotations in the chart below.[144]

### *5.3.3.1 Table of Fulfillment Formulas Quoting the Old Testament Used by Matthew in the Narrative*

| | **Matthew's Citation in his gospel** | **Expression for "fulfill" (*plēroō*)** | **Old Testament citation** |
|---|---|---|---|
| 1) | 1:22–23 | *plērōthē* | Isa 7:14: Angelic announcement of virgin conception |
| | | "so that what was spoken by the Lord through the prophet might be fulfilled, saying" | |
| 2) | 2:15 | *plērōthē* | Hos 11:1: The son is called out of Egypt |
| | | "so that what was spoken by the Lord through the prophet might be fulfilled, saying" | |
| 3) | 2:17–18 | *eplērōthē* | Jer 31:15: Weeping and wailing in Ramah |
| | | "then what was spoken through Jeremiah the prophet was fulfilled, saying"" | |
| 4) | 2:23 | *plērōthē* | Generally, "through the prophets, that he would be called a Nazarene" (cf. Isa 11:1— נֵצֶר *netzer* (Branch) |
| | | "so that what was spoken through the prophets might be fulfilled" | |
| 5) | 4:14–16 | *plērōthē* | Isa 8:23–9:1: Jesus ministers in Galilee of the gentiles |
| | | "so that what was spoken through Isaiah the prophet might be fulfilled, saying" | |
| 6) | 8:16–17 | *plērōthē* | Isa 53:4: He took infirmities and bore diseases |
| | | "so that what was spoken through Isaiah the prophet might be fulfilled, saying" | |
| 7) | 12:17–21 | *plērōthē* | Isa 42:1–4: Jesus Messiah is the servant |
| | | "so that what was spoken through Isaiah the prophet might be fulfilled, saying" | |
| 8) | 13:34–35 | *plērōthē* | Ps 78(77):2: Jesus Messiah speaks in parables |
| | | "so that what was spoken through the prophets might be fulfilled, saying" | |
| 9) | 21:4–5 | *plērōthē* | Isa 62:11; Zech 9:9: The King arrives in Jerusalem |
| | | "so that what was spoken through the prophet might be fulfilled, saying" | |
| 10) | 27:9–10 | *eplērōthē* | Zech 11:12–13 (cf. Jer 32:6–15): Judas's blood money |
| | | "then what was spoken through Jeremiah the prophet was fulfilled, saying" | |

144. For a comparison in tables, see Turner, *Matthew*, 19–21; Davies and Allison, *Matthew*, 1:29–58; Gundry, *Use of the Old Testament*, 89–127; Hagner, *Matthew 1–13*, liv–lvii; Soares-Prabhu, *Formula Quotations*, 50–52; Deines, "Jesus and Scripture," 43–48. For other discussion, see Nolland, *Matthew*, 29–36; Luz, *Matthew 1–7*, 125–31.

These fulfillment-formula quotations span the entire Gospel of Matthew. Four involve the events of Jesus's birth (1:22–23; 2:15, 17–18, 23), and one each involve his entry into Galilee and the inauguration of his public ministry (4:14–16), his healing ministry (8:16–17), his compassion and gentleness (12:17–21), his communication in parables (13:34–35), his climactic entry into Jerusalem (21:4–5), and his passion and death (27:9–10).

Two of the fulfillment-formula quotations indicate the divine source of the quotations. In 1:22 and 2:15 Matthew uses the prepositional phrases "by the Lord" (*hypo kyriou*) and "through the prophet" (*dia tou prophētou*) to underline the divine agency implicit in the participial phrase "what was spoken" (*to rhēthen*): "what was spoken *by the Lord* through the prophet" (2:15 NASB). As we discussed in Chapter 1, this points to the dual authorship of Scripture, where the human prophet is the channel through whom God communicates with his people.[145]

I indicated above that at times Matthew records a prediction prophecy being fulfilled. The Old Testament prophet or prophecy indicated foresight of a future event, in which the events of Jesus's earthly life and ministry brings to actualization predictive prophecy (e.g., 2:4–6). More often, however, Matthew indicates that "fulfill" specifies the way Jesus's earthly life and ministry is a divinely orchestrated analogical or typological correspondence or recapitulation of the nation of Israel's history (e.g., 2:15, 17–18). In this, an event from the Old Testament serves as a pattern for the New Testament event that it anticipated. Together they indicate the providential outworking of God's plan.

The ten fulfillment-formula quotations are a powerful indication of the way that Matthew sees God's plan providentially unfolding in Jesus's life and ministry.

### *5.3.3.2 The Birth and Early Life of the Messiah Fulfills Old Testament Expectations (1:22–23; 2:15, 17–18, 23)*

Of Matthew's ten fulfillment quotations, a prominent four occur in the infancy narrative of chapters one and two (1:22–23; 2:15, 17–18, 23).

**(1) Virgin conception and birth (1:22–23).** The first prominently declares that the conception and birth of Jesus Immanuel fulfills Isaiah's prophecy (citing Isa 7:14). The sign that was given to Ahaz and the house of Judah ("you" in Isa 7:14 is plural) was God's miraculous prediction of military salvation from the attack of Pekah and Rezin, but it was also a prediction of a future messianic figure who would provide spiritual salvation from sin. Isaiah's sign functioned as an indication of the way that a boy named Immanuel would be an indication to Ahaz and the house of David of

145. Turner, *Matthew*, 21; Feinberg, *Light in a Dark Place*, 183–228.

God's promised deliverance from invasion, but it also anticipates the future virgin-born messianic deliverer named Immanuel, truly God with us.[146]

**(2) Historical exodus prepares for Jesus (2:13–15).** In the context of his prophecy, Hosea recounts how God had faithfully brought Israel out of Egypt in the exodus.[147] Matthew's point of comparison is the corporate solidarity between the nation Israel as God's son being rescued and delivered by God, and Jesus as the One who will be revealed to be God's Son *par excellence*.[148] Old Testament authors consistently reminded the nation of Israel to look back to their redemption by God when he brought them out of Egypt.[149] As mentioned above, the yearly Passover was a reminder, but also a promise, that God had provided a sacrificial lamb for his people Israel. As Matthew harks back to Hosea's recounting of God faithfully bringing Israel out of Egypt under divine protection (Hos 11:1), he points out how Jesus's infancy corresponds analogically to Israel's history. The life of Jesus is the historical completion of the process of redemption. No threat from any public official can thwart the process. Jesus coming out of Egypt is the recapitulation of the promise to Israel that redemption is at hand (see above at 5.3.1.2). Jesus is the actualization of the promise to the nation Israel of redemption that was initiated with the exodus and Passover. Craig Evans calls Matthew's use of the Hosea passage an exegesis of typology and "resignification"—finding a new element or dimension in the older tradition. "This aspect of his exegesis conforms completely with what is observed in the Jewish exegesis of his day. Matthew has (re)interpreted Scripture in light of what God has accomplished (or 'fulfilled') in his Messiah."[150]

**(3) Weeping and wailing in Ramah (2:17–18).** Matthew's use of the Jeremiah narrative is similar to the way that he earlier cited the prophet Micah (cf. 2:15). This is not fulfillment in the sense of prediction-accomplishment as we see in the birth to the virgin in Bethlehem,[151] but rather is another case of analogical correspondence.[152] As Herod attempts to eliminate the newborn king of the Jews, the events of Jesus's earthly life correspond analogically to an earlier attempt by a foreign power to wipe out God's chosen people. But the advent of Jesus's life also marks the arrival of the comfort that

146. R. Watts, "Immanuel," 92–113; Wegner, "How Many Virgin Births Are in the Bible?," 467–84; Evans, *Matthew*, 46–48.

147. As discussed above, Matthew gives both the ultimate origin and agency of the prophecy expressed with ὑπό "by" ("by the Lord" *hypo kyriou*) and the immediate agent of prophecy expressed with διά "through" ("through Jeremiah the prophet" *dia Ieremiou tou prophetou*) as in 1:22.

148. Kaiser, *Messiah in the Old Testament*, 35. The quote is most likely from the Hebrew text of Hos 11:1, which states: "When Israel was a child, I loved him, and out of Egypt I called my son" (NIV). The LXX has "his children," not "my son."

149. E.g., Pss 78; 81; 105–106; Jer 2:6; 7:22–25; Ezek 20:1–20; Mic 6:1–4; etc.

150. Craig A. Evans, "New Testament Use of the Old Testament," in *A Handbook on the Jewish Roots of the Christian Faith*, ed. Craig A. Evans and David Mishkin (Peabody, MA: Hendrickson, 2019), 99–100, Kindle.

151. Matt 1:23 and 2:6. See Kai Akagi, "The Quotation of Jer. 31.15 in Mt. 2.18 Within Christological Patterning of Matthew's Nativity According to the Joseph Story," *JSNT* 45.4 (2023): 405–28, who refers to this as the "New Testament's use of the Old Testament's use of the Old Testament," 428.

152. Richard Hays refers to this as an example of Matthew's figural reading of Jeremiah: Hays, "Figural Exegesis," 38–39.

had been promised to the Jews sent into exile in Babylon. God's power is greater than the sorrow-bringing forces, so with God's sovereign protection of the infant Messiah he brings to completion the experience of the weeping at both the exile and Bethlehem. The promised messianic deliverer has arrived to inaugurate the new covenant promised by Jeremiah (Jer 31:31–35).[153]

**(4) He shall be called a Nazarene (2:23).** Collective, unnamed Old Testament prophetic strands point to significant, recognizable Old Testament themes, which Matthew draws upon: "So was fulfilled what was said through the prophets, that he would be called a Nazarene" (2:23). Matthew's reflection upon Jesus's early life intends for his readers to see a double meaning in the expression "Jesus the Nazarene." On the one hand, Jesus is the fulfillment of the hope for a messianic *netser*—the "branch" out of the line of David. On the other hand, Jesus's association with the lowly town of Nazareth gives notice that his coming is not in glory. He has come as the promised Branch of David, but his coming is in lowly surroundings, not in the grandeur and glory that Herod has claimed in a human attempt to be king. As the Branch from the royal line, Jesus would be "hacked down to a stump and reared in surroundings guaranteed to win him scorn."[154] Used by his followers, the expression "Jesus the Nazarene" was an expression of faith in him as the messianic deliverer (Acts 2:22; 3:6; 10:38). But used by his enemies it was a title of scorn utilized to deny his messianic identity (Matt 26:71; Mark 14:67).[155]

### *5.3.3.3 Jesus Ministers in Galilee of the Gentiles (4:14–16)*

Jesus's arrival in Zebulun and Naphtali in Galilee provides a fertile place of ministry and fulfills another Old Testament prophecy, Isa 9:1–7. This is the fifth quotation of an Old Testament prophecy introduced by the distinctive Matthean fulfillment formula: "to fulfill what was said through the prophet Isaiah" (4:14). Matthew recognizes that Jesus's ministry will extend far beyond the physical confines of Jewish Galilee. It will influence those traveling through the region, people from beyond the Jordan, and ultimately the gentiles.

### *5.3.3.4 Healings as Fulfillment of Isaiah 53:4 (8:17)*

Matthew once again emphasizes that Jesus's life and ministry is the fulfillment of the Old Testament, specifying that his healing ministry fulfills the prophecy of Isa 53:4: "Surely he took up our infirmities and carried our sorrow." This is another allusion to the servant of Isaiah's prophecy,[156] now focusing on the servant's role as the one who

153. Bob Becking, "'A Voice was Heard in Ramah': Some Remarks on Structure and Meaning of Jeremiah 31,15–17," *Biblische Zeitschrift* 38.2 (1994): 242; Steve Willis, "Matthew's Birth Stories: Prophecy and the Magi," *ExpTimes* 105.2 (1993): 43–45.

154. Carson, "Matthew," 125–26.

155. Wilkins, "Isaiah 53 in the Four Gospels," 115–19; August, "'He Shall be Called a Nazarene,'" 63–74.

156. See 2:23, the "Branch" of Isa 53:2; cf. Matt 12: 15–21; 26:28; 27:12; 27:38.

will bring healing. The Greek text of Matthew's quotation gets at the heart of the meaning of the prophecy, in which both sin and sickness are in view. Matthew follows more closely the MT than the LXX and so most likely gives his own translation of the passage.[157] The quotation is from the larger Servant Song of Isa 52:13–53:12, which has substitutionary atonement as one of its central themes. The servant bears the sicknesses of others through his own suffering and death. Matthew draws upon this prophecy to link Jesus's healing ministry with the substitutionary theme. Jesus does not himself become ill but takes and removes illness by his healing power.

While this does not yet explicitly introduce Jesus's vicarious suffering and death for sin, it certainly prepares the way for it.[158] Jesus came to save his people from their sins (1:21), and his healings point beyond themselves to the cross and his initiation of the new covenant in his blood that is poured out for the forgiveness of sin (26:27–28).

#### *5.3.3.5 Jesus Messiah's Ministry of Spirit-Empowerment, Mercy, and Justice Fulfills Israel's Mission (12:17–21)*

Matthew uses his typical fulfillment formula to introduce the longest Old Testament quotation in his Gospel, which identifies Jesus with the messianic servant of Isa 42:1–4 (Matt 12:17–18). The context in Isaiah's prophecy is the section often called the Servant Songs (Isa 40–52). The identity of the servant is perplexing because it vacillates between the nation Israel as the servant (41:8–10; 44:1–3, 21; 45:4 [49:3?]) and an individual who leads the nation (42:1–4; 49:5–7). That individual emerges as the servant Messiah who has a ministry and mission both to Israel and the nations.[159] In this fulfillment quotation, Matthew harks back to Isaiah's prophecy to give one of the clearest declarations of Jesus's intent as Messiah: he is the gentle, Spirit-endowed suffering servant who advances a mission of justice to the nations.[160]

This servant has an unexpected demeanor. Far from painting a picture of an imposing figure of conquest, Matthew continues his citation of the theme of a suffering servant from Isaiah's prophecy. This is a picture of a gentle servant Messiah, who will not brazenly demand allegiance with his proclamation of justice but who will gently and humbly invite those who are the most in need, both in Israel and in all the nations (cf. 11:28–30).[161]

#### *5.3.3.6 "Greater than the Temple . . . Lord of the Sabbath" (12:1–8)*

In the midst of a debate with the religious leaders over Jesus's disciples' transgression of the Sabbath, Jesus's reply puts the Pharisees on the defensive because he uses the Old

157. Gundry, *Matthew*, 150; cf. Brown, "Matthew's Christology and Isaiah's Servant," 102–3; Witherington, *Isaiah Old and New*, 243–54.

158. Erickson, *Christian Theology*, 763–68.

159. For brief overviews of this complex subject, see Kaiser, *Messiah in the Old Testament*, 173–81; Gerard Van Groningen, *Messianic Revelation in the Old Testament* (Grand Rapids: Baker Book House, 1990), 575–618.

160. Richard Beaton, "Messiah and Justice: A Key to Matthew's Use of Isaiah 42.1–4?," *JSNT* 75 (1999): 5–23.

161. See J. Brown, "Matthew's Christology and Isaiah's Servant," 98–101.

Testament itself, of which the Pharisees prided themselves as experts, to combat their accusations against his disciples. Instead of rebuking his disciples, as they may have expected, Jesus cites two different Old Testament examples that render ineffective the Pharisees' charge (12:2; cf. 12:4–5) and then gives a third response that clarifies his use of the Old Testament examples (12:7–8). He is not entering into the interparty rabbinic analogical debate but will, like in the Sermon on the Mount, show how his authoritative arrival and teaching has fulfilled the Law: "I tell you that something greater than the temple is here" (12:6).

Jesus concludes the argument with another remarkable clarification of his identity and authority: "For the Son of Man is Lord of the Sabbath" (12:8). The arrival of the greater work of the gospel of the kingdom is centralized in Jesus as the Lord of the Sabbath, which gives a further clarification of his identity through this Son of Man saying (see 8:19). Jesus has revealed himself to Israel as their long-anticipated Messiah, the one who has come to fulfill the Law (5:17–20). In similar fashion to the way that Jesus points in the Sermon on the Mount, the Sabbath Law has been fulfilled in the rest brought by Jesus's yoke of discipleship (11:25–30). The principal of Sabbath rest continues, fulfilled not simply in external obedience but in obedience to its intent and motive. The messianic Son of Man has supremacy over the temple, and he has the authority to give the true interpretation of the Law (5:17–48), including the role of the Sabbath. Jesus does not challenge the Sabbath Law itself, but the prevailing Pharisaic interpretation of it.

Jesus answers the charge against his disciples by showing from each of the three sections of the Old Testament—the Law, the Prophets, and the Writings—that the Sabbath was not fulfilled by the scrupulous observance of the Pharisees but in living out the intent and motive of the Sabbath, which was designed to bring rest.[162] Increased sacrifice brought greater burden. As the Lord of the Sabbath, Jesus gives the true interpretation of its intent, bringing rest under his easy yoke and light burden of discipleship (cf. 11:28–30).

### *5.3.3.7 Jesus Messiah's Parables Test the Hearts of Israel (13:14–15)*

Jesus concludes his messages to the crowd with a parable, his primary means of communicating to them (13:34). This emphasizes Jesus's relationship to the crowd, which he had previously clarified to the disciples (see 13:10–17). The crowd has had the opportunity to hear Jesus's proclamation of the gospel of the kingdom. Now they need to respond. The parables are one of the means by which Jesus tests the heart of those in the crowd, prompting them either to be with him or against him (12:30). Their day of opportunity is nearly over. The time is coming when there will be no middle ground. The parables have been a primary means of forcing their decision either for him or against him.

162. Keener, *Matthew* (2009), 357.

Matthew draws upon an Old Testament precedent for Jesus's relationship to the crowd. "So was fulfilled what was spoken through the prophet: 'I will open my mouth in parables, I will utter things hidden since the creation of the world'" (13:35). Matthew's standard fulfillment-formula quotation indicates that Jesus was revealing in his parables the secrets of the kingdom of heaven that have been hidden since the beginning.[163] All of the Old Testament has looked forward to the arrival of Jesus with the inauguration of the kingdom of heaven, and in his ministry he has drawn together the many strands of prophetic hope that seemed disparate to some.[164] Jesus's revelation of the secrets of the kingdom of heaven in parables has brought to the light God's program of salvation and redemption. The significance for the crowd is their response. Those spiritually alive will come to Jesus for clarification and understanding and become his disciples. Those spiritually deadened will turn away. The crowd has had their opportunity.

#### *5.3.3.8 Jesus Messiah's Climactic Arrival in Jerusalem Fulfills the Hope of Deliverance for Jerusalem (21:4–5)*

The fulfillment phrase here, "This took place to fulfill what was spoken through the prophet" (21:4), could be Jesus's commentary, or it is more likely Matthew's comment that Jesus's entrance to Jerusalem upon a colt fulfills the prophecy: "Your king comes to you, gentle and riding on a donkey" (21:5). The time has now come for Jesus to declare openly that he is the righteous Davidic Messiah, fulfilling the messianic prophecy of "the prophet," which appears to be a combination of Isa 62:11 and Zech 9:9.[165] There may be also an allusion to Gen 49:8–12, where Jacob prophesies of the kingly descendant of Judah. Jacob's prophecy is made in the context of a promise to Judah of a permanent kingly line in his descendants, who will extend the rule to include the obedience of the nations.

The Zechariah prophecy indicates the nature of Jesus's arrival: he comes as the righteous one who offers salvation, not as a conquering military leader. He comes with reconciliation, as did rulers who sometimes rode a donkey in times of peace (Judg 5:10; 1 Kgs 1:33). Jesus delineates from the moment of his entrance that he has not come to bring military conquest.

#### *5.3.3.9 Judas's Blood-Money Fulfills the Betrayal of Jesus Messiah (27:9–10)*

Matthew summarizes his narration of Judas's death and the chief priests' hard-hearted business deals with his final fulfillment quotation. Matthew says that he is quoting from the prophet Jeremiah, but the quotation is largely from Zech 11:13.[166]

163. Morris, *Matthew*, 354–55.

164. Akio Ito, "Matthew and the Community of the Dead Sea Scrolls," *JSNT* 15.48 (1992): 23–42, esp. 29–30.

165. Osborne, *Matthew*, 754–55.

166. For extended discussion of the difficulties, see Douglas J. Moo, "Tradition and Old Testament in Matt 27:3–10,"

This is similar to the way that Matthew earlier conflates messianic "branch" themes of several prophets (2:23) and the way that Mark conflated quotations from Isaiah and Malachi but only cites Isaiah as the more prominent prophet (cf. Mark 1:2; Isa 40:3; Mal 3:1). Although he is named nowhere else in the New Testament, Jeremiah is the more prominent of the two prophets, especially in Matthew's Gospel, where he is named three times (Matt 2:17; 16:14; 27:9).

Drawing on the combination of the prophets Jeremiah and Zechariah, Matthew demonstrates that the events surrounding Jesus's fateful journey to the cross are not the random tragedies of history but are prophesied actions in which God superintends the redemption of humanity. As repulsive and tragic are the betrayal and demise of Judas and the duplicity and hard-hearted manipulations of the chief priests, they are foreseen by God. The betrayal price figures prominently as a theme of judgment upon Israel's leadership.[167] Whether it is in the days of Zechariah, Jeremiah, or Jesus, Israel rejects good leaders and suffers under bad leaders, but the bad leaders who refuse to act justly will experience God's justice.

### 5.3.4 Summary

Intertwined in Matthew's use of the Old Testament in quotations, allusions, and echoes of the Old Testament is his emphasis upon the "fulfillment" of the Old Testament. For Matthew, fulfillment is a central concern, especially highlighted in our discussion of Jesus's own usage of the Old Testament and Matthew's interpretations of the Old Testament. The revelation of God in the Old Testament is thus fulfilled in Jesus's life and ministry. And as we have now seen, the Old Testament is a precious gem field from which Matthew draws incredible riches.

However, the ways in which the Old Testament is understood to have relevance for believers today is debated. Since Jesus has fulfilled the Law and the Prophets (5:17), are the Old Testament and the Law thus no longer relevant for daily life of Christians today? Or is there continuing relevance? We will discuss this more fully with reference to Israel and the church in Chapters 12 and 13, but in the next chapter we begin our discussion of the relevance of the Law for disciples of Jesus and life with him and others in the kingdom of heaven.

---

in *Studies in Midrash and Historiography*, ed. R. T. France and David Wenham, vol. 3 of *Gospel Perspectives* (Sheffield: JSOT, 1983), 157–75; Michael Knowles, *Jeremiah in Matthew's Gospel: The Rejected-Prophet Motif in Matthean Redaction*, JSNTSup 68 (Sheffield: Sheffield Academic, 1993), 15, 52–81.

167. Knowles, *Jeremiah in Matthew's Gospel*, 77–81; L. Nortjé, "Matthew's Motive for the Composition of the Story of Judas's Suicide in Matthew 27:3–10," *Neotestamentica* 28.1 (1994): 41–51.

*Chapter 6*

# THE LAW AND JESUS MESSIAH IN MATTHEW'S GOSPEL

*Pronouncement*

## BIBLIOGRAPHY

**Bird, Michael F.** "Jesus as Law-Breaker." Pages 3–26 in *Who Do My Opponents Say That I Am? An Investigation of the Accusations Against the Historical Jesus*. Edited by Scot McKnight and Joseph B. Modica. LNTS 327. London: T&T Clark, 2008. **Brown, Jeannine K.** "Jesus Messiah as Isaiah's Servant of the Lord: New Testament Explorations." *JETS* 63.1 (2020): 51–69. **Carter, Warren.** "Evoking Isaiah: Matthean Soteriology and an Intertextual Reading of Isaiah 7–9 and Matthew 1:23 and 4:15–16." *JBL* 119.3 (2000): 503–20. **Crossley, James G.** "Matthew and the Torah: Jesus as Legal Interpreter." Pages 29–52 in *Matthew Within Judaism: Israel and the Nations in the First Gospel*. Edited by Anders Runesson and Daniel M. Gurtner. ECL 27. Atlanta: Society of Biblical Literature Press, 2020. **Cuvillier, Élian.** "Torah Observance and Radicalization in the First Gospel. Matthew and First-Century Judaism: A Contribution to the Debate." *NTS* 55.2 (2009): 144–59. **Deines, Roland.** "Jesus and the Torah According to the Gospel of Matthew." Pages 295–328 in *The Gospel of Matthew in Its Historical and Theological Context: Papers from the International Conference in Moscow, September 24 to 28, 2018*. Edited by Mikhail Seleznev, William R. G. Loader, and Karl-Wilhelm Niebuhr. WUNT 459. Tübingen: Mohr Siebeck, 2021. **Evans, Craig A.** "Fulfilling the Law and Seeking Righteousness in Matthew and in the Dead Sea Scrolls." Pages 102–14 in *Jesus, Matthew's Gospel and Early Christianity: Studies in Memory of Graham N. Stanton*. Edited by Daniel M. Gurtner, Joel Willitts, and Richard A. Burridge. LNTS 435. London: T&T Clark, 2011. ———. "The Place of Jewish Scripture in Jesus' Teaching." Pages 79–94 in *The Message of Jesus: John Dominic Crossan and Ben Witherington III in Dialogue*. Edited by Robert B. Stewart. Minneapolis: Fortress, 2013. **Ferda, Tucker S.** "The Historical Jesus and the Law: The Form of His Activity and the Impact of Social Reputation." *CBQ* 80.1 (2018): 62–80. **Hagner, Donald A.** "Law, Righteousness and Discipleship in Matthew." *WW* 18.4 (1998): 364–71. ———. "Righteousness in Matthew's Gospel." Pages 101–20 in *Worship, Theology and Ministry in the Early Church: Essays in Honor of Ralph P. Martin*. Edited by Michael J. Wilkins and Terence

Paige. JSNTSup 87. Sheffield: Sheffield Academic, 1992. **Luz, Ulrich.** "The Fulfillment of the Law in Matthew (Matt. 5:17–20)." Pages 185–218 in *Studies in Matthew*. Grand Rapids: Eerdmans, 2005. **Moo, Douglas J.** "Jesus and the Authority of the Mosaic Law." *JSNT* 20 (1984): 3–49. ———. "Law." Pages 450–61 in *DJG*[1]. **Neudecker, Reinhard.** *Moses Interpreted by the Pharisees and Jesus: Matthew's Antitheses in the Light of Early Rabbinic Literature*. SubBi 44. Rome: Gregorian and Biblical Press, 2012. **Ng, Esther Yue L.** "Matthew 5:17–20 and 'A Tale of Two Missions'?" Pages 105–21 in *New Testament Theology in Light of the Church's Mission: Essays in Honor of I. Howard Marshall*. Edited by Jon C. Laansma, Grant R. Osborne, and Ray F. Van Neste. Eugene, OR: Cascade, 2011. **Olmstead, Wesley G.** "Jesus, the Eschatological Perfection of Torah, and the *imitatio Dei* in Matthew." Pages 43–58 in *Torah Ethics and Early Christian Identity*. Edited by Susan Wendel and David Miller. Grand Rapids: Eerdmans, 2016. **Ryan, Jordan.** "The Sermon on the Mount as Synagogue Teaching." Pages 53–74 in *Matthew Within Judaism: Israel and the Nations in the First Gospel*. Edited by Anders Runesson and Daniel M. Gurtner. ECL 27. Atlanta: Society of Biblical Literature, 2020. **Schreiner, Thomas R.** *40 Questions About Christians and Biblical Law*. 40 Questions Series. Grand Rapids: Kregel, 2010. **Sim, David C.** "The Rise and Fall of the Gospel of Matthew." *ExpTim* 120.10 (2009): 478–85. **Snodgrass, Klyne R.** "Matthew and the Law." Pages 101–36 in *Treasures New and Old: Recent Contributions to Matthean Studies*. Edited David R. Bauer and Mark Alan Powell. Atlanta: Scholars, 1996. **Strecker, Georg.** *The Sermon on the Mount: An Exegetical Commentary*. Nashville: Abingdon, 1988. **Trout, Bradley M.** "The Nature of the Law's Fulfilment in Matthew 5:17–20: An Exegetical and Theological Study." MA diss., North-West University, South Africa, 2014. **Wengst, Klaus.** "Keine 'Antithesen,' sondern Auslegung der Tora: Zu Mt 5,17–48." *ZNT* 18.36 (2015): 12–21. **Westerholm, Stephen.** "The Law in the Sermon on the Mount: Matt 5:17–48." *CTR* 6.1 (1992): 43–56. ———. *Law and Ethics in Early Judaism and the New Testament*. WUNT 383. Tübingen: Mohr Siebeck, 2017. **Wilkins, Michael J.** "Israel According to the Gospels." Pages 87–102 in *The People, the Land, and the Future of Israel: Israel and the Jewish People in the Plan of God*. Edited by Darrell L. Bock and Mitch Glaser. Grand Rapids: Kregel, 2014.

## 6.1 JESUS'S PRONOUNCEMENT REGARDING THE LAW: THE RELEVANCE OF THE LAW FOR LIFE IN THE KINGDOM OF HEAVEN

The Old Testament holds a prominent position in Matthew's Gospel, as we have seen in the preceding chapter. We looked at quotations, allusions, and echoes of the Old Testament found in Matthew's Gospel, and how Jesus's use of the Old Testament, and Matthew's understanding of the Old Testament, fulfill historical patterns and prophetic oracles of the Old Testament.

### 6.1.1 The Law in Matthew's Gospel

But what of the Law? What is Matthew's understanding of the Law, and what does he understand to be the relevance of the Law for discipleship to Jesus for his community and for discipleship to Jesus today? This topic is centrally important to all of the New Testament, but Matthew gives special significance to this theme in his Gospel.

The English word "law" translates the Hebrew term *torah* (תּוֹרָה) and the Greek term *nomos*. The term *nomos* occurs eight times in Matthew, seven times spoken by Jesus and one time spoken by a person addressing Jesus.[1] We can generally categorize these eight occurrences of "law" in Matthew in ways consistent with much of the usage in the Old Testament and elsewhere in the New Testament.

In the narrowest sense, "Law" can refer to the first five books of the Bible—the Pentateuch, Torah—that God gave to Moses on Mount Sinai. This was established by God in his directive to Joshua: "Keep this Book of the Law (*torah*) always on your lips; meditate on it day and night, so that you may be careful to do everything written in it. Then you will be prosperous and successful" (Josh 1:7–8).

The Torah expressed God's will for his people as given through Moses. Obedience to the Mosaic Law was the issue in Jesus's statement regarding Sabbath duty (Matt 12:5; cf. Exod 20:8) and his rebuke of the scribes and Pharisees regarding lesser and more important matters of the Law (Matt 23:23; cf. tithes, Lev 27:30–33; mercy, Lev 19:15). It was not enough only to know Torah—one must obey the Law as given by God through Moses.

In a related sense, "Law," when linked with other expressions such as "the Prophets," is a way of referring to the entire Hebrew Scriptures. "Do not think that I have come to abolish the Law or the Prophets; I have not come to abolish them but to fulfill them" (5:17; cf. 7:12; 11:13; 22:40). In the Second Temple period this expression was used to designate the Jewish Scriptures (e.g., 2 Macc 15:9; 4 Macc 18:10). "Law" denotes the Torah (the writings of the Pentateuch) and "the Prophets" refers to the writings of the Former Prophets (Joshua, Judges, 1–2 Samuel, 1–2 Kgs) and the Latter Prophets (three Major and twelve Minor Prophets).[2] As used by Jesus and elsewhere in the New Testament, "the Law and the Prophets,"[3] or "Moses and the Prophets,"[4] or "Moses, the Prophets, and the Psalms" (Luke 24:44) are shorthand expressions for the Hebrew Scriptures as a whole. "The Law" or "Moses" indicates the commanding and legislative aspects of the Old Testament, and "the Prophets" indicate the historical and foretelling aspects of the Old Testament, and together they indicate all of the Hebrew Scriptures.

In a still wider sense, "Law" can refer to the Old Testament Scriptures as a whole

1. By Jesus: 5:17, 18; 7:12; 11:13; 12:5; 22:40; 23:23. By the lawyer: 22:36.

2. Neusner and Green, "Law and Prophets," *DJBP* 379–80.

3. Matt 5:17; 7:12; 11:13; 22:40; Luke 16:16; Acts 13:15; 24:14; 28:2; Rom 3:21.

4. E.g., Luke 16:29, 31; 24:27.

(5:18). This broader shorthand expression for the entire Old Testament is what is meant by the "expert in the law" (*nomikos*) when he asks Jesus, "Teacher, which is the greatest commandment in the Law?" (22:36). In this expression the entire Old Testament is meant to indicate the system of legislation as revealing the divine will.

Hence, the "law" is what God has required of his people as expressed in his commands, statutes, and regulations. As we have seen, when we consider the "law" we can be thinking of the Old Testament Scriptures themselves. However, the Hebrew Scriptures as a whole express aspirations, hopes, songs, history, prophecies, promises, and much more. When we refer specifically to the Old Testament law we are focusing upon a specific aspect of the Hebrew Scriptures—commands, statutes, and regulations that God has given his people to obey that bring them into a healthy relationship with God. The "law" is God's will for his people to obey as expressed in the written Scriptures of the Old Testament.[5]

But we find in the First Gospel an intriguing phenomenon—Matthew shows attitudes to the Law that seem to move in opposite directions.[6] On the one hand, Matthew appears to emphasize continuity of the Old Testament law with the New Testament age. Jesus does not abolish the Law and the Prophets but is intent on fulfilling them (5:17). He upholds the commandments (*entolē*) to the degree that the smallest components, the jot and tittle, will not pass away until all is accomplished (5:17). Jesus advocates obeying what Moses commanded (8:4; cf. 19:17–18), including praying that flight from danger would not take place on the Sabbath, which some interpreters take to mean that Jesus upholds Sabbath regulations (24:20). Jesus's disciples are expected to give alms (6:2–4), and in order not to cause offense they should pay the temple tax (17:24–27). Jesus strongly condemns "lawlessness" (*anomia*: 7:23; 13:41; 23:28; 24:12), and he upholds the authority of the Pharisees and teachers of the law in interpreting the Law (23:2–3).

Yet, on the other hand, there are passages in Matthew where Jesus adjusts the disciples' performance of the Old Testament law, suggesting some discontinuity between the Old Testament and the current age. The new wine brought with Jesus's ministry is not appropriate for old wineskins but must be placed into new wineskins (9:14–17). When Jesus clarifies that Moses's permission to divorce continues, Matthew indicates that Jesus also included the "exceptive" clause, which limits divorce to *porneia* ("except for *porneia*"; 5:32 and 19:19). Elsewhere, although Matthew omits Mark's editorial aside—"In saying this, Jesus declared all foods clean" (15:20; cf. Mark 7:19)—he also clearly records Jesus's declaration that food does not make a person unclean, demonstrating discontinuity with the food laws in the Mosaic Law (cf. Lev 11:1–44; Deut 14:3–21). Sabbath restrictions and regulations must be interpreted according

5. For brief discussion of the variegated understanding of the "law" in early Judaism, see Neusner and Green, "Torah," *DJBP* 637–41; Hindy Najman, "Torah and Tradition," *EDEJ* 1316–17.

6. T. Schreiner, *New Testament Theology*, 625–27.

to the ministry of Jesus, who is Lord of the Sabbath (Matt 12:1–14). The revered Old Testament institution, the temple, and requirements regarding it, must now be understood in the light of Jesus, who is greater than the temple (12:5–6). Although Jesus and his disciples pay the temple tax so as not to give offense, they are no longer subject to temple requirements and are free not to pay the tax (17:24–27). Jesus foresees a time when the temple would be destroyed (Matt 24), which indicates that the temple requirements must be adjusted in the light of who Jesus is and what he has done in his ministry.

It is important to carefully balance the elements of continuity and discontinuity in the Matthean view of the Law. Thomas Schreiner states, "The whole of the law finds its fulfillment in Christ, but the time of fulfillment means that believers are not under the prescriptions of the law in the same way as before."[7]

### 6.1.2 Jesus Messiah Fulfills the Law: The Messianic Kingdom in Relation to the Law (5:17–48)

How then does Matthew understand the relevance of the Old Testament law for his community and discipleship to Jesus today? Perhaps this is most clearly seen in Jesus's programmatic statements regarding the Law in the Sermon on the Mount, particularly Matt 5:17–48. We discussed briefly above Jesus's statement regarding his coming to "fulfill the Law and the Prophets" (5:17), but here we attempt to make clear Jesus's relationship to the Old Testament law and the inauguration of the kingdom and discipleship to Jesus.[8]

Jesus's implicit and explicit criticism of the religious establishment brought increasing tension and outright opposition (12:22–32). At the center of the tension is the suspicion that Jesus is not fully orthodox in his commitment to the Old Testament law. So, in his first major discourse, Jesus makes clear his understanding of and commitment to the Old Testament law.

But he will not simply affirm one of the interpretative schools of thought. He will not offer just another application of the ancient law to his contemporary circumstances. Instead, he will demonstrate how he himself, in his ministry and proclamation of the kingdom of heaven, fulfills the Old Testament law's intentions, elevating himself above all the rabbinic debates. The first four verses of the passage (5:17–20) provide the crucial key to the interpretation of the Sermon, but also in many ways the crucial key

7. T. Schreiner, *New Testament Theology*, 626; see pp. 623–631 for a brief yet very helpful discussion of the law in Matthew's Gospel; see also Thomas R. Schreiner, *40 Questions About Christians and Biblical Law* (Grand Rapids: Kregel, 2010), 161–69; France, *Matthew*, NICNT, 191–97.

8. For consistency, I will use capitalized Law when referring to the Pentateuch as a division of the canon (e.g., Law and the Prophets) and lowercase law when referring to the principal of the law (e.g., Old Testament law, Jewish law, etc.); cf. *SBL Handbook of Style: For Biblical Studies and Related Disciplines*, 2nd ed. (Atlanta: SBL, 2014), 44.

to understanding Jesus's relationship to the Old Testament law and the inauguration of the kingdom. Following this declaration, Jesus gives illustrations of the way that the law is fulfilled in his ministry by taking us to the originally intended meaning and purpose of the law (5:21–48).

#### *6.1.2.1 Jesus Does Not Abolish but "Fulfills" the Law and the Prophets (5:17)*

Jesus's announcement of the arrival of the kingdom of heaven (4:17) might be interpreted by some in first-century Palestine as though he was starting a new work that would bring him into conflict with the Old Testament Scriptures. But Jesus categorically declares, "Do not think that I have come to abolish the Law and the Prophets" (5:17). The expression "Do not think" (*mē nomisēte*) reflects a contrary to fact supposition, indicating that Jesus is countering a suspicion that he is attempting to set aside God's former revelation with his announcement of the arrival of the kingdom of God. Some current scholars contend that the misunderstanding that Jesus counters is primarily potential,[9] but the polemic of the Sermon on the Mount (cf. 5:20; 6:1–18; 7:28–29) indicates that the antagonism between Jesus and the religious leaders is already well underway.[10] The religious authorities—hearing Jesus's teaching and seeing his practices of eating with tax collectors and sinners and other wicked people (9:11–13)—appear to have concluded that Jesus was a radical in regard to the law.[11] Such an attempt to set aside the Old Testament would be the ultimate mark of a heretic.[12]

It is into this scenario that Jesus declares, "Do not think that I have come to abolish the Law and the Prophets" (5:17). Jesus makes clear from the very beginning of his teaching ministry that the arrival of the kingdom does not do away with God's prior revelation through the Law and the Prophets. Instead of doing away with what God had revealed about his will for his people in the Hebrew Scriptures, Jesus's purpose for his earthly ministry is wrapped up in the formula, "I have come to fulfill them."

As we explored in the preceding chapter, the term "fulfill" (*plēroō*) has already become in Matthew's narrative an important indicator of Jesus's significance in God's historical program because Jesus's life and ministry fulfill Old Testament prophecies and expectations (e.g., 1:22–23; 2:15, 17–18, 23; 4:14–16). Throughout the New Testament various other writers look back to the Old Testament and emphasize that

9. Banks, *Jesus and the Law*, 65–70; Carson, "Matthew," 141–42.

10. Cf. Hagner, *Matthew 1–13*, 104–5; Evans, *Matthew*, 114–15.

11. A helpful investigation of this thesis is in Tucker S. Ferda, "The Historical Jesus and the Law: The Form of His Activity and the Impact of Social Reputation," *CBQ* 80.1 (2018): 62–80. Chris Keith focuses more on the challenge that the religious leaders felt to their reputations as scribal-literate interpreters of the law with the rising popularity of Jesus. Their opposition to Jesus had as its intent "to expose Jesus as an imposter to the position of interpretive authority"; see Chris Keith, *Jesus' Literacy: Scribal Culture and the Teacher from Galilee*, LHJS 8/LNTS 413 (London: T&T Clark, 2011), 190–92.

12. Keener, *Matthew* (2009), 176n46.

Jesus fulfills certain Old Testament passages regarding, for example, the Old Testament roles of prophet,[13] priest,[14] and king.[15] Here Matthew emphasizes that Jesus points in an additional direction when he declares that his eschatological person and ministry fulfills *all* of the Old Testament Scripture.[16]

Therefore, the idea of fulfillment is more than his obedience (i.e., keeping the Law) or his teaching, although they are included. Deines concludes that *plēroō* is "an exclusive Christological term, which could in the context of the First Gospel only be understood in the framework of a salvation history which reaches its peak in Jesus."[17] Jesus's fulfillment of the Law and the Prophets takes place through Jesus's entire mission, including his teaching, deeds, and messianic works, and especially his death and resurrection.[18] Jesus "fulfills" the Law and the Prophets by bringing into being the anticipated kingdom of God and the kingdom life that accompanies discipleship to Jesus Messiah. The context, especially as worked out in the "antitheses" to follow (5:21–48), indicates that Jesus not only fulfills certain anticipated roles, but that his interpretation of the Old Testament Scripture completes and clarifies God's intent and meaning through it.[19]

As we see in the "antitheses" (5:21–48), Jesus's attitude toward the Law reveals his special authority. Michael Bird states, "He is uniquely ranked and can mandate what God truly requires of his people . . . he speaks about the Law and acts about the Law as if he is, in some sense, to be identified with the God who legislated it."[20] As his ministry unfolds, Jesus will reveal clearly that he alone has that authority. Thomas Schreiner emphasizes, "Fulfillment centers on Jesus Christ and thus should be understood in terms of the newness that is realized in Christ. As the Law points to him, Jesus fulfills the Law. Jesus's life, ministry, teaching, death, and resurrection explicate the true meaning of the Law."[21]

### *6.1.2.2 The Lasting Validity of the Old Testament (5:18)*

Jesus emphatically affirms the lasting validity of "the law" (now a summary statement for the entire Hebrew Scriptures) as the revealed will of God for his people until the end of this age brings a consummation of all that God had purposed. Jesus confirms

---

13. See Deut 18:15–19; Matt 21:11; Acts 3:22.

14. See Lev 16:11–19; Isa 56:7; Matt 21:13; Heb 2:17–18; 4:14–16; 5:1–10; 7:24–25; 9:11–14.

15. See Isa 62:11; Zech 9:9; Matt 2:2; 21:5; Luke 2:11; 1 Tim 6:15; Rev 17:14; 19:16.

16. For a creative study of the ways in which early Christianity and formative Judaism perceive the fulfillment of the Hebrew Scriptures, see Jacob Neusner, Bruce D. Chilton, and Baruch A. Levine, *Torah Revealed, Torah Fulfilled: Scriptural Laws in Formative Judaism and Earliest Christianity* (London: T&T Clark, 2008).

17. Deines, "Not the Law," 74.

18. Deines, "Not the Law," 75. See also Deines, "Jesus and the Torah," 295–328; Evans, "Fulfilling the Law and Seeking Righteousness," 102–14.

19. For guides to the literature, see Guelich, *Sermon on the Mount*, 138–42; Charles, "Greatest or the Least in the Kingdom?," 139–62; Pennington, *Sermon on the Mount*, 169–79.

20. Michael F. Bird, "Jesus as Law-Breaker," in *Who Do My Opponents Say That I Am? An Investigation of the Accusations Against the Historical Jesus*, ed. Scot McKnight and Joseph B. Modica, LNTS 327 (London: T&T Clark, 2008), 26.

21. T. Schreiner, *Christians and Biblical Law*, 161.

the full authority of the Old Testament as Scripture for all ages (cf. 2 Tim 3:15–16), even down to the smallest components of the written text. Those components are the "smallest letter" (Gr. *iota*; KJV "jot") of the Hebrew alphabet (*yod*), and "the least stroke of a pen" (Gr. *keraia*, "horn"; KJV "tittle"[22]).

This has implications for understanding Jesus's view of the inspiration of Scripture. According to this statement, the inspiration and authority of the Old Testament extends to the actual words, even letters and parts of words. This is in accord with a "verbal plenary" view of inspiration, i.e., the very words, and all of the words, are inspired. Scripture does not simply contain the Word of God; the words of Scripture are the very Word of God.[23]

And this has further implications for understanding Jesus's view of salvation history. The final phrase of 5:18, "until all is accomplished," should be interpreted like *plērōsai*, "to fulfill," in 5:17, "in a way that takes salvation history and eschatology into account and refers to the messianic mission of Jesus. . . . The will of God cannot pass away without realization."[24] The Old Testament endures forever as a revelation of God's will for humans throughout history. While some of the specifics of God's will have been accomplished in Jesus's ministry to this point, the Old Testament Scripture that stands behind it remains as a valid principle. For example, the teaching of death and the shedding of blood to atone for sin is no longer expressed through temple sacrifices but rather has been "fulfilled/accomplished" once for all in Jesus's atonement on the cross (cf. Heb 9:11–14). The expression of God's will through the temple has been accomplished in Jesus's ministry and is no longer legally binding as a practice. Nevertheless, the Old Testament principle of penalty and payment for sin remains valid and needs to be taught and understood as God's will.[25]

### *6.1.2.3 Doing and Teaching the Commandments (5:19)*

"Therefore" (*oun* 5:19), the consequences of one's treatment of the Old Testament are immense. The rabbis recognized a distinction between "light" and "weighty" Old Testament commandments, and advocated obedience to both (m. Avot 2:1; 4:2). Light commandments are those such as the requirement to tithe on produce (cf. Lev 27:30; Deut 14:22), and weighty commandments are those such as profaning the name of God or the Sabbath or matters of social justice (Exod 20:2–8; Mic 6:8). Since the Old

22. Such as the lower hook or projection on the English letter "j" which distinguishes it from the letter "i."

23. For a lengthy discussion, see Feinberg, *Light in a Dark Place*, 231–425; for overviews, see John W. Wenham, "Christ's View of Scripture," in *Inerrancy*, ed. Norman L. Geisler (Grand Rapids: Zondervan, 1980), 1–36; Grudem, *Systematic Theology*, esp. 62–108.

24. Deines, "Not the Law," 76–77.

25. David A. Dorsey, "The Law of Moses and the Christian: A Compromise," *JETS* 34.3 (1991): 321–34. Dorsey's article attempts, commendably, to clarify the continuity and discontinuity of the law for the Christian.

Testament remains as the valid expression of the will of God, even down to the "jot and tittle," Jesus likewise demands a commitment to both the least of the commandments as well as the greatest but condemns those who would pervert the light into weighty (cf. Matt. 23:23).[26]

Jesus directs his comments specifically to his own followers. The "least" (*elachistos*) and "great" (*megas*) "in the kingdom of heaven" indicate those who have responded to his announcement of the gospel of the kingdom. Jesus drives home for his disciples the binding authority of Scripture. Since he does not "abolish" (*katalusai*) the Law and the Prophets but fulfills them (5:17), his disciples likewise must not "abolish" or "break" (*lysē*) the commandments but instead must practice and teach them (5:19).

The wordplay warns his disciples how to conduct themselves with regard to the Old Testament *as he now fulfills it*. Jesus's disciples must recognize that all of the Old Testament is the expression of God's will, and it is to be obeyed and taught from the perspective of how Jesus "fulfills" it through his life and ministry and his interpretation of its intent and meaning.[27]

A disciple's status in the kingdom of heaven accords with whether he or she trifles with the revealed will of God or whether he or she obeys and teaches it as truly the Word of God. The rank of "least" should not be taken to indicate exclusion from the kingdom, because in the next verse Jesus makes a distinction between those inside and outside of the kingdom. "Least" and "great" are not to be understood as referring to eternal ranks (cf. 20:1–16) but are ways in this present life to acknowledge those who have been faithful in word and deed to the revealed will of God as it is taught by Jesus.

### *6.1.2.4 "Inside-Out" Righteousness (5:20)*

From a warning and commendation to his disciples, Jesus next turns his attention to the broader audience—those who are not in the kingdom of heaven at all. "For I tell you that unless your righteousness surpasses that of the Pharisees and the teachers of the Law, you will certainly not enter the kingdom of heaven" (5:20). This may have been Jesus's most shocking statement, because the teachers of the Law and the Pharisees were the epitome of ethical righteousness.[28] Their scrupulous adherence to the written and oral law was legendary in Israel, yet Jesus says that it did not gain them entrance to the kingdom of heaven. How could anyone possibly surpass their righteousness?

26. Charles, "Greatest or Least in the Kingdom," 154–56. For a refutation of the claim that Matthew is issuing an anti-Paul polemic here in 5:19, see Angelika Strotmann and Markus Tiwald, "Das Matthäusevangelium–eine Paulus-Polemik? Überlegungen zum Toraverständnis des ersten Evangelisten," *Kontroverse Stimmen im Kanon*, ed. Martin Ebner, Gerd Häfner, and Konrad Huber, Quaestiones Disputatae 279 (Freiburg, Germany: Herder, 2016), 64–106, esp. 106.

27. Deines, "Not the Law," 77–80.

28. For helpful perspectives, see Joseph Sievers and Amy-Jill Levine, eds. *The Pharisees* (Grand Rapids: Eerdmans, 2021).

Jesus's disciples are called to a different *kind* and *quality* of righteousness, not an increased quantity. As was recognized in both Jesus's interaction with John the Baptist (3:15) and the statement of the Beatitudes (5:6), righteousness in the preaching of Jesus is not primarily a personal attainment of ethical purity. Righteousness belongs in the realm of grace.

This is not a new principle, however. The people of God knew that external acts of righteousness could not take away sin nor gain favor with God unless those acts were preceded by a repentant heart that is open to God's inner work of purification. Psalm 51 is perhaps the archetype, where David seeks inner cleansing and purification of his heart after his dreadfully sinful actions against Bathsheba (Ps 51:2, 7, 10). His understanding of the inside-out operation is explicit in Ps 51:16–17. David *would* later give temple sacrifice and offerings, and he would receive God's favor, but he knew they must be preceded by inner repentance and God's work of inner cleansing and purification.

But throughout Israel's history there was a tendency to reverse the operation, as was the case with the scribes and the Pharisees of Jesus's day. The assumption seemed to be that if one worked hard enough to clean up the outside, then the inside was automatically clean. Jesus later condemned this procedure explicitly when he said, "On the outside you appear to people as righteous but on the inside you are full of hypocrisy and wickedness" (Matt 23:27–28).

Jesus leads the audience to recognize that since entrance to the kingdom of heaven is not gained by external acts of righteousness, then they must seek a different kind—an inner righteousness that begins with a transformation of the heart, an undertaking David knew long ago could only be accomplished by God (Ps 51:10).

The arrival of the kingdom of heaven produces spiritual transformation in the disciple's heart, which will ultimately produce transformation in the disciple's external ethical life (15:16–20). If entrance to the kingdom of heaven can only be accomplished by an inner work of transformation, so also personal growth within the kingdom must proceed from the inside to the out. That principle underlies the next series of examples Jesus uses to explain how he fulfills the Old Testament. His disciples themselves will fulfill God's intention and will as revealed in Scripture as they conform their inner life to his Word, and then have that inner transformation guide their external behavior.

Jesus's declaration in 5:20 is an interpretative key to the entire Sermon on the Mount, and by extension, to life in the kingdom of heaven. And it is the reality that underlies and anticipates the apostle Paul's teaching on justification and sanctification. So, Jesus in no way sets aside or abolishes the Old Testament law but fulfills it and affirms its full authority. What he contrasts in the antitheses to follow is his internal, spiritual interpretation, which will produce in his disciples an inside-out transformation in true righteousness, with the external, legalistic interpretation of the Pharisees, which dead-ends in an external, superficial self-righteousness.

### *6.1.2.5 Matthew and Paul*

Based upon the stringent attitude toward the law found in these words of Jesus, critical scholars have often tried to pit Matthew and Paul against one another, as though Paul advocated a gospel of grace that was antinomian, which Matthew intentionally countered with a gospel of law.[29] But the contrast between Paul and Matthew is far overplayed.[30]

While Matthew records Jesus's sayings, which uphold the binding validity of the Law (5:17–20), he also has strong language of rebuke for the Pharisees who legalistically applied the Old Testament in such a way that they were cutting people off from the kingdom of heaven (e.g., 23:13–15), and he focuses on Jesus's message of transformation from the heart (e.g., 15:1–20). And Paul upholds the Law as holy and righteous and good (Rom 7:12), censuring the Judaizing legalists (e.g., Gal 1:8). Paul emphasizes salvation by grace alone (e.g., Eph 2:8–9).

Both Matthew and Paul go back to Jesus for the declaration that the Old Testament Scripture is the written, revealed will of God. The Old Testament is and will remain the will of God as Scripture (2 Tim 3:16), but it now must be understood as Jesus fulfills its salvation-historical goals and brings it to its intended meaning and end.

Matthew prepared his readers well for Jesus's staggering pronouncement, "I have not come to abolish the Law and the Prophets . . . but to fulfill them" (Matt 5:17), by consistently pointing to the way that Jesus fulfills certain Old Testament prophecies or themes. Now comes the overwhelming pronouncement that Jesus fulfills *all* of the Old Testament. Rampant must have been the rumors that Jesus and his followers had set aside the Old Testament. So, Matthew points out directly to his readers that Jesus fulfills all of the Old Testament. But the way in which Jesus fulfills the Law takes us in a slightly different direction than in the prophecy–fulfillment in the first two chapters. There specific Old Testament prophecies of a coming messianic deliverer were fulfilled in Jesus's life and ministry (1:22–23, 2:5–6, 15, 17–18, 23). And the way Jesus fulfills the Law builds upon the way in which Jesus's life and actions in baptism fulfill the salvation-historical program of God in "fulfilling all righteousness" (3:15).

Here Jesus brings to fulfillment all that the Old Testament had revealed about God's will for humanity. This means first that Jesus's life of perfect obedience to the will of God as revealed in the Law will enable him to be the perfect sacrifice for sins in his death (this is related to the "salvation-historical" aspect).

And second, his obedience provides the means by which his disciples are enabled

29. E.g., Frances W. Beare, *The Gospel According to Matthew: Translation Introduction and Commentary* (San Francisco: Harper and Row, 1981), 141.

30. For a recent study that unifies Paul and Matthew, see Esther Yue L. Ng, "Matthew 5:17–20 and 'A Tale of Two Missions'?," in *New Testament Theology in Light of the Church's Mission: Essays in Honor of I. Howard Marshall*, ed. Jon C. Laansma, Grant Osborne, and Ray Van Neste (Milton Keynes, UK: Paternoster; Eugene, OR: Cascade, 2011), 105–21.

to live lives of obedience to God's will revealed in the Law, because he will take his followers to understand and obey God's original intention of the Law. It will not be enough to conform one's behavior to an external obedience of any particular law. Rather, Jesus's disciples will understand the realities to which the Law pointed and will have a heart transformation and obedience that is accomplished through new covenant life in the Spirit that the prophet Ezekiel had prophesied (Ezek 36:25–27; cf. Jer 31:31–34).

Matthew's narrative clarifies that the arrival of new covenant promises are inaugurated with Jesus's impending death. In the upper room scene Matthew records, "This is my blood of the covenant, which is poured out for many for the forgiveness of sins" (26:27–28). And the apostle Paul clarifies that in Jesus's ministry, those promises have become concrete (Titus 3:4–7). Neither Jesus nor Matthew uses Paul's explicit language of justification and sanctification, but Matthew's narrative of Jesus's ministry establishes the historical foundation that sets the trajectory for Paul's theological explication.[31]

Jesus guides his disciples into the true intention of the Law, which focuses on inner righteousness as opposed to mere external righteousness. They gain entrance to the kingdom by repenting and confessing their sins (cf. 3:1–6; 4:17; 5:20), which allows the Spirit to enter into their lives to bring purification through applying Jesus's atoning righteousness to their hearts. In this way, Jesus's disciples are more righteous than the scribes and the Pharisees because they have received regeneration as they enter the kingdom. And they progress in righteousness through their transformation into the image of Christ.

#### *6.1.2.6 A Radicalization of the Old Testament in Jesus's Disciples (5:21–48)*

The next section of the SM is commonly called "the antitheses," because six times we hear similar recurring statements, "You have heard it said . . . but I say to you." Jesus's declaration is the antithesis of what has gone before. This has been mistakenly interpreted to mean that Jesus makes his teaching the antithesis of the Old Testament itself.[32] But if we look closely at each, we will see that Jesus is contrasting his interpretation of the Old Testament with faulty *interpretations* and/or *applications* of the Old Testament.[33] In each of the antitheses, Jesus demonstrates how the Old Testament is to be properly interpreted and applied, and thus, how the Law and the Prophets are

---

31. For a similar discussion attempting to understand Paul's concept of the "righteousness of God" and Matthew's perspective of righteousness here, see Reinhard Feldmeier and Hermann Spieckermann, *God of the Living: A Biblical Theology*, trans. Mark E. Biddle (Waco, TX: Baylor University Press, 2011), 307–8.

32. E.g., Luz, *Matthew*, 1:277–79. Some have attempted to show both continuity and discontinuity, but tend to emphasize discontinuity between the Mosaic Law and Jesus's teaching; e.g., Banks, *Jesus and the Law*, 203–26.

33. E.g., see T. Schreiner, *Christians and Biblical Law*, 165–69.

fulfilled (cf. 5:17). This elevates Jesus above all interpreters, making his pronouncements equivalent with Scripture itself.[34] Such a self-claim will be incredibly difficult for his followers to comprehend fully, and will become a grievous point of theological contention with his enemies in the religious establishment.

The historical level is important to keep before us. Jesus is speaking into a religious context in which the scribes and Pharisees held sway over the lives of the common people. The Pharisees had mapped out what they considered to be the proper course for attaining righteousness through their interpretation and application of the Old Testament. An overall lack in their interpretations was a tendency to require legalistic, external obedience to the Law without calling attention to an inner-heart obedience. They were therefore "hypocrites" in their practice of the Law (see 6:1–18) and were responsible for leading the people into hypocritical practices. Jesus looks at several examples of how they had done this and demonstrates how correct interpretation and application of the Law must be based upon proper *intent* and *motive*. Jesus is not negating the Old Testament, but the people's understanding and application of it. He confronts faulty interpretation of the scribes and Pharisees by giving his authoritative pronouncement, showing the original intention of the Old Testament.[35] By living with the intent and motive of the Law, those in the kingdom of heaven will continually live a righteousness that surpasses that of the scribes and Pharisees.

### 6.1.2.6.1 A Basic Pattern Emerges in the Antitheses

A basic pattern emerges in Jesus's declarations. (1) Jesus introduces an Old Testament saying or passage with the distinctive expression, "It was said to the people long ago." The passive form of the verb "it was said" (*errēthē*) occurs in each of the six antitheses. It is an example of the "divine passive,"[36] implying that God is the one who spoke the command to the Old Testament author, who in turn gave it to the people. The entire phrase occurs in the first antithesis (5:21) and recurs in the fourth antithesis (5:33), but it likely is understood in each of the six.

(2) Then Jesus apparently either cites (e.g., 5:43) or alludes to a current popular interpretation or traditional practice of the Old Testament passage he has quoted. The current understanding was causing the people to apply the Law in a faulty manner.[37]

(3) Then Jesus gives his authoritative pronouncement that takes his audience to

34. Élian Cuvillier, "Torah Observance and Radicalization in the First Gospel: Matthew and First-Century Judaism: A Contribution to the Debate," *NTS* 55.2 (2009): 144–59.

35. Carson (*Sermon on the Mount: An Evangelical Exposition of Matthew 5–7* [Grand Rapids: Baker Book House, 1982], 40) states, "Jesus appears to be concerned with two things: (1) overthrowing erroneous traditions, and (2) indicating authoritatively the real direction toward which the OT Scriptures point."

36. On the divine passive, see Wallace, *Greek Grammar*, 437–38.

37. Neudecker, *Moses Interpreted by the Pharisees and Jesus*, 39–42; Carson, *Sermon on the Mount*, 40; Stephen Westerholm, *Jesus and Scribal Authority*, ConBNT 10 (Lund: Gleerup, 1978), 113.

the intended meaning of the Old Testament passage. Jesus will not abrogate the Law but will bring it to its fulfillment. This did not always mean something completely unexpected or unknown. We should be able to expect to find persons within the Old Testament and Judaism who understood the intention of the Law and were moving in that direction. Jesus's declarations are a form of radicalization of the Law, bringing it to its fulfillment, in which he counters current misinterpretations and misapplications. Stephen Westerholm contends, "Something there was about Jesus' words and deeds which could be construed as a setting aside of the Law; but that, Matthew wants us to know, is a misconstruction. Jesus represents, not the Law's abrogation, but its 'fulfillment' (5:17)." [38]

With Matthew's purpose to lay out the words of Jesus so that his disciples will have a guideline for their continual growing obedience to God's will, he has distilled in the five discourses in his Gospel the very essence of discipleship to Jesus. The Sermon on the Mount, the first of the discourses, is the key directive to understanding the way that kingdom life will transform Jesus's disciples. In Jesus's declarations he reassures his listeners, and chastens his opponents, who may believe that Jesus's announcement of the arrival of the kingdom of heaven will abolish the Law and the Prophets. Rather than abolishing the Old Testament, Jesus radicalizes the Old Testament in the lives of his disciples as their continual transformation fulfills its intent, motive, and purpose. The antitheses provide crucial examples of how the Law and Prophets are fulfilled in Jesus's disciples and provide key directives for disciples of all ages.

### 6.1.2.6.2 A Brief Summary of the Antitheses

Jesus likely gave many authoritative interpretations that confronted faulty interpretations and applications of the Old Testament, but Matthew was led to record these six remarkable antitheses. A brief summary of each illustrates the direction Jesus takes discipleship in the kingdom of heaven.

1. True disciples not only avoid murder but are transformed so that they do not strip away the personhood and identity of others through anger or defamation (5:21–23), and they continually produce reconciliation in offended relationships (5:23–26).
2. Disciples of Jesus not only shun physical acts of adultery, but they are so completely committed to God's purpose for marriage that they have eyes and

38. See Stephen Westerholm, "The Law in the Sermon on the Mount: Matt 5:17–48," *CTR* 6.1 (1992): 43–56, see 44 for the quotation. See also Davies and Allison, *Matthew* 1:486–87; Olmstead, "Jesus, the Eschatological Perfection of Torah," 48–49. For further clarification, see J. Wenham, "Jesus and the Law," 92–96; Charles, "Garnishing with the 'Greater Righteousness,'" 8–10; Konradt, *Israel, Church, and the Gentiles*, 17; Deines, "Not the Law," 82–85; Neudecker, *Moses Interpreted by the Pharisees and Jesus*, 39–42 and passim; Klaus Wengst, "Keine 'Antithesen,' sondern Auslegung der Tora: Zu Mt 5,17–48," *ZNT* 18.36 (2015): 12–21.

hands only for their spouse (5:27–28) and discipline their every sexual thought and action to be singly focused on their spouse alone (5:29–30).

3. Disciples of Jesus not only respect the purity of the marital relationship, but they have God's values for the original design for marriage and are unreservedly committed to its permanence and sanctity (5:31–32).
4. Jesus's disciples do not need to give an oath as an additional confirmation of their trustworthiness because their faithful lives continually confirm the reliability of their word (5:33–37).
5. Disciples of Jesus are so secure in their transformed kingdom identity that when they are wronged, they do not merely adhere to legal retribution but use every opportunity to serve others, both good and evil people, so that the reality of God's grace in their lives woos others to the kingdom of heaven (5:38–42).
6. Jesus's disciples not only love what God loves and hate what God hates, but they have the renewed heart of God, which enables them to love the world of sinners for whom Jesus will eventually give his life (5:43–48).

And climactically, Jesus's disciples have experienced the powerfully life-changing presence of the kingdom of heaven in such a way that their progressive transformation into the image of Jesus the Son of God secures their progressive growth into the very perfection of God the Father (5:48).

### *6.1.2.7 The Pursuit of Perfection (5:48)*

The conjunction "therefore" (*oun*) introduces a powerful concluding charge: "Be perfect, therefore, as your heavenly Father is perfect" (5:48). It is a fitting conclusion to the sixth antithesis, because the perfect love of God toward his creatures is the example of the love that Jesus's disciples are to display toward their enemies and those who persecute them. God always acts perfectly toward his creatures in love because he is love (cf. 1 John 4:16). In the same way, if Jesus's disciples strive to have the Father's love for all humans, they will always give to others precisely what they need from God's perspective.

At the same time, Jesus's statement in 5:48 serves as a fitting conclusion to all of the antitheses in 5:21–47. To love one's enemies is to pursue a primary characteristic of God (5:45), but Jesus's disciples are to emulate God in every area of life. In the antitheses, Jesus used representative selections from the Old Testament to clarify the intent of the Old Testament as God's will for his people. The Old Testament is a reflection of God himself as he has made known his will for his people. Therefore, as the disciples pursue the intent and motive of the Old Testament as Jesus has clarified it, they are in fact pursuing the perfection of God himself.

Interestingly, Matthew uses a future tense of the verb in the indicative mood here—"you shall be (*esesthe*) perfect." We might think that the future tense indicates a prediction of what will take place in the future—the disciples *will be perfect* like their heavenly Father is perfect. But as the rendering of the NIV indicates, it fits the context of ethical exhortations in 5:21–47 much better to understand the verb to have an imperatival force—Jesus charges his disciples to "be perfect."[39]

This is typical Hebrew language. The Septuagint also translates the Hebrew of each of the commands of the Decalogue with a future indicative: "You shall not . . ."[40] These are not the "Ten Predictions" about the behavior of the people of Israel, because their history is spotted with violations of each of them. Instead, they are the "Ten Commandments," where the future indicatives functionĕ as demands upon their behavior. This is precisely the case in the imposing Old Testament saying, "Be holy for I, the Lord your God, am holy," where the identical future indicative form occurs in the LXX (*esesthe*; Lev 19:2 LXX).[41] God is not making a prediction, or else he would have been quite wrong about the future holiness of the nation. He is giving a command, similar to Jesus's charge that concludes the antitheses (Matt 5:48). Matthew is the only New Testament author to use the future indicative as an imperative relatively frequently, which is consistent with the Hebrew flavor that permeates his Gospel.[42]

But we may also see something of a goal and a promise in the future indicative. A present imperative, "Keep being perfect" or "Be continually perfect," would place an impossible demand upon Jesus's disciples. Instead, the future indicative holds out an emphatic *goal* that is to shape the disciple's entire life—they are to set nothing less than the perfection of God as the ultimate objective of their behavior, thoughts, and will. Further, the future indicative also implies a *promise* because the Father is not only the divine goal but also the divine enabler. Leon Morris states, "Jesus puts his command in such a way that disciples may look for divine help as they press toward God's goal for them."[43]

Jesus's disciples are to pursue the perfection that is God himself, which is restated in a slightly different fashion in the Old Testament saying cited above, "Be holy for I, the Lord your God, am holy" (Lev 19:2). The adjective "perfect" (*teleioi*) is also used in the LXX in Deut 18:13: "You shall be perfect before your God." The Hebrew adjective

---

39. The indicative mood in the future tense is used for volitive expressions when rendering specific OT injunctions or themes (Wallace: "cohortative indicative"). The "imperatival future" has a universal, timeless, and/or solemn force that distinguishes the use of the future tense from the simple imperative (see BDF, 183, §362; Turner, *Syntax*, 86, §8; Wallace, *Greek Grammar*, 452–53, 569, 718–19).

40. E.g., Exod 20:3, "you shall not have" (οὐκ ἔσονταί σοι, *ouk esontai soi*; woodenly, "other gods shall not be to you [i.e., 'yours']"); Exod 20:4, "you shall not make" (οὐ ποιήσεις, *ou poiēseis*); etc.

41. Peter brings over the future indicative in his citation of the passage: ἅγιοι ἔσεσθε, *hagioi esesthe* (1 Pet 1:16).

42. For other examples of future indicatives used (and often translated) as imperatives, seel:21; 4:7, 10; 5:21, 27, 33, 43, 48; 6:5; 19:18; 20:26, 27; 21:3; 22:37, 39; 27:4, 24 (also in Mark 9:35; Luke 1:31; 17:4; Acts 18:15; Rom 7:7; 13:9; Gal 5:14; Jas 2:8; 1 Pet 1:16). For comparison, note that the future indicative is used in a purely predictive fashion in 1 John 3:2: "we shall be (*esometha*) like him."

43. Morris, *Matthew*, 133.

is *tāmîm*, which is used for the idea of wholeness or completeness,[44] specifying the soundness of sacrificial animals (Exod 12:5) and the complete commitment of a person to God, including ethical blamelessness.[45] The Greek term *teleioi* carries the same connotations. It can indicate the "end," the "completion," or "the complete thing,"[46] that which is made "whole," that which is "perfect."[47] It can also be used to indicate a person who has attained spiritual "maturity."[48] But with the Father as the goal, Jesus is not saying "Be mature as your heavenly Father is mature." He is saying, "Be perfect, like your heavenly Father." The disciples are to pursue the Father's perfection as the goal of their lives.

So, Jesus's saying is *a command, a promise, and a statement of hope*. His disciples are engaged in the process of transformation, now made objectively real in a revolutionary way with the arrival of the kingdom of heaven. The necessity of the new birth to enter the kingdom of heaven (cf. John 3:1–7) makes possible, and real, his disciples' transformation into his image (Matt 10:24–25; 1 Cor 3:18; Rom 8:29). Since Jesus is both the perfection of the image of God in humans as a full human being, and the perfect image of the invisible God as the divine Son of God (Col 1:15–20), he is the ultimate example for his disciples to follow as they hear the command, "Be perfect . . . as your heavenly Father is perfect" (Matt 5:48). That statement implies a realistically ideal goal that Jesus's disciples are to pursue with restful dissatisfaction in this life until their final transformation in eternity.

Since the Old Testament is God's revealed will for his people, Jesus's clarification of the intended meaning of the Old Testament sets before the disciples an example of the way in which they can direct themselves to be in line with God's will for their lives. The ultimate goal is not perfect obedience to the Law but perfect likeness to the heavenly Father. They shall be like him as they give themselves over to the radical transformation that accompanies the arrival of the kingdom of heaven in the ministry of Jesus.

## 6.2 The Christian's Relation to the Law

The issues surrounding the Christian's relationship to the Old Testament law are complex, and in many ways the conclusions that we reach lead to various extant

44. Leviticus 23:15, 30; Josh 10:13.

45. Genesis 6:9; 17:1; Deut 18:13; 2 Sam 22:24–27. The Qumran community put special weight upon walking with perfection in God's ways—Rule of the Congregation (1QS) I, 13; II, 2; III, 9; IV, 22; IX, 5–9; see Ito, "Matthew and the Community of the Dead Sea Scrolls," 48.

46. Tasker (*Matthew*, 70) is uneasy about using "perfect" to render Matt 5:48, commenting that it is a "misleading translation of *teleios*, and is largely responsible for the erroneous doctrine of 'perfectionism.'"

47. The Greek word group includes the adjective *teleioi* (5:48), the noun *telos*, "end" (e.g., 10:22), and the verb *teleioō*, "I bring to completion" (e.g., Phil 3:12); the verb *teleioō* does not occur in Matthew.

48. E.g., 1 Cor 14:20; Eph 4:13; Heb 5:14; 6:1. This is the meaning adopted by William Hendriksen, *Exposition of the Gospel According to Matthew*, NTC (Grand Rapids: Baker, 1973), 317–19.

theological systems (e.g., Reformed, Dispensationalism, New Covenant, Lutheranism).[49] Some contend that none of the Old Testament applies unless it is explicitly reaffirmed in the New Testament, while others would say that all of the Old Testament applies unless it is explicitly revoked in the New Testament. Both of these extremes should be avoided in the light of Jesus's statements in 5:17–20.[50]

While a full discussion of the issues of the role of the Old Testament for understanding Matthew's Gospel is beyond what we can address here, some basic principles can be suggested.

1. The law is a revelation of God's will for humanity. It reveals a standard of God's perfect righteousness. We trifle with the will of God if we set aside some aspects of the Word of God. For example, it may be commendable to oppose abortions, but when anti-abortion activists resort to violence and murder, they have set aside God's commands.
2. It is important to understand God's purpose for giving the law if we are going to rightly understand the law itself. The law had several purposes. It was designed to instruct God's people in his will, so that they might fulfill his purpose for them as "a kingdom of priests and a holy nation" (Exod 19:6). But they were not to rely on its requirements as the means of finding forgiveness (Ps 51:14–17). The law was given to point out humanity's sinfulness and need for God (Rom 7:7) and to lead humanity to Christ by whom they can be justified by faith (Gal 3:24).[51]
3. When reading the Gospels in general, and the antitheses in particular (Matt 5:21–48), we keep in mind that Jesus was objecting to misinterpretations of the Law, not the Law itself. A tendency existed in Pharisaic Judaism to make the interpretations and traditions of the scribes and Pharisees just as binding as the Law itself. Jesus rejected their practices, not the Law. He continued to uphold the Law as the will of God. Thomas Schreiner notes, "The Old Testament commands in Matthew 5:21–48 were not set aside by Jesus. Rather, he provided the proper interpretation of those commands and applied them in a penetrating way to the lives of his disciples."[52]
4. Jesus fulfilled the law and proved to be the perfect God-Man who is therefore able to become the means of our justification, or right standing with God (Matt 5:17–20; Rom 5:18–21; Heb 5:7–10). Therefore, we are not under the law as a means of gaining salvation.

49. See, e.g., Wayne G. Strickland, ed., *Five Views on Law and Gospel* (Grand Rapids: Zondervan, 1999); T. Schreiner, *Christians and Biblical Law*, 13–14.

50. Blomberg, *Matthew*, 103–4; Moo, "Jesus and the Mosaic Law," 28–30; Carmen Joy Imes, *Bearing God's Name: Why Sinai Still Matters* (Downers Grove, IL: InterVarsity, 2019), 5.

51. Joe M. Sprinkle, "Law," *EDBT* 470.

52. T. Schreiner, *Christians and Biblical Law*, 169.

5. At the same time, Jesus is the interpreter of the law, showing what is binding principle and what is the temporary symbolic ritual (Matt 12:1–8; Heb 9:11–10:13). We should seek Jesus's mind for a proper interpretation and application of the Law and understand the Old Testament in the light of the new covenant that he inaugurates. Jesus emphasized that ultimately the law was given to aid humans to live life the way God intended it to be lived, not to keep us under a binding set of religious rules (Matt 12:3–5; 9–14). As Jesus gives his interpretation of the law, he reveals the intent and motive of the law that was lost behind the external legalism of the scribes and Pharisees. He then demonstrates how principles of the law are valid guidelines to show God's will for his people (5:21–48).[53]
6. Jesus demonstrates that the entire Old Testament hangs on love for God and neighbor (22:38–39), similar to the responsibility of the Golden Rule, which Jesus said is a summary of the Law and the Prophets (7:12). This truly brings to fulfillment all of the Old Testament. While it is not the sole hermeneutical key to Jesus's understanding of the Old Testament, the "law of love" becomes an important key to determine how the Christian is to live out the will of God, beginning with heart transformation (5:21–22, 27–28, 38–39, 43–44, etc.). The kingdom life that Jesus inaugurates fulfills the deepest inclination of humans who are created in the image of God. Kingdom life enables Jesus's disciples to live life the way God intended it to be lived, which means living responsibly in relationship to God and others. As such, the entire Old Testament hangs on love for God and others, and truly brings to fulfillment the Law and the Prophets. Carson notes, "The entire biblical revelation demands heart religion marked by total allegiance to God, loving him and loving one's neighbor. Without these two commandments the Bible is sterile."[54]

Love for God and neighbor is not understood to be simply an emotional attachment. Rather, love indicates a concrete responsibility, the act of being useful and beneficial to God and to one's neighbors, both Jew and gentile (cf. Lev 19:18, 34).[55] It may be helpful here to draw on a definition of "love" that I have developed from Matthew's Gospel: *love is an unconditional commitment to an imperfect person in which I give myself to bring the relationship to God's intended purposes.*[56]

53. Dorsey, "The Law of Moses and the Christian, 331. For a helpful discussion of "principlism" in applying the OT, see Klein, Blomberg, and Hubbard, *Introduction to Biblical Interpretation*, 278–83; and J. Daniel Hays, "Applying the Old Testament Law Today," *BSac* 158 (2001): 21–35; cf. John Goldingay, "The Old Testament and Christian Faith: Jesus and the Old Testament in Matthew 1–5: Part 2," *Them* 8.2 (1983): 12.

54. Carson, "Matthew," 524.

55. See Abraham Malamat, "Love Your Neighbor as Yourself," *BAR* 16.4 (1990): 50–51.

56. Wilkins, *Matthew*, NIVAC (Grand Rapids: Zondervan, 2004), 726.

The persons who love God with all of their being—heart, soul, and mind (Matt 22:37)—will understand that God's will for life is revealed in the Old Testament and will gladly, eagerly obey the Old Testament because they know that in doing so they are living life the way that God has designed it to be lived. In turn, their obedience to Jesus's fulfillment of the Old Testament—commitment to his person and his revelation of inside-out obedience—continues the transformation of their entire being—heart, soul, and mind—into the image of God so that they are more like what God had intended for them in creation.

And loving neighbor as self means giving ourselves to other humans to help them to live the way that God intended life to be lived—assisting them in their transformation. These are the greatest commandments because they go to the essence of the way God has created humans to live: giving ourselves to God and others to fulfill God's purposes for us as the crown of his creation in displaying in our lives the glory of God's kingdom on earth. Jesus's fulfillment of the Law and the Prophets in his inauguration of the kingdom of heaven enables this to be a concrete reality for us as his disciples.

*Chapter 7*

# CHRISTOLOGY IN MATTHEW'S GOSPEL

## *Jesus Immanuel Is More Than a Man*

### BIBLIOGRAPHY

**Bakhos, Carol.** *The Family of Abraham: Jewish, Christian, and Muslim Interpretations.* Cambridge, MA: Harvard University Press, 2014. **Bateman, Herbert W., IV, Darrell L. Bock, and Gordon H. Johnston.** *Jesus the Messiah: Tracing the Promises, Expectations, and Coming of Israel's King.* Grand Rapids: Kregel, 2011. **Bauer, David R.** *The Gospel of the Son of God: An Introduction to Matthew.* Downers Grove, IL: InterVarsity, 2019. ———. "The Kingship of Jesus in the Matthean Infancy Narrative: A Literary Analysis." *CBQ* 57.2 (1995): 306–23. **Beaton, Richard.** *Isaiah's Christ in Matthew's Gospel.* SNTSMS 123. New York: Cambridge University Press, 2004. **Bird, Michael F.** *Jesus Is the Christ: The Messianic Testimony of the Gospels.* Downers Grove: InterVarsity, 2012. **Blanton, Thomas R., IV.** "Saved By Obedience: Matthew 1:21 in Light of Jesus' Teaching on the Torah." *JBL* 132.2 (2013): 393–413. **Bock, Darrell L., and James H. Charlesworth,** eds. *Parables of Enoch: A Paradigm Shift.* Jewish and Christian Texts 11. London: T&T Clark, 2011. **Burridge, Richard A.** *Four Gospels, One Jesus? A Symbolic Reading.* 3rd ed. Grand Rapids: Eerdmans, 2014. **Byrskog, Samuel.** *Jesus the Only Teacher: Didactic Authority and Transmission in Ancient Israel.* ConBNT 24. Stockholm, Sweden: Almquist & Wiksell, 1994. **Cabrido, John Aranda.** *A Portrayal of Jesus in the Gospel of Matthew: A Narrative-Critical and Theological Study.* Lewiston, NY: Edwin Mellen, 2010. **Carlston, Charles E., and Craig A. Evans.** *From Synagogue to Ecclesia: Matthew's Community at the Crossroads.* WUNT 334. Tübingen: Mohr Siebeck, 2014. **Chae, Young S.** *Jesus as the Eschatological Davidic Shepherd: Studies in the Old Testament, Second Temple Judaism, and in the Gospel of Matthew.* **Charlesworth, James H.,** ed. *The Messiah: Developments in Earliest Judaism and Christianity.* WUNT 2/216. Tübingen: Mohr Siebeck, 2006. Minneapolis: Fortress, 1992. **Crowe, Brandon D.** *The Last Adam: A Theology of the Obedient Life of Jesus in the Gospels.* Grand Rapids: Baker Academic, 2017. ———. *The Obedient Son: Deuteronomy and Christology in the Gospel of Matthew.* BZNW 188. Berlin: de

Gruyter, 2012. **Deutsch, Celia M.** *Hidden Wisdom and the Easy Yoke: Wisdom, Torah, and Discipleship in Matthew 11:25–30*. Sheffield: JSOT Press, 1987. **———.** *Lady Wisdom, Jesus, and the Sages: Metaphor and Social Context in Matthew's Gospel*. Philadelphia: Trinity Press International, 1996. **Dvořáček, Jiří.** *The Son of David in Matthew's Gospel in the Light of the Solomon as Exorcist Tradition*. WUNT 2/415. Tübingen: Mohr Siebeck, 2016. **Gerhardsson, Birger.** "The Christology of Matthew." Pages 14–32 in *Who Do You Say That I Am? Essays on Christology; In Honor of Jack Dean Kingsbury*. Edited by Mark Allan Powell and David R. Bauer. Louisville: Westminster John Knox, 1999. **Grindheim, Sigurd.** *Christology in the Synoptic Gospels: God or God's Servant?* London: T&T Clark, 2012. **Ham, Clay Alan.** *The Coming King and the Rejected Shepherd: Matthew's Reading of Zechariah's Messianic Hope*. New Testament Monographs 4. Sheffield: Sheffield Phoenix, 2006. **Hengel, Martin.** *The Son of God: The Origin of Christology and the History of Jewish-Christian Religion*. Translated by John Bowden. Philadelphia: Fortress, 1976. **Horbury, William.** *Messianism Among Jews and Christians: Biblical and Historical Studies*. 2nd ed. London: T&T Clark, 2016. **Huizinga, Leroy A.** *The New Isaac: Tradition and Intertextuality in the Gospel of Matthew*. NovTSup 131. Leiden: Brill, 2009. **Hurtado, Larry W.** *Lord Jesus Christ: Devotion to Jesus in Earliest Christianity*. Grand Rapids: Eerdmans, 2003. **Hurtado, Larry W., and Paul L. Owen,** eds. *Who Is This 'Son of Man'? The Latest Scholarship on a Puzzling Expression of the Historical Jesus*. LNTS 390. London: T&T Clark, 2011. **Irons, Charles Lee, Danny André Dixon, and Dustin R. Smith.** *The Son of God: Three Views of the Identity of Jesus*. Eugene, OR: Wipf & Stock, 2015. **Jipp, Joshua W.** *The Messianic Theology of the New Testament*. Grand Rapids: Eerdmans, 2020. **Kammler, Hans-Christian.** "Sohn Gottes und Kreuz: Die Versuchungsgeschichte Mt 4,1–11 im Kontext des Matthäusevangeliums." *ZThK* 100.2 (2003): 163–86. **Keith, Chris.** *Jesus' Literacy: Scribal Culture and the Teacher from Galilee*. LHJS 8/LNTS 413. London: T&T Clark, 2011. **Keith, Chris, and Larry Hurtado,** eds. *Jesus Among Friends and Enemies: A Historical and Literary Introduction to Jesus in the Gospels*. Grand Rapids: Baker Academic, 2011. **Kingsbury, Jack Dean.** *Matthew: Structure, Christology, Kingdom*. Philadelphia: Fortress, 1975. **Kuhn, Karl A.** "The 'One like a Son of Man' Becomes the 'Son of God'." *CBQ* 69.1 (2007): 22–42. **Kupp, David D.** *Matthew's Emmanuel: Divine Presence and God's People in the First Gospel*. SNTSMS 90. Cambridge: Cambridge University Press, 1996. **Loke, Andrew Ter Ern.** *The Origin of Divine Christology*. SNTSMS 169. Cambridge: Cambridge University Press, 2017. **Lucass, Shirley.** *The Concept of the Messiah in the Scriptures of Judaism and Christianity*. LSTS 78. London: T&T Clark, 2011. **McKnight, Scot.** *Jesus and His Death: Historiography, the Historical Jesus, and Atonement Theory*. Waco, TX: Baylor University Press, 2005. **Mowery, Robert L.** "Son of God in Roman Imperial Titles and Matthew." *Bib* 83 (2002): 100–10. **Neusner, Jacob.** *Messiah in Context: Israel's History and Destiny in Formative Judaism*. Philadelphia: Fortress, 1984. **Novakovic, Lidija.** *Messiah, the Healer of the Sick: A Study of Jesus as the Son of David in the Gospel of Matthew*.

WUNT 2/170. Tübingen: Mohr Siebeck, 2003. **Novenson, Matthew V.** *Christ Among the Messiahs: Christ Language in Paul and Messiah Language in Ancient Judaism*. Oxford: Oxford University Press, 2012. **O'Donnell, Douglas Sean.** "Insisting on Easter: Matthew's Use of the Theologically Provocative Vocative (κύριε) in the Suppliant Narratives." Pages 185–200 in *The Earliest Perceptions of Jesus in Context: Essays in Honour of John Nolland on His 70th Birthday*. Edited by Aaron W. White, Craig A. Evans, and David Wenham. LNTS 566. London: Bloomsbury T&T Clark, 2018. **Peppard, Michael.** *Son of God in the Roman World: Divine Sonship in Its Social and Political Context*. Oxford: Oxford University Press, 2011. **Piotrowski, Nicholas G.** *Matthew's New David at the End of Exile: A Socio-Rhetorical Study of Scriptural Quotations*. NovTSup 170. Leiden: Brill, 2016. **Porter, Stanley E.** *Sacred Tradition in the New Testament: Tracing Old Testament Themes in the Gospels and Epistles*. Grand Rapids: Baker Academic, 2016. **Porter, Stanley E., and Bryan R. Dyer.** *Origins of New Testament Christology: An Introduction to the Traditions and Titles Applied to Jesus*. Grand Rapids: Baker Academic, 2023. **Riesner, Rainer.** *Messias Jesus: Seine Geschichte, seine Botschaft und ihre Überlieferung*. Gießen, Germany: Brunnen, 2019. **Sargent, Benjamin.** *David Being a Prophet: The Contingency of Scripture upon History in the New Testament*. BZNW 207. Berlin: de Gruyter, 2014. **Schreiner, Patrick.** *Matthew, Disciple and Scribe: The First Gospel and Its Portrait of Jesus*. Grand Rapids: Baker Academic, 2019. **Steinmann, Andrew E.** "What Did David Understand About the Promises in the Davidic Covenant." *BSac* 171 (2014): 19–29. **Van Aarde, Andries G.** "ΙΗΣΟΥΣ, the Davidic Messiah, As Political Saviour in Matthew's History." Pages 7–31 in *Salvation in the New Testament: Perspectives on Soteriology*. Edited by Jan G. Van Der Watt. Leiden: Brill, 2005. **Wellum, Stephen.** *Christ Alone—The Uniqueness of Jesus as Savior: What the Reformers Taught . . . and Why It Still Matters*. The Five Solas Series. Grand Rapids: Zondervan, 2017. **Wick, Peter.** "Die Bergpredigt: Synagogale Toraauslegung in Vollmacht." Pages 116–21 in *Schriftgelehrsamkeit und Toraethik: Die Bergpredigt im Kontext des Matthäusevangeliums*. Edited by Jens-Christian Maschmeier. Stuttgart: Kohlhammer, 2021. **Wilkins, Michael J.** "Peter's Declaration of Jesus' Identity in Caesarea Philippi." Pages 293–381 in *Key Events in the Life of the Historical Jesus: A Collaborative Exploration of Context and Coherence*. Edited by Darrell L. Bock and Robert L. Webb. WUNT 2/247. Tübingen: Mohr Siebeck, 2009. **Willitts, Joel.** *Matthew's Messianic Shepherd-King: In Search of 'The Lost Sheep of the House of Israel.'* BZNW 147. Berlin: de Gruyter, 2007. **Winter, Bruce W.** "The Messiah as the Tutor: The Meaning of καθηγητής in Matthew 23:10." *TynBul* 42.1 (1991): 152–57. **Witherington, Ben, III.** *The Christology of Jesus*. Minneapolis: Fortress, 1990. **Yieh, John Yueh-Han.** *One Teacher: Jesus' Teaching Role in Matthew's Gospel Report*. BZNW 124. Berlin: de Gruyter, 2004. **Zacharias, H. Daniel.** *Matthew's Presentation of the Son of David: Davidic Tradition and Typology in the Gospel of Matthew*. London: Bloomsbury T&T Clark, 2017. **Zolondek, Michael Vicko.** *We Have Found the Messiah: How the Disciples Help Us Answer the Davidic Messianic Question*. Eugene, OR: Pickwick, 2016.

## 7.1 Introduction to Christology in Matthew's Gospel: Jesus Immanuel Is More Than a Man

From the first verse, the incipit, of Matthew's Gospel, we are struck by the centrality of Jesus Messiah and his Gospel: "The book of the genealogy of Jesus Christ, the son of David, the son of Abraham" (1:1, ESV). Matthew introduces his Gospel with language reminiscent of the book of Genesis. The Greek word that the ESV and NIV render "genealogy" in Matt 1:1 is from the noun *genesis*, "beginning," which is also the title of the Septuagint of Genesis, where it implies that it is a book of "beginnings" or "origins." The term also appears in 1:18. The first use of *genesis* in 1:1 is concerned with the origins of Jesus in relation to the larger history of God's people, while the second use in 1:18 focuses on how Jesus gained his specific origin in human history.[1]

The expression *genesis* appears to function as a heading not only for the genealogy in 1:2–17[2] but also for the beginning narrative of Jesus's infancy in 1:18–2:23.[3] A case can also be made that the expression functions as a title for the entire book of the story about Jesus to follow.[4] As the book of Genesis gave the story of one beginning—God's creation and covenant relations with Israel—so the Gospel of Matthew gives the story of a new beginning—the arrival of Jesus the Messiah and the kingdom of God.

The theological topic of this chapter and the next—Christology—is central to understanding the theology of Matthew. It is the heart of the four Gospels, and indeed the heart of New Testament theology as a whole. We are often familiar with Jesus, perhaps even too familiar. Those who witnessed Jesus's earthly ministry were astounded by him. Some heard his stupendous claim to uniqueness and hardened their hearts against him. Some understood his claim yet lodged the charge of blasphemy against him. Some understood what he was saying and bowed down in worship of his deity.

The church has consistently drawn upon Matthew's Gospel as a foundational clarification of the identity of Jesus Messiah, who is the Son of God, the King of Israel, and the Lord of the church.[5] Matthew focuses on Jesus's identity as the incarnate Son of God the Father, yet Matthew also gives focused perspective on Jesus as the promised King of Israel, who came to inaugurate the kingdom of heaven, even though life in this kingdom would be of a very different sort than many had expected. Life in the kingdom of heaven is especially centered on an intimate, ongoing relationship of Jesus

1. Nolland, *Matthew*, 71.

2. Gundry, *Matthew*, 13.

3. Carson, "Matthew," 99.

4. Davies and Allison, *Matthew*, 1:149–54, argue convincingly that the expression *biblos geneseōs* is a title for the entire book. They argue that the proximity to the genealogy in 1:2–17 argues for the phrase to include reference to the genealogy and to the book. See also Morris, *Matthew*, 19.

5. Mark Allan Powell, *Matthew: An Interpretation Bible Commentary* (Louisville: Westminster John Knox, 2023), 61–62.

with his disciples throughout the ages, disciples who—only in Matthew's Gospel—are designated to become the church that Jesus himself will build and superintend.[6]

## 7.2 The Titles/Designations of Jesus Messiah

Matthew's opening narrative reveals a special emphasis upon God's mission to fulfill his covenantal promises to Israel. In the incipit of 1:1, Jesus Messiah is introduced, and his name and lineage is brimming with significance for Israel, and the nations. "This is the genealogy of Jesus the Messiah the son of David, the son of Abraham" (1:1). Matthew's opening would have special importance to a Jewish audience, which traced its ancestry through the covenants God made with Israel. The expressions "son of David" and "son of Abraham" stand in apposition to "Jesus Christ" indicating that the titles are a further explanation of Jesus Messiah's identity.[7]

In this Chapter we seek to understand the meaning of Jesus's names, titles, and descriptions. France observes that the areas of thought to which Jesus's names and titles point may be roughly summed up under two basic questions: "What was Jesus's mission?" and "Who is Jesus?"[8] And Douglas O'Donnell explains that while the titles used for Jesus in the Gospel of Matthew do not express Jesus's whole identity and mission, they do summarize precisely central aspects of the evangelist's storyline and theological vision. "Each title—Christ, son of David, Son of Man, Lord and so on—adds its own unique colour to the narrative tapestry Matthew has masterly woven together."[9] The basic names and titles that occur in Matthew are Jesus (152 times), Christ (17 times), Immanuel (1 time), S/son (89 times), Son of David (10 times), Son of Abraham (1 time), Son of God (9 times), Son of Man (30 times), Lord (80 times), and rabbi (4 times). We will explore other designations for Jesus as we unfold this chapter on Christology.

In the following chapter we will continue our study of Matthew's christological perspective, but there we will focus on Matthew's perspective of Jesus's offices and relationship to the Father and the Holy Spirit.

### 7.2.1 Jesus (*Iēsous*)

In the biblical world, a human "name" typically signifies the designation of a person that reflects the character and hoped-for or anticipated mission in the life of the person. In common practice, a person had a single personal name, which often carried some religious significance. The name "Jesus" translates the Greek term *Iēsous*, which renders

6. For a helpful popular-level treatment of the identity and mission of Jesus, see Brant Pitre, *The Case for Jesus: The Biblical and Historical Evidence for Christ* (New York: Image, 2016).

7. Turner, *Matthew*, 56–7.

8. France, *Matthew: Evangelist and Teacher*, 298.

9. Douglas Sean O'Donnell, "Insisting on Easter: Matthew's Use of the Theologically Provocative Vocative (κύριε) in the Suppliant Narratives," in White, Evans, and Wenham, *Earliest Perceptions of Jesus*, 185–200, here 185.

the Hebrew *Yeshua*, "Yahweh saves" (Neh 7:7), which is a shortened form of Joshua (*Yəhošuaʿ*), "Yahweh is salvation" (Exod 24:13).[10] The name Jesus was quite popular in Judaism of the first century, given to sons as a symbolic hope for Yahweh's anticipated sending of salvation. A widely held expression of this hope was the expectation of a Messiah who would save Israel from Roman oppression and purify his people (e.g., Pss. Sol. 17).

The name Jesus occurs some 152 times in Matthew's Gospel and has profound notions of salvation associated with it in Jesus's life and ministry.[11] But the angel announcing the birth of Jesus draws upon a less popular, although perhaps more important theme: salvation from sin is the basic need of Israel (cf. Ps 130:8; Pss. Sol. 18:3–5): "She will give birth to a son, and you are to give him the name Jesus, because he will save his people from their sins" (1:21).[12] This salvation is now at hand, so Matthew points his readers to the central purpose of Jesus's earthly life and ministry—he himself will save his people from their sins by giving his life a ransom for many (cf. 20:28).

The term for "people" in the expression "save his people" is *laos*, which normally indicates the people of Israel in Matthew's narrative (e.g., 4:16; 27:25). The expression draws the reader back to the genealogy and the established royal status of Jesus as the Davidic Messiah, heir to David's throne over the people of Israel (1:6, 16). But the description "his people" (*ton laon autou*, 1:21) anticipates going beyond only Israel and ultimately point to the salvation that Messiah offers to the entire world as the son of Abraham (1:1; cf. 2:6; 3:9; 8:11; 16:18).[13] This salvation brought by Jesus will be the basis of the righteousness of the kingdom of heaven that he inaugurates as the one who proclaims the gospel of the kingdom of heaven (cf. 4:12–23; 5:17–20).[14]

### 7.2.2 Christ/Messiah (*Christos/Māšîaḥ*)[15]

Matthew's first designation for the primary figure in his Gospel is "Jesus Christ." To many of us in the modern world that may sound like a first and last name. But on closer inspection we see that "Jesus" is his personal *name*, and "Christ" is the personal *title*. The name is the personal designation, while a "title" designates the status, role, or mission of the person. And in the biblical world, a title designates a person appointed by God for a specific role, and the dignity, honor, distinction, or preeminence attached to

10. Leonard S. Wallmark, "Name," *EDBT* 550.

11. Cf. Gerhardsson, "Christology of Matthew," 16–17.

12. Some recent scholars try to point to other aspects of "save his people from their sins," such as torah obedience (e.g., Thomas R. Blanton IV, "Saved by Obedience: Matthew 1:21 in Light of Jesus' Teaching on the Torah," *JBL* 132.2 [2013]: 393–413) or the political ramifications of their sins (e.g., Wayne S. Baxter, "Missing Matthew's Political Messiah: A Closer Look at His Birth and Infancy Narratives," *BBR* 27.3 [2017]: 333–50). Such attempts miss the stated purpose: "he will save his people from their sins" (1:21), i.e., Jesus will save them from their personal sins.

13. Erickson, "Joseph and the Birth of Isaac," 35–51.

14. David R. Bauer, "The Kingship of Jesus in the Matthean Infancy Narrative: A Literary Analysis," *CBQ* 57.2 (1995): 306–23.

15. This section draws on my earlier work: Wilkins, "Peter's Declaration," here 349–50.

a person by virtue of rank, office, precedent, privilege, attainment, or lands.[16] In Jesus's case, his primary title is "Christ," then expanded to designate Jesus Christ as the "Son of David" and "Son of Abraham," all found in the incipit of 1:1.

The absolute form "the Messiah," without an accompanying genitive or possessive pronoun, occurs rarely and primarily in late first-century BC texts (1 En. 48:10; 52:4; 2 Bar 30:1; 70:9; 4 Ezra 7:28, 29; 12:32).[17] When it does occur, it usually refers to the eschatological Davidic king. A royal Messiah, the *māšîaḥ* of Israel, representing the royal line of David, and a priestly Messiah, the *māšîaḥ* of Aaron, representing the high-priestly house, with the former subject to the latter, are mentioned in both the Dead Sea Scrolls[18] and the Testaments of the Twelve Patriarchs.[19] Prophets also could be called "Yahweh's anointed" or "anointed ones."[20] Although the Davidic messianic hope is often considered the most prominent, it is necessary to clarify what kind of Messiah was expected in Israel.

A common theme in early Jewish texts from just before or during the first century BC is that Messiah would come to judge and/or destroy the wicked,[21] deliver God's people,[22] and reign over a blessed kingdom.[23] Given the fact that messianism arose in Israel in the context of exile, alienation, and oppression during the Second Temple period, it is not surprising to find this common theme.[24] Andrew Chester proposes a definition of the concept of "messiah" within first-century BC Jewish messianic expectations: "A messiah is a figure who acts as the agent of the final divine deliverance, whether or not he is specifically designated as 'messiah' or 'anointed.'"[25]

One of the distinctive features separating the various sects of first-century Judaism is that they tended to focus on one strand of messianic expectation, sometimes to the exclusion of other strands. For example, many focused on scriptural statements of a kingly conqueror who would sit on David's throne (e.g., 2 Sam 7:11–16). Some focused on statements of a great prophet like Moses who would give the authoritative

16. Michael F. Bird, "Christ," *DJG*[2] 115–16. See also *Encyclopedia Britannica*, "Title," accessed May 4, 2023, https://www.britannica.com/topic/Title.

17. See S. Talmon, "The Concepts of *Māšîaḥ* and Messianism in Early Judaism," in *The Messiah: Developments in Earliest Judaism and Christianity*, ed. James H. Charlesworth (Minneapolis: Fortress, 1992), 79–115; Marinus de Jonge, "The Earliest Christian Use of *Christos*: Some Suggestions," *NTS* 32.3 (1986): 321–43, which draws upon his earlier article, de Jonge, "The Use of the Word 'Anointed' in the Time of Jesus," *NovT* 8 (1966): 132–48.

18. 1QS IX, 10–11; 1QSa II, 12–13; cf. CD XII, 22–23; XIII, 20–22; XIX, 9–11 [VII, 20–21]; XX, 1; Talmon, "Concepts of *Māšîaḥ* and Messianism in Early Judaism," 104–5.

19. T. Reu. 6:5–12; T. Levi 18:2–9; David E. Aune, "Christian Prophecy and the Messianic Status of Jesus," in Charlesworth, *Messiah*, 404–22; esp. 409.

20. Ps 105:15; CD II, 12; VI, 1; 1QM XI, 7–8; 11QMelch II, 18.

21. Pss. Sol. 17–18; 4 Ezra 12; 2 Bar. 40:72.

22. Pss. Sol. 17; 4 Ezra 12.

23. Pss. Sol. 17.

24. Ben Witherington III, *The Many Faces of the Christ: The Christologies of the New Testament and Beyond*, Crossroad Companions to the New Testament (New York: Crossroad, 1998), 15.

25. Andrew Chester, *Messiah and Exaltation: Jewish Messianic and Visionary Traditions and New Testament Christology*, WUNT 207 (Tübingen: Mohr Siebeck, 2007), 201. For a helpful study of the historical context see Rainer Riesner, *Messias Jesus: Seine Geschichte, seine Botschaft und ihre Überlieferung* (Gießen: Brunnen, 2019).

interpretation of God's Law (Deut 18:15–18). Still others looked at scriptural priestly passages and expected a mysterious figure like Melchizedek to have a messianic function (Gen 14:18–20; Ps 110:4).

However, we do find evidence that at least some in Israel held these strands together in tension. A trilogy of messianic proof-texts in a single document from the Qumran community speaks first of an eschatological prophet like Moses,[26] then of a departing kingly star and an arising kingly scepter from Israel who will crush their enemies,[27] and finally of a priestly figure like Levi whom Moses blessed.[28] However, this probably is an indication that the Qumran community expected more than one messiah. A famous passage in the Rule of the Community awaits the arrival of a complex of messianic figures: "until the prophet comes, and the Messiahs of Aaron and Israel" (1QS IX, 11 [Garcia]).[29]

Nolland suggests that "Jesus is identified as the royal figure of Davidic descent through whom God will restore the fortunes of his people as long promised."[30] We shall see how Matthew continues to use this title.

#### *7.2.2.1 Jesus Is the Christ/Messiah*

The term "Christ" therefore is best understood to be a title.[31] Matthew points to this title as rightly belonging to Jesus because of his lineage as a descendant of David (1:16–18). The English term "Christ" is the transliteration of the Greek term *Christos*, which in turn is a translation of the Hebrew term *māšîaḥ*, "anointed." Similar to usage in Second Temple Judaism, the term *māšîaḥ* occurs no less than thirty-nine times in the Old Testament to describe kings (2 Sam 1:14, 16; cf. 1QSa II, 14, 20), priests (Exod 28:41; cf. 1QS IX, 11) and prophets (Ps 105:15; cf. CD II, 12; V, 21–VI, 1; 1QM XI, 7, 8).

Further, when considering messianic expectations, the scope broadens. William Horbury contends that "'Messianism' can stand for all biblically inspired Jewish communal hope, spiritual and political, with or without a messiah figure."[32] The focus of many Jewish messianic texts connects the coming Messiah "not just with David, but with the whole series of Jewish kings and rulers, including the judges."[33] This diverse

26. 4QTest 1–8; cf. Deut 5:28–29; 18:18–19.

27. 4QTest 9–13; cf. Num 24:15–17.

28. 4QTest 14–22; cf. Deut 33:8–11. See Géza G. Xeravits, *King, Priest, Prophet: Positive Eschatological Protagonists of the Qumran Library*, STDJ 47 (Leiden: Brill, 2003).

29. For discussion, see J. Collins, *Scepter and the Star*, 74–101.

30. Nolland, *Matthew*, 665.

31. A full-length treatment of this discussion, especially focusing on Paul and ancient Judaism, is found in Matthew V. Novenson, *Christ Among the Messiahs: Christ Language in Paul and Messiah Language in Ancient Judaism* (New York: Oxford University Press, 2012). Bringing that study up to date and concluding that *Christos* is a title indicating "the Messiah of God and the Messiah of God's people," is Eckhard J. Schnabel, "Ἰησοῦς Χριστός, Jesus Messiah," *TynBul* 73 (2022): 1–21.

32. William Horbury, "Messianism in the Old Testament Apocrypha and Pseudepigrapha," in *Messianism Among Jews and Christians: Biblical and Historical Studies*, 2nd ed. (London: T&T Clark, 2016), 1.

33. Horbury, "Messianism," 81.

usage contributed to the diversity of messianic expectations, which contributed to the difficulty of accepting how Jesus could fulfill this diversity of offices.

The genealogy that immediately follows Matthew's incipit concentrates on the kings of Judah (e.g., 1:6) and the expression "king of the Jews" in 2:2 makes it clear from the onset that "Christ" is being used in connection with some form of royal messianism.[34] By this we see that Matthew has devoted significant effort in establishing the Jewish credentials and Davidic pedigree of Jesus as Messiah. Michael Bird states, "Such a task is undertaken with a view to demonstrating that the faith of Jesus-believers is not a departure from Judaism; rather, it is the very fulfillment of it. The Matthean Jesus holds together the new and the old revelation (Matt 9:17; 13:52)."[35] Graham Stanton concludes, "I take 'messianism' to refer to the expectation of a divinely anointed royal Davidic person who will fulfill Scripture and inaugurate a new age."[36]

#### *7.2.2.2 Jesus Messiah Performs the Deeds of the Messiah (11:2–6)*

Early in his narrative Matthew pointed to the arrest of John the Baptist as the impulse for Jesus to begin his Galilean ministry (4:12). John had been imprisoned by Herod Antipas at the fortress Machaerus, where ultimately he was put to death (see 14:1–14). As he awaited his fate, John wanted clarification about Jesus's identity and ministry as the Messiah. Having been imprisoned for a year or more, John sends his disciples to query Jesus about the messianic program, which does not seem to be unfolding as John had expected.

##### 7.2.2.2.1 John the Baptist Questions Jesus Through His Disciples (11:2–6)

John's disciples, along with John, were increasingly alarmed as to the future of the messianic program. Earlier they had questioned Jesus about the incongruity of their own practice of fasting with Jesus's disciples lack of participation in that activity (Matt 9:14–17). There is a bit of disconnect between their understanding of the prophet's message about the coming Messiah's ministry and Jesus's display of the messianic ministry.

John instructed his disciples to ask of Jesus, "Are you the one who was to come, or should we expect someone else?" (11:3). The expression "the one who was to come" (*ho erchomenos*) is an allusion to the Messiah, the Coming One, the expression that John had used to refer to Jesus at the beginning of the public ministry (3:11).

John's question seems out of character with the prophet's earlier bold and courageous declaration of Jesus as the Coming One (cf. 3:1–14). Most likely, John's present

34. Nolland, *Matthew*, 72.

35. Bird, *Jesus Is the Christ*, 2. Similarly, see Piotrowski, *Matthew's New David*.

36. Graham Stanton, "Messianism and Christology: Mark, Matthew, Luke and Acts," in *Redemption and Resistance: The Messianic Hopes of Jews and Christians in Antiquity*, ed. Markus Bockmuehl and James Carleton Paget (London: T&T Clark, 2007), 78–96; here 79.

experience does not match the message that he had given about the Coming One's arrival, which promised blessing on those who repent and judgment on those who do not. John needed to have his understanding of the messianic program reconfirmed.[37]

#### 7.2.2.2.2 Jesus Responds to John's Questions (11:4–6)

Jesus reiterates to John's disciples that the way his ministry has unfolded (chs. 8–9) is in line with the prophetic promises: "Go back and report to John what you hear and see" (11:4).[38] In Jesus's ministry as the Coming One are fulfilled Isaiah's prophecies that described the coming messianic ministry in these very terms:

- the blind receive sight (Matt 9:27–32; 20:30–34; cf. Isa 29:18; 35:5)
- the lame walk (Matt 15:30–31; cf. Isa 35:6)
- those who have leprosy are cured (Matt 8:1–4; cf. Isa 53:4)
- the deaf hear (Mark 7:32–37; 9:25; cf. Isa 29:18–19; 35:5)
- the dead are raised (Matt 10:8; Luke 7:11–17; John 11:1–44; cf. Isa 26:18–19)
- the good news is preached to the poor (Matt 5:3; Luke 14:13, 21; cf. Isa 61:1)

Therefore, Jesus explicitly confirms that in his ministry the messianic age of blessing has arrived: Jesus is the "Coming One." But the implications are even more profound because the miracles accomplished by Jesus fulfill expectations previously associated with God and the eschatological day of the Lord. Jesus indicates that he has come in the place of God performing the work of God.[39]

### *7.2.2.3 Peter's Understanding of Jesus as "the Messiah"*

Midway through Matthew's Gospel he records one of the most significant interactions between Jesus and his disciples regarding their understanding of his identity. In response to Jesus's query to the disciples, "Who do people say the Son of Man is?" (16:13), Simon Peter answered, "You are the Messiah, the Son of the living God" (16:16). Prior to this the expression, *Christos* has occurred only in Matthew's narrative, but now it is used for the first time by a person to address Jesus directly within his historical ministry.

*Christos* came to be an expression linked in the Jewish mind to David as the anointed king of Israel and with the promise of the "anointed one" who would be the light of hope for the people of Israel. In spite of David's shortcomings, God had promised

37. Ben Witherington III, *The Christology of Jesus* (Minneapolis: Fortress, 1990), 43.

38. W. Wilson, *Healing in the Gospel of Matthew*, passim.

39. Edward Meadors, "The 'Messianic' Implications of the Q Material," *JBL* 118.2 (1999): 259.

the king through Nathan the prophet that the house and throne of David would be established forever (2 Sam 7:11b–16).[40] That promise became a fixture of the hope of a coming age of blessing for the nation (e.g., Isa 26–29; 40) inaugurated by a figure who would bring to reality the promise of the eschatological reign of David's line (cf. Ps 2:2; Dan 9:25–26). By the time of the first century, the term *Messiah* or *Christ*, although understood in a variety of ways,[41] came in the minds of many Jews to refer to a kingly figure who, like David, would triumph in the last days over Israel's enemies (e.g., 1QS II, 14, 20).[42]

Jesus accepted the designation from Peter and in so doing was claiming to be God's "Anointed" agent in establishing the kingdom. He was the Christ, the messianic king in its fullest sense. Jesus was careful to define or restrict the use of the term to designate the kind of messianic deliverer he was to be (4:12–17). "Then he ordered his disciples not to tell anyone that he was the Messiah" (16:20). His hesitation, or reservation in using the title to refer to himself (26:63–64), had only to do with the popular use of the term, which often carried political and militaristic overtones in the minds of some of the people. The crowds would likely reject Jesus because he was not the kind of Messiah that they wanted (cf. 27:17, 22).

Peter's confession is not the first recognition of Jesus as Messiah, but it is the fullest to this point. The proper sense of Jesus as the Messiah/Christ is only understood in conjunction with Peter's additional statement that he is the "Son of the living God" (16:16). Jesus has a special relationship to God that sets him apart from any other kind of messianic figure. Jesus is Messiah with a unique status as the Son of the living God. This is reiterated by Jesus when he refers to "my Father in heaven" (16:17).[43]

Although Jesus accepts Peter's declaration that he is the Messiah, he qualifies the use of the title to include the kind of Messiah that he intended to be, not what Peter expected him to be. Peter confesses more than he really understands about Jesus's identity. And he does not yet fully understand Jesus's mission, because he will attempt to deter Jesus from his redemptive objective (cf. 16:22). But Peter's understanding is certainly increasing, as is that of the rest of the Twelve, as they pay attention to God's revelation of who Jesus is, and what he has come to accomplish, instead of paying attention to their own expectations and popular conceptions.

40. Andrew E. Steinmann, "What Did David Understand About the Promises in the David Covenant," *BSac* 171 (2014): 19–29.

41. E.g., priests (e.g., 1QS IX, 11) and prophets (e.g., CD II, 12; V, 21–VI, 1; 1QM XI, 7, 8).

42. See, e.g., Lawrence H. Schiffman, *The Eschatological Community of the Dead Sea Scrolls: A Study of the Rule of the Congregation*, SBLMS 38 (Atlanta: Scholars, 1989); Craig A. Evans, "Prophet, Sage, Healer, Messiah, and Martyr: Types and Identities of Jesus," in vol. 2 of *HSHJ*, ed. Tom Holmén and Stanley E. Porter (Leiden: Brill, 2011), 1217–44.

43. Keener, *Matthew* (1999), 424–25n72.

### *7.2.2.4 Jesus's Messianic Mission*

Although Jesus did not refer to himself with the explicit term Messiah/Christ in order to avoid the varied messianic expectations found in the ancient world of Judaism, the nature of his mission was messianic. And various means served to legitimate Jesus's messianic ministry and message. The confirmation by the eschatological prophet John the Baptist, Jesus's proclamation of the imminent arrival of the kingdom of God, the miracle tradition, the calling and sending of twelve apostles with an eschatological message of judgment, and his prophetic/messianic actions (e.g., climactic entry to Jerusalem; the temple incident), all constituted forms of legitimation of his messianic mission.[44]

However, Jesus's messianic ministry was misinterpreted by the crowds to mean that he was the eschatological Prophet/King who was the agent of divine political/militaristic deliverance. And ironically, Jesus was executed by the Romans as "king of the Jews" because he was misperceived as stirring the crowds to rebellion. The strongest "historical" evidence that Jesus claimed to be the Messiah is the undeniable fact that he was crucified by the Romans as a messianic pretender. If Jesus had denied he was the Messiah, his crucifixion is unexplainable. At the crucifixion there was a *titulus* that stated the reason for death. In all four Gospels, the charge against Jesus is a political one: he claimed to be "king of the Jews," i.e., the Messiah.

While Jesus did not accept the political conception, he did accept the title of Messiah. Bird affirms, "It is the contention of this study that the messianic identity of Jesus is the earliest and most basic claim of early Christology. What is more, it is precisely the testimony to Jesus as the Messiah that is arguably the most defining Christological affirmation of the canonical Gospels."[45] Darrell Bock concurs, "Thus this scene at Caesarea Philippi and what follows it are crucial to appreciating why the Gospels do what they do with the term 'Messiah.' It is a key confessional term for those who follow Jesus, but only when properly appreciated as involving suffering as well as glory."[46]

The term *Christos* has provided the church with its most widely used title for Jesus. The fact that the believers in Jesus were at an early stage described as "Christians" is eloquent testimony to the importance of the concept in their minds. The full name using the transliterated form, "Jesus Christ," is accurate and traditional. But since in common present-day usage it can be misunderstood to be a first and last name, we might render the full name "Jesus Messiah" in writing and speaking, as does the NIV in sixty-six of the more than five hundred times *christos* appears in the Greek New

44. Aune, "Christian Prophecy and the Messianic Status of Jesus," 412–13.

45. Bird, *Jesus Is the Christ*, 4.

46. Darrell L. Bock, "The Identity of Jesus as the Christ in His Ministry," in Herbert W. Bateman IV, Darrell L. Bock, and Gordon H. Johnston, *Jesus the Messiah: Tracing the Promises, Expectations, and Coming of Israel's King* (Grand Rapids: Kregel, 2011), 331–458, here 449.

Testament, to draw on the Hebrew background, and to create cognitive dissonance in English readers and hearers.

### 7.2.3 Immanuel (*Emmanouēl*)

When Joseph discovered that his betrothed Mary was pregnant, the angel of the Lord appeared to Joseph to provide knowledge of the Holy Spirit-conceived baby. The angel instructed Joseph to name the child Jesus (1:21), which is what we find him called through his earthly life, and by the early church.

Matthew further comments, "The virgin will conceive and give birth to a son, and they will call him Immanuel' (which means 'God with us')" (1:23). We have no record of Jesus ever being called "Immanuel"[47] by his family or followers. Instead, as Matthew translates it for us, we see that the name is intended as a title to indicate Jesus's divine messianic identity: "God with us." According to Peter Stuhlmacher, the best way to understand Jesus Immanuel's arrival in history is not primarily through critical questioning but through reflection on the early Christian expectation of salvation and the divine participation in the miracle of the birth of Immanuel.[48]

Both his common name and his titular name indicate profound truths: *Jesus* specifies what he does ("God saves"), and *Immanuel* specifies who he is ("God with us"). These are highly charged names that will speak of a profound christological orientation by Matthew. Richard Bauckham states, "Jesus is thus more than the Lord who saves his people; he saves them by being the divine presence with his people, as Yahweh is with his people in the biblical history of Israel."[49]

Jesus's entrance to history is encapsulated in the name Immanuel, "God with us" (1:23). His presence is assured when even two or three of his disciples are gathered in his name, "there am I among them" (18:20 ESV). And his abiding presence with his disciples throughout history is pronounced in his concluding assurance, "I am with you always, to the very end of the age" (28:20 NIV). This threefold emphasis upon the presence of Jesus indicates that Immanuel is not a mere addendum but rather is a primary christological concept of Matthew's Gospel.[50] In Jesus Messiah, God is with us indeed.

47. The spelling of the name is given in English translations both as Immanuel (NIV) and Emmanuel (NRSVue). The Hebrew spelling is עִמָּנוּ אֵל, which is usually transliterated *Immanuel*. The LXX transliterated the term into Greek as Ἐμμανουήλ, which is the Greek spelling found in Matt 1:23, and is transliterated *Emmanouēl*. Therefore, following the Hebrew, the English spelling is "Immanuel," whereas following the Greek, the English spelling is "Emmanuel." The NIV and the majority of English translations go with "Immanuel" in both Isa 7:14 and Matt 1:23. The KJV went Immanuel in Isa 7:14 but with Emmanuel in Matt 1:23.

48. Peter Stuhlmacher, *Die Geburt des Immanuel: Die Weihnachtsgeschichten aus dem Lukas- und Matthäusevangelium* (Göttingen: Vandenhoeck & Ruprecht, 2005), esp. 13–22; 65–76.

49. Richard J. Bauckham, "Christology," *DJG*² 130.

50. Bockmuehl, "Gospels on the Presence of Jesus," 92; Charles L. Quarles, *Matthew*, EBTC (Bellingham, WA: Lexham Academic, 2023), 764.

A true Israelite would proclaim only God to be eternal and omnipresent, so here Matthew records a concluding claim by Jesus to his deity, as he is with his disciples forever. Keener notes, "Jesus' continuing presence with his followers even after his departure (28:20) suggests his omnipresence—an attribute limited to deity alone."[51] Therefore, Matthew begins and concludes his Gospel with the crucial element of discipleship: the presence of the Master.[52] Luz states that "Jesus' promise means that his presence is experienced not only in spectacular miracles; it can also happen in more quiet and non-ostentatious ways."[53]

- Jesus is with his disciples in his incarnation (1:21).
- Jesus is with his disciples in the hearing of prayers (6:7–15).
- Jesus is with his disciples in overcoming fear and doubt (14:28–31).
- Jesus is with his disciples in the celebration of the Lord's Supper (26:26–29; cf. 14:13–21).
- Jesus is with his disciples as we go throughout the nations with the gospel of the kingdom of heaven, inviting all to become Jesus's disciples (28:19).
- Jesus is with his disciples as we obey all that he commanded us (28:20a).
- Jesus is with his disciples until the end of the age (28:20b).

This is the promise that has sustained discipleship to Jesus for all his followers throughout the last twenty-one centuries.

We worship and follow a risen Master who is with us constantly. All that he commanded in word and deed that is necessary for our growth as his disciples is included in the written documents of Scripture, but his very real presence comforts our individual needs and sustains us through all of our days, whether in our weakness, sorrow, joy, power, or pain. To the "very end of the age" or until the completion of God's plans for this age, Jesus promises to be the sustaining presence that assures us that history is not out of control, that the kingdom of God has indeed been inaugurated, that he is a very present help in times of trouble, and that the work that he accomplished on the cross to bring salvation to humanity is continually available through his risen and ascended ministry.

We may be keenly aware that Jesus is not here with us in a bodily fashion. But he is with us moment by moment as our omnipresent God—the always present risen Jesus Messiah. Bockmuehl states forcefully, "Between the two endpoints of his great *inclusio* of 'God with us' (1:23–28:20), the cumulative effect of his narrative delivers an affirmation of presence far stronger and richer than the religious commonplace

51. Keener, *Matthew* (2009), 718.

52. For discussion of the "I am with you" theme here, see Kupp, *Matthew's Emmanuel*, 176–200.

53. Luz, *Matthew 21–28*, 635.

of anonymous divine providence or assistance."[54] This wonderful promise of Jesus's continual presence invites us as readers into the story. We are the ongoing chapter of this gospel story, walking receptacles of the presence of the risen Jesus and living demonstrations of the power of the kingdom of God in our lives.[55]

### 7.2.4 Son (*huios*)

The meaning of the Greek term *huios* in the broader Greco-Roman world is almost completely limited to physical descent: a "son" of a physical father. It is often interchangeable with the more comprehensive expression *pais* or *paides*, "small boy, children."[56]

The Hebrew *bēn* is quite different. It is the most common term of relationship in the Old Testament. In contrast to *huios*, it not only designates physical descent but is a widespread expression of subordination, describing younger companions, pupils and members of a group, or membership of a people or profession.[57] A "son" (*bēn*) in biblical usage was a male descendant, including those beyond the first generation (e.g., Gen 31:28; Exod 12:24).[58] "Son" is also a generic name for children, and is sometimes used to categorize groups—e.g., an entire nation, male and female ("sons of Israel," Gen 32:32); a community defined by a geographical designation ("sons of Zion," Ps 149:2); or a class or profession ("the sons of the prophets," 2 Kgs 2:3).[59]

In the extended sense, "son" (*bēn*) was used in a number of ways in the Old Testament *to express belonging to God.* First, "sons of God" can refer to members of the heavenly assembly (Job 1:6; Ps 89:5–6 [6–8]) or angels (Dan 3:25). Second, "son(s) of God" is used to refer to God's people. God calls Israel his firstborn son (Exod 4:22), and Israel's king is also called God's son (2 Sam 7:14; Ps 2:7).[60] The role of the son was of great importance in the ancient biblical social order. The standard inheritance pattern for transference of property was from father to son, with distinct significance given to the firstborn (e.g., Gen 27:19; Deut 21:15–17).[61]

When we come to the New Testament, and Matthew's Gospel in particular, the term and concept of "son" plays an important christological role. The most common Greek term for "son" is *huios*, which occurs eighty-nine times in eighty-one verses in Matthew's Gospel. In its most basic sense, fifteen times *huios* refers to human sons of

54. Bockmuehl, "Gospels on the Presence of Jesus," 87.

55. Michael Green, *The Message of Matthew: The Kingdom of Heaven*, BST (Downers Grove, IL: InterVarsity, 2000), 322–23.

56. Martin Hengel, *The Son of God: The Origin of Christology and the History of Jewish-Christian Religion*, trans. John Bowden (Philadelphia: Fortress, 1976), 21; W. von Martitz and Georg Fohrer, υἱός *TDNT* 8: 335–45, here 335–36.

57. Hengel, *Son of God*, 21.

58. For a helpful overview, see William D. Mounce, ed., *Mounce's Complete Expository Dictionary of Old and New Testament Words* (Grand Rapids: Zondervan, 2006), 667–70.

59. This varied usage of "son" is referred to in social scientific studies of Matthew's Gospel as "plurisignification." See Duling, *Marginal Scribe*, 93.

60. Hengel, *Son of God*, 21–22.

61. Robin Gallaher Branch and Lee E. Klosinski, "Son," *EDB* 1241.

human fathers (e.g., 7:9; 17:15) or the sons of Israel (27:9) or the male foal/son of a donkey (27:9). Three times *huios* refers to human sons of God (5:9, 45) or sons of the kingdom (13:38), while four times *huios* refers to human sons of the evil one (13:38) or sons of hell (23:15; cf. 23:31), evil sons of the kingdom who will be thrown into the outer darkness (8:12). One time, and this relates to our christological discussion, *huios* is used to describe Joseph, the legal father of Jesus, as "son of David" (1:20).

The most widespread use of *huios* in Matthew's Gospel, sixty-six times, is to specify some aspect of Jesus. In the opening verse Jesus is referred to as "son of David" and "son of Abraham" (1:1). This is the only time that Matthew refers to Jesus as "son of Abraham," but elsewhere nine times he refers to Jesus as "son of David." Three times in the opening chapter Jesus is referred to as Mary's son (1:21, 23, 25), and one time in a later incident Jesus is specified by the Nazareth townspeople as "the carpenter's son" (13:55). Besides the nine times that Jesus is specified as "son of David," the other two most prominent titles to refer to Jesus are "Son of Man" (thirty times) and "Son of God" (twenty-one times).

The most significant titles using "son" for understanding Matthew's christological perspective of Jesus Messiah are "son of David," "son of Abraham," "Son of God" and "Son of man." We briefly explore each of those expressions.

### 7.2.5 Son of David (*huios David*)

In the incipit to his Gospel (1:1), immediately following the expression Jesus Christ/Messiah, Matthew points to Jesus to indicate what kind of Messiah Jesus is: he is the son of David.[62] Matthew uses the name of the great king seventeen times, more than any other book of the New Testament. King David was the revered conquering warrior of Israel's history. But we will see that Jesus as the Son of David is quite different than what many in Israel were hoping for.

#### *7.2.5.1 Davidic Messiah (1:1)*

The wording "son of David" expresses a promised figure who would perpetuate David's throne, thereby pointing to Messiah's lineage and royal expectation: "Your house and your kingdom will endure forever before me; your throne will be established

62. For helpful overviews, see Lidija Novakovic, "Jesus as the Davidic Messiah in Matthew," *HBT* 19.2 (1997): 148–91; Charles E. Carlston and Craig A. Evans, *From Synagogue to Ecclesia: Matthew's Community at the Crossroads*, WUNT 334 (Tübingen: Mohr Siebeck, 2014), 8–23; Joshua W. Jipp, "The Son of David Who Saves His People from Their Sins: The Gospel of Matthew," in *The Messianic Theology of the New Testament* (Grand Rapids: Eerdmans, 2020), 39–91. For full-length treatments, see Hengel, *Son of God*; Lidija Novakovic, *Messiah, the Healer of the Sick: A Study of Jesus as the Son of David in the Gospel of Matthew*, WUNT 2/170 (Tübingen: Mohr Siebeck, 2003); Young S. Chae, *Jesus as the Eschatological Davidic Shepherd: Studies in the Old Testament, Second Temple Judaism, and in the Gospel of Matthew*, WUNT 2/216 (Tübingen: Mohr Siebeck, 2006); Ham, *The Coming King and the Rejected Shepherd*; Joel Willitts, *Matthew's Messianic Shepherd-King: In Search of 'The Lost Sheep of the House of Israel,'* BZNW 147 (Berlin: de Gruyter, 2007); Michael Vicko Zolondek, *We Have Found the Messiah: How the Disciples Help Us Answer the Davidic Messianic Question* (Eugene, OR: Pickwick, 2016); Zacharias, *Matthew's Presentation of the Son of David*.

forever" (see 2 Sam 7:11b–16). It naturally evoked images of a Messiah who would rule, and the expectation was that he would be a mighty warrior like David who would destroy Israel's enemies and reestablish the throne in Jerusalem and the kingdom of Israel like in the golden days of David.

The psalmist records that promise: "The LORD swore an oath to David, a sure oath he will not revoke: 'One of your own descendants I will place on your throne. If your sons keep my covenant and the statutes I teach them, then their sons will sit on your throne for ever and ever'" (Ps 132:11–12). The promise is basic to the prophetic predictions regarding the messianic kingdom. It explains how the messianic hope of a restored kingdom was seen to be a fulfillment of the divine promise to David and expresses the hope that finds its fulfillment in Jesus as the promised one.

The first-century BC Psalms of Solomon expresses a combined hope of son and king: "Behold, O Lord, and raise up unto them their king, the son of David, at the time you have foreseen, O God, to rule over Israel your servant" (Ps. Sol. 17:21). The Florilegium from the Qumran community, when commenting upon 2 Sam 7:12–14, says, "This refers to the 'branch of David', who will arise with the Interpreter of the law who will rise up in Zion in the last days" (4QFlor 1 I, 10–12).[63]

What kind of Messiah is Jesus? He is the Davidic Messiah.[64] The expression "son of David" occurs ten times in Matthew's Gospel in diverse ways to refer to the Davidic Messiah.[65] Jesus Messiah is the Son of David (1:1), who heals (9:27; 15:22; 20:30, 31; 21:14), who exorcises demons (12:23; 15:22–28), who enters Jerusalem (21:9, 15), called the city of David in the Old Testament (2 Sam 5:7), to pronounce judgment on the temple authorities and heal the blind and the lame (21:14), and who is the Son and Lord of King David (22:42, 45).[66] Jesus is the Davidic Messiah, but as we continue to explore Matthew's perspective, we will see that Jesus is a very different kind of Davidic Messiah than many in Israel were expecting.

### 7.2.5.1.1 Jesus's Genealogy in Matthew's Gospel

In the genealogy immediately following the incipit, Matthew demonstrates Jesus's legal claim to the throne of David (1:2–17). David's greater Son, the anticipated Davidic messianic king, has arrived with the birth of Jesus.[67] One of the most significant

63. The translation is from Florentino García Martínez and Eibert J. C. Tigchelaar, *The Dead Sea Scrolls: Study Edition*, 2 vols. (Leiden: Brill, 1997–1998), 1:354. For an overview, see Marinus de Jonge, "Messiah," *ABD* 4:777–88; for an evaluation of the concept, as well as explicit terminology, see Meadors, "'Messianic' Implications," 253–77.

64. See Brown and Roberts, *Matthew*, 303–5.

65. Matt 1:1, 20; 9:27; 12:23; 15:22; 20:30, 31; 21:9, 15; 22:42; and cf. 22:45. For a helpful, brief overview of Matthew's use of "son of David," see Stanton, "Messianism and Christology," 78–96. From a social-scientific perspective that is overall not as helpful, see Duling, "Matthew's Plurisignificant 'Son of David,' in Social-Scientific Perspective," in *Marginal Scribe*, 91–119.

66. Zacharias, *Matthew's Presentation of the Son of David*, passim.

67. Cf. 22:41–46; 2 Sam. 7:12–16; Pss 89:19–29, 35–37; 110:1–7; 132:11–12.

features of Matthew's record of the genealogy is the emphasis upon Jesus's kingly lineage. David is not simply the son of Jesse, as he is stated to be in Luke's genealogy (Luke 3:31–32), but is "David the king" (Matt 1:6), an explicit emphasis upon royalty in the genealogy of Jesus.[68] From here Matthew maintains an emphasis upon kingship, using the word "king" twenty-two times, more than any other book in the New Testament. Throughout his Gospel, Matthew maintains a focus upon Jesus as the "king of the Jews."[69]

#### 7.2.5.1.2 Matthew's View of Jesus's Messianic Identity

Matthew, however, has a view of Jesus's messianic identity that differs from what some were hoping for in the arrival of the Messiah. Some were hoping for worldwide victory through the king and the subjugation of the gentile nations through war.

Joshua Jipp argues that New Testament texts, including Matthew, go in a different direction. He remarks, "NT texts consistently read the Davidic kingship texts through the lens of the particular history of Jesus the Messiah, a history that the earliest Christians believed initiated God's kingdom through the particular life of one man's peace, justice, enemy-love, and crucifixion."[70] He states further, "NT texts reject a notion of God's kingdom coming through violence."[71] Jesus, the Davidic Messiah, will be much different than what many were hoping for in the arrival of the promised son of David.

The genealogy indicates that "the birth of Jesus the Messiah" (1:18) represents a confirmation of the prophecies to the house of David. This is authenticated by Matthew's use of the prophecy of Jesus's origins in Bethlehem (Mic 5:1–4). As Micah prophesied, so Matthew emphasizes, that Jesus is the ruler who will shepherd God's people. In Matthew's Gospel, Jesus is shown to be the divine Shepherd-King who seeks, saves, refines, and judges his flock (Matt 10:6; 14:14; 15:24, 32; 25:31–46).

This picture of an eschatological shepherd/ruler who will lead the flock of Israel with justice and compassion is similar to that found in Ezekiel (Ezek 34; cf. 37:24). Unlike the corrupt leaders in Ezekiel's day, Matthew presents Jesus as the divine Shepherd-King who sees the crowds and "had compassion on them, because they were harassed and helpless, like sheep without a shepherd" (9:36).[72] He is also the human shepherd-king who is struck, causing the sheep to be scattered (26:31; cf. Zech 13:7). But his vindication will lead to the regathering of the sheep. What are separate strands of hope in

68. P. Schreiner, *Matthew, Disciple and Scribe*, esp. 65–101.

69. See 2:2; 27:11, 29, 37, 42. This is likewise emphasized by the contrast with King Herod and his son Archelaus (2:1–23), the mention of the king in the parable (22:1–13), and the Son of Man seated as King on the throne on judgment day (25:31–46).

70. Jipp, *Messianic Theology*, 25.

71. Jipp, *Messianic Theology*, 25.

72. Blomberg, *New Testament Theology*, 345.

the Old Testament, a divine and human shepherd, are dramatically brought together in the New Testament in one person, Jesus Messiah, the son of David.[73]

Of the varied expectations of a coming Messiah, Jesus is the Davidic Messiah who shepherds his people.[74] But Matthew will also show Jesus the Davidic Messiah to be more.

### *7.2.5.2 The Healing/Exorcistic Davidic Messiah (9:27; 12:23; 15:22; 20:30, 31; 21:15)*

Matthew also emphasizes Jesus Messiah, the Son of David, to be the healing/exorcistic Son of David. Of the ten explicit occurrences of the title, at least six emphasize Jesus's healing and exorcism activities.[75] These include four instances of healing those who were blind (9:27; 12:22; 20:30–31; 21:14), one instance causing those who were mute to talk (12:22), one instance of healing the lame to be able to walk (21:14–15), two instances of exorcising those who were demon-possessed (12:22; 15:22), and one instance of healing a demon-possessed girl suffering terribly (15:22, 28). Some of these incidents are accounts of people with multiple ailments.

It is especially noticeable that almost every use of the title "son of David" in Matthew's recounting of Jesus's ministry is in direct connection with his healing and exorcism power, either requested (9:27; 15:22; 20:30, 31) or experienced (12:23; 21:15). This unexpected link between the title Son of David and Jesus's concern for the suffering and oppressed counters any triumphalistic notion of Jesus's messianic identity.[76] Jesus shifts messianic expectations of those within Israel from the political to the spiritual. Luz notes, "[Jesus] is a liberator of simple people, a liberator from disease and spiritual want."[77] And we can see that those who use the title "son of David" in Matthew's Gospel are predominantly people of no social, political, or theological importance.[78]

73. Andrew T. Abernethy and Gregory Goswell, *God's Messiah in the Old Testament: Expectations of a Coming King* (Grand Rapids: Baker Academic, 2020), 226–27.

74. See John Aranda Cabrido, *A Portrayal of Jesus in the Gospel of Matthew: A Narrative-Critical and Theological Study* (Lewiston, NY: Edwin Mellen, 2010).

75. Matthew 9:27; 12:23; 15:22; 20:30–31; 21:15. The occurrence of the title in 21:9 is in the broader context of healing in 21:14–16. For a very "creative" approach to Jesus as exorcist who is re-creative, providing deliverance from the limitations of evil powers, see Sean M. McDonough, *Christ as Creator: Origins of a New Testament Doctrine* (Oxford: Oxford University Press, 2009), esp. ch. 2.

76. France, *Matthew: Evangelist and Teacher*, 285–86.

77. Luz, *Theology of the Gospel of Matthew*, 71. This is in contrast to Baxter, "Missing Matthew's Political Messiah," 333–50, who contends that Matthew believed that national-political liberation was an integral part of Jesus's messianic mission and that Jesus will save his people from the political ramifications of their sins. This is somewhat similar to Andries G. Van Aarde ("ΙΗΣΟΥΣ, the Davidic Messiah, as Political Saviour in Matthew's History," in *Salvation in the New Testament: Perspectives on Soteriology*, ed. Jan G. Van Der Watt [Leiden: Brill, 2005], 7–31), who reads Matthew as a story that retells the "history" of how God sent Joshua from Egypt as Moses's successor to save Israel. God "heals" Israel through Jesus, God's Son, Israel's Davidic Messiah. As Messiah Jesus healed all of Israel; healing in this context is to be released from "political" stress (Van Aarde, "ΙΗΣΟΥΣ, The Davidic Messiah," 7). I would have to reject this reading because Van Aarde thus strips the literal healings of Jesus and turns them into socio-political phenomena.

78. France, *Matthew: Evangelist and Teacher*, 286.

### 7.2.5.2.1 The Two Blind Men Can See (9:27)

After healing the synagogue leader's daughter (9:22–26), two blind men understand Jesus's messianic identity, as they call out, "Have mercy on us, Son of David!" (9:27).[79] The messianic age promised to bring healing to the blind (Isa 29:18; 35:5; 42:7), which Jesus told John the Baptist was one of the signs that he indeed was the expected Coming One (Matt 11:5). In all of the Old Testament no healing of blindness was ever recorded,[80] and none of Jesus's followers is ever recorded to have healed the blind.[81] But Jesus's healing of the blind is one of the most frequent of his miracles,[82] which is an unduplicated sign of his messianic identity. These men have profoundly connected Jesus with the prophecies of the Son of David who would heal blindness (cf. 12:22–23; 21:14–15) and ask for the gift of messianic mercy that would heal them.

### 7.2.5.2.2 The Demon-Possessed Blind and Mute Man Can See and Talk (12:22)

The Sabbath controversies with the Pharisees (12:1–14) come to a head as a demon-possessed man who is blind and mute is brought to Jesus. Jesus heals the man, "so that he could both talk and see" (12:22). In this situation demon possession resulted in blindness and inability to speak, so as Jesus heals the man, he is exorcizing the demon. A similar situation occurs with the epileptic boy; when Jesus exorcises the demon, the boy is healed of the epilepsy (17:18).

The people are astonished at Jesus's healing of the blind and mute demoniac, so they exclaim, "Could this be the Son of David?" (12:23). The different sectarian groups had difficulty putting together all of the varied messianic promises of the Old Testament (e.g., prophet, priest, king). The common people ("crowds" *hoi ochloi*) especially seemed to focus on one strand of the prophecies. In their mind, because King David was a warrior, the messianic son of David would be a liberator. As Jesus heals by exorcising the demon, they are perplexed, and seem to be asking, "Could the coming Messiah be both a liberator and an exorcist?"

Although David was not considered a miracle worker, he is the only person recorded to have exorcised a demon in the Old Testament (1 Sam 16:14–23). Solomon, an ancient son of David (2 Sam 12:24–25; Prov 1:1; Eccl 1:1), is viewed in some Jewish literature as an exorcist (Testament of Solomon 1:1–130; Jos. *Ant.* 8.45–47). Some see a possible allusion here also to Solomon as the son of David, although the Jesus-link is most

79. Nolland, *Matthew*, 400, states, "We are clearly meant to take Son of David as a royal messianic designation."

80. In the deuterocanonical books, Tobit is cured of blindness with the gall of a fish by his son Tobias (Tobit 11:7–15).

81. The "scales" that fell from Saul's eyes when Ananias laid hands on him could be an exception, although this seems quite different, because Ananias did not pray for healing, but rather arrived as the conduit for the giving of the Holy Spirit (Acts 9:17–19).

82. Matthew 9:27–31; 12:22–23; 15:30–31; 20:30–34; 21:14–15.

directly to David himself.[83] The Son of David would bring a time of eschatological fulfillment, including the healing of all illness and exercising control over all the evil forces. It is perhaps stretching the crowds' understanding to comprehend that the gentle healing servant Messiah (8:17; 12:18–21) is indeed the Son of David who will shepherd his people and bring the time of covenantal peace (Ezek 34:23–31; 37:24–28).

#### 7.2.5.2.3 A Gentile Girl Suffering Terribly from Demon Possession Finds Relief (15:22)

A significant account of Jesus being called "Son of David" comes in the gentile region of Tyre and Sidon (15:21). Intriguingly, a gentile woman demonstrates familiarity with Jewish messianic tradition by calling Jesus "Son of David" and calling for his merciful, miraculous ministry of exorcism for her daughter. She may have been a God-fearer or proselyte to use such language, which demonstrates an exemplary Jewish faith.[84] Here the sole focus is on Jesus, the son of David, whom the woman is "addressing *as the Messiah of Israel* and . . . it is precisely from this one that she now expects healing/salvation."[85] A temple dedicated to Eshmun, a god of healing, was five kilometers northwest of Sidon, so this woman was quite likely familiar with the pagan deity. But Jesus's reputation has preceded him, and she comes to Jesus for her daughter's healing instead of Eshmun. She uses "Lord" three times in the interaction (15:22, 25, 27), probably as a title of great respect, but she is saying more than she realizes, and Matthew's readers would understand the full meaning of Jesus as the Lord of creation who controls illness and the demonic forces of evil.[86]

#### 7.2.5.2.4 Two Blind Men Can See (20:30–31; cf. Bartimaeus in Mark 10:46)

Jesus, now journeying to Jerusalem for his final days, encounters two more blind men. The blind men understand Jesus to be the "Son of David." The messianic age promised to bring healing to the blind (Isa 29:18; 35:5; 42:7), which Jesus told John the Baptist was one of the signs that he indeed was the expected one (Matt 11:2–6), so these blind men ask for the gift of messianic mercy that would heal their blindness. Jesus's healing ministry has been an exercise of his role as the messianic son of David and has been recognized as such by the physically blind but spiritually insightful.[87] Jesus continues to have compassion on those in greatest need, so he touches their eyes, and they are healed.

83. E.g., Witherington, *Matthew*, 245; passim. For discussion, see Dennis C. Duling, "Solomon, Exorcism, and the Son of David," *HTR* (1975): 235–52. Jiří Dvořáček also recently argues that the title "son of David" could have referred to Solomon, who in some Jewish literature was a great exorcist and healer. He attempts to establish how Matthew's portrait of the son of David as a merciful, messianic, healing king, in his wisdom, healings, and exorcisms, surpasses David's son Solomon: Jiří Dvořáček, *The Son of David in Matthew's Gospel in the Light of the Solomon as Exorcist Tradition*, WUNT 2/415 (Tübingen: Mohr Siebeck, 2016). This thesis appears to me to stretch too far the Matthean evidence.

84. Osborne, *Matthew*, 597; Nolland, *Matthew*, 632.

85. Konradt, *Matthew*, 240; his emphasis.

86. Osborne, *Matthew*, 598.

87. Nolland, *Matthew*, 828.

### 7.2.5.2.5 The Blind Can See and the Lame Can Walk in the Temple Area (21:14–15)

Matthew alone mentions the healings that Jesus performs in the temple after his disruption of the commercial practices, and the ensuing confrontation with the chief priests and the scribes (21:14–16). The blind and lame were restricted from full access to temple activities to symbolize the purity that was expected to be displayed in those approaching God (cf. Lev 21:18–19). The Qumran community employed these restrictions when prescribing the rules for admission to their covenantal fellowship (CD XV, 15–17). As Jesus heals the blind and the lame, he displays his authority to create purity in all those desiring to worship God, demonstrating that as the one who is greater than the temple (12:6), he fulfills the Old Testament prescriptions for cleansing that the temple practices required to come into the presence of God.[88]

Jesus's healing activities prompt children in the temple courts to mimic the chant "Hosanna to the Son of David" that they had heard earlier from the crowd during Jesus's dramatic entry into Jerusalem (21:9, 15). Jesus's actions in the temple in pronouncing judgment and then healing the blind and lame should have caused the religious authorities to acknowledge his messianic authority as the Messiah, the very Son of David the children innocently and unwittingly identify.[89]

But instead, the religious authorities become indignant at Jesus's challenge to their authority and agenda (21:15). They recognize that Jesus will be a threat to their positions of religious prominence. Jesus acknowledges the honor so unwittingly bestowed on him by the children, and links it to Ps 8:2, chiding the religious leaders for something they should have known if they truly knew the biblical witness. The psalmist applies the praise of children to God, but here the children are ascribing the praise to Jesus as the Son of David. Jesus acknowledges his messiahship in receiving the praise and goes beyond what even the children knew by receiving personally what was applicable in the psalm only to God (21:16).[90]

### *7.2.5.3 The Savior Davidic Messiah (21:7–16)*

Matthew also emphasizes Jesus Messiah, the Son of David, to be the Savior Son of David. Matthew does not distinguish between the various groups in attendance for Jesus's triumphal entry to Jerusalem, but narrates generally that the crowds shout out, "Hosanna," which is the transliteration of the Hebrew expression that means "O save" (cf. 2 Sam 14:4; 2 Kgs 6:26).

88. Schweizer, *Matthew*, 408.

89. Schnackenburg, *Matthew*, 203.

90. France, *Matthew*, NICNT, 302–3; Keener, *Matthew* (1999), 502–3.

### 7.2.5.3.1 A Different Kind of Savior

This draws the crowd to make a connection to the Hallel (Pss 113–118) sung during the Passover season, especially expressing the messianic hopes of Israel as voiced in Psalm 118:19–29 (esp. 118:25: "O Lord, save us"). They further cry out to Jesus as "Son of David" (Matt 21:9). Linked with the cry "Hosanna," the title "Son of David" is unmistakably messianic. The crowd acknowledges what Jesus has already stated in his fulfillment of Zech 9:9: he is the Davidic Messiah, whom they call upon to save them out of their oppression.[91]

Matthew narrates that the crowds respond generally to the question, "Who is this?" (21:10): "This is Jesus, the prophet from Nazareth in Galilee" (21:11). The answer indicates the mixed nature of those attending Jesus's entrance. Some in the crowd call him a prophet, which many in his ministry saw him to be (16:14; 21:46). This does not seem to imply that they understand him to be *the* eschatological Prophet of Moses's prophecy (Deut 18:15–18),[92] but rather the prophet who has been creating such a stir in Galilee, whose hometown was Nazareth. Others who have called out "Hosanna" to the "son of David" seem to expect Jesus to bring liberation as had the kings of ancient Israel and the Maccabees of more recent times.

But Jesus has undertaken a very different kind of "triumphal entry" than many among the crowd expected. Jesus will triumph over sin, bringing salvation to his people (Matt 1:21) through his righteous sacrifice on the cross that looms ahead. Many among the crowd could only think of physical and military liberation because of their oppression. They cry "Hosanna!" now but soon will see that Jesus is not bringing the freedom they desire, and will ultimately cry out, "Crucify him!" (27:22). Although the crowd gives great acclaim to the Son of David, Jesus knows why they were really welcoming him. He knows their nationalistic ambitions and fickleness.

### 7.2.5.3.2 Pronouncement of Judgment

As the son of David, Jesus enters the temple courts and drives out all who were buying and selling there. Overturning the tables of the money changers and the benches of those selling doves, he says, "It is written, . . . 'My house will be called a house of prayer,' but you are making it 'a den of robbers'" (21:12–13). This has often been called a "cleansing" of the temple, implying that Jesus is attempting to purify the temple from corrupt practices and restore it to proper usage as intended by God. While corrupt practices are certainly being rebuked, Jesus goes beyond cleansing to enact an intentionally symbolic act of judgment against the religious leadership of Israel.[93] Nolland refers to

91. See Ian J. Vaillancourt, "Psalm 118 and the Eschatological Son of David," *JETS* 62.4 (2019): 721–38.

92. Cf. John 6:14; 7:40, 52; Acts 3:22; 7:37.

93. France, *Matthew*, TNTC, 300–303; Morris, *Matthew*, 525–26; Davies and Allison, *Matthew*, 3:133–37; Sanders, *Jesus and Judaism*, 61–69.

this as "prophetic symbolism."[94] This is a dramatic statement on Jesus's authority over the purposes of the temple sacrificial practices, a statement which, with his impending crucifixion, will be fulfilled in his death, as is so dramatically announced by God in the tearing of the veil at his death (27:51).[95]

### *7.2.5.4 The Son and Lord Davidic Messiah (22:41–46)*

Matthew also emphasizes Jesus Messiah, the son of David, to be both the "Son" and "Lord." In Matthew's narrative of the Holy Week controversies, Jesus takes the initiative to press the debate in a critical direction. He goes on the offensive as he poses a question to the Pharisees. The Pharisees were the biblical experts of the day and were the most outspoken in their criticism of Jesus, since he had declared himself to be the authoritative interpreter of the Old Testament Scriptures (cf. 5:17–48). Jesus goes to the heart of the issue, challenging their ability to rightly interpret one of the most important messianic texts in the Old Testament. If they cannot rightly interpret this text, they cannot possibly rightly understand his identity. So, he prods them with a question, "What do you think about the Messiah? Whose son is he?" (22:41–42).[96]

This must have seemed like a simple question to the Pharisees, who answer, "The son of David" (22:42). This is the automatic reply, based on common knowledge that the prophesied Messiah was from the line of David.[97]

But Jesus presses them further to plumb the depths of their understanding of the true identity of the Messiah from the Old Testament prophecies. Specifically, he asks, "How is it then that David, speaking by the Spirit, calls him 'Lord'?" (22:43).

The Pharisees recognized this psalm as a messianic prophecy by David under the inspiration of the Holy Spirit.[98] In this passage David refers to the coming messianic ruler—his descendant, his "son"—as *kyrios*, "lord." Familial respect would not expect an older person, such as David, to refer to his offspring as "lord"; rather, the offspring, "son," should refer to David, his "father," as "lord." The LXX, which is almost verbatim to what Matthew records here, has *kyrios* in both instances of the word "Lord." The Hebrew, however, has Yahweh (*yhwh*) for the first and Adon (*ʾadoni*; lit., "my Lord") for the second occurrence of "Lord."[99]

In other words, Jesus uses their own Scriptures to point out the obvious implication of these combined points, which the Pharisees cannot avoid. "If then David calls him 'Lord,' how can he be his son?" (22:45). David says that the coming Messiah is one

94. Nolland, *Matthew*, 844.

95. Peterson, *Engaging with God*, 87–90.

96. For a defense of the historicity of the exchange, see Benjamin Sargent, *David Being a Prophet*, 92–128.

97. Matt 1:1; cf. 2 Sam 7:12–14; Ps 89:4; Isa 11:1, 10; Jer 23:5: cf. Ps. Sol. 17:21.

98. Barry C. Davis, "Is Psalm 110 a Messianic Psalm?," *BSac* 157 (2000): 160–73.

99. See Hagner, *Matthew 14–28*, 651.

who is not just his special human descendant but is his "Lord." This further indicates that his descendant bears a unique relationship to Yahweh—he is seated at the highest position of privilege and authority at the right hand of Yahweh, and Yahweh will subject all his enemies to him. This bears striking similarity to Daniel's prophecy where the Son of Man was led into the presence of the Ancient of Days and "was given authority, glory and sovereign power; all nations and peoples of every language worshiped him. His dominion is an everlasting dominion that will not pass away, and his kingdom is one that will never be destroyed" (Dan. 7:14).

The Messiah is more than what the Pharisees have understood the "son of David" to be. He is more than a human descendant of David. Jesus demonstrates that since the Pharisees do not adequately understand the Old Testament prophecies regarding the Messiah, they cannot possibly understand Jesus's identity. They did not understand the depth of the personal identity of the Messiah in relationship to Yahweh, so they cannot understand the relationship of Jesus to Yahweh. Messiah is identified as the Adon, the son of Yahweh, the "son of Man" who is given authority by the Ancient of Days (Dan 7:13–14), a dramatically deeper understanding of the son of David than the Pharisees have recognized.

Jesus prods the Pharisees to acknowledge what they should have understood all along. The Jews did not generally believe that the Messiah would be divine, but a human descendant of David. Jesus does not dismiss that common messianic expectation but goes beyond it. Jesus shows that as David called Messiah "Lord," he adds to the common expectation that Messiah is David's human descendant. In the Spirit, David declares that Messiah sustains a divine relationship to Yahweh as Lord seated at Yahweh's right side.[100] The question answered only partially by the Pharisees was answered fully earlier by Simon Peter: "You are the Messiah, the Son of the living God" (16:16).

Throughout Jesus's ministry, his relationship to God has been increasingly revealed and clarified. He is the unique Son of God (Matt 3:17; 4:3, 6; 10:32–33, 40; 11:27), a most amazing truth that his disciples have increasingly come to recognize (14:33). This had earlier formed the pinnacle of their understanding when Peter confessed that Jesus is the Christ, the son of David, but he is uniquely "the Son of the Living God" (16:16).

Jesus has given increasing clarification of his identity everywhere in these controversies. He has revealed clearly his identity and his authority. He now will rebuke the religious leaders severely in the series of "woes" (ch. 23) for not accepting him for who he has revealed himself to be, their long-anticipated Messiah, David's "son" and "Lord."

And, as we will explore below, as the Davidic Messiah he sustains a matchless relationship to Yahweh as the unique Son of God, who is the prophesied Son of man.

100. See also Craig A. Evans, *Mark 8:27–16:20*, WBC 34B (Nashville: Thomas Nelson, 2001), 272–75. For a helpful presentation of arguments that support a divine understanding in some OT texts related to the expectation of a future Davidic Messiah, see Markus Zehnder, "The Question of the 'Divine Status' of the Davidic Messiah," *BBR* 30.4 (2020): 485–514.

### 7.2.6 Son of Abraham (*huios Abraam*)

The incipit, which focuses on the "beginnings of Jesus Messiah, the son of David, the son of Abraham" (1:1), would have great relevance to a Jewish audience who were the recipients of the gospel that proclaimed that Jesus is the long-awaited Messiah, the fulfillment of the promises to King David that a son would sit on his throne forever (2 Sam 7:12–16). The incipit would have further relevance to that Jewish audience when seeing the fulfillment of the promises to the patriarch Abraham that his descendants would be a blessing also to the world (see Gen 12:1–3; 13:14–16; 15:4–12; 17:4–16).

In that light, the incipit would have great relevance to a gentile audience, who would recognize that they were included in the blessings of the gospel of Jesus Messiah as the "son of Abraham." Matthew mentions David here in the incipit and more than fifteen other times,[101] but he also mentions Abraham seven times in his Gospel (Matt 1:1, 2, 17; 3:9 [2x]; 8:11; 22:32). In tracing Jesus Messiah's ancestry not only to David but also to Abraham, Matthew holds a light of hope to the entire world. The covenant God made with Abraham established Israel as a chosen people, but it also was a promise that his line would be a blessing to all the nations (Gen 12:1–3; 22:18).[102] Carol Bakhos notes, "The significance of linking Jesus and Abraham cannot be overstated. Jesus Christ, seen by Christians as the fulfillment of God's promise of salvation for humankind, is understood here as the fulfillment of the covenantal promise, the seed of Abraham through whom all nations will be blessed."[103] Jesus is the fulfillment not only of the Davidic messianic covenant but also the Abrahamic covenant. As Matthew grounds the genealogy of Jesus in Abraham, it relates Jesus to the father of the Jews.[104] Jesus is the Jewish Messiah and the Savior of all the nations as the physical and spiritual descendant of Abraham.[105]

Matthew's opening verse gives an important clue to the overall purpose and perspective that he will take in the writing of his Gospel. It would have had special meaning for those with a Jewish background, attempting both to awaken the faith of Jews and to strengthen the faith of Jewish-Christians in Jesus as the "Messiah," the "son of David," the heir to the promises of Israel's throne through King David. But additionally, we can see in the heading that this Gospel is also intended to awaken and to strengthen the faith of those from a gentile background. Gentiles and gentile Christians would

101. Matthew 1:1, 6, 17, 20; 9:27; 12:3, 23; 15:22; 20:30, 31; 21:9, 15; 22:42, 43, 45.

102. See, e.g., Carroll, "Blessing the Nations," 35–51.

103. Carol Bakhos, *The Family of Abraham: Jewish, Christian, and Muslim Interpretations* (Cambridge, MA: Harvard University Press, 2014), 65.

104. Leroy Huizenga speculates that Isaac might be in view here as the promised son of Abraham representing the covenant. If that is Matthew's intention, then right from the beginning of this Gospel messianic expectation is joined with a divinely ordained sacrificial death; see Leroy A. Huizenga, *The New Isaac: Tradition and Intertextuality in the Gospel of Matthew*, NovTSup 131 (Leiden: Brill, 2009). Huizenga explores well the extrabiblical material regarding the relationship of Isaac as the promised son of Abraham, but the argument from silence regarding such a role for Isaac in Matthew's Gospel weakens this theory.

105. Bakhos, *Family of Abraham*, 65–66. For a brief, broad perspective of the biblical Abrahamic theme, see James M. Hamilton, "Seed of the Woman and the Blessing of Abraham," *TynBul* 58.2 (2007): 253–73.

find tremendous hope in seeing that as the "son of Abraham" Jesus brings fulfillment to the promises to all the nations of the world, because he is the heir to the universal covenantal blessing established through the patriarch.[106]

Consequently, the ancestry of Jesus serves at the very beginning as an indication of an important key to interpreting this Gospel. Matthew emphasizes the way in which Jesus's ministry brought fulfillment of God's covenant to the particular people of Israel (e.g., Matt 10:6; 15:24) but also brought fulfillment of God's promise to bring universal hope to all the nations (cf. 8:5–13; 21:43). This theme of promise to all the nations will become increasingly pronounced in Matthew's Gospel and will come to a climax in the concluding commission (cf. 28:18–20).

### *7.2.6.1 The Son of Abraham as the Coming One (3:10)*

John the Baptist clarifies what he believes will occur with the arrival of the kingdom of heaven: (1) it will bring wrath on those who do not repent (3:8–10); and (2) it will be inaugurated with the arrival of the Coming One, with his baptism of the Holy Spirit and fire (3:11–12). The coming of the kingdom of heaven will be accompanied by the wrath of God and the fire of eternal punishment (3:8, 10). Those who respond to John's message and repent will escape God's wrath. But it must be an individual's personal response to God; one's religious or ethnic heritage to Abraham as father will not help. Jesus Messiah, the Coming One, who is the true son of Abraham, has opened the door to the kingdom of heaven to all who truly repent.

To the Pharisees and Sadducees, the Baptist makes clear that it does not matter that they had religious credentials as official leaders in Israel. It does not matter that they had ethnic credentials as ones born under the covenant made by God to the people of Israel through their forefather Abraham. They must come to God as repentant individuals without prior religious claims to advantage with God. This is therefore not a call solely for those living in blatant sin, as if repentance was only for "backsliders" or the "marginal." It is a call of repentance for all in Israel, including the religious leaders. Unfortunately, religious activity and pedigree can often blind a person to the deficiency of his or her own life before God.

The Baptist is not attempting to subvert the official leadership of Judaism by publicly ridiculing them. Rather, he is calling the leadership to their proper responsibility as examples for the nation. Of all people, they should be the ones who honestly and openly prepare their hearts for the coming of the Messiah. They have had the privilege of studying Scripture more carefully. They should have been the first to prepare themselves to receive kingdom life. Instead, they will receive judgment.

106. Abraham is the father of the three traditions, Judaism, Christianity, and Islam. For a helpful discussion of the unifying yet divisive figure of Abraham in each of these traditions, see Bakhos, *Family of Abraham*, passim.

### *7.2.6.2 The Coming One and Wrath (3:10)*

John the Baptist fully expects that the axe of the judgment of God is quickly to be laid at the dead wood that does not bear the life and the fruit of the kingdom of heaven. And the expected coming Davidic messianic deliverer,[107] to whom John gives public testimony, will wield that axe. Here we get to the core of John's ministry. He did not come simply to gain a following. John came to point ahead and beyond himself to another. John had a powerful place in God's history of salvation, but he knew that it was only preparatory to the main event. Calling the nation to repentance was not the main issue. The main event was the appearance of the one who would actually inaugurate God's kingdom on earth. Although there is continuity between their messages and ministry, John emphasized especially the contrast between himself and the Coming One. That contrast is seen in the Coming One's identity: Jesus Messiah is both the Son of David and the Son of Abraham, who announces the arrival of the kingdom of heaven and an open invitation to enter the kingdom.

## 7.2.7 Son of God (*huios tou theou*)

The title "Son of God" is a powerful designation in the New Testament to reveal Jesus Messiah's true identity.[108] Adam Winn states that "'Son of God' is perhaps the most well-known title for Jesus both inside and outside the church, and arguably it is the most important christological title in the NT."[109] It is no less significant in Matthew's Gospel. The expression bears witness to a bond that characterizes the relationship between Jesus and God the Father and the work of the Holy Spirit throughout Matthew's narrative. Geerhardus Vos indicates that there are a small group of statements in Matthew's Gospel that give us a glimpse of the relation existing between Jesus Messiah's deity and his redemptive function in the incarnate state. "It is the name Son of God which holds these two aspects in his life, the eternal aspect and the temporal aspect, together in a common designation."[110] We will explore that below once we have considered some of the background to the designation son of God in the ancient world.

### *7.2.7.1 Son of God in the Ancient World*

Jesus's unique sonship is antithetical to concepts of sonship popular in the ancient world.[111] In Hellenism, people believed a man could be a "son of the gods" in many ways.

In mythology, cohabitation of a god such as Zeus with a woman could produce

107. For a thorough analysis of the messianic implications, see Richard J. Bauckham, "The Messianic Interpretation of Isa. 10:34 in the Dead Sea Scrolls, 2 Baruch and the Preaching of John the Baptist," *DSD* 2.2 (1995): 202–16.

108. Matthew 2:15; 3:17; 4:3, 6; 8:29; 11:27 [3x]; 14:33; 16:16, 17; 17:5; 21:37 [2x], 38; 22:2; 24:36; 26:63; 27:40, 43, 54; 28:19.

109. Adam Winn, "Son of God," *DJG*[2] 886.

110. Geerhardus Vos, *The Self-Disclosure of Jesus: The Modern Debate About the Messianic Consciousness*, ed. Johannes G. Vos, 2nd ed. (1926; repr., Phillipsburg, NJ: P&R, 2002), 187.

111. "Son of God," *TBD* 1212.

offspring imagined to be superhuman. In medicine, a physician was called "son of Asclepius," the Greco-Roman god of medicine. The expression "son of God" was related to extraordinarily gifted men—miracle workers, healers, or wise men—grouped under the general designation of *theios aner*, or "divine man." A person with mysterious powers or qualities was given the title or reputation of "divine man."[112] In politics, generals and emperors were given high honor of being called a son of god in the cult of Roman emperor worship. The Greco-Roman world bestowed the title Son of God on Caesar.[113]

The expression for Jesus, *theou huios*, unique to Matthew among NT writers, exactly parallels the two-word "son of god" formulas found in the Greek titulature of Augustus, Tiberius, Nero, Titus, and Domitian. The Roman imperial formula *theou huios* designating the emperor in the imperial cult as "son of god" was found on inscriptions in highly visible locations throughout the empire. It was also found on legends on coins of the Matthean community. For the disciples of Jesus addressed by Matthew in his Gospel, "the Matthean formula θεοῦ υἱός [*theou huios*] would have evoked not only an awareness that Jesus had been given the same title as the emperor but also the recognition that the θεοῦ υἱός [*theou huios*] whose Father is 'Lord of heaven and earth' (Matt 11,25) is not the emperor but Jesus."[114]

### *7.2.7.2 Son/s of God in the Old Testament and Judaism*

In the Old Testament, certain men before the days of Noah (Gen 6:1–4), "the angels" or "heavenly beings" including Satan (Job 1:6; 2:1; 38:7), and other "heavenly beings" (Pss 29:1; 82:6; 89:6) are called "sons of the Most High" or "sons of God." These "sons of God" are inferior to God. Apparently, God has a council or cabinet of these "sons of God" or "holy ones" (see 1 Kgs 22:19; Jer 23:18, 22; Ps 89:5–7), who serve as messengers to carry out his orders. Not every one of them is good because 1 Kings 22:20–23 speaks of a "spirit" willing to be a lying spirit in the mouths of all Ahab's prophets. Satan was among them or perhaps even their leader.[115]

Several Old Testament passages call God the "father" of Israel (Deut 32:6; Isa 64:8; Jer 31:9), and others refer to Israel or Ephraim as God's "son" (Exod 4:22–23; Jer 31:9; Hos 11:1). The people of Israel are called God's sons and daughters (Deut 32:19; Isa 43:6; Hos 1:10).[116] Israel as a people was the chosen son of God. This "corporate sonship" became the basis of Israel's redemption from Egypt: "This is what the LORD says: Israel is my firstborn son" (Exod 4:22; cf. Jer 31:9).

112. Hengel, *Son of God*, 22–33; "Son of God," *BEB* 1981; Walter L. Liefeld, "The Hellenistic 'Divine Man' and the Figure of Jesus in the Gospels," *JETS* 16.4 (1973): 195–205.

113. Robert L. Mowery, "Son of God," *EDB* 1241.

114. Robert L. Mowery, "Son of God in Roman Imperial Titles and Matthew," *Bib* 83 (2002): 100–110, here 110.

115. Robert L. Alden, *Job*, NAC 11 (Nashville: Broadman & Holman, 1993), 53.

116. Mowery, "Son of God," 1241.

Corporate sonship was the context for personal sonship in the divine affirmation of David as king and firstborn (Ps 89:27–29): "I will be his father, and he will be my son" (2 Sam 7:14; cf. 1 Chr 17:13; 22:10; 28:6). David's "adoptive sonship" was by divine declaration: "I will proclaim the LORD's decree: He said to me, 'You are my son; today I have become your father'" (Ps 2:7).

This declaration of adoptive sonship was "the prophetic prototype of the 'essential' sonship of Jesus, David's royal son (Matt 3:17; Mark 1:11; Luke 3:22; Acts 13:33; Heb 1:5; 5:5)."[117] Other messianic prophecies ascribe divine names to the Davidic Messiah: "Immanuel" (Isa 7:13, 14), "Mighty God, Everlasting Father" (Isa 9:6, 7). Matthew indicates that these prophecies find fulfillment in Jesus (Matt 1:23; 21:4–10; 22:41–45).[118]

Intertestamental Jewish sources call the angels sons of God (Wis 5:5)[119] and identify the suffering righteous man as God's son (Wis 2:16–18;[120] Sir 4:10[121]).[122] The first-century BC Psalms of Solomon express a combined hope of son and king: "See, Lord, and raise up for them their king, the son of David, to rule over your servant Israel in the time known to you, O God" (Pss. Sol. 17:21).[123]

Texts from Qumran provide important Palestinian Jewish background for the titles "Son of God" and "Son of the Most High" (cf. 4QFlor 1 I, 11–13; 1QSa II, 11).[124] The Florilegium from the Qumran community, when commenting upon 2 Sam 7:12–14, says,

> And YHWH de[clares] to you that he will build you a house. I will raise up your seed after you and establish the throne of his kingdom [forev]er. I will be a father to him and he will be a son to me. This (refers to the) "branch of David," who will arise with the Interpreter of the law who [will rise up] in Zi[on in] the last days. (4QFlor 1 I, 10–12 [Martínez and Tigchelaar])[125]

And especially the debated Aramaic text 4QapocrDan ar I 7–9; II 1–3,[126] which says,

---

117. "Son of God," 1212.

118. "Son of God," *TBD* 1212.

119. "Why have they been numbered among the children of God? And why is their lot among the holy ones?" (NRSVue)

120. "For if the righteous man is God's child, he will help him and will deliver him from the hand of his adversaries" (Wis 2:18, NRSVue).

121. "Be a father to orphans, and be like a husband to their mother; you will then be like a son of the Most High, and he will love you more than does your mother" (NRSVue).

122. Mowery, "Son of God," 1241.

123. R. B. Wright, trans., "Psalms of Solomon," in *The Old Testament Pseudepigrapha*, 2 vols., ed. James H. Charlesworth (Garden City, New York: Doubleday, 1985), 2:667.

124. Mowery, "Son of God," 1241.

125. Florentino García Martínez and Eibert J. C. Tigchelaar, eds., *The Dead Sea Scrolls Translated: The Qumran Texts in English*, 2nd ed. (Grand Rapids: Eerdmans, 1996), 136. For an overview, see de Jonge, "Messiah," 4:777–88; for an evaluation of the concept, as well as explicit terminology, see Meadors, "'Messianic' Implications," 253–77; Adela Yarbro Collins and John J. Collins, *King and Messiah as Son of God: Divine, Human, and Angelic Messianic Figures in Biblical and Related Literature* (Grand Rapids: Eerdmans, 2008), 65–74; Tucker S. Ferda, "Naming the Messiah: A Contribution to the 4Q246 'Son of God' Debate," *DSD* 21.2 (2014): 150–75. For a dissenting voice, see Joseph A Fitzmyer, *A Wandering Aramean: Collected Aramaic Essays*, SBLMS 25 (Missoula, MT: Scholars Press, 1979), 102–7.

126. 4QapocrDan ar, the Aramaic Apocryphon (or Apocalypse) of Daniel, is commonly referred to as the "Son of God" text.

> and he will be great over [ . . . ] the earth [ . . . ] they will do, and all will serve [ . . . ] great will he be called and he will be designated by his name . . . . He will be called son of God, and they will call him son of the Most High. Like the sparks of a vision, so will their kingdom be. They will rule several years over the earth and crush everything. (Martínez and Tigchelaar)

Joseph Fitzmyer notes the debated identity of this "Son of God." Some suggest it is an antichrist, others an eschatological savior of heavenly character; still others suggest it is collective, equivalent to the Jewish people. Others suggest that the titles are those of a Messiah.[127] Hengel muses that it is possible the riddle of the identity of this Son of God may never be satisfactorily solved. But he goes on to say, "However, it makes one thing clear, that the title 'Son of God' was not completely alien to Palestinian Judaism."[128]

#### *7.2.7.3 Son of God in Matthew's Gospel*

The expression "Son of God" is a commanding designation in Matthew's Gospel to reveal Jesus Messiah's true nature and identity.[129] The expression throughout Matthew's narrative indicates the relationship between Jesus and God the Father. In Matthew's Gospel Jesus refers to himself as the Son of the Father and to God as his Father, and Jesus is declared by others to be the Son of God. Stanley Porter and Bryan Dyer state, "The evidence is overwhelming that Jesus and others believed from the outset that he was the Son of God."[130]

Nine times Matthew explicitly uses the title "Son of God" (*huios tou theou*), more than twice the four times the expression occurs in Mark's Gospel (Mark 1:1; 3:11; 5:7; 15:39). Luke has the expression seven times (Luke 1:32, 35; 4:3, 9, 41; 8:28; 22:70), and John eight times (John 1:34, 49; 3:18; 10:36; 11:4, 27; 19:7; 20:31).[131]

The expression "Son of God" in Matthew's Gospel can be a profession of faith in Jesus by his own disciples (Matt 14:33; 16:16) or by witnesses of his death (27:54), or a declaration by his enemies or skeptics: the devil (4:3, 6), demons (8:29), the high priest (26:63), or mockers at the cross (27:40, 43). At least another twelve times Matthew refers to Jesus as the "Son" (*huios*) in relationship to the Father, whether expressed by the Father from heaven (3:17; 17:5) or by the Father in a fulfillment scriptural context

127. Joseph A. Fitzmyer, "Aramaic Apocalypse," *EDSS*, 1:51. See also Fitzmyer, "4Q246: The 'Son of God' Document from Qumran," *Bib* 74 (1993): 153–74.

128. Hengel, *Son of God*, 45.

129. For the development of the theme "Son of God" in Matthew, see Carlston and Evans, *From Synagogue to Ecclesia*, 48–59; France, *Matthew: Evangelist and Teacher*, 292–98; Davies and Allison, *Matthew*, 1:339–40; Luz, *Matthew*, 1:144–46; Blomberg, *New Testament Theology*, 348–49; Turner, *Matthew*, 34–35; Donald J. Verseput, "The Role and Meaning of the 'Son of God' Title in Matthew's Gospel," *NTS* 33.4 (1987): 532–56.

130. Stanley E. Porter, and Bryan R. Dyer, *Origins of New Testament Christology: An Introduction to the Traditions and Titles Applied to Jesus* (Grand Rapids: Baker Academic, 2023), 88–89.

131. Graeme Goldsworthy, *The Son of God and the New Creation*, SSBT (Wheaton, IL: Crossway, 2016), 28; David L. Bartlett, *Christology in the New Testament*, Core Biblical Studies (Nashville: Abingdon, 2017), 29–32.

(2:15), or by Jesus to refer to himself (11:27 [3x]; 24:36; 28:19) or by Jesus to refer to himself in parables (21:37 [2x], 38; 22:2).

A generation ago, a significant group of Matthean scholars contended that the preeminent title in Matthew's Gospel was "Son of God." A leading figure was the influential Jack Dean Kingsbury, for whom "'Son of God' is the central christological title of Matthew."[132] In his seminal study, *Matthew: Structure, Christology, Kingdom*, Kingsbury works through Matthew's Gospel attempting to establish his thesis, studying every title and activity of Jesus in context.[133] Kingsbury's influence was significant at that time, and continues to this day. In his recent historical, literary, and theological introduction to the Gospel of Matthew, entitled *The Gospel of the Son of God*, David Bauer claims that, "Of all the christological titles Matthew employs, Son of God is the most central."[134] Carlston and Evans concur: "The central Christological title for Matthew seems to be, as Kingsbury rightly argues, the Son of God."[135]

Most scholars would agree that Son of God and related expressions are highly significant in Matthew's unfolding picture of Jesus. R. T. France states, "Few are likely to quarrel with the assertion that the presentation of Jesus as the Son of God is central to Matthew's christological enterprise."[136] France emphasizes that the titles of Jesus give indicators of who Jesus is, yet they must be supplemented by the narratives and other indicators of Jesus's life and ministry to rightly understand who he is and what is his mission. He states, "To agree that [Son of God] is a central concept is not necessarily to accept that it dominates all other themes and titles."[137]

An early critic of Kingsbury's thesis was David Hill, who states, "No rationale is provided for the view that one christological title needs to be understood as 'most exalted,' 'foremost,' 'principal' or 'preeminent' . . . , yet this seems to serve as a methodological presupposition of the investigation."[138] Hill does not intend to dispute the prominence of the "Son of God" title in Matthean Christology, "but to question the accuracy and adequacy of Kingsbury's claim that 'Son of God' has such primacy in Matthew that all other christological themes and titles require to be regarded as secondary to it or as subsumed under it."[139]

Donald Senior contends that titles, events, and themes combine, with no one title, theme, or event as preeminent or able to adequately communicate the richness and depth of Jesus's true identity. He states, "Matthew presents Jesus as a figure whose divine authority and mysterious presence goes beyond any fixed titles or categories."[140]

132. Kingsbury, *Matthew: Structure, Christology, Kingdom*, 40.

133. Kingsbury, *Matthew: Structure, Christology, Kingdom*, 40–122.

134. Bauer, *Gospel of the Son of God*, loc. 4177, Kindle.

135. Carlston and Evans, *From Synagogue to Ecclesia*, 48.

136. France, *Matthew: Evangelist and Teacher*, 292.

137. France, *Matthew: Evangelist and Teacher*, 292–93n37.

138. David Hill, "Son and Servant: An Essay on Matthean Christology," *JSNT* 6 (1980): 2–16; here 4.

139. Hill, "Son and Servant," 4.

140. Senior, *What Are They Saying About Matthew?*, 87. Similarly, see the discussion in Leim, *Matthew's Theological Grammar*, 176–77n2.

With that caveat in mind, I affirm a central place that the title Son of God has in Matthew's Gospel, yet it must also be studied in the light of other titles, themes, and events in Matthew's narrative.

We now turn to see how Matthew unfolds this magnificent title, Son of God.

Jesus is uniquely God's Son by way of conception (1:21–23), as is fulfilled in Jesus's return from Egypt (2:15), reiterated by the Father at Jesus's baptism (3:17), challenged by the devil at the temptations (4:3, 6), and acknowledged by demons who are about to be exorcised (8:29). Throughout Matthew's narrative Jesus continually lays claim to a unique relationship to his heavenly Father.[141] This also points back to the profound prophecy of David's line, "I will be his father, and he will be my son" (2 Sam 7:14), which spoke immediately of Solomon, but also of the future messianic line. The successor to the line was to be God's Son, as the Old Testament and later Jewish writings reveal. Psalm 2, one of the grand royal psalms that speaks of the anointing and coronation of the Lord's anointed, the Davidic king, declares, "I will proclaim the decree of the LORD: He said to me, "You are my Son; today I have become your Father" (Ps 2:7; cf. 89:27).

The importance of the title in Matthew's Gospel is seen not only in its explicit use (e.g., Matt 8:29; 14:33; 16:16; cf. 3:17 and 17:5) but also where it is implied: e.g., "'The virgin will conceive and give birth to a son, and they will call him Immanuel' (which means 'God with us')" (1:23). Jesus refers to God as his Father some twenty-three times in Matthew, fifteen of which are unique to this Gospel. Peter confesses Jesus as "the Christ, the Son of the living God" (16:16), the most exalted title in Matthew. The confession is made only by believers (except where its intent is blasphemous) and only by revelation (11:27; 16:7; cf. 13:11). The Fourth Gospel makes explicit the ontological sonship of Jesus, while Matthew assumes it as the foundation of the relationship. Jesus is the divine Son of the heavenly Father.

In Matthew's Gospel, Jesus's identity as the Son of God has a remarkable fullness as it is revealed in four distinct ways: covenant sonship, messianic sonship, incarnate sonship, and preexistent, personal sonship.[142]

#### 7.2.7.3.1 Covenant Sonship

The first aspect of Jesus Messiah's sonship is his *covenant sonship*. Covenant sonship focuses on Jesus living his earthly life in a positive covenant relationship to God as his heavenly Father. Jesus shares sonship with all the children of God, because God pronounces through Moses to his covenant people this identity: "You are the children

141. Matthew 7:21; 10:32–33; 11:25–27; 12:50; 15:13; 18:35; 20:23; 24:36; 25:34; 26:39, 42; 26:53; 28:19.

142. A similar fourfold emphasis is in the influential work of early last century by one of the Princeton biblical theologians, Geerhardus Vos, in his *Self-Disclosure of Jesus*, 141–42, 191–94. See also France, *Matthew: Evangelist and Teacher*, 292; Hengel, *Son of God*, 57–83; "Son of God," *BEB* 1981–83.

of the LORD your God . . . you are a people holy to the LORD your God. Out of all the peoples on the face of the earth, the LORD has chosen you to be his treasured possession" (Deut 14:1–2).

In this sense, Jesus is the fulfillment of the covenant people of Israel. When recounting the infant Jesus's return from Egypt with his family, Matthew states, "And so was fulfilled what the Lord had said through the prophet: 'Out of Egypt I called my son'" (Matt 2:15). Here Matthew interprets Hosea 11:1 as fulfilled in Jesus's young life: "When Israel was a child, I loved him, and out of Egypt I called my son." This interpretation depends on Matthew's "assumption that Jesus is God's 'Son' in a unique way that simultaneously associates him closely with God as Father as well as with Israel, the national 'son' to God (cf. Exod 4:22)."[143]

The incipit (Matt 1:1), the ancestry of Jesus (1:2–17), the conception narrative (1:18–25), and the infancy scene (2:1–23) serve at the very beginning of the Gospel of Matthew as an indication of an important key to interpreting this Gospel: the interplay of "particularism" and "universalism."[144] By "particularism" we understand that Matthew emphasizes that Jesus's life and ministry brings fulfillment of God's covenantal promises through Moses and David to the particular people of Israel (Exod 19–24; 2 Sam 7). By "universalism" we mean that Matthew also emphasizes that Jesus's life and ministry brings to fulfillment God's covenantal promises through Abraham (Gen 12:1–3; 22:18) to produce universal hope for all peoples (cf. Matt 24:14; 28:19).

Jesus's life exhibited a perfect relation to God and example for humanity in that he could both pray "My Father" (Matt 26:39) and also teach his disciples to pray "Our Father" (6:9). The way that Jesus uses "*my* Father" (11:27) to address his heavenly Father is exceptional because Jesus is the unique Son (cf. 3:17). But by calling his disciples to share in the kingdom of heaven, they now have entered a relationship with his Father as well. This image is prevalent throughout the Sermon on the Mount.[145] He is "*our* Father," expressing the relationship Jesus's disciples have to one another, members of one family. As covenant children Jesus's disciples share the same Father with Jesus Messiah, which means he is our covenant brother (12:49–50).

#### *7.2.7.3.1.1 Covenant Obedience*

The baptism of Jesus by John the Baptist brings with it a voice from heaven, "This is my Son, whom I love; with him I am well pleased" (3:17). We will discuss this below with reference to Jesus's messianic identity, but here we see that, as Jesus is obedient to be baptized to "fulfill all righteousness," he pleases his heavenly Father (3:15–17).

143. Blomberg, *Theology*, 349.

144. See Hagner, *Matthew*, 1:lxvi–lxviii; Paschke, *Particularism and Universalism*, esp. chs. 1–4.

145. Cf. 5:16, 45, 48; 6:26, 33; 7:11. Cf. "sons of God" (5:9) and "sons of your Father who is in heaven" (5:45) (ESV).

Luz notes that the Son of God is for Matthew not only the one who was revealed from heaven (cf. 2:15; 16:16; 17:5), but he is especially the obedient one who subjects himself to God's will. It is the obedient Son of God who gives the whole Gospel the christological frame, from Jesus's baptism (3:13–17), to the temptations that follow immediately (4:1–11), to the end of the passion narrative, where Matthew presents once more the same interpretation of Jesus's sonship with God the Father (27:43; cf. 27:54). Jesus is the obedient and humble one.[146] Hans-Christian Kammler pursues the same theme. He emphasizes that in the temptation story and also in the baptismal scene, the obedience of Jesus is not given an *ethical-paradigmatic* meaning. Rather, both texts are concerned with the ***unique***, ***soteriological*** obedience of the Son of God to the mission entrusted to him by the Father.[147]

The standard of covenantal obedience required of God's people Israel was never attained in the Old Testament storyline. Matthew articulates the story of Jesus in contrast to Israel, using "Son of God" as a primary means for conveying an asymmetrical correspondence. Matthew demonstrates that Jesus fulfills God's design for Israel, and in so doing is able to mediate his sonship to his disciples and enable their own obedience. Jesus, the obedient Son of God, grants the privilege of sonship also to his disciples, who are therefore called to follow in his path of filial obedience.[148] Brandon Crowe thus concludes, "The obedience of Jesus as the fulfillment of God's requirements for Israel thereby enables those who are unable themselves to 'fulfill all righteousness' to be part of God's family through the Son who has proven obedient on their behalf."[149]

#### *7.2.7.3.1.2 Jesus's Disciples as Sons of the Father*

Jesus's disciples have been called for the purpose of being the light of the world: "Let your light shine before others, that they may see your good deeds and glorify your Father in heaven" (5:16). Jesus's disciples cannot be hidden, for their very nature, the kingdom life within them, is everyday living testimony to those in the world who do not yet have that light-life. Their good works are produced by the light-life from God, not of their own making, because those who see them in action will glorify their Father in heaven, not them (cf. the motive of the religious leaders in 6:1). The title "Father" is used in Matthew now for the first time, introducing the special relationship that exists between God and Jesus's disciples. Jesus has been declared to be the beloved Son (3:17),

146. Luz, *Matthew 1–7*, 144. See also Oscar Cullmann, *The Christology of the New Testament*, trans. S. Guthrie and C. Hall, rev. ed. (Philadelphia: Westminster, 1963), 272–305.

147. Hans-Christian Kammler, "Sohn Gottes und Kreuz: Die Versuchungsgeschichte Mt 4,1–11 im Kontext des Matthäusevangeliums," *ZThK* 100.2 (2003): 163–86, here 184.

148. For full-length treatments of the theme of obedience and sonship, and also its implications for discipleship to Jesus, see Brandon D. Crowe, *The Obedient Son: Deuteronomy and Christology in the Gospel of Matthew*, BZNW 188 (Berlin: de Gruyter, 2012), passim, here 229–30; Crowe, *Last Adam*, esp. ch. 3.

149. Crowe, *Obedient Son*, 230.

and now those who have received the kingdom light-life are children of the heavenly Father as well (cf. John 1:7–13).[150]

Jesus's disciples possess kingdom life, which produces good deeds from a changed life. Bearing the light of the gospel in both message and life will bring people to know that the kingdom of heaven truly is in the world, and they will glorify their heavenly Father. The Beatitudes hinted at this direction, but the metaphors of "salt" and "light" are the first explicit indication that the presence of the kingdom produces changed lives. Changed lives, including bearing the life of the gospel through good works, are by-products and evidence of kingdom life in a disciple.

#### 7.2.7.3.2 Messianic Sonship

The second aspect of Jesus's sonship is his *official messianic sonship*. As the representative of God, the Messiah bears the title of Son of God. In this official sense, God declared to David that his messianic descendant would be the son to him. Jesus is the Father's Son and representative, whose earthly mission is to establish the kingdom of God. At his baptism, he began his mission with the Father's pronouncement: "This is my beloved Son, with whom I am well pleased" (3:17 ESV; cf. Ps 2:7). Jesus received a similar pronouncement from heaven at his transfiguration: "This is my beloved Son, with whom I am well pleased; listen to him" (17:5 ESV). As the messianic Son, Jesus perfectly completed the redeeming work given him to do by his Father.[151]

##### *7.2.7.3.2.1 Jesus Messiah the Son of God Is Baptized (3:16–17)*

Imagine the following scene. John the Baptist has declared openly and firmly his expectations about the judgment to accompany the powerful Coming One. The people have banked their future on the hope of the coming of the kingdom of God. And now the One recognized by John to embody those dreams simply goes into the waters of the Jordan River to be baptized like any of the people. It seems so anticlimactic and even paradoxical. But out of that unassuming scene will come a dramatic enactment of God to present Jesus for his messianic mission.

The descent of the Spirit is intended to allude to the anointing of the servant by the Spirit in Isa 42:1—which will be the words quoted by the heavenly voice in 3:17 (cf. 12:18)—and the anointing of the Davidic Branch by the Spirit in Isa 11:2. Jesus's anointing by the Spirit is both the coronation of Israel's Messiah and the commissioning of God's righteous servant for the work that he will now carry out in the power and

150. The use of the expression "Father" has metaphorical significance (e.g., Aída Besançon Spencer, "Father-Ruler: The Meaning of the Metaphor 'Father' for God in the Bible," *JETS* 39.3 [1996]: 433–42), but here it is laden with theological significance to underscore the relationship between the Father and Son, and even between the Father and Jesus's disciples.

151. "Son of God," *TBD* 1213–14.

presence of the Spirit.[152] The one who is to baptize with the Spirit (Matt 3:11), who will be guided and empowered by the Spirit (4:1), who will inaugurate the messianic age of salvation through the Spirit (12:18–21),[153] is now anointed by the Spirit for his public messianic ministry.

This is not to suggest that in the baptism Jesus receives the Spirit for the first time. Jesus's conception itself was "from the Holy Spirit" (1:20), which is an indication that even as John the Baptist was filled with the Spirit from the womb (Luke 1:15), so was Jesus. Rather, the descent of the Spirit in the baptism is a formal anointing that inaugurates Jesus's public ministry. John the Baptist declares elsewhere that the descent of the Spirit on Jesus is what confirmed for him that Jesus is indeed the Son of God (John 1:32–34). This is the visible, confirming sign that Jesus was the long-expected Messiah, the one for whom John has been preparing the way.

The symbolism of the dove is made explicit as a voice sounds out from heaven. For the Jewish people of the time, although they considered that prophecy had ceased with Malachi, a voice from God (Heb. *bat qôl*, woodenly, "the daughter of the voice") could still be heard. But that voice was indirect and did not have binding authority.[154] Now sounds out a voice that is far different. With his presence the Messiah brings the direct voice from God with all of its authority. With the arrival of the prophetic figure John the Baptist, with the descent of the Spirit on the anointed Messiah, and with the voice from the Father, God was in fact resuming direct communication. The Voice gives a dual pronouncement of the identity and nature of Jesus through citing excerpts of two messianically significant Old Testament passages: Ps 2:7 and Isa 42:1.

The statement "This is my Son, whom I love" (Matt 3:17; 17:5) calls to mind the well-known image of father and son in Ps 2:7: "I will proclaim the decree of the LORD: He said to me, 'You are my Son'" (NIV84). The designation "son of God" and the expression "anointed one" had messianic significance prior to Jesus's ministry (cf. 4QapocrDan ar II, 1; 4QFlor 1 I, 10–13, 18–19; 4QpsDan$^a$ ar).[155] The expression "whom I love" (*mou ho agapētos*, "my loved one"; Matt 3:17; 17:5) denotes the relationship which is declared between Jesus and the Voice from the Father.

Nothing is said here of when that relationship began, but Matthew has already led us to understand that Jesus's conception has marked him out as of divine origin (1:20, 23; cf. 2:15). This is not the language of adoption but of confirmation of an existing relationship of divine love between Father and Son. We will see below that Matthew

152. For an intertextual analysis that draws upon the themes of judgment, deliverance, and suffering in the Jewish tradition images of the dove (e.g., Gen 8; Ps 74:19; 2 Esdras 5:21–6:34), see David B. Capes, "Intertextual Echoes in the Matthean Baptismal Narrative," *BBR* 9 (1999): 37–49; cf. Wright, *Jesus and the Victory of God*, 536–37.

153. Cf. Isa 42:1–4; 61:1.

154. For background and discussion, see Davies and Allison, *Matthew*, 1:335–36.

155. For an overview, see Géza G. Xeravits, "Son of God," *EDEJ* 1248-49; Witherington, *Christology of Jesus*, 148–55.

understands Jesus to be the preexistent Son of God, hence his relationship with the Father is from eternity. The baptism of Jesus is widely recognized as the moment when he was anointed by the Spirit in order to undertake his office as the Messiah. But according to the heavenly voice, he was already God's beloved Son and pleasing to the Father before he was chosen and appointed to be the Messiah. Therefore, Ladd notes that "sonship and messianic status are not synonymous. Rather, sonship is the prior ground and the basis of Jesus's election to fulfill his messianic office."[156] He goes on to note that the Father's statement, "This is my beloved Son," "describes the permanent status of Jesus. He does not *become* the Son; he *is* the Son."[157]

The statement "in whom I am well-pleased" takes our understanding of Jesus's mission one step further by drawing upon Isa 42 (cf. Tg. Isa. 42:1) for another messianically significant figure—the "servant." In the declaration of the Father, Jesus is heralded as the servant who is enabled by the Spirit's anointing to bring justice to the nations. This link will be made explicit as the narrative unfolds, when Matthew cites Isa 42:1–4 in the context of clarifying the purpose of Jesus's ministry (cf. Matt 12:17–21).

As the background to the Father's declaration, these passages point out two distinct emphases of Jesus's identity, self-understanding, and mission. He is the divine Son and the suffering servant, a pronouncement that recalls the double entendre of the Nazarene allusion (2:23) and will be repeated by the voice in the transfiguration (17:5). The Father has placed into the hands of his beloved Son the mission of the servant to bring salvation to the nations (Isa 42:1, 4). Love and obedience will sustain the relationship and actualize the mission because the Father's will for the beloved Son must include obedience to the cross as the Son takes upon himself the iniquity of his people (26:39, 42; cf. Isa 53).

#### *7.2.7.3.2.2 Jesus Messiah the Son of God Is Transfigured (17:1–8)*

Matthew indicates that while Jesus is on the mountain with Peter, James, and John, he is "transfigured" (17:1–8; cf. Mark 9:2–10; Luke 9:28–36). It is a reminder of Jesus's preincarnate, divine glory (John 1:14; 17:5; Phil 2:6–7) and a preview of his coming exaltation (2 Pet 1:16–18; Rev 1:16). Jesus is transfigured to reveal his divine nature and to radiate the glory that is his as God. That glory designates the royal presence, for in his person the kingdom of God is with his people.

The transfiguration of Jesus that reveals his divine glory is seconded by the appearance of two of the greatest Old Testament figures, Moses and Elijah. Their arrival represents the Law and the Prophets witnessing to Jesus as the Messiah who fulfills the Old Testament (cf. 5:17) and who has the eschatological role of initiating the kingdom of God (4:17). Both are mentioned together in the final verses of the Old Testament—the

156. Ladd, *Theology*, 163–64.

157. Ladd, *Theology*, 164; emphasis original.

giving of the Law through God's servant Moses and the sending of the prophet Elijah before the coming day of the Lord (Mal 4:4–6). Their appearance on the mountain with Jesus indicates the greatness of Jesus, who transcends them both as the One who will be declared the Son of God. Peter did not grasp fully the stature of Jesus; he is not another Old Testament figure equal to Moses and Elijah. Jesus is superior in every way, and his transfiguration confirms the eschatological inauguration of the kingdom of God.[158] Jesus has fulfilled both the Law and the Prophets (cf. 5:17), now made clear in that he is superior to Moses and Elijah, whose revelations were pointing ultimately to Jesus, as they now do by attending him on the mountain.[159]

#### 7.2.7.3.3 Incarnate Sonship

The third aspect of Jesus as Son of God is his *incarnate sonship*. The incarnation of Jesus is traced to the direct, spiritual fatherhood of God. Jesus is the Son of God because his incarnation and birth into the human race was by conception "of the Holy Spirit" (1:20).

##### *7.2.7.3.3.1 Immanuel, "God with Us" (1:21)*

As Matthew translates Immanuel for us, we see that the name is intended as a title to indicate Jesus's messianic identity: "God with us." In the use of this name Matthew intends to make the equation: "Jesus is God." Morris notes, "The quotation and the translation of the Hebrew name underline the fact that in Jesus none less than God came right where we are."[160]

Both his common name and his titular name indicate profound truths: *Jesus* specifies what he does ("God saves"), and *Immanuel* specifies who he is ("God with us"). These are highly charged names that will speak of a profound christological orientation by Matthew. Jesus's divine sonship is prominently featured, and perhaps as Kingsbury has asserted, central to all that the author wishes to affirm.[161] At least three examples highlight this incarnate Son of God christological orientation in Matthew's Gospel.

##### *7.2.7.3.3.2 Worship of Jesus in His Earthly Ministry*

In Matthew, the verb *proskyneō* involves worship directed toward Jesus. Matthew uses the verb with Jesus as object at least ten times,[162] whereas Mark uses it this way only twice (Mark 5:6; 15:19), and Luke only once (Luke 24:52). The verb is used involving worship of Jesus from his infancy (Matt 2:2, 8, 11), onward to his adult ministry by a

158. Verseput, "'Son of God' Title," 532–56.

159. Cf. Öhler, "Expectation of Elijah."

160. Morris, *Matthew*, 31.

161. See above p. 301XXX, as we have noted on Kingsbury, *Matthew: Structure, Christology, Kingdom*, 84–127.

162. Matthew 2:2, 8, 11; 8:2; 9:18; 14:33; 15:25; 20:20; 28:9, 17.

leper, synagogue leader, and gentile woman (8:2; 9:18; 15:25), and his disciples (14:33; 20:20), and into his post-resurrection appearances (28:9, 17) in a manner not to indicate deferential respect but rather worship of the divine.

In the story of Jesus walking on the water (14:22–33), once Jesus calms the wind Matthew narrates, "Then those who were in the boat worshiped him, saying, 'Truly you are the Son of God'" (14:33). Jesus has performed a miraculous calming of nature, an act that only God can perform. In Matthew's Gospel, the title "Son of God" expresses Jesus's unique relationship to the Father (11:27) and Jesus's relationship with the Father and the Spirit (28:19–20).[163] The worship of the disciples presages the worship of the church.[164]

#### *7.2.7.3.3.3 Worship of the Resurrected Jesus*

Twice in the post-resurrection narratives Jesus's followers give this reverence to the risen Jesus: the women hurrying away from the tomb (28:8), and the eleven disciples meeting Jesus on the mountain in Galilee (28:17). Of the scenes of worship of Jesus—in the boat, at the empty tomb, and on the mountain—Larry Hurtado notes, "Jesus' transcendent status and power are indicated, and it seems undeniable that the intended readers were to take the scenes as paradigmatic anticipations of the reverence for Jesus that they offered in their worship gatherings."[165] This is worship, as in baptism, that is offered "in the name of the Father and of the Son and of the Holy Spirit" (28:19).

#### *7.2.7.3.3.4 The Exalted Jesus with His People*

Matthew's emphasis upon the presence of Jesus as the exalted Christ who is envisaged among his people in 28:19–20 indicates a divine Jesus, and reflects the practice of the worship of Jesus Messiah in the church.[166] In a striking declaration, Jesus himself assumes the place of the divine presence among his disciples, guaranteeing that when his followers reach a consensus as they ask in prayer for guidance in matters of church discipline, his Father in heaven will guide them as they carry it out. The basis of the assurance is Jesus's continual presence among his disciples who gather in his name, Jesus Messiah, the Son of the Father.

Matthew will likewise conclude his Gospel with the same theme of the presence of Jesus, where Jesus promises his disciples, "I am with you always" (28:20). The presence of Jesus is not metaphorical[167] but literal in Jesus's resurrected presence.[168]

163. Quarles, *Matthew*, 371.

164. Nolland, *Matthew*, 603. See also Richard J. Bauckham, *Jesus and the God of Israel:* God Crucified *and other Studies on the New Testament's Christology of Divine Identity* (Grand Rapids: Eerdmans, 2008), 131; Leim, *Matthew's Theological Grammar*, 234.

165. Larry W. Hurtado, *Lord Jesus Christ: Devotion to Jesus in Earliest Christianity* (Grand Rapids: Eerdmans, 2003), 338.

166. Bauckham, *Jesus and the God of Israel*, 131.

167. *Contra* Davies and Allison, *Matthew*, 2:790.

168. For discussion of the "I am with you" theme here, see Kupp, *Matthew's Emmanuel*, 176–200.

The correspondence between "God is with us" in 1:23 and "I am with you" in 28:20 allows us to find an allusion to the divine name in the "I am" of the latter. In Jesus Messiah, God is with us indeed.[169]

#### 7.2.7.3.4 Preexistent, Personal Sonship

The fourth aspect of Jesus Messiah as Son of God in Matthew's Gospel is his *preexistent, personal sonship*. The milieu in which Matthew writes of Jesus's sonship is influenced by a number of factors, two of which I mention here. The first is Matthew's own personal experience of having witnessed Jesus's life and ministry and teaching as his disciple. The second is having experienced the developing Jesus tradition in the early church. He is thus in a particularly unique position to reflect and write upon Jesus's life and ministry and to reflect and to write about Jesus as Son of God, and specifically about Jesus's preexistent, personal sonship, as we explore here. The second factor will be addressed first, but the first factor will be the primary focus of this section.

##### *7.2.7.3.4.1 Preexistent, Personal Sonship in the Early Church*

I touch first briefly on the second factor: Matthew's personal experience of the developing Jesus tradition in the earliest days of the church until he wrote his Gospel, a matter of some thirty years. Having preached the gospel and recounted the life and teaching of Jesus over and over to many different audiences, Matthew would have had significant time to reflect and clarify his understanding of the preexistent, personal sonship of Jesus, even in interaction with the other eyewitness apostles.

And as Paul became an increasingly influential apostle in his preaching to the Jews and then to the gentiles, and as he began writing his epistles through the revelation of God and under the inspiration of the Spirit, Matthew would have had access through Paul to an increasing clarification of the stunning person of Jesus Messiah, the preexistent, personal Son of God.

I note momentarily two passages. The first passage, Phil 2:6–8, for many scholars constitutes the highest point of christological reflection in the New Testament: "Certainly for a number the so-called 'Philippians hymn' is the clearest statement of preexistence."[170] It reads of Christ,

> who, though he was in the form of God, did not count equality with God a thing to be grasped, but emptied himself, by taking the form of a servant, being born in the likeness of men. And being found in human form, he humbled himself by becoming obedient to the point of death, even death on a cross. (Phil 2:6–8 ESV)

169. Morris, *Matthew*, 31–32.

170. Simon J. Gathercole, *The Pre-existent Son: Recovering the Christologies of Matthew, Mark, and Luke* (Grand Rapids: Eerdmans, 2006), 24.

Simon Gathercole notes that the hymn speaks of Christ at the outset as "in the *form* of God" and then "taking the *form* of a servant." There is a dramatic sequence in these two parallel statements that implies a prior state, or preexistence, "in the form of God," and then a subsequent "form of a servant." The term "form" (*morphē*) does not refer simply to external appearance but to what underlies it and pictures the preexistent Christ in divine majesty and glory. This corresponds with John 17:5 with Jesus the Son praying to his Father regarding "the glory I had with you before the world began." And this reminds us of Heb 1:3 with reference to the Son's preexistence: "The Son is the radiance of God's glory and the exact representation of his being."[171]

In the "form of a servant," Christ was not merely externally human but rather taking on true human nature. Moisés Silva comments that the divine and preexistent Christ did not regard the advantage of his deity as grounds to avoid the incarnation; on the contrary, "he was willing to regard himself as nothing by taking on human form. Then he further lowered himself in servanthood by obeying God to the point of ignominious death."[172] Gathercole notes, "The point still stands, then, that we have in Philippians 2 active, personal preexistence."[173]

The second passage is 2 Cor 8:9: "For you know the grace of our Lord Jesus Christ, that though he was rich, yet for your sake he became poor, so that you through his poverty might become rich." This statement is "clear evidence of preexistence."[174] The traditional and prevailing view is that *plousios* ("rich") describes the glory of heavenly existence and *eptōcheusen* ("became poor") points to the relative lowliness and destitution of earthly existence.[175] Christ chose to exchange his glorious, eternal status in heaven for a slave's destitute, temporary status on earth. Murray Harris states, "He surrendered all the insignia of divine majesty and assumed all the frailty and vicissitudes of the human condition."[176] In 2 Cor 8:9, as is common in Paul, "the incarnation and cross are telescoped into a single action reinforcing the point . . . that Paul sometimes employs preexistence in order to emphasize the gracious character of the work of Christ on the cross."[177]

Gathercole cites H.-C. Kammler approvingly: "The pre-existence of Christ in Paul . . . is conceived as *absolute, real and personal*."[178] Gathercole adds his own conclusion, "Because of Paul's widespread influence in earliest Christianity, it is

171. See Peter T. O'Brien, *The Epistle to the Philippians*, NIGTC (Grand Rapids: Eerdmans, 1991), 210–11.

172. Moisés Silva, *Philippians*, 2nd ed., BECNT (Grand Rapids: Baker Academic, 2005), 99.

173. Gathercole, *Pre-existent Son*, 25. For a very helpful discussion of the issues, see Andrew Ter Ern Loke, *The Origin of Divine Christology*, SNTSMS 169 (Cambridge: Cambridge University Press, 2017), 33–41.

174. Gathercole, *Pre-existent Son*, 26.

175. Murray J. Harris, *The Second Epistle to the Corinthians*, NIGTC (Grand Rapids: Eerdmans, 2005), 579.

176. Harris, *Second Epistle to the Corinthians*, 579.

177. Gathercole, *Pre-existent Son*, 26.

178. Gathercole, *Pre-existent Son*, 31; citing H.-C. Kammler, "Die Prädikation Jesus Christi als 'Gott' (Röm 9,5b)," *ZNW* 94 (2003): 164–80, here 176; emphasis is Kammler's in the German original.

difficult to imagine that these conceptions of preexistence were not also held much more widely."[179] Kammler also points to widespread conceptions of preexistence in the New Testament. I include Matthew and his Gospel.

#### *7.2.7.3.4.2 Preexistent, Personal Sonship in Matthew's Gospel*

As noted above, Matthew's personal experience as a disciple of Jesus gave him years of eyewitness access to Jesus's life, ministry, and teaching. His Gospel reflects his own historical recollections, his theological reflections, and the inspiration of the Spirit.[180] These passages lift the veil slightly and give us a glimpse into the divine relationship that always existed between the Father and the Son and the Holy Spirit.[181]

##### 7.2.7.3.4.2.1 Jesus Will Save His People from Sin, and He Is Immanuel, "God with Us" (1:18–25)

In the person of Jesus Immanuel, the eternal God has become human through the conception of the baby by the Holy Spirit. Both his common name and his titular name indicate profound truths: *Jesus* specifies what he does ("God saves"), and *Immanuel* specifies who he is ("God with us"). The eternal God has entered human history as the preexistent Jesus miraculously conceived in Mary. His name Jesus alerts us to one massive aspect of his life mission: to forgive sins. Only God can forgive sins, and in Jesus's birth God has become human to bring salvation from sin. This is explicitly carried out later in Matthew's Gospel, when Jesus says to the paralytic, "Take heart, son; your sins are forgiven" (Matt 9:2). The eternal God in the preexistent Jesus has entered history miraculously as the God-Man to save his people from their sins. And more.

##### 7.2.7.3.4.2.2 Peter's Declaration (16:16–17)

Matthew invests significance in Peter's declaration of Jesus's identity more than found in Mark ("You are the Messiah"; Mark 8:29) or Luke ("God' Messiah"; Luke 9:20). In Matthew Peter declares, "You are the Messiah, the Son of the living God" (Matt 16:16). Jesus declares that this knowledge is not simply from human insight. We have seen that spiritual beings know Jesus as God's Son (e.g., Matt 4:3, 6; 8:29), but divine revelation is necessary for humans.[182] Quarles demonstrates that in Matthew the title "Son of God" is far more than a mere messianic title as the ultimate king: "The title recalls Jesus's unique and miraculous conception by the Holy Spirit in 1:18–25. The attentive reader of the Gospel will know that 'Son of God' identifies Jesus as Deity

179. Gathercole, *Pre-existent Son*, 31

180. See Aquila H. I. Lee, *From Messiah to Preexistent Son: Jesus' Self-Consciousness and Early Christian Exegesis of Messianic Psalms*, WUNT 2/192 (Tübingen: Mohr Siebeck, 2005), esp. 181–201.

181. Charles Lee Irons, "A Trinitarian View: Jesus, the Divine Son of God," in *The Son of God: Three Views of the Identity of Jesus* (Eugene, OR: Wipf & Stock, 2015), 3–22, here 6.

182. Grindheim, *Christology*, 106.

incarnate, the Immanuel, who was born as a human child and yet bears the title 'mighty God' (Isa 9:6)."[183] Thus the Christ/Messiah, is also Son of God, with a transcendent connotation clearly included.[184]

7.2.7.3.4.2.3 Jesus's Identification of Himself at His Trial (26:62–65)

At his bogus trial before the chief priests and the Sanhedrin where they could find no legitimate witnesses against Jesus, the high priest finally demands,

> "I charge you under oath by the living God: Tell us if you are the Messiah, the Son of God." "You have said so," Jesus replied. (26:63–64; cf. Mark 14:61–62)

In Matthew's and Mark's accounts, Jesus states that he is the Son of Man and that his audience will see him seated at God's right hand (the right hand of power) and coming with the clouds of heaven (a combination of Dan 7:13 and Ps 110:1).

Here Jesus defines what it means to be the Messiah and the Son of God as the Son of Man, thereby making clear that the Son of Man is a divine figure who accompanies God as God comes to judge the world. This is a remarkably strong statement about what it means to be the Son of God: "The high priest concurs, as he tears his robes and declares that there is no need for additional witnesses to Jesus's blasphemy, since Jesus has condemned himself. Jesus has declared that being the Son of Man means being the Son of God—and being God himself."[185] Jesus was the personal, preexistent Son of God.

7.2.7.3.4.2.4 Jesus's Claim of Unity of Knowledge and Oneness with the Father (11:27)

Jesus follows his brief prayer (Matt 11:25–26) with an astonishing statement to his disciples and the crowds of his relationship to the Father. In this statement, which George Ladd calls "the most important passage for the study of Synoptic Christology,"[186] Jesus declares, "All things have been committed to me by my Father. No one knows the Son except the Father, and no one knows the Father except the Son and those to whom the Son chooses to reveal him" (11:27). This verse reveals a profound divine self-consciousness by Jesus, but all along Matthew has emphasized Jesus's divine self-awareness as the "Son." As we have noted, the Son theme is one of the central highpoints of Matthew's Christology, as well as Synoptic Christology generally.[187]

We find in 11:27 Jesus explicitly claiming that the Father has handed all things to the Son, and therefore only the Son and those whom he permits have knowledge

183. Quarles, *Matthew*, 411–12. Cf. Nolland, *Matthew*, 655–66.

184. Hurtado, *Lord Jesus Christ*, 339.

185. Porter and Dyer, *Origins of New Testament Christology*, 86.

186. Ladd, *Theology*, 164.

187. Stein, *Method and Message*, 131–35.

of the Father.[188] As the Son, Jesus is the sole mediator to whom "all things have been committed" (11:27), which refers to the revelation of the knowledge of the Father, to which Jesus referred in the preceding prayer (11:25–26).

In both his incarnate and eternal state as Son, Jesus and the Father know each other in an exclusive way, which in biblical language means that they enjoy an exclusive relationship. For Jesus as Son, the Father is "my Father."[189] They enjoy a direct, intuitive, and immediate knowledge that is grounded in their relationship as Father and Son, which implies that it is on the level of divine knowledge. As such, what the Father and Son share stands apart from all human relationships and all human knowledge.[190] So, Jesus's sonship involves more than a unique filial consciousness; it involves a unique and exclusive, essential relationship between Father and Son.[191]

In his incarnate state, Jesus has received from the Father the exclusive authority to reveal the Father, which does not imply the Son's inferiority to the Father but the process of revelation.[192] Humans can know the Father only through the sovereign will of the Son's revelation. Therefore, a crucial element of Jesus's messianic mission is to impart to people a mediated knowledge of God, which indicates that sonship and messiahship are not the same. Sonship precedes messiahship and is the basis for the entire messianic mission. God's program of salvation history derives from the unique, divine relationship of Father and Son.

The relation of Father and Son in the Godhead is something that is not simply figurative, but something that defines them from eternity. Blomberg notes of the christological significance of this passage that "the theology is not yet Trinitarian but prepares the way for the references to the Father and Son in the baptismal formula of 28:19."[193] Grindheim adds, "'God's Son' is no longer merely an honorary title; it describes the intimate relationship between Father and Son, a relationship between equals."[194]

#### 7.2.7.3.4.2.5 Jesus's Personal Preexistence Is Recognized by the Devil (4:3, 6) and Demons (8:29)

At Jesus's temptations, the tempter comes to him and says, "If you are the Son of God," and indicates he knows of the miraculous power of Jesus the Son of God (4:3, 6). The demons exorcised by Jesus cry out, "What do you want with us, Son of God? . . . Have you come here to torture us before the appointed time?" (8:29). The demons immediately recognize Jesus's true identity as the "Son of God," as did Satan (4:3, 6). This is a title that eventually the disciples will use (14:33; 16:16; cf. 27:54) as they gain

188. Winn, "Son of God," 891.

189. Not "the Father"; cf. also 7:21; 10:32, 33; 12:50; 16:17; 18:10, 19; 20:23; 25:34; 26:39, 42, 53.

190. Ladd, *Theology*, 165–66.

191. Ladd, *Theology*, 166.

192. Guthrie, *New Testament Theology*, 307.

193. Blomberg, *Matthew*, 193.

194. Grindheim, *Christology*, 111.

increased clarity of his uniqueness as the one whom the Father has revealed to be his "beloved Son" (3:17; 17:5). But from the demons, the use of the title trumpets their recognition that another stronghold of Satan, the sphere of the spirit world is being invaded and overpowered.

This is not simply a matter of the demons knowing about Jesus, but that they know him as the Son of God who has come from the God-side of the heaven-earth divide and has divine authority to destroy them. The demons' knowledge of Jesus was not acquired by witnessing his baptism or consulting with other demons: "Rather, the demons know Jesus because they know his origins, his identity, his power, and his purpose, and it literally scares them off the human bones they inhabit."[195]

#### 7.2.7.3.4.2.6 Jesus's Declaration of Oneness in Name as Son with the Father and Spirit (28:19)

Jesus instructs the disciples to baptize new disciples "in the name of the Father and of the Son and of the Holy Spirit." A "name" is a matter of identity and not merely function. This is a baptism "into fellowship with" or "into the lordship of" the Godhead, expressing a new relationship of new disciples with the triune Godhead. The use of *name* is common in Scripture for God's power and authority.[196] Jews were not baptized in the name of a person. Baptism in the "name" (note the singular) of the Father, Son, and Holy Spirit associates the three as personal distinctions, an early indication of the Trinitarian Godhead, and an overt proclamation of Jesus's deity. While this is not an explicit indication of Jesus's preexistence, being identified with Father God and the Holy Spirit, who are noted to be preexistent in the Old Testament (e.g., Gen 1:1–2; Isa 63:16) prepares for understanding the preexistence of Jesus Immanuel. Grindheim concludes his evaluation of Son of God in Matthew's Gospel by stating,

> Matthew's development of the Son of God theme has combined the picture of Jesus as the obedient representative Israelite with the picture of the Son who stands in a unique relationship to the Father, a relationship so close that Jesus can be seen as God's equal and as his presence on earth. Consequently, he can be worshiped as the Son of God.[197]

### 7.2.7.3.5 Jesus Was Not an "Adopted" Son but Is the "Eternal" Son

Jesus's divine sonship is argued by many as one of, if not the most characteristic of Christian claims about him. On the other hand, one of the most potent heresies of

195. Bird, *Jesus the Eternal Son*, 79.

196. E.g., *onoma* in LXX Exod 3:13–15; Prov 18:10; cf. Jub. 36:7.

197. Grindheim, *Christology*, 111.

the second and third centuries AD was adoptionism, which reduced Jesus to a human figure who had acquired divine status by merit. The early church said that Jesus's sonship preceded the incarnation, whereas adoptionists argued that Jesus's sonship had a historical beginning at some time after his birth as a human: at his birth, baptism, or resurrection.[198]

Taken as a whole, the New Testament paints a picture of Jesus that defies the standard adoptionist view.[199] The New Testament records a picture of Jesus, the Son of God, as an eternal figure having a special relationship with God from eternity, prior to his incarnation. And his resurrection and ascension into heaven are displayed as an affirmation of and a return to his glorious position at God's right hand. Adoptionism must answer two separate but interrelated questions: When did Jesus become divine, and how did Jesus become divine? "The traditional orthodox answer is that Jesus was preexistent as God, shared God's nature from eternity, and had that nature when he was incarnated."[200]

### 7.2.8 Son of Man (*ho huios tou anthrōpou*)

The title "Son of Man" is found some thirty times in Matthew's Gospel,[201] and some eighty times in all of the Gospels (Mark 14x; Luke 26x; John 10x). The expression is used by Jesus, and only by Jesus, in a somewhat mysterious, indirect way to speak about himself. For example, when traveling through the region of Caesarea Philippi, Jesus asked his disciples, "Who do people say the Son of Man is?" (16:13). When they gave various answers, Jesus then asked the disciples directly, "'But what about you?' he asked. 'Who do you say I am?'" (16:15). Jesus here uses the title in an indirect way to refer to himself, and to elicit a response from the disciples as to their understanding of his identity.

In all the texts where the expression occurs, Jesus is always the speaker, and no other person addresses him as "Son of Man." In some texts the reference is enigmatic enough for some interpreters to contend that Jesus is speaking about another person.

198. For evaluation, see Bird, *Jesus the Eternal Son*, 7; Porter and Dyer, *Origins of New Testament Christology*, 228–29. For a recent emphasis upon Jesus as the "adopted, messianic son of God" in the Gospel of Mark, and the "idealized human" in the NT generally, including Matthew's Gospel, see Kirk, *A Man Attested by God*: in Mark's Gospel, 210, and in Matthew's Gospel, 237–58, 359–87. Kirk contends that the Synoptic Gospels present Jesus not as divine but as an idealized human figure. His intent is to assert Jesus's humanity, but he does so at the expense of Jesus's deity. For a recent four-views discussion of Jesus's identity in Mark's Gospel, including Kirk's view, which is also instructive for Christology in Matthew's Gospel, see Anthony Le Donne, ed., *Christology in Mark's Gospel: Four Views* (Grand Rapids: Zondervan, 2021).

199. A helpful refutation of adoptionism is set forth in Matthew W. Bates, *The Birth of the Trinity: Jesus, God, and Spirit in New Testament and Early Christian Interpretation of the Old Testament* (Oxford: Oxford University Press, 2015), 11, passim.

200. Porter and Dyer, *Origins of New Testament Christology*, 88–89. For a helpful theological examination, see Oliver D. Crisp, *Divinity and Humanity: The Incarnation Reconsidered*, Current Issues in Theology (Cambridge: Cambridge University Press, 2007). See also for a brief refutation of adoptionism, Loke, *Origin of Divine Christology*, 83.

201. Matt 8:20; 9:6; 10:23; 11:19; 12:8, 32, 40; 13:37, 41; 16:13, 27, 28; 17:9, 12, 22; 19:28; 20:18, 28; 24:27, 30 [2x]; 24:37, 39, 44; 25:31; 26:2, 24 [2x], 45, 64.

However, most interpreters draw the conclusion that Jesus used the term as a messianic title for himself with considerable originality because the expression was not loaded with popular misconceptions concerning messiahship.[202]

Those who heard the expression would recall its use in Ezekiel, where God refers to the prophet with the expression "son of man" over ninety times (e.g., Ezek 2:1, 3, 6, 8; cf. Dan 8:17), pointing to Ezekiel's frailty as a human before the mighty God revealed in the vision.[203]

But those hearing it also would recall how the expression "Son of Man" was used in Daniel's prophecy to refer to a glorified Sovereign, the apocalyptic messianic figure who rules forever with the Ancient of Days (Dan 7:13–14). This latter sense of the expression found its way into use in Second Temple Judaism, because it occurs in the pseudepigraphal writings 1 Enoch and 2 Esdras 13 (or 4 Ezra 13).[204] The reference in 1 Enoch is particularly interesting, because it probably precedes the time of Jesus:

> Pain shall seize them when they see that Son of Man sitting on the throne of his glory. (These) kings, governors, and all the landlords shall (try to) bless, glorify, extol him who rules over everything, him who has been concealed. For the Son of Man was concealed from the beginning, and the Most High One preserved him in the presence of his power; then he revealed him to the holy and the elect ones. (1 Enoch 62:5–7)[205]

But the title Son of Man was not widely used and would not have produced immediate impressions as would other titles.

During his earthly ministry the expression would have struck a relatively ambiguous chord, but the title "Son of Man" may be the most significant to get at Jesus's clarification of his self-identity. The title occurs in Matthew's Gospel in contexts that span the full range of gospel events: Jesus's servanthood (20:28), his authority to forgive sins (9:6), as a friend of sinners (11:19), as "Lord of the Sabbath" (12:8), as suffering, dying and rising servant (17:12, 22; 20:18; 26:2), and as final judge coming in glory (10:23; 13:41; 16:27–28; 19:28; 24:27, 30, 37, 39, 44; 25:31). Who really is this Son of Man?

With such a general ambiguity, "Son of Man" is for Jesus a convenient vehicle to teach his messianic identity. It did not have popular associations attached to it, such as were attached to titles like "Messiah," or "Son of David," "Son of Abraham," or even

202. Elwell, "Son of Man," *BEB* 1983.

203. Leslie C. Allen, *Ezekiel 1–19*, WBC 29 (Dallas: Word, 1994), 38.

204. Published too late to be included here for discussion, but promising helpful background, is Richard Bauckham, *Early Jewish Literature*, vol. 1 of *"Son of Man,"* 2 vols. (Grand Rapids: Eerdmans, 2023).

205. Although the dating of this portion of Enoch is debated, current scholarly opinion dates it at around the time of Herod the Great; cf. E. Isaac, trans., "1 (Ethiopic Apocalypse of) Enoch," in *The Old Testament Pseudepigrapha*, 2 vols., ed. James H. Charlesworth (Garden City, New York: Doubleday, 1983), 1:7.

"Son of God." Instead, Jesus can teach the meaning of his true identity by referring to himself with the expression "Son of Man." No one else uses the expression to refer to Jesus, and in the rest of the New Testament the title is used of Jesus only once (Acts 7:56), except for three Old Testament references or quotations (Heb 2:6 = Ps 8:5; Rev 1:13 and 14:14 = Dan 7:13). In every instance within the Gospels except two, the title is found only on the lips of Jesus, but even in these exceptions it should be noted that the audience used this title because Jesus had previously used it as a self-designation (John 12:23), and the angel is simply repeating Jesus's own words (Luke 24:7).

With a general threefold progression, Jesus uses the expression to clarify exactly who he is and what is his ministry.[206]

1. *The Son of Man is the* humble servant *who in his earthly ministry has come to forgive sins of common sinners.*[207] The first time that Jesus uses the title in Matthew's Gospel is in response to a scribe who came to him and said, "Teacher, I will follow you wherever you go." Jesus's reply to the scribe is instructive: "Foxes have dens and birds have nests, but the Son of Man has no place to lay his head" (8:19–20). By using the title Son of Man, Jesus announces that his status is one of humility with nowhere to lay his head, an incongruous picture of the kind of messianic figure that many of the people hoped to see arrive (8:20). Because the Son of Man dined and drank with tax collectors and sinners instead of the self-righteous religious leaders, he was accused of being a glutton and drunkard (11:19). But dramatically he assumes the place of God in forgiving sins and states of himself as the Son of Man, "'But I want you to know that the Son of Man has authority on earth to forgive sins.' So he said to the paralyzed man, 'Get up, take your mat and go home'" (9:6)
2. *The Son of Man is the* suffering servant *whose atoning death and resurrection will redeem his people as the Messiah who will be crucified.*[208] In the scene at Caesarea Philippi where Jesus asks questions regarding the peoples' understanding of the identity of the Son of Man (16:15), Jesus uses the title in an indirect way to refer to himself and to elicit a response from the disciples as to their understanding of his identity. And then dramatically, "Jesus began to explain to his disciples

206. For a helpful overview by an evangelical scholar, see Robert H. Stein, *The Method and Message of Jesus' Teaching*, rev. ed. (Louisville: Westminster John Knox, 1994), 135–51. For an interesting discussion by a Jewish scholar, see Flusser, *Jesus*, 124–33. For a monograph that surveys the history of debate but ends on a note of skepticism regarding the authenticity of Jesus's usage, see Delbert Burkett, *The Son of Man Debate: A History and Evaluation*, SNTSMS 107 (Cambridge: Cambridge University Press, 1999). And for a view that "Jesus' claim was not that he was identical with the Son of Man, but that he was intimate with the Son of Man," see Bruce Chilton, "(The) Son of (the) Man, and Jesus," in *A Comparative Handbook to the Gospel of Mark: Comparisons with Pseudepigrapha, the Qumran Scrolls, and Rabbinic Literature*, ed. Bruce Chilton et al., NTGJC 1 (Leiden: Brill, 2010), 533–60, here 558.

207. Matthew 8:20; 9:6; 11:19; 12:8; 12:32; 12:40.

208. Matthew 16:13, 27–28; 17:9, 12, 22; 20:18, 28; 26:2, 24, 45.

that he must go to Jerusalem and suffer many things at the hands of the elders, chief priests and teachers of the law, and that he must be killed and on the third day be raised to life" (16:21). As the Son of Man, Jesus is able to forgive sins, something that only God can do (9:6). Jesus declares that as Son of Man he is greater than the temple (12:6, 8), greater than the prophet Jonah (12:40–41), and greater than wise king Solomon (12:42). In this way, Matthew emphasizes that Jesus's person, proclamation, and inauguration of the kingdom is greater than, and therefore the fulfillment of, the three greatest institutions in Israel—priest, prophet, king. Jesus's arrival as the Son of Man with the kingdom of God has exceeded all that Israel has witnessed in her history but he will be delivered into the hands of men who will kill him, and then he will be raised to life (17:22–23) for forgiveness of sins.

3. *The Son of Man is the glorious King and Judge who will return to bring fully the kingdom of heaven to earth.*[209] Jesus's mission was not always understood because of the misperceptions and faulty expectations of the people, the religious leaders, and even his own disciples. But at the end, after he has used the sufficiently ambiguous title "Son of Man" to clarify his identity and ministry, as he uses it for the last time at his trial before Caiaphas and the Sanhedrin, it is perfectly clear that he is claiming to be the divine Messiah of Israel (cf. 26:63–68). The Son of Man will return before the mission to Israel is completed (10:23), at the end of this age with great power and glory on the clouds of the sky (24:27, 30). At this spectacular appearance of the Son of Man, all the nations will mourn, and he will send his angels to gather the elect (24:30–31) and to bring judgment upon the sons of the evil one (13:37–43). The Son of Man as King is a title of majesty, with the ultimate goal of his mission as establishing the kingdom. After his humiliation and suffering he will receive from his Father the vindication, enthronement, glory, and judgment which are given to "one like a son of man" in Dan 7:13.[210]

Daniel Boyarin, the highly respected Jewish scholar, evaluated texts such as Dan 7, 1 Enoch, and 4 Ezra and established the justification for a messianic-divine "Son of Man" deeply embedded in Jewish thought and expectation. He comes to this conclusion:

> Many Israelites at the time of Jesus were expecting a Messiah who would be divine and come to earth in the form of a human. Thus the basic underlying thoughts

209. Matthew 10:23; 13:37, 41; 19:28; 24:27, 30, 37, 39, 44; 25:31; 26:64.

210. For recent interaction with the apocalyptic view of Jesus, see Justin Meggitt, "Putting the Apocalyptic Jesus to the Sword: Why Were Jesus's Disciples Armed?" *JSNT* 45.4 (2023): 371–404.

> from which both the Trinity and the incarnation grew are there in the very world into which Jesus was born and in which he was first written about in the Gospels.[211]

In agreement with Boyarin, I contend that Matthew's Gospel reflects directly the Jewish expectations of a divine messianic "Son of Man."

Son of Man was for Jesus a convenient title to reveal his true identity and mission. Other titles that he might have rightfully claimed and used, such as Messiah or Son of David or Son of God, evoked popular militaristic and political images among the people that could have caused them to overlook his uniqueness and the message of spiritual salvation and liberation that he proclaimed in his announcement of the arrival of the kingdom of heaven. Instead, he can teach the meaning of his true identity by referring to himself with the expression "Son of Man," which indeed is his favorite self-designation. This title, Son of Man, became his teaching device to reveal Jesus's true, manifold identity.

### 7.2.9 Lord (*kyrios*)

The term *kyrios*, often rendered "lord," occurs some eighty times in seventy-three verses in Matthew's Gospel, and is used in several different ways, but most important for our study are the ways in which it is used in relationship to Jesus. The term *kyrios* is far more common in Matthew in both its general and specialized use than in either Mark or Luke.[212]

*Kyrios* is used *generally* to refer to a "lord" or "master," such as in Jesus's saying, "No one can serve two masters [*kyrioi*]. Either you will hate the one and love the other, or you will be devoted to the one and despise the other. You cannot serve both God and money" (Matt 6:24; cf. 20:8; 24:48). It is also used generally as a respectful designation in addressing persons of varying social or political rank, equivalent to our "sir," as when the chief priests and the Pharisees address Pilate as "Sir" (*kyrios*) (27:63). The term is also used in this general way in Jesus's parables when servants address their "master" or "owner" (13:27).[213]

*Kyrios* is also used in a specialized sense, which is the subject of our study here. It can be used as a designation of God, both directly and indirectly, as when Jesus addresses his Father, "I praise you, Father, Lord [*kyrios*] of heaven and earth" (11:25), and in Matthew's reference to God, "All this took place to fulfill what the Lord [*kyrios*] had said through the prophet" (1:22).[214]

211. Daniel Boyarin, *The Jewish Gospels: The Story of the Jewish Christ* (New York: New Press, 2012), 5–6.

212. Carlston and Evans, *From Synagogue to Ecclesia*, 60–61.

213. See in parables also: 18:25, 27, 31, 32, 34; 20:8; 21:3, 40.

214. 1:22; 2:15; 4:7, 10; 5:33; 9:38; 11:25; 21:9, 42; 22:37, 44; 23:39.

Most strikingly, *kyrios* is a designation that increasingly reveals Jesus's identity and mission.[215] Sometimes during his ministry the term is used by people simply as a title of respect (e.g., 8:21; 18:21; 26:22). But the use of the designation in Matthew's Gospel also has much more significance. We find that "Lord" is the designation that is regularly used by people who approach Jesus in search of divine aid,[216] including his own disciples when they need divine assistance: "The disciples went and woke him, saying, 'Lord, save us! We're going to drown!'" (8:25; cf. 14:30). On four occasions Matthew uses *kyrios* where Mark has "Teacher" (using roughly equivalent terms: *didaskale, rabbi, rabbouni*).[217] In these cases Matthew seems to indicate that *kyrios*, "Lord," more so than "Teacher," is particularly appropriate for expressing the relationship between Jesus and the disciples.[218]

As Jesus's ministry unfolds, his disciples use the title *kyrios* with increasing deference, because he is turning out to be more than they had originally understood him to be. He is connected with God's power and has a relationship with God as the Son that can only be addressed with a title used specially for God, "Lord" (e.g., 14:28; 15:25; 17:4). Thus, in the use of the title *kyrios* Matthew draws the Father and Son together as the ones uniquely worthy of being called "Lord." This is particularly momentous when the disciples see Jesus's miraculous deeds, call upon him as "Lord," and then worship him (14:33), an activity reserved solely for deity. Hak Chol Kim contends that the Gospel of Matthew can be characterized by its special emphasis on the worship of the Lord Jesus. In the scenes where he is worshiped, "Jesus was depicted as the king of the Jews, Christ/Messiah, the 'I am' (ἐγώ εἰμι), and the Divine Being holding authority both in heaven and on earth, thus being worthy of worship."[219]

Therefore, like we have seen in "Son of Man," "Lord" is one of the titles that Jesus uses to refer to himself in a way that increasingly reveals his divine identity.[220] As the only one who refers to God in heaven as "my Father" (e.g., 7:21; cf. 11:25–27) and the one who has authority to banish false prophets to eternal judgment (7:22–23), Jesus is more than any mere respected master; he is the Lord who is worshiped as having all authority in heaven and on earth (28:16–20).

### 7.2.10 Rabbi (*rabbi*)

The attempt to understand Jesus's identity within his first-century setting leads to various conclusions. One attempt—found among popular preachers and teachers as

215. See the charting in Carlston and Evans, *From Synagogue to Ecclesia*, 60–61.

216. E.g., 8:2, 5; 9:28; 15:22, 25; 17:15; 20:30, 31, 33.

217. Matt 8:25 (cf. Mark 4:38); Matt 17:4, 15 (cf. Mark 9:5, 17); Matt 20:33 (cf. Mark 10:51).

218. Carlston and Evans, *From Synagogue to Ecclesia*, 61. So also Blomberg, *Theology*, 550. See below our discussion of "Teacher."

219. Hak Chol Kim, "The Worship of Jesus in the Gospel of Matthew," *Bib* 93.2 (2012): 227–41, here 241.

220. Matthew 9:38; 21:3; 22:43–45; 23:38; 24:42; 25:37, 44. France, *Matthew: Evangelist and Teacher*, 287–88.

well as among some New Testament scholars—is to understand Jesus as a Jewish rabbi. Some understand this to mean that Jesus was an early form of synagogue rabbi, with similarity to the Pharisaic rabbis.[221]

However, Jesus as a Jewish rabbi has much broader connotations than we might first suspect. The terms *rabbî* (from *rab*: "lord, master"; *rabbî*: "my lord") and *rabbounî* (a heightened or intensified form of *rabbî*) refer to a teacher, master, or lord.[222] Of the seventeen times that they occur in the New Testament (only in the Gospels), fourteen times they refer to Jesus. Twelve of those times they are used by Jesus's disciples to designate him, once by blind Bartimaeus, and once by Nicodemus. Twice Jesus refers to Jewish leaders (scribes and Pharisees) as rabbis, and once John the Baptist is referred to as rabbi.

This is a broad use of "rabbi" in the New Testament to indicate a teacher, master, or lord. We should note in particular the wide range of perspectives of Jesus as rabbi. Two former disciples of John the Baptist—Andrew (and John the apostle?)—approach Jesus, call him "rabbi," seek to be with him and become his disciples, then declare Jesus to be the Messiah (John 1:38–41). Nathanael calls Jesus rabbi but then declares Jesus to be the Son of God, the King of Israel (John 1:49). Nicodemus, a member of the Jewish ruling council, approaches Jesus, calls him "rabbi," and comments on the miraculous signs that Jesus had performed, which prompts him to ask about spiritual things concerning the kingdom of God (John 3:2). Peter witnesses Jesus's transfiguration alongside Moses and Elijah and hears the Father call Jesus his beloved Son but then calls Jesus "rabbi" (Mark 9:5). Jesus is observed performing miraculous signs and is approached by blind Bartimaeus for healing, who says, "Rabbi, I want to see" (10:51). Peter comments to Rabbi Jesus that the fig tree that Jesus miraculously cursed had withered (11:21). Mary Magdalene witnesses the risen Jesus, whom she calls "Rabbouni" (John 20:16).

The term rabbi is found four times in Matthew's Gospel and these are dark: twice prominently used by the traitor Judas to address Jesus (Matt 26:25, 49) and twice used by Jesus to criticize the Pharisees for their love of status, which Jesus's disciples are not to emulate (23:7, 8).[223]

---

221. On the more popular side is Stephen D. Jones, *Rabbi Jesus: Learning from the Master Teacher* (Macon, GA: Peake Road, 1997); Ray Vander Laan, *In the Dust of the Rabbi: Becoming a Disciple*, Discovery Guide, Faith Lessons 6 (Grand Rapids: Zondervan, 2006); Rob Bell, "Dust," in *Velvet Elvis: Repainting the Christian Faith* (Grand Rapids: Zondervan, 2005), 123–36Andrew

(and John the apostle?)—approach. On the more scholarly side is Brad H. Young, *Meet the Rabbis: Rabbinic Thought and the Teachings of Jesus* (Peabody, MA: Hendrickson), 2007. A semi-popular/scholarly treatment is found in Ann Spangler and Lois Tverberg, *Sitting at the Feet of Rabbi Jesus: How the Jewishness of Jesus Can Transform Your Faith* (Grand Rapids: Zondervan, 2009). For a creative, scholarly—yet, in my view not very helpful—reconstruction, see Bruce Chilton, *Rabbi Jesus: An Intimate Biography* (New York: Doubleday, 2000).

222. For helpful, brief overviews of the rabbi in Jewish society, see Neusner and Green, "Rabbi," *DJBP* 516–18; Richard Kalmin, "Rabbis," *EDEJ* 1132–34.

223. Chris Keith, *Jesus Against the Scribal Elite: The Origins of the Conflict* (Grand Rapids: Baker Academic, 2014), 18.

### *7.2.10.1 Jesus Had Characteristics of a Jewish Rabbi*

Jesus had many of the characteristics of other Jewish rabbis. He taught in their synagogues and on the Sabbath, he taught in accordance with Jewish customs, he was given respect due a teacher of the law, his disciples followed him around, and he is even called "rabbi" (Matt 26:49; Mark 9:5; John 1:49). The apparent normal pattern in Israel was for a prospective disciple to approach a rabbi and ask to study with him. Joshua ben Perahyah said, "Set up a master for yourself and get you a fellow disciple" (m. Avot 1:6 [Neusner]), which Gamaliel echoed: "Set up a master for yourself. Avoid doubt" (m. Avot 1:16 [Neusner]; cf. Matt 8:19). Later rabbinic disciples followed their master around, often physically imitating the master's teaching of Torah because imitating the master is imitating Moses' imitation of God.[224]

### *7.2.10.2 Jesus Developed a Master-Disciple Relationship Unlike Other Jewish Rabbis*

But as Jesus's ministry unfolds, he begins to establish a form of master-disciple relationship that is unlike other rabbis within Judaism or the wider Greco-Roman world. We will discuss this more fully below. But here we make some preliminary observations.

Jesus's ministry of calling, training, and sending out disciples stands as a captivating historical phenomenon. There have been numerous attempts at classifying his ministry according to other types of philosophical/social/religious movements of the first century AD (e.g., as a Sophistic philosopher, wandering charismatic, Zealot brigand, Cynic philosopher, Qumran/Essene separatist, Jewish rabbi, apocalyptic scribe, Israelite prophet figure), which probably have revealed some authentic, parallel characteristics.[225]

In a general sense a disciple is *a committed follower of a great master.* When Jesus arrived on the scene in the first century there were many masters with their disciples. A disciple was a person who had committed himself or herself to a master and the master's expectations. The form of discipleship varied significantly according to the goals of the master.

On the surface, Jesus's disciples appeared to be similar to other forms of Jewish disciples because he took a commonly occurring phenomenon—a master-disciple relationship—and used it as an expression of his kind of relationship with his followers.[226]

---

224. Jacob Neusner, *Invitation to the Talmud: A Teaching Book* (New York: Harper & Row, 1973), 7. The translations are from Jacob Neusner, *The Mishnah: A New Translation* (New Haven, CT: Yale University Press, 1988).

225. E.g., Dean O. Wenthe, "The Social Configuration of the Rabbi-Disciple Relationship: Evidence and Implications for First Century Palestine," in *Studies in the Hebrew Bible, Qumran, and the Septuagint: Presented to Eugene Ulrich*, ed. Peter W. Flint, Emanuel Tov and James C. Vanderkam, VTSup 101 (Leiden: Brill, 2006), 143–74.

226. Catherine Hezser, "Followers, Servants, and Traitors: The Representation of Disciples in the Synoptic Gospels and in Ancient Judaism," in *Christian Origins and the Establishment of the Early Jesus Movement*, ed. Stanley E. Porter and Andrew W. Pitts, TENTS 12 (Leiden: Brill, 2018), 71–88.

But Jesus's particular form of discipleship defies classification according to other existing first-century paradigms. The title "rabbi," when it is applied to Jesus, especially by his followers, implies much more than simply a synagogue rabbi.[227] This is consistent with Matt 9:14//Mark 2:18, where there is mention of diverse disciples of diverse masters: the disciples of John the Baptist (cf. John 1:35; 3:25), disciples of the Pharisees (cf. Matt 22:15–16), and disciples of Jesus. The designation "disciple" (*mathētēs*) came from the type of master, and these are distinctly different masters.

In the specific sense of a disciple of Jesus we have a much more focused definition than found among other types of rabbis. Throughout his ministry Jesus clarified the goals and characteristics of his form of discipleship, so that we can say that a disciple of Jesus is *a person who has been called by Jesus to eternal life, has claimed him as Savior and God, and has embarked upon the life of following him.*[228] Jesus developed a unique form of master-disciple relationship that was inaugurated with his announcement of the arrival of the kingdom of God and summoning men and women to be his followers.

#### *7.2.10.3 Responding to the Call by Jesus*

With Jesus, the initiative lay with his call and his choice (Matt 4:19; 9:9; Mark 1:17; 2:14; cf. Luke 5:10–11, 27–28; John 15:16) of those who would be his disciples. The response to the call involves recognition and belief in Jesus's identity (Matt 9:9–17; John 2:11; 6:68–69), obedience to his summons (Matt 4:18–22; Mark 1:18, 20), and counting the cost of full allegiance to him (Matt 19:23–30; Luke 14:25–28). Jesus's call was to enter the kingdom of heaven and experience the life transformation that accompanied the new birth by the Spirit of God, experience the beginning restoration of the image of God that had been marred by sin, and embark on the journey of transformation into the image of Jesus.

#### *7.2.10.4 Jesus Is Always Master*

Among other forms of master-disciple relationships, including the Pharisees and their rabbi-disciple relationships, the goal of the disciple was to successfully pass the course of instruction so that one day the disciple would become a rabbi. But with Jesus's disciples, they would always remain disciples. When critiquing the Pharisees, Jesus stated it plainly (23:6–10): Jesus's disciples are not to seek out personal authority as "instructor" or "master" over other disciples, because as "the Messiah" Jesus alone is Master (*kathēgētēs*). He is the sole one with personal authority to guide his disciples (28:18, 20). The admonition is to avoid the desire for personal distinction among Jesus's

227. For a helpful attempt at understanding Jesus in relationship to the scribal-literate culture, see Keith, *Jesus Against the Scribal Elite*, passim, but here especially "Teachers in the Time of Jesus: Scribal Literacy and Social Roles," 17–37.

228. For discussion see Wilkins, *Following the Master*, chs. 2–6.

disciples. The more that Jesus's disciples exalt him as the Messiah, the less they will think of magnifying themselves over others.

Matthew uses a word found only here in the New Testament to describe the third title that Jesus's disciples are to avoid—*kathēgētēs* (23:10).[229] It is a near equivalent for "teacher" (*didaskalos*; 28:8), but it carries an additional sense of "leader" (NASB).[230] The term *kathēgētēs* does not occur in the LXX, but does occur in Greek literature to designate especially a private tutor, which may point to the individual authority an instructor has over the student.[231] Some have suggested that Jesus may have originally used the term *môreh*, "guide,"[232] which was used to refer to the Teacher of Righteousness at Qumran,[233] although a direct allusion by Jesus to the sect is unlikely.[234] Since Jesus seems to be alluding to various titles that one might take, perhaps a better rendering might be "master."[235] Jesus became a problem to the religious authorities because he taught with divine authority, not scribal authority.

### 7.2.11 Teacher (*didaskolos*)

In the Jewish world of rabbis and the Greco-Roman world of various masters and teachers, Jesus stands singularly significant as the one who would always be the Master and Teacher. In later decades, Rabbinic Judaism moved toward a textual constitution of thought, discipline, and life in the Mishnah. By way of contrast, disciples of Jesus had long before moved into a position of maintaining in their Master's name that Jesus Messiah was the only true Guide (23:10).[236] There was between Jesus and the rabbis not a difference in degree as between two different teachers. There was a significant degree in principle. Jesus taught as someone specially authorized by God and therefore his word was God's word. Jesus was a teacher far different from the synagogue rabbis.[237]

It is here that we can note the subtle difference Matthew's Jesus has made in 23:8

229. They are to avoid *rabbi* . . . *patēr* . . . *kathēgētēs* ("rabbi . . . father . . . instructor").

230. Although the NIV translates *kathēgētēs* "teacher," and the ESV renders it "instructor," the term appears to carry more of the sense of "leader," coming as it does from *kata* and *hēgeomai*, to form *kathēgeomai* "I go before, lead or guide" (Abbott-Smith, *A Manual Greek Lexicon*, 223).

231. E.g., Dionysius of Halicarnassus, *Thuc.* 3.4; Plutarch, *Mor.* 327; Vettius Valens, *Anthologiarum libri* 115.18; P.Giess. 80.7; 11; P.Oxy. 930.6, 20 ("καθηγητής," BDAG, 490). See Bruce W. Winter, "The Messiah as the Tutor: The Meaning of καθηγητής in Matthew 23:10," *TynBul* 42.1 (1991): 152–57.

232. The medieval Jewish philosopher and codifier Moses ben Maimon (Maimonides; AD 1135–1204) wrote the famous *Môrêh Nevukhim*, "Guide for the Perplexed," in which he acted as a personal tutor through his writings for those "perplexed" by the contradiction between the teachings of Torah and philosophy; see "Moses ben Maimon," *EJR* 271–72.

233. A direct allusion to the original leader of the Qumran community was first suggested by C. Spicq, "Une Allusion au Docteur de Justice dans Matthieu, XXIII, 10?," *RB* 66.3 (1959): 387–96, but followed recently by several others, including M. Eugene Boring, "Gospel of Matthew," NIB 8, 432.

234. Most commentators doubt a direct allusion, including Davies and Allison, *Matthew*, 3:278.

235. E.g., Robertson, *Grammar*, 138.

236. B. D. Chilton et al., "Rabbi as a Title of Jesus," in *A Comparative Handbook to the Gospel of Mark* (Leiden: Brill, 2010), 566.

237. Hengel, *Charismatic Leader*, 50. Hengel goes on to say, "For reasons of clarity, therefore, we should desist altogether from the description of Jesus as 'rabbi'" (*Charismatic Leader*, 50). Hengel provides a needed caution of not fashioning Jesus after rabbinic rabbis because of current trends we noted above (n232XXX).

between being called rabbi and having one Teacher: "But you are not to be called 'Rabbi,' for you have one Teacher, and you are all brothers." The ultimate goal of a disciple of a rabbi was to become a rabbi himself at the end of his course of study and initiation. Later rabbinic literature is insightful to the aspirations of a student, who would traverse the levels from the basic "disciple" (*talmîd*), to "distinguished student" (*talmîd wātîq*), to "disciple-associate" (*talmîd ḥābēr*), to "disciple of the wise" (*talmîd ḥākām*). At the later stages a disciple became a rabbi himself, with the ultimate goal to become a master of Torah with disciples studying under him.[238]

With Jesus a new form of discipleship emerges. A disciple of Jesus would always and forever be only a disciple because Jesus alone is Teacher.[239] The ultimate authority within the community of disciples is Jesus as Teacher, which eliminates the struggle for authoritative teaching positions among his followers. They are brothers of one family, all of whom are equal in status.

In the restriction against being "called rabbi," Jesus is emphasizing not to be called by honorific titles or being curried as a "great one" (i.e., *rabbi*). A disciple may *be* a teaching person in the church, but teaching *honor* should be reserved for the "*one*" (*heis*, emphasized) Teacher, Jesus. Jesus warns his disciples against giving each other "honorary titles that would set them apart from or above others."[240]

As Burridge explores the passages unique to Matthew he concludes, "These verses reveal Matthew's particular interests, and, in this, the most Jewish of gospels, Jesus is not just the rabbi, but the human face of God, the revealer who has dominion and authority as the Son of God."[241] Matthew features Jesus as the authoritative Teacher of God's will to his disciples.[242] As the Messiah and the Son of God, Jesus is the one Teacher of his disciples, who can never duplicate his unique role. The disciples' own mission is to "make disciples . . . teaching them to obey everything that [Jesus has] commanded" (Matt 28:19–20).[243]

When Jesus interprets the Law (cf. 5:17–48; cf. 19:3–9), he does so with a sovereign authority ("I say to you") that puts him in a position like that of God, who gave the Law, rather than that of Moses, who mediated it. There are obvious recognizable correspondences between Jesus's proclamations in the Sermon on the Mount and Moses's

238. See Wilkins, *Discipleship in the Ancient World*, 116–24.

239. Samuel Byrskog, *Jesus the Only Teacher: Didactic Authority and Transmission in Ancient Israel*, ConBNT 24 (Stockholm: Almquist & Wiksell, 1994), 300; Hagner, *Matthew 14–28*, 661.

240. Frederick Dale Bruner, *Churchbook*, 437. See also Witherington, *Matthew*, 426; Samuel Byrskog, "Jesus the Only Teacher: Further Thoughts," in *Treasures New & Old: Essays in Honor of Donald A. Hagner*, ed. Carl S. Sweatman and Clifford B. Kvidahl, GlossaHouse Festschrift Series 1 (Wilmore, KY: GlossaHouse, 2018), 36–46. Appearing too late for discussion here but looking to be an excellent addition to the conversation is Charles L. Quarles and Charles Nathan Ridlehoover, eds., *Jesus as Teacher in the Gospel of Matthew*, LNTS (London: T&T Clark, 2023).

241. Richard A. Burridge, *Four Gospels, One Jesus? A Symbolic Reading*, 3rd ed. (Grand Rapids: Eerdmans, 2014), 68.

242. John Yueh-Han Yieh, *One Teacher: Jesus' Teaching Role in Matthew's Gospel Report*, BZNW 124 (Berlin: de Gruyter, 2004), 327. Yieh may make too much of Jesus's *identity* as Teacher. Rather, as he has in his subtitle, Jesus's *role* as Teacher is probably better to emphasize.

243. Yieh, *One Teacher*, 330.

authoritative declarations in the Sinai narrative, but Jesus does not give a new law but rather interprets Moses with divine authority: "You have heard that it was said to the people long ago . . . But *I* tell you" (e.g., 5:21–22; emphasis added). Peter Wick disputes the widespread hypothesis that Matthew views Jesus is a "new" or "second" Moses. He acknowledges obvious parallels between the Sinai account and the Sermon on the Mount, but he concludes that Jesus does not give a new Law but rather "exposits Moses with divine authority" as a sermon directed both to the Jewish people and to the disciples of Jesus.[244] This would cohere with other indications of Jesus's divine identity in Matthew.[245]

### 7.2.12 God's Spirit-Anointed Servant (*ho pais mou*)

The title "servant" is used widely in contemporary Christian settings to refer to Jesus. Yet the title "servant" (*pais*) to designate Jesus is found only once in Matthew's Gospel, and in the rest of the New Testament only in Acts 3:13, 26; 4:27, 30.[246] However, the significance of the title and how Matthew understands Jesus's identity and person as God's Spirit-anointed servant goes beyond this one passage as a theme of Matthew's theological perspective.

#### *7.2.12.1 The Messianic Servant (Isa 42:1–4 and Matt 12:15–21)*

Matthew uses his typical fulfillment formula (cf. 1:22; 2:15, etc.) to introduce the longest Old Testament quotation in his Gospel, which identifies Jesus with the messianic servant of Isa 42:1–4: "This was to fulfill what was spoken through the prophet Isaiah: 'Here is my servant whom I have chosen, the one I love, in whom I delight; I will put my Spirit on him, and he will proclaim justice to the nations'" (Matt 12:17–18). The context in Isaiah's prophecy is the section often called the Servant Songs (Isa 40–53). The identity of the servant is perplexing because it vacillates between the nation Israel as the servant (41:8–10; 44:1–3, 21; 45:4 [49:3?]) and an individual who leads the nation (42:1–4; 49:5–7). That individual emerges as the servant Messiah who has a ministry and mission both to Israel and the nations.[247] Jesus "proclaims justice" through his message of the arrival of the kingdom of heaven, which is a humble invitation to harassed and helpless people, as well as a sentence of judgment on the rulers of this world.[248]

244. For a helpful discussion that contests the prevalent theory that Matthew presents Jesus as a "new" or "second" Moses, see Peter Wick, "Die Bergpredigt: Synagogale Toraauslegung in Vollmacht," in *Schriftgelehrsamkeit und Toraethik: Die Bergpredigt im Kontext des Matthäusevangeliums*, ed. Jens-Christian Maschmeier (Stuttgart: Kohlhammer, 2021), 116–21, here 117–18.

245. Bauckham, "Christology," *DJG*$^2$ 129–30.

246. France, *Matthew*, NICNT, 471. Other terms for servant or slave, *doulos* (e.g., 18:26) and *diakonos* (e.g., 20:26), likewise are not used to refer to Jesus.

247. For brief overviews of this complex subject, see Kaiser, *The Messiah in the Old Testament*, 173–81; Van Groningen, *Messianic Revelation in the Old Testament*, 575–618.

248. See Brown and Roberts, *Matthew*, 359–67.

This servant has an unexpected demeanor. Far from painting a picture of an imposing figure of conquest, Matthew continues his citation of the theme of a suffering servant from Isaiah's prophecy: "He will not quarrel or cry out; no one will hear his voice in the streets. A bruised reed he will not break, and a smoldering wick he will not snuff out, till he has brought justice through to victory. In his name the nations will put their hope" (Matt 12:19–21). This is a picture of a gentle servant Messiah who will not brazenly demand allegiance with his proclamation of justice but who will gently and humbly invite those who are the most in need (11:28–30).[249]

The double metaphor of a bruised reed and smoldering wick emphasizes that the suffering servant will compassionately care for those who have been abused and who are about to expire because of misuse. This harkens us back to the harassed and helpless (9:36) and the weary and burdened (12:28) who have been oppressed not only by the foreign invading forces of Rome, but also by the legalistic burdens from Israel's religious establishment.

The suffering servant's advance of justice will not break those who are abused, nor will it smother those who are nearly out of resources. Rather, it will provide the ultimate victory for those who respond to the invitation to enter the kingdom of heaven. The strong and the mighty often are victorious in this life because they advance their own causes by abusing others and withholding care from those who are needy. But even as Isaiah knew that evil would not have the ultimate victory, so Matthew points to Jesus and declares that victory is at hand for those who seek God's justice.

But it is not only for Israel, for "in his name the nations will put their hope" (12:21). All the nations will put their hope in the name of this servant, the one whom Matthew declares is none other than Jesus of Nazareth (cf. 2:23). Jesus Messiah is a suffering servant who is Spirit-endowed and who offers hope, because the advance of the kingdom of heaven promises victory for all the nations of the world.[250]

### *7.2.12.2 The Theme of Jesus as Servant*

Although the title "servant" is found only here in Matthew's Gospel, the *theme* of Jesus as servant is found more widely.[251] The phrase "the one I love, in whom I delight" (12:18) takes the reader back to Jesus's baptism and forward to Jesus's transfiguration, where the Father expresses the same delight in his beloved Son (3:17; 17:5). The "servant" is the "Son of God," tying both titles together in Jesus Messiah.

249. See Brown, "Matthew's Christology and Isaiah's Servant," 93–106; Hayes, "The One Who Brings Justice," 143–52.

250. Porter, *Sacred Tradition*. Porter helpfully argues that the suffering servant connection with Jesus goes back to Jesus himself (Porter, *Sacred Tradition*, 94–95). See also Nickel, "Jesus, the Isaianic Servant Exorcist."

251. Grindheim, *Christology*, 103.

### 7.2.12.2.1 Predictions by Jesus of His Forthcoming Suffering, Death, and Resurrection

The series of dramatic predictions by Jesus of his forthcoming suffering, death, and resurrection (16:21; 17:22–23; 20:17–19; 26:2) draw from Isa 53:10–12 the purpose of Jesus as the suffering servant. But as much as he tries to get his disciples to understand the necessity of his mission, they continually misapprehend its significance. Instead of being a revolutionary liberator, as many hoped he would be, Jesus will be a suffering Messiah, something that even his own disciples, let alone the crowds, had great difficulty fathoming. By claiming the necessity of suffering death at the hands of the religious leadership of Jerusalem, Jesus begins to reveal the ultimate purpose for his life ministry. And nothing must deter him from his mission.

### 7.2.12.2.2 Jesus Came to Serve and Give His Life as a Ransom for Many (20:17–28)

The fact that Jesus came to serve is clear: "The Son of Man did not come to be served, but to serve, and to give his life as a ransom for many" (20:28). Jesus's statement came in the context of the two brothers' ambition to sit at Jesus's right and left in his kingdom (20:21). Jesus gathers them together to overturn their strictly human ambitions by making a contrast between the world's conception of greatness and that in the kingdom of heaven. To pursue positions of power and authority is a form of ambition that is valued highly among the typical power structures of the world.

But Jesus gives a different, and quite shocking, sort of ambition that must be the chief value among his disciples. "Not so with you. Instead, whoever wants to become great among you must be your servant, and whoever wants to be first must be your slave" (20:26–27). The servant (*diakonos*) worked for hire to maintain the master's home and property, while the slave (*doulos*) had been forced into service. In human eyes serving is not dignified. The formula of the Sophist, "How can a man be happy when he has to serve someone?" (Plato, *Gorgias*, 491e; cf. 492b),[252] expresses the basic Greek attitude. These were two of the lowest positions in society's scale, yet Jesus reverses their status in the community of disciples to being "great" and "first."

The ideal servant or slave lived to care for and protect and make better the lives of those over him or her. Jesus's disciples had the ambition to be great (18:1) and to be in the first and highest positions (20:21), so Jesus gives them the means by which they can do so according to the values of the kingdom of God, not the kingdoms of the world. They must arrange their lives with the ambition to give themselves for the benefit of others. It is no coincidence that Paul adopts these titles to describe himself[253] and those

252. Cited in Hermann W. Beyer, "διακονέω, διακονία, διάκονος," *TDNT* 2:82.

253. E.g., *diakonos*: 2 Cor 3:6; Eph 3:7; Col 1:23; *doulos*: Rom 1:1; Gal. 1:10.

others[254] who would give their lives for the welfare of humanity and the church. John will later call himself a slave of Jesus (Rev 1:1), as will Peter (2 Pet 1:1) and Jesus's own brothers (Jas 1:1; Jude 1).

The ultimate example for the disciples is Jesus's own life: "just as the Son of Man did not come to be served, but to serve, and to give his life as a ransom for many" (20:28). As the Son of Man, in which he had been revealed to be the Messiah, the Son of God (e.g., 16:16–17), to whom all glory and honor should be paid, Jesus had willingly set aside that prerogative for a higher purpose—to serve by giving his life as a ransom for many. This statement gives an explicit indication of his self-understanding of the purpose of the crucifixion that he has been predicting he will soon suffer (16:21; 17:22–23; 20:17–19).

"Ransom" (*lytron*) means "the price of release,"[255] often used of the money paid for the release of slaves. But in the New Testament the meaning of "redemption" or "release" as a theological concept is based on the experience of Israel's release from the slavery of Egypt. The term may also contain an allusion to the suffering servant passage of Isa 53, especially verse 6b: "And the LORD has laid on him the iniquity of us all." The phrase "for many" (*anti pollōn*, Matt 20:28) does not mean "on behalf of" but "in place of." This signifies the notion of exchange substitution for all those who will accept Jesus's payment for their sins.[256] This saying of Jesus is the basis of the doctrine of substitutionary atonement as the work of his sacrifice on the cross, which involves the greatest cost of all, the life of the Son of Man.[257]

In 12:15–21, we see Jesus functioning as the obedient servant of Isa 42:1–4 who is non-confrontational with his enemies, but whose mission ultimately brings forth justice for the whole earth regardless of opposition. As Isa 42 is filled out by later chapters, especially Isaiah 53, Matthew understands Jesus as the servant of Yahweh whose lifelong obedience culminates in his self-giving on the cross as a ransom for many: "Example and atonement are woven together as a total mission to 'save his people from their sins' (1:21)."[258]

---

254. E.g., *diakonos*: Phoebe, Rom 16:1; Tychicus, Eph 6:21; Epaphras, Col 1:23; *doulos*: Epaphras, Col 4:12.

255. Cf. "λύτρον," BDAG 605–6.

256. The preposition *anti* virtually never means "on behalf of," but demands the use "in place of" (cf. Wallace, *Greek Grammar*, 365–67). The "many" (*pollōn*) has been understood to have either an exclusive sense, "many, but not all," restricting the application to the community of the elect (e.g., 1QS VI, 1–23), or to have an inclusive sense, "many, the totality which embraces many individuals," opening the application to all without limitation. In my view, the most convincing historical and linguistic argument affirms the latter; cf. Joachim Jeremias, "πολλῶν," *TDNT* 6:536–45.

257. Cf. Sydney H. T. Page, "Ransom Saying," *DJG*[1] 660–662; Scot McKnight, "Jesus and His Death: Some Recent Scholarship," *CurBS* 9 (2001): 185–228; McKnight, *Jesus and His Death: Historiography, the Historical Jesus, and Atonement Theory* (Waco, TX: Baylor University Press, 2005).

258. France, *Matthew: Evangelist and Teacher*, 302.

### 7.2.12.2.3 Words at the Last Supper about His Blood Shed for Many (26:26–29)

It is widely believed that it was the third cup, after the supper, that Jesus took and said, "This is my blood of the covenant,[259] which is poured out for many for the forgiveness of sins" (Matt 26:28). The third cup was often called the cup of redemption, corresponding to God's third promise, "*I will redeem you* with an outstretched arm and with mighty acts of judgment" (Exod 6:6). The death of the Passover lamb and the smearing of its blood opened the way for the redemption of God's people from Egypt, but the shedding of Jesus's blood, which this cup foreshadows, opens the way for all humanity to enter into a new covenant relationship with God.[260]

With this statement Jesus indicates that he is instituting the fulfillment of the new covenant that was promised to the people of Israel. Of that new covenant the prophet Jeremiah spoke especially of the forgiveness of sins (Jer 31:31, 34). The prophet Ezekiel likewise spoke of the forgiveness that would accompany the new covenant, but he focused further on the personal transformation of those who responded to its inauguration: "I will give you a new heart and put a new spirit in you; I will remove from you your heart of stone and give you a heart of flesh. And I will put my Spirit in you and move you to follow my decrees and be careful to keep my laws" (Ezek 36:26–27).[261]

### 7.2.12.2.4 The Age of the Spirit and Judgment/Justice

That Jesus came to serve is a reflection not only of Jesus's crucifixion and death but also of what Matthew's audience will know of the divine activity in the dying and rising servant.[262] In the fulfillment quotation of 12:17–21, Matthew harks back to Isaiah's prophecy to give one of the clearest declarations of Jesus's intent as Messiah: he is the gentle, Spirit-endowed suffering servant who advances a mission of justice to the nations.[263]

The "judgment/justice" (*krisis*) that Jesus brings to the "nations" (*ta ethnē*) combines the sense of grace and judgment that has characterized the theme of inward righteousness that accompanies the arrival of the kingdom of heaven (e.g., 5:20).[264] The servant will pronounce the arrival of the kingdom that is an invitation to kingdom life but that is also a sentence of judgment upon the rulers of this world. The *krisis* Jesus brings is

259. "New" does not occur in the best MSS, but it does in Luke 22:20 (cf. Metzger, *TCGNT*, 54). However, the allusions to the Old Testament prophecies of a "new covenant" are clear.

260. Routledge, "Passover and Last Supper," 219.

261. Cf. Clay Hamm, "The Last Supper in Matthew," *BBR* 10.1 (2000): 53–69.

262. Carlston and Evans, *From Synagogue to Ekklesia*, 46.

263. Beaton, "Messiah and Justice," 5–23.

264. Many commentators and translations focus primarily upon *krisis* as positive "justice" (e.g., NIV, ESV, NASB; Beaton, *Isaiah's Christ in Matthew's Gospel*, 143–45; France, *Matthew*, NICNT, 471; Morris, *Matthew*, 310n48). A minority focus upon *krisis* as negative "judgment" (e.g., KJV; Quarles, *Matthew*, 291–94). Nolland combines judgment and justice which Jesus brings, and observes that as in 5:21, *krisis* refers primarily to the activity of judging (negative), and then derivatively to the bringing of justice (positive); Nolland, *Matthew*, 493.

the initiation of justice under God in lieu of the unmistakable injustices of this age. The focus is on "the establishment of a just order under God in place of the manifest injustices of the present life."[265]

### 7.2.13 Wisdom (*sophia*)

"Wisdom" is a topic that is debated among Matthean scholars. Some contend that Wisdom is a Matthean christological title or theme, while others contend that it simply connects to the Old Testament literary theme. Some suggest that it is a central theme, while others consider it a minor topic. Most agree that there are three primary appearances of "wisdom" in Matthew's Gospel: 11:19; 11:25–30; 23:34–39.

Wisdom, using the feminine term *sophia*, was often personified in Judaism as a woman giving her children practical guidance in everyday affairs (cf. Job 8). This personification of Wisdom appears most prominently in the book of Proverbs in the Old Testament; e.g., "Does not wisdom call out? Does not understanding raise her voice?" (Prov 8:1 [ca. 970–930 BC]). This personification was followed by its appearance in the apocryphal Wisdom of Ben Sirach: e.g., "When I was young and innocent, I sought wisdom. She came to me in her beauty, and until the end I will cultivate her" (Sir 51:13–14, NABRE; cf. Sir 51:13–30 [ca. 180s BC]). In the second century BC, the apocryphal Wisdom of Solomon also personified wisdom: "I will tell you what wisdom is and how she came to be, and I will hide no secrets from you, but I will trace her course from the beginning of creation, and make knowledge of her clear, and I will not pass by the truth" (Wis Sol 6:22, NRSVue; cf. Wis Sol 7–8 [ca. 50 BC]). This personification exemplified the way in which those who are guided by God's practical approach to life will make right decisions.

The apostle Paul used the formulation "wisdom of God" to describe Jesus Christ (1 Cor 1:24: "Christ the power of God and the wisdom of God") and God's plan of salvation. The wisdom of God is personified in Christ. The message of the gospel is "God's wisdom" (1 Cor 2:7), divine wisdom obtained from the Creator whose previously hidden plan of salvation has become reality through the crucifixion (1 Cor 2:8).[266]

This describes the wisdom milieu in which Matthew wrote his Gospel. The theme of "wisdom" occurs in three primary passages in Matthew's Gospel, to which we turn to see if they add to our understanding of Matthew's perspective of Christology.

#### *7.2.13.1 Wisdom Is Proved Right by Her Deeds (11:19)*

The first is Matt 11:19: "The Son of Man came eating and drinking, and they say, 'Here is a glutton and a drunkard, a friend of tax collectors and sinners.' But wisdom is proved right by her deeds." The saying here by Jesus appears to be a proverbial aphorism.

---

265. Nolland, *Matthew*, 493.

266. Eckhard J. Schnabel, "Wisdom," *DPL* 970.

### 7.2.13.1.1 Jesus Messiah Is Personified Wisdom

It has been interpreted by some to be christological, with Jesus identified as Wisdom incarnate.[267] As I have noted, elsewhere in the New Testament Jesus is referred to as "the wisdom of God" (1 Cor 1:24, 30) because the message of the gospel is "God's wisdom" (1 Cor 2:7), which has become reality through Jesus's death on the cross (1 Cor 2:8).[268] In this view, as Wisdom incarnate, Jesus's deeds (*erga*; cf. Matt 11:2, 19), including those which have been criticized by his opponents, will ultimately vindicate him. It is notable that when Jesus commends his teaching, he does so in words based on those of God's Wisdom personified (11:28–30; cf. Sir 24:9; 51:23–26). Bauckham observes that "this is the clearest indication of a Wisdom Christology in Matthew, which some scholars consider a broader characteristic of this Gospel."[269]

In this view, the expression "wisdom is vindicated by her deeds" (*erga*) is said to match the reference to "the deeds [*ta erga*] of the Messiah" in 11:2, forming an *inclusio* for 11:2–19, suggesting that Jesus as Messiah can be characterized as the embodiment of Wisdom, since the Messiah's deeds are Wisdom's deeds.[270] Wisdom is portrayed in 11:19 as a person who is falsely accused but is vindicated, or "proved right" (*edikaiōthē*), by her deeds. Wisdom is personified in Proverbs as one who "was formed long ages ago, at the very beginning, when the world came to be" (Prov 8:23), who was "there when he set the heavens in place" (8:27), and who "was constantly at his side" during the work of creation "like a master workman" (8:30 ESV). This view assumes that Jesus's hearers and Matthew's first readers would have understood that Jesus identified himself as this personified Wisdom.[271]

### 7.2.13.1.2 God's Wisdom Is Justified in the Ministries of Both John the Baptist and Jesus Messiah

However, the *inclusio* of "deeds" (11:2, 19) includes both "the deeds of the Messiah" (11:2) and the "deeds" of wisdom (11:19). In the former, "the deeds of the Messiah" are his alone in validating his messianic identity, as Jesus directly proves to John the Baptist's disciples. In the latter, both the activities of John the Baptist and Jesus Messiah

267. Especially, M. Jack Suggs, *Wisdom, Christology, and Law in Matthew's Gospel* (Cambridge: Harvard University Press, 1970), 36–58; Celia M. Deutsch, *Hidden Wisdom and the Easy Yoke: Wisdom, Torah, and Discipleship in Matthew 11:25–30* (Sheffield: JSOT Press, 1987), esp. 103–30; Deutsch, *Lady Wisdom, Jesus, and the Sages: Metaphor and Social Context in Matthew's Gospel* (Philadelphia: Trinity Press International, 1996). See also Boring, "Matthew," 269; Davies and Allison, *Matthew*, 2:264–65; Hagner, *Matthew 1–13*, 311; Keener, *Matthew* (1999), 343; Quarles, *Theology of Matthew*, 138–42.

268. For a brief discussion of the wisdom motif, see Eckhard J. Schnabel, "Wisdom," *NDBT* 843–48.

269. Bauckham, "Christology," *DJG*² 130.

270. Brown and Roberts, *Matthew*, 115; Carlston and Evans, *From Synagogue to Ekklesia*, 84–85; Witherington, *Matthew*, 234–36.

271. Quarles, *Matthew*, 274–75. And more fully, Quarles, *Theology of Matthew*, 138–42. See also Celia M. Deutsch, "Jesus as Wisdom: A Feminist Reading of Matthew's Wisdom Christology," in *A Feminist Companion to Matthew*, ed. Amy-Jill Levine with Marianne Blickenstaff (Cleveland, OH: Pilgrim, 2001), 98–107, here 98–101; Brown and Roberts, *Matthew*, 115; Konradt, *Matthew*, 178.

are emphasized. God's wisdom will be "proved right" (*edikaiōthē*; NIV), "justified" (ESV), or "vindicated" (NASB) by her actions (cf. "children" in the parallel in Luke 7:35) in the righteous activities of both John and Jesus Messiah. Their deeds prove their wisdom.

Additionally, since the emphasis in the passage is not primarily christological but salvation-historically attuned to the developing ministries of John the Baptist and Jesus, it is better to understand wisdom here in its more usual sense in association with God's wisdom. Wisdom is the application of knowledge to life in such a way that a person's activities are a concrete example of a life lived well in the presence of God; it is the right ordering of life as ordained by God, validating a commonsense approach to life. If this generation had taken John the Baptist and Jesus Messiah for who they said they were, the knowledge of who they were as forerunner (John the Baptist) and Messiah (Jesus) would have been proved right by their actions, as seemingly opposite as were their lifestyles.[272] Carson notes that wisdom, already personified in the Old Testament and developed into a quasi-personal hypostasis in heaven, does sometimes serve in the New Testament as a vehicle for Christology. But here wisdom is best understood in its more traditional association with God. He concludes, "Not only is this interpretation coherent and contextually suitable, but it wraps up the preceding section in which Jesus has been exonerating the Baptist by explaining his role in redemptive history and simultaneously castigating the people for their spiritual dullness."[273] Turner further emphasizes, "The use of wisdom language to describe Jesus's mission does not justify the identification of Jesus with wisdom hypostatized. . . . Wisdom is not used metaphysically but as a metaphor for Jesus's and John's credible ministries."[274]

### *7.2.13.2 "Take My Yoke upon You and Learn from Me" (11:25–30)*

The continuation of the preceding (11:19) into 11:25–30 provides the second passage that some believe yields Wisdom Christology. We noted above several times the importance of this passage for insights to Jesus as Son of God, but does this passage reveal Jesus as Wisdom personified?

#### 7.2.13.2.1 Jesus Is Wisdom Incarnate

Some say yes, this passage reveals Jesus as Wisdom personified. The passage has been described as "one of the most crucial passages for understanding the character of this Gospel and its presentation of Jesus as both sage and Wisdom incarnate."[275]

272. Evans, *Matthew*, 241.

273. Carson, "Matthew," 314. See further, D. A. Carson, "Matthew 11/Luke 7:35: A Test Case for the Bearing of Q Christology on the Synoptic Problem," in *Jesus of Nazareth: Lord and Christ—Essays on the Historical Jesus and New Testament Christology*, ed. Joel B. Green and Max Turner (Grand Rapids: Eerdmans, 1994), 128–46.

274. Turner, *Matthew*, 296–97. Cf. Carson, "Matthew," 314; France, *Matthew*, TNTC, 197; Osborne, *Matthew*, 427–28.

275. Witherington, *Matthew*, 237.

In 11:25–27 Jesus offers revelatory wisdom that is hidden from the conventionally wise and intelligent, yet it is revealed even to infants.[276] Yet others do not see the wisdom elements as prominent. Carlston and Evans comment that if 11:25–27 were not attached to 11:28–30, the wisdom elements could hardly be noted, much less made central to the Matthean Jesus. Neither the theme of thanksgiving nor the revelation to "infants" is confined to the wisdom tradition.[277]

In 11:28–30 the wisdom motifs become somewhat clearer, where Jesus calls the weary to take up his yoke, to learn from him, and there find rest for their souls. In parallels in Sirach, Wisdom does the same as Jesus in calling and offering rest (e.g., Sir 6:18–31; 51:17, 24–28).[278] Some suggest that since the Wisdom of Sirach was quite popular in early Judaism, some of Jesus's audience may have known the writing and would have concluded that Jesus was here speaking as the incarnation of God's Wisdom.[279]

#### 7.2.13.2.2 Jesus Is the Son Incarnate Who Is the Teacher of Wisdom

Others say, "Yes, but . . . " Jesus teaches similarly to Sirach of personified wisdom, but the primary emphasis in 11:25–30 is on the incarnation of the Son of God and his relationship to the Father. Parallels to wisdom themes show the multifaceted nature of the Son, who now embodies wisdom. The passage is not focused on wisdom but rather on sonship, and wisdom characterizes the Son's relationship with the Father and the relationship with those he calls to find rest. In this passage the Son is the Teacher of wisdom. The phrase "learn from me" shapes the image of the Teacher of wisdom to place the emphasis on obedience to instruction. Jesus delivers on wisdom's promises. Nolland notes, "It is with him [Jesus] that ultimate wisdom is to be found. At some level this probably makes Jesus 'Wisdom incarnate,' but while Matthew exploits the wisdom imagery, he is not specifically investing in a wisdom Christology."[280] And Matthais Konradt, commenting on 11:19 and the proverbial aphorism "wisdom is proved right by her deeds," states, "Jesus's works are manifestations of divine wisdom. However, this motif flows in rather casually. Matthew did not develop it into a substantial wisdom Christology."[281]

### *7.2.13.3 Therefore I Am Sending You Prophets and Sages and Teachers (23:34–39)*

This current passage for our consideration, 23:34–39, has been declared "the *locus classicus* of the theory that Matthew includes a wisdom Christology in his Gospel."[282]

276. Witherington, *Matthew*, 237.
277. Carlston and Evans, *From Synagogue to Ekklesia*, 86.
278. Carlston and Evans, *From Synagogue to Ekklesia*, 86.
279. Witherington, *Matthew*, 239.
280. Nolland, *Matthew*, 475.
281. Konradt, *Matthew*, 178.
282. Carlston and Evans, *From Synagogue to Ekklesia*, 86–87.

A primary point of support is found in Matthew's opening statement, where Jesus states: "Therefore I am sending you prophets and sages and teachers" (23:34). Luke's parallel passage offers an important perspective: "Therefore also the Wisdom of God said, 'I will send them prophets and apostles'" (Luke 11:49 ESV). In Luke, it is not Jesus speaking and sending but rather the Wisdom of God. It has been claimed that Matthew has this saying in the voice of Jesus because "he envisions Jesus, not someone else or some abstract entity or personification, as the Wisdom of God."[283] However, France points out that in Matthew there is no verbal echo of a known wisdom passage, and the alleged Wisdom Christology depends entirely on the silence of Matthew as compared with Luke:[284] "As far as Matthew is concerned, this is a declaration by Jesus in his own right, not an echo of an unknown wisdom saying."[285]

### *7.2.13.4 Conclusion: Wisdom Christology in Matthew's Gospel?*

We have found some evidence of Wisdom Christology in Matthew's Gospel, especially in 11:25–30. Jesus teaches similarly to Sirach of personified wisdom, but the primary emphasis in 11:25–30 is on the incarnation of the Son of God and his relationship to the Father. Parallels to wisdom themes show the multifaceted nature of the Son, who now embodies wisdom. The passage is not focused on wisdom, but rather on sonship, and wisdom characterizes the Son's relationship with the Father, and the relationship with those he calls to find rest. Rather than seeing Jesus as the personification of wisdom, it is better to see Jesus as a "teacher of wisdom." In this passage, the Son is the Teacher of wisdom.[286]

Therefore, I conclude that wisdom is a theme evident in Matthew's Gospel but not central, and not a central christological theme.[287] Carlston and Evans conclude their section on wisdom in Matthew by stating, "That wisdom is not central to the Matthean Christology is evident from the material already presented in this chapter. But it too has its part to play in the entire portrait."[288] Sigurd Grindheim concludes, "It is unwarranted, therefore, to conclude that Jesus is outright identified with wisdom. But it would also be unwarranted to rule out wisdom influence altogether. It appears that Matthew has found wisdom ideas as one motif among several others that were useful in painting his picture of Jesus."[289] And Luz likewise observes that the Matthean texts that indirectly identify Jesus with Wisdom (11:19, 28–30) are so few, so unclear, and so scattered in the Gospel that in his judgment no coherent christological model is visible

283. Witherington, *Matthew*, 432–33.

284. France, *Matthew*, NICNT, 879.

285. France, *Matthew*, NICNT, 880. Deutsch finds Wisdom themes throughout 23:34–39; cf. Deutsch, *Lady Wisdom*, 68–75; Deutsch, "Jesus as Wisdom," 104. But these are primarily based on making an explicit connection of Jesus's saying in 23:34 and Wisdom speaking in Luke 11:49.

286. For an expansion on this theme, see Patrick Schreiner, "Jesus as a Teacher of Wisdom," in *Matthew, Disciple and Scribe*, 12–20.

287. See similarly the excursus "What of Wisdom?" in Leim, *Matthew's Theological Grammar*, 232–33.

288. Carlston and Evans, *From Synagogue to Ekklesia*, 88.

289. Grindheim, *Christology*, 113.

behind them. Luz ends, "I conclude that like many others, Matthew may in some way have identified Jesus with divine Wisdom, but it is in no way an issue for him. In my judgment, Jesus-Sophia is not at all a determining element of his Christology."[290]

This concludes our study of the various designations—especially names and titles—for Jesus Messiah in Matthew's Gospel. In the next chapter we continue to explore Matthew's perspective of Christology, now focusing briefly on his perspective of Jesus Messiah's offices and relationship to the Father and Holy Spirit.

290. Luz, *Matthew*, 3:153. See also McDonough, who shows more broadly that Jesus is not normally identified with Wisdom; rather, he *has* divine Wisdom, which is only "one of the tributaries of the river of Christology" (McDonough, *Christ as Creator*, 84). Similarly, Eva Günther, *Wisdom as a Model for Jesus' Ministry: A Study on the "Lament over Jerusalem" in Matt 23:37–39 Par. Luke 13:34–35*, WUNT 2/513 (Tübingen: Mohr Siebeck, 2020).

*Chapter 8*

# JESUS IMMANUEL: OFFICES AND RELATIONSHIP TO THE FATHER AND HOLY SPIRIT

## *Incipient Trinitarianism*

### BIBLIOGRAPHY

**Bates, Matthew W.** *The Birth of the Trinity: Jesus, God, and Spirit in New Testament and Early Christian Interpretation of the Old Testament.* Oxford: Oxford University Press, 2015. **Bauckham, Richard J.** *Jesus and the God of Israel:* God Crucified *and Other Studies on the New Testament's Christology of Divine Identity.* Grand Rapids: Eerdmans, 2008. **Beaton, Richard.** *Isaiah's Christ in Matthew's Gospel.* SNTSMS 123. New York: Cambridge University Press, 2004. **Bird, Michael F.** *Jesus the Eternal Son: Answering Adoptionist Christology.* Grand Rapids: Eerdmans, 2017. **Boyarin, Daniel.** *The Jewish Gospels: The Story of the Jewish Christ.* New York: New Press, 2012. **Burke, Trevor J., and Keith Warrington,** eds. *A Biblical Theology of the Holy Spirit.* Eugene, OR: Cascade, 2014. **Collins, John J., and Adela Yarbro Collins.** *King and Messiah as Son of God: Divine, Human, and Angelic Messianic Figures in Biblical and Related Literature.* Grand Rapids: Eerdmans, 2008. **Crowe, Brandon D., and Carl R. Trueman,** eds. *The Essential Trinity: New Testament Foundations and Practical Relevance.* Phillipsburg, NJ: P&R, 2017. **Gathercole, Simon J.** *The Pre-existent Son: Recovering the Christologies of Matthew, Mark, and Luke.* Grand Rapids: Eerdmans, 2006. **Grindheim, Sigurd.** *Christology in the Synoptic Gospels: God or God's Servant?* London: T&T Clark, 2012. **Hurtado, Larry W.** *Lord Jesus Christ: Devotion to Jesus in Earliest Christianity.* Grand Rapids: Eerdmans, 2003. **Kirk, J. R. Daniel.** *A Man Attested by God: The Human Jesus of the Synoptic Gospels.* Grand Rapids: Eerdmans, 2016. **Lee, Aquila H. I.** *From Messiah to Preexistent Son: Jesus' Self-Consciousness and Early Christian Exegesis of Messianic Psalms.* WUNT 2/192. Tübingen: Mohr Siebeck, 2005. **Leim, Joshua E.** *Matthew's Theological Grammar: The Father and the Son.* WUNT 2/402. Tübingen: Mohr Siebeck, 2015. **Loke, Andrew Ter Ern.** *The Origin of Divine Christology.* SNTSMS 169. Cambridge: Cambridge University Press, 2017. **Macchia, Frank D.** *Jesus the Spirit Baptizer: Christology in Light of Pentecost.* Grand Rapids: Eerdmans, 2018. **McDonough,**

**Sean M.** *Christ as Creator: Origins of a New Testament Doctrine.* Oxford: Oxford University Press, 2009. **Sanders, Fred.** *The Triune God.* NSD. Grand Rapids: Zondervan, 2016. **Smith, Brandon D.,** ed. *The Trinity in the Canon: A Biblical, Theological, Historical, and Practical Proposal.* Brentwood, TN: B&H, 2023. **Stuhlmacher, Peter.** *Die Geburt des Immanuel: Die Weihnachtsgeschichten aus dem Lukas- und Matthäusevangelium.* Göttingen: Vandenhoeck & Ruprecht, 2005. **Witherington, Ben, III.** *The Christology of Jesus.* Minneapolis: Fortress, 1990. **Zehnder, Markus.** "The Question of the 'Divine Status' of the Davidic Messiah." *BBR* 30.4 (2020): 485–514.

## 8.1 Jesus Immanuel: Prophet, Priest, and King

Matthew presents the activities of Jesus Messiah's life and ministry to indicate the way that Jesus fulfills the various prophesied roles of the anticipated Messiah. Jesus fulfills Old Testament prophesied hope by performing the functions of prophet, priest, and king.[1] Gavin Ortlund observes that this three-pronged approach to understanding Christ's messianic work became standardized after Calvin, although a careful survey of church history can find it as far back as Eusebius. Prophets, priests, and kings were the anointed leaders among God's people in the Old Testament, so it is fitting that the Messiah (i.e., the Anointed One) should embrace all of these offices in his person. "These offices are often called Christ's *triplex munus* and sometimes teased out in terms of Christ's work as mediator."[2]

### 8.1.1 Prophet

Many within Israel looked to the prophets who spoke for God and declared God's will for his people, both in their present time and for the future. They looked for the Messiah to be the voice of God, the greatest prophet, who would fulfill Moses's prophecy of the eschatological Prophet (Deut 18:15–18).

Jesus was not acknowledged as a prophet in his hometown of Nazareth (Matt 13:57). But his final arrival in Jerusalem prompted people in the crowd to herald him as "the prophet from Nazareth in Galilee" (21:11). Many in Jesus's ministry saw him to be a prophet like John the Baptist, Elijah, Jeremiah, or others of the prophets (16:14). The crowd's response at Jesus's triumphal entry to Jerusalem does not seem to imply that they understand him to be *the* eschatological Prophet of Moses's prophecy (Deut 18:15–18)[3] but rather the prophet who has been creating such a stir in Galilee and whose hometown was Nazareth. Others who have called out "Hosanna" seem to

1. See Glenn R. Kreider, "Jesus the Messiah as Prophet, Priest, and King," *BSac* 176 (2019): 174–87.

2. Gavin Ortlund, "Resurrected as Messiah: The Risen Christ as Prophet, Priest and King," *JETS* 54.4 (2011): 749–66, esp. 751.

3. Cf. John 6:14; 7:40, 52; Acts 3:22; 7:37.

expect Jesus to bring liberation as had the kings of ancient Israel and the Maccabees of more recent times.

However, as some had earlier begun to see,[4] Jesus was indeed that great Prophet to whom Moses had pointed, the Prophet who revealed and explained the Father to his people (John 1:18). As a prophet Jesus claims divine authority, so his coming is a threat not only to the Roman political power but also to the religious authority lodged in the temple priesthood and Sanhedrin (Matt 21:46): "The people of the city have every reason to see trouble ahead as the unruly Galilean crowd bring 'their' prophet into Jerusalem in a royal procession."[5]

### 8.1.2 Priest

The priestly line of the Old Testament represented Israel to God to seek his forgiveness of sin. The Qumran community illustrates those within first-century Judaism who expected a priestly Messiah, which is especially seen in the phrase "the anointed one of Aaron" (e.g., 1QS IX, 11). Jesus's activities in the temple and his declaration of judgment upon those who have perverted the temple's function announce that he is the actualization of the priestly hopes.[6] The unfolding activities of the Passion Week, culminating in his cries from the cross and the tearing of the curtain veil, proclaim that he has fulfilled the priestly hopes (Matt 27:50–54).

The priestly presentation of Jesus in Matthew's Gospel indicates that he is the self-sacrificing priest who offers his body for the sins of the world. In his ministry one greater than the temple has arrived (12:6). The tearing of the temple curtain testifies that Jesus's sacrifice on the cross has fulfilled the hopes that had been expressed in Israel's years and years of temple sacrifice.[7] Jesus is the great high priest whose sacrifice is the permanent satisfaction of God's wrath upon humanity's sin (cf. Heb 4:14–5:10).[8] The tearing of the temple curtain from top to bottom testifies to God's activity in Jesus's death of removing the separation between God and his people.

No longer is only the high priest allowed access to the holiest of holy places to commune with God. Jesus's sacrifice on the cross fulfills God's righteous demand for the punishment and atonement for sin. Jesus is the permanently accessible new temple in whom all people who turn to him are reconciled to the Father. But he is also the healer, purifier, and teacher of God's law. In all he does, from his baptism to his closing prayers on the cross, he stands as the priestly mediator between God and humanity, setting the pattern for his church to follow.[9]

4. Cf. John 6:14; 7:40, 52; Acts 3:22; 7:37.

5. See France, *Matthew*, NICNT, 781–82.

6. For a monograph that attempts to unpack the historical Jesus as Israel's "high-priestly" Son of God, Son of David, and Son of Man, see Perrin, *Jesus the Priest*, summary in 282–89.

7. See Daniel M. Gurtner, *The Torn Veil: Matthew's Exposition of the Death of Jesus*, SNTSMS 139 (Cambridge: Cambridge University Press, 2007).

8. Cf. Keener, *Matthew* (2009), 686–87.

9. Uche Anizor and Hank Voss, *Representing Christ: A Vision for the Priesthood of All Believers* (Downers Grove, IL: InterVarsity, 2016), 45.

### 8.1.3 King

The patriarch Jacob prophesied of a kingly Messiah that would come from the tribe of Judah and reign as king: "The scepter will not depart from Judah, nor the ruler's staff from between his feet, until he to whom it belongs shall come" (Gen 49:10). This theme was continued and expanded in classic messianic passages where David's line comprises a dynasty from which the Anointed One would arise to vanquish his enemies and rule his people on an eternal throne in Jerusalem (2 Sam 7:16; cf. Ps 2:6; 110). But the distinctive strain of these prophecies was that this Anointed One extended the rule of God, not the rule of humans: "One of the central and defining features of the NT writings is their articulation of Jesus as the singular messianic king."[10]

Matthew emphasizes that Jesus is referred to as "king of the Jews" and receives worship from foreign magi even as a child (Matt 2:1–12). Matthew's opening genealogy trumpets Jesus's Davidic kingship (1:2–17). The foremost declaration of Jesus and feasibly the central theme throughout Matthew's Gospel is the "kingdom" of heaven/God, which has come near in the person of Jesus Messiah (3:1–12; 4:17, 23; 5:3, etc.).[11]

Jesus's dramatic entry to Jerusalem brings these kingship strains together. He is the divine-human king who has fulfilled the Davidic prophecies of a future king but who also has established the kingdom of heaven in a spiritual way that will allow him to reign in his followers' hearts throughout this age (Eph 3:17). Additionally, as the human representative, Jesus fulfills the intended goal for humanity that was created to rule this world for God (cf. Gen 1:26–28; Ps 8:3–8).[12]

Matthew emphasizes the kingly aspects of Jesus's messianic identity as he narrates the final week of Jesus's mission, although he will often present these details tragically, as Jesus is accused of treason for claiming the title of king of the Jews (27:11–14) and as the crowds mock his kingship (e.g., 27:29).[13]

From its beginning until the end, the Gospel of Matthew portrays Jesus as the messianic Son of David and Son of God who is Israel's true and final king. Jesus's messianic role is accomplished in his saving Israel and humankind from their sins, authoritatively fulfilling God's Torah, providing mercy and compassion through his messianic deeds, and enabling his disciples to share in his messianic ministry and activities as they make disciples of all the nations.[14]

---

10. Jipp, *Messianic Theology*, 19. See also Joshua W. Jipp, *Christ Is King: Paul's Royal Ideology* (Minneapolis: Augsburg Fortress, 2015). Similarly exploring messiah language in ancient Judaism, see Novenson, *Christ Among the Messiahs*, esp. 34–97; and Shirley Lucass, *The Concept of the Messiah in the Scriptures of Judaism and Christianity*, LSTS 78 (London: T&T Clark, 2011).

11. Jipp, *Messianic Theology*, 39.

12. For background, see Bock, "Identity of Jesus," 441–58.

13. Ham, *Coming King*, 121–26.

14. Cf. Jipp, *Messianic Theology*, 81.

### 8.1.4 The Three Offices of Prophet, Priest, and King Coalesce in the One Person of Jesus Messiah

The Old Testament messianic roles of prophet, priest, and king were primarily understood in Judaism to be fulfilled by separate individuals. Therefore, if one person fulfilled all three offices, he would have to be an extraordinary person, more than anyone could conceive. And that extraordinary nature is precisely how the Gospel writers present him and is a special focus of Matthew's clarification of Jesus's messianic identity and mission. All three offices coalesce in the one person of Jesus Messiah, but the way that he fulfills these offices confounds the people of Israel.

- He pronounces judgment on Israel like the prophets of old, not simply to restore order but, as the *Prophet* who has fulfilled the Old Testament, to enable his nation of disciples to live kingdom-empowered lives as his witnesses during this age.
- He clears the temple, not simply to restore the institutional and ethical integrity of the priestly order but to announce that he is the *Priest* who will offer the final sacrifice that will make open and permanent the access of all humans to God.
- He enters Jerusalem as the *King*, not to establish the monarchy but to bring peace between God and humanity and between humans and humans through his own death.

Therefore, our discipleship to Jesus must understand him to be more than a spokesman for God, more than a cleric for God, and more than a warrior for God.[15] J. I. Packer catches the essence of this as he declares of Jesus that, as prophet, priest, and king, it is his glory, given him by the Father, to be in this way the all-sufficient Savior. "We who believe are called to understand this and to show ourselves his people by obeying him as our king, trusting him as our priest, and learning from him as our prophet and teacher. To center on Jesus Christ in this way is the hallmark of authentic Christianity."[16]

Matthew shows us that Jesus is the Messiah who fulfills all of the hopes for humanity and offers an entirely new way of living with him as prophet, priest, and king.[17]

15. These three aspects of Jesus's work are found together in the book of Hebrews, where Jesus is the messenger who is the ultimate revelation of God (1:1–14; 3:1), the great high priest who offered himself to God as a sacrifice for our sins (2:17; 4:14–5:10; chs. 7–10), and the messianic king who is exalted to his throne (1:3, 13; 2:9; 4:16).

16. J. I. Packer, *Concise Theology* (Wheaton, IL: Tyndale, 1993), 133.

17. For helpful recent studies with implications for the church, see Richard P. Belcher Jr., *Prophet, Priest, and King: The Roles of Christ in the Bible and Our Roles Today* (Philipsburg, PA: P&R, 2016); and the forthcoming, Michael S. Horton, Elizabeth W. Mburu, Justin S. Holcomb, eds., *Prophet, Priest, and King: Christology in Global Perspective* (Grand Rapids: Zondervan, 2025).

In Jesus Messiah alone all our needs are met completely and perfectly. Our need for truth is found in Jesus as the final prophet and revelation of God. Our need for a righteous standing before God is achieved by him as our priestly representative, substitute, and new covenant head. And "our need to have our rebel hearts subdued, our enemies defeated, and the new creation inaugurated and ultimately consummated is accomplished by him as our conquering king."[18] Such is Matthew's view of Jesus, our Prophet, Priest, and King.

## 8.2 MATTHEW'S INCIPIENT TRINITARIANISM

This foray into Matthew's understanding of Christology leads us finally to what I understand to be Matthew's incipient Trinitarianism. "Incipient Trinitarianism" indicates the beginning attestation of the revelation in history of the relationship of the Father, Son, and Spirit that was recorded in the biblical text but is not yet fully developed or articulated in a theological doctrine. To explain the development of the doctrine of the Trinity in the early church, Brandon Smith uses these terms: *Incipient Trinitarianism* (**ca. AD 30–96;** the beginning of development); *Proto-Trinitarianism* (**ca. AD 96–325;** a precursor to the Nicene/Nicene-Constantinopolitan creeds); and *Pro-Nicene Trinitarianism* (**ca. AD 325–381**; the final form we have in the creeds of Nicaea and Constantinople).[19]

The stage of *Incipient Trinitarianism* (**ca. AD 30–96**) materialized in the revelation of Jesus's teachings and activities in his historical ministry and between the resurrection of Jesus and the end of the writings of the biblical canon. This stage was directly informed by the authors' reflections, memories, and repeated traditions of the Father's activities, Jesus's actions and teaching, and the Spirit's ministry. The revelation of the Trinity occurred in the historical sending of the Son in the incarnation and the sending of the Spirit at Pentecost. The writings of the New Testament are inspired attestation of the revelation that had already occurred in the historical appearances of the Son and Spirit.[20]

For example, in the case of Matthew, John, or Paul, the language for the Trinitarian persons is not fully systematized. They were passing on their faithful and Spirit-inspired memories. Sigurd Grindheim refers to this as "the fountainhead of later Trinitarian theology."[21] The biblical writers understood that their view of monotheism needed

18. Stephen Wellum, "The Threefold Office of Christ Alone: Prophet, Priest, King," in *Christ Alone—The Uniqueness of Jesus as Savior: What the Reformers Taught . . . and Why It Still Matters*, Five Solas (Grand Rapids: Zondervan, 2017), 127–55, here 155.

19. Brandon D. Smith, "Trinitarian Language in the Early Church," *Credo Magazine*, March 4, 2020, https://credomag.com/2020/03/Trinitarian-language-in-the-early-church/. See, for example, Matt 1–3; Mark 3:28–30; John 1:1–14; 5:17–23; 1 Cor 8:6; Col 1:15–20; 1 Pet 1:2; Rev 1:4–18.

20. Fred Sanders, "Trinitarian Exegesis," in *Triune God*, NSD (Grand Rapids: Zondervan, 2016), 185.

21. Sigurd Grindheim, *God's Equal: What Can We Know About Jesus' Self-Understanding in the Synoptic Gospels?*, LNTS 446 (London: T&T Clark, 2011), 221.

to be rearticulated—but not abandoned—in the light of Jesus's resurrection and the sending of the Holy Spirit. While the New Testament writers do not articulate a fully developed "doctrine of the Trinity," the implicitly Trinitarian thought forms of the teaching of Jesus found in the writings of Matthew, John, Luke, and Paul (especially) provide much of the basis for those later formulations.[22]

I briefly offer here some of Matthew's recollections that informed later theological formulations of the Trinity.[23] Fred Sanders encourages us "to embrace the doctrine of the Trinity wholeheartedly and without reserve, as a central concern of evangelical Christianity."[24]

### 8.2.1 Immanuel, "God with Us": A Declaration of Jesus's Origin and Identity

At the beginning of Matthew's narrative of Jesus's life and ministry, we discover the historical origin of the incarnation and the true identity of Jesus Messiah. When Joseph discovered that his betrothed Mary was pregnant, the angel of the Lord appeared to provide knowledge of the Holy Spirit-conceived baby. The angel instructed Joseph to name the child Jesus (1:21), and Matthew records that "all this took place to fulfill what the Lord had said through the prophet: 'The virgin will conceive and give birth to a son, and they will call him Immanuel'" (1:22–23). As Matthew translates it, we see that the name Immanuel is intended as a title to indicate Jesus's divine identity: "God with us."

Jesus's entrance into history is encapsulated in the name Immanuel, "God with us" (1:23). His presence is assured when even two or three of his disciples are gathered in his name: "There am I among them" (18:20 ESV). And his abiding presence with his disciples throughout history is pronounced in his concluding assurance, "I am with you always, to the very end of the age" (28:20). Therefore, the theme of "God with us" begins and concludes this Gospel, and links Jesus's earthly ministry to his risen life, linking his death to his resurrected life among his disciples. This threefold emphasis upon the presence of Jesus (1:23; 18:20; 28:20) indicates that Immanuel is not a mere addendum but rather is a primary christological concept of Matthew's Gospel.[25]

22. Max Turner and G. McFarlane, "Trinity," *NBD*³ 1211.

23. For brief overviews of incipient Trinitarianism in Matthew's Gospel, see Brandon D. Crowe, "The Trinity and the Gospel of Matthew," 25–43; Jonathan T. Pennington, "Matthew," in *The Trinity in the Canon: A Biblical, Theological, Historical, and Practical Proposal*, ed. Brandon D. Smith (Brentwood, TN: B&H, 2023), 83–114.

24. Fred Sanders, *The Deep Things of God: How the Trinity Changes Everything* (Wheaton, IL: Crossway, 2010), 7. Recent works on the Trinity that are helpful readings include Sanders, *Triune God*; Sanders, *Deep Things of God*; Bates, *Birth of the Trinity*; Crowe and Trueman, eds., *Essential Trinity*; Brandon D. Smith, *The Biblical Trinity: Encountering the Father, Son, and Holy Spirit in Scripture* (Bellingham, WA: Lexham, 2023); Smith, *Trinity in the Canon*. For recent assertions of eternal generation of the Son, see Fred Sanders and Scott R. Swain, eds., *Retrieving Eternal Generation* (Grand Rapids: Zondervan, 2017); Michael F. Bird and Scott Harrower, eds., *Trinity Without Hierarchy: Reclaiming Nicene Orthodoxy in Evangelical Theology* (Grand Rapids: Kregel, 2019).

25. Bockmuehl, "Gospels on the Presence of Jesus," 92; Quarles, *Matthew*, 764.

Jesus is placed in closest relationship with the Father and Spirit (28:19), and he is with us always as the divine Immanuel.[26] Jesus's earthly origin is nothing less than from the Holy Spirit, and he is assigned a name, Immanuel, that specifies his heavenly identity. He did not become God in the incarnation, but rather he took on human nature as the one who was God. Both his common name and his titular name indicate profound truths: *Jesus* specifies what he does ("God saves"), and *Immanuel* specifies who he is ("God with us"). These are highly charged names that will speak of a profound christological and incipient Trinitarian orientation by Matthew.

### 8.2.2 Jesus's Baptism: Theophany at the Jordan River

In this one passage (Matt 3:16–17), we have the voice of the Father and the Spirit of God descending like a dove on Jesus the Son. As Leon Morris states, "Matthew has certain trinitarian interest."[27] And Sanders states, "Jesus' baptism in the Jordan River by John is widely recognized as a Trinitarian manifestation of a special character."[28]

#### *8.2.2.1 Jesus and the Holy Spirit: A Power-Filled Relationship*

John the Baptist announced that the soon arriving One, Jesus Messiah, would baptize with the Holy Spirit and fire (3:11). Now in his baptism Jesus is anointed by the Spirit of God (3:16). This inaugurates the age of the Spirit foretold by the prophet Joel (Joel 2:28–29). Matthew passed over most of Jesus's early years, but some later apocryphal writers conjectured, sometimes rather wildly, about Jesus's early life. Some created fanciful stories, such as the boy Jesus fashioning sparrows out of clay and clapping his hands to have them come to life and fly away[29] or changing mischievous little children into goats and then back into children.[30] This kind of speculation usually displays a faulty understanding of Jesus's incarnation.

The consistent christological picture in the New Testament reveals Jesus as a person who was fully divine in his essence and attributes during his time on earth, yet he did not operate in glorious display of his deity. Rather, he lived a fully human life in the power of the Spirit, giving his followers the ultimate example of a Spirit-led and empowered life, the example of how true human life is to be lived. The emphasis upon the Holy Spirit as the effective power in Jesus's conception (1:20) has the inference of attributing it to God.[31] Matthew usually describes the Spirit as the Holy Spirit, but in his designation of the "Spirit of God" (3:16) at Jesus's baptism, this points to the divine nature of the Spirit. This triadic emphasis of both Jesus's baptism by John the Baptist

26. Crowe, "Trinity and the Gospel of Matthew," 40.
27. Morris, *Matthew*, 68.
28. Sanders, *Triune God*, 195–96.
29. Infancy Gospel of Thomas 2.1–5.
30. Arabic Gospel of the Infancy 40.
31. Hurtado, *Lord Jesus Christ*, 329. See also Keith Warrington, "The Synoptic Gospels," in *A Biblical Theology of the Holy Spirit*, ed. Trevor J. Burke and Keith Warrington (Eugene, OR: Cascade, 2014), 84–103, here 88–89, 93–94.

and Jesus's command to baptize new disciples in the name of the Father, Son, and Holy Spirit (28:19) point to a profound incipient Trinitarianism.[32]

The following chart displays the occurrence of the Holy Spirit in Matthew's Gospel.

| **The Holy Spirit in Matthew's Gospel** | |
|---|---|
| 1:18, 20 | Jesus Messiah is conceived in Mary by the Holy Spirit |
| 3:11 | Jesus Messiah, the Coming One, will baptize with the Holy Spirit and fire |
| 3:16 | Jesus Messiah is baptized, and the Spirit of God descends like a dove and comes to rest on him |
| 4:1 | Jesus Messiah is led by the Spirit into the wilderness to be tempted by the devil |
| 10:20 | The Spirit of their Father will speak through Jesus Messiah's disciples when mistreated |
| 12:18 | God will put his Spirit on his beloved Jesus Messiah, the servant, and he will proclaim justice to the nations (Isa 42:1) |
| 12:28 | Jesus Messiah drives out demons by Spirit of God, evidencing that the kingdom of God has come upon Israel |
| 12:31–32 | Jesus Messiah warns that blasphemy against the Holy Spirit will not be forgiven |
| 22:43 | David, in the Spirit, calls Messiah, Lord |
| 28:19 | Jesus Messiah commissions his disciples to go and make disciples of all nations, baptizing them in the name of the Father and of the Son and of the Holy Spirit |

In all of these, "Jesus is consistently depicted as surrounded by the person and work of the Holy Spirit."[33]

The reality of Jesus as the incarnate Son of God empowered by the Holy Spirit and loved by God the Father is a mind-boggling truth, if we allow ourselves to reflect deeply upon the story that Matthew unfolds. It truly is the only sufficient answer to the hopes of the Jewish people in the first century and the hopes of all people today.[34] And as we reflect upon this truth, we will find that the story will reshape our own expectations of what kingdom life is all about for us as we live in the presence and power of the Trinitarian Father, Son, and Holy Spirit.

### *8.2.2.2 The Son and the Heavenly Father: A Beloved Filial Relationship*

At the baptism, the voice gives a dual pronouncement of the identity and nature of Jesus through citing excerpts of two messianically significant Old Testament passages: Ps 2:7 and Isa 42:1.

The statement "This is my Son, whom I love" (Matt 3:17) calls to mind the

32. Gundry, *Matthew*, 52; Crowe, "Trinity and the Gospel of Matthew, 40–41.

33. Sanders, *Triune God*, 193.

34. For an overview of the historical NT christological development, see Martin Hengel, "Christological Titles in Early Christianity," in *The Messiah: Developments in Earliest Judaism and Christianity*, ed. James H. Charlesworth (Minneapolis: Fortress, 1992), 425–48. For a theological overview of "God's Three-in-Oneness: *The Trinity*," see Erickson, *Christian Theology*, 291–313.

well-known image of father and son in Ps 2:7: "I will proclaim the LORD's decree: He said to me, 'You are my Son.'" The voice here refers to Jesus as "my Son," implying the title "Son of God," which is introduced here and immediately picked up in the next chapter (4:3, 6).[35] The title had clear messianic significance prior to Jesus's ministry (cf. 4QFlor 1 I, 10–13; 4QpsDan[a] ar).[36]

The expression "whom I love" (*mou ho agapētos*, "my loved one") affirms the relationship that is declared between Jesus and the voice. Jesus is the Son, the voice is from the Father, and at the heart of their relationship is love. Nothing is said here of when that relationship began, but Matthew has already led us to understand that Jesus's conception has marked him out as of divine origin (1:20, 23; cf. 2:15). This is not the language of adoption but of confirmation of an existing relationship of divine love between Father and Son. The Fourth Gospel makes explicit the ontological sonship of Jesus, while Matthew assumes it here as the foundation of the relationship. Jesus is the divine Son of the heavenly Father.[37]

The statement "in whom I am well pleased" takes our understanding of Jesus's mission one step further by drawing upon Isa 42:1 (cf. Tg. Isa. 42:1) for another messianically significant figure—the "servant." In the declaration of the Father, Jesus is heralded as the servant who is enabled by the Spirit's anointing to bring justice to the nations. This link will be made explicit as the narrative unfolds, when Matthew cites Isa 42:1–4 in the context of clarifying the purpose of Jesus's ministry (cf. Matt 12:17–21).

As mentioned above (7.2.7.3.2.1), these passages point out two distinct emphases of Jesus's identity, self-understanding, and mission. He is the divine Son and the suffering servant, a pronouncement that recalls the double entendre of the Nazarene allusion (2:23) and will be repeated by the voice in the transfiguration (17:5). The Father has placed into the hands of his beloved Son the mission of the servant to bring salvation to the nations (Isa 42:1, 4). Love and obedience will sustain the relationship and actualize the mission because the Father's will for the beloved Son must include obedience to the cross as the Son takes upon himself the iniquity of his people (26:39, 42; cf. Isa 53).

The Father through the anointing by the Spirit formally inaugurates Jesus into his public ministry as the unique Son. And this Son is the triumphant messianic King (Ps 2) yet the humble servant (Isa 42). He will accomplish the will of his Father in coming to his people Israel (Matt 10:6; 15:24), yet he brings hope to the nations (28:18). These are the themes that will characterize the unfolding story of Jesus Messiah. Frank Macchia observes, "As the faithful Son of the Father, Jesus bears the Spirit without measure and permanently, for he will offer his life by the Spirit at the cross and rise up by the Spirit to be the Spirit Baptizer."[38]

35. Carson, "Matthew," 138.
36. See Witherington, *Christology of Jesus*, 148–55.
37. Carson, "Matthew," 138.
38. Frank D. Macchia, *Jesus the Spirit Baptizer: Christology in Light of Pentecost* (Grand Rapids: Eerdmans, 2018), 242.

For Matthew, the reality of the incarnation now makes clear God's revelation through the prophets: Jesus is the divine Son of God the Father and conceived and empowered by the Spirit for his salvation-historical mission.[39] This is not modalism, but the simultaneous existence of all three persons of the Godhead for the anointing of Jesus for his messianic ministry:[40] "The baptism of Christ draws attention to the interaction between Christ and the Holy Spirit in the economy of salvation and spurs investigation into the eternal Trinitarian ground and implications of their relationship within salvation history."[41] This is the powerful incipient Trinitarianism that will guide the early church in its future formulations of Trinitarian doctrine.

Some find similarity of the evidence of Trinitarianism at Jesus's baptism in the scene at the transfiguration. There we see the Father, the glory cloud, and the Son all present at the same time as Jesus heads to the cross (17:5). The Spirit is not mentioned explicitly in the same way as at the baptism, but some argue that there is scriptural warrant for connecting the theophanic glory cloud in Matt 17 with a manifestation of the Holy Spirit. This draws on the wording of the divine voice at the transfiguration, which is so similar to the baptism account, where the Spirit descends as a dove.[42]

While reading this transfiguration text in a Trinitarian fashion is appreciated, Graham Cole suggests that without explicit evidence for the appearance of the Spirit here, we should give the passage its explicit emphasis, which is christological. The story is about the Father and the Son, and the preincarnate glory of the Son with the Father, and an anticipatory transformation of Jesus in the light of the glory to come in the resurrection.[43]

### 8.2.3 The Disciples' Baptism in the Threefold Name of the One God

We are all probably a bit too familiar with Jesus to recognize how difficult it was for people in the first century, including even his own disciples, to comprehend fully who he was. We have learned from our earliest years in Sunday school and youth groups and Bible studies that Jesus is both God and human. We have recited doctrinal creeds and heard myriad sermons discuss Jesus's divine and human natures. We have heard just as often of God being three-in-one. But our familiarity with the truth quite likely numbs us to the reality. As Malcolm Muggeridge says, "The coming of Jesus into the world is the most stupendous event in human history."[44]

It is not just the religious significance of Jesus's ministry to which Muggeridge refers.

39. See Kaiser, *Messiah in the Old Testament*, for a discussion of the chronological unveiling of the messianic prophecies of the OT.

40. Crowe, "Trinity and the Gospel of Matthew," 41–42.

41. Sanders, *Triune God*, 196.

42. Walter C. Kaiser Jr., "The Pentateuch," in *A Biblical Theology of the Holy Spirit*, ed. Trevor J. Burke and Keith Warrington (Eugene, OR: Cascade, 2014), 5; Crowe, "Trinity and the Gospel of Matthew," 42.

43. Graham A. Cole, *He Who Gives Life: The Doctrine of the Holy Spirit*, FET (Wheaton, IL: Crossway, 2007), 163–64.

44. Muggeridge, *Jesus*, 1.

He refers especially to the mind-boggling truth that God actually became a human and lived among us. It will remain for Paul and the apostle John in their writings to explain the significance of the incarnation for human redemption, and it will remain for the early church fathers to formulate Trinitarian doctrine. Matthew writes to recount the good news of the incarnation's reality. He has already given his readers a behind the scenes understanding of Jesus's identity as he unfolded the messianic pedigree (1:1–17) and narrated accounts of the divine conception by the Holy Spirit (1:18–25) and prophetically anticipated messianic infancy (ch. 2). Matthew gives further insight to Jesus's true Trinitarian identity in his baptism as the beloved Son of the Father and the one anointed by the descending and alighting Spirit of God (3:13–17).

#### 8.2.3.1 *"In the Name of the Father, the Son, and the Holy Spirit"*

At the conclusion of Matthew's Gospel, the disciples encounter the risen Jesus, and appropriately their response is to worship him (28:17). All along Jesus has been leading them to understand his true identity as the Son of God, a fact in his earthly ministry that was difficult for them to comprehend. But now he has been raised, which is the declaration that he is indeed God's Son, and they have received at least two to three appearances from the risen Jesus prior to this in Jerusalem. They were prepared to give him the homage that is due him, the immanent presence of God among his people (cf. 1:23).[45]

In this finale to Matthew's narrative, the risen Jesus Messiah commissions his disciples, "Therefore go and make disciples of all nations, baptizing them in the name of the Father and of the Son and of the Holy Spirit" (28:19). Sanders notes that "this dominical utterance is the central text of Trinitarian theology,"[46] and Blomberg refers to "the Great Commission's incipient Trinitarianism."[47]

The uniqueness of Jesus's form of baptism is emphasized as he says that new disciples are to be baptized "in the name of the Father and of the Son and of the Holy Spirit" (28:19).[48] The use of *name* is common in Scripture for God's power and authority.[49] Jews were not baptized in the name of a person. Baptism in the "name" (singular) of the Father, Son, and Holy Spirit associates the three as personal distinctions, an early indication of the Trinitarian Godhead and overt proclamation of Jesus's deity. The definite article (*tou*, "of the") is repeated before each person of the Trinity to emphasize that the three names are grammatically absolute: "of *the* Father," "of *the* Son," "of *the* Holy Spirit."[50] This is the clearest Trinitarian language in the Gospels and sums up

45. Cf. Leim, *Matthew's Theological Grammar*, 242–43.
46. Sanders, *Triune God*, 200.
47. Blomberg, *Theology*, 349.
48. See Brown and Roberts, "Thinking Theologically with Matthew: The Holy Spirit," in *Matthew*, 315–33, esp. 322–25.
49. E.g., *onoma* in LXX Exod 3:13–15; Prov 18:10; cf. Jub. 36:7.
50. Sanders, *Triune God*, 200.

Jesus's teaching. Our understanding therefore of Jesus in Matthew must be related to this Trinitarian saying Jesus gives in his final words.[51] And Sanders remarks, "The whole development of Trinitarian doctrine in the church thus stands on the verbal foundation of this passage."[52]

This saying of Jesus is often accused of being a later theological "formula" inserted by Matthew, because it is purported to be too theologically developed to have been used by Jesus at this stage.[53] However, this is not the earliest such Trinitarian expression in the New Testament (cf. Gal 4:4–7; 1 Cor 12:4–6; 2 Cor 13:14),[54] and even in Jesus's earlier ministry and teaching we catch beginning hints of the plurality of the nature of the Godhead (e.g., Matt 3:17; 11:27; 12:28). We have noted regularly how difficult it was for Jesus's followers to move from strict theological monotheism to recognize the plurality of the Godhead in the person of Jesus in relation to his heavenly Father.

Now, however, in his risen state the cognitive dissonance is so profound that the shock has enabled a more complete paradigm shift to occur. This alone likewise explains the rapid movement of the strict monotheistic Pharisee Paul upon confrontation by the risen Lord Jesus to grasp the plurality in the nature of the Godhead. It is well known that a profound paradigm shift in one's worldview almost always occurs with some revolutionary event or thought.[55] The revolution has occurred in Jesus's resurrection and prepares the way for Paul to begin clarifying the Trinitarian nature of the Godhead as Father, Son, and Holy Spirit.

The risen Jesus Messiah is at the heart of the Christian life and the tangible picture of the living God. Jesus is not so much giving a formula as he is emphasizing a theological truth that is symbolized with baptism. Baptism is the mode of ceremonial entry into the family of God, the family of the new covenant, so what one does in the name of Jesus one does in the name of the Father, Son, and Holy Spirit.[56] Explicitly, the apostle Paul links baptism in particular to what the living God has accomplished in Jesus's resurrection.[57] Baptism marks the profound truth that with the new covenant all new disciples are brought into a new existence that is fundamentally determined by God. That new existence is the expression of the will of the Father as mediated by the Son through the power of the Spirit:[58] "As God's presence on earth, Jesus promises his disciples his eternal, personal presence."[59]

51. Crowe, "Trinity and the Gospel of Matthew," 42–43.

52. Sanders, *Triune God*, 204–5.

53. E.g., J. R. Daniel Kirk, *A Man Attested by God: The Human Jesus of the Synoptic Gospels* (Grand Rapids: Eerdmans, 2016), 359–87.

54. Although the "Father" expression is not precisely parallel, the "Son" motif argues for Paul's early recognition; cf. N. T. Wright, *The Resurrection of the Son of God*, vol. 3 of *Christian Origins and the Question of God* (Minneapolis: Fortress, 2003), 644n38.

55. E.g., classically advanced by Thomas S. Kuhn, *The Structure of Scientific Revolutions* (Chicago: University of Chicago Press, 1970).

56. The use of *name* is common in Scripture for God's power and authority (e.g., *onoma* in LXX Exod 3:13–15; Prov 18:10; cf. Jub. 36:7).

57. Cf. N. T. Wright, *Resurrection of the Son of God*, 644–45.

58. Hagner, *Matthew 14–28*, 888.

59. Grindheim, *Christology*, 88.

When Matthew juxtaposes the word "God" in the phrase "God with us" (1:23) with the christological "I" of 18:20 and 28:20, the reader is well equipped to understand the unity-in-distinction between "God" and "Jesus." The narrative impels us to include Jesus Messiah within the identity of the one God of Israel.[60] Hurtado notes: "It is clear that the theological developments that led to the doctrine of the Trinity were to some significant degree prompted and even made unavoidable by the dyadic devotional pattern and the triadic shape of discourse about God that we see amply attested in the New Testament texts."[61] As God's Messiah, now revealed to be divine, Jesus wields all authority given him by the Father, and the mode by which that authority is exercised is through the Spirit.

#### *8.2.3.2 Baptism in the Name of the Father, the Son, and the Holy Spirit*

Jesus's commission regarding baptism is also congruent with what we find in the rest of the New Testament.[62] In the book of Acts baptism is normally "in" the name of Jesus (e.g., 2:38 *epi*; 8:16 *eis*; 10:48 *en*; 19:3–5 *eis*), and in Paul's writings "in" Christ (e.g., Rom 6:3; Gal 3:27; both with *eis*). These forms highlight different aspects of the same baptism event.[63] The risen Jesus Messiah is at the heart of the Christian life and the tangible picture of the living God. Jesus is not so much giving a formula as he is emphasizing a theological truth that is symbolized with baptism. Hagner states, "In contrast to John's baptism, this baptism brings a person into an existence that is fundamentally determined by (i.e., ruled by) Father, Son, and Holy Spirit."[64] This new existence is the expression of the will of the Father as mediated by the Son through the power of the Spirit.

This is not full-blown Nicene Trinitarian theology, but it is in line with other expressions of incipient Trinitarianism in the New Testament.[65] Even though Matthew does not demonstrate developed Trinitarian theology, Jesus is here placed on the same level as the Father and the Holy Spirit, and this prepares the way for the early church's Trinitarian formulations.

60. Leim, *Matthew's Theological Grammar*, 243

61. Larry W. Hurtado, "Observations on the 'Monotheism' Affirmed in the New Testament," in *The Bible and Early Trinitarian Theology*, ed. Christopher A. Beeley and Mark E. Weedman, CUA Studies in Early Christianity (Washington, DC: Catholic University of America Press, 2018), 50–68, here 64.

62. Cf. Davies and Allison, *Matthew*, 3:685. For the use of *eis* with *onoma* in the sense of "in" employed here, not meaning *into*, see 18:20; cf. 10:41–42.

63. Cf. the practice of the early church to use the expressions interchangeably: Did. 7:1, 3 (Holmes): "in [*eis*] the name of the Father and the Son and the Holy Spirit"; Did. 9:5 (Holmes): "in [*eis*] the name of the Lord."

64. Hagner, *Matthew 14–28*, 888.

65. Osborne, *Matthew*, 1081. Cf. 1 Cor 12:4–6; 2 Cor 13:14; Eph 4:4–6; 2 Thess 2:13–14; 1 Peter 1:2; Jude 20–21; Rev 1:4–5.

*Chapter 9*

# THE KINGDOM OF HEAVEN COMES TO EARTH IN MATTHEW'S GOSPEL

## *The Internal That Transforms the External*

### BIBLIOGRAPHY

**Bateman, Herbert W., IV,** ed. *Three Central Issues in Contemporary Dispensationalism: A Comparison of Traditional and Progressive Views.* Grand Rapids: Kregel, 1999. **Beasley-Murray, George R.** *Jesus and the Kingdom of God.* Grand Rapids: Eerdmans, 1986. **Blaising, Craig A., and Darrell L. Bock.** *Progressive Dispensationalism.* Grand Rapids: Baker Academic, 1993. **Blumenthal, Christian.** *Basileia im Matthäusevangelium.* WUNT 416. Tübingen: Mohr Siebeck, 2019. ———. "*Basileia* is Gaining Space: God's Will, Mimesis of Christ and the Spatial Shaping of the *Basileia* in Matthew's Gospel." Pages 345–64 in *The Gospel of Matthew in Its Historical and Theological Context: Papers from the International Conference in Moscow, September 24 to 28, 2018.* Edited by Mikhail Seleznev, William R. G. Loader, and Karl-Wilhelm Niebuhr. WUNT 459. Tübingen: Mohr Siebeck, 2021. **Brown, Jeannine K., and Kyle Roberts**. "Thinking Theologically with Matthew: Kingdom." Pages 270–92 in *Matthew.* THNTC. Grand Rapids: Eerdmans, 2018. **Chilton, Bruce.** *Jesus' Prayer and Jesus' Eucharist: His Personal Practice of Spirituality.* Valley Forge, PA: Trinity Press International, 1997. **Clark, David.** *On Earth as in Heaven: The Lord's Prayer from Jewish Prayer to Christian Ritual.* Minneapolis: Fortress, 2017. **Cole, Graham A.** *Against the Darkness: The Doctrine of Angels, Satan, and Demons.* FET. Wheaton, IL: Crossway, 2019. **Foster, Robert L.** "Why on Earth Use 'Kingdom of Heaven'? Matthew's Terminology Revisited." *NTS* 48.4 (2002): 487–99. **Goldsworthy, Graeme.** *Gospel and Kingdom: A Christian Interpretation of the Old Testament.* Exeter, UK: Paternoster, 1981. **Green, Joel B.** "Kingdom of God/Heaven." *DJG*[2] 468–81. **Grindheim, Sigurd.** *Living in the Kingdom of God: A Biblical Theology for the Life of the Church.* Grand Rapids: Baker Academic, 2018. **Guelich, Robert A.** *The Sermon on the Mount: A Foundation for Understanding.* Waco, TX: Word, 1982. **Hafemann, Scott.** "Eschatology and Ethics: The Future of Israel and the Nations in Romans 15:1–13." *TynBul* 51.2 (2000):

161–192. **Hagner, Donald A.** "Righteousness in Matthew's Gospel." Pages 101–120 in *Worship, Theology and Ministry in the Early Church: Essays in Honor of Ralph P. Martin*. Edited by Michael J. Wilkins and Terence Paige. JSNTSup 87. Sheffield: Sheffield Academic, 1992. **Hays, Richard B.** *The Moral Vision of the New Testament—Community, Cross, New Community: A Contemporary Introduction to New Testament Ethics*. San Francisco: HarperSanFrancisco, 1996. **Hoekema, Anthony A.** *The Bible and the Future*. Grand Rapids: Eerdmans, 1974. **Kiley, Mark.** "The Lord's Prayer and Matthean Theology." Pages 15–27 in *The Lord's Prayer and other Prayer Texts from the Greco-Roman Era*. Edited by James H. Charlesworth with Mark Harding and Mark Kiley. Valley Forge, PA: Trinity Press International, 1994. **Ladd, George Eldon.** *The Gospel of the Kingdom: Scriptural Studies in the Kingdom of God*. Grand Rapids: Eerdmans, 1973. ———. *The Presence of the Future: The Eschatology of Biblical Realism*. 2nd ed. Grand Rapids: Eerdmans, 1974. **Mamić, Vinko.** *Matthew's Response to an Early Missionary Issue: Meaning and Function of the Parable of the Workers in the Vineyard (Matt 20:1–16)*. TGST 219. Rome: Gregorian and Biblical Press, 2016. **McKnight, Scot.** *Kingdom Conspiracy: Returning to the Radical Mission of the Local Church*. Grand Rapids: Brazos, 2014. **Mowery, Robert L.** "The Matthean References to the Kingdom: Different Terms for Different Audiences." *ETL* 70.4 (1994): 398–405. **Pamment, Margaret.** "The Kingdom of Heaven According to the First Gospel." *NTS* 27 (1981): 211–32. **Pennington, Jonathan T.** *Heaven and Earth in the Gospel of Matthew*. NovTSup 126. Leiden: Brill, 2007. ———. "The Kingdom of Heaven in the Gospel of Matthew." *Southern Baptist Journal of Theology* 12.1 (2008): 43–51. ———. *The Sermon on the Mount and Human Flourishing: A Theological Commentary*. Grand Rapids: Baker Academic, 2017. **Perrin, Nicholas.** *The Kingdom of God: A Biblical Theology*. BTL. Grand Rapids: Zondervan, 2019. **Quarles, Charles L.** *Sermon on the Mount: Restoring Christ's Message to the Modern Church*. NAC Studies in Bible & Theology. Nashville: B&H, 2011. **Ridlehoover, Charles Nathan.** *The Lord's Prayer and the Sermon on the Mount in Matthew's Gospel*. LNTS 616. London: T&T Clark, 2020. **Saucy, Mark.** *The Kingdom of God in the Teaching of Jesus in Twentieth Century Theology*. Dallas: Word, 1997. ———. "*Regnum Spiriti*: The Role of the Spirit in the Social Ethics of the Kingdom." *JETS* 54.1 (2011): 89–108. **Saucy, Robert L.** *The Case for Progressive Dispensationalism: The Interface Between Dispensational and Non-Dispensational Theology*. Grand Rapids: Zondervan, 1993. ———. *The Church in God's Program*. Chicago: Moody, 1972. **Schreiner, Patrick.** *The Body of Jesus: A Spatial Analysis of the Kingdom in Matthew*. LNTS 555. London: T&T Clark, 2016. ———. *The Kingdom of God and the Glory of the Cross*. SSBT. Wheaton, IL: Crossway, 2018. **Wilkins, Michael J.** "The Consideration of a Future for Israel in the Light of the Apparently Bleak Consequences for Negative Responses to Jesus's Ministry in the Gospel of Matthew." Pages 313–40 in *The Future Restoration of Israel: A Response to Supersessionism*. Edited by Stanley E. Porter and Alan E. Kurschner. McMaster Biblical Studies 10. Eugene, OR: Wipf & Stock; Hamilton, Ontario: McMaster Divinity College Press, 2023. ———. "Prayer." Pages 941–48 in *DLNTD*. **Willard, Dallas.** *Living in Christ's Presence: Final Words on Heaven and the Kingdom of God*. Downers Grove, IL:

InterVarsity, 2014. **Witherington, Ben, III.** *The Individual Witnesses*. Vol. 1 of *The Indelible Image: The Theological and Ethical Thought World of the New Testament*. Downers Grove, IL: InterVarsity, 2009. **Yarbrough, Robert W.** "The Kingdom of God in the New Testament: Matthew and Revelation." Pages 95–124 in *The Kingdom of God*. Theology in Community. Edited by Christopher W. Morgan and Robert A. Peterson. Wheaton, IL: Crossway, 2012.

## 9.1 INTRODUCTION: THE KINGDOM OF HEAVEN COMES TO EARTH IN MATTHEW'S GOSPEL

After his temptations by the devil, the first recorded message by Jesus as he embarks upon his public ministry is, "Repent, for the kingdom of heaven has come near" (Matt 4:17). This leads Joshua Jipp to declare, "The primary proclamation of Jesus and perhaps the central theme throughout Matthew's Gospel is, of course, the kingdom of heaven/God."[1] He goes on to clarify, "One aspect of Matthew's use of the phrase kingdom of heaven is its contrast with all of the rest of the kingdoms of the earth."[2]

This may surprise some Christians, because in certain circles today the expression "kingdom of heaven/God" is a somewhat ambiguous idea. Indeed, Brown and Roberts point to what is for Matthean scholars "the complexity and, at times, elusiveness of what kingdom meant for Matthew, for Jesus, and for Matthew's communities."[3] We might ask ourselves, why did Jesus not say, "The church is here," or, "Salvation is now here," or "The Holy Spirit is coming upon you," or something else? Each of those have their rightful place in Jesus's preaching and mission and in Matthew's theological perspective, but in the central position is that "the kingdom of heaven" has arrived. The ambiguity of this concept is deeply integral to the meaning of the kingdom of heaven, especially reflecting the kingdom's profoundly eschatological nature. The kingdom of heaven as it is revealed in Matthew's Gospel relates to the reign of God "as it intersects with creation, touches history, and transfigures reality."[4]

Perhaps a step back for some biblical-historical perspective may help.

### 9.1.1 God's Purpose for Creation and Humanity

God's purpose for humanity from the very beginning was to create a place where he would show himself in a tangible way in relationship with his creatures. This was to be called his *kingdom*. God is the universal King over all of his kingdom creation. But men and women were to be his representatives on the earth to rule for him in what could have been an ideal place. In the initial creation account God said,

1. Jipp, *Messianic Theology*, 65: e.g., Matt 4:17, 23; 5:3, 10, 19, 20; 6:10, 13, 33.

2. Jipp, *Messianic Theology*, 66.

3. Brown and Roberts, *Matthew*, 271.

4. Brown and Roberts, *Matthew*, 271.

> "Let us make mankind in our image, in our likeness, so that they may *rule* over the fish in the sea and the birds in the sky, over the livestock and all wild animals, and over all the creatures that move along the ground." So God created mankind in his own image, in the image of God he created them; male and female he created them. God blessed them and said to them, "Be fruitful and increase in number; fill the earth and subdue it. *Rule* over the fish in the sea and the birds in the sky and over every living creature that moves on the ground." (Gen 1:26–28; emphasis added)

The language of Gen 1:26–28 reflects the idea of humans created as royal figures representing God to "rule" (*rādâ*; LXX *archō*) over his creation. Gordon Wenham states, "Because man is created in God's image, he is king over nature. He rules the world on God's behalf."[5] Humanity is God's appointed ruler over his creation. Only humans have been given dominion to rule in God's creation. The term "rule" (*rādâ*) in 1:26, 28, is used commonly of royal dominion[6] and here speaks of human rule over life in the skies, waters, and land.[7] Wenham goes on to note that this is of course no license for the unbridled exploitation and subjugation of nature. Humans are "commissioned to rule nature as a benevolent king, acting as God's representative over them and therefore treating them in the same way as God created them . . . companions."[8]

Although humanity failed at the start with the fall of Adam and Eve (Gen 3), God's purposes throughout history have centered on establishing his kingdom, with humans created to "rule" his kingdom on the earth. The term "kingdom" (*mamlākâ*; LXX *basileios*, "royal") occurs first when God established his covenant with Moses and the people on Mount Sinai: "'Now if you obey me fully and keep my covenant, then out of all nations you will be my treasured possession. Although the whole earth is mine, you will be for me a *kingdom* of priests and a holy nation.' These are the words you are to speak to the Israelites" (Exod 19:5–6; emphasis added).

Out of the general world of people, God separates his chosen people, Israel, to be the core of establishing his kingdom plan for the earth. In the biblical plan of redemption this is the beginning of God's intention to bring to himself a people that will be his kingdom. The people of Israel were to be at once priest-kings and royal priests (Isa 61:6)—*everyone* in the whole nation was to be God's kingdom on earth.[9] "Israel was to be kings and priests to God on behalf of the nations . . . and they were to be partakers in the present aspects and coming reality of the 'kingdom of God.'"[10]

5. Gordon J. Wenham, *Genesis 1–15*, WBC 1 (Waco, TX: Word, 1987), 33.

6. E.g., 1 Kgs 4:24[5:4]; Pss 8:5–6[6–7]; 72:8; 110:2; Isa 14:2.

7. John H. Sailhamer, "Genesis," in *Genesis, Exodus, Leviticus, Numbers*, EBC 2 (Grand Rapids: Zondervan, 1990), 37; Kenneth A. Mathews, *Genesis 1–11:26*, NAC 1A (Nashville: B&H, 1996), 168.

8. G. Wenham, *Genesis 1–15*, 33.

9. Walter C. Kaiser Jr., "Exodus," in *Genesis, Exodus, Leviticus, Numbers*, EBC 2 (Grand Rapids: Zondervan, 1990), 416; Douglas K. Stuart, *Exodus*, NAC 2 (Nashville: B&H, 2006), 422.

10. Kaiser, "Exodus," 416.

But most importantly there is a decided emphasis on the preeminent kingship of God, the "Great King" who rules over his people.[11] God is king over his people Israel in a special sense, by virtue of his covenantal relationship to them, but his kingship is at the same time universal, extending to all nations and peoples and even the natural environment.

It became clear that it was God's design to establish the human institution of kingship in his sovereign plan for the redemption of his people, and ultimately for the universal triumph of peace and justice on the earth. Kingship in Israel was not unanticipated. God provided for it in antecedent revelation as Abraham was told that "kings" would arise among his descendants (Gen 17:6) and Jacob proclaimed that royalty would arise from the tribe of Judah (Gen 49:10).

The kingdom of God extends throughout the universe (the heavens and the earth), but the primary focus in the Old Testament is on the land. The whole earth (land) is God's (Exod 9:29; 19:5). The scope narrows to focus on a portion of this earth that eventually God gives to his chosen people to settle. The land is not to be sold permanently because it does not belong to its inhabitants, who are "foreigners and strangers" (Lev 25:23). Israel only holds the land for its true owner, Yahweh (Lev 25:23–24).[12]

In the Old Testament record of human kingship, no one was more significant than David, the second king of Israel after Saul. David led Israel as a kingdom to its apex in power and glory as a nation. And he became the ideal of a future leader that ultimately found fulfillment in his descendant—Jesus Messiah. But David's failures as a husband, father, and king present him as an imperfect human whom God both chastened and blessed.

Thus arose kings in Israel and Judah over the kingdom of Israel. But the history of these kings is mostly a history of failure to live up to the covenantal ideal. The kings of the north have done "evil in the eyes of the Lord" (cf. 1 Kgs 15:26, 34) because they continued the worship of the golden calves begun by Jeroboam I, the Northern Kingdom's first king (1 Kgs 12:26–33). Even among the kings of the Southern Kingdom of Judah, only Hezekiah and Josiah receive unqualified praise (2 Kgs 18:3–7; 22:2).[13]

Now Israel's prophets began to speak of a future king who would occupy the throne of David. This king will come as the fulfillment of the promise to David that "your house and your kingdom will endure forever before me; your throne will be established forever" (2 Sam 7:16).[14] This future king will not only be a descendant of David but is also identified with deity (Isa 7:14; 9:6–7; Jer 23:5–6; Ezek 36:24–28). During the

---

11. Exod 15:18; Deut 33:5; 1 Sam 8:7; 12:12; 1 Chr 17:14; 28:5; Ps 114:2.

12. Bruce R. Reichenbach, "Genesis 1 as a Theological-Political Narrative of Kingdom Establishment," *BBR* 13.1 (2003): 47–69, here 51. See also Norman C. Habel, *The Land Is Mine: Six Biblical Land Ideologies* (Minneapolis: Augsburg Fortress, 1995), 39.

13. J. Robert Vannoy, "King, Kingship," *EDBT* 450.

14. Cf. 2 Sam 7; 23:1–7; Pss 89; 132:11–12; Isa 55:3–5.

reign of this future king in the future kingdom on earth wars will cease and peace and justice will be established on the earth (Isa 2:1–5; 11:1–10; Amos 9:11–15). This future king came to be known as "Messiah" ("the Anointed One") and living with the hope of his future appearance came to be known as messianic expectation.[15]

The New Testament authors, including especially Matthew, carried forward the kingship theme and resolved many of its ambiguities—Jesus fulfilled the royal messianic promises of the Old Testament. In Jesus Messiah, who was revealed to have been conceived as the God-Man, human and divine kingship are united in one person: "In Jesus the duality of sovereigns present in the Old Testament period is eliminated."[16]

### 9.1.2 Jesus's Initial Message in Matthew's Gospel: "The Kingdom of Heaven Is at Hand" (4:17; cf. Mark 1:14–15; Luke 4:43)

Matthew records Jesus's initial message as, "From that time Jesus began to preach, saying, 'Repent, for the kingdom of heaven is at hand'" (Matt 4:17, ESV). Notice the way that Mark records the same message: "Now after John was arrested, Jesus came into Galilee, proclaiming the gospel of God, and saying, 'The time is fulfilled, and the kingdom of God is at hand; repent and believe in the gospel'" (Mark 1:14–15, ESV). The use of the expression "is fulfilled" (*peplērōtai*) suggests that this kingdom answers to well-known expectations based on past promises.[17] And notice the way in Luke that Jesus clarifies his purpose for coming to earth: "But he said to them, 'I must preach the good news of the kingdom of God to the other towns as well; for I was sent for this purpose.'" (Luke 4:43 ESV). The presence and coming of the kingdom of God is noted by many scholars as the central message of Jesus.[18] This is the overall message of the kingdom in the four Gospels. We now focus on the emphasis in Matthew's Gospel.

### 9.1.3 "Kingdom" (*basileia*) in Matthew's Gospel

The term "kingdom" (*basileia*) occurs 157 times in 149 verses of the New Testament and occurs fifty-five times in fifty-three verses (the term occurs twice in 5:19 and 24:7) in Matthew's Gospel. In the chart placed at the end of this chapter, I have noted all fifty-five of these occurrences. For clarity, I have accented the term "**kingdom**" in bold font, the qualifier "<u>**of God**</u>" (4x or 5x) in bold underlined font, and the qualifier "***of heaven***" (32x) in bold italics font. Nineteen times "kingdom" occurs alone without any qualifiers. Six occurrences of "kingdom" refer either to human kingdoms or to the kingdom of Satan (4:8; 8:12 [?]; 12:25–6; 24:7 [2x]).[19]

The expression "kingdom of God" occurs four or five times in Matthew (6:33;

15. Vannoy, "King, Kingship," *EDBT* 450–51.
16. Vannoy, "King, Kingship," *EDBT* 451.
17. Graeme Goldsworthy, "Kingdom of God," *NDBT* 616.
18. E.g., George Eldon Ladd, *The Gospel of the Kingdom: Scriptural Studies in the Kingdom of God* (Grand Rapids: Eerdmans, 1973), 14–15.
19. See also Quarles, *Theology of Matthew*, 85n3.

12:28; 19:24; 21:31, 43), fourteen times in Mark, thirty-two times in Luke, twice in John (3:3, 5), six times in Acts, eight times in Paul, and once in Revelation (12:10). Matthew prefers the expression "kingdom of heaven" (lit., "of the heavens"), which he uses some thirty-two times in his Gospel, while "kingdom of heaven" does not occur elsewhere in the New Testament. Matthew primarily uses the expression "kingdom of heaven," and the other Gospel writers (notably Luke) use the expression "kingdom of God."

What is to be made of the difference of usage between Matthew's "kingdom of heaven" and the other evangelists' use of "kingdom of God"?

## 9.1.4 Why Does Matthew Use "Kingdom of Heaven"?

Matthew chose to use the expression "kingdom of heaven" whereas no other New Testament author used it. Twelve times "kingdom of heaven" is used in Matthew's Gospel when "kingdom of God" occurs in parallel passages in Mark and/or Luke. Of those, four times "kingdom of heaven" occurs when "kingdom of God" is used in both Mark and Luke (Matt 13:11, 31; 19:14, 23), once when kingdom of God occurs only in Mark (Matt 4:17), and seven times "kingdom of heaven" occurs when "kingdom of God" occurs only in Luke (Matt 5:3; 8:11; 10:7; 11:11, 12; 13:33; 22:2).[20]

In the past, some scholars have tried to maintain a distinction between the kingdom of heaven and the kingdom of God and/or other referents. At least the following explanations have been offered.

### *9.1.4.1 A Reverent Circumlocution for "Heaven" so as Not to Mistakenly Blaspheme the Name "God"*

A widespread assumption among Matthean scholarship is that the expression "kingdom of heaven" is Matthew's reverential Jewish circumlocution for "kingdom of God." While Matthew does occasionally use the expression "kingdom of God" (12:28; 19:24; 21:31, 43), his record of John the Baptist and Jesus preaching the "kingdom of heaven" reflects common Jewish practice.[21] Since overusing God's name was equivalent to taking it in vain, thus violating the third of the Ten Commandments, many Matthean scholars suggest that the substitution of "heaven" was so as not to mistakenly blaspheme the name "God.[22]

The term "heaven" in Matthew's expression "kingdom of heaven" is actually plural (*hē basileia tōn ouranōn*: "the kingdom of the heavens"), a typical Jewish conception of the world above that includes the air one breathes, the starry world, the realm of

20. Pennington, *Heaven and Earth*, 350.

21. Vermes, *Religion of Jesus the Jew*, 120–37.

22. E.g., Morris, *Matthew*, 53; Turner, *Matthew*, 107; Hagner, *Matthew 1–13*, 47–48; Hill, *Matthew*, 90; Kingsbury, *Matthew*, 134; Luz, *Matthew 1–7*, 167; John P. Meier, *Matthew*, NTM 3 (Wilmington, DE: Michael Glazier, 1980), 23; Osborne, *Matthew*, 110n9.

spirits, but also the throne of God.[23] Matthew's "kingdom of heaven" reflects the Hebrew expression *malkût shāmayim*, found abundantly in Jewish literature (e.g., m. Berakhot 2.2, 5). Some scholars have noted that a feeling of reverence, and not wishing to blaspheme inadvertently the name of God (Exod 20:7), led the Jews at a very early date to avoid as far as possible all mention of the name of God. "Heaven" is one of the usual substitutions for the name of God (e.g., 1 Macc 3:18–19; 4:10; 12:15; m. Avot 1:3, 11). Expressions like "kingdom of heaven," "sake of heaven," "fear of heaven," and others are frequently found in later rabbinic literature.

However, Matthew's "the kingdom of heaven" is functionally the same as "the kingdom of God" in Mark and Luke, and frequently occurs in direct parallel to it. Matthew may mean by "kingdom of heaven" that the kingdom extends beyond this earth, and that the Son has part in it as well as the Father.[24] Since Matthew seems to have no inhibitions about speaking of God by name elsewhere, to avoid its use in the expression "kingdom of heaven" France suggests "is hardly an adequate explanation."[25] He offers that "kingdom of heaven" may be simply a stylistic preference, which then requires no explanation.[26] That may be the case, but we explore below explanations offered by others.

### *9.1.4.2 The Kingdom of Heaven/the Son of Man Is Distinguished from the Kingdom of the Father*

Some interpreters make a distinction between the kingdom of the Son of Man (Matt 13:41) and the kingdom of the Father (13:43). In large part this derives from Jesus's explanation of the parable of the weeds in the field. "The *Son of Man* will send out his angels, and they will weed out of *his kingdom* everything that causes sin and all who do evil. They will throw them into the blazing furnace, where there will be weeping and gnashing of teeth. Then the righteous will shine like the sun in the *kingdom of their Father*" (13:41–43; emphases added).

According to this view, the kingdom of the Son of Man is the kingdom of the present time, where the good coexist with the wicked. The kingdom of the Father refers to the eschatological community of the chosen ones. Luz indicates that the kingdom of the Father is to be distinguished from the kingdom of the Son of Man in that after the destruction of all the evil ones, the kingdom of the Son of Man is changed into the kingdom of the Father (cf. 1 Cor 15:24–28).[27]

Vinko Mamić states that this distinction is overstated, a conclusion with which I concur. The kingdom of the Son of Man ("his kingdom") in this Matthean usage

23. Vermes, *Religion of Jesus the Jew*, 120–37.
24. Morris, *Matthew*, 53.
25. France, *Matthew*, NICNT, 101.
26. France, *Matthew*, NICNT, 101. So also Turner, *Matthew*, 39.
27. Luz, *Matthew 8–20*, 270.

is an obvious synonym for the "kingdom of the Father."[28] As Jesus consummates his kingdom on the earth, he will send his angels to remove all sin and sinners from this world, now called for the first time "his kingdom" (13:41). His divine sovereignty is now established visibly over all creatures of this world. Judgment of the sons of the evil one will commence in the fiery furnace (cf. 3:11; 5:22), where there will be "weeping and gnashing of teeth" (13:42; cf. 8:12). These are Jesus's typical expressions of eternal judgment.

At that time the righteous—Jesus's disciples who have experienced the inner transformation that accompanies their entrance to the kingdom (see discussion on 5:20), who are the wheat that has grown up throughout this age—will experience the full manifestation of the kingdom's glory and "will shine like the sun" (13:43). Jesus's disciples are the light of the world during this age while they await the consummation of this age (6:14–16), but at that time they will shine with unhindered brilliance. A similar expression describes Jesus's transfigured glory, perhaps a preview of the eschatological glory that all disciples will share.[29]

The expression "their Father's kingdom" is not to suggest that there is a distinction between the kingdom of the Son and another kingdom of the Father but that the Father's will has been fully accomplished on earth through the activity of the Son. There is full congruence between the will and activity of Father and Son. Witherington states, "The kingdom of the Father and the kingdom of the Son are one and the same, and what is envisioned is the final realization of what is prayed for in the Lord's Prayer—God's Dominion come on earth once and for all."[30] Jesus's instruction on prayer to the Father for the coming of the kingdom and the establishment of his will on earth (6:10) is now answered in full. The frequent reference by Jesus to God as the disciples' Father now is clear: the kingdom of the Father is the goal to which the hard road of discipleship must eventually lead.[31] Carson notes that even when the mediation of the kingdom ceases once it is halted by the destruction of the last enemy (1 Cor 15:24–26), "in Matthew's terminology it is still appropriate to call Jesus Messiah the King (20:31; 25:34; cf. 26:64), for the kingdom remains no less his."[32]

#### *9.1.4.3 An Intentional Contrast Between the "Kingdom of Heaven" and "Kingdom of God"*

Some suggest that there is an intentional contrast between the "kingdom of heaven" and the "kingdom of God." Margaret Pamment offers that the *kingdom of God* is a present reality of the kingdom experienced in the lives of Jesus and his disciples, which

28. Vinko Mamić, *Matthew's Response to an Early Missionary Issue: Meaning and Function of the Parable of the Workers in the Vineyard (Matt 20:1–16)*, TGST 219 (Rome: Gregorian and Biblical, 2016), 267n273.

29. Davies and Allison, *Matthew*, 2:431.

30. Witherington, *Matthew*, 270.

31. France, *Gospel of Matthew*, 537.

32. Carson, "Matthew," 374.

prepares individuals for the eschatological *kingdom of heaven*, a totally future, though imminent, reality.[33]

Some traditional dispensationalists contended that the expression "kingdom of heaven," found only in Matthew, is intentionally contrasted with "kingdom of God," an expression found in all four Gospels. The *Scofield Reference Bible* advanced five distinctions between the kingdom of God and the kingdom of heaven.

1. The kingdom of God is universal, including all moral intelligences willingly subject to the will of God, whether angels, the church, or saints of past or future dispensations. The kingdom of heaven is messianic, mediatorial, and Davidic, and has for its object the establishment of the kingdom of God on the earth.
2. The kingdom of God is entered only by the new birth, internal regeneration. The kingdom of heaven during this age is the sphere of a profession, which may be real or false.
3. Since the kingdom of heaven is the earthly sphere of the universal kingdom of God, the two have almost all things in common. For this reason, many parables and other teachings are spoken of the kingdom of heaven in Matthew and of the kingdom of God in Mark and Luke. It is the omissions that are significant. The parables of the wheat and tares, and of the net (Matt 13:24–30, 36–43, 47–50) are not spoken of the kingdom of God. In the kingdom of God there are neither tares nor bad fish.
4. The kingdom of God is not external ("is not something that can be observed"; Luke 17:20) but is chiefly that which is inward and spiritual (Rom 14:17), while the kingdom of heaven is organic and is to be manifested in glory on the earth.
5. The kingdom of heaven merges into the kingdom of God when Christ, having "put all enemies under His feet," "shall have delivered up the kingdom to God, even the Father" (1 Cor 15:24–28).[34]

Traditional dispensationalists suggested that "kingdom of God" referred to the moral rule of God in the hearts of those subject to him. The kingdom of God is the sphere of reality which encompassed only those who were genuine believers. The kingdom of God is everlasting in extent. On the other hand, in this view the "kingdom of heaven" was thought to be the covenant made to David, in which God promised to establish the kingdom of his Son on the earth.

In this view some also viewed the "kingdom of God" as cosmic and universal in its dimensions, having authority over all creation, while the kingdom of heaven was limited

33. Margaret Pamment, "The Kingdom of Heaven According to the First Gospel," *NTS* 27 (1981): 211–232; similarly, see Allen, *Matthew*, lxvii–lxviii, 232.

34. *Scofield Reference Bible* (1909), 1003.

to the earth.[35] This view has largely been rejected by Matthean scholars, including most progressive dispensationalists.[36] We will discuss some of the reasons for the rejection of this view in the next section.

#### *9.1.4.4 The Expressions "Kingdom of Heaven" and "Kingdom of God" Are Virtually Synonymous*

Most scholars today, including most progressive dispensationalists, recognize the expressions as virtually synonymous.[37] The purported distinction between "kingdom of God" and "kingdom of heaven" is untenable for at least the following reasons.

First, one passage in Matthew is particularly instructive, because both "kingdom of heaven" and "kingdom of God" appear together: "Then Jesus said to his disciples, 'Truly I tell you, it is hard for someone who is rich to enter the *kingdom of heaven*. Again I tell you, it is easier for a camel to go through the eye of a needle than for someone who is rich to enter the *kingdom of God*'" (19:23–24; emphases added).

Blomberg points to the overall synonymous parallelism of these two back-to-back sentences, parallelism which strongly suggests that "kingdom of heaven" and "kingdom of God" remain synonyms for Matthew.[38] This is made even clearer when it is observed that "kingdom of God" appears in both verses in the Markan and Lukan counterparts (i.e., Mark 10:24–25; Luke 18:24–25).[39]

Second, a comparison of parallel synoptic texts reveals that Matthew often uses the expression "kingdom of heaven" when Mark and/or Luke use the expression "kingdom of God." Matthew uses the phrase "kingdom of heaven" for Mark's "kingdom of God" in six passages,[40] and Matthew wrote "kingdom of heaven" in seven passages whose Lukan parallels refer to the "kingdom of God."[41] It thus seems best to conclude that the expressions "kingdom of heaven" and "kingdom of God" mean essentially the same thing—they are virtual synonyms.[42]

35. E.g., Lewis Sperry Chafer, *Systematic Theology*, 8 vols. (Dallas: Dallas Theological Seminary Press, 1948), 7:223–24; John F. Walvoord, *Matthew: Thy Kingdom Come* (Chicago: Moody, 1974), 30.

36. E.g., Herbert W. Bateman IV, "Dispensationalism: Yesterday and Today," in *Three Central Issues in Contemporary Dispensationalism: A Comparison of Traditional and Progressive Views*, ed. Herbert W. Bateman IV (Grand Rapids: Kregel, 1999), 21–60, here 23–31; Ed Glasscock, *Matthew*, Moody Gospel Commentary (Chicago: Moody, 1997), 70; Craig A. Blaising and Darrell L. Bock, *Progressive Dispensationalism* (Grand Rapids: Baker Academic, 1993), 54; R. Saucy, *Case for Progressive Dispensationalism*, 19; Charles C. Ryrie, *Dispensationalism Today* (Chicago: Moody, 1965), 170–71.

37. For example, Ladd, *Gospel of the Kingdom*, 32; France, *Gospel of Matthew*, 101–2; Brown and Roberts, *Matthew*, 270n2; Carson, "Matthew," 128–30.

38. Blomberg, *New Testament Theology*, 306. See also France, *Gospel of Matthew*, 737; Brown and Roberts, *Matthew*, 181; Turner, *Matthew*, 39; Morris, *Matthew*, 493.

39. France offers that the parallelism of the two verses makes clear that the reference "kingdom of heaven" and "kingdom of God" is the same, yet the change from "heaven" to "God" in the two Matthean verses may be that the more personal expression "kingdom of God" is chosen by Matthew to emphasize the opposition between the two "kings," God and Mammon: France, *Gospel of Matthew*, 737.

40. Matt 4:17//Mark 1:15; Matt 13:11//Mark 4:11; Matt 13:31//Mark 4:30; Matt 18:3//Mark 10:15; Matt 19:14//Mark 10:14; Matt 19:23//Mark 10:23.

41. Matt 5:3//Luke 6:20; Matt 8:11//Luke 13:28; Matt 10:7// Luke 9:2; Matt 11:11//Luke 7:28; Matt 11:12//Luke 16:16; Matt 13:33//Luke 13:20, 21; Matt 19:14// Luke 18:16.

42. For a similar discussion, see Turner, *Matthew*, 39–41.

Third, the idea that Matthew used the expression "kingdom of heaven" instead of "kingdom of God" because he was reverently avoiding writing the noun "God" does not follow from his use elsewhere. Matthew writes the noun "God" upward of fifty times in his Gospel.[43] The first occurrence of the noun "God" in Matthew's Gospel is in the words "'The virgin will conceive and give birth to a son, and they will call him Immanuel' (which means 'God with us')" (1:23), observably appraising these references to "Immanuel" and "God" in a positive manner. Other references to "God" are certainly used in a reverent and careful manner. The sixth beatitude promises that the pure in heart will see "God" (5:8), and the seventh declares that the peacemakers will be called "sons of God" (5:9). Both beatitudes provide positive references to "God." Various other examples could be cited, indicating that Matthew did not avoid using the noun God. Therefore, it appears that Matthew did not piously avoid using the expression "kingdom of God."[44]

#### *9.1.4.5 While Interchangeable, Matthew Intends an Additional Aspect in His Use of the Phrase "Kingdom of Heaven"*

It thus seems best to conclude with a majority of scholars that in the Gospels the expressions "kingdom of heaven" and "kingdom of God" are essentially synonymous. Davies and Allison contend that Matthew's use of "kingdom of heaven" is simply a stylistic variation similar to the use of the expression "kingdom" or "kingdom of the Father," and that "kingdom of God" refers to the same reality in Matthew and the other Gospels.[45]

However, this still fails to explain why Matthew's Gospel is the only canonical Gospel to use the phrase "kingdom of heaven." While the majority of commentators concur that the expressions are interchangeable, some have suggested that Matthew intends an additional aspect in his use of the phrase "kingdom of heaven."

In fact, there has been a revolution of sorts in seeing an expanded understanding of Matthew's view of the kingdom of heaven, although it bears surprising similarity in some respects to traditional dispensationalism.

A significant salvo marking this current revolution came from Robert Foster. Foster notes in a stimulating article the prevalence of another distinctively Matthean phrase, "your Father in heaven." Rather than Matthew employing the phrase "kingdom of heaven" as a circumlocution for the divine name, Foster argues that by analyzing Matthew's rhetorical and sociological strategies that "kingdom of heaven" combines with other "heavenly" language (especially "Father in heaven") to reaffirm the readers' identity as the true people of God. He further argues that the expression "kingdom of heaven"

43. Robert L. Mowery, "The Matthean References to the Kingdom: Different Terms for Different Audiences," *ETL* 70.4 (1994): 398–405, here 404.

44. Mowery, "Matthean References to the Kingdom," 404–5.

45. Davies and Allison, *Matthew*, 1:391–92.

served to differentiate Jesus's "heavenly" messianic mission from more "earthly" ideas of the role of the Davidic Messiah. This "heavenly" language defends Jesus as a Davidic messiah, showing that he came to establish a heavenly, not earthly, kingdom. Additionally, the "heavenly" language reinforces the disciples' commitment to Jesus in the midst of persecution, reminding them that their identity, affirmation, and goal are in heaven.[46]

Perhaps the most influential salvo has come from Jonathan Pennington.[47] His conclusions bear similarity to Foster's, in that he contends that while the expression "kingdom of heaven" *denotes* the same thing as the "kingdom of God," it *connotes* many other things. For Pennington, Jesus's, and Matthew's, use of "kingdom of heaven" especially serves one overriding theological purpose: "to highlight the tension that currently exists between heaven and earth or God and humanity, while looking forward to its eschatological resolution."[48] Particularly, God's (heavenly) ordering of life and society is radically different than the ways of sinful earth. With the dawning of the new creation or new genesis (see 19:28) through Christ, those who follow Jesus as his disciples must align themselves with this coming radical heavenly kingdom. And as Jesus's disciples do so, we stand to inherit the greatest reward, God's presence through Christ (cf. 1:23; 28:20): "In this time of waiting and hoping, the Christian's stance can be summed up in the great prayer that Jesus teaches his disciples to pray: 'Let your name be sanctified, let your kingdom come, let your will be done *on earth even as it is in heaven*' (Matt 6:9–10)."[49]

Instead of a circumlocution for the kingdom of God, the kingdom of heaven is a metonymy, where a word that is associated with something is used to refer to that thing (as when *crown* is used to mean "king" or "queen"). Matthew's expression "kingdom of heaven" is likely due to the association of heaven as God's realm, with God himself. "*Matthew's choice to regularly depict the kingdom as τῶν οὐρανῶν* ["of heaven"] *is designed to emphasize that God's kingdom is not like earthly kingdoms, stands over against them, and will eschatologically replace them (on earth).*"[50]

Pennington's work, combined with that of Foster, has influenced at least in part many Matthean scholars.[51] One that stands out to me is a former student of Pennington, Patrick Schreiner. Schreiner has built on Pennington's study of the cosmological language of "heaven and earth" in Matthew but spends concentrated time on the implications of the spatial reality of the kingdom.[52] He contends that Matthew presents the space of earth under construction. The earth is tilled and turned over via Jesus's

46. Robert L. Foster, "Why on Earth Use 'Kingdom of Heaven'? Matthew's Terminology Revisited," *NTS* 48.4 (2002): 487–99.

47. Pennington, *Heaven and Earth*; Pennington, "The Kingdom of Heaven in the Gospel of Matthew," *SBJT* 12.1 (2008): 43–51.

48. Pennington, *Heaven and Earth*, ix.

49. Pennington, "Kingdom of Heaven," 50 (emphasis original).

50. Pennington, *Heaven and Earth*, 321 (emphasis original).

51. E.g., Carson, "Matthew," 129; Turner, *Matthew*, 39; Brown and Roberts, *Matthew*, 12–13n17, 270n2; Quarles, *Theology of Matthew*, 86; Sigurd Grindheim, *Living in the Kingdom of God: A Biblical Theology for the Life of the Church* (Grand Rapids: Baker Academic, 2018), 44–45.

52. P. Schreiner, *Body of Jesus*, xi.

incarnation: "Through Jesus' body, he contests the space of earth, installing the kingdom of heaven on earth. Matthew forges a bond between heaven and earth through the presence of Jesus."[53]

I believe that these recent developments are helpful alternatives to the circumlocution theory. While the expressions "kingdom of God" and "kingdom of heaven" are essentially synonymous, the expression *kingdom of heaven* connotes the powerful truth that God's kingdom has come to earth in the person of Jesus Messiah and will ultimately come to earth to replace all other kingdoms.

### 9.1.5 "Kingdom" in the Modern World

But how does the meaning of "the kingdom of heaven" described in 9.1.4.5 above impact discipleship to Jesus in our modern world and the world to which Jesus Messiah came to impact with his message, "Repent, for the kingdom of heaven is at hand" and "Come, follow me" (4:17, 19)? What is the biblical meaning of the kingdom of heaven, and what does this mean for our discipleship to Jesus and its impact on our present-day life in this world?

What comes to your mind when you hear the expression "kingdom"? We might possibly think of something like Great Britain, which is called the "United Kingdom." We might think of a king and/or queen. And of course, we might think of the subjects of the kingdom, the people whom the king or queen rules.

There are at least forty-five kinds of "kingdoms" or "monarchies" today in which a ruler has dominion over a country, ranging from absolute power to constitutional. An example is the "United Kingdom," but there are others, such as the Kingdom of Tonga, the Kingdom of Swaziland, or the Kingdom of Saudi Arabia. We might have good images, of a sweet little old lady like the late Queen Elizabeth, who was more of a figurehead. But examples of kingdoms such as the Kingdom of Saudi Arabia or Bahrain may cause some to think of kingdoms with nearly absolute political and military authority over those in their kingdoms.

They are all quite different from one another, but they are all important images in our daily world. And they all influence the way we think when we hear Jesus's first message: "Repent, for the kingdom of heaven is at hand" (4:17).

### 9.1.6 "Kingdom" in the Ancient World

An equally important issue is to try to imagine what came to the minds of those in the first century who first heard Jesus's message, "the kingdom of heaven is at hand" (Matt 3:2; 4:17; 10:7, ESV). It certainly influenced the way that many people heard Jesus when he first arrived preaching this message.

53. P. Schreiner, *Body of Jesus*, 36–37.

The people of Israel used to have a king, King David, and they had a kingdom, the kingdom of Israel. In the Old Testament the traditions of a king and kingdom were central issues, especially when the conquest by the Assyrians and the Babylonians resulted in the end of the kings and kingdom. The people of Israel by this time had experienced too much of other kingdoms and rulers dominating them. They wanted a return to the glories of the ancient monarchy under David and Solomon and their descendants. They had a brief, tantalizing experience of semi-independence during the Maccabean revolt and the rule of the Hasmoneans, but that had ended less than one hundred years earlier. The celebration of Hanukkah had been instituted to remember those golden days. But once again another power, Rome, ruled over them. The thirst for independence was strong in Israel. The prophecies of David's house and kingdom enduring forever (2 Sam 7:11–16) seemed like they would never be actualized.

John the Baptist ignited those hopes anew by preaching, "Repent, for the kingdom of heaven is near" (Matt 3:2). John the Baptist's mission is like that of a courier who precedes his king to proclaim the coming, and the need for the citizens to ready themselves for the soon-arriving king. Their readiness was indicated by their repentance from sin and sinful ways to await the kingdom. But what kind of kingdom did they expect? What did John expect would occur now that the kingdom of God was near? As the story unfolds, we will have to look closely to separate the various expectations from what God actually intended to accomplish. The people of Israel were wanting a return to the time when they had a king, and a kingdom. That is what many heard in Jesus's message, but when Jesus did not give them the kind of king and kingdom they wanted, they had second thoughts, as we will see.

### 9.1.7 Crucial Elements of the Kingdom of Heaven/God

The kingdom of heaven/God is the domain where all things are put right the way that God intended things to be as he originally created the world. The kingdom of heaven/God is comprised of several elements that must be held at once in balance.[54]

- It has a *revelatory* element in that it is the announcement of the gospel, the good news that God is now entering history in the person of Jesus and establishing his authority over all creation (4:23; 9:35; 13:11, 19). It is this element of the kingdom that Jesus's disciples are to proclaim (10:7; 24:14) and to set as the highest priority above all else (6:33). But it is also this revelatory element that many of those in the religious establishment opposed, which ultimately led to Jesus's execution (11:12; cf. 26:63–67).

54. Cf. Garland, *Theology of Mark's Gospel*, 337.

- It has a *temporal* element. In the preaching of John the Baptist and Jesus, the message that the kingdom has drawn near marks a chronological advance of God's program (3:2; 4:17). The operation of the kingdom was tangibly evident in Jesus's ministry (12:28). Yet he taught the disciples to pray that the kingdom would come in the future to establish God's will on earth as it is in heaven (6:10). Jesus further taught that there will be a future element to the kingdom when in the future all true believers will dine together with Jesus (8:10–11) and when Jesus drinks the cup with his disciples in the Father's kingdom (cf. 26:29). To use a well-known phrase, the kingdom of God is "already-but-not-yet" here.
- It has an *evocative* element, in that Jesus's announcement and commencement of the kingdom of heaven evokes responses from God's subjects—responses of either allegiance or rebellion that provide the basis for royal judgment (12:30):[55] "There was no middle ground, no neutral zone."[56]
- It has a *spatial* element, because one can enter it and live within it (5:20; 7:21; 16:19; 18:3; 19:23–24; 23:13; cf. Mark 9:47; 10:15, 23–25). In this sense it is the sphere where God's authority is experienced, which one can enter; therefore, often scholars refer to this as the "realm" of the kingdom of God that is experienced as one does the will of the Father in heaven (Matt 7:21). This element is related to the temporal in that John the Baptist, the greatest among those born of women, did not have the privilege of entering the kingdom because he belonged to the earlier era (11:11). But all those now responding to the gospel of the kingdom enter the kingdom through the agency of the church, as Peter displayed in employing the "keys of the kingdom of heaven" (16:19; cf. 21:43).

It is also a kingdom that is among people in the presence of Jesus (cf. Luke 17:20–21). The KJV rendered the Greek phrase *hē basileia tou theou entos hymōn estin* as "the kingdom of God is within you" (Luke 17:21 KJV). In the New Testament the term *entos* functions as a preposition with the genitive to mean "inside" as in Matt 23:26, contrasting the "inside" of a cup/Pharisees with the "outside." However, in Luke 17:21 it most likely should be rendered "among" you, "in your midst," since the kingdom of God was not "inside" of the Pharisees, but rather was among them in the person of Jesus. Jesus is saying that the kingdom is already here, but not in a political or militaristic manner. Jesus is speaking of the presence of the kingdom of God among humans, something within their grasp if they will only take hold of it. This saying fits in with other sayings that speak of the kingdom having reached humans in the sense that its saving benefits are now available for them (10:9; 11:20):[57] "It is through

55. Joel B. Green, "Kingdom of God/Heaven," *DJG*² 472.
56. Quarles, *Matthew*, 297.
57. See I. Howard Marshall, *The Gospel of Luke: A Commentary on the Greek Text*, NIGTC (Grand Rapids: Eerdmans, 1978), 655–56.

the body of Jesus the structures of the earth begin to change. Jesus forms space through his body."[58]

- It has a *ruling* element in that the expression "kingdom of heaven" is dynamic: it points us to God as doing something, as actively ruling.[59] In addition to an area and a group of people over whom Jesus is sovereign, the kingdom of heaven is something that happens. The kingdom of heaven is active in the world today in addition to purely existing as an entity. This point leads us to understand a central orientation of Jesus's conception of the kingdom of heaven, because it takes us to the very purpose for being created as humans. We saw earlier that one of God's purposes for creating humans was that we would be caretakers of his kingdom, the creation: that we would "rule" this earth for him. Not for ourselves but for him (Gen 1:26–28).

  The conception of ruling, before sin entered this world, was that of serving God's creation so that it would be what God created it to be. The kingdom of God/heaven is therefore the domain where all things are put right the way that God intended things to be as he originally created the world to be. We are responsible for helping all the rest of creation be what God intended.
- It has a *community* element in that the kingdom belongs to those who have entered its realm, such as the "poor in spirit" (5:3), "those persecuted because of righteousness" (5:10), and the "little children" (18:1–5; 19:14). And this "belongingness" creates a new family of disciples who have left all other hopes of being saved to obey the will of the Father and find eternal life and eternal reward (12:46–50; 19:23–30).
- It has an *experiential* element in the present existence of those who encounter Jesus's transformational kingdom rule. The Gospels clearly locate Jesus in the actualization of the messianic hope and God's rule. The advent of Jesus as God's Messiah—the anointed king—"is both simply and profoundly the decisive disclosure of God's royal rule, together with the consequent unmasking of all rules, all authorities, all powers that would compete with Jesus's authority (28:20).[60] This is the present experience of Jesus's disciples who await its full manifestation at his return.
- It has a *supernatural spiritual* element that most importantly produces a transformational righteousness that surpasses the righteousness of the Pharisees and scribes (5:20), separates it from the kingdoms of this world (4:8–10), subdues the demonic powers of this world (12:24–28), and declares Jesus as the beloved Son

58. P. Schreiner, *Body of Jesus*, 37.

59. Joel Marcus, "Entering into the Kingly Power of God," *JBL* 107 (1988): 663–75. When considering the concept of the *basileia* in Matthew's Gospel and the assignment of Jesus's royal rule to the royal rule of God, see Christian Blumenthal, *Basileia im Matthäusevangelium*, WUNT 416 (Tübingen: Mohr Siebeck, 2019), passim; esp. 186–266.

60. Green, "Kingdom of God/Heaven," 472.

of the Father as he comes in his kingdom (16:28; cf. 17:5). At the final judgment Jesus will establish his kingdom on the earth and those who have followed him and obeyed him will inherit the kingdom prepared for them from the foundation of the world (25:34).

### 9.1.8 Defining/Describing the Kingdom of Heaven/God

The expression "kingdom of heaven" evokes among modern readers as well as Jesus's initial hearers and Matthew's audiences a variety of images and concepts. We have seen above the multifaceted elements and dimensions, which have led to a variety of definitions of the kingdom of God/heaven.

Last century at the outset of evangelical scholars' engaging with the concept of the kingdom of heaven/God, George Ladd defined the kingdom of God as

> the redemptive reign of God dynamically active to establish his rule among men [humans], and . . . this Kingdom, which will appear as an apocalyptic act at the end of the age, has already come into human history in the person and mission of Jesus to overcome evil, to deliver men [humans] from its power, and to bring them into the blessings of God's reign. The Kingdom of God involves two great moments: fulfillment within history, and consummation at the end of history.[61]

More recently Nicholas Perrin defines or, more exactly, describes the "kingdom of God" this way: "Creationally engaged, universally focused, and eschatologically oriented, the kingdom of God is a transcendent sphere of reality that conspires with a community of human image-bearers in the task of restoring creation to the worship of the one true creator God."[62]

My engagement with this topic leads me to describe the kingdom of heaven/God in the following way, keeping in mind our discussion of the additional aspects found in Matthew's unique phrase, "kingdom of heaven":

> The kingdom of heaven/God is the ruling authority of God brought dynamically into human history in the person and mission of Jesus Messiah to establish the realm of God's rule and to put all things right in the way that he originally intended for his earthly creation. This is accomplished through Jesus Messiah in the power of the Holy Spirit, (1) by overcoming evil and delivering humans from the power of sin and death through redemption and reconciliation with God, (2) by beginning to restore

61. George Eldon Ladd, *The Presence of the Future: The Eschatology of Biblical Realism*, 2nd ed. (Grand Rapids: Eerdmans, 1974), 218.

62. Nicholas Perrin, *The Kingdom of God: A Biblical Theology*, BTL (Grand Rapids: Zondervan, 2019), 52.

the image of God in humans in the transformation of new covenant regeneration and renewal of life in the Spirit so that humans would rule God's creation with him through servanthood, and (3) by bringing humans into the blessings of God's ruling authority in present human history and ultimately and completely in all creation in the body of Christ in the eschatological replacement of all earthly kingdoms in the consummation of the kingdom of God/heaven at the end of history.

## 9.2 Jesus's Messianic Ministry of Bringing the Kingdom of Heaven to Earth

A central focus of Matthew's Gospel is on Jesus Messiah bringing the kingdom of heaven to earth. We can see clearly from the beginning and throughout his Gospel that Jesus is inaugurating in his life and ministry the present reality of the kingdom of heaven. But it comes and is operative in ways that are significantly different from what many in Israel expected. In his birth, messages, miracles, and especially in his death, resurrection, and final commission Jesus establishes and clarifies what the kingdom of heaven is all about—it is the fulfillment of the hopes of humanity.

### 9.2.1 John the Baptist's Message of the Soon-Arriving Kingdom of Heaven (3:2–3)

John the Baptist had one central message, in which he urgently calls the people to repent because the kingdom of heaven is at hand (Matt 3:2). This will be the same message Jesus will announce at the beginning of his public ministry (4:17) and the same message the Twelve will preach on their missionary tour through Israel (10:5).

As similar as was John's message to the Old Testament prophets, there was a distinctly new sound to it. He called the people to repent because the kingdom of heaven was not off in the future; it was near! The kingdom of heaven has come near to people in the soon-arriving Messiah. John was the one foretold by Isaiah who would be privileged to prepare the way for the Lord's arrival and his kingdom (3:3; cf. Isa 40:3). John was not just another religious zealot drumming up support for a new following. As a road must be cleared of obstacles before an approaching king, John is calling for the people to clear the obstacles out of their lives that would hinder their reception of the Lord. He is calling for the people to get themselves ready—to prepare their heart and life—for the arrival of the Coming One with the kingdom of heaven.

### 9.2.2 Jesus's Announcement of the Presence of the Kingdom of Heaven in His Person and Ministry (4:17–23)

Matthew's summary of Jesus's message is the same as his summary of John the Baptist's: "Repent, for the kingdom of heaven is near" (4:17; cf. 3:2). In neither case was the arrival of the kingdom defined, probably indicating that certain expectations about the arrival of the kingdom came to mind among those who heard the Baptist and Jesus preach.[63] But the way in which Jesus developes his ministry and the response of many to him reveal different understandings and expectations of the way that God's kingdom "is near" (*ēngiken*).

The way in which various groups within Israel had anticipated the arrival of the prophesied kingdom of God differed. Donald Gowan underscores a generally consistent prophetic hope that lent itself to a variety of expectations within Israel. "God must transform the human person; give a new heart and a new spirit. . . . God must transform human society; restore Israel to the promised land, rebuild cities, and make Israel's new status a witness to the nations. . . . And God must transform nature itself."[64] Robert Yarbrough suggests that there were two broad variations within Israel for understanding the kingdom of God: one variant is an imminent, political-military manifestation of God's kingdom, perhaps through the restoration to power of the house of David; the other emphasizes an eschatological manifestation "in which the kingdom would be revealed in opposition to all that is merely political and historical."[65]

Jesus, however, has his own agenda. He will indeed bring a form of judgment as the wrath of God remains on those who do not obey him and as he judges the ruler of this world (cf. John 3:36; 16:11). He also will bring a form of restoration as he presents the kingdom to Israel (cf. Matt 10:5–7; 15:24). He initiates a form of restoration righteousness as a qualification for entrance to the kingdom of heaven (5:20). But the way in which this fulfills the Old Testament prophetic hope is different than what many in Israel expected.

The crux of Jesus's inauguration of the kingdom of heaven has to do with how people respond to him as their Messiah.[66] He is the Coming One prophesied by John (cf. 3:13–17; 11:2–6), but he preaches the "good news" of the kingdom for all who come to him. As Jesus remains faithful to his mission, people are forced to make a decision. They will either be with him, requiring that they adjust their expectations to accept what he reveals to be God's present program, or they will be against him. The tragedy of the latter choice is fully exposed at the Roman trial when the crowd chooses the revolutionary brigand Barabbas over Jesus. Jesus has bitterly disappointed

63. The definitional silence assumes that Jesus and his forerunner, John the Baptist, would be understood by those who heard them preach, and that certain associations with the announcement of the kingdom would be called to mind. See Dale Patrick, "The Kingdom of God in the Old Testament," in *The Kingdom of God in Twentieth Century Interpretation*, ed. Wendell Willis (Peabody, MA: Hendrickson, 1987), 71.

64. Donald E. Gowan, *Eschatology in the Old Testament* (Philadelphia: Fortress, 1986), 2.

65. Robert W. Yarbrough, "The Kingdom of God in the New Testament: Matthew and Revelation," in *The Kingdom of God*, ed. Christopher W. Morgan and Robert A. Peterson (Wheaton, IL: Crossway, 2012), 106.

66. C. E. B. Cranfield, *The Gospel According to St Mark*, CGTC (Cambridge: Cambridge University Press, 1972), 68.

the crowd's expectations of what the kingdom should bring, so they turn against him (see 27:15–26).[67]

God's ways are not always what humans expect. Jesus will indeed fulfill the prophetic hope. But he will bring this hope to complete fulfillment only when he returns as the Son of Man in glory (cf. 24:29–31).[68] This dual phenomenon is what scholars today generally refer to as the *already-not-yet* nature of the presence of the kingdom. Jesus has *already* inaugurated the kingdom, but it has *not yet* reached its final form.[69] The kingdom is now present with the arrival of the messianic king of the line of David, and its arrival will challenge a variety of expectations among those who encounter its force. What some expected to occur immediately—especially full judgment and restoration—awaits future final fulfillment.

### 9.2.3 Jesus Messiah Calls Fishers of Men for the Kingdom of Heaven (4:17–25)

The primary focus of this incident is on Jesus and the kingdom of heaven that he has announced. Jesus is the Spirit-anointed messianic Son, in whom the kingdom has arrived. The only appropriate response is to obey immediately.[70] In this scene, Jesus is enlisting workers to join him in his kingdom mission. It is important to note that the call and response of the four brothers is based upon an extended prior relationship that they had enjoyed with Jesus.[71] While the emphasis of the story is primarily upon calling the four to join in Jesus's kingdom mission, that task is accomplished above all as an outgrowth of their relationship to Jesus: "'Come, follow me,' Jesus said" (4:19). Allegiance to his person is *the* decisive act.[72]

Discipleship to Jesus was going to be different than what many might have anticipated. It was not going to be simply a program through which Jesus will run his disciples. Discipleship was a life that began in relationship with the Master and moved into all areas of their experience. This is the beginning of kingdom life.[73]

---

67. For a refutation of the theory that Jesus saw himself as, and was, seditious, see Jesse P. Nickel, *The Things That Make for Peace: Jesus and Eschatological Violence*, BZNW 244 (Berlin: de Gruyter, 2021).

68. Some critical scholars deny virtually any future final fulfillment of this hope; e.g., Marcus J. Borg, *Conflict, Holiness & Politics in the Teachings of Jesus*, SBEC 5 (New York: Edwin Mellin, 1984), 45.

69. While there is diversity of opinion as to what was fulfilled in Jesus's first advent and what awaits his second, the already-not-yet general position has a large consensus. For a survey of positions, see Mark Saucy, *The Kingdom of God in the Teaching of Jesus in Twentieth Century Theology* (Dallas: Word, 1997). For a brief overview of widely held evangelical perspectives, see George R. Beasley-Murray, "The Kingdom of God in the Teaching of Jesus," *JETS* 35.1 (1992): 19–30; response by Craig Blomberg (31–36); rejoinder by Beasley-Murray (37–38); and separate article by Carl F. H. Henry, "Reflections on the Kingdom of God," 39–49.

70. Kingsbury, "On Following Jesus," 49.

71. Scot McKnight, *Turning to Jesus: The Sociology of Conversion in the Gospels* (Louisville: Westminster John Knox, 2002), 40–42. I discuss the developing relationship of the disciples to Jesus more fully elsewhere: Wilkins, *Following the Master*, ch. 6.

72. See Leon Morris, "Disciples of Jesus," in *Jesus of Nazareth: Lord and Christ–Essays on the Historical Jesus and New Testament Christology*, ed. Joel B. Green and Max Turner (Grand Rapids: Eerdmans, 1994), 116; Eduard Schweizer, *Lordship and Discipleship*, rev. ed., SBT 28 (Naperville, IL: Allenson, 1960), 20.

73. Wilkins, *Following the Master*, 100–109, 124–25.

At the core of all Jesus's teaching and preaching is the message of the "gospel of the kingdom" (4:23). Matthew uses the noun "gospel" (*euangelion*) only four times, and three of those four occur in phrase, "gospel of the kingdom," a phrase found only in Matthew.[74] The real "good news" is that the age of the kingdom of God has finally dawned in the ministry of Jesus.

This good news of the kingdom is not only taught and preached, but it is also *demonstrated* as Jesus was "healing" (*therapeuō*) every disease and sickness among the people. Healing once again signals that Jesus has authority over the powers of this world and confirms the reality of the arrival of the kingdom of heaven (11:4–6). Matthew will note later that as Jesus drove out spirits and healed the sick, he fulfilled the prophetic hope of one who "took up our infirmities and carried our diseases" (8:16–17; cf. Isa 53:4). The phrase "every disease and sickness" (4:23) indicates that nothing was beyond Jesus's ability to heal, an authority he will likewise give to the Twelve on their mission tour in Israel (Matt 10:1). Matthew specifies that these healings took place "among the people" (4:23), using the term *laos* again, a term that specifies the people of Israel. Both proclamation and miracle announce that Israel's hoped-for kingdom-promise is at hand.

### 9.2.4 The Beatitudes of the Kingdom of Heaven (5:3–12)

The Beatitudes open the Sermon on the Mount with a sober yet dazzling vision of the operation of the kingdom of heaven among God's people. More than simply a formal literary introduction,[75] the Beatitudes give a summarizing declaration of the essence of the Sermon's message, giving in a nutshell the way in which the kingdom of heaven makes its impact upon the lives of those who respond to it. The character of this kingdom life contravenes the values that most people hold dear because God's blessing rests upon the unlikely ones—the poor in spirit, the mourners, the meek, and the persecuted. Jesus's disciples embody God's alternative reality through these character qualities of the Beatitudes of the kingdom of heaven.[76]

#### *9.2.4.1 The Structure of the Beatitudes*

The overall structure of the Beatitudes gives an important clue to their theme. The first and the eighth beatitudes (5:3, 10) form a pair of bookends, an example of the common Hebrew literary device called an *inclusio*,[77] because the causal clause of the first beatitude is repeated in the last beatitude—"for theirs *is* the kingdom of heaven" (cf. 5:3, 10).

The repetition of the present tense clause signals the main theme of the Beatitudes:

74. Matthew 4:23; 9:35; 24:14.

75. Betz, *Sermon on the Mount*, 92: "As a musical masterpiece begins with an introitus, the SM opens with an extraordinary sequence of statements, the so-called Beatitudes."

76. Hays, *Moral Vision of the New Testament*, 321.

77. The *inclusio* is found in both narrative (see on 4:23; 9:35) and poetry, as here; cf. W. G. E. Watson, *Classical Hebrew Poetry*, JSOTSup 26 (Sheffield: JSOT, 1984), 282–87.

the blessedness of the kingdom of heaven is a present possession and operation among those who respond to Jesus's ministry. However, the second through seventh beatitudes (5:4–9) have a future tense in the causal clause of each beatitude (e.g., 5:4–"for they *will be* comforted"), indicating that the kingdom is a future expectation and hope as well as a present possession.

### *9.2.4.2 Interpreting the Beatitudes*

When approaching the Beatitudes we must avoid sliding into various extremes, a caution to be observed in the Sermon on the Mount as a whole. In the first place, we must not conclude that Jesus is calling his listeners to a meritorious attempt at earning salvation by living out these character qualities in order to enter the kingdom. Jesus's Beatitudes are statements of grace, not of law. In the second place, we must avoid making these into burdensome, ethical demands on those who are members of the kingdom. There are no imperatives here, except to "rejoice" when one experiences the blessing of God in the middle of persecution (5:12). In the third place, we must not conclude that these are eschatological blessings that only will be realized at the end of the age. The kingdom blessings are found in both the present tense (5:3, 10) and the future tense (5:4–9).[78] Jesus uses the Beatitudes to speak to a variety of listeners and to communicate several messages about the kingdom of heaven at one time. Specifically, he makes a pronouncement about the kingdom to Israel as a whole, and at the same time he gives instruction about the nature of kingdom life to his disciples.

While the Beatitudes are not entrance requirements, they do offer an invitation to the crowd to respond to Jesus's announcement of the kingdom of heaven. There are only two choices: the way of the kingdom or the way of the religious establishment. As Jesus pronounces the availability of the kingdom to all, he offers the way to life. But the door is to life is narrow—as narrow as Jesus (cf. 7:13–14). All must come through him.

The Beatitudes are statements of reality about the kind of characteristics that will be produced in the disciple who participates in kingdom life. These are not self-induced but are products of the kingdom life that dwells within each disciple. Therefore, they are not imperatives or required standards disciples must perform in order to procure God's approval. If that were the case, they would not be much different than the rigorous demands for purity found among the scribes and Pharisees, and they would lead to the same kind of religious hypocrisy that Jesus condemns.

But the Beatitudes do provide guidelines for the kind of characteristics that God will produce in his disciples. The qualities highlighted here echo the qualities that exemplified the truly godly person in the Old Testament. However, with the arrival of

78. For discussion see Robert A. Guelich, "The Beatitudes: 'Entrance Requirements' or 'Eschatological Blessings'?," in *The Sermon on the Mount: A Foundation for Understanding* (Waco, TX: Word, 1982), 109–11.

the work of the kingdom of heaven in the life of each disciple, these character qualities become a concrete reality. This is the link between Jesus's teaching on discipleship and later New Testament authors' discussions of regeneration and sanctification through the work of the Holy Spirit. The life made possible through the arrival of the kingdom of heaven is, for example, later described by the apostle Peter as the transformational process of the person who has been born anew by the living and enduring word of God (1 Pet 1:22–2:3).

The individual characteristics of the Beatitudes are not self-produced, nor can we simply learn or emulate them in an attempt to bring them about in our lives. They are products of a life energized by the Spirit of God. They are, like the listing Paul gives in Gal 5:22–23, the fruit of the Spirit. They are a wholistic view of what the Spirit will produce in the life of a disciple of Jesus who is walking in his ways and is being transformed into his image.

As such, the Beatitudes contrast Jesus's values of the kingdom of heaven with the values of the world and offer an indictment of the values of the religious establishment that takes pride in its accomplishments apart from the life of the kingdom of heaven. The values of the kingdom of heaven, its blessings, and the counter-values of the religious establishment of Jesus's day can be displayed in the following way:

| **Jesus's Kingdom of heaven values** | ***Jesus's Kingdom of heaven blessings*** | ***Counter-values of the religious establishment and earthly kingdoms***[79] |
|---|---|---|
| Poor in spirit | humbly receive the blessings of the kingdom of heaven | self-confident, competent, self-reliant |
| Mourn | experience God's comforting presence | self-seeking; pleasure-seeking, self-satisfied |
| Meek | gently encounter God's will come to earth as his servants | proud, domineering, aggressive, harsh, and tyrannical, self-important |
| Hunger and thirst for righteousness | experience justice, ethical virtue, God's promised salvation | satisfied, self-righteous, mollified |
| Merciful | receive forgiveness, and kindness for the hurting and needy | merciless, harsh and condemning of those not meeting their standards |
| Pure in heart | undivided devotion will encounter God in Jesus | external religious ritualism, attend to all exterior purification ceremonies |
| Peacemakers | completeness and wholeness in every area of life, including relationships with God, neighbors, and nations | competitive, aggressive, divisive |
| Persecuted because of righteousness | undeserved maltreatment is rewarded by life in the kingdom of heaven | persecuting in the name of self-righteousness the very people who stood for true righteousness; adaptable, popular |

79. See also Lawrence O. Richards, *The Teacher's Commentary* (Wheaton, IL: Victor, 1987), 541.

The Beatitudes are bold statements of the nature of kingdom life. It begins with abandoning pride in one's spiritual accomplishment before God and proceeds as one allows God to produce his kingdom life in his disciples in their everyday lives.

### 9.2.5 The Kingdom Prayer for Jesus's Disciples in Intervening History (6:9–10)

Jesus's disciples now have the privilege of living in the kingdom of heaven (Matt 11:11). But what does that look like? Jesus's explanations are given throughout Matthew's Gospel but are especially seen in what are referred to as the Lord's Prayer (here)[80] and the parables of the mysteries of the kingdom of heaven (ch. 13; see 9.2.10).

The prayer begins by invoking God: "Our Father in heaven" (6:9). The way that Jesus uses "*my* Father" (11:27) to address his heavenly Father is exceptional because Jesus is the unique Son (cf. 3:17). But by calling his disciples to share in the kingdom of heaven, we now have entered a relationship with his Father as well. This image is prevalent throughout the Sermon on the Mount.[81] He is "*our* Father," expressing the relationship we have to one another as disciples, members of one family, expressing the relationship we have to Jesus as our brother, and expressing the corporate intimacy we have together with the same Father.

The first petition is directed toward God's name, "Hallowed be your name" (6:9), or "Let it be made holy" (*hagiasthētō*). The purpose of hallowing the name (the name signifies the person and signifies something essential about the bearer[82]) is that God would be "sanctified" or set apart as holy among all people and in all actions; that he would be treated with the highest honor. This affirms the typical Jewish expectation that God would be treated with the highest honor. To hallow God's name means to hold it in reverence; hence, to hold *him* in reverence, to honor, glorify and exalt *him*.[83]

The second petition expresses the hope of God's people throughout all of history: "Your kingdom come" (6:10). The Jewish Qaddish prays similarly, "May he rule his kingdom in your lifetime and in your days and in the lifetime of the whole house of Israel, speedily and soon."[84] Israel looked for God to send his anointed one to rule the earth, and now that Jesus has inaugurated the kingdom of heaven, his disciples live with the anticipation of the completion of that program. God's anointed Messiah is here and at work, bringing the sovereign and saving rule of God. As we pray "your kingdom come," we align ourselves with Jesus's own practice of prayer and join his

80. Scot McKnight, *The Sermon on the Mount*, SGBC (Grand Rapids: Zondervan, 2013), 170.

81. Cf. 5:16, 45, 48; 6:26, 33; 7:11. For the structure and the role of the prayer in the Sermon on the Mount as a whole, see Ridlehoover, *Lord's Prayer*, loc. 2518–92, Kindle.

82. Black, *Lord's Prayer*, 84.

83. Neusner and Green, "Name," *DJBP* 448.

84. Benedict T. Viviano, "Hillel and Jesus on Prayer," in *Hillel and Jesus: Comparisons of Two Major Religious Leaders*, ed. James H. Charlesworth and Loren L. Johns (Minneapolis: Fortress, 1997), 449–50. See also Gupta, *Lord's Prayer*, 3–12.

kingdom movement and seek God's power in furthering its ultimate fulfillment.[85] In this petition, Jesus is preparing his disciples to understand that there would be an extended time of living in the already-not-yet epoch of the kingdom until his return in glory.

The third petition speaks of God's will coming to pass: "Your will be done on earth as it is in heaven" (6:10). This appeal is intended to be linked with the preceding petition. Wherever the kingdom of heaven exerts its presence, the will of God is experienced. God reigns in heaven absolutely, which means that all of heaven experiences his perfect will. Jesus prays that earth would experience that same rule of God. The term for "will" is *thelēma*, which here expresses God's will of command, as in the psalmist's exclamation, "I desire to do your will, my God; your law is within my heart" (Ps 40:8). With the inauguration of the kingdom of heaven, those who carry out the will of the Father in Jesus's ministry become his disciples (Matt 12:50) and display the reality of the kingdom of heaven as they remain faithful to God's will for their lives (cf. 5:13–16). The complete experience of God's will on earth occurs only when his kingdom has come to earth in its final form, causing an overthrow of all evil rule (Rev 20:1–10) and completing the regeneration of this earth (cf. Rom 8:18–25). But Jesus's disciples are the present living testimony to the world that God's will can be experienced today.

The invocation and first three petitions give Jesus's disciples the right priorities, because we are less likely to pray frivolously or selfishly for God's will if we have first, and meaningfully, glorified God as "Father" and entreated him to bring his kingdom to earth.[86] Then the final three petitions can be properly focused on the needs of the individual disciples—our sustenance, our sin, and our spiritual battle.

The fourth petition focuses on the disciples' sustenance: "Give us today our daily bread" (6:11). The reference to "bread" is an example of synecdoche, a part-whole figure of speech for "food" (4:4), but here extending to all of the believer's needs—physical and spiritual. Disciples are to rely on God for all of our needs.[87] The adjective translated "daily" (*epiousion*) occurs in the New Testament only here and in the parallel in Luke 11:3. Its connection with "bread" has been broadly debated,[88] but it most likely means "for the present day." In the same way that manna was only given one day at a time, disciples are to rely upon daily provision for life from God, helping us to develop a continuing, conscious dependence upon him. If God cares for us today, then surely he will provide for us every day of our lives. The best way to prevent anxiety is to

85. Black, *Lord's Prayer*, 108–34; N. T. Wright, "Lord's Prayer," 135.

86. Turner, "Prayer in the Gospels and Acts," 65.

87. See Grant R. Osborne, *The Hermeneutical Spiral: A Comprehensive Introduction to Biblical Interpretation* (Downers Grove: InterVarsity, 1991), 100–101, 108.

88. For overviews, see Gupta, *Lord's Prayer*, 91–103; Betz, *Sermon on the Mount*, 396–399; Davies and Allison, *Matthew*, 1:607–610; Hagner, *Matthew 1–13*, 149–50; Morris, *Matthew*, 146n43.

consciously trust God for today's bread and tomorrow trust him for tomorrow's bread (cf. Matt 6:34; Phil 4:6). Jesus does not renounce responsible activity of his disciples in taking care of their needs and those of their loved ones, as he indicates in his sound rebuke of the Pharisees when they avoided providing for parental needs (Matt 15:3–6). He only denounces his disciple's anxiety about the future. We are to rely on God for all physical sustenance, but to be concerned only one day at a time.

The fifth petition addresses the disciples' debt of sin: "Forgive us our debts, as we also have forgiven our debtors" (6:12). The word for "debt" is *opheilēmata*. In Luke's parallel prayer the term used is *hamartias*, "sins" (Luke 11:4). These are basically equal expressions, but with the additional nuance in Matthew that humans owe obedience to God. Sin creates an obligation or "debt" to God that humans cannot possibly repay. Jesus's disciples have responded to his charge to repent, and their sins are now forgiven. But we are not simply to relish our own state of forgiveness; we are to forgive others. Those who have received forgiveness are so possessed with gratitude to God that we in turn will eagerly forgive those who are "debtors" to us. This does not teach that humans must forgive others before they can receive forgiveness but rather that forgiveness of others is *proof* that a disciple's sins are forgiven and he or she possesses salvation (cf. Matt 18:21–35). The evidence that a person has truly been forgiven of his or her debt of sin is the willingness to forgive others.[89] If we do not forgive, it is evidence that we have not experienced forgiveness ourselves.

The final petition addresses the disciples' battle with evil forces: "And lead us not into temptation, but deliver us from the evil one" (6:13). Since God is not one who tempts his people to do evil (Jas 1:13), and the word rendered "temptation" (*peirasmos*) can be used for either temptation or test (cf. Matt 4:1–11; Jas 1:12–13), the petition indicates that the disciples should pray either that God removes tests of their faith, such as when manna was given to test Israel (Exod 16:4; Deut 8:16; 1 Pet 1:7), or else they should pray that their testing would not become an occasion for temptation. Jesus directed the disciples to pray this way in the garden of Gethsemane, "Watch and pray so that you will not fall into temptation. The spirit is willing, but the body is weak" (26:41). Jesus teaches his disciples that they need to rely on God not only for physical sustenance and forgiveness of sins, but also to depend upon him for moral triumph and spiritual victory in all of the spiritual battles of life.[90]

### 9.2.6 Entrance to the Kingdom: "Inside-Out" Righteousness (5:20)

A statement of Jesus in the Sermon on the Mount gives his proclamation of entrance to, and exclusion from, the kingdom of heaven: "For I tell you that unless

89. See P. S. Cameron, "Lead Us Not into Temptation," *ExpTimes* 101 (1990): 299–301.

90. Bruce Chilton, *Jesus' Prayer and Jesus' Eucharist: His Personal Practice of Spirituality* (Valley Forge, PA: Trinity Press International, 1997), 46–47.

your righteousness surpasses that of the Pharisees and the teachers of the law, you will certainly not enter the kingdom of heaven" (5:20). This may be one of Jesus's most astounding statements because the teachers of the Law and the Pharisees were the epitome of ethical righteousness. The teachers of the law, or scribes (*grammateis*), were not only curators of the text of the Old Testament but also taught the Law (7:29), held themselves responsible to interpret and preserve the Law (Mark 7:5–8), elaborate doctrine from the Law (Matt 17:10), and gather around themselves disciples whom they could train to carry on the profession and their teachings.

The Pharisees were members of the sect that was committed to fulfilling the demands of the Old Testament through their elaborate oral tradition. Their scrupulous adherence to the written and oral law was legendary in Israel, yet Jesus says that it did not gain them entrance to the kingdom of heaven. How could anyone possibly surpass their righteousness? If the scribes and the Pharisees had not gained entrance, what hope was there for anyone else? Does this mean an intensification of a doctrine of salvation by works? Does this mean that they must out-count the scribes and the Pharisees in performing the 613 commandments,[91] and do them one better?[92]

No. Jesus's disciples are called to a different *kind* and *quality* of righteousness that gains them entrance to the kingdom of heaven, not an increased quantity. In both Jesus's interaction with John the Baptist (3:15) and the statement of the Beatitudes (5:6), righteousness in the preaching of Jesus is not primarily a personal attainment of ethical purity. Righteousness belongs in the realm of grace.

Deines states that we may summarize the Matthean concept of righteousness as "Jesus-righteousness," because righteousness is not possible without Jesus. "Those who obey his call to discipleship get a share of this righteousness, and thus can be addressed concerning *their* righteousness, as in 5:20 and 6:1. The righteousness of the disciples, however, stays focused on Jesus as its foundation as well as its consequences."[93]

In responding to Jesus's invitation to the kingdom of heaven, individuals acquire "Jesus-righteousness," which then means that they have entered the kingdom of heaven. This is the gracious invitation of "the good news of the kingdom" (4:23). Jesus's proclamation of good news is that the kingdom of heaven is now available to those who respond to him. The shock of that declaration strips away precedents current among some in Judaism for gaining favor with God and serves as an introduction to the "antitheses" to follow (5:21–48).

91. Six hundred thirteen is the traditional number of combined commandments and prohibitions reckoned by the rabbis. Rabbi Simlai stated: "613 commandments were revealed to Moses at Sinai, 365 being prohibitions equal in number to the solar days of the year, and 248 being commands corresponding in number to the parts of the human body" (b. Makkot 23b).

92. Thomas G. Long, *Matthew*, Westminster Bible Companion (Louisville: Westminster John Knox, 1997), 54.

93. Deines, "Not the Law," 76–77. Hagner argues for God's salvific deliverance in 3:15 and 5:6, which could also be applied here (Hagner, *Matthew 1–13*, 109). See also Moloney, "Matthew 5:17–18 and the Matthean use of ΔΙΚΑΙΟΣΥΝΗ," 33–54.

It also serves as a disclosure of the most central principle of life in the kingdom of heaven—kingdom righteousness operates from the inside out, not the outside in. God's saving activity has arrived on the earthly scene to deliver his people, and this will produce a radical change in their lives from the inside out as they acquire Jesus-righteousness and enter the kingdom of heaven. Jesus's proclamation of good news is that the kingdom of heaven is now available to those who respond to him. God's saving activity has arrived on the earthly scene to deliver his people, and this will produce a radical change in their lives from the inside out, not the outside in.[94]

This is not a new principle, however. The people of God knew that external acts of righteousness could not take away sin nor gain favor with God unless those acts were preceded by a repentant heart that is open to God's inner work of purification. Psalm 51 is perhaps the prime example, where David seeks inner cleansing and purification of his heart after his outrageously sinful actions against Bathsheba (Ps 51:2, 7, 10). His understanding of the inside-out operation is unequivocal:

> You do not delight in sacrifice, or I would bring it;
> you do not take pleasure in burnt offerings.
> My sacrifice, O God, is a broken spirit;
> a broken and contrite heart
> you, God, will not despise. (Ps 51:16–17)

David *did* later offer sacrifices and offerings, and he did receive God's favor, but he knew they had to be preceded by inner repentance and God's work of cleansing and purification. But throughout Israel's history there was a tendency to reverse the operation, as was the case with the scribes and the Pharisees of Jesus's day. The assumption seemed to be that if one worked hard enough to clean up the outside, then the inside was automatically clean. Jesus later condemned this procedure explicitly when he pronounced woes on teachers of the law and Pharisees: "On the outside you appear to people as righteous but on the inside you are full of hypocrisy and wickedness" (Matt 23:27–28). Jesus leads the audience to recognize that since entrance to the kingdom of heaven is not gained by external acts of righteousness, then they must seek a different kind—an inner righteousness that begins with a transformation of the heart, an undertaking David knew could only be accomplished by God (Ps 51:10).

The arrival of the kingdom of heaven produces spiritual transformation of the disciple's heart, which will ultimately produce transformation in the disciple's external ethical life (Matt 15:16–20). If entrance to the kingdom of heaven can only be

94. Hagner, "Righteousness in Matthew's Gospel," 101–20, here 116–17. Hagner sees primarily the element of ethical righteousness in 5:20, but his argument for God's salvific deliverance in 3:15 and 5:6 could also be applied here, which he does more directly in his commentary (Hagner, *Matthew 1–13*, 109).

accomplished by an inner work of transformation, so also personal growth within the kingdom must proceed from the inside to the out. That principle underlies the next series of examples Jesus uses to explain how he fulfills the Old Testament (5:21–48). His disciples themselves will fulfill God's intention and will as revealed in Scripture as they conform their inner life to his Word, and then have that inner transformation guide their external behavior.

Jesus's declaration in 5:20 is an interpretative key to the entire Sermon on the Mount and, by extension, to life in the kingdom of heaven. What he contrasts in the antitheses to follow is his internal, spiritual interpretation, which will produce in his disciples an inside-out transformation in true righteousness in the kingdom of heaven, with the external, legalistic interpretation of the Pharisees, which dead-ends in an external, superficial self-righteousness.

### 9.2.7 The Greatness of Those in the Kingdom of Heaven (11:11)

Jesus defends John the Baptist by pointing to the greatness of his ministry, yet he gives a surprising twist to the argument by pointing to the greatness of those in the kingdom of heaven: "Truly I tell you, among those born of women there has not risen anyone greater than John the Baptist; yet whoever is least in the kingdom of heaven is greater than he" (11:11).

*The contrast is not between human accomplishments but between eras.* The arrival of the kingdom of heaven ushers in an incomparably greater era than any preceding it. John the Baptist is a transitional figure who prepared the way for the Coming One, but the implication is that John will not live to see and experience the full arrival of the kingdom's establishment.[95] Jesus's institution of the new covenant in his blood, which is poured out for the forgiveness of sin, is a dividing line. The complex of events including the cross, resurrection, ascension, and sending of the Spirit at Pentecost brings the arrival of the kingdom of heaven's redemptive life, by which time John had been executed. John is the greatest of those born during the Old Testament era because of his crucial role in preparing the way for the Messiah and his kingdom. John's mission was great because of the greatness of the one he introduced. But those in the kingdom of heaven are greater because of their privilege to have actually entered the kingdom of heaven. However, the greatness of those in the kingdom of heaven is not because of a privileged position. Greatness is measured primarily in the same way as John's—the

95. The majority of interpreters follow this reasoning, including Blomberg, *Matthew*, 187; Carson, "Matthew," 307–8; France, *Matthew*, 194–95; Hagner, *Matthew 1–13*, 305–6; Morris, *Matthew*, 280–81. A minority view is represented by Witherington, *Christology of Jesus*, 46–47, who attempts to include John in the kingdom of heaven by suggesting that the comparison is between two ways of evaluating the human condition that are not mutually exclusive. But this misses the intended comparison of the stages of redemptive history; cf. Flusser, *Jesus*, 261–64.

honor of pointing to the Messiah. Even the least in the kingdom of heaven can point to Jesus as the messianic deliverer more clearly than John.

And further, the least in the kingdom of heaven have experienced firsthand the forgiveness of their sins and the transformation of regeneration by the Spirit that characterizes this age. Greatness according to Jesus is not related to accomplishment, which is the prevailing yardstick of the world. Jesus measures greatness in one's reception of the redemptive work of Jesus and one's service to others in advancing the cause of the kingdom (cf. 18:1–4; 20:20–28). This does not in any way demean John; rather, it elevates Jesus and his redemptive work in establishing the kingdom of heaven.[96]

## 9.2.8 Violence and the Kingdom of Heaven (11:12)

Jesus continues his tribute to John by harking back to the beginning stages of his announcement that the kingdom of heaven will soon arrive in the ministry of the Coming One.[97] "From the days of John the Baptist until now, the kingdom of heaven has been forcefully advancing, and forceful men lay hold of it" (11:12, NIV84). This saying of Jesus has been widely debated, with the difficulties arising primarily because the verb *biazō* (NIV84 "forcefully advancing") and the noun *biastēs* (NIV84 "forceful men") can be taken in either a positive or negative way.[98]

The first clause probably indicates opposition from the religious establishment generally, while the second clause probably points to the forces of evil people specifically, such as Herod Antipas, who has even now imprisoned John. Since the announcement of its arrival in John's ministry, the kingdom of heaven has received opposition from the religious establishment of Israel generally, and now John has received opposition from Herod Antipas, an evil, violent man who will put John to death violently. The saying foreshadows the gathering opposition to Jesus, who will be opposed generally by the religious establishment (26:59; 27:1), but that opposition will be personalized in his arrest, trial, and execution by the Jewish high priest Caiaphas (26:57) and the Roman governor, Pontius Pilate (27:2).

## 9.2.9 The Work of the Spirit and the Presence of the Kingdom of Heaven (12:28)

### *9.2.9.1 The Divided Kingdom (12:25–28)*

When Jesus exorcised and healed a demon-possessed man who was blind and mute, the Pharisees heard of it and said, "It is only by Beelzebul, the prince of demons, that

96. See Keener, *Matthew* (1999), 337–39.

97. The expression "from the days of . . . until now" can refer to a person's entire life story, but here with John still alive, Jesus is most likely harking back to the beginnings of John's ministry.

98. Davies and Allison, *Matthew*, 2:254–55, list no less than seven different interpretations. For the history of interpretation, see P. S. Cameron, *Violence and the Kingdom: The Interpretation of Matthew 11:12* (Frankfurt: Peter Lang, 1984).

this fellow drives out demons" (12:24). The power behind an exorcism could come from either God or Satan. Since the Pharisees have already concluded that Jesus is not God's agent (cf. 12:14), in their minds the source of power that he demonstrates must come from Satan. They assume that since a demon came out of the man it must be evidence that the demon was obeying Satan as the ruler of the demons.

But Jesus shows the illogical nature of their thinking (12:25–26). If Satan was wanting to maintain rulership of this world, he would not work against himself by exorcising a demon that had control of a person. That would be counteracting his attempt to maintain control of this world, as the prince of the powers of the air (cf. Eph 2:1–3).[99] The logical conclusion should be that if the man was liberated from a demon and he was healed of blindness and enabled to speak, it is an indication that the source of Jesus's power is God's fighting against Satan's kingdom.[100]

### *9.2.9.2 The Present Reality of the Kingdom of God (12:28)*

Jesus is the Spirit-anointed servant (12:18) whose exorcisms evidence the arrival of the kingdom of God.[101] This is one of the clearest statements in Matthew's Gospel about the present reality of the kingdom of God. Only seldom does the expression "kingdom of God" occur in Matthew's Gospel (19:24; 21:31, 43), who usually prefers stylistically the expression "kingdom of heaven." These are equivalent expressions (see earlier discussion), but here it may emphasize the opposition between God and Satan. The power of the Spirit of God operating through Jesus in exorcising Satan's demons is tangible confirmation that the kingdom of God has arrived.[102] Christian Blumenthal observes that in Matt 12:28, the Matthean Jesus claims that in his exorcisms the rule of God breaks into earthly reality and begins to gain space. "With this he irreversibly initiates a process of earthly transformation, at the end of which the complete assertion of the divine *basileia* on earth will be achieved."[103]

At the same time, in the mission of Jesus the miracles are not absolutely compelling proofs. The cities of Chorazin, Bethsaida, and Capernaum did not repent, even though they witnessed the majority of his miraculous deeds (11:20–24), and these Pharisees, who are eyewitnesses, do not believe. The true significance of the exorcism as evidence of the arrival of the kingdom of God is recognizable only by faith in the person of Jesus Messiah. They exorcisms are, as it were, "chinks in the curtain of the Son of God's hiddenness."[104] The exorcisms do reveal the reality of the arrival of the kingdom of God,

99. Davies and Allison, *Matthew*, 2:337–38.

100. Cole, *Against the Darkness*, 146–47.

101. Meadors, "'Messianic' Implications of the Q Material," 262–63.

102. Meier, *Matthew*, 135.

103. Christian Blumenthal, "*Basileia* is Gaining Space: God's Will, Mimesis of Christ and the Spatial Shaping of the *Basileia* in Matthew's Gospel," in Seleznev, Loader, and Niebuhr, *The Gospel of Matthew in Its Historical and Theological Context*, WUNT 459 (Tübingen: Mohr Siebeck, 2021), 345–64, here 350.

104. Cranfield, *Mark*, 83.

but hearts that are hardened against Jesus's messianic identity are even more blinded than the man from whom Jesus just exorcised the demon.

### 9.2.10 Mysteries of the Kingdom of Heaven in Parables: Clandestine-Kingdom Disciples (13:1–58)

The center discourse, the Parabolic Disclosure (Matt 13), develops what it means for Jesus's disciples to be clandestine-kingdom disciples during this age. It acts as a transition from simple presentation of the gospel of the kingdom to a time of examination of the crowd following Jesus around, and also to a time of instruction for Jesus's disciples about the surprising nature of the kingdom of heaven.

#### *9.2.10.1 Clandestine-Kingdom Disciples*

At a crucial juncture in his earthly ministry Jesus once again develops in discourse his plan for the ages to come. Not only will his disciples exhibit in their daily lives a consistent pattern of kingdom righteousness as he declared in the Sermon on the Mount (chs. 5–7) and be charged with an ongoing mission to reach both Jew and gentile with the gospel message (ch. 10), but we will also live out our discipleship in a manifestation of the kingdom of heaven that is clandestine.

Many of the people in the crowd that followed Jesus around were hoping for the arrival of the kingdom with an overt display of a political and militaristic might. Their attraction to Jesus was not based so much on what Jesus's intention was in announcing the arrival of the kingdom but in what they expected to get out of it—the blessings of the messianic age. Hoping for the blessings was not bad, but it did misguide them to overlook the real message that Jesus was announcing.

In fact, the hope for physical and material blessings hardens them from recognizing their own spiritual condition. They are increasingly being influenced by the religious leaders, especially the Pharisees, who pride themselves on their own accomplishments and ignore their own spiritual destitution. Eventually this influence will so harden the crowd will be so hardened against Jesus's form of the kingdom of heaven that they will call for his execution in preference for the rebel leader Barabbas who was involved with plotting the overthrow of Rome and the establishment of a physical kingdom of Israel (see p. XXX on 27:20).

Jesus's own followers still did not understand fully the uniqueness of the manifestation of the kingdom of heaven that Jesus was instituting. While imprisoned, John the Baptist, his privileged prophetic forerunner, had questioned Jesus's messianic identity because his kingdom program didn't coincide with what John had anticipated (cf. 11:2–6).

So, in this third major discourse Jesus develops what it means to be clandestine-kingdom disciples. Through his parables Jesus tests the hearts of the crowd to reveal whether the message of the kingdom of heaven has taken root and is producing fruit, or whether it has been unproductive (13:18–23). They must decide whether they are with him or against him. And through these parables Jesus also reveals to his disciples the mysteries of the kingdom of heaven, making known that during this age the kingdom will exist in a hidden form. It will be an undercover kingdom, not the overpowering political, militaristic, and dominant cultural manifestation of God's rule that many expected (13:31–33). Therefore, the parables reveal what it means for Jesus's disciples to live as kingdom subjects in a world that has not yet experienced the fully consummated kingdom of God.

Therefore, Jesus's disciples are to give closest attention to the priority of the kingdom of heaven in their lives, so that they will continue to be the treasure of revelation to a watching world (13:51–52). In this remarkable series of parables, Jesus reveals that the kingdom of heaven has arrived with power, but it is a hidden, spiritual, transformational power. This is what discipleship to Jesus will be like in this age of the clandestinely inaugurated, but not fully consummated, kingdom of heaven.[105]

### *9.2.10.2 The Mysteries of the Kingdom of Heaven (13:11)*

Jesus states that the reason he speaks to the crowd in parables is because God has given the mysteries of the kingdom of heaven to the disciples, not to the crowd, to know. "Mysteries" ("secrets" NIV) is the Greek *mystēria*, which draws upon a Semitic background that speaks of an eschatological mystery (Aram. *rāz*) passed on in veiled speech to God's chosen. The term is found explicitly in the Old Testament in Daniel: "During the night the mystery was revealed to Daniel in a vision" (2:19; cf. 2:27–30, 47; 4:9). The idea of God revealing his mystery is also found elsewhere as a powerful theme in the Old Testament (e.g., Amos 3:7; Ps 25:14; Prov 3:32; Job 15:8).

Jesus's message from the beginning of his ministry declared that the kingdom of heaven had arrived, but it had not always been apparent to those observing. Jesus gives to his disciples an understanding of the kingdom of heaven as it is now, and will be, existing and operating in the world. The kingdom of heaven is present, but not in its fully manifested power. The mystery is an innovative disclosure of God's purpose for the establishment of his kingdom. The new truth, now given to humans by revelation in the person and mission of Jesus, "is that the Kingdom that is to come finally in apocalyptic power, as foreseen in Daniel, has in fact entered into the world in advance in a hidden form to work secretly within and among humans."[106]

The mysteries are not that God would establish his kingdom, which was a well-known prophetic hope within Israel, but that it has arrived in a form different than

105. For a helpful application of the parables to present-day kingdom life, see Lee-Barnewall, *Surprised by the Parables*.

106. Ladd, *Theology of the New Testament*, 92.

what had been anticipated. This is a secret now being revealed in veiled speech to God's chosen, Jesus's disciples.[107]

So, on the one hand the parables reveal to the disciples how the kingdom of God will operate in this world before its final, powerful manifestation, which he will reveal further in the final discourse in Matthew (chs. 24–25). But on the other hand, the truth that is revealed to the disciples is concealed from the crowd because of their spiritual unresponsiveness (13:12–13).

A continued contrast is drawn between the disciples and the crowd. The beginning understanding of the mysteries of the kingdom of heaven that the disciples now have, as given by God through Jesus, will be enlarged upon, so that they will have full understanding. But whatever understanding the crowd has, even that will be taken away. The implication is that Jesus's parables will be the means by which what they have is taken away. Not only do the parables *not* reveal truth to the crowd but they also take away what the crowd already has.

Therefore, we can say generally that with the parables Jesus accomplishes two important feats.

***(1) The parables test the heart of the listener.*** They act as a spiritual examination, prompting a response from the listener that will indicate whether the person's heart is open to Jesus's message or hardened. If the person's heart is hardened to Jesus's message, the parable will stimulate confusion or outright rejection and prompt the listener to turn away from Jesus and the truth (13:11–15). If the person's heart is open to Jesus's message, the listener will come to Jesus for further clarification about its meaning, like the disciples do (13:10), who eventually understand the truth embedded in the parables (13:51). Jesus's revelation of truth and the disciples' obedient receptivity is the required distinction in understanding and not understanding.[108]

***(2) The parables give instruction to those who are responsive.*** The individual parables clarify the mysteries of the kingdom of heaven by showing how the kingdom of heaven operates in this world in a very different way than expected by the religious leaders and the crowds. By this parabolic teaching Jesus gives indications of the development of the kingdom. The disciples' positive response prompts them to ask for further explanation (13:10, 36), the reward of which is Jesus's explanation of the parables (13:18–23, 37–43) and parabolic teaching directed to them that reveals additional truth about the mysteries of the kingdom (13:44–52). While the disciples are not perfect in understanding, they possess the potential and desire to progress. Ultimately, they *will* understand because they have been obedient to listen and hear (13:51).[109]

107. Osborne, *Matthew*, 509.

108. Turner, *Matthew*, 339; Osborne, *Matthew*, 509.

109. Brown and Roberts, *Matthew*, 128–30; Osborne, *Matthew*, 509; Turner, *Matthew*, 339; Trotter, "Understanding and Stumbling," 93–96.

### *9.2.10.3 Responding to the Truths of the Parables of the Mysteries of the Kingdom of Heaven*

We now focus on the specific theological truth that Jesus intended to communicate in each parable. Since some of the seven primary parables about the mysteries of the kingdom of heaven in the discourse overlap in the truth that they communicate, we can summarize them under four primary headings: (1) the kingdom of heaven's transforming power; (2) its looming judgment; (3) its surprising appearance; and (4) its incalculable value.

#### 9.2.10.3.1 The Transforming Power of the Kingdom of Heaven: The Parable of the Sower and Soils (13:1–9, 18–23)

This parable in many ways is a parable about the parables. It illustrates how the truth that is embedded in the parables will impact the life of those who hear its message. Although the gospel of the kingdom of heaven will be preached and taught indiscriminately in this world (4:23–25; 9:35–38), there are varied responses to it. The external response indicates the inward spiritual condition of a person's life. The life-giving force is in the seed, not in the soil, so how the soil responds to the seed indicates the impact of the life of the kingdom of heaven in a person's heart. This includes whether it is rejected outright by a hard heart, or received in a shallow fashion without becoming fully rooted, or choked out by competing priorities. Only the person who receives the message deep into his or her heart has allowed the life-giving gospel of the kingdom to take root and produce fruit.

Since the primary focus is not on the sower but on the soils, we can safely assume that the one sowing the message of the gospel in this world applies not only to Jesus in his historical ministry but also to the Twelve as they went out on the short mission tour (10:5–15) and to disciples throughout this age who carry the gospel message (10:16–42; 28:16–20).

This teaches us that as Jesus had varied responses to his message, so will we. Faithfulness in sowing the gospel message is paramount, not the numbers that respond. Likewise, it may be appropriate to recognize that the disproportionate response of those who do not respond fully to the gospel in comparison with those who bear fruit is consonant with Jesus's statement that many enter the broad gate and way to destruction while only a few enter the narrow gate and way to life (7:13–14). The results are ultimately in the hands of God, as well as the choice of the individual.

There is a distinction made between those who are outright hardened against the gospel message in the first soil and those who produce fruit in the fourth soil. But there is a perplexing middle ground in those who initially receive the word but who then fall away. Some hear the word and fall away due to the trials and hardships of life (13:20–21), and others get sucked into the priorities of the world over kingdom values (13:22). This is a warning to those who respond to the kingdom to guard against and be prepared for those things that would prevent them from producing fruit. Ultimately, it is the ongoing production of fruit that differentiates those who have truly responded to the kingdom and those who have not.

And it is that very fruit that gives us the hope of personal transformation. The person who receives the gospel of the kingdom into his or her heart will experience the transformation of kingdom life, the very life that Jesus described in the Sermon on the Mount (e.g., 5:3–16, 21–48). So, we should not just *hope* for transformation but *expect* it as a result of the life-giving power of the gospel of the kingdom as energized by the Spirit of God.

The fruit produced is the outward evidence of the transformational reality of the inward life of the kingdom of heaven. Seed sown on good soil will yield to the maximum that it has been created to produce, with varying amounts that reflect individual potential. The various amounts of fruit produced represent various capacities in various believers. The primary point is that fruit *will* be produced. We should perhaps extend the analogy one step further to note that the responsibility for the production of fruit lies in the life-giving operation of the Spirit-empowered gospel. But that does not eliminate the disciple's own responsibility.

#### 9.2.10.3.2 The Looming Judgment of the Kingdom of Heaven: The Parables of the Wheat and Weeds and the Dragnet (13:24–30, 36–43, 47–50)

These parables emphasize that the kingdom of heaven has been inaugurated in this world through the sowing of the gospel of the kingdom of heaven and the resultant production of sons of the kingdom—i.e., Jesus's disciples. However, the arrival of the kingdom has not vanquished the enemy nor prevented the survival of evil people in this world. From a distance or from the surface Jesus's disciples may not look that different from others in this world, but there is an inherent difference as a result of the transformation that is produced by the impact of the kingdom of heaven in a person's life. The wheat and fish of the kingdom of heaven are "good" (13:38, 48) and "righteous" (13:43, 49). This is the righteousness of the kingdom of heaven that produces personal transformation (cf. 5:20).

But these parables make another important point. We will not see the uprooting or eliminating of evil until the end of this age. There is going to be a mixed nature to the world, indicating one of the mysteries of the kingdom of heaven. It will continue in a form that seems counterintuitive to contemporary notions of God's reigning kingdom. Jesus does not give a full theodicy with the parable but only a rock-solid basis for hope. Evil derives from the evil one, not from God. We should expect spiritual warfare throughout this age while we live in an environment that is contaminated by evil. But on the horizon of history looms certain rescue for Jesus's disciples and certain judgment for those who are aligned with the evil one.

There is no thought here of the kingdom eradicating evil in this world during this age. Jesus's disciples are not called out of the world during this age, but we are promised to have Jesus's continual prayer for the Father's protecting hand upon us (cf. John 17:15–19). We are to be wary while living in this world, because evil surrounds us, but we are promised the Father's protecting care and the sure rescue of the kingdom of heaven at its consummation.

While the parables speak of the coexistence of the sons of the evil one and sons of the kingdom in this world, there is secondary application to the church. The parable of the wheat and weeds allows us to be aware of the plans of the enemy. In the way that Satan will infiltrate this world, he will also attempt to infiltrate the church. We must be aware of how to be on guard, which should encourage us to pray against the plans of Satan. Although Satan will operate in this world until the judgment, we can reduce his influence by not allowing sinful activities that give a foothold to Satan in our communities (Eph 4:27) and by dealing effectively and quickly with sin within the community (Matt 18:15–20). And like a large dragnet, the kingdom of heaven will have all sorts respond to it in the preaching of "fishers of men" (4:19). The true nature of those who are gathered in will not always be readily apparent, as Judas Iscariot will so sadly exemplify. Only at the judgment will the full implication be known.[110]

#### 9.2.10.3.3 The Surprising Appearance of the Kingdom of Heaven: The Parables of the Mustard Seed and Yeast (13:31–33)

The parables of the mustard seed and the yeast combine to emphasize one of the primary mysteries of the kingdom of heaven—it has come in a surprisingly hidden form. Jesus does not deny the greatness and glory that the kingdom will ultimately manifest but emphasizes that during this age it will exist in a hidden and inconspicuous form. This contrasts the partial inauguration of the kingdom with its final consummation. During this age the beginning presence of the kingdom will be inauspicious, yet it will permeate this world and operate with hidden transformation in the hearts of the sons and daughters of the kingdom.

These parables should caution us about the popularity of our faith. In centuries past these parables were assumed to point to the way that the church would start small and insignificant but then would become great and transform the world. The church has experienced remarkable growth at various periods of time in the world's history but often at the expense of contamination from the world.

This should again caution us against equating the kingdom of heaven and the church. It is only with the arrival of the Son of Man that the kingdom will be established in visible power and glory. We live at a time when the popularity of the church wanes

110. Cf. Keener, *Matthew* (1999), 393.

in much of the Western world but is dynamically alive in much of the majority world. The parables of the mustard seed and yeast caution us against expecting during this age the popularity of the kingdom of heaven. It will remain inconspicuous and hidden except to eyes of faith, awaiting its final manifestation. The secret of the kingdom of heaven is that it will influence this world in a mighty way as it operates through the church. But we must not equate growth of the church automatically with the influence of the kingdom. Some growth is simply manmade; some is superficial. As citizens of the kingdom, we are the salt of the earth and the light of the world (5:13–16) and seek to bring people into a loving community within the church, but our popularity is never to be the final gauge of the real influence of the kingdom of heaven.

#### 9.2.10.3.4 The Incalculable Value of the Kingdom of Heaven: The Parables of the Hidden Treasure and Costly Pearl (13:44–46)

The parables of the hidden treasure and costly pearl focus our attention on the incalculable value of the kingdom of heaven. Continuing the thought of the inconspicuousness of the mustard seed and yeast (13:31–32, 33), the parable of the hidden treasure emphasizes that the kingdom of heaven has a value that far outweighs what anyone looking upon an open field might have expected. And the parable of the costly pearl emphasizes that the well-trained expert will discover upon finding the reality of the kingdom of heaven that nothing is comparable in value. Whatever cost a person expends is nothing in comparison to the value of belonging to the kingdom of heaven. Salvation and the righteousness of the kingdom is a greater treasure than all that the world has to offer. And it is the source of greatest joy (13:44).

## 9.2.11 The Agency of the Kingdom of Heaven on Earth (16:18; 21:43; 24:14)

We will discuss much more fully the nature of the church, both universal and local, in Chapter 11: The "CHURCH," and the "CHURCH." Here we will briefly attempt to clarify the relationship of the "CHURCH" and "Israel" and the "kingdom of heaven."

### *9.2.11.1 Peter, Jesus, the Church, and the Kingdom of Heaven (16:18–19)*

Jesus's saying to Peter gives a prediction of Jesus's new community, the church, and entrance to the kingdom of heaven: "And I tell you that you are Peter, and on this rock I will build my church, and the gates of Hades will not overcome it. I will give you the keys of the kingdom of heaven; whatever you bind on earth will be bound in heaven, and whatever you loose on earth will be loosed in heaven" (16:18–19).

Matthew is the only evangelist to use the term "church" (*ekklēsia*; cf. 18:18), which brings to mind the "assembly (or "community"; Heb. *qāhāl*) of the Lord" (Deut 23:3; cf. 5:22). In the selection of the twelve disciples/apostles to bear his message of fulfillment to Israel (Matt 10:1–6), who will judge the tribes of Israel (19:28), Jesus points ahead to the time when his disciples, his family of faith (12:48–50), will be called "my church." This will be the fellowship of disciples who, unlike national Israel, will believe in Jesus's identity as the Messiah, the Son of the living God (16:16), and leave all other allegiances behind as they receive mercy and forgiveness of sin, and likewise demonstrate toward each other mercy and forgiveness (18:15–35).

The building metaphor leads naturally to a discussion of "keys" in this third and final pronouncement about Peter. Once again Peter is addressed personally in the second-person singular pronoun ("I will give *you*"; *soi*) and verbs ("whatever *you bind* [*dēsēs*]"; "whatever *you loose* [*lysēs*]"). The "keys" metaphor could point to a "generic power" given to Peter alone,[111] or to his "authority" over the house of God,[112] but the building metaphor of the preceding saying more closely prepares for Jesus to pronounce Peter's role in opening or shutting the doors to the kingdom of heaven.[113] This saying gives a declaration about entrance to the kingdom, but authority is not too far removed: Peter is given the authority to admit entrance to the kingdom of heaven.[114]

In this way Peter is contrasted to the scribes and Pharisees who shut off entrance to the kingdom and who do not enter in themselves (23:13).[115] The apostles had been told by the risen Jesus to wait for the empowering of the Holy Spirit, after which they would be his witnesses to the three people groups: Jews in Jerusalem and Judea, Samaritans in Samaria, and gentiles to the ends of the earth (Acts 1:8).

Peter, as the representative disciple who gives the first personal declaration of the Messiah's identity, is the one in the book of Acts who opens the door of the kingdom of heaven to all these peoples. On each of three occasions, it is through Peter's authoritative preaching and presence that the door to the kingdom is opened, first to Jews (Acts 2), then to Samaritans (Acts 8), and finally to gentiles (Acts 10). The entrance image is foremost in view, and therefore "the keys refer to the fact that chronologically Peter, acting as the representative of Jesus, was the first to announce the message."[116] Even though the Samaritans had "believed" through the preaching of Philip (Acts 8:4–13), it was necessary for Peter to go there in order for them to receive the Holy Spirit as

111. Raymond E. Brown, Karl P. Donfried, and John Reumann, eds., *Peter in the New Testament: A Collaborative Assessment by Protestant and Catholic Scholars* (Minneapolis: Augsburg, 1973), 96, 100–101.

112. T. W. Manson, *The Sayings of Jesus*, 2nd ed. (London: SCM, 1999), 205; Stendahl, "Matthew," 787.

113. Pierre Bonnard, *L'évangile selon Saint Matthieu*, 2nd ed., Commentaire du Nouveau Testament 1, 2nd series, (Neuchatel, Switzerland: Delachaux, & Niestle, 1970), 246; Jack Dean Kingsbury, "The Figure of Peter in Matthew's Gospel as a Theological Problem," *JBL* 98 (1979): 67–83, here 76n27.

114. This is preferred to the view of Francis Wright Beare (*The Gospel According to Matthew: Translation, Introduction and Commentary* [San Francisco: Harper and Row, 1981], 355) that sees Peter as a chief rabbi exercising discipline over the established community. The tenor of the passage is establishment and entrance to the new, not regulation of the already established.

115. Dietrich Müller and Colin Brown, "κλείς," *NIDNTT* 2:732; Guthrie, *New Testament Theology*, 714.

116. Guthrie, *New Testament Theology*, 714.

confirmation to the early church that God has now included the Samaritans in the kingdom of heaven (Acts 8:14–17).[117]

Peter was the special medium through whom the proclamation of the gospel was first made or confirmed, which opened the kingdom of heaven to all peoples. Once Peter has functioned in that leadership role to use the keys to open the door to the kingdom of heaven, he passes from the scene. The door to the kingdom now stands open throughout the age, so keys are no longer needed. The door stands open to all people who accept the gospel message and receive forgiveness of sins.

This points to the way in which the church in this age is the body of Christ which is given the responsibility to declare the gospel that points the way to the open door to the kingdom of heaven. Matthew does not conflate kingdom with church,[118] but rather the church is the instrument God uses to declare the reality and presence of the kingdom of heaven and offer the invitation to enter the kingdom. Once a person enters the kingdom of heaven, he or she is then an appendage of the body of Christ as the church and becomes an instrument in demonstrating and proclaiming the gospel of the kingdom of heaven.

### *9.2.11.2 Jesus and Israel*

One mark of God's purposes in this age is the relationship of Jesus to Israel. Jesus came as a Jew to the Jewish people with the offer of the kingdom of heaven. But Israel as a whole is now seen to be rejecting both Jesus and his message about the kingdom. Nonetheless, a substantial group within Israel did respond in faith. Discipleship to Jesus was commitment to him, which meant that a new disciple was allowed to enter into the presence of the kingdom of heaven in the person of Jesus. The kingdom of heaven therefore has entered history in the person of Jesus and its blessings are being demonstrated in the lives of Jesus's disciples.[119] While some suggest that, as the recipients of messianic salvation, they replace Israel,[120] several passages lead us to recognize that Israel will still have a role in the future. We will see that the role of carrying out God's purposes through the kingdom of God has been taken away from the nation of Israel in the present age, and that Jesus's disciples currently enjoy both the blessings of the kingdom of heaven and the role of carrying the message of the gospel of the kingdom (21:43). But Israel is still kept in view as receiving in the future the eschatological fulfillment of the promises of the kingdom (10:23; 23:37–39; cf. Rom 11:25–32; 15:7–13; Rev 7:1–8).[121] The Twelve

117. Müller and Brown, "κλείς," *NIDNTT* 2:732; Guthrie, *New Testament Theology*, 714.

118. Brown and Roberts, *Matthew*, 283.

119. Cf. Ladd, *Theology of the New Testament*, 104–6.

120. Ladd is representative of this view: "Jesus' disciples are the recipients of the messianic salvation, the people of the Kingdom, the true Israel" (*Theology of the New Testament*, 106).

121. E.g., Scott Hafemann, "Eschatology and Ethics: The Future of Israel and the Nations in Romans 15:1–13," *TynBul* 51.2 (2000): 161–92.

represent the fulfillment in part of the promises to Israel, but they do not replace Israel nor become Israel.

#### 9.2.11.2.1 Instructions for the Short-Term Mission to Israel (10:5–15)

The instructions for the disciples'/apostles' mission are the second of the five major discourses in Matthew's Gospel. Jesus begins the mission discourse with a surprising prohibition: "Do not go among the Gentiles or enter any town of the Samaritans. Go rather to the lost sheep of Israel" (10:5–6). The full expression is "lost sheep of the house of Israel," which does not mean one separate part of Israel that is lost but rather that the whole of Israel is lost and is being called to make a decision about the gospel of the kingdom. The key to the prohibition is found in the directive to go only to Israel. This is a special mission of Jesus's disciples during his historical ministry to the crowds of Israel, who are like harassed and helpless sheep without a shepherd (9:36).

Jesus goes first to Israel (cf. 15:21–28) to fulfill the salvation-historical order that God established with Israel being the tool that God will use to bring blessing to the world.[122] Then he will charge the Eleven to continue the historical outworking by going to the nations (28:19–20). The Twelve symbolize the continuity and theological salvation-history priority of Israel in God's program.[123] Paul later saw this as the priority of the Jews in salvation, but also in judgment, as God's plan throughout salvation history will be "first for the Jew, then for the Gentile" (Rom 1:16; 2:9–10).[124] Jesus's singular attention to Israel underscores God's faithfulness to his covenant promises, the continuity of his purposes, and that his plan for Israel is still unfinished.

Jesus is dispelling any doubt that his disciples or any in the audience may have had as to whether he truly was the Messiah coming in fulfillment of the promises given to Israel and dispelling any doubts that he is fulfilling God's program of salvation history. But there is also a warning in the prohibition. The eschatological ingathering is beginning. This is Israel's opportunity, and from here on it will be fully responsible for its own decision. In Jesus's commission to the Twelve to go to Israel alone there is an apologetic of his faithfulness to God's program directed to the disciples and crowds, but there is also an oblique warning directed to Israel.[125]

The disciples are to go to Israel with the same message that both John the Baptist and Jesus preached: "The kingdom of heaven has come near" (10:7; see on 3:2; 4:17). They also go with the same authority as Jesus (10:1) as they "heal the sick, raise the dead, cleanse those who have leprosy, drive out demons" (10:8). Jesus likewise performed each of these miracles. The power of the Twelve is clearly an extension

122. E.g., Gen 12:2–3; 22:18.

123. Scott, "Gentiles and the Ministry of Jesus," 161–69.

124. Douglas J. Moo, *The Epistle to the Romans*, NICNT (Grand Rapids: Eerdmans, 1996), 69, 139; Brindle, "'To the Jew First,'" 221–33.

125. Kingsbury, *Matthew*, 22–23.

of Jesus's own power and will be exercised in the same manner. The commission to raise the dead harks back to Jesus's stupendous miracle of raising Jairus's daughter (9:25–26).

#### 9.2.11.2.2 "Going Through the Cities of Israel Before the Son of Man Comes" (10:23)

During his mission discourse, with the mention of the end (10:22) Jesus culminates the prophetic aspect of the commissioning with a remarkable statement: "Truly I tell you, you will not finish going through the towns of Israel before the Son of Man comes" (10:23). This has been described as one of the most difficult verses in the Bible to interpret. The difficulty comes especially in trying to understand the temporal context.[126] Some suggest that Jesus was promising the disciples that they would witness the eschatological coming of the Son of Man while they were on their first Palestinian mission, or at his resurrection, or at Pentecost, or at the destruction of Jerusalem in AD 70.[127] Others contend that this is to be associated with the coming of the Son of Man at the end of the age.

The latter seems to fit the larger context here. While the Jews have priority of salvation (10:6) and of judgment (10:15), their judgment does not permanently exclude them from God's eschatological promises. The ongoing mission to the nations continues to include both Jew and gentile (see on 28:18–20). As Jesus offers comfort to the mission-disciples about their ultimate salvation unto the end (10:22), he warns them not to abandon Israel. When persecuted in one city, they should flee to the next because the mission to Israel will not conclude before the Son of Man returns. There will be a continuing mission to Israel alongside of the mission to the gentiles until the parousia.[128]

In spite of Israel's hardheartedness, God will remain faithful to his covenant promises to her. And in spite of the difficulties of the mission for the disciples, they must remain faithful to their calling to bring the message to both Jew and gentile. It will bring persecution, family alienation, and ostracism (10:21–22), but those who endure to the end will be saved. This is a powerful apologetic to the Jews both those involved in Jesus's ministry and those within hearing of Matthew's Gospel; God has not abandoned his covenantal promises. It is also a challenging yet sober call to the mission-disciples to hold steadfast to the mission to proclaim the message of the gospel to all peoples—both Jew and gentile—until the very end.

126. Ben Witherington III, *Jesus, Paul, and the End of the World: A Comparative Study in New Testament Eschatology* (Downers Grove: InterVarsity, 1992), 39–42.

127. For discussion of these and other views, see Carson, "Matthew," 290–93, who holds to the lattermost.

128. Blomberg, *Matthew*, 176; Davies and Allison, *Matthew*, 2:189–90. So also Gundry, *Matthew*, 194, though he doubts the authenticity of the saying.

### *9.2.11.3 The Kingdom Is Taken Away from Israel (21:43)*

In his final week before his crucifixion, Jesus climaxes his indictment of the religious leadership with a stinging pronouncement: "Therefore I tell you that the kingdom of God will be taken away from you and given to a people who will produce its fruit" (21:43).[129] We will interact with this saying more fully in Chapter 12, "Israel, Disciples, and Church in Matthew's Gospel: Stewards of the Kingdom in God's Timing," but a few observations are relevant here.

This unique Matthean statement gives Jesus's unambiguous conclusion to the preceding parable. The leaders did not fulfill the obligations to God for which they were responsible, neither in their lives nor in leading the nation of Israel. They had not repented at the arrival of the kingdom of God but instead rejected the very Son who had announced its arrival. This is a statement to them personally of the judgment that they will receive, which had been enacted to the disciples symbolically in Jesus's cursing of the fig tree for not bearing fruit (21:18–21).

The context of the parable indicates that the privileged role of the religious leaders in caring for God's "vineyard" is now being taken away. But this is also a hint that Israel's privileged role in the establishment of God's kingdom will be taken away and given to another people. "People" is the singular *ethnos,* which prepares for the time when the church, a nation of gathered people, will include both Jew and gentile in the outworking of God's kingdom in the present age. All those who become individual disciples out of the plural "nations" (28:19; *ethnē*) will be brought together as one new "nation." Peter will later also use the singular *ethnos* in the context of the "stone" passage to refer to the church (1 Pet 2:9). This will not abolish the promises made to Israel nationally (cf. Rom 11:25–33),[130] but it does point to the transition of leadership and prominence that will be given to the church in the outworking of God's kingdom program in the present age.

### *9.2.11.4 Preaching the Gospel of the Kingdom to All Nations (24:14)*

Jesus cautioned the disciples against false assumptions about what will signal the end (24:6, 8), but he gives an explicit indicator of the activity that must be accomplished before the end of this age: "And this gospel of the kingdom will be preached in the whole world as a testimony to all nations, and then the end will come" (24:14). The expression "gospel of the kingdom" is unique to Matthew (cf. 4:23; 9:35), combining the good news of salvation with the arrival of the kingdom of heaven. This is testimony or a witness to the reality of God's presence in the ministry of Jesus and his followers (cf. 8:4; 10:18). Although the increase of events in 24:9–13 is some indication that

129. For more extended discussion, see Wilkins, "Consideration of a Future for Israel," 313–40, here esp. 326–28.

130. Those who contend that in some way Israel has a national future are quite diverse; see below in Chapter 12.

the parousia is near, the only explicit condition to be met will be the proclamation of the gospel of the kingdom in the entire world to all the nations. After that gospel proclamation has occurred, the end will come.

But the urgency of worldwide missionary activity is demanded by recognizing that the final fulfillment of Jesus's statement in 24:14 awaits the eschatological arrival of the events of great tribulation. Jesus's disciples are to give themselves urgently to the task of preaching the gospel of the kingdom throughout this present age, because we cannot fully discern when it has finally reached into all of the world to all of the nations.[131] Each new generation of nations does bring with it a new mission field. But once this proclamation has been fulfilled in God's timing, the beginning of the time of tribulation on the earth will begin.

#### *9.2.11.5 New Covenant with Jesus's Death and the Arrival of the Spirit (26:26–40)*

Jesus gives a surprising twist to the occasion of celebrating the Passover with his disciples as he states, "I tell you, I will not drink from this fruit of the vine from now on until that day when I drink it new with you in my Father's kingdom" (26:29). The fourth cup was associated with God's promise, "I will take you as my own people" (Exod 6:7). It was poured and, following the conclusion of the antiphonal singing of the second part of the Hallel (Pss 115–118), drunk together by all.

Jesus's words hold out a poignant promise. It is a glad announcement that his sacrificial death will bring forgiveness of sins and a sad indication that he will have to go away, but a sure assurance that he will return. When he comes again and brings the final establishment of the kingdom on earth, he will accomplish the fulfillment of the time of peace and redemption that his disciples confidently await and bring to Israel their long-awaited consolation. Until then the Lord's Supper is a memorial and perpetual reminder of the new and greater exodus by which all those who embrace its significance and historical accomplishment find release from sin's bondage and deliverance into new and everlasting life.[132] The blessings of the kingdom of heaven that have been inaugurated now through the finished work of Christ on the cross are a permanent reminder that he is coming again to bring the final establishment of the kingdom of heaven to those who await his fellowship.

### 9.2.12 Jesus Messiah's Reign over the Kingdom of Heaven on Earth

The final scene in the Olivet Discourse is unique to Matthew's Gospel. The emphasis is squarely upon judgment of those who are excluded from the kingdom and on the

131. E.g., Davies and Allison, *Matthew*, 3:344; Morris, *Matthew*, 602.

132. Merrill, "Remembering," 27–36.

reward for those who are admitted to the kingdom (Matt 25:34). The scene involves the glorious coming of the Son of Man. He is accompanied in his glory by all the angels, and he sits upon his throne of glory (25:31–33). The "throne" (v. 31) draws on the motif of the ruler of the kingdom before whom all of the nations will be gathered (25:32).

### *9.2.12.1 The King and the Kingdom (25:31–34)*

The debated expression "the nations" (*ta ethnē*) has been interpreted to mean the church, all humanity, all non-believers, etc., but within the Matthean context most likely it is intended to mean both Jews and gentiles who throughout this age are the combined object of the Great Commission (see on 24:14; 28:18–20). The nations as entities are not judged, but rather the "people" (NIV) within them: "And he will separate the people one from another as a shepherd separates the sheep from the goats" (25:32).

The King gives the explanation for the separation as he says to those on his right, "Come, you who are blessed by my Father; take your inheritance, the kingdom" (25:34). The King is understood to be the Son of Man sitting on the throne (25:31), bringing to mind the prophecy of Dan 7:13–14 where the Son of Man receives the kingdom from the Ancient of Days. This is one of the rare times that Jesus refers to himself as King, although the theme has been there throughout Matthew's Gospel (e.g., Matt 1:1–17; 2:2; 4:17; 21:5; 27:11, 29, 37, 42).

The King addresses the sheep on his right as "blessed by my Father" (25:34). The blessing consists of their inheritance, which is the kingdom that they now receive, not because they have earned it through their own efforts, but because it is a gift of their relationship with the Father and the Son. God's assured purpose is carried out as the blessing of the inheritance of the kingdom for the sheep is realized.

### *9.2.12.2 Eternal Punishment and Eternal Life in the Kingdom (25:46)*

Jesus concludes the dramatic judgment scene by stating, "Then they will go away to eternal punishment, but the righteous to eternal life" (25:46). Daniel's prophecy of a future time of great tribulation that will come on the earth also leads to a prophecy of eternal life and punishment (Dan 12:1–3; cf. 2 Bar. 51:5–6). Daniel's prophecy echoes here in the final words of Jesus's concluding discourse in Matthew's Gospel.

Those who have responded to Jesus's announcement and have become his disciples have all along been noted to be "people of the kingdom" (13:38), but now they enter into the full blessing and experience of life in the kingdom. Many, whatever their understanding of a literal earthly thousand-year reign of Christ and his kingdom, understand this judgment scene to be the same as that occurring at the end of this earthly age, just prior to the eternal state (Rev 20:11–13).[133] Many others understand this judgment to take place prior to the inauguration of the earthly millennial kingdom by Jesus, who now will rule over those who are blessed to enter that reign with him.[134]

The evidence is scanty either way in Matthew's Gospel, but the important point throughout this scene is clear—judgment will come.[135]

## 9.3 LIFE IN THE KINGDOM OF HEAVEN

"To live in the kingdom of God and to bring the message of the kingdom of God to the people who are there in a loving, attractive, forceful way is the gift that comes to every person who is a follower of Jesus Christ."[136] Those words were published just shortly after Dallas Willard passed into the presence of his Savior. I knew Dallas for over thirty-five years, and I can say with great love that he lived those words as clearly as most any person I have ever known. And he would want for us that gift of life in the kingdom of God. As we have noted, the concept of the kingdom of God/heaven is ambiguous because we cannot see it, touch it, or hear it, except through people who live in it. The kingdom of heaven is the domain where all things are put right the way that God intended things to be as he originally created the world to be.

For many who had good experiences with the concept of "kingdom," our thoughts when hearing of the kingdom of God are positive. But for those raised in oppressive, or dysfunctional, or abusive earthly kingdom experiences, it might strike a negative note, or fear. The misconceptions that we can have, and that those in the first century had, are clarified by Jesus and the Gospel writers. The following passages in Matthew's Gospel lead us to recognize what the kingdom of heaven *is not* but also what it *is*.

### 9.3.1 What the Kingdom of Heaven *Is Not*

Here is what the kingdom of God is *not*.

- The kingdom of heaven is not entered through religious righteousness (5:20; cf. 21:30).
- The kingdom of heaven is not fully consummated (established) in this age. Jesus taught his disciples to pray for the kingdom to come (6:9–10).
- Jesus's kingdom of heaven is not run by rulers who lord it over others, but by servants who serve others (20:26–28).

133. Erickson, *Christian Theology*, 1102–3. Hagner, *Matthew 14—28*, 742–43; Blomberg, *Matthew*, 376; Morris, *Matthew*, 634–35.

134. E.g., Pond, "Background and Timing," 201–20; R. Saucy, *Case for Progressive Dispensationalism*, 130.

135. See Sim, *Apocalyptic Eschatology*, 130–39; James M. Hamilton Jr., *God's Glory in Salvation Through Judgment: A Biblical Theology* (Wheaton, IL: Crossway, 2010).

136. Dallas Willard, *Living in Christ's Presence: Final Words on Heaven and the Kingdom of God* (Downers Grove, IL: InterVarsity, 2014), 69.

- The full blessings of the of the kingdom of heaven will not be experienced until the kingdom comes to earth (26:29).
- Jesus is "king of the Jews," but his kingdom is not of this world. Jesus's kingdom does not operate politically nor militarily like the kingdoms of this world, like Rome (John 18:33–37).
- Jesus will not be made into the kind of king that the people want (John 6:14–15).
- The coming of the kingdom of God is not something that can be observed externally (Luke 17:20–21).

### 9.3.2 What the Kingdom of Heaven *Is*

- Those who enter the kingdom are saved from their sins by Jesus Immanuel, ransomed from death by Jesus's death, and they enjoy forgiveness of sins through his poured-out blood (Matt 1:21; 20:28; 26:28).[137]
- The kingdom of heaven is here in the presence of Jesus, and we enter the kingdom as we repent and become his disciples (4:17).
- Jesus calls men and women to follow him as his disciples to experience new life in the kingdom of heaven (4:18–22).
- Faith is empty without a corresponding change of life, hence disciples in the kingdom of heaven will experience radical change in their lives (5:3–12).[138]
- Jesus taught his disciples to place the kingdom of heaven and his righteousness as their highest priority. All else will then fall into place (6:33).
- The kingdom of God is here in the power of the Holy Spirit over the spirit world (12:28).
- The kingdom of heaven is here in the disciples who serve each other. The kingdom of God is made up of servants who serve one another (20:25–28).
- The kingdom of God is here, but not here in full (6:9–10).
- The kingdom of God will arrive in full at the end of the age (24:14).
- Faith in this life is rewarded with the fullness of the kingdom of heaven at the end of this world (8:10–12).
- We will experience the fullness of the kingdom at the end of this age when we drink the cup of the new covenant with Jesus in the Father's kingdom (26:29).

### 9.3.3 The Guardian and Steward of the Kingdom of Heaven

The juxtaposition of sayings concerning the church (16:18) and the kingdom of heaven (16:19) gives us clarification about God's purposes during this present age. As we saw hinted at earlier in Jesus's ministry, although the kingdom has been inaugurated,

137. Thomas R. Schreiner, *The King in His Beauty: A Biblical Theology of the Old and New Testaments* (Grand Rapids: Baker Academic, 2013), 447.

138. T. Schreiner, *King in His Beauty*, 447.

a full establishment of the kingdom awaits a future arrival of the King in glory. Therefore, Matt 16:18–19 helps us to understand four points about the relationship of the kingdom and the church.

In the first place, the kingdom of God is not the same as the church. Matthew does not conflate kingdom with church.[139] The kingdom of heaven is the presence of the king who has come to inaugurate the fulfillment of God's salvation-historical redemptive plan by establishing the new covenant blessings of the Spirit. One's confession of sin and God's forgiveness of it allows one to enter into the kingdom.

Second, the arrival of the kingdom with its salvation-historical fulfillment of God's plan of redemption creates the church. Jesus's message of the arrival of the kingdom of heaven challenged men and women to respond to him and enter the kingdom (5:20), which brought them into a new discipleship fellowship in Jesus (12:46–50). The fellowship community that Jesus created and will build in this age is the church, which is made up of people who have responded to his invitation and entered into the kingdom of heaven in the name of the king and now enjoy the messianic blessings of the new covenant. The activity of God in the person of the king and the power of the Spirit brought salvation to earth and the beginning of the promises of Old Testament kingdom blessings. Those who respond to the invitation to the kingdom of heaven and receive the work of the Spirit in their lives in regeneration and sanctification in this age are those members who make up the body of Christ, the church.

Third, the church is the collective witness and has as its central mission to proclaim the reality of the presence of kingdom of heaven. One of the main tasks of the church is to display in this present evil age the life and fellowship of the reality of the kingdom of heaven, which is an anticipatory witness to the full establishment of the kingdom in power in the age to come. Mark Saucy states that "we see the church as the sphere in which the coming eschatological Kingdom's power is active. This power of the Kingdom is today visible in the church."[140] This witness is especially evident in (1) the humility that disciples display as they serve others, not themselves (20:20–28), and (2) the forgiveness that disciples who have been forgiven display as they forgive others (18:23–35).

Fourth, the church is the guardian and steward of the kingdom. The declaration to Peter that he will be given the keys to the kingdom of heaven indicates that Peter will be the one who offers the message that allows entrance to the kingdom of heaven. The keys were employed initially by Peter to open the doors of the kingdom to all people (16:18); that was a one-time act in history. However, the same principle is employed by all disciples as they carry out the Great Commission (28:18–20), declaring the terms under which God forgives sin and allows entrance to the kingdom of heaven

139. Brown and Roberts, *Matthew*, 283.

140. M. Saucy, *Kingdom of God*, 347.

(cf. 18:15–20; John 20:22–23). The disciples of Jesus went out with the same message and ministry as did Jesus, healing the sick and casting out demons (10:1–5), and their work prepares for the way in which the church during this age will be the instrument by which the presence of the kingdom of heaven is made known through the work of the Spirit.[141] And with the resurrection of Jesus the power of death is broken, a sure promise that the gates of Hades will not prevail against the church (16:18).

The selection of twelve disciples/apostles shows both continuity with Israel and discontinuity. The church, no longer Israel, is the primary witness to and steward of the gospel message in this present age. However, this does not deny Israel its future role as witness (e.g., Rev 7:1–8), nor does it replace Israel's promise of being recipients of the gospel message as a nation (Matt 10:23; 23:37–39; Rom 11:25–33; 15:7–13). At a future time in the outworking of the kingdom of God, repentant Israel[142] will once again play a central role, but in this age the church as the body of Christ, made up of Jewish and gentile believing disciples of Jesus, is the visible manifestation of the reality of kingdom life.

### 9.3.4 Life in the Kingdom of Heaven Today in the Power of the Spirit

What we have in Matthew's Gospel is Jesus's proleptic view of the kingdom of heaven on earth today as it anticipates what will be made clear in the rest of New Testament revelation. Matthew has given his faithful record of Jesus's teaching and activities in establishing the kingdom of heaven on earth in his public ministry. We also have Matthew's reflections on Jesus's revelation, which anticipates the fuller revelation in the rest of the New Testament.

The bridge from the mission of Jesus establishing the kingdom of heaven to the rest of the New Testament, especially in its already-and-not-yet character, is principally grounded in the new covenant's provision for the final resolution of the sin problem. This is the fundamental ground of renewal that begins in the human heart and ultimately transforms all human society and the world of nature itself.[143]

I conclude the study of this chapter with my definition/description of the kingdom of heaven I gave earlier in this chapter:

> The kingdom of heaven/God is the ruling authority of God brought dynamically into human history in the person and mission of Jesus Messiah to establish the realm of the kingdom of heaven and to put all things right in the way that he originally intended for his earthly creation. This is accomplished through Jesus Messiah in the power of the Holy Spirit,

141. Cf. Ladd, *Theology of the New Testament*, 106–14.

142. E.g., Zech 12:10–14.

143. Mark Saucy, "*Regnum Spiriti*: The Role of the Spirit in the Social Ethics of the Kingdom," *JETS* 54.1 (2011): 89–108; here 105–6.

1. by overcoming evil and delivering humans from the power of sin and death through redemption and reconciliation with God,
2. by beginning to restore of the image of God in humans in the transformation of new covenant regeneration and renewal of life in the Spirit so that humans would rule God's creation with him through servanthood, and
3. by bringing humans into the blessings of God's ruling authority in present human history and ultimately and completely in all creation in the body of Christ in the eschatological replacement of all earthly kingdoms in the consummation of the kingdom of God/heaven at the end of history.

One of my close colleagues, J. P. Moreland, is a philosopher who has been captured throughout his life by the truths of Jesus and his teachings about the kingdom of God/heaven. He gives this challenge: "The crisis of our age requires nothing less than a revolution of those who live in, proclaim, and seek to advance the Kingdom that was not made with hands."[144] Such is the challenge that Matthew has recorded in his Gospel regarding Jesus announcing the reality of the presence of the kingdom of heaven.

**"KINGDOM" (*BASILEIA*) IN MATTHEW'S GOSPEL**

| |
|---|
| (1) 3:2 "Repent, for the **kingdom *of heaven*** has come near." |
| (2) 4:8 "Again, the devil took him to a very high mountain and showed him all the **kingdoms** of the world and their splendor." |
| (3) 4:17 "From that time on Jesus began to preach, 'Repent, for the **kingdom *of heaven*** has come near.'" |
| (4) 4:23 "Jesus went throughout Galilee, teaching in their synagogues, proclaiming the good news of the **kingdom**, and healing every disease and sickness among the people." |
| (5) 5:3 "Blessed are the poor in spirit, for theirs is the **kingdom *of heaven***." |
| (6) 5:10 "Blessed are those who are persecuted because of righteousness, for theirs is the **kingdom *of heaven***." |
| (7) 5:19 "Therefore anyone who sets aside one of the least of these commands and teaches others accordingly will be called least in the **kingdom *of heaven***, but whoever practices and teaches these commands will be called great in the **kingdom *of heaven***." |
| (8) 5:20 "For I tell you that unless your righteousness surpasses that of the Pharisees and the teachers of the law, you will certainly not enter the **kingdom *of heaven***." |
| (9) 6:10 ". . . your **kingdom** come, your will be done, on earth as it is in heaven. |
| (10) 6:33 "But seek first his **kingdom** [**of God**][145] and his righteousness, and all these things will be given to you as well." |

*continued*

144. J. P. Moreland, *Kingdom Triangle: Recover the Christian Mind, Renovate the Soul, Restore the Spirit's Power* (Grand Rapids: Zondervan, 2007), 14.

145. ℵ and B omit τοῦ θεοῦ, which is followed by the NIV, NASB, NET, and others as representing the original text; see Osborne, *Matthew*, 252n17. On the other hand, the ESV, NRSVue, and KJV include "of God," suggesting that τοῦ θεοῦ was in the original text; for discussion see France, *Gospel of Matthew*,

| |
|---|
| (11) 7:21 "Not everyone who says to me, 'Lord, Lord,' will enter the **kingdom *of heaven***, but only the one who does the will of my Father who is in heaven." |
| (12) 8:11 "I say to you that many will come from the east and the west, and will take their places at the feast with Abraham, Isaac and Jacob in the **kingdom *of heaven***." |
| (13) 8:12 "But the subjects of the **kingdom** will be thrown outside, into the darkness, where there will be weeping and gnashing of teeth." |
| (14) 9:35 "Jesus went through all the towns and villages, teaching in their synagogues, proclaiming the good news of the **kingdom** and healing every disease and sickness." |
| (15) 10:7 "As you go, proclaim this message: 'The **kingdom *of heaven*** has come near.'" |
| (16) 11:11 "Truly I tell you, among those born of women there has not risen anyone greater than John the Baptist; yet whoever is least in the **kingdom *of heaven*** is greater than he." |
| (17) 11:12 "From the days of John the Baptist until now, the **kingdom *of heaven*** has been subjected to violence, and violent people have been raiding it." |
| (18) 12:25 "Every **kingdom** divided against itself will be ruined, and every city or household divided against itself will not stand." |
| (19) 12:26 "If Satan drives out Satan, he is divided against himself. How then can his **kingdom** stand?" |
| (20) 12:28 "But if it is by the Spirit of God that I drive out demons, then the **kingdom of God** has come upon you." |
| (21) 13:11 "Because the knowledge of the mysteries of the **kingdom *of heaven*** has been given to you, but not to them." |
| (22) 13:19 "When anyone hears the message about the **kingdom** and does not understand it, the evil one comes and snatches away what was sown in their heart." |
| (23) 13:24 "The **kingdom *of heaven*** is like a man who sowed good seed in his field." |
| (24) 13:31 "The **kingdom *of heaven*** is like a mustard seed, which a man took and planted in his field." |
| (25) 13:33 "The **kingdom *of heaven*** is like yeast that a woman took and mixed into about sixty pounds of flour until it worked all through the dough." |
| (26) 13:38 "The field is the world, and the good seed stands for the people of the **kingdom**. The weeds are the people of the evil one," |
| (27) 13:41 "The Son of Man will send out his angels, and they will weed out of his **kingdom** everything that causes sin and all who do evil." |
| (28) 13:43 "Then the righteous will shine like the sun in the **kingdom** of their Father." |
| (29) 13:44 The **kingdom *of heaven*** is like treasure hidden in a field. |
| (30) 13:45 "Again, the **kingdom *of heaven*** is like a merchant looking for fine pearls." |
| (31) 13:47 "Once again, the **kingdom *of heaven*** is like a net that was let down into the lake and caught all kinds of fish." |

264n8; so also Hagner, *Matthew 1–13*, 161 note i. Metzger notes that "the textual data are susceptible to quite diverse evaluations" and therefore, the editorial committee explained the absence of the modifier as being due to accidental scribal omission. In the light of the conflicting interpretations, the committee thought it best to include the words in the text, enclosed within square brackets; Metzger, *TCGNT*[2], 15–16.

| |
|---|
| (32) 13:52 "Therefore every teacher of the law who has become a disciple in the **kingdom *of heaven*** is like the owner of a house who brings out of his storeroom new treasures as well as old." |
| (33) 16:19 "I will give you the keys of the **kingdom *of heaven***;" |
| (34) 16:28 "Truly I tell you, some who are standing here will not taste death before they see the Son of Man coming in his **kingdom**." |
| (35) 18:1 "Who, then, is the greatest in the **kingdom *of heaven***?" |
| (36) 18:3 "Truly I tell you, unless you change and become like little children, you will never enter the **kingdom *of heaven***." |
| (37) 18:4 "Therefore, whoever takes the lowly position of this child is the greatest in the **kingdom *of heaven***." |
| (38) 18:23 "Therefore, the **kingdom *of heaven*** is like a king who wanted to settle accounts with his servants." |
| (39) 19:12 "For there are eunuchs who were born that way, and there are eunuchs who have been made eunuchs by others—and there are those who choose to live like eunuchs for the sake of the **kingdom *of heaven***." |
| (40) 19:14 "Let the little children come to me, and do not hinder them, for the **kingdom *of heaven*** belongs to such as these." |
| (41) 19:23 "Truly I tell you, it is hard for someone who is rich to enter the **kingdom *of heaven***." |
| (42) 19:24 "Again I tell you, it is easier for a camel to go through the eye of a needle than for someone who is rich to enter the **kingdom of God**." |
| (43) 20:1 "For the **kingdom *of heaven*** is like a landowner who went out early in the morning to hire workers for his vineyard." |
| (44) 20:21 "Grant that one of these two sons of mine may sit at your right and the other at your left in your **kingdom**." |
| (45) 21:31 "Truly I tell you, the tax collectors and the prostitutes are entering the **kingdom of God** ahead of you." |
| (46) 21:43 "Therefore I tell you that the **kingdom of God** will be taken away from you and given to a people who will produce its fruit." |
| (47) 22:2 "The **kingdom *of heaven*** is like a king who prepared a wedding banquet for his son." |
| (48) 23:13 "Woe to you, teachers of the law and Pharisees, you hypocrites! You shut the door of the **kingdom *of heaven*** in people's faces. You yourselves do not enter, nor will you let those enter who are trying to." |
| (49) 24:7 "Nation will rise against nation, and **kingdom** against **kingdom**. There will be famines and earthquakes in various places." |
| (50) 24:14 "And this gospel of the **kingdom** will be preached in the whole world as a testimony to all nations, and then the end will come." |
| (51) 25:1 "At that time the **kingdom *of heaven*** will be like ten virgins who took their lamps and went out to meet the bridegroom." |
| (52) 25:34 "Come, you who are blessed by my Father; take your inheritance, the **kingdom** prepared for you since the creation of the world." |
| (53) 26:29 "I tell you, I will not drink from this fruit of the vine from now on until that day when I drink it new with you in my Father's **kingdom**." |

*Chapter 10*

# DISCIPLESHIP IN MATTHEW'S GOSPEL

## *Salvation, Righteousness, and Transformation*

### BIBLIOGRAPHY

**Bauer, David R.** "Perfection of Disciples in Matthew's Gospel: An Examination of a Central Concept in Matthean Kingdom Ethics." Pages 3–20 in *Kingdom Rhetoric: New Testament Explorations in Honor of Ben Witherington III.* Edited by T. Michael W. Halcomb. Eugene, OR: Wipf & Stock, 2013. **Bayer, Hans F.** *Apostolic Bedrock: Christology, Identity, and Character Formation According to Peter's Canonical Testimony.* PBM. Milton Keynes, UK: Paternoster, 2016. **Bockmuehl, Markus.** "The Gospels on the Presence of Jesus." Pages 87–102 in *OHC.* **Brown, Jeannine K.** *The Disciples in Narrative Perspective: The Portrayal and Function of the Matthean Disciples.* AcBib 9. Atlanta: Society of Biblical Literature, 2002. ———. "Living Out Justice, Mercy, and Loyalty: Discipleship in Matthew's Gospel." Pages 9–26 in *Following Jesus Christ: The New Testament Message of Discipleship for Today. A Volume in Honor of Michael J. Wilkins.* Edited by John K. Goodrich and Mark L. Strauss. Grand Rapids: Kregel, 2019. ———. "Matthew's Characterization of the Disciples." Pages 85–104 in *The Gospels as Stories: A Narrative Approach to Matthew, Mark, Luke, and John.* Grand Rapids: Baker Academic, 2020. **Carey, Holly J.** *Women Who Do: Female Disciples in the Gospels.* Grand Rapids: Eerdmans, 2023. **Cohick, Lynn H.** *Women in the World of the Earliest Christians: Illuminating Ancient Ways of Life.* Grand Rapids: Baker Academic, 2009. **Cooper, Ben.** *Incorporated Servanthood: Commitment and Discipleship in the Gospel of Matthew.* LNTS 490. London: T&T Clark, 2013. **Deines, Roland.** "The Description of Faith in the Gospel of Matthew." Pages 125–164 in *Treasures New & Old: Essays in Honor of Donald A. Hagner.* GlossaHouse Festschrift Series 1. Edited by Carl S. Sweatman and Clifford B. Kvidahl. Wilmore, KY: GlossaHouse, 2018. ———. "Not the Law but the Messiah: Law and Righteousness in the Gospel of Matthew—an Ongoing Debate." Pages 53–84 in *Built upon the Rock: Studies in the Gospel of Matthew.* Edited by Daniel M. Gurtner and John Nolland. Grand Rapids: Eerdmans, 2008. **Dunn, James D. G.** *Jesus' Call to Discipleship.* Cambridge: Cambridge University Press, 1992. **Eklund, Rebekah.** "Matthew, the Cross, and the Cruciform Life." Pages 16–30 in *Cruciform Scripture: Cross,*

*Participation, and Mission*. Edited by Christopher W. Skinner, Nijay K. Gupta, Andy Johnson, and Drew J. Strait. Grand Rapids: Eerdmans, 2021. **Eubank, Nathan.** *Wages of Cross-Bearing and Debt of Sin: The Economy of Heaven in Matthew's Gospel*. BZNW 196. Berlin: de Gruyter, 2013. **Foster, Paul.** *Community, Law and Mission in Matthew's Gospel*. WUNT 2/177. Tübingen: Mohr Siebeck, 2004. **Goodrich, John K., and Mark L. Strauss,** eds. *Following Jesus Christ: The New Testament Message of Discipleship for Today. A Volume in Honor of Michael J. Wilkins*. Grand Rapids: Kregel, 2019. **Gupta, Nijay K.** "The Spirituality of Faith in the Gospel of Matthew." Pages 108–24 in *Matthew and Mark Across Perspectives: Essays in Honour of Stephen C. Barton and William R. Telford*. Edited by Kristian A. Bendoraitis and Nijay K. Gupta. LNTS 538. London: Bloomsbury T&T Clark, 2016. **Hengel, Martin.** *The Charismatic Leader and His Followers*. Translated by J. C. G. Greig. New York: Crossroad, 1981. ———. *Saint Peter: The Underestimated Apostle*. Translated by Thomas H. Trapp. Tübingen: Mohr Siebeck, 2006. Repr., Grand Rapids: Eerdmans, 2010. **Hezser, Catherine.** "Followers, Servants, and Traitors: The Representation of Disciples in the Synoptic Gospels and in Ancient Judaism." Pages 71–88 in *Christian Origins and the Establishment of the Early Jesus Movement*. Edited by Stanley E. Porter and Andrew W. Pitts. TENTS 12. Leiden: Brill, 2018. **Keener, Craig S.** *The Historical Jesus of the Gospels*. Grand Rapids: Eerdmans, 2009. **Keith, Chris.** *Jesus' Literacy: Scribal Culture and the Teacher from Galilee*. LNTS 413. London: T&T Clark, 2011. **Kinney, Robert S.** *Hellenistic Dimensions of the Gospel of Matthew: Background and Rhetoric*. WUNT 2/414. Tübingen: Mohr Siebeck, 2016. **Konradt, Matthias.** "Following Jesus and Fulfilling the Law: Considerations on the Ethical Conception of the Gospel of Matthew." Pages 275–294 in *The Gospel of Matthew in Its Historical and Theological Context: Papers from the International Conference in Moscow, September 24 to 28, 2018*. Edited by Mikhail Seleznev, William R. G. Loader, and Karl-Wilhelm Niebuhr. WUNT 459. Tübingen: Mohr Siebeck, 2021. **Lang, David,** ed., *Transforming the Nations: Perspectives on Discipleship Today*. Singapore: Singapore Bible College Press, 2015. **Lészai, Lehel.** "The Disciples in Hellenism and Rabbinism." Pages 78–91 in *From Movement to Inheritance: Hidden Assets from the Treasury of Hungarian Reformation*. Edited by Olga Lukács, Alpár Csaba Nagy, and István Péter. R5AS 59. Göttingen: Vandenhoeck & Ruprecht, 2019. **Longenecker, Richard L.,** ed. *Patterns of Discipleship in the New Testament*. Grand Rapids: Eerdmans, 1996. **Lunde, Jonathan.** *Following Jesus, the Servant King: A Biblical Theology of Covenantal Discipleship*. Grand Rapids: Zondervan, 2010. **Luz, Ulrich.** "The Disciples in the Gospel According to Matthew." Pages 115–48 in *The Interpretation of Matthew*. Edited by Graham N. Stanton. 2nd ed. SNTI. Edinburgh: T&T Clark, 1995. ———. *Studies in Matthew*. Translated by Rosemary Selle. Grand Rapids: Eerdmans, 2005. **Markley, John R.** *Peter—Apocalyptic Seer: The Influence of the Apocalypse Genre on Matthew's Portrayal of Peter*. WUNT 2/348. Tübingen: Mohr Siebeck, 2013. **McKnight, Scot.** "Jesus and the Twelve." *BBR* 11.2 (2001): 203–31. ———. "Jesus and the Twelve." Pages 181–214 in *Key Events in the Life of the Historical Jesus: A Collaborative Exploration of Context and Coherence*. Edited by Darrell L. Bock and Robert L. Webb. WUNT 247. Tübingen: Mohr Siebeck, 2009.

**Meier, John P.** *Companions and Competitors*. Vol. 3 of *A Marginal Jew: Rethinking the Historical Jesus*. ABRL. New York: Doubleday, 2001. **Neudecker, Reinhard.** "Master-Disciple/Disciple-Master Relationship in Rabbinic Judaism and in the Gospels." *Gregorianum* 80 (1999): 245–61. **Pattarumadathil, Henry.** *"Your Father in Heaven": Discipleship in Matthew as a Process of Becoming Children of God*. AnBib 172. Rome: Pontificio Istituto Biblico, 2008. **Przybylski, Benno.** *Righteousness in Matthew and His World of Thought*. SNTSMS 41. Cambridge: Cambridge University Press, 1980. **Rengstorf, Karl H.** "μαθητής." *TDNT* 4:415–61. **Runesson, Anders.** "Judging Gentiles in the Gospel of Matthew: Between 'Othering' and 'Inclusion.'" Pages 133–151 in *Jesus, Matthew's Gospel and Early Christianity: Studies in Memory of Graham N. Stanton*. Edited by Daniel M. Gurtner, Joel Willitts, and Richard A. Burridge. LNTS 435; London: T&T Clark, 2011. **Segovia, Fernando F.**, ed. *Discipleship in the New Testament*. Philadelphia: Fortress, 1985. **Shin, In-Cheol.** "Matthew's Designation of the Role of Women as Indirectly Adherent Disciples." *Neotestamentica* 41.2 (2007): 399–415. **Siker, Jeffrey.** "Sin in the Gospel of Matthew." Pages 51–67 in *Sin in the New Testament*. EBS. Oxford: Oxford University Press, 2019. **Vaitusi, Nofoaiga.** *A Samoan Reading of Discipleship in Matthew*. IVBS 8. Atlanta: SBL Press, 2017. **Vickers, Brian.** "What Does Justification Have to Do with the Gospels?" Pages 179–212 in *The Doctrine on Which the Church Stands or Falls: Justification in Biblical, Theological, Historical, and Pastoral Perspective*. Edited by Matthew Barrett. Wheaton, IL: Crossway, 2019. **Viljoen, Francois P.** "Righteousness and Identity Formation in the Sermon on the Mount." *HvTSt* 69.1 (2013). 10.4102/hts.v69i1.1300. **Vine, Cedric E. W.** *Jesus and the Nations: Discipleship and Mission in the Gospel of Matthew*. Eugene, OR: Pickwick, 2022. **Wenthe, Dean O.** "The Social Configuration of the Rabbi-Disciple Relationship: Evidence and Implications for First Century Palestine." Pages 143–74 in *Studies in the Hebrew Bible, Qumran, and the Septuagint: Presented to Eugene Ulrich*. Edited by Peter W. Flint, Emanuel Tov, and James C. Vanderkam. VTSup 101. Leiden: Brill, 2006. **Wiarda, Timothy J.** *Peter in the Gospels: Pattern, Personality and Relationship*. WUNT 2/127. Tübingen: Mohr Siebeck, 2000. **Wick, Peter.** "Verborgenes und Befohlenes: Schriftgelehrsamkeit und Jüngerschaft bei Matthäus. Exegetische Beobachtungen zum Verhältnis von Theorie und Praxis und Perspektiven für die Ausbildung in den kirchlichen Dienst im heutigen (hoch)schulpolitischen Umfel." Pages 132–44 in *Schriftgelehrsamkeit und Toraethik: Die Bergpredigt im Kontext des Matthäusevangeliums*. Edited by Jens-Christian Maschmeier. Stuttgart: Kohlhammer, 2021. **Wilkins, Michael J.** *The Concept of Disciple in Matthew's Gospel: As Reflected in the Use of the Term* Μαθητής. NovTSup 59. Leiden: Brill, 1988. ———. "Disciples and Discipleship." *DJG*² 202–12. ———. *Following the Master: A Biblical Theology of Discipleship*. Grand Rapids: Zondervan, 1992. ———. *In His Image: Reflecting Christ in Everyday Life*. Colorado Springs, CO: NavPress, 1997. Repr., Eugene, OR: Wipf & Stock, 2019. ———. "Peter's Declaration of Jesus' Identity in Caesarea Philippi." Pages 293–381 in *Key Events in the Life of the Historical Jesus: A Collaborative Exploration of Context and Coherence*. Edited by Darrell L. Bock and Robert L. Webb. WUNT 247. Tübingen: Mohr Siebeck, 2009. ———. "Temptation of Jesus."

*DJG*[2] 952–59. ———. "Women in the Teaching and Ministry of Jesus." Pages 91–112 in *Women and Men in Ministry: A Complementary Perspective.* Edited by Robert L. Saucy and Judith K. TenElshof. Chicago: Moody, 2001. **Willitts, Joel.** "The Twelve Disciples in Matthew." Pages 166–79 in *Jesus, Matthew's Gospel and Early Christianity: Studies in Memory of Graham N. Stanton.* Edited by Daniel M. Gurtner, Joel Willitts, and Richard A. Burridge. LNTS 435. London: T&T Clark, 2011. **Witherington, Ben, III.** *Women and the Genesis of Christianity.* Edited by Ann Witherington. Cambridge: Cambridge University Press, 1990. ———. *Women in the Ministry of Jesus: A Study of Jesus' Attitudes to Women and Their Roles as Reflected in His Earthly Life.* SNTSMS 51. Cambridge: Cambridge University Press, 1984. **Wyant, Jennifer S.** *Beyond Mary or Martha: Reclaiming Ancient Models of Discipleship.* ESEC 21. Atlanta: SBL Press, 2019.

## 10.1 INTRODUCTION TO DISCIPLESHIP IN MATTHEW'S GOSPEL

As Jesus concludes his earthly mission, and as Matthew concludes his Gospel, Jesus declares his well-known Great Commission—"Make disciples of all the nations" (28:19). Jesus (and Matthew) assume that we know what kind of disciple this would be. But what is not always recognized by modern readers is that the first-century world displayed a variety of religious, philosophical, and political leaders, all of whom had followers who were committed to their cause, teaching, and beliefs. While several different terms designated these followers, *disciple* was one of the most commonly used, and *discipleship* referred to the process of growth and development as a disciple.

Jesus expected his disciples to know what was involved "mak[ing] disciples" and what the goal was in "teaching them to obey all that I commanded you" (28:20).

What is the kind of disciple that those who are committed to carrying out the Great Commission expected to make? What kind of disciple are they, and we, to be? How are Jesus's disciples similar to, or different from, other forms of discipleship in the ancient world, such as the disciples of the prophet John the Baptist, or the disciples of the studious Pharisees or the politically oriented Sadducees, or the revolutionist disciples of the Zealots?

And how are disciples of Jesus today similar to or different from other forms of followers? Ideological, political/militaristic, charismatic leaders in the recent past such as extremists Adolf Hitler or Karl Heinrich Marx, or today like Vladimir Putin, have their own obsessive enthusiasts. If those seem far away, but what of political extremists in our own backyard? Each group has its own obsessive enthusiasts or, we might say, "disciples."

How are we as disciples of Jesus different, and how does the world view us in the light of other religious or political or militaristic disciples? I came to know Jesus in the days when many of us were viewed as "Jesus freaks." I did have a radical conversion and transformation of life and lifestyle, with long hair, wild clothes, and driving an old beat-up Volkswagen van with Jesus-stickers all over it. I was "saved" and was a genuine, radical disciple of Jesus. How did I, and how do I now, without long hair and wild clothes and driving a modest Honda SUV, differ from other types of disciples of other types of political/religious/militaristic leaders?

To understand the genuine identity of disciples of Jesus is a central concern for us in this chapter. The concern is not simply to complete our theological task, but to help push us all to become more like Jesus and establish a firm understanding of what helping others become more like Jesus means, whether in our marriages and families, churches, neighborhood communities, or throughout the world in our careers and journeys.

In this chapter we will first take an overview of master-disciple relationships in the ancient world generally. Then we will survey how the disciples of Jesus came into existence historically, and how Jesus developed his unique form of discipleship. Then a large section will focus on Matthew's theological perspective of Jesus's form of discipleship and Matthew's purposes as laid out in his Gospel.

This will include zeroing in on the issues of *salvation* in relationship to discipleship and the kingdom of heaven, what it means to display *righteousness* in our walk with Jesus, and then *transformation* as a disciple of Jesus and its reality as an expression of kingdom life in the present world as exhibited in Matthew's Gospel.

Following the investigation of Jesus's disciples on the historical horizon, and then Matthew's perspective of Jesus's disciples on the theological horizon, we will expectantly have a clearer perspective of what discipleship to Jesus means from our modern-day horizon.

## 10.2 DISCIPLESHIP TERMINOLOGY AND CONCEPTS IN THE ANCIENT WORLD[1]

The English word *disciple* normally designates a "follower," "adherent," or "student" of a great master, religious leader, or teacher. In the ancient Jewish and Greco-Roman world *disciple* is the word used most commonly to translate the Greek word *mathētēs* (μαθητής) and the Hebrew words *talmîd* (תַּלְמִיד) and *limmûd* (לִמּוּד).[2]

1. Much of the following material is adapted from my prior books and articles: Wilkins, *Concept of Disciple in Matthew's Gospel*; *Following the Master*; "Disciples" and "Discipleship," *DJG*[1] 176–89; and "Disciples, Discipleship," *DJG*[2] 202–12. Here I give discussion and expanded analysis of the literature.

2. Wilkins, *Concept of Disciple*, see chs. 1–3; see also Paul Trebilco, *Self-Designations and Group Identity in the New Testament* (Cambridge: Cambridge University Press, 2012), 208–18.

### 10.2.1 Discipleship in the Greek-Speaking World

Discipleship was a common phenomenon in the ancient Mediterranean world. In the earliest classical Greek literature, *mathētēs* was used in three ways: (1) with a general sense of a "learner," in morphological relation to the verb *manthanō*, "to learn";[3] (2) with a technical sense of "adherent" to a great teacher, teaching, or master;[4] (3) and with a more restricted sense of an "institutional pupil" of the Sophists.[5] Sophists such as Protagoras were among the first to establish an institutional relationship in which the master imparted virtue and knowledge to the disciple through a paid educational process.

Socrates and Plato objected to such a form of discipleship on epistemological grounds, advocating instead a relationship in which the master directs dialogue to draw out innate knowledge from his followers. Therefore, Plato records that Socrates (and those opposed to the Sophists) resisted using *mathētēs* for his followers in order to avoid Sophistic mis-associations.[6]

But Socrates used the term freely to refer to "learners"[7] and "adherents"[8] where there was no danger of misunderstanding. Hippocrates likewise rejected charging fees for passing on medical knowledge, but vowed in the famous Hippocratic Oath that, in the same way that his teachers and gods passed on the art of medicine to him, his intention was "to impart precept, oral instruction, and all other instruction to my own sons, the sons of my teacher, and to indentured pupils (*mathētai*) who have taken the Healer's oath, but to nobody else."[9]

In the Hellenistic period at the time of Jesus, *mathētēs* continued to be used with general connotations of a learner,[10] but it was used more regularly to refer to an adherent.[11] The type of adherence was determined by the master, ranging from being the follower of a great thinker and master of the past like Socrates,[12] to being the pupil of a philosopher like Pythagoras,[13] to being the devotee of a religious master like Epicurus.[14]

The relationship assumed the development of a sustained commitment of the disciple to the master and to the master's particular teaching or mission, and the relationship extended to imitation of the conduct of the master as it impacted the personal life of the disciple. In Hellenism the intellectual factor was a constituent part of the idea

3. E.g., Isocrates, *Panath.* 16.7.
4. E.g., Xenophon, *Mem.* 1.6.3, 4.
5. E.g., Demosthenes, *Lacr.* 35.41.7.
6. Plato, *Soph.* 233.B.6–C.6.
7. Plato, *Crat.* 428.B.4.
8. Plato, *Symp.* 197.B.1.
9. Hippocrates, *The Oath* (Jones, LCL), 1:298–99.
10. Diodorus Siculus, *Bib. hist.* 23.2.1.13, 26. One who emphasizes this perspective is Kinney, *Hellenistic Dimensions*, esp. chs. 7–8.
11. Dio Chrysostom, *1 Regn.* 38.6.
12. Dio Chrysostom, *Hom.* (*Or.* 53) 1.2.
13. Diodorus Siculus, *Bib. hist.* 12.20.1, 3.
14. Plutarch, *Suav. Viv.* 1100.A.6.

of discipleship, but ultimately imitating the master's behavior, lifestyle, and mission gained preeminence.[15]

A disciple in the ancient Greek-speaking world was primarily an adherent to a particular master and was often in training to become a master with his/her own disciples.

### 10.2.2 Discipleship in the Old Testament

Disciple terminology is strikingly scarce in the Old Testament, but other evidence points to master-disciple relationships within the national life of Israel. The single occurrence of *talmîd* in the Old Testament (*mathētēs* does not occur in the LXX) indicates a student or apprentice in musical instruction (1 Chr 25:8). The prophet Isaiah refers to the group gathered around him as "my disciples" (Isa 8:16; *limmûday*), and their relationship is characterized by an educational process accentuating speaking and listening (*limmûdîm* [Isa 50:4]). The term *limmûdîm* was used by Isaiah to specify the "disciples" of Yahweh (Isa 54:13), indicating that *limmûdîm* could be disciples of both Yahweh and a human master.

The existence of master-disciple relationships within the social structure of Israel is witnessed in and by the prophets associated with Samuel (1 Sam 19:20–24), the sons of the prophets associated with Elisha (2 Kgs 4:1, 38; 9:1), the writing prophets Jeremiah and Baruch (Jer 36:32), Ezra and the scribal tradition (Ezra 7:6, 11), and the wise counselors within the wisdom tradition (Prov 22:17; 25:1; Jer 18:18). Each of these institutions was involved in the process of the communication of the revelation of Yahweh (prophecy, law, wisdom), and the suggested intimacy of the relationship indicates mutual support of master and disciple in the task of revealing the word of God to the nation.

However, a unique form of discipleship in the Old Testament is most clearly seen as Israel is in relationship to God and as the people follow God: "I will walk among you and be your God, and you will be my people" (Lev 26:12). When the nation fulfills its commitment to the covenant it is said to be following God[16] and walking in his ways.[17] The leaders of the people, such as Joshua and Caleb (Num 32:12; Josh 14:8, 9, 14), were evaluated by the criterion of whether or not they were following God and walking in his ways. David is the supreme example of the king whose life was characterized by following God: "my servant David, who kept my commands and followed me with all his heart, doing only what was right in my eyes" (1 Kgs 14:8).

15. See also on this Lehel Lészai, "The Disciples in Hellenism and Rabbinism," in *From Movement to Inheritance: Hidden Assets from the Treasury of Hungarian Reformation*, ed. Olga Lukács, Alpár Csaba Nagy, and István Péter, R5AS 59 (Göttingen: Vandenhoeck & Ruprecht, 2019), 78–91, here esp. 79–83.

16. E.g., Deut 4:1–14; 1 Sam 12:14.

17. E.g., Deut 10:12.

The Old Testament theme of God with his people prepares for Matthew's focus on Jesus as Immanuel, "God with us [i.e., his people]" (Matt 1:23), who would develop a following of disciples unique to his messianic status.[18]

### 10.2.3 Discipleship in Judaism at the Time of Jesus

Within Judaism of the first century AD several different types of individuals were called "disciples," using the essentially equivalent terms *mathētēs* and *talmîd*.[19] The terms designated adherents or followers who were committed to a recognized leader, teacher or movement. Relationships ran the spectrum from philosophical[20] (Philo), to technical (rabbinical scribes[21]), to sectarian (Pharisees[22]), to revolutionary (Zealot-like nationalists[23]).

We find evidence of discipleship relationships in the writings from Philo, the Qumran community, the Gospels, Josephus, and the rabbinical literature. Each of these relationships reflects the religious/cultural influence surrounding the writer(s).[24] Philo's conception of discipleship reflects diaspora Judaism with Greek influence upon Jews who were scattered throughout the Mediterranean world. The conception of discipleship found within the Qumran writings reflects an ascetic community that had withdrawn from the rest of Judaism and saw itself as the true Israel. The conception of discipleship in Josephus reflects a person with a Palestinian-Jewish background who has gone over to become a part of the Roman establishment and who now tries to write an apologetic for traditional Jewish ways to his Roman audience. The conception of discipleship found in the rabbinical literature reflects relationships established in the wake of the fall of Jerusalem and the development of rabbinical Judaism.

The Gospel writers indicate types of discipleship within Judaism viewed from both the Jewish social perspective as well as the perspective of discipleship to Jesus.

#### *10.2.3.1 Disciples of Israel's Religious Heritage: Disciples of Moses*

The apostle John in his Gospel recorded an incident in which being a "disciple of Moses" indicated commitment to God and his revelation. The "Jews"[25] who questioned the parents of the man born blind (John 9:18–34) attempted to scorn the man by saying that, although the blind man was a disciple of Jesus, *they* were disciples of Moses (9:28).

18. See Wilkins, *Following the Master*, 51–69.
19. Wenthe, "Social Configuration," 143–74.
20. Philo, *Sacr.* 7; 64; 79.
21. m. Avot 1:1; b. Shabbat 31a.
22. Josephus, *Ant.* 13:289; 15:3, 370.
23. Midr. Shir Hashirim Zuṭa.
24. Cf. Max Wilcox, "Jesus in the Light of His Jewish Environment," *ANRW* 25.1:159–85.
25. A consensus in Johannine studies is that the expression "the Jews" stands for the religious leaders of Judaism; see Klink, *John*, ZECNT, 127–28; Köstenberger, *John*, e.g., 15; C. K. Barrett, *The Gospel According to St. John*, 2nd ed. (1955; repr., Philadelphia: Westminster, 1978), 171–72; Morris, *Gospel According to John*, 130–32.

Their claim was to a direct line with the revelation of God to Moses through Torah (cf. 9:29). While this is similar to some Greek forms of discipleship (e.g., "disciples of Socrates," who lived long after his death) and later specialized rabbinic use,[26] in this context there is no specialized meaning of discipleship. Rather, the emphasis is upon following a type of teaching: i.e., following a person known to receive a revelation of God (Moses), or one who claims it (Jesus). Here discipleship is a personal commitment to a type of teaching as represented in a person who is known to speak for God. Any true Jew would have called himself/herself a "disciple of Moses" in this sense, regardless of any secondary sectarian commitments (e.g., to John, the Pharisees, Sadducees, Essenes, Qumran, etc.). Therefore, as a development from the Old Testament portrait of discipleship to God, the ideal of Judaism was that every Israelite was a disciple to Moses and to Torah.[27] These are Jews who focused on their privileged position as those to whom God had revealed himself through Moses.[28]

#### *10.2.3.2 Disciples of a Rabbi and Religious Institution: Disciples of the Pharisees*

We also find the "disciples of the Pharisees." Matthew tells us that the disciples of the Pharisees (along with the disciples of John the Baptist) were concerned about the question of fasting (9:14; cf. Mark 2:18). Matthew also tells us that the disciples of the Pharisees were involved in a dispute about another important Pharisaic issue: paying taxes to Caesar (Matt 22:15–16).[29] These passages accentuate key ingredients of Pharisaism. The Pharisees were committed to an intense study of the Scriptures, and additionally the oral tradition, but they were also fully committed to living out the Law and the tradition.[30] Hagner suggests that "Pharisaism was at heart, though tragically miscarried, a movement for righteousness. It was this concern for righteousness that drove the Pharisees to their legalism with such a passion."[31] All through the Gospels the Pharisees are portrayed as concerned with fidelity to the Scripture, the traditions, and the unblemished practice of both. Therefore, it would be expected that their disciples were students of the Law and tradition, and that they were practitioners of legalistic adherence to both.

26. See Karl H. Rengstorf, "μαθητής," *TDNT* 4:415–61, 437 for examples. The rabbinic use became specialized because it signified a rabbinic-type study of the Law of Moses and the oral tradition concerning it.

27. Emil Schürer, *The History of the Jewish People in the Age of Jesus Christ (175 B.C.–A.D. 135)*, rev. ed., ed. Geza Vermes, Fergus Millar, and Matthew Black, 3 vols. (Edinburgh: T. & T. Clark, 1973–1987), 1:332.

28. See Lészai, "Disciples in Hellenism and Rabbinism," 78–91.

29. See b. Pesahim 112b and Bava Qamma 113a–b and 114a. See Hill, *The Gospel of Matthew*, 304.

30. For a recent analysis of the Pharisees by a wide spectrum of scholars, see Sievers and Levine, eds., *The Pharisees*, including two chapters devoted to Matthew's Gospel: Henry Pattarumadathil, "Pharisees and Sadducees Together in Matthew," 224–40, and Adela Yarbro Collins, "Polemic Against the Pharisees in Matthew 23," 241–71.

31. Donald A. Hagner, "Pharisees," *ZPEB* 4:752.

The disciples of the Pharisees were students of the Pharisaic rabbis and were in training to become rabbis themselves. The Pharisees lived among everyday Jews and were often situated in the synagogues of local communities. The disciples of the Pharisees were committed to the study of Torah and to imitation of the lifestyle of the rabbi. The Pharisees were prominent throughout Palestine, especially using the local synagogues as their base of influence. Gamaliel, a prominent religious leader in Israel, was a Pharisee, a "teacher of the Law" (cf. Acts 5:34; *nomodidaskalos*). He belonged to one of the rabbinical schools and was the one under whom the apostle Paul had studied before he followed Jesus (Acts 5:34; 22:3).

The Pharisaic master-disciple relationship is the forerunner of the later talmudic rabbinic master-disciple relationships that evolved into a formal educational system for training rabbis that especially involved passing on the oral law.[32] This is heard in a saying attributed to the Great Synagogue, which became a standard of Israel: "Be prudent in judgment. Raise up many disciples. Make a fence around the Torah" (m. Avot 1:1 [Neusner]).

### *10.2.3.3 Disciples of a Prophet: Disciples of John the Baptist*

We also see in the Gospels the disciples of John the Baptist (Matt 9:14; cf. Mark 2:18), that fiery prophet who lived out in the wilderness of Judea and announced the arrival of the kingdom of heaven. He demanded repentance in the light of the coming wrath and the arrival of Jesus Messiah, whom he declared would baptize with the Holy Spirit and unquenchable fire (Matt 3:1–12). John the Baptist's disciples had committed themselves to John's preaching and lifestyle. They also had left Jewish society to follow the eschatological prophet. After John was imprisoned by Herod Antipas, his disciples remained near John. He sent his disciples to ask Jesus, "Are you the one who is to come, or should we expect someone else?" (11:2–3).

The circle of disciples around John did not include all those who came for baptism but may have initially been a group who assisted him in baptizing the crowds, similar to the way Jesus's disciples assisted him (John 4:1–2). There is no mention of John expounding Scripture to his disciples, although his disciples did call him rabbi, recorded at least once (John 3:26), and at least once John teaches the multitudes, tax collectors, and soldiers (Luke 3:10–18). He did teach his disciples a special prayer (Luke 5:33; 11:1), and they appear to have had their own fasting practices (Matt 9:14; Mark 2:18). John's disciples centered their lives on the practice of piety as had John. The prophetic and eschatological form of his activity was a vivid expression of ancient Judaism.[33]

32. See Neusner, *Invitation to the Talmud*, 79–80.

33. Hengel, *Charismatic Leader*, 35–37.

Since John was preparing the way for Jesus and the messianic age, Günther Bornkamm perceptively stresses that the disciples of John represent the closest analogy to the disciples of Jesus, even though they are not exactly parallel.[34]

## 10.3 Historical Disciples of Jesus

The type of discipleship found in Judaism depended upon the kind of master or group to which the disciple belonged. On the surface Jesus's disciples appeared to be similar to other forms of Jewish disciples. Jesus took a commonly occurring phenomenon—a master with disciples—and used it as an expression of his kind of relationship that he would develop with his followers.

But Jesus would mold and shape that relationship to form a unique form of discipleship, far different than others.[35] Some press too far the similarities between Jesus and other forms of master-discipleship relationships. For example, later forms of rabbinic master-disciple relationships are sometimes read back too closely into Jesus's relationship with his disciples.[36] Jesus held scribal authority, but it was not derived from formal education within the scribal/rabbinic traditions.[37]

There was a wide spectrum of other types of master-disciple relationships in existence that may have more relevance for understanding Jesus's form.[38] John the Baptist and his disciples appear more closely related to Jesus and his disciples than to the Pharisaic or later rabbinic system.

But even in comparison to John the Baptist and his disciples, Jesus developed a relationship with his disciples that was unique to his status as the messianic Son of God, whose disciples would ultimately worship him, an action reserved solely for God with his people (Matt 28:16–17).[39]

Discipleship in the ancient world was primarily *professional or vocational* for a small group of insiders who were in training to become masters themselves with their own disciples.

Discipleship to Jesus is *kingdom transformational* for all who obey his call to come to him for life in the kingdom of God. Disciples of Jesus would always remain disciples

34. Günther Bornkamm, *Jesus of Nazareth*, trans. Irene and Fraser McCluskey with James M. Robinson (London: Hodder and Stoughton, 1960), 145. In my view, an overplay of the distinction between John the Baptist and Jesus and their respective disciples is found in Albert I. Baumgarten, "An Ancient Debate of Disciples," in *Perceiving the Other in Ancient Judaism and Early Christianity*, ed. Michal Bar-Asher Siegal, Wolfgang Grünstäudl, and Matthew Thiessen, WUNT 394 (Tübingen: Mohr Siebeck, 2017), 1–18.

35. See Trebilco, *Self-Designations and Group Identity in the New Testament*, 218–24; Meier, *Companions and Competitors*, ch. 25.

36. E.g., Reinhard Neudecker, "Master-Disciple/Disciple-Master Relationship in Rabbinic Judaism and in the Gospels," *Gregorianum* 80 (1999): 245–61. On a popular level pressing this comparison, see Vander Laan, with Sorenson and Sorenson, *In the Dust of the Rabbi*. For a sympathetic view of Jesus within the Judaism of his day, but that at times may press the comparison too far, see Young, *Meet the Rabbis*, esp. 29–37.

37. See Keith, *Jesus' Literacy*, 189–92.

38. See Hengel, *Charismatic Leader*, 42–57.

39. See Morris, "Disciples of Jesus," 112–27.

of their Master, Jesus. The new birth initiates life-transformation in the heart of Jesus's disciples, which then directs from the inside-out the transformation of the mind, body, and relationships so that Jesus's disciples are now more like God had originally intended them from creation. New disciples embark on the journey of transformation into the image of Jesus, who is the true image of God.

The following are some of the unique aspects of his form of discipleship.

### 10.3.1 First Disciples of Jesus: The First Jesus Movement

From the beginning of his public ministry Jesus had followers. His first followers, according to the Johannine tradition, were originally disciples of John the Baptist. Since the Baptist's ministry prepared the way for Jesus, it is natural that some of John's disciples would make the transition to following Jesus. The first disciples of John to become followers of Jesus were Andrew and another unnamed disciple (possibly the apostle John). Andrew, convinced that Jesus was the Messiah, brought his brother, Simon Peter, to Jesus. Philip, another person from the same hometown as Andrew and Peter, was next called by Jesus, and he in turn brought Nathanael to Jesus (cf. John 1:35–49). These first followers were likely "his disciples" (*hoi mathētai autou*; 2:2) who next traveled with Jesus to the wedding celebration at Cana, experienced the first miraculous sign, and believed in Jesus (2:11).

This early movement to follow Jesus gained momentum as the news of Jesus traveled through social relationships in a relatively localized area. Since Jesus focused his ministry in the Galilee region, the early disciples were drawn from an existing network of relatives,[40] business partners,[41] and neighbors or acquaintances.[42]

The Jesus movement accelerated rapidly. In the early stages of his ministry a great company of disciples attached themselves to Jesus (Luke 6:17; 10:1; John 6:60). Jesus appealed to the multitude of people, and a groundswell of followers came after him to become his disciples. But the early company of disciples was apparently a mixed sort. In John's Gospel there is a unique record of disciples who had followed Jesus for some period of time, but after a discourse by Jesus that they found particularly hard to accept, they left and no longer followed him (cf. John 6:60–66). Apparently, they had followed Jesus because he was an exciting new miracle worker and teacher (cf. 2:23–25). They made some kind of a commitment to Jesus, but when his teaching did not conform to their expectations, they left him. They were only loosely attached to the movement.[43]

40. E.g., brothers: Andrew and Simon Peter; John and James.

41. E.g., Peter and Andrew were partners in the fishing industry with James and John (Luke 5:10).

42. E.g., most of the Twelve disciples were from Capernaum and Bethsaida.

43. Wilkins, *Following the Master*, ch. 6; Meier, *Companions and Competitors*, ch. 25; Jeannine K. Brown, "Disciple, Discipleship: New Testament," *EBR* 1:887–89.

### 10.3.2 Jesus's Disciples and the Crowds

Two groups were in attendance for much of Jesus's ministry: the disciples (*hoi mathētai*) and the "crowds," or "multitudes" (*hoi ochloi*).[44] The disciples were those who obeyed Jesus's call to come out of the crowd and follow him. The disciples believed in Jesus as their master[45] and committed themselves to his mission of establishing the kingdom of God and to the salvation that he offered (Matt 19:16–29).

The crowds were those to whom Jesus continued to offer a call. The crowds were a neutral, though curious, group who were not attached in a serious way to Jesus. Although they followed Jesus (Matt 4:25), the crowds did not exhibit the twin prerequisites of discipleship: the cost of giving up their old lives and committing themselves to Jesus (e.g., Mark 8:34–38). They followed only in a physical sense, not in the true sense of devoting themselves to Jesus. They were the people of Israel who were the object of Jesus's evangelistic ministry. They flocked to him for healing (Matt 15:29–31) and teaching (5:28–29) but could not understand (13:10–15) because they were not true believers. Making disciples from among the crowd was the object of Jesus's ministry in Israel (9:35–38), and the worldwide commission he gave to his disciples before he ascended was to make disciples of the nations (28:18).

### 10.3.3 The Twelve Disciples/Apostles of Jesus

The four Gospels witness that, in the ebb and flow of the popularity of the Jesus movement, a core of twelve disciples were called by Jesus into a special relationship with him.[46] Although the Twelve are *disciples*, paradigms of what it means to be a believer in Jesus, they also are designated as *apostles*, leaders among the disciples. Luke states that Jesus "called his disciples to him, and chose twelve of them, whom he also named apostles" (Luke 6:13).

The distinction between the general group of disciples and the specific group of the Twelve has to do with function or role, not with status or worth. All disciples are equal with regard to their discipleship to Jesus, which speaks of their entrance into salvation and the kingdom of God. The role of the Twelve as apostles is functionally oriented toward leadership. But this function did not elevate them to a higher status. Rather, the calling to leadership as an apostle is a calling to servanthood (Matt 20:25–28; Luke 22:24–30). As "disciples" the Twelve are paradigms of what Jesus accomplishes in believers; as "apostles" the Twelve are also set apart as the leaders within this new movement to come.[47]

44. Cf. Wilkins, *Following the Master*, ch. 6; Meier, *Companions and Competitors*, ch. 24.

45. Matt 4:18–22; Mark 1:16–20; cf. Luke 5:1–11.

46. Cf. Scot McKnight, "Jesus and the Twelve," in Bock and Webb, *Key Events in the Life of the Historical Jesus*, 181–214; Wilkins, *Following the Master*, ch. 8; Meier, *Companions and Competitors*, chs. 26–27.

47. Peter K. Nelson, *Leadership and Discipleship: A Study of Luke 22:24–30*, SBLDS 138 (Atlanta: Scholars Press, 1994), 255–64; Jeannine K. Brown, "Apostle: New Testament," *EBR* 2:472–76.

### *10.3.3.1 The Twelve Disciples*

In answer to the prayer for the Lord of the harvest to send out workers into his harvest field (9:38), Jesus called his twelve disciples to him (10:1). Although this is the first time that Matthew has mentioned the Twelve explicitly, the informal way in which they are introduced suggests that the Twelve became a recognized group earlier.[48]

Matthew is the only New Testament writer to refer to "the twelve disciples" (11:1; 20:17; 26:20), although the title "the Twelve" occurs regularly elsewhere.[49] Twelve has obvious salvation-historical significance. The number corresponds to the twelve patriarchs of Israel, the sons of Jacob, from whom the tribes of Israel descended. The twelve disciples symbolize the continuity of salvation history in God's program, as Jesus sends them out to proclaim to the lost sheep of the house of Israel that the kingdom of heaven has arrived (cf. 10:5–6).[50]

But there is a form of discontinuity as well, because the Twelve will sit on twelve thrones judging the house of Israel (cf. 19:28).[51] The arrival of the kingdom of heaven in Jesus's ministry demands an appropriate response from his chosen people Israel. In the gathering of twelve disciples, we find the hint that Jesus is indeed the messianic king of Israel who has come to unite the people of God in all ages.[52]

The same authority that characterized Jesus's ministry in Matt 8–9 is now given to the Twelve. All that the Twelve will accomplish—whether powerful works or powerful preaching of the gospel of the kingdom—is based on having received Jesus's authority. Disciples of every era will find their own authority only in their submission to Jesus's authority. As the Twelve cast out demons and heal disease and sickness, it is external validation of the reality of the presence of the kingdom of heaven, and people should now turn to Jesus as the messianic deliverer. But their authoritative mission is also an exercise of control over Satan's realm of rule on this earth. No longer is Satan the uncontested ruler of this world. He has met his match, and more, in the arrival of the Jesus. Satan's evil forces have also met their match, and more, as Jesus's emissaries go out with his authority to bring release to those held captive.

### *10.3.3.2 The Twelve Apostles (10:2)*

Not only are the twelve "disciples" (10:1), they are also "apostles" (10:2). The term *apostle* has a significantly different meaning than the word *disciple. Disciple* is the term used to designate all those who have believed in Jesus, while the title *apostle* designates

48. For discussions of the historicity of the Twelve within Jesus's ministry, see Scot McKnight, "Jesus and the Twelve," *BBR* 11.2 (2001): 203–31; John P. Meier, "The Circle of the Twelve: Did It Exist During Jesus' Public Ministry?," *JBL* 116.4 (1997): 635–72; Meier, *Companions and Competitors*, 125–63.

49. E.g., Matt 10:5; 26:14; Mark 3:14, 16; Luke 6:13; 8:1; John 6:67, 70; Acts 6:2; etc.

50. Cf. McKnight, "Jesus and the Twelve," 220–31; Karl H. Rengstorf, "δώδεκα," *TDNT* 2:326.

51. Cf. Meier, *Companions and Competitors*, 251–52.

52. Cf. Seán Freyne, *The Twelve: Disciples and Apostles. A Study in the Theology of the First Three Gospels* (London: Sheed and Ward, 1968), 23–48.

those who have been commissioned to be his representatives. This is a clue to the role of the Twelve. As *disciples*, the Twelve are the examples of what Jesus accomplishes in all believers; as *apostles*, the Twelve are set aside as the leaders within the new movement. Further, this is a clue that the Twelve will transition from the time of Jesus's historical earthly ministry when they are sent out as disciples to Israel (10:5–15), to the time of his ascended ministry when they are sent out as apostles to the nations (10:16–23).

Matthew uses the word "apostle" only here, and he is the only Gospel writer to use the expression "the twelve apostles" (cf. Rev 21:14). *Apostle* has narrow and wide meanings in the New Testament. The narrow sense, as here, is the usual meaning, signifying the special authoritative representatives chosen by Jesus to play a foundational role in the establishment of the church.[53] The apostle Paul normally used the term to refer to the Twelve but includes himself among them as a special apostle to the gentiles (1 Cor. 15:8–10). The wide sense of apostle derives from the common verb *apostellō*, "I send" (e.g., Matt 10:5), and therefore can mean merely "messenger" (John 13:16), or refer to Jesus as "the apostle and high priest whom we confess" (Heb 3:1), or designate an individual such as Barnabas, Titus, or Epaphroditus within the group of missionaries that is larger than the Twelve and Paul.[54]

The Twelve do not function as a permanent organizational group, however. Although the Twelve provided continuity in God's salvation-historical program, the absence of the title in the later developing church gives us a clue that they do not provide permanent organizational leadership as a group.[55] Four times a listing of the Twelve occurs in the New Testament.

### *10.3.3.3 Lists of the Twelve Disciples/Apostles*[56]

| Matthew 10:2–4 | Mark 3:16–19 | Luke 6:13–16 | Acts 1:13 |
|---|---|---|---|
| ***First group of four*** | | | |
| *1. first, Simon (who is called Peter)* | *Simon (to whom he gave the name Peter)* | *Simon (whom he named Peter)* | *Peter* |
| 2. his brother Andrew | James son of Zebedee | Andrew | John |
| 3. James son of Zebedee | John | James | James |
| 4. his brother John | Andrew | John | Andrew |

53. Cf. Gal 1:17, 19; 1 Cor 9:1–5; 15:7; Eph 2:19–22.

54. Barnabas in Acts 14:4, 14; Titus in 2 Cor 8:23; Epaphroditus in Phil 2:25; probably Timothy and Silas also in 1 Thess 1:1; 2:7; cf. Andronicus and Junias in Rom 16:7. James the brother of Jesus seems to be included among the apostles in Jerusalem as a "pillar of the church" (Gal 1:17; 2:9).

55. Cf. McKnight, "Jesus and the Twelve," 209–10; Rengstorf, "δώδεκα," *TDNT* 2:326–28.

56. For discussion of the Twelve see Wilkins, *Following the Master*, ch. 8; Wilkins, "Disciples," *DJG*[1] 179–81. See also Meier, *Companions and Competitors*, ch. 27. For discussions of the apocryphal traditions about the Twelve, see Edgar Hennecke, *New Testament Apocrypha*, 2 vols., ed. Wilhelm Schneemelcher (Philadelphia: Westminster, 1963–1965).

| Matthew 10:2–4 | Mark 3:16–19 | Luke 6:13–16 | Acts 1:13 |
|---|---|---|---|
| ***Second group of four*** | | | |
| *5. Philip* | *Philip* | *Philip* | *Philip* |
| 6. Bartholomew | Bartholomew | Bartholomew | Thomas |
| 7. Thomas | Matthew | Matthew | Bartholomew |
| 8. Matthew the tax collector | Thomas | Thomas | Matthew |
| ***Third group of four*** | | | |
| *9. James son of Alphaeus* | *James son of Alphaeus* | *James son of Alphaeus* | *James son of Alphaeus* |
| 10. Thaddaeus | Thaddaeus | Simon the Zealot | Simon the Zealot |
| 11. Simon the Zealot | Simon the Zealot | Judas son of James | Judas son of James |
| 12. Judas Iscariot, who betrayed him. | Judas Iscariot, who betrayed him | Judas Iscariot, a traitor. | |

### 10.3.4 The Twelve Disciples and Other Disciples

Mark gives evidence of disciples of Jesus outside the circle of the Twelve (Mark 3:13–15), and Matthew specifically speaks of them (Matt 8:19, 21) and alludes to a wider circle of disciples (10:24, 25, 42), even acknowledging through the verb *mathēteuō* that Joseph of Arimethea had "become a disciple of Jesus" (27:57). Luke indicates that Jesus chose the Twelve from among a much larger number of disciples (cf. Luke 6:13–17), and John indicates that from the large group of disciples many abandoned their commitment to Jesus and left him (cf. John 6:60–66).

"Following Jesus" (e.g., Mark 14:51) is a technical expression for being his disciple. Some disciples physically followed Jesus around as disciples in his itinerant ministry (e.g., the Twelve), while a wider group of disciples followed Jesus in a more figurative sense and stayed within their own communities. The latter was comprised of, among others, common masses of people (Luke 6:13), a variety of men and women (8:2–3; 23:49, 55; 24:13, 18, 33), tax collectors (19:1–10), scribes (Matt 8:18–21), and religious leaders (27:57; John 19:38–42). The prophetic demand to follow Jesus provided entrance of his disciples into the family of mother and brother and sister around Jesus (cf. Matt 3:31–34) but must be balanced by Jesus's admonition to observe biological family obligations (cf. Mark 7:9–13).[57]

Following Jesus meant togetherness with him while traveling on "the Way" (Acts 9:2; cf., e.g., Matt 20:17), but that following could be manifested in either a physical or figurative sense. The difference between the Twelve and the broader group of disciples is the role to which they were called.

57. Cf. David Catchpole, *Jesus People: The Historical Jesus and the Beginnings of Community* (Grand Rapids: Baker Academic, 2006), 64.

The broader group of disciples left all in a figurative sense and carried out a role of living life with Jesus and exemplifying kingdom life in the Spirit within their own communities. To the possessed man whose demons had been exorcized by Jesus and begged Jesus to go with him, Mark tells us that Jesus did not permit him but said to him, "'Go home to your own people and tell them how much the Lord has done for you, and how he has had mercy on you.' So the man went away and began to tell in the Decapolis how much Jesus had done for him. And all the people were amazed" (Mark 5:19–20). The broader group of disciples were called to the role of living within their communities and exemplifying the kingdom life that the Spirit produces.[58]

On the other hand, the Twelve were called to be coworkers with Jesus in broadcasting the kingdom message outside of their home communities. Leaving all literally to follow Jesus was a necessary sacrifice in order to join with him in the proclamation of the kingdom (Matt 10:1–15), and as a training time for their future role as apostles in the church (19:23–30).

### 10.3.5 The Women Disciples Who Followed Jesus

The Gospels and Acts give prominence to various women who were disciples of Jesus.[59] These women were part of the wider group of disciples around him, but some of them physically accompanied Jesus during his itinerancy. On a preaching tour through Galilee, Jesus had "with him" the Twelve and several women who had been healed by Jesus and who were now contributing to the support of Jesus and the Twelve (Luke 8:1–3). While parallels can be found for women supporting synagogues, rabbis, and their disciples out of their own money, property, or foodstuffs,[60] the wording indicates that these women were actual disciples of Jesus (Matt 12:49–50; Luke 8:19–21).[61] A great master with female disciples was an unusual occurrence in Palestine of the first century, yet these women exhibited the twin characteristics of Jesus's disciples: they had given up their old lives and had committed themselves to Jesus (cf. Mark 8:34–38).[62]

58. Catchpole, *Jesus People*, 60–67.

59. Ben Witherington III, *Women in the Ministry of Jesus: A Study of Jesus' Attitudes to Women and Their Roles as Reflected in His Earthly Life*, SNTSMS 51 (Cambridge: Cambridge University Press, 1984), esp. ch. 4; Witherington, *Women and the Genesis of Christianity* (Cambridge: Cambridge University Press, 1990), esp. chs. 7, 13–14; Meier, *Companions and Competitors*, 78–80; Michelle Lee-Barnewall, *Neither Complementarian nor Egalitarian: A Kingdom Corrective to the Evangelical Gender Debate* (Grand Rapids: Baker Academic, 2016), esp. 93–101; Holly J. Carey, *Women Who Do: Female Disciples in the Gospels* (Grand Rapids: Eerdmans, 2023).

60. E.g., Josephus, *Ant.* 17.41–44; see Lynn H. Cohick, *Women in the World of the Earliest Christians: Illuminating Ancient Ways of Life* (Grand Rapids: Baker Academic, 2009), chs. 5 and 9.

61. Witherington, *Women in the Ministry of Jesus*, 116–25; Witherington, *Women and the Genesis of Christianity*, 110–22; Lee-Barnewall, *Neither Complementarian nor Egalitarian*, 93–101. Contra Shin, "Matthew's Designation," 399–415, here 413.

62. See Lee-Barnewall, *Neither Complementarian nor Egalitarian*, 93–101. For a variety of other perspectives, including some feminist and some non-feminist, see Dorothy A. Lee, *The Ministry of Women in the New Testament: Reclaiming the Biblical Vision for Church Leadership* (Grand Rapids: Baker Academic, 2021); Susan E. Hylen, *Women in the New Testament World*, EBS (Oxford: Oxford University Press, 2019); Lynn Japinga, *From Daughters to Disciples: Women's Stories from the New Testament* (Louisville: Westminster John Knox, 2021); Witherington, *Women in the Ministry of Jesus*, passim; Witherington, *Women and the Genesis of Christianity*, passim. Amy-Jill Levine attempts to challenge the

This group of women followed Jesus to Jerusalem, attended the crucifixion, and were the first ones to arrive at the empty tomb. They are thus displayed in the Gospels as exemplary disciples of Jesus (Luke 23:49, 55; 24:9).[63] Holly Carey notes, "In all of their stories, the actions of these women are portrayed as models of the kind of discipleship that Jesus calls for—a discipleship that is faithful, risky, persistent, and willing to embrace suffering as the cost of following him."[64]

Later, in the book of Acts, women had significant roles in the early church.[65] Luke uses the feminine form of the word for disciple (*mathētria*, Acts 9:36) in a casual way, indicating that women believers like Tabitha were commonly called "disciples."[66]

Jesus's teaching about, and ministry to, women is both radical and conservative. It is radical because he challenges and rehabilitates some of the prevailing mindsets about women that were found within Judaism in the first century. He offers spiritual life and opens doors of ministry that many in Israel would have denied women, even in including women as his disciples.

But Jesus was conservative as well, because he was carrying forward God's will for women that had been revealed in the Old Testament from the beginning narratives of Genesis (e.g., Gen 1:26–28). Jesus's earthly mission was intended to fulfill the Law and the Prophets (Matt 5:17), which meant to bring to completion what God had intended from the very beginning.

Where the people of his day had deviated from God's will for women, Jesus stands out as a radical revolutionary who challenges the status quo of the religious elite as he asserts his authoritative statement about women and their roles. Where the people of his day had correctly sustained God's will for women, Jesus will appear to be a firm conservative who reasserts attitudes and roles for women already extant within Israel.

Ultimately, Jesus brings a dignity, value, and significance to women and their roles that God had intended from the very beginning, when God created humans as male and female and gave the mandate of being complementarian co-laborers in ruling God's world for him (Gen 1:26–28). Where women lack this because of misinterpretation of the Old Testament, or because of cultural bias, Jesus will bring restoration. Where the people of Israel had been correct in their interpretation, Jesus will bring confirmation.

---

consensus that women accompanied Jesus; see Amy-Jill Levine, "Women Itinerants, Jesus of Nazareth, and Historical-Critical Approaches: Reevaluating the Consensus," in *Gender and Second-Temple Judaism*, ed. Kathy Ehrensperger and Shayna Sheinfeld (Lexington, MD: Lexington/Fortress Academic, 2020), 45–64.

63. See Richard Bauckham, *Gospel Women: Studies of the Named Women in the Gospels* (Grand Rapids: Eerdmans, 2002), 109–202, 257–310. Stuart L. Love, *Jesus and Marginal Women: The Gospel of Matthew in Social-Scientific Perspective*, Matrix 5 (Eugene, OR: Cascade, 2009).

64. Carey, *Women Who Do*, 123.

65. After discussing the roles of Mary and Martha as sketched in Luke 10:38–42, Jennifer S. Wyant (*Beyond Mary or Martha: Reclaiming Ancient Models of Discipleship*, ESEC 21 [Atlanta: SBL, 2019]) traces the interpretation of this passage and the roles of women as disciples of Jesus throughout history.

66. Witherington, *Women and the Genesis of Christianity*, ch. 13.

Therefore, we find in the first place that Jesus restores and reaffirms to women their dignity and worth as persons who are fully equal to men as humans created in the image of God. Women are called to be disciples of Jesus alongside of male disciples. In the second place, Jesus preserves the male-female distinction of humans, so that they are restored and affirmed in the different roles that God had intended from the beginning. And in the third place, he restores and affirms to women the status of co-laborers with men in God's plan for the outworking of his will on this earth.[67]

### 10.3.6 Disciples in the Early Church

The term *mathētēs* is used regularly in Luke-Acts to designate persons who have placed their faith in Jesus the Messiah. In Luke 6:13, 17, reference is made to a great multitude of disciples. These disciples of Jesus were convinced believers in Jesus's messiahship and are set in contrast with the "great throng of people" (Luke 6:17) who were interested in Jesus but not committed to him.

This can be compared with Luke's usage of *mathētēs* in Acts, where he speaks of the multitude of believers (Acts 4:32) and the multitude of "disciples" (6:2). In Luke's writings the expressions "those who believe" and "the disciples" signify the same group of people (cf. 6:7; 9:26; 11:26; 14:21–22). As Acts records, by the time of the early church the term *disciple* had become synonymous with the true believer—all those who confessed Jesus as the Messiah—or, as Luke records, "The disciples were called Christians first at Antioch" (11:26).[68]

## 10.4 JESUS'S UNIQUE FORM OF DISCIPLESHIP

Jesus's ministry of calling, training, and sending out disciples stands as a captivating historical phenomenon. There have been numerous attempts at classifying his ministry according to other types of social/religious movements of the first century AD (e.g., as a wandering charismatic, Zealot brigand, Cynic philosopher, Qumran/Essene separatist, Jewish rabbi, apocalyptic scribe, Israelite prophet figure), which probably have revealed some authentic, parallel characteristics.[69]

In a general sense, a disciple is *a committed follower of a great master*. When Jesus arrived on the scene in the first century there were many masters with their disciples. John the Baptist had his disciples (e.g., John 1:35; 3:25), the Pharisees had their disciples (Matt 22:15–16), and various other kinds of religious and political masters had their disciples. A disciple was a person who had committed himself or herself to a master

67. For a more extensive treatment of women as disciples of Jesus, see Wilkins, "Women in the Teaching and Ministry of Jesus," 91–112, here 91–92. The final paragraphs of this section were excerpted with adaptations.

68. Wilkins, *Following the Master*, ch. 13.

69. E.g., Wenthe, "Social Configuration," 143–74; Kinney provides an added perspective on the Homeric and Hellenistic parallels: Kinney, *Hellenistic Dimensions*, esp. ch. 8.

and the master's expectations. The form of discipleship varied significantly, according to the goals of the master.

But the goal of the disciple in most cases was—after a significant time of training and study—to become a master with his own disciples.

On the surface, Jesus had many of the characteristics of a Jewish rabbi. As mentioned above (7.2.10), the terms "*rabbi*" and "*rabbouni*"[70] refer to a teacher, master, lord. Of the seventeen times that terms for "rabbi" occur in the New Testament, fourteen times they refer to Jesus. Twelve of those times they are used by Jesus's disciples to designate him, once by blind Bartimaeus, and once by Nicodemus. Then, twice Jesus refers to Jewish leaders (scribes and Pharisees) as rabbis, and once John the Baptist is called rabbi by his disciples. Jesus taught in their synagogues and on the Sabbath, he taught in accordance with Jewish customs, he is given respect due a teacher of the law, his disciples followed him around, and he is called "rabbi" (Matt 26:49; Mark 9:5; John 1:49). On the surface Jesus had appearances of a rabbi.

The apparent normal pattern in Israel was for a prospective disciple to approach a rabbi and ask to study with him. Joshua ben Perahyah said, "Set up a master for yourself. And get you a fellow disciple" (m. Avot 1.6 [Neusner]), which Gamaliel echoed, "Set up a master for yourself. Avoid doubt" (m. Avot 1.16 [Neusner]; cf. Matt. 8:19). Later rabbinic disciples followed their master around, often physically imitating the master's teaching of Torah because imitating the master is imitating Moses' imitation of God.[71] Thus, in general within the world of Judaism a disciple of a rabbi was a person in training to become a rabbi.

In the specific sense of a *disciple of Jesus*, we have a much more focused definition than other forms of master-disciple relationships. In its essence, Jesus's form of discipleship was radically different. Throughout his ministry Jesus clarified the goals and characteristics of his form of discipleship, so that we can say that a disciple of Jesus is *a person who has been called by Jesus to eternal life, has claimed him as Savior and God, and has embarked upon the life of following him alone and always.* Therefore, Jesus was starkly different from other synagogue rabbis, and his disciples were likewise starkly different from other forms of disciples. In the following ways Jesus developed a unique form of discipleship that was inaugurated with his announcement of the arrival of the kingdom of God and summoning men and women to be his disciples.

### 10.4.1 Called by Jesus

In the first place, Jesus *called* those who would be his followers. It was a voluntary commitment with other forms of discipleship. In rabbinic circles and in Greek

70. ῥαββί from רַב, "lord, master," רַבִּי, "my lord'; ῥαββουνί, a heightened or intensified form of *rabbi*, ῥαββί (cf. "ῥαββουνί," BDAG 902).

71. Neusner, *Invitation to the Talmud*, 79–80.

philosophical schools, a person made a voluntary decision to join the school of the master and in so doing became a disciple. As Jesus's ministry unfolds, he begins to establish a form of discipleship that is unlike the rabbis.[72]

With Jesus, the initiative lay with his call (Matt 4:19; 9:9; Mark 1:17; 2:14; cf. Luke 5:10–11, 27–28) and his choice (John 15:16) of those who would be his disciples. Jesus's call established the high mark of his form of discipleship. That call must be understood within the broader biblical concept of "calling,"[73] because it is a call that demands a decision of life commitment from those who are curious.[74] The call focused people on making a commitment to Jesus, summoning them to place their unreserved faith in him as the one coming with the proclamation of the kingdom. The call at this stage meant commitment to Jesus personally. It also included some sense of joining with Jesus in his announcement that the kingdom of God had arrived. For some this meant that they were to accompany Jesus physically, but not all were called to follow Jesus around physically.

### 10.4.2 Responding to the Call to Follow Jesus

The response to Jesus's call involves recognition and belief in his identity (John 2:11; 6:68–69), obedience to his summons (Mark 1:18, 20), and counting the cost of full allegiance to him (Matt 19:23–30; Luke 14:25–28). Responding to his call is the beginning of something new. It means losing one's old life (Matt 8:34–37; Luke 9:23–25) and finding new life in the family of God through obeying the will of the Father (Matt 12:46–50).[75]

During Jesus's earthly ministry the disciple was to "follow" Jesus, an allegiance to his person which is regarded as the decisive act, whether it is a literal or figurative attachment. The outward "following" of a disciple after Jesus in ethical behavior is always motivated by the inward obedience of the heart. It is an inside-out transformation that characterizes the disciple who follows Jesus.[76]

### 10.4.3 Counting the Cost of Eternal Life

The theme of "counting the cost" provides a primary emphasis in Jesus's ministry (e.g., Matt 19:16–23; cf. Luke 9:57–62; 18:24–30). The call to eternal life was extended to all who would come after him. It was given to individuals and to the crowds of people who had not yet made a decision to enter into eternal life and discipleship to Jesus.

72. Hezser, "Followers, Servants, and Traitors," 71–88.

73. K. L. Schmidt, "*kaleō*, κ.τ.λ.," *TDNT* 3:487–536; L. Coenen, "Call; *kaleō*," "Church, Synagogue; *ekklēsia*," *NIDNTT* 1:271–76, 291–307.

74. Kingsbury, "On Following Jesus," 49.

75. Craig S. Keener, *The Historical Jesus of the Gospels* (Grand Rapids: Eerdmans, 2009), esp. 196–213. See also Lehel Lészai, *Discipleship in the Synoptics* (Cluj-Napoca, Romania: Cluj University Press, 2017), 301.

76. Matthias Konradt, "Following Jesus and Fulfilling the Law: Considerations on the Ethical Conception of the Gospel of Matthew," in Seleznev, Loader, and Niebuhr, *Gospel of Matthew*, 275–94; here 294.

The "god" of the rich young man's life was his wealth (Matt 19:16–23). Jesus knew his heart and challenged him with exchanging wealth as his god for Jesus as his God. The rich young man could not give up his wealth for Jesus as his God, and Matthew comments insightfully, "he went away sad, because he had great wealth" (19:22). He had preferred his great wealth over the wealth of Jesus as his Master and God and entering the kingdom of heaven (19:23).

Possessions all too often become one's source of security, one's badge of self-worth, one's means of personal power. Jesus challenges the crowd to find their security, self-worth, and power in him. They must count the cost of what a wholehearted commitment to Jesus requires and exchange the god of their life for Jesus as the God of their life and entering the kingdom of heaven.[77]

### 10.4.4 Personalized Cost and Cross

However, the cost of each person's following Jesus in discipleship was personalized in keeping with the inclinations of the heart of the individual and the will of the Father. Although the rich young man was called to give up his riches, Nicodemus and Joseph of Arimathea, who became disciples of Jesus sometime during his earthly ministry (cf. John 3:1–14; 19:38–42), remained within the religious establishment and retained their wealth. When demonstration of their faith and allegiance to Jesus was required, they came forward to claim the body of Jesus (27:57–60). Although they were wealthy individuals, apparently wealth was not the same kind of personal "god" that it was for the rich young man. Their wealth and influence were used later for the great privilege of supplying a new tomb for the crucified Jesus to occupy until his resurrection. Nicodemus and Joseph of Arimathea were courageous in remaining in the religious establishment of Israel while at the same time exemplifying what it is to be bold disciples of Jesus.[78]

Jesus is not here asking all within the crowd to give away everything in order to become disciples, because other followers continued to retain possessions while becoming disciples of Jesus: for example, Peter and Andrew retained a house after their calling (Mark 1:29), Joseph of Arimathea was a wealthy disciple (Matt 27:57; Luke 23:50–53), and the women followers supported Jesus out of their own possessions (cf. Luke 8:1–3; 14:33).

Each person must count the cost of allegiance to Jesus, but that cost is personalized by Jesus to each individual. I refer to these as the "gods" of our lives that must be rejected in place of having Jesus as our God. Jesus knows the heart of each one whom he calls, but the cost remains for each. The "cost" of discipleship is one's life.

77. Norval Geldenhuys, *Commentary on the Gospel of Luke*, NICNT (Grand Rapids: Eerdmans, 1951), 398–99.

78. For a treatment of the ambiguity of the evangelists' portrayal of Nicodemus and Joseph of Arimathea, see David M. Allen, "Secret Disciples: Nicodemus and Joseph of Arimathea," in Keith and Hurtado, *Jesus Among Friends and Enemies*, 149–69.

## 10.4.5 Jesus Breaks Down Barriers of Status, Religion, Gender, Nationalism

Unlike the some of the sectarians within Judaism, Jesus broke through the barriers that separated the clean from the unclean, the obedient from the sinful. He summoned the common fisherman as well as the traitorous tax collector, and even a zealous revolutionary. He indicated that Jews and gentiles would join him in the future kingdom banquet (Matt 8:10–12). Both men and women were his closest followers (e.g., Luke 8:1–3; 23:55). A decisive factor in his form of discipleship is that Jesus called to himself those who, in the eyes of sectarians, did not seem to enjoy the necessary qualifications for fellowship with him (Matt 9:9–13; Mark 2:13–17).[79] In calling the despised to himself (Matt 9:9), in sitting down to a meal with tax collectors and sinners (9:10), and in having women among his circle of disciples (12:49–50), Jesus demonstrates that they have been adopted into discipleship to him and fellowship with God.[80]

## 10.4.6 Transformational Kingdom Discipleship

Discipleship is the ongoing process of growth as a disciple; it means becoming like Jesus in every area of life. As individuals responded to Jesus's call to kingdom life and became his disciples, they entered into a transformational kingdom life of discipleship. I define this transformational discipleship as "living a fully human life in this world in union with Jesus Christ and his people, growing in conformity to his image, and helping others to become like Jesus."[81]

We will discuss this more fully below as we explore Matthew's unique perspective of discipleship, but this is a preview of how unique Jesus's form of discipleship was in the first century and today.

## 10.4.7 Attachment to Jesus: A Disciple of Jesus Is Always a Disciple of Jesus

Jewish disciples followed their master around, often literally imitating him. The goal of Jewish disciples was someday to become masters, or rabbis, themselves and to

79. For a discussion of the social background of Jesus and disciples, see Ekkehard W. Stegemann and Wolfgang Stegemann, *The Jesus Movement: A Social History of Its First Century*, trans. O. C. Dean Jr. (Minneapolis: Fortress, 1999), esp. 187–220. For a somewhat non-stereotypical perspective on the women in Matthew's Gospel as epitomized by the anointing woman (26:6–13), Levine suggests that women in Matthew's Gospel are independent, with access to their own funds, unconcerned with potential scandal or criticism, and free to do what they want; see Amy-Jill Levine, "The Gospel of Matthew: Between Breaking and Continuity," in *Gospels: Narrative and History*, ed. Mercedes Navarro Puerto and Marinella Perroni; English edition ed. Amy-Jill Levine, *The Bible and Women: An Encyclopaedia of Exegesis and Cultural History*, The Bible and Women: New Testament 2.1 (Atlanta: Society of Biblical Literature, 2015), 121–44; here 142.

80. Dunn, *Jesus' Call to Discipleship*, ch. 4. For a colorful treatment of the varied characters around Jesus, see Greg Carey, *Sinners: Jesus and His Earliest Followers* (Waco, TX: Baylor University Press, 2009).

81. See Wilkins, *Following the Master*, 41–42; Michael J. Wilkins, *In His Image: Reflecting Christ in Everyday Life* (Colorado Springs, CO: NavPress, 1997; repr., Eugene, OR: Wipf & Stock, 2019), 55.

have their own disciples who would follow them. But Jesus's disciples were to remain disciples of their master and teacher and to follow him only (cf. Matt 23:1–12). For Jesus, discipleship was not simply an academic or religious program. Discipleship was a life that began in relationship with him as master and moved into all areas of their experience. Even though his disciples were to be taught to obey all that Jesus commanded (Matt 28:20) and it is probable that they memorized much of his teaching and passed it on as the tradition of the church, the disciples were committed to his person.[82] Following Jesus means togetherness with him and service to him in his mission.

### 10.4.8 Continuing to Count the Cost

Even as initially committing oneself to Jesus required the would-be disciple to count the cost, so following Jesus requires disciples to continue to count the cost (Mark 8:34). Discipleship *begins* through entrance to the way of salvation; discipleship *advances* as one travels along the way each day with Jesus. Luke reveals to us that self-denial, taking up the cross, and following Jesus not only characterize entrance into the way, but also characterize life on the way. "Then he said to them all: 'Whoever wants to be my disciple must deny themselves and take up their cross *daily* and follow me'" (Luke 9:23, emphasis added). With the inclusion of "daily" to the cross-bearing proclamation, the Lukan account specifies that denial of one's own will and taking up the will of the Father to follow the Master is something that must occur on a daily basis.

It is possible for one not to be a true disciple while externally traveling with Jesus. For example, Judas Iscariot followed Jesus throughout his ministry, and there were many of Jesus's disciples who followed him about for some period of time, but when Jesus confronted them, he declared that some of them did not truly believe, at which time many of these disciples no longer followed Jesus (John 6:60–66). Apparently, these disciples were following Jesus because he was an exciting new miracle worker and teacher (cf. 2:23–25). When Jesus's teaching did not conform to their expectations, they left him. These individuals had attached themselves as "disciples" to the Jesus movement, but they were not truly in line with Jesus's goals. Therefore, the challenge to count the cost is directed not only to the crowd but also to the disciples (cf. Mark 8:34–9:1; Matt 10:37–39; 16:24–26; Luke 9:23–27).

Salvation is a gracious gift from God. We must count the cost of the future journey along the way, then be prepared for a lifetime of paying the cost of an all-or-nothing discipleship to Jesus.

82. Rengstorf, "μαθητής," *TDNT* 4:415–61.

### 10.4.9 Traveling Along the Way

Jesus's life is continually set before the disciples as the example of the life that is given over to fulfilling the will of God. Therefore, the blessed life on the way is the one who hears and obeys the Word of God (Luke 11:27–28). Not all who walk on the way truly belong to the Way. External statements of commitment must be judged by the fruit of one's life (6:43–49; 19:11–27). That fruit consists, at least in part, in loving and doing good to others (6:17–36), proper stewardship of material possessions (6:35; 8:3), servanthood (22:24–30), prayer (10:2; 11:1; 18:1–8), and testimony to the Way (9:1–6; 10:1–12, 17–20; 12:8–12; 14:23–24; 24:44–49).

Through the incident of some disciples leaving, Jesus establishes a definition of what it means to be his disciple. Once the disciples leave, Jesus turns to the Twelve and asks, "You do not want to leave too, do you?" Simon Peter steps forward and gives a statement which is a hallmark of true discipleship to Jesus: "Lord, to whom shall we go? You have the words of eternal life. We have come to believe and know that you are the Holy One of God" (John 6:67–69). Peter functions as a spokesperson for the definition of true discipleship. Jesus's true followers, his true disciples, are people who make a true faith commitment to him (although some continue to do so falsely, like Judas: 6:70–71). Ben Cooper describes this true faith commitment as a "theocentric commitment" and may be summarized as *incorporated servanthood*. He explains, "To be committed to God is to be a disciple of Jesus, incorporated into the divine Servant program for the world."[83]

At this stage of the Jesus movement the contrast between true and false discipleship is starkly drawn, and faith in Jesus clearly shifts to faith in him for eternal life. Those disciples who left did not rightly understand Jesus's messianic ministry and did not truly believe on him. They were following Jesus with earthly expectations. Peter speaks for the other disciples by stating that true discipleship means basing one's hope of eternal life on Jesus as the Holy One of God. Discipleship for Peter and the other disciples was a matter of life with Jesus both now and for eternity.[84]

### 10.4.10 Becoming Like Jesus

Jesus declared that to be a disciple is to become like the master (Matt 10:24–25; Luke 6:40).[85] Becoming like Jesus includes going out with the same message, ministry, and compassion (10:5–23), practicing the same religious and social traditions (12:1–8; Mark 2:18–22), belonging to the same family of obedience (Matt 12:46–49), exercising the same selfless servanthood (20:26–28; Mark 10:42–45; John 13:12–17), and experiencing the same suffering (Matt 10:16–25; Mark 10:38–39).

83. Cooper, *Incorporated Servanthood*, 252.
84. Wilkins, *Following the Master*, 114–16.
85. See Konradt, "Following Jesus and Fulfilling the Law," esp. 290–94.

Analogous to other master-disciple relationships, Jesus's disciples would become like him and carry out the same ministry as he did. But Jesus's disciples would become like him in a unique way. The spiritual unity that would be established between Jesus and his disciples—Jesus in them and they in Jesus (cf. John 17:13–26)—guaranteed a likeness quite unknown in any other kind of discipleship relationship.[86] This aspect of discipleship to Jesus prepares the way for the "transformation" language found prominently in the Pauline letters, where the ultimate goal of the believer's life is to be transformed and conformed to the image of Christ (cf. Rom 8:29; 2 Cor 3:18; Gal 4:19).

### 10.4.11 Commissioned by Jesus

Jesus committed his earthly ministry to "making disciples" within Israel (cf. John 4:1), and he commissioned his disciples to "make disciples" among the nations (Matt 28:16–20). They do so by proclaiming the gospel message among those who have not yet received forgiveness of sins, with the intent of them becoming Jesus's disciples (cf. Luke 24:46–47; John 20:21).[87] The command finds remarkable verbal fulfillment in the activities of the early church (e.g., Acts 14:21), where disciples went from Jerusalem to Judea, to Samaria, to the ends of the earth proclaiming the message of Jesus and making disciples. In the early church, to believe in the gospel message was to become a disciple (cf. Acts 4:32 with 6:2). Jonathan Lunde refers to this as "covenantal discipleship," which he describes as "learning to receive and respond to God's grace and demand, which are mediated through Jesus, the Servant King, so as to reflect God's character in relation to him, to others, and to the world, in order that all may come to experience this same grace and respond to this same demand."[88]

## 10.5 Gospel Portraits of Jesus and the Disciples

Jesus developed a unique form of discipleship in his earthly ministry that carries on to us today. In this next section we will focus on Matthew's theological perspective of discipleship to Jesus and how that informs the way in which Matthew's community, including believers like us today, are transformed members of Jesus's kingdom community.

Students of the four Gospels have long recognized that each Gospel presents the record of Jesus's life from a different perspective. Richard Burridge comments how the early church drew on the symbolism of Ezek 1:10 and Rev 4:7 of four living creatures around the divine throne to represent the emphases of the four Gospels—the human,

86. Niebuhr, "Matthew's Idea of Being Human," 333–35.

87. Lehel Lészai, "The Mission of the Disciples," *Sacra Scripta* 9.1 (2011): 65–83.

88. Jonathan Lunde, *Following Jesus, the Servant King: A Biblical Theology of Covenantal Discipleship* (Grand Rapids: Zondervan, 2010), esp. 276–87.

the lion, the ox, and the eagle.[89] These four pictures stood for the Gospels and the imagery was used for summaries of the gospel message. The images varied over the centuries but overall attempted to portray that Jesus was born as a man, sacrificed like an ox, rose again triumphant like a lion, and ascended like an eagle, extending his wings to protect his people.[90]

If each Gospel has different perspectives about Jesus, we might expect to find different perspectives about his closest companions, the disciples. And such is indeed the case—each Gospel records a unique perspective of Jesus's disciples. Each focuses on distinctive features that help us understand Jesus's purpose in calling and training his disciples.[91] Joseph Fitzmyer states, "We have in the four canonical Gospels portraits of Jesus with lines, shadows, colors, and *chiaroscuro* [contrasted light and shadows in painting] that differ. The Marcan Jesus acts differently from the Lukan Jesus; the Matthean Jesus speaks differently from the Johannine Jesus. Correspondingly, the role of discipleship differs in the four Gospels."[92]

The scene that depicts disciples following Jesus around during his earthly ministry dominates the Gospel panorama. That vision of discipleship demands our attention, both on a historical as well as a personal level. Discipleship can be understood narrowly as a technical discussion of the historical master-disciple relationship. It can also be understood in a broader way as Christian experience and what such a way of life requires, implies, and entails.[93] To understand fully the gospel portrait of discipleship, one must keep in view (a) the moment within the early life of Jesus in which the challenge of discipleship is given to and lived out by the disciples, and (b) the moment within the church's life when the would-be disciple is tested.[94]

Elsewhere I have displayed the portraits of the disciples of Jesus as they are found in the four individual Gospel records.[95] This gives us the broadest perspective of Jesus's form of discipleship as seen from the four evangelists' perspectives. Each Gospel focuses on distinctive features that help us understand Jesus's purpose in calling and training his disciples. Combined, the sketches of the disciples in each Gospel give us a well-rounded perspective of what Jesus intended discipleship to mean.

89. Burridge, *Four Gospels, One Jesus?*, 25–33.

90. Burridge, *Four Gospels, One Jesus?*, 30.

91. See John K. Goodrich and Mark L. Strauss, eds. *Following Jesus Christ: The New Testament Message of Discipleship for Today. A Volume in Honor of Michael J. Wilkins* (Grand Rapids: Kregel, 2019), chs. 1–4; Paul D. Hanson, *The People Called: The Growth of Community in the Bible* (San Francisco: Harper & Row, 1986), 430–38.

92. Joseph A. Fitzmyer, *Luke the Theologian: Aspects of His Teaching* (New York: Paulist, 1989), 118.

93. See Richard L. Longenecker, ed., *Patterns of Discipleship in the New Testament* (Grand Rapids: Eerdmans, 1996), 1–7; Fernando F. Segovia, "Introduction: Call and Discipleship—Toward a Re-examination of the Shape and Character of Christian Existence in the New Testament," in *Discipleship in the New Testament*, ed. Fernando F. Segovia (Philadelphia: Fortress, 1985), 2. See also Ernest Best, *Disciples and Discipleship: Studies in the Gospel According to Mark* (Edinburgh: T&T Clark, 1986), 1–2.

94. John J. Vincent, "Discipleship and Synoptic Studies," *ThZ* 16 (1960), 464. For various expositions of this theme by a broadly evangelical, leading German NT scholar, see Ernst Käsemann, *On Being a Disciple of the Crucified Nazarene: Unpublished Lectures and Sermons*, ed. Rudolf Landau and Wolfgang Kraus, trans. Roy A. Harrisville (Grand Rapids: Eerdmans, 2010).

95. Wilkins, *Following the Master*, chs. 9–12.

| Matthew | Mark | Luke | John |
|---|---|---|---|
| **The Transformed Disciple** (12:46–50; 28:18–20) | **The Servant Disciple** (10:45) | **The Costly Disciple** (14:25–33) | **The Evidential Disciple** (8:31–32; 13:34–35; 15:7–8) |
| *Transformed Paradigms with a Commission* | *Servants of the Redemptive Servant* | *Followers on the Costly Way* | *Believers Marked by Jesus* |

## 10.6 MATTHEW'S PORTRAIT OF JESUS'S DISCIPLES: TRANSFORMED PARADIGMS WITH A COMMISSION

Our primary intention in this section is to accentuate Matthew's perception of discipleship.[96] I have observed that Matthew's portrait of Jesus's disciples gives the overall perspective of "Transformed Paradigms with a Commission."

At least four options present themselves to us as we try to understand Matthew's intention in his portrayal of the disciples. Readers could decide on one of four ways of viewing the disciples in Matthew's Gospel.[97]

1. **No one should identify with the disciples in Matthew's narrative.** The disciples have a unique role in history that applies only to them. Georg Strecker places the disciples strictly within the moment of the earthly life of Jesus, thus idealizing the disciples in the past.[98] This is explained as an "idealization" or

96. The literature on discipleship in Matthew is substantial. I have alluded to other scholars who have studied Matthew's perception of discipleship in our discussion above and will interact with others below. We also will pay special attention to commentaries on Matthew, where the study of discipleship is a necessary pursuit. A few articles and monographs that deserve particular mention are the following, from various perspectives: Goodrich and Strauss, *Following Jesus Christ*; Brown, *Disciples in Narrative Perspective*; Brown, "Living Out Justice, Mercy, and Loyalty: Discipleship in Matthew's Gospel," in Goodrich and Strauss, *Following Jesus Christ*, 9–26; Carey, *Women Who Do*, esp. 104–35; Cooper, *Incorporated Servanthood*; Roland Deines, "Description of Faith in the Gospel of Matthew," in Sweatman and Kvidahl, *Treasures New & Old*, 125–64; Dunn, *Jesus' Call to Discipleship*; Terence L. Donaldson, "Guiding Readers—Making Disciples: Discipleship in Matthew's Narrative Strategy," in Longenecker, *Patterns of Discipleship*, 30–49; Richard A. Edwards, "Uncertain Faith: Matthew's Portrait of the Disciples," in Segovia, *Discipleship in the New Testament*, 47–61; Edwards, *Matthew's Narrative Portrait of Disciples: How the Text-Connoted Reader Is Informed* (Harrisburg, PA: Trinity Press International, 1997); Rebekah Eklund, "Matthew, the Cross, and the Cruciform Life," in *Cruciform Scripture: Cross, Participation, and Mission*, ed. Christopher W. Skinner, Nijay K. Gupta, Andy Johnson, and Drew J. Strait (Grand Rapids: Eerdmans, 2021), 16–30; Luz, "Disciples in the Gospel"; Henry Pattarumadathil, *"Your Father in Heaven": Discipleship in Matthew as a Process of Becoming Children of God*, AnBib 172 (Rome: Pontificio Istituto Biblico, 2008); P. Schreiner, *Matthew, Disciple and Scribe*; Cedric E. W. Vine, *Jesus and the Nations: Discipleship and Mission in the Gospel of Matthew* (Eugene, OR: Pickwick, 2022); Wilkins, *Concept of Disciple*, esp. chs. 4–5 and "Conclusion"; Wilkins, *Following the Master*, 147–93; Joel Willitts, "The Twelve Disciples in Matthew," in Gurtner, Willitts, and Burridge, *Jesus, Matthew's Gospel and Early Christianity*, 166–79.

97. For a helpful discussion, see Hank Voss, *The Priesthood of All Believers and the* Missio Dei*: A Canonical, Catholic, and Contextual Perspective*, PTMS 223 (Eugene, OR: Pickwick, 2016), loc. 3175–97, Kindle. I have dealt with this discussion more fully in Wilkins, "Discipleship Models," in *Following the Master*, 24–47. See also Willitts, "Twelve Disciples in Matthew," 166–79, who calls for rendering the twelve disciples at one and the same time uniquely historical and historically transcendent.

98. Strecker, *Der Weg der Gerechtigkeit*, 86–122, 191–98.

"historicizing" tendency: "The disciples, like the person of Jesus, are placed in the unrepeatable, holy past."[99]

2. **Only truly committed believers can identify with the disciples in Matthew's narrative.** Several scholars and teachers suggest that a disciple is a committed Christian, a believer who has made a commitment to follow Jesus and obey his radical demands of discipleship.[100] Dwight Pentecost asserts, "There is a vast difference between being saved and being a disciple. Not all men who are saved are disciples although all who are disciples are saved. In discussing the question of discipleship, we are not dealing with a man's salvation. We are dealing with a man's relationship to Jesus Christ as his teacher, his Master, and his Lord."[101]
3. **Only the leaders of the Christian community should identify with the disciples in Matthew's narrative.** Matthew presents the disciples as leaders, and only leaders should identify with them.[102] Commenting on a similar phenomenon in Mark's Gospel, Dennis Sweetland states that everyone is called to participate in the reign of God, but only some are called to be followers of Jesus. "The disciple of Jesus is called to serve other members of the eschatological community (cf. Mk 1:31) and, through the missionary enterprise, those outside the community as well."[103]
4. **All followers of Jesus should identify with the disciples in Matthew's narrative.** Matthew presents the disciples of Jesus in their unique historical setting but also so that they become examples of how Jesus transforms and uses all disciples in the outworking of his will throughout history. Matthew had a desire to pass on faithfully the historical story of Jesus and his disciples, but he also had a desire to interpret that history from his own perspective for

99. Strecker, *Der Weg der Gerechtigkeit*, 194: "Idealisierung": "Die Jünger sind wie die Person Jesus der unwiederholbaren, heiligen Vergangenheit eingeordnet." For discussion of this view, see Luz, "Disciples in the Gospel," 115–48.

100. E.g., Zane C. Hodges, *The Gospel Under Siege: A Study on Faith and Works* (Dallas: Redención Viva, 1981), 36–45; Hodges, *Absolutely Free: A Biblical Reply to Lordship Salvation* (Grand Rapids: Zondervan; Dallas: Redención Viva, 1989), 67–87; Allan Coppedge, *The Biblical Principles of Discipleship* (Grand Rapids: Zondervan, 1989), 40–42; Bruce Stopher, *Disciples Who Make Disciples: Honest Questions Real Answers* (San Antonio: Seven Servants, 2019), 49; Lucas Kitchen, *Salvation and Discipleship: Is There A Difference?* (Longview, TX: Lucas Kitchen, 2017), esp. chs. 1–3; Leroy Eims, *The Lost Art of Disciple Making* (Grand Rapids: Zondervan; Colorado Springs: NavPress, 1978), 61–83, 181–188; Walter A. Henrichsen, *Disciples Are Made—Not Born* (Wheaton, IL Victor, 1974), 18, 40; Gary W. Kuhne, *The Dynamics of Discipleship Training: Being and Producing Spiritual Leaders* (Grand Rapids: Zondervan, 1978), 15; Juan Carlos Ortiz, *Disciple* (Carol Stream, IL: Creation House, 1975), 9; 14; Paul W. Powell, *The Complete Disciple* (Wheaton, IL: Victor, 1982), 11–12; J. Oswald Sanders, *Spiritual Maturity* (Chicago: Moody, 1962), 108–9.

101. J. Dwight Pentecost, *Design for Discipleship* (Grand Rapids: Zondervan, 1971), 14.

102. Paul S. Minear, "The Disciples and the Crowds in the Gospel of Matthew," *AThRSup* 3 (1974): 28–44; Mark Sheridan, "Disciples and Discipleship in Matthew and Luke," *Biblical Theology Bulletin* 3 (1973), 235–55; Raymond Thysman, *Communaute et directives ethiques: la catechese de Matthieu*, Recherches et Synthèses: Section d'exegese 1 (Gembloux, Belgium: Duculot, 1974).

103. Dennis M. Sweetland, *Our Journey with Jesus: Discipleship According to Mark*, GNS 22 (Wilmington, DE: Michael Glazier, 1987), 17, 35.

> the needs of his audience.[104] John Yueh-Han Yieh states, "Matthew presents Jesus' disciples as a paradigm of discipleship. As characters in the story, their interaction with Jesus functions as a mirror allowing the readers to evaluate their own relationships with Jesus."[105] As the Messiah and the Son of God, Jesus is the only teacher in the church. The church should be a community of Jesus's disciples—teaching, learning, and obeying all that he has commanded.[106] An approximation of this balanced view occurs in Robert Guelich's statement: "The evangelist's genuine interest in the past, as seen by his consistent use of the disciples as the Twelve, has a present application. The past tradition is not merely preserved; rather, it is used in terms of the context and concerns of the present situation."[107]

I propose that this fourth view is the most accurate way of interpreting the portrait of the disciples in Matthew's Gospel. **In this latter view, a disciple is the true believer who enters the life of discipleship at the time of conversion.** In this paradigm, conversion is the beginning point of becoming a disciple, and discipleship is vitally linked to it as the natural result. Discipleship is not a second step in the Christian life but rather is synonymous with the Christian life. Discipleship is not something reserved solely for leaders or leaders in training but is the expression of the normal Christian life. At conversion, one becomes a disciple of Jesus, and the process of growth as a Christian is called discipleship.

This view of discipleship emphasizes that as Jesus called men and women to himself, and as he sent his disciples out to make other disciples, he was calling men and women into a saving relationship with himself that *would* make a difference in the new disciple's life. Therefore, Jesus's purpose in the Great Commission included both conversion and growth, i.e., "making disciples" meant that one became a disciple at the moment of conversion and growth in discipleship was the natural result of the new disciple's life. As a paradigm, Jesus's disciples become a very practical and realistic display of what one must be to be called a disciple (28:16, 18).[108]

We now turn to exploring that endeavor. The following discussion will attempt to display Matthew's portrayal of disciples of Jesus as "transformed paradigms with a commission." As readers of Matthew's Gospel, this is encouragement to all of us in our discipleship to Jesus.

---

104. This has been described by Gerhard Barth as "transparency": "an equating of the time of the Church with the time of the earthly activity of Jesus"; Gerhard Barth, "Matthew's Understanding of the Law," in *Tradition and Interpretation in Matthew*, ed. Günther Bornkamm, Gerhard Barth, and Heinz Joachim Held, trans. Percy Scott (Philadelphia: Westminster, 1963), 58–164, here 111. For discussion of this view, see Luz, "Disciples in the Gospel," 115–48.

105. Yieh, *One Teacher*, 302.

106. Yieh, *One Teacher*, 330.

107. Guelich, *Sermon on the Mount*, 53.

108. Voss, *Priesthood of All Believers*, loc. 3197, Kindle.

### 10.6.1 Matthew's Perspective of Jesus's Disciples as "Saved," "Righteous," and "Transformed"

Matthew displays Jesus's disciples and would-be disciples with various expressions that designate their relationship to Jesus and the kingdom of heaven. Three expressions have significant importance for Matthew's portrait of the disciples: "saved," "righteous," and "kingdom transformed."

#### *10.6.1.1 Save His People from Their Sins (1:21)*

The explicit terms for "salvation" (*sōtēria*) and "Savior" (*sōtēr*) are not found in Matthew's Gospel. However, the related term *sōzo*, meaning "save," "rescue," "deliver" is significant for understanding the concept of salvation in Matthew's Gospel.

Early in the narrative of the arrival of Jesus Messiah through miraculous conception, Matthew records how an angel of the Lord appeared to Joseph in a dream and said, "Joseph son of David, do not be afraid to take Mary home as your wife, because what is conceived in her is from the Holy Spirit. She will give birth to a son, and you are to give him the name Jesus, because he will save his people from their sins" (Matt 1:20–21).

"Sins" (*hamartiai*) refers to the violation or transgression of a normative standard prescribed by God in thought, word, or action (or inaction). Sin is alienation from God and ultimately is at the root of death, both temporal and eternal. "Sin" is understood by Matthew not only as a theological abstraction but also as a real reflection upon human thought and behavior that violated right relationships with both other human beings and with God.[109] Hence, Jesus will "save" his people from their sins that have caused alienation and death.

The word for "save" (*sōzō*) has both a theological and physical sense. In its physical sense *sōzō* is used primarily to rescue from physical death (8:25; 14:30; 27:40, 42, 49). In its theological sense (1:21; 16:25), *sōzō* denotes, negatively, deliverance from sin, death, and divine wrath. Positively, *sōzō* denotes the bestowal of far-ranging spiritual blessings both temporal and eternal. Jesus Messiah's people are promised both deliverance and blessings.[110]

The term "people," in the expression "he will save his people from their sins," is *laos*, which in Matthew's Gospel consistently refers to the people of Israel (e.g., 2:6; 27:25).[111] God is initiating the salvation of his covenant people Israel by sending Jesus to bring to them the long-awaited and promised salvation.[112]

Jesus Messiah came to save his people from their sins. But how? Matthew does not

---

109. Siker, *Sin in the New Testament*, 51.

110. Bruce Demarest, *The Cross and Salvation: The Doctrine of Salvation*, FET (Wheaton, IL: Crossway, 1997).

111. Luz, *Matthew 1–7*, 95; Nolland, *Matthew*, 98.

112. Siker, *Sin in the New Testament*, 23.

answer that question explicitly here, but the reader within Matthew's community, near and far, already understands that Jesus will save his people from their sins by offering his life in death upon the cross. The reader anticipates that Jesus's salvific birth will culminate in his salvific death and resurrection. The statement of Jesus at the Last Supper recapitulates what was announced at the outset of the Gospel: "This is my blood of the covenant, which is poured out for many for the forgiveness of sins" (26:28). Thus, the salvific death of Jesus is already announced in his birth story (1:21), and this becomes a beacon that sets a trajectory for Matthew's Gospel (e.g., 3:1–6; 9:2–8; 20:28; 26:26).[113] Salvation from their sins is central to Jesus's mission to "his people."

As Matthew's Gospel unfolds, it becomes increasingly clear that "his people" will include all those who believe in Jesus Messiah, because he is the Son of Man who has come "to give his life as a ransom for many" (20:28). Saving his people from their sins will be realized in the forgiveness of the sins of a paralyzed man in Jesus's own town (9:1–8), in the calling of sinners, not the righteous (9:13), in the forgiveness sins in Jesus's community of the church (18:21–35), in the forgiveness of the sins of many through the pouring out of Jesus's blood (26:26–29), and in making disciples of all the nations (28:18–20). Thus, Matthew provides a statement of hope for the present and future salvation from sins for his people Israel and for the new community of faith.[114]

### *10.6.1.2 Surpassing Righteousness and the Kingdom of Heaven*

In addition to his disciples being saved "from their sins" (Matt 1:21) Matthew uses the noun "righteousness" (*dikaiosynē*) as an expression that designates disciples in their relationship to Jesus and the kingdom of heaven. The term occurs seven times in Matthew's Gospel (3:15; 5:6, 10, 20; 6:1, 33; 21:32), more than in any other writing of the New Testament, except for Romans and 2 Corinthians. Five of the seven occur in the Sermon on the Mount. Guelich states: "It is evident from its distribution that *righteousness* (δικαιοσύνη) is both Matthean and one of his key concepts in the Sermon."[115] Betz remarks, "Within the SM [Sermon on the Mount], the term δικαιοσύνη occupies a place of central importance."[116] Davies and Allison

113. Siker, *Sin in the New Testament*, 53. Cf. Davies and Allison, *Matthew*, 1:210; France, *Gospel of Matthew*, 54; Gundry, *Matthew*, 23–24; Hagner, *Matthew*, 1:19; Nolland, *Matthew*, 98–99; Turner, *Matthew*, 67–68; Luz, *Matthew*, 1:95; Luz, *Theology of the Gospel of Matthew*, 71. Contra Baxter, "Missing Matthew's Political Messiah," who contends that Matthew believed that national-political liberation was an integral part of Jesus's messianic mission and that Jesus will save his people from the political ramifications of their sins.

114. See, e.g., Turner, *Matthew*, 68; Nolland, *Matthew*, 98; Boris Repschinski, "'For He Will Save His People from Their Sins' (Matthew 1:21): A Christology for Christian Jews," *CBQ* 68.2 (2006): 248–67; Siker, *Sin in the New Testament*, 53–54. Perhaps stretching too far the role of the disciples in this endeavor is Eubank, *Wages of Cross-Bearing*, e.g., chs. 3–4; here 209: "Jesus is introduced as the one born to save his people from their sins (1:21), and throughout the Gospel he does this by teaching them how to find debt forgiveness and store up treasure in the heavens in order to acquire eternal life."

115. Guelich, *Sermon on the Mount*, 84.

116. Betz, *Sermon on the Mount*, 130.

take that further to suggest, "The word 'righteousness' . . . expresses the essence of the sermon on the mount."[117]

Several decades ago Benno Przybylski explored the controversy regarding the meaning of the overall Matthean concept of righteousness, which he argues revolved around the question: Does the term "righteousness" (*dikaiosynē*) refer to God's gift to humans or God's demand upon humans?[118] That controversy continues to this day, as we explore the debate in the following way: Is righteousness in Matthew's Gospel the pursuit of ethical righteousness ("demand") or the reception of kingdom righteousness ("gift")? Or is there a combination of both for a range of possible senses?[119]

Matthew also uses the cognate adjective *dikaios* to designate a person who is "righteous" or "just" or "faithful to the law" as an expression that designates the character of a person.[120] The debate here is similar to that of the noun. How does a person become "righteous" or "just"?

We do not have space to address each passage where the noun *dikaiosynē* and adjective *dikaios* occur, but we can give some summarizing comments. We will examine all seven uses of the noun *dikaiosynē*, leaving discussion of its use in 5:20 as our final focal point, since it is highly debated and central to our understanding of Jesus's and Matthew's view of righteousness. We will also discuss selected occurrences of the adjective *dikaios*.

### 10.6.1.2.1 Joseph Was Righteous (1:19)

In the opening scene where Joseph discovers that his betrothed Mary was pregnant, we discover the beginning richness of "righteous/righteousness" in Matthew's Gospel. Joseph emerges as righteous (*dikaios*) in an initial decision to divorce Mary secretly to prevent her from incurring shame. But even more surprisingly, at the urging of an angel he takes her home to be his wife in spite of the knowledge that Mary was pregnant, but not by him. As the first person designated as *dikaios* in this Gospel, "Joseph proves to be a prototype of righteousness for Matthew's version of the Christ-movement."[121] This is not righteous simply by being law-abiding, but righteous from the heart by attempting to do the right thing by his betrothed, and then even more so by obedience to the revealed will of God through the angel.

117. Davies and Allison, *Matthew*, 1:499.

118. Benno Przybylski, *Righteousness in Matthew and his World of Thought*, SNTSMS 41 (Cambridge: Cambridge University Press, 1980), 1. Representative of the"demand" position evaluated by Przybylski is Strecker, *Der Weg der Gerechtigkeit*, 86–122, 191–98. Representative of the"gift" position cited by Przybylski is M. J. Fiedler, "Der Begriff δικαιοσύνη im Matthaus-Evangelium, auf seine Grundlagen untersucht," 2 vols. (Ph.D. diss., Martin-Luther-Universitat, Halle-Wittenberg, 1957).

119. See Hagner, "Righteousness in Matthew's Gospel," 115–19. See also Jeannine K. Brown, "Justice, Righteousness," *DJG*[2] 494.

120. Matthew 1:19; 5:45; 9:13; 10:41; 13:17, 43, 49; 20:4; 23:28, 29, 35; 25:37, 46; 27:19.

121. Philip F. Esler, "The Righteousness of Joseph: Interpreting Matt 1.18–25 in Light of Judean Legal Papyri," *NTS* 68.3 (2022): 326–43; here 343.

### 10.6.1.2.2 Fulfill All Righteousness in Jesus's Baptism (3:15)

Jesus states explicitly that in his baptism he and John will fulfill all righteousness. Some suggest that Jesus means this in an ethical sense, that the baptism will fulfill all of the righteous expectations of the Law, similar to what Jesus will declare in the Sermon on the Mount (cf. Matt 5:17).[122] However, the present context does not imply an ethical submission to God's commands. Nowhere in the Old Testament is there a divine command to submit to John's baptism. Therefore, submission to his baptism can hardly be thought of as an act of righteousness, and certainly not thought of as fulfilling *all* righteousness.

More likely Jesus means this in a salvation-historical sense. God's saving activity prophesied throughout the Old Testament is now being fulfilled with the inauguration of Jesus's ministry, culminating in his death on the cross (cf. Isa 53:11).[123] Jesus is obedient to God's plan of salvation that has been revealed in the Scriptures.[124]

### 10.6.1.2.3 Hunger and Thirst for Righteousness (5:6)

In the Beatitudes of the Sermon on the Mount, Jesus states, "Blessed are those who hunger and thirst for righteousness" (Matt 5:6). In the context of the preceding beatitudes, righteousness includes several facets. (1) It includes "justice" for those who have been downtrodden or who have experienced injustice. (2) It also includes the idea of personal ethical righteousness for those who desire a life lived above the entanglements of sin. These are the persons in Jesus's day who live a life in accord with the Law. (3) But further, as in Jesus's statement at his baptism by John the Baptist (3:15), this "righteousness" especially includes the salvation-historical sense of God's saving activity. Those who hunger and thirst for righteousness desire to see justice executed on earth, they long to experience a deeper ethical righteousness in their own lives, and most of all they crave God's promised salvation come to the earth. Persons who "hunger and thirst" are in dire need. They could perish if they are not filled. Such is the passion of those who desire righteousness.[125]

And the ultimate source of this kind of righteousness is to be found only in God himself (cf. Pss 42:1–2; 63:1). His gift of kingdom life is the only true satisfaction for those who long to see and experience true justice, personal righteousness, and transformative salvation. His enablement is the only satisfaction for those who long for his standard of righteousness written in his law (Ps 119:10–11, 20, etc.).[126] Although the scribes and the Pharisees focused on attaining righteousness in studying and interpreting the law, their efforts resulted for some in self-righteousness, which will not enable

122. Przybylski, *Righteousness in Matthew*, 91–94.

123. Hagner, "Righteousness in Matthew's Gospel," 115–19.

124. Keener, *Matthew*, 132; Wilkins, *Matthew* (2009), 139–44.

125. Wilkins, *Matthew*, 207–8. For discussion see Hagner, "Righteousness in Matthew's Gospel," 111–15.

126. See Morris, *Matthew*, 99–100.

them to enter the kingdom of heaven (cf. Matt 5:20). But for those who deeply long for God's multifaceted righteousness, they will be filled. That divine satisfaction will come in a final sense in God's future reign, but it will be experienced in the present by those who respond to Jesus's invitation to kingdom life and enter into a relationship with him as he fills their deepest personal hunger and thirst for righteousness (cf. 12:1–8; 26:26–29; John 4:13–15; 6:35–40).

Jesus's disciples see firsthand the contrast between the self-righteousness of some of the religious leaders and God's righteousness in Jesus's life and ministry. As they continue to experience the transformation that accompanies life in the realm of the kingdom of heaven, their hunger and thirst for God's righteousness remains real as they live in the already-not yet of the present age, experiencing a passionate concern for the right things in kingdom living. This passionate pursuit of righteousness flows from a transformed heart. Jesus's disciples will be vessels of God's righteousness as they strive for justice, as they exemplify a life of righteousness, and as they bring God's gift of salvation to a world that still is held in the sway of the evil one (cf. Eph 2:1–10).

#### 10.6.1.2.4 Blessed Are Those Who Are Persecuted Because of Righteousness (5:10)

The eighth beatitude makes it clear that the Beatitudes are not entrance requirements to the kingdom of God, or else Jesus would be sanctioning torture or martyrdom as a way of earning one's entrance to the kingdom. On the other hand, this makes clear that the Beatitudes are not ethical demands for personal behavior, or else Jesus would be implying that it would be good for his disciples to seek out persecution in order to gain his blessing.

Instead, in the eighth beatitude Jesus comforts those who have suffered undeserved persecution. Persecution for one's own sin or foolishness may be deserved,[127] but the people Jesus addresses here were persecuted because of their stand for righteousness.[128] "The godly character and behavior described in the Sermon on the Mount may incite resentment that results in persecution."[129] This implicates once again the religious leadership of Jesus's day, who persecuted those who did not adopt their particular brand of righteousness. Persecution can take the form of physical or verbal abuse, or even both, but especially points to the way that the religious leaders hounded the populace, and excluded from their fellowship any who did not meet their standards (cf. Luke 6:22; Matt 23:34).[130] Sadly, and ironically, the religious leaders were persecuting in the name of their self-righteousness the very people who stood for true righteousness.

But as difficult as is the persecution, the reward far outweighs the hazard for Jesus's

127. Cf. 1 Pet 2:20; 3:14; 4:14–15.
128. Hagner, *Matthew 1–13*, 94.
129. Quarles, *Matthew*, 166.
130. Gundry, *Matthew*, 72.

disciples, because "theirs is the kingdom of heaven," where the causal clause of the first beatitude is repeated in the last beatitude (cf. 5:3, 10). Jesus here gives hope to the people of his day who have stood up and contended for God's form of righteousness against the self-righteousness of the religious leaders. Although they have been persecuted for it, Jesus says that the kingdom of God belongs to them, not the religious leaders, and all they need to do now is to respond to his invitation to join the kingdom.[131]

### 10.6.1.2.5 Practicing Righteousness in Front of Others (6:1)

Jesus addresses the arena of public religion because this is the place where a person's spirituality is developed and tested. "Be careful not to do your 'acts of righteousness' before men, to be seen by them" (6:1, NIV84). The public religious life is crucial for the development of one's spirituality, because it is here that the people of God gather for worship, gain instruction in the Scriptures, and encourage one another in personal piety. But this arena is also hazardous because public religious practices can be carried out not for the primary purpose of developing one's spiritual life before God but for the purpose of being seen by people.

Although they are not mentioned by name, the "teachers of the law and the Pharisees" are the most likely objects of this censure, because they are the implicit objects of denunciation in the Beatitudes and are the explicit objects in 5:20. They were the most public and influential religious figures among the common people, so Jesus denounces them for their faulty example. Some of them perform religious acts in the public arena not for the value that could be had in developing their personal life with God but to receive the respect of their peers and the admiration of the common people (see 6:2, 5, 16, 18).[132]

### 10.6.1.2.6 Seek First His Kingdom and His Righteousness (6:33)

The use of the present imperative "seek" (*zēteite*) does not mean to look for something not present because Jesus has already announced the arrival of the kingdom. In this context it means that they are to make the kingdom of heaven the center of their continual, daily priorities. Jesus's disciples have entered the kingdom of heaven already, and are to live with that reality, drawing upon God's ordering of their daily lives.[133]

In doing so they will "seek . . . his righteousness" (6:33), which means that they are to pursue their experiential growth of transformational righteousness—to pursue the increasing perfection of the Father (5:48) through their practice of "acts of righteousness" (6:1, NIV84).

131. Wilkins, *Matthew*, 210.

132. Wilkins, *Matthew*, 270.

133. Thomas E. Schmidt, "Burden, Barrier, Blasphemy: Wealth in Matt. 6:33, Luke 14:33, and Luke 16:15," *TrinJ* NS 9 (1988): 171–89, esp. 174–75.

### 10.6.1.2.7 "I Have Not Come to Call the Righteous, but Sinners" (9:13)

One of the most undeniably distinctive features of Jesus's message and ministry is the promise of salvation to "sinners."[134] But in an incisive play on terms, Jesus shows the Pharisees that he has a different view of what it means to be a sinner than they do. From the standpoint of the Pharisees, a sinner was a person who had violated the law according to their interpretations. But from the standpoint of Jesus, a sinner was any person who remained opposed to the will of God. The Pharisees consider themselves to be righteously healthy before God because they define righteousness by their observance of the law—their "sacrifice." But they are blind to their real sinfulness before God.

Therefore, Jesus declares: "But go and learn what this means: 'I desire mercy, not sacrifice.' For I have not come to call the righteous, but sinners" (9:13). The motley crew assembled with Jesus cannot avoid their own sinfulness. Matthew had been one of them, but he had experienced Jesus's merciful call to salvation, so now he brings his former sinful companions to Jesus. He desires for his friends to find that healing for their souls as well. It is to these that Jesus has come to bring his message of mercy. Jesus's offer of salvation to sinners apart from factional observances threatens the foundation and way of life of the Pharisees yet is at the heart of the gospel he has come announcing.[135] This continues the emphasis in Matthew's Gospel upon a call to the righteousness that is not self-induced but is Jesus's gracious offer of kingdom life.

### 10.6.1.2.8 The Righteous Will Shine (13:43)

The explanation of the parable of the wheat and weeds (13:36–43) is unique for the way in which Jesus explains the events that will transpire at the end of the age. At that time the "righteous" (*dikaios*)—Jesus's disciples who have experienced the inner transformation that accompanies their entrance to the kingdom, who are the wheat that has grown up throughout this age—will experience the full manifestation of the kingdom's glory: "Then the righteous will shine like the sun in the kingdom of their Father" (13:43). Jesus's disciples are the light of the world during this age while they await the consummation of this age (6:14–16), but at that time they will shine with unhindered brilliance.

A similar expression describes Jesus's transfigured glory, perhaps a preview of the eschatological glory that all disciples will share.[136] The expression "the kingdom of their Father" (13:43) is not to suggest that there is a distinction between the kingdom of the Son and another kingdom of the Father, but that the Father's will has been

134. Sanders, *Jesus and Judaism*, 174.
135. Wilkins, "Sinner," *DJG*[1] 760.
136. Davies and Allison, *Matthew*, 2:431.

fully accomplished on earth through the activity of the Son. There is full congruence between the will and activity of Father and Son. Jesus's instruction on prayer to the Father for the coming of the kingdom and the establishment of his will on earth (6:10) is now answered in full.

### 10.6.1.2.9 The Way of Righteousness (21:32)

The important point for the study of "righteousness" in Matthew is in 21:32: "For John came to you to show you the way of righteousness, and you did not believe him, but the tax collectors and the prostitutes did. And even after you saw this, you did not repent and believe him" (21:32). The "way of righteousness [*dikaiosynē*]" here probably evokes John the Baptist and "the way for the Lord" (3:3) and carries on the salvation-historical sense that Jesus referred to earlier (3:15).[137] Rather than suggesting the pursuit of ethical righteousness, Jesus focuses on repentance and the reception of kingdom righteousness. Sinners who repent will obey God and by it show their repentance. It does not matter if they once turned their back on God. God wants obedience. The Jewish leaders were hypocritical in that they talked but did not live up to their talk. In the final analysis, it is the fruit of one's life that proves whether or not we are submissive to God's message through his messengers.

### 10.6.1.2.10 Outside Appear as Righteous but on the Inside Full of Hypocrisy and Wickedness (23:25–28)

The fifth and sixth "woes" that Jesus pronounces on the scribes and Pharisees condemns the practice of hiding inner greed, self-indulgence, and impurity with external displays of righteousness and virtue (23:25–28).

External displays of purity without internal purity are hollow deceptions. Jesus here alludes to the practice of his day where ornate ossuaries (small bone-box receptacles) made of white limestone are used to retain the bones of deceased ancestors.[138] The teachers of the law and the Pharisees that Jesus indicts are like these ossuaries—on the outside they were deceptively ornate, but inside there is nothing but impure death. Jesus makes his point plain—the teachers of the law and Pharisees have given themselves the appearance of having avoided unrighteousness by their attention to their many legal requirements, but they are instead inwardly unrighteous, because they have not attended to the transformation of the heart that could have come by responding to Jesus (cf. 5:20; 15:17–20). External displays of righteous deeds and activities are nothing without originating from inner righteousness.

---

137. Hagner, "Righteousness in Matthew's Gospel," 114. So also J. Brown, "Justice, Righteousness," 494.

138. For pictures and discussion of the practice, see Michael J. Wilkins, "Matthew," *ZIBBC*, 1:144, 160.

### 10.6.1.2.11 Surpassing Righteousness and Entering the Kingdom of Heaven (5:20)

Having surveyed the usage of the noun *dikaiosynē* and the adjective *dikaios* in Matthew's Gospel, we now turn to a crucial occurrence of *dikaiosynē* in Jesus's Sermon on the Mount that most scholars consider determinative for understanding Jesus's and Matthew's teaching on "righteousness."

From a warning and commendation to his disciples, Jesus turns his attention to the broader audience—those who are not in the kingdom of heaven. "For I tell you that unless your righteousness surpasses that of the Pharisees and the teachers of the law, you will certainly not enter the kingdom of heaven" (5:20). This may have been Jesus's most astonishing assertion because the teachers of the law and the Pharisees were the quintessence of ethical righteousness. This saying of Jesus has received widespread attention in recent years and is extensively debated as to its meaning. Here we will focus on the two primary perspectives, which have numerous variations.[139]

#### *10.6.1.2.11.1 Pursuit of Ethical Righteousness of the Kingdom*

On the one hand are those who argue that the righteousness of the kingdom is, in some way or another, a demand to pursue ethical conduct. For example, Davies and Allison state, "'Righteousness' is therefore Christian character and conduct in accordance with the demands of Jesus—right intention, right word, right deed."[140] Likewise, Francois Viljoen argues that Matthew uses "righteousness" in an ethical sense to refer to the proper behavioral norms and attitudes for his community. He states that righteousness is a goal for Jesus's disciples to pursue. "In the Sermon on the Mount, δικαιοσύνη is related to Matthew's emphasis on 'doing the will of God' (cf. Mt 7:21; 12:46-50). Righteousness gives expression to Matthew's understanding of the practice of true discipleship."[141]

Viljoen goes on further to contend that commitment to Jesus forms the central focus of the Matthean community's identity. Their discipleship is demonstrated by doing the will of God as defined and interpreted by Jesus, which becomes the distinguishing mark of the community. In doing so they would surpass the righteousness of the scribes and Pharisees.[142] Similarly, Betz indicates that the very purpose of the Sermon on the Mount was to demonstrate that Jesus's teachings are the greater righteousness. Mere compliance

139. For an excellent overview, see Guelich, "*Excursus*: Righteousness in Matthew 5–7," in *Sermon on the Mount*, 84–87. For an ongoing discussion in one publication between these two basic positions, see Manuel Vogel, "Die Ethik der 'besseren Gerechtigkeit' im Matthäusevangelium," *ZNT* 36.18 (2015): 57–63, and Roland Deines, "Gerechtigkeit, die zum Leben führt: Die christologische Bestimmtheit der Glaubenden bei Matthäus," *ZNT* 36.18 (2015): 45–55.

140. Davies and Allison, *Matthew*, 1:499.

141. Francois P. Viljoen, "Righteousness and Identity Formation in the Sermon on the Mount," *HvTSt* 69.1 (2013): 1–10; here, 9, https://doi.org/10.4102/hts.v69i1.1300.

142. Viljoen, "Righteousness and Identity Formation," 10.

with written statutes of law is inadequate morally and ethically. Obedience to Jesus's teachings is the "greater righteousness" and indicates eschatologically the condition for entering into the kingdom of God.[143]

Taking this even further, Thomas Blanton contends that this ethical pursuit is focused on obedience to Jesus's interpretation of the Law. He states that "Jesus functions as YHWH's emissary who is able to save those who listen to him by calling them to pursue the 'better righteousness' that may be obtained only by those who scrupulously observe the Torah."[144] Rejecting "standard" interpretations, Blanton declares that Jesus "saves his people from their sins" not primarily by forgiving sin or by his death on the cross but by exhorting his audience to follow the Torah with perfect obedience. He argues, "The recognition of Jesus' salvific role as Torah teacher helps to place Matthew's portrait of Jesus more firmly within its first-century Jewish context and serves as a corrective to exegesis that is unduly influenced by later Christian theologies of atonement, in which the cross plays a central role."[145] According to Blanton, "Jesus saves, at least in part, by teaching people to follow the Torah."[146]

#### *10.6.1.2.11.2 Reception of the Gift of Kingdom Righteousness*

On the other hand are those who argue that salvation does not come by observing torah, but by confessing Jesus as God's Messiah who offers entrance to the kingdom of heaven through his sacrificial death on the cross. Matthew supports in his Gospel the double-love command, deeds of mercy, and the avoidance of offenses. Yet the most important demand is discipleship to Jesus. And what counts in this respect is trust and faith in Jesus, not purity and tithes.

Deines addresses the question of whether the foundation for the righteousness that is valid in the kingdom of heaven lies in observance of the Torah or in the work and word of the Messiah. He declares, "That is why I think that it is appropriate to summarize the Matthean concept of righteousness as Jesus-righteousness. The intention of this phrase is to point out that this righteousness is not possible without Jesus."[147] He takes this further to note that those who obey Jesus's call to discipleship get a share of this righteousness and thus can be addressed concerning *their* righteousness (as in 5:20 and 6:1).[148] Élian Cuvillier concurs: "The pillar which sustains Matthew's theology—and therefore his religious identity—is no longer primarily the law and obedience to its commandments, but the Messiah and his teaching."[149]

Guelich expands upon this to suggest that *righteousness* in the Sermon on the Mount

143. Betz, *Sermon on the Mount*, 197.
144. Blanton, "Saved by Obedience," 393–413; here 413.
145. Blanton, "Saved by Obedience," 413.
146. Blanton, "Saved by Obedience," 411.
147. Deines, "Not the Law," 53–84; here 81.
148. Deines, "Not the Law," 81.
149. Cuvillier, "Torah Observance," 144–59; here 159. Somewhat uniquely, but similarly, is Philip La Grange Du Toit, "The Fulfilment of the Law According to Matthew 5:17: A Dialectical Approach," *Acta Theologica* 38.2 (2018): 49–69.

is soteriological, ethical, and christological. Righteousness is *soteriological* in that it connotes the "gift" of a new relationship between God and the individual (5:6; 6:33). Righteousness is *ethical* in that it connotes the demand for conduct in keeping with the will of God in relationship to others (5:20, 21–48) and to God (6:1–18), a conduct concomitant with the "gift." And finally, and for Guelich most importantly, Matthew's use of righteousness in the Sermon is *eschatological* or, more accurately, *christological*, because it expresses the commensurate conduct growing out of the new relationship with Jesus and demanded by Jesus. Guelich states, "Such relationships and such conduct are characteristic of the age of salvation and are part of Jesus's coming as the fulfillment of the Old Testament promise, the Messiah Son of God who comes declaring the Kingdom present and future."[150]

#### *10.6.1.2.11.3 Inside-Out Righteousness, not Outside-In*

From my perspective, the latter understanding of righteousness is more all-encompassing and most expressive of Matthew's overall emphases, yet the former view's emphasis upon ethical conduct will ultimately be included in the disciple's life. I would underscore that due regard for the transformation of kingdom-righteousness in the life of Jesus's disciples will recognize the reality of ethical righteousness that will result from the reception and gift of the transformation of the heart.

The shock of Jesus's declaration strips away practices among some of the scribes and Pharisees for gaining favor with God. It serves both as an introduction to the "antitheses" to follow (5:21–48) and as a revelation of the fundamental principle of life in the kingdom of heaven—namely, kingdom righteousness operates from the inside-out, not from the outside-in. However, this is not a new principle. God's people knew that external acts of righteousness could not take away sin or gain favor with God unless they were preceded by a repentant heart. Psalm 51 is perhaps the archetype, where David seeks inner cleansing and purification of his heart after his dreadfully sinful action against Bathsheba (Ps 51:2, 7, 10).

The Gospel of Matthew makes clear from the outset that Jesus was born to save his people from their sins (1:21). In part, this salvation comes from heeding Jesus's demand for what Siker calls the "interiorization of righteousness"[151] and a renewed prophetic focus on the disposition of one's heart (5:21–45; 25:31–46). But Jesus's ministry will culminate in his death, which Matthew's Jesus declares is the pouring out of his blood for the forgiveness of sins (26:28). This atoning death will give way to the resurrected Jesus in Matthew's Gospel, with the risen Jesus sending the disciples out to baptize new members into the community of forgiven sinners (28:16–20).[152]

150. Guelich, *Sermon on the Mount*, 87.
151. Siker, *Sin in the New Testament*, 13.
152. Siker, *Sin in the New Testament*, 13.

Jesus's disciples are called to a different kind and quality of righteousness, not an increased quantity.[153] Don Garlington emphasizes that in terms of sheer quantity it would be virtually impossible to top the 613 commands of the Torah, not to mention the multitudinous halakoth of the various enclaves of the Second Temple period.[154] As France states forthrightly, "Jesus is not talking about beating the scribes and Pharisees at their own game, but about a different level or concept of righteousness altogether."[155] As was recognized in both Jesus's interaction with John the Baptist (3:15) and the statement of the Beatitudes (5:6), righteousness in the preaching of Jesus is not primarily a personal attainment of ethical purity, although that will become the result of the operation of the Spirit of God in a disciple's life in the kingdom of heaven.[156] Pennington emphasizes the priority of internal disposition over external purity and defines righteousness in Matthew as *whole-person behavior that accords with God's nature, will, and coming kingdom*.[157]

Righteousness belongs in the realm of grace. Jesus's proclamation of good news is that the kingdom of heaven is now available to those who respond to him. God's saving activity has arrived on the earthly scene to deliver his people, and this will produce a radical change in their lives.[158] Deines remarks, "It is the eschatological, overflowingly rich righteousness that Jesus fulfilled and made available to his disciples that from now on opens the way into the kingdom of God."[159] As Nijay Gupta emphasizes, "But though the Gospel's power works 'inside out', it must finally come 'out' to fulfill its purpose of cosmic redemption."[160] He then goes on to conclude, "The Gospel according to Matthew, and the nature of its spirituality, is about becoming something new by God's grace by faith."[161]

#### 10.6.1.2.12 Jesus and Matthew Prepare for Paul

In Chapter 5 ("The Old Testament and Jesus Messiah in Matthew's Gospel: Fulfillment") we touched upon a related issue that is debated in studies of Matthean theology—the relationship of Matthew and the apostle Paul. Based on what some

153. The verb *perisseuō* ("surpass") can be understood as "qualitative" or "quantitative." According to "περισσεύω," BDAG 805, the latter is more dominant in the NT, yet instances of the former are also present. Because of its usage in the present text, we ought to emphasize the *qualitative* component. For helpful discussions, see Quarles, *Sermon on the Mount*, 101–4; Deines, "Not the Law," 80–81; Don Garlington, "The 'Better Righteousness': Matthew 5:20," *BBR* 20.4 (2010): 479–502; here 488.

154. Garlington, "'Better Righteousness,'" 488–89.

155. France, *Matthew*, NICNT, 189.

156. For similar discussion, see Moloney, "Matthew 5:17–18."

157. Pennington, *Sermon on the Mount*, 177, 179; his emphasis.

158. Hagner, "Righteousness in Matthew's Gospel," 116–17. Hagner sees primarily the element of ethical righteousness in 5:20, but his argument for God's salvific deliverance in 3:15 and 5:6 could also be applied here, which he does more directly in his commentary (Hagner, *Matthew 1–13*, 109).

159. Deines, "Not the Law," 80–81; Cuvillier, "Torah Observance," 155.

160. Nijay K. Gupta, "The Spirituality of Faith in the Gospel of Matthew," in *Matthew and Mark Across Perspectives: Essays in Honour of Stephen C. Barton and William R. Telford*, ed. Kristian A. Bendoraitis and Nijay K. Gupta, LNTS 538 (London: Bloomsbury T&T Clark, 2016), 108–24; here 124.

161. Gupta, "Spirituality of Faith," 124.

perceive as the stringent attitude toward God's Law found in the words of Jesus in 5:17–20, various critical scholars have tried to pit Matthew and Paul against each another, as though Paul advocated a gospel of grace that was antinomian, which Matthew intentionally countered with a gospel of law.[162]

But the contrast between Paul and Matthew is overstated.[163] I concur with Paul Foster, who states that "Matthew's Gospel is primarily written to tell the story of Jesus in order to command faith in that person as God's Messiah. It does not reveal its support for or opposition to Pauline perspectives in any unambiguous way."[164] Graham Stanton states, "Matthew's Gospel as a whole is neither anti-Pauline, nor has it been strongly influenced by Paul's writing; it is simply un-Pauline."[165]

While Matthew records Jesus's sayings that uphold the binding validity of the Law (5:17–19), he also has strong language of rebuke for some Pharisees who legalistically applied the Old Testament in such a way that they were cutting people off from the kingdom of heaven (e.g., 23:13–15). Matthew focuses on Jesus's message of defilement or purity that comes from the heart, not observing traditions of humans that nullify the word of God (e.g., 15:1–20).

Paul upholds the Law as holy, righteous, and good (Rom 7:12) but has strong words of condemnation for the Judaizing legalists (e.g., Gal 1:8), focusing on salvation by grace alone (e.g., Eph 2:8–9). Both Matthew and Paul hark back to Jesus for the declaration that the Old Testament Scripture is the written, revealed will of God. The Old Testament is and will remain Scripture, and Jesus brings it to its intended meaning and goal.

Jesus fulfills the Law by his life and ministry, ultimately giving his life as a ransom for many (Matt 20:28) and as a sacrificial atonement for the sins of his people in the new covenant in his blood (26:26–28). This prepares the way for Paul's explication of Jesus's sacrifice as righteousness that is imputed to believers and transformational righteousness that is imparted to obedient disciples. Rather than being an artificial harmonization,[166]

162. Especially, Sim, *Gospel of Matthew and Christian Judaism*, esp. 188–213; Sim, "Matthew 7.21–23: Further Evidence of Its Anti-Pauline Perspective," *NTS* 53 (2007): 325–43. For a direct critique of Sim, see Joel Willitts, "The Friendship of Matthew and Paul: A Response to the Recent Trend in the Interpretation of Matthew's Gospel," *HvTSt* 65.1 (2009): 1–8, art. #151, https://doi.org/10.4102/hts.v65i1.151.

163. For rejection of an "anti-Pauline polemic" in Matthew's Gospel, see Strotmann and Tiwald, "Das Matthäusevangelium—eine Paulus-Polemik?," 64–106. See also Moloney, "Matthew 5:17–18." For an insightful blog on salvation in Matthew and its relationship to the apostle Paul, see Fred Sanders, "Salvation in Matthew (with an Assist from Paul)," *The Scriptorium*, January 11, 2013, https://www.patheos.com/blogs/scriptorium/2013/01/salvation-in-matthew-with-an-assist-from-paul/.

164. Paul Foster, "Paul and Matthew: Two Strands of the Early Jesus Movement with Little Sign of Connection," in *Paul and the Gospels: Christologies, Conflicts and Convergences*, ed. Michael F. Bird and Joel Willitts, LNTS 411 (London: Bloomsbury T&T Clark, 2011), 86–115; here 86.

165. Stanton, *Gospel for a New People*, 314.

166. E.g., Daniel Harrington refers to "our largely canon-influenced tendency to harmonize Paul and Matthew"; Daniel J. Harrington, "Matthew and Paul," in *Matthew and His Christian Contemporaries*, ed. David C. Sim and Boris Repschinki, LNTS 333 (London: T&T Clark, 2008), 11–26, here 25.

this helps us to see that Paul looks back and explains what Jesus did. Matthew and Paul are one—Paul explains what Jesus accomplished.[167]

The historical Jesus and Matthew's historical recollections and theological reflections prepare the way for Paul's theological formulations. Jesus's perspective toward the Law prepares for what Paul will formulate in his epistles and theology. It is the same reality that underlies what will later become Paul's understanding of justification and sanctification.

Neither Jesus nor Matthew are influenced by Paul's perspective of righteousness, but rather, Paul looks back upon the developing oral traditions of Jesus's teachings and ministry, which are the bases for the doctrines that he develops. These will be the special emphases of the former "righteous" Pharisee, the apostle Paul.[168] Richard Hays observes, "Small wonder Paul, that most faultless of Pharisees (Phil. 3:4–6), when he came to understand the Gospel of Christ, considered his spiritual assets rubbish. His new desire was to gain Christ, not having a righteousness of his own that comes from the law, but one which is from God and by faith in Christ (Phil. 3:8f.)."[169]

### 10.6.2 Salvation and Righteousness Produce Kingdom Transformation in Jesus's Disciples

Matthew emphasizes that to be saved and considered righteous are not simply abstract theological concepts. Rather, they are experienced spiritual realities that are the beginnings of personal and community kingdom transformation. Grindheim states, "The righteousness of the Pharisees and the teachers of the law reached only to their actions (Mt. 23.1–33), but the righteousness of the disciples reaches to the heart and to their inward attitude."[170]

Karl-Wilhelm Niebuhr suggests that Matthew's idea of being human is an important part of his Jesus story. Matthew not only tells about Jesus Christ, the Son of God, and about Jesus's fate on the cross and about his mighty rising from the dead, but his Gospel is also about people. As individuals responded to Jesus's call to kingdom life and became his disciples, they entered into a transformational kingdom life of discipleship that fulfills their creation as humans.[171]

Earlier in this chapter I defined this transformational discipleship as "*living a fully*

167. Brian Vickers, "What Does Justification Have to Do with the Gospels?," in *The Doctrine on Which the Church Stands or Falls: Justification in Biblical, Theological, Historical, and Pastoral Perspective*, ed. Matthew Barrett (Wheaton, IL: Crossway, 2019), 179–212, esp. 186.

168. Wilkins, *Matthew*, 230–35.

169. Hays, *Moral Vision of the New Testament*, 326.

170. Grindheim, *Introducing Biblical Theology*, 140–41. See also Robert Morgan, "Towards a Critical Appropriation of the Sermon on the Mount: Christology and Discipleship," in *Christology, Controversy, and Community: New Testament Essays in Honour of David R. Catchpole*, ed. David G. Horrell and Christopher M. Tuckett, NovTSup 99 (Leiden: Brill, 2000), 157–91; here 186. One who stresses the vastness and breadth of salvation is Tom Greggs, *The Breadth of Salvation: Rediscovering the Fullness of God's Saving Work* (Grand Rapids: Baker Academic, 2020).

171. Karl-Wilhelm Niebuhr, "Matthew's Idea of being Human: God's Righteousness and Human Responsibility according to the Gospel of Matthew," in Seleznev, Loader, and Niebuhr, *The Gospel of Matthew in Its Historical and Theological Context*, WUNT 459 (Tübingen: Mohr Siebeck, 2021), 329–44; here 342.

*human life in this world in union with Jesus Christ and his people, growing in conformity to his image, and helping others to become like Jesus.*"[172] Jesus's birth and human development establishes a model for us as his disciples. Healthy discipleship ultimately is full human development, as intended in our original creation in the image of God: the entire person is brought into conformity to the image of Jesus Christ. A severely limiting view of discipleship restricts it simply to one or two areas of human life. Some view discipleship simply as a mental exercise of study. Others view discipleship as a "spiritual" exercise somehow separate from the social dimension of life. We will see that discipleship means developing like Jesus in every area of our lives. Full discipleship is to be taught to obey everything Jesus commanded in his life and words (cf. 28:19–20).

### 10.6.3 Characteristics of Transformational Discipleship in Matthew's Gospel

In Jesus's announcement of the arrival of the kingdom of heaven he has introduced his unique form of discipleship in which his disciples experience salvation, righteousness and kingdom transformation. With that Jesus's disciples become transformed paradigms with a commission. The following chart unfolds several characteristics of transformational disciples to Jesus Messiah that are found in Matthew's Gospel.

| **MATTHEW'S VIEW OF JESUS'S DISCIPLES**<br>**Transformed Paradigms with a Commission (Matt 12:46–50; 28:18–20)**<br>***Jesus's Disciples Experience Salvation, Righteousness and Kingdom Transformation*** |
|---|
| Jesus's Disciples Are "with Him" in Kingdom Allegiance |
| Jesus's Disciples Experience Purity from a New Covenant Heart |
| Jesus's Disciples Are Paradigms of Christian Life |
| Simon Peter Is First Among Equal Disciples |
| Jesus's Disciples are Commissioned to Make Disciples |
| Matthew's Gospel Is a Manual on Discipleship |

#### *10.6.3.1 Jesus's Disciples Are "with Him" in Kingdom Allegiance*

In the beginning days of the Jesus movement great crowds, including a large number of disciples, followed Jesus around. Matthew is well aware of this large number of disciples, but focusing on the small group of disciples gives us special insight into Matthew's distinctive view of discipleship. Matthew is helping his readers to understand how discipleship to Jesus means that we are with him in kingdom allegiance.[173]

172. See Wilkins, *Following the Master*, 41–42; Wilkins, *In His Image*, 55.

173. Wilkins, *Concept of Disciple*, 126–72.

### 10.6.3.1.1 The Small Group of Disciples Around Jesus

Examination of parallel passages indicates that on several occasions Matthew focuses only on a small group of disciples around Jesus when in Luke and John and even in Mark there are indications of a much larger group of disciples (cf. Luke 6:17; 10:1; 19:31; John 6:60, 66; Mark 3:13–19). Either as an eyewitness or as one privy to the same oral tradition as the other Synoptic Gospels, Matthew surely would have been aware of a larger number of disciples who had followed Jesus in his earthly ministry (e.g., Luke's "a great multitude of his disciples"; Luke 6:17). However, in his story Matthew consistently has only a small group of disciples around Jesus.

Some scholars interpret the small group around Jesus to be an indication that only a small group of supremely committed individuals were able to become disciples. Gerd Theissen suggests that the incident of the rich young man indicates that only through the process of accomplishing a "better righteousness" can one become a disciple. Theissen suggests that traversing a graduated series of norms was necessary to pass from being one who was in sympathy with Jesus, to being one who was a fully committed disciple. Hence, only a small group of radically committed individuals were able to become disciples.[174]

### 10.6.3.1.2 Discipleship Is to Be "with Jesus"

Theissen raises an issue that we must be very clear about. He rightly emphasizes the commitment of the disciples to Jesus. But in my view the commitment has to do with obtaining eternal life, not with attaining an advanced stage of the Christian life. The rich young man whom Theissen cites came with the question, "Teacher, what good thing must I do to get *eternal life*?" (Matt 19:16; emphasis mine). A person becomes a disciple through a faith commitment to Jesus, not a work commitment. We must be clear about this issue.

Jesus made a sharp distinction between those who would follow him as his disciple. "Whoever is not with me is against me, and whoever does not gather with me scatters" (12:30).[175] A person is either with Jesus or against him. The disciples made the commitment to be with Jesus for eternal life. When they confessed Jesus as their Master and Savior they became disciples. Only the disciples, his brothers and sisters who do the will of God, are "with Jesus" as his followers after the resurrection (cf. 12:49–50; 28:10, 16).

The disciples are not idealized believers who rise above the masses in the church[176]

174. Theissen, *Sociology of Early Palestinian Christianity*, 18–21. This same position was held early last century by the influential Matthean scholar Benjamin Bacon, *Studies in Matthew*, 87–89, 240. This is also a widely held view among other scholars: cf. M. L. Held, "Disciples," *New Catholic Encyclopedia*, 15 vols. (New York: McGraw-Hill, 1967), 4:895. See also Sheridan, "Disciples and Discipleship in Matthew and Luke," 237; Strecker, *Der Weg der Gerechtigkeit*, 191–92.

175. Matthew and Luke (Luke 11:23) record the pronouncement as it is found here. Mark and Luke also have the reverse saying, "Whoever is not against us is for us" (cf. Mark 9:40; Luke 9:50). The saying here is more restrictive.

176. So Bacon, *Studies in Matthew*, 87–89, 240.

or the priestly class in the church serving the lay people.[177] Rather, the disciples are Jesus's true followers, the religious leaders are Jesus's enemies, and the crowd is the mass of people who continue to be the object of Jesus's saving ministry. In his earthly ministry Jesus went to the crowds himself. He preached to them, he taught them, and he healed them. Then he prepared his disciples to go to them (10:5–42; 14:14–19; 15:29–36). In his ascended ministry Jesus sends the disciples to a larger crowd, the nations, to make disciples of them (28:16–20).

Ultimately, following Jesus for eternal life is not always the popular way.

#### 10.6.3.1.3 Jesus's Disciples Are a Paradigm of Christian Life

Matthew portrays the disciples as they really were so that they can be an example or paradigm of what discipleship should be for his church. Not that he has intended an idealistic paradigm. He shows both the positive and negative. The positive aspect, which is especially present in the discipleship teachings, shows what will happen to true disciples who fully obey and follow Jesus (cf. 25:14–30).[178] The negative traits show what can happen to disciples who do not identify with Jesus in obedience to the will of the Father—e.g., they stumble (16:23), flee (26:56), fall asleep (26:40, 45), and act in brash boldness (26:35).

Portrayed both positively and negatively (15:23; 16:5–12, 19; 17:6–7; 19:13–15), the disciples become paradigms of imperfect followers of Jesus who are taught to advance in their life with Jesus. And, as a paradigm for Matthew's church, they become a very practical and realistic display of what it means to be called a "disciple" (28:19)—what would later be called a "Christian."[179] Luke records, "And in Antioch the disciples were first called Christians" (Acts 11:26, ESV; cf. 26:28; 1 Pet 4:16). True disciples remain committed to Jesus and grow in their discipleship to him, even in an often-hostile world.[180]

#### 10.6.3.1.4 Jesus Is "with" His Disciples (28:20) So That We Can Remain "with Him"

The beginning of Matthew's Gospel introduced us to Jesus Immanuel, "God with us" (1:23). In the center of this Gospel Jesus proclaims that where two or three gather in his name he is there "with them" (18:20). And the final saying of Jesus in this Gospel is what gives us the greatest assurance that we can carry out his purpose in our lives because he promises unconditionally: "And surely I am with you always, to the very end

177. So Thysman, *Communauté et directives éthiques*; Minear, "Disciples and the Crowds," 31–32, 40–42; Sheridan, "Disciples and Discipleship," 237–39.

178. See Dogara Ishaya Manomi, "'Good and Faithful Slave': Social Identity, Virtue, and Human Flourishing in the Parable of the Talents (Matt 25:14–30)," *NovT* 64.4 (2022): 413–31.

179. Wilkins, *Concept of Disciple*, 169.

180. David Horrell states: "The distinctive name 'Christian' emerges from the context of hostility, initially voiced as an accusation by outsiders, then proudly claimed by ingroup members and eventually coming to serve as the fundamental group-designator" (David Horrell, "'Becoming Christian:' Solidifying Christian Identity and Content," in *Handbook of Early Christianity: Social Science Approaches*, ed. Anthony J. Blasi, Paul-André Turcotte, and Jean Duhaime [Walnut Creek, CA: AltaMira, 2002], 309–35; here 328).

of the age" (28:20). This points to the dramatic reality that completes one of the key christological truths of Matthew's Gospel: "the omnipresence of Christ with his new kingdom community."[181] This premise joins the Shekinah glory of the Old Testament and the divine comfort of Yahweh's presence among his people—and not just divine presence but divine assistance.[182] The power and courage and resources necessary to remain with Jesus comes from the fact that Jesus is with us always as our ever-present Immanuel until the end of the age.

### *10.6.3.2 Jesus's Disciples Experience Purity from a New Covenant Heart*

The Pharisees and teachers of the law from Jerusalem lodged a charge against the disciples that "they don't wash their hands before they eat!" (Matt 15:2). Bodily cleanliness was valued highly in the ancient world.[183] The heat and dust made frequent washing necessary for both health and refreshment. Within ancient Israel, a host provided travelers with water for their feet so that they could be refreshed and cleansed from their journey and be ready for a meal (Gen 18:4; 19:2; 1 Sam 25:41; cf. John 13:1–10). The hands were a particular concern for cleanliness, as something unclean could be transmitted to oneself and others, so the priests were required to wash their hands and feet prior to offering their service (Exod 30:18–21).

The Pharisees and later rabbis adapted the concern for hygienic cleanliness to ceremonial purity and applied it to common Israelites, with the purpose that they would consume everyday food as though it were a sacrifice to God at the temple altar. A small measure of water[184] was poured over the hands up to the wrists prior to the consumption of food, which demonstrates that the concern for this washing was ceremonial, not hygienic (m. Yadaim 1:1).[185]

But Jesus explains to the disciples the central role that the spiritual heart plays in spiritual purity: "For out of the heart come evil thoughts—murder, adultery, sexual immorality, theft, false testimony, slander. These are what defile a person; but eating with unwashed hands does not defile them" (Matt 15:19–20). Food that goes into the mouth does not affect the spiritual heart; it simply goes through the digestive system and is excreted (15:17). Ceremonial purification rites attendant to eating food do not affect a person's spiritual purity. These traditions of the elders have nothing to do with true spiritual cleanness because they only focus on external physical activities. These do not make a person unclean before God.

God's evaluative judgment concerns the behavior that originates in the heart of a person. The implication is that the spiritual heart is naturally evil (cf. 7:11) and needs the transformative righteousness that Jesus has initiated with the arrival of the

181. Osborne, *Matthew*, 1082.

182. Osborne, *Matthew*, 1082. See also Quarles, *Matthew*, 764.

183. "καθαρός et al.," NIDNTTE 2:568–74.

184. A "quarter-log of water," which is equal in bulk to an egg and a half; Danby, *Mishnah*, 778n9.

185. Neusner and Green, "Washing of Hands," *DJBP* 667.

kingdom of heaven. Inward, spiritual defilement is more deadly than outward, ceremonial defilement. The spiritual heart is evil, and it must first be cleansed, which will then produce lives that exemplify righteous purity in word, thought, motivation, deed, and relationships.[186]

The person who responds to Jesus's invitation to the kingdom receives the new heart and the Spirit promised by God through the prophet Ezekiel (Ezek 36:26–27). This is the transformation that is the product of being saved from the power of sin and having the surpassing righteousness of God bestowed in our inner person as one enters the kingdom of heaven.

Out of this new heart will come the opposite of what comes out of the old heart. Out of this new heart will come noble deliberations, restoration, marital faithfulness, sexual purity, charity, truthfulness, praise. As demonstrated in the parable of the talents (Matt 25:14–30), the Matthean Jesus redefines social identity from a social status to a virtue status, from the quantity of one's giftings to the quality of one's character, and from a mere sense of belonging to a pursuit of human flourishing through virtue.[187]

Jesus reveals that this transformation is impelled by a new heart in a renewed inner person that is empowered by the Spirit of God.

### *10.6.3.3 Simon Peter Is First Among Equals*

Matthew's Gospel gives special attention to the apostle Peter.[188] He is mentioned first among the original four called by Jesus (4:18–22) and he is designated explicitly as "first" in the listing of the Twelve (10:2). Matthew narrates five incidents in five central chapters in which Peter figures prominently that are found nowhere else in the Gospels (14:28–31; 15:15; 16:17–19; 17:24–27; 18:21). Three incidents especially highlight Peter's leadership role: (1) Peter getting out of the boat to walk on the water

186. Thomas H. McCall, *Against God and Nature: The Doctrine of Sin* (Wheaton, IL: Crossway, 2019), loc. 1738–39, Kindle.

187. Manomi, "'Good and Faithful Slave,'" 413–31.

188. The literature on Peter in the NT and in Matthew's Gospel is immense, including Oscar Cullmann, *Peter: Disciple, Apostle, Martyr: A Historical and Theological Essay*, trans. Floyd V. Filson, 2nd ed. (Philadelphia: Westminster, 1962); the seminal studies in the ecumenical project in the latter part of the twentieth century, "Peter in the Gospel of Matthew," in *Peter in the New Testament: A Collaborative Assessment by Protestant and Catholic Scholars*, ed. Raymond E. Brown, Karl P. Donfried, and John Reumann (Minneapolis: Augsburg, 1973), 75–107; Kingsbury, "Figure of Peter," 47–61; Edwards, "Uncertain Faith," in *Discipleship in the New Testament*, 67–83; Edwards, *Matthew's Narrative Portrait of Disciples*; Caragounis, *Peter and the Rock*,; Arlo J. Nau, *Peter in Matthew: Discipleship, Diplomacy, and Dispraise*, GNS 36 (Collegeville, MN: Liturgical, 1992); Kari Syreeni, "Peter as a Character and Symbol in the Gospel of Matthew," in *Characterization in the Gospel: Reconceiving Narrative Criticism*, ed. David Rhoads and Kari Syreeni, JSNTSup 184 (Sheffield: Sheffield Academic, 1999), 106–52; Wiarda, *Peter in the Gospels*; Wilkins, "Peter's Declaration," 293–381; Martin Hengel, *Saint Peter: The Underestimated Apostle*, trans. Thomas H. Trapp (Grand Rapids: Eerdmans, 2010); Markus Bockmuehl, *The Remembered Peter in Ancient Reception and Modern Debate*, WUNT 262 (Tübingen: Mohr Siebeck, 2010); *Simon Peter in Scripture and Memory: The New Testament Apostle in the Early Church* (Grand Rapids: Baker Academic, 2012); Verheyden, "Rock and Stumbling Block," 263–311; Markley, *Peter*; Helen K. Bond and Larry W. Hurtado, eds., *Peter in Early Christianity* (Grand Rapids: Eerdmans, 2015); Robert H. Gundry, *Peter: False Disciple and Apostate According to St. Matthew* (Grand Rapids: Eerdmans, 2015); Bayer, *Apostolic Bedrock*; Judith M. Lieu, ed. *Peter in the Early Church: Apostle—Missionary—Church Leader*, BETL 325 (Leuven: Peeters, 2021).

to meet Jesus (14:22–33), (2) Peter's declaration at Caesarea Philippi of Jesus's messianic identity and Jesus's declaration of Peter's role in the church (16:16–19), and (3) the unique story of Jesus telling Peter to find the temple tax in the fish's mouth (17:24–27).

After the arrest of Jesus, Matthew records that Peter follows Jesus from afar (26:58) and ends up sitting in the courtyard of the high priest (26:69). Then come Peter's denials (26:73–75). Matthew states that the second denial is "with an oath," and that Peter claims, "I don't know the man" (26:72). Finally, Matthew adds that Peter went out and wept "bitterly" (26:75). This is an intensification of the self-condemnation that Peter now experiences. These changes deepen the dark denial that Peter made and with which Peter has to live. This is the last time Peter is mentioned in Matthew; therefore, Peter is left on a negative note.

Jesus called Peter first, established him as the first of the disciples/apostles, and set him as the rock (16:18), the first member of the church to come.[189] But Peter is deemphasized near the end of Matthew's Gospel. The church was not to exalt him as a supreme rabbi because Jesus declares, "You are all brothers" (23:8). Peter is only one of the group of disciples. Even though he is their leader, he is *primus inter pares*—first among equals—and is never detached from the group. Jesus creates a new community where all disciples are brothers, and Jesus alone is their Teacher and Master (23:8–10).

This is why the strengths and weaknesses of Peter are portrayed. Just like all the other disciples, Peter has strengths and weaknesses and is instructed by Jesus so that he can progress and understand Jesus's mission. Almost everything that is said of Peter is elsewhere said of the disciples. Peter is one of the disciples, but he also must carry out his specific role as leader of the Twelve and rock of the church. This does not exalt him or separate him; it is a functional role through which Jesus uses him. In like manner the Eleven (Peter included) are given the age-long commission to make disciples. Peter is to function as the rock and user of the keys, but once his role is performed, he ceases to be significant. He is like any other of the nameless disciples. This may have been Matthew's way of avoiding ongoing preeminence among the disciples. Since the nameless eleven disciples on the mountain in Galilee were the ones who were given the commission (28:16–20), the work of making disciples must be carried out throughout the age by all future disciples.

Peter plays an important role as a leader and spokesman for the disciples in the several incidents in Matthew's Gospel. But even as Matthew emphasizes Peter's leadership role, he also shows how Peter is an imperfect leader who is in process of development, as Jesus prepares him for the early days of the church ahead. For example, in the first

189. For my full treatment of Matthew's theological portrait of Peter and his developing leadership role, see Wilkins, "Matthew's Theological Understanding of Simon Peter," 173–216, 264.

of these incidents, Peter demonstrates tremendous courage when he requests to walk to Jesus on the water, something none of the great Old Testament figures had ever done. Yet at the same time, Peter's courage to go to Jesus on the water becomes the occasion for failure when he begins to sink.

#### 10.6.3.3.1 Peter Is an Example for Other Disciples

Since the disciples function in Matthew's Gospel as an example, both positive and negative, of what it means to be a disciple, the portrait of Simon Peter in Matthew's Gospel provides a personalized example of discipleship for Matthew's church. Most of the time Matthew presents the disciples as a nameless, faceless, collective unity. Peter stands out in sharp relief against this backdrop of anonymity, being the only named disciple to become the focus of special attention. He functions as a paradigm much like the disciples do as a group. In his strengths and in his weaknesses, he can be a paradigm to Matthew's church; so Matthew accentuates the truly human element in Peter. The church would find much in common with Peter's typically human characteristics. In his likeness to ordinary believers, with their highs and lows, he provides a means for instructing the church in the path of discipleship.[190]

#### 10.6.3.3.2 Peter Is an Example for Other Leaders

Peter likewise serves this function for the leaders of Matthew's church. In his success and failure as a leader Peter provides an instructive case study for the leadership of Matthew's church. In several instances the questions and responses that Peter voices to Jesus on behalf of the disciples were issues that still spoke to the church of Matthew's day—e.g., external purity (15:11–20), paying taxes (17:24–27), and forgiving brother or sister (18:21–35). As Jesus instructs Peter, instruction is provided for the church and its leaders. Peter will have a foundational role in establishing the church, but the focus is still on Jesus, who says, "I will build my church" (16:18). As Jesus had called Peter, corrected him and instructed him, so Jesus would do with leaders in the church.[191]

The following graph of events in Matthew's Gospel demonstrate how Peter is up and down in his discipleship to Jesus yet how he is continually led forward to be a leader among the Twelve.

---

190. One of the seminal studies to establish this thesis was in the ecumenical project in Brown, Donfried, and Reumann, *Peter in the New Testament*, 75–107, the chapter entitled "Peter in the Gospel of Matthew." See also the recent work of Bruce Henning, who "has shown that the kind of person allowed not only in the kingdom but as a high ranking person there can nonetheless be as flawed as the Matthean Peter"; Bruce Henning, "Stretching the Scope of Salvation in Matthew: The Significance of the Great Peter's Failings" *NTS* 68.4 (2022), 474–86; here 486.

191. Wilkins, *Concept of Disciple*, ch. 5; Wilkins, "Disciples, Discipleship," 208; Meier, *Companions and Competitors*, 221–45; more broadly on Peter, see Wiarda, *Peter in the Gospels*. As this negatively affects attempts at recreating the community identity and Peter's role, see Vine, *Audience of Matthew*, esp. chs. 3–6.

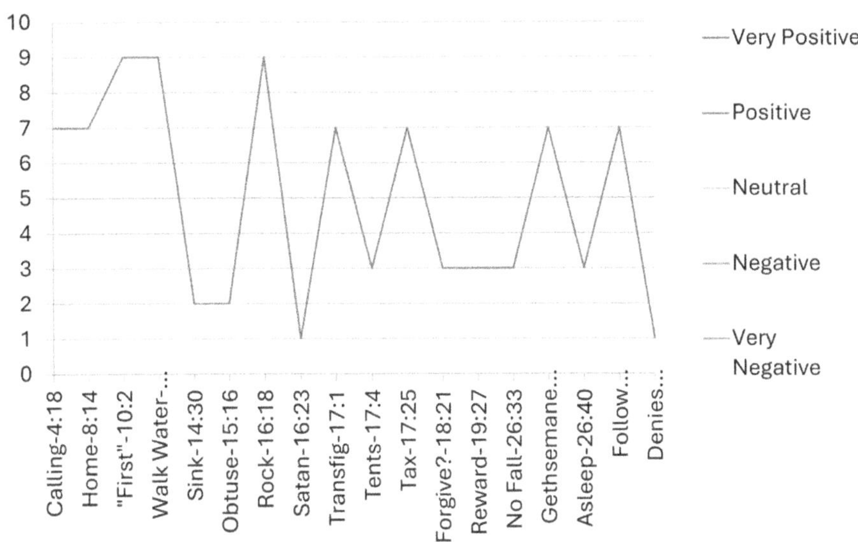


### *10.6.3.4 Jesus's Disciples Are Ambassadors of the Great Commission*

Jesus's training and teaching time with his followers in his earthly ministry resulted in the kind of disciple, and definition of disciple, that set his form of discipleship apart from other forms in Judaism and the Greco-Roman world. So, in the Great Commission, he said that his disciples were to make more of what he had made of them. The Commission encapsulates a significant aspect of Jesus's purpose for coming to earth. In addition, the placement of the Commission at the conclusion of Matthew's Gospel has long been recognized as an indication of Matthew's overall purpose for writing his Gospel.[192] It is especially crucial for our understanding of the role of the disciples in Matthew's Gospel. As the risen Jesus meets with those disciples who have been with him in his earthly ministry, now called "the eleven disciples" (28:16), he declares, "All authority in heaven and on earth has been given to me. Therefore go and make disciples of all nations, baptizing them in the name of the Father and of the Son and of the Holy Spirit, and teaching them to obey everything I have commanded you" (28:18–20).

This commissioning points once again to the uniqueness of Jesus's form of discipleship. Jesus's call was at the same time an invitation to salvation and a summons to service. Understood within the broader biblical concept of "calling," Jesus summoned his disciples in a way similar to the way God called Israel to be the blessed people and to be a blessing for others. Even as Israel was called not only to be God's people and to

192. For discussion, see B. Rod Doyle, "Matthew's Intention as Discerned by His Structure," *Revue Biblique* 95.1 (1988): 34–54; Bauer, *Structure of Matthew's Gospel*, esp. 109–28.

enjoy his blessing but also to be the source of blessing to all the nations of the earth, so also when Jesus issued his call it meant both a call to enter into a discipleship relationship with him and to become fellow workers with him in the kingdom.

Men and women were called into a relationship with Jesus, which secured their own salvation and secured the ongoing proclamation of the good news. While some passages seem to emphasize one element more than the other, Jesus's call to follow him—whether it was the Twelve or the broader group of disciples[193]—meant that those who responded would join him in both the blessings of the gospel message and the future proclamation of the gospel message.

Jesus committed his earthly ministry to making disciples within Israel (cf. John 4:1). In his ascended ministry, he commissions his disciples to "make disciples" among the nations (Matt 28:16–20). The obvious meaning of "making disciples" is to proclaim the gospel message among those who have not yet received forgiveness of sins.

All nations, now including both gentiles and Jews, receive the opportunity to become Jesus's disciples. Although some suggest that "all the nations" means only gentiles, not the Jews, since Matthew invariably only refers to gentiles by this title,[194] most recognize Matthew's overall intention is to include the Jews. The full expression "all the nations" is used four times in Matthew in settings that more naturally comprise all peoples, including Jews (24:9, 14; 25:32), as here.

Therefore, in the commission Matthew returns to the universal theme of the introductory verse of the Gospel (1:1). There the blessings promised to Abraham and through him to all people of the earth (Gen 12:3) are said now to be fulfilled in Jesus the Messiah. Matthew's purpose has been to show how Jesus is the Messiah of all peoples. His theme of universal salvation through Jesus (e.g., Matt 1:1; 2:1–12; 4:15–16; 8:5–13; 10:18; 13:38; 24:14) thus climaxes in the command to "make disciples of all the nations."[195] When we see Matthew's commission to make disciples of "all the nations" in the light of Luke's commission, that "repentance for the forgiveness of sins will be preached in his name to all nations, beginning at Jerusalem" (Luke 24:47), we understand that Jesus's ministry in Israel was to be the beginning point of what would be later a universal offer of salvation to all the peoples of the earth.[196]

193. Luke especially allows us to see the involvement of the broader circle of disciples in Jesus's earthly mission. In the ministry of the seventy (Luke 10:1–20) and the women who accompanied Jesus (8:1–3), Luke shows that disciples other than the Twelve went on mission with Jesus.

194. E.g., Stephen Hre Kio, "Understanding and Translating 'Nations' in Mt 28:19," *The Bible Translator* 41.2 (1990): 230–39; Douglas R. A. Hare, *The Theme of Jewish Persecution of Christians in the Gospel According to St. Matthew* (Cambridge: Cambridge University Press, 1967); Douglas R. A. Hare and Daniel J. Harrington, "Make Disciples of All the Gentiles," *CBQ* 37 (1975): 359–69.

195. Osborne, *Matthew*, 1080–83; Carson, "Matthew," 666–70; Alfred Plummer, *An Exegetical Commentary on the Gospel According to St. Matthew* (1915; repr., Grand Rapids: Baker, 1982), 430.

196. Cf. John P. Meier, "Nations or Gentiles in Matthew 28:19?," *CBQ* 39.1 (1977): 94–102; Joseph A. Fitzmyer, *The Gospel According to Luke (X–XXIV)*, AB 28A (Garden City, NY: Doubleday, 1985), 1583–84; Osborne, *Matthew*, 1079–80n25; Wilcox, "Jesus in the Light of His Jewish Environment," 169.

But Jesus's Great Commission implies more than securing salvation as Jesus's disciple. It also includes the process of growth as a disciple.[197] As he addresses the disciples and commands them to "make disciples of all the nations," Jesus tells them to make more of what he has made of them. The process will not be exactly the same as what Jesus did with them because the circumstances after Jesus's death and resurrection and Pentecost will change the process. However, the process will be similar in many ways.

Specifically, the process of growth is implied in the phrases "baptizing them in the name of the Father and of the Son and of the Holy Spirit, and teaching them to obey everything I have commanded you" (Matt 28:19–20). As a person responds to the invitation to come out of the nations to start life as a disciple, she or he begins the life of discipleship through baptism and through obedience to Jesus's teaching. The participle "baptizing" (*baptizontes*) describes the activity by which the new disciple identifies with Jesus and the community of disciples, and the participle "teaching" (*didaskontes*) introduces the activities by which disciples new and old grow in discipleship as they are obedient to what Jesus commanded.[198]

## 10.6.4 Matthew's Gospel as a Manual on Discipleship

As Matthew concludes his Gospel with Jesus's Commission to "make disciples of all the nations" (28:18–20), Jesus is telling the disciples to continue the disciple making that he began with them. The primary emphasis of the Great Commission is found in the *imperative* "make disciples" (*mathēteusate*), which implies both the call to discipleship and the process of growth in discipleship. Even as men and women are called from among the nations to start life as a disciple, they must in turn follow Jesus through baptism and through being taught to obey all that Jesus commanded.[199] The *participle* "go" (*poreuthentes*) points to the obligation of disciples to reach out to all the nations, and the *participles* "baptizing" (*baptizontes*) and "teaching" (*didaskontes*) describe activities through which new disciples grow in discipleship. Growth in discipleship includes both identification with Jesus's death and resurrection ("baptism") and obedience to all that Jesus had commanded the disciples in his earthly ministry ("teaching them to obey all that I have commanded").

197. Grant R. Osborne, *The Resurrection Narratives: A Redactional Study* (Grand Rapids: Baker Book House, 1984), 91; Moisés Silva, "New Lexical Semitisms?," *ZNTW* 69 (1978): 256n9.

198. Richard DeRidder, *Discipling the Nations* (Grand Rapids: Baker Book House, 1975), 190. For discussion of the meaning of baptism as "adherence," see William B. Badke, "Was Jesus a Disciple of John?," *Evangelical Quarterly* 62.3 (1990): 195–204.

199. In my view, in his unique and creative study Cedric Vine places too much emphasis upon existing "national structures," in which a small cadre of individuals (prophet, righteous person, disciple/teacher, wise person, scribe) adopt different discipleship roles to establish divine sovereignty of the kingdom of God; see Vine, *Jesus and the Nations*, passim; e.g., 25–27. Rather than "national structures," I suggest that the primary emphasis of the imperative "make disciples" (*mathēteusate*) in 28:19 is upon a universal offer of salvation to all the peoples of the earth, which then produces transformation of individuals as Jesus's disciples; so also Osborne, *Matthew*, 1080–83; Carson, "Matthew," 666–70; Peter Stuhlmacher, "Matt 28:16–20 and the Course of Mission in the Apostolic and Postapostolic Age," in *The Mission of the Early Church to Jews and Gentiles*, ed. Jostein Ådna and Hans Kvalbein, WUNT 2/127 (Tübingen: Mohr Siebeck, 2000), 17–43.

This leads to the conclusion that Matthew's Gospel is, at least in part, a manual on discipleship. Several factors point to Matthew's intention to provide in his Gospel resources for discipleship:

1. the major discourses are directed at least in part to the disciples;[200]
2. most of the sayings directed to the disciples are in fact teaching on discipleship;
3. the disciples are portrayed primarily in a positive, yet realistic, light; and
4. the disciples are called, trained and commissioned to carry out their own climactic mandate to "make disciples" (28:19).

The goal of the believer's life of faith is made clear, and the disciple is equipped to make more disciples.

The final participial phrase in Jesus's Great Commission, "teaching," like the second, "baptizing," is subordinate to the imperative "make disciples" and indicates the process by which disciples of Jesus are continually transformed through the discipleship and discipling process. *Discipleship* is the process by which a disciple (Christian) is transformed, while *discipling* is the involvement of one disciple helping another disciple to grow in his or her discipleship.

The basic elements of this final participial phrase are packed with significance (28:20).

### *10.6.4.1 "Them"*

The pronoun "them" (*autous*) in the phrase "teaching *them* to obey" includes that idea that everyone who has become a disciple of Jesus is to be involved in the process of discipleship. This is one of the key distinctives of the form of discipleship that Jesus initiated. Access to education by an esteemed rabbi was normally reserved for privileged men in rabbinic Judaism. Some rabbis denied young girls even the basics of torah instruction, such as Eliezer who says: "Whoever teaches Torah to his daughter is as if he teaches her sexual satisfaction" (m. Sotah 3:4 [Neusner]). But Jesus once again breaks down all barriers to indicate that all of his disciples—women and men, gentile and Jew, poor and rich—are to be taught to obey everything he commanded. This means that everyone who has heard the gospel message and has responded by believing on Jesus for eternal life is a *disciple/Christian/believer*, all of which are virtually synonymous terms (cf. Acts 2:44; 4:32; 5:14; 6:1, 7; 11:26; 26:28).

Today some incorrectly use the title "disciple" to refer to a person who is more committed than other Christians or to refer only to those who are involved in special "discipleship programs." But Jesus's commission emphasizes that a person becomes

200. Matt 5:1–2; 10:1–2; 13:10; 18:1; 23:1–3.

a disciple of Jesus when she or he believes the gospel message and attaches to Jesus. Therefore, all Christians are disciples. It is just that some are obedient disciples while others are not. That leads us to the next elements of this participial phrase.

### *10.6.4.2 "To Obey"*

The activity of discipleship is involved with "teaching them *to obey*" (*didaskontes autous tērein*). New disciples are to be taught the rudimentary elements of the Christian life, while more advanced teaching is given to mature disciples as they advance in the Christian life. But the emphasis is not simply upon acquisition of knowledge; the distinguishing feature is always that disciples are to "obey" or "conform" their lives to the teaching. Obedience was the hallmark of Jesus's disciples (12:49–50).

### *10.6.4.3 "Everything I Have Commanded You"*

All disciples, new and mature, are to be taught "to obey everything that I [Jesus] have commanded [*eneteilamēn*]," so that they increasingly become like him (cf. 10:24–25; Rom 8:29; 2 Cor 3:18). The verb *entellomai* does not imply only specific "commands" Jesus gave (as in the Old Testament understanding of "giving the law"). Rather, it includes Jesus's entire verbal ministry. Jesus is not pointing to particular commands but rather to the full explication in his life and ministry for disciples.[201] All that Jesus communicated by word of mouth is included in his commands, whether they are teachings, proverbs, blessings, parables, directives, or prophecies.

But we should go even further to suggest that all of Jesus's *life* is included in *entellomai*. The verb unifies Jesus's words and deeds and therefore recalls the entire Gospel of Matthew. Davies and Allison emphasize the all-inclusiveness of the expression, indicating that more than verbal revelation is involved, for verbal revelation cannot be separated from Jesus's life, which is itself a command. They state, "ἐνετειλάμην accordingly unifies word and deed and so recalls the entire book: everything is in view. The earthly ministry as a whole is an imperative."[202] And David Bauer perceptively notes that if we take seriously the inclusive language "all," we will not limit missional catechesis to the five great discourses, even if we give to them pride of place. "It must include the entirety of Jesus' instructions throughout the Gospel. Indeed, it is not limited even to what Jesus said, but encompasses also what he did. For, in Matthew's Gospel, Jesus instructs as much through actions as through speech."[203]

201. Gottlob Schrenk, "ἐντέλλομαι, ἐντολή," *TDNT* 2:545.

202. Davies and Allison, *Matthew*, 3:686. See also Hubert Frankemölle, "Zur Theologie der Mission im Matthäusevangelium," in *Mission im Neuen Testament*, ed. Karl Kertelge, Questiones Disputatae 93 (Freiburg, Germany: Herder & Herder, 1982), 93–129; here 127–28.

203. David R. Bauer, "The Theme of Mission in Matthew's Gospel from the Perspective of the Great Commission," *The Asbury Journal* 74.2 (2019): 240–76.

Thus, in the expression "teaching them to obey everything I have commanded you," the content of "commanded" is the complete expression of all that Jesus said and did. For the purposes of the context of the Great Commission, we can say that the content is Matthew's Gospel itself. All disciples, new and mature, are to study Jesus's authoritative life and words as found in this Gospel—indeed throughout Scripture—and they must be taught to obey it, follow it, observe it, and practice it in their own lives.[204]

### *10.6.4.4 A Manual on Discipleship*

Since "all I have commanded you" is so all-encompassing, in the five discourses and the alternating narratives of Jesus's life that are recorded in his Gospel, Matthew has prepared a compendium of the material that Jesus had initially given his first disciples in his life and words. Diverse perspectives contend that the five discourses signal some form of intended structure in Matthew's Gospel. Combined, the *narratives* of Jesus's life provide Jesus's example to follow, and the *discourses* give Jesus's instructions to obey, and together they are the basis of our ongoing transformation to become like Jesus.

Dale Allison points to the structure of alternating narratives and discourses and suggests that this provides an overall story where Jesus's oral instructions and imperatives are incarnated in Jesus's own life and ministry. Jesus's example lives out what he preached: "Jesus, in the First Gospel, embodies his sentences; the Lord lives as he speaks and speaks as he lives."[205] What Jesus did in making disciples of his first followers, succeeding generations of the church will do in the making of new disciples of Jesus.

Therefore, in the Great Commission it would be inappropriate for Jesus to state, "teaching them to obey everything I *taught* you." He did more than teach. He gave a new authoritative basis for life as a disciple in this age. We are to obey all Jesus commanded or authoritatively revealed as binding upon our lives as God's will for us, especially as Matthew has structured it in the six narratives and five discourses.

I therefore maintain that Matthew's Gospel is intended, at least in part, as a resource tool to help Jesus's disciples in their task of making and developing future disciples. Matthew's Gospel became a catechetical tool in the early church for next generations of disciples of Jesus. And for much of church history, the Gospel of Matthew was used as one of the primary catechetical tools for teaching disciples to obey all that Jesus commanded.[206] Matthew points to Jesus to be the supreme Lord and Teacher of the disciples, and emphasizes that Jesus's life and teaching produced in them obedience to

204. Peter Wick, "Verborgenes und Befohlenes: Schriftgelehrsamkeit und Jüngerschaft bei Matthäus," in *Schriftgelehrsamkeit und Toraethik: Die Bergpredigt im Kontext des Matthäusevangeliums*, ed. Jens-Christian Maschmeier (Stuttgart: Kohlhammer, 2021), 132–44. Wick argues that Jesus offers his disciples teaching "*Theorie*" that they must transform into real-world "*Praxis*" that is applicable in training for church service today (Wick, "Verborgenes und Befohlenes," 140).

205. Allison, "Structure, Biographical Impulse, and the *Imitatio Christi*," 154–55.

206. Guthrie, *New Testament Introduction*, 21.

and understanding of the truth of God's revelation.[207] That same obedience and understanding will continue to be the hallmark of disciples in the ongoing age. Therefore, Matthew's Gospel can be called "a manual on discipleship."

Here is where we can learn from history and heed Matthew's purpose for writing. With its alternating sections of narrative and discourse, this Gospel gives one of the most complete pictures of Jesus's *actions* and collections of his *sayings* available to us, an indispensable base from which the church will teach disciples to obey all that Jesus commanded.[208]

Matthew did not collect every action of Jesus, nor every word that Jesus uttered, but he was guided and superintended by the Holy Spirit to record what was needed for discipleship to Jesus throughout this age. Since discipleship is basically equivalent to teaching on spiritual formation and sanctification that we find elsewhere in Scripture, Matthew has provided us an invaluable tool for our growth in discipleship, which is the Christian life.

Jesus's life, in both word and deed, is the center of what his disciples are to deliberately teach new and experienced disciples to obey, and their lives will reflect the transforming will of God in their own every word and deed.[209] So, Matthew organizes his story of Jesus in alternating sections of narratives and discourses to reveal Jesus as the Messiah in deed and the Messiah in word.[210]

- In the six *narratives*, Matthew reveals Jesus's true identity in his deeds and introduces themes that will provide a picture of the divine/human Jesus Messiah who lived his life in the power and leading of the Spirit (cf. 1:18, 20; 3:16; 4:1; 12:18, 28). The Spirit will also empower and lead of Jesus's disciples who have obeyed the gospel summons to enter the kingdom (cf. 3:11; 10:20; 12:31; 28:19).[211] The narratives provide the example of Spirit-led humanity, and Jesus's disciples are to be taught to obey all that this divine-human Jesus Messiah commanded.
- In the five *discourses*, Matthew records Jesus's teachings (chs. 5–7), commands (ch. 10), parables (ch. 13), church directives (ch. 18), and prophecies (chs. 24–25) that will guide his followers in their discipleship to Jesus until the end of the age. Among other clues, Matthew signals these discourses by the way that he concludes them with the recurring phase, "And when Jesus had finished . . ." (*kai egeneto hote etelesen ho Iēsous*: 7:28; 11:1; 13:53; 19:1; 26:1). The five major

207. For a helpful emphasis on Jesus teaching the church through Matthew's Gospel and the discourses, and present-day relevance, see David P. Scaer, *Discourses in Matthew: Jesus Teaches the Church* (St. Louis: Concordia, 2004). See also Wick, "Verborgenes und Befohlenes," 132–44.

208. Cf. Nienhuis, *Concise Guide*, 22–24; Allison, "Structure, Biographical Impulse," 135–55.

209. Carson, "Matthew," 669–70.

210. Wilkins, "Disciples, Discipleship," 208.

211. Roland Deines, "The Holy Spirit in Matthew's Gospel," in White, Evans, and Wenham, *Earliest Perceptions of Jesus*, 213–35.

> discourses are intended as instruction in, and clarification of, what it means to be Jesus's unique kind of disciple.[212] The basic thrust of each discourse points to intentional well-roundedness.

The *narratives* and *discourses* provide a holistic presentation of the kind of discipleship that was to be taught to disciples as the basis for full-orbed obedience to Jesus Messiah and became the basis for Christian catechesis within the church throughout its history.

In my earlier discussion of the structure of Matthew's Gospel, I partially developed the following chart. It displays the narratives and *discourses* of Matthew's Gospel and my understanding of what each reveals about Jesus Messiah in deed and *Jesus Messiah in word.*

| **"TEACHING THEM TO OBEY EVERYTHING I HAVE COMMANDED YOU" (MATT 28:20)**<br>**Matthew's** Narrative-*Discourse* **Structure of the**<br>Life and Ministry of Jesus Messiah as the Transformational Model of Discipleship **and**<br>***Jesus's Oral Guidance for Discipleship to Jesus Messiah in the Kingdom of Heaven*** | |
|---|---|
| Narrative One (chs 1–4): | Jesus Immanuel: The Messiah of Israel and the Hope of Gentiles (chs. 1–4).<br>Jesus Messiah arrives in history to save his people from their sins (1:21), to be called a Nazarene (2:23), to fulfill all righteousness in his baptism (3:15), to be tempted as the divine-human Son of God (4:1–11), and to begin advancing the messianic kingdom as he calls his first followers (4:12–25). |
| *Discourse One* (chs. 5–7). | *Kingdom Discipleship to Jesus Messiah: The Sermon on the Mount* (chs. 5–7) develops what it means to be ***kingdom-life disciples***. Jesus expounds the reality of a radical everyday discipleship lived in the presence and power of the kingdom of God within the disciples' everyday world. As his disciples, we will be a living demonstration of the reality of the kind of life that is available to the world. |
| Narrative Two (chs. 8–9) | Jesus Messiah Demonstrates the Power of the Kingdom of Heaven in his Miraculous Ministry (chs. 8–9). The authoritative power of Messiah is demonstrated as the miracle-working Son of God (8:1–9:38) |
| *Discourse Two* (ch. 10). | *Mission-Driven Discipleship in the Kingdom of Heaven: The Mission Mandate* (ch. 10) develops what it means to be ***mission-driven disciples***. Jesus commissions all his disciples to go out to share and live the good news of the kingdom of heaven to an alien and often hostile world until his return. |
| Narrative Three (chs. 11–12) | Jesus Messiah Experiences Opposition from the Religious Leadership of Israel (chs. 11–12). Jesus Messiah is the Lord of the Sabbath and humble Son of the Father who confronts the religious leaders of Israel. But they plotted how they might kill Jesus (12:14). |
| *Discourse Three* (ch. 13) | *Clandestine Kingdom Discipleship in the Kingdom: Parables of the Mysteries of the Messianic Kingdom* (ch. 13). The *Parabolic Disclosure* develops what it means to be ***clandestine-kingdom disciples***. Through parables Jesus tests the hearts of the crowd to reveal whether the message of the kingdom of heaven has taken root and is producing fruit, or whether it has been unproductive. Through parables Jesus also reveals to his disciples what it means for Jesus's them to live as kingdom subjects covertly in a world that has not yet experienced the fully consummated kingdom of heaven. |

212. Dunn, *Jesus According to the New Testament*, 35.

| | |
|---|---|
| Narrative Four (chs. 14–17) | Jesus Messiah's Divine Identity is Demonstrated—He is the Son of God Who Will Be the Crucified Messiah. (chs. 14–17). The full identity of Jesus Messiah is revealed as the Son of God is worshiped (13:54–16:20) and the suffering of the Messiah is revealed (16:21–17:27). |
| *Discourse Four* (ch. 18) | *Community Discipleship within the Church and the church: The Community Prescription* (ch. 18). The Community Prescription for Jesus Messiah's Church (ch. 18) develops what it means to be ***church-oriented disciples***, members of the universal Church that Jesus builds (16:18) and the local church community of disciples (ch. 18). Discipleship to Jesus is expressed through a church that is characterized by humility, responsibility, purity, accountability, discipline, forgiveness, reconciliation, and restoration. |
| Narrative Five (chs. 19–23) | Jesus Messiah Asserts Divine Authority over Israel and Its Leadership (chs. 19–23). The community of the Messiah is demonstrated (19–20), and Jesus Messiah asserts his authority over Jerusalem and Israel's leaders. The triumphant King of Israel enters Jerusalem, clears the temple of hypocritical religious activity, and pronounces judgment on the leadership of Israel (chs. 21–23). |
| *Discourse Five* (chs. 24–25) | *The* Eschatological Forecast focuses on the expectant preparation for Jesus's return with power. This Olivet Discourse develops what it means to be ***expectant-sojourner disciples*** (chs. 24–25). Jesus looks down the long corridor of time and prophesies to his disciples of his return, the end of the age, and the establishment of his messianic throne. This discourse culminates Jesus's teaching on discipleship by describing how his disciples are to live each day in this age of the already-not-yet consummation of the kingdom of God in expectant preparation for his return with power. As Jesus's disciples, we are to *live* as though Jesus was coming back tonight but *plan* as though he is not coming back for a hundred years. |
| Narrative Six (chs. 26–28) | Jesus Messiah Is Crucified and Risen with a Divine Commission (chs 26–28) Jesus Messiah is betrayed and abandoned by his own disciples, vilified by Israel, crucified by Rome, and rises with a divine Commission to make disciples of all the nations. The crucified yet risen Messiah is with his disciples until the end of the age as we make disciples of all the nations. |

With an intentional strategy to develop this kind of disciple, Matthew's Gospel becomes a God-given guideline for intentional development. I once heard someone say that the church is filled with "undiscipled disciples." That is, although we may be committed to missions to the extent that we are fully committed to *going* to the world and participating in *evangelism*, which produces disciples, and *baptism*, which enfolds disciples, we have not fulfilled Jesus's purposes until we are likewise fully committed to carrying out the rest of the Great Commission, which is *teaching disciples to obey all that Jesus commanded*. That is a central purpose behind the writing of Matthew's Gospel, and it is the purpose of the resurrected Jesus in calling us to carry out fully his Great Commission.

When understood within the context of the first-century AD social and religious setting, the Great Commission allows us to see that Jesus was calling for a distinct form of discipleship. Becoming Jesus's disciple was not a vocational change, nor a political attachment, nor even a new stirring of God. Deciding on responding to the call to be Jesus's disciple meant being faced with the eternal decision of whether one would follow Jesus as the way to eternal life and personal transformation. Any other attachment, whether familial or religious or economic, was substituting another master for Jesus.

The final saying of Jesus in this Gospel is what gives us the assurance that we can carry out his purpose in our lives, because he promises unconditionally: "And surely I am with you always, to the very end of the age" (28:20). Our discipleship to the risen Jesus continues to be our greatest source of comfort, power, and security.

As Matthew has demonstrated over and over in this Gospel, the arrival of Jesus began the greatest revolution that history has ever known. It is a revolution that begins in the heart, where Jesus enters in and begins the transformation of regenerated righteousness. But then it extends to every area of our lives, so that our physical, emotional, mental, and relational life is impacted by the power of the Spirit of God to produce the righteousness of the kingdom of heaven.

As the new disciple is baptized and taught to obey all that Jesus commanded, Jesus is present. Those obeying the command are comforted by the awareness that the risen Jesus will continue to transform all his disciples. Jesus Immanuel is always present for his disciples to follow, to be transformed, and to offer this same hope to all the nations.

*Chapter 11*

# THE "CHURCH" AND THE "CHURCH" IN MATTHEW'S GOSPEL

## *Jesus Builds His C/CHURCH Universally and Locally*

### BIBLIOGRAPHY

**Allison, Gregg R.** *Sojourners and Strangers: The Doctrine of the Church*. FET. Wheaton, IL: Crossway, 2012. **Bayer, Hans F.** *Apostolic Bedrock: Christology, Identity, and Character Formation According to Peter's Canonical Testimony*. PBM. Milton Keynes, UK: Paternoster, 2016. **Bockmuehl, Markus.** *Simon Peter in Scripture and Memory: The New Testament Apostle in the Early Church*. Grand Rapids: Baker Academic, 2012. **Bond, Helen K., and Larry W. Hurtado,** eds. *Peter in Early Christianity*. Grand Rapids: Eerdmans, 2015. **Brown, Raymond E., Karl P. Donfried, and John Reumann,** eds. *Peter in the New Testament*. Minneapolis: Augsburger; New York: Paulist, 1973. **Burgess, Joseph A.** *A History of the Exegesis of Matthew 16:17–19 from 1781 to 1965*. Ann Arbor, MI: Edwards Brothers, 1976. **Caragounis, Chrys C.** *Peter and the Rock*. BZNW 58. Berlin: de Gruyter, 1990. **Cullmann, Oscar.** *Peter: Disciple, Apostle, Martyr: A Historical and Theological Essay*. Translated by Floyd V. Filson. 2nd ed. Philadelphia: Westminster, 1962. **Dunn, James D. G.** *Unity and Diversity in the New Testament: An Inquiry into the Character of Earliest Christianity*. 2nd ed. London: SCM; Philadelphia: Trinity, 1990. **Fitzmyer, Joseph.** "Aramaic *Kepha'* and Peter's Name in the New Testament." Pages 121–32 in *To Advance the Gospel*. New York: Crossroad, 1981. **Foster, Paul.** "The Church in the Gospel of Matthew." Pages 128–33 in *The Cambridge Companion to the New Testament*. Edited by Patrick Gray. CCR. Cambridge: Cambridge University Press, 2021. ———. *Community, Law and Mission in Matthew's Gospel*. WUNT 2/177. Tübingen: Mohr Siebeck, 2004.**France, R. T.** "Matthew's Gospel and the Church." Pages 242–78 in *Matthew: Evangelist and Teacher*. Grand Rapids: Zondervan, 1989. **Gruen, Erich S.** "Synagogues and Voluntary Associations as Institutional Models: A Response to Richard Ascough and Ralph Korner." *JJMJS* 3 (2016): 125–31. **Hanson, Paul D.** *The People Called: The Growth of Community in the Bible*. San Francisco: Harper & Row, 1986. **Hengel, Martin.** *Saint Peter:*

*The Underestimated Apostle*. Translated by Thomas H. Trapp. Grand Rapids: Eerdmans, 2010. **Hiers, Richard H.** "'Binding' and 'Loosing': The Matthean Authorizations." *JBL* 104 (1985): 233–50. **Hurtado, Larry W.** "The Apostle Peter in Protestant Scholarship: Cullmann, Hengel, and Bockmuehl." Pages 1–15 in *Peter in Early Christianity*. Edited by Helen K. Bond and Larry W. Hurtado. Grand Rapids: Eerdmans, 2015. **Kingsbury, Jack Dean.** "The Figure of Peter in Matthew's Gospel as a Theological Problem." *JBL* 98 (1979): 67–83. **Korner, Ralph J.** *The Origin and Meaning of* Ekklēsia *in the Early Jesus Movement*. AJEC 98. Leiden: Brill, 2017. **Lap, F.** *Peter: The Myth, the Man and the Writings: A Study of the Early Petrine Text and Tradition*. JSNTSup 239. London: Sheffield Academic, 2003. **Last, Richard.** "*Ekklēsia* Outside the Septuagint and the *Dēmos*: The Titles of Greco-Roman Associations and Christ-Followers' Groups." *JBL* 137.4 (2018): 959–80. **Lewis, Jack P.** "'The Gates of Hell Shall Not Prevail Against It' (Matt 16:18): A Study of the History of Interpretation." *JETS* 38.3 (1995): 349–367. **Lim, Eunyung.** *Entering God's Kingdom (Not) Like a Little Child: Images of the Child in Matthew, 1 Corinthians, and Thomas*. BZNW 243. Berlin: de Gruyter, 2021. **Lohfink, Gerhard.** *Jesus and Community: The Social Dimension of Christian Faith*. Philadelphia: Fortress, 1984. **Macaskill, Grant.** *The New Testament and Intellectual Humility*. Oxford: Oxford University Press, 2018. **McClister, David.** "'Where Two or Three Are Gathered Together': Literary Structure as a Key to Meaning in Matt 17:22–20:19." *JETS* 39.4 (1996): 549–60. **McIver, Robert K.** "The Parable of the Weeds Among the Wheat (Matt 13:24–30, 36–43) and the Relationship Between the Kingdom and the Church as Portrayed in the Gospel of Matthew." *JBL* 114.4 (1995): 643–59. **Merkle, Benjamin L.** "The Meaning of Εκκλησία in Matthew 16:18 and 18:17." *BSac* 167 (2010): 281–91. **Nickelsburg, George W. E.** "Enoch, Levi and Peter: Recipients of Revelation in Upper Galilee." *JBL* 100.4 (1981): 590–606. **Pennington, Jonathan T.** "Are We Missing the Point of Matthew 18?" *Christianity Today Pastors: His Body Endures* (March 29, 2022): 58–61. **Perkins, Pheme.** *Peter: Apostle for the Whole Church*. SPNT. Columbia, SC: University of South Carolina Press, 1994. **Runesson, Anders.** *The Origins of the Synagogue: A Socio-Historical Study*. Coniectanea Biblica, New Testament 37. Stockholm, Sweden: Almquiest & Wiksell, 2001. **Ryan, Jordan J.** *The Role of the Synagogue in the Aims of Jesus*. Minneapolis: Fortress, 2017. **Trebilco, Paul.** *Self-Designations and Group Identity in the New Testament*. Cambridge: Cambridge University Press, 2012. **Wiarda, Timothy J.** *Peter in the Gospels: Pattern, Personality, and Relationship*. WUNT 2/127. Tübingen: Mohr Siebeck, 2000. **Wilcox, Max.** "Peter and the Rock: A Fresh Look at Matthew XVI. 17–19." *NTS* 22 (1976): 73–88. **Wilkins, Michael J.** "Matthew's Theological Understanding of Simon Peter." Pages 173–224 in *The Concept of Disciple in Matthew's Gospel: As Reflected in the Use of the Term* Μαθητής. NovTSup 59. Leiden: Brill, 1988. ———. "Peter's Declaration of Jesus' Identity in Caesarea Philippi." Pages 293–381 in *Key Events in the Life of the Historical Jesus: A Collaborative Exploration of Context and Coherence*. Edited by Darrell L. Bock and Robert L. Webb. WUNT 247. Tübingen: Mohr Siebeck, 2009.

## 11.1 INTRODUCTION: THE "CHURCH" AND THE "CHURCH" IN MATTHEW'S GOSPEL

Surrounding the ceiling of St Peter's Basilica in Rome is a Latin quotation from Matthew's Gospel in letters six feet high: *Tu es Petrus et super hanc petram aedificabo ecclesiam meam*, translated in English: "You are Peter, and on this rock I will build my church" (16:18). The passage cited in the Vatican Basilica refers to the "CHURCH" universal; its other occurrences in Matthew's Gospel refer to the local "CHURCH" congregation of Christians (18:17 twice). As Ian Boxall notes, "This is one major reason—Matthew's popularity in the early Church is another—why Matthew has inherited the title of 'the Gospel of the Church.'"[1]

Matthew's Gospel is unique among the canonical Gospels in the use of the term *ekklēsia*. We noted that it occurs three times in Matthew's Gospel but nowhere else in the canonical Gospels. These occurrences in Matthew's Gospel are highly significant. Some scholars suggest that this terminology emerged in a post-Easter setting as believers in Jesus identified their corporate communities while differentiating their new groups from Judaism, which described their own corporate gatherings as "synagogues."[2] But in my view, Davies and Allison are moving in the right direction when they contend that there is no reason to regard 16:17–19 as the product of post-Matthean interpolation.[3] These words of revelation are best seen as Jesus's prophecies about Peter's future role in the Jesus movement.[4] In 16:18 Jesus refers to the *universal* CHURCH, while Jesus's statement in 18:17 refers to the *local* CHURCH.[5] In this chapter we will render *ekklēsia* as CHURCH and CHURCH, the large capital letters and small capital letters indicating the difference between the *universal* "CHURCH" and the *local* "CHURCH."

## 11.2 THE CHURCH: JESUS BUILDS THE UNIVERSAL "CHURCH"

The first of occurrence of *ekklēsia* is in the context of Peter's declaration at Caesarea Philippi of Jesus's identity. Peter steps forward once again as a leader and spokesperson for the others (cf. 10:2)[6] and declares, "You are the Messiah, the Son of the living God" (16:16).

1. Boxall, *Discovering Matthew*, 134.

2. See Paul Foster, "The Gospel of Matthew," in *The Cambridge Companion to the New Testament*, CCR (Cambridge: Cambridge University Press, 2021), 128; Luz, *Matthew 8–20*, 355–59; Perkins, *Peter*, esp. 1–14; F. Lap, *Peter: The Myth, the Man and the Writings: A Study of the Early Petrine Text and Tradition*, JSNTSup 239 (London: Sheffield Academic, 2003), esp. 237–53.

3. Davies and Allison, *Matthew*, 2:621. See also Keener, *Matthew* (2009), 423–24; Benjamin L. Merkle, "The Meaning of Εκκλησία in Matthew 16:18 and 18:17," *BSac* 167 (2010): 281–91.

4. E.g., Keener, *Matthew* (2009), 425; Osborne, *Matthew*, 626–30; Gundry, *Matthew*, 330–31; Nolland, *Matthew*, 620–27; Morris, *Matthew*, 424–25; Wiarda, *Peter in the Gospels*, esp. 206–28; Hengel, *Saint Peter*, esp. 1–35; Bockmuehl, *Simon Peter in Scripture and Memory*, esp. 3–32.

5. Davies and Allison, *Matthew*, 2:785.

6. Since the question was posed by Jesus to the group of disciples ("He said to *them* [plural], 'But who do *you* [plural] say I am?"; 16:15, ESV), Peter functions at least in part as spokesman for the Twelve.

### 11.2.1 Jesus's Pronouncements About Peter (16:17–19)

Once Peter makes his grand declaration of whom he understands Jesus to be, Jesus in turn makes a grand beatitude and pronouncement about Peter.[7] These verses (16:17–19) have an obvious parallelism Matthew employs that helps in understanding Jesus's words. There are three parallel groups of three clauses (tristichs), with the first line of each unit setting the theme or making a pronouncement about Peter, and the second and third lines of each (composed in antithetic parallelism) forming an explanation or consequence of the respective first line.[8]

1. Blessed are you, Simon son of Jonah,
   for this was not revealed to you by flesh and blood,
   but by my Father in heaven. (16:17)
2. And I tell you that you are Peter,
   and on this rock I will build my church,
   and the gates of Hades will not overcome it. (16:18)
3. I will give you the keys of the kingdom of heaven;
   whatever you bind on earth will be bound in heaven,
   and whatever you loose on earth will be loosed in heaven. (16:19)

#### *11.2.1.1 Peter Is the Recipient of Blessed Revelation (16:17)*

Jesus's first statement to Peter is a beatitude. The Greek word for "blessed' (*makarios*) is the same as found in the Beatitudes of the Sermon on the Mount. As in the Beatitudes, this is not a *conferral* of blessing but an *acknowledgment* that Peter has been blessed personally by a revelation from God, Jesus's Father (cf. 5:3–11; 11:6; 13:16; 24:46).[9] Jesus contrasts what humans have discerned about him on their own ("Who do people say the Son of Man is?"), with what his disciples have gleaned through Jesus's instruction and the Father's revelation.

Although Peter apparently acts as spokesman for the group, Jesus's reply is directed to Peter personally. Each of the pronouncements about Peter are in the second person singular: "'Blessed are *you* [*ei*], Simon son of Jonah, for this was not revealed to *you* [*soi*] by flesh and blood, but by my Father in heaven" (16:17). Peter is the *personal* recipient of revelation from the Father, which is a *personal* blessing to Peter. On the other hand, what Peter confesses has already been confessed by all the disciples (cf. 14:33),[10] and

7. For an overview of Protestant scholars focusing on Simon Peter, see Larry W. Hurtado, "The Apostle Peter in Protestant Scholarship: Cullmann, Hengel, and Bockmuehl," in *Peter in Early Christianity*, ed. Helen K. Bond and Larry W. Hurtado (Grand Rapids: Eerdmans, 2015), 1–15.

8. See Wilkins, *Concept of Disciple*, 186–87.

9. Cf. Bonnard, *Matthieu*, 244.

10. Most commentators agree that the significant feature concerned the declaration of Jesus as "Son of God," which is the similar declaration of 14:33; cf. Kingsbury, "Figure of Peter,"

the expression of blessedness is like that already attributed to all the disciples, who had received a revelation of the mysteries of the kingdom of heaven (cf. 13:11, 16).[11]

Peter is obviously singled out, but he is still within the circle of disciples. The revelation given to him by the Father is a blessing personally but not so far as to set him apart from or above the rest of the disciples.[12] Indeed, as spokesman he represents the common view of the group, and the blessing and revelation may be obliquely directed to the group as well. His declaration is an answer *for* the disciples (16:15, 16) and provokes a charge *to* all the disciples (16:20). Perhaps it is best to say that Peter is individually singled out for his act of leadership in making the declaration, yet his leadership role is from *within* the circle of disciples. He is blessed personally yet representationally as well. The personal address continues with Peter as special focus: "And I tell *you* [*soi*] that *you are Peter* [*sy ei Petros*] . . . I will give *you* [*soi*] . . . whatever *you bind* [*dēsēs*] . . . whatever *you loose* [*lysēs*]" (16:18–19). But even with the pronouncement about the special role that Peter will play, the rest of the disciples will also be included in similar roles (e.g., 18:18–20).

### *11.2.1.2 Peter, the Rock, and the Everlasting Church (16:18)*

The second tristich begins with the statement, "And I tell you that," a phrase that carries a tone of consequence stemming from the prior statement of Peter. Peter made an extremely important declaration about Jesus, and in response to this Jesus makes a significant pronouncement to, and about, Peter. Jesus calls Peter here by the name that he had given him, which is transliterated from Aramaic in John 1:42 as *Kēphas*. As John specifies, the name Peter (*Petros*) is the Greek equivalent for *Kēphas* (Aramaic). Some understand this to be the occasion of the giving of the name,[13] but more likely this is a pronouncement prompted by the declaration of Peter who already bears the name.[14]

This is one of the most discussed and debated verses in Scripture[15] and contains three significant features that must be interpreted to understand clearly Jesus's intention for Peter and the Church to come: (a) the relationship of Peter to "this rock," (b) the nature of the "Church," and (c) the meaning of the "gates of Hades" in relationship to the Church.

---

74n25, and *Matthew*, 78–83; Carson, "Matthew," 416; Gundry, *Matthew*, 330; Schweizer, *Matthew*, 340; Hill, *Matthew*, 260; Tasker, *Matthew*, 159.

11. M. D. Goulder, *Midrash and Lection in Matthew* (London: SPCK, 1974), 387.

12. Contra Beare, *Matthew*, 354; Manson, *Sayings of Jesus*, 204.

13. E.g., Schweizer calls this the Matthean bestowal of the name: Schweizer, *Matthew*, 341.

14. Cf. Osborne, *Matthew*, 626–27; Wilhelm Mundle, "πέτρα," *NIDNTT* 3:383; Josef Blank, "The Person and Office of Peter in the New Testament," in *Truth and Certainty*, ed. Edward Schillebeeckx and Bas van Iersel, trans. Erika Young, Concilium 83 (New York: Herder and Herder, 1973), 50.

15. For an overview of the history of this discussion see Cullmann, *Peter*, 155–70; Joseph A. Burgess, *A History of the Exegesis of Matthew 16:17–19 from 1781 to 1965* (Ann Arbor, MI: Edwards Brothers, 1976); Raymond E. Brown, Karl P. Donfried, and John Reumann, eds., *Peter in the New Testament* (Minneapolis: Augsburg; New York: Paulist, 1973).

*11.2.1.2.1 Peter and the Rock*

The first feature of the saying to Peter has a well-known wordplay in Greek: "You are Peter [*Petros*], and on this rock [*petra*] I will build my church." In Aramaic, almost certainly the language that Jesus spoke on this occasion, the same word, *kêphāʾ*, would have been used for both "Peter" and "rock." Translating the wordplay into Greek, Matthew would most naturally use the feminine noun *petra*, because it is the most common and closest equivalent to *kêphāʾ*, which is a common noun in Aramaic texts found in the Qumran caves, meaning "rock" or "crag," or "a part of a mountainous or hilly region."[16] But when it came to recording the wordplay in Greek for his Gospel, Matthew was required to use the less common noun *petros* in the first half of the wordplay because it is a masculine noun, for he would not refer to Peter with a feminine noun.[17] But the use of the two different Greek words would not change the basic meaning of the wordplay, because *petros* and *petra* were at times used interchangeably.[18]

The natural wordplay in Aramaic, using one word, is best served in Greek by the two different words, because the masculine form would lend itself as a more likely designation of the *person* Peter, and the feminine form (a literary variant) for a *feature* of him suggested by the sense of the Aramaic *kêphāʾ*.[19] With the same Aramaic word used in both halves of the wordplay, the meaning would be, "You are Rock, and on this rock I will build my Church."

This helps interpret the meaning of the wordplay, which has been interpreted in three primary ways.

1. Drawing on the close relationship of the terms in both Aramaic and Greek and the syntactical prominence of the person confessing, one view stresses that the most obvious intent of the wordplay is to refer to Peter. Peter will play a foundational role in the establishment of Jesus's CHURCH.[20]
2. The second view rejects any notion of the CHURCH being built upon a human person and argues that the Greek wordplay makes a distinction between *Petros* and *petra* and that the demonstrative pronoun "this" (*tautē*) points away from

16. Joseph Fitzmyer, "Aramaic *Kephaʾ* and Peter's Name in the New Testament," in *To Advance the Gospel* (New York: Crossroad, 1981), 115.

17. Cullmann, *Peter*, 18–19; Mundle, "πέτρα," *NIDNTT* 3:383.

18. Colin Brown, "πέτρα," *NIDNTT* 3:386.

19. Fitzmyer suggests that *kêphāʾ* may have nuances that are reflected in the two Greek terms. This would not mean the stark differences of "stone" and "bedrock," but subtle differences, like the man himself and "an aspect of him that was to be played upon" ("*Kephaʾ*," 119). This specific nuance remains to be tested, but his suggestion is helpful.

20. This was the interpretation of most of the early church fathers, although very early many fought against its use for establishing any kind of papacy (e.g., Ignatius, Justin, Origen, Tertullian, Cyprian, Firmilian; see Cullmann, *Peter*, 159–62). This became the view of the Roman Catholic Church and is held today by scholars such as those represented in Brown, Donfried, Reumann, *Peter*, 92–93. It is also the dominant view held of those of a broader confessional background, such as Albright and Mann, *Matthew*, 647; Carson, "Matthew," 418–20; France, *Gospel of Matthew*, 254–55; Morris, *Matthew*, 422–24; Stendahl, *School of St. Matthew*, 787.

Peter as a person and specifies an *aspect* of him.[21] In this view it is the truth of the declaration,[22] or the faith[23] of Peter expressed in the declaration that is the rock upon which the CHURCH will be built.

3. The last view likewise claims that Jesus intends a contrast between *Petros* and *petra*, but it differs by observing that other New Testament passages refer to Christ as the "rock"[24] and the "foundation"[25] and that Jesus refers to *himself* as the rock upon which the CHURCH will be built. This view likewise contends that the demonstrative pronoun "this" points away from Peter and to Jesus himself.[26]

Each view has its strengths, but several considerations combine to point to the first view as the preferred interpretation—Jesus intended Peter as the antecedent to "this rock" upon which he will build his CHURCH. In the first place, Jesus's pronouncement is directed toward Peter personally, both before and after the wordplay, and it is unlikely that a change of reference would have been made without some explicit indication. The second person singular verbal form and personal pronouns, plus the specification of his human name, indicate that the stress is on Peter personally: "And I tell *you* [*soi*] that *you are* Peter [*sy ei Petros*] . . . I will give *you* [*soi*] . . . whatever *you bind* [*dēsēs*] . . . whatever *you loose* [*lysēs*]" (16:18–19).

Second, the copulative "and" (*kai*) more naturally signals *identification* of the halves of the wordplay than *contrast*: "You are Peter *and* upon this rock." Contrast is necessary if the saying points to the declaration or Christ.

Third, "Peter" is the nearest explicit antecedent to "rock," and the nearest explicit antecedent is preferred over an implied or more distant antecedent unless something in the context specifies another referent. No other referent is specified in the passage.

Fourth, the Aramaic substratum almost certainly identifies Peter as the intended antecedent (as does the interchangeability of the terms *petros* and *petra*). Jesus's speaking Aramaic on this occasion is much more probable than positing that Jesus was speaking Greek.[27]

21. This view was held early in church history by John Chrysostom and attested to by Origen, Eusebius, Ambrose, and Theodore of Mopsuestia (cf. Cullmann, *Peter*, 162; Brown, Donfried, and Reumann, *Peter*, 93 and n216). More recently this has been proposed by Allen, *Matthew*, 176; McNeile, *Matthew*, 241; Mundle, "πέτρα," *NIDNTT* 3:384–85, and Caragounis, *Peter and the Rock*.

22. Caragounis, *Peter and the Rock*, esp. 88–119.

23. This is a view held by Luther (cited in Cullmann, *Peter*, 162), and early in the twentieth century by A. B. Bruce, "The Gospel According to Matthew," in *The Expositor's Greek Testament*, (n.d.; repr., Grand Rapids: Eerdmans, 1976), 1:224; cf. also Tasker, *Matthew*, 162.

24. E.g., Matt 21:42, but the term used is *lithos*; cf. 1 Cor 10:4, where the term used is *petra*.

25. E.g., 1 Cor 3:11; 1 Pet 2:4–8.

26. This view was held as early as Origen and Augustine (cf. Cullmann, *Peter*, 162; Brown, Donfried, and Reumann, *Peter*, 93n216). This was also the major view of Luther, Calvin, and many of the Reformers (cf. Cullmann, *Peter*, 162–63). More recently, some who hold to the Matthean creation of the passage in Greek have also proposed that the reference is to Christ and/or his words (e.g., Max Wilcox, "Peter and the Rock: A Fresh Look at Matthew XVI. 17–19," *NTS* 22 [1976]: 73–88; Gundry, *Matthew*, 334).

27. See Carson, "Matthew, 416–20, for other valuable support.

Thus, the most natural reading of the wordplay is to see that Jesus points to Peter as one who will play a foundational role in the establishment of his CHURCH. This is a notion consistent with the way in which from the beginning Peter was spokesman and leader of the Twelve. The leadership role he was beginning to assume at the time of the declaration is recognized by Jesus and is promised to be extended in laying the foundation of the CHURCH.

This is borne out in the historical record. Jesus appeared to Peter after the resurrection and gave him special encouragement to feed Jesus's sheep (John 21). Peter held a leadership position among the disciples prior to Pentecost (Acts 1:15–26) and was the leading figure/preacher at Pentecost and beyond.[28] Peter is given a unique function and position in the foundation of the CHURCH. This does not mean that Peter builds the church (Jesus says "*I* will build my church") but that he is important in the first days of its foundation. Actually, he disappears from the narrative of Acts after the foundation is laid (Acts 16 and on).[29]

Although Peter's foundational role was later taken to an extreme by the Roman Catholic Church to invest Peter with an authority and a succession of leadership,[30] we should not react and go to the opposite extreme and deny the natural reading of the wordplay. As Carson notes, "If it were not for Protestant reactions against extremes of Roman Catholic interpretation, it is doubtful whether many would have taken 'rock' to be anything or anyone other than Peter."[31]

#### *11.2.1.2.2 Peter, Jesus, and the* CHURCH

The second phrase of this first saying to Peter gives a prediction of Jesus's new community, the universal CHURCH. Matthew is the only evangelist to use the term *ekklēsia* (cf. 16:18; 18:18 [2x]). The two words in the Old Testament regularly used for the "congregation" of Israel in the exodus period are the Hebrew terms *ʿdh* and *qhl*. In the LXX *ʿdh* is mostly translated *synagōgē* and never *ekklēsia*. The term *qhl* is mostly translated *ekklēsia*, but also quite often *synagōgē*. Both terms involve the concept of a gathered group.[32] At Qumran both terms are used of the Qumran community (cf. 1QM IV, 9–10; 1QSa II, 4), which France understands as "probably with reference to seeing themselves as the counterpart to the Exodus congregation of Israel."[33] This then brings to mind the "community/assembly [*qahal*] of the Lord" (Deut 23:3; cf. 5:22).

In the selection of the twelve disciples/apostles to go with his message of fulfillment to Israel (Matt 10:1–6), who will judge the tribes of Israel (19:28), Jesus points

28. Acts 2:14, 37, 38; 3:4, 6, 12; 4:8; 5:3–32; 8:14, 18–25; 9:32–43; 10:9–48; 11:2–18; 12:3–19; 15:6–11.

29. Cf. Oscar Cullmann, "Πέτρος," *TDNT* 6:108.

30. This is referred to by some as a prime example of biblical exegesis losing to theological eisegesis. For an emphasis upon appropriate exegesis, see Cullmann, *Peter*, 214–17; Konradt, *Matthew*, 254–55.

31. Carson, "Matthew," 418.

32. France, *Gospel of Matthew*, 672–73.

33. France, *Gospel of Matthew*, 673.

ahead to the time when his disciples, his family of faith (12:48–50), will be called "my CHURCH." This will be the fellowship of disciples who, unlike national Israel, will believe in Jesus's identity as the Messiah, the Son of the living God (16:16), and leave all other allegiances behind as they receive mercy and forgiveness of sin, and likewise demonstrate toward each other mercy and forgiveness (see below on 18:15–35).

Jesus will build his CHURCH, and it will come about through the foundational activity of the apostles and prophets (Eph 2:20). Peter will be the leader among the apostles who will play a foundational role in the early CHURCH, but once he has fulfilled that role, he will pass off the scene. He does not hold a permanent position that is passed on to others. And it will soon be seen that unless Peter continues to be open to the leading of Jesus's Father, he will compromise his leadership role.

But even though Peter appears to be the antecedent to "this rock," the reference should not be understood too narrowly. The purpose of wordplay is to accent specific characteristics between like sounding, or meaning, words. In this situation the person alone is not accented, otherwise the wordplay would have been unnecessary. Rather, by calling him "Peter," Jesus suggests that more than just the person is played upon.

Those characteristics that make Simon a "rocky ledge" comprise the elements that make for the wordplay. The demonstrative "this" (*tautē*) accents this even more: Peter, as the one who is now functioning as the rock, *this* is the rock upon which Jesus will build his CHURCH. And what is *this rock? This rock* is everything that Peter is at this very moment. *This rock* includes Peter as the courageous confessor who steps forward, Peter as the representative spokesman for the disciples, Peter as the blessed recipient of revelation, Peter as the first individual to make a public declaration of Christ, and Peter as the one who leads the disciples forward into realms of expression of faith. Upon *this Peter* Jesus will build his CHURCH. Hans Bayer concludes, "The meaning of the entire phrase is that Jesus builds his invincible church upon Peter's confession *and* his transformed person as the primary, apostolic 'rock'-witness."[34] If Simon functions in this way, he is the rock; if he does not, he can become a stumbling stone (16:23).

At the same time, Jesus's pronouncement is not a conferral of unique, individual supremacy. Peter is given a special recognition for all he is and is to be, but he is never placed above or apart from the disciples. This is also borne out in history. Although crucial in New Testament church history, Peter is almost always together with other disciples. Early in Acts he appears as the recognized leader (Acts 2; 3; 5; 8), but at the Jerusalem Council James shares the leadership (cf. Acts 15:13–29). Thereafter Peter disappears from the narrative and Paul is the one who is given special notice for continuing the work of the CHURCH. Peter is crucial for his role in the foundation of the CHURCH, but he is not the only part of the foundation. The CHURCH is "built

34. Bayer, *Apostolic Bedrock*, 58; his emphasis.

on the foundation of the apostles and prophets" (Eph. 2:20). Thus, Peter appears as a unique person yet also as a prototype or representative for all disciples, both then and now.[35]

### *11.2.1.2.3 Jesus and His Everlasting CHURCH (16:18)*

As Jesus looks down the long corridor of history, and even at his own corridor that will lead him to the cross, he gives an absolute promise that his CHURCH will endure to the end of the age: "I will build my church, and the gates of Hades will not overcome it" (16:18). Hades (Heb. Sheol) is the realm of the dead, and "gates," which are essential to the security and might of a city, indicate power. So, the expression "gates of Hades" in the Old Testament and later Jewish literature,[36] which is basically the same as the "gates of death,"[37] referred to the realm and power of death.[38] Jesus thus promises that death will not overpower the CHURCH, his own family of faith (cf. Matt 12:48–50). Davies and Allison state, "The promise is that even the full fury of the underworld's demonic forces will not overcome the church."[39]

In just a short while Jesus will give the first of four predictions of his coming death. This will be hard for his disciples to handle, so here Jesus gives not only an enigmatic allusion to his coming death but also to his power over death. Even though his own death will be brought about by his enemies, death will not prevail over him.[40] This was included in Peter's own first powerful sermon at Pentecost, when he declares that in Jesus's resurrection the reality of the prophetic hope of the conquest of Hades ("death" in NIV) has occurred (Acts 2:31). And even though the new community will face martyrdom and persecution, the CHURCH will never die. Jesus will conquer death through his own resurrection, which will be proof that he lives to continue to build his CHURCH against all the forces of death.[41] This is a passing allusion to the forces of Satan as well, whose very existence conjures up the thought of Hades. The CHURCH will not die.

## 11.2.2 Peter, the Keys, and Binding and Loosing (16:19)

The building metaphor of the preceding pronouncement leads naturally to a discussion of keys in this third and final pronouncement about Peter. The first line sets the theme of the pronouncement: "I will give you the keys of the kingdom of heaven"

35. Brown and Roberts, *Matthew*, 152.

36. Isa 38:10; Wis 16:13; 3 Macc. 5:51; Pss. Sol. 16:2.

37. Job 38:17; Ps 9:13; 107:18; cf. 1QH[a] VI, 24–26.

38. E.g., "For a moment my soul was poured out to death; (I was) near the gates of Hades with the sinner. Thus my soul was drawn away from the Lord God of Israel, unless the Lord had come to my aid with his everlasting mercy" (Pss. Sol. 16:2 [Wright in *OTP*, 265]).

39. Davies and Allison, *Matthew*, 2:633

40. McNeile, *Matthew*, 242.

41. For a historical overview of this saying, see Jack P. Lewis, "'The Gates of Hell Shall Not Prevail Against It' (Matt 16:18): A Study of the History of Interpretation," *JETS* 38.3 (1995): 349–67.

(16:19). The second and third lines explicate the theme: "and whatever you bind on earth shall be bound in heaven, and whatever you loose on earth shall be loosed in heaven." Once again Peter is addressed personally in the second person pronoun ("I will give *you*" [*soi*]) and verbs ("whatever *you bind*" [*dēsēs*] . . . "whatever *you loose*" [*lysēs*]).

### *11.2.2.1 The Keys of the Kingdom of Heaven*

The keys metaphor could point to a "generic power" given to Peter alone[42] or to his "authority" over the house of God,[43] but the building metaphor of the preceding saying more closely prepares for Jesus to pronounce Peter's role in opening or shutting the doors to the kingdom of heaven.[44] This saying gives a declaration about entrance to the kingdom, but authority is not too far removed: Peter is given the authority to admit entrance to the kingdom of heaven.

In this way Peter is contrasted to the scribes and Pharisees who shut off entrance to the kingdom and who do not enter in themselves (23:13).[45] The Pharisees compassed land and sea to make proselytes (23:15), and Peter also has a mission to carry out to give people access to the kingdom, and this mission specially involves his preaching of the gospel.[46] The apostles had been told by the risen Jesus to wait for the empowering of the Holy Spirit, after which they would be his witnesses to the three people groups: Jews in Jerusalem and Judea, Samaritans in Samaria, and gentiles to the ends of the earth (Acts 1:8).

Peter—as the representative disciple who gives the first personal declaration of the Messiah's identity—is the one in the book of Acts who opens the door of the kingdom to all these peoples. On each of three occasions, it was through Peter's authoritative preaching and presence that the door to the kingdom was opened, first to Jews (Acts 2), then to Samaritans (Acts 8), and finally to gentiles (Acts 10).

The entrance image is foremost in view, and therefore "the keys refer to the fact that chronologically Peter, acting as the representative of Jesus, was the first to announce the message."[47] Even though the Samaritans had believed through the preaching of Philip (Acts 8:4–13), it was necessary for Peter to go there in order for them to receive the Holy Spirit as confirmation to the early CHURCH that God has now included the Samaritans in the kingdom of heaven (Acts 8:14–17).[48] Peter was the special medium through whom the proclamation of the gospel was first made or confirmed, which

42. Brown, Donfried, and Reumann, *Peter*, 96, 100–101.

43. Blank, "Peter," 51; Manson, *Sayings*, 205; Stendahl, "Matthew," 787.

44. Julius R. Mantey, "Distorted Translations in John 20:23; Matthew 16:18–19," *RevExp* 78.3 (Summer 1981): 409–16; Bonnard, *Matthieu*, 246; Kingsbury, "Peter," 76n27; Osborne, *Matthew*, 628–9.

45. Cf. a similar saying in Luke 11:52, where Jesus charges the scribes and Pharisees with taking away the "keys of knowledge"; see Dietrich Müller and Colin Brown, "κλείς," *NIDNTT* 2:732; Guthrie, *New Testament Theology*, 714.

46. Müller and Brown, "κλείς," *TDNT* 732.

47. Guthrie, *New Testament Theology*, 714.

48. Müller and Brown, "κλείς," *TDNT* 732; Guthrie, *New Testament Theology*, 714.

opened the kingdom to all peoples—Jews, then Samaritans, and finally gentiles. Once Peter functioned in that leadership role to use the keys to open the door to the kingdom of God, he passes from the scene. The door to the kingdom now stands open throughout the age, so keys are no longer needed. The door stands open to all people who accept the gospel message and receive forgiveness of sins.

### *11.2.2.2 Binding and Loosing*

Since the rabbinic literature customarily uses "binding and loosing" to describe the authority of the rabbis in teaching and discipline to declare what is forbidden or permitted, and thus to impose or remove an obligation by a doctrinal decision,[49] some suggest that the saying conceives of Peter as a "supreme rabbi" who applies halakoth ("binding interpretations") in the life of the church[50] or one who exorcises demons.[51]

However, since the keys metaphor suggests that Peter is given authority to open the door to the kingdom of heaven, the binding and loosing metaphor continues that theme by indicating that Peter is the one who was given authority to declare the terms under which God grants entrance to, and exclusion from, the kingdom. The syntax and logic of these three pronouncements about Peter is understood best by the continuation and elucidation of the first line in the second and third, because the second and third lines are syntactically related to the first as an explanation of the theme introduced in the first. Based upon the conclusion that the keys refer to entrance, the binding and loosing also refer to entrance but with an added element of ongoing discipleship.

Peter's authority is tied directly to his declaration. Through the revelation of the Father and the personal declaration of Jesus as the Messiah, the Son of the living God, Peter receives blessing and becomes the foundation of the CHURCH. His declaration is a condensation of the gospel, and through Peter's preaching of the gospel, and the preaching of others who followed him, sins are forgiven and entrance gained to the kingdom.

Two passages that help clarify the meaning are Matt 18:18 and John 20:22b–23.

(i) The first passage (Matt 18:18) describes forgiveness or retention of sins within the CHURCH and illustrates that the disciples as a whole have responsibility for declaring the terms under which sins are forgiven or a brother excluded from the fellowship of the local CHURCH. As parallel statements, these sayings of Jesus are the basis for entrance or banishment from the kingdom (16:19) and the local CHURCH (18:18). Both sayings relate to forgiveness of sin.

(ii) John 20:22b–23 also concerns the forgiveness of sins and is a threefold saying of almost identical construction to Matt 16:19. The periphrastic future tense indicates

49. See Friedrich Buchsel, "δέω (λύω)," *TDNT* 2:60, who cites Str.-B., I, 739, b. Mo'ed Qaṭ 16a; b. Menaḥ 34b.

50. E.g., Stendahl, "Matthew," 787; Beare, *Matthew*, 355.

51. For this view see, Richard H. Hiers, "'Binding' and 'Loosing': The Matthean Authorizations," *JBL* 104 (1985): 233–50.

that what Peter and the disciples do in this present age has already been determined by God.[52] Peter is only an instrument God uses because God alone can grant forgiveness of sin and entrance to the kingdom. Peter is an instrument through whom God the Father grants forgiveness of sin. The passive voice of the verbs "will have been bound" and "will have been loosed" and the phrase "in heaven" are Semitic circumlocutions for describing the action of God.[53] In John 20:22b–23 the reception of the Holy Spirit by all the disciples will enable them to declare the terms under which God has forgiven or retained sins. Seen in this light, the role given to Peter in Matt 16:19 of "binding and loosing" must point in the same direction: Peter (and by extension all disciples of Jesus in this age) is given authority to declare the terms under which God either forgives or retains sins.[54]

However, the "binding and loosing" are not merely a reduplication of the use of "keys." As we will see in 18:18, "binding and loosing" include entrance and exclusion, but also refer to the application of all that Jesus taught and exemplified to the lives of his disciples. The thrust of the binding and loosing brings together the image of evangelism with the life of ongoing discipleship: "i.e., the authority of Peter and the church to declare the kingdom truths as they interpret and proclaim Jesus's teaching, guiding the new community regarding what is forbidden and what is permitted in both doctrine and conduct."[55] What Peter has learned to do from Jesus he applies to the Church: "It is Peter's role to see that all that Jesus taught is brought to bear on people's lives; Peter binds and looses only as he has learned to do so from Jesus."[56] The Church has authority to apply the truths of Jesus Messiah's life and teaching and live them. There is an ethical dimension to binding and loosing, which means authenticating right living and discipling those who fail to live according to Jesus Messiah's teaching (cf. 18:17–18; 28:20).[57]

This third pronouncement isolates both the unique and representative roles of Peter. Peter alone is given the keys because once the door to the kingdom of heaven is unlocked there is no more need for keys. This points to a temporally limited, functional role for Peter alone. The saying implies that once Peter opens the doors to Jews (Acts 2), Samaritans (Acts 8), and gentiles (Acts 10), all the disciples will continue to proclaim

52. Gundry, *Matthew*, 335; see the excellent discussion in Carson, "Matthew," 421–26.

53. Brown, Donfried, Reumann (*Peter*, 96n220) cite C. H. Dodd, *Historical Tradition in the Fourth Gospel* (Cambridge: Cambridge University Press, 1963), 347–49. They also note that the Johannine parallel three-phrase pronouncement (John 20:22b–23) has the passive voice ("are forgiven," "are held fast"), which is also a circumlocution for God; cf. also Gundry, *Matthew*, 335.

54. Cf. Bonnard, *Matthieu*, 246; Carson, "Matthew," 420–24; Cullmann, *Peter*, 205; Müller and Brown, "κλείς," 733; George W. E. Nickelsburg, "Enoch, Levi and Peter: Recipients of Revelation in Upper Galilee," *JBL* 100.4 (1981): 575–600; here 594–95. Guthrie, *New Testament Theology*, 714, points out that Peter was the first person historically to proclaim a loosing from sins (Acts 2:38) and a binding (Acts 5:3).

55. Osborne, *Matthew*, 629. Cf. France, *Gospel of Matthew*, 682.

56. Nolland, *Matthew*, 682.

57. Hagner, *Matthew 14–28*, 473; Carson, "Matthew," 421–26; Morris, *Matthew*, 426; France, *Gospel of Matthew*, 625–26; Nolland, *Matthew*, 681–82; Osborne, *Matthew*, 631; Keener, *Matthew* (2009), 429–30; Konradt, *Matthew*, 254–55.

the gospel because the authority of "binding and loosing" is shared by all (cf. Matt 18:18; John 20:22b–23). The response of people to the gospel message preached by Jesus's disciples will determine their eternal fate and their destiny in this life. People who receive the gospel message will be loosed from their sins so that they can enter the open door to the kingdom and advance in their discipleship to Jesus as their lives are conformed to his image (Matt 10:24–25). People who reject the gospel message will be bound in their sins, which will prevent them from entering the kingdom.

### *11.2.2.3 The Distinction Between the CHURCH (16:18) and the Kingdom of Heaven (16:19)*

The sayings in 16:18–19 draw a distinction between the "CHURCH" (16:18) and the "kingdom of heaven" (16:19). Peter is the rock upon whom Jesus will build his CHURCH (16:18), and Peter is the one to whom Jesus will give the keys to the kingdom of heaven (16:19). In this age the CHURCH universal and the kingdom of heaven are closely related, but the kingdom is not to be equated with the CHURCH. "The kingdom has reference to the divine rule; the church to the people of God."[58]

The present manifestation of the *kingdom of heaven* is the "already" rule of God on earth where believers experience the power of God that releases us from the evil of this world and allows us to experience forgiveness of sin and the joy of fellowship with God, the oneness of our fellowship in Christ, and the power of the Spirit in our daily lives. The "not yet" manifestation of the kingdom of heaven awaits the return of Jesus Messiah.

The *universal CHURCH* is the visible manifestation of the *kingdom of heaven* where "kingdom-believers" in Jesus Messiah experience joy, oneness, and power in fellowship with other believers throughout the world. With the arrival and proclamation of the kingdom of heaven in Jesus Messiah we understand the inaugurated perspective of the kingdom on earth with the emphasis on "already."

The CHURCH is the steward or custodian of the present kingdom.[59] In Chapter 12 we will discuss Matt 21:43 more fully, but here we can anticipate that discussion by observing that Jesus was taking away the stewardship of the kingdom of heaven from the nation of Israel and giving responsibility for stewardship of the kingdom of heaven to the CHURCH.

First, this means that the CHURCH has responsibility to declare the terms under which God will grant entrance to or exclusion from the kingdom of heaven. The *universal CHURCH* is called to stewardship of the kingdom of heaven to declare throughout

58. Morris, *Matthew*, 425. See also Robert K. McIver, "The Parable of the Weeds Among the Wheat (Matt 13:24–30, 36–43) and the Relationship Between the Kingdom and the Church as Portrayed in the Gospel of Matthew," *JBL* 114.4 (1995): 643–59.

59. Cf. Davies and Allison, *Matthew*, 2:637n127. For a similar expression, see Gregg R. Allison, *Sojourners and Strangers: The Doctrine of the Church*, FET (Wheaton, IL: Crossway), 82–100.

the world the terms of entrance to the kingdom of heaven. With the parallel saying on binding and loosing occurring in a CHURCH discipline passage (18:16–18), the requirement for entrance and exclusion is the same for both: forgiveness of sins.

Similarly, Jesus states, "Woe to you, teachers of the law and Pharisees, you hypocrites! You shut the door of the kingdom of heaven in people's faces. You yourselves do not enter, nor will you let those enter who are trying to" (23:13). Just as the responsibility for the stewardship of the kingdom is taken from the Jewish nation and given to the church (21:43), so are the keys of the kingdom taken from the Jewish leaders and given to Peter (16:19).[60] Peter was given a foundational role to employ the keys that opened the doors of the kingdom of heaven to all peoples on earth. Employing the keys was the declaration of the terms of entrance to the kingdom, namely, to repent and believe in the gospel message for the forgiveness of sins. Disciples of Jesus throughout history are called to declare those same terms of entrance to those already open doors.

Second, the CHURCH has authority to take the truths of Jesus Messiah and live them, authenticating right living and discipling those who fail to live according to Jesus Messiah's teaching (cf. 18:17–18; 28:20a).[61] Osborne notes, "Matthew centers on ethics (. . . chs. 5–7), the 'righteous' living that must characterize the citizens of the kingdom. Here the teaching office of the church is given authority by Christ to understand and apply his kingdom ethics."[62]

This is the "already" aspect of the kingdom of heaven. We await the full manifestation of the rule of God on earth until the "not yet" aspect of the kingdom of heaven on earth is established with the return of Jesus Messiah.

## 11.3 THE CHURCH: JESUS BUILDS THE LOCAL "CHURCH" COMMUNITIES

Matthew records a significant discourse of Jesus regarding the future community of disciples. With Jesus's impending absence from his disciples as he journeys to the cross, he now spends time instructing them about the kind of community life that will characterize their relationships with one another and with the world at large. This extended instruction comprises the fourth of five discourses by Jesus that Matthew has recorded in his Gospel (chs. 5–7, 10, 13, 18, 24–25). This fourth discourse (ch. 18) is understood by most evangelical Matthean scholars as a prophecy by Jesus that develops what it means to be *community-based disciples.* This community is referred to as the "CHURCH" because within the discourse we find the occurrence of the term *ekklēsia,*

60. Davies and Allison, *Matthew,* 2:639.

61. Osborne, *Matthew,* 631; Keener, *Matthew* (2009), 429–30.

62. Osborne, *Matthew,* 631.

which appears in the canonical Gospels only in Matthew, here for the second and final time (18:17 [2x]; cf. 16:18).

In the earlier section of this chapter, we noted that *ekklēsia* can be rendered as "CHURCH" and "CHURCH," the large and small capitals indicating the difference between the *universal* "CHURCH" and the *local* "CHURCH." Davies and Allison clarify that in distinction from Jesus's saying in 16:18, which refers to the CHURCH universal, Jesus's statement in 18:17, refers to the local CHURCH. "The local community is here meant, not the church universal."[63]

The broad prescription of the CHURCH's community life continues from chapters 18 through 20, until Matthew begins to narrate Jesus's final passion week. But the core is found in chapter 18, with the conclusion of the discourse proper set off by the distinctively recurring formula, "When Jesus had finished . . ." (19:1; cf. 7:28; 11:1; 13:53; 26:1).

### 11.3.1 A New Identity as the "CHURCH"

In 16:17–19 Jesus speaks of Peter's role in the foundational days of the universal CHURCH, while in 18:15–18 Jesus addresses group discipline in a localized setting. In this context, a local gathering of disciples of Jesus is pictured, which is instructed how to deal with a sinning member. The *ekklēsia* terminology differentiates the gathering of Jesus's disciples from the Jewish practice of referring to local groups as "synagogues." This is an example of the Matthean Jesus foreseeing a new identity for both the universal and local disciples of Jesus Messiah as the *ekklēsia*.[64]

An interesting phenomenon occurs in Matthew's Gospel where, on five separate occasions, Matthew refers to "their synagogue/s" (*synagōgē/ais autōn*) when denoting the first-century Jewish institution (4:23; 9:35; 10:17; 12:9; 13:54) and once to "your synagogues" (*synagōgais hymōn*) (23:34). Two of these are on the lips of the Matthean Jesus (10:17; 23:34). By contrast, Matthew uses the term *ekklēsia* when there would have been a noticeable opportunity to speak of "our synagogue/s," had he so intended.

The language of "their synagogues" has been interpreted differently. Some contend that the expression "their synagogues" does not have to mean distancing. On this reading, the expression only means that Jesus visited the synagogues of Galilee whenever an opportunity arose.[65] On the other hand, this may reflect the time of Matthew's writing, when Christians have already begun to meet separately from their Jewish compatriots to worship in a distinctly Christian setting, and "may reflect the distancing of Matthew's community from the synagogues."[66]

63. Davies and Allison, *Matthew* 2:785.

64. P. Foster, "Matthew," 129.

65. Maier, *Matthäus, Kapitel 1–14*, 225–26.

66. Hagner, *Matthew 1–13*, 80; Luz, *Matthew 1–7*, 166. Davies and Allison (*Matthew*, 1:413–14) lean toward this view but leave the conclusion open.

Additionally, in my view, it may reflect the distinction that occurred very early between Jewish identity and leadership and Jesus's own ministry and his disciples. The religious leaders, especially the Pharisees and scribes who had their greatest following from the synagogues, early on set themselves in opposition to Jesus and his message. The phrase "their synagogues" may show the separation between the Jewish leaders and Jesus that Matthew saw developing in Jesus's own ministry. This then paved the way for Matthew to view a continuing distinction between the local CHURCH and the local synagogue.[67]

In this latter view, we then see in 18:17 the development of an identity that is breaking from Jewish self-definitional labels related to the institution of the synagogue and a new self-identity seen in the adoption of the institution of the *ekklēsia*.[68] P. Foster notes, "In this way, the Gospel of Matthew signals its connection with the larger early Christian movement and its shared understanding of being a new movement, which ultimately derives its identity from its connection to Jesus and the recognition of him as the Christ, the son of the living God."[69]

## 11.3.2 The Character and Characteristics of the "CHURCH"

Much of our understanding of the character and characteristics of the community of Jesus's disciples as the "local CHURCH" is unique to Matthew's Gospel among the evangelists. In this fourth discourse, Jesus delineates the local CHURCH as the community of disciples that witness to the reality of the presence of the kingdom of heaven. This is a look ahead by Jesus to the future functioning of his family of disciples as the CHURCH, the local community of believers in this present age. What is it that characterizes a "successful" local CHURCH? We often think of numbers, popularity, profitability, and flourishing leadership. By way of contrast, the successful witness of the local CHURCH that Jesus delineates in this discourse comes both through their declaration of the gospel message and through their example of living out the gospel message as a family of faith that is characterized by humility, purity, accountability, discipline, reconciliation, forgiveness, and restoration.[70]

---

67. Morris, *Matthew*, 86.

68. For discussion of *ekklēsia* in the light of the ideal of cohesiveness among members and corporate identity, see Richard Last, "*Ekklēsia* outside the Septuagint and the *Dēmos*: The Titles of Greco-Roman Associations and Christ-Followers' Groups," *JBL* 137.4 (2018): 959–80. For examples of the ongoing voluminous debate regarding the relation of the *ekklēsia* to the *synagōgē*, see Trebilco, *Self-Designations*; Anders Runesson, *The Origins of the Synagogue: A Socio-Historical Study*, Coniectanea Biblica, New Testament 37 (Stockholm: Almquiest & Wiksell, 2001); Ralph J. Korner, *The Origin and Meaning of* Ekklēsia *in the Early Jesus Movement*, AJEC 98 (Leiden: Brill, 2017); Erich S. Gruen, "Synagogues and Voluntary Associations as Institutional Models: A Response to Richard Ascough and Ralph Korner," *JJMJS* 3 (2016): 125–31; Jordan J. Ryan, *The Role of the Synagogue in the Aims of Jesus* (Minneapolis: Fortress, 2017).

69. P. Foster, "Matthew," 130.

70. For related discussion see Wilkins, *Matthew*, 611–39.

### *11.3.2.1 Humility: The Greatness of Kingdom Life in the* CHURCH *(18:1–4)*

Matthew tells us that the event that precipitates the community discourse is a surprising question from Jesus's disciples.[71] "At that time the disciples came to Jesus and asked, 'Who, then, is the greatest in the kingdom of heaven?'" (18:1). The disciples are still developing an understanding of what it means to be Jesus's particular type of disciple, which is different than other forms of master-disciple relationships within Judaism and the wider Greco-Roman world at that time. Discipleship in the ancient world often involved a significant commitment to a rigorous course of study and disciplined lifestyle in order to attain to the master's level of expertise.[72]

The ambition to achieve greatness is a pursuit central to human accomplishment, and on the strictly natural level it is not an inappropriate pursuit. But the disciples have a very different type of greatness in mind than Jesus meant. When Jesus had spoken of John the Baptist's greatness and the greatness of the person who is the least in the kingdom of heaven, he had meant the honor of serving God by preparing for the Messiah and of experiencing the arrival of the blessings of the new covenant through his blood (see 11:11). The disciples had understood him to mean primarily the greatness that comes from human endeavor and heroic accomplishments. One of the primary topics Jesus undertakes throughout this community discourse will be to try to revise their understanding of "greatness" to think the way that God thinks about greatness, not the typical way that humans think.[73] This is a shocking foretelling of a characteristic of the CHURCH to come.

Jesus begins the revising of their thinking with a visual aid by calling a little child and having him stand among them. He then makes a startling statement: "I tell you the truth, unless you change and become like little children, you will never enter the kingdom of heaven" (18:3). Jesus is not commending an inherent innocence of children. The Old Testament has a balanced view of both the sinfulness and the value of children from birth. The psalmist knows of his sinfulness from conception (Ps 51:5), yet he also knows that he is a wonderful creation of God (139:13–14). Jewish tradition regarded children as a blessing and gift from God (127:3–5; 128:3–4; Pss. Sol. 1:3).

#### 11.3.2.1.1 The Humility of a Child

Instead of pointing to the innocence of a child, Jesus uses the little child as an object lesson on their humility that comes from their vulnerability. "Therefore, whoever

71. As is typical in Matthew's Gospel, the mention of "disciples" calls to mind the Twelve, but the wider circle of Jesus's disciples is in view as well. The wider circle includes all who have responded to his invitation to kingdom life (cf. Wilkins, *Concept of Disciple*, 163–72).

72. For discussion of ancient forms of master-disciple relationships in the ancient Greco-Roman and Jewish world, see above Ch. 10, "Discipleship in Matthew's Gospel: Salvation, Righteousness, and Transformation."

73. For a study that emphasizes the disciples' consistent lack of understanding Jesus's message and mission in Matthew, see Brown, *Disciples in Narrative Perspective*, esp. 147–52.

humbles himself like this child is the greatest in the kingdom of heaven" (18:4, ESV). In the ancient world children were often valued primarily for the benefit that they would bring to the family by enhancing the work force, adding to the defensive power, and guaranteeing the future glory of the house. Children were without rights or significance apart from their future value to the family and were among the most powerless in society. The humility of a child consists of the inability to advance his or her own cause apart from the help and direction and resources of a parent. Additionally, when the Greek word *mikros* ("small, little") is used in a spiritual sense, it refers to "a state of humility."[74]

Jesus celebrates the humility that comes from the child's weakness, defenselessness, and vulnerability. The child can really do nothing for himself or herself and would die if left to his or her own resources. The child who tries to take care of herself or himself is destined for disaster. It is this kind of humility that Jesus's uses as a visual aid to contrast the world's form of greatness to the greatness of the kingdom of heaven. Like the values established in the Beatitudes (5:3–10), this is an explicit pronouncement of grace to those who seemingly are unworthy of the kingdom, but it is also a pronouncement of condemnation upon those who thought themselves to be worthy but actually were not. If persons wish to enter the kingdom, they must turn away from their own power, aggressiveness, and self-seeking, and in childlike humility of weakness, defenselessness, and vulnerability call upon God's mercy to allow them to enter the kingdom of heaven. The child becomes a metaphor of the values of discipleship to Jesus that are to characterize the CHURCH.[75]

Therefore, childlikeness is a characteristic of all true disciples because it is only through the mercy of God that a person can enter the kingdom of God and find the "greatness" that comes from having one's sins forgiven and being invested with kingdom life. Jesus declares that greatness is not achieved according to one's accomplishments, but in one's humility in receiving God's grace. The pattern of the world is to count one's accomplishments, especially if it involves personal sacrifice in order to accomplish some significant feat. The disciples had committed themselves to that kind of effort for the kingdom of heaven and were now looking to see who had accomplished the most and therefore who had become the greatest among them in the kingdom according to the values of the world (18:1).

#### 11.3.2.1.2 The Greatness of Humility

But Jesus turns that value upside down as he demonstrates through the example of a little child that the truly transformed life cannot be achieved by one's efforts, but only by humbly allowing God to bring his spiritual renewal within a person's life.

74. G. Scott Gleaves, "Humility," *LTW*.

75. Carter, *Households and Discipleship*, 96–97.

That renewing activity of God brings a person into the realm of the kingdom of heaven. This is much the same message as the Beatitudes, where those who have cast aside all self-effort at achieving status before God will be enabled to receive the gift of kingdom life (cf. 5:3–16). As one humbly receives this gift of life, he or she becomes Jesus's disciple and is privy to all the "greatness" that comes from an intimate relationship to Jesus and to his Father (18:4).[76] Jesus extended the invitation to kingdom life because he himself was humble: "Come to me, all you who are weary and burdened, and I will give you rest. Take my yoke upon you and learn from me, for I am gentle and humble in heart, and you will find rest for your souls. For my yoke is easy and my burden is light" (11:28–30).

Likewise, it is not what you or I have done that brings greatness but what God has done in our lives to bring us into the kingdom of heaven. From that beginning point we are able to dedicate our lives to following Jesus's pattern of servanthood for the sake of the kingdom that allows us to progress in that kind of humble greatness (cf. 20:25–28). Jesus acclaims the humility that comes from disciples who acknowledge their weakness, defenselessness, and vulnerability in order to rely on their Master, Jesus.

Humility is a grateful awareness that life is a gift, and it is manifested as an ungrudging acknowledgment of absolute dependence upon God.[77] Humility is the opposite of arrogance and pride, which are hostile behaviors toward other people based on a belief in one's own superiority or greater importance. Thus *hyperēphania* (cf. Mark 7:22), "arrogance" or "pride," is a conscious effort to appear conspicuously above others, leading to boastfulness and insolence.[78]

Grant Macaskill notes that "humble people think and act in ways that gratefully acknowledge dependency on God, patiently submit to his will, and recognize the seductive power of sin."[79] And humility often is associated with "servanthood," especially with reference to Jesus's humility. Macaskill expands upon Jesus's humility and servanthood to emphasize that Jesus's humility is defined or even constituted by a volitional commitment to serve the needs of others through an act of personal condescension. In this Jesus makes himself present with them in their need, as the embodiment of divine wisdom. "This willingness to condescend into the position of a servant, sacrificing self and status, can be considered a characteristic of God's own humility of mind, of his humble way of thinking."[80]

76. Eunyung Lim suggests that the child here symbolizes "the socially marginalized, economically disadvantaged, and politically oppressed" whom disciples of Jesus are to emulate, in contrast to the children of the kings of the earth in the preceding story of Peter and the four-drachma coin in the fish's mouth (17:25–27); see Eunyung Lim, *Entering God's Kingdom (Not) Like A Little Child: Images of the Child in Matthew, 1 Corinthians, and Thomas*, BZNW 243 (Berlin: de Gruyter, 2021), 67. But this appears to overemphasize a sociological interpretation at the expense of the stated theme of spiritual "humility"; see Luz, *Matthew 8–20*, 429; Davies and Allison, *Matthew*, 2:754–60; Hagner, *Matthew 14–28*, 517–18; Osborne, *Matthew*, 670–71.

77. Elwell and Comfort, "Humility," *TBD* 618.

78. Friberg et al., "ὑπερηφανία, ας, ἡ," *ALGNT*, loc. 27445; Manser et al., eds., "Arrogance," *ZDBT*, loc. 5793; Walter M. Dunnett, "Pride [Arrogance]," *EDBT* 630–31.

79. Grant Macaskill, *The New Testament and Intellectual Humility* (Oxford: Oxford University Press, 2018), 7.

80. Macaskill, *New Testament and Intellectual Humility*, 7.

Humility is therefore a crucial element of the local CHURCH as Jesus envisions it operating in this age and world. As Jesus humbly served his disciples by giving his life as a ransom for many (20:28), so we as his disciples humbly serve him by humbly serving each other. Humility simply recognizes that others in the community need us, and that the Lord has gifted us uniquely to serve him by serving them.

#### *11.3.2.2 Purity: A Heart with Complete Devotion to God (18:5–9)*

A second characteristic of the local CHURCH is "purity." Purity indicates the state of heart where there is complete devotion to God. The pure heart is the undivided heart where there is no conflict of loyalties, no division of interests, no mixture of motives, no hypocrisy, and no insecurity. It is whole-heartedness God-ward.[81] Jesus reverses the tradition of the Pharisees and scribes regarding ceremonial purity and transfers the state of defilement—and so of purity—entirely from the outer person to the inner person (15:1–20). "Purity in this sense may be said to be a state of heart reserved completely for God and freed from all worldly distractions."[82]

Jesus demonstrates that his community has responsibility to pattern a life of purity for others that will not lead them to sin. Since the context concerns individual efforts to achieve greatness (18:1–4), we can assume that this is Jesus's starting point. "One of these little ones" (18:6), perhaps especially indicating new disciples, who have become weak, defenseless, and vulnerable as they have humbly entered the kingdom of heaven. They look at the pattern of those disciples who have preceded them and they are highly susceptible to following their example.

Although all disciples must enter the kingdom by becoming like a humble child (18:3), the world's pattern of greatness is a dangerous temptation to those within the community of disciples. Members of the community may start counting their accomplishments, comparing their achievements, and condemning their brothers' and sisters' endeavors, all in the pursuit of greatness according to the world's standards. If I pursue greatness according to the world's definition, then I will dedicate myself to maximizing my own potential, sacrificing all that is necessary so that I can accomplish my intended goals.

If this is the pattern that has been adopted by the community, new disciples are vulnerable to pattern their new life of discipleship after that model. Therefore, Jesus declares that we must take seriously our responsibility for other disciples because if they follow a faulty pattern they will be led into the sin of worldly greatness instead of kingdom humility.

---

81. R. A. Finlayson, "Purity," *NBD*[3] 991.

82. Finlayson, "Purity," *NBD*[3], 991.

So, a core value for the community of faith is responsibility for other disciples' purity of life, starting perhaps first with one's attitude of personal greatness, from which flow all other areas of life. This is apparently why Jesus's warnings are directed both to our responsibility for others' sinful behavior (18:5–7) as well as responsibility for our own behavior (18:8–9). The world's pattern is to primarily look out for oneself, but all that we do within the community of faith will impact everyone else. Therefore, it should be a high value within the community to develop a pattern of life in which all disciples are committed to living out our responsibility to each other's purity.

### *11.3.2.3 Accountability: For Our Own and Each Other's Walk with Jesus (18:10–14)*

Accountability means being held responsible to God and each other in the local CHURCH for our own walk with Jesus and each other's walk with Jesus. Blomberg states of accountability, "One places oneself under the authority of a group of believers who will follow a stipulated process of intervention to produce repentance and restoration to full fellowship whenever possible."[83] Jesus calls for the disciples to make the connection between the angelic care for the "little ones" and the following parable of the sheep ("What do you think?"). The key is his concern for his humble followers who have gone astray through others causing them to sin (18:6–7) or through their own sinful choices (18:8–9). The Father not only will send angels to try to bring them back to the path of discipleship but will himself expend every effort to bring about their safe return.

#### 11.3.2.3.1 Accountability for Restoration

Following on the responsibility that the community bears for each other's purity is the accountability that we share for the restoration of those who have gone astray.

The parable of the lost sheep (18:10–14) reveals God's heart. The shepherd could have settled for bringing back ninety-nine sheep. That is a pretty high percentage. Loss of some of the flock is expected in the wilds of nature. He would not have been condemned for losing only one. But in the same way that God sends protecting angels over each of his little disciples (18:10), he considers each wayward disciple non-expendable. We might assume that the leadership of the community bears significant responsibility for bringing back those who have gone astray, but all of the members are accountable for whatever lengths that we can go to restore wayward brothers and sisters.

It is sometimes easier to beat a brother or sister when they have fallen, punishing them for their lack of faithfulness or getting back at them for the way that they have hurt us. But what they need is for us to accept them back into the community so that

83. Blomberg, *New Testament Theology*, 377.

they can be strengthened by our unity and faithfulness. The community is accountable to the Shepherd to give unreserved commitment to restoring those who have gone astray.

#### 11.3.2.3.2 Accountability Overcomes Independence and Creates Community

The fierce independence that many desire in the modern world is evidence of a subtle sinfulness. We really don't want to have to think about anyone else. But what overcomes that independency is a proper sense of accountability—others need us. The community discourse prescribes how an appropriate accountability to the needs of others can overcome an unhealthy independence from others. Once we gain God's heart for his children, which prompts him to provide ministering angels for their every need (18:10), our own eyes are opened to the needs of those for whom he has given us responsibility, and an accountability relationship is established that creates God's kind of community.

The parable of the lost sheep (18:12–14) is connected to this type of care but carries it over to the spiritual well-being of disciples in the community. When we love individuals and desire to treat them with the respect their kinship in the kingdom entitles them, we care very much about the direction of their lives. The parable is often interpreted to imply going after unbelievers. That is the thrust of the Lukan parallel, but in Matthew's context it implies that disciples are to go after fallen brothers or sisters, knowing that this is what God himself desires for that individual. The tone of this passage is that we go after those who have strayed, because God himself cares immensely that none in his fold would perish (18:14).

### *11.3.2.4 Discipline: Correcting Wayward Disciples (18:15–17)*

This pericope, which is unique to Matthew's Gospel, follows logically from the preceding warnings about sin committed by disciples. In this passage Jesus gives (1) four steps of discipline (18:15–17) and (2) the method of confirmation that the community must apply to the sinful situation (18:18–20).

Jesus begins by specifying the problem: "If your brother sins against you . . ." (18:15 NIV84). The "little one" who went astray is now called a "brother" who has committed sin. "Brother" harks back to the scene where Jesus emphasizes that his disciples, who have obeyed the will of the Father by following Jesus, are his mother, and brother, and sister (cf. 12:46–50). The gender of the disciple is not so much in view as is the emphasis upon the family relationship of disciples. "Sister" could have just as easily been used (hence the NIV renders "brother or sister"), so this is a principle of discipline that applies to any member of the family of faith. This—the first of only three times that the verb "sin" (*hamartanō*; cf. 18:15, 21; 27:4) occurs in Matthew's Gospel—is an indication that the offense in view is significant. Jesus addresses in a very practical manner what the community of disciples must do if one in the family commits a sin.

The basis of the process is rooted in Lev 19:15–18, as Jesus's reference to the passage in 18:16 indicates. The Leviticus passage also stands behind a three-stage process of discipline found in the Qumran community, which includes individual confrontation, witnesses, and if necessary, final judgment by the community leaders.[84]

The church has responsibility to protect its purity from those who have brought sinful activity into the fellowship. It is sometimes easier to compromise the purity of the community than to confront the sin. Or, as is often the maxim of the world, it is easier to "live and let live" because of the difficulty of sustaining absolute standards. "Who am I to judge when I'm not perfect myself?" is often another guideline. But courageous concern for members of the community of faith will take seriously the plight of the individual who is practicing sin, and the purity of the community that allows the sin to infect the fellowship.

Jesus goes on to enunciate four steps for dealing with a sinning member of the discipleship community, with the intended goal the restoration of the sinning brother or sister to a state of purity and the reestablishment of the fellowship of the body.

#### 11.3.2.4.1 Personal Confrontation (18:15)

First, "go and point out their fault, just between the two of you. If they listen to you, you have won them over" (18:15). Either the person who has been offended, or a member of the community who has knowledge of the brother's sin, must go to the person who has sinned and lay out his fault. Jesus emphasizes that the entire encounter is sensitive. It must be undertaken with privacy so that if it is resolved, there will not be undue attention given to the tragedy of committed sin by a member of the community.[85] The ultimate objective of the encounter is not punishment, but *restoration*—winning over a straying member with the result of restoration to the faithful path of discipleship.

#### 11.3.2.4.2 Witnesses to the Confrontation (18:16)

Second, if the first step does not result in repentance, one or two other members of the community should go back to witness the confrontation (not that they were eyewitnesses to the original sin) and the sinning brother's refusal to repent. They would be able to help arbitrate, or in the case of stubborn rebellion, become witnesses of non-repentance.[86] This follows the guideline provided in Deut 19:15: "One witness is not enough to convict anyone accused of any crime or offense they may have committed. A matter must be established by the testimony of two or three witnesses."

84. 1QS V, 24–VI, 1; cf. also CD IX 2–4; see F. Garcia Martinez, "La reprension fraterna en Qumran y Mt 18,15–17," *FiloNT* 2.1 (1989): 23–40. Martinez demonstrates how Jesus derives his process of discipline from the Leviticus passage, and not from the Qumran community.

85. Nolland, *Matthew*, 746; Keener, *Matthew* (2009), 453.

86. France, *Gospel of Matthew*, 693; Nolland, *Matthew*, 746–47.

### 11.3.2.4.3 Involvement of the CHURCH (18:17)

The third step, in the case of non-repentance, is to bring the complaint before the CHURCH: "If they still refuse to listen, tell it to the church" (Matt 18:17). This verse contains the second and third occurrences of the word "church" (*ekklēsia*) in Matthew's Gospel, all used by Jesus, and these three are the only occurrences in the canonical Gospels. This is a look ahead by Jesus to the future functioning of his family of disciples as the community of believers in this present age (16:18).

As with the goal of finding and restoring wayward disciples ("sheep"; 18:12–14), the intent of including the CHURCH in the disciplining process is to involve the broader body of believers in trying to get the sinning brother to acknowledge his sin. Those who have shared the fellowship of the community may persuade the sinning brother to accept responsibility for his action(s).[87]

The way in which this was carried out in the small home CHURCHES of the early CHURCH may be quite different than today. Such a sin would become immediately evident to the community. Today some CHURCHES actually publish a list or make an announcement from the pulpit. I personally have seen this work more effectively when the church leaders are made aware of the situation and are brought into the process of attempted restoration rather than making a public announcement. In many cases this will work, but when it does not, a fourth step is necessary.

### 11.3.2.4.4 Treat as an Unbeliever (18:17)

The fourth step of discipline is to treat the sinning brother who refuses to repent like a pagan (lit. "gentile," *ethnikos*) or tax collector, the common titles for those who are consciously rebellious against God and his people. "If they still refuse to listen, tell it to the church; and if they refuse to listen even to the church, treat them as you would a pagan or a tax collector" (18:17). The Old Testament prescriptions for exercising punishment (Deut 25:1–3) were later applied by Judaism to the responsibility of the synagogue. The synagogue was not only the place of worship, instruction, and fellowship but also the place of discipline. Extreme discipline included flogging and expulsion from the community (m. Makkot 3.1–2; see Matt 10:17). Jesus does not call for physical punishment but instead focuses on spiritual exclusion from the fellowship of the CHURCH, which is symbolic of spiritual death.

Again, the way that this is carried out today must be determined by the individual circumstances. Some suggest that the person is not to be allowed to participate in any activities of the CHURCH. However, since unbelievers, such as "pagans and tax collectors," are encouraged to come to the assembly to hear the gospel message, it must mean something other than strict removal. Rather, this is best carried out when the church

87. Osborne, *Matthew*, 686; France, *Gospel of Matthew*, 693.

considers the sinning individual not to be a believer. Confessing disciples who live with unconfessed sin indicate by their lives that they are not truly members of Jesus's spiritual family and are not to be allowed to enjoy the fellowship of the family. They should be treated like non-believers, with the same compassion and urgency of having them exercise repentance, yet not extended the same openness to the inner fellowship of the community that is reserved for fellow disciples.[88]

### *11.3.2.5 Reconciliation: Consensus on Community Discipline and Life (18:18–20)*

After giving the four steps of dealing with the discipline of a sinning brother by the CHURCH, Jesus emphasizes that the responsibility of the community of disciples is to come to a corporate consensus in which there is correspondence between heaven and earth in carrying out the will of the Father.

#### 11.3.2.5.1 Consensus in Discipline (18:18)

That means in the first place to seek the Father's will about the activities of brothers and sisters who are accused of sinful behavior, and then to seek to bring God's will to bear on the situation. Jesus states, "Truly I tell you, whatever you bind on earth will be bound in heaven, and whatever you loose on earth will be loosed in heaven" (18:18). This saying is virtually identical to the pronouncement made of Peter's role in the foundation of the CHURCH (see on 16:19), except with the striking difference that here the verbs are plural, indicating that Peter's foundational, functional authority is extended to the entire community of disciples.[89] In this context the community of disciples, the CHURCH, is given authority to declare the terms under which God forgives or refuses to forgive the sin of wayward disciples.

#### 11.3.2.5.2 Consensus in Praying for God's Will in the Community (18:19)

Second, the correspondence sought in the community of disciples between earth and heaven not only functions as God's sanction on the process of discipline but also promises to guide the community's attempt generally to carry out the will of the heavenly Father on earth (cf. 6:10; 26:39–42). Jesus states, "Again, truly I tell you that if two of you on earth agree about anything they ask for, it will be done for them by my Father in heaven" (18:19). The confirmation of the action of the community in binding and loosing the sins of community members is expressly related to the action of the Father in carrying out the requests of the community. The unity of the community's requests is intended to reflect the will of the Father.[90]

88. Turner, *Matthew*, 445; Nolland, *Matthew*, 747–48; Osborne, *Matthew*, 686–87.

89. Brown and Roberts, *Matthew*, 170–71.

90. See David McClister, "'Where Two or Three Are Gathered Together': Literary Structure as a Key to Meaning in Matt 17:22–20:19," *JETS* 39.4 (1996): 549–60; here 556–57.

### 11.3.2.5.3 Consensus in Experiencing Jesus's Presence Within the Community (18:20)

Jesus's third statement expands upon the first two, indicating that the fellowship that the community enjoys in reaching consensus about disciplining a brother is actually brought about by the presence of Jesus: "For where two or three come together in my name, there am I with them" (18:20). Jewish councils required a minimum of three judges to come to a decision regarding minor cases in the local community, assuming that the Shekinah remains with a just court.[91] Likewise, when two men gathered to discuss the law, the Shekinah was present: "But two who are sitting, and words of the Torah pass between them—the Presence is with them" (m. Avot 3:2 [Neusner]).

But in a striking declaration, Jesus himself assumes the place of the divine presence among his disciples, guaranteeing that when his followers reach a consensus as they ask in prayer for guidance in matters of discipline, his Father in heaven will guide them as they carry it out. The basis of the assurance is Jesus's continual presence among his disciples who gather in his name. This looks ahead to the promise that he will be with his disciples forever (Matt 28:20), not metaphorically like Paul promises that he will be with the church at Corinth (1 Cor. 5:3–5),[92] but in reality in his resurrected presence.[93]

Two of the most important guidelines for exercising discipline within the community are the intended goal and the ultimate source of discipline. *The intended goal is reconciliation.* If a brother or sister accepts discipline and is won over, then the goal is achieved (18:15). The goal is not punishment, but reconciliation. A disciple who continues in sin is alienated both from God and from pure fellowship with other believers. When he or she confesses that sin, the fellowship with God and with other believers is restored.

A second important guideline for all exercise of discipline within the community is that *the ultimate source of the discipline is God himself.* God alone can forgive or retain sin, so it is the responsibility of the community to understand God's standards, seek for the unity of the Spirit that leads to an understanding of God's will, and follow the leading of the presence of Jesus within the community (18:18–20).

The community that disciplines its own members displays the love and compassion and purity of God the Father that draws its members together truly as brothers and sisters in Christ.

### *11.3.2.6 Forgiveness: In the CHURCH toward Sinning Disciples (18:21–35)*

Forgiveness in the CHURCH toward sinning disciples means withdrawing punishment for a recognized sin when the sinner acknowledges the sin and seeking to have

91. Cf. m. Sanhedrin 1:1; b. Berakhot 6a.

92. Contra Davies and Allison, *Matthew*, 2:790.

93. For discussion of the "I am with you" theme here, see Kupp, *Matthew's Emmanuel*, 176–200.

punishment—whether it is physical, emotional, or spiritual—no longer dispensed to the sinner. We are to forgive when asked and no longer dispense punishment.

### 11.3.2.6.1 Repeated Forgiveness (18:21–22)

Restoration of a sinning brother or sister to the path of discipleship is the purpose of discipline within the CHURCH, as was specified at the first stage of the process: "If they listen to you, you have won them over" (18:15). The CHURCH is to be ready to forgive and restore a person who repents. But the wise disciple recognizes that those who apparently are repenting and seeking forgiveness may only be putting on a show and will soon scurry back to their sinful ways. Those conducting such a sham can cause considerable damage in other people's lives and disrupt the proper functioning of the CHURCH. In this brief interaction that is unique to Matthew's Gospel, Peter seems to be thinking this way as he approaches Jesus and asks, "Lord, how many times shall I forgive my brother when he sins against me? Up to seven times?" (18:21).

Jesus's astonishing response is that Peter must forgive not the magnanimous number of seven times but times without counting: "I tell you, not seven times, but seventy-seven times" (18:22). The meaning of the number that Jesus uses is unclear (*hebdomēkontakis hepta*). One might read "seventy-seven times," which is the same wording found in the LXX of Gen 4:24,[94] or the less likely "seventy times seven."[95] The teaching within Judaism, based on Amos 1:3; 2:6 and Job 33:29, 30, that three times was enough to show a forgiving spirit did not go as far as did Peter. Peter was being extraordinarily generous by more than doubling that amount. But Jesus means him to understand that he should go on forgiving without counting, even as God has fully forgiven those who have responded to the invitation to the kingdom of heaven, including forgiving Peter.[96] Nolland notes, "The number is designed to break through any notion that there are limits to forgiveness: one is to keep on forgiving far beyond the point where one has lost count of the wrongs."[97]

Forgiveness is not to be based on mere generosity. Jesus seems to be saying that the number does not matter. Peter and the rest of the disciples are to continue to forgive without keeping count. The reason for such an unheard of thought is given in the parable that immediately follows—Peter should go on forgiving without counting because the reality of his own forgiveness is demonstrated in the way in which he forgives others (18:23–35).

94. "If Cain is avenged seven times, then Lamech seventy-seven times [*hebdomēkontakis hepta*]," which renders the Hebrew שִׁבְעִים וְשִׁבְעָה, "seventy and seven," i.e., seventy-seven. Theodotian's recension renders unambiguously with *hebdomēkonta kai hepta* to match the Hebrew.

95. BDF, §248(2), 130.

96. Brown and Roberts, *Matthew*, 172–75.

97. Nolland, *Matthew*, 755.

### 11.3.2.6.2 Deserved Punishment (18:31–34)

The quisling servant in the concluding parable could not get away with his treachery because other servants of the king were grieved when they saw the unfair treatment and went to tell the king (18:31). The true nature of the servant is revealed, as he is called "wicked" by the king (18:32).

The lesson is revealed in the king's words "Shouldn't you have had mercy on your fellow servant just as I had on you?" (18:33). The mercy and benevolence of the master's treatment of the first servant should have so impacted his life and values that he would shower mercy and benevolence on others. Instead, his wicked nature has only taken selfish advantage of the master. Now he will receive the punishment that he deserved in the first place. He is handed over to the "torturers" (handed over to the "jailers to be tortured," NIV), which indicates those jailors in a debtor's prison who not only guarded against escape but who inflicted torture on inmates.[98] Since it would be impossible for the servant to repay the vast amounts he owed, the scene concludes with the grim certainty that he will experience that punishment forever, a harsh metaphorical allusion to an eternal destiny of judgment (cf. 8:12; 10:28; 13:42, 49–50; 18:34; 22:13; 24:51).[99]

### 11.3.2.6.3 The Parable's Principle (18:35)

The core of the meaning of the parable is found in the final verse: "This is how my heavenly Father will treat each of you unless you forgive your brother or sister from your heart" (18:35). Mercy is *not giving* to a person what he deserves, while grace is *giving* to a person what he *does not* deserve. This takes us to a central principle of the kind of kingdom life that Jesus has inaugurated. A person who has truly experienced the mercy and grace of God by responding to the presence of the kingdom of God will be transformed into Jesus's disciple, which, in a most fundamental way, means to experience a transformed heart that produces a changed life that gives the same mercy and grace and forgiveness that he or she has received from God (cf. Isa 40:2).

Such a transformation will be evident in the words and actions of a disciple's life (12:33–37; 13:8, 23; 15:17–20). A person who has not truly experienced and appropriated the grace and mercy of God will not experience his forgiveness. He will, like the first servant, accept the personal benefits, but it will be only superficial. It will not penetrate to his hard and wicked heart to produce transformation. Such a person has not received God's forgiveness and therefore will experience the eternal condemnation for his or her sins. Jesus's disciples will be living demonstrations of forgiveness because through the grace and mercy of God they have experienced God's forgiveness.

98. See Karel van der Toorn, "Prison," *ABD* 5:468–69.

99. For a scholarly discussion of fiery judgment in Matthew's Gospel, see Sim, *Apocalyptic Eschatology*, esp. 130–39.

We are to be "wise as serpents and harmless as doves" (10:16). We are to be wise and not be foolish and deceived by people who would harm and manipulate us. But we are to be harmless and not seek revenge and retaliate against those who have harmed us when they ask for forgiveness. I have often heard the expression "God forgives and forgets." I think it is important to clarify that this does and does not reflect an accurate understanding of God and forgiveness. On the one hand, we recognize that God cannot forget sin, because he remains omniscient. But on the other hand, God removes the punishment when we ask to be forgiven and he does not hold our sin against us. This is where the psalmist reflects on God's forgiveness: "For as high as the heavens are above the earth, so great is his steadfast love toward those who fear him; as far as the east is from the west, so far does he remove our transgressions from us" (Ps 103:11–12).

#### 11.3.2.6.4 Unlimited Forgiveness from the Heart (18:35)

Perhaps the kingdom value that is most difficult for the world to comprehend is the kind of forgiveness that Jesus articulates in the discourse. It is not a conditional acceptance but an unqualified and unlimited removal of all that we hold against others.[100] At least one reason why the world cannot really understand this value is that hurt is real in offended relationships. And when we have been hurt, we do not want to be hurt again. We will not allow ourselves to be used. We want to get even with those who have abused us. If we do forgive others, it is often conditionally based upon the actions of the one we are forgiving.

But what Jesus shows is that when we experience God's unqualified and unlimited forgiveness, it will influence all that we are and will impact all of our relationships. Mercy experienced will produce mercy demonstrated.

This is what ties the community discourse together. The individual who has experienced the mercy of God and has received his forgiveness has humbly entered the life of the kingdom of heaven. All the former values of the world are now turned upside down. I no longer need to be on top. I do not need to be the greatest. Because when I do, I am estranged from others who also want to be the greatest. Unhealthy competition and comparison are now eliminated from our fellowship because I am here now to seek your best, not my own. I can elevate your good as my aspiration to serve.

There is something powerful in the concluding parable that gets emphasized in the contrast between the two debts. The first man who is forgiven by his master is forgiven such a large amount that it should truly affect the way that he responds to others' infractions against him. The implication is that this great debt is the type of debt that we have been forgiven by the Father. Our sins were such that we never would have been able to pay them, and we were granted a reprieve simply in the asking.

100. Nolland, *Matthew*, 754.

Likewise, we should be just as willing to forgive infractions against us, which end up being qualitatively much less in comparison. The key to forgiveness is to stop focusing on what others have done *to* us and focus on what Jesus has done *for* us.

The obvious relevance is that we are quick to forgive those who sin against us. But it is much more than simply a head nod and a toleration of that person. It is a forgiveness "from the heart" (18:35). True reconciliation is not simply a tolerant attitude toward one another in the same living space. It is a real, personal, loving connection between individuals that Jesus desires, and without a heart attitude of forgiveness, this type of connection is not even possible. Often our forgiveness of others points people toward God's forgiveness of them. Forgiveness not only sustains the intimacy of the community, but it is a powerful device that allows people to make change in their own lives and move on toward deeper intimacy with God.

Peter and the other disciples are thus brought face to face with an incomprehensible truth that will mark their lives forever. As they continue to see Jesus's life and ministry come to a close, and then come to understand the significance of the events of the cross and empty tomb, they will be gripped by the compassionate forgiveness, mercy, and grace of God that was demonstrated in their loving Savior Messiah, their Master, Jesus. And such a transformation will occur in their own lives that the mercy and forgiveness of God will be a preeminent characteristic of the community of disciples, the CHURCH. Peter will later write, "Once you were not a people, but now you are the people of God; once you had not received mercy, but now you have received mercy" (1 Pet 2:10).

### *11.3.2.7 Restoration: You Have Won Them Over (18:21–35)*

Restoration is at the heart of God's plan for fallen humanity, and it provides a rubric that the CHURCH is called to emulate in dealing with wayward disciples. The Old Testament and New Testament use terms such as "restore" and "renew" to picture God's handling of history and the believer's spiritual life.

#### 11.3.2.7.1 The Figurative Usage of "Restoration"

The figurative usage of "restoration" falls into three basic areas.

First, there is personal spiritual restoration. In Ps 23 the psalmist acknowledges God's restorative powers in times of trials: "He restores my soul. He leads me in paths of righteousness for his name's sake" (Ps 23:3, ESV). In 51:12 David seeks restoration in the light of his grievous sin against God: "Restore to me the joy of your salvation and grant me a willing spirit, to sustain me."

Second, Paul calls for mature believers to identify their areas of strength and to mentor back to spiritual health another ailing believer: "Brothers and sisters, if someone is caught in a sin, you who live by the Spirit should restore that person gently. But watch yourselves, or you also may be tempted" (Gal 6:1).

Third, there are references to an eschatological restoration: "Jesus replied, 'To be sure, Elijah comes and will restore all things'" (Matt 17:11; cf. 19:28; Acts 1:6; 3:21).

#### 11.3.2.7.2 Not Punishment but Winning Over a Brother or Sister

It is that second figurative sense of restoration that Jesus alludes to in the CHURCH community discourse of Matt 18. The ultimate objective of discipline is not punishment but winning over a brother or sister so that he/she would be restored to the faithful path of discipleship within the forgiving community. "If your brother or sister sins, go and point out their fault, just between the two of you. If they listen to you, you have won them over" (18:15).

The discipline of brothers and sisters is not a pleasant task, but as we follow Jesus's teaching it will help contribute to a community of disciples that is a faithful witness to the presence of the risen Lord Jesus in our midst. And it is important always to keep in mind that the goal is not discipline itself, or even punishment. The intended goal of all discipline is restoration of the sinning brother or sister to a state of purity and the reestablishment of the fellowship of peace within the body.[101]

### 11.3.3 A Flourishing Community

Jonathan Pennington is a Matthean scholar who is a New Testament professor, but he is also a faithful pastor of a local church. He wrote an article in which he focused on the biblical functioning of the local church in Matt 18. When he came to vv. 15–20 he made this insightful comment: "This supposed 'church discipline' text is really part of the great theme of forgiveness as the primary mark of the Christian community. The central ethical exhortation in Matthew is the call to be merciful."[102] He then emphasizes that showing mercy is a two-sided virtue: merciful compassion toward those in need (6:2–4; 9:12–13; 12:7) and merciful forgiveness toward those who have wronged us (5:7, 9; 6:14–15; 18:21–35). Therefore, in his view—and I think that he is right on target—when we focus solely on church discipline, we miss Jesus's emphasis in the church discourse on the church as a flourishing community.[103]

A non-flourishing community is one that does not live in relationship to the reality of the cross and resurrection of Jesus. A non-flourishing community lives according to the prevailing secular cultural paradigm of values. We might try to gather around like interests, or geographical location, or even political ideologies.

101. For a practical application, see Ken Sande, *The Peacemaker: A Biblical Guide to Resolving Personal Conflict*, 3rd ed. (Grand Rapids: Baker, 2004).

102. Jonathan T. Pennington, "Are We Missing the Point of Matthew 18?," *Christianity Today* (29, 2022), 61.

103. Pennington, "Are We Missing the Point of Matthew 18?," 59.

But the kind of community that Jesus envisions addresses the whole person and the healing and restoration that arrives with the gospel of the kingdom of heaven in the mission of Jesus. That wholistic restoration creates the kind of community that provides healing of body, soul, spirit, and mind. Steven Porter recently issued a powerful reminder that the mental health issues that are so prominent in today's society must be addressed by the church. "It bears reminder that Christian spirituality importantly includes the human mind. Referring to Christianity as '*mentally healthy* Christianity' and the church as a '*mentally healing* church' should appear redundant. Pursuing the health and healing of the human mind is just what it is to be a Christian and to be a church."[104] Christian community is based on having received mercy and forgiveness and restoration of the whole person, which in turn will impel us to demonstrate mercy and forgiveness and provide restoration of body, soul, spirit, and mind to our fellow church disciples.

That is what is so unique about the community that Jesus has established, which today is visible as the CHURCH/church, the body of Christ. Whatever else we may use as guidelines for the health of the church, Jesus says that his community of disciples is the primary witness to the reality of the presence of the kingdom throughout this age. And our witness comes both through our declaration of the gospel message and through our example of living out the gospel message as a family of faith. And what will characterize our fellowship as the CHURCH/church is humility, purity, accountability, discipline, reconciliation, forgiveness, and restoration.

## 11.4 The CHURCH and the church in Matthew's Gospel

The idea of discipleship was one of the first emphases of Jesus's earthly mission and Matthew's Gospel. We have seen that Jesus's first message was, "Repent, for the kingdom of heaven has come near" (4:17). And, not long after, Jesus called his first followers into a discipleship relationship with himself: "Come, follow me" (4:19).

This solidifies in the minds of many people a one-on-one relationship with Jesus: "I am a disciple of Jesus, and to grow in discipleship means to develop that relationship by becoming more like him." That certainly is an important truth because we have seen in Matthew's Gospel where Jesus called individuals to follow him, serve him, and grow in relationship with him (e.g., Peter, Andrew, John, James, Matthew, Mary Magdalene, Mary the mother of James and Joseph, the mother of Zebedee's sons, Joseph of Arimathea, etc.).

104. Steven L. Porter, "Mentally Healthy and Healing Church: Spiritual Formation and Soul Care as Ecclesiology," editorial introduction, *JSFSC* 15.1 (2022): 3–5; here 3; emphasis his.

One of the great truths of the Christian faith that attracted me to it so many years ago was the claim that God in Jesus had come to earth to offer and establish a personal relationship with individuals. I eagerly responded to that offer and entered into a personal discipleship relationship with Jesus that has been at the center of my daily life ever since then.

However, pushed to an extreme, as with so many issues in life, individual discipleship often overshadows an equally important biblical truth, the idea of "the church as community."[105] From the earliest times of the biblical record, God called his people to community, whether in the early patriarchal families, in the wandering people of Israel, in the kingdom of Israel, in the group of Twelve, or in the CHURCH/CHURCH.[106]

Jesus did indeed call men and women into a deep personal relationship with himself, yet if we focus exclusively on the individual in our growth in discipleship, we run the danger of separating the individual from the CHURCH, the community of faith. One-on-one discipleship pushed too far can easily develop into the kind of unhealthy independency that marks our modern culture.[107] That kind of unhealthy individualism deceives us into separating ourselves from others, it encourages us to pride ourselves on not needing anyone, and it makes us reluctant to have anyone need us. David Gill has wisely said:

> We must have the community to support and correct our discipleship in the world. This seems so obvious, but our practice is so frequently individualistic. . . . We must resist the individualism of our culture and cultivate deep and strong relationships with others. The challenges we face are formidable; without community they become impossible.[108]

"The challenges we face are formidable; without community they become impossible." Do we really believe that statement? I know that in my younger years I did not. Whether it was cultural background, my own particular environment, or my own prideful independency, I preferred to walk alone, to need no one, and to have no one need me. In my early years right out of high school I gloried in my independency, my ability to make

105. The idea of the church as "community" is a concept that is difficult to define. However, as James Dunn recognizes, this term, somewhat better than related terms (e.g., "congregation" or "sect"), implies two essential ingredients: relations and structured organization; cf. James D. G. Dunn, *Unity and Diversity in the New Testament: An Inquiry into the Character of Earliest Christianity*, 2nd ed. (London: SCM; Philadelphia: Trinity, 1990), 398n2a.

106. The initiation and development of Israel and the church as a called community is extensively documented in the study of Hanson, *People Called*.

107. Gerhard Lohfink gives a powerful account of the heritage of liberal theological "individualism" in Germany in the twentieth century, which in turn has affected secular German society. That account is equally applicable to Europe in general, North America, industrialized Asian society, the emerging majority world, and, indeed, much of twentieth- and twenty-first-century culture as a whole; see Gerhard Lohfink, *Jesus and Community: The Social Dimension of Christian Faith* (Philadelphia: Fortress, 1984), 1–5.

108. David W. Gill, *The Opening of the Christian Mind: Taking Every Thought Captive to Christ* (Downers Grove, IL: InterVarsity, 1989), 135–36.

it on my own through life. My theme was Simon and Garfunkel's song "I Am a rock" and its following lyric: "I am an island."

But challenges of life, and coming to know Jesus, broke down my cocky self-sufficiency. I came to realize that other people, including my wife and young children, relied on me. I came to understand the necessity of community like never before. The challenges we faced were formidable; without community they became impossible.

That is why individual disciples must function as a CHURCH community, the family of God. The disciples spent three years with Jesus as they obeyed his call, listened to his teaching, and witnessed his ministry. At the end of their training came the darkest moment of their experience: Jesus's trial and crucifixion. As they huddled in the upper room in the shadow of the empty cross, all they had hoped for appeared lost; all they had endured appeared to have been in vain; all they had sacrificed appeared to be wasted. Where was their Master? Who would lead the way now?

But out of the darkness came the brightness of a new hope—the resurrection—and a new creation—the CHURCH/CHURCH. Jesus's followers now embarked upon a dimension of their discipleship journey to which Jesus had pointed but which they had only dimly perceived. The prophecy of Jesus, found only in Matthew's Gospel, of the coming universal CHURCH and the local CHURCH community, was now stunningly real.

The small band of disciples around Jesus during the darkest moments exploded to thousands in Jerusalem within days of Pentecost and soon became countless throughout the Roman world. The disciples were now empowered by the Holy Spirit to proclaim boldly in the remotest parts of the earth the gospel message that Jesus had inaugurated in Israel.

And these disciples were now joined together to form the CHURCH/CHURCH, the body of their risen Master, Jesus Messiah. Jesus called individuals to discipleship; yet responding to that call brought disciples into a community of faith—the CHURCH universal and CHURCH local. Jesus no longer was with his disciples physically, yet he promised to be with them always (28:20). Stanley Hauerwas concludes his comments on Jesus's community discourse by saying, "Throughout his ministry Jesus teaches us what it means to be a disciple. Our task is to learn how to be for one another exemplifications of what he has taught."[109] Through the Spirit, the CHURCH/CHURCH community will now provide the fellowship, encouragement, edification, and mutuality necessary for following the Master in the new era.[110]

109. Stanley Hauerwas, *Matthew*, BTCB (Grand Rapids: Brazos, 2006), 167.

110. I have developed this theme more fully in Wilkins, *Following the Master*, 244–80, esp. 243–48.

*Chapter 12*

# Israel, Disciples, and Church in Matthew's Gospel

## *Stewards of the Kingdom in God's Timing*

### Bibliography

**Blaising, Craig A.** "A Theology of Israel and the Church." Pages 85–100 in *Israel, the Church, and the Middle East: A Biblical Response to the Current Conflict*. Edited by Darrell Bock and Mitch Glaser. Grand Rapids: Kregel, 2018. **Block, Daniel I.** *Covenant: The Framework of God's Grand Plan of Redemption*. Grand Rapids: Baker Academic, 2021. **Boyarin, Daniel.** *The Jewish Gospels: The Story of the Jewish Christ*. New York: New Press, 2012. **Broadhead, Edwin K.** *Jewish Ways of Following Jesus: Redrawing the Religious Map of Antiquity*. WUNT 266. Tübingen: Mohr Siebeck, 2010. **Bruno, Chris, Jared Compton, and Kevin McFadden**. *Biblical Theology According to the Apostles: How the Earliest Christians Told the Story of Israel*. NSBT 52. Downers Grove, IL: InterVarsity, 2020. **Bryan, Steven M.** "Jesus and Israel's Eschatological Constitution." Pages 2835–54 in vol. 3 of *HSHJ*. Edited by Tom Holmén and Stanley E. Porter. 4 vols. Leiden: Brill, 2011. **Cuvillier, Élian.** "Torah Observance and Radicalization in the First Gospel. Matthew and First-Century Judaism: A Contribution to the Debate." *NTS* 55.2 (2009): 144–59. **Dennert, Brian C.** *John the Baptist and the Jewish Setting of Matthew*. WUNT 2/403. Tübingen: Mohr Siebeck, 2015. **Donaldson, Terence L.** *Jews and Anti-Judaism in the New Testament: Decision Points and Divergent Interpretations*. Waco, TX: Baylor University Press, 2010. **———.** "'Nations,' 'Non-Jewish Nations,' or 'Non-Jewish Individuals.'" Pages 169–94 in *Matthew Within Judaism: Israel and the Nations in the First Gospel*. Edited by Anders Runesson and Daniel M. Gurtner. ECL 27. Atlanta: Society of Biblical Literature Press, 2020. **Esler, Philip F.** "Ethnic Identities in the Dead Sea Legal Papyri and Matthew: Reinterpreting Matthew 25:31–46." Pages 195–209 in *Matthew Within Judaism: Israel and the Nations in the First Gospel*. Edited by Anders Runesson and Daniel M. Gurtner. ECL 27. Atlanta: Society of Biblical Literature Press, 2020. **Evans, Craig A. and David Mishkin,** eds. *A Handbook on the Jewish Roots of the Christian Faith*. Peabody, MA: Hendrickson, 2019. **Harvey, Richard S.** *Mapping Messianic Jewish Theology*. Studies in Messianic Jewish Theology Series. Carlisle, UK: Paternoster, 2009. **Hamilton, Catherine**

**Sider.** *The Death of Jesus in Matthew: Innocent Blood and the End of Exile.* SNTSMS 166. Cambridge: Cambridge University Press, 2017. **Holmén, Tom, and Stanley E. Porter,** eds. *HSHJ.* 4 vols. Leiden: Brill, 2011. **Kaiser, Walter C., Jr.** *The Promise-Plan of God: A Biblical Theology of the Old and New Testaments.* Grand Rapids: Zondervan, 2008. **Kinzer, Mark S.** *Post-Missionary Messianic Judaism: Redefining Christian Engagement with the Jewish People.* Grand Rapids: Brazos, 2005. **Konradt, Matthias.** *Israel, Church, and the Gentiles in the Gospel of Matthew.* Translated by Kathleen Ess. BMSEC. Waco, TX: Baylor University Press, 2014. **———.** "Matthäus im Kontext: Eine Bestandsaufnahme zur Frage des Verhältnisses der matthäischen Gemeinde(n) zum Judentum." Pages 3–42 in *Studien zum Matthausevangelium.* Edited by Alida Euler. WUNT 358. Tübingen: Mohr Siebeck, 2016. **Köstenberger, Andreas J., with T. Desmond Alexander.** *Salvation to the Ends of the Earth: A Biblical Theology of Mission.* 2nd ed. NSBT 53. Downers Grove, IL: InterVarsity, 2020. **Levine, Amy-Jill.** "Jesus in Jewish-Christian Dialogue." Pages 175–88 in *Soundings in the Religion of Jesus: Perspectives and Methods in Jewish and Christian Scholarship.* Edited by Bruce Chilton, Anthony Le Donne, and Jacob Neusner. Minneapolis: Fortress, 2012. **———.** *The Social and Ethnic Dimensions of Matthean Salvation History.* SBEC 14. Lewiston, NY: Edwin Mellen, 1988. **Lieu, Judith M.** *Neither Jew nor Greek: Constructing Early Christianity.* 2nd ed. London: T&T Clark, 2016. **McDermott, Gerald**, ed. *Understanding the Jewish Roots of Christianity: Biblical, Theological, and Historical Essays on the Relationship Between Christianity and Judaism.* SSBT. Bellingham, WA: Lexham, 2021. **Olmstead, Wesley G.** "A Gospel for a New Nation: Once More, the ἔθνος of Matthew 21.43." Pages 115–32 in *Jesus, Matthew's Gospel and Early Christianity: Studies in Memory of Graham N. Stanton.* Edited by Daniel M. Gurtner, Joel Willitts, and Richard A. Burridge. LNTS 435. London: T&T Clark, 2011. **Paschke, Boris.** *Particularism and Universalism in the Sermon on the Mount: A Narrative-Critical Analysis of Matthew 5–7 in the Light of Matthew's View on Mission.* NTAbh, NS 56. Münster: Aschendorff, 2012. **Repschinski, Boris.** *The Controversy Stories in the Gospel of Matthew: Their Redaction, Form and Relevance for the Relationship Between the Matthean Community and Formative Judaism.* FRLANT 189. Göttingen: Vandenhoeck & Ruprecht, 2000. **Runesson, Anders.** *Divine Wrath and Salvation in Matthew: The Narrative World of the First Gospel.* Minneapolis: Fortress, 2016. **———.** "Judging Gentiles in the Gospel of Matthew: Between 'Othering' and Inclusion." Pages 133–51 in *Jesus, Matthew's Gospel and Early Christianity: Studies in Memory of Graham N. Stanton.* Edited by Daniel M. Gurtner, Joel Willitts, and Richard A. Burridge, LNTS 435. London: T&T Clark, 2011. **Runesson, Anders, and Daniel M. Gurtner,** eds. *Matthew Within Judaism: Israel and the Nations in the First Gospel.* ECL 27. Atlanta: Society of Biblical Literature Press, 2020. **Saldarini, Anthony J.** *Matthew's Christian-Jewish Community.* Chicago: University of Chicago Press, 1994. **Senior, Donald.** "Viewing the Jewish Jesus of History Through the Lens of Matthew's Gospel." Pages 81–96 in *Soundings in the Religion of Jesus: Perspectives and Methods in Jewish and Christian Scholarship.* Edited by Bruce Chilton, Anthony Le Donne, and Jacob Neusner. Minneapolis: Fortress, 2012. **Sim, David C.** *The Gospel of Matthew and Christian*

*Judaism: The History and Social Setting of the Matthean Community*. SNTW. Edinburgh: T&T Clark, 1998. **Turner, David L.** "His Glorious Throne: Israel and the Gentiles in Mission and Judgment in the Gospel of Matthew." Pages 135–68 in *Matthew Within Judaism: Israel and the Nations in the First Gospel*. Edited by Anders Runesson and Daniel M. Gurtner. ECL 27. Atlanta: SBL, 2020. ———. *Israel's Last Prophet: Jesus and the Jewish Leaders in Matthew 23*. Minneapolis: Fortress, 2015. **Wilkins, Michael J.** "The Consideration of a Future for Israel in the Light of the Apparently Bleak Consequences for Negative Responses to Jesus's Ministry in the Gospel of Matthew." Pages 313–40 in *The Future Restoration of Israel: A Response to Supersessionism*. Edited by Stanley E. Porter and Alan E. Kurschner. McMaster Biblical Studies 10. Eugene, OR: Wipf & Stock; Hamilton, Ontario: McMaster Divinity College Press, 2013. ———. "Isaiah 53 in the Four Gospels." Pages 109–32 in *The Gospel According to Isaiah 53: Encountering the Suffering Servant in Jewish and Christian Theology*. Edited by Darrell L. Bock and Mitch Glaser. Grand Rapids: Kregel, 2012. **Willitts, Joel.** "Zionism in the Gospel of Matthew." Pages 107–40 in *The New Christian Zionism: Fresh Perspectives on Israel and the Land*. Edited by Gerald R. McDermott. Downers Grove, IL: InterVarsity, 2016. **Yango, Emo.** "God-Talk with Insiders and Outsiders." Pages 142–46 in *The Church in a Changing World: An Asian Response; Challenges from the Malang Consultation on Globalization*. Edited by Bruce Nichols, Theresa Roco Lua, and Julie Belding. Quezon City, Philippines: Asia Theological Association, 2010.

## 12.1 Introduction: Israel, Disciples, and Church in Matthew's Gospel

We do not reshape our theology in accordance with contemporary cultures, but rather seek by God's grace to *transform* our cultures and societal behaviour to conform to Jesus Christ, and according to the Scriptures."[1] Those were guiding words for a recent consultation in Malang, Indonesia, that sought to help form global leaders for international churches in the face of current international challenges—ethnic, gender, national, migrancy, environmental, religious, etc. The papers that resulted from that consultation reflect the diversity but unity in Christ that characterized their joint effort.

One short paper had an intriguing title: "God-Talk with Insiders and Outsiders." The "insider" is Ahmad, a Muslim believer who has entered the kingdom of God but who still self-identifies with his Muslim family and community, and he still practices the rituals of Islam. The "outsider" is Kuya Bon, a non-Christian Muslim whose non-Christian son had been stabbed several times by members of a militant Filipino

1. Theresa Roco Lua, "The Challenge of Malang," *The Church in a Changing World: An Asian Response; Challenges from the Malang Consultation on Globalization*, ed. Bruce Nichols, Theresa Roco Lua, and Julie Belding (Quezon City, Philippines: Asia Theological Association, 2010), 9–14, here, 10.

Christian militia. The author, Emo Yango, asks the questions, "How do we do 'God-talk' in mission? More specifically, how is theologizing happening in that context?"[2] These are some of the current challenges of evangelism, mission, and the development of the church in that international setting.

The church of the twenty-first century is not so different from the church of the first century.[3] I present that situation as an introduction to the next two chapters, where we consider the people of Israel, the disciples of Jesus, and the first-century church, with its "insiders" and "outsiders" in the Gospel of Matthew. Anders Runesson introduces his study of the problem of gentiles and "othering" in the Gospel of Matthew by stating, "If we can identify Matthew's relationship to non-Jews, this would implicitly say something about the context in which this text was authored, revealing who was regarded as an insider and outsider respectively, and why. As we shall see, Matthew's relationship to the gentile world was complex."[4]

And that is what we undertake here. In this chapter and the next we attempt to understand one of the most complex issues in God's program of history. Specifically, what is the place and role of ethnic Israel in relationship to God's unfolding plan of history, including Israel's relationship to Jesus Messiah, the kingdom of heaven, torah, gentiles, Jesus's disciples, the church, and the future? Matthew's Gospel is especially significant in addressing these issues because Matthew has special interest in Israel, perhaps more so than any of the other Gospels.[5]

### 12.1.1 Salvation-Historical "Particularism" and "Universalism"

The terms "particularism" and "universalism" indicate that Matthew's Gospel lays striking emphasis upon both the fulfillment of the promises of salvation to a particular people, Israel, and also the fulfillment of the universal promise of salvation to all the peoples of the earth.[6] The church, made up of every nationality, has cherished this Gospel because Matthew aims to record the continuation of the history of salvation to all of the nations. His introductory statement, that Jesus Christ is both the "son of

2. Emo Yango, "God-Talk with Insiders and Outsiders," in *Church in a Changing World: An Asian Response; Challenges from the Malang Consultation on Globalization*, ed. Bruce Nichols, Theresa Roco Lua, and Julie Belding (Quezon City, Philippines: Asia Theological Association, 2010), 142–46.

3. From this point on I will use lower case "church" for both the universal and local church.

4. Anders Runesson, "Judging Gentiles in the Gospel of Matthew: Between 'Othering' and Inclusion," in Gurtner, Willitts, and Burridge, *Jesus, Matthew's Gospel and Early Christianity*, 133–51, here 135.

5. This chapter draws upon some of my earlier research and writing. For a somewhat popular approach, see Michael J. Wilkins, "Israel According to the Gospels," in *The People, the Land, and the Future of Israel: Israel and the Jewish People in the Plan of God*, ed. Darrell L. Bock and Mitch Glaser (Grand Rapids: Kregel, 2014), 87–102. For a mid-range readership, see Wilkins, "The Theology of the Land in the Gospels," in *A Handbook on the Jewish Roots of the Gospels*, ed. Craig A. Evans and David Mishkin (Peabody, MA: Hendrickson, 2021), 436–55. For a scholarly audience, see Wilkins, "The Consideration of a Future for Israel in the Light of the Apparently Bleak Consequences for Negative Responses to Jesus's Ministry in the Gospel of Matthew," in *The Future Restoration of Israel*, ed. Stanley E. Porter and Alan E. Kurschner (Eugene, OR: Wipf & Stock; Hamilton, Ontario: McMaster Divinity College Press, 2013), 313–40.

6. See, e.g., Paschke, *Particularism and Universalism*, 3–4.

David" and the "son of Abraham" (1:1), is the preliminary indication that salvation promises made both through David to God's chosen people, Israel (e.g., 2 Sam 7:8–17), and through Abraham to all peoples (Gen 12:1–3; 22:18), have been fulfilled through the life and ministry of Jesus Messiah, the promised Savior of all nations.

Matthew's Gospel alone points explicitly to Jesus's intention to go first to the lost sheep of the house of Israel (Matt 10:5–6; 15:24), showing historically how God's promise of salvation to Israel was indeed fulfilled. And yet the promises made to Abraham that he would be a blessing to all the nations are also fulfilled as Jesus extends salvation to the gentiles (cf. 21:44; 28:19). The church throughout the ages has found assurance in Matthew's Gospel that God truly keeps his promises to his people.

### 12.1.2 Fulfillment

Within this matrix of issues is the concept of "fulfillment." As we saw in Chapters 5 and 6, Matthew focuses on the way in which Jesus's life and ministry fulfills the Old Testament and the Law. But what does that mean with respect to Israel? What does "fulfillment" indicate about the relevance and practice of Torah and the Old Testament? What is the value of the Old Testament and the Law now for disciples of Jesus? What is its value for Jews? For Jewish Christians? As Matthew focuses on "fulfillment," does he indicate that the role ethnic Israel has played in God's program of salvation history has come to an end? What is Jesus's attitude toward Israel, and what is the relationship between Israel and the Church as presented in Matthew's Gospel? Answers to these kinds of questions have helped in large measure to shape various theological systems. The differing perspectives in Matthew's Gospel toward Israel and the nations have caused diverse interpretations. We will not be able to resolve the larger issues here that are found elsewhere in the New Testament because that is beyond our purview, but a survey of Matthew's perspective of ethnic Israel may help move us closer to understanding these thorny interpretative issues.[7]

### 12.1.3 Complex Perspectives of Israel in Matthew's Gospel

Matthew's Gospel has long been noted for having complex perspectives of the nation of Israel—e.g., we noted above a particularistic emphasis and yet a universal outreach, a positive reception of Jesus's initial ministry yet an increasingly negative reaction to his later ministry, a positive role of Israel in God's program of salvation history and yet an often negative function of Israel in the ministry of Jesus Messiah. Focusing on these complex perspectives, Matthias Konradt commences his important study of

7. For an overview of current issues and their relationship to Matthew's Gospel, see Terence L. Donaldson, *Jews and Anti-Judaism in the New Testament: Decision Points and Divergent Interpretations* (Waco, TX: Baylor University Press, 2010), esp. 12–25 and 30–54. For a wider study, see Michael J. Vlach, *Has the Church Replaced Israel? A Theological Evaluation* (Nashville: B&H, 2010).

Matthew's theological underpinnings by surfacing the question: "How is the reader to understand the progression from the exclusive focus of Jesus's ministry on Israel—as formulated programmatically in Matthew 15.24 and in the corresponding instruction to his disciples in 10.6—to the universal commission in 28.18b–20?"[8] That is, Jesus declares to the gentile woman the focus of his mission: "I was sent only to the lost sheep of the house of Israel" (15:24 ESV). And he gives specific instructions to his Jewish disciples on their short-term mission, "Go nowhere among the Gentiles and enter no town of the Samaritans, but go rather to the lost sheep of the house of Israel" (10:5–6 ESV). But then in his final Great Commission to his eleven Jewish disciples, Jesus declares, "Go therefore and make disciples of all nations" (28:19 ESV).

Additionally, how do we understand Matthew's record of Jesus's earliest ministry that was exclusively concentrated on Israel, "Jesus went throughout Galilee, teaching in their synagogues, proclaiming the good news of the kingdom, and healing every disease and sickness among the people" (4:23), in the light of Matthew's unique record of Jesus's dramatic statement to the Jewish people and leaders in the temple area, "Therefore I tell you that the kingdom of God will be taken away from you and given to a people who will produce its fruit" (21:43)?

Interpreting Matthew's diverse perspectives is important for the consideration of ethnic Israel in God's program of history. In what follows, we explore how Jesus Messiah's arrival and ministry fulfills the lineage promises to both David and Abraham, which emphasizes a unique particularity of Israel as the recipients of Jesus's invitation to the kingdom of heaven. As a result of this particularity, many in Israel respond positively to Jesus Messiah. However, surprisingly, many in Israel, both leaders and common people, respond negatively to Jesus's ministry. Matthew records sayings of Jesus that portend ominously grim consequences for Israel's negative responses to Jesus. What becomes of the nation of Israel in the final theological perspective of Matthew?

As we explore these varied understandings of Matthew's view of the place in history of ethnic Israel, we additionally see that several modern issues have precipitated current studies of Israel in relationship to God's program.

### 12.1.4 Modern Issues Precipitating Studies of Israel and the Church

The relationship of ethnic Israel and the church to God's program of history is one of the most important discussions among scholars today. Among the precipitating matters that brought about the current concentration of scholarship on the role of ethnic Israel are at least the following interlocking issues.[9]

8. See, e.g., Matthias Konradt, *Israel, Church, and the Gentiles*, 1.

9. Similarly, Markus Bockmuehl, "Seeing the Son of David," in *Seeing the Word: Refocusing New Testament Study*, Studies in Theological Interpretation (Grand Rapids: Baker Academic, 2006), 189–232.

### *12.1.4.1 The Shoah/Holocaust*

In modern Hebrew, the term *Shoah* means "catastrophe." *Shoah* refers to the systematic, deliberate murder of nearly six million Jews by Nazi Germany and its collaborators during the Second World War. Eva Fleischner, a Jewish-Catholic scholar who fled Nazi Germany in her teens, states, "No statistic can convey even remotely the horror of the genocide that exterminated one-third of the world's Jews for no other reason than that they were Jews."[10] The expression "Final solution to the Jewish question" (in German: "Endlösung den Judenfrage") refers to the Nazi plan for destruction of the Jews. English-speaking countries now more commonly use the word Holocaust, which is Greek for "sacrifice by fire."[11]

The concept "anti-Semitism" indicates hostility toward or discrimination against Jews on the basis of race or ethnicity. Nazi anti-Semitism, which culminated in the Holocaust, had a racist dimension in that it targeted Jews because of their supposed biological characteristics.[12] The concept of anti-Judaism is usually understood as opposition against Jews' religious convictions or customs, although there is a trend to use them somewhat interchangeably.[13] Paula Fredriksen attends to definitions within the context of their historical development. She asks the question,

> Is anti-Judaism, then, the same as anti-Semitism and anti-Zionism? I do not think so. The first is a theological position; the second, a racist one; the third, a political one. But, without question, the long centuries of Christianity's anti-Judaism soaked into the soil of Western culture, preparing the ground for these more recent avatars.[14]

After the horrors of the Shoah/Holocaust, many within the church have reassessed their biblical and theological positions regarding ethnic Israel.[15] Many have attempted to ascertain whether there may be latent anti-Judaism or anti-Semitism or anti-Zionism within their theological systems. And there are many in the post-Holocaust world

10. Eva Fleischner, "The Shoah and Jewish-Christian Relations," in *Seeing Judaism Anew: Christianity's Sacred Obligation*, ed. Mary C. Boys (Lanham, MD: Rowman & Littlefield, 2005), 3.

11. From the Mémorial de la Shoah in Paris: http://www.memorialdelashoah.org/en/archives-and-documentation/what-is-the-shoah.html. See also Barry R. Leventhal, "The Holocaust and the Sacred Romance," in *To the Jew First: The Case for Jewish Evangelism in Scripture and History*, ed. Darrell L. Bock and Mitch Glaser (Grand Rapids: Kregel, 2008), 122–54.

12. *Encyclopedia Britannica*, "Anti-Semitism," by Michael Berenbaum, accessed June 27, 2021, https://www.britannica.com/topic/anti-Semitism.

13. John G. Gager, *The Origins of Anti-Semitism: Attitudes Toward Judaism in Pagan and Christian Antiquity* (Oxford: Oxford University Press, 1985), 1–34.

14. Paula Fredriksen, "The Birth of Christianity and the Origins of Christian Anti-Judaism," in *Jesus, Judaism and Anti-Judaism: Reading the New Testament After the Holocaust*, ed. Paula Fredriksen and Adele Reinhartz (Louisville: Westminster John Knox, 2002), 24.

15. For a sensitive treatment of this issue, see Brown and Roberts, "Reading Judaism Ethically in the Post-Holocaust Era," in *Matthew*, 506–22. For a brief overview of the theological issues, see Jennifer Rosner, "Post-Holocaust Jewish-Christian Relations: Challenging Boundaries and Rethinking Theology," in *Understanding the Jewish Roots of Christianity: Biblical, Theological, and Historical Essays on the Relationship between Christianity and Judaism*, ed. Gerald McDermott, SSBT (Bellingham, WA: Lexham, 2021), 142–60.

who address the question of whether anti-Judaism/anti-Semitism/anti-Zionism is to be found in the Bible itself.[16]

Regarding our study of Matthew's theology, the question is raised whether Matthew's Gospel is anti-Semitic/anti-Jewish. One key verse that has regularly been cited as evidence of Matthew's anti-Jewish stance is Matt 27:25. At the trial of Jesus, the crowd in Jerusalem demands that Pilate release Barabbas and crucify Jesus. When Pilate washes his hands in an attempt to declare himself innocent of the responsibility for Jesus's death, Matthew records, "And all the people answered, 'His blood be on us and on our children!'" (27:25 ESV). We will see below that some Jewish scholars have seen this verse as the base of anti-Semitic/anti-Jewish activity throughout the centuries. Jewish scholar Herbert Basser declares that in Matthew the Jews seem to invite, as well as accept, retribution for Jesus's death upon themselves and their descendants.[17] He states, "While some see an oath here that extended to only two generations, there can be little doubt that the text conveys the understanding that Jews incriminated themselves and all future generations of Jews."[18]

Are Matthew and his Gospel anti-Jewish? The range of conclusions is wide. Scot McKnight contends that Matthew is not anti-Semitic but is "a loyal critic."[19] Amy-Jill Levine reluctantly concludes that Matthew is "anti-Jewish" but does not see Matthew as condemning Jews as a people or race—they are still part of the missionary purview.[20] But Douglas R. A. Hare concludes that the acid of anti-Judaism pervades Matthew's Gospel and Matthew displays an "extreme pessimism concerning the Jews."[21] Gerd Lüdemann contends that at several points in the Matthean narrative it is "Matthew's intention to foist blame for the death of Jesus on the Jewish people. . . . Israel has forfeited its election."[22] Richard Burridge recognizes the difficulties of interpreting Matthew's perspective, and strikes a moderating posture:

> If Matthew is properly understood in literary terms as a form of ancient biography, not only is its subject clearly depicted as the Jewish Messiah, but also allegations that the Gospel itself is anti-Semitic cannot be sustained. But this does not mean

16. This includes those engaged in what Magus Zetterholm has called the "radical new perspective on Paul." See Magnus Zetterholm, *Approaches to Paul: A Student's Guide to Recent Scholarship* (Minneapolis: Fortress, 2009), loc. 2901–12, 2917–33, Kindle.

17. Herbert W. Basser, with Marsha B. Cohen, *The Gospel of Matthew and Judaic Traditions: A Relevance-Based Commentary*, BRLA 46 (Leiden: Brill, 2015), 696.

18. Basser, *Matthew and Judaic Traditions*, 696.

19. Scot McKnight, "A Loyal Critic: Matthew's Polemic with Judaism in Theological Perspective," in *Anti-Semitism and Early Christianity: Issues of Polemic and Faith*, ed. Craig A. Evans and Donald A. Hagner (Minneapolis: Fortress, 1993), 55–79.

20. Amy-Jill Levine, "Anti-Judaism and the Gospel of Matthew," in *Anti-Judaism and the Gospels*, ed. William R. Farmer (Harrisburg, PA: Trinity Press International, 1999), 36.

21. Douglas R. A. Hare, "The Rejection of the Jews in the Synoptic Gospels and Acts," in *Antisemitism and the Foundations of Christianity*, ed. Alan T. Davies (Mahwah, NJ: Paulist, 1979), 43, 45.

22. Gerd Lüdemann, *The Unholy in Holy Scriptures: The Dark Side of the Bible*, trans. John Bowden (Louisville: Westminster John Knox, 1997), 92–93; cf. 90–98.

> that we are absolved from the responsibility of interpreting, teaching and depicting this Gospel with extreme sensitivity and care.[23]

In Chapter 2 I have interacted with Burridge's assertion that Matthew, in literary terms, is a form of ancient biography, an assertion that I have slightly tweaked. But I believe that he is spot-on to say that Jesus is clearly depicted as the *Jewish Messiah*. And further, we need to be as sensitive and caring as possible when interpreting Matthew's perspective regarding Israel.

There are widely divergent conclusions regarding Matthew's assessment of Israel, and the ones mentioned above are just a sampling of the many scholarly perspectives. So, it is necessary for us in our post-Holocaust world to attempt to understand accurately Matthew's intentions. Such will be our focus below.

#### *12.1.4.2* **"Intra muros"/"Extra muros"** ***and "The Parting of the Ways"***

A related, significant issue in Matthean studies, and biblical studies generally, concerns the relationship of the Christian community to the Jewish community.[24] Early church fathers indicate that Matthew was in direct contact with the Jewish community. Eusebius includes a statement from Irenaeus (ca. AD 130–202) that indicates close knowledge of the Jewish community: "Now Matthew published among the Hebrews a written gospel also in their own tongue" (Eusebius, *Hist. eccl.* 5.8.2 [Lake, LCL] = *Haer.* 3.1.1). This may indicate that Matthew communicated the gospel both orally and in written form to the Jewish and/or Jewish-Christian community. Eusebius also notes Origen's (ca. AD 184–253) understanding that Matthew wrote "for those who from Judaism came to believe, composed as it was in the Hebrew language" (Eusebius, *Hist. eccl.* 6.25.4 [Lake, LCL]). Eusebius himself (ca. AD 323) also indicated his view that "Matthew had first preached to Hebrews, and when he was on the point of going to others he transmitted in writing in his native language the Gospel according to himself" (Eusebius, *Hist. eccl.* 3.24.5–6 [Lake, LCL]).

But early in church history the fathers indicated a rift was occurring between the Jewish and Christian communities. Ignatius, writing around AD 110, is believed by many to be the first to note a schism between Judaism and Christianity. While being taken to Rome under arrest to be executed in the Roman persecution,[25] he writes to

23. Richard A. Burridge, "Matthew's (Portrayal of) Jesus: A Jewish Messiah in an Anti-Semitic Gospel?," in *Treasures New & Old: Essays in Honor of Donald A. Hagner*, ed. Carl S. Sweatman and Clifford B. Kvidahl, GlossaHouse Festschrift Series 1 (Wilmore, KY: GlossaHouse, 2018), 107–24; here, 124. See also Paul Foster, "Jews and the Jewish Law in the Gospel of Matthew," in *The Cambridge Companion to the New Testament*, ed. Patrick Gray, CCR (Cambridge: Cambridge University Press, 2021), 115–33.

24. As noted in Ch. 2, a helpful, brief overview of recent scholarship on the relationship of Matthew's community to the Jewish community is found in Dennert, *John the Baptist*, esp. 2–7. More extensively, see McIver, *Mainstream or Marginal?*, and Donaldson, *Gentile Christian Identity*, esp. ch. 4.

25. See discussion by Bart D. Ehrman, "Letters of Ignatius," *The Apostolic Fathers I*, LCL (Cambridge, MA: Harvard University Press), 206–9.

the church in Magnesia on the Meander in ancient Ionia in Asia Minor: "Do not be deceived by false opinions or old fables that are of no use. For if we have lived according to Judaism until now, we admit that we have not received God's gracious gift" (Ign. *Magn.* 8:1 [Ehrman, LCL]). He goes on to say squarely, "It is outlandish to proclaim Jesus Christ and practice Judaism. For Christianity (*Christianismos*) did not believe in Judaism (*Ioudaismos*), but Judaism in Christianity" (Ign. *Magn.* 10:3; cf. *Phld.* 6:1 [Ehrman, LCL]). The identity of *Ioudaismos* in Ignatius is debated, whether he indicates the Jewish community proper,[26] Jesus-believing Jews,[27] or heretical views held by Christians.[28] Either way, as Heikki Räisänen states it, "Ignatius understands Judaism to be something clearly different from the new faith."[29]

#### 12.1.4.2.1 Is Matthew's Community *Intra muros* or *Extra muros*?

The issues at hand are often expressed in two metaphors: *Intra muros* or *Extra muros* ("within the walls or outside the walls") and the "parting of the ways." In the 1985 German edition of his monumental commentary on Matthew, Ulrich Luz could declare, "The Matthean church, whose mission in Israel has come to an end, no longer belongs to the Jewish synagogue association. The break between the congregation and the synagogue is final. The attempt to settle [the church] within the Jewish synagogue association must now be considered a failure."[30] But in the 2007 English translation, in which Luz had almost completely rewritten the commentary after the explosion of scholarship addressing the relationship of Matthew's church to Judaism, he declares, "The total picture is complicated."[31] So our task here is to attempt to make sense of the complication.

The first metaphor concerns Matthew's community and the Jewish community: Is Matthew's community *intra muros* or *extra muros*—that is, is Matthew's community within the walls of the Jewish synagogue, or outside the walls and operating as a new community, the church? This debate is especially highlighted by a resurgence of *intra muros* interpretations in which Matthew's community is understood as still located *within the walls* of the Jewish community, existing as a kind of sect or subgroup within

26. The traditional view is that Ignatius addresses the differences between Judaism proper and Christianity proper in his use of the terms *Ioudaismos* and *Christianismos*; see Schoedel, *Ignatius of Antioch*, 119, 126–27; Ehrman, "Ignatius," 207.

27. Magnus Zetterholm, *The Formation of Christianity in Antioch: A Social-Scientific Approach to the Separation Between Judaism and Christianity* (New York: Routledge, 2003), 185–235.

28. See discussion by Daniel Boyarin, "Why Ignatius Invented Judaism," in *The Ways That Often Parted: Essays in Honor of Joel Marcus*, ed. Lori Baron, Jill Hicks-Keeton, and Matthew Thiessen (Atlanta: SBL Press, 2018), 309–24.

29. Heikki Räisänen, *The Rise of Christian Beliefs: The Thought World of Early Christians* (Minneapolis: Fortress, 2010), 277.

30. Ulrich Luz, *Das Evangelium nach Matthäus*, EKKNT, 4 vols. (Zürich: Neukirchen-Vluyn, 1985), 1:70: "Die matthäische Gemeinde, deren Mission in Israel zu Ende gekommen ist, gehört nich mehr dem judischen synagogenverband an. Der Bruch zwischen Gemeinde und Synagoge ist endgültig. Der Versuch, [die Gemeinde] sei innerhalb des jüdischen Synagogenverbandes anzusiedeln, muß inzwischen als gescheitert gelten" (my translation).

31. Luz, *Matthew*, 1:48.

the larger world of Judaism.[32] By way of contrast, other studies suggest that although the Matthean community originated in the synagogue environment, at the time of the writing of the Gospel the group had broken away from its former religious setting and was operating as an independent entity.[33] Still other scholars suggest mediating positions, such as Matthew's community was "on its way out"[34] or that Matthew's community is "caught in between" being *intra muros* and *extra muros*.[35]

This very complicated debate of whether the Matthean community was *intra muros* or *extra muros* may conceal an issue about which there does seem to be more of a consensus: Matthew's Gospel, and therefore his community, belongs in a Jewish milieu. Brian Dennert contends that the issue is not whether the Matthean community is Jewish but "what kind" of Jewish group it is and how it perceives itself in relation to other Jewish groups. He goes on to suggest that "this current scholarly opinion is in a sense a refinement of the 'traditional' position, as the document is once again being read in the light of a Jewish social matrix and viewed as an attempt to relate a Jewish group's beliefs about Jesus to its heritage and current situation."[36] Our discussion in this chapter will help us determine the relationship of Matthew's community to the Jewish community, that is, the relationship of Matthew's church to the Jewish synagogue. Are they within the same walls, or outside?[37]

#### 12.1.4.2.2 When Did the *Parting of the Ways* Between Christianity and Judaism Occur?

The second metaphor is related but usually focuses on the larger question of the relationship of Christianity as a whole to Judaism as a whole: When did the *parting of*

32. Donaldson, *Gentile Christian Identity*, 310–11. Examples of this resurgence of *intra muros* interpretations include Amy-Jill Levine, *The Social and Ethnic Dimensions of Matthean Salvation History*, SBEC 14 (Lewiston, NY: Edwin Mellen, 1988), 2, 185–97; J. Andrew Overman, *Matthew's Gospel and Formative Judaism: The Social World of the Matthean Community* (Minneapolis: Fortress, 1990); Saldarini, *Matthew's Christian-Jewish Community*; Sim, *Gospel of Matthew and Christian Judaism*; Boris Repschinski, *The Controversy Stories in the Gospel of Matthew: Their Redaction, Form and Relevance for the Relationship Between the Matthean Community and Formative Judaism*, FRLANT 189 (Göttingen: Vandenhoeck & Ruprecht, 2000); Frederick. J. Murphy, "The Jewishness of Matthew: Another Look," in *When Judaism and Christianity Began: Essays in Memory of Anthony J. Saldarini*, ed. Alan Jeffery Avery-Peck, Daniel J. Harrington, and Jacob Neusner, 2 vols., SJSJ 85 (Leiden: Brill, 2004), 2:377–403; Anders Runesson, "Re-thinking Early Jewish-Christian Relations: Matthean Community History as Pharisaic Intragroup Conflict," *JBL* 127.1 (2008): 95–113; Runesson, *Divine Wrath and Salvation*. For an analysis of the sociological concept of "sect" and the denial of its application to the early Christians generally and Matthew's community in particular, see Eyal Regev, "Were the Early Christians Sectarians?," *JBL* 130.4 (2011): 771–93; esp. 782–83.

33. Foster, *Community, Law and Mission*; Stanton, *Gospel for a New People*; Wesley J. Olmstead, *Matthew's Trilogy of Parables: The Nation, the Nations and the Reader in Matthew 21.28–22.14*, SNTSMS (Cambridge: Cambridge University Press, 2003); Roland Deines, *Die Gerechtigkeit der Tora im Reich des Messias: Mt 5,13–20 als Schlüsseltext der matthäischen Theologie*, WUNT 177 (Tübingen: Mohr Siebeck, 2004).

34. Evert Jan Vledder and A. G. van Aarde, "The Social Location of the Matthean Community," *HvTSt* 51 (1995): 388–408.

35. Senior, "Matthew at the Crossroads," 6–15; here 15. Also see Wim Weren, "The History and Social Setting of the Matthean Community," in *Matthew and the Didache: Two Documents from the Same Jewish-Christian Milieu?*, ed. Huub van de Sandt (Minneapolis: Fortress, 2005), 51–62.

36. Dennert, *John the Baptist*, 7.

37. For a clear explanation of the debate, but showing the difficulty of categorization, see Boxall, *Discovering Matthew*, 61–75, esp. 65–68.

*the ways* between Christianity and Judaism occur? Like the *intra/extra muros* debate, the debate about the timing and location of the parting of the ways between Christians and Jews is very complex. James Dunn was one of the earliest modern scholars to tackle the issue in his *The Partings of the Ways Between Christianity and Judaism and Their Significance for the Character of Christianity.*[38] The progression of the debate is found in some of the important titles that have recently addressed the topic.

- *Jews and Christians: The Parting of the Ways, A. D. 70 to 135*[39]
- *The Ways That Never Parted*[40]
- *The Ways That Often Parted*[41]
- "Jewish Christians: The Parting of the Ways"[42]
- "The Parting of the Ways: Theological Construct or Historical Reality?"[43]
- *The Separated Ways of Romans, Jews and Christians*[44]
- *Jews and Christians—Parting Ways in the First Two Centuries CE? Reflections on the Gains and Losses of a Model*[45]

When did the separation between Matthew's community and the Jewish community ensue? Annette Yoshiko Reed describes the various perspectives of the parting(s) "as an inexorable development from Jesus' revolutionary teachings, Paul's preaching of a law-free Gospel for the gentiles, and/or the de-Judaization of the church's base of converts in the wake of the Jewish revolts against Rome."[46]

38. James D. G. Dunn, *The Partings of the Ways Between Christianity and Judaism and Their Significance for the Character of Christianity*, 2nd ed. (London: SCM, 2006).

39. James D. G. Dunn, ed., *Jews and Christians: The Parting of the Ways, A. D. 70 to 135*, The Second Durham-Tubingen Research Symposium on Earliest Christianity and Judaism (Durham, September, 1989), WUNT 66 (Tübingen: Mohr Siebeck, 1992).

40. Adam H. Becker and Annette Yoshiko Reed, eds., *The Ways That Never Parted: Jews and Christians in Late Antiquity and the Early Middle Ages* (Minneapolis: Fortress, 2007). From the perspective that "Jewish Christianity" continued to exist throughout antiquity, see Edwin K. Broadhead, *Jewish Ways of Following Jesus: Redrawing the Religious Map of Antiquity*, WUNT 266 (Tübingen: Mohr Siebeck, 2010).

41. Lori Baron, Jill Hicks Keeton, and Matthew Thiessen, eds., *The Ways That Often Parted: Essays in Honor of Joel Marcus*, ECL 24 (Atlanta: Society of Biblical Literature Press, 2018).

42. From a Jewish perspective, see Gedaliah Alon, "Jewish Christians: The Parting of the Ways," in *The Jews in Their Land in the Talmudic Age, 70–640 C.E.*, ed. and trans. Gershon Levi (1980; repr., Cambridge, MA: Harvard University Press, 1989), 288–307.

43. Judith M. Lieu, "The Parting of the Ways: Theological Construct or Historical Reality?," in *Neither Jew nor Greek? Constructing Early Christianity*, 2nd ed. (London: T&T Clark, 2016), 31–49.

44. Udo Schnelle, *Die getrennten Wege von Römern, Juden und Christen: Religionspolitik im 1. Jahrhundert n. Chr.* (Tübingen: Mohr Siebeck, 2019).

45. Jens Schröter, Benjamin A. Edsall, and Joseph Verheyden, eds., *Jews and Christians—Parting Ways in the First Two Centuries CE? Reflections on the Gains and Losses of a Model*, BZNW 253 (Berlin: de Gruyter, 2021).

46. Annette Yoshiko Reed, "'Jewish Christianity' After the 'Parting of the Ways': Approaches to Historiography and Self-Definition in the Pseudo-Clementines," in *The Ways That Never Parted: Jews and Christians in Late Antiquity and the Early Middle Ages*, ed. Adam H. Becker and Annette Yoshiko Reed (Minneapolis: Fortress, 2007), 189–231; here 191–92. Reed herself contends that Christianity's relationship to Judaism continued to shape Christian self-definition for centuries after the so-called "parting of the ways." See Reed, "'Jewish Christianity,'" 230.

I am persuaded that the supreme factor that led to the parting between Judaism and Christianity is the person of Jesus.[47] Jesus did not intend to start a new religion, because he and early Christianity arose out of Judaism. The Gospels emphasize that Jesus saw himself, and was remembered as, fulfilling God's promises to Israel as the long-awaited Messiah. But the Gospels also indicate a significant dispute between Jesus and the Jewish leaders (e.g., Mark 10:2–9//Matt 19:3–9; Mark 12:13–40//Matt 21:33–46), which is probably best viewed from the perspective of internal debates within Judaism, as various groups rivaled each other for leadership. Michael Bird states it this way: "I am advocating instead that several of Jesus' controversial attitudes and actions sowed seeds of division that would eventually evolve into a prickly hedge that partitioned off his later followers from other Jewish groups."[48]

The expansion of "the Way" in its initial years as narrated in the book of Acts (cf. Acts 9:2; 19:2, 9, 23; 24:14, 22) repeatedly highlights conflicts between Jews who were not following Jesus and Jews who were following Jesus. We can see in Acts already the beginnings of the parting of the ways, a parting that is probably already an element of the evangelists' perspectives.[49] From the Jewish viewpoint, liberal inclusion of gentiles into the church and the deification of Jesus would be root causes of the early Jewish-Christian rift. Craig Evans suggests that the fundamental sticking points for many Jewish people accepting Jesus's and the early church's claims were the simple facts that Jesus had been put to death and the kingdom of God had failed to materialize.[50] From the Jewish perspective, Jesus's and the early church's claims are false. As such this would have been an early cause of the parting of the ways between the early church and the Jewish synagogue. Jason Maston avers, "As soon as the first Christians announced that the crucified Jesus was God's anointed one and made him an object of worship, the Way was on a path to distinction from Judaism."[51] And Donald Hagner maintains that "the point of contention that has always been decisive in the Jewish-Christian dialogue has been the person of Jesus. If we have now begun to see through historical Jesus studies that Jesus Christ binds Jews and Christians together, it is also clear that he remains the main dividing point between Jews and Christians."[52]

The discussion that we will engage below focuses on the combination of these two debated metaphors—*intra/extra muros* and the "parting of the ways"—as we entertain how Matthew viewed the relationship of Jesus and his followers to Israel. The emerging

47. E.g., Jason Maston, "Parting of the Ways," in *A Handbook on the Jewish Roots of the Christian Faith*, ed. Craig A. Evans and David Mishkin (Peabody, MA: Hendrickson, 2019), 361–68; Bird, "Jesus and the 'Partings of the Ways,'" 1183–215; Craig A. Evans, "Root Causes of the Jewish-Christian Rift from Jesus to Justin," *Christian-Jewish Relations Through the Centuries*, ed. Stanley E. Porter and Brook W. Pearson, JSNTSup 192 (Sheffield: Sheffield Academic, 2000), 20–35.

48. Bird, "Jesus and the 'Partings of the Ways,'" 1189.

49. Maston, "The Parting of the Ways," 367.

50. Evans, "Root Causes of the Jewish-Christian Rift," 20–21.

51. Maston, "Parting of the Ways," 367.

52. Donald A. Hagner. "The Jesus Quest and Jewish-Christian Relations," in *HSJS*, 4 vols., ed. Tom Holmén and Stanley E. Porter (Leiden: Brill, 2011), 2:1055–77; here 1055.

perspective—that Matthew and his Gospel are firmly localized within Judaism—will be given due regard, but as Konradt claims, this perspective requires significant adjustment.[53]

#### *12.1.4.3 Supersessionism/Replacement*

A third issue concentrating scholarship on the role of ethnic Israel in relationship to the church is "supersessionism." In common usage, to say that one thing supersedes another is to say that the one comes to replace the previous. With respect to Jewish-Christian relations, supersessionism refers to the idea that the church has superseded or replaced ethnic Israel of the Old Testament as the new people of God, because Israel as a nation and its leaders have rejected Jesus as their Messiah.[54] We will see below that supersessionism has a long narrative in the history of the church, some tracing its appearance to the post-apostolic era.

With the introductory and concluding emphases upon the nations in Matthew's Gospel, some scholars contend that Matthew intends his readers to see that the promises to Israel are now fulfilled through Jesus's mission, and the church replaces Israel in God's economy. Additionally, negative statements about Israel in Matthew's Gospel have been used to support a supersessionist perspective. One such statement is Jesus's stark declaration to the Jewish audience in the temple area in Matt 21:43: "Therefore I tell you that the kingdom of God will be taken away from you and given to a people who will produce its fruit." William Hendrickson asserts that the object of the invective is "the nation, namely, the old unconverted Israel, the rejectors of the Messiah."[55] He goes on to clarify that "in the place of the old covenant people there would arise . . . a church international, gathered from both Jews and Gentiles."[56] Matthew's Gospel has long been interpreted as promoting the view that the church has superseded Israel as God's people, taking the place of ethnic Israel in the future plan of God.

Both the defense of supersessionism and its rejection have been at the forefront of much scholarly debate in recent decades, which we will explore below.

#### *12.1.4.4 The Geopolitical Nation of Israel*

A fourth precipitating issue that has impelled the concentration of scholarship on the role of ethnic Israel in relationship to the church is the appearance of Israel as a nation in the twentieth century. The Balfour Declaration was a public statement issued by the British government in 1917 during the First World War announcing support

53. Matthias Konradt, "Matthew Within or Outside of Judaism? From the 'Parting of the Ways' Model to a Multifaceted Approach," in *Jews and Christians—Parting Ways in the First Two Centuries CE? Reflections on the Gains and Losses of a Model*, ed. Jens Schröter, Benjamin A. Edsall, and Joseph Verheyden, BZNW 253 (Berlin: de Gruyter, 2021), 121–50; here 121–22.

54. For definitions and discussion, see Donaldson, *Jews and Anti-Judaism*, 20–25.

55. William Hendrickson, *Exposition of the Gospel According to Matthew*, NTC (Grand Rapids: Baker, 1973), 786.

56. Hendrickson, *Matthew*, 786.

for the establishment of a "national home for the Jewish people" in Palestine, then an Ottoman region with a small minority Jewish population. The Balfour Declaration was endorsed by the major Allied powers and was included in the British mandate over Palestine, formally approved by the newly created League of Nations on July 24, 1922.[57] On May 14, 1948, on the day in which the British Mandate over Palestine expired, the Jewish People's Council gathered at the Tel Aviv Museum and approved the Declaration of the Establishment of the State of Israel.[58] After this remarkable restoration of the nation of Israel in *Eretz-Israel*, the land of Israel, after centuries-long dispersion, there was, and is, a worldwide necessity to deal with Israel as a geopolitical nation.

Together with the preceding issues, the presence of the geopolitical nation of Israel in the Middle East today is one of the most volatile and controversial issues in the modern world. There is a necessity to provide balance between support of Israel and legitimate concern for Palestinians. In celebration of Israel's seventieth anniversary, Darrell Bock and Mitch Glaser edited a volume in which scholars and practitioners engaged in church/Israel/Arab studies and activities surface and address the most relevant issues from a biblical perspective.[59] In my view, among the many issues that need to be addressed are (1) Israel's biblical right to the land, (2) the existence of Palestinians and their right to exist, (3) the existence of Israeli Christians and Palestinian Christians attempting peaceful negotiations (see the Kairos Document[60]), (4) the two-state or one-state solution,[61] (5) the difficulty of overcoming supersessionism, (6) a way of ending the violence, because much of the conflict between Israel and the Palestinians and surrounding Muslim neighbors in the region is caused by a fundamental rejection of Israel's right to exist as a Jewish nation, (7) the distinction between the biblical and the current nation of Israel, and perhaps most importantly, (8) a more carefully articulated understanding of the role of Israel in God's plan. Bock believes that there is "a way forward—which begins with a deeper understanding of the role of Israel in God's plan. Once Israel's role becomes clear, an understanding of God's plans for the nations comes easier, as does the path to real and comprehensive reconciliation."[62]

57. *Encyclopaedia Britannica*, "The Balfour Declaration," https://www.britannica.com/event/Balfour-Declaration.

58. The text of the Declaration of the Establishment of the State of Israel can be found at the website of the Israel Ministry of Foreign Affairs: https://www.mfa.gov.il/mfa/foreignpolicy/peace/guide/pages/declaration%20of%20establishment%20of%20state%20of%20israel.aspx.

59. Darrell L. Bock and Mitch Glaser, eds., *Israel the Church and the Middle East: A Biblical Response to the Current Conflict* (Grand Rapids: Kregel, 2018). For discussion of these issues from a Christian Roman Catholic theologian's perspective, see Matthew Levering, *Engaging the Doctrine of Israel: A Christian Israelology in Dialogue with Ongoing Judaism*, Engaging Doctrine (Eugene, OR: Cascade, 2021). From a conservative Jewish theologian's perspective, see David Novak, *Zionism and Judaism: A New Theory* (Cambridge: Cambridge University Press, 2015).

60. See https://www.kairospalestine.ps/index.php/about-kairos/kairos-palestine-document.

61. See the thoughtful and insightful study by Michael Brown, "Is It Sinful to Divide the Land of Israel?," in *Israel, the Church and the Middle East: A Biblical Response to the Current Conflict*, ed. Darrell Bock and Mitch Glaser (Grand Rapids: Kregel, 2018), 217–26.

62. Darrel L. Bock, "A Conclusion and Way Forward," in Bock and Glaser, *Israel, the Church and the Middle East*, 267.

#### *12.1.4.5 Israel in God's Program of History*

It is beyond our scope to pursue a full New Testament examination of these issues. But Matthew's emphasis on the way Jesus's life and ministry fulfills the Old Testament provides insight to God's program of history, and the way in which Jesus understood the role of ethnic Israel in his day and in the future. Davies and Allison emphasize that the fulfillment of the Jewish Scriptures in Jesus's life and ministry testifies to the authenticity of Matthew's story "and simultaneously shows that Matthew's religion is not a repudiation of the past but instead the goal of a long history: there is a unity between the old and new, a unity grounded in the divine purpose."[63]

Matthew has much to say about God's purposes, which is the overall intention of this Chapter. But first, providing a bit of an Old Testament context may be helpful.

## 12.2 THE OLD TESTAMENT, HUMANITY'S PURPOSE, AND ETHNIC ISRAEL

The Old Testament provides the beginning of God's purpose for humanity. It provides the beginning context for Jesus Messiah's entrance to history and his beginning establishment of the kingdom of heaven on earth.

### 12.2.1 Abraham and the Promise

With Abraham a new development in divine revelation to humans commences, which focuses on God's word of blessing and promise—God promises that Abraham would be a blessing to the world (see Gen 12:1–3; 13:14–16; 15:4–12; 17:4–16). Walter Kaiser suggests that the core of the covenant between God and Abraham consisted of a promise that was basically threefold: (1) a "seed" (*zeraʿ*), (2) a "land" (*ʾereṣ*), and (3) a "blessing (*berakah*) to all of the nations of the earth."[64]

First, through Abraham's seed/descendants God promises to make a great nation (*gôy*), which would become the nation of Israel. As God will emphasize to Moses, "Now if you obey me fully and keep my covenant, then out of all nations you will be my treasured possession. Although the whole earth is mine, you will be for me a kingdom of priests and a holy nation." These are the words you are to speak to the Israelites" (Exod 19:5–6). Kaiser emphasizes, "Israel was more than a family or God's son; Israel had also become a *gôy*, a 'nation.'"[65]

Second, the promise of the land to Abraham, Isaac, and Jacob and their seed runs through the narratives related to the patriarchs.[66] The borders of this promised land

63. Davies and Allison, *Matthew*, 3:577.

64. Walter C. Kaiser Jr., *The Promise-Plan of God: A Biblical Theology of the Old and New Testaments* (Grand Rapids: Zondervan, 2008), 54.

65. Kaiser, *Promise-Plan of God*, 71.

66. Gen 12:1, 7; 13:15, 17; 15:7–8, 18; 17:8; 24:7; 26:3–5; etc.

are specified: "On that day the LORD made a covenant with Abram, saying, 'To your offspring I give this land (*eretz*), from the river of Egypt to the great river, the river Euphrates'" (Gen 15:18). The land promise and the promise of a seed are binding aspects of God's message to the patriarchs as an "everlasting covenant" (17:7, 13, 19) and an "everlasting possession" (17:8; 48:4).[67] These promises were fulfilled in the later settlement of the land under Joshua, and this was the signal that the people of Israel would inhabit the land so that they would be an everlasting steward of God's blessing to all of the nations. The promise of the land of Israel (*eretz Israel*) operated "as a formative, dynamic, seminal force in the history of Israel."[68]

Third, through the nation of Israel the final aspect of God's promise to Abraham was that his seed would be a blessing for all nations. On five separate instances the patriarchs were allocated to be a blessing for all nations: Abraham (Gen 12:3; 18:18; 22:17–18), Isaac (26:3–4), and Jacob (28:13–14).[69] This becomes an important emphasis in Matthew's Gospel as is seen in the incipit (Matt 1:1), where Jesus Messiah is son of David and son of Abraham—a promise of blessing and fulfillment to the nation of Israel, David's seed, and to the world, through Abraham's seed.

### 12.2.2 God's Own Land Granted to Israel

In the Torah, Yahweh speaks of the land of Canaan as his own land: "The land shall not be sold in perpetuity, for *the land is mine*" (Lev 25:23; emphasis added). But throughout the Hebrew Bible Yahweh makes clear that "Canaan is YHWH's land grant to Israel."[70] The land of Israel was a basic component of Jewish belief and religious practice as found in the Old Testament. Walter Brueggemann argues that "land is a central, if not *the central theme* of biblical faith. Biblical faith is a pursuit of historical belonging that includes a sense of destiny derived from such belonging."[71] From this land God will use Israel as an instrument of blessing to the whole earth. Even after the sinfulness of the people caused them to lose the land for a period of time in the catastrophes of the fall of Samaria in 722 BC and in the fall of Jerusalem in 586 BC, this land, *Eretz Israel*, continues to be the geographical platform on which the story of the Bible is staged. Ronald Allen states emphatically, "No other land on the planet is as important in terms of God's work of salvation as the little land of Israel."[72] God granted this one area of land to Israel to be a base of blessing to all of God's created earth.

67. Kaiser, *Promise-Plan of God*, 54–64.

68. W. D. Davies, *The Gospel and the Land: Early Christianity and Jewish Territorial Doctrine* (Berkeley: University of California Press, 1974), 18.

69. Kaiser, *Promise-Plan of God*, 54.

70. Norman C. Habel, *The Land is Mine: Six Biblical Land Ideologies*, OBT (Minneapolis: Augsburg Fortress, 1995), loc. 533, Kindle.

71. Walter Brueggemann, *The Land: Place as Gift, Promise, and Challenge in Biblical Faith*, 2nd ed., OBT (Minneapolis: Augsburg Fortress, 2002), loc. 313, Kindle; emphasis original.

72. Ronald B. Allen, "The Land of Israel," in *Israel, The Land and the People: An Evangelical Affirmation of God's Promises*, ed. H. Wayne House (Grand Rapids: Kregel, 1998), 18–19.

### 12.2.3 David and the Throne in Jerusalem

This promise is reiterated in the covenant God makes with David, with a set of promises that Bruce Waltke argues also pertain to the remote future: (1) David's house (i.e., his dynasty) will endure forever; (2) his kingdom will endure forever; and 3) his throne will be established forever (2 Sam 7:16).[73] As seen in 2 Sam 7 and Ps 89, God makes a commitment to maintain the Davidic dynasty forever, but he preserves the divine freedom to punish individual members of the dynasty who rebel against the God's sovereign rule.[74] Kaiser comments: "Rascals there may be, but the blessing would never be revoked from the family; thus it was an 'everlasting covenant.'"[75] Consequently the throne of David in Jerusalem is secured by an everlasting covenant.

### 12.2.4 The Promised New Covenant

The promised new covenant (Jer 31:31–34; Ezek 36:25–35) also is made with Israel, and the descendant of David functions as the mediator of the new covenant. This includes the repossession of the promised land (Jer 24:6; 31:28; 32:41; Amos 9:15), the reuniting of Israel in one kingdom ruled by one king (Jer 50:4; Ezek 34:23; 37:22), and a rebuilt sanctuary in Jerusalem (Ezek 34:23–28; 37:22–27).[76]

In the announcement of the new covenant the prophet Jeremiah spoke especially of the forgiveness of sins: "'The days are coming,' declares the LORD, 'when I will make a new covenant with the house of Israel and with the house of Judah. . . . For I will forgive their wickedness and will remember their sins no more'" (Jer 31:31, 34). This harks back to God's promise to Israel in the exodus: "I will redeem you with an outstretched arm and with great acts of judgment" (Exod 6:6, ESV). The death of the Passover lamb and the smearing of its blood opened the way for the redemption of God's people from Egypt, but the shedding of Jesus's blood, which this cup foreshadows, opens the way for the redemption of all humanity to enter into a new covenant relationship with God.

The prophet Ezekiel likewise spoke of the forgiveness that would accompany the new covenant, but he focused further on the personal transformation of those who responded to its inauguration: "I will give you a new heart and put a new spirit in you; I will remove from you your heart of stone and give you a heart of flesh. And I will put my Spirit in you and move you to follow my decrees and be careful to keep my laws" (Ezek 36:26–27).[77]

73. Waltke, *Old Testament Theology*, 661.

74. J. J. M. Roberts, "Davidic Covenant," in *Dictionary of the Old Testament: Historical Books*, ed. Bill T. Arnold and H. G. M. Williamson (Downers Grove, IL: InterVarsity, 2005), 210.

75. Kaiser, *Promise-Plan of God*, 122.

76. Ralph H. Alexander, "A New Covenant—An Eternal People (Jeremiah 31)," in *Israel, The Land and the People: An Evangelical Affirmation of God's Promises*, ed. H. Wayne House (Grand Rapids: Kregel, 1998), 169–206; Kaiser, *Promise-Plan of God*, 199–203; 209–11.

77. Cf. Hamm, "Last Supper in Matthew," 53–69.

## 12.3 JESUS MESSIAH ARRIVES IN ISRAEL

The promises to ethnic Israel listed above are the milieu into which Jesus was born and ministered and into which Matthew wrote his Gospel.

### 12.3.1 Jesus Messiah Comes as the Fulfillment of the Lineage of David and Abraham

From the beginning narratives, Matthew places special focus on Israel in the arrival of Jesus Messiah, who is the fulfillment of the lineage of and God's covenants with David, the ancient king of Israel, and Abraham, the ancient patriarch of Israel: "This is the genealogy of Jesus the Messiah the son of David, the son of Abraham" (Matt 1:1). As "the son of David," Jesus's arrival fulfills the covenant that God made with David of a promised figure who would perpetuate David's throne, thereby pointing to Messiah's lineage and royal expectation (see 2 Sam 7:11–16).[78] As "the son of Abraham," Jesus's arrival also fulfills the covenant God made with Abraham, which included the promise that his line would be a blessing not just to Israel, but to all the nations (Gen 12:1–3; 22:18).[79]

#### *12.3.1.1 Jesus Messiah Is the Son of David*

Matthew's emphasis that Jesus is the son of David also naturally evoked images of a Messiah who would come conquering—a mighty warrior like David who would destroy Israel's enemies and reestablish the throne in Jerusalem and the kingdom of Israel like in the golden days of David. The idea that Messiah would be a king out of the Davidic line can be traced back to the word of the Lord through the prophet Nathan to David (2 Sam 7:16). Matthew then demonstrates that this prophecy is fulfilled in the subsequent genealogical narration—Jesus Messiah is the fulfillment of the lineage of the kingly line of Israel (Matt 1:2–17). The promise is basic to the prophetic predictions regarding the messianic kingdom and the messianic hope of a restored kingdom (2 Sam 7:11–16).[80]

As the Gospel unfolds, almost every use of the title "son of David" in Matthew's recounting of Jesus's ministry is in direct connection with Jesus's healing power, either requested or experienced. France suggests that this aspect of messianic identity serves to counterbalance any triumphalistic notion of Jesus's messianic role with his concern

78. For a careful study of "son of David" in the incipit (and throughout), see Zacharias, *Matthew's Presentation of the Son of David*, 29–52; also Baxter, "Healing and the 'Son of David,'" 36–50.

79. E.g., Carroll, "Blessing the Nations," 35–51; Hamilton, "Seed of the Woman," 253–73. Ulrich Luz links the expression with the genealogy to follow but adds that "son of Abraham" acts as a sort of "blank slate" to be filled in by the readers as they journey through the Gospel; see Luz, *Theology of the Gospel of Matthew*, 24.

80. Cf. Runesson, "Judging Gentiles," 139–40.

for the suffering and oppressed. Healing and exorcisms may not have been the "deeds of Messiah" linked with "son of David" in many Jewish minds, so Matthew makes this explicit.[81]

#### *12.3.1.2 "He Will Save His People from Their Sins"*

When the angel announces that the conceived infant is from the Holy Spirit (Matt 1:20), he further instructs Joseph, "You are to give him the name Jesus, because he will save his people from their sins" (1:21). The term "people" is *laos*, which in Matthew's Gospel consistently refers to the people of Israel. The use of the term here in the beginning narrative is significant. As Nolland notes, "The messianic and salvation history focus of Mt. 1 thus far requires that 'his people' be referred not to a new Christian people of God, but to the historic people of God. 'His' points to Jesus's own embeddedness within this people: the people to whom he belongs."[82]

### 12.3.2 The Unique Particularity of Israel, Yet the Universal Hope for All Nations

We see, therefore, that the incipit (1:1), the ancestry of Jesus (1:2–17), and the conception narrative (1:18–25) serve at the very beginning of the Gospel of Matthew as an indication of an important key to interpreting this Gospel: the interplay of "particularism" and "universalism."[83]

#### *12.3.2.1 The Great Light of God's Deliverance in Jesus*

At the initiation of Jesus's public ministry, Israel is in focus as the prophet John the Baptist arrives heralding to Israel the appearance of the kingdom of heaven and the "Coming One" who is more powerful than John (3:11). Jesus then appears preaching the same message as John to the inhabitants of Galilee: "Repent, for the kingdom of heaven is at hand" (4:17, ESV). Non-Jewish populations surrounded the tribes of Israel in the north on three sides, so the region was described as "Galilee of the Gentiles" (4:15–17; cf. Isa 9:1–2). The inhabitants are called "the people living in darkness" (Matt 4:16), a description of Jews who await deliverance while living among the hopelessness of the gentiles. We noted above that the term "people" (*laos*) is consistently used in Matthew to refer to Israel.[84] Here, where the darkness is most dense and so far-removed from the center of Jewish religious life in Jerusalem, these Jews are the first to see the

81. France, *Matthew: Evangelist and Teacher*, 285–86. See also Luz, *Theology of the Gospel of Matthew*, 70–75; Zacharias, *Matthew's Presentation of the Son of David*, 79–103.

82. Nolland, *Matthew*, 98.

83. See Hagner, *Matthew 1–13*, lxvi–lxviii; Paschke, *Particularism and Universalism*, 1–4.

84. Fourteen times Matthew uses *laos* to designate Israel and the people of Israel: 1:21; 2:4, 6; 4:16, 23; 13:15; 15:8; 21:23; 26:3, 5, 47; 27:1, 25, 64.

great light of God's deliverance in Jesus. It will bring hope to those who understand most clearly the hopelessness of death. This light presages the universal message of hope because from this same region of "Galilee of the Gentiles" Jesus will send out the disciples to carry out the commission to make disciples of all the nations (28:18).[85]

#### *12.3.2.2 The Twelve Disciples/Apostles*

The leaders of Israel in Jesus's day had not fulfilled their responsibility to guide and protect the people, and therefore the people were harassed and helpless (9:36). So, Jesus calls twelve disciples (Matt 10:1) / apostles (10:2) to go to Israel with the gospel message. The number "twelve" has obvious salvation-historical significance.[86] The number corresponds to the twelve patriarchs of Israel, the sons of Jacob, from whom the tribes of Israel descended. The twelve disciples/apostles symbolize the continuity of salvation history in God's program, as Jesus sends them out to proclaim to the lost sheep of the house of Israel that the kingdom of heaven has arrived (cf. 10:5–6).[87]

But there is a form of discontinuity as well, because the Twelve will sit on twelve thrones judging the house of Israel (cf. 19:28).[88] We will address that connection between the twelve apostles and the twelve tribes of Israel below, but here we see that the arrival of the kingdom of heaven in Jesus's ministry demands an appropriate response from his chosen people Israel.

In the gathering of twelve disciples/apostles, we find the hint that Jesus is indeed the messianic king of Israel, but he is also the son of the living God, who will build his church through the foundational work of the apostle Peter and the Twelve (16:18–19). The twelve disciples/apostles have continuity with the twelve tribes of Israel, yet at this early point we see an indication that they are differentiated as well.[89]

#### *12.3.2.3 The Twelve Disciples/Apostles Go to the Lost Sheep of Israel*

Before Jesus—"the Lord of the harvest"—sends out his workers/disciples into his harvest field (9:38), he initiates his mission discourse to the disciples with a prohibition that has profound significance for Israel: "These twelve Jesus sent out with the following, instructing them, 'Go nowhere among the gentiles and enter no town of the Samaritans, but go rather to the lost sheep of the house of Israel'" (10:5–6 ESV). Jesus's historical ministry is intended to fulfill the promises of salvation coming first to Israel.

---

85. See Andreas J. Köstenberger, with T. Desmond Alexander, *Salvation to the Ends of the Earth: A Biblical Theology of Mission*, 2nd ed., NSBT 53 (Downers Grove, IL: InterVarsity, 2020), 43–47.

86. Daniel J. Pfeifer, "Which Came First, the Symbol or the Referent? A Study of the Historical Twelve," *BSac* 172 (2015): 433–49.

87. Cf. McKnight, "Jesus and the Twelve," 181–214; Rengstorf, "δώδεκα," *TDNT* 2:326.

88. Cf. Meier, *Companions and Competitors*, 251–52. For an emphasis on the Twelve as both disciples and rulers, see Joel Willitts, "Twelve Disciples in Matthew," 166–79.

89. Wilkins, *Concept of Disciple*, 126–72.

The expression "lost sheep of the house of Israel" can be interpreted as either a partitive genitive or an explicative genitive.[90] If the former, the disciples' mission is limited to a portion of Israel, perhaps the sinners and outcasts, or perhaps as one scholar suggests, to Jews in the first century living in rural areas of Galilee and the northern region of Israel who were remnants of the ancient Israelite population of the former Northern Kingdom of Israel.[91]

Davies and Allison represent the majority view, which interprets the phrase as an explicative genitive: "The disciples are being sent to all Israel, and the people as a whole are characterized as lost sheep."[92] They argue, "Not only does 'the lost sheep of the house of Israel' stand over against 'the Gentiles' (all of them) and 'the Samaritans' (all of them), but in Isa 53.6; Jer 50.6; and Ezek 34 all the people of Israel are lost sheep."[93] I follow the lead of Davies and Allison in seeing that the Matthean Jesus indicates that the whole of Israel is lost and is being called to make a decision about Jesus's proclamation of the gospel of the kingdom.[94] As Isaiah states it, "We all, like sheep, have gone astray, each of us has turned to our own way; and the Lord has laid on him the iniquity of us all" (Isa 53:6).

This is a special mission of Jesus's disciples during his historical ministry to the people of Israel. Jesus goes first to Israel (cf. also 15:21–28) to fulfill the salvation-historical order that God established with Israel being the tool that God will use to bring blessing to the world (e.g., Gen 12:2–3; 22:18). The Twelve symbolize the continuity and theological salvation-historical priority of Israel in God's program.[95] Jesus's singular attention to Israel underscores God's faithfulness to his covenant promises, the continuity of his purposes, and that his plan for Israel is still unfinished. Jesus dispels any doubt as to whether he is truly the Messiah coming in fulfillment of the promises given to Israel. This is an important message that Matthew clarifies for his readers.

### 12.3.3 Many in Israel Respond Positively to Jesus Messiah

Throughout his narrative, Matthew records a positive response from many of the people of Israel, and from many gentiles, to the ministry of Jesus Messiah.

90. Davies and Allison, *Matthew*, 2:167.

91. Willitts, *Matthew's Messianic Shepherd-King*, 182. Willitts's thesis has not convinced all Matthean scholars: e.g., Donald Senior, "Review of Joel Willitts, *Matthew's Messianic Shepherd-King: In Search of "The Lost Sheep of the House of Israel,"* *RBL* 8 (2009); John Kampen, *Matthew Within Sectarian Judaism*, AYBRL (New Haven, CT: Yale University Press, 2019), 248n9. Nonetheless, Willitts's study is an important contribution to the discussion of the christological and geographical features of Matthew's Gospel and the implications for future Israel.

92. Davies and Allison, *Matthew*, 2:167.

93. Davies and Allison, *Matthew*, 2:167.

94. See also Carson, "Matthew," 275, 283–85; France, *Gospel of Matthew*, 372–73, 381–82; Keener, *Matthew* (2009), 315–16; Konradt, *Israel, Church, and the Gentiles*, 38–39.

95. Scott, "Gentiles and the Ministry of Jesus," 161–69; Turner, *Matthew*, 264.

### *12.3.3.1 Positive Response to John the Baptist's Announcement of the Kingdom of Heaven*

The first announcement of the arrival of the kingdom of heaven came from John the Baptist: "Repent, for the kingdom of heaven is at hand" (Matt 3:2 ESV). Matthew records a resoundingly positive response: "Then Jerusalem and all Judea and all the region about the Jordan were going out to him" (3:5, ESV). Among those that went out to hear John were some of the official religious leadership of Judaism, including Pharisees and Sadducees (3:7).[96] Despite the historical actuality that Pharisees and Sadducees were often opposed to one another (cf. Acts 23:7–8), they are united in coming to where John was baptizing.[97] On the surface they appear to join with the crowds who are responding to John's call to repent. Perhaps they are claiming as the official leadership of Israel to validate John's ministry, but we will see below that he saw through their hypocrisy. Thus, very early in the announcement of the arrival of the kingdom of heaven there is a mixed reception.

### *12.3.3.2 Positive Response to Jesus's Announcement of the Kingdom of Heaven*

There is also a positive response to Jesus Messiah himself as he continues the announcement that John the Baptist began: "Repent, for the kingdom of heaven is at hand" (Matt 4:17, ESV). Large crowds from Galilee, the Decapolis, Jerusalem, Judea and the region across the Jordan followed him (4:25).

### *12.3.3.3 Positive Response to the Sermon on the Mount*

Large crowds were there for Jesus's first discourse, the Sermon on the Mount (5:1). But it is his disciples, who have come out of the crowd, who are the primary audience of the sermon (5:1–3). They are Jewish people who have believed in Jesus's message of the gospel of the kingdom of heaven—they are now the heirs to the promises made to the people of Israel.[98] Those who responded positively to his offer of the kingdom became his disciples. Discipleship entailed unreserved commitment to him, which meant that a new disciple entered the kingdom of heaven in the person of Jesus (5:2–16, 20).

At the conclusion of the Sermon, Matthew records, "When Jesus had finished saying these things, the crowds were amazed at his teaching, because he taught as one who had authority, and not as their teachers of the law" (7:28–29). The crowds have not made the step of allegiance to Jesus to become his disciples, yet they are positively inclined toward

96. Josephus, *Jewish War* 2.119, 164–66; *Antiquities* 13.171–73, 293–98; 18.11, 16–17; 20.199; *Life* 10–11.

97. Matthew will note other occasions when the Pharisees and Sadducees are listed together in their opposition to Jesus (16:1–12).

98. Keener, *Matthew* (2009), 163–68.

him, at least at this point. Large crowds of the people of Israel continue to show up to hear and experience Jesus's messianic preaching and powers (e.g., 8:1, 16–17; 9:35–36).

#### *12.3.3.4 Positive Response in the Feeding of the Five Thousand*

One of the last major gatherings in Galilee where Jesus addressed the people of Israel resulted in the feeding of the five thousand (14:15–21). Matthew is the only evangelist to note that the number five thousand associated with the feeding counted only men, not women and children who were there (14:21). The total number may have stretched to ten thousand or more, far larger than the populations of most villages surrounding the Sea of Galilee.[99] John's Gospel points out that when Jesus performed this miracle the crowd surged forward to make him their king, but he withdrew from them (John 6:14–15). The crowd apparently thought that Jesus was now going to restore the throne to Israel.

After this incident Matthew's narrative indicates that Jesus increasingly moves away from the people of Israel to turn to gentile regions. But in his climactic entry to Jerusalem for his final week, once again large crowds greet him enthusiastically (Matt 21:8–12).

#### *12.3.3.5 Positive Responses in Jesus's Final Days*

The concluding narratives of Matthew's Gospel also demonstrate positive responses to Jesus's ministry. Striking among these are many women who become followers of Jesus as he travels from Galilee to Jerusalem for his encounter with the cross (27:55). These women are exemplary in their commitment to Jesus, which sets a trajectory for a unique form of discipleship to Jesus not found elsewhere in ancient Judaism.[100] We also find one of the leadership of Israel, Joseph of Arimathea, a member of the Sanhedrin, whom Matthew says "had himself become a disciple of Jesus" (27:57). We are not told when or how he had become a disciple of Jesus, but he demonstrates courage in claiming the body of Jesus from Pilate and the Roman authorities. Although Joseph is called a disciple, he is not one of the Twelve but, like the women, is among the wider circle of Jesus's adherents. These are courageous examples of the positive response to Jesus within Israel.

### 12.3.4 Many in Israel Respond Negatively to Jesus's Ministry

But from the earliest narratives of Matthew's Gospel there are indications that many in Israel—both leaders and people—respond negatively to Jesus's arrival and ministry.

---

99. Hagner, *Matthew 14–28*, 418.

100. Cf. Wilkins, *Matthew*, 908–9.

### *12.3.4.1 Negative Response from King Herod and "All Jerusalem"*

When the gentile magi arrive seeking the one born king of the Jews, Herod, the puppet king installed by Rome over Israel, is disturbed, and all Jerusalem with him (2:3). The people of Israel had long waited for the rightful heir to the throne. An expectation circulated in the world of the first century that a ruler would arise from Judea. Suetonius writes, "There had spread over all the Orient an old and established belief, that it was fated at that time for men coming from Judaea to rule the world."[101] Israel's prophets had long spoken of a period of world peace and prosperity that was to be instituted by a future Davidic deliverer (e.g., Ezek 34:23–31). This belief had penetrated beyond the borders of Israel, so that others, such as these gentile magi, also looked for a ruler(s) who would arise from the land of Judea. Through the Jewish community in their homeland, the magi would have become familiar with Balaam's prophecy, "A star will come out of Jacob; a scepter will rise out of Israel" (Num 24:17). In many quarters within Judaism this prophecy was understood to point to a messianic deliverer (e.g., CD VII, 18–26; 4QTest 9–13).

Apparently, Herod heard in the inquiry from the magi of the birth of "the king of the Jews" a potential threat to his rule, and with him "all Jerusalem" heard. The name "Jerusalem" is not only the designation for the holy city (Matt 4:5; 27:53) but also represents the religious and political leadership of Israel and the people of Israel associated with the city and leadership.

The reaction of the leadership most likely gives a clue to the spiritual health of Israel's governance. They had aligned themselves politically with Herod, and if his power base was threatened, so was theirs. One would expect the religious leadership to celebrate at the report of the birth of the king of Israel, but the arrival of the true king of the Jews presents a threat to Israel's corrupt religious and political power. From the outset of Matthew's story, Jerusalem is potentially negative toward Jesus and will join forces with those who will attempt to kill him (2:16, 20).[102] Herod attempted to kill the infant Jesus Messiah to eliminate him as a challenge to the throne (2:13), and his son Archelaus similarly was considered to be life-threatening to Jesus (2:22).

### 12.3.4.2 John the Baptist Rebukes Jerusalem for Their Negative Responses

But this is just the beginning of negative responses from Jerusalem. David Turner notes, "As Matthew's story proceeds, this same Jerusalem establishment will unite in diametrical opposition to the born-king of the Jews (see 15:1; 16:21; 20:17–18; 21:1, 10; 23:37)."[103] The designation "Jerusalem" next appears in the throngs that went out to be

---

101. Suetonius, *Vespasian* 5 (Rolfe, LCL).

102. Peter W. L. Walker, *Jesus and the Holy City: New Testament Perspectives on Jerusalem* (Grand Rapids: Eerdmans, 1996), 33–34; Bauer, "Kingship of Jesus," 306–23.

103. Turner, *Matthew*, 81.

baptized by John the Baptist: "Then Jerusalem and all Judea and all the region about the Jordan were going out to him" (3:5 ESV). We saw above that some of the religious leadership, including Pharisees and Sadducees, appear to join with the crowds who are responding to John the Baptist's call to repent.

But John sees through their hypocrisy. He has grim words for these religious leaders, calling them a "brood of vipers" (3:7), the same expression that Jesus uses to castigate the Pharisees later (12:34; 23:33). Crafty and deceptive, vipers become the analogy of the approach of these religious leaders who have come to John with ulterior motives.

The Jerusalem leadership may be attempting to ingratiate themselves with the crowds who were drawn by John the Baptist. But more likely they were coming out with more sinister motives, possibly to see if they could find fault in this prophetic figure that was outside their circles. Attracting such a following was a threat to both of these common enemies. The expression "all Jerusalem" in Matt 2:3 set the stage for Matthew's focus upon the religious leaders of Israel, here the Pharisees and Sadducees, being duplicitous in coming to John for baptism, and who will eventually be shown to be to blame for leading the people of Israel to reject Jesus and take his blood on their heads (cf. 27:20, 25).[104]

#### 12.3.4.3 Jerusalem's Leadership Influences the Crowds of Israel to Respond Negatively to Jesus

As Matthew narrates Jesus's unfolding public ministry, he highlights how the leaders increasingly respond negatively to Jesus. They say that Jesus's preaching and powers are blasphemous (9:3) and satanically inspired (9:33–34) and that he deserves death (12:14). Matthew will clearly implicate the religious leaders of Israel in their opposition to Jesus, but he will also clearly indicate that the people of Israel succumb to the influence of the leaders and also reject Jesus.

The dramatic place where this is laid clear by Matthew is in his third discourse, the parables of the mysteries of heaven, where the crowds are the primary object of the parables. The parables are designed in part to test the hearts of those in the crowd to see whether or not they are spiritually responsive to Jesus's invitation to the kingdom of heaven. Regarding those in the crowd who turn away from the invitation, Jesus uses Isaiah's indictment of ancient Israel (Isa 6:9–10) to indicate that even as the people (*laos* in Isa 6:9, LXX) of Israel had a long background of unbelief and rejection of God's prior prophets, so the crowd is now hardened against him (Matt 13:14–15).

104. Witherington, *Matthew*, 79; Yamasaki, *John the Baptist*, 86.

#### 12.3.4.4 The Crowds of Israel Respond Negatively to Jesus's Parables

The crowd mirrors the people of Israel to whom the prophet Isaiah ministered. They rejected the message because they were spiritually deadened. The parables are given after the increasing rejection and opposition by both the leaders and people of Israel. God does not force anyone to accept the message of the kingdom, so the crowd's response to the parables is dictated by the nature of their heart. If a person in the crowd has no spiritual ears to hear Jesus's invitation to the kingdom, his or her heart will be increasingly hardened, and he or she will turn away from Jesus and the healing that comes with the arrival of the kingdom of heaven (13:15).[105]

#### 12.3.4.5 The Crowds of Israel Are Persuaded by Israel's Leadership to Reject Jesus

The negative responses to Jesus's ministry will continue until their culmination in Matthew's narrative of the passion week. After the confrontation between Jesus and the authorities in the temple area (chs. 21–23) comes the plotting by the chief priests, the elders of the people, and the high priest, Caiaphas, to have Jesus arrested, tried, convicted, and executed (cf. 26:3–4). One of Jesus's own, Judas Iscariot, plots to betray Jesus and turns him over for arrest and trial by the religious leaders (26:14–16). They convict him of blasphemy (26:65–68), then plot to turn him over to the Roman authorities for execution (27:1–2).

The disastrous story culminates in the trial of Jesus before Pilate. The religious leaders of Israel persuade the crowds to demand that Barabbas be released and that Jesus be crucified (cf. 27:20–25). Matthew then records the tragic declaration that as one "people" (*laos*) they answer, "His blood is on us and on our children!" (27:25). What will be the consequences for Israel?

## 12.4 Grim Consequences for Israel's Negative Responses to Jesus

Matthew carefully narrates that these negative responses to Jesus Messiah's ministry result in grim consequences for both the leaders and the people of Israel.[106] We will not go into great detail upon each but primarily will allow for their cumulative effect.

### 12.4.1 John the Baptist's Declaration of Coming Judgment for the Unrepentant People and Leadership of Israel (3:1–12)

John the Baptist clarifies what he believes will occur with the coming of the kingdom: (1) it will bring wrath on those who do not repent (3:8–10), and (2) it will be

105. Cf. Osborne, *Matthew*, 511–12.

106. For similar discussion, yet with somewhat different conclusions, see Konradt, "Consequences of Negative Reactions," 167–264.

inaugurated with the arrival of the Coming One, with his baptism of the Holy Spirit and fire (3:11–12). The coming of the kingdom of heaven will be accompanied by the wrath of God and the fire of eternal punishment (3:8, 10).

Those who respond to John's message and repent will escape God's wrath. But it must be an individual's personal response to God; one's religious or ethnic heritage will not help. It does not matter that they had religious credentials as official leaders in Israel. It does not matter that they had ethnic credentials as ones born under the covenant made by God to the people of Israel through their forefather Abraham. They must come to God as repentant individuals without prior religious claims to advantage with God.

This is therefore not a call solely for those living in blatant sin, as if repentance was only for flagrant sinners. It is a call of repentance for all in Israel, including the people of Israel and the religious leaders of Israel. Unfortunately, religious activity and pedigree can often blind a person to the deficiency of his or her own life before God.

The Coming One will baptize the repentant with the blessing of the Holy Spirit. But the unrepentant, those who are not receptive to the Coming One, he will baptize with the judgment of eternal fire (cf. Joel 2:28–29). This is a heavy indictment of the unrepentant, especially here the religious leadership of Israel.[107]

### 12.4.2 Religious Leaders Who Do Not Acquire Jesus's Form of Righteousness Will Not Enter the Kingdom of Heaven (5:20)

Another major negative consequence is revealed in Jesus's first discourse, the Sermon on the Mount. The disciples are the primary audience of the Sermon, but crowds were also within hearing of Jesus's words, which included an invitation to enter the kingdom of heaven (5:1–3). In a contrasting, dramatic statement, Jesus infers that the righteousness of the scribes and Pharisees has not qualified them to enter the kingdom: "For I tell you, unless your righteousness exceeds that of the scribes and Pharisees, you will never enter the kingdom of heaven" (5:20, ESV). This may have been one of Jesus's most staggering announcements because the scribes and the Pharisees were the archetype of ethical righteousness. Yet Jesus states that the scribes and Pharisees stand outside of the kingdom of heaven.

Jesus's invitation to the kingdom is addressed to those who are called to a different *kind* and *quality* of righteousness, not an increased quantity. As is recognized in both Jesus's interaction with John the Baptist (3:15) and the statement of the Beatitudes (e.g., 5:6), righteousness in the preaching of Jesus is not primarily a personal attainment of external ethical purity. We have seen in earlier chapters that righteousness is an internal

107. See Osborne, *Matthew*, 115–16. Some reject the notion of two baptisms, one for the repentant and one for the unrepentant, and say that this is a single immersion in God's judgment of unrepentant Israel; see Daniel W. McManigal, *A Baptism of Judgment in the Fire of the Holy Spirit: John's Eschatological Proclamation in Matthew 3*, LNTS 595 (London: Bloomsbury, 2019), passim.

transformation that results from the radical change of one's heart. Jesus condemned the Pharisees for having hearts that were defiled and far away from God. What gains a person entrance to the kingdom of heaven is an internal heart transformation that results in external transformation (cf. 15:1–20). Jesus's proclamation of good news is that the kingdom of heaven is now available to those who respond to him with this kind of openness to God. God's saving activity has arrived on the earthly scene to deliver his people, and this will produce a radical change in their lives.[108]

At this early stage of Jesus's ministry, he infers that the scribes and Pharisees have not responded appropriately, and the negative consequence is that they have not entered the kingdom of heaven.

### 12.4.3 Sons of the Kingdom Without Faith in Jesus Will Be Thrown into the Outer Darkness (8:10–12)

In the interaction between Jesus and a gentile centurion who asks Jesus to heal his servant, Matthew presents a radical example of faith. The centurion believes that what Jesus has expressed he can do, he will do. That is the basis of his faith, which Israel has not enacted. Jesus's declaration that the "sons of the kingdom will be thrown into the outer darkness" (8:12, ESV; "subjects of the kingdom," NIV) sounds an ominous note. The "sons of the kingdom" are the Jewish people who live in Israel, to whom, it was supposed, belongs the kingdom of God. Living in the land of Israel in itself was thought to be a blessing, which should have indicated that they would be the first to benefit in the restoration of Israel.[109] But the people of Israel have not responded to Jesus's message and ministry; hence, dire consequences await them in the final judgment.

We find in this narrative a staggering reversal of ethnic and religious expectations. Here at this very early stage of Jesus's ministry and Matthew's narrative, a gentile is healed, a promise of gentile inclusion to the kingdom of heaven is revealed, and the people of Israel are warned of exclusion from God's program of redemption if they do not repent. This certainly must have shocked Jesus's audience and is a stark reminder to Matthew's readers of the nature of salvation and discipleship to Jesus.

Jesus will continue to appeal to Israel to repent and enter the kingdom of heaven. This fulfills the covenantal promises to Israel made through Abraham, Isaac, and Jacob. But attendance at the eschatological banquet requires one primary requirement for all of God's children, regardless of ethnic identity—faith in the message and ministry of Jesus as Messiah. Gentiles who believe will join Jews who believe.[110]

108. For a scholarly and pastoral interaction with this crucial saying of Jesus, see Bruner, *Christbook*, 203–5.

109. Evans, *Matthew*, 189.

110. Carson, "Matthew," 240.

Those who do not turn to him in faith as the messianic deliverer will receive their just punishment, whether they are Jew or gentile. The gentile mission has not yet been declared, but Jesus's reply to the centurion indicates that the door to the kingdom is open to whoever believes.[111]

### 12.4.4 It Will Be More Bearable for Sodom and Gomorrah on the Day of Judgment than for Those Among the Lost Sheep of the House of Israel Who Reject the Message of the Gospel (10:5–15)

When Jesus sent his twelve disciples on a short-term mission, he gave them explicit instructions that they were not to go to the gentiles or to the Samaritans but to go exclusively to the lost sheep of the house of Israel (10:5). This is a special mission of Jesus's disciples during his historical ministry to the crowds of Israel, who are like harassed and helpless sheep without a shepherd (9:36). As the Twelve proclaim the message "The kingdom of heaven has come near" (10:7), they are functioning as stewards of the kingdom of heaven, the role that Israel as a nation was called to perform. Israel is being called to join the Twelve in that role by responding in repentance to the gospel message. The Twelve symbolize the continuity and theological salvation-history priority of Israel in God's program.[112] Jesus's singular attention to Israel underscores God's faithfulness to his covenant promises, the continuity of his purposes, and that his plan for Israel is still unfinished.

But there are dire consequences for those among the house of Israel who reject the gospel message. Jesus declares, "If anyone will not welcome you or listen to your words, leave that home or town and shake the dust off your feet. Truly I tell you, it will be more bearable for Sodom and Gomorrah on the day of judgment than for that town" (10:14–15).

The preaching of the gospel becomes for Israel both a "threat" as well as a "promise."[113] Increased light of God's revelation makes for increased responsibility, and those who have been exposed to the opportunity of Jesus's ministry and the witness of the disciples will have greater responsibility for that privilege. The whole scene exudes urgency because the time of Jesus's earthly ministry is short and the blessings of the kingdom, as well as the punishment of judgment, are awaiting an expected decision from Israel.

111. Charles H. H. Scobie, "Israel and the Nations: An Essay in Biblical Theology," *TynBul* 43.2 (1992): 283–305; here 293–94; Carson, "Matthew," 240.

112. Scott, "Gentiles and the Ministry of Jesus," 169.

113. Ladd, *Theology of the New Testament*, 88.

### 12.4.5 The Unrepentant Cities of Israel with the Greatest Revelation of Jesus's Ministry Will Receive Ultimate Condemnation on the Day of Judgment (11:20–24)

Capernaum, Chorazin, and Bethsaida were the cities in which most of Jesus's miracles had been performed (11:20). They have had the greatest privilege and opportunity both to hear the gospel message and to see it validated by miracles, but with that privilege comes greater accountability and responsibility. These cities are denounced because they did not repent when they saw Jesus's mighty works. The privilege of witnessing Jesus's miraculous ministry should have moved the people within this Jewish region to repent and accept the invitation to the kingdom of heaven (11:21). Capernaum, Jesus's own city (9:1, 9; cf. 4:13), had been privileged to be the headquarters of his Galilean ministry, and many of his earliest miracles were performed there as scores brought their sick and demon-possessed to him (e.g., 8:5–17; 9:2–8, 18–33). Its prideful self-exaltation at being the locus of Jesus's miraculous ministry will instead result in its being condemned to Hades. Jesus uses a strikingly familiar reference to prideful ancient Babylon (Isa 14:12–15) to emphasize the consequence of Capernaum's satanically stimulated refusal to repent.

Even the most prideful and arrogant pagan cities, such as Tyre and Sidon and Sodom (Matt 11:21–23), would have repented if they had been exposed to the privilege of the revelation of the gospel brought by Jesus. Repentance is the appropriate response to Jesus's miracles, which are a validation of his message of the gospel of the kingdom (cf. 4:23; 9:35). The gradation of punishment for these pagan cities in comparison to the cities of Israel indicates that punishment will accord with the light of revelation received (cf. 11:22, 24). These cities of Israel should have been gripped by the reality of the gospel of the kingdom and repented. Now they are under the judgment of God and will go down to Hades.[114]

### 12.4.6 Blasphemy Against the Spirit Will Not Be Forgiven, Even for Religious Leaders (12:30–32)

The Pharisees had been mounting charges of blasphemy against Jesus (9:3), but Jesus shows that all of their charges are actually blasphemy themselves (12:31). The Old Testament regarded deliberate, defiant sin against God and his ordinances to be blasphemy (Num 15:30–31). Such defiant sin was considered within Judaism to be unforgivable (Jub. 15:34).

Rejection of Jesus's ministry as validated by the Spirit is the same sort of defiant,

114. France, *Gospel of Matthew*, 436–39; Konradt, *Israel, Church, and the Gentiles*, 208–19.

deliberate sin. By attributing the work and power of the Spirit to Satan, the religious leaders were displaying the highest dishonor to God. Since the reality of the presence of the kingdom of heaven is evidenced through exorcisms and healings and miracles, all of which are produced through the Spirit with which Jesus has been anointed, to reject this evidence is to reject the kingdom's offer of forgiveness of sins (Matt 9:1–8). This is a heart sin of unchangeable rejection whereby the Jewish leaders rejected the ministry of the Holy Spirit in their lives. As long as the Pharisees continue to reject that evidence and attribute the working of the Spirit to Satan, they cannot enter the kingdom and receive forgiveness: "Anyone who speaks a word against the Holy Spirit will not be forgiven, either in this age or in the age to come" (12:32).

### 12.4.7 The Spiritually Unresponsive Crowds in Israel Will Not Receive the Mysteries of the Kingdom of Heaven, and Their Hearts Will Be Hardened (13:1–16)

The crowds of Israel have shown interest and even enthusiasm for Jesus's message and ministry (e.g., 5:24–25; 12:23; 22:33), but an individual who is still a part of the crowd has not yet made the step of faith to become a disciple of Jesus (cf. 19:16–22).[115] At this crucial place in Jesus's ministry he gives the crowds parables that test their responsiveness to the gospel message. The disciples have already responded positively, but the parables prompt them to seek understanding (13:10–17).

Jesus's parables stimulate a hardening in those not believing, which prevents them from turning for God to heal them. The unbelievers among the crowd are like the Pharisees who have committed the unpardonable sin (12:31–32) and have sinned away their day of opportunity. The parables are given after the increasing rejection and opposition by both the leaders and people of Israel. The crowd's response to the parables is dictated by the nature of their heart. If a person in the crowd has no spiritual ears, his or her heart will be increasingly hardened and will turn away from Jesus and the healing that comes with the arrival of the kingdom of heaven. Many in the crowd have joined the leaders in rejecting Jesus; hence he states that the harsh consequences are directed toward the "people" of Israel, once again using *laos*: "For this people's [*laos*] heart has become calloused" (13:15). This is a further indictment of the "people" of Israel, along with the leaders of Israel for their lack of obedience to Jesus's preaching of the gospel. Judgment is inevitable for hardness of heart and an unwillingness to hear.[116]

115. See Cousland, *Crowds in the Gospel of Matthew*, 3–30.

116. Snodgrass, *Stories with Intent*, 161. Undervaluing Snodgrass's emphasis upon obedience is Nathan Eubank, "Merit and Anti-Judaism in Matthew's Parables since Jülicher," in *Matthew Within Judaism: Israel and the Nations in the First Gospel*, in *Matthew Within Judaism: Israel and the Nations in the First Gospel*, ed. Anders Runesson and Daniel M. Gurtner, ECL 27 (Atlanta: Society of Biblical Literature Press, 2020), 425–46.

## 12.4.8 The Kingdom of God Is Taken Away from "You" (*hymōn*), and Given "to a People/Nation" (*ethnei*) (21:43)

We now come to one of the most debated passages in Matthew's Gospel regarding the ancient people of Israel. Following Jesus's dramatic entry to Jerusalem and the clearing of the temple, he was teaching via parables in the temple courts.

In the midst of his parables comes a devastating declaration from Jesus, which Graham Stanton has stated "is as important as any other verse in the gospel for our understanding of the relationship of Matthew's community to Judaism."[117] Jesus declares: "Therefore I tell you that the kingdom of God will be taken away from you and given to a people who will produce its fruit" (21:43). This unique Matthean statement gives Jesus's conclusion to the preceding parable of the wicked tenants, who were charged with caring for the master's vineyard, who had beaten, killed, and stoned the master's servants when they came to collect fruit from the vineyard (21:35), and who finally killed the master's son.

We can only briefly surface the most important issues at stake in this passage, which are: Who are the "you" (*hymōn*) from whom the kingdom of God is taken? Who are the "people" ("nation" NASB) (*ethnos*) to whom the kingdom of God is given? What are the implications for understanding the future restoration of Israel?[118] There are three primary positions that emerge in answering these questions.

### *12.4.8.1 The Kingdom of God Is Taken from the Nation of Israel and Given to the Church*

For much of church history this saying of Jesus has been interpreted to mean that the "you" (*hymōn*) from whom the kingdom of God is taken is the nation of Israel. The leaders in the narrative are addressed personally, but they are addressed as representative of the people of Israel as a whole.[119]

The "people/nation/community" (NIV; *ethnei*) to whom the kingdom of God is given in this context are obedient disciples of Jesus, those within Israel who have responded positively to Jesus's announcement of the arrival of the kingdom, and those believing Jews and gentiles in the future who bear the fruit of kingdom life. The singular *ethnei* here should be understood as "people," or "nation," or perhaps "community," which contrasts with the usual plural *ta ethnē* as found in the Great Commission, where it indicates the "nations" or "peoples" of the world (28:19). France concludes, "This

117. Stanton, *Gospel for a New People*, 118.

118. For extended discussion, see Konradt, *Israel, Church, and the Gentiles*, 172–93.

119. See, e.g., France, *Gospel of Matthew*, 816–17; Hagner, *Matthew 14–28*, 617, 623–24; Luz, *Matthew 21–28*, 42–44; van Tilborg, *Jewish Leaders*, 26; Meier, *Matthew*, 242–45; Schnackenburg, *Matthew*, 212. For a recent study that sees Israel, including leaders and people, experiencing judgment and sent into a new exile, see Chris Bruno, Jared Compton, and Kevin McFadden, *Biblical Theology According to the Apostles: How the Earliest Christians Told the Story of Israel*, NSBT 52 (Downers Grove, IL: InterVarsity, 2020), 40–57.

'nation' is neither Israel nor the gentiles, but a new entity, drawn from both, which is characterized not by ethnic origin but by faith in Jesus."[120] These obedient Jewish disciples, including the Twelve (once Judas is replaced) and all other men and women who have followed Jesus, will receive the blessings of the kingdom of God and are the foundation of the church that will include both Jewish and gentile believers.

Matthean scholars Davies and Allison observe that "the dominant interpretation in Christian history"[121] of these harsh sayings was that the leaders represented the nation of Israel and that the nation is therefore condemned for rejecting and having Jesus killed. Luz is representative of this view as he suggests that at the least the thought implied by 21:43 is that "the entire nation loses its election."[122] Luz continues, "Thus Matthew is in fact one of the fathers of the 'succession theory' that later became dominant and according to which the church has taken Israel's place as the chosen people."[123]

Wesley Olmstead contends that the scene in 21:43 paradoxically includes judgment and fulfillment. Judgment is being meted out to the people and leaders together for joining hands in spilling the innocent blood of Israel's last and greatest prophet, the Son (21:33–46). Olmstead asserts that Matthew is stressing that YHWH's people have filled up their cup of rebellion (27:15–25; cf. 23:29–36) and so provoked YHWH's judgment—the suspension of national privilege. But on the other hand, there is fulfillment, "because in reconstituting Israel around Jesus, Israel's God was maintaining covenant fidelity with Abraham in the most surprising of ways, by sweeping the nations into that nation he promised to make great. This is a gospel for a new *nation*."[124]

### *12.4.8.2 The Leaders of Israel*

In a different direction, there is a growing interpretative movement among Matthean scholars who contend that the "you" (*hymōn*) from whom the kingdom of God is taken are the "leaders" of the nation of Israel but that the nation of Israel itself is not included in this condemnation.[125] The first parable (21:28–31a) was addressed to the chief priests

120. France, *Gospel of Matthew*, 817.

121. Davies and Allison, *Matthew*, 3:189n79. Davies and Allison reject a supersessionist reading of 21:43: "While many exegetes have found in our passage the final dismissal of the Jews, that is eisegesis" (3:190). For a careful reading of church history and supersessionism, see Vlach, *Has the Church Replaced Israel?*, 27–76.

122. Luz, *Matthew 21–28*, 44.

123. Luz, *Matthew 21–28*, 44.

124. See Wesley G. Olmstead, "A Gospel for a New Nation: Once More, the ἔθνος of Matthew 21.43," in Gurtner, Willitts, and Burridge, *Jesus, Matthew's Gospel and Early Christianity*, 115–32; here 131–32.

125. E.g., Boxall, *Matthew Through the Centuries*, 322; Brown and Roberts, *Matthew*, 199–200; Evans, *Matthew*, 375; Daniel J. Harrington, "Matthew's Christian-Jewish Community," in *Introduction to Messianic Judaism: Its Ecclesial Context and Biblical Foundations*, ed. David Rudolph and Joel Willitts (Grand Rapids: Zondervan, 2013), 116–66, here 165–66; Keener, *Matthew* (2009), 510–11; Mark S. Kinzer, *Post-Missionary Messianic Judaism: Redefining Christian Engagement with the Jewish People* (Grand Rapids: Brazos, 2005), 106–8; Konradt, *Israel, Church, and the Gentiles*, 174–202; Nolland, *Matthew*, 878–79; Rodney Reeves, *Matthew*, Story of God Bible Commentary (Grand Rapids: Zondervan, 2017), 425–29; Anthony Saldarini, "Reading Matthew Without Anti-Semitism," in *The Gospel of Matthew in Current Study*, ed. David Aune (Grand Rapids: Eerdmans, 2001), 166–84; Sim, *Gospel of Matthew and Christian Judaism*, 148–49; Turner, *Israel's Last Prophet*, 236–51; Daniel Daley, *God's Will and Testament: Inheritance in the Gospel of Matthew and Jewish*

and the elders of the people (21:23), whom Jesus directly condemns: "The tax collectors and the prostitutes are entering the kingdom of God ahead of you. For John came to you to show you the way of righteousness, and you did not believe him, but the tax collectors and the prostitutes did. And even after you saw this, you did not repent and believe him" (21:31b–32).

The context of the second parable indicates that the privileged role of the religious leaders in caring for the kingdom of God is now being taken away from them (21:43). The religious leaders did not fulfill the obligations to God for which they were responsible, neither in their own lives nor in leading the nation of Israel. They had not repented at the arrival of the kingdom of God but instead rejected the very Son who had announced its arrival. This is a statement to the religious leaders personally of the judgment that they will receive, which had been enacted to the disciples symbolically in Jesus's cursing of the fig tree for not bearing fruit (21:18–21).

In this view the "people" (*ethnei*, ἔθνει) to whom the kingdom is given are Jesus's disciples, those who have responded positively to the invitation to the kingdom, and who now become the leaders of the kingdom and are responsible for proclaiming the arrival of the kingdom and living lives that have been transformed by life in the kingdom of God.

This view has become somewhat of a consensus among Matthean scholars, especially attempting to avoid a replacement interpretation. But this view has its critics who suggest that Jesus's rebuke includes not only the leadership of Israel but the people and nation itself as culpable of unrepentance, unbelief, and rejection of Jesus's invitation to the kingdom.[126]

### *12.4.8.3 Stewards of the Kingdom*

A third view, which is my own, attempts to balance the above two by suggesting that Jesus is referring to the stewardship of the kingdom of God. Israel had been granted the privilege of living out and proclaiming to the world the blessings of God's kingdom.[127] But now that privilege is being given to the collective disciples of Jesus, which is made up of believing Jews and gentiles.[128]

*Tradition* (Waco, TX: Baylor University Press, 2021), see esp. Ch. 5, "Inheritance in the Gospel of Matthew," and Ch. 6, "Conclusion: Matthew and the Promise of Discipleship."

126. See the work of Wesley Olmstead who refutes the argument of Saldarini and others that *ethnos* refers only to new leaders for Israel: Olmstead, *Matthew's Trilogy of Parables*, 89–95. For other challenges to this consensus, see Foster, *Community, Law and Mission*, esp. ch. 2; Josef Schmidt, *Gesetzesfreie Heilsverkündigung im Evangelium nach Matthäus: Das Apostelkonzil (Apg 15) als historischer und theologischer Bezugspunkt für die Theologie des Matthäusevangeliums*, FzB 113 (Würzburg: Echter, 2007).

127. For a helpful discussion see France, *Gospel of Matthew*, 816–17.

128. For one who attempts to balance the tension found in these issues, see Russell Pregeant, *Matthew*, Chalice Commentaries for Today (St. Louis: Chalice, 2004), 156–58.

### 12.4.8.3.1 Israel Is Culpable

With the first view, we have seen already in Matthew's narrative that some of both the people and leaders of Israel have responded positively to Jesus's announcement of the arrival of the kingdom of heaven. But as a whole they have responded negatively to Jesus's announcement of the arrival of the kingdom. Grim consequences have been declared by Jesus for both the people and the leaders of Israel who have responded negatively.[129] The privilege of the kingdom of God is now declared to be taken away from those who have responded negatively, and the nation no longer enjoys aspects of its privileged position.

Recent Matthean scholarship has largely shifted away from a replacement or supersessionist interpretation since it does not appear to take seriously enough the everlasting Abrahamic covenant which we saw above promises for Israel a "seed," a "land," and to be a "blessing to all of the nations of the earth."

### 12.4.8.3.2 The Leaders of Israel Are Culpable

In agreement with the second view, we will see that the leaders of the nation are especially culpable for not taking proper responsibility for leadership of the nation. This unique Matthean statement in 21:43 gives Jesus's unambiguous conclusion to the preceding parable. The context of the parable indicates that the privileged role of the religious leaders in caring for God's "vineyard" is now being taken away. The leaders did not fulfill the obligations to God for which they were responsible, neither in their lives nor in leading the nation of Israel. They had not repented at the arrival of the kingdom of God but instead rejected the very Son who had announced its arrival. This is a statement to them personally of the judgment that they will receive, which had been enacted to the disciples symbolically in Jesus's cursing of the fig tree for not bearing fruit (21:18–21). This goes back to Jesus's observation of the leaders' dereliction of responsibilities to the people of Israel (9:36). Now Jesus condemns these disobedient shepherd/leaders.

Although this view that Jesus is taking away from the leaders the kingdom of God has found widespread acceptance among Matthean scholars, it does not take seriously enough the culpability that the people of Israel themselves must own as Matthew records their rejection of Jesus's gospel message.

---

129. For a helpful attempt to balance judgment and restoration, see Steven M. Bryan, "Jesus and Israel's Eschatological Constitution," in vol. 3 of *HSHJ*, ed. Tom Holmén and Stanley E. Porter (Leiden: Brill, 2011), 2835–54. On the one hand he claims that Israel experienced judgment through their unbelief: "Jesus' calling of twelve disciples suggest both that Jesus identified the community being called into existence by God's eschatological action *as Israel* and that participation in that community was possible even now" (2852; my emphasis). On the other hand, he concludes, "As those who claim to be Jesus' followers and heirs to privileges which have come to them because of Israel's judgment, Christians must still come to grips with the theological, social and political implications of the fact that Jesus' aims were focused on the *national restoration of Israel*" (2853; my emphasis). It is a bit unclear to me as to how Bryan brings those two emphases together. For his detailed discussion of Jesus's parables of national judgment, see Bryan, *Jesus and Israel's Traditions*, 46–81.

#### 12.4.8.3.3 The People Bearing Fruit Are Now Stewards of the Kingdom

Perhaps the balance that I am seeking comes from recognizing that Israel—including the leaders and the people—is not losing its covenantal privilege as God's chosen people but is losing its privileged position as stewards of God's kingdom in the present age. Israel's privileged role in the establishment and stewardship of God's kingdom will be taken away and given to another people. The singular *ethnos* indicates a new "people" or "nation" or "community," which indicates those who have responded positively to Jesus's gospel message and who in the present age enjoy new covenant blessings (26:28), which will include regeneration (cf. 15:18–20) and the bearing of fruit (13:23) through the Spirit (3:11; 10:20). This prepares for the time when the church, a community/people/nation of gathered disciples of Jesus will include both Jews and gentiles in the outworking of God's kingdom in the present age. All those who become individual disciples out of the plural "nations" (28:19; *ethne*) will be brought together as one new "nation/people/community."

Peter will later also use the singular *ethnos* in the context of the "stone" passage to refer to the church (1 Pet 2:9). This will not abolish the promises made to Israel nationally (Matt 5:17; cf. Rom 11:25–33), but it does point to the transition of leadership and stewardship that will be given to repentant, believing, and fruitful disciples of Jesus as the church in the outworking of God's kingdom program in the present age.[130]

The role of being stewards of the kingdom has been promised to Peter and all disciples. Peter is the one who held the keys to the kingdom of heaven (16:18–19), opening the door to the kingdom to Jews, Samaritans, and gentiles (Acts 1:8; chs. 2, 8, 10), and once that door is opened, it remains open and access to it is proclaimed by disciples of Jesus as they announce the gospel of the kingdom of God. Matthew is the only gospel writer to mention the church, and in combining Matt 16:18–19 with 21:43 he records sayings that prepare for the role and nature of believing disciples, the church, as being given stewardship of the kingdom of God. Jesus's disciples currently enjoy both the blessings of the kingdom of God and the responsibility of the role of carrying the message of the gospel of the kingdom and demonstrating the reality of the presence of the kingdom as they are transformed by obedience to everything Jesus commanded (21:43; 28:18–20).

The nature of this "people" (*ethnos*) to whom the kingdom of God is given is found in the description, "who will produce its fruit" (21:43). John the Baptist had earlier warned the religious leaders and the crowds who wanted to be baptized by him to produce fruit in keeping with repentance (3:7–10; cf. Luke 3:3–8).

The kingdom of God will produce its fruit in this new people of Jesus's disciples who

130. For somewhat similar yet differently nuanced views, see Turner, *Matthew*, 518–19; Osborne, *Matthew*, 790–94.

have repented and believed in Jesus, which points to the work of the Holy Spirit in the establishment of the new covenant. The fruit produced is God's presence reigning in his regenerated people who demonstrate the power of God through lives that are distinguished by the fruit of righteousness (Matt 5:20; cf. Rom 1:17) and good works (Matt 5:16; cf. Col 1:5–10), the fruit of Spirit-produced transformation of character (Matt 3:11; cf. Gal 5:21–24), and the fruit of new generations of disciples (Matt 28:18–20; cf. John 15:16) that will bear witness to the reality of the kingdom on earth.[131]

If this third view has explanatory value, what then has become of the promised covenantal relationship of ethnic/national Israel to God and his outworking of the kingdom of God on earth?[132] To that we will shortly turn in the next chapter.

### 12.4.9 Warnings and Woes upon the Leadership and the Desolation of the House of Israel (23:1–38)

Following the debates in the temple area with the various leadership groups of Israel, Jesus warns the crowds and his disciples about the destructive example of the scribes and the Pharisees because they give accurate teaching yet hypocritical personal application (23:1–12). "So you must be careful to do everything they tell you. But do not do what they do, for they do not practice what they preach" (23:3). Jesus's statement follows from the religious leaders' position as expounders of Moses' teaching (23:1).[133] Jesus gives a scathing denunciation against them, yet he recognizes their official capacity when exercised in the proper manner.[134]

Then he addresses these leaders of Israel directly and pronounces a series of seven "woes" upon them, which flesh out the condemnation that Jesus has directed to them

---

131. I vacillate on which term is best to use—"nation/people/community"—but perhaps all three are appropriate when recognizing the varied use in Matthew. "Nation" is helpful to use here in the light of the singular/plural distinction between *ethnos* in 21:43 and the plural *ethnē* in 28:19. But we want to avoid "nationalistic" implications in the use of "nation."

"People" is appropriate to use when we emphasize that this new entity is not ethnically or geopolitically oriented but is created by faith in Jesus. However, "people" is often used to translate the term *laos* (λαός), which Matthew regularly uses to designate the "people" of Israel (e.g., 2:6; 27:25), in distinction from the term *ochlos* (ὄχλος), which Matthew regularly uses to refer to the general "crowd[s]" who are interested in, but not committed to, Jesus (see on 5:1–2, 28–29; 27:24–25).

"Community" is perhaps appropriate because it has neither geopolitical nor ethnic implications but rather emphasizes a group drawn together out of the larger world by common interests and commitments, here, discipleship to Jesus by faith in his person and mission. But we will want to avoid the implication that this is a localized community but rather recognize that it is a worldwide community of disciples of Jesus.

With these cautions in mind, it is perhaps appropriate to use all three where applicable.

132. Vlach, *Has the Church Replaced Israel?*, 142, provides a variation on the above views of 21:43 by suggesting that "the kingdom of God would be taken away from the current unbelieving nation of Israel and given to a future nation of Israel that would believe."

133. For discussion of Matthew's heightened polemic with the Jewish leaders, see Turner, *Israel's Last Prophet*, passim; Newport, *Sources and Sitz im Leben*, esp. ch. 2. See also the work of Ja, *Pharisees in Matthew 23 Reconsidered*, who sees that Matt 23 reflects both Pharisaic practice in the setting of Jesus and continuing debate in the period after the destruction of the temple (p. 167). I disagree with the latter but affirm her work on the former, the setting of Jesus.

134. See Noel S. Rabbinowitz, "Matthew 23:2–4: Does Jesus Recognize the Authority of the Pharisees and Does He Endorse Their Halakhah?," *JETS* 46.3 (2003): 423–47.

throughout his ministry. They are least aware of the judgment that awaits them. Their woeful condition lies especially in their hypocrisy and blindness, in which they have disfigured the truth of God's revelation through their self-deception and inconsistency. But their woefulness also results from abusing their responsibility for leadership in the nation. They have refused the invitation to the kingdom of God and have led the people of Israel to the doom that was prophesied of Chorazin, Bethsaida, and Capernaum (11:20–24).

The final invective against the religious leaders is a culminating pronouncement of judgment (23:33–36), which begins with a profound exclamation: "You snakes! You brood of vipers! How will you escape being condemned to hell?" (23:33). Jesus's lament is one of judgment against "this generation" (23:36) and on "Jerusalem" whose house is left desolate (23:37–38). Scholars have been divided as to the intended recipients of Jesus's invective. France is representative of those who understand this to be Jesus's final appeal to the people of Jerusalem, who represent the nation as a whole, and as a lament, knowing that they will not repent.[135] Konradt is representative of those who understand the invective against Jerusalem as a reference to the religious authorities, the leadership of Israel.[136]

The generation of Israel's history that Jesus addresses has been privileged to witness the culmination of salvation history. They have had the opportunity of accepting the gospel of the kingdom and seeing God establish his righteousness in Israel. But instead, like those other wicked people in Israel's history who have spilled innocent blood, the religious authorities of this generation will continue spilling innocent blood—Jesus's and his messengers. And the crowds will follow their lead in asking for Jesus's death (27:20), with the result that the people of Israel of that generation declare, "His blood is on us and on our children!" (27:25). Israel cannot deny her responsibility for shedding innocent blood. "Truly I tell you, all this will come on this generation" (23:36).

### 12.4.10 The Leadership and People of Israel in the First Century Are Culpable with Rome for the Death of Jesus (27:24–25)

Matthew narrates an important scene at the trial of Jesus that is one of the most difficult passages in all of Scripture with respect to understanding the role of ethnic Israel in God's program of history.

> When Pilate saw that he was getting nowhere, but that instead an uproar was starting, he took water and washed his hands in front of the crowd. "I am innocent

135. France, *Gospel of Matthew*, 882–85; R. T. France, "Matthew and Jerusalem," in *Built upon the Rock: Studies in the Gospel of Matthew*, ed. Daniel M. Gurtner and John Nolland (Grand Rapids: Eerdmans, 2008), 108–27; here, 120–21. See also Luz, *Matthew 21–28*, 93, 153.

136. Konradt, *Israel, Church and the Gentiles*, 230–39. See also Turner, *Matthew*, 562–63; Yair Furstenberg, "Jesus against the Laws of the Pharisees: The Legal Woe Sayings and Second Temple Intersectarian Discourse," *JBL* 139.4 (2020): 769–88.

> of this man's blood," he said. "It is your responsibility!" All the people answered, "His blood is on us and on our children!" (27:24–25)

The term "crowd" (*ochlos*) has been the normal word Matthew uses to designate the masses of people who have been witnessing the trial (27:15–19). Now the crowd is persuaded by the chief priests and the elders to ask for the release of Barabbas and the crucifixion of Jesus (27:20–24). As Matthew switches to a different word, "people" (*laos*), in the expression "All the people answered" (27:25), he emphasizes that the crowd and the religious leaders have joined in asking for Jesus's death. "People" (*laos*) is the word that Matthew normally uses to designate Israel (e.g., 1:21; 2:6; 4:16; 15:8).

Used here, the implications are ominous for the nation. The Jewish leaders and the crowds whom they have manipulated have joined together as the people of Israel to claim responsibility for Jesus's death as they declare boldly, "Let his blood be on us and on our children!" (27:25, NIV84).[137] Blood on a person (or "on the head") is a common idiom to indicate responsibility for someone's death.[138] The expression "on our children" indicates the familial solidarity of generations within Israel (e.g., Gen 31:16). The crowd is so convinced that Jesus deserves death that they brashly proclaim their responsibility for his death and extend that responsibility to their descendants.

This statement by the people has been called "the darkest and hardest verse in this gospel"[139] because it may appear that Matthew puts the responsibility for Jesus's crucifixion directly on the Jewish people.

Early in church history this verse was used to pronounce God's judgment on the people of Israel. Jerome says that this verse is the basis of the conviction that God no longer claims the Jewish people as Israel: "For an eternal curse remains on those who say, 'His blood be upon us and upon our sons' [Matt 27:25]; and God does not rule over them, nor is his name invoked upon them, so long as they are not called the people of God" (*Comm. Isa.* 17.32).[140]

Modern New Testament scholar Kenneth Newport states that it is not just the Jewish leaders who have rejected Jesus but the "crowds" too, because it is the crowds who, at the instigation of the chief priests and the elders, call for Jesus's crucifixion (27:22–23) and acknowledge their own guilt with the words "His blood be on us and on our children" (27:25). "Throughout the Gospel the Jews are portrayed as an evil and wicked generation who have set themselves in constant opposition to God."[141]

137. See Newport, *Matthew 23*, 74.

138. E.g., Lev 20:9; Josh 2:19; 2 Sam 1:16; Ezek 18:13; Acts 5:28; 18:6.

139. Robert H. Smith, "Mt 27:25—The Hardest Verse in Matthew's Gospel," *Currents in Theology and Missiology* 17.6 (1990): 421.

140. St. Jerome, *Commentary on Isaiah–Origen Homilies 1–9 on Isaiah*, trans. Thomas P. Scheck, Ancient Christian Writers 68 (New York: Newman, 2015), 812.

141. Newport, *Matthew 23*, 74.

The Jewish exegete C. G. Montefiore exclaims bitterly, "A terrible verse, a horrible invention. . . . This is one of those phrases which been responsible for oceans of human blood and a ceaseless stream of misery and desolation."[142] Jewish scholar Herbert Basser avows that there can be little doubt that the text conveys the understanding that Jews incriminated themselves and all future generations of Jews.[143] Daniel Marguerat declares that by this cry Israel erased itself from the history of salvation.[144] And John Kampen states, "In terms of derogatory and vicious treatment of Jews throughout Christian history, the bloodguilt of Matthew 27:25 has been most ubiquitous."[145]

However, it must be remembered that in this passage Matthew is simply recording what the people have declared. Leon Morris clarifies that "we should bear in mind that this was no more than a thoughtless assumption of responsibility by an unruly mob. They had no authority to commit their nation for the evil thing that they were doing. And even if they could do this, they could not bind God to punish subsequent generations of the chosen people."[146] The religious leaders and the crowds of that day share responsibility with the Romans for the death of Jesus. Pilate tried to escape the responsibility, but he cannot wash his hands of the matter. By not finding any guilt and still ordering Jesus to be executed, Pilate was guilty of the death of an innocent man. The people of that day, as in any day, are responsible for their own actions but cannot bind future generations.[147]

The apostle Peter in his first public sermon at Pentecost indicts the religious leaders, the Jewish crowds, and the Romans for Jesus's death.

> Fellow Israelites, listen to this: Jesus of Nazareth was a man accredited by God to you by miracles, wonders and signs, which God did among you through him, as you yourselves know. This man was handed over to you by God's deliberate plan and foreknowledge; and you, with the help of wicked men, put him to death by nailing him to the cross (Acts 2:22–23; cf. 2:36; 3:17–19).

Guilt is attributed to that generation and judgment exacted with the destruction of the temple and the city of Jerusalem in AD 70.

But only that generation of Roman officials and Israel's leaders and people are implicated. Morris goes on to say rightly, "This verse has been greatly misused throughout the centuries, being made a proof text to justify all manner of horrific practices against the Jews."[148]

---

142. C. G. Montefiore, *The Synoptic Gospels*, 2nd ed., 2 vols. (1927; repr., New York, KTAV, 1968), 2:346. Cited in Luz, *Matthew 21–28*, 506.

143. Basser, *Matthew and Judaic Traditions*, 696.

144. Daniel Marguerat, *Le Jugement dans l'évangile de Matthieu*, 2nd ed., Le Monde de la Bible 6 (1981; repr., Geneva: Labor et Fides, 1995), 376: "*Par ce cri, Israël s'est effacé lui-même de l'histoire du salut.*"

145. Kampen, "Problem of Christian Anti-Semitism," 372.

146. Morris, *Matthew*, 708.

147. Konradt, *Matthew*, 417–19.

148. Morris, *Matthew*, 708.

Nolland states that even though they crucified their own Messiah, God takes their grievous deed and provides the opportunity for salvation for them and for the world.[149] To those who acknowledge their guilt Peter's sermon also extends an offer of forgiveness of sins and salvation (2:37–41; 3:19–4:4). Thousands of Jewish people, including many priests, received that offer of forgiveness of sins and salvation in the first days after Pentecost (2:41; 4:4; 6:7). Everyone is responsible for his or her own actions, but God's forgiveness awaits any who repent. It is not all Jews everywhere and forever who experienced judgment but only those in Jerusalem or the land of Israel, and only that generation, which experienced judgment in AD 70.[150] Catherine Sider Hamilton maintains, "Jesus's blood means an end to the temple; the Shekinah and the outworking of the faith of Israel now rest in him and in the community that meets in his name."[151]

Church father Chrysostom provides relevant commentary upon the actions and statements of the people of Israel: "They acted with unutterable madness. They acted both against themselves and against their children! Yet this lover of humanity did not hold their own sentence against them. . . . Rather he received both from them and from their children those who repented. He counted them worthy of good things beyond number."[152]

And the theologian, exegete, and esteemed church father Augustine provides a further expansion:

> Many of those who said, **His blood be upon us and upon our children** (27:25), later on came to believe the apostles bringing them the good news of the resurrection. His blood was indeed upon them, but it was to wash them, not to destroy them; it was upon some to destroy them, upon others to cleanse them; upon those to be destroyed, in justice; upon those to be cleansed, in mercy.[153]

Matthew's Gospel does indeed have complex perspectives toward the nation of Israel, ending on ominous (21:43; 27:25) yet hopeful notes (28:19–20).

In the next chapter we explore Matthew's perspective of Jesus Messiah's relationship to Israel and its future, especially as to the functional shift of Israel's role as stewards of the kingdom in God's timing.

149. John Nolland, "Matthew and Anti-Semitism," in *Built upon the Rock: Studies in the Gospel of Matthew*, ed. Daniel M. Gurtner and John Nolland (Grand Rapids: Eerdmans, 2008), 154–69; here esp. 163–69.

150. Osborne, *Matthew*, 1021.

151. Catherine Sider Hamilton, "'His Blood Be upon Us': Innocent Blood and the Death of Jesus in Matthew," *CBQ* 70.1 (2008): 100. For discussion of the "innocent blood" tradition in Israel (Cain and Abel; Zechariah; and later, e.g., in 1 En. 6–11) and Matthew's Gospel (Matt 2:16–18; 27:25; cf. 23:35; 26:28), see Catherine Sider Hamilton, *The Death of Jesus in Matthew: Innocent Blood and the End of Exile*, SNTSMS 166 (Cambridge: Cambridge University Press, 2017), esp. 32–44, 231–36.

152. Chysostom, *The Gospel of Matthew, Homily 86.2*, in ACCSNT Ib, ed. Manlio Simonetti (Downers Grove, IL: InterVarsity, 2002), 282.

153. Augustine, *Miscellanea Agostiniana* 1.471–72—cited in Williams, *Matthew*, 504 (emphasis Williams's). See also Timothy B. Cargal, "'His Blood Be upon Us and Our Children': A Matthean Double Entendre?," *NTS* 37.1 (1991): 101–12.

*Chapter 13*

# JESUS MESSIAH'S RELATIONSHIP TO ISRAEL AND ITS FUTURE IN MATTHEW'S GOSPEL

## *A Functional Shift of Stewardship*

### BIBLIOGRAPHY

**Blaising, Craig A.** "The Future of Israel as a Theological Question." *JETS* 44.3 (2001): 435–50. ———. "A Theology of Israel and the Church." Pages 85–100 in *Israel the Church and the Middle East: A Biblical Response to the Current Conflict*. Edited by Darrell Bock and Mitch Glaser. Grand Rapids: Kregel, 2018. **Blomberg, Craig L.** "Freedom from the Law Only for Gentiles? A Non-Supersessionist Alternative to Mark Kinzer's 'Postmissionary Messianic Judaism.'" Pages 41–56 in *New Testament Theology in Light of the Church's Mission: Essays in Honor of I. Howard Marshall*. Edited by Jon C. Laansma, Grant R. Osborne, and Ray F. Van Neste. Eugene, OR: Cascade, 2011. **Bock, Darrell L., and Mitch Glaser,** eds. *Israel the Church and the Middle East: A Biblical Response to the Current Conflict*. Grand Rapids: Kregel, 2018. **Boyarin, Daniel.** *Border Lines: The Partition of Judaeo-Christianity*. Philadelphia: University of Pennsylvania Press, 2005. **Bryan, Steven M.** *Jesus and Israel's Traditions of Judgement and Restoration*. SNTSMS. Cambridge: Cambridge University Press, 2002. **Clark, Kenneth W.** "The Gentile Bias in Matthew." *JBL* 66 (1947): 165–72. **Cuvillier, Élian.** "'Juifs', 'Israël' et 'people' dans le premier évangile: à la recherche d'un nouveau paradigm." Pages 137–58 in *Juifs et chrétiens au premier siècle: Identités, dialogues, dissidences*. Edited by Dan Jaffé. Judaïsme ancien et christianisme primitive. Paris, Cerf, 2019. **Donaldson, Terence L.** *Gentile Christian Identity from Cornelius to Constantine: The Nations, the Parting of the Ways, and Roman Imperial Ideology*. Grand Rapids: Eerdmans, 2020. **Evans, Craig A., and David Mishkin,** eds. *A Handbook on the Jewish Roots of the Gospels*. Peabody, MA: Hendrickson, 2021. Kindle edition. **Habel, Norman C.** *The Land is Mine: Six Biblical Land Ideologies*. OBT. Minneapolis: Augsburg Fortress, 1995. **Harrington, Daniel J.** "Matthew's Christian-Jewish Community." Pages 116–66 in *Introduction to Messianic Judaism: Its Ecclesial Context and Biblical Foundations*. Edited by David Rudolph and Joel Willitts. Grand Rapids: Zondervan, 2013. **Harvey, Richard S.** "Messianic

Jewish Theology: A Preliminary Typology." *Norsk Tidsskrift for Misjonsvitenskap* (*Norwegian Journal of Missiology*) 73.3–4 (2019): 69–83. **House, H. Wayne.** *Israel, the Land and the People: An Evangelical Affirmation of God's Promises.* Grand Rapids: Kregel, 1998. **Konradt, Matthias.** *Israel, Church, and the Gentiles in the Gospel of Matthew.* Translated by Kathleen Ess. BMSEC. Waco, TX: Baylor University Press, 2014. ———. "Matthew Within or Outside of Judaism? From the 'Parting of the Ways' Model to a Multifaceted Approach. Pages 121–50 in *Jews and Christians—Parting Ways in the First Two Centuries CE? Reflections on the Gains and Losses of a Model.* Edited by Jens Schröter, Benjamin A. Edsall, and Joseph Verheyden. BZNW 253. Berlin: de Gruyter, 2021. **Kvalbein, Hans.** "Has Matthew Abandoned the Jews? A Contribution to a Disputed Issue in Recent Scholarship." Pages 45–62 in *The Mission of the Early Church to Jews and Gentiles.* Edited by Jostein Ådna and Hans Kvalbein. WUNT 127. Tübingen: Mohr Siebeck, 2000. **Levine, Amy-Jill.** *The Misunderstood Jew: The Church and the Scandal of the Jewish Jesus.* San Francisco: HarperSanFrancisco, 2006. **Martin, Oren R.** *Bound for the Promised Land: The Land Promise in God's Redemptive Plan.* NSBT 34. Downers Grove, IL: InterVarsity, 2015. **Nolland, John.** "Matthew and Anti-Semitism." Pages 154–69 in *Built upon the Rock: Studies in the Gospel of Matthew.* Edited by Daniel M. Gurtner and John Nolland. Grand Rapids: Eerdmans, 2008. **Novak, David.** "Supersessionism Hard and Soft." *First Things* 290 (2019): 27–31. **Runesson, Anders.** *Divine Wrath and Salvation in Matthew: The Narrative World of the First Gospel.* Minneapolis: Fortress, 2016. **Schröter, Jens, Benjamin A. Edsall, and Joseph Verheyden,** eds. *Jews and Christians—Parting Ways in the First Two Centuries CE? Reflections on the Gains and Losses of a Model.* BZNW 253. Berlin: de Gruyter, 2021. **Sigal, Phillip.** "Aspects of Dual Covenant Theology: Salvation." *HBT* 5.2 (1983): 1–48. ———. *The Halakhah of Jesus of Nazareth According to the Gospel of Matthew.* SBL 18. Atlanta: Society of Biblical Literature, 2007. **Soulen, Richard Kendall.** *The God of Israel and Christian Theology.* Minneapolis: Fortress, 1996. **Turner, David L.** "Matthew 21:43 and the Future of Israel." *BSac* 159 (2002): 46–61. **Vlach, Michael J.** *Has the Church Replaced Israel? A Theological Evaluation.* Nashville: B&H, 2010. **Wilkins, Michael J.** "The Consideration of a Future for Israel in the Light of the Apparently Bleak Consequences for Negative Responses to Jesus's Ministry in the Gospel of Matthew." Pages 313–40 in *The Future Restoration of Israel.* Edited by Stanley E. Porter and Alan E. Kurschner. Eugene, OR: Wipf & Stock; Hamilton, Ontario: McMaster Divinity College Press, 2013. ———. "Israel According to the Gospels." Pages 87–102 in *The People, the Land, and the Future of Israel: Israel and the Jewish People in the Plan of God.* Edited by Darrell L. Bock, and Mitch Glaser. Grand Rapids: Kregel, 2014.

## 13.1 Jesus Messiah's Relationship to Israel and Its Future in Matthew's Gospel

There is no mistaking the grim consequences that Matthew narrates will fall upon the unrepentant nation of Israel. Of the ten passages that we have surveyed in the preceding chapter, three are unmistakably focused on the grim consequences to fall on the religious leaders of Israel (Matt 5:20; 12:30–32; 23), four are clearly focused on the people of Israel in that generation (8:12; 10:5–15; 11:20–24; 13:1–16), and at least three appear to include both the leaders and the people (3:1–12; 21:43; 27:24–25). The future does look grim for ethnic Israel in Matthew's Gospel.

## 13.2 EVIDENCE OF A FUTURE FOR ETHNIC ISRAEL

But is there hope? Yes. The promises to Abraham of a future for his seed, the future for Israel in the land, and that his seed would be a blessing for all nations are binding aspects of God's promise to the patriarchs as an "everlasting covenant" (17:7, 13, 19) and an "everlasting possession" (17:8; 48:4).[1] These promises were actualized in the settlement of the land under Joshua, and this settlement was the signal that the people of Israel would inhabit the land so that their seed would be an everlasting instrument of God's blessing to all of the nations.

Matthew does not appear to focus explicitly on the future of ethnic Israel as a theological agenda. That will await other New Testament authors such as the apostles Paul and John,[2] but we do see implicit evidence throughout his Gospel of a future for ethnic Israel. That evidence is what we now explore.

### 13.2.1 Jesus Will Save His People from Their Sins (1:21)

Matthew records the announcement by the angel to Joseph that Mary will bear the child of hope to the people of Israel: "She will give birth to a son, and you are to give him the name Jesus, because he will save his people from their sins" (1:21). The term "people" is *laos*, which we have seen in Matthew's Gospel consistently refers to the people of Israel (e.g., 2:6; 13:15; 15:8; 26:5; 27:25).[3] God is initiating the salvation of his covenant people Israel.

But as Matthew's Gospel unfolds, it becomes increasingly clear that his people will include all those who believe in Jesus Messiah because he is the Son of Man who has come "to give his life as a ransom for many" (20:28). Saving his people from their sins will be realized in the forgiveness of the sins of a paralyzed man in Jesus's own town (9:1–8), in the forgiveness of the sins in Jesus's community of the church (18:21–35), and in the forgiveness of the sins of many through the pouring out of Jesus's blood

1. Kaiser, *Promise-Plan of God*, 54–64.

2. Those who contend that Israel has a national future, in some way, are quite diverse; see, e.g., David L. Turner, "Matthew 21:43 and the Future of Israel," *BSac* 159 (2002): 46–61; Craig A. Blaising, "The Future of Israel as a Theological Question," *JETS* 44.3 (2001): 435–50. The general theme of the restoration of Israel is important for Sanders, *Jesus and Judaism*, and Wright, *Jesus and the Victory of God*, although it differs significantly. See also Matthias Konradt, *Israel, Kirch und die Völker im Matthäusevangelium*, WUNT 2/215 (Tübingen: Mohr Siebeck, 2007), e.g., 203, 393–95, who emphasizes that Israel retains its place as God's elect people, but also shares in God's salvation through the unique and necessary death and resurrection of Jesus.

3. Luz, *Matthew 1–7*, 95.

(26:26–29). Thus, Matthew provides a statement of hope for the present and future salvation of sins for his people Israel *and* for the new community of faith.[4]

### 13.2.2 Jesus Messiah Has the Eschatological Role of Shepherding "My People Israel" (2:6)

Matthew 2:6 is an instructive text concerning Matthew's understanding of the eschatological role of Jesus. "But you, Bethlehem, in the land of Judah, are by no means least among the rulers of Judah; for out of you will come a ruler who will shepherd my people Israel" (2:6). Matthew cites Mic 5:2 to the effect that Jesus will be the "s/Son of David" (e.g., 1:1; 9:27; 15:22; 21:9), the messianic ruler who will shepherd his people (*laos*) Israel.[5] Nolland suggests that Matthew's language borrowed from 2 Sam 5:2, for the final line expresses the conviction held by "all the tribes of Israel" (2 Sam 5:1) that David is destined to be king and leads to the anointing of David as king over Israel at Hebron (2 Sam 5:3). Nolland contends that in this way Matthew is underlining the Davidic connection.[6] "The text is here applied typologically to the king of messianic expectation. The reference to 'shepherd my people Israel' can hardly avoid evoking the eschatological expectation of the ingathering of the twelve tribes of Israel."[7]

### 13.2.3 There Is a Continuing Mission to Israel in the Land During This Age Until the Coming of the Son of Man (10:23)

We saw in the preceding chapter that Jesus commissioned the twelve disciples to go "to the lost sheep of the house of Israel" with the message that "the kingdom of heaven is at hand" (Matt 10:6, 7, ESV). This is a short-term mission by the Twelve to Israel during Jesus's earthly mission (10:5–15). He also prophesies of a mission to the gentiles that will occur throughout this age (10:16–22). It is today the disciples of Jesus, the church, comprised of Jews and gentiles alike, that assumes a position of stewardship in proclaiming the gospel of the kingdom of God.

Jesus culminates the prophetic aspect of the commissioning with a remarkable statement: "Truly I tell you, you will not finish going through the towns of Israel before the Son of Man comes" (10:23). This has been described as one of the most difficult verses in the Bible to interpret.[8] One difficulty comes from trying to discern whether

---

4. See, e.g., Turner, *Matthew*, 68; Nolland, *Matthew*, 98; Repschinski, "'For He Will Save,'" 248–67; Siker, *Sin in the New Testament*, 53–54.

5. Evans, *Matthew*, 55; Davies and Allison, *Matthew*, 1:243; see also David L. Turner, "His Glorious Throne: Israel and the Gentiles in Mission and Judgment in the Gospel of Matthew," in Runesson and Gurtner, *Matthew Within Judaism*, ECL 27 (Atlanta: SBL, 2020), 152.

6. Nolland, *Matthew*, 115.

7. Nolland, *Matthew*, 115. So also Davies and Allison, *Matthew*, 1:243–44. See Ezek 34:4–16; 37; Hos 2; Micah 5:1–9; 2 Esdr. 13:34–50; 2 Bar. 77–86; Ps. Sol. 17; 4 Ezra 13:34–50; m. Sanhedrin 10:3; cf. Matt 19:28.

8. Davies and Allison, *Matthew*, 2:187–92; Evans, *Matthew*, 224; Carson, "Matthew," 290.

going through the cities of Israel is mission oriented (10:11), with a potentially positive reception, or is to be seen as flight from persecution. The former is preferred by most commentators. The mission to Israel will continue.[9]

Another significant difficulty is found in trying to understand the temporal context. Was Jesus promising the disciples that they would witness the eschatological coming of the Son of Man while they were on their first Palestinian mission, or at his resurrection, or at Pentecost, or at the destruction of Jerusalem in AD 70?[10] Others contend that this is to be associated with the coming of the Son of Man at the end of the age.[11]

The latter appears to fit the larger context here: the mission to Israel will continue until Jesus comes at the end of the age. Following the mission to Israel during Jesus's earthly mission (10:5–15) there will be a mission to the world, to both Jews and gentiles, that will occur throughout this age (10:16–22).[12] While the Jews have priority of salvation (10:6) and of judgment (10:15), their judgment does not permanently exclude them from God's eschatological promises. As Jesus offers comfort to the missionary disciples about their ultimate salvation unto the end (10:22), he warns them not to abandon Israel. There will be a continuing mission to Israel alongside of the mission to the gentiles until Jesus returns at the end of this age (see on 28:18–20).[13] This verse "reflects Matthew's concern that the mission to God's people Israel not be abandoned."[14] Therefore, Matt 10:23 anticipates an ongoing mission to Israel until the second coming of Jesus Messiah.[15]

And the mission to Israel will be conducted in the cities of the land of Israel. For hundreds of years Israel as a nation was not in the land. But in the return to the land in the twentieth century, this saying of Jesus acknowledges the blessed place Israel has in God's providence. In spite of Israel's hardheartedness, God will remain faithful to his covenant promises to her. This is a powerful apologetic to the Jews both those involved in Jesus's ministry and those within hearing of Matthew's Gospel, both in the first century and today, that God has not abandoned his covenantal promises to Israel in the land.[16] Israel will still be in the land until the coming of the Son of Man, and then beyond (cf. 19:28).[17]

9. E.g., Nolland, *Matthew*, 426–27; Turner, *Israel's Last Prophet*, 193–95.

10. For discussion of these and other views, see Carson, "Matthew," 290–93, who holds to the latter.

11. E.g., Blomberg, *Matthew*, 176; Davies and Allison, *Matthew*, 2:189–90; Keener, *Matthew* (2009), 324–25; Nolland, *Matthew*, 428–29; Turner, *Israel's Last Prophet*, 193–95. Turner ("His Glorious Throne," 164) has recently again concluded that "the most likely understanding of Matt 10:23 involves ongoing mission to the Jews."

12. Turner, "His Glorious Throne," 164–65.

13. Kvalbein, "Has Matthew Abandoned the Jews?," 45–62; Konradt, *Israel, Church and the Gentiles*, 74–87. We will discuss this further in Ch. 15, "Mission and Commission in Matthew's Gospel: Transformational Discipling of the Nations."

14. Davies and Allison, *Matthew*, 2:192.

15. See Blomberg, *Matthew*, 176; Davies and Allison, *Matthew*, 2:189–90; Keener, *Matthew* (2009), 324–25; Nolland, *Matthew*, 428–29; Turner, *Israel's Last Prophet*, 193–95; Turner, *Matthew*, 277.

16. Konradt, *Israel, Church, and the Gentiles*, 82–87. Contra Luz, who states: "It seems more likely to me that for Matthew not only 10:5–6 but also 10:23 were corrected by the Great Commission"; Luz, *Matthew 1–7*, 94.

17. Paige Patterson, "Israel and the Great Tribulation," in *The Return of Christ: A Premillennial Perspective*, ed. David L. Allen and Steve W. Lemke (Nashville: B&H, 2011), loc. 1600–1828, Kindle.

### 13.2.4 The Twelve Apostles Will Sit on Twelve Thrones "Judging" the Twelve Tribes of Israel (19:28)

In the context of a discussion between Jesus and Peter and the other disciples regarding the cost of discipleship (19:23–27), Jesus refers to the future eschatological time of renewal, a hope that is basic to Jewish expectation of Israel's future national restoration.[18] "Jesus said to them, 'Truly I tell you, at the renewal of all things, when the Son of Man sits on his glorious throne, you who have followed me will also sit on twelve thrones, judging the twelve tribes of Israel'" (19:28). The expression "judging" is the rendering of most translations of the term *krinō* (e.g., NIV, ESV, NASB, NRSVue, KJV, etc.). The meaning of *krinō* in 19:28 has been debated.[19] Some scholars contend that "judging" indicates condemnation of Israel for rejecting Jesus as national Messiah.[20] Luz declares, "There is no good future for an Israel that rejects Jesus, not even at the coming Son of Man's judgment of the world."[21]

However, others counter that meaning of *krinō* in 19:28 should be understood as "ruling" or "governing." Matthew uses *krinō* elsewhere only twice to indicate a ruling in a small-claims court (5:40) and inappropriate discernment or evaluation of another person (7:1–2), while *katakrinō* describes an ominous verdict (12:41; 20:18; 27:3).[22] This is also the distinction between *krinō* and *katakrinō* in 1 Cor 11:32.[23] In Matt 19:28 the idea of the Twelve ruling or governing with Jesus as the Son of Man is paramount, which Nolland notes it is likely to be inspired by the paralleling in Dan 7 of a Son of Man and the saints of the Most High.[24] Condemning Israel would bring no great pleasure to the disciples, but reward would, which was the point of Peter's request (19:27).[25] Evans suggests that "judge" here has the sense as in the book of Judges, where "judges functioned as leaders and administrators who ruled Israel's tribes with justice, and who on occasion defended the tribes from foreign aggression."[26]

Jesus indicates a future time of renewal when the twelve apostles will participate in the final establishment of the kingdom of God on the earth, when Israel will be restored to the land and the Twelve will rule with Jesus Messiah over the renewal of

18. Cf. Sanders, *Jesus and Judaism*, 103; David C. Sim, "The Meaning of *palingenesia* in Mt 19.28," *JSNT* 50 (1993): 3–12.

19. Blaine Charette, *The Theme of Recompense in Matthew's Gospel*, JSNTSup 79 (Sheffield: JSOT Press, 1992), 113–14.

20. Charette, *Theme of Recompense*, 113–14; Carson, "Matthew," 481; Luz, *Matthew 8–20*, 517; cf. Beasley-Murray, *Jesus and the Kingdom of God*, 275–76. Similarly, Basser, *Matthew*, 507–9, although he argues that this is Matthew's creation.

21. Luz, *Matthew 21–28*, 164.

22. Cf. Wilkins, *Matthew*, 263–65, 308–10; Turner, "His Glorious Throne," 151–53n47.

23. See also Konradt, *Israel, Church, and the Gentiles*, 262n494

24. Nolland, *Matthew*, 801; see Dan 7:9, 13–14, 18, 22, 27, esp. vv. 14, 27; cf. Luke 22:30; 1 Cor 6:2; Rev 2:26–27; 3:21; 20:6; Wis 3:8. See also Gundry, *Matthew*, 392–93; Davies and Allison, *Matthew*, 3:55–58; Konradt, *Israel, Church, and the Gentiles*, 259–63; Philip F. Esler, "Ethnic Identities in the Dead Sea Legal Papyri and Matthew: Reinterpreting Matthew 25:31–46," in Runesson and Gurtner, *Matthew Within Judaism*, 195–209; here 203–4.

25. See Konradt, *Israel, Church, and the Gentiles*, 259–63; Konradt, *Matthew*, 295–96. Contra Osborne, who links this saying with the following verse (19:29) to suggest that a literal understanding of the Twelve and Israel is doubtful, so 19:29 connects these promises with "everyone" in the church as the new Israel (Osborne, *Matthew*, 722).

26. Evans, *Matthew*, 348.

all things. Some have seen this as a case of "Israel" being enlarged to include non-Jewish, gentile believers,[27] but there is nothing in Matthew's use of the term "Israel" to indicate such a broadening of the expression[28] (see above on Matthew's use of "Israel" in, e.g., 2:6, 20–21, etc.). The twelve apostles will judge the twelve tribes in the sense of shepherding them (cf. Pss. Sol. 17:26), not punishing them.[29] This is the conclusion reached by a diverse array of Matthean scholars.[30] David Turner argues that "Matt 19:28 speaks of the Twelve as future rulers of Israel, not as those who preside over Israel's condemnation."[31] This apparently speaks to the political reconstitution of a twelve-tribe nation-state in the restored Davidic kingdom.[32] The terminology, here focusing on the twelve tribes of Israel, is remarkable (cf. Luke 22:30; Rev 21:12), linked as it is to the description of the eschaton as a time of regeneration.[33] Matthew does not offer us details, but this is a potent expectation of the future restoration of Israel. "The παλιγγενεσία [*palingenesia*] for him meant the world in which Christ reigns, a world with a redeemed Israel."[34]

### 13.2.5 Israel Will Be in the Land of Jerusalem Until They Bless the Coming One (23:37–39)

Matthew records extended controversies between Jesus and the religious leadership of Israel that occurred in the temple area during the passion week (Matt 21–22). These controversies revealed beyond any doubt that the religious establishment, especially the Pharisees, will not lead the people of Israel in repentance and accept Jesus's invitation to the kingdom of heaven. So, Jesus unleashes blistering critiques (23:1–12) and "woes" (23:13–36) upon the scribes and the Pharisees for their hypocrisy and faulty leadership. Jesus's statement to "Jerusalem" includes a prophecy of judgment upon the leadership and people of Israel for its current and past transgressions (23:37–39).[35]

---

27. Colin Chapman, *Christian Zionism and the Restoration of Israel: How Should We Interpret the Scriptures?* (Eugene, OR: Cascade, 2021), 68.

28. Davies and Allison, *Matthew*, 1:242–44; 3:54–58.

29. Keener, *Matthew* (2009), 479–80; Evans, *Matthew*, 348.

30. Cf., e.g., Davies and Allison, *Matthew*, 3:55–58; Gary Gromacki, "The Fulfillment of the Abrahamic Covenant," *The Journal of Ministry and Theology* 18.2 (2014): 77–119; Gundry, *Matthew*, 392–93; Keener, *Matthew* (2009), 479–80; Konradt, *Israel, Church, and the Gentiles*, 259–63; Runesson, *Divine Wrath and Salvation in Matthew*, 45–46n16; 310n244; R. Saucy, *Progressive Dispensationalism*, 267–69; Willitts, *Matthew's Messianic Shepherd-King*, 119–21; Witherington, *Matthew*, 371–72.

31. Turner, "His Glorious Throne," 167.

32. Willitts, "Zionism in the Gospel of Matthew," 138.

33. Turner, *Matthew*, 475; cf. Sim, "Meaning of *palingenesia*," 3–12.

34. Davies and Allison, *Matthew*, 3:57–58.

35. When considering the different settings of the saying in Luke 13:33–35 and Matt 23:37–39, Eva Günther suggests that since the original context is uncertain, it is therefore uncertain whether the pre-Synoptic logion first appeared in Q or goes back to a dominical saying; see Günther, *Wisdom as a Model*, 7–10. But since Jesus as prophet warned Jerusalem several times in different settings of forthcoming judgment, those who argue for this as an original dominical saying include Martin Hengel, "Jesus as Messianic Teacher of Wisdom and the Beginnings of Christology," in *Studies in Early Christology* (London: T&T Clark, 2004), 73–119, here 76, 86; Darrell L. Bock, *Luke 9:51–24:53*, BECNT 3B (Grand Rapids: Baker Books, 1996), 1246–51; France, *Gospel of Matthew*, 882–85.

However, it appears that while Jesus is pronouncing judgment on that generation of Israel, he is also offering hope to future generations of the people of Israel. Thus Jesus, as prophet, has repeatedly spoken of forthcoming judgment but also of his desire to gather Jerusalem under his protective care.[36] Jesus's tone combines the denunciation of the religious leaders with a compassionate lament—"O Jerusalem, Jerusalem"—and concludes his address to the people of Israel—which in this context in the temple has included the crowds and the religious leaders—with a dramatic prophecy: "For I tell you, you will not see me again until you say, 'Blessed is he who comes in the name of the Lord'" (23:39).

This prophecy is the climax of Jesus's public ministry to Israel and it takes the reader from the sadness of Israel's rejection of Jesus to their soulful cry at seeing Jesus again as they quote the fragment from Ps 118:26: "Blessed is he who comes in the name of the Lord." How should this quotation be understood? Luz understands the complexities of interpreting the "difficult verse," and distills the interpretative options to three, all of which have had their advocates in the history of the church's interpretation: (1) a word of judgment, (2) a condition to be met, (3) a promise to be fulfilled.[37]

### *13.2.5.1 A Word of Judgment*

The most common interpretation—in the ancient church, throughout most of church history, and in the early modern period—understood 23:39 as a word of judgment. At the parousia, ethnic Israel will greet Jesus *against their will* as the one who comes in the name of God. Their greeting is not an expression of faith, but obeisance, that is compelled by the obvious might of the parousia-Christ. Luz cites Juan de Maldonat, a Spanish Jesuit theologian and exegete (1533–1583), who gives a drastic explanatory example: "A king says to a man who does not acknowledge his rule: 'I will string you up, and then you will say that I am king!'"[38] So it will be with Israel: acknowledging Jesus Messiah at the parousia will no longer help them.[39]

This is Luz's preferred interpretation. He explains that at the parousia the people of Jerusalem, who represent Israel that has rejected him, will greet the Judge of the world as the one who comes in the name of the Lord, but then it will be too late.[40] John Calvin likewise states, "He says He will not come to them until they cry out in fear—too late—at the sight of His terrible Majesty, 'truly He is the Son of God.'"[41]

---

36. For a sensitive treatment of this passage as pronouncing judgment and offering hope, see Bruner, *Churchbook*, 458–64.

37. Luz, *Matthew 21–28*, 162–65. I have here reversed his order of presenting these interpretative options.

38. Juan de Maldona, *Commentarii in quator Evangelistas*, ed. Johann Michael Raich (Moguntiae: Sumptibus Francisci Kirchheim, 1874), 1:467; cited in Luz, *Matthew 21–28*, 163n59.

39. Luz, *Matthew 21–28*, 163.

40. Luz, *Matthew 21–28*, 164.

41. John Calvin, *A Harmony of the Gospels Matthew, Mark and Luke*, trans. A. W. Morrison, Calvin's Commentaries, 22 vols. (repr., Grand Rapids: Eerdmans, 1972), 3:71.

### *13.2.5.2 A Condition to Be Met*

Another interpretation understands the "until" clause as a condition: "until you say" (*heōs an eipēte*). Then 23:39 might be paraphrased: "You will see me again only when [if] you say 'Blessed is he who comes in the name of the Lord'"—that is, when you accept Jesus as the Messiah.[42] This interpretation was also represented in the ancient church and is found among modern interpreters.[43] Davies and Allison suggest that the text does not mean "when the Messiah comes his people will bless him," but rather, "when his people bless him, the Messiah will come." They state, "While Israel's redemption may be, on the basis of both Old Testament promises and 19:28, a firm hope, its date is contingent upon Israel's acceptance of Jesus."[44] They understand 23:39 not to be a pronouncement of condemnation but instead a promise of redemption: the Messiah will come when his people repent (cf. Acts 3:19–20).[45]

France takes it a step further. He also understands the phrase "*until you say*" as a conditional statement but also as an example of an unreal condition. There is an assumption of an untruth for the sake of argument; i.e., "They will not see him again *until* they welcome him, but the indefinite phrasing of the second clause gives no assurance that such a welcome will ever be forthcoming."[46]

### *13.2.5.3 A Promise to Be Fulfilled*

A third view, which I affirm, suggests that Jesus is pointing to an eschatological experience where at the parousia there will be a national turning of Israel to Jesus Messiah. This view suggests that Paul articulated this in his epistle to the Romans:

> I do not want you to be ignorant of this mystery, brothers and sisters, so that you may not be conceited: Israel has experienced a hardening in part until the full number of the Gentiles has come in, and in this way all Israel will be saved. As it is written: "The deliverer will come from Zion; he will turn godlessness away from Jacob." (Rom 11:25–26)

Following this interpretation of Paul, the notion of a fulfilled promise is found in the early church fathers. Cyril of Alexandria points to Paul's expectation of the time when "the fullness of the nations comes in" (Rom 11:25) and they believe in Christ, "then the Jews who believe after these things see the beauty of the divine nature of Christ.

42. Luz, *Matthew 21–28*, 4:163–64.

43. See examples from the ancient church in Luz, *Matthew 21–28*, 163–64. Among the modern interpreters, see Dale C. Allison Jr., "Matt. 23.39=Luke 13.35b as a Conditional Prophecy," *JSNT* 18 (1983): 75–84; Davies and Allison, *Matthew*, 323–24; Evans, *Matthew*, 399.

44. Davies and Allison, *Matthew*, 323–24.

45. Davies and Allison, *Matthew*, 323–24. So also Daniel J. Harrington, *Matthew*, 328–29: "The preposition *heōs* seems to have a conditional sense: Only if and when Jerusalem recites Ps 118:26, will the Son of Man come."

46. France, *Gospel of Matthew*, 885. He draws upon the emphatic negation of *ou mē* with *heōs an* and the subjunctive *eipēte*.

They behold the Father in the Son and declare him to be the Redeemer proclaimed through the prophets."[47]

Leon Morris reasons along the same lines that it is best to take Jesus's words as pointing to "an eschatological reality." "When the final kingdom is set up in all its glory, Jesus will be greeted as him *who comes in the name of the Lord*. Not until then will the inhabitants of Jerusalem recognize the reality of the divine visitation that took place when Jesus came to them."[48]

Nolland rejects the view that the fragment from Ps 118:26 will be uttered by those facing judgment. He argues that blessing belongs to welcoming and celebrating, not to fear and despair. He further argues that "the one who says, 'Blessed is the one who comes in the name of the Lord,' is involved in joyful welcome of one whose significance is appreciated."[49]

Nolland further rejects the syntax as conditional. The conditional view maintains that there is a delay of the coming of the Son of Man until a time when there will be a proper reception for him in Jerusalem. Jesus will wait in heaven until the circumstances are right. But Nolland counters, "Despite the attractions of this view, it is not easy to imagine the Matthean Jesus quite saying: 'You were not ready for me at this point. Never mind. I will go off and wait quietly in heaven until you are ready.'"[50]

Rather, Matt 23:39 appears to be a prophetic announcement by Jesus that when he returns remorseful Israel will utter in sincere repentance the words, "Blessed is he who comes in the name of the Lord." This is God's merciful offer of hope to his people.[51] This is in line with the statement in Zechariah: "And I will pour out on the house of David and the inhabitants of Jerusalem a spirit of grace and supplication. They will look on me, the one they have pierced, and they will mourn for him as one mourns for an only child, and grieve bitterly for him as one grieves for a firstborn son" (Zech 12:10; cf. John 19:34–37). Robert Gundry believes that this "implies a conversion of Israel at the parousia . . . and a return of the kingdom to Israel at the parousia."[52]

This is the last time that Jesus will address the crowds, who have had their opportunity for repentance. The christological implications of Jesus's quotation of Ps 118:26 are profound. The same words were cited in Matt 21:9 at Jesus's entrance to Jerusalem, shouted by those who were identifying him as the messianic Son of David. Now as Jesus cites the same passage, he identifies himself with God's Messiah, Israel's Savior, the "Coming One," who will in the future once again come to his people after a time of great judgment, when they will have no other choice but to acknowledge him as

47. Cyril of Alexandria, *Fragments on Matthew* 264," as cited in Manlio Simonetti, *Matthew 1–13*, ACCSNT Ib, (Downers Grove, IL: InterVarsity, 2002), 185.

48. Morris, *Matthew*, 592, emphasis original. See also Blomberg, *Matthew*, 351.

49. Nolland, *Matthew*, 952–53.

50. Nolland, *Matthew*, 953.

51. Turner, *Israel's Last Prophet*, 328.

52. Gundry, *Matthew*, 474. So also Keener, *Matthew* (2009), 558–59.

Lord, either in great joy or in great sorrow.[53] Matthew's perspective on the city of Jerusalem and the temple implies both God's judgment on them in AD 70, and his future restoration of repentant Israel when Jesus returns.[54]

### 13.2.6 A Future Preaching of the Gospel, the Desolation of Sacrilege in the Holy Place, and Emphasis upon the Land of Judea Indicate a Future Role of Israel in the Land (24:14–16)

In Jesus's eschatological discourse (Matt 24–25), he first cautions the disciples against false assumptions about what will signal the end (24:6, 8), but then he gives an explicit indicator of the activity that must be accomplished before the end of this age: "And this gospel of the kingdom will be preached in the whole world as a testimony to all nations, and then the end will come" (24:14). The expression "gospel of the kingdom" is unique to Matthew (cf. 4:23; 9:35), combining the good news of salvation with the arrival of the kingdom of God. Although the increase of events in 24:9–13 is some indication that the parousia is near, the only explicit condition to be met will be the proclamation of the gospel of the kingdom in the entire world to all the nations. After that gospel proclamation has occurred, the end will come.

With the mention of "the abomination that causes desolation," both Matthew (24:15–22) and Mark (13:14–20) shift the focus to activities at the end of the age. Jesus is giving a mixture of prophetic elements that speak both to his present generation and to the future. Jesus's prophecy includes both the destruction of Jerusalem and the temple in AD 70, but he looks beyond to a future time when another abomination that causes desolation will arise in Jerusalem to lead astray God's people and bring destruction upon those who resist him.[55] When these signs of the end of the age appear, those waiting for the arrival of the Son of Man are to recognize that their redemption is drawing near (Luke 21:28). This refers both to repentant Israel and to unrepentant wicked people.

Jesus warns of first-century historical judgment on Israel for rejecting the invitation to the kingdom but he also provides future guidance for his disciples and future Israel. Jesus anticipates the fulfillment of the covenantal promises to Israel to be restored to the land, with an apparently (and seemingly implausible[56]) rebuilt temple and attendant desecration, which ushers in the messianic kingdom.[57]

53. Turner, *Matthew*, 562.

54. Willitts, "Zionism in the Gospel of Matthew," 132.

55. Ladd (*Theology*, 198) suggests that the historical and eschatological elements are purposely intertwined under a kind of "prophetic foreshortening." The near event, the destruction of Jerusalem, serves as a symbol for the far event as Jesus sees beyond that day to the entire age and his coming in power and glory at the end of the age. For another attempt to balance the two, see Turner, "Structure," 3–27.

56. Turner, *Matthew*, 580; Patterson, "Israel and the Great Tribulation," loc. 1600–1828.

57. Cf. Evans, *Matthew*, 406; Hafemann, "Eschatology and Ethics," 161–92.

### 13.2.7 The Imperative of the Great Commission to "Make Disciples of All the Nations" Includes a Continuing Mission to Israel (28:19–20)

Some argue that in Jesus's imperative "make disciples of all the nations," "all the nations" means only "gentiles," not the "Jews," since Matthew normally refers to gentiles by this title.[58] Kenneth Clark is representative of this view, in which he contends that Jesus's command to the Eleven that they "make disciples of all the gentile peoples" serves as the capstone and climax of a gentile bias that has been building throughout the gospel as a whole. Matthew's perspective is that "Judaism as such has definitely rejected Jesus as God's Messiah, and God has finally rejected Judaism."[59] Others often appeal to this view because of Jesus's harsh statements about taking the kingdom away from the Jewish nation (e.g., 21:43).[60]

Donaldson offers a unique view that has gained traction among some Matthean scholars. He suggests tentatively that Matthew envisages two ongoing, complementary, and coterminous missions—one to "the lost sheep of the house of Israel" (10:5–15; 15:24) and the other to "all the (non-Jewish) *ethnē*" (28:18–20), which continues until the coming of the Son of man (10:23). In this view, at some level the categories Jew and gentile, or Israel and the non-Jewish *ethnē*, continue to have a significant place within the new *ekklēsia* of Jesus.[61] We will address some of the implications of this view below, but as I have discussed above, most scholars understand the mission Jesus gave to the disciples in 10:5–15—namely, to go "only to the lost sheep of the house of Israel," to which he alludes in 15:24—as a short-term mission in Jesus's earthly ministry that fulfilled his offer of the kingdom of heaven to ethnic Israel.

Most scholars, then, contend that Jesus's overall intention is to include Jews and gentiles in his Commission, and Matthew intends his readers to understand their inclusion (cf. 24:9, 14; 25:32).[62] This becomes the joint object of the imperative "make disciples." *Panta ta ethnē* includes a universal mission to all the peoples of the world. Nolland is representative as he states, "Matthew uses ἔθνη alone when referring to the Gentiles, but when he speaks of 'all the ἔθνη', he no longer uses ἔθνη to distinguish Gentiles from Jews but rather refers to the whole of humanity."[63] The rest of the New Testament clearly has in view the evangelism of Jews as a part of missionary strategies (e.g., Acts 2:22; 13:38–39; Rom 1:16; Eph 2:11–16). For Matthew, Jesus's universal

58. E.g., Kenneth W. Clark, "The Gentile Bias in Matthew," *JBL* 66 (1947): 165–72; Hare, *Theme of Jewish Persecution of Christians*, 326–27; Kio, "Understanding and Translating 'Nations,'" 230–39.

59. Clark, "Gentile Bias in Matthew," 166.

60. See the discussion at 12.4.8 above and Chapter 15 below.

61. Terence L. Donaldson, "'Nations,' 'Non-Jewish Nations,' or 'Non-Jewish Individuals,'" in Runesson and Gurtner, *Matthew Within Judaism*, 188–94.

62. E.g., see Davies and Allison, *Matthew*, 3:684; Keener, *Matthew* (2009), 719–20; Morris, *Matthew*, 746; Turner, "His Glorious Throne," 157–58.

63. Nolland, *Matthew*, 1266.

lordship entails a universal mission, including Israel with the other nations, and an eventual universal judgment.[64]

Although ethnic Israel is not at present functionally the steward and witness of the outworking of the kingdom of God (21:43), individual Jews are still invited to participate in the salvation brought by Jesus with the arrival of the kingdom of heaven, which makes them disciples of Jesus, and are included in the church. Together Jewish believers in Jesus and gentile believers in Jesus are disciples of Jesus, who now comprise the *ekklēsia* of Jesus that together are engaged in making disciples of the *ethnē* of the world.

### 13.2.8 Summary of Matthew's Perspective on a Future for Ethnic Israel

Our survey has noted that Matthew has recorded quite positive responses to Jesus within Israel: individuals like the prophet John the Baptist, the twelve diverse disciples, tax collectors and "sinners," women and religious leaders like Joseph of Arimathea. Indeed, Jews and gentiles are included in the worldwide mission (28:18–20).

Our survey has also demonstrated quite negative responses to Jesus's offer of the kingdom of heaven, which resulted in significant grim consequences for Israel. I concluded that the stewardship of God's kingdom in this age has been taken away from Israel.

Although Israel is not at present functionally the steward and witness of the outworking of the kingdom of God (21:43), individual Jews are invited to participate in the salvation brought by Jesus with the arrival of the kingdom and become included in discipleship to Jesus that includes Jews and gentiles, men and women, commoner and elite (28:18–20). Matthew's recounting of grim consequences for Israel's rejection of Jesus does not preclude his clear vision of a future for ethnic Israel.

We now turn our attention to various attempts at interpreting the grim consequences of Israel's rejection of Jesus Messiah alongside evidence of a future for ethnic, national Israel.

## 13.3 Interpreting the Grim Consequences Alongside Evidence of a Future for Ethnic, National Israel

In this final section of this chapter, we explore briefly a sampling of the myriad viewpoints that attempt to understand and interpret the grim consequences of national Israel's negative responses to Jesus and his earthly ministry, yet their is evidence of a

64. Turner, "His Glorious Throne," 158. See also Konradt, *Israel, Church, and the Gentiles*, esp. 311–17; Donaldson, *Gentile Christian Identity*, 310–311.

future for ethnic Israel. Since this is a theology of Matthew's Gospel, we focus on the evidence in Matthew, with only tangential reference to the rest of the New Testament. This will naturally cause our conclusions to be tentative.

Our discussion occurs at a time when the relationship of Matthew's Gospel within Judaism of the first century is a pressing and widespread topic within the scholarly world[65] and beyond. The relationship of Israel and the church has been a controversial and painful topic through much of church history. Especially in recent considerations, that relationship has been bitterly disputed, in large part due to the events we briefly discussed earlier: the Shoah/Holocaust, the existence of various forms of supersessionism/replacement theology, and the birth and continuing existence of the modern geopolitical nation of Israel.

Within evangelicalism the discussion has been carried on hopefully with less animus than has been found elsewhere, such as in some secular settings. Also, hopefully in evangelical circles the discussion has been maintained with Spirit-guided scholarship and humility. Examples can be found in some of the various "views" books recently published,[66] and by some scholars in the messianic Jewish movement.[67]

We now turn to various views raised by current scholarship regarding Matthew's perspective of Israel. We will see that there is a significant range in understanding the role of ethnic, national Israel in God's program of history.

### 13.3.1 Some Contend That the Grim Consequences Indicate That Ethnic Israel Is Permanently Rejected

The negative statements about Israel in Matthew's Gospel have been interpreted by some to indicate that for Matthew and Matthew's Jesus, Israel has been rejected by God in his salvation-historical program. It has been argued that Israel has been rejected as God's people, and a new entity/nation has replaced Israel as the people of God. With the introductory and concluding emphases upon the nations, a range of scholars contend that Matthew intends his readers to see that the promises to Israel are now fulfilled through Jesus's mission and that the disciples of Jesus or the church have replaced Israel in God's economy. Peter Stuhlmacher comments, "A future hope of

65. E.g., see the recent volume by Runesson and Gurtner, *Matthew Within Judaism*.

66. E.g., Chad O. Brand, *Perspectives on Israel and the Church* (Nashville: B&H, 2015); Louis Goldberg, ed., *How Jewish Is Christianity? 2 Views on the Messianic Movement* (Grand Rapids: Zondervan, 2003); Jared Compton and Andrew David Naselli, eds., *Three Views on Israel and the Church: Perspectives on Romans 9–11* (Grand Rapids: Kregel, 2018).

67. A current voice in addressing the various forms of messianic Jewish theology has been sounded by Richard Harvey, himself a messianic Jew, whose doctoral work in religious studies at the University of Wales (Lampeter), led to his dissertation, "Mapping Messianic Jewish Theology: A Constructive Approach," which was supervised by Rabbi Professor Dan Cohn-Sherbok. His dissertation was published for a broader audience in which he maps the diverse theological terrain of the young messianic Jewish movement. See Richard S. Harvey, *Mapping Messianic Jewish Theology*, Studies in Messianic Jewish Theology (Carlisle, UK: Paternoster, 2009). For a recent summary of the book, see Richard S. Harvey, "Messianic Jewish Theology: A Preliminary Typology," *Norsk Tidsskrift for Misjonsvitenskap* (*Norwegian Journal of Missiology*) 73.3–4 (2019): 69–83.

salvation for all Israel in the sense of Romans 11:25–27 cannot be found in the Gospel of Matthew. According to the evangelist's presentation, Israel has forfeited its privilege of election by rejecting and killing Jesus."[68] This is often referred to as "supersessionism" or "replacement" of Israel, as we noted before.

#### *13.3.1.1 Ancient Supersessionists*

What appears to be an early example of supersessionism emerges in the Epistle of Barnabas, probably written between the destruction of the Second Temple (70 BC) and the second Jewish revolt against the Romans (AD 135), possibly around AD 130.[69] In this anonymous treatise, the author firmly asserts that the Jewish religion is and always has been in error and that Jews have misinterpreted their own Scriptures, and therefore Christianity has replaced their practices.[70] The author states of Jewish temple practices: "And so he nullified these things that the new law of our Lord Jesus Christ, which is without the yoke of compulsion, should provide an offering not made by humans" (Barn. 2:6 [Ehrman, LCL]).

Justin Martyr wrote the *Dialogue with Trypho the Jew* somewhere perhaps between AD 155 and 160, in which he tries to prove the truth of Christianity to a learned Jew named Trypho. Justin attempts to demonstrate that the new covenant has superseded the old covenant of God with the Jewish people and that the gentiles have been chosen to replace Israel as God's chosen people.[71] Justin draws upon the Old Testament figure Abraham and states,

> For as he believed the voice of God, and it was imputed to him for righteousness, in like manner we [Christians] having believed God's voice spoken by the apostles of Christ, and promulgated to us by the prophets, have renounced even to death all the things of the world. Accordingly, He promises to him a nation of similar faith, God-fearing, righteous, and delighting the Father; but it is not you [Jews], "in whom is no faith." (Justin Martyr, *Dial.*, 119)

Justin is perhaps the earliest figure in Christian history to deny Jews the status of children of Abraham, instead reserving it for Christians alone.[72] But the worst accusation of all was the charge that the Jews killed Christ, and therefore God. The well-known Antiochian preacher John Chrysostom (ca. AD 347–407) contends:

68. Stuhlmacher, *Biblical Theology*, 612.

69. Bart D. Ehrman, ed. and trans., *The Apostolic Fathers*, LCL 25 (Cambridge, MA: Harvard University Press, 2003), 2:6–8.

70. Ehrman, *Apostolic Fathers*, 2:8–9.

71. *Encyclopedia Britannica*, "St. Justin Martyr," revised by Melissa Petruzzello, accessed November 1, 2017, https://www.britannica.com/biography/Saint-Justin-Martyr.

72. Cf. Jeffrey S. Siker, *Disinheriting the Jews: Abraham in Early Christian Controversy* (Louisville: Westminster/John Knox, 1991), 14.

> Tell me this. If a man were to have slain your son, would you endure to look upon him, or accept his greeting? Would you not shun him as a wicked demon, as the devil himself? They slew the Son of your Lord; do you have the boldness to enter with them under the same roof? . . . For I am persuaded to call the fasting of the Jews a table of demons because they slew God. If the Jews are acting against God, must they not be serving the demons?[73]

Christoph Markschies comments that John Chrysostom was not particularly original with his vicious attacks. Historians have documented that these terrible allegations were already found long before Chrysostom in the Christian literature of antiquity.[74]

### *13.3.1.2 Modern Matthean Supersessionists*

Such supersessionist sentiments are likewise found among modern Matthean scholars. Commenting on the parable of the vineyard (21:33–45) and Jesus's stark statement in Matt 21:43, "Therefore I tell you that the kingdom of God will be taken away from you and given to a people who will produce its fruit," R. V. G. Tasker, a British evangelical New Testament scholar, states that because of the rejection of Jesus the Messiah, which came as the climax of a long series of rejections of the prophets God had sent to it (21:35–36), Jesus points to the old Israel, which forfeits the right to receive the blessings relating to the kingdom of God. "These blessings would in consequence be made available to a less exclusive people of God which would contain men of all races and nations (43); and the murderers of God's Son would themselves be destroyed (41)."[75]

American evangelical New Testament scholar Robert Mounce similarly comments: "By rejecting the message of the prophets and finally by rejecting the Son, Israel has demonstrated that they are incapable of producing the kind of conduct and life that is appropriate in God's Kingdom. The Kingdom is taken from Israel and given to the Gentiles."[76] American Roman Catholic New Testament scholar John Meier declares, "The Kingdom was once given to Israel. But, because Israel has rejected the Son of God, the Kingdom has been taken from her and given to the new people of God, non-Israel, the church."[77] Luz finds the roots of Christian anti-Judaism here in Matthew's text as the "disinheriting of Israel."[78]

Matthew's Gospel has long been interpreted as promoting the view that the Church

73. John Chrysostom, *Adv. Jud.* 1.7.5 (Harkins, FOTC).

74. Christoph Markschies, "From 'Wide and Narrow Way' to 'The Ways that Never Parted'? Road Metaphors in Models of Jewish-Christian Relations in Antiquity," in Schröter, Edsall, and Verheyden, *Jews and Christians*, 11–32; here 21–22.

75. Tasker, *Matthew*, 204.

76. Robert H. Mounce, *Matthew*, GNC (San Francisco: Harper & Row, 1985), 205.

77. John P. Meier, *The Vision of Matthew: Christ, Church, and Morality in the First Gospel*, Theological Inquiries (New York: Paulist, 1978), 17.

78. Luz, *Matthew 21–28*, 44.

has superseded Israel as God's people, taking the place of ethnic Israel in the future plan of God. Some interpret the Gospel of John similarly.[79] This has led to the theological notion of "supersessionism." Supersessionism refers to the idea that the church has superseded or replaced ethnic Israel of the Old Testament as the new people of God because Israel as a nation and its leaders have rejected Jesus as their Messiah.[80] Luz contends that Matthew is one of the fathers of supersessionism, "which became dominant and according to which the church has taken Israel's place as the chosen people."[81] The implications of this view, as Luz notes, are staggering, because it has been used to denigrate the people of Israel for centuries. Peter Ochs describes it this way: "Here *supersessionism*—or *replacement theology*—refers to a Christian belief that with the incarnation of God in Jesus Christ, Israel's covenant with God was superseded and replaced by God's presence in the church as the body of Christ."[82] The church (the people of "the new covenant") has replaced Israel (the people of "the old covenant") as the people of God.[83]

### *13.3.1.3 Expressions of Supersessionism*

Richard Soulen provides an overview in which he classically articulates three distinct expressions of supersessionism.[84] (1) "Economic supersessionism" describes those who emphasize that it was God's plan for Israel's role as the people of God to expire with the coming of Christ and to be replaced by the church: "Everything that characterized the economy of salvation in its Israelite form becomes obsolete and is replaced by its ecclesial equivalent."[85] In this expression, Israel's role in the economy of redemption is to prepare for salvation in its spiritual and universal form. (2) "Punitive supersessionism" suggests that God abrogates his covenant with Israel because of their rejection of Jesus Christ and the gospel: God is punishing Israel for their rejection of Christ.[86] "Because the Jews obstinately reject God's action in Christ, God in turn angrily rejects and punishes the Jews."[87] (3) "Structural supersessionism" suggests that the Old Testament Scriptures are largely indecisive in the formulation of the canonical narrative of salvation history and God's work as Consummator and Redeemer.[88] "So construed, Israel's

79. For overviews of the issues in John's Gospel, see Reimund Bieringer, Didier Pollefeyt, and Frederique Vandecasteele-Vanneuville, eds., *Anti-Judaism and the Fourth Gospel* (Louisville: Westminster John Knox, 2001); Ruth Sheridan, "Issues in the Translation of οἱ Ἰουδαῖοι in the Fourth Gospel," *JBL* 132.3 (2013): 671–695.

80. For definitions and discussion, see Donaldson, *Jews and Anti-Judaism*, 20–25. For discussion of supersessionism and messianic Judaism, see Philip du Toit, "Does the New Testament Support Messianic Judaism?," *Conspectus* 22 (2016): 81–123.

81. Luz, *Matthew 21–28*, 44.

82. Peter Ochs, *Another Reformation: Postliberal Christianity and the Jews* (Grand Rapids: Baker Academic, 2011), 1.

83. For historical overviews, see Ronald E. Diprose, *Israel and the Church: The Origin and Effects of Replacement Theology* (Bucks, UK: Authentic Media, 2004), esp. 175–92.

84. Richard Kendall Soulen, *The God of Israel and Christian Theology* (Minneapolis: Fortress, 1996), 28–33.

85. Soulen, *God of Israel*, 29.

86. Soulen, *God of Israel*, 30–33.

87. Soulen, *God of Israel*, 30.

88. Soulen, *God of Israel*, 31–33.

story contributes little or nothing to understanding how God's consummating and redemptive purposes engage human creation in universal and enduring ways."[89]

There are, therefore, variations among supersessionists, as Soulen emphasizes and as we will see below. What may be described as "strong supersessionism" holds that national Israel has no future in the plan of God. What may be described as "moderate supersessionism" sees a divine plan for the future salvation of the Jews but not their national restoration. This latter view holds that Israel is the object of God's irrevocable gift of calling and grace but that guarantees them no national role; it promises them only their becoming part of the church as the people of God.

A modern expression of moderate supersessionism is articulated in the widely respected work of Millard Erickson, who states that there is a future for national Israel. They are still the special people of God. Their future is bright, as Paul indicates: "And in this way all Israel will be saved" (Rom 11:26). But Erickson goes on to note that Israel will be saved by entering the church, just as do the gentiles. He emphasizes that there is no statement anywhere in the New Testament that there is any other basis of salvation. He sums up his view by stating that the church is the new Israel: the church occupies the place in the new covenant that Israel occupied in the old. "Whereas in the Old Testament the kingdom of God was peopled by national Israel, in the New Testament it is peopled by the church. There is a special future coming for national Israel, however, through large-scale conversion to Christ and entry into the church."[90]

### 13.3.2 Some Contend That Israel Is in a Dual Covenant with New Covenant Disciples of Jesus

On the other extreme from those who hold to some form of supersessionism are those who contend that the positive response to Jesus by many in Israel, and the evidence in Matthew's Gospel of a future for Israel, indicate that Israel is in a "Dual Covenant" with new covenant disciples of Jesus. It is argued that Israel continues as God's chosen people, but side by side with the church in this age as a different people of God.

#### *13.3.2.1 Jewish Dual-Covenant Scholars*

"Dual-covenant theology" or "two-covenant theology" has taken a variety of forms, but its most general sense is widely held as a reaction against supersessionism/replacement and a rejection of anti-Judaism and the horrors of the Holocaust. Current advocates point to the Jewish philosopher Franz Rosenzweig early in the twentieth

89. Soulen, *God of Israel*, 32.

90. Erickson, *Christian Theology*, 965–66. A similar perspective may be found in the very positive work of Benjamin L. Gladd, *From Adam and Israel to the Church: A Biblical Theology of the People of God*, ESBT (Downers Grove, IL: InterVarsity, 2019). In Gladd's view, national Israel has no future in God's plan, but individuals within Israel who repent and turn to Christ enter the church and join the people of God (Gladd, *From Adam and Israel*, esp. 58–74).

century as a formative representative of this position. He is regarded among some experts as "one of the most original Jewish thinkers of the modern period."[91] And in what some scholars regard is "arguably the greatest work of modern Jewish philosophy: *The Star of Redemption*,"[92] Rosenzweig claims that the Jewish people did not need the gospel of Jesus Christ to experience salvation because God's covenant with Abraham, renewed at Sinai and mediated by Moses, assured them of salvation, and the Mishnah states explicitly that every member of "Israel" has a portion in the world to come (m. Sanhedrin 10:1).[93] Rosenzweig alludes to Jesus's parable of the prodigal son where the father says to the eldest son after the youngest son returned, "My son, . . . you are always with me, and everything I have is yours" (Luke 15:31). Rosenzweig states,

> We are wholly agreed as to what Christ and his church mean to the world: no one can reach the Father save through him. No one can reach the Father! But the situation is quite different for one who does not have to reach the Father because he is already with him. And this is true of the people of Israel.[94]

Rosenzweig emphasizes that a Jew is born into the faith community that was instituted between God and Israel on Sinai—it is a natural phenomenon. By way of contrast, pagans have to undergo a rebirth in coming to faith in Jesus. A Christian is made, not born.[95] As for the Jew, "the individual is born a Jew."[96]

Following the early lead of Rosenzweig was Eugene Borowitz. Borowitz is considered by many as the most original and influential Reform Jewish thinker in recent years. Borowitz began to develop an understanding of the commanding nature of covenant and to introduce and explore the idea of dual-covenant theology in his most comprehensive work on theology, *Renewing the Covenant* (1991). Jewish author Abel Bibliowicz follows the lead of Borowitz and expresses dual-covenant theology unambiguously as displacing supersessionism: "Supersession theology no longer needs to be an insurmountable theological anchor. Only the embrace of multiple, separate, and equally valid tracks to the Divine will diffuse the ever-present danger of supersession theology. All else is derivative."[97]

Jewish scholar Phillip Sigal also developed his own theory of dual-covenant theology,

91. See *The Stanford Encyclopedia of Philosophy*, "Franz Rosenzweig," by Benjamin Pollock, updated Spring 2019, ed. Edward N. Zalta, https://plato.stanford.edu/archives/spr2019/entries/rosenzweig/.

92. Pollock, "Franz Rosenzweig."

93. Nahum Glatzer, *Franz Rosenzweig: His Life and Thought* (Indianapolis: Hackett, 1998), ix–xxxviii.

94. Rosenzweig in a letter to Rudolph Ehrenberg, quoted in Glatzer, *Franz Rosenzweig*, 341.

95. For a helpful historical overview, see Kai Kjær-Hansen, "One Way for Jews and Gentiles in the New Millennium," in *To the Jew First: The Case for Jewish Evangelism in Scripture and History*, ed. Darrell L. Bock and Mitch Glaser (Grand Rapids: Kregel, 2008), 298.

96. Glatzer, *Franz Rosenzweig*, 27–28.

97. Abel Mordechi Bibliowicz, *Jews and Gentiles in the Early Jesus Movement: An Unintended Journey* (New York: Palgrave Macmillan, 2013), 113.

namely, that "God intended there be two tributaries of the covenant with Abraham: the Judaic, expressed in rabbinic Judaism; and the Christian."[98] He emphasizes that "salvation as understood by John and Jesus was the salvation offered by Judaism: the world to come, the time of God's sovereignty or *malkhut shamayim* [*kingdom of heaven*]. For this salvation, repentance was a prerequisite. God's grace would be extended only to the penitent."[99] He indicates that the positive perspective toward Israel in Matthew's Gospel leads to seeing the continuation of Israel and the church side by side as a different people of God who participate in dual covenants with God. Sigal states, "Judaism sees its roots in the covenant with Abraham renewed at Sinai, mediated by Moses, and Christianity sees its roots in these covenants renewed in the eucharist, mediated by Jesus."[100] He further explains that to understand covenant theology from the perspective of dual-covenant theology "is to entertain the plausibility of a purposeful action on the part of God of having graced his people with parallel tracks on which to attain salvation."[101]

### *13.3.2.2 Christian Dual-Covenant Scholars*

Dual-covenant theology soon found its way into left-leaning Christian circles as well.[102] One example is the Christian Scholars Group on Christian-Jewish Relations.[103] Their interpretation suggests that in addition to the new covenant, ethnic Israel continues in relationship to God in a second, parallel covenant and embraces a separate and equally valid track to God and salvation. Their formal statement on Christian-Jewish relations contains the following affirmation on salvation:

> **6. Affirming God's enduring covenant with the Jewish people has consequences for Christian understandings of salvation.** Christians meet God's saving power in the person of Jesus Christ and believe that this power is available to all people in him. Christians have therefore taught for centuries that salvation is available only through Jesus Christ. With their recent realization that God's covenant with the Jewish people is eternal, Christians can now recognize in the Jewish tradition the redemptive power of God at work. If Jews, who do not share our faith in Christ, are in a saving covenant with God, then Christians need new ways of understanding the universal significance of Christ.[104]

98. Phillip Sigal, *The Halakhah of Jesus of Nazareth According to the Gospel of Matthew*, SBL 18 (Atlanta: Society of Biblical Literature, 2007), x.

99. Phillip Sigal, "Aspects of Dual Covenant Theology: Salvation," *HBT* 5.2 (1983): 1–48; here 11.

100. Sigal, "Aspects of Dual Covenant Theology," 1.

101. Sigal, "Aspects of Dual Covenant Theology," 1.

102. See John T. Pawlikowski, *Christ in the Light of the Christian-Jewish Dialogue*, Studies in Judaism and Christianity (1982; repr., Eugene, OR: Wipf & Stock, 2001), esp. 8–35.

103. See https://www.bc.edu/content/dam/files/research_sites/cjl/sites/partners/csg/history.htm.

104. Mary C. Boys, ed., *Seeing Judaism Anew: Christianity's Sacred Obligation* (Lanham, MD: Rowman & Littlefield, 2005), loc. 76, Kindle. See also the influential Rosemary Radford Ruether, *Faith and Fratricide: The Theological Roots of Anti-Semitism* (New York: Seabury, 1974), esp. 226–61.

One of the original members of the organization was Roman Catholic scholar John Pawlikowski, who states that Christology, as developed in the latter strata of New Testament materials, especially in Pauline literature and in the Gospel of John, constitutes in the end the fundamental uniqueness of the revelation through Jesus. "This revelation does not invalidate the earlier revelation given to the people Israel at Sinai; nor does it in any way signify a displacement of Jews by Christians in the covenantal relationship. Rather, it involves the creation of a second, parallel covenant which retains deep roots in the past."[105]

Dual-covenant theology has circulated for some years among non-evangelicals and even among some conservative Christians. If you have ever been told that Jews do not need Jesus because they "already have a covenant with God," then you are hearing this theory of salvation. This is becoming an ascendant view among a wide group of scholars who are trying to acknowledge a place for Israel's uniqueness.

#### *13.3.2.3 Evangelical Rejection of Dual-Covenant Theology*

But dual-covenant theology has the inherent danger of abandoning the uniqueness of Jesus's saving work for both Jew and gentile. This is a highly problematic feature, which is a challenge to the uniqueness of Jesus Messiah's person and work.[106] Christology is the central issue in this discussion, although at times it appears to be marginalized by some who wish to be more inclusive than is warranted.[107]

The New Testament is clear that the new covenant is universal and leaves no room for a people related to God by other covenantal means. Craig Blaising states, "The church in the New Testament sees itself proclaiming new covenant blessings that flow from the covenant made with Abraham (Gal. 3:6–14). The New Testament sees both Jew and Gentile in Messiah, united in this new covenant blessing (Gal. 3:26–29)."[108]

105. John T. Pawlikowski, "Christology in Light of the Jewish-Christian Dialogue: The Revolution in Christian–Jewish Understanding," *Proceedings of the Catholic Theological Society of America* 49 (1994): 120–34, https://ejournals.bc.edu/index.php/ctsa/article/view/3891/3456. See also Pawlikowski, *Christian-Jewish Dialogue*, 8–35. With similar sympathies, see Saldarini, "Reading Matthew Without Anti-Semitism," 166–84.

106. For helpful, brief overviews and critique, see the entire issue of *Mishkan* 11, edited by Ole Chr. Kvarme: "Two Covenant Theology," *Mishkan* 11 (1989), with helpful articles by Maurice G. Bowler, Louis Goldberg, David W. Torrance, Arnulf H. Baumann, Mitch Glaser, and Tormod Engelsviken. More recently, see David Mishkin, *Jewish Scholarship on the Resurrection of Jesus* (Eugene, OR: Pickwick, 2017), 103–17; Craig A. Blaising, "The Future of Israel as a Theological Question," in *To the Jew First: The Case for Jewish Evangelism in Scripture and History*, ed. Darrell L. Bock and Mitch Glaser (Grand Rapids: Kregel, 2008), 102–21; Craig A. Blaising, "A Theology of Israel and the Church," in *Israel the Church and the Middle East: A Biblical Response to the Current Conflict*, ed. Darrell Bock and Mitch Glaser (Grand Rapids: Kregel, 2018), 85–100.

107. Boris Repschinski has at times self-identified with those who see the Matthean groups as one among many others within Judaism, but he rightly recognizes that such attempts often seem to downplay the importance of the Christology of the gospel; see Boris Repschinski, "Shift the Issue and Win the Fight? Rhetorical Strategies of Dealing with Conflicts in the Gospels of Matthew and John," *ZKT* 139.4 (2017): 387–410; here esp. 388n.2.

108. Blaising, "Future of Israel as a Theological Question," in *To the Jew First*, 109. The Manila Manifesto of the Second Lausanne Congress on World Evangelism, 1989, gave a clear evangelical rejection of dual-covenant theology. It reads in part as follows: "It is sometimes held that in virtue of God's covenant with Abraham, Jewish people do not need to acknowledge Jesus as their Messiah. We affirm that they need him as much as anyone else, that it would be a form of anti-Semitism, as well as being

### 13.3.3 Avoiding the Extremes of Supersessionism and Dual-Covenant Theology

Many scholars have reassessed the Matthean understanding of God's role for Israel, and the supersessionist perspective of God's role for Israel in history is being reevaluated by many today. Has God really abrogated his covenant with Israel and replaced her with the church? Many think not.[109] But at the same time, does this mean that we are we to understand that God has developed dual covenants with humans, one for Israel and one for the rest of humanity? Many think not.[110] So this leaves me, and many others, attempting to find a mediating position in which we disavow supersessionism yet at the same time decline dual-covenant theology.[111]

Matthew's Gospel has challenged me as a scholar to come to a mediating position that avoids the extremes of supersessionism and dual-covenant theology. But I also am challenged to understand the bases of each of these extremes.

I understand the harsh and grim consequences enumerated above that we see in Matthew's Gospel that Jesus addressed to national Israel for not repenting and responding to his call to enter the kingdom of heaven. Those cannot be ignored. And I understand the significant place that the disciples play in the church that Jesus is building to advance the kingdom of God. The consequences of having the kingdom taken away from "you" (*hymōn*)—Israel—and given "to a people" (*ethnei*) who produce the fruit of the kingdom (21:43)—true disciples of Jesus who comprise the church—likewise cannot be ignored. Supersessionism bases itself at least in part on Israel's rejection of the unique person and work of Jesus Messiah and the openness of discipleship to all the nations.

At the same time that I work to understand these harsh and grim consequences for Israel, I also work to understand the deep compassion and passion that Jesus Messiah

disloyal to Christ, to depart from the New Testament pattern of taking the gospel to 'the Jew first. . . . ' We therefore reject the thesis that Jews have their own covenant which renders faith in Jesus unnecessary" (https://lausanne.org/content/manila-1989-documents).

109. Among those attempting to move beyond supersessionism is the group "The Society for Post-Supersessionist Theology" (https://www.spostst.org/); the group *Yachad BeYeshua* (Together in Jesus) (https://www.yachad-beyeshua.org/); the Roman Catholic Church's Second Vatican Council (Vatican II) (1962–1965), where Pope Paul VI promulgated the Conciliar Declaration *Nostra Aetate*.

110. I have noted above those evangelicals who reject dual-covenant theology. Blomberg argues that the dual-covenant or two-covenant perspective has hovered around the fringes of messianic Jewish congregations for years, but today it is common enough that it is dividing the Jewish-Christian movement down the middle. He critiques Mark Kinzer in that light, suggesting that "although Kinzer never refers to his view as a form of the two-covenant theory it is precisely that—very sophisticated, intricate and subtle, and it deserves serious engagement by the world of NT scholarship." Craig L. Blomberg, "Freedom from the Law Only for Gentiles? A Non-Supersessionist Alternative to Mark Kinzer's 'Postmissionary Messianic Judaism,'" in *New Testament Theology in Light of the Church's Mission: Essays in Honor of I. Howard Marshall*, ed. Jon C. Laansma, Grant R. Osborne, and Ray F. Van Neste (Eugene, OR: Cascade, 2011), 41–56, here 42.

111. Terence Donaldson has written a helpful article that deals with the issue of supersessionism and the need for a more nuanced typology when considering Christ-groups in the first and second centuries. See Terence L. Donaldson, "Supersessionism and Early Christian Self-Definition," *JJMJS* 3 (2016): 1–32. See also Broadhead, *Jewish Ways of Following Jesus*.

has for his people Israel. Matthew plainly records that Jesus entered history as the divine-human Messiah who is Immanuel ("God with us"), who came to save his "people" (*laos*) from their sins (1:21–23). He went first to the lost sheep of the house of Israel with the message of the arrival of the kingdom of heaven (10:6–7; 15:24). And even when the people and the leaders of Israel rejected him, Matthew records the hope of a future for Israel (10:23; 19:28; 23:37–39; 24:14–16; 28:19–20). Israel remains an object of God's love as his people with whom he had made an eternal covenant. Dual-covenant theology bases itself at least in part on God's love for Israel and clinging to the eternal covenant with Abraham as mediated by Moses.

As Jesus Messiah shared his final Passover meal with his disciples, he initiated the new covenant with his body and blood for the forgiveness of sins (26:19–29) that brought to fulfillment all of the hopes that the original Passover represented. And thus, Jesus Messiah initiated the basis for his Great Commission to make disciples of all the nations, Israel and gentiles alike. Thus, there is only one covenant for salvation.

I believe that this calls for a mediating position that acknowledges the bases of the extremes but seeks a way of avoiding each extreme's excesses. Supersessionism as an extreme abrogates God's covenant with Israel. Dual-covenant theology as an extreme rejects the uniqueness of Jesus's person as the divine-human Messiah and his exclusive atoning sacrifice for all of humanity, Israel included.

### 13.3.4 Stewards of the Kingdom of Heaven in God's Timing

I thus emphasize "fulfillment" rather than "replacement."[112] "Fulfill" indicates the way in which the value of the law and the temple continues but is brought to its intended full meaning in Jesus. Each of these still hold a valuable place in salvation history and God's dealings with humanity. Torah is fulfilled in Jesus but not done away with (5:17–20). Torah still has value as God's Word but now needs to be understood in the light of Jesus's fulfillment of it. We are to be "Torah readers in Jesus Messiah" to understand salvation history.

A mediating position that I broached above, which I believe acknowledges the bases of these positions but avoids these extremes, recognizes that Israel and the church are seen in Matthew's Gospel as stewards or instruments used by God in bearing witness to the kingdom of heaven but at differing times in salvation history. Matthew points to a spiritual oneness of gentile and Jew in Christ that is permanent. However, Matthew

112. "Fulfillment" is likewise the emphasis of Piotrowski, *Matthew's New David*, 244n45: "And this joining to Israel of Gentile converts is the church, Jesus' people. Hence no 'replacement' is in effect, but an inclusion into the old as 'fulfillment'." But Piotrowski also seems to exclude ethnic Israel from a present or future role in God's program of history: "As the narrative progresses, especially on the scaffolding of the prologue-quotations, Matthew brings these two groups—'Israel' and Jesus-followers—into confluence. Thus, to Matthew, those who have responded to Jesus' call—now made through the Jewish disciples to all the nations (28:16–20)—can claim this coveted theological title, 'Israel'" (Piotrowski, *Matthew's New David*, 239–40).

points to functional distinctions for the nation of Israel and the church in the plan and purpose of God. We have seen in Matthew's narrative and record of Jesus's teachings that Israel and the church will be used at differing times as the stewards or instruments God will use to proclaim and further the impact of the kingdom of heaven on earth.

This is what I refer to as the "stewards of God's kingdom in God's timing." I have selected the term "steward" (*oikonomos*) because in biblical usage it has a literal/basic sense of one put in charge of a household or estate that belongs to another (e.g., Luke 12:42; Gal 4:2) and, by extension, a figurative sense of one entrusted by God with spiritual authority and administration of what belongs to God (e.g., 1 Cor 4:1; Titus 1:7; 1 Pet 4:10).[113] While the precise phrase "stewards of the kingdom of God" does not occur in Scripture, I believe that the phrase has a biblical base and it helpfully expresses the relationship of certain human groups to the activities of God. Paul states of himself and other leaders, "This is how one should regard us, as servants of Christ and stewards [*oikonomous*] of the mysteries of God" (1 Cor 4:1, ESV), and Peter says to the churches of Asia Minor, "Each of you should use whatever gift you have received to serve others, as faithful stewards [*oikonomoi*] of God's grace in its various forms" (1 Pet 4:10).

It is here that we see the relationship of Israel, the disciples of Jesus, and the church. In the Old Testament, Abraham and his descendants and David and his descendants are a blessing to the world as the nation of Israel as stewards of the kingdom of God. In the New Testament, Jesus's disciples are gathered first to give the message of the gospel of the kingdom of God to Israel, and then become the church that is commissioned to go make disciples of Jesus from all the nations as stewards of the kingdom of God. The steward does not own the kingdom of God but is one who cares for what belongs to God. Israel, Jesus's disciples, and the church act for God as the stewards of God's kingdom in God's timing.

As the recipients of his messianic salvation, Jesus's disciples become his new nation of witnesses to the reality of the kingdom, producing the fruit of the kingdom, enabling them to be the stewards of the kingdom of God (Matt 21:43).

As those who have acknowledged Jesus's person and work in bringing the kingdom of heaven to earth, Jesus's disciples are now the stewards of the kingdom of heaven. Israel is still God's chosen "ethnic" people that will be used again in the future. This is what Paul anticipated when he declared that "all Israel will be saved" (Rom 11:26). In the context of Rom 9–11 and the clear allusions to Jer 31:33–34, the identity of "all Israel" is clear. This is the nation of Israel, the physical descendants of Abraham who will at some distant time again function as stewards of the kingdom of God. Daniel Block clarifies his perspective of what it means that "all Israel will be saved." He notes that like the prophets, Paul anticipated this as a climactic occurrence in the distant

113. "οἰκονόμος," BDAG, 698.

future, at the end of the ages, when the fullness of the gentiles has been realized. They all looked ahead to the time when "all Israel will be saved." He states that it is not clear whether this involves a millennial reality, as some dispensationalists propose, or is a part of the picture of the new heavens and the new earth.

> However, whatever the role of Israel will be when God's redemptive plan has been fully accomplished and instituted, for Paul—and for Moses and Jeremiah and Ezekiel before him—a future without a people identifiable as the physical descendants of Abraham was inconceivable.[114]

Such is the hope that lies at the basis of Matthew's expectation of a future for Israel. But at the present time Jesus's disciples are the stewards of God's kingdom in God's timing, made up of ethnic Jews and ethnic gentiles who are disciples of Jesus, the church.

## 13.4 CONCLUSION

We noted in beginning this chapter that Matthew's Gospel has long been noted for having complex perspectives of the nation of Israel—e.g., particularistic and universal, positive and negative. Throughout the Old Testament the concept of God's kingdom includes the universal reign of God over the universe (Ps 103:19; 1 Chr 29:11–12) and the coming kingdom when God's glory would be manifest on the earth (Isa 24:23). The prophets continue that theme and emphasize that while God is King, both of Israel[115] and of all the earth,[116] he shall become King and shall rule in a tangible way over his people.[117] This leads many to the conclusion that "while God is the King, he must also become King, i.e., he must manifest his kingship in the world of human beings and nations."[118] Therefore, God's kingdom includes both his activity of his reign and the realm of his reign.

The people of Israel were God's chosen children through whom he covenanted to establish his kingdom on the earth. They were not to be the sole heirs of the kingdom but rather were to be the center of God's witness of his reality. This has been described as God's centripetal mission to the world, as the people would come to Israel to hear and witness God's revelation of his purposes for humanity.[119] The final eschatological hope revealed in the prophets is still centripetal, where God's purposes for all humanity are realized as they come to Jerusalem. This is classically pictured by Isaiah.

114. Block, *Covenant*, 515.
115. E.g., Exod 15:18; Num 23:21; Deut 33:5; Isa 43:15.
116. E.g., 2 Kgs 19:15; Isa 6:5; Jer 46:18; Pss 29:10; 99:1–4.
117. E.g., Isa 24:23; 33:22; 52:7; Zeph 3:15; Zech 14:9–21.
118. Ladd, *Theology of the New Testament*, 58.
119. Cf. Köstenberger, with Alexander, *Salvation to the Ends of the Earth*, 129–30.

> In the last days the mountain of the LORD's temple will be established as highest among the mountains; it will be exalted above the hills, and all nations will stream to it. Many peoples will come and say, "Come, let us go up to the mountain of the LORD, to the house of the God of Jacob. He will teach us his ways, so that we may walk in his paths."
>
> The law will go out from Zion, the word of the LORD from Jerusalem. (Isa 2:2–3)

Jesus came to Israel with the announcement that the kingdom of heaven had arrived. Israel continued as God's chosen recipients of the kingdom mission and witness. To and through Israel Jesus ministered throughout his earthly life, calling Israel to repent and receive his kingdom offer so that the centripetal concept would continue as gentiles stream to Zion to worship on the holy mountain.

But the final events of Jesus Messiah's earthly ministry bring to a critical juncture his relationship to Israel and the role that they would play during this age. The events also clarify further the relationship and role for the disciples that Jesus has been gathering around him. Throughout Matthew's narrative we have seen an uneasy tension between Jesus's compassion for the people of Israel (e.g., Matt 9:35–38) yet the continual opposition to him by Israel's leadership (e.g., 12:24). We have also seen a puzzling tension between Jesus's commitment only to go to Israel (e.g., 10:5–6; 15:24) yet a tender responsiveness to the faith of gentiles (8:10; 15:28). We have seen an emphasis upon the present fulfillment of the covenantal promises of the kingly Davidic line (1:17; 2:2–6) yet an emphasis upon the future fulfillment of the covenantal promises of the universal Abrahamic line (8:11–12). These tensions now prepare for some critical changes in God's kingdom program. The narrative of these final chapters begins to clarify the process that led to these changes.[120]

Since the days of Matthew's community, Jews and Christians have shared a very large amount of their theology—in fact, a much greater amount than is usually expected. The first Christians, who were all Jewish, believed that their faith was the fulfillment of the Jewish Scriptures. They believed that they were beginning to receive what had been promised in the covenants and the prophets. Hagner states, "They thought of their faith not as a new religion but as the true Judaism."[121] Nevertheless, there was a key dividing point between the earliest Christians. "It centered in the Christian confession of the crucified Jesus as both Messiah and Lord, as the one who had inaugurated a new era in the history of salvation, an era of eschatological fulfillment."[122]

---

120. For an overview of these issues, see Ladd, *Theology of the New Testament*, 104–6. I agree in large part with Ladd's perspective but differ where he emphasizes that the church now replaces and becomes Israel, seemingly permanently.

121. Hagner, "Jesus Quest and Jewish-Christian Relations," 2:1055

122. Hagner, "Jesus Quest and Jewish-Christian Relations," 2:1055

This study of Matthew's narrative of Jesus and his disciples in relationship with Israel produces the following points:

1. Jesus's arrival proclaims the past, present, and future promise to save his repentant and believing people, Israel, from their sins (1:21). Jesus came as a Jew to the Jewish people to fulfill the salvation-historical promises to Israel (1:1, 21–23; 10:5–6; 15:24).
2. Although Jesus's ministry was particularistic in its attention to Israel, it responded to the faith of gentiles and held promise of a future universalistic outreach and the offer of discipleship to the repentant from the believing nations (8:5–13; 15:21–28; 28:18–20).
3. A substantial group responded to exercise faith in Jesus Messiah. Matthew recorded quite positive accounts of responses to Jesus within Israel: individuals like the prophet John the Baptist, the twelve diverse disciples/apostles, tax collectors and "sinners," courageous women like Mary Magdalene who served Jesus in his public ministry and death, and religious leaders like Joseph of Arimathea who served Jesus in his burial. Indeed, Jews and gentiles are included in the worldwide mission (28:18–20). Those who responded positively to his offer of the kingdom became his disciples. Discipleship entailed unreserved commitment to him, which meant that a new disciple entered the kingdom of heaven in the presence of the person of Jesus and that they now bear the fruit of kingdom life (5:2–16, 20; 7:16–20).
4. However, Israel as a whole, including both the leaders and the people, rejected both Jesus and his message about the kingdom (12:25–32, 38–39; 13:10–17; 27:25).
5. Jesus declares in the events of the temple, the cursing of the fig tree, and the parables directed to the religious leaders who have questioned his authority, that the responsibility for being stewards of the kingdom of God is taken away from Israel (21:43).
6. The constituent elements of the rift between Israel and the Jesus-followers find their germinal roots in the historical Jesus. The reasons the leaders of Israel give for Jesus's death—that he was a false prophet, he committed blasphemy, and that he was presuming to be the Messiah—and his debates with the leaders of Israel that touched upon the pillars of Judaism (God, torah, election, and temple) illustrate the primary points of contention. Although Jesus himself remained within the orbit of a "common Judaism," his attitudes and actions pushed those boundaries to the point that he incurred violent opposition from other Jews.[123]

123. Bird, "Jesus and the 'Partings of the Ways,'" 2:1183–215.

7. Jesus did not call "sinners" to become his followers and then require them to be law-observant in a way that the Pharisees or early rabbis would find acceptable. Rather, against tendencies in recent Matthean research, according to Matthew's understanding of Jesus it is precisely the scribes and Pharisees who desperately need to re-study the Scriptures (9:13; 12:3, 5, 7; 19:4; 21:42).[124]
8. The recipients of his messianic salvation, the disciples of Jesus, become his new nation of witness to the reality of the presence and the transformative power of the kingdom of God. This new nation of disciples, the church, made up of Jews and gentiles, now has the responsibility of being the stewards of the kingdom of God (16:17–19; 18:12–20; 21:43).
9. The mission now becomes centrifugal instead of centripetal. This means that instead of the gentiles coming to Israel to hear God's message, Jesus's disciples are to go to all the nations with the gospel of the kingdom of heaven to make more disciples (28:18–20).[125]
10. Israel will have a presence in the cities/land of Israel and will experience the preaching of the gospel until the parousia (10:23).
11. Jesus anticipates the fulfillment of the covenantal promises to Israel to be restored to the land, with an apparently (and seemingly implausible) rebuilt temple and attendant desecration, which will usher in the messianic kingdom (24:15).[126]
12. Jesus gives what appears to be a prophetic announcement that when he returns, remorseful Israel will utter in sincere repentance the words, "Blessed is he who comes in the name of the Lord" (23:39). This is God's merciful offer of hope to his people.
13. The twelve apostles will sit on twelve thrones "judging" the twelve tribes of Israel. Matthew gives indications that since the Twelve will sit on twelve thrones judging the twelve tribes of Israel, in the future restored Davidic kingdom the twelve disciples will govern over Israel's restored tribal territories (19:28). This indicates the future role of the twelve apostles and the existence of the twelve tribes of the nation of Israel in God's purposes.[127]

124. Cf. Deines, "Not the Law," 53–84; here 70; Matthias Konradt, "Matthäus im Kontext: Eine Bestandsaufnahme zur Frage des Verhältnisses der matthäischen Gemeinde(n) zum Judentum," in *Studien zum Matthausevangelium*, ed. Alida Euler, WUNT 358 (Tübingen: Mohr Siebeck, 2016), 3–42; here 39–40; Tuckett, "Matthew," 99–129: "But the fundamental basis is *not* the Law as such but *Jesus'* teaching" (127, emphasis original). For a rather idiosyncratic study see Herman C. Waetjen, *Matthew's Theology of Fulfillment, Its Universality and Its Ethnicity: God's New Israel as the Pioneer of God's New Humanity*, T&T Clark Biblical Studies (London: Bloomsbury T&T Clark, 2017), esp. 1–17.

125. Christopher J. H. Wright, *The Mission of God: Unlocking the Bible's Grand Narrative* (Downers Grove, IL: InterVarsity, 2006), 523–25. Wright agrees with the broad level of truth in the distinction between centripetal and centrifugal missions but qualifies the distinction by pointing to centrifugal elements in the OT (e.g., God's salvation will go to the ends of the earth) and centripetal elements in the NT (e.g., the nations are gathered in to Christ) (C. Wright, *Mission of God*, 523).

126. It is interesting to note that there is a very active movement within Judaism in Israel to rebuild the temple, which would be the Third Temple. E.g., see the following website: www.templeinstitute.org. See Ch. 16 for more discussion.

127. See above on 10:23 (13.2.3) and 19:28 (13.2.4).

14. Although ethnic Israel is not at present functionally the instrument, witness, and steward of the outworking of the kingdom of God (21:43), individual Jews are invited to participate in the salvation brought by Jesus with the arrival of the kingdom, to be incorporated in discipleship to Jesus in the church that includes Jews and gentiles, men and women, commoner and elite; and to become participants in the missional outreach to all the nations (28:18–20).

The role of carrying out God's purposes through the kingdom of God has been taken away from the nation of Israel in the present age, and Jesus's disciples currently enjoy both the blessings of the kingdom of God and the responsibility of the role of carrying the message of the gospel of the kingdom (21:43; 28:18–20). Jesus's disciples represent the fulfillment in part of the promises to Israel, and they now functionally perform the role that Israel had performed, but they do not replace Israel nor become Israel. Israel is still kept in view as receiving in the future the eschatological fulfillment of the promises of the kingdom (10:23; 23:37–39; cf. Rom 11:25–32; 15:7–13; Rev 7:1–8).[128] As F. F. Bruce notes, the apostle Paul held hope of the ultimate blessing of ethnic "Israel of God" (Gal. 6:16).[129]

In spite of Matthew's recounting of grim consequences for Israel's rejection of Jesus, he has a vision of a future for ethnic Israel in God's plan of salvation. Israel is not removed from its place as God's elect people, but it shares in God's salvation through the unique and necessary death and resurrection of Jesus Messiah. And there is a future for ethnic, national Israel in God's plan of history. Matthias Konradt concludes that Matthew did not have the church take Israel's place—more exactly, the church appears as a new entity that causes the significance and role of Israel as the people of God to shift.[130] Konradt states, "The role of Israel becomes focused in being the special—but, after Easter, no longer the exclusive—addressee of the offer of salvation or the messianic ministry, whereby it is certain for Matthew that the "'lost sheep of the house of Israel' find salvation from their sins only within the ecclesia."[131]

There remains a role for Israel in the future stewardship of the kingdom of God, although at present the church is the primary steward of the kingdom. Israel experiences individual salvation within the stewardship of the church but experiences the knowledge that she is still God's treasured possession (Exod 19:5).

128. Cf. Hafemann, "Eschatology and Ethics," 161–92.

129. F. F. Bruce, *The Epistle to the Galatians: A Commentary on the Greek Text*, NIGTC (Grand Rapids: Eerdmans, 1982), 275. For a recent discussion of the grammatical issues, especially the connective *kai* in *kai epi ton Israēl tou theou* (Gal. 6:16) that acts to specify ethnic Israel in distinction from the church, see Michael H. Burer, *Galatians*, EEC (Bellingham, WA: Lexham, 2024), 534–36.

130. Konradt, *Israel*, 379.

131. Konradt, *Israel*, 379.

*Chapter 14*

# THE DEATH AND RESURRECTION OF JESUS MESSIAH IN MATTHEW'S GOSPEL

## *Forgiveness and New Life*

## BIBLIOGRAPHY

**Allen, David.** *According to the Scriptures: The Death of Christ in the Old Testament and the New.* London: SCM, 2018. **Bauckham, Richard, and Trevor Hart.** *At the Cross: Meditations on People Who Were There.* Downers Grove, IL: InterVarsity, 1999. **Beilby, James, and Paul R. Eddy,** eds. *The Nature of the Atonement: Four Views.* Downers Grove, IL: InterVarsity, 2006. **Berg, Inhee C.** *Irony in the Matthean Passion Narrative.* Minneapolis: Fortress, 2014. **Bock, Darrell L., with Benjamin I. Simpson.** *Jesus According to Scripture: Restoring the Portrait from the Gospels.* 2nd ed. Grand Rapids: Baker Academic, 2017. **Bockmuehl, Markus.** "The Gospels on the Presence of Jesus." Pages 87–102 in *OHC.* **Botner, Max, Justin Harrison Duff, and Simon Dürr,** eds. *Atonement: Jewish and Christian Origins.* Grand Rapids: Eerdmans, 2020. **Boyd, Gregory A.** *Crucifixion of the Warrior God: Interpreting the Old Testament's Violent Portraits of God in Light of the Cross.* 2 vols. Minneapolis: Fortress, 2017. **Bray, Gerald L.** *God Is Love: A Biblical and Systematic Theology.* Wheaton, IL: Crossway, 2012. **Brown, Raymond E.** *The Death of the Messiah: From Gethsemane to the Grave. A Commentary on the Passion Narratives in the Four Gospels.* 2 vols. ABRL. New York: Doubleday, 1994. **Bryan, Christopher.** *The Resurrection of the Messiah.* Oxford: Oxford University Press, 2011. **Carrier, Brian.** *Earthquakes and Eschatology in the Gospel According to Matthew.* WUNT 2/534. Tübingen: Mohr Siebeck, 2020. **Carroll, John T., and Joel B. Green.** *The Death of Jesus in Early Christianity.* Peabody, MA: Hendrickson, 1995. **Carson, D. A.** *Scandalous: The Cross and Resurrection of Jesus.* Wheaton, IL: Crossway, 2010. **Craig, William Lane.** *Assessing the New Testament Evidence for the Historicity of the Resurrection of Jesus.* Lewiston, NY: Edwin Mellin, 1989. ———. *Atonement and the Death of Christ: An Exegetical, Historical, and Philosophical Exploration.* Waco, TX: Baylor University Press, 2020. ———. "Did Jesus Rise from the Dead?" Pages 142–76 in *Jesus Under Fire: Modern Scholarship Reinvents the Historical Jesus.* Edited by

Michael J. Wilkins and J. P. Moreland. Grand Rapids: Zondervan, 1995. ———. "On the Organic Connection Between Jesus' Atoning Death and Resurrection." Pages 89–104 in *Raised on the Third Day: Defending the Historicity of the Resurrection of Jesus. Essays in Honor of Dr. Gary R. Habermas.* Edited by W. David Beck and Michael R. Licona. Bellingham, WA: Lexham Press, 2020. **Crisp, Oliver D.** *Participation and Atonement: An Analytic and Constructive Account.* Grand Rapids: Baker Academic, 2022. **Crisp, Oliver D., and Fred Sanders,** eds. *Locating Atonement: Explorations in Constructive Dogmatics.* LATCS 3. Grand Rapids: Zondervan, 2015. **Crowe, Brandon D.** *Why Did Jesus Live a Perfect Life? The Necessity of Christ's Obedience for Our Salvation.* Grand Rapids: Baker Academic, 2021. **Davis, Stephen T.** *Risen Indeed: Making Sense of the Resurrection.* Grand Rapids: Eerdmans, 1993. **Demarest, Bruce.** *The Cross and Salvation: The Doctrine of Salvation.* FET. Wheaton, IL: Crossway, 1997. **Dennis, John A.** "Death of Jesus." *DJG*[2] 172–93. **Edwards, J. Christopher.** *The Ransom Logion in Mark and Matthew: Its Reception and Its Significance for the Study of the Gospels.* WUNT 2/327. Tübingen: Mohr Siebeck, 2012. **Eklund, Rebekah.** *Jesus Wept: The Significance of Jesus' Laments in the New Testament.* LNTS 515. London: Bloomsbury T&T Clark, 2015. **Evans, Craig A.** "'He Laid Him in a Tomb' (Mark 15:46): Roman Law and the Burial of Jesus." Pages 52–66 in *Matthew and Mark Across Perspectives: Essays in Honour of Stephen C. Barton and William R. Telford.* Edited by Kristian A. Bendoraitis and Nijay K. Gupta. LNTS 538. London: Bloomsbury T&T Clark, 2016. ———. "The Testimony of Josephus and the Burial of Jesus." Pages 89–104 in *Raised on the Third Day: Defending the Historicity of the Resurrection of Jesus. Essays in Honor of Dr. Gary R. Habermas.* Edited by W. David Beck and Michael R. Licona. Bellingham, WA: Lexham Press, 2020. **Gathercole, Simon J.** "The Cross and Substitutionary Atonement." *SBET* 21.1 (2003): 152–65. ———. *Defending Substitution.* ASBT. Grand Rapids: Baker Academic, 2015. **Gorman, Michael J.** *The Death of the Messiah and the Birth of the New Covenant: A (Not So) New Model of the Atonement.* Eugene, OR: Cascade, 2014. ———. "The Work of Christ in the New Testament." Pages 72–86 in *OHC.* **Green, Joel B.** *The Death of Jesus: Tradition and Interpretation in the Passion Narratives.* WUNT 2/33. Tübingen: Mohr Siebeck, 1988. **Gurtner, Daniel M.** *The Torn Veil: Matthew's Exposition of the Death of Jesus.* SNTSMS 139. Cambridge: Cambridge University Press, 2007. **Hamilton, Catherine Sider.** *The Death of Jesus in Matthew: Innocent Blood and the End of Exile.* SNTSMS 167. Cambridge: Cambridge University Press, 2017. ———. "'His Blood Be upon Us': Innocent Blood and the Death of Jesus in Matthew." *CBQ* 70.1 (2008): 82–100. **Hamilton, James M., Jr.** *God's Glory in Salvation Through Judgment: A Biblical Theology.* Wheaton, IL: Crossway, 2010. **Hamm, Clay.** "The Last Supper in Matthew." *BBR* 10.1 (2000): 53–69. **Hart, John-Mark.** "Triune Beauty and the Ugly Cross: Towards a Theological Aesthetic." *TynBul* 66.2 (2015): 293–312. **Hastings, W. Ross.** *The Resurrection of Jesus Christ: Exploring Its Theological Significance and Ongoing Relevance.* Grand Rapids: Baker Academic, 2022. **Hengel, Martin.** *The Atonement: The Origins of the Doctrine in the New Testament.* Translated by John Bowden. Philadelphia: Fortress, 1981. ———. *Crucifixion: In the Ancient World and the Folly of the Message of the Cross.* ET.

Philadelphia: Fortress, 1977. **Johnson, Adam J.** *Atonement: A Guide for the Perplexed.* Guides for the Perplexed. London: Bloomsbury T&T Clark, 2015. ———, ed. *Five Views on the Extent of the Atonement.* Counterpoints. Grand Rapids: Zondervan, 2019. ———, ed. *T&T Clark Companion to Atonement.* Bloomsbury Companions 5. London: Bloomsbury, 2017. **Johnson, Raymond M.** *I See Dead People: The Function of the Resurrection of the Saints in Matthew 27:51–54.* RAD. Phillipsburg, NJ: P&R, 2019. **Licona, Michael R.** *The Resurrection of Jesus: A New Historiographical Approach.* Downers Grove, IL: InterVarsity, 2010. **Loke, Andrew Ter Ern.** *Investigating the Resurrection of Jesus Christ: A New Transdisciplinary Approach.* Routledge New Critical Thinking in Religion, Theology and Biblical Studies. London: Routledge, 2020. **Longenecker, Richard N.**, ed. *Life in the Face of Death: The Resurrection Message of the New Testament.* Grand Rapids: Eerdmans, 1998. **McKnight, Scot.** *A Community Called Atonement.* Living Theology. Nashville: Abingdon, 2007. ———. *Jesus and His Death: Historiography, the Historical Jesus, and Atonement Theory.* Waco, TX: Baylor University Press, 2005. ———. "Jesus and His Death: Some Recent Scholarship." *CurBR* 9 (2001): 185–228. **Mishkin, David.** *Jewish Scholarship on the Resurrection of Jesus.* Eugene, OR: Pickwick, 2017. **Moltmann, Jürgen.** *The Crucified God.* Translated by John Bowden and R. A. Wilson. London: SCM, 1974. ———. *The Trinity and the Kingdom of God.* Translated by Leonard Swidler. Philadelphia: Fortress, 1981. **Morris, Leon.** *The Cross of Christ.* Grand Rapids: Eerdmans, 1988. **Novakovic, Lidija.** "The Resurrection of the Saints as a Prolepsis of the Resurrection of Jesus: A Reassessment of Matthew's Portrayal of the Risen Jesus." Pages 347–70 in *Matthew Within Judaism: Israel and the Nations in the First Gospel.* Edited by Anders Runesson and Daniel M. Gurtner. ECL 27. Atlanta: SBL, 2020. **Packer, J. I., and Mark Dever.** *In My Place Condemned He Stood: Celebrating the Glory of the Atonement.* Wheaton, IL: Crossway, 2007. **Pinnock, Clark H.** *Flame of Love: A Theology of the Holy Spirit.* Forward and Commentary by Daniel Castelo. 2nd ed. Downers Grove, IL: InterVarsity, 2022. **Senior, Donald.** *The Passion of Jesus in the Gospel of Matthew.* The Passion Series 1. Collegeville, MN: Liturgical Press, 1990. **Sim, David C.** "The 'Confession' of the Soldiers in Matthew 27:54." *HeyJ* 34.4 (1993): 401–24. **Stott, John R. W.** *The Cross of Christ.* 20th anniversary special ed. Downers Grove, IL: InterVarsity, 2006. **Stuhlmacher, Peter.** *Reconciliation, Law, and Righteousness: Essays in Biblical Theology.* Translated by Everett R. Kalin. Philadelphia: Fortress, 1986. **Tidball, Derek.** *The Message of the Cross: Wisdom Unsearchable, Love Indestructible.* BST. Downers Grove, IL: InterVarsity, 2001. **Troxel, Ronald L.** "Matthew 27.51–54 Reconsidered: Its Role in the Passion Narrative, Meaning, and Origin." *NTS* 48.1 (2002): 30–47. **Venard, Olivier-Thomas**, ed. *La passion selon saint Matthieu: Matthieu 26–28.* 2 vols. La Bible en ses Traditions 4. Leuven: Peeters, 2021. **Wenham, John W.** "When Were the Saints Raised? A Note on the Punctuation of Matthew xxvii. 51–53." *JTS* 32.1 (1981): 150–52. **Wilkins, Michael J.** "Women in the Teaching and Example of Jesus." Pages 91–112 in *Women and Men in Ministry: A Complementary Perspective.* Edited by Robert L. Saucy and Judy TenElshof. Chicago: Moody, 2001. **Wright, N. T.** *The Resurrection of the Son of God.* Vol. 3 of *Christian Origins and the Question of God.*

Minneapolis: Fortress, 2003. **Wright, N. T., Simon Gathercole, and Robert B. Stewart.** *What Did the Cross Accomplish? A Conversation About the Atonement.* Louisville: Westminster John Knox, 2021. **Yarbrough, Oliver Larry,** ed. *Engaging the Passion: Perspectives on the Death of Jesus.* Minneapolis: Fortress, 2015.

## 14.1 INTRODUCTION: THE DEATH AND RESURRECTION OF JESUS MESSIAH IN MATTHEW'S GOSPEL[1]

Matthew's narrative of the passion events comprises the two longest chapters in his Gospel (26:1–75; 27:1–66), which alerts us to the importance of the arrest, trials, flogging, crucifixion, death, and burial for the core message of Jesus's life and ministry. And then in a stunningly short narrative Matthew recounts the resurrection scene with the concluding Great Commission (28:1–20). The succession of events leading to and including the crucifixion and the resurrection stimulated numerous echoes in later reception history, becoming a sweeping foundation of Western literature, arts, and religious expression.[2] Matthew's narrative of the passion became a fountainhead of religious and cultural expression throughout the world.

When Christians speak of the "passion" of Jesus, subtle layers of meaning in the word help illustrate significant issues. "Passion" derives from the Latin words *patior* ("to suffer") and *passio* ("suffering"). The Latin translations of the New Testament adopted the term *passio* to point to the Gospel narratives of Jesus's suffering and the attending events. When we speak of Christ's "passion" we refer to the suffering and death that he endured. But "passion" has other connotations in English. It can mean intense emotion, feeling, even commitment. People can do things "with a passion." Donald Senior notes that both sides of the term "passion" come into play in the Gospels. He notes that on the one side of "passion," Jesus Messiah was condemned to die by the Roman authorities—the cross was imposed on him. In this sense Jesus of Nazareth was a victim of suffering and death. But the other side of "passion" is present too. The crucifixion was no surprise, as if it fell on Jesus like a tile off a roof. The Gospels are clear that the hostility against Jesus was a result of Jesus's own mission. "Because of his unyielding commitment, his 'passion,' Jesus put himself on a collision course with

1. Elements of this Chapter were first explored in my commentary on Jesus's final week culminating in his death and resurrection, especially in the Bridging Contexts section of each passage. All has been significantly reworked and updated; see Wilkins, *Matthew*, 681–972.

2. Olivier-Thomas Venard, ed., *La passion selon saint Matthieu: Matthieu 26–28*, 2 vols., La Bible en ses Traditions 4 (Leuven: Peeters, 2021), 46–47. For examples in Matthew's passion narrative, and also from a somewhat broader perspective, see Oliver Larry Yarbrough, ed., *Passion: Contemporary Writers on the Story of Calvary* (Maryknoll, NY: Orbis, 2015); Yarbrough, *Engaging the Passion: Perspectives on the Death of Jesus* (Minneapolis: Fortress, 2015).

certain powerful forces in society. From this perspective Jesus' death was the outcome of his life; he 'chose' death. In the language of the Gospel, he 'took up the cross.'"[3]

Those are difficult words to understand, but as we look at the death of Jesus in this Chapter, we will also look at the resurrection of Jesus Messiah. It is only as we consider the death and resurrection together that we will enter fully into the *passion* that marked Jesus Messiah's bodily incarnation, crucifixion, and resurrection.

Was the risen Jesus Messiah of the Gospel of Matthew present or absent to the early Christian believer? To state the question more directly, is the crucified Jesus Messiah personally here with us now or is he away elsewhere until he returns as ruler and judge? Mark concludes his Gospel somewhat unresolved on these questions; Matthew is clearer. He does not keep us guessing about an unfulfilled Galilean resurrection encounter or about Jesus Messiah's abiding presence. The theme of "God with us" (Matt 1:23) begins and concludes this Gospel, which links Jesus's earthly ministry to his risen life, linking his death to his resurrected life.[4]

## 14.2 THE CRUCIFIXION AND DEATH OF JESUS MESSIAH

In the final section of the passion narrative we find the crucifixion, death, and burial of Jesus (27:45–61), which leads to the stunningly brief resurrection narrative (28:1–20). Matthew's treatment of these events indicates the central place that Jesus's death and resurrection holds in God's plan of salvation, which should alert us to the central place that they should hold for us in the development of our historical and theological foundation, in the practice of our corporate worship and personal growth in Christ, and in the message that we proclaim to a waiting world.

A crucified Messiah was an anomaly to common Jewish expectations, but it became one of the bedrock historical factors in the most basic preaching and teaching in the early church. A crucified Messiah can also seem like an anomaly to modern people, Christian and non-Christian alike, who want a more sanitized kind of "good news." But the blood of Jesus Messiah's cross is a fact of history that offers the only good news, that the incarnate Son of God willingly endured an ignominious death so that humanity can experience a glorious life that is liberated from sin's death grip.

### 14.2.1 Crucifixion in the Ancient World

Matthew does not focus on the details of Jesus's crucifixion, probably because it was such a well-known horrific practice that he did not like to dwell on the details, but also because it would be too painful to recount the suffering of his Lord. Recent

3. Donald Senior, *The Passion of Jesus in the Gospel of Matthew*, The Passion Series 1 (Collegeville, MN: Liturgical Press, 1990), 7–8.

4. Bockmuehl, "Gospels on the Presence of Jesus," *OHC*, 92.

historical and archaeological studies have helped bring a realistic sense of its horrors for us who live so far removed from the practice.[5] Crucifixion was used both as a means of execution and for exposing an executed body to shame and humiliation. A tragic crucifixion scene that occurred in Israel over one hundred years earlier than Jesus's is recorded in the Qumran Nahum Pesher, which refers to an act of Alexander Jannaeus, a king of Judah during the Hasmonean dynasty (103–76 BC) who hanged eight hundred Pharisees on one occasion.[6] The Qumran community had apparently seen its horrors.[7]

Crucifixion involved a painful and slow means of execution, which the Romans adopted from the Assyrians and Phoenicians.[8] It was viewed by ancient writers as the cruelest and most barbaric of punishments, and was intended as a public spectacle to warn others who may consider the same crime as that committed by the victim.[9] Matthew notes that the site of crucifixion was not far from a public thoroughfare; those passing by hurled insults at the crucified one (27:39). The victim usually died after agonizing days—of thirst, exhaustion, and exposure. Roman executioners placed victims in various positions to maximize torture and humiliation. Seneca wrote that "some hang their victims with head toward the ground, some impale their private parts, others stretch out their arms on fork-shaped gibbet."[10] The hands were often nailed and/or tied to the crossbeam (*patibulum*), which was then hoisted up and affixed to the upright stake (*palus*), to which the feet were then nailed. The crossbeam was placed either on top of the *palus* (like a "T") or in the more traditional cross shape (†). Nailing the placard over his head (27:37) probably indicates the latter.

### 14.2.2 The Crucifixion of Jesus Messiah (27:45–50)

In the passion narrative, Matthew takes us to the very heart of his Gospel about Jesus Messiah. The crucifixion narrative culminates a critical theme of this Gospel, a theme that marks a central purpose of Jesus's entire earthly mission: Jesus brings salvation from sin. The infancy narrative commenced with the announcement that the soon-to-be-born child would be named Jesus "because he will save his people from their sins" (Matt 1:21). As the narrative unfolds, Jesus makes pronouncements about forgiving sins (9:1–8) and about providing a ransom for many (20:28). At least four times Jesus predicted he would be handed over by the Jewish leaders to be killed at the hands of the gentiles (16:21; 17:22–23; 20:17–19; 26:2).

5. A helpful historical study is Hengel, *Crucifixion*. See also Chapman, *Ancient and Christian Perceptions of Crucifixion*; Samuelsson, *Crucifixion in Antiquity*; Chapman and Schnabel, *Trial and Crucifixion of Jesus*; Cook, *Crucifixion in the Mediterranean World*. For a helpful exegetical and theological exploration, see Fleming Rutledge, *The Crucifixion: Understanding the Death of Jesus Christ* (Grand Rapids: Eerdmans, 2015).

6. 4QpNah 3–4 I, 6–9.

7. James C. VanderKam, *The Dead Sea Scrolls Today* (Grand Rapids: Eerdmans, 1994), 49–50.

8. Cf. Hengel, *Crucifixion*, 22–32.

9. Hengel, *Crucifixion*, 29–32.

10. Seneca, *Dialogue* 6 (*On Consolation To Marcia*) 20.3.

For Matthew's readers, those Old Testament passages that spoke so darkly of a suffering servant who would bring forgiveness of sin are now crystal clear (e.g., Isa 42:1–4; 52:13–53:12). They point to the crucifixion of their Messiah, who brings true redemption in his sacrifice on the cross. Matthew narrates these events starkly, with little commentary about their meaning. But for his readers the meaning is clear—Jesus is the crucified Messiah whose death liberates his people through the unimaginable horror of dying for their sins in their place. Somberly, with deepest sorrow, yet with unimaginable joy, Matthew's audience watches the Savior go to the cross.

Matthew observes that the tone of mockery at Golgotha from the witnesses (Matt 27:39–44) suddenly turns somber as darkness comes over the land from the sixth hour until the ninth hour (27:45). The most widely accepted method of calculating the time of the day throughout much of the ancient world was to begin with sunrise, which is approximately 6:00 a.m. (cf. Let. Aris. 303). All three Synoptic Gospels employ that timeframe in their narratives (cf. 27:45; Mark 15:33; Luke 23:44).[11] Therefore, the sixth hour is 12:00 noon and the ninth hour is 3:00 p.m. According to Mark, Jesus had already been on the cross for about three hours because he was crucified at the third hour, or 9:00 a.m. (Mark 15:25).

## The Events of Jesus's Crucifixion and Jesus's Seven Cries from the Cross

1. Arrival at Golgotha (Matt 27:33)
2. Jesus rejects the soldiers' offer of wine mingled with gall (27:34)
3. Soldiers divide Jesus's clothes (27:35)
4. Soldiers place a placard over Jesus's head reading, "THIS IS JESUS, THE KING OF THE JEWS" (27:37)
5. Crucifixion between the two insurrectionists (27:38)
6. The *first cry* from the cross, "Father, forgive them, for they do not know what they are doing" (Luke 23:34)
7. Jesus is mocked by all passing by (Matt 27:39–44)
8. The conversation with the insurrectionists (Luke 23:39–43)
9. The *second cry* from the cross, to the insurrectionist, "I tell you the truth, today you will be with me in paradise" (Luke 23:43)
10. The *third cry*, Jesus says to his mother, "Dear woman, here is your son," and to the disciple, "Here is your mother" (John 19:26–27)

11. There was some variation, with evidence for later Roman practice beginning the day at midnight, as is now the system in most modern societies, and with Jewish day-keeping beginning the calendar day with sundown.

11. Darkness overtakes the scene at Golgotha (Matt 27:45)
12. The *fourth cry*, "My God, my God, why have you forsaken me?" (27:46)
13. The *fifth cry*, "I am thirsty" (John 19:28)
14. The *sixth cry*, "It is finished" (John 19:30)
15. The *seventh cry*, "Father, into your hands I commit my spirit" (Luke 23:46)[12]
16. Jesus bows his head and gives up his spirit (Matt 27:50; cf. John 19:30)

Pilate likely had little concern for the religious arguments that had turned the Jerusalem priesthood against Jesus. However, as the Roman administrator of Israel he was responsible to keep the peace and was persuaded by the accusations from the Jerusalem leadership that Jesus had pronounced himself "king of the Jews." Pilate condemned him to crucifixion, the routine capital punishment ordered by the Romans for radical agitators or insurrectionists.

Once at the crucifixion site, the soldiers may have tied and nailed Jesus's hands to the crossbeam that he and Simon of Cyrene had carried (27:32).[13] Then they nailed his ankles to the upright beam, possibly with a spike driven through the bones and into the beam between them. Death was sometimes hastened by breaking the legs, but not in Jesus's case, who had been so weakened by the earlier flogging that he was already near death when nailed to the cross (cf. John 19:33).

### 14.2.3 The Theological Meaning of Jesus Messiah's Death

Nowhere does Jesus or Matthew give a full exposition of the meaning of the suffering of the cross that Jesus predicted awaited him in Jerusalem. That full theological explanation awaits especially the apostle Paul and the rest of the New Testament authors. But throughout his life Jesus gave hints of the cross's meaning, and then in the cataclysmic events surrounding the crucifixion the meaning of Jesus's death on the cross is illustrated.[14]

Matthew immediately records several events that follow upon the death of Jesus, all of which give significant historical and theological testimony to explain the impact of Jesus's death.

12. Of the seven cries of Jesus from the cross, three are recorded by Luke (nos. 1, 2, 7) and three by John (nos. 3, 5, 6). Matthew and Mark record only the fourth saying.

13. See Frederick T. Zugibe, "Two Question About Crucifixion: Does the Victim Die of Asphyxiation? Would Nails in the Hands Hold the Weight of the Body?" *Bible Review* 5.2 (1989): 34–43.

14. The most thorough study of the passion of Jesus Messiah is Brown, *Death of the Messiah*. See also Joel B. Green, *The Death of Jesus: Tradition and Interpretation in the Passion Narratives*, WUNT 2/33 (Tübingen: Mohr Siebeck, 1988). For a sweeping attempt at placing the cross at the center NT theology, see Gregory A. Boyd, *Crucifixion of the Warrior God: Interpreting the Old Testament's Violent Portraits of God in Light of the Cross*, vol. 1: *The Cruciform Hermeneutic*, vol. 2: *The Cruciform Thesis* (Minneapolis: Fortress, 2017).

### *14.2.3.1 Allusions to the Meaning of Jesus's Death in His Earthly Ministry*

From Jesus's first announcement of the arrival of the kingdom of heaven (4:17), it was obvious that his ministry would be different. Right away the difference was seen in the unique authority he possessed (5:17). And his authority began pointing to the significant contrast between his own ministry and that of Israel's religious establishment. Even as ominous clouds concerning Jesus's safety gathered as he confronted the religious authorities, his vulnerability increasingly indicated that his life would realize the people's hopes of salvation.

He was named "Jesus" to indicate that he would save his people from their sins (1:21), and as his life unfolded it was clear that he would save them in a unique and costly manner. The Son of Man has authority to forgive sins (9:6), which pits him against the sacerdotal authority of the religious system. He is greater than the temple, which puts him at odds with the temple authorities and the Pharisaic traditions (12:1–6). As the gentle suffering servant he brings justice to victory, causing the nations to put their hope in him, not the nation of Israel (12:18–21).

#### 14.2.3.1.1 "The Son of Man Did Not Come to Be Served, but to Serve, and to Give His Life as a Ransom for Many" (20:28)

At the culmination of Jesus's life, he predicted his future suffering on the cross, which contains allusions to the cross's meaning. He is a threat to Israel's religious establishment because he is gaining a widespread following with his open invitation to the kingdom of heaven. He is a threat to the Roman military and political machine because he is being perceived as the king of the kingdom of heaven. He is able to offer salvation to Israel's most prestigious leaders, but he does so in a way that denies their own religious attainments and in a way that commands their unswerving loyalty to himself (19:16–30).

Jesus's way of power is not in self-serving but in serving others, which he will illustrate in his life becoming a "ransom for many" (20:28), a theme that has inherently ominous connotations.[15] But his way of power also indicates the means of liberating those people enslaved to sin. Because he suffers at the hands of wicked men (21:38–41), his death hints of his own righteousness. And as he promises a new era of kingdom life on the earth, he does so by signaling the temporary end of the functional role of Israel and the beginning of a new nation of his own fruit-bearing disciples that will come into being even as he is rejected and killed (21:42–44).[16]

The ultimate example of selfless servanthood for the disciples is Jesus's own life

---

15. France, *Gospel of Matthew*, 760–61. For an important discussion of the authenticity of the ransom logion, see Stuhlmacher, *Reconciliation, Law, and Righteousness*, ch. 2. For a full treatment of the exegesis and early reception history of the ransom logion, see J. Christopher Edwards, *The Ransom Logion in Mark and Matthew: Its Reception and Its Significance for the Study of the Gospels*, WUNT 2/327 (Tübingen: Mohr Siebeck, 2012).

16. France, *Gospel of Matthew*, 814–17.

(20:28). As the Son of Man, in which he had been revealed to be the Messiah, the Son of God (e.g., 16:16–17), to whom all glory and honor should be paid, Jesus had willingly set aside that prerogative for a higher purpose—to serve by giving his life as a ransom for many. This statement gives an explicit indication of his self-understanding of the purpose of the crucifixion that he has been predicting he will soon suffer (16:21; 17:22–23; 20:17–19; 26:2).

Jesus will give his life as a "ransom" (*lytron*), which means "the price of release,"[17] often used of the money paid for the release of slaves. But in the New Testament meaning, "redemption" or "release" as a theological concept is based on the experience of Israel's release from the slavery of Egypt. The term also contains an allusion to the suffering servant passage of Isa 53, especially v. 6b: "And the LORD has laid on him the iniquity of us all." Jesus's use of "ransom" indicates that his death is the means to secure the freedom of those who come to him from the domineering grip of sin.

The human analogy of a ransom payment does not fit the atonement of Jesus Messiah in every detail. There was no ransom paid either to "sin" or to Satan, for they did not have the power to demand such a payment. Grudem notes, "It is sufficient to note that a price was paid (the death of Christ) and the result was that we were 'redeemed' from bondage."[18] Erickson states, "Christ's death, then, was indeed God's triumph over the forces of evil, but only because it was a substitutionary sacrifice."[19]

Oliver Crisp observes that as an atonement model, substitutionary sacrifice provides a helpful way of thinking about one aspect of Christ's reconciling work.[20] The phrase "for many" (*anti pollōn*) in Jesus's statement is loaded with significance. The preposition *anti* virtually never means "on behalf of" but demands the use "in place of,"[21] signifying the notion of exchange substitution for all those who will accept his payment for their sins. The "many" (*pollōn*) has been understood to have either an exclusive sense, "many, but not all," restricting the application to the community of the elect (e.g., 1QS VI, 1–23), or to have an inclusive sense, "many, the totality which embraces many individuals," opening the application to all without limitation.

The most convincing historical and linguistic argument affirms the latter.[22] This saying of Jesus is the basis of the doctrine of substitutionary atonement as the work of his sacrifice on the cross, which involves the greatest cost of all, the life of the Son of Man.[23] He was so secure in his identity as the Son of God that he could give himself unconditionally, in spite of the appearance of any of his earthly circumstances, to serve

17. Cf. "λύτρον," BDAG 605; A. T. Robertson, *A Grammar of the Greek New Testament in the Light of Historical Research* (Nashville: Broadman, 1934), 572–74; Wallace, *Greek Grammar*, 365–67.

18. Grudem, *Systematic Theology*, 722–23. See here Grudem's important caveat on using the "ransom" analogy.

19. Erickson, *Christian Theology*, 751.

20. Oliver D. Crisp, *Participation and Atonement: An Analytic and Constructive Account* (Grand Rapids: Baker Academic, 2022), 6; see 77–94.

21. Cf. Wallace, *Greek Grammar*, 365–67.

22. Joachim Jeremias, "πολλοί," *TDNT* 6:536–545.

23. Cf. Page, "Ransom Saying," *DJG*[1] 660–62; McKnight, "Jesus and His Death," 185–228.

us. The paradigm of power is turned upside down, so that in the apparent weakness of a human on a cross is the greatest display of power that the world has ever known. In that single substitutionary act of service, all the greatest needs of humanity were met as Jesus became the ransom for sin.[24] And that act stands before us as the single example of the servanthood to which we are called within the reciprocating community of disciples and to a stupefied waiting world.[25]

#### 14.2.3.1.2 "This Is My Blood of the Covenant, Which Is Poured Out for Many for the Forgiveness of Sins" (26:28)

Matthew narrates Jesus's celebration of the Passover with his disciples, which provides an important hermeneutical lens for understanding Jesus's death. In the same way that the life of the Passover lamb was exchanged for the life of a firstborn Israelite son (Exod 12:1–3), Jesus's life will be exchanged for humanity's life to obtain their redemption. The analogy is made explicit in Jesus's words, "This is my blood of the covenant, which is poured out for many for the forgiveness of sins" (26:28).[26] He offers himself as a *substitute* for the many. "His death was a *sacrifice* typified by the Old Testament sacrificial system."[27]

The traditional cups of the Passover celebration offer another stunning illustration for Jesus to show that his sacrificial life is the fulfillment of all that for which the historical ritual had hoped. It is widely believed that it was the third cup, after the supper, which Jesus took and said, "This is my blood of the covenant,[28] which is poured out for many for the forgiveness of sins" (26:28). The third cup was often called the cup of redemption, corresponding to God's third promise, "*I will redeem you* with an outstretched arm and with mighty acts of judgment" (Exod 6:6; emphasis added). The death of the Passover lamb and the smearing of its blood opened the way for the redemption of God's people from Egypt.

The forgiveness of sins evokes the images of Exod 24, Jer 31, and Isa 53. It also draws upon the significant theme introduced in the opening verses of Matthew's Gospel, where the angel instructs Joseph regarding the naming of Mary's child, "She will give birth to a son, and you are to give him the name Jesus, because he will save his people from their sins" (Matt 1:21). Jesus's entire earthly ministry as portrayed in Matthew's Gospel is enclosed with reference to the theme of forgiveness of sins.[29]

---

24. Hagner, *Matthew 14–28*, 583.

25. For a clear and convincing presentation, see Thomas R. Schreiner, "Penal Substitution," in *The Nature of the Atonement: Four Views*, ed. James Beilby and Paul R. Eddy (Downers Grove, IL: InterVarsity, 2006), 67–98; here 90–92.

26. Brown and Roberts, *Matthew*, 368–69.

27. Erickson, *Christian Theology*, 738.

28. "New" does not occur in the best manuscripts, but it does occur in Luke 22:20 (cf. Metzger, *TCGNT*, 54). However, the allusions to the Old Testament prophecies of a "new covenant" are clear.

29. Jonathan T. Pennington, "The Lord's Last Supper in the Fourfold Witness of the Gospels," in *The Lord's Supper: Remembering and Proclaiming Christ Until He Comes*, ed. Thomas R. Schreiner and Matthew R. Crawford, NACSBT 10 (Nashville: B&H, 2010), 31–67; here 59.

The shedding of Jesus's blood, which this cup foreshadows, opens the way for the redemption of all humanity to enter into a new covenant relationship with God.[30] With this statement Jesus indicates that he is instituting the fulfillment of the new covenant that was promised to the people of Israel. Of that new covenant the prophet Jeremiah spoke especially of the forgiveness of sins: "'The days are coming,' declares the LORD, 'when I will make a new covenant with the house of Israel and with the house of Judah. . . . For I will forgive their wickedness and will remember their sins no more'" (Jer 31:31, 34). The prophet Ezekiel likewise spoke of the forgiveness that would accompany the new covenant, but he focused further on the personal transformation of those who responded to its inauguration: "I will give you a new heart and put a new spirit in you; I will remove from you your heart of stone and give you a heart of flesh. And I will put my Spirit in you and move you to follow my decrees and be careful to keep my laws" (Ezek 36:26–27).[31]

Throughout his ministry Jesus based his invitation to the kingdom of heaven and the attendant forgiveness of sins and promise of regeneration upon the initiation of the new covenant (cf. 5:17–20). The time has come for its inauguration with the cross and the coming of the Spirit at Pentecost. Those who receive Jesus's gracious invitation to partake of his sacrificial death live in the blessing of the new covenant. We experience forgiveness of sins and the beginnings of transformation into the image of Jesus Messiah that accompanies our regeneration through the Holy Spirit (cf. Titus 3:4–7; 2 Cor 3:18).

### 14.2.3.1.3 "My Father, If It Is Possible, May This Cup Be Taken from Me. Yet Not as I Will, but as You Will" (26:39)

In Gethsemane Jesus asks the inner group of three to share with him this overwhelming time of sorrow and trouble as he faces the cross (Matt 26:36–38). He did not ask them to pray, but to watch. As he grievously anticipates his looming death, his overwhelming sorrow reveals a heart broken almost to the point of death itself, because he knows that he will experience being forsaken by his Father (27:46).

#### *14.2.3.1.3.1 Jesus's First Prayer (26:39)*

Jesus goes a little farther away from the trio of disciples to be alone because he must plead with his Father privately, although having his closest followers near provided necessary human support. There alone "he fell with his face to the ground and prayed" (Matt 26:39). In this typical posture of abject humility in prayer, Jesus lays his life before his Father in utter honesty and trust. Matthew reveals in this scene one of the most profound insights into the intimacy between Father and Son. In this time of

30. Routledge, "Passover and Last Supper," 203–21; here 219.

31. Cf. Hamm, "Last Supper in Matthew," 53–69.

prayer that lasted an hour (26:40), Jesus probably reiterated various expressions of this central theme, which accounts for the variation between the four evangelists.

With urgency and trustfulness, Jesus lays his life in his Father's safe keeping as he calls out with tender intimacy, "My Father" (26:39). This continues Matthew's unique insight into the special relationship of Son and Father in this Gospel (cf. 7:21; 10:32–33). To his Father, Jesus pleads, "If it is possible, may this cup be taken from me. Yet not as I will, but as you will" (26:39). Jesus is facing a very real temptation, the most severe of his life. He started his earthly ministry by being tempted by the devil in the wilderness (4:1–11), and he was variously tempted by satanic devices at other points in his earthly ministry (e.g., 16:22–23). The significant feature of the earlier temptations was the satanic attempt to deter Jesus from the cross (cf. 4:8–9; 16:21–23). Now at the moment when he is ready to accomplish his life's mission, the temptation is intensified to its maximum. This is the devil's last-ditch effort to attempt to convince Jesus that the cross is not necessary.

In the Old Testament the "cup" has associations of suffering and of the wrath of God (e.g., Ps 11:6; Isa 51:17; Ezek 23:33), and the same kind of symbolism is found here. Jesus's death meant suffering, and because it was a death for sin there are connotations of the wrath of God connected to it.[32] But Jesus has demonstrated his complete confidence in his Father's sovereign power and his Father's perfect will throughout his life, so at this moment of greatest temptation, he turns to his Father for guidance. Jesus has prophesied that he must endure this cup of crucifixion to accomplish redemption of humanity (cf. 20:22–23, 28; 26:27), but Satan's temptation is to get him to believe that it is not absolutely necessary.

Jesus lays the temptation out to his Father, but he is not asking to shirk what has been revealed to be his destiny. He wants primarily to obey his Father's will. This is the landmark example of honesty and trustfulness in prayer. The Father will not respond to the petition in the way requested, but it does not reflect any fault in the one requesting. The Father did hear the Son's plea, but it was the Son's obedience to the Father's answer to continue to the cross that brought salvation to humanity (Heb 5:7–10)

Jesus was a brave person who had before faced down perilous challenges to his life (e.g., Luke 4:28–30; John 8:59). Many men and women of lesser obvious courage have faced death calmly. It was not death itself that evoked this plea from Jesus but the *kind* of death. Jesus faces the most intense suffering imaginable as he endures not simply death but a divinely sustained human death in which he suffers punishment for the sins of humanity. The overwhelming sorrow (*perilypos*, Matt 26:38) comes from the grievous anticipation of separation from his Father that he will experience in his human consciousness (2 Cor 5:21). Although dreading the prospect of pain and death on the

32. Morris, *Matthew*, 668–69.

cross, the prospect of separation from the Father was a greater horror, and a greater sorrow (Matt 27:46). But doing the will of the Father was Jesus's only motivation because, in enduring his own forsakenness from his Father, he knew that millions of men and women before and after his triumph over sin at the cross would be reconciled to the Father through his death.

##### *14.2.3.1.3.2 The Second and Third Prayers and the Disciples' Failures (26:42–44)*

Matthew indicates that as Jesus goes away to pray a second and third time, he prays the same thing (26:44). However, in the second prayer there is a slight but significant variation. Now he states, "My Father, if it is not possible for this cup to be taken away unless I drink it, may your will be done" (26:42). Now there is the conscious recognition that it is not possible for the cup to be taken and that Jesus is the one who must drink its wrathful onslaught. There is a conscious submission to that destiny as he states, "May your will be done." Jesus here duplicates the wording of his earlier prayer (6:9b–13), revealing a theme of his earthly mission to do the will of his Father (cf. Heb 5:8).[33]

But the disciples have not yet learned this obedience, because once again Jesus goes back to find the trio sleeping, "because their eyes were heavy" (Matt 26:43). They have not learned the discipline of spirit over flesh. So, Matthew tells us that Jesus left them. Matthew records no interaction with them, but Mark states that "they did not know what to say to him" (Mark 14:40), which may imply that Jesus chided them once again.

As he goes away to pray again, Matthew states that he "prayed the third time, saying the same thing" (Matt 26:44). Although there may be some development in Jesus's understanding of the nature of Satan's temptation and the Father's will for him, Matthew allows us to see that even from the start there was no deficiency in Jesus's prayer. He continues only to seek the Father's will.

#### *14.2.3.2 The Declaration of "Innocent/Righteous Blood" (23:35; 27:4–8, 19, 24–25)*

Jesus's pronouncement of "my blood of the covenant" (26:28) surfaces important themes for Matthew.[34] Derek Tidball notes that "Matthew draws our attention to the blood of Christ more than any of the Gospel writers."[35] And John Carroll and Joel Green state graphically, "The motif of the blood of Jesus weaves its way as a bright red thread through the Matthean passion account, riveting readers' attention on the

33. Contra the view that Gethsemane has been assimilated to the Lord's Prayer, held by Neumann, "Thy Will Be Done," 161–82.

34. Exploring the meaning of Jesus's death and innocent blood, see C. Hamilton, "Death of Judas in Matthew," 419–37. See also C. Hamilton, *The Death of Jesus in Matthew*, esp. 32–44, 231–36.

35. Derek Tidball, *The Message of the Cross: Wisdom Unsearchable, Love Indestructible*, BST (Downers Grove, IL: InterVarsity, 2001), 123.

question of responsibility for the death of Jesus but at the same time enabling readers to probe the deeper layers of the event's meaning."[36]

Matthew has gone to great lengths to establish that Jesus is innocent of Roman and Jewish charges against him. Matthew emphasizes that Pilate, along with the Jewish leadership of Israel, is responsible for the death of Jesus. In the expression "All the people answered, 'His blood is on us and on our children!'" (27:25), Matthew emphasizes that the crowd and the religious leaders have joined in asking for Jesus's death. "People" (*laos*) is the word that Matthew normally uses to designate Israel (e.g., 1:21; 2:6; 4:16; 15:8). Used here, the implications are ominous for the nation. The Jewish leaders and the crowds whom they have manipulated have joined together as the people of Israel to claim responsibility for Jesus's death as they declare boldly, "Let his blood be on us and on our children!" (NIV84).[37] Blood on a person (or "on the head") is a common idiom to indicate responsibility for someone's death.[38] The expression "on our children" indicates the familial solidarity of generations within Israel (e.g., Gen 31:16). The crowd is so convinced that Jesus deserves death that they brashly proclaim their responsibility for his death and extend that responsibility to their descendants.

The religious leaders and the crowds of that day share responsibility with the Romans for the death of Jesus. Pilate tried to escape the responsibility, but he cannot wash his hands of the matter. By not finding any guilt and still ordering Jesus to be executed, Pilate was guilty of the death of an innocent man.[39] The people of that day, as in any day, are responsible for their own actions.[40]

We noted in an earlier Chapter (section XXX) that the apostle Peter in his first public sermon at Pentecost indicts the religious leaders, the Jewish crowds, and the Romans for Jesus's death (Acts 2:22–23; cf. Acts 2:36; 3:17–19). Guilt is attributed to that generation and judgment exacted with the destruction of the temple and the city of Jerusalem in AD 70. But only that generation of Roman officials and Israel's leaders and people are implicated.[41] To all those who acknowledge their guilt Peter's sermon extends an offer of forgiveness of sins and gospel salvation (2:37–41; 3:19–4:4). Thousands of Jewish people, including many priests, received that offer in the first days after Pentecost (2:41; 4:4; 6:7). Everyone is responsible for his or her own actions, but God's forgiveness awaits any who repent. It is not all Jews everywhere and forever who experiences judgment, but only those in Jerusalem or the land of Israel, and only that generation, which experienced judgment in AD 70.[42]

36. John T. Carroll and Joel B. Green, *The Death of Jesus in Early Christianity* (Peabody, MA: Hendrickson, 1995), 39.

37. See Newport, *Matthew 23*, 74.

38. E.g., Lev 20:9; Josh 2:19; 2 Sam 1:16; Ezek 18:13; Acts 5:28; 18:6.

39. Boyd, *Crucifixion of the Warrior God*, 558–59.

40. Konradt, *Gospel According to Matthew*, 417–19.

41. For an excellent discussion, see Brown and Roberts, *Matthew*, 516–21. Also Helen K. Bond, *Pontius Pilate in History and Interpretation*, SNTSMS 100 (Cambridge: Cambridge University Press, 1998), 129–37.

42. Osborne, *Matthew*, 1021.

### *14.2.3.3 The Darkness at the Crucifixion (27:45)*

Darkness often accompanies the conception of death in Scripture (cf. Job 10:21–22). This was not a solar eclipse, for the Passover was at the full moon, and a lunar eclipse would not produce darkness on the earth.[43] Instead this was some unknown act of God indicating the judgment of God on the sins of the world. The darkness that came over the land at the crucifixion scene displays a limitation on the power of Satan (cf. Luke 22:53), God's displeasure on humanity for crucifying his Son, and most importantly God's judgment on evil.[44]

### *14.2.3.4 Jesus's Cry from the Cross: "My God, My God, Why Have You Forsaken Me?" (27:46)*

At about the ninth hour, or 3:00 p.m., Jesus has been on the cross for six hours. Since early in the morning, he has endured flogging, crucifixion, and mockery. His tortured body is now nearly lifeless. From out of the darkness surrounding Golgotha, Jesus's voice cries out, "'*Eli, Eli, lama sabachthani*?' (which means, 'My God, my God, why have you forsaken me?')" (27:46). The connection between the darkness and Jesus's cry is very close—the darkness is a symbol of the agonizing content of the cry.[45] The crucifixion scene recalls the lament of King David in Ps 22:[46]

> My God, my God, why have you forsaken me?
> Why are you so far from saving me,
> so far from my cries of anguish?
> O my God, I cry out by day, but you do not answer,
> by night, but I find no rest. (Ps 22:1–2; cf. Matt 27:35, 39, 43)

David goes on to recount his vindication (Ps 22:22–23 [LXX 21:23–24]), but Jesus's cry does not go that far. Matthew's readers, who know the full story, can think of the entirety of Ps 22 as a preview of Jesus's vindication by the resurrection. But Matthew focuses on Jesus's abandonment, a theme that pervades the narrative.[47] Although Jesus

43. A lunar eclipse can produce a reddish darkening of the moon, but not the earth. For an unconvincing attempt to justify a reconstruction of the chronology of Jesus's crucifixion based upon a lunar eclipse, see Colin J. Humphries and W. G. Waddington, "The Jewish Calendar, A Lunar Eclipse and the Date of Christ's Crucifixion," *TynBul* 43.2 (1992): 331–51.

44. Wilkins, "Darkness," *EDBT* 142–43; Conzelmann, "σκότος, κ.τ.λ.," *TDNT* 7:423–45; Hahn, "Darkness," *NIDNTT* 1:420–425. For a discussion of the possible (new) covenant ratification aspect of the darkness of the death scene, see Forbes, "Darkness over All the Land," 83–96.

45. Hendricksen, *Matthew*, 970.

46. The entire saying in Mark's gospel is a transliteration of the Aramaic, which would most likely have been what Jesus would have spoken on the cross. The saying in Matthew's Gospel is a transliteration which is partly Hebrew (ηλι ηλι) and partly Aramaic (λεμα σαβαχθανι) (Metzger, *TCGNT*, 2nd ed., 58–59, 99–100), although it is possible that the entire saying is a variation of Aramaic, since the Aramaic targum to Ps 22:1 has ηλι ηλι (see Davies and Allison, *Matthew*, 3:624).

47. E.g., Boring, "Matthew," 492.

will in truth be vindicated in his resurrection, Matthew calls us to ponder deeply his abandonment.[48]

Of the seven cries of Jesus from the cross, this is the only one that Matthew and Mark record, the meaning of which is profoundly difficult to grasp fully.[49] Hagner says of this cry of Jesus, "This is one of the most impenetrable mysteries of the entire Gospel narrative," and "Perhaps it is best simply to let the words stand as they are—stark in their impenetrability to us mortals."[50] Morris points out, "Pious and earnest Christians have always found these words very difficult."[51] And Blomberg comments, "All kinds of theological questions are raised that the text simply doesn't answer."[52]

Matthew does not interpret the meaning, but Jesus's cry does not indicate that his death caught him by surprise, nor does he now see his life as a failure. The mockers think they are laughing at Jesus with clever irony, but Matthew reveals a deeper irony. Matthew and the readers know, and God knows, that Jesus *does* trust in God. The deep irony of this scene (Matt 27:41–43) is that the mockers are speaking better than they know: Jesus does trust God.[53] Neither is this the same cry of victory that will ultimately come from the completion of his atoning sacrifice, which John records (John 19:30).

Matthew's intention is to give us a singular focus upon Jesus's abandonment on the cross. Jesus not only feels abandoned, but he actually is at that infinitely significant moment abandoned by God. Jesus is being subjected to the separation from the Father that must accompany bearing the sin of his people (Matt 1:21; 20:28; 26:28). He now bears the divine retribution and punishment for sin, as the Father's cup of wrath is poured out on him in divine judgment of sin. This is Jesus's realization of his vicarious sacrifice. "He has become the sin offering, and at this dark moment God must turn away from sin."[54]

Not only did Jesus bear the load of humanity's sin, but he became sin on humanity's behalf. In the apostle Paul's words, "God made him who had no sin to be sin for us, so that in him we might become the righteousness of God" (2 Cor 5:21), and, "Christ redeemed us from the curse of the law by becoming a curse for us, for it is written: 'Cursed is everyone who is hung on a pole'" (Gal 3:13).

Jesus's abandonment is horrific, but it is not without purpose.[55] From later theological reflection we understand that Jesus's forsakenness by the Father did not affect

48. Cf. Davies and Allison, *Matthew*, 3:624–25.

49. For a detailed discussion of how Jesus perceived his own death, see McKnight, "Jesus and His Death," 185–228.

50. Hagner, *Matthew 14–28*, 845–46.

51. Leon Morris, *The Cross of Christ* (Grand Rapids: Eerdmans, 1988), 67.

52. Blomberg, *Matthew*, 419.

53. D. A. Carson, *Scandalous: The Cross and Resurrection of Jesus* (Wheaton, IL: Crossway, 2010), 33. For another focus on irony in Matthew's narrative of the passion, see Berg, *Irony in the Matthean Passion Narrative*.

54. Osborne, *Matthew*, 1037–38. Carson gives an insightful treatment of this passage that is especially helpful for lay readers and full of devotional insights for scholars ("The Ironies of the Cross: Matthew 27:27–51a," in *Scandalous*, 13–37).

55. See the helpful study of Eklund, *Jesus Wept*, 42–45.

their ontological relationship; i.e., Jesus was not separated in his essence or nature or substance from the Father. They retained full ontological unity, so the separation did not affect the Trinitarian relationship of the members of the Godhead.[56] Rather, Jesus's divinely sustained humanity experienced consciously the full penalty of death for the sins of humanity. Later theological reflection on Jesus Messiah's divine/human natures as God incarnate help therefore to understand Jesus's very real agony.[57] Earlier he had indicated to the disciples that the purpose of his life's mission was to be a "ransom for many" (Matt 20:28). Here we see that fateful prediction being carried out. This lays the foundation for the theological doctrine of atonement in which Jesus's sacrifice on the cross is one of penal substitution or vicarious atonement—Jesus suffers our punishment for our sin. The penalty for sin is death (Rom 6:23), and in Jesus's separation from God he experiences deathly punishment for the sins of humanity.[58] The cross is the ultimate expression of God's love for humanity.[59]

But even in the depth of Jesus's abandonment to his atoning sacrifice, he still knew that this experience was not one of despair—he still calls the Father "my God, my God." The relational separation while bearing the sins of humanity could not separate him entirely from God because his consummate trust in the Father's will expects that he will not be abandoned forever and because the oneness of their ontology is indissoluble. John-Mark Hart states, "The Father's eternal love for and delight in the Son in the fellowship of the Spirit is the perfection of all beauty, and this divine love has been made known to the world pre-eminently in the vicarious death of Jesus for the redemption of sinners."[60] Hart suggests that the close connection between the concepts of beauty and glory in Scripture reveals how a cruciform theological aesthetic can illuminate our understanding of God, humanity, and salvation—God's triune beauty is most fully revealed in the ugly spectacle of the cross.[61]

#### *14.2.3.5 Jesus Gives Up His Spirit (27:50)*

Now at the very end, Jesus knows that his suffering is nearing its completion. He cries out again in a loud voice. Neither Matthew nor Mark give the content of Jesus's final cry, but the implication is that this is one final agonizing experience of separation

56. Osborne, *Matthew*, 1037–39; contra Jürgen Moltmann, *The Trinity and the Kingdom of God*, trans. Leonard Swidler (Philadelphia: Fortress, 1981), e.g., 77–78, and Moltmann, *The Crucified God*, trans. John Bowden and R. A. Wilson (London: SCM, 1974), e.g., 222–23. For an important critique of Moltmann's view, see Dennis W. Jowers, "The Theology of the Cross as Theology of the Trinity: A Critique of Jurgen Moltmann's Staurocentric Trinitarianism," *TynBul* 52.2 (2001): 245–66.

57. Venard, *La passion selon saint Matthieu*, 36–42, 373.

58. For discussion of the doctrine of the atonement, see the listing of various resources below under 14.2.5, "Theological Reflections on the Meaning of the Death of Jesus Messiah"; also Erickson, *Christian Theology*, 713–68; Grudem, *Systematic Theology*, 707–25.

59. For a very helpful overview of Jesus's ministry culminating in the cross as an act of love, see Bray, *God Is Love*, 559–602.

60. See John-Mark Hart, "Triune Beauty and the Ugly Cross: Towards a Theological Aesthetic," *TynBul* 66.2 (2015): 293–312, here 311.

61. Hart, "Triune Beauty," 301–5, 311–12.

from the Father as he bears humanity's sin punishment. And then "he gave up his spirit" (27:50). Matthew's expression (*aphēken to pneuma*) is the equivalent of Mark's "breathed his last" (*exepneusen*) (Mark 15:37). This is a shorthand representation for the experience of death, but none of the evangelists describes Jesus's death in the usual way of saying that he died, a clue that they viewed his death as singularly unique. Matthew shows that even to the very end Jesus maintained volitional control over his destiny. Jesus approaches his death willingly, which is an indication that there is an important element of voluntariness in his death (cf. John 10:17–18). This points to what John's Gospel makes explicit, that Jesus has come to the recognition that he had paid in full the debt for sin—with a shout of victory Jesus cries out, "It is finished" (John 19:30). John uses a single word in Greek (*tetelestai*) to record this triumph, used often on receipts in this sense of "paid in full."[62] The redemption that Jesus came to achieve was accomplished once for all. As Jesus calls out again with a great cry from the cross, this is one final agonizing experience of separation from the Father as he bears humanity's sin-punishment. And then "he gave up his spirit" (Matt 27:50). This is the final voluntary demonstration of his divine dignity, in which he gives the irrevocable expenditure of his life for the sins of his people.

### 14.2.4 Testimonies to the Theological Meaning of Jesus Messiah's Death

Matthew records several events that follow upon the death of Jesus, all of which give significant historical and theological testimony to explain the impact of Jesus's death. These are spectacular and supernatural replies to Jesus's cry to his Father, "My God, my God, why have you forsaken me?" (27:46): the tearing of the temple veil, an earthquake, the splitting of the rocks and the opening of the tombs, the resurrection of the saints and their appearances to many in Jerusalem (27:51–53).[63] "They are awesome, cosmic signs of God's answer to the prayer of Jesus. With the exception of the tearing of the temple veil, these 'signs' are unique to Matthew's account and reveal his special interpretation of the death of Jesus."[64]

#### *14.2.4.1 Testimony of the Temple's Torn Veil (*Velum Scissum*) (27:51)*

The first testimony comes from the temple, where at the moment of Jesus's death, "the curtain of the temple was torn in two from top to bottom" (27:51). The word for curtain (*katapetasma*) is used in the LXX sometimes of the curtain between the holy place and the most holy place[65] and sometimes of the curtain over the entrance to the

62. "τελέω," LSJ 1772, II.1.b.
63. Tidball, *Message of the Cross*, 134.
64. Senior, *Passion of Jesus*, 141.
65. E.g., Exod 26:31–35; 27:21; 30:6; 2 Chr 3:14.

holy place.[66] The former is more likely here, as its usage elsewhere in the New Testament indicates (Heb 6:19; 9:3; 10:20).[67]

The curtain was an elaborately woven fabric of seventy-two twisted plaits of twenty-four threads each, and the veil was sixty feet high and thirty feet wide (cf. m. Sheqalim. 8.5).[68] It would take a significant rift to tear this imposing veil, so the incident gives momentous testimony to the meaning of Jesus's death on the cross. This tearing of the curtain (*velum scissum*) that separated the holy of holies from the rest of the temple signifies the removal of the separation between God and the people and is a further sign of God's judgment on Israel's temple activity (cf. Matt 21:12–22). The sixty-foot-high curtain was split from top to bottom, which is a sign that God himself abolished the separation from the holy of holies, signifying that the new and living way was now open for all people to enter into the presence of God through the sacrifice of Jesus on the cross (see Heb 10:20; Eph 2:11–22). Since only the priestly aristocracy would have known about the tearing of the veil, when a number of priests only a few weeks later became believers (Acts 6:7), they would have informed the Christian community of the events firsthand.[69]

Jesus's consistent emphasis upon "fulfillment" here reaches its pinnacle. He fulfills all righteousness as he undertakes his earthly ministry (Matt 3:15–17), he fulfills the Law and the Prophets as he authoritatively pronounces its intended meaning (5:17–48), and in his ministry one greater than the temple has arrived (12:6). The tearing of the temple curtain testifies that Jesus's sacrifice on the cross has fulfilled the hopes that had been expressed in Israel's years and years of temple sacrifice. Jesus is the great high priest whose sacrifice is the permanent satisfaction of God's wrath upon humanity's sin (Heb 4:14–5:10). Jesus is the permanently accessible new temple in whom all people who turn to him are reconciled to the Father.

The tearing of the temple curtain from top to bottom testifies to God's activity in Jesus's death of removing the separation between God and his people. No longer is only the high priest allowed access to the holiest of holy places to commune with God. Jesus's sacrifice on the cross fulfills God's righteous demand for the punishment and atonement for sin. No longer are any high priestly sacrifices necessary (Heb 10:10–22). All those who are cleansed from sin by the blood of Jesus are a holy priesthood to God (1 Pet 2:5) and live in his presence constantly through the indwelling of Jesus in our hearts and the ever-present comfort of God's Spirit (Eph 2:11–22; 3:16–17). The tearing of the temple veil (27:51–53) is symbolic of revelation and transformation, which conveys the message of a new era that begins with Jesus's death and resurrection.[70]

66. E.g., Exod 27:37; Num 3:26.

67. The most detailed study of this and the following incidents in 27:51–54 is by Gurtner, *Torn Veil*.

68. Josephus gives a detailed description of the curtain in his *Jewish Wars* (5.212–13).

69. Cf. Keener, *Matthew* (2009), 686–87.

70. Regev, *Temple in Early Christianity*, 198.

### *14.2.4.2 Testimony of Old Testament Holy People Who Are Raised (27:51b–53)*

The second testimony is a complex of earthquakes, splitting rocks, and raised bodies.[71] Matthew says first that "the earth shook, the rocks split" (27:51b). The word for "rocks" is *petrai* (27:51), referring to large rocks, while the word for the "stone" that they rolled in front of Jesus's tomb is *lithos* (27:60). The same word (kiʾpoʾ) is used in the Syriac translations to render both terms.[72] Matthew's language implies that this is a significant earthly reaction to the divine events on the cross. The entire region sits on a major seismic rift. One of the chief geological characteristics of Palestine has been its proneness to earthquakes, especially because the Jordan Rift Valley is part of a very large fault zone that stretches northward from the entrance of the Gulf of Aqaba for over 683 miles to the foot of the Taurus range.[73] An earthquake would not be an unusual event, but coupled with the rocks splitting to open the tombs, this is another significant testimony to the meaning of the events of Jesus's crucifixion. Another earthquake will soon testify to a further significant divine event—Jesus's resurrection (cf. 28:2).[74]

Matthew continues the narration of the events that witness to the significance of Jesus's death by retelling an incident that is found in none of the other gospels: "The tombs broke open and the bodies of many holy people who had died were raised to life. They came out of the tombs, and after Jesus's resurrection they went into the holy city and appeared to many people" (27:52–53). Earthquakes in the Jerusalem region are not infrequent and could easily cause damage to the thousands of tombs in the area because these are tombs carved out of stone, with rocks that block the entrance rather than modern graves beneath mounds of earth. But raising the bodies within can only be attributed to God's direct action, which implies that God is behind the earthquake as well.

Matthew's unique record of these events emphasizes the victory over death that Jesus's sacrifice on the cross accomplished. These who are raised are described literally

71. For a recent thorough study of these events that views them as historical with literary and theological significance, see Johnson, *I See Dead People*. For a study that affirms that 27:52–53 belongs to the earliest text of Matthew, see Charles L. Quarles, "Matthew 27:52–53 as a Scribal Interpolation: Testing a Recent Proposal," *BBR* 27.2 (2017): 207–26. In a somewhat different direction that contends that since these events are not found in Mark or Q, Matthew invented the earthquakes in retelling this story, "but he also thought that they actually had occurred," see Joel Marcus, "Did Matthew Believe His Myths?," in *An Early Reader of Mark and Q*, ed. Joseph Verheyden and Gilbert Van Belle, BTS 21 (Leuven: Peeters, 2016), 217–49. An example of one who doubts the historical basis of these incidents is Ronald L. Troxel, "Matt 27.51–54 Reconsidered: Its Role in the Passion Narrative, Meaning and Origin," *NTS* 48.1 (2002): 30–47.

72. The same term is used to translate both "Peter" and "rock" in 16:18, additional support that the same Aramaic term kēʾpāʾ lies behind them both, since Syriac is a cognate language of Aramaic.

73. See the drawings showing the primary faults in D. R. Bowes, "Earthquake," *ZPEB* 2:178–80.

74. For a careful study of Matthew's emphasis upon earthquakes, see Brian Carrier, *Earthquakes and Eschatology in the Gospel According to Matthew*, WUNT 2/534 (Tübingen: Mohr Siebeck, 2020). Carrier suggests that Matthew contains eight references to seismic activity (8:24; 21:10; 24:7, 29; 27:51, 54; 28:2, 4), the majority of which are found only in Matthew's Gospel; Carrier, *Earthquakes and Eschatology*, 1–35; passim.

as "who had fallen asleep" (27:52, ESV), a common New Testament idiom for a person who has died but whose eternal destiny is secure.[75] Since this is the only record of this incident in Scripture, the exact chronology is difficult to determine, but the supernatural significance is obvious. As with the preceding miraculous testimonies, the supernatural raising of the bodies of these holy ones and their appearances in Jerusalem is striking testimony to Jesus's accomplished work on the cross, and thereafter his resurrection.

The expression "holy people" probably refers to pious Old Testament figures: heroes and martyrs from Israel's history selected to bear miraculous testimony to these events.[76] We might think of the way in which Moses and Elijah were selected to appear with Jesus on the Mount of Transfiguration (17:1–8). But in this case, it is a resurrection of the bodies of these holy people. The references to "holy people" and "holy city" in this context assumes Jewish saints and Jerusalem, respectively, which allows the reader to see that even with the acted judgment of Jesus on the temple leadership and the condemnation of the leadership of Israel in Matt 23–24, Israel remains in God's plans.[77]

The NIV placement of a comma after the phrase "they came out of the tombs" along with the insertion of the conjunction "and" (27:53, NIV84) can imply that the bodies were raised at the time of the earthquake and splitting rocks, and then they later appeared in Jerusalem.[78] It would seem strange to have raised bodies remaining in a tomb for days until they make their appearance. However, the Greek text has no punctuation, and the conjunction does not follow "out of the tombs"[79] (cf. NIV, "They came out of the tombs after Jesus' resurrection").

A better explanation is that a full stop should be placed after the phrase "the tombs broke open" (27:52a), with a new sentence beginning with the next phrase. As such it would then read, "And the bodies of many holy people who had died were raised to life, and, coming out of the tombs after Jesus's resurrection, they went into the holy city and appeared to many people."[80] With this rendering, Matthew indicates a specific sequence: (1) the tombs are opened by earthquakes at Jesus's crucifixion; (2) Jesus is raised three days later; (3) the bodies of these holy ones are raised and they enter the city and appear to many. In this way the miraculously opened tombs at the time of Jesus's death are a prolepsis of the resurrection of Jesus and the bodies of the holy people to follow in a mere three days.[81] Once Jesus is raised and their resurrection

75. E.g., 1 Cor 11:30; 15:18, 20; 1 Thess 4:13–15.

76. Davies and Allison, *Matthew*, 3:633.

77. See Blomberg, *Matthew*, 421.

78. This is the conclusion of Johnson, *I See Dead People*, 62–63; Charles L. Quarles, "Matthew 27:51–53: Meaning, Genre, Intertextuality, Theology, and Reception History," *JETS* 59.2 (2016): 271–86; here 274–76.

79. Remembering that there is no punctuation in the original Greek manuscripts.

80. Cf. John W. Wenham, "When Were the Saints Raised? A Note on the Punctuation of Matthew xxvii. 51–53," *JTS* 32.1 (1981): 150–52; Carson, "Matthew," 650–51; Blomberg, *Matthew*, 421; France, *Matthew*, 1081–82. Osborne, *Matthew*, 1046.

81. For discussion, see Lidija Novakovic, "The Resurrection of the Saints as a Prolepsis of the Resurrection of Jesus: A Reassessment of Matthew's Portrayal of the Risen Jesus," in Runesson and Gurtner, *Matthew Within Judaism*, ECL 27 (Atlanta: SBL, 2020), 347–70.

follows, their appearance to people in Jerusalem is a witness to the efficaciousness of Jesus's work on the cross and the declaration of his victory over death in his—and their—resurrection. This anticipates Paul's teaching on Jesus being the firstfruits of the dead (1 Cor 15:20–23). These raised Old Testament holy people are a powerful testimony to Jesus's work and identity and of the reality of the future, final resurrection.

Some brand this incident as legend,[82] or at best only theological narrative, i.e., theology set forth as history.[83] This is advanced especially because some scholars cannot understand the historical plausibility of these events, which seem to make more sense theologically than historically.[84] However, there is little within any of the events surrounding Jesus's crucifixion that make sense on the normal historical level. These are all unique events that uniformly testify to the most unique acts of God in human history—Jesus's vicarious death on the cross and his vindicated resurrection from death. The darkness of the crucifixion scene, the thirty-foot-high temple curtain being torn from top to bottom, an earthquake that opens tombs, and the resurrection of Old Testament saints are all extraordinary, supernatural testimonies and "confirmation that Jesus is who he had claimed to be and that his ministry stands vindicated before the nation."[85]

Matthew here recalls the imagery of Ezekiel, who prophesied that the Sovereign Lord would open graves and resurrect people to life in the valley of dry bones: "Therefore prophesy and say to them: 'This is what the Sovereign Lord says: My people, I am going to open your graves and bring you up from them; I will bring you back to the land of Israel'" (Ezek 37:12; cf. 11–14).[86] Matthew lets this event stand unadorned because its meaning is clear. Derek Tidball relates, "The raising of these holy ones is a foretaste of the resurrection to which all believers can look forward. Through the death of Jesus a new day has arrived, a day when death has been defeated by death, and resurrection to life eternal has been made possible."[87] Matthew does not answer all the questions that we would like answered about these miraculous events that occur with Jesus's death, but in narrating them he presents a unified testimony to the supernatural confirmation of Jesus's identity and mission. Because of Jesus's death, salvation is a possibility. Because of Jesus's and the holy people's resurrection, victorious life over death is a reality.

82. E.g., Robert J. Miller, "Response: What Do Stories About Resurrection(s) Prove?," in *Will the Real Jesus Please Stand Up? A Debate Between William Lane Craig and John Dominic Crossan*, ed. Paul Copan (Grand Rapids: Baker Books, 1998), 77–98.

83. E.g., Allen, *According to the Scriptures*, 66; Troxel, "Matthew 27.51–54 Reconsidered," 30–47; Boring, "Matthew," 493; Hagner, *Matthew 14–28*, 851; Gundry, *Matthew*, 576–77; Donald Senior, "The Death of Jesus and the Resurrection of the Holy Ones (Mt 27:51–53)," *CBQ* 38 (1976): 312–29.

84. Cf. Hagner, *Matthew 14–28*, 851.

85. Darrell L. Bock with Benjamin I Simpson, *Jesus According to Scripture: Restoring the Portrait from the Gospels*, 2nd ed. (Grand Rapids: Baker Academic, 2017), 391. See also J. Wenham, "When Were the Saints Raised?," 151.

86. Cf. Moyise, *Jesus and Scripture*, 48.

87. Tidball, *Message of the Cross*, 133.

### *14.2.4.3 Testimony from Gentile Soldiers (27:54)*

The third testimony following the death of Jesus is that of the centurion and the guards at the crucifixion scene. The centurion, as his title indicates, is the officer in charge of one hundred soldiers in his company (see on 8:5).[88] He could have been in attendance of the events since Jesus's Roman trial and subsequent flogging and mocking by the soldiers. He had probably witnessed many crucifixions, but the cataclysmic events of the earthquake and opened tombs, plus the manner of Jesus's death, combined to evoke the statement from him and those with him, "Surely he was the Son of God!" (27:54). Mark's statement is quite similar, "Surely this man was the Son of God!" (Mark 15:39), while Luke records that he praised God and said, "Surely this was a righteous man" (Luke 23:47).

Opinions vary as to what the centurion and those with him meant by this exclamation.

*(1) A pagan reaction.* Some suggest that this was a pagan reaction to the dramatic events unfolding, but it does not indicate true faith. They suggest that the expression could best be rendered, "Truly this was a son of a god." The centurion and those with him viewed Jesus merely as a typical Greco-Roman "divine-man" figure, a great human hero deified upon his death. However, the centurion and his men are more likely commenting upon the current Jewish charges against Jesus, not the association with far removed Greco-Roman deities.

*(2) A response of fear.* Others suggest that the soldiers' statement is an acknowledgment of guilt and defeat in the face of the divine. They are greatly terrified (*ephobēthēsan sphodra*), an expression that implies dread much more than worship. These soldiers are the same ones who are explicitly identified by Matthew as the brutalizers and executioners of Jesus, and they are wicked characters right through the passion narrative. "The resurrection of the saints foreshadows the eternal life in store for all the righteous, while the terror and subsequent cry of defeat on the part of the evil soldiers prefigures the attitude of the wicked on the day of reckoning as they learn of the horrible fate in store for them."[89] However, the positive way in which this confession is reported leads Matthew's readers to understand that the centurion and his men are not simply terrified, but are recognizing that Jesus is "surely" or "truly" (*alēthōs*) the Son of God.

*(3) A beginning confession of faith.* A more satisfactory understanding of the centurion's and his men's statement is that as little as they may have really understood, this was a true step of faith. The centurion was gaining an insight to Jesus's true identity. The charge of blasphemy from the Sanhedrin was in part lodged against Jesus's claim

88. Matthew and Luke both have the Greek translation for the title "ruler of a hundred" (*hekatontarchos*), while Mark has a transliteration of the Latin title (*kentyrion*),

89. David C. Sim, "The 'Confession' of the Soldiers in Matthew 27:54," *HeyJ* 34.4 (1993): 401–24. Cf. Shiner, "Ambiguous Pronouncement," 3–22.

to be the Son of God, to which Jesus had responded with an affirmative (26:63–64). The centurion was certain to have known the various charges against Jesus because the military chain of command necessitates that he know about potential uprisings to rescue the convicted Jesus. As he watches the events unfold, the centurion and his men are overwhelmed by the realization that the identification was truthful. He recognizes that Jesus is a man innocent of the contrived charges (Luke 23:47), which then leads to the logical conclusion that he is truly who he claimed to be—the Son of God who sustains a divine relationship to the Ancient of Days as the Son of Man. This is the claim for which Jesus was convicted of blasphemy by the Sanhedrin (Matt 26:63–65). In this Jewish context, the centurion was struck by the confirmation that Jesus has a filial relationship to Israel's God.[90] The meaning of the genitive construction *huios theou* ("son of God") points in the direction of declaring that Jesus is "*the* Son of God," not "*a* son of God" or "*a* son of *a* god.[91]

However much the centurion and his men understood by these words, Matthew's point is clear. He emphasizes for his readers that the reaction of the centurion and his men—"they were terrified"—is the same as that experienced by the disciples at the transfiguration (17:6), and their confession is nearly identical to the conclusion drawn by the disciples at the calming of the sea (14:33). Therefore, the evaluative point of view of these Roman guards agrees with that of God the Father (3:17; 17:5) and Peter (16:16), a confession that is now given publicly.[92]

Matthew has given increasing emphasis to Jesus as Son of God since the Jewish trial that evinced cries of blasphemy (26:63–65). The centurion's evocation is in dramatic distinction from the religious leaders and the bystanders at the cross who had mocked Jesus for his claim to be the Son of God (27:40–43). It is a striking picture for Matthew's readers. The cataclysmic events surrounding the crucifixion testify to Jesus's true identity, and the centurion and his men make a step of faith to acknowledge the truth of that testimony.[93] Turner notes, "Although they do not grasp all that 'Son of God' means in Matthew, their positive response to Jesus implies openness to further Christian witness. Perhaps some will become disciples."[94]

### 14.2.5 Theological Reflections on the Meaning of the Death of Jesus Messiah

Jesus's death is not simply a meaningless fact of history. There is profound meaning in his death, which Matthew has hinted at in his narration of these singularly

90. Nolland, *Matthew*, 1220–21.

91. For a technical discussion of Colwell's Rule and Apollonius's Corollary (to Apollonius's Rule), which point in the direction of the construction being rendered "the Son of God," see Wallace, *Greek Grammar*, 256–70.

92. Kingsbury, *Matthew as Story*, 90

93. Nolland, *Matthew*, 1220–21.

94. Turner, *Matthew*, 671

momentous events. The Gospels are often referred to as theology enacted, whereas the Epistles are theology explained. In the Gospels we find God acting in history in the person of his Son, Jesus Messiah, to accomplish salvation for his people. In the Epistles we find the early church leaders reflecting back and giving inspired theological explanation of what God did in history. Throughout church history believers have had the privilege to reflect both upon the activities of God in Jesus's ministry that accomplished salvation and upon the theological formulations of New Testament authors. This is often referred to as the "work of Christ," which Michael Gorman states is "standard theological shorthand for the saving activity of Jesus of Nazareth—a vast topic, with nearly every verse of the NT and every work of NT scholarship relating to it."[95]

The narrative that Matthew unfolds of the death of Jesus leads to the following theological reflection. The word that is used repeatedly by theologians to capture the meaning of Jesus's death is "atonement" (Heb. *kippur/kippurim*; Gr. *hilastērion*). Robert Yarbrough observes, "'Atonement' may be defined as God's work on sinners' behalf to reconcile them to himself. It is the divine activity that confronts and resolves the problem of human sin so that people may enjoy full fellowship with God both now and in the age to come."[96] Andrew Trotter suggests that the Bible's central message is atonement: "that is, that God has provided a way for humankind to come back into harmonious relation with him. . . . From the first stories in Genesis to the last visions of Revelation, God seeks to reconcile his people to himself."[97] And Scot McKnight states, "The atonement . . . is the good news of Christianity—it is our gospel. It explains how that gospel works."[98]

Oliver Crisp applies it to the next logical question that drives his study of atonement: "*What is the mechanism by means of which Christ's work reconciles fallen human beings to God?*"[99] Atonement is instituted by God to reconcile humans with himself. Moses said to Aaron, "Come to the altar and sacrifice your sin offering and your burnt offering and make atonement for yourself and the people; sacrifice the offering that is for the people and make atonement for them, as the LORD has commanded" (Lev 9:7). Everyone is guilty of sin, including the high priest, and needs atonement that can only be provided by God himself. The Day of Atonement (Heb. *yôm [hak]kippūrîm*, Lev 23:27–28) was the most solemn holy day of all the feasts and festivals God gave to Israel.[100] The high priest carried out elaborate rituals to atone for the sins of the people (16:1–34).[101]

95. Michael J. Gorman, "The Work of Christ in the New Testament," *OHC*, 72–86, here 72.

96. Robert F. Yarbrough, "Atonement," *NDBT* 388.

97. Andrew H. Trotter Jr., "Atonement," *EDBT* 42.

98. Scot McKnight, *A Community Called Atonement*, Living Theology (Nashville: Abingdon, 2007), 1.

99. Crisp, *Participation and Atonement*, 3, his emphasis.

100. Neusner and Green, "Atonement," "Yom Kippur," *DJBP* 65, 684.

101. Mark F. Rooker, *Leviticus*, NAC 3A (Nashville: Broadman & Holman, 2000), 218.

In the New Testament the word "atonement" (*hilastērion*) occurs only three times (Rom 3:25; Heb 2:17; 9:5) and "atoning" (*hilasmos*) only twice (1 John 2:2; 4:10), but the concept of atonement is found in ideas with a wide range of words and their cognates, among them ransom, redemption, covenant, sacrifice, reconciliation, representation, victory, and substitution.[102] Although terms in the Old Testament (*kippūr*; LXX *exilaskomai*) and epistles of the New Testament (*hilastērion*; *hilasmos*) that specify atonement do not occur in Matthew's Gospel, the concept is found throughout. Atonement was a part of the everyday world of Matthew's Gospel.[103] Wayne Grudem defines atonement as "*the work Christ did in his life and death to earn our salvation*,"[104] which broadens the scope of atonement to include all of Jesus's life and death.[105] This encourages us to view all of Matthew's treatment of Jesus's life and death in order to understand the concept of atonement.

Grudem summarizes the atoning work of Jesus's life and death in four expressions that express four needs of humanity as sinful people:[106]

1. We deserve to *die* as the penalty for sin.
2. We deserve to *bear God's wrath* against sin.
3. We are *separated* from God by our sins.
4. We are in *bondage to sin* and to the kingdom of Satan.

These four needs are met by Jesus's life and death in the following ways as found in the narratives of Matthew's Gospel and in the explanations of the Epistles:

---

102. These ideas have resulted in numerous theories as to *how* God accomplished atonement through Jesus's death, among them "Example," "Moral-Influence, "Governmental," "Christus Victor," "Ransom," "Satisfaction," "New Covenant," "Representation," and "Penal Substitution." See Erickson, *Christian Theology*, 714–30; Yarbrough, "Atonement," 389. For a wide-ranging debate concerning "atonement," see Beilby and Eddy, eds., *The Nature of the Atonement: Four Views*. The four views debated are "Christus Victor" by Gregory A. Boyd; "Penal Substitution" by Thomas R. Schreiner; "Healing," by Bruce R. Reichenbach; and "Kaleidoscopic," by Joel B. Green.

103. See John A. Dennis, "Death of Jesus," *DJG*[2] 172–93, here 182–84.

104. Grudem, *Systematic Theology*, 705; his emphasis.

105. Grudem, *Systematic Theology*, 705, 722–24. See also Martin Hengel, *The Atonement: The Origins of the Doctrine in the New Testament*, trans. John Bowden (Philadelphia: Fortress, 1981); William Lane Craig, *Atonement and the Death of Christ: An Exegetical, Historical, and Philosophical Exploration* (Waco, TX: Baylor University Press, 2020); Crisp, *Participation and Atonement*. Other helpful discussions are found in John R. W. Stott, *The Cross of Christ*, 20th anniversary special ed. (Downers Grove, IL: InterVarsity, 2006); J. I. Packer and Mark Dever, *In My Place Condemned He Stood: Celebrating the Glory of the Atonement* (Wheaton, IL: Crossway, 2007); Michael J. Gorman, *The Death of the Messiah and the Birth of the New Covenant: A (Not So) New Model of the Atonement* (Eugene, OR: Cascade, 2014); Tidball, *Message of the Cross*; Carson, *Scandalous*; David L. Allen, *Atonement*; Adam J. Johnson, *Atonement: A Guide for the Perplexed*, Guides for the Perplexed (London: Bloomsbury T&T Clark, 2015); Johnson, ed., *T&T Clark Companion to Atonement*, Bloomsbury Companions 5 (London: Bloomsbury, 2017); Johnson, ed., *Five Views on the Extent of the Atonement*, Counterpoints (Grand Rapids: Zondervan, 2019); Max Botner, Justin Harrison Duff, and Simon Dürr, eds., *Atonement: Jewish and Christian Origins* (Grand Rapids: Eerdmans, 2020); N. T. Wright, Simon Gathercole, and Robert B. Stewart, *What Did the Cross Accomplish? A Conversation about the Atonement* (Louisville: Westminster John Knox, 2021). For a full theological treatment see Demarest, *Cross and Salvation*.

106. Grudem, *Systematic Theology*, 722.

1. *Sacrifice.* Jesus died as a sacrifice for us to pay the penalty of death that we deserved because of our sin (Matt 16:21; 26:26–28; cf. Rom 3:25; Heb 2:17; 9:5, 26).
2. *Propitiation.* Jesus died as an offering for our sins to remove us from the wrath of God that we deserved (Matt 27:46; cf. John 3:36; 1 John 2:2; 4:10).
3. *Reconciliation.* Jesus experienced death and separation from God to overcome our separation from God. He provided reconciliation for us to be brought back into fellowship with God (Matt 26:28, 37–45; 27:46; cf. 2 Cor 5:18–19).
4. *Redemption.* Jesus died to pay the penalty for our sin, and we were redeemed from bondage to sin and Satan so that we now live in newness of life in the Spirit in the kingdom of the beloved Son (Matt 1:21; 20:28; cf. Rom 6:11, 14; Col 1:13; Heb 2:15; 1 John 5:19).[107]

As much as the suffering of Jesus upon the cross baffles our limited understanding, serious reflection yields powerful insights to this which is God's central act of mercy on humankind. The *meaning* of Jesus's suffering and death on the cross is essential for our understanding of the good news of the kingdom of heaven that he announced and that we have the privilege to both proclaim and experience. This leads me to the conclusion that from a biblical-theological perspective that is informed by a systematic-theological perspective, the view of Jesus's life and death as expressed in Matthew's Gospel is most clearly understood as *penal substitution*, i.e., "Christ's death in our place, instead of us."[108] Similarly, James Hamilton concludes, "The center of Matthew's theology is the glory of God in salvation through judgment, supremely manifested in the cross of Christ."[109]

This is my understanding of the *meaning* Jesus's death on the cross. The *results* of Jesus's suffering and death likewise are worthy of our most serious contemplation, to which we now turn.

107. Grudem, *Systematic Theology*, 723–25.

108. Simon J. Gathercole, *Defending Substitution*, ASBT (Grand Rapids: Baker Academic, 2015), 15; Gathercole, "The Cross and Substitutionary Atonement," *SBET* 21.1 (2003): 152–65. See also Packer and Dever, *In My Place Condemned He Stood*; this collection of essays includes the classic and crucial essay by J. I. Packer, "What Did the Cross Achieve? The Logic of Penal Substitution," 53–100; see also Steve Jeffery, Michael Ovey, and Andrew Sach, *Pierced for Our Transgressions: Rediscovering the Glory of Penal Substitution* (Wheaton, IL: Crossway, 2007). For a solid philosophical and theological defense of the suffering of Jesus Messiah as a substitutionary, representational, and redemptive act that satisfies divine justice, see Craig, *Atonement and the Death of Christ*. Entering the systematic theological debate is beyond the scope here of our exploration of a *Matthean* biblical theology, but see the works listed above. For an excellent constructive discussion in which atonement is related to various other systematic categories, see Oliver D. Crisp and Fred Sanders, eds., *Locating Atonement: Explorations in Constructive Dogmatics*, Los Angeles Theology Conference 3 (Grand Rapids: Zondervan, 2015). Penal substitution has been questioned seriously in recent years, and many have undertaken what Crisp and Sanders (*Locating Atonement*, 13) refer to as a sort of *egalitarian approach to atonement doctrine* in which the various models are synthesized (see e.g., Joshua M. McNall, *The Mosaic of Atonement: An Integrated Approach to Christ's Work* [Grand Rapids: Zondervan, 2019]). Brandon Crowe responds to some of what he perceives to be misunderstandings of this model with one central question: "Is *perfect* obedience necessary for eternal life?" He emphasizes that Jesus's unique obedience leads to imputation to us of his perfect righteousness; i.e., our justification before God; see Brandon D. Crowe, *Why Did Jesus Live a Perfect Life? The Necessity of Christ's Obedience for Our Salvation* (Grand Rapids: Baker Academic, 2021), here loc. 233–71.

109. Hamilton, *God's Glory in Salvation*, 380.

### 14.2.6 The Results of Jesus's Death: Boundary-less Discipleship (27:54–66)

The results of Jesus's suffering on the cross are inextricably linked with the meaning of his suffering—his sacrifice for sin, his propitiation of the wrath of God on sin, his reconciliation of sinners to fellowship with God, and his redemption of lost sinners from sin's grip. But here specifically we look at three sets of people who illustrate the results of Jesus's suffering in their lives and point to a central tenet of the life of the kingdom of God in this age—*boundary-less discipleship to Jesus*. And what this teaches us is that, to quote the late Billy Graham, "*the ground is level at the foot of the cross.*"[110] We find a oneness and an equality at the cross that transcends national, cultural, ethnic, gender, social, and political boundaries. In the middle of all the rejection of the passion narrative, these "individuals who do not reject Jesus stand out: the Roman centurion confesses Jesus as Son of God (27:54), women who watch the crucifixion are named (27:55), and Joseph of Arimathea provides Jesus with a tomb (27:57ff.)."[111] Jesus the Son of God is the Messiah for all peoples, who calls all into a personal discipleship to him.

#### *14.2.6.1 Gentiles and Powerful (27:54)*

The first group that seizes our attention is made up of the Roman centurion and his men. These men are gentiles, and they are powerful. They represent the most powerful military and political machine of that time, and one of the most significant of all human history. The centurion is responsible for carrying out the orders of Pilate, who represents the power of the Roman Empire. The centurion is likely the one who supervised Jesus's flogging, who allowed the guards to ridicule Jesus, who ordered the nails to be driven into Jesus's body, who watched with amusement as his guards taunted Jesus with the sour drink, who heard Jesus's own people mock and taunt him, and who had probably watched with some anxiousness about the uprising that might occur. This one being crucified had just a few days earlier been seen as a threat to the peace of Roman-occupied Jerusalem as he entered the city with fanfare.

But as the centurion and his men watch Jesus die and hear his eerie cry to God about his forsakenness, and as they watch the supernatural darkening of the sky, as the temple curtain is torn, the earth shaken and the tombs opened, they are struck with the realization that Jesus just may be who he said he was. And in awe they pronounce, "Surely he was the Son of God!" (Matt 27:54). If this was his beginning confession of trust in Jesus, the centurion came as a pagan and, like the insurrectionist who believed, came to belief as Jesus hung upon the cross and experienced death. Richard Bauckham and Trevor Hart refer to the centurion as "an accidental witness" to the true identity of

110. Franklin Graham, with Donna Lee Toney, *Billy Graham in Quotes* (Nashville: Thomas Nelson, 2011), 90. My emphasis.

111. David B. Howell, *Matthew's Inclusive Story: A Study in the Narrative Rhetoric of the First Gospel*, JSNTSup 42 (Sheffield: JSOT Press, 1990), 158.

Jesus Messiah. They write, "Maybe it was the evident sincerity and pain poured out in those words from the cross that broke through the callus built up by years of exposure to death and degradation and pierced the heart and spirit of the centurion."[112] The cataclysmic events surrounding the crucifixion testify to Jesus's true identity, and the centurion and his men make a step of faith to acknowledge the truth of that testimony, however much is their full understanding.

As a result of these gentile Roman soldiers' acclamation, in principle the way is now open for the task to go and make disciples of all nations (28:19).[113] Matthew has hinted at the salvation of gentiles from the very first verse of his Gospel as he recalled Jesus fulfilling the Abrahamic covenant (1:1). A Roman centurion early in Jesus's ministry had expressed faith in Jesus's ability to heal his servant (8:5–13), and now another centurion steps forward to give a profound declaration of faith in Jesus's true identity. This pagan centurion, representing the most powerful military and political force on earth at that time, has humbly taken a step toward following Jesus.

### *14.2.6.2 Women and Marginalized (27:55–56, 61)*

Not only are gentiles and the powerful among those who move toward Jesus, but we also find that women and marginalized are among Jesus's closest disciples. Women and men were originally created by God as humans who were equal and complementary coworkers in ruling God's creation for him (Gen 1:26–28). But as we saw in my earlier chapter on "Discipleship in Matthew's Gospel" (Ch. 10), in some circles within Judaism, because of misinterpretation of Scripture and cultural bias, women had lost their dignity, value, and worth. Josephus states, "The woman, says the Law, is in all things inferior to the man,"[114] apparently interpreting Gen 3:16 to indicate that women are not only under the authority of men but also have a lower personal status. A widely cited rabbinic prayer reflects an attitude prevalent at least among some of the rabbis: "'Praised [be Thou O Lord . . .] who did not make me a gentile'; 'Praised [be Thou O Lord . . .] who did not make me a boor'; 'Praised [be Thou O Lord . . .] who did not create me a woman.'"[115]

One direct result of Jesus's ministry was the restoration and affirmation of women that God intended from the beginning of creation, as is demonstrated in the following ways:

- Women were equally worthy of Jesus's saving activity (e.g., John 4:1–42).
- Women were called to be Jesus's disciples (Matt 12:48–50).
- Women received instruction and nurture as Jesus's disciples (Luke 10:38–42).

112. Richard Bauckham and Trevor Hart, *At the Cross: Meditations on People Who Were There* (Downers Grove, IL: InterVarsity, 1999), 99.

113. Kingsbury, *Matthew as Story*, 90.

114. Josephus, *Against Apion* 2.201 (Thackeray, LCL).

115. Tosefta Berakhot 6:18 (Neusner).

- Women were part of his ministry team (Matt 27:55–56; Luke 8:1–3).
- Because of their courageous presence at the cross and the empty tomb, women were designated as the first to testify to the reality of Jesus's resurrection (Matt 28:10; Mark 16:7; John 20:17).

For women to be disciples of a great master was certainly an unusual circumstance in Palestine of the first century. Yet here we find another instance of the unique form of discipleship Jesus instituted. While women were not part of the Twelve, several of these women disciples traveled with Jesus and had a significant part in his earthly ministry. Jesus restores and reaffirms to women their dignity and worth as persons who are fully equal to men as humans created in the image of God.[116] He also preserves the male-female distinction of humans, so that they are restored and affirmed in the different roles that God had intended from the beginning. Distinctions among Jesus's disciples relate to function, not spiritual standing or commitment or essential personal worth. Jesus restores and affirms to women the status of being co-laborers with men in God's plan for working out his will on earth.[117]

The following chart notes the Gospels' records of the women at the crucifixion and burial scene, and prepares for their significant role in the resurrection scenes.

| **The Crucifixion** | | | | **Galilee mission** |
|---|---|---|---|---|
| ***Matthew 27:55–56*** | ***Mark 15:40–41*** | ***Luke 23:49*** | ***John 19:25*** | ***Luke 8:1–3*** |
| Many women . . . followed Jesus from Galilee to care for his needs | Some women . . . Many other women who came up with him to Jerusalem were also there. | The women who had followed him from Galilee | Near the cross of Jesus | Jesus traveled about . . . The Twelve were with him, and also some women: |
| 1) Mary Magdalene | 1) Mary Magdalene | | 4) Jesus's mother | 1) Mary called Magdalene, out of whom seven demons were cast |
| 2) Mary the mother of James and Joses | 2) Mary the mother of James the younger and Joses | | 3) Jesus's mother's sister | 5) Joanna, wife of Cuza |
| 3) Mother of Zebedee's sons | 3) Salome | | 2) Mary the wife of Clopas | 6) Susanna |
| | | | 1) Mary of Magdala | Many others |

*continued*

116. See Witherington, *Women in the Ministry of Jesus*, esp. ch. 4; Witherington, *Women and the Genesis of Christianity*, esp. chs. 7, 13–14.

117. This material is developed more fully in Wilkins, "Women in the Teaching and Example of Jesus," 91–112.

| The Burial | | | | |
|---|---|---|---|---|
| ***Matthew 27:61*** | ***Mark 15:47*** | ***Luke 23:55*** | ***John*** | |
| 1) Mary Magdalene | 1) Mary Magdalene | The women who came with Jesus from Galilee | | |
| 2) The other Mary | 2) Mary the mother of Joses | | | |

### *14.2.6.3 Wealthy and Religious (27:57–60, 62–66)*

Gentiles and women, powerful and marginalized, and also the wealthy and religious stand together before the crucified Jesus Messiah. The rich man from Arimathea, named Joseph, requests the body of Jesus and gives it proper burial. Because Joseph is a rich man and a member of the council, his tomb becomes the fulfillment of the proper place for a burial spot for Jesus (Isa 53:9).[118] Matthew's account of the burial of Jesus should be viewed in the light of what Josephus states: during peacetime "even malefactors who have been sentenced to crucifixion are taken down and buried before sunset."[119] Joseph's courage in asking for the body and his service to Jesus are exemplary of what a disciple should do. And as Jesus's disciple, Joseph is a fitting foil for the disciples who had forsaken Jesus. An earlier rich man had walked sadly away when he realized that Jesus must be his sole Master, and that any other "god" of his life, which was his great wealth, must yield to him (Matt 19:16–22). It is harder for a rich man to be saved than it is for a camel to go through the eye of a needle, but as Jesus had declared then, all things are possible with God (19:23–26). And so we see here that God had enabled Joseph to yield to Jesus as Master, become his disciple, and be saved.

This is a remarkable disciple of Jesus. He bucked the religious establishment, he put his life on the line, and he gave over his own family tomb to his Master. This makes a striking contrast to the religious leaders who recall that Jesus had given them the "sign of Jonah" (12:40) and then join forces with Pilate to see to it that a guard secures the tomb (27:62–66). Their aim was to prevent Jesus's disciples, now among them Joseph, from stealing his body and proclaiming a resurrection (27:64). Accordingly, not content to bring Jesus to the cross, the Jewish leaders continue their active opposition against Jesus even after he has died. The example of Joseph is loud testimony that even the

---

118. Focusing on Mark's account, the following article is also helpful in viewing Matthew's account of Jesus's burial: see Craig A. Evans, "'He Laid Him in a Tomb' (Mark 15:46): Roman Law and the Burial of Jesus," in *Matthew and Mark Across Perspectives: Essays in Honour of Stephen C. Barton and William R. Telford*, ed. Kristian A. Bendoraitis and Nijay K. Gupta, LNTS 538 (London: Bloomsbury T&T Clark, 2016), 52–66.

119. Josephus, *Jewish Wars* 4.317 (Thackeray, LCL). For discussion, see Craig A. Evans, "The Testimony of Josephus and the Burial of Jesus," in *Raised on the Third Day: Defending the Historicity of the Resurrection of Jesus. Essays in Honor of Dr. Gary R. Habermas*, ed. W. David Beck and Michael R. Licona (Bellingham, WA: Lexham, 2020), 143–58, here 158.

wealthy and religious, indeed a member of the council, are welcome to the cross and discipleship to Jesus.

### 14.2.7 Conclusion

Matthew's narrative of the death of Jesus Messiah is powerfully transformative as we the audience enter into the experience of Jesus himself but also into the experience of those who were eyewitnesses. Scot McKnight concludes his masterful study of Jesus and his death with these words:

> The death of Jesus protects the followers of Jesus from condemnation and ushers them into being right with God—so that, as an *ecclesial body*, they may worship God, love him, and serve him on earth while they await the final day when they will receive the total redemption of their bodies.[120]

We now turn to the confirmation of the reality of the atonement in Jesus's resurrection: "He has risen, just as he said" (28:6).

## 14.3 THE RESURRECTION OF JESUS MESSIAH

In one of the shortest narratives of his Gospel, Matthew tells a stunning account of Jesus Messiah's resurrection from the dead (28:1–20). The brevity of the resurrection account is almost anti-climactic to the extensiveness of Matthew's overall Gospel account. But like the brevity of the announcement of Jesus Messiah's conception, the resurrection is a well-accepted historical fact for Matthew's readers, so there is no need for extensive narrative. The resurrection is the declaration that Jesus is who he said that he was, that what he came to accomplish at the cross was efficacious, and that he now lives to be the faithful Companion, Master, and Lord to all those who respond to his great commission.

That is what brings the ultimate peace, the forgiveness of sins that reconciles humans to God and humans to humans, a revolution that all of the Roman Empire could never crush. The *pax Romana*, the famed "peace of Rome," was a surface condition imposed by Caesar Augustus and the Roman military might. The kingdom of heaven brings real peace, *pax Dei*, the "peace of God" that transcends all understanding (Phil 4:7), which is a heart and life condition brought about by Jesus's reconciling work on the cross, which has begun for all those who dare to become Jesus's disciples.

Matthew's concluding chapter climaxes the amazing story of Jesus Messiah. He was conceived in a miraculous manner as the Savior of his people. He lived a sensational life

120. McKnight, *Jesus and His Death*, 372, emphasis original.

in the power of the Spirit announcing the arrival of the kingdom of heaven. But he had been tragically betrayed by his own people and crucified by the Roman government. Would that be the end of the story? Indeed not! Jesus Messiah is found missing from his grave. Various explanations are set forth, but Matthew tells in convincing fashion that the only viable explanation for the empty tomb is that Jesus has been raised, just as he had predicted. The angel announces the resurrection, his women followers are the first to witness both the empty tomb and the risen Jesus, the authorities try to concoct a tale to counteract the miracle, and all of his followers now have the commission to proclaim the invitation to enter into a relationship with the risen Jesus as his disciples.[121]

As the astonishing verification of his divine identity as Son of God (Rom 1:4) and of the efficaciousness of his atoning work on the cross, Jesus's resurrection figures prominently in all four Gospels. While we do not have enough of the details to resolve all of the differences between the various accounts of the resurrection found in the Gospels and in Paul (esp. 1 Cor 15:1–8), their variations strengthen the truth that the evangelists are independent witnesses and that they are not attempting to reproduce a concocted deception.[122] The variation has produced numerous counterproposals among skeptics, but as N. T. Wright declares, "The proposal that Jesus was bodily raised from the dead possesses unrivalled power to explain the historical data at the heart of early Christianity."[123] Therefore, each writer should be allowed to present his unique perspective, which adds to the historical plausibility of this most momentous event of history.[124]

---

121. For a helpful overview of Matthew's account of the resurrection of Jesus Messiah, see Kevin L. Anderson, "Resurrection," *DJG*[2] 774–89; esp. 783–84.

122. Cf. Morris, *Matthew*, 733; Hagner, *Matthew 14–28*, 868.

123. Wright, *Resurrection of the Son of God*, 718.

124. The literature on the resurrection is massive, but the following will give the reader a head start. For thorough studies of the historical and exegetical issues, see N. T. Wright, *Resurrection of the Son of God*; Longenecker, *Life in the Face of Death*; Licona, *Resurrection of Jesus*; Christopher Bryan, *The Resurrection of the Messiah* (Oxford: Oxford University Press, 2011); Bruce D. Chilton, *Resurrection Logic: How Jesus' First Followers Believed God Raised Him from the Dead* (Waco, TX: Baylor University Press, 2019); Andrew Ter Ern Loke, *Investigating the Resurrection of Jesus Christ: A New Transdisciplinary Approach*, Routledge New Critical Thinking in Religion, Theology and Biblical Studies (London: Routledge, 2020). Published too late to be evaluated fully, but which looks to be immensely helpful is Gary Habermas, *Evidences*, vol. 1 of *On the Resurrection* (Brentwood, TN: B&H, 2024). The historical reliability of the resurrection narratives is set forth by Blomberg, *Historical Reliability of the Gospels*, 100–110; Craig, "Did Jesus Rise from the Dead?," 142–76; and at a more scholarly level, William Lane Craig, *Assessing the New Testament Evidence for the Historicity of the Resurrection of Jesus* (Lewiston, NY: Edwin Mellin, 1989). On a popular, apologetic level are Gary R. Habermas, *The Resurrection of Jesus: An Apologetic* (Grand Rapids: Baker Book House, 1980); George Eldon Ladd, *I Believe in the Resurrection of Jesus* (Grand Rapids: Eerdmans, 1975); and Josh McDowell and Sean McDowell, *Evidence for the Resurrection: What It Means for Your Relationship with God* (Ventura, CA: Regal, 2009). The theological distinctives of each Gospel are explored by Osborne, *Resurrection Narratives*; Bryan, *The Resurrection of the Messiah*, esp. 45–158; and Anderson, "Resurrection," *DJG*[2] 774–89; For a discussion of the philosophical issues, see Stephen T. Davis, *Risen Indeed: Making Sense of the Resurrection* (Grand Rapids: Eerdmans, 1993); at a more scholarly level, Peter Carnley, *The Structure of Resurrection Belief* (Oxford: Clarendon, 1987). For a skeptical brief overview by a leading Jewish scholar, see Geza Vermes, *The Resurrection: History and Myth* (New York: Doubleday, 2008). For a scholarly book by a Jewish believer in Jesus Messiah that explores various aspects of the Jewish response to the resurrection of Jesus, see Mishkin, *Jewish Scholarship on the Resurrection of Jesus*.

### 14.3.1 The Empty Tomb

Matthew presents the women as coming to the tomb owned by Joseph of Arimathea where Jesus had been laid (Matt 27:58–61) after the end of the Sabbath: "After the Sabbath, at dawn on the first day of the week, Mary Magdalene and the other Mary went to look at the tomb" (28:1). "Dawn" means the first sunrise of the new week. This is in line with the other Gospel accounts, with the women coming early Sunday morning, which is the root of the later practice of Christians gathering on Sunday morning to worship the risen Jesus (e.g., 1 Cor 16:2).[125]

As noted earlier, Jesus repeatedly said that he would be raised "on the third day" (Matt 16:21; 17:23; 20:19). Keeping in mind that the Old Testament regularly reckoned a part of a day as a whole day,[126] which is carried over into early rabbinic thought where a part of a day was considered to be a whole day,[127] we understand that Jesus was in the tomb for part of three days. Dying at approximately 3:00 p.m. on Friday, he was placed in the tomb before sundown (one day). He remained in the tomb all day Saturday (second day),[128] and from sundown Saturday until his resurrection on Sunday morning (third day). So, he was raised on the third day, as he prophesied, and was in the tomb for parts of three days and three nights (see 12:40; 26:16).

### 14.3.2 The Resurrection Appearances of Jesus Messiah

Three elements are common to all four Gospels' resurrection accounts: the empty tomb, the announcement of the resurrection to the women, and the meeting of the disciples with the risen Jesus.[129] When we compile all of the resurrection traditions in the four canonical Gospels, the book of Acts, and Paul's account, there are upward of thirteen actual resurrection appearances. A plausible synchronization of the events surrounding Jesus's resurrection and appearances found in the four Gospel versions, Acts, and Paul's account is as follows in the numbered events. The *resurrection appearances* are starred (*). The events and resurrection appearances found in Matthew's Gospel are placed in **bold**.[130]

125. Cf. Carson, "Matthew," 652–54; Davies and Allison, *Matthew*, 3:663; France, *Matthew*, 406; Hagner, *Matthew 14–28*, 868–69; Keener, *Matthew* (1999), 700; Morris, *Matthew*, 734n3.

126. Cf. Gen 42:17–18; 1 Sam 30:12–13; 1 Kgs 20:29; 2 Chr 10:5, 12; Esth 4:16; 5:1.

127. "A day and a night constitute a עונה (a full day), and part of a עונה counts as a whole עונה" (y. Shabbat, 12a, 15, 17; cf. b. Nazir 5b; b. Pesahim 4.2); cited in Gerhard Delling, "ἡμέρα," *TDNT* 2:949–50.

128. For a unique and helpful study of Jesus Messiah's descent to the dead, see Matthew Y. Emerson, *"He Descended to the Dead": An Evangelical Theology of Holy Saturday* (Downers Grove, IL: InterVarsity, 2019).

129. Morris, *Matthew*, 733; Hagner, *Matthew 14–28*, 868; Osborne, *Matthew*, 1051–57.

130. This reconstruction is suggested in part by J. Wenham, *Easter Enigma*, 139 and passim. For a similar reconstruction see Craig L. Blomberg, *Jesus and the Gospels: An Introduction and Survey* (Nashville: Broadman and Holman, 1997), 354–55; and Walvoord, *Jesus Christ Our Lord*, 239. For a listing of eleven resurrection appearances, see Osborne, *Matthew*, 1054. For scholarly discussion of the appearances in Luke and John (Luke 24:37–42; John 20:25–27; 21:13–15), see J. D. Atkins, *The Doubt of the Apostles and the Resurrection Faith of the Early Church: The Post-Resurrection Appearance Stories of the Gospels in Ancient Reception and Modern Debate*, WUNT 495 (Tübingen: Mohr Siebeck, 2019).

## Sequence of Jesus's Post-Resurrection Appearances and Surrounding Events from the Four Canonical Gospels, Acts, and 1 Corinthians

While we do not have all of the details to make an exhaustive reconciliation of the four Gospels' accounts of Jesus's resurrection appearances and surrounding events, a plausible synchronization of their versions follows:

**(1) Jesus is raised from the dead; a great earthquake; an angel rolls away the stone from the tomb (Matt 28:1)**

**(2) Guards fearful (Matt 28:4); then make report to chief priests (28:11–15)**

**(3a) A group of women come to the tomb near dawn, with Mary Magdalene possibly arriving first (Matt 28:1; Mark 16:1–3; Luke 24:1; John 20:1).**

**(3b) The women are met by two young men who actually are angels, one of whom acts as the spokesman and announces Jesus's resurrection (Matt 28:2–7; Mark 16:4–7; Luke 24:2–8).**

**(4a) The women leave the garden tomb with a mixture of fear and joy, at first unwilling to say anything but then resolve to report to the disciples (Matt 28:8; Mark 16:8).**

(4b) Mary Magdalene may have dashed on ahead, telling Peter and John in advance of the arrival of the other women (John 20:2).

(5) The rest of the women tell of the empty tomb but are not believed (Luke 24:8–11).

(6) Peter and John run to the tomb, having heard the report by Mary Magdalene and the women, and discover it to be empty (John 20:3–5; Luke 24:12).

(7) Mary also returns to the tomb after Peter and John have left, and she sees the angels (John 20:11–13).

(8)* Jesus appears to Mary, although at first she supposed him to be a gardener. Mary wants to cling to Jesus but leaves to report to the disciples that she saw Jesus (John 20:14–18).

**(9)* Jesus meets the remaining women, who worship him. He confirms their commission to tell the disciples, with the reminder of his promise of meeting them in Galilee. The women obey (Matt 28:9–11; Luke 24:8–11).**

(10)* Jesus appears to Peter individually, in or near Jerusalem on the Sunday afternoon of the resurrection day (Luke 24:34; 1 Cor. 15:5).

**(11) Sometime after Jesus's resurrection, the bodies of the holy ones Matthew mentions are raised and they enter the city and appear to many, giving additional testimony to Jesus's resurrection (Matt 27:51b-53).**

(12)* Jesus appears to Cleopas and his unnamed companion on the road to Emmaus. They return to Jerusalem to tell the Eleven (Luke 24:13–35; Mark 16:12–13).

(13)* That same resurrection Sunday evening, Jesus appears to the ten disciples (the Twelve minus Judas and Thomas) and others behind locked doors in the upper room in Jerusalem (Luke 24:36–43; John 20:19–25).

(14)* Sunday evening a week later Jesus appears to the Eleven at the same place in Jerusalem, with Thomas now present (John 20:24–31; 1 Cor 15:5; Mark 16:14).

(15)* Perhaps three days later Jesus appears to seven of the disciples beside the Sea of Galilee (John 21:1–14).

**(16)* Jesus gives his climactic Great Commission to the Eleven (and others?) on a mountain in Galilee, commanding them to make disciples throughout the world (Matt 28:16–20; Mark 16:15–18).**

(17)* Jesus appears to the apostles as well as about five hundred brethren in the hills of Galilee (1 Cor 15:6). Further appearances and teaching by Jesus (Luke 24:44–47; Acts 1:3; 1 Cor 15:6).

(18)* Probably during this time in Galilee, Jesus appears to James, his half-brother (1 Cor 15:7).

(19)* In Galilee and perhaps in Jerusalem, Jesus gives teaching of the things concerning the kingdom of God to his followers that take place over a forty-day period (Luke 24:43–49; Acts 1:3–8).

(20)* Back in the Jerusalem area, Jesus gives his parting instructions to the disciples to await the coming Holy Spirit. He ascends into heaven near Bethany on the Mount of Olives, outside of Jerusalem (Luke 24:50–53; Acts 1:9–12; [Mark 16:19–20]).

(21) The eleven disciples select a replacement for Judas (Acts 1:12–26); gather in upstairs room with the women, Mary the mother of Jesus, and his brothers (Acts 1:12–14).

(22) Fifty days after Passover on Pentecost the Spirit descends on the gathering of believers (Acts 2:1–13).

(23)* Jesus appears to Saul/Paul on the Damascus road some three to five years later (1 Cor 15:8; Acts 9:1–38).

### 14.3.3 Reflections on the Theological Meaning of the Resurrection of Jesus Messiah

For three long hours a great darkness came over the land as Jesus hung upon the cross (Matt 27:45). From the perspective of Jesus's disciples who were hidden away, the darkness must have seemed like a cruel joke. Death seems to have won. Matthew had narrated the beginning of Jesus's ministry in Galilee with a bright promise (4:15–17), but as Jesus hung upon the cross for those three long hours, the bright light went out. The shadow of death once more claimed the land, not just in Galilee of the Gentiles but throughout the earth. The bright hope of salvation that Jesus announced seemed to have been extinguished.

#### *14.3.3.1 Jesus Messiah's Resurrection Is the Confirmation That Death Has Been Conquered, and the Beginning of New Life for All Who Dare to Follow Him*

But the light was not extinguished. At the dawn, or at the shining forth (*epiphoskō*; 28:1) of the new week, the bright light of the sun, the brilliant light of the angel, and the glorious light of the risen Savior greeted the world. And the blessed women disciples could only, appropriately, draw near, hold tight to Jesus's feet, and worship him (28:9). And that was all of the answer they needed. The risen Jesus dispelled all darkness, all fear of death, all of the wearisome burden of sin, and pain, and sorrow. Because he lives, they can face tomorrow.

For twenty chapters Matthew recounted the most wonderful life ever conceived and lived on the face of this earthly planet. Thirty-some wonderful years narrated in twenty mind-boggling chapters. And then Matthew slowed the pace for seven very long chapters to walk with Jesus, almost ponderously, through all of the events of the passion week. Six short days from the triumphal entry to the cross narrated in seven long, painful chapters. And then in one brief chapter, the second shortest in his Gospel, Matthew recounts simply, but elegantly, the resurrection of Jesus Messiah. Twenty short verses declare the really good news that humanity needs to hear—Jesus is alive; it is not a hoax, and he is triumphing over history.

The light of the gospel of the kingdom of heaven was not extinguished with Jesus's death. Indeed, the resurrection of Jesus has overcome the darkness, and the light of his life lived through his disciples is going throughout the world through all of history. This is the message that Matthew presents in his final chapter. We might wish for more details of those final days that the risen Jesus spent with his disciples before his ascension, but Matthew has given us what we need to hear—death is vanquished. Richard Longenecker states, "Death is a stark and haunting reality that is very much a part of the personal story of us all."[131] That was the dark reality that stung the hopes of Jesus's followers and seemed to extinguish them all when he died upon that cross. But in the brief verses of the resurrection story, Matthew dispels the darkness and reignites the hopes with the

131. Richard N. Longenecker, "Introduction," in *Life in the Face of Death: The Resurrection Message of the New Testament*, ed. Richard N. Longenecker (Grand Rapids: Eerdmans, 1998), 1.

only truth that is needed: "Do not be afraid, for I know that you are looking for Jesus, who was crucified. He is not here; he has risen, just as he said" (28:5–6).

It is vital to grasp the truth of the resurrection, as well as Matthew's perspective in giving it to us. The work of the cross culminates Jesus's atoning purpose for his incarnate life and ministry on this earth. That is why Matthew slowed the pace of his narrative. However, the fast-paced resurrection story is the simple but profound confirmation that Jesus's death on the cross succeeded in carrying out his life's work. Once we grasp that truth, we recognize that Matthew need say no more. Indeed, the rest of the New Testament, and our lives, are the rest of the story. Because Jesus lives, *we* can face tomorrow.

As victorious as was Jesus's own resurrection, we too have been raised with him in newness of life. The apostle Paul understood this truth deeply, and declared victoriously, "Don't you know that all of us who were baptized into Christ Jesus were baptized into his death? We were therefore buried with him through baptism into death in order that, just as Christ was raised from the dead through the glory of the Father, we too may live a new life" (Rom 6:3–4).

The resurrection is the confirmation that the darkness of death has been conquered, and that Jesus offers the beginning of new life for all who dare to follow him. That theme is unfolded in Matthew's concluding narrative in a few brief scenes.

#### *14.3.3.2 The Resurrection of Jesus Messiah Fulfills the Deepest Hopes of Humanity*

The expectations of a resurrection of the righteous to new life and the wicked to punishment are well attested in the Old Testament (e.g., Isa 26:19; Dan 12:2) and Second Temple Jewish literature (e.g., 2 Macc 7; 1 En. 102; 2 Bar. 49–51). Resurrection in rabbinic Judaism refers to the concept of all the dead being brought back to life by God on the day of judgment, giving eternal life to the righteous, and consigning the wicked to gehenna. This was a central part of rabbinic belief from the first century after the destruction of the temple in AD 70, with the decline of the Sadducees, who rejected the notion of resurrection (Matt 22:23; Acts 23:8), and the ascendance of Pharisaism, which placed resurrection as a central blessed hope.[132] Belief in the resurrection plays a prominent role in synagogue liturgy, including Amidah (Standing Prayer), with the Shemoneh Esre or Tefillah (Eighteen Benedictions, Prayers), which are recited in all worship services. The prayer of the second benediction praises God as the one who resurrects the dead: "Who is like You, almighty, and who is compared to you, King, who kills and gives life and brings salvation to spring up? And You are reliable to give life to the dead. Praised are You, Lord, who gives life to the dead."[133]

132. E.g., m. Sanhedrin 10:1; b. Rosh Hashanah 16b–17a.

133. See Neusner and Green, "Amidah," "Resurrection," *DJBP* 30–31, 526–27,

But the resurrection of Jesus Messiah has even more far-reaching implications. With his resurrection Jesus is declared with power to be the Son of God (Rom 1:2–6), through whom all peoples of the world now gain access to salvation through his sacrifice on the cross. And with his resurrection this new era of the gospel of salvation is inaugurated with the sending of the Spirit of God at Pentecost. In his life and death and resurrection, Jesus is the exemplar of the new people that will be regenerated and transformed into his image (1 Cor 15; 2 Cor 3:18; Rom 6:1–11; 8:29).[134] What Jesus began with his disciples will be continued as new disciples are made of all the nations because the risen Jesus is ever with us as our Master and Lord (Matt 28:18–20).

### *14.3.3.3 Jesus Messiah's Resurrection Restores Men and Women to Equality of Discipleship to Him*

The crucifixion and resurrection accounts tell us a final number of things about God's purposes for women in the life and ministry of Jesus. We have seen throughout his ministry that Jesus was restoring men and women to a place of equality that had been denied many women in first century Israel (see Matt 12:46–50; 27:55–56).

Matthew focuses only on Mary Magdalene and the "other Mary" (27:61) in his resurrection narrative. Mary Magdalene apparently hailed originally from Magdala (or Tarichaea in Greek). Luke tells us that she is the one "from whom seven demons had come out" (Luke 8:2). Mary Magdalene figures prominently at the crucifixion scene, and even more here in the resurrection scenes, especially in John's account. She is the only woman to appear in all lists of the women who witnessed the crucifixion and resurrection, and she is normally listed first in any listing of the women followers of Jesus.[135] Being listed first demonstrates her prominence in the days of Jesus's ministry, as she was quite likely a leader among the women.

"The other Mary" at the resurrection scene is the mother of James and Joses and is quite possibly to be identified as Mary the wife of Clopas (John 19:25). Her prominent listing implies that she was a woman of some significance within the discipleship band.

We saw above that in Jesus's commissioning of the women as the first witnesses of and to his resurrection, we have one of the bedrock authentications of the resurrection narratives (28:10). Several attendant points are important to note.

First, God was bestowing a special honor on these women. They are exemplary of true discipleship to Jesus, and because of their faithfulness and courage, they are

134. See Carrier, *Earthquakes and Eschatology*, 180–210, who suggests that Matthew's emphasis upon seismic activity leads to the conclusion that collectively they indicate that the life, death, and resurrection of Jesus together represent the partial fulfillment of the OT eschatological day of the Lord.

135. Luke names no women at the crucifixion but does at the resurrection. Interestingly, John reverses the order to have Mary Magdalene last, with Mary Jesus's mother first, but Mary Magdalene is the only woman to be named in John's resurrection account.

| **The Women at the Resurrection** | | | | **Galilee mission** |
|---|---|---|---|---|
| ***Matthew 28:1*** | ***Mark 16:1*** | ***Luke 24:1, 10–11*** | ***John 20:1–18*** | ***Luke 8:1–3*** |
| | | The women (24:1) | | |
| 1) Mary Magdalene | 1) Mary Magdalene | 1) Mary Magdalene (24:10–11) | 1) Mary Magdalene | 1) Mary called Magdalene |
| 2) The other Mary | 2) Mary the mother of James | 5) Joanna | | 5) Joanna, wife of Chuza |
| | 3) Salome | 2) Mary the (mother?) of James | | 6) Susanna |
| | | the others (feminine) with them who told this to the apostles | | |

given the special honor of first witnesses to the empty tomb and the post-resurrection appearances of Jesus. Many scholars consider God's choice of these women as the first witnesses of Jesus's resurrection to be one of the bedrock authentications of the resurrection narratives and the historicity of the resurrection itself.[136] Jesus's appearances to these women with debated status lend credibility to the account because they would be unlikely selections for a fictionalized account trying to be understood as believable. It was only rarely that women were allowed to be witnesses in a Jewish court of law.[137] For these reasons and more, the selection of women as the first witnesses yields high credibility to the resurrection narratives, and to the resurrection itself.[138]

Second, women are restored in Jesus's community of faith to their original status as equal with men because they were both created in the image of God (Gen 1:26–28). The mention of "my brothers" likewise reiterates that all Jesus's disciples are equal in value within the family of faith. And the return to Galilee harks back to the region of "Galilee of the Gentiles" (cf. Matt 4:15–16), preparing the way for Jesus's commission to make disciples of all the nations. The historical precedence of going to Israel (10:5–6; 15:24) has been fulfilled. Now the family of faith includes all those who are Jesus's disciples, from every gender, every ethnicity, and every religion.

Third, women are validated as worthy of the most privileged service in the community of faith, bearing witness to the reality of the risen Lord Jesus. This is an indication that women are restored as co-laborers with men in the community of faith, a role they had been assigned from the beginning of creation (Gen 1:26–28). In Matt 12:49–50,

136. E.g., Osborne, "Women in Jesus' Ministry," 270.

137. Darrell L. Bock, "A Note on Women as Witnesses and the Empty Tomb Resurrection," in *Raised on the Third Day: Defending the Historicity of the Resurrection of Jesus. Essays in Honor of Dr. Gary R. Habermas*, ed. W. David Beck and Michael R. Licona (Bellingham, WA: Lexham Press, 2020), 257–61, here 260. Citing esp. Robert Gordon Maccini, *Her Testimony Is True: Women as Witnesses According to John*, JSNTSup 125 (Sheffield: Sheffield Academic, 1996), esp. 77–79, 161–71, 225–33.

138. For discussion of the broader issues, see Craig, "Did Jesus Rise From the Dead?," 151–55.

Jesus's disciples are called his "brother, and sister, and mother," indicating not only their relationship to him but also their relationship to each other. They are now brothers and sisters of one family of faith. There will still be functional differences within the family, especially with reference to positions of leadership within the family of faith (e.g., 16:16–19; 1 Tim 3:1–15; 5:17–20; Heb 13:17; 1 Pet 5:1–5). But the emphasis is placed upon the equality of all brothers and sisters in Christ. All those who believe on Jesus as the risen Savior are his disciples, his brothers and sisters and serve as co-laborers in the kingdom of heaven.

Fourth, the women are the first to worship the risen Jesus Messiah. The risen Jesus meets the women to confirm the reality of their hopes. He "suddenly" appears to them and gives an ordinary address, "Greetings" (*chairete*), one they must have heard him utter on many occasions but that now prompts them to fall at his feet to worship him. The presence of the risen Jesus turns their fear into worship. By mentioning that they "clasped his feet" (Matt 28:9), Matthew subtly emphasizes that this is no mere spiritual vision but a physical resurrection. And their recognition of that fact tells the women something about Jesus that evokes their most profound adoration. The term used for "worship" (*proskyneō*) in Matthew can either indicate kneeling before an esteemed religious figure (e.g., 8:2) or, when linked with the action of grasping of feet, indicate worship. By allowing this act of worship here and in 28:17, something that neither angels (Rev 22:8–9) nor apostles will allow (Acts 10:25–26; 14:11–15), Jesus accepts the acknowledgment of his deity. Only God is to be worshiped (cf. Matt 4:9–10; 14:33; Rev 22:9), and these women now prostrate themselves before the Risen One who is rightly to be accorded that honor.

These women are exemplary of what it means to be faithful disciples of Jesus Christ, who battle through the fears and the uncertainties to be obedient to God's will for their lives. As such, they are held up, along with the Twelve and other very human disciples like Joseph of Arimathea and Nicodemus, and Mary and Martha and Lazarus, as examples of what is to be accomplished in Jesus's final commission, to "make disciples of all the nations."

### *14.3.3.4 Jesus Messiah's Resurrection Outlives Hoaxes*

Matthew wants his readers to know that from the very beginning there were attempts to cover the truth of Jesus's resurrection. No one could deny the stark reality of an empty tomb. Therefore, those who had the most to lose were forced to come up with a story to account for the empty tomb.

The chief priests had much to lose because Jesus's resurrection went against their Sadducean theology that denied the resurrection (Matt 22:23). Their commitment to their theology forced them to deny anything that went contrary to it. So, they denied the accounts of Jesus's bodily resurrection. It also threatened their personal security.

If it really was true that Jesus was the Messiah, the people would turn on them for having him executed. And it threatened their position of authority as religious leaders.

The guards also had much to lose. All that the guards knew was that the tomb was empty. They only had hardly believable stories of an earthquake, the stone being rolled back, and some bright, shiny creature confronting them. After that they had no recollection. They had become like dead men, which implies that they had either fainted dead-away, or that they were so gripped with terror and shock that they were incapacitated. Either way, they had committed a serious dereliction of duty and were facing the most severe punishment—execution—for failing to secure an enemy site while in occupied territory. Their desperation forced them to cooperate with the Jewish leaders' ruse.

Matthew writes upward of thirty years after these events, and yet he states, "And this story has been widely circulated among the Jews to this very day" (28:15). This Matthean aside indicates that there was an active attempt by the Jewish leaders to counteract the increasingly widespread declaration that Jesus had been raised from the dead in vindication of his claim to be Messiah. Had Matthew simply invented the story to try to perpetuate a mythic resurrection, all the religious leaders needed to do was to produce Jesus's body. Nearly a century later the rumor was still being spread among the Jews, as is evident in the writings of Justin Martyr (*Dial.* 108.2).[139] The truth is often harder for a person to believe than a lie, and many then, and even now, still fall for this conspiracy to avoid the radical truth of Jesus's resurrection. The empty tomb continued to stare blankly in the face of the Jewish leaders, who could only hope that some are foolish enough to prefer their pathetic rumor over the history-altering truth of Jesus's resurrection.

### *14.3.3.5 The Risen Master Continues to Disciple His Disciples Through Matthew's Manual on Discipleship*

Jesus's thundering Great Commission which, in its unique emphases, graces the conclusion to Matthew's Gospel. We have discussed the Great Commission earlier in Ch. 10 on Discipleship in Matthew's Gospel, but here we offer a few concluding thoughts on the Great Commission as outward-, inward-, and upward-looking.

***Outward-looking.*** The Great Commission is obviously outward-looking because of its impelling missionary thrust to make disciples of all nations. The world out there

139. Evidence of disparaging stories about Jesus circulating in Jewish circles occurs even much later. One example is Sefer Toledot Yeshu (The Book of the Life of Jesus), which has accounts of Jesus's disgraceful death and concocted stories of Jesus's resurrection which are undermined by discovering Jesus's body. Scholars debate whether Toledot Yeshu is an ancient or medieval work, but many suggest that it displays evidence of being an antique tradition as well as being a medieval and early modern text. See discussion in Michael Meerson and Peter Schäfer, eds. and trans., *Toledot Yeshu: The Life Story of Jesus*, 2 vols. and database, Texts and Studies in Ancient Judaism 159 (Tübingen: Mohr Siebeck, 2014), esp. 3–27, 92–103.

is lost and dying without a Savior. Jesus's final Great Commission makes sure that we do not become ingrown or complacent or callous. We must turn and look outward and bring the good news of the gospel of the kingdom of heaven to the people of all the nations that alone will save them. Matthew's Gospel is a powerful recounting of how Jesus Messiah entered history with the purpose of redeeming lost humanity. His life mission to the world becomes our example as we go out with his passionate love for lost people.

***Inward-looking.*** The Great Commission is also inward-looking because it speaks to the ongoing transformation of those who have become disciples of Jesus from out of the world. It is inward because individual disciples consider their own personal discipleship transformation as they are united in baptism to Jesus and to his community of faith and as they yield their obedience to all that Jesus commanded. Only this obedience will produce transformation into the likeness of Jesus.

But this cannot be accomplished alone. More mature disciples are to teach other disciples how it is that they are to obey all that Jesus commanded. The community of disciples looks within itself to provide modeling, physical examples, compassionate encouragement, structured and informal teaching of Jesus's life and words, in the process of teaching other disciples how to obey all that Jesus commanded. All the other Gospels, and the rest of New Testament, and indeed all of Scripture is a ready resource.

But Matthew's Gospel is an essential manual of discipleship because its very structure of alternating narrative and discourse lays before individual disciples and the discipleship community the most extensive collection of Jesus's commands in word and deed to be found anywhere in the New Testament.

***Upward Looking.*** The Great Commission is also upward-looking because disciples are to have only the risen and ascended Jesus as Master, Teacher, and Lord. No other master is ever to supplant Jesus, and we are never to consider ourselves to be masters of any other disciples. That is one of the radical departures of Jesus's form of discipleship from other forms in the ancient world (cf. Matt 23:8–10). What makes this possible is that Jesus promises to be with us always, to the very end of the age (28:20). Matthew's Gospel assures us that as we walk with Jesus through this world and throughout this age, he continually provides for us the example of life, and the guidance of his words, and the supply of his power, to transform continually our lives from the inside-out until he comes again in power and glory to establish fully his kingdom on the earth. Until he comes, he alone is our ever-present Master and Lord.

#### *14.3.3.6 The Risen Jesus Messiah Is with Us, His Disciples, Always, to the Very End of the Age*

Jesus's entrance to history is encapsulated in the name Immanuel, "God with us" (1:23), and when even two or three of his disciples are gathered in his name, "there [is he] among them" (18:20, ESV), and his abiding presence with his disciples throughout history is pronounced in his concluding assurance, "I am with you always, to the very end of the age" (28:20). A true Israelite would proclaim only God to be eternal and omnipresent, so here Matthew records a concluding claim by Jesus to his deity, as he is with his disciples forever. Therefore, Matthew concludes his Gospel with the crucial element of discipleship: the presence of the Master.[140] Both those who obey the Commission and those who respond to the Commission are comforted by the awareness that the risen Jesus will continue to fashion all his disciples, which points to the timeless abiding fact of Jesus with us that sustains our discipleship throughout the extent of this age.

We worship and follow a risen Master who is with us constantly. All that he commanded in word and deed that is necessary for our growth as his disciples is included in the written documents of Scripture, but his very real presence comforts us and sustains us through all of our days, whether in our weakness, sorrow, joy, power, or pain. To the "very end of the age" or until the completion of God's plans for this age, Jesus promises to be the sustaining presence that assures us that history is not out of control, that the kingdom of heaven has indeed been inaugurated, that he is a very present help in times of trouble, and that the work that he accomplished on the cross to bring salvation to humanity is continually available through his risen and ascended ministry.

We may be keenly aware that Jesus is not here with us in a bodily fashion. But he is with us moment by moment as our omnipresent God—the always present risen Jesus Messiah. Matthew affirms Jesus as always present. He never articulates precisely how this is, and, as Bockmuehl states it, Matthew refuses to materialize or localize that presence with any narrowly sacramental focus. "Nevertheless, between the two endpoints of his great *inclusio* of 'God with us' (1:23–28:20), the cumulative effect of his narrative delivers an affirmation of presence far stronger and richer than the religious commonplace of anonymous divine providence or assistance."[141]

This wonderful promise of Jesus's continual presence invites us as readers into the story. This should not evoke fear or a guilty conscience but rather should spur all his disciples on to proclaim the good news of the presence of the kingdom of God in our lives. We are the ongoing chapter of this gospel story, walking receptacles of the presence of the risen Jesus and living demonstrations of the power of the kingdom of God in our lives.[142] May we be faithful and obedient disciples of Jesus Messiah as we walk in the closest intimacy with him and proclaim this good news that he is with us, in all that includes, to the very end of the age.

140. For discussion of the "I am with you" theme here, see Kupp, *Matthew's Emmanuel*, 176–200.

141. Bockmuehl, "Gospels on the Presence of Jesus," 87.

142. M. Green, *Message of Matthew*, 322–23.

## 14.4 Conclusion: Jesus Messiah Is the Crucified One Who Now Lives as the Risen One

The angel's message to the women disciples is designed to dispel the darkness that the pall of death held over them. They had witnessed firsthand Jesus's death on the cross and his body being carried away and placed in a tomb. Now as they approach the tomb in the murkiness of dawn, an earthquake rocks the area, the stone is discovered rolled away, fearsome Roman guards lie like dead men on the ground, and a brilliantly lit angelic figure appears to them.

Their whole world had come crashing down with the death of their Master, but now the angelic figure says, "Do not be afraid, for I know that you are looking for Jesus, who was crucified" (28:5). It is not enough to seek a crucified leader. Perhaps the followers of the insurrectionists between whom Jesus had been crucified likewise sought the place where their crucified leaders had been buried on the late afternoon before the Sabbath. They likewise would fear retribution for seeking their executed leaders. The women disciples of Jesus had come to seek him in whom they had placed their hopes of being the Coming One to whom John the Baptist had pointed but who is now merely Jesus, the Crucified One.

But the brilliantly lit angelic figure adds the message that will dispel the women disciples' fear, and the fear of Jesus's followers for all of history: "He is not here; he has risen, just as he said. Come and see the place where he lay" (28:6). The resurrection of Jesus—bodily, physically—is held out as the only hope that will dispel their fears and bring a new hope in the one whom they had trusted Jesus to be.

It is important to see the relationship between the resurrection and crucifixion. According to the apostle Paul, Jesus as the Crucified One was the center of his message to the Corinthians (see 1 Cor 2:2, where a similar form is used)—Jesus remains the Crucified One. Matthew has demonstrated how powerful the significance of the cross is, and he does not negate that fact. Although the angel announces that Jesus has been raised, this does not mean that he was un-crucified.

The women were seeking Jesus as the one who had been crucified, but he is no longer there in that state. He is not there solely as the Crucified One; he has departed as the Risen One. Still, later Christian reflection continues to acknowledge Jesus as the crucified Christ, a central focus of the gospel message (cf. 1 Cor 1:23; 2:2; Gal 3:1).

Without the resurrection we who believe in Jesus are to be pitied, because there is no confirmation that the crucifixion was efficacious. But without the crucifixion we are hopeless because there is no forgiveness of sins. The apostle Paul declares: "If Christ has not been raised, your faith is futile; you are still in your sins. Then those also who have fallen asleep in Christ are lost. If only for this life we have hope in Christ, we are to be pitied more than all men" (1 Cor 15:17–19). The Crucified One is victorious because he is the Risen One, and we are no longer in our sins because Jesus is both crucified and risen, and because he is both, we have a tangible, real hope.[143] Paul says that Jesus "was delivered over to death for our sins and was raised to life for our justification" (Rom 4:25). Gavin Ortlund declares starkly, "Our salvation consists of both a bloody cross and an empty tomb, both a Friday afternoon's agony and a Sunday morning's vindication—and the latter is not merely proof of the gospel, but part of the gospel."[144] The line of reasoning is that Jesus acted vicariously on our behalf not only in dying but in living and in rising as well. In this way we will speak not only of the vicarious death of Jesus Messiah but also comprehensively of the vicarious resurrection of Jesus Messiah.[145]

Therefore, on a penal substitutionary understanding of the atonement, the resurrection of Jesus is organically connected with his atoning death. Jesus's resurrection is a dramatic divine ratification of the efficacy of Jesus's atoning death, but Jesus's resurrection is also more directly a necessary consequence of his complete satisfaction of divine justice on our behalf.[146] William Lane Craig states, "The penalty of death having been fully paid, Jesus can no longer be justly held by it: he must rise from the dead."[147] The resurrection is not just proof of Jesus Messiah's deity or confirmation of his sacrifice. It foretells the transformation of the world. By the resurrection Jesus became the cause of salvation and transformation. Those who die with him share life with him.[148] Clark Pinnock asserts, "The resurrection inaugurated—first for Jesus, then for us—the new creation. The resurrection states that the forces of evil will not prevail. It gives a glimpse of new creation and signifies a glorified existence in human nature in a new environment where what we were meant to be can be realized."[149]

Those are powerful words about the most powerful events of history. Matthew's Gospel spells out clearly that Jesus Messiah is the Crucified One who now lives as the Risen One. And because he lives, we too now truly live.

143. For a very helpful recent treatment of this resurrection theme, see W. Ross Hastings, *The Resurrection of Jesus Christ: Exploring Its Theological Significance and Ongoing Relevance* (Grand Rapids: Baker Academic, 2022).

144. Ortlund, "Resurrected as Messiah," 751.

145. Clark H. Pinnock, *Flame of Love: A Theology of the Holy Spirit*, foreword and commentary by Daniel Castelo, 2nd ed. (Downers Grove, IL: InterVarsity, 2022), 110–11.

146. William Lane Craig, "On the Organic Connection Between Jesus' Atoning Death and Resurrection," in Beck and Licona, *Raised on the Third Day* (Bellingham, WA: Lexham Press, 2020), 89–104, here 104.

147. Craig, "Organic Connection," 104.

148. Pinnock, *Flame of Love*, 112.

149. Pinnock, *Flame of Love*, 112. Similarly, Stephen T. Davis, "Resurrection and Meaning," in *Risen Indeed: Making Sense of the Resurrection* (Grand Rapids: Eerdmans, 1993), ch. 10. Comparably, Jeff Brannon emphasizes that in the biblical narrative the biblical-theological categories of creation, fall, and redemption correspond with the themes of life, death, and resurrection: M. Jeff. Brannon, *The Hope of Life After Death: A Biblical Theology of Resurrection*, ESBT (Downers Grove, IL: InterVarsity, 2022), loc. 76–89, Kindle.

*Chapter 15*

# MISSION AND COMMISSION IN MATTHEW'S GOSPEL

## *Transformational Discipling of the Nations*

### BIBLIOGRAPHY

**Ådna, Jostein.** "The Mission to Israel and the Nations: The Understanding of Mission in the Gospel of Matthew Reconsidered." Pages 45–60 in *The Church and Its Mission in the New Testament and Early Christianity: Essays in Memory of Hans Kvalbein*. Edited by David E. Aune and Reidar Hvalvik. WUNT 404. Tübingen: Mohr Siebeck, 2018. **Akin, Daniel L., Benjamin L. Merkle, and George G. Robinson.** *40 Questions About the Great Commission*. 40 Questions Series. Grand Rapids: Kregel, 2020. **Allison, Dale C., Jr.** "Deconstructing Matthew." Pages 237–49 in *Studies in Matthew: Interpretation Past and Present*. Grand Rapids: Baker Academic, 2005. **Balabanski, Vicky.** "Mission in Matthew against the Horizon of Matthew 24." *NTS* 54.2 (2008): 161–75. **Bauer, David R.** "The Theme of Mission in Matthew's Gospel from the Perspective of the Great Commission." *The Asbury Journal* 74.2 (2019): 240–76. **Bird, Michael F.** *Jesus and the Origins of the Gentile Mission*. LNTS 331. London: T&T Clark, 2006. **Brands, Michael.** *The Life and Ministry of Jesus as Enactment of the Great Commission: A New Proposal for Interpreting Matthew 28:16–20 in Light of Matthew's Gospel*. Lewiston, NY: Mellen, 2015. **Brindle, Wayne A.** "'To the Jew First': Rhetoric, Strategy, History, or Theology." *BSac* 159 (2002): 221–33. **Brown, Schuyler.** "The Mission to Israel in Matthew's Central Section (Mt 9:35–11:1)." *ZNW* 69 (1978): 73–90. **Chan, Sam.** *Evangelism in a Skeptical World: How to Make the Unbelievable News About Jesus More Believable*. Grand Rapids: Zondervan, 2018. **Clark, Kenneth W.** "The Gentile Bias in Matthew." *JBL* 66 (1947): 165–72. **Donaldson, Terence L.** *Gentile Christian Identity from Cornelius to Constantine: The Nations, the Parting of the Ways, and Roman Imperial Ideology*. Grand Rapids: Eerdmans, 2020. ———. "'Nations,' 'Non-Jewish Nations,' or 'Non-Jewish Individuals': Matthew 28:19 Revisited." Pages 169–94 in *Matthew Within Judaism: Israel and the Nations in the First Gospel*. Edited by Anders Runesson and Daniel M. Gurtner. ECL 27. Atlanta: SBL Press, 2020. **Foster, Paul.** *Community, Law and Mission in Matthew's Gospel*. WUNT 2/177. Tübingen: Mohr Siebeck, 2004. **Freyne, Seán.** *The Twelve: Disciples and Apostles. A Study in the Theology of the First Three Gospels*. London:

Sheed and Ward, 1968. **Hare, Douglas R. A.** *The Theme of Jewish Persecution of Christians in the Gospel According to St. Matthew.* Cambridge: Cambridge University Press, 1967. **Hare, Douglas R. A., and Daniel J. Harrington.** "Make Disciples of All the Gentiles." *CBQ* 37 (1975): 359–69. **Jackson, Glenna S.** *Have Mercy on Me: The Story of the Canaanite Woman in Matthew 15.21–28.* JSNTSup 228. London: Sheffield, 2002. **Juel, Donald.** "The Mission Theology of Matthew." Pages 233–54 in *The Biblical Foundations for Mission.* Edited by Donald Senior and Carroll Stuhlmueller. Maryknoll, NY: Orbis, 1983. **Keener, Craig S.** "Matthew's Missiology: Making Disciples of the Nations (Matthew 28:19–20)." *Asian Journal of Pentecostal Studies* 12.1 (2009): 3–20. **Kio, Stephen Hre.** "Understanding and Translating 'Nations' in Mt 28:19." *The Bible Translator* 41.2 (1990): 230–39. **Klauber, Martin I. and Scott M. Manetsch,** eds. *The Great Commission: Evangelicals and the History of World Missions.* Nashville: B&H, 2008. **Kok, Jacobus, Tobias Nicklas, Dieter T. Roth, and Christopher M. Hays,** eds. *Sensitivity to Outsiders: Exploring the Dynamic Relationship between Mission and Ethics in the New Testament and Early Christianity.* WUNT 2/364. Tübingen: Mohr Siebeck, 2013. **Konradt, Matthias.** *Israel, Church and the Gentiles in the Gospel of Matthew.* Translated by Kathleen Ess. BMSSEC. Waco, TX: Baylor University Press, 2014. **Köstenberger, Andreas J., with T. Desmond Alexander.** *Salvation to the Ends of the Earth: A Biblical Theology of Mission.* 2nd ed. NSBT 53. Downers Grove, IL: 2020. **Kvalbein, Hans.** "Has Matthew Abandoned the Jews? A Contribution to a Disputed Issue in Recent Scholarship." Pages 44–62 in *The Mission of the Early Church to Jews and Gentiles.* Edited by Jostein Ådna and Hans Kvalbein. WUNT 2/127. Tübingen: Mohr Siebeck, 2000. **Larkin, William J., Jr.** "Mission." *EDBT* 534–38. **Lészai, Lehel.** "The Mission of the Disciples." *Sacra Scripta* 9.1 (2011): 65–83. **Levine, Amy-Jill.** *The Social and Ethnic Dimensions of Matthean Salvation History: "Go Nowhere Among the Gentiles" (Matt 10:5b).* SBEC 14. Lewiston, NY; Queenston, Canada; Lampeter, UK: Edwin Mellen, 1988. **Meier, John P.** "Salvation-History in Matthew: In Search of a Starting Point." *CBQ* 37 (1975): 203–15. **———.** "Nations or Gentiles in Matthew 28:19?" *Catholic Biblical Quarterly* 39.1 (1977): 94–102. **Ng, Esther Yue L.** "Matthew 5:17–20 and 'A Tale of Two Missions'?" Pages 201–21 in *New Testament Theology in Light of the Church's Mission: Essays in Honor of I. Howard Marshall.* Edited by Jon C. Laansma, Grant Osborne, and Ray Van Neste. Eugene, OR: Cascade, 2011. **Park, Eugene Eung Chun.** *The Mission Discourse in Matthew's Interpretation.* WUNT 2/81. Tübingen: J. C. B. Mohr (Paul Siebeck), 1995. **———.** "Cynic Itinerant Philosophers and Galilean Wandering Missionaries in Matthew." Pages 125–139 in *Reading a Tendentious Bible: Essays in Honor of Robert B. Coote.* Edited by Marvin L. Chaney, Uriah Y. Kim, and Annette Schellenberg. Hebrew Bible Monographs 66. Sheffield: Sheffield Phoenix, 2014. **Paschke, Boris.** *Particularism and Universalism in the Sermon on the Mount: A Narrative-Critical Analysis of Matthew 5–7 in the Light of Matthew's View on Mission.* NTAbh NS 56. Münster: Aschendorff, 2012), 45–57. **Powell, Mark Allan.** *God With Us: A Pastoral Theology of Matthew's Gospel.* Minneapolis: Fortress, 1995. **Repschinski, Boris.** "'For He Will Save His People from Their Sins' (Matthew 1:21): A Christology for

Christian Jews." *CBQ* 68.2 (2006): 248–67. **Sarma, Bitrus A.** *Hermeneutics of Mission in Matthew: Israel and the Nations in the Interpretive Framework of Matthew's Gospel*. Carlisle, UK: Langham, 2015. **Schmidt, Frederick W.** "Jesus and the Salvation of the Gentiles." Pages 97–105 in *Through No Fault of their Own? The Fate of Those Who Have Never Heard*. Edited by William V. Crockett and James G. Sigountos. Grand Rapids: Baker, 1991. **Schnabel, Eckhard J.** "The First Gospel and Matthew's Mission: Narrative, Theological and Historical Perspectives." Pages 1–20 in *Society of Biblical Literature 2005 Seminar Papers*. SBLSP 44. Atlanta: Society of Biblical Literature, 2005. ———. *Jesus and the Twelve*. Vol. 1 of *Early Christian Mission*. 2 vols. Downers Grove, IL: InterVarsity, 2004. **Scott, J. Julius.** "Gentiles and the Ministry of Jesus: Further Observations on Matt. 10:5–6; 15:21–28." *JETS* 33.2 (1990): 161–69. **Senior, Donald, and Carroll Stuhlmueller.** *The Biblical Foundations for Mission*. Maryknoll, NY: Orbis, 1983. **Sim, David C.** "The Gospel of Matthew and the Gentiles." *JSNT* 17.57 (1995): 19–48. ———. "Matthew, Paul and the Origin and Nature of the Gentile Mission: The Great Commission in Matthew 28:16–20 as an Anti-Pauline Tradition." *HvTSt* 64.1 (2008): 377–92. **Stuhlmacher, Peter.** "Matt 28:16–20 and the Course of Mission in the Apostolic and Postapostolic Age." Pages 17–43 in *The Mission of the Early Church to Jews and Gentiles*. Edited by Jostein Ådna and Hans Kvalbein. WUNT 2/127. Tübingen: Mohr Siebeck, 2000. **Tanner, J. Paul.** "The 'Outer Darkness' in Matthew's Gospel: Shedding Light on an Ominous Warning," *BSac* 174 (2017): 445–59. **Tucker, Brian J.** "Matthew's Missional Particularism and the Continuation of Gentile Social Identity." *Canadian-American Theological Review* 5.1 (2016): 15–24. **Vine, Cedric E. W.** *Jesus and the Nations: Discipleship and Mission in the Gospel of Matthew*. Eugene, OR: Pickwick, 2022. **Von Dobbeler, Axel.** "Die Restitution Israels und die Bekehrung der Heiden: Das Verhältnis von Mt 10,5b–6 und Mt 28,18–20 unter dem Aspekt der Komplementarität: Erwägungen zum Standort des Matthausevangeliums." *ZNW* 91 (2000): 18–44. **White, Benjamin L.** "The Eschatological Conversion of 'All the Nations' in Matthew 28.19–20: (Mis)reading Matthew through Paul." *JSNT* 36.4 (2014): 353–82. **Wick, Peter.** "Verborgenes und Befohlenes: Schriftgelehrsamkeit und Jüngerschaft bei Matthäus. Exegetische Beobachtungen zum Verhältnis von Theorie und Praxis und Perspektiven für die Ausbildung in den kirchlichen Dienst im heutigen (hoch)schulpolitischen Umfel." Pages 132–44 in *Schriftgelehrsamkeit und Toraethik: Die Bergpredigt im Kontext des Matthäusevangeliums*. Edited by Jens-Christian Maschmeier. Stuttgart: Kohlhammer, 2021. **Wilcox, Max.** "Jesus in the Light of his Jewish Environment." *Aufstieg und Niedergang der Römischen Welt, II*, 25, 1. Edited by H. Temporini and W. Haase. Berlin: de Gruyter, 1982. **Wilkins, Michael J.** "The Consideration of a Future for Israel in the Light of the Apparently Bleak Consequences for Negative Responses to Jesus's Ministry in the Gospel of Matthew." Pages 313–40 in *The Future Restoration of Israel: A Response to Supersessionism*. Edited by Stanley E. Porter and Alan E. Kurschner. McMaster Biblical Studies 10. Hamilton, Ontario: McMaster Divinity College Press, 2023. **Willitts, Joel.** "The Friendship of Matthew and Paul: A Response to a Recent Trend in the Interpretation of Matthew's Gospel." *HvTSt* 65.1 (2009): art. #151. https://doi.org

/10.4102/hts.v65i1.151. **Wright, Christopher J. H.** *The Mission of God: Unlocking the Bible's Grand Narrative.* Downers Grove, IL: InterVarsity, 2006. ———. *The Mission of God's People: A Biblical Theology of the Church's Mission.* BTL. Grand Rapids: Zondervan, 2010. **Ziethe, Carolin.** *Auf seinen Namen werden die Volker hoffen: Die matthäische Rezeption der Schriften Israels zür Begründung des universalen Heils.* BZNW 233. Berlin: de Gruyter, 2018.

## 15.1 Introduction: Mission and Commission in Matthew's Gospel

Missiologist and biblical scholar Christopher Wright states, "*The whole Bible is itself a 'missional' phenomenon.*"[1] He goes on to clarify his statement: "The writings that now comprise our Bible are themselves the product of and witness to the ultimate mission of God. The Bible renders to us the story of God's mission through God's people in their engagement with God's world for the sake of the whole of God's creation."[2]

Furthering that thought, I understand the Gospel of Matthew to be a witness to the mission of Jesus Messiah to his people Israel, and it is a witness of the beginnings of the mission of Jesus's disciples to all the nations. That is the grand narrative of Matthew's Gospel. In this chapter we consider the concept, activity, and theology of "mission" in Matthew's Gospel. Eckhardt Schnabel observes, "The theme of 'mission' has long been recognized as one of the fundamental interests of the author of the First Gospel."[3] More generally, Andreas Köstenberger asserts, "The Gospel of Matthew provides a crucial contribution to a biblical theology of mission."[4] Paul Foster states, "Mission, or the spread of the gospel, is an important theme in Matthew's narrative and references to this topic increase in the final third of the gospel."[5] And David Bauer contends, "The Gospel of Matthew has mission as a central focus, even though Matthean scholars often overlook this focus."[6]

I heartily concur with these conclusions. The concept of *mission* in Matthew's Gospel is prominent as a theological theme and as a pressing mandate from Jesus in his discourses and a special focus in Matthew's narrative.[7]

1. C. Wright, *Mission of God*, 22, emphasis original.

2. C. Wright, *Mission of God*, 22.

3. Eckhard J. Schnabel, "The First Gospel and Matthew's Mission: Narrative, Theological and Historical Perspectives," *Society of Biblical Literature 2005 Seminar Papers*, SBLSP 44 (Atlanta: Society of Biblical Literature, 2005), 1–20, here 1; https://www.sbl-site.org/meetings/AMseminarpapers.aspx.

4. Köstenberger, with Alexander, *Salvation to the Ends of the Earth*, 43.

5. Foster, *Community, Law and Mission*, esp. 218–52, here 248.

6. Bauer, "Theme of Mission," 240–76.

7. Included in those focusing on "mission" in Matthew's Gospel with the above cited works, see Ådna, "Mission to Israel and the Nations," 45–60; France, *Matthew: Evangelist and Teacher*, 206–41; Michael Brands, *The Life and Ministry of Jesus as Enactment of the Great Commission: A New Proposal for Interpreting Matthew 28:16–20 in Light of Matthew's Gospel* (Lewiston, NY: Mellen, 2015), passim; Konradt, *Israel, Church and the Gentiles*, 327–54; Bitrus A. Sarma, *Hermeneutics of Mission in Matthew: Israel and the Nations in the Interpretive Framework of Matthew's Gospel* (Carlisle, UK: Langham, 2015); Donald Juel, "The Mission Theology of Matthew," in *The Biblical Foundations for Mission*, ed. Donald Senior and Carroll Stuhlmueller (Maryknoll, NY: Orbis, 1983), 233–54; Mark Allan Powell, *God With Us: A Pastoral Theology of Matthew's Gospel* (Minneapolis: Fortress, 1995), 1–27.

But we should consider one caveat before we undertake our study: the word "mission" is not found in standard English translations of Matthew's Gospel.[8] And further, in the New Testament as a whole the English term "mission" is found only in several English translations of Acts 12:25[9] and in one translation of Acts 13:25.[10] The term in Acts 12:25 rendered "mission" is the Greek *diakonia*, which indicates the dedicated "service" that Barnabas and Saul conducted in carrying a gift to the Jerusalem church during the famine (cf. 11:27–30). The term in Acts 13:25 rendered "mission" is the Greek term *dromos*, which indicates the "course" or "career" of the life of John the Baptist as he preached repentance and baptism to all the people of Israel (cf. 13:24).

The English term *mission* comes from the Latin feminine noun *missio*, meaning "a sending off, sending away," which derives from the Latin verb *mitto*, "to send, let go."[11] Therefore, the word *mission* signifies being sent from one place to another for a specific purpose, especially in reference to a divine assignment. Matthew tells us in his opening narrative that Jesus's coming to earth had a specific purpose: to "save his people from their sins" (Matt 1:21). This was a central purpose of Jesus's mission. Jesus's calling of his disciples indicates their future mission: "Follow me, and I will make you fishers of men" (4:19 ESV). It is this broad understanding of mission that will guide us in this chapter.

Therefore, although the specific term "mission" is scarce in Matthew's Gospel, the concept will be found throughout. *Mission* refers to the specific act of Jesus sending out his disciples, some later called apostles, for explicit tasks that Jesus spells out in the mission discourse, Great Commission, and elsewhere in Matthew's Gospel.[12] *Missionaries* are those who are sent out by Jesus (and subsequently by early Christian communities) for specific tasks. This definition will guide us in this Chapter as we explore Matthew's theology of mission.

William Larkin, an evangelical New Testament scholar and missiologist, offers us a definition of mission: "Mission is the divine activity of sending intermediaries, whether supernatural or human, to speak or do God's will so that his purposes for judgment or redemption are furthered."[13] Eckhard Schnabel, also a prominent evangelical New Testament scholar and one of the foremost experts in the technical study of mission in the Bible, gives the following definition of mission:

8. E.g., NIV, ESV, NASB, KJV, CSB, NRSVue, NLT, NET.

9. E.g., NIV: "When Barnabas and Saul had finished their *mission*, they returned from Jerusalem, taking with them John, also called Mark" (Acts 12:25). See similarly NASB, CSB, NRSVue, NLT, NET.

10. E.g., NET: "But while John was completing his *mission*, he said repeatedly, 'What do you think I am? I am not he. But look, one is coming after me. I am not worthy to untie the sandals on his feet!'" (Acts 13:25, NET, italics added).

11. D. P. Simpson, *Cassell's New Latin Dictionary*, 5th ed. (London: Cassell & Company, 1968), 375.

12. For discussion, see Park, "Cynic Itinerant Philosophers," 125–39; here 125n1.

13. William J. Larkin Jr., "Mission," *EDBT* 534–38; here 534.

> the activity of individuals (or of a community of faith) who distinguish themselves from the society in which they live both in terms of religious conviction (theology) and social behavior (ethics), who are convinced of the truth of their belief, and who actively work to win other people to their convictions and way of life.[14]

He notes that Jesus understood himself to be sent by the Father (the mission of Jesus), and Jesus called disciples, trained them as his envoys (missionaries), and sent them into the towns and villages of Galilee and eventually into Judea, Samaria, and beyond (the mission of the Twelve).[15]

Schnabel demonstrates that the semantic field of "mission" permeates the New Testament. He lists no less than 143 terms that demonstrate the range of missionary concepts and activities in the New Testament. The terms listed are not technical terms for mission but describe missionary activity. He groups the terms according to twelve subject matters.[16] I have adopted his twelve subject matters and selected some of these terms for our examination of mission in Matthew's Gospel. I have incorporated some terms not included in Schnabel's table so that the following chart is representative of my understanding of Matthew's view of mission.

| **TERMS FOR MISSIONARY ACTIVITY IN MATTHEW'S GOSPEL[17]** | |
|---|---|
| **(1) Subjects of missionary work:**<br>• fisher (*halieus*, Matt 4:19)<br>• disciple (*mathētēs*, 10:1)<br>• apostle (*apostolos*, 10:2)<br>• worker (*ergatēs*, 10:10)<br>**(2) Addressees of missionary work:**<br>• sinners (*hamartōloi*, 9:13)<br>• men (*anthrōpoi*, 8:27)<br>• the nations (*ta ethnē*, 28:19)<br>• Israel (*Israēl*, 10:6, 23; 15:24)<br>• people (*laos*, 4:16)<br>• crowds (*ochloi*, 4:25)<br>**(3) Place of missionary work:**<br>• earth (*gē*, 24:30)<br>• world (*kosmos*, 26:13)<br>• Galilee (*Galilaia*, 4:23)<br>• darkness (*skotos*, 4:16)<br>• Syria (*Syria*, 4:24)<br>• country, region, place (*chōra*, 4:16) | **(7) Goal of the proclamation:**<br>• repent (*metanoeō*, 4:17)<br>• follow (*akoloutheō*, 4:20, 22)<br>• make disciples (*mathēteuō*, 28:19)<br>• see . . . hear . . . understand . . . turn . . . be healed (*oraō . . . akouō . . . suniēmi . . . epistrephō . . . iaomai*, 13:15)<br>• believe (*pisteuō*, 9:28; 18:16; 21:22)<br>• save (*sōzō*, 1:21)<br>• answered prayer (*proseuchē*, 21:22)<br>• answered prayer (*aiteō*, 18:19)<br>**(8) Proclamation by deed:**<br>• raise the dead (*egeirō nekros*, 10:8)<br>• drive out unclean spirits (*ekballō pneumatōn akathartōn*, 10:1)<br>• heal (*therapeuō*, 10:1)<br>• harvest (*therismos*, 9:37)<br>• heal (*iaomai*, 13:15)<br>• cleanse lepers (*katharizō*, 10:8)<br>• build (*oikodomeō*, 16:18) |

14. Eckhard J. Schnabel, "Mission," *DJG*[2] 604. See similarly, Schnabel, *Early Christian Mission*, 1:11.

15. Schnabel, "Mission," 604.

16. Schnabel, *Early Christian Mission*, 1:36–37.

17. Adapted from the broader study of Schnabel, *Early Christian Mission*, 1:36–37.

| TERMS FOR MISSIONARY ACTIVITY IN MATTHEW'S GOSPEL | |
|---|---|
| **(4) Sending and position of the missionaries:**<br>• send out (*apostellō*, 10:5, 16; 15:24)<br>• apostle (*apostolos*, 10:2)<br>• servant (*pais*, 12:18; *diakonos*, 20:26)<br>**(5) Proclamation by word:**<br>• proclaim (*kēryssō*, 4:23; 10:7)<br>• teaching (*didaskō*, 4:23)<br>• make disciples (*mathēteuō*, 28:19)<br>**(6) Content of the proclamation:**<br>• the kingdom of heaven has come near (*ēngiken gar basileia tōn ouranōn*, 4:17)<br>• follow me (*deute opisō mou*, 4:19)<br>• follow me (*akolouthei moi*, 9:9)<br>• call (*kaleō*, 4:21; 9:13; 22:3, 4, 8–9)<br>• the gospel of the kingdom of heaven (*to euangelion tēs basileias*, 4:23)<br>• the mysteries of the kingdom of heaven (*ta mystēria tēs basileias tōn ouranōn*, 13:11) | **(9) Execution of the missionary task:**<br>• do not go among Gentiles or . . . Samaritans (*aperchomai*, 10:5)<br>• sent out (*apostellō*, 10:5)<br>• the sower sowed seed (*ho speirōn tou speirein*, 13:3–23)<br>**(10) Interpretation of missionary work:**<br>• fisher of people (*halieus anthrōpōn*, 4:19)<br>• harvest (*therismos*, 9:37–8)<br>• build (*oikodomeō*, 16:18)<br>• sheep (*probata*, 9:36; 10:6; 15:24; 18:12)<br>• the sower sowed seed (*ho speirōn tou speirein*, 13:3–23)<br>• Father planted (*phyteuō*, 15:13)<br>**(11) The effort of missionary work:**<br>• work (*ergazomai*, 21:28)<br>• being hated (*esesthe misoumenoi*, 10:22)<br>**(12) Misunderstandings:**<br>• deceive (*planaō*, 25:5) |

From this brief overview, we turn directly to our study of mission in Matthew's Gospel. In this Chapter we will take the following approach.

First, we will undertake a journey through Matthew's Gospel as he unfolds his narrative of Jesus's mission and Matthew's unique emphasis upon the mission of Jesus as he touches upon it in Jesus's discourses. This will include an examination of the particularistic thrust of mission in Matthew's Gospel, where Matthew underscores the mission of Jesus to Israel. Simultaneously we will note the universalistic thrust of mission in Matthew's Gospel, where Matthew underscores the mission of Jesus to all the nations. Oftentimes these two Matthean missional thrusts are examined separately, but I have found that examining them simultaneously gives a more authentic perspective on Matthew's authorial objectives.

Our second task will be an attempt to understand how the tension between these two missional thrusts—particularism and universalism—is resolved. This will build on our earlier Chapters 12 and 13 regarding Israel, disciples, and church. Our third undertaking is to explore some significant themes regarding mission in Matthew's Gospel. We will conclude this chapter with summary and final observations.[18]

## 15.2 Particularism and Universalism in Mission in Matthew's Gospel

A dual thrust surfaces one of the well-known difficulties of studying mission in Matthew's Gospel, namely, attempting to understand the tension between the

18. Some material here draws from Wilkins, *Matthew*.

particularistic thrust, where Jesus emphasizes a mission only to the lost sheep of the house of Israel (10:6; 15:24), and the universalistic thrust, where Jesus emphasizes a mission to all the nations (24:14; 28:19).[19] We use the term "particularism" in the sense that Matthew emphasizes the mission of Jesus to Israel as God's "particular" chosen people. "Particularism restricts the offer of salvation to the people of Israel (cf. Mt 10:5–6)."[20] Our use here of "universalism" indicates Matthew's emphasis upon Jesus's mission to all peoples and nations with the opportunity of salvation for all. "Universalism offers salvation to all people (cf. Mt 28:19)."[21]

On the one hand, we see a distinctive development as Matthew focuses on Jesus's mission to Israel in the first half of his Gospel with a very positive emphasis, which then turns increasingly negative. On the other hand, we see another distinctive development as Matthew focuses on Jesus's mission to all the nations, which is at the first somewhat subtle but becomes increasingly pronounced as we near the end of Matthew's Gospel.[22] Paul Foster notes that "the first two passages (Matt 10.5–23; 15.21–28) present the most restricted attitude, however after ch. 15 there is almost without exception a positive attitude displayed to bringing Gentiles into the community."[23]

We can only be selective, but our attempt is to surface passages representative of Matthew's understanding of the mission to Israel and the mission to all the nations. Since Matthew's view of mission is developed chronologically through his narrative of Jesus's life and ministry and teaching, we see a distinct progression as he focuses on Jesus's particularistic mission to Israel and then as he focuses on Jesus's universal mission to all peoples. We will follow that historical progression selectively as we work our way through Matthew's Gospel and his understanding of the mission.[24]

19. For valuable discussions, see France, *Matthew: Evangelist and Teacher*, 206–41; C. Wright, *Mission of God*, 222–64; Levine, *Social and Ethnic Dimensions*, passim; Paschke, *Particularism and Universalism*, passim; C. J. Moore, "Can We Hasten the Parousia? An Examination of Matt 24:14 and Its Implications for Missional Practice," *Them* 44.2 (2019): 291–311. For one who sets aside what he calls the problematic terms "universalism" and "particularism" as being more prone to obscuring than to clarifying what is at stake, see Anders Runesson, "Beyond Universalism and Particularism: Rethinking Paul and Matthew on Gentile Inclusion," in *Paul and Matthew Among Jews and Gentiles: Essays in Honor of Terence L. Donaldson*, ed. Ronald Charles, LNTS 628 (London: T&T Clark, 2020), 99–112, here 109.

20. Paschke, *Particularism and Universalism*, 1. See also "Particularism," Oxford Languages online: https://www.oed.com/search/dictionary/?scope=Entries&q=particularism.

21. Paschke, *Particularism and Universalism*, 1. See also *Encyclopedia Britannica*, "Christianity: The Relation of the Early Church to Late Judaism," by Jaroslav Jan Pelikan, accessed August 29, 2022, https://www.britannica.com/topic/Christianity.

22. See Carolin Ziethe, *Auf seinen Namen werden die Volker hoffen: Die matthäische Rezeption der Schriften Israels zür Begründung des universalen Heils*, BZNW 233 (Berlin: de Gruyter, 2018), 380. Ziethe throughout focuses on the theme of fulfillment of Scripture for Israel and also the offer of universal salvation in the developing narrative of Matthew's Gospel.

23. Foster, *Community, Law and Mission*, 220.

24. For a discussion of the dual emphasis upon Israel and nations in Matthew's developing narrative, see Levine, *Social and Ethnic Dimensions*, passim; Eugene Eung-Chun Park, *The Mission Discourse in Matthew's Interpretation*, WUNT 2/81 (Tübingen: J. C. B. Mohr [Paul Siebeck], 1995), esp. 167–86.

### 15.2.1 The Mission of Jesus Messiah, the Son of David, the Son of Abraham (1:1)

Matthew's opening verse gives important clues to the mission of Jesus Messiah and the overall purpose and perspective that Matthew will take in the writing of his Gospel: "The book of the genealogy of Jesus Christ, the son of David, the son of Abraham" (1:1, ESV). Matthew's Gospel will have special significance to those in his audience with a Jewish background, who traced their ancestry through the covenants God made with Israel. Matthew writes to record and demonstrate how Jesus Messiah's mission at least in part was to fulfill God's promises to his ancient people, Israel.

From the outset Matthew calls Jesus "Messiah" (Gr. *Christos*). The designation harks back to David as the anointed king of Israel's past and was associated with the covenant promise God gave through Nathan the prophet to David, a promise of an "anointed one" who would be the hope for Israel's future (2 Sam 7:11–16).

Matthew also calls Jesus Messiah the "son of David," the descendant from David's royal lineage who would reestablish the throne in Jerusalem and the kingdom of Israel. Jesus is the long-anticipated Messiah, the son of David, whose mission is to bring the kingdom on earth in fulfillment of the promises to the Davidic line and the people of Israel.

And further, Matthew refers to Jesus Messiah as the "son of Abraham" (Matt 1:1). Matthew will have a special focus in his Gospel on the fulfillment of the covenantal assurances of blessing and promise that God gave to Abraham as the father of Israel that are now fulfilled in the arrival of Jesus Messiah (1:2). With Abraham, a new development in divine revelation to humans commenced, which focused on God's word of blessing and promise. The core of the covenant between God and Abraham consisted of a promise that was basically threefold: (1) a "seed" (*zera'*), (2) a "land" (*eretz*), and (3) a "blessing" (*berakah*) through Israel to all of the nations of the earth.[25] Christopher Wright emphasizes that the Abrahamic covenant begins in a singular blessing of particularity to Abraham but ends in profound universality of blessing to all of the nations of the earth.[26]

We see here a significant emphasis for Matthew: Jesus's mission is to fulfill that promise to Abraham as the father of Israel, but also there is the implication that he will fulfill the promise of blessing to all of the nations of the earth (e.g., Gen 17:1–5; 18:18). Betz emphasizes, "The fact that Jesus' ancestry was Abrahamic determined his line of Judaism and led consistently to the inclusion of the Gentiles into the Kingdom of God."[27]

25. Kaiser, *Promise-Plan of God*, 54.

26. Christopher J. H. Wright, *The Mission of God's People: A Biblical Theology of the Church's Mission*, BTL (Grand Rapids: Zondervan, 2010), 71.

27. Hans Dieter Betz, *Essays on the Sermon on the Mount* (Philadelphia: Fortress, 1985), 272–73.

We will see that emphasis running throughout Matthew's narrative: fulfillment to Israel, yet a subtle but significant emphasis upon inclusion of gentiles in fulfillment of God's promises to all of the nations of the earth.

### 15.2.2 Jesus Messiah's Mission Is to Save His People from Their Sins (1:21)

In the conception-announcement scene, Matthew records the announcement by the angel to Joseph that Mary will bear the child of hope to the people of Israel: "She will give birth to a son, and you are to give him the name Jesus, because he will save his people from their sins" (Matt 1:21). The term "people" is *laos*, which we have seen in Matthew's Gospel consistently refers to the people of Israel (e.g., 2:6; 13:15; 15:8; 26:5; 27:25).[28] God is initiating the salvation of his covenant people Israel.

But as Matthew's Gospel unfolds, it becomes increasingly clear that "his people" will come to include all those who believe in Jesus Messiah because he is the Son of Man who has come "to give his life as a ransom for many" (20:28). Saving his people from their sins will be realized in the forgiveness of the sins of a paralyzed man in Jesus's own town (9:1–8), in the forgiveness sins in Jesus's community of the church (18:21–35), and in the forgiveness of the sins of many through the pouring out of Jesus's blood (26:26–29). Thus, Matthew provides a universal statement of hope for the present and future salvation of sins for his people Israel and for the anticipated new community of faith of all those who believe on Jesus.[29]

### 15.2.3 Jesus Messiah's Mission as the Ruler Who Will "Shepherd My People Israel" (2:6)

The mission to Israel will continue eschatologically as Jesus Messiah shepherds the people of Israel (2:6). Matthew cites Mic 5:2 to the effect that Jesus will be the "Son of David," the messianic ruler who will shepherd his people (*laos*) Israel.[30] Matthew's language borrowed from 2 Sam 5:2 expresses the conviction held by "all the tribes of Israel" (2 Sam 5:1) that David is destined to be king, which leads to the anointing of David as king over Israel at Hebron (2 Sam 5:3). Nolland suggests that Matthew is underlining the Davidic connection in that the text is here applied typologically to the king of messianic expectation. Matthew's reference to "shepherd my people Israel" evokes the eschatological expectation of the ingathering of the twelve tribes of Israel.[31]

28. Luz, *Matthew 1–7*, 95.

29. See e.g., Turner, *Matthew*, 68; Nolland, *Matthew*, 98; Repschinski, "'For He Will Save,'" 248–67; Siker, *Sin*, 53–54.

30. Evans, *Matthew*, 55; Davies and Allison, *Matthew*, 1:243; Turner, "His Glorious Throne," 152.

31. Nolland, *Matthew*, 115. So also Davies and Allison, *Matthew*, 1:243–44. See Ezek 34:4–16; 37; Hos 2; Mic 5:1–9; 2 Esdr 13:34–50; 2 Bar. 77–86; Ps. Sol. 17; 4 Ezra 13:34–50; m. Sanhedrin 10:3; cf. Matt 19:28.

## 15.2.4 John the Baptist's and Jesus's Mission to Jews Who Await Deliverance (4:12–25)

John the Baptist arrives on the scene of history with a mission from the wilderness of Judea to Israel that begins with the message: "Repent, for the kingdom of heaven has come near" (Matt 3:2). People from Jerusalem and all Judea and the whole region of the Jordan went out to be baptized by him, indicating that Israel recognized its need to confess their sins and repent (3:5–6). The leaders of Israel likewise went out to John, but he recognized their hypocrisy and rebuked them (3:7–12). At the beginning of Matthew's record of the mission to Israel, this is a joyful response from the people but an ominous evaluation of the leadership of Israel.

### *15.2.4.1 Jesus and His Mission*

That negative evaluation of Israel's leadership is heightened when Matthew records John's arrest (4:12–13). Jesus then initiates his public mission in Galilee. The inhabitants are called "*the people* sitting in darkness" (4:16, my translation), a description of Jews who await deliverance while living among the hopelessness of the gentiles. These Jews are the first to see the great light of God's mission of deliverance in Jesus. It will bring hope to those who understand most clearly the hopelessness of death.

### *15.2.4.2 Jesus's Message and the First Responses to His Mission*

It is here that Jesus commences his mission with the same message as John the Baptist: "'Repent, for the kingdom of heaven has come near'" (4:17). As he walks along the Sea of Galilee he sees two men, Peter and Andrew. Jesus approaches these men as they are conducting their customary fishing activities and calls out, "Come, follow me, and I will make you fishers of men" (4:19, ESV). Leaving all means primarily a commitment to Jesus and his mission. They are heeding Jesus's call to change their primary occupation from fishing for fish to fishing for human souls. They have now joined Jesus in his mission.

As with Peter and Andrew, Jesus interrupts the brothers James and John in their busy activities and calls them. By obeying Jesus's call, they are relinquishing commitment to the family business, their assets, and their livelihood, surely having an impact on varied family relationships, responsibilities, and obligations. They also have now joined Jesus in his mission.

## 15.2.5 Jesus Messiah's Mission of Evangelism and Instruction (Chs. 5–7)

These four brothers are presumably among the disciples who are the focus of Jesus's instruction in the Sermon on the Mount (cf. 5:1–2). Matthew's wording to specify the audience of the Sermon on the Mount is important. Jesus sees the crowds, then goes up on the mountain and sits down. Matthew specifies that Jesus leaves the crowds so that he can teach his disciples.[32]

We have noted in Chapter 10 that Matthew specifies three primary groups of people around Jesus in his earthly ministry: his disciples, the religious leaders, and the crowds. The *disciples* are those who have made a commitment to Jesus as the Messiah. The *religious leaders* are Jesus's opponents for much of his ministry, represented especially by the Pharisees (12:22–32). The *crowd* is the basically neutral though curious group of people who are astounded by his teaching and ministry (7:28–29) but who have not yet made a commitment to him. The disciples are *with* Jesus, the religious leaders are *against* him, and the crowd stands in the middle as not yet having made a decision for or against him.[33] Jesus's objective was to make disciples from among the crowd. As he teaches and preaches, the sign of faith is when one comes out of the crowd to call Jesus "Lord," at which time the person becomes a disciple/believer (cf. 8:18, 21; 17:14, 15).[34]

We see here in the Sermon on the Mount a continuing blend of an explicit note of particularism with a hint of Jesus's universal gospel message. The Jewish disciples, crowds, and religious leaders are privy to Jesus's explicit instruction and invitation to the kingdom (5:1–2, 17–20), yet there is universal application of those who become disciples from all the nations in Jesus's final Great Commission (28:16–20). We can hear universal overtones in the Beatitudes where the "merciful" (5:7) and "peacemakers" (5:9) are not expressly limited to Israel. And there are hints of universal inclusive language where the disciples are "the salt of the earth" and "the light of the world" and where *others* "may see your good deeds and glorify your Father in heaven (5:13, 14, 16).[35] Having concluded that *gē* here means "the earth," Nolland notes, "Though Matthew continues to tell a very Jewish story, the universal significance of what Jesus has set in motion is allowed to show through."[36]

### 15.2.6 Jesus Messiah's Mission Foresees a Universal Banquet and Judgment for Unrepentant Israel (8:11–13)

In three brief scenes, Matthew demonstrates how Jesus's messianic mission brings restoration to people who were often marginalized within Jewish culture: lepers (8:1–4); gentiles (8:5–13), and women (8:14–15). In this way Jesus breaks down boundaries of purity, ethnicity, and gender so that all may respond to his invitation to the kingdom of heaven.

The healing of the centurion's servant transcends ethnic boundaries. The centurion

32. Davies and Allison, *Matthew*, 1:421.

33. Wilkins, *Concept of Disciple*, esp. 163–72; Wilkins, *Following the Master*, 179–83. For similar perspectives, see Paschke, *Particularism and Universalism*, 45–57; Cousland, *Crowds in the Gospel of Matthew*, passim.

34. For Jesus's and the early church's mission to the Pharisees and scribes, see Ng, "Matthew 5:17–20," 201–21.

35. Paschke, *Particularism and Universalism*, 70–102; Davies and Allison, *Matthew*, 1:450; Hagner, *Matthew 1–13*, 99–101.

36. Nolland, *Matthew*, 213.

is an officer of the Roman legion who comes to Jesus requesting help for his servant who lies at home paralyzed, suffering terribly. The centurion displays remarkable sensitivity for Jewish traditions when he considers himself unworthy to receive Jesus, a Jewish teacher, into his gentile home. Entering the home of a gentile renders a Jew ceremonially unclean (cf. Acts 10:28).

The centurion displays exemplary faith in Jesus, recognizing Jesus to be the messianic deliverer who can heal on the authority of his word alone. This faith results in his servant's healing. This faith is what many in Israel lacked. This is one of several passages that has in view members of the nations other than Israel who will be participants in the messianic banquet, as per the prophetic texts in the eschatological pilgrimage tradition that speak of the gentiles coming into Jerusalem (e.g., Isa 2:2–3; 60:3–4; Mic 4:1–2; Zech 8:20–23).[37] Gentile peoples across the world who believe in Jesus will join Israel's patriarchs in ultimate celebration in the kingdom of heaven (cf. Isa 25:6–9; 56:3–8). But the original "subjects of the kingdom"—descendants of the patriarchs—will lose their place and face judgment unless they follow the path of faith that the centurion has exemplified.[38]

### 15.2.7 Jesus Messiah Sends His Messengers to Further His Mission to Israel: The Mission Discourse (9:35–10:42)

Jesus's own mission is at this point well established. Now is the time to expand his influence by sending out his disciples with the same message and power, because opposition is building (Matt 9:3–4, 34; chs. 11–12). Jesus will send them first to his people Israel (10:5–15). But he will also prepare his disciples for a worldwide mission among the gentiles (10:16–23). And Jesus's training will address directly the discipleship characteristics that the disciples will need to embody while they carry out the mission (10:24–42).[39]

#### *15.2.7.1 Jesus Messiah's Mission to Israel Brings Healing for Physical and Spiritual Needs in Israel (9:35–36)*

As Jesus's mission unfolds, the crowds in Israel continue to be the object of Jesus's gospel message, and the motivating force is his compassion. "When he saw the crowds, he had compassion for them" (9:36). The word "had compassion" is *splanchnizomai*, "to be moved in the inward parts," which usually indicates the heart and affections.[40]

The need that Jesus sees in this instance is that the crowds "were harassed and helpless, like sheep without a shepherd" (9:36). The leaders in Israel's history had been likened to shepherds. Joshua was appointed leader after Moses, so that "the LORD's

37. Osborne, *Matthew*, 892 and nn21, 22; France, *Matthew*, 195; P. Foster, *Community, Law, and Mission*, 60.

38. See Tanner, "'Outer Darkness,'" 445–59.

39. For helpful discussion of the delimitation of the text, see Park, *Mission Discourse in Matthew's Interpretation*, esp. ch. 2.

40. "σπλαγχνίζομαι," BDAG 938.

people will not be like sheep without a shepherd" (Num 27:17).[41] That is what Israel was like in Jesus's day. The leaders had not fulfilled their responsibility to guide and protect the people, and therefore they were harassed and helpless.

In the preceding miracle stories (Matt 8–9), Jesus's mission involved healing the diseased and sick, raising the dead, calming the stormy sea, and exorcising powerful demons. Those immediate needs are hugely important, but woven throughout the scenes is Jesus's recognition that an underlying destitution is far worse.

In a word, the problem is "sin." Jesus's mission also includes that he is the promised suffering servant, who will take upon himself the infirmities of his people, but also their sins (8:17; cf. Isa 53:4, 5). The deeper illness of the paralytic and the spiritual sickness of tax collectors and Pharisees alike is their sin (Matt 9:2, 13). So, the real downfall of the leaders of Israel is that they are not giving proper care to the spiritual needs of the people. Their religious rituals and traditions were beating the people down and leaving them helplessly burdened (cf. 23:4, 13–15). Jesus sees deeply into the real need of the crowds and moves to bring healing to both body and soul.[42]

### *15.2.7.2 Jesus Messiah Enlists Coworkers in His Mission (9:37–38)*

The metaphor changes from sheep that are harassed and helpless and in need of a shepherd to a bountiful harvest in need of harvesters. Although the metaphor changes, the meaning remains the same. The "harvest" (9:37) is the crowds within Israel who have such tremendous needs, but this theme will provide guidance throughout the present era of mission outreach, as the following mission discourse will make clear (esp. 10:5–23). Even as Jesus's life mission is to bring the gospel of the kingdom to the needy, he wants his disciples to join him in that mission because "the harvest is plentiful but the workers are few" (9:37).

While Matthew normally emphasizes a small group of disciples around Jesus, it need not be restricted to the Twelve here. The disciples are all those who have responded to his summons to the kingdom of heaven. Jesus will send out the Twelve on a special mission within Israel (10:1–15), but as long as there are needy crowds he calls disciples throughout the ages to become harvest workers (10:16–23). Jesus will draw upon the harvest metaphor elsewhere in an eschatological context, but there it is harvest time of judgment (13:30, 39).

The disciples are to "ask the Lord of the harvest, therefore, to send out workers into his harvest field" (9:38). The "Lord of the harvest" is God, who will respond to their prayer for harvest workers. But dramatically it is Jesus who steps forward in answer to their prayers to commission the Twelve to go out to minister to the harvest. The harvest mission includes the immediate assignment of the Twelve to take the gospel message

41. "Sheep, Shepherd," *DBI* 782–85.

42. Turner, *Matthew*, 262–63.

only to Israel (10:1–15) but also the long-range mission of the disciples throughout the age until the Son of Man returns (10:16–23).

### *15.2.7.3 Commissioning the Twelve for Mission (10:1–4)*

In answer to the prayer for the Lord of the harvest to send out workers into his harvest field (9:38), Jesus called his twelve disciples to him (10:1), the highest of christological clues to Jesus's divine identity: Jesus himself is the Lord of the harvest.[43] "Twelve" has obvious salvation-historical significance. The number corresponds to the twelve patriarchs of Israel, the sons of Jacob from whom the tribes of Israel descended. The twelve disciples symbolize the continuity of salvation history in God's mission program, as Jesus sends them out to proclaim to the lost sheep of the house of Israel that the kingdom of heaven has arrived (cf. 10:5–6).[44] But there is a form of discontinuity as well because the Twelve will sit on twelve thrones judging the house of Israel (cf. 19:28).[45] The arrival of the kingdom of heaven in Jesus's ministry demands an appropriate response from his chosen people Israel. In the gathering of twelve disciples, we find the hint that Jesus is indeed the messianic king of Israel who has come to unite the people of God in all ages.[46]

The same authority that characterized Jesus's mission in Matt 8–9 is now given to the Twelve. Like Jesus, this authority enables them to drive out evil spirits and to heal every kind of disease and sickness (10:1; cf. 4:23; 9:35). All that the Twelve will accomplish—whether powerful works or powerful preaching of the gospel of the kingdom—is based on having received Jesus's authority. Disciples of every era will find their own authority in mission only in their submission to Jesus's authority. In the authoritative call, disciples are conscripted to kingdom service (4:18–22). In the authoritative instruction of the Sermon on the Mount, disciples learn how to live the kingdom life (chs. 5–7; esp. 7:29). And in the authoritative commission, disciples go out with the power and message of the kingdom (10:1–5; cf. 9:6, 8; 28:18–20).[47]

Evil or unclean spirits are mentioned only one other time in Matthew's Gospel (12:43), but they are the same malevolent spirit beings that are called demons elsewhere (e.g., 8:28–32). The advance of the kingdom of heaven in Jesus's mission continually encounters spiritual warfare. Unclean spirits are in rebellion against God and are capable of inflicting mental, moral, and physical harm upon humans. Demon-possessed people are healed right alongside of other illnesses (e.g., 4:25), and demons being cast out are an indication that the time of God's judgment has begun upon the evil stranglehold over this world (8:16, 17, 29).

As the Twelve cast out demons and heal disease and sickness, it is external validation

43. Schweizer, *Matthew*, 235–36; Filson, *Matthew*, 125.

44. Cf. McKnight, "Jesus and the Twelve," 220–31; Rengstorf, "δώδεκα," *TDNT* 2:326.

45. Cf. Meier, *Companions and Competitors*, 251–52.

46. Cf. Freyne, *The Twelve*, 23–48.

47. Hagner, *Matthew 1–13*, 265.

of the reality of the presence of the kingdom of heaven, and people should now turn to Jesus as the messianic deliverer. But their authoritative mission is also an exercise of control over Satan's realm of rule on this earth. No longer is Satan the uncontested ruler of this world. He has met his match, and more, in the arrival of the Jesus. And Satan's evil forces have met their match, and more, as Jesus's emissaries go out with his authority to bring release to those held captive.

### *15.2.7.4 Instructions for the Short-Term Mission to Israel (10:5–15)*

The instructions for the disciples'/apostles' mission is the second of the five major discourses in Matthew's Gospel. This mission discourse is divided into three basic sections: missionary instructions for the immediate historical context (10:5–15), a preview of the disciples' role as missionaries in the future age (10:16–42), and principles of discipleship for disciple-missionaries of every era (10:24–42)

#### 15.2.7.4.1 A Surprising Prohibition and the Focus of the Mission (10:5–6)

Jesus begins the mission discourse with a surprising prohibition: "Do not go among the Gentiles or enter any town of the Samaritans. Go rather to the lost sheep of Israel" (10:5–6). The mission apparently was restricted to Jewish Galilee, which was surrounded on all sides by gentile country, except to the south, where lay Samaria.[48] The full expression is "lost sheep of the house of Israel," which does not mean one separate part of Israel that is lost but rather that the whole of Israel is lost and is being called to make a decision about the gospel of the kingdom.

The key to the prohibition is found in the directive to go only to Israel. This is a special mission of Jesus's disciples during his historical ministry to the crowds of Israel, who are like harassed and helpless sheep without a shepherd (9:36). Jesus goes first to Israel (cf. 15:21–28) to fulfill the salvation-historical order that God established with Israel being the tool that God will use to bring blessing to the world.[49] Then he will charge the Eleven to continue the historical outworking by going to the nations (28:19–20). The Twelve symbolize the continuity and theological salvation-history priority of Israel in God's program.[50] Paul later saw this as the priority of the Jews in salvation, but also in judgment, as God's plan throughout salvation history will be "first to the Jew, then to the Gentile" (Rom 1:16; 2:9–10).[51] Jesus's singular attention to Israel underscores God's faithfulness to his covenant promises, the continuity of his purposes, and that his plan for Israel is still unfinished.

48. Hill, *Matthew*, 184–45; Morna D. Hooker, "Uncomfortable Words X: 'The Prohibition of Foreign Missions (Mt. 10:5–6),'" *ExpTim* 82 (1971): 364.

49. E.g., Gen 12:2–3; 22:18.

50. Scott, "Gentiles and the Ministry of Jesus," 161–69.

51. Moo, *Romans*, 69, 139; Brindle, "'To the Jew First,'" 221–33.

We might wonder why Jesus would even bother to give such a prohibition, given that the Twelve would not likely go to gentiles and Samaritans.[52] The early church did not accept a universal mission easily (cf. Acts 10; 11:1–4; 15), so it is doubtful that the Twelve would have been eager to go to the gentiles or Samaritans at this early date (e.g., John 4:27; Luke 9:51–54; Matt 15:23). More likely, Jesus is dispelling any doubt that his disciples or any in the audience may have had as to whether he truly was the Messiah coming in fulfillment of the promises given to Israel and dispelling any doubts that he is fulfilling God's program of salvation history.

But there is also a warning in the prohibition. The eschatological ingathering is beginning. This is Israel's opportunity, and from here on it will be fully responsible for its own decision. In Jesus's commission to the Twelve to go to Israel alone is an apologetic to the disciples and crowds of his faithfulness to God's program but also an oblique warning to Israel. The eschatological ingathering is beginning. This is Israel's opportunity, and from here on it will be fully responsible for its own decision.[53]

### 15.2.7.4.2 The Message and Miracles of the Mission (10:7–8a)

The disciples are to go to Israel with the same message that both John the Baptist and Jesus preached: "The kingdom of heaven is near" (10:7; cf. 3:2; 4:17). They also go with the same authority as Jesus (10:1) as they "heal the sick, raise the dead, cleanse those who have leprosy, drive out demons" (10:8). Jesus likewise performed each of these miracles. The power of the Twelve is clearly an extension of Jesus's own power and will be exercised in the same manner. The commission to raise the dead harks back to Jesus's stupendous miracle of raising Jairus's daughter (9:25–26).

### 15.2.7.4.3 The Equipment for the Mission (10:8b–10)

The disciples have been the beneficiaries of the gift of the kingdom of heaven—in the message they have believed, in the authority over unclean spirits and disease and sickness they have been given, and in the commission that they now have received. They likewise are to give this ministry of the gospel freely to the lost sheep of the house of Israel. "Freely you have received; freely give" (10:8). They are not to accept payment from those to whom they minister, which would otherwise make it a mercenary venture. Jesus gave them their authoritative power as a gift, so they must not take payment for performing miracles.

They are instructed further, "Do not get any gold or silver or copper to take with you in your belts—no bag for the journey, or extra shirt or sandals or a staff; for the worker is worth his keep" (10:9–10). Jesus is not prohibiting them from owning these

52. Contra Joachim Jeremias, *Jesus' Promise to the Nations*, Studies in Biblical Theology 24 (London: SCM, 1958), 16–28.

53. Kingsbury, *Matthew: Structure, Christology, Kingdom*, 22–23; Broadus, *Matthew*, 219.

items but rather is stressing the urgency and requirements of the mission. Mark's account assumes that they have basic necessities, such as a walking staff and sandals (Mark 6:8–9). Matthew's account also assumes that they already have these items but stresses that the Twelve are not to spend time procuring extra supplies as though they are going to be gone to foreign lands for an extended period of time.

There are two reasons for this prohibition. In the first place, they are going out on a relatively quick preaching tour through the Galilean countryside. To procure extensive supplies is unnecessary. In the second place, Jesus explains, "For the worker is worth his keep" (10:10). On this brief mission tour the Twelve are to accept the hospitality that will be extended to them as traveling missionaries, so they will have no need to take along money or extra clothing or equipment. It is the responsibility of those to whom they minister to support their mission (10:10).[54] The apostle Paul will call upon this principle as a rationale for the support of full-time Christian workers (1 Cor 9:14; 1 Tim 5:18; cf. Did. 13:1–2). In 1 Tim 5:18 he quotes the parallel passage in Luke 10:7, giving it the stature of "Scripture." Although they are not to charge for their ministry, the Twelve are to accept the hospitality extended to them as traveling missionaries (Matt 10:11), so they will have no need to take along money ("gold or silver or copper") or extra clothing or typical traveling equipment (10:9–10). To receive aid from the unconverted might give the appearance of selling the gospel, reducing the missionaries to the level of various popular philosophers and religious preachers who sought payment for their services. It is the responsibility of those to whom they minister to support their mission (10:10; cf. 3 John 5–8).

### 15.2.7.4.4 Worthy of the Mission (10:11–14)

Jesus indicates that while the Twelve are on the mission journey, they will look for worthy persons. "Whatever town or village you enter, search for some worthy person there and stay at his house until you leave. As you enter the home, give it your greeting." (10:11). The term for the person who is "worthy" (*axios*) in 10:10 is the same term translated "deserving" in 10:13. It does not point to a person who has a high moral or religious stature but indicates the person who responds positively to the gospel message proclaimed by the disciples.[55] An individual, a house, or a city (10:11, 12, 14) that receives the greeting, which Luke tells us is "Peace be to this house" (Luke 10:5; see Matt 5:47), and the peace or benediction of the missionaries (see 2 John 10), recognizes that the Twelve are emissaries of God and has received their message.

If the household does not receive God's message and messengers, then the missionaries are to shake the dust off their feet when they leave. It was a sign used by Jews when leaving gentile regions that they have removed completely unclean elements

54. Plummer, *Matthew*, 149.

55. Albright and Mann, *Matthew*, 212.

(b. Sanhedrin 12a). For the missionaries it is an acted parable of judgment on those rejecting the mission message.[56] Paul practiced this symbol when leaving regions where his message was rejected (Acts 13:51).

#### 15.2.7.4.5 Judgment for Rejecting the Mission (10:15)

The element of judgment that has been implied in the mission is now explicit. "Truly I tell you, it will be more bearable for Sodom and Gomorrah on the day of judgment than for that town" (Matt 10:15). The preaching of the gospel becomes for Israel a "threat" as well as a "promise."[57] Increased light of God's revelation makes for increased responsibility, and those who have been exposed to the opportunity of Jesus's mission and the witness of the disciples will have greater responsibility for that privilege. Jesus pronounces a similar note of judgment on the Galilee towns of Chorazin, Bethsaida, and Capernaum (11:20–24). The whole scene exudes urgency because the time of Jesus's earthly ministry is short and the blessings of the kingdom, as well as the punishment of judgment, are awaiting an expected decision from Israel.

### *15.2.7.5 Instructions for the Long-Term Mission to the World (10:16–23)*

Up to this point in the mission discourse Jesus has emphasized a mission of the Twelve that would take place during his own historical mission (10:5–15). Now Jesus gives expanded instruction that equips the Twelve and all future disciples for the mission that will take them beyond Jesus's earthly ministry (10:16–23).

How do we know? This shift is seen at least in the following.

(1) *The change from present tense to future tense.* In the first part of the mission discourse the present tense is used to commission the Twelve, indicating the present mission within Jesus's earthly ministry. In the second part, however, the future tense is used, marking off a distinctively different future ministry.

(2) *A witness to gentiles.* The future ministry will involve a witness to "Gentiles" (10:18), to whom the Twelve were warned not to go in their short-term mission (10:5). This indicates the worldwide mission of the Great Commission (28:18–20).

(3) *The disciples' persecution.* Throughout the second section Jesus prepares the disciples for intense persecution. However, there is no evidence that the Twelve experienced this kind of persecution during Jesus's earthly ministry. Therefore, Jesus is preparing them for the persecution and suffering that will characterize mission-disciples throughout the age.

(4) *Eschatological references.* The appearance of some of these warnings in Mark's (13:9–13) and Matthew's (e.g., 24:9–13) records of Jesus's eschatological message

56. Ladd, *Theology of the New Testament*, 88.

57. Ladd, *Theology of the New Testament*, 88.

indicates that Jesus is here including warnings about treatment that missionary disciples will endure until the coming of Jesus and the end of the age.

(5) *No results of the mission.* In Matthew's mission charge there is no reference to the Twelve either going out or returning from the mission, giving no results of the mission. In this way the commission is sufficiently open-ended to include both instructions for the immediate mission to Israel and the ongoing mission to the nations until the end of the age. Together, these all indicate that the original historical setting of Jesus's sending of the Twelve to the people of Israel provided an occasion for him also to lay down instruction for the future Christian mission to all the nations.

#### 15.2.7.5.1 Jesus's Missionary Disciples Are Sheep Among Wolves (10:16)

The theme of judgment upon the towns in Israel for rejecting the mission of the Twelve leads to a surprising reversal of the sheep metaphor: "I am sending you out like sheep among wolves" (10:16). Up to now the disciples were to go to the sheep, who are the crowds that are harassed and helpless, the lost people of Israel (9:36: 10:6). But now the disciples themselves are the sheep who are sent out among wolves. Why this reversal? Because, as we noted above, in this section Jesus undertakes a different subject. In the first part of the commissioning, he gave instructions to the disciples about their short-term mission to Israel during his earthly ministry (10:5–15). In this second part he gives instructions to the disciples/apostles about their long-term mission throughout the world until his return, which will include stiff opposition and even persecution, so they are to be aware (10:16–23).

#### 15.2.7.5.2 Jesus's Missionary Disciples Are to Be Wise as Serpents, yet Harmless as Doves (10:16)

Along with the reversal of the sheep metaphor to indicate future danger, Jesus warns the disciples that wariness, yet innocence, will be necessary in the future mission. They must venture out as defenseless sheep in the midst of ravenous wolves, but what will keep them alert to the dangers is to be "wise as serpents and innocent as doves" (10:16, ESV). The serpent was the emblem of wisdom or shrewdness and intellectual keenness (Gen 3:1; Ps 58:5), while the dove represented simple innocence (Hos 7:11). This is a difficult but necessary balance to maintain. Without innocence the keenness of the snake is crafty, a devious menace; without keenness the innocence of the dove is naïve, helpless gullibility (cf. Rom 16:19). As one commentator notes, "The caution of the disciples is to consist not in clever diplomatic moves but in the purity of a life that is genuine and wears no masks."[58]

58. Schweizer, *Matthew*, 240.

### 15.2.7.5.3 Jesus's Missionary Disciples Will Endure Flogging in the Jewish Synagogue (10:17)

Jesus's warning is now explicit: "Be on your guard against men; they will hand you over to the local councils and flog you in their synagogues" (Matt 10:17). The language echoes Jesus's prophetic statement of the way that the Jewish religious leaders will mistreat missionaries (cf. 23:33–34). The synagogue was not only the place of assembly for worship but was also an assembly of justice where discipline was exercised (cf. John 9:35). The place of judgment in individual cities in the Old Testament was in "the gate" (e.g., Ruth 4:1), which may be linked to "councils" (Matt 10:17). Apparently, the synagogue became the central place of authority in individual cities after the exile. Note that it is not "our" or "your" synagogues; it is "their" synagogues. Here the synagogue belongs to those opposed to Jesus's disciples. There is no record of this occurring during the time of the first mission to Israel, so it points to a future persecution.

The Old Testament gave prescriptions for exercising discipline and punishment (Deut 25:1–3), which later Judaism applied to the responsibility of the synagogue. Flogging was prescribed as a punishment for various sins, such as slandering a woman (Deut 22:13–19), incest (Lev 20:17–21), or entering the temple while unclean (Num 5:1–4) (see m. Makkot 3.1–2). An example might be the lifting of the ban upon eating certain meats (e.g., Acts 10:9–16), which would make a Jewish convert to Christ unclean in the eyes of the synagogue officials and subject to flogging (m. Makkot 3.2).

### 15.2.7.5.4 Jesus's Missionary Disciples Will Be Witnesses to Gentiles (10:18)

The future mission of the disciples will take them to high places. "On my account you will be brought before governors and kings as witnesses to them and to the Gentiles" (Matt 10:18). This was the experience of the early church. The book of Acts records times in which early church leaders were first called before Jewish officials of the national council,[59] later before the ruling authorities in Israel,[60] and finally before the rulers of the Roman world.[61] At the time of their trials the mission-disciples will give a witness to these ruling figures of the truthfulness of the gospel message brought by Jesus.

During the first mission they had a general message related to the arrival of the kingdom of heaven (10:7), but when delivered over to trial in the future mission there will be a specific message for the occasion (10:19–20). Persecution will become an opportunity for testimony to the gospel message, but they will not be speaking on their own. Jesus promises that the Spirit will speak through them in the moment of their most difficult scenes of opposition. The Spirit is the creative, empowering, guiding force

59. Acts 4:1–22; 5:17; 7:12.
60. Matt 1:27–23:11.
61. Matt 14:5; 16:19–34; 17:1–9; 18:12–17; 23:24–26:32; 28:17–31.

in Jesus's own life (1:18, 20; 3:11, 16; 4:1; 12:18, 28). It is under the Spirit's influence that Jesus as the servant proclaims justice (12:18), and it is through this same Spirit that Jesus's disciples will find their own empowering and guidance to give the witness required at the time of their greatest need.

### 15.2.7.5.5 Jesus's Missionary Disciples Will Encounter Opposition (10:21–22)

Not only will opposition come from Jewish and gentile officials, but it will also come from the disciples' closest family relations. "Brother will betray brother to death, and a father his child; children will rebel against their parents and have them put to death" (10:21). It is quite possible that Jesus was misperceived by Jewish officials to be a *mesith*,[62] a beguiler of the people, one who entices individuals and even whole towns into idolatry. Moses had warned the people that even if one's own brother or sister, or wife or closest friend tries to beguile a person into idolatry, the *mesith* is to be stoned (Deut 13:6–11). In the future there will be those who think that the disciples are leading the people into idolatry with their call to worship Jesus, and the consequences will be that the mission-disciples will be delivered over to persecution and death.[63] This will be for everyone a tragic misperception of Jesus's identity and message.

Along with family betrayal because of their commitment to Jesus's exclusivity, his disciples will feel the wrath and alienation from humanity for following Jesus and proclaiming his message: "You will be hated by everyone because of me" (Matt 10:22). The same expression is found in the eschatological discourse (24:9), where all the "nations" hate Jesus's disciples. An element of hyperbole may be included, but the statement indicates that there is an unavoidable consequence that comes from attachment to Jesus and his message. The phrase "because of me" is literally "because of my name" (*dia to onoma mou*) and is an important christological expression (cf. 5:11; 24:9) that harks back to the Old Testament significance of God's name as the representation of his person as the sole focus of Israel's worship and allegiance (e.g., Exod 3:15; 6:3; 9:16; 20:7). Jesus's disciples will have the privilege of carrying his name, but it also brings with it suffering because the antagonism and hatred that is directed to him will naturally fall on his followers.[64]

### 15.2.7.5.6 Jesus Messiah's Missionary Disciples Who Endure Will Be Saved (10:22)

But Jesus promises that "he who stands firm to the end will be saved" (Matt 10:22; see also 24:13). By this statement Jesus gives great assurance that in spite of an increase

62. Or *massith*; see *DTBYML*, "יָסַת" 1:583.

63. See D. Neale, "Was Jesus a *Mesith*? Public Response to Jesus and His Ministry," *TynBul* 44.1 (1993): 89–101, esp. 94–98.

64. Cf. John 15:21; 2 Tim 3:12; 1 Pet 4:13–14.

in persecution, the hatred of humanity will not overcome his disciples. Active resistance may be included in standing firm, but much more in view is their enduring fortitude under any circumstance, including the most hateful persecution. Those who endure until the end of the age, when the Son of Man comes, or to the end of their lives, will be saved.

"Will be saved" (10:22) does not speak of rescue from death because many Christians have experienced martyrdom. Instead, Jesus gives both a concrete promise and a cautionary reminder. His *promise* is that the one who remains committed to his name to the end will not be consumed by the persecution but will experience the full blessing and peace of the kingdom's salvation. The *reminder* is that the test of a disciple's real commitment to Jesus is whether he or she remains steadfast to the end. Jesus through his Spirit will provide the resources to withstand whatever difficulties may come (10:19–20); in fact, Jesus himself will be with them to the end of the age to see them through (28: 20).

#### 15.2.7.5.7 Jesus Messiah's Missionary Disciples Have an Ongoing Mission to Israel (10:23)

With the mention of the end (10:22), Jesus culminates the prophetic aspect of the commissioning with a remarkable statement: "Truly I tell you, you will not finish going through the cities of Israel before the Son of Man comes" (10:23). This is one of the most problematic verses in the Bible. One difficulty comes from trying to discern whether going through the cities of Israel is mission oriented (10:11), with a potentially positive reception, or if this is to be seen as flight from persecution. The former is preferred by most commentators. The mission to Israel will continue.[65]

Another significant difficulty is found in trying to understand the temporal context. What does "before the Son of Man comes" mean in this context?[66] Some suggest that Jesus was promising the disciples that they would witness the eschatological coming of the Son of Man while they were on their first Palestinian mission, or at his resurrection, or at Pentecost, or at the destruction of Jerusalem in AD 70.[67] Others contend that this is to be associated with the coming of the Son of Man at the end of the age.

The latter seems to fit the larger context here. While the Jews have priority of salvation (10:6) and of judgment (10:15), their judgment does not permanently exclude them from God's eschatological promises. The ongoing mission to the nations continues to include both Jew and gentile (28:18–20). As Jesus offers comfort to the mission-disciples about their ultimate salvation unto the end (10:22), he warns them not to abandon Israel. When persecuted in one city, they should flee to the next because the mission

65. E.g., Nolland, *Matthew*, 426–27; Turner, *Israel's Last Prophet*, 193–95.

66. Witherington, *Jesus, Paul, and the End*, 39–42.

67. For discussion of these and other views, see Carson, "Matthew," 290–93, who holds to the latter.

to Israel will not conclude before the Son of Man returns. There will be a continuing mission to Israel alongside of the mission to the gentiles until the Son of Man returns.[68]

Despite Israel's hardheartedness, God will remain faithful to his covenant promises to her. And despite the difficulties of the mission for the disciples, they must remain faithful to their calling to bring the message to both Jew and gentile. It will bring persecution, family alienation, and ostracism (10:21–22), but those who endure to the end will be saved. This is a powerful apologetic to the Jews both those involved in Jesus's ministry and those within hearing of Matthew's Gospel—God has not abandoned his covenantal promises. It is also a challenging yet sober call to the mission-disciples to endure to the end with the message of the gospel to all peoples—both Jew and gentile.

Concluding his mission instructions to the disciples as to their short-term mission to Israel and the long-term mission to the world, Jesus resumes his own mission to Israel, and increasingly now to gentiles.

### 15.2.8 Jesus Messiah's Mission Includes Denouncing the Privileged Unrepentant Cities of Israel (11:20–23)

Having rebuked "this generation" (11:16–19) for not responding to John's and his missions, Jesus turns up the heat by denouncing those who have rejected the gospel message (11:20–24). Matthew narrates that Capernaum, Chorazin, and Bethsaida, what some call the "evangelical triangle," were the cities in which most of Jesus's miracles had been performed (11:20). They have had the greatest privilege and opportunity both to hear the gospel message and to see it validated by miracles, but with that privilege comes greater accountability and responsibility. They have rejected Jesus's mission, so upon them each are pronounced a series of "woes." "'Woe to you' is not a grim call for vengeance, but an expression of regret . . .; it combines warning and compassion."[69] But each city has brought this fate upon itself.

The privilege of witnessing Jesus's miraculous mission should have moved the people within the Jewish region of Capernaum, Chorazin, and Bethsaida to repent and accept the invitation to the kingdom of heaven because even the most prideful and arrogant pagans would have repented if they had been exposed to the privilege of the revelation of the gospel brought by Jesus (11:21). Repentance is the appropriate response to Jesus's miracles, which are a validation of his message of the gospel of the kingdom (cf. 4:23; 9:35).

The contrast is heightened. Capernaum, Jesus's own city (9:1, 9; cf. 4:13), had been privileged to be the headquarters of his Galilean ministry, and many of his earliest miracles were performed there, as scores brought their sick and demon-possessed

68. Blomberg, *Matthew*, 176; Davies and Allison, *Matthew*, 2:189–90. So also Gundry, *Matthew*, 194, who, however, doubts the authenticity of the saying.

69. Morris, *Matthew*, 288.

to him.[70] Its prideful self-exaltation at being the locus of Jesus's miraculous ministry will instead result in its being condemned to Hades. Jesus uses a strikingly familiar reference to prideful ancient Babylon (Isa 14:12–15) to emphasize the consequence of Capernaum's satanically stimulated refusal to repent.

### 15.2.9 Jesus Messiah's Mission Receives from Jerusalem's Leadership Opposition That Influences the People of Israel to Respond Negatively (9:3, 33–34; 12:14)

As Matthew narrates Jesus's unfolding public mission, he highlights how the leaders increasingly respond negatively to Jesus, saying that Jesus's preaching and powers are blasphemous (9:3) and satanically inspired (9:33–34) and that he deserves death (12:14). Matthew will clearly implicate the religious leaders of Israel in their opposition to Jesus, but he will also clearly indicate that the people of Israel will succumb to the influence of the leaders and will also reject Jesus.

### 15.2.10 Jesus Messiah's Mission Is to Bring Justice and Hope to the Nations (12:17–21)

Matthew informs us that not only was Jesus healing all those who came, but he was "warning them not to tell who he was" (12:16, NIV84). A regular aspect of Jesus's ministry was to demand secrecy about his identity and activity (8:4; cf. 12:16; 16:20; 17:9) because he carefully avoided stirring up in the crowds a misunderstanding of his messianic identity and mission. The typical person in Israel hoped for liberation from his or her oppression by the Roman occupation and the fulfillment of the promise of a Messiah who would restore the dignity of the Davidic kingdom to Israel. Jesus wanted the people to see that his purpose in coming will not always meet their expectations.

As Matthew now clarifies, Jesus is indeed the Messiah, but he has come meekly to bring justice to the gentiles. Although miracles will attest the authenticity of his gospel message about the arrival of the kingdom of heaven, Jesus does not want crowds clamoring for the miracles alone. They could easily misunderstand his message to mean that he had come to effect only national and military liberation.

Matthew uses his typical fulfillment formula (cf. 1:22; 2:15, etc.) to introduce the longest Old Testament quotation in his Gospel, which identifies Jesus with the messianic servant of Isa 42:1–4 (Matt 12:17–18). The context in Isaiah's prophecy is the section often called the Servant Songs (Isa 40–52). The identity of the servant is perplexing because it vacillates between the nation Israel as the servant (41:8–10; 44:1–3, 21; 45:4 [49:3?]) and an individual who leads the nation (42:1–4; 49:5–7).

70. Matthew 8:5–17; 9:2–8, 18–33; etc.

That individual emerges as the servant Messiah who has a ministry and mission both to Israel and the nations.[71] The phrase "the one I love, in whom I delight" (Matt 12:18) takes the reader back to Jesus's baptism and forward to Jesus's transfiguration, where the Father expresses the same delight in his beloved Son (3:17; 17:5).

In this fulfillment quotation, Matthew harks back to Isaiah's prophecy to give one of the clearest declarations of Jesus's intent as Messiah: he is the gentle, Spirit-endowed, suffering servant who advances a mission of justice to the nations.[72] Later Peter will proclaim that God had anointed Jesus with the Holy Spirit, which in the incarnation was Jesus's source of power for doing good and healing (Acts 10:37–38). Ultimately the same Spirit impelled Peter to go to the gentile centurion Cornelius with the message of the gospel (Acts 10:44–48). The age that Jesus inaugurated with the arrival of the kingdom of heaven is the age of the Spirit. Therefore, to speak against the working of the Spirit is blasphemy, which is the sin that cannot be forgiven (see on Matt 12:28, 31–32). In 12:18, the "justice" (*krisis*) that Jesus brings to the "nations" (*ta ethnē*) combines the sense of grace and judgment that has characterized the theme of inward righteousness that accompanies the arrival of the kingdom of heaven (e.g., 5:20). The servant will pronounce the arrival of the kingdom that is an invitation to kingdom life but which is also a sentence of judgment upon the rulers of this world.

This servant has an unexpected demeanor. Far from painting a picture of an imposing figure of conquest, Matthew continues his citation of the theme of a suffering servant from Isaiah's prophecy (12:19–21). This is a picture of a gentle servant Messiah who will not brazenly demand allegiance with his proclamation of justice but who will gently and humbly invite those who are the most in need (11:28–30). Even as Isaiah knew that evil would not have the ultimate victory, so Matthew points to Jesus and declares that victory is at hand for those who seek God's justice.

But it is not only for Israel. All the nations will put their hope in the name of this servant, the one whom Matthew declares is none other than Jesus of Nazareth (cf. 2:23; 12:21). The "name" stands for the whole of the person, including his identity and mission. Jesus Messiah is a suffering servant who is Spirit-endowed and who offers hope, because the advance of the kingdom of heaven promises victory for all the nations of the world. Michael Bird argues that the origin of the gentile mission is found in Jesus's own mission: "The propulsion and momentum for the origin of the various gentile missions in the early church ultimately derives from the effective history of the historical Jesus."[73]

71. For brief overviews of this complex subject, see Kaiser, *Messiah in the Old Testament*, 173–81; Van Groningen, *Messianic Revelation in the Old Testament*, 575–618.

72. Beaton, "Messiah and Justice," 5–23.

73. Michael F. Bird, *Jesus and the Origins of the Gentile Mission*, LNTS 331 (London: T&T Clark, 2006), 177.

## 15.2.11 Jesus Messiah's Mission Is to Test the Hearts of the People of Israel (13:14–15)

The dramatic place of Jesus's mission in this age—as it concerns the disciples and the crowds—is laid clear by Matthew in his third discourse, the parables of the mysteries of heaven. Here Jesus's parables are designed in part to test the hearts of those in the crowd to see whether they are spiritually responsive to Jesus's invitation to the kingdom of heaven (13:2, 10–17). Jesus uses Isaiah's indictment of ancient Israel to indicate that even as the people (*laos* in Isa 6:9 LXX) of Israel had a long background of unbelief and rejection of God's prior prophets, so the people of Israel in Jesus's day are now hardened against him (Matt 13:14–15).

The indictment of the "people" of Israel may be accentuated when Matthew switches from "crowds" (*ochloi*, 13:2) as the audience of Jesus's parables to "people" (*laos*, 13:15), which we have seen is a common designation in Matthew's Gospel for the people of Israel (e.g., 1:21; 2:6; 4:16; 26:5; 27:25).

The people of Israel in Jesus's day mirrors the people of Israel to whom the prophet Isaiah ministered. They rejected the message because they were spiritually deadened. Jesus's parables are given after the increasing rejection and opposition by both the leaders and people of Israel. God does not force anyone to accept his mission with the message of the kingdom, so the people's response to the parables is dictated by the nature of their heart. If a person does not have spiritual ears to hear Jesus's invitation to the kingdom, his or her heart will be increasingly hardened and he or she will turn away from Jesus and the healing that comes with the arrival of Jesus's mission with the gospel of the kingdom of heaven.[74]

## 15.2.12 Jesus Messiah's Mission to Israel Will Include Healing for a Gentile Woman's Child (15:21–28)

Jesus may have stayed for some time in the Jewish region of Gennesaret on the northwest coast of the Sea of Galilee (14:34), but he now explicitly withdraws to gentile territory, and the infamous cities of Tyre and Sidon. The Jews of Galilee have been privileged to hear and see first Jesus's mission, with the message of the gospel and the miracles that authenticated his announcement of the arrival of the kingdom of heaven (4:12–17). But their lack of repentance is their condemnation (11:20–24). Jesus and his disciples proceed with a mission to gentile regions, and then finally he will set his sights on Judea and the final destination, Jerusalem.

74. Cf. Osborne, *Matthew*, 511–12.

### *15.2.12.1 The Gentile Woman Acknowledges Jesus as the Son of David (15:22–23)*

Jesus's first encounter in the mission in the gentile region is with a Canaanite woman. The expression "Canaanite," which is found only here in the New Testament, indicates a woman from the region that was a virtual stereotype in the Old Testament and rabbinic literature of pagan non-Jews (e.g., m. Qiddushin 1.3).

Intriguingly, this pagan woman demonstrates familiarity with Jewish messianic tradition by calling Jesus "Son of David" (see Matt 1:1; 9:27) and calling for his merciful, miraculous ministry of exorcism for her daughter. A temple dedicated to Eshmun, a god of healing, was excavated five kilometers northwest of Sidon.[75] This woman was quite likely familiar with the pagan deity, but Jesus's reputation has preceded him, and she comes to Jesus for her daughter's healing instead of Eshmun. Her use of "Lord" three times in the interaction (15:22, 25, 27) is probably for her a title of great respect, but she is saying more than she realizes.

Jesus does not reply to the woman's cry for help, which the disciples apparently take as his way of rebuffing the woman's request. So, they urge him, "Send her away, for she keeps crying out after us" (15:23). The disciples most likely remembered Jesus's mission charge that included the directive not to go to gentiles but only to the lost sheep of Israel (cf. 10:5–6). Given that prior directive, the disciples attempt to turn the woman away.

### *15.2.12.2 Jesus Messiah Reaffirms the Priority of Israel (15:24)*

In this gentile region, Jesus maintains his commitment to fulfill the mission for which he was sent as he says, "I was sent only to the lost sheep of Israel" (15:24). As we recognized in the mission discourse (cf. 10:6), "lost sheep of Israel" does not mean the lost sheep *among* Israel, as though some are lost and others not. The expression indicates the lost sheep *who are* the house of Israel. Jesus comes as the suffering servant who has come to save all of Israel. Jesus's mission dictates that he must first go to Israel with the fulfillment of the promises made to the nation (cf. Isa 53:6–8), so that the gentiles themselves would glorify God for his promises made to his people.

### *15.2.12.3 The Gentile Woman Understands God's Mission and Program of Care for All of His Creatures (15:25–26)*

The woman's great need to have her daughter exorcised drives her to be persistent, which is a sign that she knows that Jesus certainly can come to her aid. She kneels in humble obeisance before Jesus and calls him Lord a second time as she seeks his help for her daughter (Matt 15:25).

---

75. Cf. Rousseau and Arav, "Tyre and Sidon," in *Jesus and His World*, 327–28.

However, Jesus maintains his commitment to his mission to Israel. He replies, "It is not right to take the children's bread and toss it to the dogs" (15:25–26). The "children's bread" may be an allusion to the messianic banquet[76] but more likely emphasizes the care that God promised to provide for his covenant children, Israel (Deut 14:1–2; Hos 11:1). As a metaphor, "dogs" is a humiliating label for those apart from, or enemies of, Israel's covenant community (1 Sam 17:43; Ps 22:16; Prov 26:11).[77] Jesus used the metaphor similarly in the Sermon on the Mount to indicate that the holy message of the gospel of the kingdom must not be defiled by those who are unreceptive to, or have rejected, Jesus's invitation (Matt 7:6). Some suggest that the diminutive form used here (*kynarion*), but not in 7:6 (*kyon*), conjures up an image of a little puppy dog, so that Jesus is using the term as an endearing metaphor. More likely, the diminutive form parallels "children's bread" and suggests a dog that has been domesticated but is nonetheless still a dog. Jesus uses a common metaphor to indicate the contrast between God's care for those of his family and those who are not. He is not condoning the use of a derogatory title, as the response of the woman indicates.

The woman continues the metaphor but uses it to emphasize that dogs too had a caring relationship with "their master" (15:27). This very perceptive woman, who had already confessed Jesus as the messianic son of David, now presses Jesus by calling upon the extended blessings promised to the gentiles. Although Israel receives the primary blessings of the covenant, gentiles also were to be the recipient of blessing through them, a promise central to the Abrahamic covenant (Gen 12:3; see Matt 1:1; 8:5–13).[78] The woman draws upon that promise to seek the aid of Jesus Messiah.

### *15.2.12.4 Jesus Messiah Affirms the Great Faith of the Gentile Woman and Heals Her Daughter (15:28)*

This gentile woman understands the mission and program of God to go to Israel first but nonetheless persists. Jesus's reply seems somewhat harsh, given her desperate straits, but in a sense, he was testing her. Would she see through the salvation-historical distinction between Israel and the gentiles and recognize that God ultimately desires to bring healing to all people? She passes with flying colors because she acknowledges that, as the Messiah of Israel, Jesus is the master of all, and he will care for the needs of all, whether Jews ("children") or gentiles ("dogs").

Her response is called by Jesus an exercise of "great faith," which was rewarded by having her daughter healed that very hour (15:28). The vocative expression "woman" expresses Jesus's deep emotion at the woman's humble and insightful

76. Hagner, *Matthew 14–28*, 442.

77. See Neusner and Green, "Dog," *DJBP* 172; Ryken et al., "Animals," "Dogs," *DBI* 29, 213–14.

78. See F. Gerald Downing, "The Woman from Syrophoenicia, and Her Doggedness: Mark 7:24–31 (Matthew 15:21–28)," in *Women in the Biblical Tradition*, ed., George J. Brooke, Studies in Women and Religion 31 (Lewiston: Edwin Mellen, 1992), 129–49; cf. Jackson, *Have Mercy on Me*.

interaction.[79] Even though God has a program, he responds to true faith in any case.[80] The privileged people of Nazareth did not respond in faith to Jesus's mission, and so could not receive Jesus's healing ministry (see 13:58). But this gentile woman had an openness to Jesus that allowed his healing ministry to operate.

Here we understand that faith is essentially accepting the revelation and will of God as one's own reality and purpose for life. The "greatness" of faith points to the fact that in such an unlikely person—a gentile woman living outside of Israel—this mother demonstrates one of the clearest understandings of God's salvation-historical program and Jesus's participation in this mission. This is another incident where exorcism is called "healing" (cf. 12:22–23) and is a continuation of the confirmation of Jesus's messianic mission. This is also another incident in which Jesus's mission bears out the salvation-historical appropriateness of going first to Israel with the offer of salvation but in which his compassion demonstrates that he also has an eye on the ultimate ingathering of all peoples (8:5–13).[81]

### *15.2.12.5 Jesus Messiah's Mission Responds to Great Faith and Ungrateful Privilege*

In this passage it is initially shocking that Jesus seems ready to ignore the request of the woman simply because she is a non-Israelite, and some commentators have been scathing in their criticism of Jesus for his lack of ethnic sensitivity.[82] But as we noted, Jesus does not demonstrate ethnic bigotry against gentiles but salvation-historical privilege for Israel. His mission is initially to go to Israel, but the whole world eventually will be blessed through Israel. Jesus will develop this plan further, but we get a peek of the broader picture here that has as its eventual scope the entire world (28:19) and all people groups (21:43).

While there is no real evidence that Jesus lifts his particularistic priority of Israel during his earthly ministry,[83] we can see an initial hint here of Jesus's mission to reach beyond the ethnic borders of Israel to help the non-Israelite woman (cf. also the centurion's son, 8:5). And this shows his heart. In the same way that he had compassion on the harassed and helpless people of Israel, who are like sheep without a shepherd (9:36), he has compassion on a little girl and her mother, who are like dogs without a scrap of hope, and he responds. In either case his response is to those who have opened eyes of faith to see him and respond to him.

79. Wallace, *Greek Grammar*, 68.

80. Gene R. Smillie, "'Even the Dogs': Gentiles in the Gospel of Matthew," *JETS* 45.1 (2002): 73–97; esp. 93–95; T. W. Manson, *Only to the House of Israel?*, 3rd ed., Facet Books Biblical Series 9 (1955; repr., Philadelphia: Fortress, 1964), 22–23.

81. Scott, "Gentiles and the Ministry of Jesus," 161–69.

82. E.g., Beare, *Matthew*, 341–42.

83. Frederick W. Schmidt, "Jesus and the Salvation of the Gentiles," in *Through No Fault of their Own? The Fate of Those Who Have Never Heard*, ed. William V. Crockett and James G. Sigountos (Grand Rapids: Baker, 1991), 97–105.

The vast majority of those within Israel who were privileged to see and hear him first will ultimately reject him. So, this woman of great faith gives us due warning and instruction. Privilege demands accountability, and faith in Jesus's identity and mission brings the touch of the kingdom's blessing. Not simply the blessing of wealth; quite possibly the woman already had that. And not even the blessing of health, because the mother herself received nothing noted, and her little daughter would eventually die physically. Rather, like the earlier incident of the centurion, this gentile woman of great faith is a foretaste of the promise of the eschatological feast of salvation that all those from every point of the compass will enjoy who respond to Jesus's summons to the kingdom of heaven (8:10–12).

I live in great privilege, both materially and physically. I also have had a great privilege to grow up in a culture where the gospel has throughout my life been freely proclaimed. But privilege can also be a hindrance to spiritual realities. The kingdom's blessing turns upside down many of our typical conceptions of privilege. I have been remarkably touched by a different kind of privilege that I have seen in men and women of great faith around the world. The sheer delight of poor church people in the slums outside of Manila in the Philippines results from their understanding of their privilege to experience their new-found eternal life in Christ. The steadfast courage of a group of pastors from Muslim countries in central Asia results as they rejoice in their privilege to suffer for the name of Jesus. The unfathomable peace of Christian patients in intensive care wards in hospitals around the world results from their recognition that they are loved by the one who holds the health of their souls in his tender hands.

This wonderful story of the persistent mother warns and instructs us that Jesus always responds to those who have the courage to come to him with their desperate need, because true privilege comes through openness to him in faith, whether Jew or gentile.

### 15.2.13 Jesus Messiah's Mission Increasingly Turns to Gentiles (15:29–31)

Jesus returns to the region of Galilee (15:29), but Mark specifies that he goes to the Decapolis (Mark 7:31), which is in the primarily gentile region on the southeastern coast of the Sea of Galilee. Jesus performs miracles here among great crowds (Matt 15:30). When Jesus began to withdraw from Galilee great crowds had followed him to seek his healing, and now in this gentile region he continues that healing ministry, authenticating his message that the kingdom of God has arrived. When juxtaposed with the preceding story that emphasized the salvation-historical priority of Israel first, and then the gentiles, the dropping of "crumbs" to the gentile mother and daughter prepares for a turning to gentiles with the bread and fish of the miraculous feeding of the four thousand.

Gentiles increasingly become the focus of his ministry now that the religious leadership is working to turn the people away from him.[84] As Israel rejects the kingdom, gentiles increasingly come into view as recipients of his message and healing. Like the crowd in Israel, they are amazed when they see his miraculous ministry and they "praised the God of Israel" (15:31; cf. 9:33). But like Israel's crowd, it will not be enough to be amazed. They must believe on him as the Messiah of the nations and become his disciples.

### 15.2.14 Jesus Messiah's Mission Includes Feeding Four Thousand Among the Gentiles (15:32–39)

Jesus has compassion for these primarily gentile people who have listened to his mission message and received his miraculous healings for three days and have had nothing to eat (15:32). This is now the second time that Jesus feeds a crowd of thousands miraculously after spending time healing those brought to him, although now he is in the primarily gentile region of Decapolis.[85]

Some conclude that this feeding of the four thousand is a Matthean doublet of the earlier feeding of the five thousand. But the significant differences point to two separate incidents in which Jesus confirms to masses of people at one time that he is the Messiah of Israel who has come to offer redemption to the gentiles as well.[86] Matthew is emphasizing that Jesus's mission is now shifting to the gentiles.

In this feeding the number of small bread cakes is seven, and there are seven baskets left over (15:37). If the number of twelve baskets left over in the feeding of the five thousand is symbolic of Israel, as most suppose, then the number seven here, which is normally symbolic of perfection or completion, may symbolize the completion or fullness of God meeting the needs of all peoples, here now including gentiles.[87] The word for basket is *spyris* (15:37), a large, flexible basket, often with handles, that was used for carrying provisions. When compared to the feeding of the five thousand, an interesting contrast occurs. There the word for "basket" was *kophinos*, a smaller container that occurs in Jewish contexts to denote a hamper for carrying kosher foods.[88] This appears to once more distinguish the Jewish and gentile settings of the feeding miracles.[89]

84. Carson, "Matthew," 406–7.

85. For further discussion see the feeding of the five thousand in 14:13–21.

86. Morris, *Matthew*, 406–7.

87. Cf. Hagner, *Matthew 14–28*, 451–52; less convinced is Carson, "Matthew," 409.

88. Millard, "Basket," *IBD* 1:177–178; Bargil Pixner, *With Jesus Through Galilee According to the Fifth Gospel* (Israel: Corazin, 1992), 83.

89. Cf. Osborne, *Matthew*, 609.

### 15.2.15 Jesus Messiah's Mission Receives Opposition from Israel's Leadership (Esp. Chs. 11; 21–23; 26–27)

In the Matthean narrative, Jesus Messiah's mission to Israel fulfills covenantal promises, but Israel as a nation does not repent and enter the kingdom of heaven. Very early in Matthew's presentation of Jesus's mission we can see hints of condemnation of the leadership of Israel (5:20) and hints of condemnation of unrepentant people of Israel (8:11–13). The negative responses to Jesus's mission continue until their culmination in Matthew's narrative of the passion week. After the confrontation between Jesus and the authorities in the temple area (chs. 21–23), Matthew narrates the plotting by the chief priests, the elders of the people, and the high priest, Caiaphas, to have Jesus arrested, tried, convicted, and executed (cf. 26:3–4). One of Jesus's own, Judas Iscariot, plots to betray Jesus and turn him over for the arrest and trial by the religious leaders (26:47–57). They convict him of blasphemy (26:59–68) and then plot to accuse him of insurrection and turn him over to the Roman authorities for execution (27:1–2). Matthew accentuates the reality that Israel's leadership cannot escape their culpability for Jesus's death.

### 15.2.16 Israel's Leadership Persuades the People of Israel to Reject Jesus and His Earthly Mission (27:25)

The story of Jesus's earthly mission culminates in the disastrous trial of Jesus before Pilate. The religious leaders of Israel persuade the crowds to demand that Barabbas be released and that Jesus be crucified (cf. 27:20–25). Matthew then records the tragic declaration that as one "people" (*laos*) they answer, "His blood is on us and on our children!" (27:25). The crowds of Israel have joined the leadership of Israel as one people demanding the execution of Jesus Messiah.

The people of that day, as in any day, are responsible for their own actions. So only that generation of Roman officials and Israel's leaders and people are implicated in the death of Jesus.[90] But what of the mission to Israel?

### 15.2.17 Jesus Messiah's Mission Is Entrusted to His Disciples in the Great Commission (28:16–20)

We have observed above a striking emphasis in Matthew's Gospel upon Jesus's particularistic mission to Israel. But we also see in Matthew's Gospel an equally remarkable emphasis upon a universal mission to all the nations of the earth. From beginning to end Matthew emphasizes a particularistic mission to Israel and a universal mission to the gentiles. In the very first verse we see that the arrival in history of Jesus Messiah brings the fulfillment of the promise of blessing to Israel and to gentiles. The final

90. Osborne, *Matthew*, 1021.

designation of the identity of Jesus Messiah in the incipit is that he is the "son of Abraham" (1:1). This recalls the covenant promise God made with the Abraham, the father of Israel, to not only bless the nation Israel as his chosen people but also to bless all the nations of the earth through Abraham's line. And in the final verses of Matthew's Gospel, we hear the thundering Great Commission in which Jesus Messiah commands his disciples to make disciples of "all the nations" (28:19).

Jesus reserved an undisguised declaration of the universal mission until after the resurrection, but all through Matthew there are hints of its coming. This is part of Jesus's own earthly economy of salvation history, and Matthew has emphasized it for his own apologetic message to his Jewish kinsmen and Jewish-Christian community (see on 10:6).[91]

### *15.2.17.1 To Believe in the Gospel Message Was to Become a Disciple*

Jesus committed his earthly ministry to "making disciples" within Israel (cf. 4:12–25; John 4:1), and he commissioned his disciples to "make disciples" among the nations (Matt 28:16–20). The meaning of "making disciples" is to proclaim the gospel message among those who have not yet received forgiveness of sins, with the intent of them becoming Jesus's disciples (cf. Luke 24:46–47; John 20:21).[92] The command finds remarkable verbal fulfillment in the activities of the early church, where disciples went from Jerusalem to Judea, to Samaria, to the ends of the earth proclaiming the message of Jesus and "making disciples" (Acts 14:21). In the early church, to believe in the gospel message was to secure salvation and become a disciple (cf. Acts 4:32 with 6:2).

### *15.2.17.2 Jesus's Great Commission Implies Securing Salvation and the Process of Growth as a Disciple*

As mentioned in 10.6.3.4, Jesus's Great Commission implies more than securing salvation as Jesus's disciple. It also includes the process of growth as a disciple.[93] As he addresses the disciples and commands them to "make disciples of all nations" (28:19), Jesus is telling the disciples to continue the disciple making that he began with them. The *imperative* "make disciples" (*mathēteusate*) implies both the call to discipleship and the process of growth in discipleship. Even as men and women are called from among the nations to start life as a disciple, they must in turn follow Jesus through baptism and through being taught to obey all that Jesus commanded. The *participle* "go" (*poreuthentes*) points to the obligation of disciples to reach out to all the nations, and the *participles* "baptizing" (*baptizontes*, 28:19) and "teaching" (*didaskontes*, 28:19) describe activities through which new disciples grow in discipleship. Growth in discipleship

91. John P. Meier, "Salvation-History in Matthew: In Search of a Starting Point," *CBQ* 37 (1975): 203–15.

92. Lészai, "Mission of the Disciples," 65–83.

93. Osborne, *Resurrection Narratives*, 91; Silva, "New Lexical Semitisms?," 256n9.

includes both identification with Jesus's death and resurrection ("baptism") and obedience to all that Jesus had commanded the disciples in his earthly ministry ("teaching them to obey all Jesus commanded").

#### *15.2.17.3 An Invitation to Salvation and a Summons to Service*

This commissioning points once again to the uniqueness of Jesus's form of discipleship. Jesus's call was at the same time an invitation to salvation and a summons to service. Understood within the broader biblical concept of "calling," Jesus summoned his disciples in a manner similar to the way God called Israel to be the blessed people and to be a blessing for others. Even as Israel was not called solely to be God's people and to enjoy his blessing but was in turn to be the source of blessing to all the nations of the earth, so also when Jesus issued his call it meant both a call to enter into a discipleship relationship with him and to become fellow workers with him in the kingdom.

Men and women were called into a relationship with Jesus, which secured their own salvation and secured the ongoing proclamation of the good news. While some passages seem to emphasize one element more than the other, Jesus's call to follow him—whether to the Twelve or the broader group of disciples—meant that those who responded would join him in both the blessings of the gospel message and the future proclamation of the gospel message.

In the use of the full title "the eleven disciples" (28:16), Matthew addresses the solidarity of the church with the Commission, while at the same time he acknowledges the leadership role of the apostolic circle. As "the Eleven" these followers have a unique role in the foundation of the church and in salvation history (19:28). As "disciples" they represent all those who have entered into eternal life in Jesus's invitation to enter the kingdom of heaven (19:29). Therefore, as "the Eleven," the injunction of the Great Commission is given to those who have a leadership role in the church; but as "disciples," they are a paradigm for all believers. Hence, in their role as "the eleven disciples" the Great Commission is the obligation of all believers.[94]

## 15.3 THE RELATIONSHIP OF THE MISSION DISCOURSE (CH. 10) AND THE GREAT COMMISSION (28:16–20)

Reading Matthew's Gospel leads us to many texts that appear to be in tension with each other. Jesus emphatically declares that he has come "not to abolish the Law or the Prophets" (5:17), yet later he defends his disciples when they pick grain on the Sabbath (12:1–8) and defends vigorously his own healing on the Sabbath (12:9–14), stating

94. Cf. also Carson, "Matthew," 666–70.

that "something greater than the temple is here" (12:6). Jesus endorses the Decalogue's imperative to honor father and mother and criticizes scribes and Pharisees for not doing so (15:4–6; 19:17–19), yet when a would-be follower desires to bury his father, Jesus states flatly, "Follow me, and let the dead bury their own dead" (8:22). Students of Matthew's Gospel have wrestled with many ways of dealing with such tensions, as is evident by glancing through current commentaries and monographs on Matthew.[95]

In this Chapter we have addressed one such tension that is widely recognized. Matthean scholars regularly point to what is often dubbed the tension of particularism and universalism in Matthew's view of mission. In 10:5–6 Jesus confines mission to the particular people of Israel. However, in 28:18–20 Jesus expands the mission universally when he addresses the eleven disciples. How should we relieve the tension of these perspectives on mission? We have touched on related issues in earlier Chapters, where we discussed the relationship of the disciples of Jesus to Israel, so here we will build on conclusions reached there.

### 15.3.1 Three Primary Views of the Relationship of 10:5–6 and 28:18–20

In Matt 28:19, the object of the imperative "make disciples" is *panta ta ethnē*, which has occasioned a long-standing debate. Does *panta ta ethnē* mean "all the nations" or "all the gentiles?" That is, all the nations including Israel, or all the nations except Israel? Is the command of Jesus in 10:5–6 to go only to the lost sheep of the house of Israel expanded in 28:19a to include Israel and gentiles, or is it replaced by the missions command of 28:19a to exclude Israel?[96]

Luz notes, "The question is fundamental for understanding Matthean theology, because it reaches into almost all of its areas. Has the proclamation in Israel definitely failed, and is it now abandoned, or does it continue, alongside the mission to non-Jews that is now commanded by the risen Jesus?"[97] Luz queries further,

> The disciples are sent to πάντα τὰ ἔθνη [*panta ta ethnē*]. Does that mean "all nations" or "all Gentiles"—that is, all nations except Israel? Is the command of Jesus in 10:5–6 to go only to the lost sheep of the house of Israel expanded in v. 19a, or is it replaced by the "missions command" of v. 19a?[98]

Donaldson recently asks the further questions:

95. For an overview of approaches toward dealing with Matthean tensions, see Dale C. Allison Jr., "Deconstructing Matthew," in *Studies in Matthew: Interpretation Past and Present* (Grand Rapids: Baker Academic, 2005), 237–49.

96. Donaldson, "'Nations,' 'Non-Jewish Nations,' or 'Non-Jewish Individuals,'" 169.

97. Luz, *Matthew 21–28*, 628–29.

98. Luz, *Matthew 21–28*, 628.

> Does ἔθνη [*ethnē*] here have the distinctive sense of "non-Jewish nations," so that the command is to "make disciples of all the gentiles"? Or is the word to be taken in its basic sense of "nations" (a category to which Israel would also belong), so that the command is to "make disciples of all the nations (Israel included)"? Should πάντα τὰ ἔθνη be read exclusively (all the gentile nations) or inclusively (all the nations without exception)?[99]

There are at least three primary views of the relationship of 10:5–6 and 28:18–20, with numerous refinements of each.[100]

#### *15.3.1.1 Matthew 28:19 Reverses or Replaces 10:5–6 by Redirecting Mission from Jews Alone to Gentiles Alone*

The minority view is that 28:19 reverses or replaces 10:5–6 by redirecting mission from Jews alone to gentiles alone.[101] In this view, some argue that "all the nations" means only gentiles, not the Jews, since Matthew normally refers to gentiles by this title. Kenneth Clark is representative of this view, in which he contends that Jesus's command to the Eleven that they "make disciples of all the gentile peoples" serves as the capstone and climax of a gentile bias that has been building throughout the gospel as a whole. Matthew's perspective is that "Judaism as such has definitely rejected Jesus as God's Messiah, and God has finally rejected Judaism."[102] Others often appeal to this view because of Jesus's harsh statements about taking the kingdom away from the Jewish leaders or nation and giving it to a nation (*ethnei*, singular) producing its fruit (21:43).[103]

#### *15.3.1.2 Matthew 28:19 Expands the Disciples' Mission from Jews Exclusively to Include Jews and Gentiles*

The traditional or majority view is that 28:19 expands the disciples' mission from Jews exclusively in 10:5–6 to include Jews and gentiles.[104] Davies and Allison are

99. Donaldson, "'Nations,' 'Non-Jewish Nations,' or 'Non-Jewish Individuals,'" 169–94; here 169; see his full chapter for recent discussion.

100. See Luz, *Matthew 21–28*, 628–31; Turner, *Israel's Last Prophet*, 200–220; Turner, "His Glorious Throne," 162–68.

101. E.g., Clark, "Gentile Bias in Matthew," 165–72; Hare, *Theme of Jewish Persecution*; Lloyd Gaston, "The Messiah of Israel as Teacher of the Gentiles: The Setting of Matthew's Christology," *Int* 29 (1975): 24–40; Hare and Harrington, "Make Disciples," 359–69; Kio, "Understanding and Translating 'Nations,'" 230–39.

102. Clark, "Gentile Bias in Matthew," 166.

103. See discussion in Chapter 12.

104. E.g., in commentaries, see Blomberg, *Matthew*, 176; Culpepper, *Matthew*, 279–81; 757–59; Davies and Allison, *Matthew*, 2:189–90; 3:684–85; Keener, *Matthew*, 324–25; Nolland, *Matthew* (2009), 428–29. In his 2008 commentary Turner leaned toward this second view; see Turner, *Matthew*, 277. In focused essays and monographs, see Meier, "Nations or Gentiles in Matthew 28:19?," 94–102; Schuyler Brown, "The Mission to Israel in Matthew's Central Section (Mt 9:35–11:1)," *ZNW* 69 (1978): 73–90; Brown, "The Matthean Community and the Gentile Mission," *NovT* 22.3 (1980): 193–220; Eugene Eung-Chun Park, "Matthew's Theology of Mission," in *Mission Discourse in Matthew's Interpretation*, esp. ch. 5: 167–86; Stuhlmacher, "Matt 28:16–20," 17–43; Kvalbein, "Has Matthew Abandoned the Jews?," 44–62; P. Foster, *Community, Law and Mission*, esp. ch. 6: Mission in Matthew's Gospel, 218–52; Ådna, "Mission to Israel," 45–60; Brands, *Life and Ministry of Jesus*, e.g., ii, 143, 219, 341, 360.

representative of this view. They emphasize that the resurrection marks the end of the exclusive focus on Israel. But they believe that the meaning of *panta ta ethnē* includes Israel: "universal lordship means universal mission."[105] Luz presents an interesting situation, in that his comments on 10:5–6 shows a certain sympathy for the minority position but without coming to a definitive conclusion. However, in his comments on 28:16–20 he suggests that from his exegesis of 24:9, 14 and 25:31–46, the weight of the arguments has shifted for him.[106] He concludes that the mission command of the Lord of the whole world is *fundamentally* universal and is for all nations. "While it does not exclude a continuing mission to Israel, Matthew probably no longer has great hopes for it; that is shown by 22:8–10; 23:39–24:2; and 28:15. For him and his churches the separation of Israel into a majority hostile to Jesus and a minority consisting of disciples of Jesus is definitive."[107] France states of this Great Commission, "The commission is of course to go far *beyond* Israel, but that does not require that Israel be excluded."[108] Keener is more positive: "What is important to remember is that the Gentile mission extends the Jewish mission—not replaces it; Jesus nowhere revokes the mission to Israel (10:6), but merely adds a new mission revoking a previous prohibition (10:5)."[109] Nolland notes, "Though the claim is made from time to time, 28:19 does not turn from the Jews to the Gentiles; rather, it widens the scope from that of 10:5, which is in view."[110]

### *15.3.1.3 Matthew 28:19 Introduces Two Separate Missions: One to Israel and One to the Nations*

A relatively recent and unique view that has gained traction among some Matthean scholars suggests that Matthew saw two separate missions: one to Israel and one to the nations.[111] Donaldson suggests tentatively that Matthew envisages two ongoing, complementary, and coterminous missions—one to "the lost sheep of the house of Israel" (10:5–15; 15:24) and the other to "all the non-Jewish *ethnē*" (28:18–20), which continues until the coming of the Son of Man (10:23).[112] This results in an *ekklēsia* of disciples drawn from both "the house of Israel" and "all the non-Jewish *ethnē*." In this

105. Davies and Allison, *Matthew*, 3:684.

106. Luz, *Matthew 21–28*, 629.

107. Luz, *Matthew 21–28*, 631.

108. France, *Gospel of Matthew*, 1114 (emphasis original).

109. Keener, *Matthew* (2009), 719.

110. Nolland, *Matthew*, 1265–66.

111. Levine, *Social and Ethnic Dimensions*, esp. 2, 185–97; 273–78; David C. Sim, "The Gospel of Matthew and the Gentiles," *JSNT* 57 (1995): 19–48; esp. 41–44; "Matthew, Paul and the Origin and Nature of the Gentile Mission: The Great Commission in Matthew 28:16–20 as an Anti-Pauline Tradition," *HvTSt* 64.1 (2008): 377–92, https://doi.org/10.4102/hts.v64i1.28; Axel von Dobbeler, "Die Restitution Israels und die Bekehrung der Heiden: Das Verhältnis von Mt 10,5b–6 und Mt 28,18–20 unter dem Aspekt der Komplementarität: Erwägungen zum Standort des Matthausevangeliums," *ZNW* 91 (2000): 18–44; Konradt, *Israel, Church, and the Gentiles*, esp. 311–17; Runesson, *Divine Wrath and Salvation in Matthew*, 373–88; esp. 379n97; Brian J. Tucker, "Matthew's Missional Particularism and the Continuation of Gentile Social Identity," *Canadian-American Theological Review* 5.1 (2016): 15–24; esp. 24; Willitts, "Friendship of Matthew and Paul"; Donaldson, "'Nations,' 'Non-Jewish Nations,' or 'Non-Jewish Individuals,'" 169–94.

112. Donaldson, "Matthew 28:19 Revisited," 191.

view, at some level, the categories Jew and gentile, or Israel and the non-Jewish *ethnē*, continue to have a significant place within the new *ekklēsia* of Jesus.[113] Willitts likewise argues for a Jewish mission and an "all the nations" mission, because the aim of the mission of Jesus and his disciples was ethnically distinct: two different groups entailing two different missionary tasks. "The mission to Israel involved the announcement of the coming of the kingdom of God and Israel's restoration (Mt 10). In contrast, the mission to the nations meant the extension of the kingdom of God throughout the whole earth and implied the conversion of the nations to the living God (Mt 28)."[114]

### 15.3.2 Evaluation of the Primary Views of the Relationship of 10:5–6 and 28:18–20

The movement of the Matthean Jesus's particularistic focus on the mission to the "lost sheep of the house of Israel" (10:5–6, ESV) to the universalistic focus on the mission to "all nations" (28:19) is a very difficult one to interpret. Nolland states, "Matthew will not give a full answer to the question how one can get from this starting point to an unrestricted Gentile mission."[115] I have reduced my evaluation of the arguments to the following.

#### *15.3.2.1 Assessment of Views of Mission in Matthew's Gospel*

In my assessment, the primary argument of the first view is the culpability of the leaders and the people of Israel for rejecting the mission of Jesus and Jesus's taking the kingdom away from them (see on 21:43). However, as we concluded earlier, this does not mean that Jewish people cannot be part of the kingdom of heaven but rather that the responsibility for being stewards of the kingdom of heaven is taken away from Israel.[116] This convinces me that the first view is not broad enough to include Israel in the universal appeal of the Matthean Jesus.

The primary argument of the third view is that since nowhere does the Matthean Jesus rescind the mission to Israel, it remains intact, and it must have a separate fulfillment from the universal mission to all the nations. However, although the Matthean Jesus continues to appeal to Israel, we have seen in the discussion above that the movement of the Matthean Jesus is increasingly to include gentiles, and this is seen within the mission to Israel. This perceived movement convinces me that the third view draws too great a wedge between the mission to restore Israel and the mission to include the gentiles in God's salvation-historical scheme. The Matthean Jesus has one mission that in some way fulfills the priority of Israel in God's salvation-historical scheme and at the same time fulfills the promise of the inclusion of gentiles.

113. Donaldson, "Matthew 28:19 Revisited," 188–94.
114. Willitts, "Friendship of Matthew and Paul," 4.
115. Nolland, *Matthew*, 415.
116. See our discussion in Chs. 12–13.

I therefore respect the argumentation and intent of the first and third views but affirm the second view: Jesus has one mission that fulfills the covenantal priority of Israel yet within that fulfills the promise of the inclusion of the gentiles.[117]

### *15.3.2.2 Support from the Mission of the Matthean Jesus*

Some of the following incidents in my view affirm the mission of Jesus that foretells the one universal mission of the Great Commission. During his mission the Matthean Jesus focused on the lost sheep of the house of Israel, yet at the same time Matthew prepares the reader for the inclusion of gentiles.

We see this at least in part in the coming of the gentile magi (2:1–12) to worship the one born "king of the Jews." We also see in Jesus's mission an inclusion of the gentile centurion, who is representative of those who will come from the east and the west and take their places at the feast with the patriarchs of Israel—Abraham, Isaac, and Jacob—in the kingdom of heaven (8:5–13). Inclusion of gentiles in Jesus's mission is also seen in the two gentile Gadarene men from whom Jesus exorcised demons after his Jewish disciples marveled at his identity after the stilling of the storm (8:28–34).

Within Jesus's mission to Israel where he heals the Jewish crowds, and where the Jewish leaders plot to kill Jesus, Matthew tells us that Jesus is the Isaianic servant of the Lord who brings justice and hope to the gentiles (12:14–21; cf. Isa 42:1–4).

Within Jesus's mission to Israel in the regions of Galilee, Matthew tells of an incident where Jesus and his disciples are in gentile Tyre and Sidon (Matt 15:21–28). Jesus affirms the priority of the people Israel (15:24) but also affirms the faith of the gentile Canaanite woman in her plea for healing of her daughter (15:28). In his startling parabolic reply to the woman, the bread given to the Jewish "children" also results in breadcrumbs falling to gentile "dogs," speaking of Jesus's one mission that includes the priority of Israel in salvation history yet at the same time affirms the place of gentiles' accessibility to the kingdom of heaven (15:25–28).[118] Konradt observes that "She recognizes in Jesus not only the Messiah of Israel, but as the one who *as Israel's Messiah* is also the one who brings salvation to the Gentiles."[119] In this incident involving the gentile Canaanite woman, we see one mission that includes both Israel and gentiles, which retains the priority of Israel in salvation history and at the same time foretells the one universal mission of the forthcoming Great Commission.

117. Wick, "Verborgenes und Befohlenes," 132–44. Wick argues that Jesus offers his disciples teaching "*Theorie*" in the mission discourse that they must then transform into real-world "Praxis" in the worldwide mission that is applicable in training for church service today (Wick, "Verborgenes und Befohlenes," 140).

118. Osborne, *Matthew*, 599–600; Nolland, *Matthew*, 633–36.

119. Konradt, *Matthew*, 241; his emphasis.

### *15.3.2.3 Israel and Gentiles Are the Focus of "All the Nations" (28:19)*

I therefore agree with the majority opinion that Jesus's overall intention is to include Jews and gentiles in his Great Commission.[120] This becomes the joint object of the imperative "make disciples" (28:19). *Panta ta ethnē* includes a universal mission to all the peoples of the world. The full expression "all the nations" is used four times in Matthew in settings that more naturally comprise all peoples, including Jews (24:9, 14; 25:32; 28:19). Nolland is representative as he states, "Matthew uses ἔθνη [*ethnē*] alone when referring to the Gentiles, but when he speaks of 'all the ἔθνη', he no longer uses ἔθνη to distinguish Gentiles from Jews but rather refers to the whole of humanity."[121] The rest of the New Testament clearly has in view the evangelism of Jews as a part of missionary strategies (e.g., Acts 2:22; 13:38–39; Rom 1:16; Eph 2:11–16). For Matthew, Jesus's universal lordship entails a universal mission, including Israel with the other nations, and an eventual universal judgment.[122]

Individual Jews are invited to participate in the salvation brought by Jesus with the arrival of the kingdom of heaven. When they respond positively, they become disciples of Jesus and are included in the church. Together, Jewish believers in Jesus and gentile believers in Jesus are disciples of Jesus, who now comprise the *ekklēsia* of Jesus that together are engaged in making disciples of *panta ta ethnē* of the world. As with the mission of the early church, there will be differences of a sensitive approach to those of different ethnicity, gender, culture, or historical setting.

Therefore, in the Commission Matthew returns to the universal theme of the introductory verse of the Gospel (1:1). There the blessings promised to Abraham and through him to all people of the earth (Gen 12:3) are said now to be fulfilled in Jesus the Messiah. When the original covenant promise to Abraham (Gen 12:3) is reiterated (Gen 18:18; 22:18), the Septuagint uses the same words found in Matthew 28:19: "all the nations." Matthew's purpose has been to show how Jesus is the Messiah of all peoples. His theme of universal offer of salvation through Jesus (e.g., 1:1; 2:1–12; 4:15–16; 8:5–13; 10:18; 13:38; 24:14) thus climaxes this Gospel in the command to "make disciples of all the nations."[123] When we see Matthew's commission to make disciples of "all the nations" again in the light of Luke's commission, that "repentance and forgiveness of sins will be preached in his name to all nations, beginning at Jerusalem" (Luke 24:47), we understand that Jesus's ministry in Israel was to be the beginning point of what would be later a universal offer of salvation to all the peoples of the earth.[124]

---

120. E.g., see Davies and Allison, *Matthew*, 3:684; Keener, *Matthew* (2009), 719–20; Morris, *Matthew*, 746; France, *Gospel of Matthew*, 816–17; Hagner, *Matthew 14–28*, 617, 623–24; Turner, *Israel's Last Prophet*, 203; Turner, "His Glorious Throne," 157–58; Balabanski, "Mission in Matthew," esp. 174–75.

121. Nolland, *Matthew*, 1266.

122. Turner, "His Glorious Throne," 158. See also Konradt, *Israel, Church, and the Gentiles*, esp. 311–17; Donaldson, *Gentile Christian Identity*, 310–11.

123. Osborne, *Matthew*, 1080–83; Carson, "Matthew," 666–70; Plummer, *Matthew*, 430.

124. Cf. Meier, "Nations or Gentiles in Matthew 28:19?,"

Peter Stuhlmacher points to the transition of the mission of Jesus and his future followers when noting the three distinct geographical and ethnic mission fields of Matt 10:5b–6: the Jewish mission, the Samaritan mission, and the gentile mission. During Jesus's earthly mission the focus was on the first, the Jewish mission, but in his ascended mission he sends his disciples—that is, all of us—to complete the threefold Jewish, Samaritan, and gentile mission.[125] Acts 1:8 has a similar division: "But you will receive power when the Holy Spirit comes on you; and you will be my witnesses in Jerusalem, and in all Judea and Samaria, and to the ends of the earth." In fact, the entire book of Acts is structured according to the plan of 1:8. Acts chs. 2–7 focus on the mission to Jews in Jerusalem and surrounding areas. Acts chs. 8–9 focus on the mission to Samaritans in Samaria. And Acts chs. 10–28 focus on the mission to gentiles to the ends of the earth.

#### *15.3.2.4 The Double Horizon of the Mission to Israel and Then to the Nations*

The double horizon of the mission to Israel and then to the nations instructs all disciples of the mission's present universal responsibilities, as well as of its moorings in historical Israel.[126] To emphasize too heavily Matthew's particularistic themes could lead one to accuse him of ethnic prejudice, but to emphasize too heavily the universal theme could lead one to accuse him of ethnic anti-Semitism.

In my view, an appropriate balance is found in recognizing God's plan of salvation history which we see played out and articulated later by the apostle Paul—to the Jew first, and then to the nations (Rom 1:16). Matthew emphasizes that Jesus's admonition to the disciples to give singular attention to Israel (10:6) underscores God's faithfulness to his covenant promises. But by bearing witness to the gentiles (10:18) the mission accomplishes his salvific purposes for all of humanity while declaring that God's plan for Israel is still unfinished until the return of the Son of Man (10:23). Now the Old Testament's principally centripetal paradigm of mission in the Old Testament, with Jerusalem at the center and the nations streaming to it, is exchanged in the New Testament for a principally centrifugal paradigm of mission, with Jesus's disciples beginning in Jerusalem but now going out to all the nations (28:19–20).[127]

---

94–102; Fitzmyer, *Luke (X–XXIV)*, 1583–84; Osborne, *Matthew*, 1079–80n25; Wilcox, "Jesus in the Light of His Jewish Environment," 169. Cedric Vine proposes a unique, creative view by which Matthew envisages an adaptive process in which a small cadre of individuals (prophet, righteous person, disciple/teacher, wise person, scribe) adopt different discipleship roles and work within existing "national structures" to establish divine sovereignty of the kingdom of God; see Vine, *Jesus and the Nations*, passim, e.g., 25–27. Rather than "national structures," I suggest that the emphasis in Matthew is upon a universal offer of salvation to all the peoples of the earth; cf. Osborne, *Matthew*, 1080–83; Carson, "Matthew," 666–70; Stuhlmacher, "Matt 28:16–20," 17–43.

125. Stuhlmacher, "Matt 28:16–20," 17–43.

126. Kingsbury, *Matthew, Structure, Christology, Kingdom*, 35. See Sarma, *Hermeneutics of Mission in Matthew*.

127. Cf. Blomberg, *New Testament Theology*, 375; Köstenberger, "Matthew," in *Salvation to the Ends of the Earth*, 43–67.

## 15.4 CHARACTERISTICS OF MISSION IN MATTHEW'S GOSPEL

In the second of Jesus's discourses that Matthew has collected in his Gospel, the author has provided us another crucial collection of Jesus's commands that disciples are to be taught to obey (28:20). The second discourse, the mission discourse, develops what it means to be "mission-driven disciples." The mission discourse describes how Jesus's disciples are to go out to share and live the message of the gospel of the kingdom of God to an alien and often hostile world (ch. 10). A comparison of Matthew's account of the mission discourse with Mark's and Luke's reveals that Matthew gives a great deal more space to it than do either of them. Matthew's version runs to nearly one hundred lines of Greek text, while Mark's has about fourteen and Luke's has about twelve.

Additionally, as we have seen above, mission emphases are found throughout Matthew's Gospel, culminating in the Great Commission (28:18–20). We will first glean characteristics of mission from the mission discourse (ch. 10), and then we will expand our view to glean characteristics of mission from the Gospel as a whole.

### 15.4.1 The Mission Discourse (Ch. 10)

This mission discourse includes several important characteristics of mission.[128]

(1) In this discourse Jesus lays out God's salvation-historical mission of redemption. The disciples go to Israel first to fulfill God's covenantal promises (10:6), but then they are to go to the gentiles (10:18). They will continue with the two-pronged mission to Jews and gentiles throughout the age until Jesus returns (10:23). The equipping of mission-disciples must be appropriate to both phases of the mission. The urgent mission to Israel during Jesus's historical ministry required preparation and equipment that was unique to that setting (cf. 10:5–15), which should be wisely evaluated so that unwarranted application is not made to the later worldwide mission (10:16–23).

(2) The disciples are to go with the same authoritative message and power that characterized Jesus's own mission (10:1–8).

(3) Since the universal mission charge is addressed to disciples, mission in this age is a responsibility of all believers (10:24–25, 40–42), not just a special category of persons within the church. It occurs in both public confession to the world (10:32–33) as well as in private commitments to one's family (10:34–39).

(4) Like Jesus's experience, the disciples can expect opposition and persecution (10:24–25) from Jews and gentiles alike, as well as one's own closest family and

128. Cf. Wilkins, *Matthew*, 399–400; Köstenberger, *Salvation*, 43–67; Senior and Stuhlmueller, *Biblical Foundations for Mission*, 250–51.

companions (10:17–21). Jesus is the dividing line between the entire world and his disciples (10:22).

(5) The source of the disciples' power and guidance is the Spirit (10:19–20), and the source of their care and control is the sovereign will of the Father (10:28–33). Disciples therefore should have no fear (10:26–27).

(6) Mission is a community issue, as the one who receives shares the reward of the one who carries the message (10:40–42).

(7) Mission includes not only proclamation and displays of God's power but also care for the needy among them (10:42).

(8) Mission includes spiritual transformation. The centrality of Jesus in the life of the disciples is the most vital characteristic of the mission, so that the disciples increasingly grow to be like the Master (10:24).

(9) All of these issues prepare and equip Jesus's disciples to undertake with boldness and effectiveness the programmatic mission statement with which Matthew concludes his Gospel, the Great Commission (28:18–20), which is the key to understanding Matthew's overall purpose for writing his Gospel.

### 15.4.2 Mission-Driven Discipleship

An important implication concerns mission and discipleship. I emphasize three important points here.

In the first place, *every disciple is a missionary.* While the discourse does have special significance for the Twelve in their historical ministry, it has immediate relevance for disciples of every era of the church. All of Jesus's disciples are intended to identify with the original disciples. If we call ourselves Christians, we are disciples of Jesus, and this passage impels us to see that mission activity is a vital part of our discipleship to him.[129] The principles outlined in this mission discourse and throughout this Gospel are as relevant today as they were to the original disciples.[130]

Second, *every disciple is a missionary, but not every missionary goes overseas.* Even in Jesus's day many of his disciples did not go out on a mission tour. The demoniac who had demons driven out begged to go with Jesus, but Jesus sent him sent back to his home to tell his townspeople what Jesus had done for him (Luke 8:38–39). His mission field was his own hometown. The woman named Tabitha in the book of Acts was a disciple of Jesus who apparently did not leave her hometown, and yet she was a servant of God who affected the entire region, both by her actions and the miracle that was produced in her life (Acts 9:36–43). While all of us may not become full-time

129. Douglas A. Sweeney, "Introduction," in *The Great Commission: Evangelicals and the History of World Missions*, ed. Martin I. Klauber and Scott M. Manetsch (Nashville: B&H, 2008), 2.

130. See C. Wright, "God and the Nations in New Testament Mission," in *Mission of God*, 501–30.

occupational missionaries, it is clear that all disciples are called to join in mission in some fashion. The specifics of how one engages in mission should be tailored to one's giftedness and abilities, but a disciple of Jesus will see that carrying the message of salvation to the world is a vital part of our discipleship to Jesus.[131]

Lastly, *support of worldwide mission is the responsibility of all disciples.* Much of the evangelistic and teaching ministry of the early church was performed by traveling missionaries who served the various churches and who were dependent on the hospitality and gifts given by members of the churches they visited. One striking example is Gaius, in John's third epistle. Gaius was especially faithful in hospitality, and many traveling missionaries had shared with John's church how generous Gaius had been (3 John 6). The support of worldwide mission is the responsibility of all disciples. When we stay home and support those who go, we are fellow workers with them (3 John 8). God gives generously to us, so we should likewise give generously to mission-disciples who have been called to a full-time mission. They are servants of God and should not be treated like beggars. As I. Howard Marshall states it, "Christian ministers and missionaries live in the faith that God will encourage his people to provide for their needs; it is better that such provision err on the side of generosity than stinginess."[132]

### 15.4.3 Persecution and Suffering Are to Be Expected on Mission

Another repercussion concerns persecution and suffering. A primary focus in the Mission Mandate is to give instructions to disciples on how to endure persecution and suffering, because if the Master was persecuted in his mission, his disciples will be persecuted in theirs (10:24–25). Matthew is keen for us to have Jesus's perspective on persecution and suffering.

First, persecution may include rejection, alienation, being hated, and ultimately martyrdom (10:21–22, 28, 38–39).

Second, the severity of persecution and suffering requires us to give unqualified allegiance to Jesus. Jesus warns us not to give priority to any other relationship and not to deny allegiance to him because of fear of persecution. To deny Jesus here on earth is to be denied by the Father in heaven (10:33). How one bears up under persecution is basically the determination of whether one is a disciple or not, which has eternal implications (10:32–34). The disciple is not to fear those who can kill the body but only fear the one who can destroy both body and soul in hell (10:28).

Third, Jesus's disciples can expect to be maligned and to have falsehood spread about their message and character because the same was done to Jesus (10:25). But Jesus's

131. For a realistic approach to proclaiming the gospel in a skeptical world, see Sam Chan, *Evangelism in a Skeptical World: How to Make the Unbelievable News About Jesus More Believable* (Grand Rapids: Zondervan, 2018).

132. I. Howard Marshall, *The Epistles of John*, NICNT (Grand Rapids: Eerdmans, 1978), 86.

disciples are not to fear this subversive persecution because eventually the truth will be revealed, and they will be vindicated (10:26).

Fourth, and perhaps most importantly, while experiencing persecution the Spirit will provide power and guidance to speak the right words for the situation (10:19–20). And the Father will exercise sovereign control over all circumstances, so we are not to fear that the persecution is out of God's control (10:29–31).[133]

### 15.4.4 Transformational Solidarity Between Jesus and His Disciples While on Mission

Matthew has emphasized in the mission discourse that there is an incontrovertible solidarity between Jesus and his disciples, including authority (10:1), message (10:1), activity (10:7, 8), mission (10:18), suffering (10:18, 24–25, 38), confession (10:32), and reception (10:40). Since the Twelve represent the relationship that disciples throughout the ages will enjoy with Jesus (see 28:16–20), the open-ended historical nature of the discourse posits specific examples for our own mission. However, as we noted above, the Twelve's urgent mission to Israel during Jesus's earthly ministry (e.g., 5:5–15) will need to be understood historically so that we do not draw unwarranted application.

The discourse encourages us to understand that disciples who follow Jesus will engage in mission and will be transformed to meet life's demands by being continually transformed to be like the Master. Discipleship begins by taking up one's cross, which symbolizes God's will for a person's life, and following Jesus into every situation of days on this earth. The extended section on the characteristics of mission-disciples draws together those two themes. The form of discipleship that Jesus instituted explicitly connects discipleship and mission—all believers are disciples/missionaries, and each role affects the other as they carry out Jesus's mission to the world.

Since the objective of the Great Commission is to "make disciples," this includes both *initial conversion* and *lifelong transformation*. Once a person among the nations experiences initial conversion to become a disciple of Jesus, he or she embarks upon the experience of lifelong transformation. This is what full-orbed mission means. Matthew has constructed his Gospel so that the alternation of narratives of Jesus's life with records of Jesus's discourses gives the most complete record of what Jesus's disciples are being transformed into.

The five major discourses in particular are intended as instruction in, and clarification of, what it means to be Jesus's unique kind of disciple.[134] In these discourses

133. For a valuable study of these themes, see Jacobus Kok, Tobias Nicklas, Dieter T. Roth, and Christopher M. Hays, eds., *Sensitivity to Outsiders: Exploring the Dynamic Relationship Between Mission and Ethics in the New Testament and Early Christianity*, WUNT 2/364 (Tübingen: Mohr Siebeck, 2013), especially the introductory chapter by Jacobus Kok and Dieter T. Roth, "Sensitivity Towards Outsiders and the Dynamic Relationship Between Mission and Ethics/Ethos," 1–26.

134. Dunn, *Jesus According to the New Testament*, 35.

Jesus illuminates the transformation that will occur to his disciples. As we discussed in Chapter 10 on discipleship in Matthew's Gospel, the basic thrust of each discourse points to that kind of intentional well-roundedness. Examining the narratives of Jesus's life and his discourses and incorporating those lessons will provide the transformational power of growth as a disciple into the image of the Master, Jesus Messiah.

### 15.4.5 "Wise as Serpents and Harmless as Doves" (10:16)

One of the central cautions of Jesus in this mission discourse is that as his disciples live out their lives with him in the world, their hearts become vulnerable to hurt, temptation, and spiritual attacks. Jesus warns his disciples that a delicate balance must be maintained while we walk in this world as mission-disciples: we must protect or guard our heart from hurt, yet at the same time we must not go to an extreme where we develop a heart that is so protected that it becomes hardened. As Jesus gives his prophetic vision of his disciples being sent out into the world, he says, "I am sending you out like sheep among wolves. Therefore, be as shrewd as serpents and innocent as doves" (10:16).

Jesus did not call his disciples out of the world into a safe haven of rest. We must venture out as defenseless sheep in the midst of ravenous wolves. So, we must guard our heart. Guarding our heart in the world means to be wise as a serpent. We are to know the ways of the world, which means to know the traps that might await us. We are to understand clearly how people can hurt and abuse us. There are people in this world who want to dominate us to perpetuate their own self-serving agenda. One strategy of the cults is to demand obedience to a strong leader's personal direction. We must guard ourselves and those for whom we have responsibility to protect the heart. We are to be wise about the temptations that will come our way and to know how to escape. We are to protect our heart; we are to be responsibly wise.

On the other hand, we are to be innocent as a dove. We are not to allow our heart to become so protective and distrustful of the wolves in the world that we harden our heart. We are not to learn the craftiness of the snake so well that we acquire the heart of a snake. I have said many times in the past, "I don't trust anyone." That statement came from a heart that had been hurt by people. While it is true that many people cannot be trusted, I took it too far. I became so distrustful of people that I hurt them by my accusations of false motives or unfaithfulness. A dove does not hurt others. A dove brings grace and beauty. The dove is the symbol of peace.[135]

Being wise as serpents and harmless as doves in this world is a difficult yet necessary balance as mission-disciples carry the message of the gospel of the kingdom to a world that is dying, eternally, without its message of grace and salvation. I do not fancy myself

135. See Wilkins, *In His Image*, 179–80.

as a "great missionary," but I do know that I am called to unwavering commitment to bring the gospel of the kingdom to my generation and those who follow. That is the clarion call of Jesus's mission discourse to every generation of the church.

### 15.4.6 Jesus Immanuel—I Am with Mission-Driven Disciples Always

The beginning of Matthew's Gospel introduced us to Jesus Immanuel, God with us (1:23). And the final saying of Jesus in this Gospel is what gives us the greatest assurance that we can carry out his purpose in our lives because he promises unconditionally: "And surely I am with you always, to the very end of the age" (28:20). Our discipleship to the risen Jesus continues to be our greatest source of comfort, power, and security. As Matthew has demonstrated over and over in this Gospel, the arrival of Jesus began the greatest revolution that history has ever known. It is a revolution that begins in the heart, where Jesus enters in and begins the transformation. But then it extends to every area of our lives, so that our physical, emotional, thought, and relational life is impacted by the power of the kingdom of heaven. With an intentional strategy to develop this kind of disciple, Matthew's Gospel becomes a God-given guideline for intentional, transformational discipleship.

Whether or not we are professional missionaries traveling the world, all of us who are disciples of Jesus Messiah have as a central calling to make disciples of all the nations. And Matthew's Gospel shows us how. Matthew's Gospel is intended, at least in part, as a resource tool to help Jesus's disciples in their task of making and developing future disciples while on mission throughout life. Matthew points to Jesus as the supreme Lord and Teacher of the disciples and emphasizes that Jesus's life and teaching produced in them obedience to and understanding of the truth of God's revelation throughout their mission in life. That is our calling as mission-driven disciples of Jesus Messiah.

*Chapter 16*

# ESCHATOLOGY IN MATTHEW'S GOSPEL

## *Sojourning Rightly Until the Return of Jesus Messiah*

### BIBLIOGRAPHY

**Allen, David L., and Steve W. Lemke,** eds. *The Return of Christ: A Premillennial Perspective.* Nashville: B&H, 2011. **Allison, Dale C. Jr.** "Eschatology." *DJG*[1] 206–9. **Beale, G. K.** *A New Testament Biblical Theology: The Unfolding of the Old Testament in the New.* Grand Rapids: Baker Academic, 2011. **Bornkamm, Günther.** "End-Expectation and Church in Matthew." Pages 15–51 in *Tradition and Interpretation in Matthew.* Edited by Günther Bornkamm, Gerhard Barth, and Heinz Joachim Held. Translated by Percy Scott. Philadelphia: Westminster, 1963. **Bryan, Steven M.** "Jesus and Israel's Eschatological Constitution." Pages 2835–54 in vol. 3 of *HSHJ.* Edited by Tom Holmén and Stanley E. Porter. 4 vols. Leiden: Brill, 2011.———. *Jesus and Israel's Traditions of Judgement and Restoration.* SNTSMS 117. Cambridge: Cambridge University Press, 2002. **Carey, Greg.** *Death, the End of History, and Beyond: Eschatology in the Bible.* Interpretation. Louisville: Westminster John Knox, 2023. **Carrier, Brian.** *Earthquakes and Eschatology in the Gospel According to Matthew.* WUNT 2/534. Tübingen: Mohr Siebeck, 2020. **Cox, Steven.** "The Eschatology of the Gospels." Loc. 4884–5667 in *The Return of Christ: A Premillennial Perspective.* Edited by David L. Allen and Steve W. Lemke. Nashville: B&H, 2011. Kindle edition. **Esler, Philip F.** "Ethnic Identities in the Dead Sea Legal Papyri and Matthew: Reinterpreting Matthew 25:31–46." Pages 195–210 in *Matthew Within Judaism: Israel and the Nations in the First Gospel.* Edited by Anders Runesson and Daniel M. Gurtner. ECL 27. Atlanta: Society of Biblical Literature Press, 2020. **Eubank, Nathan.** *Wages of Cross-Bearing and Debt of Sin: The Economy of Heaven in Matthew's Gospel.* BZNW 196. Berlin: de Gruyter, 2013. **Gempf, Conrad.** "The Imagery of Birth Pangs in the New Testament." *TynBul* 45.1 (1994): 119–35. **Gibbs, Jeffrey A.** *Jerusalem and Parousia: Jesus' Eschatological Discourse in Matthew's Gospel.* Saint Louis: Concordia Academic, 2000. **Gowan, Donald E.** *Eschatology in the Old Testament.* Philadelphia: Fortress, 1986. **Gray, Sherman W.** *The Least of My Brothers: Matthew 25:31–42—A History of Interpretation.* SBLDS 114. Atlanta: Scholars, 1989. **Gundry, Robert H.** *The Church and the Tribulation.* Grand Rapids: Zondervan, 1973.

**Hafemann, Scott J.** "Eschatology and Ethics: The Future of Israel and the Nations in Romans 15: 1–13," *TynBul* 51 (2000): 161–92. **Hagner, Donald A.** "Apocalyptic Motifs in the Gospel of Matthew: Continuity and Discontinuity." *HBT* 7.2 (1985): 53–82. **Hoekema, Anthony A.** *The Bible and the Future*. Grand Rapids: Eerdmans, 1979. **Hultberg, Alan,** ed. *Three Views on The Rapture: Pretribulation, Prewrath, or Posttribribulation*. Grand Rapids: Zondervan, 2010. **Inbari, Motti.** "Messianic Religious Zionism and the Reintroduction of Sacrifice: The Case of the Temple Institute." Pages 256–273 in *Rethinking the Messianic Idea in Judaism*. Edited by Michael L. Morgan and Steven Weitzman. Bloomington, IN: Indiana University Press, 2015. **Keown, Mark.** "An Imminent Parousia and Christian Mission: Did the New Testament Writers Really Expect Jesus's Imminent Return?" Pages 242–63 in *Christian Origins and the Establishment of the Early Jesus Movement*. Edited by Stanley E. Porter and Andrew W. Pitts. TENTS 12. Leiden: Brill, 2018. **Kirchhevel, Gordon D.** "He That Cometh in Mark 1:7 and Matt 24:30." *BBR* 4 (1994): 105–11. **Köstenberger, Andreas J., Alexander E. Stewart, and Apollo Makara.** *Jesus and the Future: Understanding What He Taught about the End Times*. Wooster, OH: Weaver, 2017. **Kvalbein, Hans.** "Has Matthew Abandoned the Jews? A Contribution to a Disputed Issue in Recent Scholarship." Pages 45–62 in *The Mission of the Early Church to Jews and Gentiles*. Edited by Jostein Ådna and Hans Kvalbein. WUNT 127. Tübingen: Mohr Siebeck, 2000. **Ladd, George Eldon.** *The Gospel of the Kingdom: Scriptural Studies in the Kingdom of God*. Grand Rapids: Eerdmans, 1973. ———. *The Presence of the Future: The Eschatology of Biblical Realism*. 2nd ed. Grand Rapids: Eerdmans, 1974. **Lewis, Daniel J.** *3 Crucial Questions about the Last Days*. Grand Rapids: Baker, 1998. **Marguerat, Daniel.** *Le Jugement dans l'évangile de Matthieu*. 2nd ed. Le Monde de la Bible 6. Geneva: Labor et Fides, 1981. **Meadors, Edward.** "The 'Messianic' Implications of the Q Material." *JBL* 118.2 (1999): 253–77. ———. "What Did Matthew Really Care About?" Pages 24–43 in *What the New Testament Authors Really Cared About: A Survey of Their Writings*. Edited by Kenneth Berding and Matt Williams. Grand Rapids: Kregel, 2008. **Merkle, Benjamin L.** "Who Will be Left Behind? Rethinking the Meaning of Matthew 24:40–41 and Luke 17:34–35." *WTJ* 72.1 (2010): 169–79. **Nel, Marius.** "What Is 'the Sign of the Son of Man in Heaven' (Mt 24:30)?" *In die Skriflig/In Luce Verbi* 49.1 (2015): art. #1876. **Nelson, Neil D., Jr.** "'This Generation' in Matt 24:34: A Literary Critical Perspective." *JETS* 38.3 (1995): 369–85. **Pettegrew, Larry D.** "The Rapture Debate at the Niagara Bible Conference." *BSac* 157 (2000): 331–47. **Pond, Eugene W.** "The Background and Timing of the Judgment of the Sheep and Goats." *BSac* 159 (2002): 201–20. ———. "Who are 'The Least' of Jesus' Brothers in Matthew 25:40?" *BSac* 159 (2002): 436–48. **Reiser, Marius.** *Jesus and Judgment: The Eschatological Proclamation in Its Jewish Context*. Translated by Linda M. Maloney. Minneapolis: Fortress, 1997. **Saucy, Mark.** *The Kingdom of God in the Teaching of Jesus: In Twentieth Century Theology* (Dallas: Word, 1997). **Sim, David C.** *Apocalyptic Eschatology in the Gospel of Matthew*. SNTSMS 88. Cambridge: Cambridge University Press, 1996. ———. "The Meaning of *palingenesia* in Mt 19.28." *JSNT* 50 (1993): 3–12. ———. "The Rise and

Fall of the Gospel of Matthew." *ExpTim* 120.10 (2009): 478–85. **Turner, David L.** "The Structure and Sequence of Matthew 24:1–41: Interaction with Evangelical Treatments." *Grace Theological Journal* 10.1 (1989): 3–27. **Wenham, David.** *The Rediscovery of Jesus' Eschatological Discourse*. GP 4. Sheffield: JSOT, 1984. **Willitts, Joel.** "Zionism in the Gospel of Matthew." Pages 107–40 in *The New Christian Zionism: Fresh Perspectives on Israel and the Land*. Edited by Gerald R. McDermott. Downers Grove, IL: InterVarsity, 2016. **Wilson, Alistair I.** *When Will These Things Happen? A Study of Jesus as Judge in Matthew 21–25*. PBM. Carlisle, UK: Paternoster, 2004. **Winn, Adam.** "'This Generation': Reconsidering Mark 13:30 in Light of Eschatological Expectations in Second Temple Judaism." *BBR* 30.4 (2020): 540–60. **Witherington, Ben III.** *Jesus, Paul, and the End of the World: A Comparative Study in New Testament Eschatology*. Downers Grove: InterVarsity, 1992.

## 16.1 Eschatology in Matthew's Gospel: Sojourning Rightly Until the Return of Jesus Messiah

Life as we know it is going to come to an end. All of history will come to a climactic end when Jesus returns. But that end may be sooner than we think. So, be prepared. I have a life motto that expresses what I believe to be the reflection of this exhortation:

> **Live** *as though Jesus is coming back tonight;*
> **Plan** *as though he is not coming back for a hundred years.*

That is the message of the Olivet Discourse in a nutshell. Regardless of your theological persuasion with reference to the return of Jesus, that exhortation is equally relevant because life is fragile and fleeting, and we do not know when the end will come. Whether it is at the end of history as we know it with the return of Jesus, or at the end of our life with our own death, we need to be prepared. But that does not mean to withdraw and count moments. Rather, our privilege and our charge is to maximize the precious moments of life with which we have been gifted to make a difference in this life for the sake of the kingdom of heaven.

That life motto essentially came from studying eschatology in Matthew's Gospel, and especially Jesus's Olivet Discourse. Jesus warns us to have our lives in order so that at any moment if he returns, we will not be ashamed. At the same time, he exhorts us to be fully engaged in all of life so that we conscientiously care for all of our responsibilities for the long haul.

In that light, I want to have my life so straight with Jesus all through this very day—with my family, my work, my words, my thoughts—that if he returns today, I hope to hear, "Well done, good and faithful servant!" (25:21). At the same time,

I must be accountable for what I have been given responsibility over whether now or tomorrow or next year, or a hundred years from now, whatever the future might bring.

Consequently, in our study of the theology of Matthew's Gospel, we now come to the topic of eschatology, which I have found is a tremendously rewarding study in itself.

### 16.1.1 Eschatology

The term *eschatology* derives from two Greek words: the adjective *eschatos* ("last" or "end") and the noun *logos* ("word"). Accordingly, in biblical and systematic theology *eschatology* refers to "the study of last things." But what are these "last things"? In a popular vein, Michael Wittmer notes that, "when it comes to eschatology, the Christian Scriptures teach the three Rs: the Return of Christ, the Resurrection of the body, and the Restoration of all things."[1]

In a bit more technical expression, Greg Carey suggests that "eschatology" in the Bible addresses three domains: personal, historical, and cosmological.[2] There is considerable overlap of the domains that Carey surfaces, and we see each in Matthew's Gospel. Most Matthean scholars would agree that eschatology is a significant theme in the first Gospel.

#### *16.1.1.1 Personal Eschatology*

*Personal eschatology* explores the question, "Where are we as individuals headed after we die?" This question forces us to consider what happens to the material and immaterial aspects of our person after we die. Matthew's Gospel addresses both of these, although there is little explanation of either. The broadest perspective of personal eschatology includes one's personal death (6:27; 24:9), the intermediate state (the condition of the person between the time of death and the resurrection) (18:8–9; 19:16), resurrection and afterlife (22:30–32; 27:51–53; 28:5–7), heaven and afterlife (5:11–12; 6:19–21; 19:28–29), and judgment and hell (5:29–30; 18:34–35; 23:33).

#### *16.1.1.2 Historical Eschatology*

*Historical eschatology* asks the question "Where is the world heading?" This question compels us to think through what we believe about God and his involvement in history. In recent years there has been a significant emphasis by scholars on the domain of historical eschatology. Grant Osborne isolates three different aspects of historical eschatology. *Realized eschatology* stresses the present reality of kingdom blessings. *Inaugurated eschatology* stresses the tension between the already and the not yet of the presence of

1. Michael Wittmer, *Four Views on Heaven*, Counterpoints (Grand Rapids: Zondervan, 2022), 9.

2. Greg Carey, *Death, the End of History, and Beyond: Eschatology in the Bible*, Interpretation (Louisville: Westminster John Knox, 2023), 1–32.

the kingdom, as well as on the opening stages of the kingdom in the appearance of the last days.[3] *Final eschatology* stresses the consummation of history at the eschaton and last judgment.[4] Osborne observes that

> Matthew contains all three, with realized eschatology in the ethical teaching on righteousness in the Sermon on the Mount, inaugurated eschatology in the concept of reward in the Beatitudes and in the kingdom teaching of his gospel, and final eschatology in many of his parables and in portions of the Olivet Discourse.

We have discussed significant aspects of historical eschatology in our chapter on the kingdom of heaven (Ch. 9), but below we will emphasize especially final eschatology in our overview of the Olivet Discourse.

#### *16.1.1.3 Cosmological Eschatology*

The third domain, *cosmological eschatology*, asks the question, "What is ultimately real?" This last domain addresses realities that lie beyond our phenomenal world—transcendent things we cannot know through our five senses.[5]

In the Matthean context, cosmological eschatology includes belief in an afterlife, which implies convictions involving bodies and souls, heaven and hell, supernatural beings like angels and demons, and ultimately persuasions concerning the nature of God.[6] Donald Hagner contends that Matthew's eschatology has an apocalyptic orientation, since it contains an expectation not simply of "end things" but also of a radical transformation of the present order by supernatural agency in the near future, which is deeply rooted in Old Testament prophecy.[7]

In that direction, some scholars argue that Matthew's Gospel exhibits a form of *apocalyptic eschatology*, which can be broadly defined as a comprehensive worldview that emphasizes the final judgment and its aftermath within a dualistic and deterministic framework. One well-known advocate of this perspective is Sim, who argues that Matthew's Gospel embraces apocalyptic eschatology, since most of a set of major characteristics are present. These characteristics include dualism, determinism, anticipation of eschatological woes, the arrival of a savior figure, future judgment (with concentration on the fate of the wicked and of the righteous), and the prospect of an imminent end.[8]

3. See also G. K. Beale, *A New Testament Biblical Theology: The Unfolding of the Old Testament in the New* (Grand Rapids: Baker Academic, 2011).

4. Osborne, *Matthew*, 1099.

5. Carey, *Death, the End of History, and Beyond*, 9–15.

6. Carey, *Death, the End of History, and Beyond*, 20–27.

7. Donald A. Hagner, "Apocalyptic Motifs in the Gospel of Matthew: Continuity and Discontinuity," *HBT* 7.2 (1985): 53–82.

8. Sim, *Apocalyptic Eschatology*, 23–53.

### 16.1.2 The Parousia

The study of eschatology refers also to the time of Jesus's parousia. The Greek term *parousia* and the expression *hē parousia* mean "coming" or "the coming" or "the arrival." It is used as a quasi-technical expression to refer to the return of Jesus Messiah in glory at the end of this age. Among the Gospels, the idiom is found only in Matthew's Gospel, and here only four times, all in the Olivet Discourse (emphases below are mine).

- "Tell us," they said, "when will this happen, and what will be the sign of your *coming* [*parousia*] and of the end of the age?" (24:3)
- "For as lightning that comes from the east is visible even in the west, so will be *the coming* [*hē parousia*] of the Son of Man" (24:27)
- "As it was in the days of Noah, so it will be at *the coming* [*hē parousia*] of the Son of Man" (24:37)
- "That is how it will be at *the coming* [*hē parousia*] of the Son of Man" (24:39)

We will discuss the parousia below in our survey of Jesus's Olivet Discourse.

### 16.1.3 The Study of Eschatology Today

Eschatology strikes different chords in people depending upon their past experiences. To some, eschatology may seem somewhat removed from daily Christian life and a rather dry, abstract enquiry. When I first became a Christian in the early 1970s, I attended a church where the Sunday evening service was dedicated to teaching on biblical prophecy. Stretched across the front of the church were huge banners mapping out Bible teaching on end times. Some of the younger people had grown up with this type of teaching weekly and had become quite bored with it all.

#### *16.1.3.1 Fascinating Study of Events Leading Up to the End of This Age*

To others, the study of eschatology means a spellbinding attempt to figure out a timeframe of events leading up to the end of this age. Prophecy is big business in our culture. An issue of *Time* magazine had a cover story entitled, "The Bible and the Apocalypse: Why More Americans Are Reading and Talking About the End of the World."[9] The author documented the rise in attention given by the general population in North America to end-time discussions. She highlighted especially the phenomenally successful series by Tim LaHaye and Jerry Jenkins. Starting with the first book, *Left Behind*,[10] which sold nearly eighty million copies, the series has thirteen volumes. Left Behind books have been adapted into multiple films and have also spawned video games

9. Nancy Gibbs, cover story: "The Bible and the Apocalypse," *Time* (July 1, 2002): 40–48.

10. Tim LaHaye and Jerry B. Jenkins, *Left Behind: A Novel of the Earth's Last Days* (Wheaton, IL: Tyndale, 1996).

and graphic novels.[11] Alissa Wilkinson is a senior culture reporter and critic at Vox.com and an associate professor of English and humanities at The King's College.[12] In a piece for the *Washington Post*, Wilkinson notes that the Left Behind books merged popular fiction with devoutly believed prophecy. She writes that *Left Behind* is not great literature, but it is highly engaging reading for a mass market, with its fast-moving fictional elements with components drawn from sci-fi, romance, disaster porn, and political and spy novels.[13] She suggests that the genius of the Left Behind books is that they work on two levels. For the non-Christian reader, the traditional fictional genre elements and the mystery of what will happen next keep the pages turning. But for the Christian reader, reading current events into the novel's narratives is thrilling, especially "seeing how various elements of the Bible that are written as visions in Revelation (dragons, beasts, women giving birth, horsemen, fiery pits, the symbol 666) might actually work out in contemporary America and the geopolitics beyond its borders."[14] Matthew's Gospel figures importantly in the Left Behind phenomenon, as Matthew contains the longest and most extensive record of Jesus's eschatological discourse (Matt 24–25). The Left Behind books go far beyond the Matthean texts, which can be highly problematic.[15] But at the least they have roots in biblical revelation.

#### *16.1.3.2 Vengeful or Offensive Theme*

On the other hand, one prominent Matthean scholar contends that many modern Matthean scholars find the theme of eschatology in Matthew's Gospel either offensive or unsavory. Sim brands Matthew as having a "vengeful eschatology,"[16] which he suggests is at least partly to blame for what he describes as Matthew's remarkable fall from grace from its original position of priority and prominence in the church's life and scholarship.[17] He states, "The most studied and influential Gospel in the ancient Church has fallen dramatically from grace."[18] He offers that Matthew now lags behind the Gospel of John and vies with Mark's Gospel for second place. He concludes, "On the basis of informal conversations and some evidence in the scholarly literature, it was suggested that Matthew contains some features that are viewed in modern times with distaste. These elements are the Gospel's very vivid and vindictive eschatology."[19]

I am not so sure that Sim describes the present situation accurately. Matthew's

11. Camila Domonoske, "Tim LaHaye, Evangelical Legend Behind 'Left Behind' Series, Dies At 90," *NPR* (25, 2016; 6:40 PM ET).

12. Alissa Wilkinson: http://www.alissawilkinson.com/bio.

13. Alissa Wilkinson, "The Left Behind Series Was Just the Latest Way America Prepared for the Rapture," *Washington Post*, July 13, 2016, https://www.washingtonpost.com/news/act-four/wp/2016/07/13/the-left-behind-series-was-just-the-latest-way-america-prepared-for-the-rapture/.

14. Wilkinson, "Left Behind Series."

15. Anna Case-Winters (*Matthew*, Belief [Louisville: Westminster John Knox, 2015], 273–74) warns against undue speculation and fascination regarding times and signs of Jesus's return.

16. Sim, "Rise and Fall," 478–85; here 481–82.

17. Sim, "Rise and Fall," 478, passim.

18. Sim, "Rise and Fall," 478.

19. Sim, "Rise and Fall," 485.

Gospel does include some of the most difficult teaching on eschatology, especially the final judgment and the fate of the wicked in the eternal fires of gehenna (e.g., 3:7–12; 5:22; 7:19; 13:41–42, 49–50; 18:8–9; 25:30, 41). But as the Left Behind series demonstrates, there is still a fascination with eschatological themes on the popular level. And my own research experience reveals unabated scholarly interest in Matthew's Gospel, including Matthew's theology of eschatology, which we will discover in this chapter and the next.

## 16.2 A THEOLOGY OF LAST THINGS IN JESUS'S INCARNATIONAL INITIATION OF THE KINGDOM OF HEAVEN

The study of eschatology in Matthew's Gospel begins with the arrival of Jesus Messiah in history. George Ladd observed that the kingdom of God, which will appear as an apocalyptic act at the end of the age, has already come into human history in the person and mission of Jesus to overcome evil, to deliver humans from its power, and to bring them into the blessings of God's reign. "The Kingdom of God involves two great moments: fulfillment within history, and consummation at the end of history."[20] Our study of this aspect of inaugurated eschatology begins with Matthew's record of Jesus Messiah's arrival in history.

### 16.2.1 Fulfillment of Old Testament Expectations

The Old Testament holds a prominent position in Matthew's Gospel, as we have seen in Chapter 5. We looked at quotations, allusions, and echoes of the Old Testament found in Matthew's Gospel, and how Jesus's use of the Old Testament, and Matthew's understanding of the Old Testament in the light of Jesus's life and ministry, fulfill historical patterns and prophetic oracles of the Old Testament. Dale Allison notes, "These [connections to the Old Testament] constantly remind readers that Jesus fulfilled the eschatological hopes and messianic expectations of Judaism."[21] These are seen especially in the ministries and messages of John the Baptist and Jesus Messiah.

### 16.2.2 John the Baptist's Eschatological Ministry and Message

As similar as John's message was to the Old Testament prophets, there was a distinctly new sound to it. He called the people to repent because the kingdom of heaven was not off in the future; it was near (3:2)! The kingdom of heaven has come near to people in the soon-arriving person of the Coming One, the Messiah.

John clarifies what he believes will occur with the eschatological coming of the

20. Ladd, *Presence of the Future*, 218.

21. Dale C. Allison Jr., "Eschatology," *DJG*[1] 208.

kingdom: (1) It will bring wrath on those who do not repent. The coming of the kingdom of heaven will be accompanied by the wrath of God and the fire of eternal punishment (3:8–10). John the Baptist saw that the coming of the kingdom of heaven will be the inauguration of the last days. (2) The coming of the kingdom will be inaugurated with the arrival of the Coming One, with his baptism of the Holy Spirit and fire (3:11–12). Those who respond to John's message and repent will escape God's wrath. But it must be an individual's personal response to God; one's religious or ethnic heritage will not help. It was a call of repentance for all in Israel, including the religious leaders.[22]

### 16.2.3 Jesus Messiah's Initiation of the Eschatological Kingdom of Heaven

Matthew's summary of Jesus's message is the same as his summary of John the Baptist's: "Repent, for the kingdom of heaven has come near" (4:17; cf. 3:2). In neither case was the arrival of the kingdom defined, probably indicating that certain expectations about the arrival of the kingdom came to mind among those who heard them preach.[23] But the way in which Jesus developed his ministry, and the response of many to him, reveal different understandings and expectations of the way that God's kingdom "is near" (*ēngiken*).

Jesus's inauguration of the kingdom of heaven has to do with how people respond to him as their Messiah. He is the Coming One prophesied by John (cf. 3:13–17; 11:2–6), but he preaches the "good news" of the kingdom for all who come to him. God's ways are not always what humans expect. Jesus will indeed fulfill the prophetic hope. But he will bring this hope to complete fulfillment only when he returns as the Son of Man in glory (cf. 24:29–31). This twofold event is generally referred to as the *already-not yet* nature of the presence of the kingdom.[24] With its arrival, the "last things" of the kingdom of heaven is now present with the arrival of the messianic king of the line of David, and its arrival will confront a variety of expectations among those who experience its impact. But some of what others expected to occur immediately—especially full judgment and restoration—await future final fulfillment.

### 16.2.4 Adjustment of John the Baptist's Understanding of the Arrival of the Kingdom of Heaven in Jesus Messiah's Eschatological Mission

Some of the last things that Jesus has *already* inaugurated and what is *not yet* and awaits future fulfillment are revealed in an interaction of Jesus with John the Baptist and his disciples. Having been imprisoned at the fortress of Machaerus for a year or

22. See Gibbs, *Jerusalem and Parousia*, 34–41.
23. See Patrick, "Kingdom of God in the Old Testament," 71.
24. See Saucy, *Kingdom of God*, e.g., 20–22.

more, John sends his disciples to query Jesus about the messianic program and about Jesus's identity and ministry as the Messiah (11:2; cf. Luke 7:18–35).

### *16.2.4.1 John the Baptist Questions Jesus Through His Disciples (11:2–3)*

John's disciples were committed followers of the prophet. There is a bit of disconnect between their understanding of the prophet's message about the coming Messiah's ministry and Jesus's display of the messianic ministry. John the Baptist instructed his disciples to ask of Jesus, "Are you the one who was to come, or should we expect someone else?" (11:3). The expression "the one who was to come" (*ho erchomenos*) is an allusion to the Messiah, the Coming One, the expression that John had used to refer to Jesus at the beginning of Jesus's public ministry (3:11).

John's present experience does not match the message that he had given about the Coming One's arrival, which promised blessing on those who repent and judgment on those who do not. John needed to have his understanding of the eschatological messianic program reconfirmed.[25]

### *16.2.4.2 Jesus Responds to John's Questions (11:4–6)*

Jesus reiterates to John's disciples that the way his ministry has unfolded (Matt 8–9) is in line with the prophetic promises: "Go back and report to John what you hear and see" (11:4). In Jesus's ministry are fulfilled Isaiah's prophecies that describe the coming messianic ministry in these very terms:

- the blind receive sight (Matt 9:27–32; 15:30–3; cf. Isa 29:18; 35:5)
- the lame walk (Matt 15:30–31; cf. Isa 35:6)
- those who have leprosy are cured (Matt 8:1–4; cf. Isa 53:4)
- the deaf hear (Mark 7:32–37; 9:25; cf. Isa 29:18–19; 35:5)
- the dead are raised (Matt 10:8; Luke 7:11–17; John 11:1–44; cf. Isa 26:18–19)
- the good news is preached to the poor (Matt 5:3; Luke 14:13, 21; cf. Isa 61:1)

Judaism was ripe with expectations of the last things to unfold. Jesus explicitly confirms that in his ministry the messianic age of blessing has arrived. These are the beginnings of the last things.

The implications are even more profound because the miracles accomplished by Jesus fulfill expectations previously associated with God and the eschatological Day of the Lord. Jesus has come in the place of God and is now performing the work of God.[26] Jesus confirms for John that the eschatological blessings of the messianic age have

25. Witherington, *Christology of Jesus*, 43; Gibbs, *Jerusalem and Parousia*, 76–78.

26. Meadors, "'Messianic' Implications," 259.

arrived with his ministry. Each of the prophecies to which Jesus alludes as having been fulfilled in his ministry includes in the immediate context references to both blessing and judgment (Isa 35:4–6; 61:1–2). John and his disciples must use eyes of faith to recognize both blessing and judgment. Jesus has brought the blessing of healing and good news to the poor and oppressed (Matt 11:4–5), yet those who reject his ministry and message face certain judgment, which even now is being pronounced by Jesus (11:20–24; cf. John 3:31–36; 5:25–35).[27]

## 16.3 A Theology of Last Things in Jesus's Olivet Discourse in Matthew's Gospel

As Jesus sits on the Mount of Olives, perhaps pondering his prophetic forecast of the temple's fate, his disciples approach him to ask his private understanding of the incredible events to which he has just alluded (Matt 24:3).[28] Jesus's reply initiates an extended discourse, an eschatological forecast of the events that will stretch on down the course of history. This is the fifth and final major discourse recorded in Matthew's Gospel. As with the other discourses, it is directed to Jesus's disciples and is part of the body of material that new disciples will be taught to obey throughout the ages until Jesus's return (28:20). Here the material is apocalyptic revelation, an "eschatological forecast," whereas the earlier discourses included teaching (chs. 5–7), missionary mandate (ch. 10), parables (ch. 13), and sayings on community life of the church (ch. 18). Since he gave this discourse while sitting on the Mount of Olives, the traditional name came to be the "Olivet Discourse." David Wenham opines, "There are perhaps no more difficult chapters in the gospels than the chapters containing Jesus' eschatological discourse, i.e. Matthew 24, 25, Mark 13, Luke 21."[29] And of all the Synoptic Gospels, Matthew gives the fullest description of this prophecy and gives some of the most profound insights to his theology of eschatology.

The content of the discourse is in response to the disciples' questions: "'Tell us,' they said, 'when will this happen, and what will be the sign of your coming and of the end of the age?'" (24:3). Matthew's record of the disciples' query actually contains two questions: the first is "When will all these things be?" which is directed toward the timing of the destruction of the temple. The second question includes a conceptual unity of both Jesus's coming and the end of the age: "What will be the sign of your coming and the end of the age?" This is indicated in Greek by one article that

27. Yamasaki, *John the Baptist*, 106–10; Webb, "Jesus' Baptism," 305–7.

28. For a helpful survey of the Olivet Discourse and eschatology generally in the Gospels, see Steven Cox, "The Eschatology of the Gospels," in *The Return of Christ: A Premillennial Perspective*, ed. David L. Allen and Steve W Lemke (Nashville: B&H, 2011), loc. 4884–5667, Kindle.

29. David Wenham, *The Rediscovery of Jesus' Eschatological Discourse*, GP 4 (Sheffield: JSOT, 1984), 1.

governs both the phrase "sign of your coming" and the phrase "end of the age." This indicates that Jesus's "coming" (*parousia*) and the "end of the age" are descriptions of one event.[30]

Jesus's answer to the first question comes most directly in Luke's account (Luke 21:20; cf. Matt 24:15), although Matthew records that Jesus alluded to the abandonment of Jerusalem's temple in that generation in the conclusion to the woes upon the religious leadership of Israel (Matt 23:34). But the way in which the disciples ask both questions may indicate that in their minds the destruction of the temple and the parousia/end of the age are not separated, which clues us to Jesus's reply.

In Matthew's account, as well as in the other Synoptic accounts, we have historical and eschatological references, with Jesus prophesying both the fall of Jerusalem and his own eschatological parousia. Luke focuses on specific historical details of the destruction of the temple and the fall of Jerusalem that appear to point to the events of AD 70 (Luke 21:20–24), while Matthew and Mark give details that are difficult to see completely fulfilled with the first-century events and thus point to a future fulfillment (cf. Matt 24:15–22; Mark 13:14–20). The historical events, which allude to the destruction of the temple in AD 70, are given in answer to the disciples' question concerning the temple in existence then, but these events are used by Jesus to foreshadow the end-time events.

### 16.3.1 Interpreting Matthew's Perspective of Jesus's Olivet Discourse

Jesus's eschatological forecast in the Olivet Discourse has produced an almost dizzying array of interpretations.[31] The primary issue to be determined is understanding the relationship of historically fulfilled prophecy and prophecy yet to be fulfilled in the future. We can grasp one of the most important issues in the discourse by subsuming the various interpretations under three broad headings.

#### *16.3.1.1 Historicist (Preterist) View: All Fulfilled in the First Century*

On one extreme are those who suggest that virtually all of the events that Jesus prophesies in the discourse were fulfilled in the first century, primarily with the fall of Jerusalem and the destruction of the temple in AD 70. This is often called the "preterist" (past perspective) position. One proponent suggests that the fall of Jerusalem alone is in view from 24:4 through 24:35. Only at 24:36 and following does Jesus discuss the parousia. Thus, all of the *events* were fulfilled at AD 70.[32]

30. Cf. France, *Matthew*, TNTC, 337; Gundry, *Matthew*, 476; Hagner, *Matthew 14–28*, 688; Ladd, *Theology*, 196–98; Toussaint, *Matthew*, 268–69.

31. For helpful overviews see Turner, "Structure and Sequence of Matthew 24:1–41," 3–27; Ladd, *Theology*, 197–99; Carson, "Matthew," 548–57; Quarles, *Matthew*, 603.

32. France, *Matthew*, TNTC, 333–36; France, *Matthew*, NICNT, 890–94.

The strength of this view is that it takes seriously the context of Israel's judgment, which Jesus just emphasized in the temple incidents, the controversies with the religious leaders, and the woes pronounced on the teachers of the law and the Pharisees (chs. 21–23). This view also finds ready parallels in historical incidents that transpired leading up to the temple destruction in AD 70 that parallel Jesus's prophecy.[33]

The weakness of this view is that it minimizes some of the details of the discourse that were not fulfilled historically in AD 70,[34] as well as the remarkable parallels in other prophetic literature to the events recorded here that indicate a future fulfillment of those features of the discourse (e.g., Dan 9:27; 12:11).

#### *16.3.1.2 Futurist View: All Fulfilled in the Future When Israel Is Reestablished*

On the other extreme is the futurist view, the strength of which, as one might expect, is the acknowledgment of the direct fulfillment of parallel prophetic passages like Dan 9 and 12 in future events prophesied by Jesus in the Olivet Discourse. This view suggests that virtually all of the events of the discourse will be fulfilled in the future when Israel is once again reestablished in God's purposes.[35] Many who hold this view suggest that the church is "raptured" prior to the events of the great tribulation, so Israel is once again the evangelistic instrument to bear witness to the gospel of the kingdom.[36] This view takes seriously God's promises to Israel to be reestablished in the land in the complete fulfillment of Daniel's seventieth week.

A weakness of this view is that it overlooks that Jesus gives the discourse to his disciples, not to Israel, as a guide to their understanding of their own role in this age and how they are to respond to future events. The events are a guide to the church's expectations throughout this age, not solely specified to be related to Israel's future role. Another weakness is that it minimizes the way that Daniel's prophecy of the abomination of desolation has already been partially fulfilled with the defiling activities of Antiochus IV Epiphanies (Dan 11:31).

#### *16.3.1.3 Prophetic Foreshortening View: Historical and Future Events Are Intentionally Intertwined*

The resolution adopted in my interpretation is a mediating one, where there appears to be an intentional intertwining of historical and eschatological fulfillment. In this view there is comprehensive theological cohesion in the discourse between Jesus's

33. France, *Matthew*, TNTC, 336–46.

34. Ladd, *Theology*, 197–99; Robert H. Gundry, *The Church and the Tribulation* (Grand Rapids: Zondervan, 1973), 132–34.

35. See Barbieri, "Matthew," 76–78.

36. Whatever one concludes with reference to a "rapture" in the unfolding of these events, because of the scantiness of exegetical material, especially here in the discourse (if not absence of material here), that theological conclusion forms a tenuous base if it is the primary determining factor as to how the discourse is interpreted.

treatment of the fall of Jerusalem and statements regarding the parousia, but there is no clear dividing point between historical and eschatological fulfillment.[37]

George Ladd suggests that the historical and eschatological elements are purposely intertwined under a kind of prophetic foreshortening. The near event, the destruction of Jerusalem, serves as kind of a symbol for the far event.[38] Jesus intertwines his answer to both questions posed by the disciples concerning the destruction of Jerusalem and the parousia. The fall of Jerusalem in AD 70 is a forewarning of the period of great tribulation to come at the end of this age. The destruction of the temple in AD 70 is a direct answer to the disciples of that day, but Jesus sees beyond that day to the entire age and his coming in power and glory at the end of the age.[39]

In my view the events of 24:4–14 are a general description of the life of the church during this age, perhaps with some increase of activity in 24:9–14. But at 24:15 begins a double reference to events that will be partially fulfilled at AD 70 with the destruction of the temple and Jerusalem but culminate in the future fulfillment of the complex of events surrounding the return of Jesus—the abomination that causes desolation, the end of the age, and the parousia. This general mediating position has been adopted by a wide range of interpreters, perhaps "a majority of conservative sources,"[40] including those from an amillennial perspective,[41] those from a premillennial-pretribulational perspective,[42] those from a prewrath or mid-tribulational perspective,[43] and those from a premillennial-posttribulational perspective.[44]

Majority certainly does not always signify accuracy, but here it indicates that caution

37. Morris, *Matthew*, 593–94n4; Turner, *Matthew*, 566–67.

38. Ladd, *Theology*, 198. Cf. also Hagner, *Matthew 14–28*, 688; Mounce, *Matthew*, 228–30; Davies and Allison, *Matthew*, 3:330–33; Turner, *Matthew*, 566–67. For an attempt to balance the two, see Turner, "Structure and Sequence," 3–27; Turner, *Matthew*, 566–67. See also Morris, *Matthew*, 593–94.

39. Cranfield suggests that in Jesus's own view the historical and the eschatological are mingled, and that the final eschatological event is seen through the "transparency" of the immediate historical incident (Cranfield, *Mark*, 390–94).

40. Turner, "Structure and Sequence," 9. For an inductive study for laypersons that adopts this general approach, see Andreas J. Köstenberger, Alexander E. Stewart, and Apollo Makara, *Jesus and the Future: Understanding What He Taught About the End Times* (Wooster, OH: Weaver, 2017).

41. Anthony A. Hoekema, *The Bible and the Future* (Grand Rapids: Eerdmans, 1979), 130, suggests that the signs given by Jesus "had their initial fulfillment at the time of the destruction of Jerusalem; since this discourse exemplifies the principle of prophetic foreshortening, however, the signs mentioned in them will have a further fulfillment at the time of the Parousia." See also Hendrickson, *Matthew*, 852–56.

42. Turner, "Structure and Sequence," passim; Alva J. McClain, *The Greatness of the Kingdom* (Chicago: Moody, 1959), 136–39: "a hard and fast chronological scheme" should not be read into the Olivet Discourse (365). See also Glasscock, *Matthew*, 468: "The nature of eschatological revelation allows for a typological fulfillment at one level with a more complete fulfillment at another. This will be seen in the reference to Daniel's abomination of desolation."

43. See Alan Hultberg, "A Case for Prewrath Rapture," in *Three Views on The Rapture: Pretribulation, Prewrath, or Posttribribulation,* ed. Alan Hultberg (Grand Rapids: Zondervan, 2010), 109–83, passim, here 112: "Though the disciples would see a proleptic fulfillment of these events in the destruction of Jerusalem, the end of the age and the coming of the Son of Man were yet future."

44. Robert Gundry indicates that (1) the events centering around the destruction of Jerusalem in A.D. 70 did not exhaust Jesus's prophecy, with the result that a time of future tribulation immediately before the return of Christ is yet to be fulfilled and (2) the events centering around the destruction of Jerusalem did, however, constitute a fulfillment precursive to a larger and final fulfillment at the end of the age (Gundry, *Church and the Tribulation*, 129). See also Ladd, *Theology*, 198.

against going too far in either direction seems to be the wisest course of interpreting Jesus's prophecy.[45] Jesus warns of first-century historical judgment on Israel for rejecting the invitation to the kingdom but also upholds guidance for his disciples and the fulfillment of the covenantal promises to Israel to be restored to the land, which ushers in the reign of the messianic kingdom.[46] The fifth discourse is an eschatological forecast of events fulfilled partially in the first century but brought to their final fulfillment with the events surrounding the return of Jesus Messiah in glory.[47]

#### *16.3.1.4 Prophetic Foreshortening Overview of the Olivet Discourse*

We may then see five basic parts, with subsections, to Jesus's Olivet Discourse.

1. **Part One**—Jesus offers a general description of events that will transpire throughout the entire age (24:4–8), with worldwide evangelistic activity consummating the age (24:9–14).
2. **Part Two**—Jesus describes events, generally chronological, that will accompany the parousia (24:15–31).
   a. Jesus describes "great tribulation," which intertwines prophecy of the destruction of the temple in AD 70 and the final desolation at the end of the age (24:15–28).
   b. Jesus describes the coming of the Son of Man during the time of tribulation (24:29–31).
3. **Part Three**—Jesus's teaches on the nearness and watching for his coming (24:32–42).
   a. Jesus gives a general principle of "nearness" concerning the destruction and parousia (24:32–35).
   b. Jesus gives indications of general conditions of the "sign" of his coming as to why they are to "watch" (24:36–42).
4. **Part Four**—Jesus gives parabolic warnings because the time of his coming is unknown (24:43–25:30).

45. Carson ("Matthew," 556–57) and D. Wenham (*Rediscovery of Jesus' Eschatological Discourse*, 346–50) espouse a somewhat unique approach, which Turner calls a "revised preterist-futurist view" ("Structure and Sequence," 9–10). They suggest that Jesus first gives a general discussion of this time period (24:4–28), with a brief discussion of the fall of Jerusalem in AD 70 inserted as an example of God's judgment (24:15–21), and then comes the second advent (24:29–31), with the warning in 24:32–35 describing the whole tribulation period that stretches from the ascension to the second advent. While somewhat unique, it falls generally within the broad sweep of mediating positions between the extremes of historical and futuristic interpretations but avoids the significance of the temple and Israel in these tribulational scenes.

46. Hafemann, "Eschatology and Ethics," 161–92.

47. Quarles (*Matthew*, 603) adopts a preterist-futurist view in which he argues that "Matthew presents the fall of Jerusalem and the second coming as distinct events and does not imply that the events leading to Jerusalem's destruction will recur prior to the second coming. Other New Testament books indicate that the events surrounding the fall of Jerusalem foreshadow eschatological events. Matthew does not deny this; he simply does not explore this implication of Jesus's words."

   a. The parable of the thief in the night warns to be watchful by being prepared (24:43–44).
   b. The parable of the servant warns to be responsible (24:45–51).
   c. The parable of the virgins warns to be equipped (25:1–13).
   d. The parable of the servants warns to be productive (25:14–30).
5. **Part Five**—Jesus concludes the discourse with a scene of reward of eternal life and of judgment of eternal punishment at the time of his coming (25:31–46).
   a. The glorious Son of man will separate the sheep to his right and the goats to his left (25:31–33).
   b. Reward of eternal life comes to the sheep (25:34–40)
   c. Judgment of eternal punishment comes to the goats (25:41–46)

#### *16.3.1.5 Jesus's Eschatological Preparation of the Disciples*

Jesus's eschatological forecast in this final discourse in Matthew's Gospel is his most complete discussion of end-time events that surround his return in glory. But it does not cover everything. It must be understood in its historical setting. Jesus gives this during his final week with his disciples. They still have not comprehended that he will be crucified, that he will be raised, that he will ascend to the Father, and that they will soon become the kingdom community called the church with the descent of the Spirit at Pentecost. So, in this discourse Jesus gives only a rough outline of events that will transpire throughout this age until his return. The events he discusses here will be fleshed out later with further revelation given to the apostles. They will later, especially after the resurrection and arrival of the Spirit, be better prepared to handle a more complete picture of end-time events. But during this tumultuous week that will lead to his execution, and resurrection, the disciples are not yet ready for a complete picture.

Jesus quite likely gave fuller details of end-time events to the apostles during the forty days before the ascension where he spoke about the kingdom of God (Acts 1:4). Through prophetic insights and revelation from the Father through the Spirit the apostles will have many more details filled in under inspiration as they write later books of the New Testament (e.g., John's Revelation and Paul's 1–2 Thessalonians).

Later descriptions of end-time and eternal activities will fill in the details of Jesus's basic outline given here in the fifth discourse. This is similar to what Jesus provides in the missionary discourse (Matt 10) and the community discourse (ch. 18), where he gives only a rough outline that later will be filled in by New Testament writers who are inspired to give details of missionary outreach (e.g., Acts) and the structure and function of the church (e.g., Ephesians, 1–2 Timothy).

So, we must not make Jesus's eschatological forecast in the Olivet Discourse say more than what he intended to say. Further details must be supplied by other New Testament and Old Testament writings, the exhaustive study of which is not the purpose of this study of Matthew's theological perspective. Like we have done with his other discourses, we seek to understand Jesus's purpose for his disciples in giving this discourse in its historical setting, and Matthew's intention as he recorded it for his community.

This fifth discourse has a specific intention to give to Jesus's disciples a basic prophetic overview of the events to transpire in the near and distant future. But Jesus's intent is not primarily to give a timetable; he focuses especially on the attitudes and character qualities that guide their discipleship to him for the days and years ahead when he would no longer be with them physically.

### 16.3.2 Last Things *Before* the Parousia in Matthew's Record of Jesus Messiah's Olivet Discourse

In the first section of the discourse (Matt 24:4–14), Jesus gives a preview of general conditions on the earth that in some sense characterize the entire age before the coming of the Lord.

#### *16.3.2.1 The Beginning of Birth Pains (24:4–14)*

The Twelve have been warned of some of this impending persecution and suffering that they will endure on their future worldwide missionary endeavor (cf. 10:16–23), but here it is given in a discourse that anticipates suffering that will be common to all disciples as they await the return of Jesus and the end of this age. At the end of this age, referred to as "birth pains" (24:8), the time of great tribulation will commence.

#### *16.3.2.2 Sufferings Throughout the World (24:4–8)*

Jesus begins the discourse with a stern admonition: "Watch out that no one deceives you" (24:4). As he looks ahead to the future of his disciples, he warns them that many events might deceive them into thinking that the end of the age had arrived. But instead, all of these events are general characteristics of this age of birth pains. Jesus explicitly emphasizes that neither false messiahs, nor wars, nor global conflicts, nor famines nor earthquakes are to be seen as indicators of the end of the age. These are conditions that will affect the entire world throughout this age.

##### 16.3.2.2.1 False Messiahs (24:4–5)

He first warns, "Many will come in my name, claiming, 'I am the Christ,' and will deceive many" (24:5). Prophetic figures and messianic deliverers had long attempted to incite revolution against occupying forces in the Second Temple period, and they continued into the years after the foundation of the church. The second-century Jewish rebel, Simon Bar Kokhba, which means "son of a star," was so named by Rabbi Akiba, proclaiming him messiah on the basis of the star from Jacob in Num 24:17. Later rabbis rejected this identification and referred to him as Bar Kosiba, "son of a lie," a pejorative epithet reflecting the rabbinic rejection of him as messiah.[48] Throughout the ages since the first century, many have attempted to claim messianic identity. Jesus's disciples must not be deceived.

#### 16.3.2.2.2 Wars and Calamities (24:6–7)

Jesus next warns that wars and rumors of wars will recur repeatedly throughout the age, with nations and kingdoms rising against each other (Matt 24:6–7). The end is not near even though calamities may seem to indicate that it is. The Old Testament linked wars, cosmic battles, famines, earthquakes, and other catastrophic events with the end of the age, as did the apocalyptic vision of 4 Ezra 9:1–6 (2 Esdras). Note also the catastrophic events recorded in the apostle John's Revelation. But Jesus emphasizes that throughout this age these activities will be a regular and recurring part of the suffering of this life until the return of Jesus begins the redemption of all creation. There will indeed be a vast uprising of cataclysmic events at Jesus's return, but these general events of this age—including wars and calamities—do not signal his parousia.

#### 16.3.2.2.3 Birth Pains (24:8)

These are just the beginning of birth pains (Matt 24:8). "Birth pains" is a common metaphor from the Old Testament prophets to depict terrible human suffering generally (Isa 13:8; 21:3; 42:14; Jer 30:7–10; Hos 13:13) but also the suffering that Israel specifically will endure prior to her deliverance (Isa 26:17–19; 66:7–11; Jer 22:23; Mic 4:9–10). The imagery points to an expected time of suffering that would characterize the period prior to the messianic age. Although the inauguration of the kingdom of heaven brings redemption to its citizens, the whole world continues to experience birth pains as it awaits final redemption, as do even believers who have the first fruits of the Spirit (cf. Rom 8:22–23). Jesus warns that ongoing suffering will characterize this age.

We might think that the use of the expression "birth pains" contradicts Jesus's statement that the time of his coming is unknown (Matt 24:36), since pain presages the imminent birth of a baby. However, the plural term (*ōdinōn*, "birth pains") appears to have been used for a more obvious purpose to highlight a different facet of birth pains: the pain of childbirth is not steady, nor is it a steadily increasing pain, but is instead a repeated phenomenon, coming in waves over and over again.[49] The baby does not come on the first pang, but with the first all know that the inexorable process has begun. We do not know if the baby will come on the fifth, the fifteenth, the fiftieth, or the five hundredth pang. With each pang we know that the time will come, but we do not know how soon or how long. Periods of wars and rumors of wars, tragic waves of

48. Neusner and Green, "Bar Kosiba, Simon," *DJBP* 77–78.

49. Conrad Gempf, "The Imagery of Birth Pangs in the New Testament," *TynBul* 45.1 (1994): 119–35; esp. 132–34.

earthquakes and times of famine wash over the landscape of history in repeated pains. Each is a reminder that the end is coming, but no one knows when until the Son of Man appears. Throughout the labor each must remain on guard.

Some will try to mislead believers that these pains *are* the end. But Jesus warns his disciples not to be deceived. The first appearance, especially the tragedies they will witness in Jerusalem in AD 70, are the *beginning* of birth pains, but they will continue to recur and will characterize the entire age. The metaphor indicates the inescapability of the sequence of events once the process begins and also the repetitive nature of the waves of pain until the end.[50] Even as I write, the sufferings of the people of Israel and Palestine in Gaza and the sufferings of the people of Ukraine with the invasion by Russia are terrible reminders of the birth pains that continue to wrack our world.

### *16.3.2.3 Sufferings of Jesus's Disciples (24:9–13)*

"*Then* you will be handed over to be persecuted and put to death, and you will be hated by all nations because of me" (24:9; my emphasis). Some see chronological sequence in 24:9, indicating that the events of 24:9–14 will presage the parousia.[51] But a special emphasis of the adverb "then" (*tote*) here signals a change of focus.[52] Jesus switches from prophesying of the suffering that the *world as a whole* will experience throughout this age (24:4–8) to predicting suffering that his *disciples* will encounter because they are his followers (24:9–13).[53]

#### 16.3.2.3.1 Persecution (24:9–11)

Jesus warns his disciples that they will encounter persecution (24:9; cf. 10:16–24). The disciples will be handed over to *thlipsis* ("persecution, distress, tribulation"), a word that occurs four times in Matthew, three of which are found in this chapter (13:21; 24:9, 21, 29). In 24:21 and 29, *thlipsis* points to a specific future period of unparalleled "distress" (NIV) or "tribulation" (NASB). Here, as in 13:21, the term indicates a general kind of trouble or persecution. Jesus's disciples will feel wrath and alienation from humanity for following him and proclaiming his message.

The phrase "because of me" is literally "because of my name" (*dia to onoma mou*) and is an important christological expression[54] (cf. 5:11; 24:9) that harks back to the Old Testament significance of God's name as the representation of his person as the sole focus of Israel's worship and allegiance (e.g., Exod 3:15; 6:3; 9:16; 20:7). Jesus's disciples

50. Gempf, "Imagery of Birth Pangs," 133–34.

51. Some see a shift of increased persecution of the church signaled in 24:9 just prior to the parousia; e.g., Gundry, *Church and the Tribulation*, 49; Brent Kinman, *History, Design and the End of Time: God's Plan for the World* (Nashville: Broadman and Holman, 2000), 80.

52. E.g., Blomberg, *Matthew*, 354–55; Carson, "Matthew," 560; Davies and Allison, *Matthew*, 3:341; Hagner, *Matthew 14–28*, 694.

53. France, *Matthew*, TNTC, 338.

54. Hagner, *Matthew 1–13*, 278.

will have the privilege of carrying his name, but it also brings with it suffering because the antagonism and hatred that is directed to him will naturally fall on his followers.[55]

### 16.3.2.3.2 Betrayal (24:10)

Because of persecution, the faith of Jesus's followers will be tested (Matt 24:10). It is not easy to endure persecution, and those who only hold on to Jesus because of their own comfort will find that it is easier to turn away from him and avoid the suffering. They not only will seek their own escape from suffering, but they will become enemies of Jesus and turn against his followers, their former fellow disciples. They will betray them to the persecutors, and the love that formerly was the chief characteristic of the relationship between them (5:43–47; 22:34–40) will now be turned to hate as they utterly reject Jesus and his followers. Their apostasy is the evidence that they were not true disciples.

### 16.3.2.3.3 Deception (24:11)

Not only will false messiahs try to deceive the world (24:5), false prophets will surface within the community to try to deceive Jesus's disciples (24:11). The apostle John warns likewise of deceptive voices both within the church and in the world (1 John 2:18–27; 4:1–6), which are to be tested according to the criterion of acknowledging that Jesus is the Messiah incarnate from God (1 John 2:22; 4:2–3). This criterion will be employed throughout this age to test cults and false theology, but sadly, these false prophets will deceive many (Matt 24:11).

### 16.3.2.3.4 Wickedness and Lovelessness (24:12)

All the preceding—persecution, betrayal, deception—are described as the increase of wickedness, which points to the spiritual death of those who fall away and those who have attempted to deceive the community. The chief characteristic of spiritual death is that it causes love to grow cold. Jesus emphasized throughout his ministry that love is not primarily an emotion but is an active commitment to God and to others to promote God's will (cf. 5:43–47). Those who are spiritually dead cannot produce this kind of love, which reemphasizes that these apostates never knew God at all. The NIV expression "*most* will grow cold" (*tōn pollōn*) is perhaps best understood along with the other uses of the plural positive *polloi* in this chapter as "many" (24:5, 10–11),[56] with the indication that a large percentage of the community will apostatize.[57] This is a somber picture of the community of disciples being impacted by apostasy. But it is not

55. Cf. John 15:21; 2 Tim 3:12; 1 Pet 4:13–14.

56. Blomberg, *Matthew*, 355; Hagner, *Matthew 14–28*, 695.

57. The articular *tōn pollōn* can indicate majority, as in the NIV rendering; cf. "πολλύς, πολλή, πολύ," BDAG 849, §2.β.א; Davies and Allison, *Matthew*, 3:343n98; France, *Matthew*, TNTC, 338.

unlike Jesus's statements elsewhere when he emphasizes that the gate and way to life is narrow, with only a few finding it (7:13–14).

#### 16.3.2.3.5 Standing Firm (21:13)

Along with the somber picture of apostasy Jesus gives a critical promise: "but the one who stands firm to the end will be saved" (24:13). Active resistance may be included in standing firm, but much more in view is the enduring fortitude of the disciples under any circumstance, including the most hateful persecution. The identical expression occurred earlier in the mission discourse where Jesus gives great assurance that, in spite of the increase in persecution, the hatred of humanity will not overcome his missionary disciples (10:22). Here Jesus also looks to the future to promise that the disciple who endures to the end—that is, the end of the persecution with the coming of the Son of Man (10:23) or the end of a person's life—will be saved.

"Saved" does not speak of rescue from death, because many true disciples have experienced martyrdom. Instead, Jesus gives both a concrete promise and a cautionary reminder. His promise is that the one who remains committed to his name to the end will not be consumed by the persecution but will experience the full blessing and peace of the kingdom's salvation with his arrival. But Jesus likewise reminds them that the indication of a disciple's real commitment to him will be whether he or she remains steadfast to the end of the persecution or life. Jesus is faithful to provide the resources to withstand whatever difficulties may come because the same Spirit who is upon Jesus in his earthly ministry (12:18) will speak through the disciples when they are under pressure and persecution (10:19–20) and will provide the strength necessary to endure the persecution to the end. Jesus himself will be with them to the end of the age (28:20).

### *16.3.2.4 Preaching the Gospel to All Nations (24:14)*

Jesus cautioned the disciples against false assumptions about what will signal the end (24:6, 8), but now he gives an explicit indicator of the activity that must be accomplished before the end of this age: "And this gospel of the kingdom will be preached in the whole world as a testimony to all nations, and then the end will come." The expression "gospel of the kingdom" is unique to Matthew (24:14; cf. 4:23; 9:35), combining the good news of salvation with the arrival of the kingdom of God. This is testimony or a witness to the reality of God's presence in the ministry of Jesus and his followers (cf. 8:4; 10:18). Although the increase of events in 24:9–13 is some indication that the parousia is near, the only explicit condition to be met will be the proclamation of the gospel of the kingdom in the entire world to all the nations. After that gospel proclamation has occurred, the end will come.

During Jesus's earthly ministry the disciples' mission was restricted to Israel (cf. 10:5–7) in fulfillment of the Davidic covenant. The future mission shifts to all the nations, which will fulfill the Abrahamic covenant, but it will include a continued outreach to Israel (see on 10:23; 28:19).[58] This future mission is inaugurated with the risen Jesus's "Great Commission" (28:16–20), but it is prophesied both here in the Olivet Discourse and earlier in the Missionary Discourse (10:16–23).

This worldwide proclamation was fulfilled in part during the first century with the preaching of Paul throughout the then-known world (e.g., Rom 15:19), which contributes to the possibility of the imminence of Jesus's return.[59] But the urgency of worldwide missionary activity is demanded by recognizing that the final fulfillment of Jesus's statement in 24:14 awaits the eschatological arrival of the events of great tribulation, to which he now turns. Jesus's disciples are to give themselves urgently to the task of preaching the gospel of the kingdom throughout this present age because we cannot fully discern when it has finally reached into all of the world to all of the nations.[60] "Though Christians desire for Christ to come quickly, they should not cut corners to 'make it happen,' for others' eternal destinations are at stake."[61] Each new generation of nations brings with it a new mission field. But once this proclamation has been fulfilled in God's timing, the beginning of the time of tribulation on the earth will begin.

### 16.3.3 Last Things *at* the Parousia in Matthew's Record of Jesus Messiah's Olivet Discourse (24:15–31)

In this next section Jesus describes events, generally chronological, that will accompany his parousia (24:15–31). He first describes the "great tribulation" (24:15–28), which intertwines prophecy of the destruction of the temple in AD 70 and the final desolation at the end of the age (24:15–28). He then describes the coming of the Son of Man during the time of tribulation (24:29–31).

#### *16.3.3.1 Description of "Great Tribulation" (24:15–28)*

The combination of the inferential ("so, therefore") and temporal ("when") conjunctions beginning 24:15 signals a major temporal shift: "So when you see standing in the holy place . . . " (24:15). Moving from general characteristics of this age until his return, Jesus now points to the event prophesied by Daniel the prophet, "the abomination that causes desolation" (Dan 9:27). Some contend that at this point Jesus focuses exclusively on the destruction of the temple in AD 70,[62] while a wide spectrum of scholars contend that these events also presage a future time of eschatological defilement and

58. Cf. Brindle, "'To the Jew First,'" 221–33.

59. E.g., Blomberg, *Matthew*, 356–57.

60. E.g., Davies and Allison, *Matthew*, 3:344; Morris, *Matthew*, 602.

61. Moore, "Can We Hasten the Parousia?," 291–311.

62. E.g., France, *Matthew*, TNTC, 340–41; Blomberg, *Matthew*, 357–59.

destruction.[63] The latter view is preferred here, especially when it is compared with Paul's prediction of the eschatological man of lawlessness (2 Thess 2:1–12), and the Apocalypse's vision of the eschatological beast (Rev 13:11–18), which are remarkably similar to Jesus's prophecy. Together they indicate some "evil, deified figure such as the AntiChrist."[64]

If one looks only at the account in Luke (21:20–24), the focus is apparently on the fall of Jerusalem. But when we look at the Matthean (24:15–22) and Markan (13:14–20) accounts—with the mention of "the abomination that causes desolation"—we can see that the focus shifts to something that did not occur at the destruction of Jerusalem in AD 70. The reference to the abomination shifts the focus to activities at the end of the age. Jesus, therefore, is giving a mixture of prophetic elements that speak both to his present generation and to the future.

#### 16.3.3.1.1 The Abomination That Causes Desolation (24:15)

The prophecy in Daniel refers to a period of "seven," in the middle of which a ruler will set up "an abomination that causes desolation" (Dan 9:27), which is similar to the expressions in Dan 8:13, 11:31, and 12:11. During the days of the Maccabees the same expression was used to describe the sacrilege of Antiochus IV Epiphanes, the Seleucid king, when he decreed that an altar to Olympian Zeus and perhaps a statue of him was to be erected in the temple on 15 Chislev, 167 BC (1 Macc 1:54, NRSVue; cf. 2 Macc 6:2). This was one of the lowest points of Jewish history.

But the Daniel references were also brought to mind in AD 26 when Pontius Pilate arrived as prefect to govern Judea and introduced to Jerusalem military standards bearing idolatrous symbols of the emperor.[65] Others believe Daniel's prophecy was being fulfilled when Emperor Gaius (Caligula) ordered that a gigantic statue of himself be set up in the temple in Jerusalem, although he was dissuaded by King Herod Agrippa I and died in AD 41 before the order could be carried out.[66]

But rather than having been completely realized in the activities of Antiochus IV Epiphanes or any other time, Jesus now quotes Daniel directly to clarify that the fulfillment of the "abomination that causes desolation" is yet future.[67] Paul harks back to Jesus's and Daniel's prophecies as he gives his own prophetic statement of the antichrist who is yet to come (2 Thess 2:3–4), which prefigures the antichrist (the first beast) who will be set up by the false prophet (the second beast) as a god in the temple (Rev 13:11–18).

63. E.g., Davies and Allison, *Matthew*, 3:344; Gundry, *Matthew*, 485; Ladd, *Theology*, 675–76.

64. Gundry, *Matthew*, 482.

65. See Josephus, *Ant.* 10.55–59; Paul Barnett, *Jesus and the Rise of Early Christianity: A History of New Testament Times* (Downers Grove: InterVarsity, 1999), 144–48.

66. Cf. Philo, *Legatio Ad Gaium* 200–203; Josephus, *Ant.* 10.257–309; see F. F. Bruce, *New Testament History* (New York: Doubleday, 1969), 253–57.

67. For discussion of related issues, see Gleason L. Archer Jr., "Daniel," in EBC 7, 111–21.

Both Matthew and Mark include a parenthetical phrase: "let the reader understand" (Matt 24:15; Mark 13:14). This is an aside intended to get the reader of Daniel to see that in Jesus's words one will find the real fulfillment of the prophecy. With the onset of the abomination that causes desolation as spoken of by Daniel (Dan 9:27), the period of "great tribulation" begins (Matt 24:21). This desolating sacrilege is the predominant event of the period of tribulation, which corresponds to Daniel's period of "seven," in the middle of which a ruler will set up "an abomination that causes desolation" (Dan 9:27). When we look at the prophecy of Daniel (esp. 9:25–27) and the events of the book of Revelation (see the number of days of 1,260 [=3½ years] in Rev 12:6), this actually marks the second half of the seven years of tribulation, the time of "great tribulation." Apparently the first three and one-half years were a time of relative peace and quiet.

As discussed in the introduction to this chapter, Jesus's prophecy is an answer to both of the disciples' questions. He predicts the destruction of Jerusalem and the temple in AD 70, but he looks beyond to a future time when another abomination that causes desolation will arise in Jerusalem to lead astray God's people and bring destruction upon those who resist him.[68]

### 16.3.3.1.2 Flight of Believers (24:16–20)

In a series of five warnings taken from everyday life in Israel, Jesus accentuates the immediacy of danger that will accompany the fulfillment of the arrival of the abomination that causes desolation. Daniel's prophecy marks these events occurring during the second half of the seven years of tribulation. When the abomination occurs, those who have heeded the prophecies of Jesus will know that immediate and utter destruction is coming on Jerusalem, so they are to flee with the greatest haste (Matt 24:16). Many believers will be martyred during these years of great tribulation, and Jesus says that his followers should flee (24:16). The impending destruction means that there will be no time to gather provisions in the home (24:17). The outer coat was an essential garment for traveling, often used as a blanket when sleeping outdoors, and only those in the greatest hurry would think of leaving it behind (24:18). The danger of travel in this perilous time is greatest for those most at risk, especially pregnant mothers and their infants. Jesus describes their fate with a cry of "woe," emphasizing that those

68. There is an active movement within Judaism in Israel to rebuild the temple, which would be the Third Temple. E.g., see the following website: www.templeinstitute.org. For in intriguing discussion of the modern Jewish vision and movement for a "Third Temple" in modern Israel in the activities of the contemporary "Temple Institute," see Motti Inbari, "Messianic Religious Zionism and the Reintroduction of Sacrifice: The Case of the Temple Institute," in *Rethinking the Messianic Idea in Judaism*, ed. Michael L. Morgan and Steven Weitzman (Bloomington, IN: Indiana University Press, 2015), 256–73. Inbari is assistant professor of religion at the University of North Carolina at Pembroke. He states: "The growing trend of Jewish prayers on the Temple Mount and the vigorous activities of the Temple Institute, discussed above, suggest that the vision of the Third Temple has emerged as a widely accepted component of contemporary Israeli Jewish messianism" (Inbari, "Messianic Religious Zionism," 270).

who are most vulnerable and who normally can rely on the help of others will suffer the most (24:19). Flight in winter, when roads are washed out and when rivers are swollen, presents even more difficulty for those fleeing the horrors of the coming desolation. In prayer the disciples must cling to God's presence and ever-ready help, even though they may have to disrupt even the most devoutly held religious traditions, such as the Jewish Sabbath (24:20).

### 16.3.3.1.3 "Great Tribulation" (24:21)

The adverb "then" (*tote*) occurs again, here with a strong sense of temporal sequence (cf. 24:14, 16, 30), indicating that the appearance of the abomination that causes desolation launches the period of "great distress" or "great tribulation" (*thlipsis megalē*) (24:21). While the time of the siege and destruction of Jerusalem were horrible,[69] the description here in Matthew indicates a time of tribulation that did not occur during the fall of Jerusalem. The horrors that fell upon the Jewish people in the Holocaust and upon the entire world with the two World Wars of the twentieth century are a somber warning that the desolation that comes from humanity's unleashed depravity will yet be unequaled. The vision that Jesus paints must yet be ahead. The apostle John's vision reveals such a future time of incredible horror (Rev 7–19) and speaks of those martyrs who come "out of the great tribulation" (7:14) just prior to the end of the age (Rev 7:9). The unusual piling up of negatives in Matthew's narrative, "never to be equaled again" (*oud' ou mē genētai*, Matt 24:21), makes for an emphatic negation, which points both to the unequaled climax of horror and the promise of God that it will not be repeated.

### 16.3.3.1.4 The Days Cut Short (24:22)

Jesus again reiterates the terrible suffering of those future days: "If those days had not been cut short, no one would survive, but for the sake of the elect those days will be shortened (24:22). This is a proverbial way of indicating that God is in control even of these days of horror. If the wickedness of humanity and the wrath of God were allowed to run unchecked, there would be no end to the horror, and no one would survive. This is a promise that the time of tribulation would not last indefinitely, because God is in control.

The people of Israel are often referred to as "the elect" (e.g., Isa 45:4; 1 En. 1:1), but here this is a reference to believing Christians (e.g., Rom 11:7). In the time of future great tribulation, when Israel will once again be used of God for witness (e.g., Rev 7:3–8) to bring in a multitude of believers from all the nations who worship God and the Lamb (Rev 7:9–12), the expression "the elect" includes all those who believe on Christ during this period (cf. Matt 24:22, 24, 31).

69. See Josephus, *J.W.* books 5–6.

### 16.3.3.1.5 Warnings About False Messiahs (24:23–28)

Jesus once again points to the rise of false messiahs and prophets, but whereas before he noted that these charlatans would be a characteristic of the entire age until the parousia and do not signal the end of the age (see on 24:5, 11), during the time of great tribulation there will be an unprecedented rise of miracle-working false messiahs and prophets (24:24). The signs and miracles they perform are indications of supernatural activity, but believers must be careful not to be deceived into thinking that God stands behind them. Satan himself and his evil forces are able to manipulate the supernatural, so the spiritually discerning must look for the hand that lies behind the signs and miracles to see whether it truly comes from God. False messiahs and prophets who work supernatural deeds are therefore ultimately pawns in the hands of the enemy of God, the evil one.

Believers, beware (24:26). The desert had messianic overtones for diverse groups within Israel who associated the wilderness with God's forthcoming deliverance (e.g., Essenes of the Qumran community); messianic pretenders often gathered their followers in the wilderness prior to their public appearance.[70] Josephus recounts stories of rebel leaders who gathered thousands of followers to them in the desert and in the temple.[71] Jesus warns that they are not to believe those "in the wilderness" or those "in inner rooms" who say that they are the Messiah. Messiah will not come in a secretive manner only to his exclusive gang of followers. Rather, the Son of Man will come in a spectacular manner, like lightning that is visible to all (24:26–27).

The warnings about secret workings of false messiahs and the declaration of his own spectacular appearance prompts Jesus to give a puzzling saying: "Wherever there is a carcass, there the vultures will gather" (24:28). This saying is proverbial, either quoted by Jesus or created by him to make a macabre point (cf. also Luke 17:37). Here in the Matthean context it connects either with the appearance of false messiahs and prophets or connects with the coming of the Son of Man.

The proverb means one of the following. (1) It may point out that the corruption of this world will draw false messiahs and prophets to converge and feed upon those being deceived, who, therefore, really are spiritually dead. This fits best with the warnings about false prophets.[72] (2) It may mean that just as certainly as vultures gather to devour a corpse or animal carcass, so all people will be drawn to see Christ upon his return.[73] (3) It may indicate that from far and wide people can see high circling vultures

70. See Joseph Patrich, "Hideouts in the Judean Wilderness," *BAR* 15.5 (1989): 32–42. For an overview of these groups, see Horsley and Hanson, *Bandits, Prophets, and Messiahs*.

71. Josephus, *J.W.*, 5.508–15; 250–51.

72. Morris, *Matthew*, 608. This seems to make sense of the metaphor by connecting it with negative connotations, but does not really fit the context of Jesus's statement about his return.

73. Blomberg, *Matthew*, 361. This seems to make more sense of Jesus's statement in the context, but the metaphor does not really make a parallel with Jesus's coming; does this make Jesus's coming parallel a carcass?

converging on the carcass of a dead animal, and so will be the visibility of the return of the Son of Man when he comes to bring judgment on the deadness of this corrupt world.[74] This latter view seems to make most sense in the context of Jesus's allusion to his lightning-like appearance, but it is awkward in that it seems to make Jesus parallel a vulture. But such incongruities often characterize Jesus's proverbial sayings and parables for effect.

### *16.3.3.2 Description of the Coming of the Son of Man (24:29–31)*

The phrase "Immediately after the distress of those days" (24:29) introduces a temporal sequence: the Son of Man will come after the time of the tribulation of those days. Here "distress" (*thlipsis*) connects with 24:21 to point to a specific period of great tribulation. The adverbial expression "immediately after" emphasizes that the celestial signs and the coming of Jesus will occur after the time of "great tribulation" just described in 24:15–28.

Those who hold that this occurs during the fall of Jerusalem emphasize that one must resort to a "pitiful prosiness"[75] in order to have these events occur literally at the end of the age. Those who see these events occurring at the end suggest that one must "wildly spiritualize"[76] these events in order to see them occurring at the fall of Jerusalem.

Once again, the mixture of prophecy referring to both the fall of Jerusalem and the end of the age should be acknowledged. Although the judgment that was to be brought on Israel in AD 70 with the fall of Jerusalem does seem to be in Jesus's mind (cf. 23:37–39; Luke 21:20–24), the primary emphasis rests upon the end of the age when he will come as the Son of Man in great universal power.

#### 16.3.3.2.1 Heavenly Disturbances (24:29)

The end of the age will come with great disturbances in the heavens, with darkened skies, falling stars, the disruption of the forces of this age, and finally with the coming of Jesus. At his coming he will gather the elect from the ends of heaven. These events most likely refer to his coming at the end of the time of tribulation, which would correspond with the time of judgment of the nations (Matt 25:31–46).

Jesus uses typical apocalyptic imagery as he alludes to passages such as Isa 13:10 and 34:4[77] to describe his coming with a mixture of literal and figurative language (Matt 24:29). God will cause the skies to be darkened and the heavenly bodies to be

74. Hagner, *Matthew 14–28*, 707; but Hagner downplays the judgment aspect.

75. France, *Matthew*, TNTC, 344, quoting D. Lamont, *Christ and the World of Thought*, 2nd ed. (Edinburgh: T&T Clark, 1936) 266.

76. Toussaint, *Matthew*, 266.

77. Cf. Ezek 32:7; Joel 2:31; 3:15; Amos 8:9; 2 Esdras 5:4–5; 7:39; T. Mos. 10:5.

disturbed. Such language may point to both physical phenomena as well as political and spiritual disruptions.[78] The darkness at Jesus's crucifixion during his first coming was an indication that he had conquered the forces of evil on the cross, and the darkness during the second coming of the Son of Man is an indication that he will now exert his rule over all forces, especially those of the demonic prince of the powers of the air.

### 16.3.3.2.2 Heavenly Appearances (24:30–31)

Along with these heavenly disturbances will come heavenly appearances. "Then will appear the sign of the Son of Man in heaven" (24:30). There is debate as to whether the sign is some sort of heavenly ensign or banner, or whether the sign is the Son of Man himself. Many have connected the sign with the "banner" that Messiah will raise as he gathers the nations and Israel (Isa 11:10–12; 18:3) or the type of banners noted in the War Scroll that the battle formations of the congregation at Qumran raise at the final battle (cf. 1QM III, 13–IV, 17). Among the many theories of some sort of particular heavenly ensign, some, such as Chrysostom, suggested that the sign will be a cross in the sky.[79] However, since the rest of the verse points to the coming of the Son of Man himself as that which promotes mourning, the apparent reference to Dan 7:13, "one like the Son of Man," indicates that Jesus himself is the sign of the eschatological consummation of the age (see Matt 16:27; 26:64).[80]

As in his first coming, when Jesus's ministry and resurrection was a sufficient sign that he was indeed the Messiah, the Son of God,[81] so his second coming will be the sign to all the nations or tribes of the earth, who will then mourn (24:30). The term *phylai* can be rendered either "nations" (NIV) or "tribes" (NASB). Matthew regularly uses *ethnē* to refer to the nations (e.g., 24:9; 28:19), and the only other time that he uses *phylai* it refers specifically to the twelve tribes of Israel (19:28), which indicates that here it should be rendered as "tribes," calling to mind the twelve tribes of Israel. If so, "earth" refers to the land of Israel.[82] This integrates Daniel's emphasis of the time of great stress that will come upon the earth at the arrival of the Son of Man with the prophet's emphasis on the coming day of the Lord with its judgment of evil.

This language would hold special meaning to a Jewish audience, since the prophecy of Zech 12:10 speaks of the people of Israel mourning when they look on the one whom they have pierced. The apostle John applied this prophecy to those Jews who mourned the crucifixion (John 19:37), and he quotes the prophecy in Rev 1:7. Those events had

78. See Carrier, *Earthquakes and Eschatology*.

79. For discussion of the various options, see Marius Nel, "What Is 'the Sign of the Son of Man in Heaven' (Mt 24:30)?," *In die Skrilig* 49.1 (2015), art. #1876, http://dx.doi.org/10.4102/ids.v49i1.1876.

80. Cf. also the messianic expectation of a person as banner in Isa 5:26–30; see Gordon D. Kirchhevel, "He That Cometh in Mark 1:7 and Matt 24:30," *BBR* 4 (1994): 105–11.

81. The Jewish leaders had repeatedly asked for such a sign (Matt 12:38; 16:1; cf. John 2:18; 20:30–31).

82. So Blomberg, *Matthew*, 362.

great import for the people of Israel, and John uses the singular noun form *phylē* to refer to each individual tribe of the twelve of Israel (7:4–8). This is a kind of mourning that produces repentance, or else it stems from recognition of their coming judgment. But in the light of the place that Paul gives to Israel's future repentance and conversion (Rom 9–11; cf. Matt 23:39), repentance is more likely in view.

Jesus continues the description of his coming, "They will see the Son of Man coming on the clouds of the sky, with power and great glory" (24:30, ESV). Coming on the clouds with power and glory cannot easily be made to refer to Christ's coming spiritually in judgment against Israel at the time of the destruction of the temple. Rather, this is eschatological language that echoes Daniel's prophecy and points to Christ's return at the end of the age. Jesus completes his self-identity through the use of the relatively ambiguous title "Son of Man" (see 8:20 and discussion in Ch. 7 above). He is the Son of Man who displays humiliation with nowhere to lay his head (8:20), who experiences suffering as the servant who gives his life for many (20:17–19, 28), and who is now revealed as the one who will come in glorious power as the majestic sovereign designated by the Ancient of Days to receive worship as the divine King of the kingdom of God (Dan 7:13–14).

At his appearance "he will send his angels with a loud trumpet call" (24:31). Both banners and trumpets were associated in Jewish eschatological thought with the majestic arrival of the Messiah.[83] Jesus's return—accompanied as it will be by angels and the sounding trumpet—recurs in Paul's eschatological teaching (1 Cor 15:51–52; 1 Thess 4:16). Jesus refers elsewhere to the angelic host who accompany his eschatological appearance both for gathering and for bringing judgment (Matt 13:39, 41, 49; 16:27; 25:31) and who are at his disposal for his care (4:11; 26:53). The angel of the Lord appeared to announce the arrival of Jesus as the incarnate Immanuel (1:20–24) and to guide the family during his infancy (2:13:23), and an angel will announce the resurrected Jesus (28:2–5).

This picture coincides with the sovereign Son of Man, at whose disposal are the very angelic beings of heaven who "will gather his elect from the four winds, from one end of the heavens to the other" (24:31). The "elect" is another reference to all believers, both Jew and gentile, who have come to believe on him during this time of great tribulation. The gathering "from the four winds, from one end of heaven to another" has been taken to refer to the four points of the compass (cf. Ezek 37:9; Dan 8:8; 11:4) and from every place under heaven, indicating the gathering of all believers who are on the earth at the time.[84] Others have taken the expression "from one end of the heavens to another" to refer to Jesus's angels gathering and bringing with him all of the redeemed already

83. Isa 18:3; 27:13; Jer 4:21; 6:1; 51:27; 1QM III–IV; VIII; XVI; XVII–XVIII.

84. Carson, "Matthew," 568; Keener, *Matthew* (2009), 352; Morris, *Matthew*, 611.

in heaven to join with those believers on the earth (cf. Rev 19:11–16).[85] It probably should include both, so that at the end of the period of tribulation Jesus returns both to bring with him all those believers who are with him in heaven, as well as to gather those believers who are alive on the earth.[86]

## 16.3.4 Eschatological Discipleship in the Olivet Discourse: The "Nearness" and "Signs" of the Parousia (24:32–42)

A switch of emphasis now occurs. Up to this point there has been a combination of historical and eschatological features in answer to the questions about the destruction of the temple and his return and the end of the age. Jesus has given a descriptive overview of the entire age. But now he deals with attitudes that should characterize those who live during this age and await his coming. This is the description of eschatological discipleship to Jesus Messiah that is to characterize all of Jesus's disciples in these last times before the parousia.

### *16.3.4.1 The "Nearness" Concerning the Destruction of Jerusalem and the Parousia (24:32–35)*

Jesus gives several lessons that will equip people during this age in preparation for the end: the first is the parabolic lesson from the fig tree. Prior to this, the fig tree provided Jesus with an object lesson for his disciples on the irresponsibility of the Jewish leaders who should have recognized his messianic authority in announcing the arrival of the kingdom of heaven (see 21:18–22). It is possible that Jesus continues the allusion to Israel, perhaps pointing to the Messiah's future liberation of Israel and the temple from gentile dominance, with the fig tree illustration indicating the time of future blessing for Israel.[87]

But rather than pointing to Israel, Jesus more likely uses the fig tree generally as a parabolic lesson taught from nature to the disciples. It teaches a principle of nearness concerning the abomination that causes desolation of the temple and the return of the Son of Man (24:32–33). In the winter months figs lose their leaves, so buds on a branch and new leaves in spring are an indication that summer is near. So also, when the events in the preceding context occur, the disciples are to be prepared for the coming of the Son of Man. Jesus stated earlier that the general distressful events of this age must not be interpreted to mean that the Lord is near (24:1–8). However, as the end grows

85. Blomberg, *Matthew*, 363.

86. Pretribulationists contend that Jesus brings with him both the deceased and the "raptured" believers who are with him in heaven, while postribulationists contend that he brings with him only the former.

87. David Flusser, "Jesus Weeps over Jerusalem," in *Jesus* (Jerusalem: Magness, 1997), 240–43.

nearer, subtle increases of difficulty begin to mark the end. The budding tree can be overlooked; it is not spectacular and can even be unnoticed until too late.

Therefore, when his disciples see "all these things" (24:33)—that is, the beginning of the increase of distress and the accomplishment of the worldwide proclamation of the gospel of the kingdom—they should be alert that the end may be near. It is better with the NIV to render *estin* (24:33) impersonally, "it is near," which includes all aspects of the parousia. All people during this age should stay alert, because the arrival of summer can come unnoticed. But for those who are alert there are certain indications that the end is near, specifically the preaching of the gospel of the kingdom to all nations (24:14).

Therefore, "summer" (24:32) here refers to the age of blessedness and fruitfulness that will occur when Jesus has returned. This helps disciples to stay alert, because they can be prepared. But because the budding is not spectacular, only subtle, the outcomes of the parousia can be overlooked. The point is that people are to stay alert and are to be forewarned by certain signs at the very end.

#### 16.3.4.1.1 "This Generation"

The identity of "this generation" (24:34) has vexed interpreters. Some contend that the reference is to the generation of Jesus's disciples alive when he spoke, who will witness the terrible events at AD 70.[88] Another proposal understands Jesus to be talking about the present evil age and the final apostate generation that comprises it rather than a literal generation of thirty to forty years. Jesus indicates that "this generation" refers to the people of the present evil age who will remain until his second coming, and only the Father knows the timing of that coming.[89]

It is perhaps easiest to see a two-fold reference, as Jesus has done throughout the discourse. The disciples to whom Jesus spoke on the Mount of Olives most naturally will be "this generation" that sees the events of the destruction of the temple, which shows the applicability of the discourse to AD 70. Further, within the context of Jesus's statements about the coming of the Son of Man at the end of the age, there must be primary applicability to those at the end of the age who see the events surrounding the abomination of desolation occurring.[90] When these signs of the end of the age appear, those waiting for his arrival are to recognize that their redemption is drawing near (Luke 21:28). This refers both to repentant Israel and to unrepentant wicked people of this present age. But it also refers to believers who are alive at that time who see these things occurring—they will be the generation of Jesus's disciples who will see their Lord appear.

88. E.g., Davies and Allison, *Matthew*, 365–6; France, *Matthew*, TNTC, 346.

89. Adam Winn, "'This Generation': Reconsidering Mark 13:30 in Light of Eschatological Expectations in Second Temple Judaism," *BBR* 30.4 (2020): 540–60.

90. Cf. Ladd, *Theology*, 196–205.

Therefore, the saying is a word of warning to those of the generation with Jesus and those in the future who had not yet repented that the arrival of the Son of Man will bring judgment. But the saying is also a word of encouragement to his followers that tribulation will not go on forever, as it might appear to those who are suffering in it. Summer is near.

#### 16.3.4.1.2 "My Words Will Never Pass Away"

In the final words of this section, Jesus gives a profound word of assurance to all those looking down the corridors of history and seeing the incredible events he has just described: "Heaven and earth will pass away, but my words will never pass away" (24:35). This is similar to the enduring quality of the Old Testament that Jesus had declared in the Sermon on the Mount (5:18). Like there, Jesus ascribes divine, eternal qualities to his own teaching. Jesus's words are his own, and have authority for that reason (24:34), with his teaching having the same divine character as God and his words.[91] Throughout history will come birth pains and tribulation that may seem as though history is out of control. But Jesus's rock-solid prophecy of his return to establish his kingdom on the earth provides the assurance needed by his disciples to maintain hope and determination. Even though heaven and earth will not exist in the future in the form that we know them now (cf. 2 Pet 3:10; Rev 21:1), the firm foundation of discipleship to Jesus for eternity are his words of truth.

The beginning lesson on how all should await Jesus's arrival (Matt 24:32–35) will now be expanded throughout the rest of the discourse as an encouragement to Jesus's disciples to wait alertly and in expectation of reward but as a warning to the unprepared and unrepentant that Jesus's return will bring judgment.

### *16.3.4.2 The "Sign" of the Parousia (24:36–42)*

In both his direct statement and in all of the parables to follow, Jesus's primary point is the imminence of his return.[92] Although people enduring the horror of the great tribulation will surely know that they are in some of the worst incidents to have transpired on the face of the earth, disciples until that time must live with the conviction that he can return unexpectedly at any moment.

#### 16.3.4.2.1 The Day and Hour of Coming Are Unknown (24:36)

Jesus begins with a startling but central truth of the timing of his coming and the end of the age—No one knows! The expression "day or hour" is used throughout

91. Daniel Doriani, "The Deity of Christ in the Synoptic Gospels," *JETS* 37.3 (1994): 333–50, esp. 343.

92. Contra Mark Keown, "An Imminent Parousia and Christian Mission: Did the New Testament Writers Really Expect Jesus's Imminent Return?" in *Christian Origins and the Establishment of the Early Jesus Movement*, ed. Stanley E. Porter and Andrew W. Pitts, TENTS 12 (Leiden: Brill, 2018), 242–63. He answers "no" to his own question.

Scripture to indicate a general reference to time (cf. Matt 7:22; 10:19; 24:42, etc.). This includes not only a literal day and/or time of day but also the year and/or month. This is to be seen as an answer even to the putting forth of buds and new leaves in the preceding parable (24:32–35). There may be a general indication of coming, but it is so general that no one will be able to pinpoint the time. Until the budding actually occurs, no one prior to them will be able to guess the time. A person might think that the budding has begun, but even this can be mistaken.

The knowledge of his return was not given to angelic heavenly beings, whose knowledge, though superhuman, is not unlimited. Their knowledge accords with what is God's will for them to know.[93]

And neither was it given to the Son to know the time of his return. This is an important christological statement—it is an example of Jesus's voluntarily limiting his divine attributes. He willingly remains uninformed as to his return. The theological doctrine of the kenosis generally contends that in Jesus's incarnation he voluntarily limited the use of his divine attributes so that he could experience full human life. While he did not in any sense give up his deity or any of his divine attributes, Jesus voluntarily limited the use of those divine attributes so that he could experience full human life. It was only at the will of his Father that he would use his divine attributes, if it was the Father's will for him to do so. He acted primarily in his humanity and was empowered by the Spirit (see Ch. 7 on Matthew's Christology).

For example, he was not omnipresent in his human manifestation, and on other occasions there was a restriction on his omnipotence (cf. 13:58; Mark 6:5). Here he indicates that he did not know the future with regard to his return at the end of history. He did not give up his omnipresence or omnipotence, nor does this saying imply that he had given up the divine attribute of omniscience (knowing all things). Rather, as is the case with his other attributes, the independent use of his supernatural knowledge was limited to whether it was the Father's will for him to use it. In his earthly ministry Jesus came to do the will of his Father in heaven. It was not the Father's will for him to know the date of his return during his time on earth. In his human consciousness Jesus restricted himself to normal human knowledge, while he always retained the attribute of omniscience in his divine nature.[94] On other occasions he demonstrates supernatural knowledge of the present and the future, when it was the Father's will for him to know such.[95]

This saying of Jesus apparently governs the rest of the discourse and should be the

93. For an overview, see Erickson, *Christian Theology*, 410–11.

94. An overview of the theological issues can be found in any standard systematic theology, such as Erickson, *Christian Theology*, 645–49, or Grudem, *Systematic Theology*, esp. 683–90. Grudem says of Jesus's statement here, "The ignorance of the time of his return was true of Jesus' human nature and human consciousness only, for in his divine nature he was certainly omniscient and certainly knew the time when he would return to the earth" (Grudem, *Systematic Theology*, 698–99).

95. E.g., John 2:4; 4:17–18; 6:70; 11:4, 11; 13:10–11, 38.

key to interpreting the next major sections. In the light of the unknown day or hour of his return, he exhorts his disciples to watch and be prepared.

### 16.3.4.2.2 Analogy of the Days of Noah (24:37–39)

Jesus emphasizes the unexpectedness of his return by making a comparison to the time of Noah (Matt 24:37–38). The people in the days of Noah did not heed the warnings of judgment that were given to them. They continued to carry along as normal in the everyday activities of eating and drinking, marrying and giving their children in marriage. Although this was a profligate generation (Gen 6:11–12), the point that Jesus makes is not that these activities were sinful but that the people were so wrapped up in everyday activities of life that they were caught off guard because they had no concern for righteousness and spiritual realities. By contrast, Noah and his family went about with preparations for the future deluge, even though they saw no specific signs of its coming and did not know the time of its arrival until it came upon them. Jesus's return will catch off guard all those who do not heed whatever warnings are given and whatever signs might presage the end and those who are spiritually unprepared (cf. 1 Thess 5:1–6).

### 16.3.4.2.3 Some Will Be Taken, Some Left (24:40–41)

Two other scenes from typical daily life illustrate the unexpectedness of the coming of the Son of Man (Matt 24:40–41). While men are working in the field, and women are grinding grain with a hand-mill, one is prepared, and one is not. The mention of two in either case reiterates that preparedness is an either-or proposition—a person is either prepared or not prepared.

The "taking" and "leaving" are intriguing. The expressions may indicate that one is taken away to judgment (like those swept away by the flood) and the other is left to enjoy the blessing of the salvation at the arrival of the Son of Man (like Noah and his family were saved by God's warning),[96] although the verb for "taken" in 24:40, 41 (*paralambanetai*) is different than the verb for "took them all away" in 24:39 (*ēren*). Or vice versa, one is taken away to safety to enjoy the blessing of the arrival of the Son of Man (like Noah and his family in the ark) and the other is left to experience the wrath of the Son of Man (like those who died with the arrival of the flood).[97]

The latter view has in its favor that it corresponds in some sense with the angels who gather the elect at the coming of the Son of Man (24:31) and seems to be more consistent with the following parables. Also, the verb *paralambanetai* means "take to

96. E.g., Gundry, *Matthew*, 494; Blomberg, *Matthew*, 366; Benjamin L. Merkle, "Who Will Be Left Behind? Rethinking the Meaning of Matthew 24:40–41 and Luke 17:34–35," *WTJ* 72.1 (2010): 169–79.

97. E.g., Morris, *Matthew*, 614–15; Hagner, *Matthew 14–28*, 720; Davies and Allison, *Matthew*, 3:383.

safety" in 2:13, 14, 20, 21, while the verb "left" in Matthew often has a meaning of "abandon" or "forsake" (e.g., 4:20, 22; 8:22; 19:29; 23:38; 26:56).[98] The point is that the Son of Man gathers his people to him at his return to enjoy the full manifestation of the kingdom of God, while those left experience his judgment.

Jesus gives first a summarizing conclusion to the preceding paragraph (24:32–41), which also acts as an introduction to the parables to follow. "Therefore keep watch, because you do not know on what day your Lord will come" (24:42). "Watch" implies not only keeping a lookout but also includes the active dimension of being prepared. Jesus stresses the deep division between those who are prepared and those who are not. Their preparedness will mean either blessing at the coming of the Son of Man or judgment, so they must keep watch and be prepared at all times because they do not know when he will return.

#### *16.3.4.3 Disciples' Watchful Preparation for Jesus's Parousia (24:43–25:30)*

Life as we know it is going to come to an end. All of history will come to a climactic end when Jesus returns. But that end may be sooner than we think. So, be prepared. In the light of the fact that the time of his return is unknown (24:36), Jesus emphasizes that there is coming a sure separation of those who are taken and those who are left (24:37–41). It is an either-or proposition. There is no middle ground. Therefore, we should live with the sure expectation that the end is near for each of us, which will affect our daily discipleship to him. At the end of our lives, or when he returns in glory and power, we will either be with him, or we will not.

Jesus gives four parables and a judgment scene that illustrate why and how his disciples can have assurance that they have been faithful and that they will be approved when Jesus returns. But these parables and the judgment scene teach the obverse as well; they point out the judgment that awaits those who have not been faithful. On the primary level they indicate who demonstrates true life of the kingdom to receive life eternal. On the secondary level each indicates how discipleship to Jesus can be advanced.

The first parable, the homeowner and the thief (24:43–44), gives the general principle that faithful discipleship to Jesus while awaiting his return is demonstrated in those who *watch by being prepared*. The three following parables demonstrate how to watch and be prepared. Discipleship to Jesus means that his disciples will be

- *prepared* (the homeowner and the thief; 24:43–44)
- *responsible* (the two kinds of servants; 24:45–51)

98. Davies and Allison, *Matthew*, 3:383.

- *equipped* (ten virgins; 25:1–13)
- *productive* (the talents; 25:14–30)

The concluding scene of the judgment of the sheep and the goats (25:31–46) brings the eschatological forecast to a climactic conclusion by announcing that watching and being prepared throughout one's life, and throughout history, requires that we will be

- *accountable* to Jesus for our discipleship (the sheep and the goats; 25:31–46).

Blomberg notes that these parables create an interesting series of expectations, especially the first three. In the first, Christ's return is completely unexpected. In the second, sooner than expected. And in the third, later than expected. Jesus covers all expectations—Christians must remain prepared for him to come at any time. The fourth parable then explores more fully what that preparation involves—good stewardship of all God has committed to us. Jesus's eschatological discourse culminates with a "quasiparabolic picture of final judgment," elaborating the theme of Jesus's return, which each of the preceding parables has depicted more briefly.[99]

#### 16.3.4.3.1 The Parable of the Homeowner and the Thief: *Watch by Being Prepared* (24:43–44)

The parable of the homeowner and thief sets the stage for how Jesus's disciples should live their lives in the expectation that Jesus will return: we are to *watch* diligently. But watching does not mean just sitting around waiting to see what will happen next. It means that we will be *prepared* for his arrival at any time or day. For example, my wife's cat Maui watches our home diligently while we are gone. She notices everything that goes on. But she is not prepared to do anything about it. She runs and hides in the closet if she hears a sound! And some dogs certainly are not much better. But the best kind of watchdog is one that watches and is prepared to do something about an intruder.

So it is with us. We must watch, but our watching for the Lord's return must be accompanied with the appropriate kinds of preparedness. On the primary level this means that we will nurture a lively expectation of Jesus's return.[100] To do so means that our entire worldview is kingdom-oriented, as Jesus has been emphasizing throughout his ministry. Our hope lies in God's fully established kingdom on earth, not in the kingdoms that we create. We wait with all of creation for its full liberation (Rom 8:18–25), but our waiting and watching means that we are prepared by responding to

99. Blomberg, *Matthew*, 364.

100. Daniel J. Lewis, *3 Crucial Questions About the Last Days* (Grand Rapids: Baker, 1998), 135.

the invitation to the kingdom of God on earth now and experiencing the beginning of regeneration as our own souls are washed and renewed by the Holy Spirit (Titus 3:4–7). As we nurture daily the blessed hope of Jesus's return, the grace of God teaches us to say "no" to ungodliness and worldly passions "and to live self-controlled, upright and godly lives in this present age" (Titus 2:12; cf. 11, 13). When this is our daily, even hourly, focus, we watch and wait for Jesus's return fully prepared to meet him with peace and confidence.

Like many parables, one particular aspect of the parable is used as a comparison. Here, the point is the unexpectedness of a thief's attempt to break in. Other aspects of the parable are not used as comparisons; for example, Jesus is not a thief in terms of his intent to steal; he is only like the thief in the unexpectedness of his coming.[101] Alert watchfulness is important, but perhaps it is more important to stress "preparedness." Appropriate watching must be accompanied with preparedness as disciples ready themselves for the Lord's sudden appearance by making sure of their salvation, by keeping short accounts of their behavior, by continually seeking first the kingdom of God over other priorities, etc. We must watch, but our watching for the Lord's return must be accompanied with the appropriate kinds of preparedness, as stressed in the following parables that show us three ways of being prepared.

### 16.3.4.3.2 The Parable of Two Kinds of Servants: *Watch by Being Responsible* (24:45–51)

The parable of the two kinds of servants continues that theme by teaching that a person truly demonstrates that he or she is prepared with kingdom life by *responsible* behavior. Jesus indicates that a person's faithful responsibility is the external evidence of whether or not a person is truly one of Jesus's own. We are to examine ourselves as to whether or not we are true believers, which will be evidenced by the way we think, by the way we treat others, and by our righteous or unrighteous behavior. The wicked servant revealed a wicked heart when he contemplated the long delay of his master's return. He was primarily externally motivated by the master's presence; when that was removed, his wicked heart produced wicked actions.

A faithful and good heart is demonstrated regardless of circumstances. Whether we are with other believers or not, whether we think that we will be caught or not, a pure heart is intent upon producing responsible behavior (cf. 5:20; 15:18–19).

Jesus's discipleship community, the church, has been established as the primary steward by which the reality of the gospel of the kingdom is made known to a watching world. It is our responsibility to make known the gospel by all that we are and all that

101. In the proverbial saying earlier Jesus drew a comparison with a vulture to his appearance as the Son of Man (24:8). The comparison is apparently his visibility to bring judgment, not the carnivorous habits!

we say. And when we live with the blessed hope of Jesus's soon return, we are motivated to live up to our responsibilities. This means that we are ethically responsible for daily purity in the light of the expectation of Jesus's imminent coming.[102] Someone has said well, "Live each day so that you will neither be afraid of tomorrow nor ashamed of yesterday."

It also means that we take seriously our responsibility as stewards of God's world and all of his resources. Our role as spouse or parent means that we care for them as God would. Our chosen career path means that we live our lives responsibly as serving God through our work, whether it is sacred or secular (cf. Eph 6:7–8). The leadership positions that we undertake, whether we lead in business, school, or church—we serve our people by serving Jesus as our Master, and we are ultimately responsible to him for the way that we treat those for whom we have responsibility (Eph 6:9). And the more responsibly that we carry out the Master's affairs, the more responsibility we are given. Those who put off their responsibilities thinking that the Master will be delayed may discover that it is too late to make amends.[103]

The parable is not talking about rewards or punishment for believers, and it is not advocating cutting off believers who have fallen away. The parable is a contrast between true and false believers and addresses the consequences of those who show by their lives that they are deserving of hell. We must be careful not to imply that one can earn his or her salvation by watchfulness or preparedness, but rather that a person who truly is a disciple of Jesus will watch and will be prepared, because it is his or her kingdom nature to do so. The warning for professing or non-disciples is that they should not delay repenting, thinking that they will have time. Rather, their own death or the return of Jesus will find them to be unrepentant sinners who hypocritically put on a show of kingdom life but who are spiritually corrupt.

The servant performing in a faithful and wise manner alludes generally to all believers, so the reference to giving food is to be taken metaphorically to refer to caring generally for the needs of others. The good slave is the true, faithful disciple of Jesus who is responsible and wise in the outworking of his or her Christian life.

What prompts the wicked servant's wickedness is when he begins to notice that his lord is going to be away a long time. The way that one thinks about the Lord's return will eventually influence what one says and the way one acts. Perhaps the servant thought the master would never return, or perhaps that he could get away with his wickedness before he was caught. This may have been a subtle hint by Jesus that his return would be delayed,[104] which will act as a test to the heart of each person.

102. Lewis, *3 Crucial Questions*, 135–36.
103. Blomberg, *Parables*, 193.
104. Carson, "Matthew," 573.

### 16.3.4.3.3 The Parable of the Ten Virgins: *Watch by Being Equipped* (25:1–13)

The parable of the ten virgins continues the theme of watchful preparation, now indicating that disciples truly demonstrate that they are prepared with kingdom life for the Lord's coming by *being equipped* to meet him at any moment. At the end of life or at the return of Jesus it will be too late to try to get equipped. Jesus's disciples must be spiritually equipped to meet Jesus, or we will not be ready.

We are ready when our relationships, with God and others, are straightened out. We are ready when at any moment of our day, whether it is in the privacy of our home or in the apartment of our romantic interest or in the recesses of our mind, we are not ashamed to have the Lord meet us. We are also ready when we have prepared for our children to be adequately cared for, when we will not be ashamed of our credit card accounts being made public. We are ready when past grievances have been acquitted.

The Jewish custom of the bridegroom coming at an unexpected time for his bride added to the anticipation. The lack of preparation by the ten virgins is a dramatic representation of the unthinkable. In today's terms, a bride or groom who does not plan to be on time for his or her own wedding would not simply be seen as unfortunate, but emotionally deficient to appreciate the gravity and importance of the day. As disciples who love and are committed to Jesus, it would similarly be unthinkable that we do not prepare for his coming. The parable points out the personal nature of our relationship to the Lord. Our commitment and desire to see Jesus face to face when he comes for us should encourage us to prepare appropriately.

One of the most important ways of preparing ourselves to be ready is to ponder deeply the significance of being in the presence of Jesus in such a way that we act upon its surety. The apostle Paul lived his life in the light of the return of Christ. Donald Hagner states, "Uncertainty concerning the time is in a sense a non-issue; the *fact* of the future return of the Son of Man is what counts."[105] Much of Paul's writings ground ethical behavior not only in our current redeemed state but in its connection to our future life with Christ (cf. Col 3:4). This is the attitude we should have now, and we should encourage the church to have also. A suitable attitude of readiness in the church and in our own lives allows our anticipation of eternal things to make more insignificant some of our petty concerns and more manageable some of our bigger concerns.

Jesus addresses his disciples directly to drive home the lesson of the parable, "Therefore keep watch, because you do not know the day or the hour" (25:13). As in the preceding parable, this is another distinction between two types of people—those who are truly disciples of Jesus and those who are not. Disciples of Jesus will be ready for the arrival of the Son of Man. The destiny of those who are not ready is outside the shut door. The previous parable (24:50–51) and the following parable (25:29–30) both

105. Hagner, *Matthew 14–28*, 716.

speak of hell as the destiny for those who do not "watch" correctly by being properly prepared with salvation to be ready to accompany the Son of Man when he arrives. Therefore, the shut door (25:10) points to hell here as well, especially with the ominous comment from the bridegroom: "Truly I tell you, I don't know you" (25:12).

#### 16.3.4.3.4 The Parable of the Talents: *Watch by Being Productive* (25:14–30)

The parable of the talents also illustrates how watchful preparation in kingdom living demonstrates that disciples are ready for the Lord's coming by their intentional *productivity*. In common usage today "talents" (25:14–18, NIV84; "bags," NIV; Gk. *talanta*[106]) often refers to the natural endowments of a person. That is an appropriate usage, but to draw closer to the intent of the parable, the talents symbolize the giftedness that is bestowed on each person who is graced with kingdom life and how we use those talents in service of the kingdom (1 Cor 12:7).

A combined perspective is important. All that we are—whether naturally endowed or Spirit-bestowed—must be employed in service of the kingdom of God. Not everyone is born with the same talents, and not everyone is endowed with the same gifts of the Spirit, yet each of us can be productive in our own unique ways. All of our service in the kingdom of heaven is inherently valuable, whether it is in sacred or secular realms, whether it receives greater or lesser return. Our responsibility is to plan for the long haul and use our giftedness to advance the kingdom of heaven.[107]

The explicit problem with the wicked servant is his attitude about his master. This is the way that many people deal with God. Their wrong attitude about God (God is mean, God is unconcerned with our fate, etc.) results in an excuse for not being obedient to him. This starts with salvation as a first application, but it can be applied by Christians who develop wrong attitudes about God. They see God as not loving, because of their circumstances, and they then get off the path of obedience to God.

But faithfulness is contingent upon an accurate view of God. Inaccurate views of God allow us to rationalize our own irresponsibility and unfaithfulness. Therefore, it is vitally important to have a correct biblical view of God's character, his activities, and his goals for us. This is the important role of solid Bible teaching and preaching, because our view of God determines our behavior. The parable reveals the depth of the wickedness of the servant that impels him to pervert the image of his master, which then provides him with an excuse for his personal irresponsibility.

We can see this in people who tragically put off coming to Christ for salvation because they have stereotyped him and will not come to faith until they can figure out how a supposedly good God can continue to allow suffering. There are sufficient

---

106. See "τάλαντον," BDAG 988; in NT times, a *talanton* was a unit of coinage, whether of gold, silver, or copper.

107. For an attempt to demonstrate how detailed study of prophecy has historically led to productive outcomes, see Larry D. Pettegrew, "The Rapture Debate at the Niagara Bible Conference," *BSac* 157 (2000): 331–47.

biblical answers to support faith in God as good and loving, but ultimately the person's individual culpability for sin is at stake. We can also see this in people who blatantly blame God for their own laziness and irresponsibility. But we can also see this in people so caught up in their personal grief and tragedy that they cannot see the light of God's love and care.

The parable teaches us that a truthful understanding of God will bring about the productive investment of our lives. That causes me to examine my own ministry to these kinds of people. I realize that I must ultimately turn these people over to their own accountability to God, but I also realize that I must have as much patience with them as I can until they are called to give that accounting. I must enter deeply into their world to try to bring a truthful understanding of God, so that they can rightly understand God's nature, which will cause them to invest their lives productively in service of the kingdom.

In a surprising twist to the story, the master declares that the talent is to be taken from the wicked servant and given to the one who has ten, the one who had proven his industriousness. The lesson is summed up in the saying, "For whoever has will be given more, and they will have an abundance. Whoever does not have, even what they have will be taken from them" (25:29). This maxim parallels the saying in 13:12, illustrating a similar point about spiritual responsiveness; here it emphasizes that wise and conscientious use of one's God-given abilities is a responsibility that accompanies a right relationship with God.

But the punishment is not simply taking away the talent from the wicked slave, now called worthless or unprofitable (*achreios*). The master instructs that he should be thrown "outside, into the darkness, where there will be weeping and gnashing of teeth" (25:30). As has been the point throughout the other parables, the contrast is between those whose eternal destiny is salvation in the presence of the long-expected Son of Man and those whose eternal destiny is eternal damnation. The first two servants are true disciples; the third is not, as his destiny indicates. Similar to the other parables, a person's faithfulness is the external evidence of whether or not he or she is truly one of Jesus's own. As the disciples await the return of the Son of Man, they are to teach in the community that industriousness and productivity of discipleship is a testimony of one's love and trust of Jesus as Lord. But their industriousness and productivity should not come from a self-advancing motivation; it should be demonstrated in serving others as Jesus has served them (20:20–28).

We now conclude our study of Matthew's theology in the next chapter by gaining his perspective on eternity and his unique eschatological messages.

*Chapter 17*

# Eternity and Eschatological Messages in Matthew's Gospel

## Bibliography

**Carey, Greg.** *Death, the End of History, and Beyond: Eschatology in the Bible.* Interpretation. Louisville: Westminster John Knox, 2023. **Clark, John C., and Marcus Peter Johnson.** *A Call to Christian Formation: How Theology Makes Sense of Our World.* Grand Rapids: Baker Academic, 2021. **Edwards, David L., and John R. W. Stott.** *Evangelical Essentials: A Liberal-Evangelical Dialogue.* Downers Grove, IL: InterVarsity, 1988. **Eire, Carlos M. N.** *A Very Brief History of Eternity.* Princeton, NJ: Princeton University Press, 2009. **Esler, Philip F.** "Ethnic Identities in the Dead Sea Legal Papyri and Matthew: Reinterpreting Matthew 25:31–46." Pages 195–210 in *Matthew Within Judaism: Israel and the Nations in the First Gospel.* Edited by Anders Runesson and Daniel M. Gurtner. ECL 27. Atlanta: Society of Biblical Literature Press, 2020. **Eubank, Nathan.** "Prison, Penance, or Purgatory: The Interpretation of Matthew 5.25–26 and Parallels." *NTS* 64.2 (2018): 162–77. **Fairhurst, Alan M.** "Matthew's Hell: From Percy Dearmer to David Sim." *ExpTim* 110.5 (1999): 138–40. **Gladd, Benjamin L., and Matthew S. Harmon.** *Making All Things New: Inaugurated Eschatology for the Life of the Church.* Grand Rapids: Baker Academic, 2016. **Gomes, Alan W.** *40 Questions About Heaven and Hell.* 40 Questions Series. Grand Rapids: Kregel, 2018. **Green, Joel B.** "Heaven and Hell." *DJG*[2] 370–76. **Hamilton, James M., Jr.** *God's Glory in Salvation Through Judgment: A Biblical Theology.* Wheaton, IL: Crossway, 2010. **Marguerat, Daniel.** *Le Jugement dans l'évangile de Matthieu.* 2nd ed. Le Monde de la Bible 6. Geneva: Labor et Fides, 1981. **Middleton, J. Richard.** *A New Heaven and a New Earth: Reclaiming Biblical Eschatology.* Grand Rapids: Baker Academic, 2014. **Olmstead, Wesley T.** "Judgment." Pages 458–63 in *DJG*[2]. **Osborne, Grant R.** "Life, Eternal Life." *DJG*[2] 518–22. **Porter, Stanley E.** "Eternity, Eternal." *DLNT* 345–47. **Ryken, Philip Graham.** "A New Heaven and A New Earth: Revelation 21:1–22:5." Pages 119–138 in *Coming Home: Essays on the New Heaven and New Earth.* Edited by D. A. Carson and Jeff Robinson Sr. Wheaton, IL: Crossway, 2017. **Smith, Ian K.** *Not Home Yet: How the Renewal of the Earth Fits into God's Plan for the World.* Wheaton, IL: Crossway, 2019. **Sprinkle, Preston,** ed. *Four Views* *on Hell.* 2nd edition. Counterpoints: Bible and Theology. Grand Rapids: Zondervan, 2016. **Tanner, Paul J.** "The 'Outer Darkness' in Matthew's Gospel: Shedding Light on an Ominous Warning." *BSac* 174 (2017): 445–59. **Travis, Stephen H.** *Christ and the Judgement of God: The Limits of Divine Retribution in New Testament Thought.* 2nd ed. Peabody, MA: Hendrickson, 2009. ———. "Judgment." *DJG*[1] 408–11. **Turner, David L.** "His Glorious Throne: Israel and the Gentiles in Mission and Judgment in the Gospel of Matthew." Pages 135–68 in *Matthew Within Judaism: Israel and the Nations in the First Gospel.* Edited by Anders Runesson and Daniel M. Gurtner. ECL 27. Atlanta: Society of Biblical Literature, 2020. **Wax, Trevin.** *Eschatological Discipleship: Leading Christians to Understand Their Historical and Cultural Context.* Nashville: B&H Academic, 2018. **Wilson, Alistair I.** *When Will These Things Happen? A Study of Jesus as Judge in Matthew 21–25.* PBM. Carlisle, UK: Paternoster, 2004. **Wittmer, Michael E.**, ed. *Four Views on Heaven.* Counterpoints: Bible and Theology. Grand Rapids: Zondervan, 2022.

## 17.1 A THEOLOGY OF ETERNITY IN MATTHEW'S GOSPEL

Jesus concludes the Olivet Discourse with both ominous and hopeful prophecies: "Then [those on his left] will go away to eternal punishment, but the righteous to eternal life" (25:46). The next phase of our eternity begins the moment we die. We all die, and we all will experience eternity. What does that look like?

Each of us has to some degree pondered what that might look like and what our involvement as deceased humans might be in eternity. Carlos Eire, professor of history and religious studies at Yale University, from a secular perspective, attempts to demonstrate how Western culture has reached the point where the concept of eternity has essentially been disproved and discarded and how that perspective on reality informs the way those who adopt this perspective live their lives.[1]

I understand how that can affect our view of life. But I also now understand how denying eternity can be an attempt to escape from reality. As a young nineteen-year-old in combat with an army airborne-infantry unit in Viet Nam in 1968–1969, I was confronted with the possibility of a soon-arriving eternity. I was not a believer, so I was faced with the unknown. I personally did not believe in hell or heaven or eternity. But a common topic among my fellow squad members was what might happen if we were killed. Was there really a heaven and hell? I remember the horror that I felt after an intense battle when I held a dying member of my squad as he went off to eternity. Where was he now, or was he anywhere? What was he experiencing, or was he experiencing anything? Was there a heaven, or a hell?

1. Carlos M. N. Eire, *A Very Brief History of Eternity* (Princeton, NJ: Princeton University Press, 2009).

I considered the possibility of my personally spending eternity in hell. "How do I escape what might be an eternity in hell and find an eternity in heaven?" I pondered this kind of question almost daily as we engaged in deadly conflict. It spurred me to look for answers, which I did not find until over two years later in the good news of Jesus and entrance to the kingdom of heaven. And what profound peace I then experienced when facing eternity! But that peering into the unknown of eternity before I met Jesus has never really left me, and it motivates me to this day to live each moment in the light of a now-known eternity with Jesus.

### 17.1.1 The Concept of Eternity

The concept of eternity figures prominently in the Old Testament and New Testament, using especially the Hebrew noun *ʿôlām* and the Greek noun *aiōn* and adjective *aiōnios* (LXX). The Old Testament does not have a single word comparable to the English word "eternity." The concept is most closely rendered as "forever and ever," "from generation to generation," and "from age to age." Moses and the Israelites sang: "The LORD reigns for ever and ever" (Exod 15:18; Heb. *ʿôlām*; LXX *aiōn*). Qoheleth writes: "He has made everything suitable for its time; moreover, he has put a sense of past and future [Heb. *ʿôlām*; LXX *aiōn*] into their minds, yet they cannot find out what God has done from the beginning to the end" (Eccl 3:11 NRSVue). God said to Noah, "Whenever the rainbow appears in the clouds, I will see it and remember the everlasting [*aiōnios* LXX] covenant between God and all living creatures of every kind on the earth" (Gen 9:16). The apostle John writes, "The world and its desires pass away, but whoever does the will of God lives forever [Gr. *aiōn*]" (1 John 2:17).

The Old Testament concept of the age that is to be has now begun in the life and ministry of Jesus Messiah. The person who believes Jesus's gospel message and enters the kingdom of heaven now enjoys the blessings of the unlimited future age imported into the present through Jesus Messiah's redemptive work. Eternity is understood to be the unlimited and incalculable space of time bounded at its beginning by the introduction of the kingdom of God in Christ and stretching out into the unlimited future.[2]

In Matthew's Gospel, the Greek noun *aiōn*, from which is derived the word "age" or "aeon," appears eight times and can refer generally to this life or age,[3] or it can designate forever and ever.[4] The adjective *aiōnios* occurs six times, three times referring to "eternal" life[5] and three times to refer to "eternal" fire or punishment.[6]

Matthew says little about what actually happens in eternity. Matthew records twelve

2. Elwell, "Eternity," *TBD* 450.
3. Matt 12:32; 13:22; 21:19.
4. Matt 13:39, 40, 49; 24:3; 28:20.
5. Matt 19:16, 29; 25:46.
6. Matt 18:8; 25:41, 46.

times that Jesus speaks of *krisis*,[7] eight of which are warnings Jesus makes about "judgment,"[8] including several of "the day of judgment"[9] or "the judgment."[10]

The eschatological parables in Jesus's Olivet Discourse contain both assuring images of eternal life and of alarming warnings of eternal condemnation.

| **ETERNAL LIFE IN MATTHEW'S GOSPEL** |
|---|
| **Of eternal life, Jesus states:** |
| • "Truly I tell you, he will put him in charge of all his possessions" (24:47).<br>• "The virgins who were ready went in with him to the wedding banquet" (25:10).<br>• "His master replied, 'Well done, good and faithful servant! You have been faithful with a few things; I will put you in charge of many things. Come and share your master's happiness!'" (25:23).<br>• "For whoever has will be given more, and they will have an abundance" (25:29). |

These are pictures of an eternity with joyous wonders.

| **ETERNAL CONDEMNATION IN MATTHEW'S GOSPEL** |
|---|
| **Of eternal condemnation, Jesus states in his eschatological parables:** |
| • "He will cut him to pieces and assign him a place with the hypocrites, where there will be weeping and gnashing of teeth" (24:51).<br>• "And the door was shut. . . . 'Truly I tell you, I don't know you'" (25:10, 12).<br>• "Whoever does not have, even what they have will be taken from them (25:29).<br>• "And throw that worthless servant outside, into the darkness, where there will be weeping and gnashing of teeth'" (25:30). |

These are ominous pictures of an eternity with tragic portents of eternal condemnation.

Jesus concludes the Olivet Discourse with both ominous and hopeful prophecies: "Then they will go away to eternal punishment, but the righteous to eternal life" (25:46).

### 17.1.2 Interpreting Matthew's Perspective of Judgment

Eschatology is a significant theme in Matthew's Gospel, and more than the other evangelists, Matthew is concerned about the final judgment.[11] "Judgment is the process

7. Matt 5:21, 22; 10:15; 11:22, 24; 12:18, 20, 36, 41, 42; 23:23, 33; none in Mark; four times in Luke; nine times in John.

8. Matt 5:21, 22; 10:15; 11:22, 24; 12:36, 41, 42.

9. Matt 10:15; 11:22, 24; 12:36.

10. Matt 12:41, 42.

11. Significant studies on the theme of judgment in Matthew's Gospel are Günther Bornkamm, "End-Expectation and Church in Matthew," in *Tradition and Interpretation in Matthew*, ed. Günther Bornkamm, Gerhard Barth, and Heinz Joachim Held, trans. Percy Scott (Philadelphia: Westminster, 1963), 15–51; Marguerat, *Le Jugement*; Sim, *Apocalyptic Eschatology*; Gibbs, *Jerusalem and Parousia*; Nathan Eubank, "Prison, Penance, or Purgatory: The Interpretation of Matthew 5.25–26 and Parallels," *NTS* 64.2 (2018): 162–77. From the perspective of the historical Jesus and judgment more generally, see Bryan, *Jesus and Israel's Traditions*; Marius Reiser, *Jesus and Judgment: The Eschatological*

whereby God calls people to account for their behavior and allots their destinies accordingly."[12] Judgment is the moment when the righteous are distinguished from the unrighteous, and judgment concerns people both inside and outside the church. Consequently, judgment serves for Matthew as an impetus for hearing and doing God's will (see 7:21–29). This is not because Matthew endorses a "works-righteousness," as though a person might be regarded as righteous as a result of one's performance. We saw in Ch. 10 that Matthew especially eschews salvation and discipleship from works-righteousness. Matthew's representations of salvation and discipleship are more organic. In the same way that a good tree bears good fruit, and a bad tree bears bad fruit, righteous persons display in their everyday lives their transformed nature before God (see 7:15–20; 12:33). Those who have entered the kingdom of heaven show in their lives ("produce fruit"; see 3:8; 21:43) their allegiance to the king. Those who do not produce good fruit are destroyed (3:10; 7:19; 13:40, 42).[13]

Sim refers to Matthew's eschatology, which focuses on the events at the end of the age including the final judgment, as "a dominant theme in the Gospel."[14] He goes on to argue, "It is also true that much of the evangelist's view of the judgement is unpleasant in the extreme, especially with regard to the fate of the wicked."[15] He points to Matthew's portrayal of Jesus the final judge, who will cast the unworthy into the outer darkness,[16] where they will weep and gnash their teeth[17] as they are tortured[18] by the eternal fires of gehenna.[19] He reacts to this by asserting, "Matthew's liking for this subject matter is unparalleled in the remainder of the New Testament, including the Book of Revelation. It is obvious that this unattractive concentration on the fiery fate of the wicked leaves many modern readers perplexed and even offended."[20]

Such Matthean language is indeed difficult to process, and in the current inclusive culture sounds exclusivistic and archaic, and even, to many, cruel. Therefore, various attempts have been made to account for the Matthean theme of judgment in alternative interpretations. Two interpretations attempt to avoid taking this judgment language literally, while one interpretation takes judgment language literally.

#### *17.1.2.1 Paraenetic Exhortation to Matthew's Church*

The first method suggests that Matthew's focus on the judgment and its aftermath serves a paraenetic function. By using apocalyptic imagery and colorful language the evangelist warns his church that they too will face the final judgment. This imagery

---

*Proclamation in Its Jewish Context*, trans. Linda M. Maloney (Minneapolis: Fortress, 1997).

12. Stephen H. Travis, "Judgment," *DJG*[1] 408.

13. Joel B. Green, "Heaven and Hell," *DJG*[2] 373.

14. Sim, "Rise and Fall," 482.

15. Sim, "Rise and Fall," 482.

16. Matt 8:12; 22:13; 25:30.

17. Matt 8:12; 13:42, 50; 22:13; 24:51; 25:30.

18. Matt 8:29; 18:34.

19. Matt 3:7–12; 5:22; 7:19; 13:41–42, 49–50; 18:8–9; 25:41; cf. 5:29–30; 10:28; 23:15, 33.

20. Sim, "Rise and Fall," 482.

and language are not intended to be taken literally, but by using this approach Matthew exhorts his readers not to be complacent about their salvation but to live by the ethical standards and aim for the higher righteousness set down by Jesus himself. The judgment of the world applies to all nations.

Günther Bornkamm concludes, "All are gathered before the tribunal of the judge of the world and are judged by the 'one' standard, namely that of the love they have shown towards, or withheld from the humblest."[21] Daniel Marguerat contends that Matthew displays a pastoral "realism" in which his intention is to fight against spiritual drifts that his church is experiencing. The consistent warning of final judgment is intended to bring believers back to a lived Christian identity ("de fidélité chrétienne vécue").[22]

#### *17.1.2.2 Warning to the Persecuting Enemies*

A second method has been advocated by Sim.[23] He argues that Matthew's community was undergoing a number of significant crises in the aftermath of the Jewish war (AD 66–70). These included an acutely polemical interaction with other Jewish groups as well as persecution by local gentiles. Matthew responded to this situation in a mode that was both available and acceptable at the time: the adoption and propagation of a vindictive eschatology that promised the extreme eternal punishment of those responsible for his community's suffering.

Sim argues that "Matthew interpolated much of this material into his sources with the result that the Matthean Jesus became the mouthpiece for the evangelist's own ideas about the fate of the wicked."[24] He argues that the desperate plight of Matthew's community called for an even more desperate measure—the adoption and propagation of a vindictive eschatology.

#### *17.1.2.3 Eschatological Warnings and Promises of a Literal Eternal Destiny*

In advocating a third method, I maintain that the language of judgment and eternal punishment in Matthew's Gospel goes back to Jesus. Matthew has faithfully recorded and passed on Jesus's language and has adopted it as his own in his theological perspective. Wesley Olmstead argues, "However uncomfortable the notion seems to be to Western readers of the Gospels, there is little doubt that Jesus both assumed and taught the reality of divine judgment. Not only is it the case that each of the evangelists bears

21. Bornkamm, "End-Expectation and Church in Matthew," 23–24. Similarly, O. Lamar Cope, "'To the Close of the Age': The Role of Apocalyptic Thought in the Gospel of Matthew," in *Apocalyptic and the New Testament: Essays in Honor of J. Louis Martyn*, ed. Joel Marcus and Marion L. Soards, JSNTSup 24 (Sheffield: JSOT Press, 1989): 113–24.

22. Marguerat, *Le Jugement*, esp. 477–561.

23. Sim, *Apocalyptic Eschatology*, passim; see especially a condensed argument in Sim, "Rise and Fall," 482–83.

24. Sim, "Rise and Fall," 483. Similarly making a contrast between the "peaceful" historical Jesus and the violent author Matthew is David J. Neville, "Toward a Teleology of Peace: Contesting Matthew's Violent Eschatology," *JSNT* 30.2 (2007): 131–61.

witness to this, but also declarations of impending judgment are found in every layer of the Gospel tradition."[25]

The voice of Jesus in Matthew's Gospel may seem unpleasant, but I affirm the genuineness of his voice. In that way Jesus is certainly in the line of the Old Testament prophets. The psalmist and prophet Asaph says to Israel, "If my people would only listen to me, if Israel would only follow my ways, how quickly I would subdue their enemies and turn my hand against their foes! Those who hate the LORD would cringe before him, and their punishment would last forever" (Ps 81:13–15).

This is divine punishment of the sort that Jesus declared. Alistair Wilson contends that Matthew presents us with a coherent portrayal of Jesus as one who embodies the roles of both prophet and sage in his judging activity. But he is no ordinary prophet or teacher of wisdom—he is the Judge of Israel and all the nations. Wilson concludes, "If there are good reasons for believing that Matthew has carefully transmitted traditions regarding Jesus, then it surely follows that we cannot be content to regard Matthew's narrative as simply a striking literary portrayal of Jesus but must consider its significance as a witness to the 'historical Jesus.'"[26]

Since there is extensive weight in Matthew's Gospel on the last judgment, we should align our understanding of reality and the future with the voice of Jesus and Matthew's eschatological perspective. With this comes a distinctive futuristic sense of what is eternal (*aiōnios*, Matt 25:41), what brings judgment (*krisis*, 23:33), what brings life (*zōē*, 25:46), what brings punishment (*kolasis*, 25:46), and heaven (*ouranos*, 19:21) and hell (*gehenna*, 23:33).

I sympathize with the first two methods of interpretation given above because the thought of God condemning people to an eternal hell is a torturous concept. Matthew has among the most explicit statements of Jesus regarding hell as a place of punishment.

But we will now see that Matthew includes both the joy of eternal life with Jesus and the Father, and the horror of eternal condemnation away from Jesus and the Father. James Hamilton contends that Matthew emphasizes that God's glory in salvation through judgment will be shown at the end of time, when Jesus Messiah returns to judge his enemies and save all who have called on his name.[27] It is our choice to make our eternal destiny.

### 17.1.3 Eternal Life in Matthew's Gospel

The "eternal" aspect of eschatology receives significant emphasis in Matthew's Gospel.

25. Wesley T. Olmstead, "Judgment," *DJG*[2] 462. Cf. Travis, "Judgment," 409–10.

26. A. Wilson, *When Will These Things Happen?*, 255.

27. Hamilton, *God's Glory in Salvation through Judgment*, 355–441. Similarly, see Turner, "His Glorious Throne," 153–61.

### *17.1.3.1 "Eternity," "Age"* (**aiōn**; *Heb.* **⊠ôlām***)*

The Greek word for the noun "age," or "aeon," is *aiōn* and the Greek word for the adjective "eternal" is *aiōnios*. The noun *aiōn* occurs eight times in Matthew's Gospel in some significant contexts. "Age" (*aiōn*) speaks of a long but indefinite period of time, past or future. The ages, past and future, make up the whole of time.[28]

In the striking passage regarding the blasphemy against the Holy Spirit, Jesus states, "Anyone who speaks a word against the Son of Man will be forgiven, but anyone who speaks against the Holy Spirit will not be forgiven, either in this age [*aiōn*] or in the age to come" (Matt 12:32). In the parable of the good and bad fish, Jesus declares, "This is how it will be at the end of the age [*aiōn*]. The angels will come and separate the wicked from the righteous and throw them into the blazing furnace, where there will be weeping and gnashing of teeth" (13:49–50).

In Jesus's explanation of the parable of the weeds in the field we gain further clarity of the nature of this age and the end of this age (13:37–40). The harvest at the end of the age (*aiōn*) is a reference to the judgment that will accompany the coming of the Son of Man to consummate the establishment of the kingdom (24:3). The harvesters are Jesus's angels (13:39), who will accompany Jesus to establish his kingdom and bring judgment (24:31). As he consummates his kingdom on the earth, Jesus will send his angels to remove all sin and sinners from this world, here called for the first time "[my] kingdom" (13:41).

Jesus's divine sovereignty is now established visibly over all creatures of this world. Judgment of the sons of the evil one will commence in the fiery furnace (cf. 3:11; 5:22), where there will be "weeping and gnashing of teeth" (13:42; cf. 8:12). These are Jesus's typical expressions of eternal judgment. At that time the righteous—Jesus's disciples who have experienced the inner transformation that accompanies their entrance to the kingdom (5:20), who are the wheat that has grown up throughout this age—will experience the full manifestation of the kingdom's glory and "will shine like the sun" (13:43).

This use of "age" (*aiōn*) speaks of the contrast between "the present age" (an "evil age"; 12:32; cf. Gal 1:4) and "the age to come" (Matt 12:32) when in God's judgment wrongs will be righted and his people will come into their full inheritance (19:29; cf. Mark 10:30). There is a sense, however, in which it can be said that we are both living now in the end of the ages while the wheat and weeds grow up together (Matt 13:24–30; cf. 1 Cor 10:11) and that we experience "the powers of the age to come" (Matt 28:20; cf. Heb 6:5) and its life.[29]

Matthew concludes his Gospel with the words from Jesus: "And surely I am with you always, to the very end of the age [*aiōn*]" (28:20). To the "very end of the age"

28. "Age, Ages," *BEB* 36.

29. O'Donnell, *Matthew*, 377–80; Elwell, "Age, Ages," *BEB* 36.

(28:20) or until the completion of God's plans for this age, Jesus promises to be the sustaining presence that assures us that history is not out of control, that the kingdom of God has indeed been inaugurated, that he is a very present help in times of trouble, and that the work that he accomplished on the cross to bring salvation to humanity is continually available through his risen and ascended ministry.

### *17.1.3.2 "Eternal," "Everlasting"* (**aiōnios**)

The adjective *aiōnios* describes the nature of something as "enduring," "everlasting" or "eternal." It is related to the noun *aiōn* ("age"). It occurs six times in Matthew (18:8; 19:16, 29; 25:41, 46 [2x]), four times in Mark, four times in Luke, and seventeen times in John. It describes the quality of something as lasting the eon or enduring the age. Many of the instances in which this word occurs are in reference to something eternal, especially eternal (*aiōnios*) life (e.g., Matt 19:16; cf. John 4:14; Acts 13:48; Rom 2:7).[30]

- "If your hand or your foot causes you to stumble, cut it off and throw it away. It is better for you to enter life [*zōē*] maimed or crippled than to have two hands or two feet and be thrown into eternal [*aiōnios*] fire" (18:8).
- "Just then a man came up to Jesus and asked, 'Teacher, what good thing must I do to get eternal [*aiōnios*] life?'" (19:16).
- "And everyone who has left houses or brothers or sisters or father or mother or wife or children or fields for my sake will receive a hundred times as much and will inherit eternal [*aiōnios*] life" (19:29).
- "Then he will say to those on his left, 'Depart from me, you who are cursed, into the eternal [*aiōnios*] fire prepared for the devil and his angels'" (25:41).
- "Then they will go away to eternal [*aiōnios*] punishment, but the righteous to eternal [*aiōnios*] life" (25:46).

"Eternality as bounded is a temporal concept that can be readily used of a new or transferred state of the believer, such that, for example, that person enters into eternal life. Eternity as unbounded is a timeless concept that is suitably used of God and his existence."[31]

### *17.1.3.3 "Life"* (**zōē**)

With this extensive thrust upon the eternal, a strong futuristic sense of "life" is distinctive. At the conclusion to the Sermon on the Mount, we find the Jewish metaphor of the two paths, the "narrow" one that leads to "life" and the "broad" one that

30. J. A. McGuire-Moushon and Rachel Klippenstein, "Eternity," *LTW*.

31. Stanley E. Porter, "Eternity, Eternal," *DLNT* 347.

leads to destruction (7:13–14). Later, Matthew reiterates the danger of causing others to stumble (18:8–9) and the sadness of the wealthy man turning away (19:16–17) but adds to his understanding of "life" (*zōē*) two new emphases. First, to the final promise that the disciples will "sit on twelve thrones, judging the twelve tribes of Israel" (19:28), Jesus adds the promise to "inherit eternal life" (19:29). Jesus centers fully on the final or eternal aspects of God's reward for surrendering all for him. Second, he concludes the Olivet discourse with an allusion to Dan 12:2, "establishing the absolute nature of divine justice in the sense that the wicked 'will go away to eternal punishment, but the righteous to eternal life' (Mt 25:46). The emphasis is on the future and eternal nature of the two opposite destinies."[32]

### *17.1.3.4 "Soul," "Life" (***psychē***)*

Another term Matthew uses to designate life is *psychē* ("soul," "life"). Some passages speak of one's present blessings. The section on anxiety in the Sermon on the Mount begins, "Do not worry about your life [*psychē*]" (6:25), which is a clear reference to earthly existence (cf. 11:29; 12:18 [*psychē* = "I" in NIV]). Other passages use "life" to speak of one's eternal destiny. Jesus commands his followers, "Do not be afraid of those who kill the body but cannot kill the soul [*psychē*]. Rather, be afraid of the One who can destroy both soul [*psychē*] and body in hell" (10:28). Jesus sums up the discipleship sayings of the mission discourse by establishing the eternal parameters of discipleship: "Whoever finds their life [*psychē* = seeking the world's rewards] will lose it, and whoever loses their life [*psychē*] for my sake will find it [for eternity]" (10:39). "To live for present pleasure means to lose the future. The emphasis is on the eternal consequences of rejecting God, eternal punishment versus everlasting life."[33]

### *17.1.3.5 "Kingdom" (***basileia***)*

The same emphases occur in Matthew's characteristic "kingdom" theology. In Matthew's Gospel entering the kingdom of God/heaven is equivalent to the divine gift of eternal life. The metaphor is stated negatively: "Not everyone who says to me, 'Lord, Lord,' will enter the kingdom of heaven, but only the one who does the will of my Father who is in heaven" (7:21; cf. 5:20; 18:3; 23:13). And the metaphor is stated positively: "Truly I tell you, the tax collectors and the prostitutes are entering the kingdom of God ahead of you" (21:31; cf. 19:23–24). Both positive and negative statements combine facets of life in Jesus Messiah now and life eternal. With the arrival of Jesus Messiah, the kingdom has come near (3:2; 4:17) and in fact has arrived (12:28).[34] Life in the kingdom, both now and eternal, has begun.

32. Grant R. Osborne, "Life, Eternal Life," *DJG*² 519.
33. Osborne, "Life, Eternal Life," *DJG*² 519.
34. Osborne, "Life, Eternal Life," *DJG*² 519.

### *17.1.3.6 "Heaven"* **(ouranos)**

Matthew mentions "heaven" (*ouranos*) some eighty-two times in seventy-two verses, especially in the phrase "kingdom of heaven," as we might expect.[35] *Ouranos* occurs eighteen times in Mark, thirty-four times in Luke and sixteen times in John. In Matthew's Gospel, "heaven" (*ouranos*) is God's throne (5:34; 23:22) where the Father resides, the realm of known reality opposite earth (5:18). "Heaven" (*ouranos*) is used in Matthew to refer to:

1. the atmosphere directly above the earth (*sky, air, firmament*) (6:26)
2. the starry heaven (*firmament, sky*) (24:29a)
3. heaven as the dwelling place of God (5:16); the Spirit as a dove descends from heaven and twice the voice of the Father from heaven confirms Jesus's relationship to heaven (3:16, 17; 17:5);[36] the risen Son of Man sitting at the right hand of the Mighty One (26:64); and the dwelling place of the angels (22:30)
4. heaven, therefore, often seen as a synonym for God himself (cf. 23:22)
5. heaven as the place where treasures are stored for the righteous dead (6:20; 19:21)

In Matthew the "kingdom of heaven" is in part a present reality (5:19; 18:3–4), and in part a future expectation (8:11) (see Ch. 9).

There is currently a debate among theologians as to the nature of heaven.[37] A recent book entitled *Four Views on Heaven* engages this debate. Each author believes in heaven, but they disagree on what exactly is the nature of heaven.[38]

- **Traditional Heaven**—our destiny is to leave earth and live forever in heaven where we will rest, worship, and serve God.
- **Restored Earth**—the saved will live forever with Jesus on this restored planet, enjoying ordinary human activities in our redeemed state.[39]
- **Heavenly Earth**—a balanced view that seeks to highlight both the strengths and weaknesses of the heavenly and earthly views.

35. For similar tabulations, see Pennington, *Heaven and Earth*, 67–76.

36. Friberg, *Analytical Greek Lexicon*; Elwell, "Heaven," *BEB* 940.

37. For a wide-ranging study of heaven and hell, see Gomes, *40 Questions About Heaven and Hell*.

38. Michael E. Wittmer, ed., *Four Views on Heaven*, Counterpoints: Bible and Theology (Grand Rapids: Zondervan, 2022); contributors: (1) John S. Feinberg (Traditional Heaven), (2) J. Richard Middleton (Restored Earth), (3) Michael Allen (Heavenly Earth), (4) Peter Kreeft (Roman Catholic Beatific Vision).

39. For a full-length treatment of the restored earth view, see J. Richard Middleton, *A New Heaven and a New Earth: Reclaiming Biblical Eschatology* (Grand Rapids: Baker Academic, 2014).

- **Roman Catholic Beatific Vision**—stresses the intellectual component of salvation, though it encompasses the whole of human experience of joy, happiness coming from seeing God finally face-to-face.

There is little talk in Matthew's Gospel of a place in heaven where one enjoys eternal life. As noted above, "heaven" is the place where treasures are stored for the righteous dead (6:20; 19:21), but whether this speaks of the intermediate or eternal state is not declared. However, we have the assurance that entering the kingdom of heaven is a present reality for those who have entered into discipleship to Jesus. And that means "to the very end of the age" (28:20).

### 17.1.4 Eternal Judgment in Matthew's Gospel

It is true that Matthew has some of the strongest references to the judgment and punishment of unbelievers in the Gospels and in the New Testament generally.[40]

#### *17.1.4.1 "Judgment," "Punishment" (*krisis*)*

We have noted that Matthew records eight warnings Jesus makes about "judgment" (*krisis*),[41] including several of "the day of judgment"[42] or "the judgment."[43]

An example is found in Jesus's Sermon on the Mount, where judgment leads to the punishment of the "fire of hell" (5:21–22). The parable of the unforgiving and unmerciful servant (18:23–35), which is unique to Matthew's Gospel, concludes with some of the harshest language regarding judgment (18:34–35). Since it would be impossible for the unmerciful servant to repay the vast amounts owed, the scene concludes with the grim certainty that he will experience that punishment forever, a harsh metaphorical allusion to an eternal destiny of torture (cf. 8:12; 10:28; 13:42, 49–50; 24:51).

A unique term for "punishment" (*kolasis*) is found in the New Testament only in Matt 25:46 and 1 John 4:18. They read, "He will reply, 'Truly I tell you, whatever you did not do for one of the least of these, you did not do for me.' Then they will go away to eternal punishment [*kolasis*], but the righteous to eternal life" (Matt 25:45–46). "There is no fear in love. But perfect love drives out fear, because fear has to do with punishment [*kolasis*]. The one who fears is not made perfect in love" (1 John 4:18). We will discuss the Matthew passage below.

#### *17.1.4.2 "Outer Darkness," "Weeping and Gnashing of Teeth"*

Three times Matthew refers to outer darkness (8:12; 22:13; 25:30), and five times he adds the expression "weeping and gnashing of teeth" in judgment contexts (13:42,

40. Matt 3:7, 10; 5:22, 29–30; 7:13, 19, 21–23; 8:12, 29; 10:15, 28; 12:36–37, 41–42; 13:40–42, 49–50; 16:24–28; 18:8–9; 19:28–29; 22:13; 24:40–41, 51; 25:12, 30.

41. Matt 5:21, 22; 10:15; 11:22, 24; 12:36, 41, 42.

42. Matt 10:15; 11:22, 24; 12:36.

43. Matt 12:41, 42.

50; 22:13; 24:51; 25:30). No other Gospel associates "weeping" with final judgment. Only in Luke 13:28 does "gnashing of teeth" appear.[44]

Paul Tanner concludes that when all the evidence is taken into account, the best exegetical conclusion is that in Matthew's Gospel, Jesus uses "outer darkness" and "weeping and gnashing of teeth" to speak of a place of eternal torment for the wicked.[45]

### *17.1.4.3 "Hell"*

The word "hell" occurs in the English (NIV) New Testament thirteen times. Compared to the rest of the New Testament, Matthew stresses "hell" more often, rendering the term *gehenna* seven times,[46] contrasted to Mark's three times (Mark 9:43, 45, 47), Luke's once (Luke 12:5), none in John, and only two other times in the New Testament (Jas 3:6; the thirteenth occurrence of "hell" in 2 Pet 2:4 renders *tartaroō*, "hold captive in Tartarus"). The other similar term for hell in the New Testament, "Hades" (*hadēs*), is used twice by Matthew (Matt 11:23; 16:18), twice in Luke (Luke 10:15; 16:23), none in Mark or John, and in the rest of the New Testament, only in Revelation four times (Rev 1:18; 6:8; 20:13, 14).

An interesting point is made that Jesus spoke of the fate of the wicked in terms that may appear to point toward death and destruction—finality and not ongoing punishment, or, in the current debate, annihilation: "Do not be afraid of those who kill the body but cannot kill the soul. Rather, be afraid of the One who can destroy both soul and body in hell" (Matt 10:28). Preston Sprinkle suggests, "The parallel between 'kill' and 'destroy' seems to say that the punishment of the wicked will be death, the termination of life, and not an ongoing conscious existence."[47] John Nolland comments, "'Destroy' replaces 'kill' as more appropriate for the post-death situation contemplated here. 'Destroy' would naturally imply annihilation."[48] Nolland goes on to maintain that there are no Matthean texts incompatible with an understanding of annihilation. He points to "eternal fire" of 18:8 and 25:41 and concludes that they can reasonably be taken as a fire that has been kept available (and will be kept available) for its destructive role.[49] He notes there are probably some early Jewish traditions of perpetual punishment, such as the phrase "to the gloom of everlasting fire" (1QS II, 8 [García]), which may well imply unending suffering. Nolland also points to the phrase "he will send fire and worms into their flesh; they shall weep in pain forever" (*heōs aiōnos*) (Judith 16:17, NRSVue), which is likely to imply unending suffering, but he adds that "'for an age' would be a possible translation."[50]

44. Blomberg, *New Testament Theology*, 377.

45. Tanner, "'Outer Darkness' in Matthew's Gospel," 445–459; here 459.

46. Matt 5:22, 29, 30; 10:28; 18:9; 23:15, 33.

47. Preston Sprinkle, ed., *Four Views on Hell*, 2nd ed. Counterpoints: Bible and Theology (Grand Rapids: Zondervan, 2016), 12.

48. Nolland, *Matthew*, 436–37.

49. Nolland, *Matthew*, 437n94.

50. Nolland, *Matthew*, 437nn94, 95.

The nature of hell is highly debated today. Renowned evangelical theologian and pastor John Stott stunned many of us years ago when he wrote *against* the traditional doctrine of hell as eternal conscious torment. He wrote,

> I find the concept intolerable and do not understand how people can live with it without either cauterizing their feelings or cracking under the strain. As a committed Evangelical, my question must be—and is—not what does my heart tell me, but what does God's word say? And in order to answer this question, we need to survey the biblical material afresh and to open our minds (not just our hearts) to the possibility that Scripture points in the direction of annihilation.[51]

The debate is seen in the recent volume *Four Views on Hell*, where respected theologians wrestle with a Christian doctrine of hell: Do we go to heaven or hell when we die? Is hell a place of eternal, conscious torment? Or do we cease to exist? Are believers and unbelievers ultimately saved by grace in the end? These are the types of questions that led to the following positions:[52]

- **Eternal Conscious Torment.** Hell is a place where the wicked will experience everlasting conscious torment.
- **Terminal Punishment, or Annihilationism (Conditional Immortality).** Unbelievers will be punished in hell, yet that punishment will consist of death and destruction.
- **Universalism (Ultimate Reconciliation).** All creation, through the atoning work of Christ, will ultimately be reconciled to its Creator.
- **Purgatory.** Believers who are not fully sanctified in this life will finish the process of sanctification after death.[53]

As with the Counterpoints book on heaven that we noted earlier, each of the contributors believes in hell. They do not deny the *existence* of hell; they differ on the nature of hell, what hell is like. Perhaps Jesus's teaching in the Olivet Discourse will offer us some direction.

51. David L. Edwards and John R. W. Stott, *Evangelical Essentials: A Liberal-Evangelical Dialogue* (Downers Grove, IL: InterVarsity, 1988), 314–15.

52. Sprinkle, *Four Views on Hell*. Contributors: (1) Denny Burk, "Eternal Conscious Torment," (2) John Stackhouse, "Terminal Punishment, Annihilationism or Conditional Immortality," (3) Robin Parry, "Universalism or Ultimate Reconciliation," (4) Jerry Walls, "Purgatory." See also Gomes, *40 Questions About Heaven and Hell*, for a traditional view of hell as eternal conscious torment, 289–95.

53. Sprinkle, *Four Views on Hell*, 13–14.

### 17.1.5 Eternal Life in the Olivet Discourse

The final scene in the Olivet Discourse is unique to Matthew's Gospel. In this fifth part, Jesus concludes the discourse with a scene of reward of eternal life and of judgment of eternal punishment at the time of his coming (25:31–46). The concept of eternal life is linked to the use of the adjective *aiōnios* and a noun, usually the word for life, *zōē*. "Eternal life" is used of the condition of a present and/or future relationship with God based on the redemptive work of Jesus Messiah.[54] Each of the preceding four parables includes statements of judgment, but the emphasis has been upon getting one's life prepared. Now the emphasis is squarely upon judgment of those who are excluded and on the reward for those who are admitted to the eternal kingdom (25:34).

#### *17.1.5.1 Sheep Separated from Goats (25:31–33)*

This scene in the Olivet Discourse switches to the glorious coming of the Son of Man. He is accompanied in his glory with all the angels, and he sits upon his throne of glory (25:31–33). The throne draws on the motif of the ruler of the kingdom before whom all of the nations will be gathered (25:32).[55] The debated expression "the nations" (*ta ethnē*) has been interpreted to mean the church, all humanity, all non-believers, and so on, but within the Matthean context most likely it is intended to mean both Jews and gentiles who throughout this age are the combined object of the Great Commission (see 24:14; 28:18–20).[56] The nations as entities are not judged, but rather the people (Gr. *autous*, "them") within them: "and he will separate the people one from another as a shepherd separates the sheep from the goats" (25:32).[57]

The shepherd metaphor softens the judgment image but does not diminish the foreboding consequences of separating the sheep from the goats. Sheep is a consistent image of the people of God, whether the reference is specifically to Israel (9:36; 10:6; 15:24; Ezek 34) or to Jesus's disciples (Matt 10:16; cf. 26:31 quoting Zech 13:7; John 10 [15x]). "Goats" do not occur often in the New Testament, but in the Old Testament seventy percent of the references to them concern their use as animals for sacrifice, such as the goat offered for sin sacrifice and the one that was the scapegoat on the Day of Atonement (Lev 16:8–10, 26).

There does not appear to be any significant reason why the goat was selected to contrast with the sheep, except for the symbolism that will be attached to both in a surprising manner. "He will put the sheep on his right and the goats on his left" (Matt

54. Stanley E. Porter, "Eternity, Eternal," *DLNT* 347.

55. Turner, "His Glorious Throne," 156–58.

56. Turner, "His Glorious Throne," 156–61. For judging only outsiders here (i.e., non-Jews), see Runesson, "Judging Gentiles," 133–51; here 147–49. For a detailed history of interpretation as to the identity implied here, see Sherman W. Gray, *The Least of My Brothers: Matthew 25:31–42—A History of Interpretation*, SBLDS 114 (Atlanta: Scholars, 1989), although Gray argues that the judgment of the church is described in 24:45–25:30, and judgment of those outside the church is described in 25:31–46 (Gray, *Least of My Brothers*, 358–59).

57. Esler, "Ethnic Identities," 195–210, here 206–8.

25:32–33). The right-hand side is the place of honor, whether it is the king's mother at the king's right side (Judg 2:19), or King David at God's right-hand side (Ps 16:11), or the Messiah sitting at the right side of God (Ps 110:1, 5; cf. Matt 22:44). The left-hand side is not typically a place of disfavor (cf. 20:21, 23), although the context signifies it to be so here.

#### *17.1.5.2 The Reward of the Sheep (25:34–40)*

The King gives the explanation for the separation as he says to those on his right, "Come, you who are blessed by my Father; take your inheritance, the kingdom" (25:34). The King is understood to be the Son of Man sitting on the throne (25:31), bringing to mind the prophecy of Dan 7:13–14 where the Son of Man receives the kingdom from the Ancient of Days. This is one of the rare times that Jesus refers to himself as King, although the theme has been there throughout Matthew's Gospel. Matthew traces Jesus's lineage to King David (Matt 1:1–17); he narrates Jesus to be sought by the magi as the one born king of the Jews (2:2); Jesus announces the arrival of the kingdom of heaven (4:17); Jesus's earthly ministry comes to a climactic point in his triumphal entry to Jerusalem where he fulfills the expectation of Israel's king coming to her (see 21:5); he is accused by the Sanhedrin of claiming to be the king of the Jews (27:11); and he is mocked as king in his crucifixion (27:29, 37, 42).

The King addresses the sheep on his right as "blessed by my Father" (25:34). The blessing consists of their inheritance, which is the kingdom that they now receive, not because they have earned it through their own efforts but because it is a gift of their relationship with the Father and the Son. God's assured purpose is carried out as the blessing of the inheritance of the kingdom for the sheep is realized.

Kingdom inheritance is the reward for caring for Jesus's physical needs (25:35). The sheep cared for Jesus when he was in need whether hungry, thirsty, a stranger, naked, sick, or imprisoned. The precedent is found in those Old Testament admonitions where God rejects Israel's external displays of religiosity (e.g., fasting) as a sham and declares that true righteousness is displayed in caring for the needy (e.g., Isa 58:6–10).

But there is a surprised reaction from those who are rewarded (25:37–39): "Lord, when did we see you hungry and feed you . . . ? (25:37). The surprise of the "righteous" sheep (cf. 10:41; 13:43, 49; 25:41) comes from their taking literally his words, because they can recall no time when they had done this for the King. Their surprise indicates that these were not intentional meritorious acts attempting to gain access to the kingdom. Rather, these acts of mercy provide evidence that the sheep belong to the kingdom, just as the preceding parables pointed out external behavioral evidence of a person who had truly received the gift of salvation and the resulting transformation by the Spirit.

Jesus responds, "Truly I tell you, whatever you did for one of the least of these brothers of mine, you did for me" (25:40). Following on the surprise of the righteous, this statement of Jesus is a central principle of the passage—in caring for the needs of the least of these brothers of Jesus, they have served Jesus.

### *17.1.5.3 The Least of These Brothers of Mine (25:40)*

Solving the question of the identification of these "brothers and sisters" is important. The answer to that question determines what Jesus gives as the basis for one's acceptance into eternal life or departure into eternal punishment (25:46). Five primary solutions have been offered.[58] (1) *All needy persons in humanity.* This view emphasizes that mercy is to be displayed toward all persons.[59] (2) *All Christians.* Others suggest that all Christians are in view, since the most explicit reference to "brothers and sisters" in Jesus's usage in Matthew refers to his disciples.[60] (3) *Christian missionaries.* Others suggest that these are Christian missionaries, the treatment of whom determines the fate of all people. Those who receive them receive Jesus; those who reject them reject Jesus—a theme not unlike the reward offered in the Missionary Discourse (10:40–42).[61] (4) *Jewish Christians.* Some conclude Jesus is referring to Jewish Christians, especially focusing on the way that converted Christians treat converted Jews who are missionaries for him during the "Great Tribulation."[62] 5) *Tribulation martyrs.* This view suggests that Jesus refers to Christians who were martyred for the faith during the great tribulation and who will return with the risen Lord at his second coming.[63]

The consistent way that Jesus refers to his disciples as "brothers and sisters" in Matthew's narrative leads to the second view. But the expression "least" points explicitly to *needy* disciples. This makes a distinction from the sheep (disciples generally) to emphasize that needy disciples are often the ones who are excluded from care—attention is often wrongfully diverted to prominent members of the discipleship community. This is in line with the admonition Jesus gave to the disciples who were arguing about who was the greatest in the kingdom of heaven (18:1). He charged them to become like children, and receiving children in his name is like receiving Jesus himself (18:2–5). This is also in line with James's rebuke of his church for showing partiality to the rich in the assembly while dishonoring the poor in the church (cf. James 2:1).

Thus, Jesus affirms that believers are to care for one another, but especially the least and insignificant among them. This does not absolve a general mercy that Christians

58. See Gray, *Least of My Brothers*; Eugene W. Pond, "Who Are 'The Least' of Jesus' Brothers in Matthew 25:40?," *BSac* 159 (2002): 436–48.

59. This was a minority position for much of church history but has found many recent adherents. For a recent defense, see Davies and Allison, *Matthew*, 3:428–29; Schweizer, *Matthew*, 478–80; C. E. B. Cranfield, "Who are Christ's Brothers?," *Metanoia* 4 (1994): 31–39.

60. Matt 5:47; 12:49–50; 18:15–17; 23:8; 28:10. E.g., Hagner, *Matthew 14–28*, 744–45; Carson, "Matthew," 585–721.

61. Blomberg, *Matthew*, 378; Travis, "Judgment," 410–11.

62. E.g., Barbieri, "Matthew," 81; Glasscock, *Matthew*, 491–92.

63. E.g., Pond, "Who Are 'The Least,'" 443–48.

must demonstrate toward all in need. As Morris says, "Everyone in need is to be the object of Christian benevolence."[64] But perhaps the best guiding light is given by the apostle Paul, who states the principle, "Therefore, as we have opportunity, let us do good to all people, especially to those who belong to the family of believers" (Gal 6:10).

But we should reiterate that these good deeds are not the works by which one enters the kingdom; they are the substantiation of the kind of kingdom life that has been produced through the transformation of the heart of his disciples through regeneration. Their works of caring for the needy among them will confirm that they belong to Jesus. Otherwise, they are not truly his sheep because they have not been born again by the Spirit of God.

### 17.1.6 Eternal Punishment in the Olivet Discourse (25:41–45)

The scene repeats as Jesus addresses those on his left, the goats, in almost the same wording he used to commend the sheep on his right, except that the goats are condemned because they have *not* demonstrated mercy to one of the least of these brothers and sisters of Jesus.

#### *17.1.6.1 Eternal Fire Prepared for the Devil and His Angels (25:41–43)*

"Then he will say to those on his left, 'Depart from me, you who are cursed, into the eternal fire prepared for the devil and his angels" (Matt 25:41). Jesus introduces a somewhat new idea in that the eternal fire is prepared for the devil and the fallen angels aligned with him. These angels are the third of the stars of heaven seduced by the dragon (Rev 12:3–4). The devil is the dynamism behind the wicked kingdoms who persecute God's people. And human sinners join the cosmic powers in the fiery lake.[65] The devil is thrown into the lake of fire (Rev 20:10), where the beast and the false prophet had been thrown. They will all be tormented day and night for ever and ever (20:10). Likewise, Jesus says to the goats, "Depart from me, you who are cursed, into the eternal fire" (Matt 25:41).[66]

A close link is found in the parable of the weeds in the field, where the weeds or tares (*zizania*) are the people of the evil one who are sown by the devil and who are pulled up and burned in the fire at the end of the age (13:39–40). The kingdom was prepared for the sheep since "the creation of the world" (25:34), but the fire was "prepared" for the rebellious angels of the devil. "Jesus is now saying that those on his left at the judgment will find their eternal habitation in the place where the evil are, Satan and all those associated with him."[67]

64. Morris, *Matthew*, 639.

65. G. K. Beale, *The Book of Revelation: A Commentary on the Greek Text*, NIGNT (Grand Rapids: Eerdmans, 1999), 634; Osborne, *Matthew*, 938.

66. Nolland, *Matthew*, 1033; Blomberg, *Matthew*, 378–79.

67. Morris, *Matthew*, 639–40.

#### *17.1.6.2 The Punishment of the Goats (25:41–45)*

Eternal fire is the punishment for not caring for the physical needs of one of the least of these (25:41–43). The goats respond similarly to the way that the sheep have (25:44). Jesus responds in the same way as he has to the sheep, except the goats have *not* acted on behalf of "the least of these" (25:45). Jesus omits the specification "of these brothers and sisters of mine" from v. 40, but we should assume that he intends this as a shortened reference. The goats are just as surprised as the sheep, but they are surprised like those in the preceding parables. The five foolish virgins (25:1–13) and the wicked servant who did not invest his talent (25:14–30) were not condemned to eternal punishment for some externally heinous sin but for their failure to do the right thing. So here, sins of omission are also worthy of eternal damnation because they are evidence that a person has not been made righteous by association with the kingdom of God (5:20). Righteous acts spring from a heart sanctified by the Spirit of God while unrighteous acts, even of omission, indicate a heart lacking in the Spirit's work of transformation (cf. 15:19; Titus 3:1–8).

### 17.1.7 Eternal Punishment and Eternal Life in the Olivet Discourse (25:46)

Jesus concludes the dramatic judgment scene by stating, "Then they will go away to eternal punishment, but the righteous to eternal life" (Matt 25:46). Daniel's prophecy of a future time of great tribulation that will come on the earth also leads to a prophecy of eternal life and punishment: "Multitudes who sleep in the dust of the earth will awake: some to everlasting life, others to shame and everlasting contempt. Those who are wise will shine like the brightness of the heavens, and those who lead many to righteousness, like the stars for ever and ever" (Dan 12:2–3; cf. 2 Bar. 51:5–6). Daniel's prophecy echoes here in the final words of Jesus's concluding discourse in Matthew's Gospel.

A significant point to be noted is that Jesus's pronouncement emphasizes the eternality of punishment and life. The adjective "eternal" (*aiōnios*), "pertaining to an age," in a context like this designates the age to come, the age that is without end.[68] The term for "punishment" (*kolasis*) is found in the New Testament only here and in 1 John 4:18.

France suggests that the use of *kolasis* ("punishment") here in Matt 25:46 draws upon Jesus's imagery of the cursed thrown into the eternal fire prepared for the devil and his angels (25:41). In his view, the imagery of fire suggests destruction rather than punishment. He points to the parable of the wheat and the weeds, where the weeds are destroyed, not kept burning forever. Combined with 10:28 where the verb

68. Morris, *Matthew*, 641.

"destroy" (*apollymi*) is used in relation to hell, "punish" in 25:41 suggests an annihilationist theology (sometimes described as "conditional immortality"). He concludes, "The sense of 'eternal punishment' here will not be 'punishment which goes on forever' but 'punishment which has eternal consequences,' the loss of eternal life through being destroyed by fire."[69]

However, many commentators point out that it is difficult to ignore the correspondence between "eternal life" and "eternal punishment" in this passage.[70] Moisés Silva points out that whatever qualitative nuances are involved in the term *aiōnios*, few would deny that eternal life is without end. And "endless" is the most likely sense that provides a semantic match between the two phrases. "The fact is that αἰώνιος [*aiōnios*] is the most common and natural way to express the notion that something continues forever."[71] Blomberg states, "The parallel between eternal punishment and eternal life makes it difficult to see in the former any kind of annihilationism."[72]

Jesus does not describe here the specific nature of how the saved and lost will spend eternity, but rather that eternal life and eternal punishment are the consequences of how we have lived in the present age, either with Jesus or against him.[73] Those who have responded to Jesus's announcement and have become his disciples have all along been noted to be "people of the kingdom" (Matt 13:38), but now they enter into the full blessing and experience of life in the kingdom.

Many understand this judgment scene to be the same as that occurring at the end of this earthly age, just prior to the eternal state (Rev 20:11–13).[74] Others understand this judgment to take place prior to the inauguration of the earthly millennial kingdom by Jesus, who will rule over those who are blessed to enter that reign with him.[75]

The former view is in harmony with the references to the eternal life or punishment into which the sheep or goats now enter (25:41, 46). Premillennialists who hold this position have to explain how the immediacy of the coming of the Son of Man throughout the discourse gives way to a scene of judgment that occurs a thousand years later. Most do so by suggesting that Jesus has compressed future events.

The latter view is more in harmony with the consistent reference to the immediacy of the coming of the Son of Man throughout the discourse, but those holding to this view must explain the references to entering into "eternal life" at the time of the millennium—either Jesus is speaking nonchronologically and is compressing future

69. France, *Gospel of Matthew*, 967. See also Alan Fairhurst, who sees hell as the annihilation of the wicked: Alan M. Fairhurst, "Matthew's Hell: From Percy Dearmer to David Sim," *ExpTim* 110.5 (1999): 138–40. He notes that this is now the position of the Anglican Church in England.

70. E.g., Blomberg, *Matthew*, 379; Carson, "Matthew," 586–87; Morris, *Matthew*, 641; Osborne, "Matthew," 939; Luz, *Matthew 21–28*, 282.

71. Moisés Silva, "κολάζω," *NIDNTTE* 2:718.

72. Blomberg, *Matthew*, 379.

73. Luz, *Matthew 21–28*, 282.

74. Erickson, *Theology*, 1102–4; Hagner, *Matthew 14–28*, 742–43; Blomberg, *Matthew*, 376; Morris, *Matthew*, 634–35.

75. E.g., Pond, "Background and Timing," 201–20; R. Saucy, *Case for Progressive Dispensationalism*, 130.

events or, more likely, "eternal" is used here not as an experience of their final state but as a confirmation of it before the final experience.[76]

The evidence is scanty either way, but the important point throughout this scene is clear: Judgment will come.[77] In that way this judgment scene provides a dramatic conclusion to the entire discourse and a sequential culmination to the preceding parables. The presence of kingdom life will always produce evidence in the transformed speech, thought, actions, and character of Jesus's followers. The absence of transformation is proof that a person has not accepted the invitation to the kingdom. Reward or penalty is distributed according to the evidence.[78]

As has been the emphasis throughout the Olivet Discourse, and ultimately throughout this Gospel, there are only two types of people.[79] Those who have not followed Jesus are actually against him and will endure separation from him in their eternal punishment. Jesus's disciples are with him and will enjoy with him life that is eternal. This should produce the greatest joy in Jesus's disciples as we consider our eternal destiny. But the fate of the wicked should also weigh heavily upon us, provoking the same kind of anguish that the apostle Paul experienced as he considered the eternal fate of his fellow Jews who had rejected Jesus (Rom 9:1–3; 10:1–2).

## 17.1.8 The Future for Ethnic Israel

In Chapter 12 we addressed the place and role of ethnic Israel in relationship to God's unfolding plan of history, including Israel's relationship to Jesus Messiah, the kingdom of heaven, to Torah, Jesus's disciples, and the church. Matthew's Gospel is especially significant in addressing these issues, because Matthew has special interest in Israel, perhaps more so than any of the other Gospels. Here we briefly address one aspect of that issue, the eschatological future of ethnic Israel. We can summarize our findings of Chapter 12 in five brief points.

### *17.1.8.1 There Is a Continuing Mission to Israel in the Land During This Age Until the Coming of the Son of Man (10:23)*

Israel will have a presence in the cities/land of Israel and will experience the preaching of the gospel until the parousia (10:23). There will be a continuing mission to Israel alongside of the mission to the gentiles until Jesus returns at the end of this age (see on 28:18–20).[80] Matthew 10:23 "reflects Matthew's concern that the mission to God's

76. Pond, "Background and Timing," 219–20; R. Saucy, *Case for Progressive Dispensationalism*, 288n67.

77. See Sim, *Apocalyptic Eschatology*, 130–39.

78. Ladd, *Theology*, 206–7. See also Stephen H. Travis, *Christ and the Judgement of God: The Limits of Divine Retribution in New Testament Thought*, 2nd ed. (Peabody, MA: Hendrickson, 2009).

79. So also Osborne, *Matthew*, 940.

80. Kvalbein, "Has Matthew Abandoned the Jews?," 45–62; Konradt, *Israel, Church and the Gentiles*, 74–87. We have discussed this further in Chapter 15, Mission and Commission: Transformational Discipling of the Nations.

people Israel not be abandoned."[81] Therefore, this verse anticipates an ongoing mission to Israel until the second coming of Jesus Messiah.[82]

### *17.1.8.2 The Mission to Israel Will Be Conducted in the Cities of the Land of Israel (24:15)*

Jesus anticipates the fulfillment of the covenantal promises to Israel to be restored to the land, with an apparently (and seemingly implausible) rebuilt temple and attendant desecration, which will usher in the messianic kingdom (24:15). For hundreds of years Israel as a nation was not in the land. But in the return to the land in the twentieth century, this saying of Jesus acknowledges the blessed place Israel has in God's providence. In spite of Israel's hardheartedness, God will remain faithful to his covenant promises to her. This is a powerful apologetic to both those involved in Jesus's ministry and those within hearing of Matthew's Gospel in the first century and today that God has not abandoned his covenantal promises to Israel in the land.[83] Israel will still be in the land until the coming of the Son of Man, and then beyond (cf. 19:28).[84]

### *17.1.8.3 Israel Will Be in the Land of Jerusalem Until They Bless the Coming One (23:37–39)*

Jesus gives what appears to be a prophetic announcement that when he returns at the parousia, remorseful Israel will utter in sincere repentance the words, "Blessed is he who comes in the name of the Lord" (23:39). This is God's merciful offer of hope to his people.[85] This is in line with the statement in Zechariah: "They will look on me, the one they have pierced, and they will mourn for him as one mourns for an only child" (Zech 12:10; cf. John 19:34–37). Robert Gundry believes that this "implies a conversion of Israel at the parousia . . . and a return of the kingdom to Israel at the parousia."[86] As Jesus cites Ps 118:26, he identifies himself with God's Messiah, Israel's Savior, the Coming One, who will in the future once again come to his people after a time of great judgment, when they will have no other choice but to acknowledge him as Lord, either in great joy or in great sorrow.[87] Matthew's perspective on the city of Jerusalem and the temple implies both God's judgment on them in AD 70 and his future restoration of repentant Israel when Jesus returns.[88]

81. Davies and Allison, *Matthew*, 2:192.

82. See Blomberg, *Matthew*, 176; Davies and Allison, *Matthew*, 2:189–90; Keener, *Matthew*, 324–25; Nolland, *Matthew*, 428–29; Turner, *Israel's Last Prophet*, 193–95; Turner, *Matthew*, 277.

83. Konradt, *Israel, Church, and the Gentiles*, 82–87. Contra Luz, who states: "It seems more likely to me that for Matthew not only 10:5–6 but also 10:23 were corrected by the Great Commission"; Luz, *Matthew 1–7*, 94.

84. Patterson, "Israel and the Great Tribulation," loc. 1600–1828, Kindle.

85. Turner, *Israel's Last Prophet*, 328, appears to see this as a prophetic announcement by Jesus, but he seems also to maintain a conditional aspect of the saying. Nolland perceives the conditional as unnecessary.

86. Gundry, *Matthew*, 474. So also Keener, *Matthew*, 558–59.

87. Turner, *Matthew*, 562.

88. Willitts, "Zionism in the Gospel of Matthew," 132.

#### *17.1.8.4 The Twelve Apostles Will Sit on Twelve Thrones "Judging" the Twelve Tribes of Israel (19:28)*

Matthew gives indications that since the Twelve will sit on twelve thrones judging the twelve tribes of Israel, in the future restored Davidic kingdom the twelve disciples will govern over Israel's restored tribal territories (19:28). This indicates the future role of the twelve apostles and the existence of the twelve tribes of the nation of Israel in God's purposes. Jesus indicates a future time of renewal when the twelve apostles will participate in the final establishment of the kingdom of God on the earth, when Israel will be restored to the land and the Twelve will rule with Jesus Messiah over the renewal of all things. The twelve apostles will judge the twelve tribes in the sense of shepherding them (cf. Pss. Sol. 17:26), not punishing them.[89] This is the conclusion reached by a diverse array of Matthean scholars.[90] Turner argues that "Matt 19:28 speaks of the Twelve as future rulers of Israel, not as those who preside over Israel's condemnation."[91] This apparently speaks to the political reconstitution of a twelve–tribe nation state in the restored Davidic kingdom.[92] The terminology in Matt 19:28, focusing on the twelve tribes of Israel, is remarkable (cf. Luke 22:30; Rev 21:12), linked as it is to the description of the eschaton as a time of regeneration.[93] Matthew does not offer us details, but "the renewal" (19:28) expresses a potent expectation of the future restoration of Israel. "The παλιγγενεσία [*palingenesia*] for him meant the world in which Christ reigns, a world with a redeemed Israel."[94]

#### *17.1.8.5 Individual Jews Participate in the Salvation Brought by Jesus with the Arrival of the Kingdom of Heaven*

Although ethnic Israel is not at present functionally the instrument, witness, and steward of the outworking of the kingdom of God (21:43), individual Jews are invited to participate in the salvation brought by Jesus with the arrival of the kingdom, to be incorporated in discipleship to Jesus that includes Jews and gentiles, men and women, commoner and elite, and to become participants in the missional outreach to all the nations (28:18–20).

### 17.1.9 "I Am with You Always, to the Very End of the Age"

Matthew concludes his Gospel with the wonderful good news that Jesus promises, "And surely I am with you always, to the very end of the age" (28:20). The phrase

89. Keener, *Matthew* (2009), 479–80; Evans, *Matthew*, 348

90. E.g., cf. Davies and Allison, *Matthew*, 3:55–58; Gromacki, "Fulfillment of the Abrahamic Covenant," 77–119; Gundry, *Matthew*, 392–93; Keener, *Matthew* (2009), 479–80; Konradt, *Israel, Church, and the Gentiles*, 259–63; Runesson, *Divine Wrath and Salvation in Matthew*, 45–46n16; 310n244; R. Saucy, *Case for Progressive Dispensationalism*, 267–69; Willitts, *Matthew's Messianic Shepherd-King*, 119–21; Witherington, *Matthew*, 371–72; Esler, "Ethnic Identities," 195–209; here 203–4.

91. Turner, "His Glorious Throne," 167.

92. Willitts, "Zionism in the Gospel of Matthew," 138.

93. Turner, *Matthew*, 475; cf. Sim, "Meaning of *palingenesia*," 3–12.

94. Davies and Allison, *Matthew*, 3:57–58.

"always" (*pasas tas hēmeras*, "all the days") is a promise that Jesus would be with his disciples for the extent of the entire age.[95] The expression "end of the age" (*synteleia aiōnos*) is found five times in Matthew (13:39–40, 49; 24:3; 28:20) and only one other time in all of the New Testament (Heb 9:26). The thought is not only temporal but also includes that of the consummation or completion of the purpose of God. In each Matthean usage Jesus is speaking of the end of this life as we know it, the completion of all that is involved in this age.[96]

All that he commanded in word and deed that is necessary for our growth as his disciples is included in the written documents of Scripture, but his very real presence comforts our individual needs and sustains us through all of our days, whether in our weakness, sorrow, joy, power, or pain. To the "very end of the age" or until the completion of God's plans for this age, Jesus promises to be the sustaining presence that assures us that history is not out of control, that the kingdom of heaven has indeed been inaugurated, that he is a very present help in times of trouble, and that the work that he accomplished on the cross to bring salvation to humanity is continually available through his risen and ascended ministry.

## 17.2 ESCHATOLOGICAL MESSAGES IN MATTHEW'S GOSPEL: SOJOURNING RIGHTLY UNTIL THE RETURN OF JESUS MESSIAH

**Live** *as though Jesus is coming back tonight;*
**Plan** *as though he is not coming back for a hundred years.*

I opened the preceding Chapter by noting that this saying is one of the life maxims that guides my everyday life. The saying essentially came from studying Jesus's Olivet Discourse. Jesus warns us to have our lives in order so that at any moment if he returned we would not be ashamed. At the same time, Jesus exhorts us to be fully engaged in all of life so that we conscientiously care for all of our responsibilities for however long he gives us life in this world.

In the latter part of the Olivet Discourse, Jesus deals with attitudes that should characterize those who live during this age and await his coming. He gives several messages that will equip people during this age in preparation for the end (24:32–25:30). All of us need to move from speculation to utilization in our study of prophecy and eschatology because the Bible does not record prophecy of end-time activity simply for curiosity's sake or for trivial pursuits. There are certainly many who undertake a study

95. The use of the accusative in the expression "all the days" (*pasas tas hemeras*) emphasizes that it is not just that Jesus would be with his disciples *during* the present age (which would have been expressed with the genitive), but for the *extent* of the age (Wallace, *Greek Grammar*, 202).

96. Morris, *Matthew*, 356–57.

of eschatology in a vain attempt to figure out that which Jesus said was unknown—the time of the end and his return (24:36).

But prophecy about the future is always given for the purpose of affecting behavior in the present. Every passage in the Bible that I have ever studied with a message about end times always comes in the context of exhortation and warning. And that must never be forgotten whenever we undertake a study of any eschatological passage. The study in this theology of Matthew's record of Jesus's life and teaching understands that the offer and establishment of the kingdom of God is an inaugurated eschatology, *an already-not yet basis*—it is present and fully operative in the lives of those who respond, yet it awaits a final manifestation, when Jesus Messiah will reign on the earth and Israel will experience the realization of her covenantal promises. That outlook on Jesus's eschatological discourse leads to important theological messages.

### 17.2.1 Godly Living in the Present

The first theological message is that the study of the future should spur us to godly living in the present. Jesus's signal statement, "See, I have told you ahead of time" (24:25), stands in the middle of his prophecy of future events. He tells his disciples these events so they not be deceived and go after false messiahs and prophets (24:23–24, 26) but also so that they would develop godly perseverance through wars, famines, earthquakes, and persecution (24:6–7, 9–10), that our love for him and each other would not falter when wickedness surrounds us (24:12), and that the testimony of our lips and lives remains steadfast and pure even to the very end (24:13–14).[97]

Jesus's message to us in the Sermon on the Mount is that personal righteousness will result from entering the kingdom of heaven (5:20), and now he prophesies of future events so that we will discipline ourselves to maintain and expand that personal kingdom-righteousness in our daily lives no matter what the circumstances may be. He does not tell us these things so that we would be obsessed with dates and events and speculation about the minute details of his prophecy but to encourage us to godly living. Trevin Wax refers to this as "eschatological discipleship," in which Christians view the past, present, and future from a biblical perspective, which then shapes their understanding of following Jesus in the present world.[98] Ian Smith helpfully focuses on the biblical vision of life with God in his future renewed earth and how that affects life today.[99] Our study of the "last things" should radically affect our godly living in the present.

97. For a scholarly and pastoral approach, see Benjamin L. Gladd and Matthew S. Harmon, *Making All Things New: Inaugurated Eschatology for the Life of the Church* (Grand Rapids: Baker Academic, 2016).

98. Trevin Wax, *Eschatological Discipleship: Leading Christians to Understand Their Historical and Cultural Context* (Nashville: B&H Academic, 2018), 41. See also John C. Clark and Marcus Peter Johnson, *A Call to Christian Formation: How Theology Makes Sense of Our World* (Grand Rapids: Baker Academic, 2021), 163–90, who refer to doing theology as "Living Forward, Understanding Backward: The Eschatological Tension of Christian Theology."

99. Ian K. Smith, *Not Home Yet: How the Renewal of the Earth Fits into God's Plan for the World* (Wheaton, IL: Crossway, 2019).

### 17.2.2 Conviction About the Future

A second theological message is that our study of prophecy should produce conviction about what is going to happen in the future. There is the possibility that we can be wrong on certain points, which will help us avoid a narrow dogmatism, but when we have done our homework and we settle on what we believe to be the Bible's teaching, we should develop conviction—because the appropriate kind of conviction affects our character and our attitude.

People without an appropriate kind of conviction will be swayed between depression and giddiness by each change of circumstance. Superpower nations who like to flex their nuclear or biological muscles produce in people all around us the fear of unstoppable international disaster. But Jesus warns us against being alarmed when international events seem to indicate that the world is going to fall apart (24:6). When we are convinced that the end of the world will only come when Jesus returns visibly and powerfully, we can maintain hope and vigilance no matter how bad things become.

Similarly, the apostle Paul gives prophetic revelation about Jesus's return so that his readers would have hope about their loved ones who have died (1 Thess 4:13–18). One of my closest friends lost his daughter suddenly to a tragic death. It was a blow that would devastate most anyone, yet he told me that it was his unwavering conviction about her presence with the Lord, and that he would be with her one day, that gave him a blanket of peace in the cold, harsh realities of this world. And that conviction came only from a study of God's word about the future.

In our personal study and in our preaching and teaching we ought not to overlook the massive place that prophetic teaching occupies in Scripture. Even though we must guard against excess and obsession with this kind of study, we will have no peace or security without conviction about the future.

### 17.2.3 Warning of Difficult Times Ahead

There is also an important theological message in Jesus's prophecy of difficult times ahead. Jesus spent much of his time in the discourses preparing the disciples for the harsh realities of life during this age. The power of this preparation cannot be underestimated because much of our development as disciples comes in preparing ourselves before the fact.

Jesus prepares us for rejection as we go out to do missions (10:22–23). He prepares us for the mixed nature of the kingdom until his return (13:24–50). He warns us about imperfection in the Christian community until his return (18:7) and tells us how we should respond in the light of this imperfection (18:12–20). And he repeatedly tells us of the hardships and trials that come as a result of following him. The Olivet Discourse expands on this preparation, cueing us to the fact that there will be those who try to deceive us, as well as persecute us. Knowledge of this fact helps us to prepare ourselves mentally and spiritually for this reality and helps guard against disillusionment. When we fail to tell disciples about these things, there are chances that they will be deceived by messianic pretenders or will be disillusioned by the difficulty of the process. Being faithful and fruitful disciples requires intentional preparation on our part before the fact.

Jesus's prophetic words, as well as much of eschatology generally, are an encouragement for believers in the midst of persecution rather than a handbook for future prediction or simply as a hope for escape from an imperfect world. Every generation has had those who attempt to predict the time of the return of Jesus, at times even selling all worldly possessions in anticipation. These groups have been immensely disappointed—or worse—when their predictions fell flat. Prophecy is not escapism from the trials of life. The reality is that Jesus gives us this information so that we can endure and live appropriately until his return.

### 17.2.4 Warning of Impending Judgment

But there is another theological message in Jesus's eschatological forecast—a warning of impending judgment. Not only is prophecy an encouragement to godly living; it is a stimulus to repentance. I often hear media commentators speak disparagingly of preachers or evangelists as end-time doomsayers. But the fact of prophetic revelation is that judgment is coming on those who reject God's day of opportunity. Whether at the end of one's life or the end of the age, judgment is coming. Here again we must guard against excess, but most churches with which I am familiar never come close to an excess in their preaching. An appropriate preaching and teaching and evangelism from eschatological passages will have to include warning of judgment, or else the full message has been ignored. This calls for wisdom in our presentations, compassion in our approach, and urgency in our message.

### 17.2.5 Vigorous Involvement in Missions and Evangelism

The conviction of Jesus's return therefore should fuel a vigorous involvement in missions, evangelism, and church planting. Our study of prophecy moves beyond academic debate or idle curiosity when we are gripped with the fact that the souls of men and women are at stake. Our active participation in outreach to a lost world enables people across the nation and around the world to be prepared to meet Jesus Messiah when he comes in glory.

Churches and individual Christians that ignore the centrality of mission and evangelistic outreach miss an essential component to the overall plan of God. Jesus tells us that "the end" will come after the gospel has been preached as a testimony to all nations (24:14). This does not mean that we preach the gospel simply to force his return.

However, the parousia and consummation of the kingdom is very much connected with all the nations hearing the testimony of the gospel.[100]

And on a different note, there is strong encouragement in Jesus's statement. Even though at various times in history opposition appears to be insurmountable, true Christianity will assert itself in the preaching of the gospel message. The prophetic statement of Jesus assures us that nothing can stop the preaching of the gospel. To the churches around the world that persevere under governments that have legislated against evangelism or proselytizing, for example in some Islamic or communist nations, this is a powerful, immediately relevant promise. This is also a powerful promise to those in Western countries that have become increasingly secularized. No matter how bad things may get within public opinion or the political arena, no matter how much government may legislate against Christianity or how much persecution is mounted against it, the gospel cannot be stopped until the end when Jesus returns in glory and power.[101] This will sustain us until the end of time, or the end of our own time on this earth.

### 17.2.6 Eschatological Homesickness

Philip Ryken encourages us to develop what he calls "eschatological homesickness," a longing for our eternal home, the place that Jesus has prepared for us. When explaining his motivation for writing an essay on the book of Revelation, Ryken states, "My purpose in expounding the last two chapters of the Bible is to awaken greater homesickness, as well as renewed hope, so that everyone who reads these words may go out into the world like the apostles, the abolitionists, and all the other great men and women of God who had such a vision of glory that they were able to do the suffering work of the church in the world until Jesus comes again."[102]

Such is, at least in part, my purpose in exploring this magnificent theme of eschatology in Matthew's Gospel.

**Live** *as though Jesus is coming back tonight,*
**Plan** *as though he is not coming back for a hundred years.*

100. See Turner, "His Glorious Throne," 161–67.

101. Addressing the darkness and vulnerability of the circumstances of Matthew's community while called to mission, see Balabanski, "Mission in Matthew," 161–75.

102. Philip Graham Ryken, "A New Heaven and a New Earth: Revelation 21:1–22:5," in *Coming Home: Essays on the New Heaven and New Earth*, ed. D. A. Carson and Jeff Robinson Sr. (Wheaton, IL: Crossway, 2017), 119–38, here, 121.

*Part 4*

---

# FINAL MATTERS

*Chapter 18*

# CONCLUDING REFLECTIONS

AS I COME to the conclusion of this volume on a theology of Matthew's Gospel, I am profoundly overwhelmed with the magnitude of what Matthew accomplished. Developing a written document of this length in the first century was no easy task in itself, and for Matthew to develop his historical record of the life and ministry of Jesus Messiah, which then flowed into Matthew's theological understanding of God's work throughout history, is nothing short of miraculous. And such it is because it was the Spirit of God who supernaturally conceived the Son of God, Jesus Messiah, in mother Mary to accomplish salvation for Israel and all of humanity. And it was the Spirit of God who supernaturally guided and superintended Matthew's mind, heart, and hand to produce this magnificent Gospel. And I stand on the shoulders of a multitude of humble disciples of Jesus Messiah who have been privileged to preach and teach on the gospel message found in Matthew's Gospel and attempt to unfold its historical, theological, and life-changing message. I have been absorbed with Matthew's Gospel for nearly fifty years and find its riches still beyond full comprehension.

It has been my privilege and joy to have been immersed in the gospel of Jesus Christ for nearly all of my adult life. I came under the gospel message when I was twenty-one years old. As I mentioned in a previous Chapter, I had returned from combat in Viet Nam a year earlier as a rather shell-shocked and confused, angry young man. For several months I was presented with the gospel message from a variety of sources, until the Spirit of God broke through my defenses, and I willingly and gladly opened my mind and heart to the gospel. That was during the Jesus Movement in the late 1960s and early 1970s. A week later I came to know a young lady, Lynne Melia, who a year later would bless me by becoming my wife. It is to Lynne that I dedicate this volume. She is the love of my life and partner in this journey with Jesus for now over fifty years.

Only a year after our marriage began, God called us to begin a Christian education, a relationship with Talbot School of Theology, Biola University, that now stretches to over fifty years. At first it was Christian psychology, then missions, and then New Testament studies. I was immersed in a world I did not know existed, and I reveled in how the gospel enlightened all my studies. It is to the faculty, staff, and students at Talbot that I also dedicate this volume. What a privilege it has been to work side by side with all of them.

One professor, Robert Saucy, became my most important mentor, and he would later become my most trusted colleague and one of my closest friends on the faculty. When I came on the faculty, we met biweekly for nearly thirty years, where we shared lunch, friendship, and theology. Bob's keen mind and heart for God and the church forced me to think biblically. Bob was one of the leading progressive dispensationalists of the twentieth century. But that was not his hobby horse. His passion was to think biblically about theology. I had never heard of dispensationalism, and Bob did not try to coerce me. He taught me how to think biblically. His commitment to biblical theology was his entrée to his primary expertise in systematic theology, at which he excelled. Although I became a New Testament specialist, his imprint is all over the way that I think as a New Testament theologian.

I was encouraged to explore doctoral studies after seminary, and I applied to Fuller Theological Seminary. At the time it had one of the finest and strongest New Testament departments in the world. I was accepted to study under George Eldon Ladd, one of the leading experts in New Testament theology. He had grown up under the influence of traditional dispensationalism, but he had rejected it. George passed away only a year or two into my studies, but his influence on me is significant for a broad New Testament theology that is primarily committed to the text, not other systems of interpretation.

I then came under the mentorship of Ralph P. Martin. Ralph was one of the world's top New Testament specialists. He was from Great Britain and had no patience with the wranglings of American theology. I finished my doctoral studies under Ralph and also Donald Hagner. Don is uniquely a Matthean specialist but also a broadly proficient New Testament specialist and theologian. It was especially under the friendship, guidance, and stern discipline of Ralph and Don that I was guided in my scholarship.

Shortly after my seminary training and while undergoing my doctoral studies and throughout my teaching career, I have been closely involved in pastoral ministry. I have been ordained in the Evangelical Free Church of America since 1977, serving as senior pastor in two different churches. I also have served on the pastoral staff of a Presbyterian church. I am decidedly a conservative evangelical, but I associate freely as a scholar with the broader world of New Testament scholarship.

These reflections underlie my writing of this theology of Matthew's Gospel. In many ways I still live with the influence of my beginning days in the Jesus Movement. I love Jesus, my Savior, and I revel in the beauty of people who are unreservedly committed to radical discipleship to Jesus. I still feel the support, encouragement, and loving prod of Lynne to get my work done. I still live with the influence of Bob Saucy as I remain faithful to the Bible as God's word and seek to understand the grand theological patterns of Scripture. I still can hear George Ladd's rantings about closed-minded exegetes and preachers. I still feel the sting of Ralph Martin's critique of my scholarship when I allow my assumptions to overrule the biblical text, but I watch and attempt to emulate his pastoral heart as he walked with his wife Lily through personal tragedies. I still enjoy the broad understanding and support of Don Hagner to let the text of Matthew be an entrée into the world of the gospel of Jesus Messiah. And I still am careful to be responsible to the people of the church and young students in academia so that my scholarship is accessible, beneficial, and glorifying to God. Each of these people, and many other men and women, are behind my thinking and writing of this theology of Matthew's Gospel.

My great joy after all of these years is still to explore the gospel of Jesus Messiah. I have been through the dispensational debates, the inerrancy debates, the redaction-critical debates, the gender debates, the open theism debates, the critical theory debates, the ethnicity debates, and many others. The one constant throughout is the gospel of Jesus Messiah. And my avenue to explore the gospel is through the Gospel of Matthew.

Many of these debates have come to a focus in the Gospel of Matthew, so what I have written here has come through many years of allowing the text to be determinative for my thinking. Throughout this book you have found places where I interact with these various debates, but my principal focus has been on understanding Matthew's theology.

This applies to understanding Matthew's Gospel in its own right. I have resisted the pull toward reconciling Matthew's theology with the rest of New Testament theology. I live with the knowledge that Matthew is one of three Synoptic Gospels, and I revel in their common yet unique perspectives. I also revel in the unique perspective of the apostle John. I revel in the knowledge that John writes while looking back at decades of circulation of Matthew's Gospel and that John intentionally complements what the Synoptic Gospels have recorded. At times I have given a nod toward how Matthew fits with Pauline theology, such as their respective perspectives on the law. But overall, I let the reader explore those relationships as an outgrowth of having studied Matthew's theology.

I do believe that a study of the theology of Matthew's Gospel directly interacts with these debates. For example, in our day the role and future of ethnic Israel is one of the most hotly debated issues nationally and internationally in the religious and political worlds. Matthew's Gospel alone does not resolve that issue, but it is a powerful starting place from which we can move to the rest of the New Testament to see God's historical design. The rest of the authors of this series, Biblical Theology of the New Testament, I trust absolutely with their exegetical skills and biblical theological conclusions. I encourage you the readers to take this starting point in Matthew's Gospel to explore the rest of God's stupendous theology of the New Testament.

I pray that the next generations of the church, both in America and around the world, will in some small way be strengthened in commitment to the gospel through this exploration of the theology of the Gospel of Matthew.

# BIBLIOGRAPHY

THIS IS A sampling of the vast literature on Matthew's Gospel. The volumes and articles selected here are representative of the research for this volume, but this is not exhaustive. Many shorter studies, such as journal articles and chapters in books, are cited in the footnotes.


Adeyemo, Tokunboh, Solomon Andria, Issiaka Coulibaly, Tewoldemedhin Habtu, and Samuel Ngewa, eds. *Africa Bible Commentary: A One-Volume Commentary*. Nairobi, Kenya: WordAlive; Grand Rapids: Zondervan, 2006.

Ådna, Jostein, and Hans Kvalbein, eds. *The Mission of the Early Church to Jews and Gentiles*. WUNT 2/127. Tübingen: Mohr Siebeck, 2000.

Akagi, Kai. "The Quotation of Jer. 31.15 in Mt. 2.18 Within Christological Patterning of Matthew's Nativity According to the Joseph Story." *JSNT* 45.4 (2023): 405–28.

Akin, Daniel L., Benjamin L. Merkle, and George G. Robinson. *40 Questions About the Great Commission*. 40 Questions Series. Grand Rapids: Kregel, 2020.

Albright, W. F., and C. S. Mann. *Matthew*. AB 26. Garden City, New York: Doubleday, 1971.

Alexander, Ralph H. "A New Covenant—An Eternal People (Jeremiah 31)." Pages 169–206 in *Israel, the Land and the People: An Evangelical Affirmation of God's Promises*. Edited by H. Wayne House. Grand Rapids: Kregel, 1998.

Alexander, T. Desmond, Brian S. Rosner, D. A. Carson, and Graeme Goldsworthy, eds. *New Dictionary of Biblical Theology: Exploring the Unity and Diversity of Scripture*. Downers Grove, IL: InterVarsity, 2000.

Alfeyev, Hilarion. "The Gospel of Matthew in Church Tradition and Modern Scholarship." Pages 3–16 in Seleznev, Loader, and Niebuhr. *The Gospel of Matthew in Its Historical and Theological Context*. WUNT 459. Tübingen: Mohr Siebeck, 2021.

Allen, David L. *According to the Scriptures: The Death of Christ in the Old Testament and the New*. London: SCM, 2018.

Allen, David L. *The Atonement: A Biblical, Theological, and Historical Study of the Cross of Christ*. Nashville: B&H, 2019.

Allen, David L., and Steve W. Lemke, eds. *The Return of Christ: A Premillennial Perspective*. Nashville: B&H, 2011.

Allen, Ronald B. "The Land of Israel." Pages 18–33 in *Israel, the Land and the People: An Evangelical Affirmation of God's Promises*. Edited by H. Wayne House. Grand Rapids: Kregel, 1998.

Allison, Dale C., Jr. *The New Moses: A Matthean Typology*. Minneapolis: Fortress, 1993.

———. *Studies in Matthew: Interpretation Past and Present*. Grand Rapids: Baker Academic, 2005.

Allison, Gregg R. *Sojourners and Strangers: The Doctrine of the Church*. FET. Wheaton, IL: Crossway, 2012.

Anizor, Uche, and Hank Voss. *Representing Christ: A Vision for the Priesthood of All Believers*. Downers Grove, IL: InterVarsity, 2016.

Archer, Gleason L., and G. C. Chirichigno. *Old Testament Quotations in the New Testament: A Complete Survey*. Chicago: Moody, 1983.

Atkins, J. D. *The Doubt of the Apostles and the Resurrection Faith of the Early Church: The Post-Resurrection Appearance Stories of the Gospels in Ancient Reception and Modern Debate*. WUNT 495. Tübingen: Mohr Siebeck, 2019.

August, Jared M. "'He Shall Be Called a Nazarene': The Non-citation of Matthew 2:23." *TynBul* 69.1 (2018): 63–74.
Aune, David E. *The New Testament in Its Literary Environment*. LEC. Philadelphia: Westminster, 1987.
———, ed. *The Gospel of Matthew in Current Study: Studies in Memory of William G. Thompson, S.J.* Grand Rapids: Eerdmans, 2001.
Aus, Roger David. *Feeding the Five Thousand: Studies in the Judaic Background of Mark 6:30–44 par. and John 6:1–15*. Studies in Judaism. Lanham, MD: University Press of America, 2010.
———. *Matthew 1–2 and the Virginal Conception: In Light of Palestinian and Hellenistic Judaic Traditions on the Birth of Israel's First Redeemer, Moses*. Studies in Judaism. Lanham, MD: University Press of America, 2004.
Avery-Peck, Alan Jeffery, Daniel J. Harrington, and Jacob Neusner, eds. *When Judaism and Christianity Began. Essays in Memory of Anthony J. Saldarini*. 2 vols. SJSJ 85. Leiden: Brill, 2004.
Baasland, Ernst. *Parables and Rhetoric in the Sermon on the Mount: New Approaches to a Classical Text*. WUNT 351. Tübingen: Mohr Siebeck, 2015.
Bailey, Kenneth E. "Informal Controlled Oral Tradition and the Synoptic Gospels." *Asia Journal of Theology* 5.1 (1991): 34–54.
———. *Jesus Through Middle Eastern Eyes: Cultural Studies in the Gospels*. Downers Grove: InterVarsity, 2008.
Bakhos, Carol. *The Family of Abraham: Jewish, Christian, and Muslim Interpretations*. Cambridge, MA: Harvard University Press, 2014.
Balabanski, Vicky. "Mission in Matthew Against the Horizon of Matthew 24." *NTS* 54.2 (2008): 161–75.
Balch, David L. *Social History of the Matthean Community*. Minneapolis: Fortress, 1991.
Banks, Robert. *Jesus and the Law in the Synoptic Tradition*. Society for NTS Monograph Series 28. Cambridge: Cambridge University Press, 1975.
Barbieri, Louis, Jr. "Matthew." Pages 13–94 in vol. 2 of *The Bible Knowledge Commentary*. 2 vols. Edited by John F. Walvoord and Roy B. Zuck. Wheaton, IL: Victor, 1983.
Baron, Lori, Jill Hicks Keeton, and Matthew Thiessen, eds. *The Ways That Often Parted: Essays in Honor of Joel Marcus*. ECL 24. Atlanta: Society of Biblical Literature Press, 2018.
Barrett, Matthew, ed. *The Doctrine on Which the Church Stands or Falls: Justification in Biblical, Theological, Historical, and Pastoral Perspective*. Wheaton, IL: Crossway, 2019.
Bartlett, David L. *Christology in the New Testament*. Core Biblical Studies. Nashville: Abingdon, 2017.
Basser, Herbert W., with Marsha B. Cohen. *The Gospel of Matthew and Judaic Traditions: A Relevance-Based Commentary*. BRLA 46. Leiden: Brill, 2015.
Bateman, Herbert W., IV, ed. *Three Central Issues in Contemporary Dispensationalism: A Comparison of Traditional and Progressive Views*. Grand Rapids: Kregel, 1999.
Bateman, Herbert W., IV, Darrell L. Bock, and Gordon H. Johnston. *Jesus the Messiah: Tracing the Promises, Expectations, and Coming of Israel's King*. Grand Rapids: Kregel, 2011.
Bates, Matthew W. *The Birth of the Trinity: Jesus, God, and Spirit in New Testament and Early Christian Interpretations of the Old Testament*. Oxford: Oxford University Press, 2015.
———. *Salvation by Allegiance Alone: Rethinking Faith, Works, and the Gospel of Jesus the King*. Grand Rapids: Baker Academic, 2017.
Bauckham, Richard J. *Early Jewish Literature*. Volume 1 of *"Son of Man."* Grand Rapids: Eerdmans, 2023.
———. *Gospel Women: Studies of the Named Women in the Gospels*. Grand Rapids: Eerdmans, 2002.
———. "The Gospels as Testimony to Jesus Christ: A Contemporary View of Their Historical Value." Pages 55–70 in *OHC*.
———, ed. *The Gospels for All Christians: Rethinking the Gospel Audiences*. Grand Rapids: Eerdmans, 1998.
———. "James, Peter, and the Gentiles." Pages 91–142 in *The Missions of James, Peter, and Paul: Tensions in Early Christianity*. Edited by Bruce Chilton and Craig Evans. NovTSup 115. Leiden: Brill, 2005.
———. *Jesus and the Eyewitnesses: The Gospels as Eyewitness Testimony*. 2nd ed. Grand Rapids: Eerdmans, 2017.
———. *Jesus and the God of Israel:* God Crucified *and Other Studies on the New Testament's Christology of Divine Identity*. Grand Rapids: Eerdmans, 2008.
———. "The Messianic Interpretation of Isa. 10:34 in the Dead Sea Scrolls, 2 Baruch and the Preaching of John the Baptist." *DSD* 2.2 (1995): 202–16.
———. *Who Is God? Key Moments of Biblical Revelation*. ASBT. Grand Rapids: Baker Academic, 2020.
Bauckham, Richard, and Trevor Hart. *At the Cross: Meditations on People Who Were There*. Downers Grove, IL: InterVarsity, 1999.

Bauer, David R. *The Gospel of the Son of God: An Introduction to Matthew*. Downers Grove, IL: InterVarsity, 2019.

———. "The Literary and Theological Function of the Genealogy in Matthew's Gospel." Pages 129–59 in *Treasures New and Old: Recent Contributions to Matthean Studies*. Edited by David R. Bauer and Mark Allan Powell. SBLSymS 1. Atlanta: Scholars, 1996.

———. "Perfection of Disciples in Matthew's Gospel: An Examination of a Central Concept in Matthean Kingdom Ethics." Pages 3–20 in *Kingdom Rhetoric: New Testament Explorations in Honor of Ben Witherington III*. Edited by T. Michael W. Halcomb. Eugene, OR: Wipf & Stock, 2013.

———. *The Structure of Matthew's Gospel: A Study in Literary Design*. Bible and Literature Series 15; JSNTSup 31. Sheffield: Sheffield Academic, 1988.

———. "The Theme of Mission in Matthew's Gospel from the Perspective of the Great Commission." *Asbury Journal* 74.2 (2019): 240–76.

Bauer, David R. and Mark Allan Powell, eds. *Treasures New and Old: Recent Contributions to Matthean Studies*. Society of Biblical Literature Supplement Series 1. Atlanta: Scholars, 1996.

Baum, Armin D. "The Anonymity of the New Testament History Books: A Stylistic Device in the Context of Greco-Roman and Ancient Near Eastern Literature." *NovT* 50.2 (2008): 120–42.

———. "Biographies of Jesus in Old Testament and Rabbinic Style: The Genre of the New Testament Gospels." Pages 33–58 in *The Earliest Perceptions of Jesus in Context: Essays in Honour of John Nolland on His 70th Birthday*. Edited by Aaron W. White, Craig A. Evans and David Wenham. LNTS 566. London: Bloomsbury T&T Clark, 2018.

Baumgarten, Albert I. "An Ancient Debate of Disciples." Pages 1–18 in *Perceiving the Other in Ancient Judaism and Early Christianity*. Edited by Michal Bar-Asher Siegal, Wolfgang Grünstäudl, and Matthew Thiessen. WUNT 394. Tübingen: Mohr Siebeck, 2017.

Baxter, Wayne S. "Healing and the 'Son of David': Matthew's Warrant." *NovT* 48.1 (2006): 36–50.

———. "Missing Matthew's Political Messiah: A Closer Look at His Birth and Infancy Narratives." *BBR* 27.3 (2017): 333–50.

Bayer, Hans F. *Apostolic Bedrock: Christology, Identity, and Character Formation According to Peter's Canonical Testimony*. PBM. Milton Keynes, UK: Paternoster, 2016.

———. *Jesus' Predictions of Vindication and Resurrection: The Provenance, Meaning, and Correlation of the Synoptic Predictions*. WUNT 2/20. Tübingen: Mohr Siebeck, 1986.

Beale, G. K. *The Book of Revelation: A Commentary on the Greek Text*. NIGTC. Grand Rapids: Eerdmans, 1999.

———. *Handbook on the New Testament Use of the Old Testament: Exegesis and Interpretation*. Grand Rapids: Baker Academic, 2012.

———. *A New Testament Biblical Theology: The Unfolding of the Old Testament in the New*. Grand Rapids: Baker Academic, 2011.

Beale, G. K., and D. A. Carson, eds. *Commentary on the New Testament Use of the Old Testament*. Grand Rapids: Baker Academic, 2007.

Beare, Francis Wright. *The Gospel According to Matthew: Translation, Introduction and Commentary*. San Francisco: Harper and Row, 1981.

Beaseley-Murray, George R. *Jesus and the Kingdom of God*. Grand Rapids: Eerdmans, 1986.

Beaton, Richard. *Isaiah's Christ in Matthew's Gospel*. SNTSMS 123. Cambridge: Cambridge University Press, 2002.

———. "Messiah and Justice: A Key to Matthew's Use of Isaiah 42.1–4?" *JSNT* 75 (1999): 5–23.

Becker, Adam H., and Annette Yoshiko Reed, eds. *The Ways That Never Parted: Jews and Christians in Late Antiquity and the Early Middle Ages*. Minneapolis: Fortress, 2007.

Becker, Eve-Marie, and Anders Runesson, eds. *Mark and Matthew I. Comparative Readings: Understanding the Earliest Gospels in Their First Century Settings*. WUNT 271. Tübingen: Mohr Siebeck, 2011.

———. *Mark and Matthew II. Comparative Readings: Reception History, Cultural Hermeneutics, and Theology*. WUNT 304. Tübingen: Mohr Siebeck, 2013.

Beilby, James, and Paul R. Eddy, eds. *The Nature of the Atonement: Four Views*. Downers Grove, IL: InterVarsity, 2006.

Belcher, Richard P., Jr. *Prophet, Priest, and King: The Roles of Christ in the Bible and Our Roles Today*. Phillipsburg, PA: P&R, 2016.

Bendoraitis, Kristian A. *"Behold, the Angels Came and Served Him": A Compositional Analysis of Angels in Matthew*. LNTS 523. London: Bloomsbury T&T Clark, 2015.

Bendoraitis, Kristian A., and Nijay K. Gupta, eds. *Matthew and Mark Across Perspectives: Essays in Honour of Stephen C. Barton and William R. Telford*. LNTS 538. London: Bloomsbury T&T Clark, 2016.

Bennema, Cornelis. "Early Christian Identity Formation Amidst Conflict." *Journal of Early Christian History* 5.1 (2015): 26–48.

———. "The Ethnic Conflict in Early Christianity: An Appraisal of Bauckham's Proposal on the Antioch Crisis and the Jerusalem Council." *JETS* 56.4 (2013): 753–63.

Berding, Kenneth, and Jonathan Lunde, eds. *Three Views on the New Testament Use of the Old Testament*. Grand Rapids: Zondervan, 2008.

Berding, Kenneth, and Matt Williams. *What the New Testament Authors Really Cared About: A Survey of Their Writings*. Grand Rapids: Kregel, 2008.

Berg, InHee C. *Irony in the Matthean Passion Narrative*. Minneapolis: Augsburg Fortress, 2014.

Bernier, Jonathan. *Rethinking the Dates of the New Testament: The Evidence for Early Composition*. Grand Rapids: Baker Academic, 2022.

Best, Ernest. *Disciples and Discipleship: Studies in the Gospel According to Mark*. Edinburgh: T&T Clark, 1986.

Betz, Hans Dieter. *Essays on the Sermon on the Mount*. Philadelphia: Fortress, 1985.

———. *The Sermon on the Mount: A Commentary on the Sermon on the Mount, Including the Sermon on the Plain (Matthew 5:3–7:27 and Luke 6:20–49)*. Hermeneia. Minneapolis: Fortress, 1995.

*Biblia Patristica: Index des citations et allusions bibliques dans la littérature patristique*. Paris: Centre national de la recherche scientifique, 1975–.

Bingham, D. Jeffrey. *Irenaeus' Use of Matthew's Gospel in Adversus Haereses*. Traditio Exegetica Graeca 7. Leuven: Peeters, 1997.

Bird, Michael F. *Jesus and the Origins of the Gentile Mission*. LNTS 331. London: T&T Clark, 2006.

———. "Jesus and the 'Partings of the Ways.'" Pages 1183–1215 in vol. 2 of *HSHJ*. 4 vols. Edited by Tom Holmén and Stanley E. Porter. Leiden: Brill. 2011.

———. "Jesus as Law-Breaker." Pages 3–26 in *Who Do My Opponents Say That I Am? An Investigation of the Accusations Against the Historical Jesus*. Edited by Scot McKnight and Joseph B. Modica. LNTS 327. London: T&T Clark, 2008.

———. *Jesus Is the Christ: The Messianic Testimony of the Gospels*. Downers Grove, IL: InterVarsity, 2012.

———. *Jesus the Eternal Son: Answering Adoptionist Christology*. Grand Rapids: Eerdmans, 2017.

———. "New Testament Theology Re-loaded: Integrating Biblical Theology and Christian Origins." *TynBul* 60.2 (2009): 265–91.

Bird, Michael F., Craig A. Evans, Simon J. Gathercole, Charles E. Hill, and Chris Tilling. *How God Became Jesus: The Real Origins of Belief in Jesus' Divine Nature—A Response to Bart D. Ehrman*. Grand Rapids: Zondervan, 2014.

Bird, Michael F., and Scott Harrower, eds. *Trinity Without Hierarchy: Reclaiming Nicene Orthodoxy in Evangelical Theology*. Grand Rapids: Kregel, 2019.

Bird, Michael F., and Joel Willitts, eds. *Paul and the Gospels: Christologies, Conflicts and Convergences*. LNTS 411. London: Bloomsbury T&T Clark, 2011.

Black, C. Clifton. *The Lord's Prayer*. Interpretation. Louisville: Westminster John Knox, 2018.

Blaising, Craig A. "The Future of Israel as a Theological Question." *JETS* 44.3 (2001): 435–50.

———. "A Theology of Israel and the Church." Pages 85–100 in *Israel the Church and the Middle East: A Biblical Response to the Current Conflict*. Edited by Darrell Bock and Mitch Glaser. Grand Rapids: Kregel, 2018.

Blaising, Craig A., and Darrell L. Bock. *Progressive Dispensationalism*. Grand Rapids: Baker Academic, 1993.

Blanton, Thomas R., IV. "Saved By Obedience: Matthew 1:21 in Light of Jesus' Teaching on the Torah." *JBL* 132.2 (2013): 393–413.

Block, Daniel I. *Covenant: The Framework of God's Grand Plan of Redemption*. Grand Rapids: Baker Academic, 2021.

Blomberg, Craig L. "Freedom from the Law Only for Gentiles? A Non-Supersessionist Alternative to Mark Kinzer's 'Postmissionary Messianic Judaism.'" Pages 41–56 in *New Testament Theology in Light of the Church's Mission: Essays in Honor of I. Howard Marshall*. Edited by Jon C. Laansma, Grant R. Osborne, and Ray F. Van Neste. Eugene, OR: Cascade, 2011.

———. *The Historical Reliability of the Gospels*. 2nd ed. Downers Grove: InterVarsity, 2007.

———. *Matthew*. NAC 22. Nashville: Broadman, 1992.

———. "Matthew." Pages 1–109 in *Commentary on the New Testament Use of the Old Testament*. Edited by G. K. Beale and D. A. Carson. Grand Rapids: Baker Academic, 2007.

———. *A New Testament Theology.* Waco, TX: Baylor University Press, 2018.

Blumenthal, Christian. *Basileia im Matthäusevangelium.* WUNT 416. Tübingen: Mohr Siebeck, 2019.

Bock, Darrell L. *Blasphemy and Exaltation in Judaism: The Charge Against Jesus in Mark 14:53–65.* Tübingen: Mohr Siebeck, 1998. Repr., Grand Rapids: Baker Academic, 2000.

———. *Luke 1:1–9:50* and *Luke 9:51–24:53.* BECNT. Grand Rapids: Baker Books, 1994.

———. "A Note on Women as Witnesses and the Empty Tomb Resurrection." Pages 256–61 in *Raised on the Third Day: Defending the Historicity of the Resurrection of Jesus. Essays in Honor of Dr. Gary R. Habermas.* Edited by W. David Beck and Michael R. Licona. Bellingham, WA: Lexham Press, 2020.

———. "Single Meaning, Multiple Contexts and Referents: The New Testament's Legitimate, Accurate, and Multifaceted Use of the Old." Pages 105–66 in *Three Views on the New Testament Use of the Old Testament.* Edited by Kenneth Berding and Jonathan Lunde. Grand Rapids: Zondervan, 2008.

———. "The Words of Jesus in the Gospels: Live, Jive, or Memorex?." Pages 73–99 in *Jesus Under Fire: Modern Scholarship Reinvents the Historical Jesus.* Edited by Michael J. Wilkins and J. P. Moreland. Grand Rapids: Zondervan, 1995.

Bock, Darrell L., and Mitch Glaser, eds. *Israel the Church and the Middle East: A Biblical Response to the Current Conflict.* Grand Rapids: Kregel, 2018.

———, eds. *To the Jew First: The Case for Jewish Evangelism in Scripture and History.* Grand Rapids: Kregel, 2008.

Bock, Darrell L., with Benjamin I. Simpson. *Jesus According to Scripture: Restoring the Portrait from the Gospels.* 2nd ed. Grand Rapids: Baker Academic, 2017.

———. *Jesus the God-Man: The Unity and Diversity of the Gospel Portrayals.* Grand Rapids: Baker Academic, 2016.

Bock, Darrell L., and Robert L. Webb, eds. *Key Events in the Life of the Historical Jesus: A Collaborative Exploration of Context and Coherence.* WUNT 247. Tübingen: Mohr Siebeck, 2009.

Bockmuehl, Markus. "The Gospels on the Presence of Jesus." Pages 87–102 in *OHC.*

———. *The Remembered Peter in Ancient Reception and Modern Debate.* WUNT 262. Tübingen: Mohr Siebeck, 2010.

———. *Seeing the Word: Refocusing New Testament Study.* Studies in Theological Interpretation. Grand Rapids: Baker Academic, 2006.

———. *Simon Peter in Scripture and Memory: The New Testament Apostle in the Early Church.* Grand Rapids: Baker Academic, 2012.

———. "A 'Slain Messiah' in 4Q Serekh Milhamah (4Q285)?" *TynBul* 43.1 (1992): 155–69.

Bockmuehl, Markus, and Donald A. Hagner, eds. *The Written Gospel.* Cambridge: Cambridge University Press, 2005.

Bockmuehl, Markus, and James Carleton Paget, eds. *Redemption and Resistance: The Messianic Hopes of Jews and Christians in Antiquity.* London: T&T Clark, 2007.

Bond, Helen K. *Pontius Pilate in History and Interpretation.* SNTSMS 100. Cambridge, Cambridge University Press, 1998.

Bond, Helen K., and Larry W. Hurtado, eds. *Peter in Early Christianity.* Grand Rapids: Eerdmans, 2015.

Bonnard, Pierre. *L'évangile selon Saint Matthieu.* 2nd ed. Commentaire du Nouveau Testament 1. 2nd series. Neuchatel, Switzerland: Delachaux & Niestle, 1970.

Borg, Marcus J. *Conflict, Holiness & Politics in the Teachings of Jesus.* Studies in Bible and Early Christianity 5. New York: Edwin Mellin, 1984.

Borg, Marcus J., and John Dominic Crossan. *The Last Week: A Day-by-Day Account of Jesus's Final Week in Jerusalem.* New York: HarperCollins, 2006.

Boring, M. Eugene. "The Gospel of Matthew: Introduction, Commentary, and Reflections." Pages 87–505 in vol. 8 of *The New Interpreter's Bible.* Edited by Leander E. Keck. Nashville: Abingdon, 1995.

Bornkamm, Günther. "End-Expectation and Church in Matthew." Pages 15–51 in *Tradition and Interpretation in Matthew.* Edited by Günther Bornkamm, Gerhard Barth, and Heinz Joachim Held. Translated by Percy Scott. Philadelphia: Westminster, 1963.

———. "The Stilling of the Storm in Matthew." Pages 52–57 in *Tradition and Interpretation in Matthew.* Edited by Günther Bornkamm, Gerhard Barth, and Heinz Joachim Held. Translated by Percy Scott. Philadelphia: Westminster, 1963.

Bornkamm, Günther, Gerhard Barth, and Heinz Joachim Held, eds. *Tradition and Interpretation in Matthew.* Translated by Percy Scott. Philadelphia: Westminster, 1963.

Borowitz, Eugene B. *Contemporary Christologies: A Jewish Response.* New York: Paulist, 1980.

Botner, Max, Justin Harrison Duff, and Simon Dürr, eds. *Atonement: Jewish and Christian Origins.* Grand Rapids: Eerdmans, 2020.

Boxall, Ian. *Discovering Matthew: Content, Interpretation, Reception.* Discovering Biblical Texts. Grand Rapids: Eerdmans, 2015.

———. "Joseph Son of David in the Reception History of Matthew's Gospel." Pages 29–46 in Seleznev, Loader, and Niebuhr. *The Gospel of Matthew in Its Historical and Theological Context.* WUNT 459. Tübingen: Mohr Siebeck, 2021.

———. *Matthew Through the Centuries.* WBBC. Hoboken, NJ: Wiley, 2019.

Boyd, Gregory A. *Crucifixion of the Warrior God: Interpreting the Old Testament's Violent Portraits of God in Light of the Cross.* Volume 1: *The Cruciform Hermeneutic.* Volume 2: *The Cruciform Thesis.* Minneapolis: Fortress, 2017.

Brands, Michael. *The Life and Ministry of Jesus as Enactment of the Great Commission: A New Proposal for Interpreting Matthew 28:16–20 in Light of Matthew's Gospel.* Lewiston, NY: Mellen, 2015.

Brannon, M. Jeff. *The Hope of Life After Death: A Biblical Theology of Resurrection.* ESBT. Downers Grove, IL: InterVarsity, 2022.

Bray, Gerald L. *God Is Love: A Biblical and Systematic Theology.* Wheaton, IL: Crossway, 2012.

Bridge, Edward. "Christians and Jews in Antioch." Pages 208–36 in *Into All the World: Emergent Christianity in Its Jewish and Greco-Roman Context.* Edited by Mark Harding and Alanna Nobbs. Grand Rapids: Eerdmans, 2017.

Brindle, Wayne A. "'To the Jew First': Rhetoric, Strategy, History, or Theology?" *BSac* 159 (2002): 221–33.

Broadhead, Edwin K. *Jewish Ways of Following Jesus: Redrawing the Religious Map of Antiquity.* WUNT 266. Tübingen: Mohr Siebeck, 2010.

Brown, Jeannine K. "Direct Engagement of the Reader in Matthew's Discourses: Rhetorical Techniques and Scholarly Consensus." *NTS* 51.1 (2005): 19–35.

———. *The Disciples in Narrative Perspective: The Portrayal and Function of the Matthean Disciples.* AcBib 9. Atlanta: SBL Press, 2002.

———. *Matthew.* Teach the Text Commentary Series. Grand Rapids: Baker Books, 2015.

———. "Matthew, Gospel of." *DJG*[2] 570–84.

———. "Matthew's Christology and Isaiah's Servant: A Fresh Look at a Perennial Issue." Pages 93–106 in Sweatman and Kvidahl. *Treasures New & Old: Essays in Honor of Donald A. Hagner.* GlossaHouse Festschrift Series 1. Wilmore, KY: GlossaHouse, 2018.

Brown, Jeannine K., and Kyle Roberts. *Matthew.* THNTC. Grand Rapids: Eerdmans, 2018.

Brown, Raymond E. *The Birth of the Messiah: A Commentary on the Infancy Narratives in the Gospels of Matthew and Luke.* New updated ed. ABRL. New York: Doubleday, 1993.

———. *The Death of the Messiah: From Gethsemane to the Grave. A Commentary on the Passion Narratives in the Four Gospels.* 2 volumes. ABRL. New York: Doubleday, 1994.

———. *The* Sensus Plenior *of Sacred Scripture.* Baltimore: St Mary's University Press, 1955. Repr., 1960. Repr., Eugene, OR: Wipf & Stock, 2008.

Brown, Raymond E., Karl P. Donfried, and John Reumann, eds. *Peter in the New Testament: A Collaborative Assessment by Protestant and Catholic Scholars.* Minneapolis: Augsburg, 1973.

Brown, Schuyler. "The Matthean Community and the Gentile Mission." *NovT* 22.3 (1980): 193–220.

———. "The Mission to Israel in Matthew's Central Section (Mt 9:35–11:1)." *ZNW* 69 (1978): 73–90.

Brueggemann, Walter. *The Land: Place as Gift, Promise, and Challenge in Biblical Faith.* Rev. ed. OBT. Minneapolis: Augsburg Fortress, 2002.

Bruner, Frederick Dale. *Matthew: A Commentary.* 2 vols. Rev. and exp. ed. Grand Rapids: Eerdmans, 2004.

Bruno, Chris, Jared Compton, and Kevin McFadden. *Biblical Theology According to the Apostles: How the Earliest Christians Told the Story of Israel.* NSBT 52. Downers Grove, IL: InterVarsity, 2020.

Bryan, Christopher. *The Resurrection of the Messiah.* Oxford: Oxford University Press, 2011.

Bryan, Steven M. "Jesus and Israel's Eschatological Constitution." Pages 2835–54 in vol. 3 of *HSHJ.* Edited by Tom Holmén and Stanley E. Porter. Leiden: Brill, 2011.

———. *Jesus and Israel's Traditions of Judgement and Restoration.* SNTSMS 117. Cambridge: Cambridge University Press. 2002.

Burer, Michael H. *Divine Sabbath Work.* BBRSup 5. Winona Lake, IN: Eisenbrauns, 2012.

Burk, Denny, James M. Hamilton Jr., and Brian J. Vickers, eds. *God's Glory Revealed in Christ: Essays on Biblical Theology in Honor of Thomas R. Schreiner.* Nashville: B&H, 2019.

Burke, Trevor J., and Keith Warrington, eds. *A Biblical Theology of the Holy Spirit.* Eugene, OR: Cascade, 2014.

Burkett, Delbert. *The Son of Man Debate: A History and Evaluation.* SNTSMS 107. Cambridge: Cambridge University Press, 1999.

Burnet, Régis. *Exegesis and History of Reception: Reading the New Testament Today with the Readers of the Past.* WUNT 455. Tübingen: Mohr Siebeck, 2021.

Burridge, Richard A. *Four Gospels, One Jesus? A Symbolic Reading.* 3rd ed. Grand Rapids: Eerdmans, 2014.

———. "Matthew and Gospel Genre: A Critical Review of the Last 25 Years, 1993–2018." Pages 47–74 in Seleznev, Loader, and Niebuhr. *The Gospel of Matthew in Its Historical and Theological Context.* WUNT 459. Tübingen: Mohr Siebeck, 2021.

———. *What Are the Gospels? A Comparison with Graeco-Roman Biography.* 25th anniversary (3rd) ed. Waco, TX: Baylor University Press, 2018.

Byrskog, Samuel. *Jesus the Only Teacher: Didactic Authority and Transmission in Ancient Israel.* ConBNT 24. Stockholm: Almquist & Wiksell, 1994.

———. "Jesus the Only Teacher: Further Thoughts." Pages 36–46 in *Treasures New & Old: Essays in Honor of Donald A. Hagner.* Edited by Carl S. Sweatman and Clifford B. Kvidahl. GlossaHouse Festschrift Series 1. Wilmore, KY: GlossaHouse, 2018.

Cabrido, John Aranda. *A Portrayal of Jesus in the Gospel of Matthew: A Narrative-Critical and Theological Study.* Lewiston, NY: Edwin Mellen, 2010.

Calvin, John. *A Harmony of the Gospels: Matthew, Mark and Luke.* Volume 1: *Matthew, Mark and Luke.* Translated by A.W. Morrison. Edited by David W. Torrance and Thomas F. Torrance. Edinburgh: Saint Andrew Press, 1972.

Caneday, Ardel. "Biblical Types: Revelation Concealed in Plain Sight to be Disclosed—'These Things Occurred Typologically to Them and Were Written Down for Our Admonition.'" Pages 134–55 in Burk, Hamilton, and Vickers, *God's Glory Revealed in Christ.* Nashville: B&H, 2019.

Caragounis, Chrys. *Peter and the Rock.* BZNW 58. Berlin: de Gruyter, 1990.

Carey, Greg. *Death, the End of History, and Beyond: Eschatology in the Bible.* Interpretation. Louisville: Westminster John Knox, 2023.

———. *Sinners: Jesus and His Earliest Followers.* Waco, TX: Baylor University Press, 2009.

Carlston, Charles E., and Craig A. Evans. *From Synagogue to Ecclesia: Matthew's Community at the Crossroads.* WUNT 334. Tübingen: Mohr Siebeck, 2014.

Carrier, Brian. *Earthquakes and Eschatology in the Gospel According to Matthew.* WUNT 2/534. Tübingen: Mohr Siebeck, 2020.

Carroll, R. M. Daniel. "Blessing the Nations: Toward a Biblical Theology of Mission from Genesis." *BBR* 10.1 (2000): 17–34.

Carson, D. A., ed. *The Enduring Authority of the Christian Scriptures.* Grand Rapids: Eerdmans, 2016.

———. *The Gospel According to John.* PNTC. Grand Rapids: Eerdmans, 1990.

———. *Jesus the Son of God: A Christological Title Often Overlooked, Sometimes Misunderstood, and Currently Disputed.* Wheaton, IL: Crossway, 2012.

———. "Matthew." Pages 23–670 in *Matthew–Mark.* REBC 9. Rev. ed. 13 vols. Edited by Tremper Longman III and David E. Garland. Grand Rapids: Zondervan, 2010.

———. *Scandalous: The Cross and Resurrection of Jesus.* Wheaton, IL: Crossway, 2010.

———. *The Sermon on the Mount: An Evangelical Exposition of Matthew 5–7.* Grand Rapids: Baker Book House, 1982.

Carson, D. A., and Jeff Robinson Sr., eds. *Coming Home: Essays on the New Heaven and New Earth.* Wheaton, IL: Crossway, 2017.

Carter, Warren. "The Disciples." Pages 81–102 in *Jesus Among Friends and Enemies: A Historical and Literary Introduction to Jesus in the Gospels.* Edited by Chris Keith and Larry W. Hurtado. Grand Rapids: Baker Academic, 2011.

———. *Households and Discipleship: A Study of Matthew 19–20.* JSNTSup 103. Sheffield: JSOT Press, 1994.

———. "Kernels and Narrative Blocks: The Structure of Matthew's Gospel." *CBQ* 54.3 (1992): 463–81.

———. *Matthew: Storyteller, Interpreter, Evangelist.* Peabody, MA: Hendrickson, 1996.

Case-Winters, Anna. *Matthew.* Belief. Louisville: Westminster John Knox, 2015.

Catchpole, David. *Jesus People: The Historical Jesus and the Beginnings of Community.* Grand Rapids: Baker Academic, 2006.

Chae, Young S. *Jesus as the Eschatological Davidic Shepherd: Studies in the Old Testament, Second Temple Judaism, and in the Gospel of Matthew.* WUNT 2/216. Tübingen: Mohr Siebeck, 2006.

Chan, Sam. *Evangelism in a Skeptical World: How to Make the Unbelievable News About Jesus More Believable.* Grand Rapids: Zondervan, 2018.

Chanikuzhy, Jacob. *Jesus, the Eschatological Temple: An Exegetical Study of Jn 2,13–22 in the Light of the Pre 70 C.E. Eschatological Temple Hopes and the Synoptic Temple Actions.* CBET 58. Leuven: Peeters, 2012.

Chapman, David W. *Ancient Jewish and Christian Perceptions of Crucifixion.* WUNT 2/244. Tübingen: Mohr Siebeck, 2008.

———. "Perceptions of Crucifixion among Jews and Christians in the Ancient World." *TynBul* 51.2 (2000): 313–16.

Chapman, David W., and Eckhard J. Schnabel. *The Trial and Crucifixion of Jesus: Texts and Commentary.* WUNT 344. Tübingen: Mohr Siebeck, 2015.

Charette, Blaine. *The Theme of Recompense in Matthew's Gospel.* JSNTSup 79. Sheffield: JSOT Press, 1992.

Charles, J. Daryl. "Garnishing with the 'Greater Righteousness': The Disciple's Relationship to the Law (Matthew 5:17–20)." *BBR* 12.1 (2002): 1–15.

Chilton, Bruce. "The Gospel According to John's Rabbi Jesus." *BBR* 25.1 (2015): 39–54.

———. *Resurrection Logic: How Jesus' First Followers Believed God Raised Him from the Dead.* Waco, TX: Baylor University Press, 2019.

Chilton, Bruce, et al. "(The) Son of (the) Man, and Jesus." Pages 533–60 in *A Comparative Handbook to the Gospel of Mark: Comparisons with Pseudepigrapha, the Qumran Scrolls, and Rabbinic Literature.* Edited by Bruce Chilton, Darrell Bock, Daniel M. Gurtner, Jacob Neusner, Lawrence H. Schiffman, and Daniel Oden. New Testament Gospels in Their Judaic Contexts 1. Leiden: Brill, 2010.

Chilton, Bruce, Anthony Le Donne, Jacob Neusner, eds. *Soundings in the Religion of Jesus: Perspectives and Methods in Jewish and Christian Scholarship.* Minneapolis: Fortress, 2012.

Chung, Woojin. *Translation Theory and the Old Testament in Matthew: The Possibilities of Skopos Theory.* Linguistic Biblical Studies 15. Leiden: Brill, 2017.

Clark, John C., and Marcus Peter Johnson. *A Call to Christian Formation: How Theology Makes Sense of Our World.* Grand Rapids: Baker Academic, 2021.

Clark, Kenneth W. "The Gentile Bias in Matthew." *JBL* 66 (1947): 165–72.

Cohen, Akiva. *Matthew and the Mishnah: Redefining Identity and Ethos in the Shadow of the Second Temple's Destruction.* WUNT 2/418. Tübingen: Mohr Siebeck, 2016.

Cohick, Lynn H. *Women in the World of the Earliest Christians: Illuminating Ancient Ways of Life.* Grand Rapids: Baker Academic, 2009.

Cole, Graham A. *Against the Darkness: The Doctrine of Angels, Satan, and Demons.* FET. Wheaton, IL: Crossway, 2019.

———. *He Who Gives Life: The Doctrine of the Holy Spirit.* FET. Wheaton, IL: Crossway, 2007.

Collins, Adela Yarbro, and John J. Collins. *King and Messiah as Son of God: Divine, Human, and Angelic Messianic Figures in Biblical and Related Literature.* Grand Rapids: Eerdmans, 2008.

Collins, John J., and Daniel C. Harlow, eds. *The Eerdmans Dictionary of Early Judaism.* Grand Rapids: Eerdmans, 2010.

Cook, John Granger. *Crucifixion in the Mediterranean World.* WUNT 327. Tübingen: Mohr Siebeck, 2014.

Cousland, J. R. C. *The Crowds in the Gospel of Matthew.* NovTSup 102. Leiden: Brill, 2002.

Cox, Steven. "The Eschatology of the Gospels." Loc. 4884–5667 in *The Return of Christ: A Premillennial Perspective.* Edited by David L. Allen and Steve W. Lemke. Nashville: B&H, 2011. Kindle edition.

Craig, William Lane. *Assessing the New Testament Evidence for the Historicity of the Resurrection of Jesus.* Lewiston, NY: Edwin Mellin, 1989.

———. *The Atonement.* Elements in the Philosophy of Religion. Cambridge: Cambridge University Press, 2018.

———. *Atonement and the Death of Christ: An Exegetical, Historical, and Philosophical Exploration.* Waco, TX: Baylor University Press, 2020.

———. "Did Jesus Rise from the Dead?" Pages 142–76 in *Jesus Under Fire: Modern Scholarship Reinvents the Historical Jesus.* Edited by Michael J. Wilkins and J. P. Moreland. Grand Rapids: Zondervan, 1995.

Crisp, Oliver D. *Divinity and Humanity: The Incarnation Reconsidered.* Current Issues in Theology. Cambridge: Cambridge University Press, 2007.

———. *Participation and Atonement: An Analytic and Constructive Account.* Grand Rapids: Baker Academic, 2022.

Crisp, Oliver D. and Fred Sanders, eds. *Locating Atonement: Explorations in Constructive Dogmatics*. Los Angeles Theology Conference 3. Grand Rapids: Zondervan, 2015.

Crowe, Brandon D. *The Last Adam: A Theology of the Obedient Life of Jesus in the Gospels*. Grand Rapids: Baker Academic, 2017.

———. *The Obedient Son: Deuteronomy and Christology in the Gospel of Matthew*. BZNW 188. Berlin: de Gruyter, 2012.

———. *Why Did Jesus Live a Perfect Life? The Necessity of Christ's Obedience for Our Salvation*. Grand Rapids: Baker Academic, 2021.

Crowe, Brandon D., and Carl R. Truman, eds. *The Essential Trinity: New Testament Foundations and Practical Relevance*. Phillipsburg, NJ: P&R, 2017.

Cullman, Oscar. *The Christology of the New Testament*. Translated by Shirley C. Guthrie and Charles A. M. Hall. Philadelphia: Westminster Press, 1959.

———. *Peter: Disciple, Apostle, Martyr: A Historical and Theological Essay*. Translated by Floyd V. Filson. 2nd ed. Philadelphia: Westminster, 1962.

Culpepper, R. Alan. *Matthew: A Commentary*. NTL. Louisville: Westminster John Knox, 2021.

Cuvillier, Élian. *L'évangile de Matthieu*. Pages 21–151 in *Le Nouveau Testament Commenté*. Edited by Camille Focant and Daniel Marguerat. Paris: Bayard; Geneva: Labor et Fides, 2012.

———. "Torah Observance and Radicalization in the First Gospel. Matthew and First-Century Judaism: A Contribution to the Debate." *NTS* 55.2 (2009): 144–59.

Davies, W. D. *The Gospel and the Land: Early Christianity and Jewish Territorial Doctrine*. Berkeley: University of California Press, 1974.

Davies, W. D., and Dale C. Allison Jr. *A Critical and Exegetical Commentary on the Gospel According to Saint Matthew*. 3 vols. ICC. Edinburgh: T&T Clark, 1988–1997.

Davis, James F. *Lex Talionis in Early Judaism and the Exhortation of Jesus in Matthew 5.38–42*. JSNTSup 281. London: T&T Clark, 2005.

Davis, Stephen T. *Risen Indeed: Making Sense of the Resurrection*. Grand Rapids: Eerdmans, 1993.

Davis, Stephen, Daniel Kendall, and Gerald O'Collins, eds. *The Resurrection: An Interdisciplinary Symposium on the Resurrection of Jesus*. Oxford: Oxford University Press, 1997.

Deines, Roland. *Acts of God in History: Studies Towards Recovering a Theological Historiography*. Edited by Christoph Ochs and Peter Watts. WUNT 317. Tübingen: Mohr Siebeck, 2013.

———. "The Description of Faith in the Gospel of Matthew." Pages 125–64 in *Treasures New & Old: Essays in Honor of Donald A. Hagner*. Edited by Carl S. Sweatman and Clifford B. Kvidahl. GlossaHouse Festschrift Series 1. Wilmore, KY: GlossaHouse, 2018.

———. "Did Matthew Know He was Writing Scripture? Part 1." *EuroJTh* 22 (2013): 101–9.

———. "Did Matthew Know He was Writing Scripture? Part 2." *EuroJTh* 23 (2014): 3–12.

———. *Die Gerechtigkeit der Tora im Reich des Messias: Mt 5,13–20 als Schlüsseltext der matthäischen Theologie*. WUNT 177. Tübingen: Mohr Siebeck, 2004.

———. "Gerechtigkeit, die zum Leben führt: Die christologische Bestimmtheit der Glaubenden bei Matthäus." *ZNT* 36.18 (2015): 45–55.

———. "The Holy Spirit in Matthew's Gospel." Pages 213–35 in *The Earliest Perceptions of Jesus in Context: Essays in Honour of John Nolland*. Edited by Aaron White, David Wenham, and Craig A. Evans. LNTS 566. London: Bloomsbury T&T Clark, 2018.

———. "Jesus and Scripture: Scripture and the Self-Understanding of Jesus." Pages 39–70, 225–234 (notes) in *All That the Prophets Have Declared: The Appropriation of Scripture in the Emergence of Christianity*. Edited by Matthew R. Malcolm. Milton Keynes, UK: Paternoster, 2015.

———. "Jesus and the Torah According to the Gospel of Matthew." Pages 295–328 in Seleznev, Loader, and Niebuhr. *The Gospel of Matthew in Its Historical and Theological Context*. WUNT 459. Tübingen: Mohr Siebeck, 2021.

———. "Not the Law but the Messiah: Law and Righteousness in the Gospel of Matthew—An Ongoing Debate." Pages 53–84 in *Built upon the Rock: Studies in the Gospel of Matthew*. Edited by Daniel M. Gurtner and John Nolland. Grand Rapids: Eerdmans, 2008.

Demarest, Bruce. *The Cross and Salvation: The Doctrine of Salvation*. FET. Wheaton, IL: Crossway, 1997.

Dennert, Brian C. *John the Baptist and the Jewish Setting of Matthew*. WUNT 2/403. Tübingen: Mohr Siebeck, 2015.

Dennis, John A. "Death of Jesus." *DJG*[2] 172–93.

Derickson, Gary W. "Matthew's Chiastic Structure and Its Dispensational Implications." *BSac* 163 (2006): 423–37.

Deutsch, Celia M. *Hidden Wisdom and the Easy Yoke: Wisdom, Torah, and Discipleship in Matthew 11:25–30.* Sheffield: JSOT Press, 1987.

———. *Lady Wisdom, Jesus, and the Sages: Metaphor and Social Context in Matthew's Gospel.* Philadelphia: Trinity Press International, 1996.

Diehl, Judith A. "What is a 'Gospel'? Recent Studies in the Gospel Genre." *CurBR* 9.2 (2011): 171–99.

Dinkler, Michal Beth. "What Is a Genre?" Pages 77–96 in *Modern and Ancient Literary Criticism of the Gospels: Continuing the Debate on Gospel Genre(s).* Edited by Robert Matthew Calhoun, David P. Moessner, and Tobias Nicklas. WUNT 451. Tübingen: Mohr Siebeck, 2020.

Diprose, Ronald E. *Israel and the Church: The Origin and Effects of Replacement Theology.* Bucks, UK: Authentic Media, 2004.

Doane, Sébastien. "Rachel Weeping: Intertextuality as a Means of Transforming the Readers' Worldview." *JBRec* 4.1 (2017): 1–20.

Donaldson, Terence L. *Gentile Christian Identity from Cornelius to Constantine: The Nations, the Parting of the Ways, and Roman Imperial Ideology.* Grand Rapids: Eerdmans, 2020.

———. *Jesus on the Mountain: A Study in Matthean Theology.* JSNTSup 8. Sheffield: JSOT Press, 1985.

———. "'Nations,' 'Non-Jewish Nations,' or 'Non-Jewish Individuals.'" Pages 169–94 in *Matthew Within Judaism: Israel and the Nations in the First Gospel.* Edited by Anders Runesson and Daniel M. Gurtner. ECL 27. Atlanta: Society of Biblical Literature Press, 2020.

———. "The Vindicated Son: A Narrative Approach to Matthean Christology." Pages 100–21 in *Contours of Christology in the New Testament.* Edited by Richard N. Longenecker. MNTS. Grand Rapids: Eerdmans, 2005.

Donato, Christopher John, ed. *Perspectives on the Sabbath: Four Views.* Nashville: B&H, 2011.

Doriani, Daniel M. "The Deity of Christ in the Synoptic Gospels." *JETS* 37.3 (1994): 333–50.

———. *Matthew.* 2 volumes. Reformed Expository Commentary. Phillipsburg, NJ: P&R, 2008.

———. *The Sermon on the Mount: The Character of a Disciple.* Phillipsburg, NJ: 2006.

Downing, F. Gerald. "The Woman from Syrophoenicia, and Her Doggedness: Mark 7:24–31 (Matthew 15:21–28)." Pages 129–49 in *Women in the Biblical Tradition.* Edited by George J. Brooke. Studies in Women and Religion 31. Lewiston: Edwin Mellen, 1992.

Drimbe, Amiel. *The Church of Antioch and the Eucharistic Traditions (ca. 35–130 CE).* WUNT 2/529. Tübingen: Mohr Siebeck, 2020.

Duff, Paul B. *Jesus Followers in the Roman Empire.* Grand Rapids: Eerdmans, 2017.

Duling, Dennis C. *A Marginal Scribe: Studies in the Gospel of Matthew in a Social-Scientific Perspective.* Matrix: The Bible in Its Mediterranean Context 7. Eugene, OR: Wipf & Stock, 2012.

Dungan, David Laird. *A History of the Synoptic Problem: The Canon, the Text, the Composition, and the Interpretation of the Gospels.* ABRL. New York: Doubleday, 1999.

Dunn, James D. G. *Beginning from Jerusalem.* Volume 2 of *Christianity in the Making.* Grand Rapids: Eerdmans, 2009.

———. *Jesus' Call to Discipleship.* Cambridge: Cambridge University Press, 1992.

———. *Jesus Remembered.* Volume 1 of *Christianity in the Making.* Grand Rapids: Eerdmans, 2003.

———, ed. *Jews and Christians: The Parting of the Ways, A. D. 70 to 135.* The Second Durham-Tubingen Research Symposium on Earliest Christianity and Judaism (September, 1989). WUNT 66. Tübingen: Mohr Siebeck, 1992.

———. *The Oral Gospel Tradition.* Grand Rapids: Eerdmans, 2013.

———. *The Partings of the Ways Between Christianity and Judaism and their Significance for the Character of Christianity.* 2nd ed. London: SCM, 1991; 2006.

Du Toit, Philip La Grange. "The Fulfilment of the Law According to Matthew 5:17: A Dialectical Approach." *Acta Theologica* 38.2 (2018): 49–69.

———. "The Hermeneutical Dilemma Behind 'Anti-Judaism' in the New Testament: An Evangelical Perspective." *Conspectus* (2015): 43–88.

Dvořáček, Jiří. *The Son of David in Matthew's Gospel in the Light of the Solomon as Exorcist Tradition.* WUNT 2/415. Tübingen: Mohr Siebeck, 2016.

Edwards, J. Christopher. *The Ransom Logion in Mark and Matthew: Its Reception and Its Significance for the Study of the Gospels.* WUNT 2/327. Tübingen: Mohr Siebeck, 2012.

Edwards, James R. *The Hebrew Gospel and the Development of the Synoptic Tradition*. Grand Rapids: Eerdmans, 2009.

Edwards, Richard A. *Matthew's Narrative Portrait of Disciples: How the Text-Connoted Reader Is Informed*. Harrisburg, PA: Trinity Press International, 1997.

———. *Matthew's Story of Jesus*. Philadelphia: Fortress, 1985.

Ehrman, Bart D., and Zlatko Pleše. *The Apocryphal Gospels: Texts and Translations*. Oxford: Oxford University Press, 2011.

Ehrman, Bart D., Craig A. Evans, and Robert B. Stewart. *Can We Trust the Bible on the Historical Jesus?* Louisville: Westminster John Knox, 2022.

Eire, Carlos M. N. *A Very Brief History of Eternity*. Princeton, NJ: Princeton University Press, 2009.

Eklund, Rebekah. *Jesus Wept: The Significance of Jesus' Laments in the New Testament*. LNTS 515. London: Bloomsbury T&T Clark, 2015.

———. "Matthew, the Cross, and the Cruciform Life." Pages 16–30 in *Cruciform Scripture: Cross, Participation, and Mission*. Edited by Christopher W. Skinner, Nijay K. Gupta, Andy Johnson, and Drew J. Strait. Grand Rapids: Eerdmans, 2021.

Elliott, John H. *Introduction, Mesopotamia, and Egypt*. Vol. 1 of *Beware the Evil Eye: The Evil Eye in the Bible and the Ancient World*. 4 vols. Eugene, OR: Cascade, 2015.

Ellis, E. Earle. *The Old Testament in Early Christianity: Canon and Interpretation in the Light of Modern Research*. WUNT 54. Tübingen: Mohr Siebeck, 1991.

———. *Prophecy and Hermeneutic in Early Christianity: New Testament Essays*. WUNT 18. Tübingen: Mohr Siebeck, 1978.

———. "Pseudonymity and Canonicity of New Testament Documents." Pages 212–24 in *Worship, Theology, and Ministry in the Early Church: Essays in Honor of Ralph P. Martin*. Edited by Michael J. Wilkins and Terence Paige. JSNTSup 87. Sheffield: JSOT Press, 1992.

Emadi, Samuel. "Intertextuality in New Testament Scholarship: Significance, Criteria, and the Art of Intertextual Reading." *CurBR* 14.1 (2015): 8–23.

Emerson, Matthew Y. *"He Descended to the Dead": An Evangelical Theology of Holy Saturday*. Downers Grove, IL: InterVarsity, 2019.

Erickson, Millard J. *Christian Theology*. 3rd ed. Grand Rapids: Baker Academic, 2013.

Erickson, Richard J. "Joseph and the Birth of Isaac in Matthew 1." *BBR* 10.1 (2000): 35–51.

Esler, Philip F. "Ethnic Identities in the Dead Sea Legal Papyri and Matthew: Reinterpreting Matthew 25:31–46." Pages 195–210 in Runesson and Gurtner, *Matthew Within Judaism*. ECL 27. Atlanta: Society of Biblical Literature Press, 2020.

———. "The Righteousness of Joseph: Interpreting Matt 1.18–25 in Light of Judean Legal Papyri." *NTS* 68.3 (2022): 326–43.

Eubank, Nathan. "Merit and Anti-Judaism in Matthew's Parables Since Jülicher." Pages 425–46 in Runesson and Gurtner, *Matthew Within Judaism*. ECL 27. Atlanta: Society of Biblical Literature Press, 2020.

———. "Prison, Penance, or Purgatory: The Interpretation of Matthew 5.25–26 and Parallels." *NTS* 64.2 (2018): 162–77.

———. *Wages of Cross-Bearing and Debt of Sin: The Economy of Heaven in Matthew's Gospel*. BZNW 196. Berlin: de Gruyter, 2013.

———. "What Does Matthew Say About Divine Recompense? On the Misuse of the Parable of the Workers in the Vineyard (20:1–16)." *JSNT* 35.3 (2013): 242–62.

Eurell, John-Christian. *Peter's Legacy in Early Christianity: The Appropriation and Use of Peter's Authority in the First Three Centuries*. WUNT 2/561. Tübingen: Mohr Siebeck, 2021.

Evans, Craig A. "'The Book of the Genesis of Jesus Christ': The Purpose of Matthew in Light of the Incipit." Pages 61–72 in *The Gospel of Matthew*, vol. 2 of *Biblical Interpretation in Early Christian Gospels*. Edited by Thomas R. Hatina. LNTS 310. London: T&T Clark, 2008.

———. *From Prophecy to Testament: The Function of the Old Testament in the New*. Peabody, MA: Hendrickson, 2004.

———. "Fulfilling the Law and Seeking Righteousness in Matthew and in the Dead Sea Scrolls." Pages 102–14 in *Jesus, Matthew's Gospel and Early Christianity: Studies in Memory of Graham N. Stanton*. Edited by Daniel M. Gurtner, Joel Willitts, and Richard A. Burridge. LNTS 435; London: T&T Clark, 2011.

———. "'He Laid Him in a Tomb' (Mark 15:46): Roman Law and the Burial of Jesus." Pages 52–66 in *Matthew and Mark Across Perspectives: Essays in Honour of Stephen C. Barton and William R. Telford*. Edited by Kristian A. Bendoraitis and Nijay K. Gupta. LNTS 538. London: Bloomsbury T&T Clark, 2016.

———. *Matthew*. New Cambridge Bible Commentary. Cambridge: Cambridge University Press, 2012.

———. "Prophet, Sage, Healer, Messiah, and Martyr: Types and Identities of Jesus." Pages 1217–44 in vol. 2 of *HSHJ*. 4 vols. Edited by Tom Holmén and Stanley E. Porter. Leiden: Brill, 2011.

Evans, Craig A., and David Mishkin, eds. *A Handbook on the Jewish Roots of the Christian Faith*. Peabody, MA: Hendrickson, 2019.

———. *A Handbook on the Jewish Roots of the Gospels*. Peabody, MA: Hendrickson, 2021.

Evans, Craig A., and N. T. Wright. *Jesus, the Final Days: What Really Happened*. Edited by Troy A. Miller. Louisville: Westminster John Knox, 2009

Eve, Eric. *Behind the Gospels: Understanding the Oral Tradition*. Minneapolis: Fortress, 2014.

Farrar, Thomas J., and Guy J. Williams. "Diabolical Data: A Critical Inventory of New Testament Satanology." *JSNT* 39.1 (Sept 2016): 40–71.

Feinberg, John S. *Light in a Dark Place: The Doctrine of Scripture*. FET. Wheaton, IL: Crossway, 2018.

Feldmeier, Reinhard, and Hermann Spieckermann. *God of the Living: A Biblical Theology*. Translated by Mark E. Biddle. Waco, TX: Baylor University Press, 2011.

Ferda, Tucker S. "The Historical Jesus and the Law: The Form of His Activity and the Impact of Social Reputation." *CBQ* 80.1 (2018): 62–80.

———. "Naming the Messiah: A Contribution to the 4Q246 'Son of God' Debate." *DSD* 21.2 (2014): 150–75.

Fitzmyer, Joseph A. *Luke the Theologian: Aspects of His Teaching*. New York: Paulist, 1989.

———. *The One Who Is to Come*. Grand Rapids: Eerdmans: 2006.

Flusser, David. *Jesus*. Jerusalem, Israel: Magnes, 1997.

Forbes, Greg W. "Darkness over All the Land: Theological Imagery in the Crucifixion Scene." *Reformed Theological Review* 66.2 (2007): 83–96.

Foster, Paul. *Community, Law and Mission in Matthew's Gospel*. WUNT 2/177. Tübingen: Mohr Siebeck, 2004.

———. "The Gospel of Matthew." Pages 115–33 in *The Cambridge Companion to the New Testament*. Edited by Patrick Gray. CCR. Cambridge: Cambridge University Press, 2021.

———. "Ignatius of Antioch's Reception of the Gospel of Matthew." Pages 249–87 in *The Composition, Theology, and Early Reception of Matthew's Gospel*. Edited by Joseph Verheyden, Jens Schröter, and David C. Sim. WUNT 477. Tübingen: Mohr Siebeck, 2022.

———. "Paul and Matthew: Two Strands of the Early Jesus Movement with Little Sign of Connection." Pages 86–115 in *Paul and the Gospels: Christologies, Conflicts and Convergences*. Edited by Michael F. Bird and Joel Willitts. LNTS 411. London: Bloomsbury T&T Clark, 2011.

Foster, Robert L. "Why on Earth Use 'Kingdom of Heaven'? Matthew's Terminology Revisited." *NTS* 48.4 (2002): 487–99.

France, R. T. *The Gospel According to Matthew*. TNTC. Grand Rapids: Eerdmans, 1985.

———. *The Gospel of Matthew*. NICNT. Grand Rapids: Eerdmans, 2007.

———. *Jesus and the Old Testament: His Application of Old Testament Passages to Himself and His Mission*. London: Tyndale, 1971. Repr., Vancouver: Regent College Publishing, 1998.

———. "Matthew and Jerusalem." Pages 108–27 in *Built upon the Rock: Studies in the Gospel of Matthew*. Edited by Daniel M. Gurtner and John Nolland. Grand Rapids: Eerdmans, 2008.

———. *Matthew: Evangelist and Teacher*. Grand Rapids: Zondervan, 1989.

Funk, Robert W., and the Jesus Seminar. *The Acts of Jesus: The Search for the Authentic Deeds of Jesus*. San Francisco: HarperSanFrancisco, 1998.

Gadamer, Hans-Georg. *Truth and Method*. 2nd rev. ed. Translation revised by Joel Weinsheimer and Donald G. Marshall. London/New York: Continuum, 2004.

Gale, Aaron M. *Redefining Ancient Borders: The Jewish Scribal Framework of Matthew's Gospel*. London: T&T Clark, 2005.

Garland, David E. *The Intention of Matthew 23*. NovTSup 52. Leiden: Brill, 1979.

———. *Reading Matthew*. New York: Crossroad, 1993.

———. *A Theology of Mark's Gospel: Good News About Jesus the Messiah, the Son of God*. BTNT. Grand Rapids: Zondervan, 2015.

Garlington, Don. "The 'Better Righteousness': Matthew 5:20." *BBR* 20.4 (2010): 479–502.

———. "Who is the Greatest?" *JETS* 53.2 (2010): 287–316.

Gathercole, Simon J. "The Alleged Anonymity of the Canonical Gospels." *JTS* 69.2 (2018): 447–76.

———. *Defending Substitution: An Essay on Atonement in Paul*. ASBT. Grand Rapids: Baker Academic, 2015.

———. "The Earliest Manuscript Title of Matthew's Gospel (BnF Suppl. gr. 1120 ii 3 / _[4])." *NovT* 54.3 (2012): 209–35.

———. *The Gospel and the Gospels: Christian Proclamation and Early Jesus Books*. Grand Rapids: Eerdmans, 2022.

———. *The Pre-existent Son: Recovering the Christologies of Matthew, Mark, and Luke*. Grand Rapids: Eerdmans, 2006.

———. "The Titles of the Gospels in the Earliest New Testament Manuscripts." *ZNW* 104.1 (2013): 33–76.

Gaventa, Beverly Roberts. *Mary: Glimpses of the Mother of Jesus*. SPNT. Columbia: University of South Carolina Press, 1995.

Gempf, Conrad. "The Imagery of Birth Pangs in the New Testament." *TynBul* 45.1 (1994): 119–35.

Gerhardsson, Birger. "The Christology of Matthew." Pages 14–32 in *Who Do You Say That I Am? Essays on Christology; In Honor of Jack Dean Kingsbury*. Edited by Mark Allan Powell and David R. Bauer. Louisville: Westminster John Knox, 1999.

———. *The Reliability of the Gospel Tradition*. Peabody, MA: Hendrickson, 2001.

———. *The Testing of God's Son (Matt 4:1–11 & Par.)*. ConBNT 2.1. Lund: Gleerup, 1996.

Gibbs, Jeffrey A. *Jerusalem and Parousia: Jesus' Eschatological Discourse in Matthew's Gospel*. St. Louis: Concordia Academic, 2000.

———. *Matthew 1:1–11:1*. Concordia Commentary. St. Louis: Concordia, 2006.

Gibson, Jeffrey B. *The Disciples' Prayer: The Prayer Jesus Taught in Its Historical Setting*. Minneapolis: Fortress, 2015.

Gladd, Benjamin L. *From Adam and Israel to the Church: A Biblical Theology of the People of God*. ESBT. Downers Grove, IL: InterVarsity, 2019.

———. *Handbook on the Gospels*. Handbooks on the New Testament. Grand Rapids: Baker Academic, 2021.

Gladd, Benjamin L., and Matthew S. Harmon. *Making All Things New: Inaugurated Eschatology for the Life of the Church*. Grand Rapids: Baker Academic, 2016.

Glatzer, Nahum. *Franz Rosenzweig: His Life and Thought*. Indianapolis, IN: Hackett, 1998.

Goldingay, John. *Reading Jesus' Bible: How the New Testament Helps Us Understand the Old Testament*. Grand Rapids: Eerdmans, 2017.

Goldsworthy, Graeme. *Gospel and Kingdom: A Christian Interpretation of the Old Testament*. Exeter, UK: Paternoster, 1981.

———. *The Son of God and the New Creation*. Short Studies in Biblical Theology. Wheaton, IL: Crossway, 2016.

Gomes, Alan W. *40 Questions About Heaven and Hell*. 40 Questions Series. Grand Rapids: Kregel, 2018.

Goodacre, Mark. *The Case Against Q: Studies in Markan Priority and the Synoptic Problem*. Harrisburg, PA: Trinity Press International, 2002.

———. *The Synoptic Problem: A Way Through the Maze*. BibSem 80. London: Sheffield Academic, 2001.

Goodrich, John K., and Mark L. Strauss, eds. *Following Jesus Christ: The New Testament Message of Discipleship for Today. A Volume in Honor of Michael J. Wilkins*. Grand Rapids: Kregel, 2019.

Gorman, Michael J. *The Death of the Messiah and the Birth of the New Covenant: A (Not So) New Model of the Atonement*. Eugene, OR: Cascade, 2014.

Gosnell, Peter W. *The Ethical Vision of the Bible: Learning Good from Knowing God*. Downers Grove: InterVarsity, 2014.

Gowan, Donald E. *Eschatology in the Old Testament*. Philadelphia: Fortress, 1986.

Gray, Sherman W. *The Least of My Brothers: Matthew 25:31–42—A History of Interpretation*. SBLDS 114. Atlanta: Scholars, 1989.

Green, H. Benedict. *The Gospel According to Matthew: Introduction and Commentary*. The New Clarendon Bible (New Testament). Oxford: Oxford University Press, 1975.

Green, Joel B. *The Death of Jesus: Tradition and Interpretation in the Passion Narratives*. WUNT 2/33. Tübingen: J.C.B. Mohr (Paul Siebeck), 1988.

Green, Joel B., Scot McKnight, and I. Howard Marshall, eds. *Dictionary of Jesus and the Gospels*. Downers Grove: InterVarsity, 1992.

Green, Joel B., Jeannine K. Brown, and Nicholas Perrin, eds. *Dictionary of Jesus and the Gospels*. 2nd ed. Downers Grove: InterVarsity, 2013.

Green, Michael. *The Message of Matthew: The Kingdom of Heaven*. BST. Downers Grove: InterVarsity, 2000.

Greenman, Jeffrey P., Timothy Larsen, and Stephen R. Spencer, eds. *The Sermon on the Mount through the Centuries: From the Early Church to John Paul II*. Grand Rapids: Brazos, 2007.

Greidanus, Sidney. *The Modern Preacher and the Ancient Text: Interpreting and Preaching Biblical Literature*. Grand Rapids: Eerdmans, 1988.

Grindheim, Sigurd. *Christology in the Synoptic Gospels: God or God's Servant?* London: T&T Clark, 2012.

———. *God's Equal: What Can We Know About Jesus' Self-Understanding?* LNTS 446. London: T&T Clark, 2011.

———. *Introducing Biblical Theology*. London: Bloomsbury, 2013.

Grudem, Wayne. *Systematic Theology: An Introduction to Biblical Doctrine*. 2nd ed. Grand Rapids: Zondervan, 2020.

Gruen, Erich S. "Synagogues and Voluntary Associations as Institutional Models: A Response to Richard Ascough and Ralph Korner." *JJMJS* 3 (2016): 125–31.

Guelich, Robert A. *Mark 1–8:26*. WBC 34A. Dallas: Word, 1989.

———. *The Sermon on the Mount: A Foundation for Understanding*. Waco, TX: Word, 1982.

Guenter, Kenneth E. "'This Generation' in the Trilogy of Matthew 24:34–35." *BSac* 175 (2018): 174–94.

Gundry, Robert H. *The Church and the Tribulation*. Grand Rapids: Zondervan, 1973.

———. *Matthew: A Commentary on His Handbook for a Mixed Church Under Persecution*. 2nd ed. Grand Rapids: Eerdmans, 1994.

———. *Peter: False Disciple and Apostate According to Saint Matthew*. Grand Rapids: Eerdmans, 2015.

———. *The Use of the Old Testament in St Matthew's Gospel: With Special Reference to the Messianic Hope*. NovTSup 8. Leiden: Brill, 1975.

Günther, Eva. *Wisdom as a Model for Jesus' Ministry: A Study on the "Lament over Jerusalem" in Matt 23:37–39 Par. Luke 13:34–35*. WUNT 2/513. Tübingen: Mohr Siebeck, 2020.

Gupta, Nijay K. *The Lord's Prayer*. SHBCSS. Macon, GA: Smyth and Helwys, 2017.

———. "The Spirituality of Faith in the Gospel of Matthew." Pages 108–24 in *Matthew and Mark Across Perspectives: Essays in Honour of Stephen C. Barton and William R. Telford*. Edited by Kristian A. Bendoraitis and Nijay K. Gupta. LNTS 538. London: Bloomsbury T&T Clark, 2016.

Gurtner, Daniel M. "The Gospel of Matthew from Stanton to Present: A Survey of Some Recent Developments." Pages 23–38 in *Jesus, Matthew's Gospel and Early Christianity: Studies in Memory of Graham N. Stanton*. Edited by Daniel M. Gurtner, Joel Willitts, and Richard A. Burridge. LNTS 435. London: T&T Clark, 2011.

———. *The Torn Veil: Matthew's Exposition of the Death of Jesus*. SNTSMS 139. Cambridge: Cambridge University Press, 2007.

Gurtner, Daniel M., and John Nolland, eds. *Built upon the Rock: Studies in the Gospel of Matthew*. Grand Rapids: Eerdmans, 2008.

Gurtner, Daniel M., Joel Willitts, and Richard A. Burridge, eds. *Jesus, Matthew's Gospel and Early Christianity: Studies in Memory of Graham N. Stanton*. LNTS 435. London: T&T Clark, 2011.

Guthrie, Donald. *New Testament Introduction*. 3rd ed. Downers Grove, IL: InterVarsity, 1970.

———. *New Testament Theology*. Downers Grove, IL: InterVarsity, 1981.

Habel, Norman C. *The Land is Mine: Six Biblical Land Ideologies*. OBT. Minneapolis: Augsburg Fortress, 1995.

Habermas, Gary. *Evidences*. Vol. 1 of *On the Resurrection*. 2 vols. Brentwood, TN: B&H, 2024. (This was published too late to be evaluated here, but it looks to be immensely helpful.)

Hafemann, Scott J., ed. *Biblical Theology: Retrospect and Prospect*. Downers Grove, IL: InterVarsity, 2002.

———. "Eschatology and Ethics: The Future of Israel and the Nations in Romans 15:1–13." *TynBul* 51 (2000): 161–92.

———. *The God of Promise and the Life of Faith: Understanding the Heart of the Bible*. Wheaton, IL: Crossway, 2001.

Hagner, Donald A. "Apocalyptic Motifs in the Gospel of Matthew: Continuity and Discontinuity." *HBT* 7.2 (1985): 53–82.

———. "Determining the Date of Matthew." Pages 76–92 in *Jesus, Matthew's Gospel and Early Christianity: Studies in Memory of Graham N. Stanton*. Edited by Daniel M. Gurtner, Joel Willitts, and Richard A. Burridge. LNTS 435. London: T&T Clark, 2011.

———. "The Jesus Quest and Jewish-Christian Relations." Pages 1055–77 in vol. 2 of *HSHJ*. 4 vols. Edited by Tom Holmén and Stanley E. Porter. Leiden: Brill, 2011.

———. *Matthew 1–13*. WBC 33A Dallas: Word, 1993.

———. *Matthew 14–28*. WBC 33B. Dallas: Word, 1995.

Hurtado, Larry W. *Lord Jesus Christ: Devotion to Jesus in Earliest Christianity*. Grand Rapids: Eerdmans, 2003.
———. "Observations on the 'Monotheism' Affirmed in the New Testament." Pages 50–68 in *The Bible and Early Trinitarian Theology*. Edited by Christopher A. Beeley and Mark E. Weedman. CUA Studies in Early Christianity. Washington, DC: Catholic University of America Press, 2018.
———. *One God, One Lord: Early Christian Devotion and Ancient Jewish Monotheism*. Philadelphia: Fortress, 1988.
Hurtado, Larry W., and Paul L. Owen, eds. *"Who Is This Son of Man?": The Latest Scholarship on a Puzzling Expression of the Historical Jesus*. LNTS 390. London: T&T Clark, 2011.
Hylen, Susan E. *Women in the New Testament World*. EBS. Oxford: Oxford University Press, 2019.
Imes, Carmen Joy. *Bearing God's Name: Why Sinai Still Matters*. Downers Grove, IL: InterVarsity, 2019.
Inbari, Motti. "Messianic Religious Zionism and the Reintroduction of Sacrifice: The Case of the Temple Institute." Pages 256–73 in *Rethinking the Messianic Idea in Judaism*. Edited by Michael L. Morgan and Steven Weitzman. Bloomington, IN: Indiana University Press, 2015.
Irons, Charles Lee, Danny André Dixon, and Dustin R. Smith. *The Son of God: Three Views of the Identity of Jesus*. Eugene, OR: Wipf & Stock, 2015.
Ja, Layang Seng. *The Pharisees in Matthew 23 Reconsidered*. Langham Monographs. Carlisle, UK: Langham, 2018.
Jaffé, Dan, ed. *Juifs et chrétiens aux premiers siècles: Identités, dialogues, et dissidences*. Judaïsme ancient et Christianisme primitif. Paris, France: Cerf, 2019.
Japinga, Lynn. *From Daughters to Disciples: Women's Stories from the New Testament*. Louisville: Westminster John Knox, 2021.
Jason, Mark A. *Repentance at Qumran: The Penitential Framework of Religious Experience in the Dead Sea Scrolls*. Emerging Scholars. Minneapolis: Fortress, 2015.
Jeffery, Steve, Michael Ovey, and Andrew Sach. *Pierced for Our Transgressions: Rediscovering the Glory of Penal Substitution*. Wheaton, IL: Crossway, 2007
Jipp, Joshua W. *Christ Is King: Paul's Royal Ideology*. Minneapolis: Augsburg Fortress, 2015.
———. *The Messianic Theology of the New Testament*. Grand Rapids: Eerdmans, 2020.
Johnson, Adam J., ed. *Five Views on the Extent of the Atonement*. Counterpoints. Grand Rapids: Zondervan, 2019.
———, ed. *T&T Clark Companion to Atonement*. Bloomsbury Companions 5. London: Bloomsbury, 2017.
Johnson, Raymond M. *I See Dead People: The Function of the Resurrection of the Saints in Matthew 27:51–54*. RAD. Phillipsburg, NJ: P&R, 2019.
Joosten, Jan. "The Text of Old Testament Quotations in Matthew." Pages 201–16 in Seleznev, Loader, and Niebuhr. *The Gospel of Matthew in Its Historical and Theological Context*. WUNT 459. Tübingen: Mohr Siebeck, 2021.
Jorgensen, David W. *Treasure Hidden in a Field: Early Christian Reception of the Gospel of Matthew*. SBIR 6. Berlin: de Gruyter, 2016.
Kähler, Christoph. "Satanischer Schriftgebrauch: Zur Hermeneutik von Mt 4,1–11/Lk 4, 1–13." *Theologische Literaturzeitung* 119.10 (1994): 857–68.
Kaiser, Walter C., Jr. *The Messiah in the Old Testament*. Grand Rapids: Zondervan, 1995.
———. *The Promise-Plan of God: A Biblical Theology of the Old and New Testaments*. Grand Rapids: Zondervan, 2008.
———. "Single Meaning, Unified Referents: Accurate and Authoritative Citations of the Old Testament by the New Testament." Pages 45–104 in *Three Views on the New Testament Use of the Old Testament*. Edited by Kenneth Berding and Jonathan Lunde. Grand Rapids: Zondervan, 2008.
Kammler, Hans-Christian. "Sohn Gottes und Kreuz: Die Versuchungsgeschichte Mt 4,1–11 im Kontext des Matthäusevangeliums." *ZTK* 100.2 (2003): 163–86.
Kampen, John. *Matthew Within Sectarian Judaism*. AYBRL. New Haven, CT: Yale University Press, 2019.
Käsemann, Ernst. *On Being a Disciple of the Crucified Nazarene: Unpublished Lectures and Sermons*. Edited by Rudolf Landau, in cooperation with Wolfgang Kraus. Translated by Roy A. Harrisville. Grand Rapids: Eerdmans, 2010.
Kealy, Sean P. *Matthew's Gospel and the History of Biblical Interpretation*. 2 vols. Mellen Biblical Press Series 55a and 55b. Lewiston, NY: Mellen Biblical Press, 1997.
Keener, Craig S. *Acts: An Exegetical Commentary*. 4 vols. Grand Rapids: Baker Academic, 2012–2015.
———. *Christobiography: Memory, History, and the Reliability of the Gospels*. Grand Rapids: Eerdmans, 2019.
———. *A Commentary on the Gospel of Matthew*. Grand Rapids: Eerdmans, 1999.

———. "'The Dead Are Raised' (Matthew 11:5 // Luke 7:22): Resuscitation Accounts in the Gospels and Eyewitness Testimony." *BBR* 25.1 (2015): 55–79.

———. *The Gospel of Matthew: A Socio-Rhetorical Commentary.* Grand Rapids: Eerdmans, 2009.

———. *The Historical Jesus of the Gospels.* Grand Rapids: Eerdmans, 2009.

———. "Matthew's Missiology: Making Disciples of the Nations (Matthew 28:19–20)." *Asian Journal of Pentecostal Studies* 12.1 (2009): 3–20.

———. *Miracles: The Credibility of the New Testament Accounts.* 2 vols. Grand Rapids: Baker Academic, 2011.

Keith, Chris. *Jesus Against the Scribal Elite: The Origins of the Conflict.* Grand Rapids: Baker Academic, 2014.

———. *Jesus' Literacy: Scribal Culture and the Teacher from Galilee.* LHJS 8; LNTS 413. London: T&T Clark, 2011.

Keith, Chris, and Larry Hurtado, eds. *Jesus Among Friends and Enemies: A Historical and Literary Introduction to Jesus in the Gospels.* Grand Rapids: Baker Academic, 2011.

Keown, Mark. "An Imminent Parousia and Christian Mission: Did the New Testament Writers Really Expect Jesus's Imminent Return?" Pages 242–63 in *Christian Origins and the Establishment of the Early Jesus Movement.* Edited by Stanley E. Porter and Andrew W. Pitts. TENTS 12. Leiden: Brill, 2018.

Kilpatrick, George D. *The Origins of the Gospel According to St. Matthew.* Oxford: Clarendon, 1946.

Kim, Hak Chol. "The Worship of Jesus in the Gospel of Matthew." *Bib* 93.2 (2012): 227–41.

Kingsbury, Jack Dean. "The Figure of Peter in Matthew's Gospel as a Theological Problem." *JBL* 98 (1979): 67–83.

———. *Matthew as Story.* 2nd ed. Philadelphia: Fortress, 1988.

———. *Matthew: Structure, Christology, Kingdom.* 2nd ed. Minneapolis: Fortress, 1989.

Kinney, Robert S. *Hellenistic Dimensions of the Gospel of Matthew: Background and Rhetoric.* WUNT 2/414. Tübingen: Mohr Siebeck, 2016.

Kinzer, Mark S. *Post-Missionary Messianic Judaism: Redefining Christian Engagement with the Jewish People.* Grand Rapids: Brazos, 2005.

Kio, Stephen Hre. "Understanding and Translating 'Nations' in Mt 28:19." *The Bible Translator* 41.2 (1990): 230–39.

Kirk, Alan. *Q in Matthew: Ancient Media, Memory, and Early Scribal Transmission of the Jesus Tradition.* LNTS 564. London: Bloomsbury T&T Clark, 2016.

———. *Memory and the Jesus Tradition.* Reception of Jesus in the First Three Centuries 2. London: Bloomsbury, 2018.

Kirk, J. R. Daniel. "Conceptualising Fulfilment in Matthew." *TynBul* 59.1 (2008): 77–98.

———. *A Man Attested by God: The Human Jesus of the Synoptic Gospels.* Grand Rapids: Eerdmans, 2016.

Klauber, Martin I., and Scott M. Manetsch, eds. *The Great Commission: Evangelicals and the History of World Missions.* Nashville: B&H, 2008.

Klein, William W., Craig L. Blomberg, and Robert L. Hubbard, Jr. *Introduction to Biblical Interpretation.* 2nd ed. Dallas: Word, 2004.

Klink, Edward W., III, ed. *The Audience of the Gospels: The Origin and Function of the Gospels in Early Christianity.* LNTS 353. London: T&T Clark, 2010.

———. *John.* ZECNT. Grand Rapids: Zondervan, 2016.

Klink, Edward W., III, and Darian R. Lockett. *Understanding Biblical Theology: A Comparison of Theory and Practice.* Grand Rapids: Zondervan, 2012.

Knoppers, Gary N. *Jews and Samaritans: The Origins and History of Their Early Relations.* Oxford: Oxford University Press, 2013.

Knowles, Michael P. *Jeremiah in Matthew's Gospel: The Rejected-Prophet Motif in Matthean Redaction.* JSNTSup 68. Sheffield: Sheffield Academic, 1993.

———. "Scripture, History, Messiah: Scriptural Fulfillment and the Fullness of Time in Matthew's Gospel." Pages 59–82 in *Hearing the Old Testament in the New Testament.* Edited by Stanley E. Porter. MNTS. Grand Rapids: Eerdmans, 2006.

———. "Serpents, Scribes, and Pharisees." *JBL* 133.1 (2014): 165–78.

Kokkinos, Nikos. *The Herodian Dynasty: Origins, Role in Society and Eclipse.* JSPSup 30. Sheffield: Sheffield Academic, 1998.

Konradt, Matthias. *Das Evangelium nach Matthäus.* Das Neue Testament Deutsch 1. Göttingen: Vandenhoeck & Ruprecht, 2015.

———. "Following Jesus and Fulfilling the Law: Considerations on the Ethical Conception of the Gospel of Matthew." Pages 275–94 in Seleznev, Loader, and Niebuhr. *The Gospel of Matthew in Its Historical and Theological Context*. WUNT 459. Tübingen: Mohr Siebeck, 2021.

———. *The Gospel According to Matthew: A Commentary*. Translated by M. Eugene Boring. Waco, TX: Baylor University Press, 2020.

———. *Israel, Church, and the Gentiles in the Gospel of Matthew*. Translated by Kathleen Ess. BMSSEC. Waco, TX: Baylor University Press, 2014.

———. "Matthew Within or Outside of Judaism? From the 'Parting of the Ways' Model to a Multifaceted Approach." Pages 121–50 in *Jews and Christians—Parting Ways in the First Two Centuries CE? Reflections on the Gains and Losses of a Model*. Edited by Jens Schröter, Benjamin A. Edsall, and Joseph Verheyden. BZNW 253. Berlin: de Gruyter, 2021.

———. *Studien zum Matthausevangelium*. Edited by Alida Euler. WUNT 358. Tübingen: Mohr Siebeck, 2016.

Korner, Ralph J. *The Origin and Meaning of* Ekklēsia *in the Early Jesus Movement*. AJEC 98. Leiden: Brill, 2017.

Köstenberger, Andreas J. *John*. BECNT. Grand Rapids: Baker Academic, 2004.

———. *The Missions of Jesus and the Disciples According to the Fourth Gospel: With Implications for the Fourth Gospel's Purpose and the Mission of the Contemporary Church*. Grand Rapids: Eerdmans, 1998.

Köstenberger, Andreas J., with T. Desmond Alexander. *Salvation to the Ends of the Earth: A Biblical Theology of Mission*. 2nd ed. NSBT 53. Downers Grove, IL: IVP Academic, 2020.

K[illegible]stenberger, Andreas J., and Gregory Goswell. *Biblical Theology: A Canonical, Thematic, and Ethical Approach*. Wheaton, IL: Crossway, 2023. (This volume was published too late for use here but is listed for the readers' information.)

Köstenberger, Andreas J., Alexander E. Stewart, and Apollo Makara. *Jesus and the Future: Understanding What He Taught About the End Times*. Wooster, OH: Weaver, 2017.

Kreider, Glenn R. "Jesus the Messiah as Prophet, Priest, and King." *BSac* 176 (2019): 174–87.

Kuhn, Karl A. "The 'One Like a Son of Man' Becomes the 'Son of God.'" *CBQ* 69.1 (2007): 22–42.

Kupp, David D. *Matthew's Emmanuel: Divine Presence and God's People in the First Gospel*. SNTSMS 90. Cambridge: Cambridge University Press, 1996.

Kvalbein, Hans. "Has Matthew Abandoned the Jews? A Contribution to a Disputed Issue in Recent Scholarship." Pages 45–62 in *The Mission of the Early Church to Jews and Gentiles*. Edited by Jostein Ådna and Hans Kvalbein. WUNT 127. Tübingen: Mohr Siebeck, 2000.

Ladd, George Eldon. *The Gospel of the Kingdom: Scriptural Studies in the Kingdom of God*. Grand Rapids: Eerdmans, 1973.

———. *The Presence of the Future: The Eschatology of Biblical Realism*. 2nd ed. Grand Rapids: Eerdmans, 1974.

———. *A Theology of the New Testament*. Rev. ed. Edited by Donald A. Hagner. Grand Rapids: Eerdmans, 1993.

Lang, David, ed. *Transforming the Nations: Perspectives on Discipleship Today*. Singapore: Singapore Bible College Press, 2015.

Larkin, William J., Jr. "Mission." Pages 534–38 in *EDBT*.

Lap, F. *Peter: The Myth, the Man and the Writings: A Study of the Early Petrine Text and Tradition*. JSNTSup 239. London: Sheffield Academic, 2003.

Last, Richard. "*Ekklēsia* Outside the Septuagint and the *Dēmos*: The Titles of Greco-Roman Associations and Christ-Followers' Groups." *JBL* 137.4 (2018): 959–80.

Lau, Theresa Yu Chui Siang. "The Gospels and the Old Testament." Pages 155–80 in *The Content and Setting of the Gospel Tradition*. Edited by Mark Harding and Alanna Nobbs. Grand Rapids: Eerdmans, 2010.

———. "Reading the Gospel of Matthew as a Gospel of the Jerusalem Council." PhD dissertation, University of Melbourne, Centre for Jewish History and Culture, 2006.

Lee, Aquila H. I. *From Messiah to Preexistent Son: Jesus' Self-Consciousness and Early Christian Exegesis of Messianic Psalms*. WUNT 2/192. Tübingen: Mohr Siebeck, 2005.

Lee-Barnewall, Michelle. *Neither Complementarian nor Egalitarian: A Kingdom Corrective to the Evangelical Gender Debate*. Grand Rapids: Baker Academic, 2016.

———. *Surprised by the Parables: Growing in Grace through the Stories of Jesus*. Bellingham, WA: Lexham, 2020.

Leim, Joshua E. *Matthew's Theological Grammar: The Father and the Son*. WUNT 2/402. Tübingen: Mohr Siebeck, 2015.

Lemcio, Eugene E. *The Past of Jesus in the Gospels*. SNTSMS 68. Cambridge: Cambridge University Press, 1991.

Lészai, Lehel. "The Disciples in Hellenism and Rabbinism." Pages 78–91 in *From Movement to Inheritance:*

*Hidden Assets from the Treasury of Hungarian Reformation*. Edited by Olga Lukács, Alpár Csaba Nagy, and István Péter. R5AS 59. Göttingen: Vandenhoeck & Ruprecht, 2019.
———. *Discipleship in the Synoptics*. Cluj-Napoca, Romania: Cluj University Press; Leipzig: Evangelische Verlangsanstalt, 2017.
Levering, Matthew. *Did Jesus Rise from the Dead? Historical and Theological Reflections*. Oxford: Oxford University Press, 2019.
———. *Engaging the Doctrine of Israel: A Christian Israelology in Dialogue with Ongoing Judaism*. Engaging Doctrine. Eugene, OR: Cascade, 2021.
Levine, Amy-Jill. "The Gospel of Matthew: Between Breaking and Continuity." Pages 121–44 in *Gospels: Narrative and History*. Edited by Mercedes Navarro Puerto and Marinella Perroni. English ed. edited by Amy-Jill Levine. The Bible and Women: New Testament 2.1. Atlanta: Society of Biblical Literature, 2015.
———. "Jesus in Jewish-Christian Dialogue." Pages 175–88 in *Soundings in the Religion of Jesus: Perspectives and Methods in Jewish and Christian Scholarship*. Edited by Bruce Chilton, Anthony Le Donne, and Jacob Neusner. Minneapolis: Fortress, 2012.
———. "Matthew's Portrayal of the Synagogue and Its Leaders." Pages 177–94 in *The Gospel of Matthew at the Crossroads of Early Christianity*. Edited by Donald Senior. BETL 243. Leuven: Peeters, 2011.
———. *The Misunderstood Jew: The Church and the Scandal of the Jewish Jesus*. San Francisco: HarperSanFrancisco, 2006.
———. *The Social and Ethnic Dimensions of Matthean Salvation History: "Go Nowhere Among the Gentiles" (Matt 10:5b)*. SBEC 14. Lewiston, NY; Queenston, Canada; Lampeter, UK: Edwin Mellen, 1988.
———. "Women Itinerants, Jesus of Nazareth, and Historical-Critical Approaches: Reevaluating the Consensus." Pages 45–64 in *Gender and Second-Temple Judaism*. Edited by Kathy Ehrensperger and Shayna Sheinfeld. Lexington, MD: Lexington/Fortress Academic, 2020.
Levine, Amy-Jill, with Marianne Blickenstaff, eds. *A Feminist Companion to Matthew*. Cleveland, OH: Pilgrim, 2004.
Lewis, Daniel J. *3 Crucial Questions about the Last Days*. Grand Rapids: Baker, 1998.
Lewis, Jack P. "'The Gates of Hell Shall Not Prevail Against It' (Matt 16:18): A Study of the History of Interpretation." *JETS* 38.3 (1995): 349–67.
Licona, Michael R. *The Resurrection of Jesus: A New Historiographical Approach*. Downers Grove, IL: InterVarsity, 2010.
Lieu, Judith M. *Neither Jew nor Greek? Constructing Early Christianity*. Cornerstones. 2nd ed. London: T&T Clark, 2016.
———. "The Parting of the Ways: Theological Construct or Historical Reality?" Pages 31–49 in *Neither Jew nor Greek. Constructing Early Christianity*. Judith M. Lieu. Cornerstones. 2nd ed. London: T&T Clark, 2016.
———, ed. *Peter in the Early Church: Apostle—Missionary—Church Leader*. BETL 325. Leuven: Peeters, 2021.
Lim, Eunyung. *Entering God's Kingdom (Not) Like A Little Child: Images of the Child in Matthew, 1 Corinthians, and Thomas*. BZNW 243. Berlin: de Gruyter, 2021.
Lischer, Richard. *Reading the Parables*. Interpretation. Louisville: Westminster John Knox, 2018.
Litfin, Duane. "Revisiting the Unpardonable Sin: Insight from an Unexpected Source." *JETS* 60.4 (2017): 713–32.
Litwa, M. David. *How the Gospels Became History: Jesus and Mediterranean Myths*. Synkrisis. New Haven, CT: Yale University Press, 2019.
Loader, William R. G. "Did Adultery Mandate Divorce? A Reassessment of Jesus' Divorce Logia." *NTS* 61.1 (2015): 67–78.
———. *Jesus' Attitude Towards the Law: A Study of the Gospels*. WUNT 2/97. Tübingen: Mohr Siebeck, 1997. Repr., Grand Rapids: Eerdmans, 2002.
Loader, William R. G., Boris Repschinski, and Eric Wong, eds. *Matthew, Paul, and Others: Asian Perspectives on New Testament Themes*. Innsbruck, Austria: Innsbruck University Press, 2019.
Loke, Andrew Ter Ern. *Investigating the Resurrection of Jesus Christ: A New Transdisciplinary Approach*. Routledge New Critical Thinking in Religion, Theology and Biblical Studies. London: Routledge, 2020.
———. *A Kryptic Model of the Incarnation*. Ashgate New Critical Thinking in Religion, Theology and Biblical Studies. London: Routledge, 2014.
———. *The Origin of Divine Christology*. SNTSMS 169. Cambridge: Cambridge University Press, 2017.
Long, Phillip J. *Jesus the Bridegroom: The Origin of the Eschatological Feast as a Wedding Banquet in the Synoptic Gospels*. Eugene, OR: Wipf & Stock, 2013.

Longenecker, Richard N. *Biblical Exegesis in the Apostolic Period.* Grand Rapids: Eerdmans, 1975.

———, ed. *Contours of Christology in the New Testament.* MNTS. Grand Rapids: Eerdmans, 2005.

———, ed. *Patterns of Discipleship in the New Testament.* Grand Rapids: Eerdmans, 1996.

Love, Stuart L. *Jesus and Marginal Women: The Gospel of Matthew in Social-Scientific Perspective.* Matrix 5. Eugene, OR: Cascade, 2009.

Lucass, Shirley. *The Concept of the Messiah in the Scriptures of Judaism and Christianity.* LSTS 78. London: T&T Clark, 2011.

Lunde, Jonathan. *Following Jesus, the Servant King: A Biblical Theology of Covenantal Discipleship.* Grand Rapids: Zondervan, 2010.

Luz, Ulrich. "The Disciples in the Gospel According to Matthew." Pages 115–48 in *The Interpretation of Matthew.* Edited by Graham N. Stanton. 2nd ed. SNTI. Edinburgh: T&T Clark, 1995.

———. *Das Evangelium nach Matthäus (Mt 1–7).* Evangelisch-Katholischer Kommentar zum Neuen Testament. Zürich: Neukirchen-Vluyn, 1985.

———. *Matthew 1–7: A Commentary.* Translated by James E. Crouch. Hermeneia. Minneapolis: Fortress, 2007.

———. *Matthew 8–20: A Commentary.* Translated by James E. Crouch. Hermeneia. Minneapolis: Fortress, 2001.

———. *Matthew 21–28: A Commentary.* Translated by James E. Crouch. Hermeneia. Minneapolis: Fortress, 2005.

———. *Studies in Matthew.* Translated by Rosemary Selle. Grand Rapids: Eerdmans, 2005.

———. *The Theology of the Gospel of Matthew.* Translated by J. Bradford Robinson. New Testament Theology. Cambridge: Cambridge University Press, 1995.

Macaskill, Grant. *The New Testament and Intellectual Humility.* Oxford: Oxford University Press, 2018.

Macchia, Frank D. *Jesus the Spirit Baptizer: Christology in Light of Pentecost.* Grand Rapids: Eerdmans, 2018.

Maier, Gerhard. *Das Evangelium des Matthäus, Kapitel 1–14.* HTANT 5. Witten: SCM R. Brockhaus; Giessen, Germany: Brunnen, 2015.

———. *Das Matthäus-Evangelium.* Bibelkommentar. Edition C. Holzgerlingen, Germany: SCM Haenssler, 2007.

Mamić, Vinko. *Matthew's Response to an Early Missionary Issue: Meaning and Function of the Parable of the Workers in the Vineyard (Matt 20:1–16).* TGST 219. Rome: Gregorian and Biblical Press, 2016.

Mangum, Douglas, and Douglas Estes, eds. *Literary Approaches to the Bible.* Lexham Methods Series. Bellingham, WA: Lexham, 2018.

Manomi, Dogara Ishaya. "'Good and Faithful Slave.'" *NovT* 64.4 (2022): 413–31.

Manson, T. W. *The Sayings of Jesus.* 2nd ed. London: SCM, 1999.

Marcus, Joel. "History and Theology in Matthew." Pages 47–56 in *History and Theology in the Gospels: Seventh International East-West Symposium of New Testament Scholars, Moscow, September 26 to October 1, 2016.* Edited by Tobias Nicklas, Karl-Wilhelm Niebuhr, and Mikhail Seleznev, in collaboration with Judith König and Rebecca Draughon. WUNT 447. Tübingen: Mohr Siebeck, 2020.

———. *John the Baptist in History and Theology.* SPNT. Columbia: University of South Carolina Press, 2018.

Marguerat, Daniel. *Jésus et Matthieu: A la recherche du Jésus de l'histoire.* Le Monde de la Bible 70. Geneva: Labor et Fides, 2016.

———. *Le Jugement dans l'évangile de Matthieu.* 2nd ed. Le Monde de la Bible 6. Geneva: Labor et Fides, 1995.

Markley, John R. *Peter–Apocalyptic Seer: The Influence of the Apocalypse Genre on Matthew's Portrayal of Peter.* WUNT 2/348. Tübingen: Mohr Siebeck, 2013.

Markschies, Christoph. "From 'Wide and Narrow Way' to 'The Ways That Never Parted'? Road Metaphors in Models of Jewish-Christian Relations in Antiquity." Pages 11–32 in *Jews and Christians—Parting Ways in the First Two Centuries CE? Reflections on the Gains and Losses of a Model.* Edited by Jens Schröter, Benjamin A. Edsall, and Joseph Verheyden. BZNW 253. Berlin: de Gruyter, 2021.

Marshall, I. Howard. *Commentary on Luke.* NIGTC. Grand Rapids: Eerdmans, 1978.

———. *New Testament Theology: Many Witnesses, One Gospel.* Downers Grove: InterVarsity, 2004.

Martin, Ralph P. *The Four Gospels.* Vol. 1 of *New Testament Foundations: A Guide for Christian Students.* Grand Rapids: Eerdmans, 1975.

Massaux, Édouard. *The First Ecclesiastical Writers.* Vol. 1 of *The Influence of the Gospel of Saint Matthew on Christian Literature before Saint Irenaeus.* Translated by Norman J. Belval and Suzanne Hecht. Edited by Arthur J. Bellinzoni. New Gospel Studies 5/1. Macon, GA: Mercer, 1990.

Maunder, Chris, ed. *The Oxford Handbook of Mary.* Oxford Handbooks. Oxford: Oxford University Press, 2019.

Mbabazi, Isaac Kahwa. *The Significance of Interpersonal Forgiveness in the Gospel of Matthew.* Eugene, OR: Pickwick, 2013.

McCall, Thomas H. *Against God and Nature: The Doctrine of Sin*. Wheaton, IL: Crossway, 2019.

McDaniel, Karl J. *Experiencing Irony in the First Gospel: Suspense, Surprise and Curiosity*. LNTS 488. London: T&T Clark Bloomsbury, 2013.

McDermott, Gerald, ed. *Understanding the Jewish Roots of Christianity: Biblical, Theological, and Historical Essays on the Relationship Between Christianity and Judaism*. Studies in Scripture and Biblical Theology. Bellingham, WA: Lexham, 2021.

McIver, Robert K. *Mainstream or Marginal? The Matthean Community in Early Christianity*. Friedensauer Schriftenreihe Series 12. Berlin: Peter Lang, 2012.

———. "The Parable of the Weeds Among the Wheat (Matt 13:24–30, 36–43) and the Relationship Between the Kingdom and the Church as Portrayed in the Gospel of Matthew." *JBL* 114.4 (1995): 643–59.

McKnight, Scot. "The Challenge of Allegiance in the Roman Empire: Discipleship in Romans and Galatians." Pages 92–108 in Goodrich and Strauss, *Following Jesus Christ*. Grand Rapids: Kregel, 2019.

———. *A Community Called Atonement*. Living Theology. Nashville: Abingdon, 2007.

———. *Jesus and His Death: Historiography, the Historical Jesus, and Atonement Theory*. Waco, TX: Baylor University Press, 2005.

———. "Jesus and the Twelve." Pages 181–214 in *Key Events in the Life of the Historical Jesus: A Collaborative Exploration of Context and Coherence*. Edited by Darrell L. Bock and Robert L. Webb. WUNT 247. Tübingen: Mohr Siebeck, 2009.

———. *Kingdom Conspiracy: Returning to the Radical Mission of the Local Church*. Grand Rapids: Brazos, 2014.

———. *A Light Among the Gentiles: Jewish Missionary Activity in the Second Temple Period*. Minneapolis: Fortress, 1990.

———. "Matthew, Gospel of." Pages 526–541 in *DJG*[1].

———. "Matthew as 'Gospel.'" Pages 59–75 in *Jesus, Matthew's Gospel and Early Christianity: Studies in Memory of Graham N. Stanton*. Edited by Daniel M. Gurtner, Joel Willitts, and Richard A. Burridge. LNTS 435. London: T&T Clark, 2011.

———. *Sermon on the Mount*. Story of God Bible Commentary. Grand Rapids: Zondervan, 2013.

McKnight, Scot, and Joseph B. Modica, eds. *Who Do My Opponents Say That I Am? An Investigation of the Accusations Against the Historical Jesus*. LNTS 327. London: T&T Clark, 2008.

McManigal, Daniel W. *A Baptism of Judgment in the Fire of the Holy Spirit: John's Eschatological Proclamation in Matthew 3*. LNTS 595. London: Bloomsbury, 2019.

McNeile, A. H. *Gospel According to St. Matthew*. Grand Rapids: Baker Book House, 1980.

Meadors, Edward P. "The 'Messianic' Implications of the Q Material." *JBL* 118.2 (1999): 253–77.

———. "What Did Matthew Really Care About?" Pages 24–43 in *What the New Testament Authors Really Cared About: A Survey of Their Writings*. Edited by Kenneth Berding and Matt Williams. Grand Rapids: Kregel, 2008.

Meerson, Michael, and Peter Schäfer, eds. and trans. *Toledot Yeshu: The Life Story of Jesus*. 2 vols. and database. Texts and Studies in Ancient Judaism 159. Tübingen: Mohr Siebeck, 2014.

Meier, John P. "Antioch." Pages 12–86 in *Antioch and Rome: New Testament Cradles of Catholic Christianity*. Edited by Raymond E. Brown and John P. Meier. New York: Paulist, 2004.

———. *Companions and Competitors*. Vol. 3 of *A Marginal Jew: Rethinking the Historical Jesus*. ABRL. New York: Doubleday, 2001.

———. *Law and Love*. Vol. 4 of *A Marginal Jew: Rethinking the Historical Jesus*. ABRL. New Haven, CN: Yale University Press, 2009.

———. *Mentor, Message, and Miracles*. Vol. 2 of *A Marginal Jew: Rethinking the Historical Jesus*. ABRL. New Haven, CN: Yale University Press, 1994.

———. *Matthew*. New Testament Message 3. Wilmington, DE: Glazier, 1980.

———. "Nations or Gentiles in Matthew 28:19?" *CBQ* 39.1 (1977): 94–102.

———. *The Roots of the Problem and the Person*. Volume 1 of *A Marginal Jew: Rethinking the Historical Jesus*. ABRL. New York: Doubleday, 1991.

———. "Salvation-History in Matthew: In Search of a Starting Point." *CBQ* 37 (1975): 203–15.

———. *The Vision of Matthew: Christ, Church, and Morality in the First Gospel*. Theological Inquiries. New York: Paulist, 1978.

Menken, Maarten J. J. *Matthew's Bible: The Old Testament Text of the Evangelist*. BETL 173. Leuven: Peeters, 2004.

Merkle, Benjamin L. "The Meaning of Ἐκκλησία in Matthew 16:18 and 18:17." *BSac* 167 (2010): 281–91.

———. "Who Will Be Left Behind? Rethinking the Meaning of Matthew 24:40–41 and Luke 17:34–35." *WTJ* 72.1 (2010): 169–79.

Metzger, Bruce M. "The Nazareth Inscription Again." Pages 75–92 in *New Testament Studies: Philological, Versional, and Patristic*. Edited by Bruce M. Metzger. NTTS 10. Leiden: Brill, 1980.

———. *The Text of the New Testament: Its Transmission, Corruption, and Restoration*. 2nd ed. Oxford: Oxford University Press, 1968.

Middleton, J. Richard. *A New Heaven and a New Earth: Reclaiming Biblical Eschatology*. Grand Rapids: Baker Academic, 2014.

Miller, Robert J. *Helping Jesus Fulfill Prophecy*. Eugene, OR: Cascade, 2015.

———. "How Matthew Helped Jesus Fulfill Prophecy." Pages 127–42 in *The Message of Jesus: John Dominic Crossan and Ben Witherington III in Dialogue*. Edited by Robert B. Stewart. Minneapolis: Fortress, 2013.

Mishkin, David. *Jewish Scholarship on the Resurrection of Jesus*. Eugene, OR: Pickwick, 2017.

Mitchell, Margaret M. "Patristic Counter-Evidence to the Claim That 'The Gospels Were Written for All Christians.'" *NTS* 51.1 (2005): 36–79.

Montefiore, Claude Goldsmid. *The Synoptic Gospels*. 2 vols. 2nd ed. 1927. Repr., New York: KTAV, 1968.

Moffitt, David M. "Righteous Bloodshed, Matthew's Passion Narrative, and the Temple's Destruction: Lamentations as a Matthean Intertext." *JBL* 125.2 (2006): 299–320.

Moloney, Francis. "Matthew 5:17–18 and the Matthean Use of ΔΙΚΑΙΟΣΥΝΗ." Pages 33–54 in *Unity and Diversity in the Gospels and Paul: Essays in Honor of Frank J. Matera*. Edited by Christopher W. Skinner and Kelly R. Iverson. ECL 7. Atlanta: SBL Press, 2012.

Moo, Douglas J. "Jesus and the Authority of the Mosaic Law." *JSNT* 20 (1984): 3–49.

———. "Law." *DJG*[1] 450–61.

———. "Tradition and Old Testament in Matt 27:3–10." Pages 157–75 in *Studies in Midrash and Historiography*. Edited by R. T. France and David Wenham. Vol. 3 of *Gospel Perspectives*. Sheffield: JSOT Press, 1983.

Moore, C. J. "Can We Hasten the Parousia? An Examination of Matt 24:14 and Its Implications for Missional Practice." *Them* 44.2 (2019): 291–311.

Morgan, Christopher W., and Robert A. Peterson, eds. *The Kingdom of God*. Theology in Community. Wheaton, IL: Crossway, 2012.

Morgan, Michael L., and Steven Weitzman, eds. *Rethinking the Messianic Idea in Judaism*. Bloomington, IN: Indiana University Press, 2015.

Morgan, Robert. "Towards a Critical Appropriation of the Sermon on the Mount: Christology and Discipleship." Pages 157–91 in *Christology, Controversy, and Community: New Testament Essays in Honour of David R. Catchpole*. Edited by David G. Horrell and Christopher M. Tuckett. NovTSup 99. Leiden, Netherlands: Brill, 2000.

Morgan, Robert, and John Barton. *Biblical Interpretation*. Oxford Bible Series. Oxford: Oxford University Press, 1988.

Morris, Leon. "Disciples of Jesus." Pages 112–27 in *Jesus of Nazareth: Lord and Christ. Essays on the Historical Jesus and New Testament Christology*. A Volume in Honor of I. Howard Marshall on the Occasion of His Sixtieth Birthday. Edited by Joel B. Green and Max Turner. Grand Rapids: Eerdmans, 1994.

———. *The Gospel According to Matthew*. PNTC. Grand Rapids: Eerdmans, 1992.

Moses, A. D. A. *Matthew's Transfiguration Story and Jewish-Christian Controversy*. JSNTSup 122. Sheffield: Sheffield Academic, 1996.

Mounce, Robert H. *Matthew*. Good News Commentary. San Francisco: Harper & Row, 1985.

Mowery, Robert L. "From Lord to Father in Matthew 1–7." *CBQ* 59 (1997): 642–56.

———. "The Matthean References to the Kingdom: Different Terms for Different Audiences." *ETL* 70.4 (1994): 398–405.

———. "Son of God in Roman Imperial Titles and Matthew." *Bib* 83 (2002): 100–110.

Moyise, Steve. *Jesus and Scripture: Studying the New Testament Use of the Old Testament*. Grand Rapids: Baker Academic, 2010.

———. "Matthew's Bible in the Infancy Narrative." Pages 9–24 in *The Scriptures of Israel in Jewish and Christian Tradition*. Essays in Honour of Maarten J. J. Menken. Edited by Bart Koet, Steve Moyise, and Joseph Verheyden. NovTSup 148. Leiden: Brill, 2013.

Nel, Marius. "What Is 'the Sign of the Son of Man in Heaven' (Mt 24:30)?" *In die Skriflig/In Luce Verbi* 49.1 (2015): Art. #1876.

Nelson, Peter K. *Leadership and Discipleship: A Study of Luke 22:24–30*. SBLDS 138. Atlanta: Scholars Press, 1994.

Neudecker, Reinhard. "Master-Disciple/Disciple-Master Relationship in Rabbinic Judaism and in the Gospels." *Gregorianum* 80 (1999): 245–61.

———. *Moses Interpreted by the Pharisees and Jesus: Matthew's Antitheses in the Light of Early Rabbinic Literature*. Subsidia Biblica 44. Rome: Gregorian and Biblical Press, 2012.

Neumann, James N. "Thy Will Be Done: Jesus's Passion in the Lord's Prayer." *JBL* 138.1 (2019): 161–82.

Neusner, Jacob. *Invitation to the Talmud: A Teaching Book*. New York: Harper & Row, 1973.

———. *The Mishnah*. New Haven, CT: Yale University Press, 1988.

Neusner, Jacob, Bruce D. Chilton, and Baruch A. Levine. *Torah Revealed, Torah Fulfilled: Scriptural Laws in Formative Judaism and Earliest Christianity*. London: T&T Clark, 2008.

Neusner, Jacob, and William Scott Green, eds. *Dictionary of Judaism in the Biblical Period: 450 B.C.E. to 600 C.E.* Peabody, MA: Hendrickson, 1999.

Newport, Kenneth G. C. *The Sources and Sitz im Leben of Matthew 23*. JSNT 117. Sheffield: Sheffield Academic, 1995.

Ng, Esther Yue L. "Matthew 5:17–20 and 'A Tale of Two Missions'?" Pages 201–21 in *New Testament Theology in Light of the Church's Mission: Essays in Honor of I. Howard Marshall*. Edited by Jon C. Laansma, Grant Osborne, and Ray Van Neste. Eugene, OR. Cascade, 2011.

Nicholls, Bruce, Theresa Roco Lua, and Julie Belding, eds. *The Church in a Changing World: An Asian Response; Challenges from the Malang Consultation on Globalization*. Quezon City, Philippines: Asia Theological Association, 2010.

Nickel, Jesse P. "Jesus, the Isaianic Servant Exorcist: Exploring the Significance of Matthew 12,18–21 in the Beelzebul Pericope." *ZNW* 107.2 (2016): 170–85.

———. *The Things That Make for Peace: Jesus and Eschatological Violence*. BZNW 244. Berlin: de Gruyter, 2021.

Nickelsburg, George W. E. "Enoch, Levi and Peter: Recipients of Revelation in Upper Galilee." *JBL* 100.4 (1981): 575–600.

Nicklas, Tobias. "Zwischen Redaktion und 'Neuinszenierung': Vom Umgang erzählender Evangelien des 2. Jahrhunderts mit ihren Vorlagen." Pages 311–30 in *Gospels and Gospel Traditions in the Second Century: Experiments in Reception*. Edited by Jens Schröter, Tobias Nicklas, and Joseph Verheyden, in collaboration with Katharina Simunovic. BZNW 235. Berlin: de Gruyter, 2019.

Niebuhr, Karl-Wilhelm. "Matthew's Idea of Being Human: God's Righteousness and Human Responsibility According to the Gospel of Matthew." Pages 329–44 in Seleznev, Loader, and Niebuhr. *The Gospel of Matthew in Its Historical and Theological Context*. WUNT 459. Tübingen: Mohr Siebeck, 2021.

Nienhuis, David R. *A Concise Guide to Reading the New Testament: A Canonical Introduction*. Grand Rapids: Baker Academic, 2018.

Nofoaiga, Vaitusi. *A Samoan Reading of Discipleship in Matthew*. IVBS 8. Atlanta: Society of Biblical Literature Press, 2017.

Nolland, John. *The Gospel of Matthew*. NIGTC. Grand Rapids: Eerdmans, 2005.

———. "Matthew and Anti-Semitism." Pages 154–69 in *Built upon the Rock: Studies in the Gospel of Matthew*. Edited by Daniel M. Gurtner and John Nolland. Grand Rapids: Eerdmans, 2008.

Nortjé, Lilly. "Matthew's Motive for the Composition of the Story of Judas's Suicide in Matthew 27:3–10." *Neot* 28.1 (1994): 41–51.

Novak, David. "Supersessionism Hard and Soft." *First Things* 290 (2019): 27–31.

———. *Zionism and Judaism: A New Theory*. Cambridge: Cambridge University Press, 2015.

Novakovic, Lidija. "Jesus as the Davidic Messiah in Matthew." *HBT* 19.2 (1997): 148–91.

———. *Messiah, the Healer of the Sick: A Study of Jesus as the Son of David in the Gospel of Matthew*. WUNT 2/170. Tübingen: Mohr Siebeck, 2003.

———. "The Resurrection of the Saints as a Prolepsis of the Resurrection of Jesus: A Reassessment of Matthew's Portrayal of the Risen Jesus." Pages 347–70 in Runesson and Gurtner, *Matthew Within Judaism*. ECL 27. Atlanta: Society of Biblical Literature, 2020.

Novenson, Matthew V. *Christ Among the Messiahs: Christ Language in Paul and Messiah Language in Ancient Judaism*. Oxford: Oxford University Press, 2012.

Ochs, Peter. *Another Reformation: Postliberal Christianity and the Jews*. Grand Rapids: Baker Academic, 2011.

O'Donnell, Douglas Sean. *Matthew: All Authority in Heaven and on Earth*. Preaching the Word. Wheaton, IL: Crossway, 2013.

Öhler, Markus. "The Expectation of Elijah and the Presence of the Kingdom of God." *JBL* 118.3 (1999): 461–76.

Olmstead, Wesley G. "A Gospel for a New Nation: Once More, the ἔθνος [*ethnos*] of Matthew 21.43." Pages 115–32 in *Jesus, Matthew's Gospel and Early Christianity: Studies in Memory of Graham N. Stanton*. Edited by Daniel M. Gurtner, Joel Willitts, and Richard A. Burridge. LNTS 435. London: T&T Clark, 2011.

———. "Jesus, the Eschatological Perfection of Torah, and the *imitatio Dei* in Matthew." Pages 43–58 in *Torah Ethics and Early Christian Identity*. Edited by Susan Wendel and David Miller. Grand Rapids: Eerdmans, 2016.

———. *Matthew 1–14: A Handbook on the Greek Text*. BHGNT. Waco, TX: Baylor University Press, 2019.

———. *Matthew 15–28: A Handbook on the Greek Text*. BHGNT. Waco, TX: Baylor University Press, 2019.

———. *Matthew's Trilogy of Parables: The Nation, the Nations and the Reader in Matthew 21:28–22:14*. SNTSMS 127. Cambridge: Cambridge University Press, 2003.

Oppong-Kumi, Peter Yaw. *Matthean Sets of Parables*. WUNT 2/340. Tübingen: Mohr Siebeck, 2013.

Ortlund, Gavin. "Resurrected as Messiah: The Risen Christ as Prophet, Priest and King." *JETS* 54.4 (2011): 749–66.

Osborne, Grant R. *Matthew*. ZECNT. Grand Rapids: Zondervan, 2010.

Overman, J. Andrew. *Church and Community in Crisis: The Gospel According to Matthew*. Edited by Howard Clark Kee and J. Andrew Overman. New Testament in Context. Valley Forge, PA: Trinity Press International, 1996.

———. *Matthew's Gospel and Formative Judaism: The Social World of the Matthean Community*. Minneapolis: Fortress, 1990.

Packer, J. I. *Concise Theology*. Wheaton, IL: Tyndale House, 1993.

Packer, J. I., and Mark Dever. *In My Place Condemned He Stood: Celebrating the Glory of the Atonement*. Wheaton, IL: Crossway, 2007.

Page, Sydney H. T. "Ransom Saying." *DJG*[1] 660–62.

Park, Eugene Eung-Chun. "Covenantal Nomism and the Gospel of Matthew." *Catholic Biblical Quarterly* 77.4 (2015): 668–85.

———. "Cynic Itinerant Philosophers and Galilean Wandering Missionaries in Matthew." Pages 125–39 in *Reading a Tendentious Bible: Essays in Honor of Robert B. Coote*. Edited by Marvin L. Chaney, Uriah Y. Kim, and Annette Schellenberg. Hebrew Bible Monographs 66. Sheffield: Sheffield Pheonix, 2014.

———. *The Mission Discourse in Matthew's Interpretation*. WUNT 2/81. Tübingen: Mohr Siebeck, 1995.

———. "An Unintended Reader's Response to Matthew 22:34–40." *Sacra Scripta* 9.1 (2011): 7–25.

Park, Wongi. "Multiracial Biblical Studies." *JBL* 140.3 (2021): 435–59.

———. *The Politics of Race and Ethnicity in Matthew's Passion Narrative*. Cham, Switzerland: Palgrave Macmillan, 2019.

Paschke, Boris. *Particularism and Universalism in the Sermon on the Mount: A Narrative-Critical Analysis of Matthew 5–7 in the Light of Matthew's View on Mission*. NTAbh, NS 56. Münster: Aschendorff, 2012.

Pattarumadathil, Henry. *"Your Father in Heaven": Discipleship in Matthew as a Process of Becoming Children of God*. AnBib 172. Rome: Pontificio Istituto Biblico, 2008.

Pawlikowski, John. *Christ in the Light of the Christian-Jewish Dialogue*. Studies in Judaism and Christianity. New York: Paulist, 1982.

———. "Christology in Light of the Jewish-Christian Dialogue: The Revolution in Christian–Jewish Understanding." *Proceedings of the Catholic Theological Society of America* 49 (1994): 120–34. Baltimore, Maryland. June 9–12, 1994. https://ejournals.bc.edu/ojs/index.php/ctsa/article/view/3891/3456.

Pennington, Jonathan T. *Heaven and Earth in the Gospel of Matthew*. NovTSup 126. Leiden: Brill, 2007.

———. "Heaven, Earth, and a New Genesis: Theological Cosmology in Matthew." Pages 28–44 in *Cosmology and New Testament Theology*. Edited by Jonathan T. Pennington and Sean M. McDonough. LNTS 335. London: T&T Clark, 2008.

———. "The Kingdom of Heaven in the Gospel of Matthew." *SBJT* 12.1 (2008): 43–51.

———. "The Lord's Last Supper in the Fourfold Witness of the Gospels." Pages 31–67 in *The Lord's Supper: Remembering and Proclaiming Christ Until He Comes*. Edited by Thomas R. Schreiner and Matthew R. Crawford. NAC Studies in Bible and Theology 10. Nashville: B&H, 2010.

———. "Matthew." Pages 83–114 in *The Trinity in the Canon: A Biblical, Theological, Historical, and Practical Proposal*. Edited by Brandon D. Smith. Brentwood, TN: B&H, 2023.

———. "Matthew 13 and the Function of the Parables in the First Gospel." *SBJT* 13.3 (2009): 12–21.

———. *Reading the Gospels Wisely: A Narrative and Theological Introduction*. Grand Rapids: Baker Academic, 2012.

———. *The Sermon on the Mount and Human Flourishing: A Theological Commentary*. Grand Rapids: Baker Academic, 2017.

Peppard, Michael. *Son of God in the Roman World: Divine Sonship in Its Social and Political Context*. Oxford: Oxford University Press, 2011.

Perkins, Pheme. *Peter: Apostle for the Whole Church*. SPNT. Columbia: University of South Carolina Press, 1994.

Perrin, Nicholas. *Jesus the Priest*. Grand Rapids: Baker Academic, 2018.

———. *Jesus the Temple*. Grand Rapids: Baker Academic, 2010.

Pfeifer, Daniel J. "Which Came First, The Symbol or the Referent? A Study of the Historical Twelve." *BSac* 172 (2015): 433–49.

Pinnock, Clark H. *Flame of Love: A Theology of the Holy Spirit*. 2nd ed. Foreword and commentary by Daniel Castelo. Downers Grove, IL: InterVarsity, 2022.

Piotrowski, Nicholas G. *Matthew's New David at the End of Exile: A Socio-Rhetorical Study of Scriptural Quotations*. NovTSup 170. Leiden: Brill, 2016.

Pitre, Brant James. *The Case for Jesus: The Biblical and Historical Evidence for Christ*. New York: Image, 2016.

———. *Jesus, the Tribulation, and the End of the Exile: Restoration Eschatology and the Origin of the Atonement*. WUNT 2/204. Tübingen: Mohr Siebeck, 2005.

Pizzuto, Vincent A. "The Structural Elegance of Matthew 1–2: A Chiastic Proposal." *CBQ* 74.4 (2012): 712–37.

Plummer, Alfred. *An Exegetical Commentary on The Gospel According to St. Matthew*. 1915. Repr., Grand Rapids: Baker, 1982.

Pond, Eugene W. "The Background and Timing of the Judgment of the Sheep and Goats." *BSac* 159 (2002): 201–20.

———. "Who Are 'The Least' of Jesus' Brothers in Matthew 25:40?" *BSac* 159 (2002): 436–48.

Porter, Stanley E. *Sacred Tradition in the New Testament: Tracing Old Testament Themes in the Gospels and Epistles*. Grand Rapids: Baker Academic, 2016.

Porter, Stanley E., and Bryan R. Dyer. *Origins of New Testament Christology: An Introduction to the Traditions and Titles Applied to Jesus*. Grand Rapids: Baker Academic, 2023.

Porter, Stanley E., and Alan E. Kurschner, eds. *The Future Restoration of Israel: A Response to Supersessionism*. McMaster Biblical Studies Series 10. Eugene, OR: Pickwick; Hamilton, Ontario: McMaster Divinity College Press, 2023.

Porter, Steven L. "Mentally Healthy and Healing Church: Spiritual Formation and Soul Care as Ecclesiology." *Journal of Spiritual Formation and Soul Care* 15.1 (2022): 3–5.

Powell, Mark Allan. *God With Us: A Pastoral Theology of Matthew's Gospel*. Minneapolis: Fortress, 1995.

———. *Introducing the New Testament: A Historical, Literary, and Theological Survey*. Grand Rapids: Baker Academic, 2009.

———. *Matthew*. Interpretation Bible Commentary. Louisville: Westminster John Knox, 2023.

———. *Methods for Matthew*. Methods in Biblical Interpretation. Cambridge: Cambridge University Press, 2009.

———. "Toward a Narrative-Critical Understanding of Matthew's Gospel." *Int* 46.4 (1992): 341–46.

Powell, Mark Allan, and David R. Bauer, eds. *Who Do You Say That I Am? Essays on Christology; In Honor of Jack Dean Kingsbury*. Louisville: Westminster John Knox, 1999.

Pregeant, Russell. *Matthew*. Chalice Commentaries for Today. St. Louis: Chalice, 2004.

Provan, Iain, and Mark Boda, eds. *Let Us Go Up to Zion: Essays in Honour of H. G. M. Williamson on the Occasion of His Sixty-Fifth Birthday*. VTSup 153. Leiden: Brill, 2012.

Przybylski, Benno. *Righteousness in Matthew and His World of Thought*. SNTSMS 41. Cambridge: Cambridge University Press, 1980.

Puerto, Mercedes Navarro, and Marinella Perroni, eds. *Gospels: Narrative and History*. Edited by Amy-Jill Levine. The Bible and Women: New Testament 2.1. Atlanta: Society of Biblical Literature, 2015.

Quarles, Charles L. *Matthew*. Evangelical Biblical Theology Commentary. Bellingham, WA: Lexham Academic, 2022.

———. *Matthew*. Exegetical Guide to the Greek New Testament. Nashville: B&H, 2017.

———. "Matthew 27:51–53: Meaning, Genre, Intertextuality, Theology, and Reception History." *JETS* 59.2 (2016): 271–86.

———. "Matthew 27:52–53 as a Scribal Interpolation: Testing a Recent Proposal." *BBR* 27.2 (2017): 207–26.

———. *Midrash Criticism: Introduction and Appraisal.* Lanham, MD: University Press of America, 1997.

———. "The Oath Formulas of Matthew 23:16–22 as Evidence for a Pre-70 Date of Composition for Matthew's Gospel." *TynBul* 72 (2021): 1–24.

———. "The *Protoevangelium of James* as an Alleged Parallel to Creative Historiography in the Synoptic Birth Narratives." *BBR* 8 (1998): 139–49.

———. *Sermon on the Mount: Restoring Christ's Message to the Modern Church.* NAC Studies in Bible and Theology. Nashville: B&H, 2011.

———. *A Theology of Matthew: Jesus Revealed as Deliverer, King, and Incarnate Creator.* Explorations in Biblical Theology. Phillipsburg, NJ: P&R, 2013.

Rabbinowitz, Noel S. "Matthew 23:2–4: Does Jesus Recognize the Authority of the Pharisees and Does He Endorse Their Halakhah?" *JETS* 46.3 (2003): 423–47.

Reed, Annette Yoshiko. "'Jewish Christianity' after the 'Parting of the Ways': Approaches to Historiography and Self-Definition in the Pseudo-Clementines." Pages 189–231 in *The Ways That Never Parted: Jews and Christians in Late Antiquity and the Early Middle Ages.* Edited by Adam H. Becker and Annette Yoshiko Reed. Minneapolis: Fortress, 2007.

———. *Jewish-Christianity and the History of Judaism: Collected Essays.* Texts and Studies in Ancient Judaism 171. Tübingen: Mohr Siebeck, 2018; Minneapolis: Fortress, 2022.

Regev, Eyal. *The Temple in Early Christianity: Experiencing the Sacred.* AYBRL. New Haven, CT: Yale University Press, 2019.

———. "Were the Early Christians Sectarians?" *JBL* 130.4 (2011): 771–93.

Reiser, Marius. *Jesus and Judgment: The Eschatological Proclamation in Its Jewish Context.* Translated by Linda M. Maloney. Minneapolis: Fortress, 1997.

Rengstorf, Karl H. "δώδεκα." *TDNT* 2:321–28.

———. "μαθητής." *TDNT* 4:415–61.

Repschinski, Boris. *The Controversy Stories in the Gospel of Matthew: Their Redaction, Form and Relevance for the Relationship Between the Matthean Community and Formative Judaism.* FRLANT 189. Göttingen: Vandenhoeck & Ruprecht, 2000.

———. "'For He Will Save His People from Their Sins' (Matthew 1:21): A Christology for Christian Jews." *CBQ* 68.2 (2006): 248–67.

———. "Matthew's Perspective on Roman Political Authorities." Pages 9–42 in *Matthew, Paul, and Others: Asian Perspectives on New Testament Themes.* Edited by William Loader, Boris Repschinski, and Eric Wong. Innsbruck, Austria: Innsbruck University Press, 2019.

———. "Shift the Issue and Win the Fight? Rhetorical Strategies of Dealing with Conflicts in the Gospels of Matthew and John." *ZKT* 139.4 (2017): 387–410.

Ribbens, Benjamin J. "Whose 'Mercy'? What 'Sacrifice'? A Proposed Reading of Matthew's Hosea 6:6 Quotations." *BBR* 28.3 (2018): 381–404.

Riches, John. *Matthew.* T&T Clark Study Guides. London: T&T Clark, 1996.

Riches, John, and David C. Sim, eds. *The Gospel of Matthew in its Roman Imperial Context.* Early Christianity in Context. JSNTSup 276. London: T&T Clark, 2005.

Ridlehoover, Charles Nathan. *The Lord's Prayer and the Sermon on the Mount in Matthew's Gospel.* LNTS 616. London: T&T Clark, 2020.

Riesner, Rainer. *Messias Jesus: Seine Geschichte, seine Botschaft und ihre Überlieferung.* Gießen, Germany: Brunnen, 2019.

Roberts, Kyle. *A Complicated Pregnancy: Whether Mary Was a Virgin and Why It Matters.* Minneapolis: Fortress, 2017.

Robertson, O. Palmer. *Testimony of the Four Gospels.* Vol. 1 of *Christ of the Consummation: A New Testament Biblical Theology.* 3 vols. Phillipsburg, NJ: P&R, 2022.

Rodríguez, Rafael. *Structuring Early Christian Memory: Jesus in Tradition, Performance and Text.* LNTS 407. London: Bloomsbury T &T Clark, 2010.

Rohrbaugh, Richard L. "The Social Function of Genealogies in the New Testament and Its World." Pages 250–72 in *To Set at Liberty: Essays on Early Christianity and Its Social World in Honor of John H. Elliott.* Edited by Stephen K. Black. SWBA 11. Sheffield: Sheffield Phoenix, 2014.

Rosner, Brian S. "Biblical Theology." Pages 3–11 in *NDBT.*

Rosner, Jennifer. "Post-Holocaust Jewish-Christian Relations: Challenging Boundaries and Rethinking

Theology." Pages 142–60 in *Understanding the Jewish Roots of Christianity: Biblical, Theological, and Historical Essays on the Relationship Between Christianity and Judaism*. Edited by Gerald McDermott. Studies in Scripture and Biblical Theology. Bellingham, WA: Lexham, 2021.

Rousseau, John J., and Rami Arav. *Jesus and His World: An Archaeological and Cultural Dictionary*. Minneapolis: Fortress, 1995.

Ruether, Rosemary Radford. *Faith and Fratricide: The Theological Roots of Anti-Semitism*. New York: Seabury, 1974.

Runesson, Anders. "Beyond Universalism and Particularism: Rethinking Paul and Matthew on Gentile Inclusion." Pages 99–112 in *Paul and Matthew Among Jews and Gentiles: Essays in Honor of Terence L. Donaldson*. Edited by Ronald Charles. LNTS 628. London: T&T Clark, 2020.

———. *Divine Wrath and Salvation in Matthew: The Narrative World of the First Gospel*. Minneapolis: Fortress, 2016.

———. "Judging Gentiles in the Gospel of Matthew: Between 'Othering' and Inclusion.'" Pages 133–51 in *Jesus, Matthew's Gospel and Early Christianity: Studies in Memory of Graham N. Stanton*. Edited by Daniel M. Gurtner, Joel Willitts, and Richard A. Burridge. LNTS 435. London: T&T Clark, 2011.

———. *The Origins of the Synagogue: A Socio-Historical Study*. ConBNT 37. Stockholm, Sweden: Almquiest & Wiksell, 2001.

———. "Rethinking Early Jewish–Christian Relations: Matthean Community History as Pharisaic Intragroup Conflict." *JBL* 127.1 (2008): 95–132.

Runesson, Anders, and Daniel M. Gurtner, eds. *Matthew Within Judaism: Israel and the Nations in the First Gospel*. ECL 27. Atlanta: Society of Biblical Literature Press, 2020.

Rutledge, Fleming. *The Crucifixion: Understanding the Death of Jesus Christ*. Grand Rapids: Eerdmans, 2015.

Ryan, Jordan J. *The Role of the Synagogue in the Aims of Jesus*. Minneapolis: Fortress, 2017.

Ryken, Philip Graham. "A New Heaven and a New Earth: Revelation 21:1–22:5." Pages 119–38 in *Coming Home: Essays on the New Heaven and New Earth*. Edited by D. A. Carson and Jeff Robinson Sr. Wheaton, IL: Crossway, 2017.

Sailhammer, John H. "Hosea 11:1 and Matthew 2:15." *WTJ* 63 (2001): 83–92.

Saldarini, Anthony J. "Matthew." Pages 1000–1063 in *Eerdmans Commentary on the Bible*. Edited by James D. G. Dunn and John W. Rogerson. Grand Rapids: Eerdmans, 2003.

———. *Matthew's Christian-Jewish Community*. Chicago: University of Chicago Press, 1994.

———. "Reading Matthew Without Anti-Semitism." Pages 166–84 in *The Gospel of Matthew in Current Study*. Edited by David E. Aune. Grand Rapids: Eerdmans, 2001.

Samuelsson, Gunnar. *Crucifixion in Antiquity: An Inquiry into the Background and Significance of the New Testament Terminology of Crucifixion*. 2nd ed. WUNT 2/310. Tübingen: Mohr Siebeck, 2013.

Sande, Ken. *The Peacemaker: A Biblical Guide to Resolving Personal Conflict*. 3rd exp. and rev. ed. Grand Rapids: Baker, 2004.

Sanders, E. P. *Jesus and Judaism*. Philadelphia: Fortress, 1985.

Sanders, Fred. *The Deep Things of God: How the Trinity Changes Everything*. Wheaton, IL: Crossway, 2010.

———. "Salvation in Matthew (with an Assist from Paul)." *Scriptorium*. (11 January 2013). https://www.patheos.com/blogs/scriptorium/2013/01/salvation-in-matthew-with-an-assist-from-paul/.

———. *The Triune God*. New Studies in Dogmatics. Grand Rapids: Zondervan, 2016.

Sanders, Fred, and Scott R. Swain, eds. *Retrieving Eternal Generation*. Grand Rapids: Zondervan, 2017.

Sargent, Benjamin. *David Being a Prophet: The Contingency of Scripture upon History in the New Testament*. BZNW 207. Berlin: de Gruyter, 2014.

Sarma, Bitrus A. *Hermeneutics of Mission in Matthew: Israel and the Nations in the Interpretative Framework of Matthew's Gospel*. Langham Monographs. Carlisle, UK: Langham Trust, 2015.

Saucy, Mark. *The Kingdom of God in the Teaching of Jesus in 20th Century Theology*. Dallas: Word, 1997.

———. "*Regnum Spiriti*: The Role of the Spirit in the Social Ethics of the Kingdom." *JETS* 54.1 (2011): 89–108.

Saucy, Robert L. *The Case for Progressive Dispensationalism: The Interface Between Dispensational and Non-Dispensational Theology*. Grand Rapids: Zondervan, 1993.

———. *The Church in God's Program*. Chicago: Moody, 1972.

Scaer, David P. *Discourses in Matthew: Jesus Teaches the Church*. Saint Louis: Concordia, 2004.

Schiffman, Lawrence H., and James C. VanderKam, eds. *Encyclopedia of the Dead Sea Scrolls*. 2 vols. Oxford: Oxford University Press, 2000.

Schmidt, Thomas E., and Moisés Silva, eds. *To Tell the Mystery: Essays on New Testament Eschatology in Honor of Robert H. Gundry.* JSNTSup 100. Sheffield: JSOT Press, 1994.

Schnabel, Eckhard J. *Early Christian Mission.* 2 vols. Downers Grove, IL: InterVarsity, 2004.

———. "The First Gospel and Matthew's Mission: Narrative, Theological and Historical Perspectives." Matthew Section. 2005 SBLSP. Published online at https://www.sbl-site.org/meetings/AMseminarpapers.aspx.

———. *Jesus in Jerusalem: The Last Days.* Grand Rapids: Eerdmans, 2018.

Schnackenburg, Rudolf. *The Gospel of Matthew.* Translated by Robert R. Barr. Grand Rapids: Eerdmans, 2002.

Schneemelcher, Wilhelm. *New Testament Apocrypha.* 2 vols. Rev. ed. Edited by R. McL. Wilson. Louisville: Westminster John Knox, 1991.

Schnelle, Udo. *Theology of the New Testament.* Translated by M. Eugene Boring. Grand Rapids: Baker Academic, 2007.

Schoedel, William R. *Ignatius of Antioch: A Commentary on the Letters of Ignatius of Antioch.* Edited by Helmut Koester. Hermeneia. Philadelphia: Fortress, 1985.

Schreiner, Patrick. *The Body of Jesus: A Spatial Analysis of the Kingdom in Matthew.* LNTS 555. London: T&T Clark, 2016.

———. *The Kingdom of God and the Glory of the Cross.* Short Studies in Biblical Theology. Wheaton, IL: Crossway, 2018.

———. *Matthew, Disciple and Scribe: The First Gospel and Its Portrait of Jesus.* Grand Rapids: Baker Academic, 2019.

Schreiner, Thomas R. *40 Questions About Christians and Biblical Law.* 40 Questions Series. Grand Rapids: Kregel, 2010.

———. *The King in His Beauty: A Biblical Theology of the Old and New Testaments.* Grand Rapids: Baker Academic, 2013.

———. "Penal Substitution." Pages 67–98 in *The Nature of the Atonement: Four Views.* Edited by James Beilby and Paul R. Eddy. Downers Grove, IL: InterVarsity, 2006.

Schröter, Jens. *Jesus of Nazareth: Jew from Galilee, Savior of the World.* Translated by Wayne Coppins and S. Brian Pounds. BMSSEC. Waco, TX: Baylor University Press, 2014.

———. "The Quest for the Historical Jesus: Current Debates and Prospects." *Early Christianity* 11 (2020): 283–96.

Schröter, Jens, Benjamin A. Edsall, and Joseph Verheyden, eds. *Jews and Christians—Parting Ways in the First Two Centuries CE? Reflections on the Gains and Losses of a Model.* BZNW 253. Berlin: de Gruyter, 2021

Schweizer, Eduard. *The Good News According to Matthew.* Translated by David E. Green. Richmond: John Knox, 1975.

Scobie, Charles H. H. "Israel and the Nations: An Essay in Biblical Theology." *TynBul* 43.2 (1992): 283–305.

Segovia, Fernando F., ed. *Discipleship in the New Testament.* Philadelphia: Fortress, 1985.

Seleznev, Mikhail, William R. G. Loader, and Karl-Wilhelm Niebuhr, eds. Seleznev, Loader, and Niebuhr. *The Gospel of Matthew in Its Historical and Theological Context.* WUNT 459. Tübingen: Mohr Siebeck, 2021.

Senior, Donald. "Directions in Matthean Studies." Pages 5–21 in *The Gospel of Matthew in Current Study: Studies in Memory of William G. Thompson, S.J.* Edited by David E. Aune. Grand Rapids: Eerdmans, 2001.

———, ed. *The Gospel of Matthew at the Crossroads of Early Christianity.* BETL 243. Leuven: Peeters, 2011.

———. *Matthew.* ANTC. Nashville: Abingdon, 1998.

———. "Matthew at the Crossroads of Early Christianity: An Introductory Assessment." Pages 3–24 in *The Gospel of Matthew at the Crossroads of Early Christianity.* Edited by Donald Senior. BETL 243. Leuven: Peeters, 2011.

———. *The Passion of Jesus in the Gospel of Matthew.* Passion Series 1. Collegeville, MN: Liturgical Press, 1990.

———. Review of *Matthew's Messianic Shepherd-King: In Search of "The Lost Sheep of the House of Israel,"* by Joel Willitts. *Review of Biblical Literature* (2009), http://www.bookreviews.org.

———. "Viewing the Jewish Jesus of History through the Lens of Matthew's Gospel." Pages 81–97 in *Soundings in the Religion of Jesus: Perspectives and Methods in Jewish and Christian Scholarship.* Edited by Bruce Chilton, Anthony Le Donne, and Jacob Neusner. Minneapolis: Fortress, 2012.

———. *What Are They Saying About Matthew?* Rev. and exp. ed. New York: Paulist, 1996.

Shanks, Monte Allen. *Papias and the New Testament.* Eugene, OR: Pickwick, 2013.

Shelton, W. Brian. *Quest for the Historical Apostles: Tracing Their Lives and Legacies.* Grand Rapids: Baker Academic, 2018.

Shin, In-Cheol. "Matthew's Designation of the Role of Women as Indirectly Adherent Disciples." *Neot* 41.2 (2007): 399–415.

Schottroff, Luise. *Der Anfang des Neuen Testaments: Matthäus 1–4 neu entdeckt. Ein Kommentar mit Beiträgen zum Gespräch*. Edited by Frank Crüsemann, Claudia Janssen, and Rainer Kessler. Stuttgart: Kohlhammer, 2019.

Siegal, Michal Bar-Asher, Wolfgang Grünstäudl, and Matthew Thiessen, eds. *Perceiving the Other in Ancient Judaism and Early Christianity*. WUNT 2/394. Tübingen: Mohr Siebeck, 2017.

Sievers, Joseph, and Amy-Jill Levine, eds. *The Pharisees*. Grand Rapids: Eerdmans, 2021.

Sigal, Phillip. "Aspects of an Inquiry into Dual Covenant Theology." *HBT* 3 (1981): 181–209.

———. "Aspects of Dual Covenant Theology: Salvation." *HBT* 5.2 (1983): 1–48.

———. *The Halakhah of Jesus of Nazareth According to the Gospel of Matthew*. SBL 18. Atlanta: Society of Biblical Literature, 2007.

Siker, Jeffrey S. *Disinheriting the Jews: Abraham in Early Christian Controversy*. Louisville: Westminster John Knox, 1991.

———. *Sin in the New Testament*. EBS. Oxford: Oxford University Press, 2019.

Silva, Moíses, ed. *New International Dictionary of New Testament Theology and Exegesis*. 2nd ed. 5 vols. Grand Rapids: Zondervan, 2014

Sim, David C. *Apocalyptic Eschatology in the Gospel of Matthew*. SNTSMS 88. Cambridge: Cambridge University Press, 1996.

———. *The Gospel of Matthew and Christian Judaism: The History and Social Setting of the Matthean Community*. SNTW. Edinburgh: T&T Clark, 1998.

———. "The Gospel of Matthew and Galilee: An Evaluation of an Emerging Hypothesis." *ZNW* 107.2 (2016): 141–69.

———. "Matthew 7.21–23: Further Evidence of Its Anti-Pauline Perspective." *NTS* 53 (2007): 325–43.

———. "Matthew, Paul and the Origin and Nature of the Gentile Mission: The Great Commission in Matthew 28:16–20 as an Anti-Pauline Tradition." *HvTSt* 64.1 (2008): 377–92.

———. "Matthew: The Current State of Research." Pages 33–51 in Becker and Runesson, *Mark and Matthew I. Comparative Readings*. WUNT 271. Tübingen: Mohr Siebeck, 2011.

———. "The Meaning of *palingenesia* in Mt 19.28." *JSNT* 50 (1993): 3–12.

———. "The Rise and Fall of the Gospel of Matthew." *ExpTim* 120.10 (2009): 478–85.

———. "Rome in Matthew's Eschatology." Pages 91–106 in *The Gospel of Matthew in its Roman Imperial Context*. Edited by John K. Riches and David C. Sim. London, Bloomsbury, 2005.

———. *There Will Be Weeping and Gnashing of Teeth: Essays on Matthew's Apocalyptic Eschatology*. Berlin: de Gruyter, 2023.

Simonetti, Manlio, ed. *Matthew 1–13*. ACCSNT Ia. Downers Grove: InterVarsity, 2001.

Simonetti, Manlio, ed. *Matthew 14–28*. ACCSNT Ib. Downers Grove: InterVarsity, 2002.

Skarsaune, Oskar. *The Proof from Prophecy: A Study in Justin Martyr's Proof-Text Tradition: Text-Type, Provenance, Theological Profile*. NovTSup 56. Leiden, NE: Brill, 1987.

Skinner, Christopher W., and Kelly R. Iverson. *Unity and Diversity in the Gospels and Paul: Essays in Honor of Frank J. Matera*. ECL 7. Atlanta: Society of Biblical Literature Press, 2012.

Slee, Michelle. *The Church in Antioch in the First Century CE: Communion and Conflict*. JSNTSup 244. London: Sheffield, 2003.

Smillie, Gene R. "'Even the Dogs': Gentiles in the Gospel of Matthew." *JETS* 45.1 (2002): 73–97.

Smith, Brandon D. *The Biblical Trinity: Encountering the Father, Son, and Holy Spirit in Scripture*. Bellingham, WA: Lexham, 2023.

———, ed. *The Trinity in the Canon: A Biblical, Theological, Historical, and Practical Proposal*. Brentwood, TN: B&H, 2023.

Smith, Christopher R. "Literary Evidences of a Fivefold Structure in the Gospel of Matthew." *NTS* 43.4 (1997): 540–51.

Smith, Ian K. *Not Home Yet: How the Renewal of the Earth Fits into God's Plan for the World*. Wheaton, IL: Crossway, 2019.

Smith, Justin Marc. *Why Βίος? On the Relationship Between Gospel Genre and Implied Audience*. LNTS 518. London: Bloomsbury T&T Clark, 2015.

Smith, Robert H. "Mt 27:25—The Hardest Verse in Matthew's Gospel." *Currents in Theology and Missiology* 17.6 (1990): 421–50.

Snodgrass, Klyne R. "Matthew and the Law." Pages 101–36 in *Treasures New and Old: Recent Contributions to Matthean Studies*. Edited by David R. Bauer and Mark A. Powell. SBLSymS 1. Atlanta: Scholars Press, 1996.

———. *Stories with Intent: A Comprehensive Guide to the Parables of Jesus*. Grand Rapids: Eerdmans, 2008.

Soares-Prabhu, George M. *The Formula Quotations in the Infancy Narratives of Matthew*. AnBib 63. Rome: Pontifical Biblical Press, 1976.

Spadaro, Martin C. *Reading Matthew as the Climactic Fulfillment of the Hebrew Story*. Eugene, OR: Wipf & Stock, 2015.

Spicq, C. "Une Allusion au Docteur de Justice dans Matthieu, XXIII, 10?" *Revue Biblique* 66.3 (1959): 387–96.

Sprinkle, Preston, ed. *Four Views on Hell*. 2nd ed. Counterpoints: Bible and Theology. Grand Rapids: Zondervan, 2016.

*Stanford Encyclopedia of Philosophy, The*. "Franz Rosenzweig." By Benjamin Pollock. Edited by Edward N. Zalta. Rev. ed. (2019). https://plato.stanford.edu/archives/spr2019/entries/rosenzweig/.

Stanton, Graham N. "The Early Reception of Matthew's Gospel: New Evidence from Papyri?" Pages 42–61 in *The Gospel of Matthew in Current Study: Studies in Memory of William G. Thompson, S.J.* Edited by David E. Aune. Grand Rapids: Eerdmans, 2001.

———. *A Gospel for a New People: Studies in Matthew*. Edinburgh: T&T Clark, 1992.

———. *Gospel Truth? New Light on Jesus and the Gospels*. Valley Forge, PA: Trinity Press International, 1995.

———, ed. *The Interpretation of Matthew*. 2nd ed. SNTI. Edinburgh: T&T Clark, 1995.

———. "Matthew as a Creative Interpreter of the Sayings of Jesus." Pages 257–72 in *The Gospel and the Gospels*. Edited by Peter Stuhlmacher. Grand Rapids: Eerdmans, 1991.

———. "The Origin and Purpose of Matthew's Gospel: Matthean Scholarship from 1945–1980." Pages 9–75 in *Studies in Matthew and Early Christianity*. Edited by Markus Bockmuehl and David Lincicum. WUNT 309. Tübingen: Mohr Siebeck, 2013.

Stegemann, Ekkehard W., and Wolfgang Stegemann. *The Jesus Movement: A Social History of Its First Century*. Translated by O. C. Dean Jr. Minneapolis: Fortress, 1999.

Steinmann, Andrew E. "What Did David Understand About the Promises in the Davidic Covenant?" *BSac* 171 (2014): 19–29.

Stendahl, Krister. *The School of St. Matthew and Its Use of the Old Testament*. 2nd ed. Lund: Gleerup, 1954.

Stewart, Alexander E. "The Temporary Messianic Kingdom in Second Temple Judaism and the Delay of the Parousia: Psalm 110:1 and the Development of Early Christian Inaugurated Eschatology." *JETS* 59.2 (2016): 255–70.

Stott, John R. W. *The Cross of Christ*. 20th anniversary special ed. Downers Grove, IL: InterVarsity, 2006.

Strecker, Georg. *The Sermon on the Mount: An Exegetical Commentary*. Translated by O. C. Dean Jr. Nashville: Abingdon, 1988.

———. *Der Weg der Gerechtigkeit: Untersuchung zur Theologie des Matthäus*. Göttingen: Vandenhoeck & Ruprecht, 1962.

Streeter, B. H. *The Four Gospels: A Study of Origins*. 4th rev. ed. London: Macmillan: 1930.

Strotmann, Angelika, and Markus Tiwald. "Das Matthäusevangelium–eine Paulus-Polemik? Überlegungen zum Toraverständnis des ersten Evangelisten." Pages 64–106 in *Kontroverse Stimmen im Kanon*. Edited by Martin Ebner, Gerd Häfner, and Konrad Huber. Quaestiones Disputatae 279. Freiburg: Herder, 2016.

Stuhlmacher, Peter. *Biblical Theology of the New Testament*. Translated and edited by Daniel P. Bailey, with the collaboration of Jostein Ådna. Grand Rapids: Eerdmans, 2018.

———. *Die Geburt des Immanuel: Die Weihnachtsgeschichten aus dem Lukas- und Matthäusevangelium*. Göttingen: Vandenhoeck & Ruprecht, 2005.

———. "Matt 28:16–20 and the Course of Mission in the Apostolic and Postapostolic Age." Pages 17–43 in *The Mission of the Early Church to Jews and Gentiles*. Edited by Jostein Ådna and Hans Kvalbein. WUNT 127. Tübingen: Mohr Siebeck, 2000.

———. *Reconciliation, Law, and Righteousness: Essays in Biblical Theology*. Translated by Everett R. Kalin. Philadelphia: Fortress, 1986.

Stump, Eleonore. *Atonement*. Oxford Studies in Analytic Theology. Oxford: Oxford University Press, 2019.

Swain, Scott R. *The Trinity and the Bible: On Theological Interpretation*. Bellingham, WA: Lexham Academic, 2021.

Swanson, Richard W. *Provoking the Gospel of Matthew: A Storyteller's Commentary, Year A*. Cleveland: Pilgrim, 2007.

Sweatman, Carl S., and Clifford B. Kvidahl, eds. *Treasures New & Old: Essays in Honor of Donald A. Hagner.* GlossaHouse Festschrift Series 1. Wilmore, KY: GlossaHouse, 2018.

Syreeni, Kari. "Peter as a Character and Symbol in the Gospel of Matthew." Pages 106–52 in *Characterization in the Gospel: Reconceiving Narrative Criticism.* Edited by David Rhoads and Kari Syreeni. JSNTSup 184. Sheffield: Sheffield Academic, 1999.

Tabb, Brian J., and Andrew M. King, eds. *Five Views of Christ in the Old Testament: Genre, Authorial Intent, and the Nature of Scripture.* Counterpoints. Grand Rapids: Zondervan, 2022.

Talbert, Charles H. *Matthew.* Paideia. Grand Rapids Academic: Baker, 2010.

Tamfu, Dieudonné. "Jesus' Kingly Blessings for the Nations: A Missiological Understanding of Matthew 1:1." *Journal of Global Christianity* 1.1 (2015): 79–91.

Tanner, J. Paul. "The 'Outer Darkness' in Matthew's Gospel: Shedding Light on an Ominous Warning." *BSac* 174 (2017): 445–59.

Tasker, R. V. G. *The Gospel According to St. Matthew: An Introduction and Commentary.* TNTC. Grand Rapids: Eerdmans, 1961.

Thielman, Frank. *Theology of the New Testament: A Canonical and Synthetic Approach.* Grand Rapids: Zondervan, 2005.

Thiselton, Anthony C. *The Holy Spirit: In Biblical Teaching, Through the Centuries, and Today.* Grand Rapids: Eerdmans, 2013.

———. *New Horizons in Hermeneutics: The Theory and Practice of Transforming Biblical Reading.* Grand Rapids: Zondervan, 1992.

———. *The Two Horizons: New Testament Hermeneutics and Philosophical Description.* Grand Rapids: Eerdmans, 1980.

Thysman, Raymond. *Communaute et directives ethiques: la catechese de Matthieu.* Recherches et Syntheses: Section d'exegese 1. Gembloux, Belgium: Duculot, 1974.

Tidball, Derek. *The Message of the Cross: Wisdom Unsearchable, Love Indestructible.* BST. Downers Grove, IL: InterVarsity, 2001.

Toussaint, Stanley D. *Behold the King: A Study of Matthew.* Portland, OR: Multnomah, 1981.

Travis, Stephen H. *Christ and the Judgement of God: The Limits of Divine Retribution in New Testament Thought.* 2nd ed. Peabody, MA: Hendrickson, 2009.

Trebilco, Paul. *Self-Designations and Group Identity in the New Testament.* Cambridge: Cambridge University Press, 2012.

Troxel, Ronald L. "Matt 27.51–54 Reconsidered: Its Role in the Passion Narrative, Meaning and Origin." *NTS* 48.1 (2002): 30–47.

Tuckett, Christopher M. *2 Clement: Introduction, Text, and Commentary.* Oxford Apostolic Fathers. Oxford: Oxford University Press, 2012. Leuven: Peeters, 2011.

———. "Matthew: The Social and Historical Context—Jewish Christian and/or Gentile?" Pages 99–129 in *The Gospel of Matthew at the Crossroads of Early Christianity.* Edited by Donald Senior. BETL 243. Leuven: Peeters, 2011

Turner, David L. "His Glorious Throne: Israel and the Gentiles in Mission and Judgment in the Gospel of Matthew." Pages 135–168 in Runesson and Gurtner, *Matthew Within Judaism.* ECL 27. Atlanta: Society of Biblical Literature, 2020.

———. *Israel's Last Prophet: Jesus and the Jewish Leaders in Matthew 23.* Minneapolis: Fortress, 2015.

———. *Matthew.* BECNT. Grand Rapids: Baker Academic, 2008.

———. "The Structure and Sequence of Matthew 24:1–41: Interaction with Evangelical Treatments." *Grace Theological Journal* 10.1 (1989): 3–27.

Twelftree, Graham H. *Jesus the Miracle Worker: A Historical and Theological Study.* Downers Grove: InterVarsity, 1999.

Vaitusi, Nofoaiga. *A Samoan Reading of Discipleship in Matthew.* IVBS 8. Atlanta: Society of Biblical Literature Press, 2017.

Van Aarde, Andries G. *God-With-Us: The Dominant Perspective in Matthew's Story, and Other Essays.* HvTStSup 5. Pretoria, South Africa: University of Pretoria, 1994.

———. "ΙΗΣΟΥΣ, the Davidic Messiah, As Political Saviour in Matthew's History." Pages 7–31 in *Salvation in The New Testament: Perspectives on Soteriology.* Edited by Jan G. Van Der Watt. Leiden: Brill, 2005.

Van Aarde, Andries G., and Yolanda Dreyer. "Matthew Studies Today—A Willingness to Suspect and A Willingness to Listen." *HvTSt* 66.1 (2010): art. #820. https://doi.org/10.4102/hts.v66i1.820.

Van Eck, Ernest. *Parables of Jesus the Galilean: Stories of a Social Prophet.* Matrix: The Bible in Its Mediterranean Context. Eugene, OR: Wipf & Stock, 2016.

Van Groningen, Gerard. *Messianic Revelation in the Old Testament.* Grand Rapids: Baker Book House, 1990.

Van Tilborg, Sjef. *The Jewish Leaders in Matthew.* Leiden, Netherlands: Brill, 1972.

Vanhoozer, Kevin J. *Is There a Meaning in This Text? The Bible, the Reader, and the Morality of Literary Knowledge.* Grand Rapids: Zondervan, 1998.

Vearncombe, Erin K. "Redistribution and Reciprocity: A Socio-Economic Interpretation of the Parable of the Labourers in the Vineyard (Matthew 20.1–15)." *JSHJ* 8.3 (2010): 199–236.

Venard, Olivier-Thomas, ed. *La passion selon saint Matthieu: Matthieu 26–28.* 2 Volumes. La Bible en ses Traditions 4. Leuven: Peeters, 2021.

Verheyden, Joseph. "Irenaeus and the Gospel of Matthew." Pages 289–320 in *The Composition, Theology, and Early Reception of Matthew's Gospel.* Edited by Joseph Verheyden, Jens Schröter, and David C. Sim. WUNT 477. Tübingen: Mohr Siebeck, 2022.

———. "Rock and Stumbling Block: The Fate of Matthew's Peter." Pages 263–311 in *The Gospel of Matthew at the Crossroads of Early Christianity.* Edited by Donald Senior. BETL 243. Leuven: Peeters, 2011.

Verheyden, Joseph, Jens Schröter, and David C. Sim, eds. *The Composition, Theology, and Early Reception of Matthew's Gospel.* WUNT 477. Tübingen: Mohr Siebeck, 2022.

Vermes, Geza. *The Religion of Jesus the Jew.* Minneapolis: Fortress, 1993.

———. *The Resurrection: History and Myth.* New York: Doubleday, 2008.

Verseput, Donald J. "The Davidic Messiah and Matthew's Jewish Christianity." *SBLSP* 34 (1995): 102–16.

———. *The Rejection of the Humble Messianic King: A Study of the Composition of Matthew 11–12.* European University Studies 291. Frankfurt am Main: Peter Lang, 1986.

———. "The Role and Meaning of the 'Son of God' Title in Matthew's Gospel." *NTS* 33.4 (1987): 532–56.

Vickers, Brian. "What Does Justification Have to Do with the Gospels?" Pages 179–212 in *The Doctrine on Which the Church Stands or Falls: Justification in Biblical, Theological, Historical, and Pastoral Perspective.* Edited by Matthew Barrett. Wheaton, IL: Crossway, 2019.

Viljoen, Francois P. "Righteousness and Identity Formation in the Sermon on the Mount." *HvTSt* 69.1 (2013): art. #1300. https://doi.org/10.4102/hts.v69i1.1300.

Vine, Cedric E. W. *The Audience of Matthew: An Appraisal of the Local Audience Thesis.* LNTS 496. London: Bloomsbury T&T Clark, 2014.

———. *Jesus and the Nations: Discipleship and Mission in the Gospel of Matthew.* Eugene, OR: Pickwick, 2022.

Vlach, Michael J. *The Church as a Replacement of Israel: An Analysis of Supersessionism.* Edition Israelogie. Frankfurt am Main: Peter Lang, 2009.

———. *Has the Church Replaced Israel? A Theological Evaluation.* Nashville: B&H, 2010.

Vledder, Evert-Jan. *Conflict in the Miracle Stories: A Socio-Exegetical Study of Matthew 8 and 9.* JSNTSup 152. Sheffield: Sheffield Academic, 1997.

Vogel, Manuel. "Die Ethik der 'besseren Gerechtigkeit' im Matthäusevangelium." *ZNT* 18.36 (2015): 56–62.

Vos, Geerhardus. *Biblical Theology: Old and New Testaments.* Grand Rapids: Eerdmans, 1948.

———. *The Self-Disclosure of Jesus: The Modern Debate About the Messianic Consciousness.* 2nd ed. Edited by Johannes G. Vos. Phillipsburg, NJ: P&R, 2002.

Voss, Hank. *The Priesthood of All Believers and the* Missio Dei*: A Canonical, Catholic, and Contextual Perspective.* PTMS 223. Eugene, OR: Pickwick, 2016.

Waetjen, Herman C. *Matthew's Theology of Fulfillment, Its Universality and Its Ethnicity: God's New Israel as the Pioneer of God's New Humanity.* T&T Clark Biblical Studies. London: Bloomsbury T&T Clark, 2017.

Wainwright, Elaine M. *Habitat, Human, and Holy: An Eco-Rhetorical Reading of the Gospel of Matthew.* Earth Bible Commentary Series 6. Sheffield: Sheffield Phoenix, 2016.

———. "Matthew, The Gospel of." Pages 778–79 in *The Cambridge Dictionary of Christianity.* Edited by Daniel Patte. Cambridge: Cambridge University Press, 2010.

———. *Shall We Look for Another? A Feminist Rereading of the Matthean Jesus.* The Bible and Liberation Series. Maryknoll, NY: Orbis, 1998.

Wainwright, Elaine M., with Robert J. Myles and Carlos Olivares. *Matthew: An Introduction and Study Guide.*

*The* Basileia *of the Heavens in Near.* T&T Clark Study Guides to the New Testament 1. London: Bloomsbury T&T Clark, 2017.

Walker, Peter W. L. *Jesus and the Holy City: New Testament Perspectives on Jerusalem.* Grand Rapids: Eerdmans, 1996.

Waltke, Bruce K., with Charles Yu. *An Old Testament Theology: An Exegetical, Canonical, and Thematic Approach.* Grand Rapids: Zondervan, 2007.

Walvoord, John F. *Matthew: Thy Kingdom Come.* Chicago: Moody, 1974.

Warrington, Keith. "The Synoptic Gospels." Pages 84–103 in Burke and Warrington, *A Biblical Theology of the Holy Spirit.* Eugene, OR: Cascade, 2014.

Watson, Francis. *The Fourfold Gospel: A Theological Reading of the New Testament Portraits of Jesus.* Grand Rapids: Baker Academic, 2016.

———. *What Is a Gospel?* Grand Rapids: Eerdmans, 2022.

Watts, Rikki. "Immanuel: Virgin Birth Proof Test or Programmatic Warning of Things to Come (Isa 7:14 in Matt 1:23)?" Pages 92–113 in *From Prophecy to Testament: The Function of the Old Testament in the New.* Edited by Craig A. Evans. Peabody, MA: Hendrickson, 2004.

———. *Isaiah's New Exodus and Mark.* WUNT 2/88. Tübingen: Mohr Siebeck, 1997.

Wax, Trevin. *Eschatological Discipleship: Leading Christians to Understand Their Historical and Cultural Context.* Nashville: B&H Academic, 2018.

Weaver, Dorothy Jean. *The Irony of Power: The Politics of God Within Matthew's Narrative.* Studies in Peace and Scripture: Institute of Mennonite Studies. Eugene, OR: Pickwick, 2017.

———. *Matthew's Missionary Discourse: A Literary Critical Analysis.* JSNT 38. Sheffield: Sheffield Academic, 1990.

Webb, Robert L. "Jesus' Baptism: Its Historicity and Implications." *BBR* 10.2 (2000): 261–309.

———. "Jesus' Baptism by John: Its Historicity and Significance." Pages 95–150 in *Key Events in the Life of the Historical Jesus: A Collaborative Exploration of Context and Coherence.* Edited by Darrell L. Bock and Robert L. Webb. WUNT 247. Tübingen: Mohr Siebeck, 2009.

———. *John the Baptizer and Prophet: A Socio-Historical Study.* JSNTSup 62. Sheffield: JSOT Press, 1991.

Wegner, Paul D. "How Many Virgin Births Are in the Bible? (Isaiah 7:14): A Prophetic Pattern Approach." *JETS* 54.3 (2011): 467–84.

Wellum, Stephen J. *Christ Alone—The Uniqueness of Jesus as Savior. What the Reformers Taught . . . and Why It Still Matters.* The Five Solas Series. Grand Rapids: Zondervan, 2017.

———. *God the Son Incarnate: The Doctrine of Christ.* FET. Wheaton, IL: Crossway, 2016.

Wendel, Susan J., and David M. Miller. *Torah Ethics and Early Christian Identity.* Grand Rapids: Eerdmans, 2016.

Wengst, Klaus. "Keine 'Antithesen,' sondern Auslegung der Tora: Zu Mt 5,17–48." *ZNT* 18.36 (2015): 12–21.

Wenham, David. "How Do the Beatitudes Work? Some Observations on the Structure of the Beatitudes in Matthew." Pages 201–12 in *The Earliest Perceptions of Jesus in Context: Essays in Honour of John Nolland on His 70th Birthday.* Edited by Aaron W. White, Craig A. Evans, and David Wenham. LNTS 566. London: Bloomsbury T&T Clark, 2018.

Wenham, David, ed. *The Rediscovery of Jesus' Eschatological Discourse.* Vol. 4 of *Gospel Perspectives.* Sheffield: JSOT Press, 1984.

Wenham, John. *Easter Enigma: Are the Resurrection Accounts in Conflict?* 2nd ed. Grand Rapids: Baker, 1992.

———. *Redating Matthew, Mark and Luke: A Fresh Assault on the Synoptic Problem.* Downers Grove, IL: InterVarsity, 1992.

Wenthe, Dean O. "The Social Configuration of the Rabbi-Disciple Relationship: Evidence and Implications for First Century Palestine." Pages 143–74 in *Studies in the Hebrew Bible, Qumran, and the Septuagint: Presented to Eugene Ulrich.* Edited by Peter W. Flint, Emanuel Tov, and James C. Vanderkam. VTSup 101. Leiden: Brill, 2006.

Weren, Wim J. C. *Studies in Matthew's Gospel: Literary Design, Intertextuality, and Social Setting.* BibInt 130. Leiden: Brill, 2014.

Weren, Wim J. C., Huub Van de Sandt, and Joseph Verheyden, eds. *Life Beyond Death in Matthew's Gospel: Religious Metaphor or Bodily Reality?* Biblical Tools and Studies 13. Leuven: Peeters, 2011.

Westerholm, Stephen. *Jesus and Scribal Authority.* ConBNT 10. Lund: Gleerup, 1978.

———. *Law and Ethics in Early Judaism and the New Testament.* WUNT 383. Tübingen: Mohr Siebeck, 2017.

———. *Understanding Matthew: The Early Christian Worldview of the First Gospel.* Grand Rapids: Baker Academic, 2006.

White, Aaron W., Craig A. Evans, and David Wenham, eds. *The Earliest Perceptions of Jesus in Context: Essays in Honour of John Nolland on His 70th Birthday*. LNTS 566. London: Bloomsbury T&T Clark, 2018.

White, Benjamin L. "The Eschatological Conversion of 'All the Nations' in Matthew 28.19–20: (Mis)reading Matthew through Paul." *JSNT* 36.4 (2014): 353–82.

Wiarda, Timothy J. *Peter in the Gospels: Pattern, Personality, and Relationship*. WUNT 2/127. Tübingen: Mohr Siebeck, 2000.

Wick, Peter. *Schriftgelehrsamkeit und Toraethik: Die Bergpredigt im Kontext des Matthäusevangeliums*. Edited by Jens-Christian Maschmeier. Stuttgart: Kohlhammer, 2021.

Wilcox, Max. "Jesus in the Light of his Jewish Environment." *ANRW* 25.1:159–85. Part 2, Principat 25.1. Edited by H. Temporini and W. Haase. Berlin: de Gruyter, 1982.

Wilkins, Michael J. "Barabbas." *ABD* 1:607.

———. "Bartholomew." *ABD* 1:615.

———. "Belief/Believer." *ABD* 1:656–57.

———. "Brother/ Brotherhood." *ABD* 1:782–83.

———. "Christian." *ABD* 1:925–26.

———. "Imitate/Imitator." *ABD* 3:392.

———. *The Concept of Disciple in Matthew's Gospel: As Reflected in the Use of the Term* Μαθητής. NovTSup 59. Leiden: Brill, 1988.

———. "The Consideration of a Future for Israel in the Light of the Apparently Bleak Consequences for Negative Responses to Jesus's Ministry in the Gospel of Matthew." Pages 313–40 in *The Future Restoration of Israel: A Response to Supersessionism*. McMaster Biblical Studies Series 10. Edited by Stanley E. Porter and Alan E. Kurschner. Eugene, OR: Wipf & Stock; Hamilton, Ontario: McMaster Divinity College Press, 2023.

———. "Disciples." *DJG*[1] 176–81.

———. "Disciples and Discipleship." *DJG*[2] 202–12.

———. "Discipleship." *DJG*[1] 182–88.

———. *Discipleship in the Ancient World and Matthew's Gospel*. 2nd. ed. Grand Rapids: Baker, 1995.

———. *Following the Master: A Biblical Theology of Discipleship*. Grand Rapids: Zondervan, 1992.

———. *In His Image: Reflecting Christ in Everyday Life*. Colorado Springs: NavPress, 1997. Repr., Eugene, OR: Wipf & Stock, 2019.

———. "The Interplay of Ministry, Martyrdom and Discipleship in Ignatius of Antioch." Pages 294–315 in *Worship, Theology, and Ministry in the Early Church. Essays in Honor of Ralph P. Martin*. Edited by Michael J. Wilkins and Terence Paige. JSNTSup 87. Sheffield: JSOT Press, 1992.

———. "Isaiah 53 in the Four Gospels." Pages 109–132 in *The Gospel According to Isaiah 53: Encountering the Suffering Servant in Jewish and Christian Theology*. Edited by Darrell L. Bock and Mitch Glaser. Grand Rapids: Kregel, 2012.

———. "Israel According to the Gospels." Pages 87–102 in *The People, the Land, and the Future of Israel: Israel and the Jewish People in the Plan of God*. Edited by Darrell L. Bock and Mitch Glaser. Grand Rapids: Kregel, 2014.

———. "Matthew." Pages 1–203 in *Matthew, Mark, Luke*. Vol. 1 of *ZIBBC*. Edited by Clinton E. Arnold. Grand Rapids: Zondervan, 2002.

———. *Matthew*. NIVAC. Grand Rapids: Zondervan, 2004.

———. "Milk/Solid Food." *DLNTD* 736–38.

———. "Named and Unnamed Disciples in Matthew: A Literary-Theological Study." Pages 418–39 in *Society of Biblical Literature 1991 Seminar Papers*. SBLSP 30. Edited by Eugene H. Lovering Jr. Atlanta: Scholars Press, 1991.

———. "New Birth." *DLNTD* 792-95.

———. "Pastoral Theology." *DLNTD* 876–82.

———. "Peter's Declaration of Jesus' Identity in Caesarea Philippi." Pages 293–381 in *Key Events in the Life of the Historical Jesus: A Collaborative Exploration of Context and Coherence*. Edited by Darrell L. Bock and Robert L. Webb. WUNT 247. Tübingen: Mohr Siebeck, 2009.

———. "Prayer." *DLNTD* 941–48.

———. "Sinner." *DJG*[1] 757–60.

———. "Teaching/Paraenesis." *DLNTD* 1156–59.

———. "Temptation of Jesus." *DJG*[2] 952–59.

———. "The Theology of the Land in the Gospels." Pages 436–55 in *A Handbook on the Jewish Roots of the Gospels*. Edited by Craig A. Evans and David Mishkin. Peabody, MA: Hendrickson, 2021.

———. "Women in the Teaching and Ministry of Jesus." Pages 91–112 in *Women and Men in Ministry: A Complementary Perspective*. Edited by Robert L. Saucy and Judith K. TenElshof. Chicago: Moody, 2001.

Wilkins, Michael J., and J. P. Moreland, eds. *Jesus Under Fire: Modern Scholarship Reinvents the Historical Jesus*. Grand Rapids: Zondervan, 1995.

Wilkins, Michael J., and Terence Paige, eds. *Worship, Theology and Ministry in the Early Church: Essays in Honor of Ralph P. Martin*. JSNTSup 87. Sheffield: Sheffield Academic, 1992.

Wilkins, Michael J., and Erik Thoennes. *Biblical and Theological Studies: A Student's Guide*. Reclaiming the Christian Intellectual Tradition. Wheaton, IL: Crossway, 2018.

Willitts, Joel. "The Friendship of Matthew and Paul: A Response to a Recent Trend in the Interpretation of Matthew's Gospel." *HvTSt* 65.1 (2009): art. #151. https://doi.org/10.4102/hts.v69i1.1300.

———. "Matthew and *Psalms of Solomon's* Messianism: A Comparative Study in First-Century Messianology." *BBR* 22.1 (2012): 27–50.

———. *Matthew's Messianic Shepherd-King: In Search of "The Lost Sheep of the House of Israel."* BZNW 147. Berlin: de Gruyter, 2007.

———. "The Twelve Disciples in Matthew." Pages 166–79 in *Jesus, Matthew's Gospel and Early Christianity: Studies in Memory of Graham N. Stanton*. Edited by Daniel M. Gurtner, Joel Willitts, and Richard A. Burridge. LNTS 435. London: T&T Clark, 2011.

———. "Zionism in the Gospel of Matthew." Pages 107–40 in *The New Christian Zionism: Fresh Perspectives on Israel and the Land*. Edited by Gerald R. McDermott. Downers Grove: InterVarsity, 2016.

Wilson, Alistair I. *When Will These Things Happen? A Study of Jesus as Judge in Matthew 21–25*. PBM. Carlisle, UK: Paternoster, 2004.

Wilson, Walter T. *The Gospel of Matthew*. 2 vols. Eerdmans Critical Commentary. Grand Rapids: Eerdmans, 2022. (These volumes were published too late for my full interaction but are listed here for the reader's benefit.)

———. *Healing in the Gospel of Matthew: Reflections on Method and Ministry*. Minneapolis: Fortress, 2014.

Winn, Adam. "'This Generation': Reconsidering Mark 13:30 in Light of Eschatological Expectations in Second Temple Judaism." *BBR* 30.4 (2020): 540–60.

Winter, Bruce W. "The Messiah as the Tutor: The Meaning of καθηγητής in Matthew 23:10." *TynBul* 42.1 (1991): 152–57.

Witherington, Ben, III. *The Acts of the Apostles: A Socio-Rhetorical Commentary*. Grand Rapids: Eerdmans, 1998.

———. *Biblical Theology: The Convergence of the Canon*. Cambridge: Cambridge University Press, 2019.

———. *Isaiah Old and New: Exegesis, Intertextuality, and Hermeneutics*. Minneapolis: Fortress, 2017.

———. *Jesus, Paul, and the End of the World: A Comparative Study in New Testament Eschatology*. Downers Grove: InterVarsity, 1992.

———. *Matthew*. SHBC 19. Macon, GA: Smyth & Helwys, 2006.

———. *Women and the Genesis of Christianity*. Edited by Ann Witherington. Cambridge: Cambridge University Press, 1990.

———. *Women in the Ministry of Jesus: A Study of Jesus' Attitudes to Women and Their Roles as Reflected in His Earthly Life*. SNTSMS 51. Cambridge: Cambridge University Press, 1984.

Wittmer, Michael E., ed. *Four Views on Heaven*. Counterpoints: Bible and Theology. Grand Rapids: Zondervan, 2022.

Wright, Christopher J. H. *The Mission of God: Unlocking the Bible's Grand Narrative*. Downers Grove, IL: InterVarsity, 2006.

———. *The Mission of God's People: A Biblical Theology of the Church's Mission*. BTL. Grand Rapids: Zondervan, 2010.

Wright, N. T. *Jesus and the Victory of God*. Vol. 2 of *Christian Origins and the Question of God*. Minneapolis: Fortress, 1996.

———. *The Resurrection of the Son of God*. Vol. 3 of *Christian Origins and the Question of God*. Minneapolis: Fortress, 2003.

———. "Son of Man–Lord of the Temple? Gospel Echoes of Psalm 8 and the Ongoing Christological Challenge." Pages 77–96 in *The Earliest Perceptions of Jesus in Context: Essays in Honour of John Nolland on His 70th Birthday*. Edited by Aaron W. White, Craig A. Evans and David Wenham. LNTS 566. London: Bloomsbury T&T Clark, 2018.

Wright, N. T., and Michael F. Bird. *The New Testament in Its World: An Introduction to the History, Literature, and Theology of the First Christians.* Grand Rapids: Zondervan, 2019.

Wright, N. T., Simon Gathercole, and Robert B Stewart. *What Did the Cross Accomplish? A Conversation about the Atonement.* Louisville: Westminster John Knox, 2021.

Wright, Stephen I. *Jesus the Storyteller.* London: SPCK, 2014; repr., Louisville: Westminster John Knox, 2015.

Wyant, Jennifer S. *Beyond Mary or Martha: Reclaiming Ancient Models of Discipleship.* ESEC 21. Atlanta: SBL Press, 2019.

Yamasaki, Gary. *John the Baptist in Life and Death: Audience-Oriented Criticism of Matthew's Narrative.* JSNTSup 167. Sheffield: Sheffield Academic, 1998.

Yang, Yong-Eui. *Jesus and the Sabbath in Matthew's Gospel.* JSNTSup 139. Sheffield: Sheffield Academic, 1997.

Yarbrough, Oliver Larry, ed. *Engaging the Passion: Perspectives on the Death of Jesus.* Minneapolis: Fortress, 2015.

———, ed. *Passion: Contemporary Writers on the Story of Calvary.* Maryknoll, NY: Orbis, 2015.

Yarbrough, Robert W. "The Kingdom of God in the New Testament: Matthew and Revelation." Pages 95–123 in *The Kingdom of God.* Edited by Christopher W. Morgan and Robert A. Peterson. Theology in Community. Wheaton, IL: Crossway, 2012.

———. *The Salvation Historical Fallacy? Reassessing the History of New Testament Theology.* History of Biblical Interpretation Series 2. Leiderdorp, NL: Deo, 2004.

———. "Salvation History." Pages 45–58 in *God's Glory Revealed in Christ: Essays on Biblical Theology in Honor of Thomas R. Schreiner.* Edited by Denny Burk, James M. Hamilton Jr., and Brian Vickers. Nashville: B&H, 2019.

Yieh, John Yueh-Han. *Conversations with Scripture: The Gospel of Matthew.* Anglican Association of Biblical Scholars Study Series. New York: Morehouse, 2012.

———. *One Teacher: Jesus' Teaching Role in Matthew's Gospel Report.* BZNW 124. Berlin: de Gruyter, 2004.

Young, Brad H. *Meet the Rabbis: Rabbinic Thought and Teachings of Jesus.* Peabody, MA: Hendrickson, 2007.

Zacharias, H. Daniel. *Matthew's Presentation of the Son of David: Davidic Tradition and Typology in the Gospel of Matthew.* T&T Clark Biblical Studies. London: Bloomsbury T&T Clark, 2017.

Zehnder, Markus. "The Question of the 'Divine Status' of the Davidic Messiah." *BBR* 30.4 (2020): 485–514.

Ziethe, Carolin. *Auf seinen Namen werden die Volker hoffen: Die matthäische Rezeption der Schriften Israels zür Begründung des universalen Heils.* BZNW 233. Berlin: de Gruyter, 2018.

Zimmermann, Ruben. "Parables in Matthew: Tradition, Interpretation, and Function in the Gospel." Pages 159–86 in *An Early Reader of Mark and Q: New and Old on the Composition, Redaction, and Theology of the Gospel of Matthew.* Edited by Joseph Verheyden and Gilbert van Belle. Biblical Tools and Studies 21. Leuven: Peeters, 2016.

———. *Puzzling the Parables of Jesus: Methods and Interpretation.* Minneapolis: Fortress, 2015.

Zolondek, Michael Vicko. *We Have Found the Messiah: How the Disciples Help Us Answer the Davidic Messianic Question.* Eugene, OR: Pickwick, 2016.

# Scripture Index

## Old Testament

**Jeremiah**



**Lamentations**



**Ezekiel**



**Daniel**

**Mark**

**Romans**

# Extrabiblical Literature Index

## GRECO-ROMAN LITERATURE

# Subject Index

# Author Index